Rick Steves'

GERMANY

2012

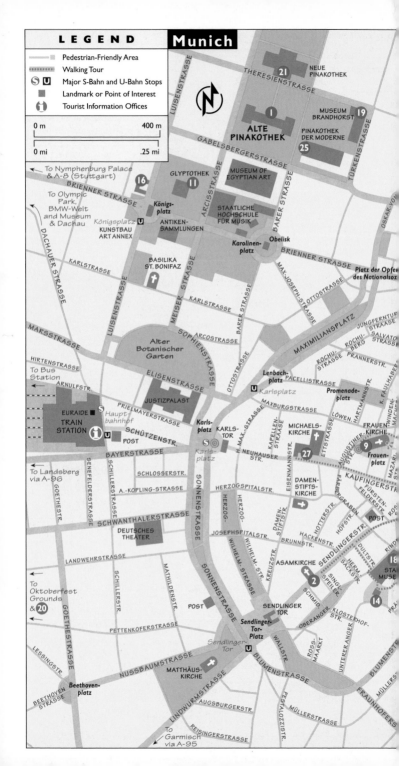

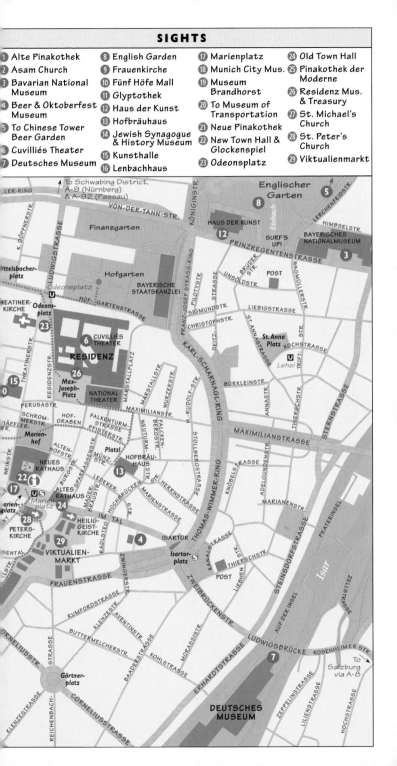

SIGHTS

1 Alte Pinakothek
2 Asam Church
3 Bavarian National Museum
4 Beer & Oktoberfest Museum
5 To Chinese Tower Beer Garden
6 Cuvilliés Theater
7 Deutsches Museum
8 English Garden
9 Frauenkirche
10 Fünf Höfe Mall
11 Glyptothek
12 Haus der Kunst
13 Hofbräuhaus
14 Jewish Synagogue & History Museum
15 Kunsthalle
16 Lenbachhaus
17 Marienplatz
18 Munich City Mus.
19 Museum Brandhorst
20 To Museum of Transportation
21 Neue Pinakothek
22 New Town Hall & Glockenspiel
23 Odeonsplatz
24 Old Town Hall
25 Pinakothek der Moderne
26 Residenz Mus. & Treasury
27 St. Michael's Church
28 St. Peter's Church
29 Viktualienmarkt

SIGHTS

1. Alexanderplatz
2. Bebelplatz
3. Berlin Cathedral
4. Berlin Wall Memorial
5. Bode Museum
6. Brandenburg Gate
7. City Hall
8. DDR Museum
9. Erotic Art Museum
10. Gemäldegalerie
11. Gendarmenmarkt
12. German Cathedral
13. German History Museum
14. German Resistance Mem.
15. Hackeschen Höfe
16. Hauptbahnhof (Main Train Station) & EurAide
17. Jewish Museum Berlin
18. KaDeWe Department Store
19. Kaiser Wilhelm Memorial Church
20. Käthe Kollwitz Museum
21. The Kennedys Museum
22. Memorial to the Murdered Jews of Europe
23. Museum of Decorative Arts
24. Museum of the Wall at Checkpoint Charlie
25. Musical Instruments Museum
26. Natural History Museum
27. Neue Wache Memorial
28. Neues Museum & Egyptian Collection
29. New National Gallery
30. New Synagogue
31. Old National Gallery
32. Pergamon Museum
33. Philharmonic Concert Hall
34. Potsdamer Platz & Sony Center
35. Reichstag
36. Spree River Cruises
37. Stasi Museum
38. Topography of Terror
39. TV Tower
40. Zoo

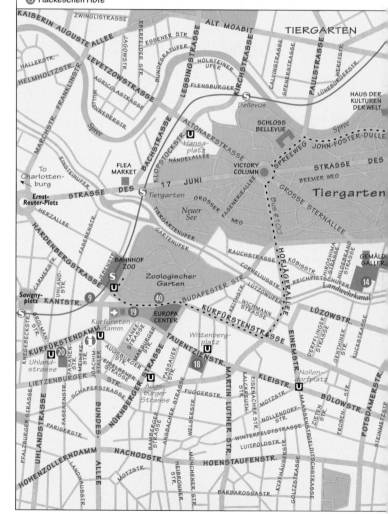

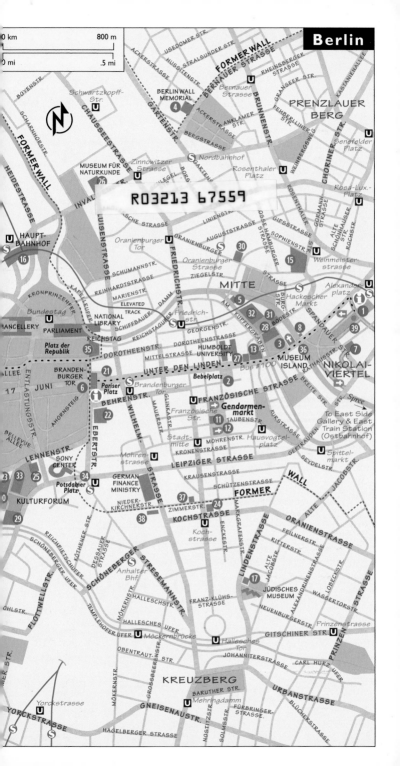

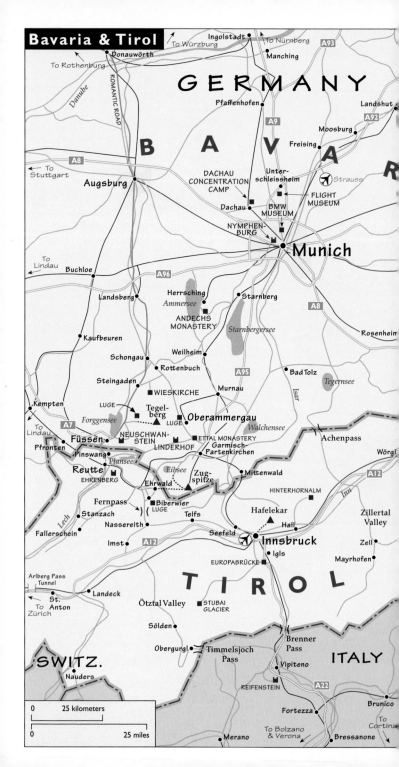

CONTENTS

Germany

Deutschland

Germany is blessed with some of
Europe's most high-powered sights.
There's spectacular scenery—the jagged
Alps, flower-filled meadows, rolling hills
of forests and farms, and rivers such as
the raging Rhine and moseying Mosel.
Germany has hundreds of castles, some
ruined and mysterious; others stout,
crenellated, and imposing; and still others
right out of a Disney fairy tale. In this
land of the Protestant Reformation—and
Catholic Counter-Reformation—churches
and cathedrals are another forte.
Austere Lutheran houses of worship
tower silently next to exuberantly
overripe Baroque churches dripping with
curlicues.

Deutschland is energetic, efficient, and organized. It's
Europe's muscleman, both economically and wherever people
line up (Germans have a reputation for pushing ahead). It's the
European Union's most populous country and biggest economy, with a geographic diversity and cultural richness that
draw millions of visitors every year.

Germany's dark side is recalled in eerie Nazi remnants
(stern office buildings, thoughtfully presented "documentation
centers," haunting concentration camps) and chilling reminders of the Cold War (embodied in a few quickly disappearing

sites—such as scant fragments of the notorious Berlin Wall). And of course there are the cultural clichés, kept alive more by tradition-loving Germans than by tourist demand. The country is dotted with idyllic half-timbered villages where you can enjoy strudel at the bakery or sip a stein of beer while men in lederhosen play oompah music. Peruse a wonderland of chocolates, stock up on Hummels and cuckoo clocks, and learn how to polka.

All of these traditions stand at sharp contrast with the "real" Germany of today. Despite its respect for the past, this truly is a 21st-century country. At the forefront of human progress, Germany is a world of high-tech trains, gleaming cities, social efficiency, and world-class museums celebrating history's greatest cultural achievements.

Modern Germany bustles. Its cities hold 75 percent of its people, and average earnings are among the highest in the world. Most workers get at least a month of paid vacation, and during the other 11 months, this land that's roughly the size of Montana creates a Gross Domestic Product (GDP) that's about one-quarter of the United States'. Germany has risen from the ashes of World War II to become the world's fifth-largest industrial power.

People all over the world enjoy the fruits of Germany's labor. Their cars are legendary—BMW, Mercedes-Benz, Volkswagen, Audi, and Porsche. We ride German elevators and trains (ThyssenKrupp and Siemens AG), take German medicines (Bayer), use German cosmetics (Nivea)…and eat German goodies (Haribo's Gummi Bears).

Germany beats out all but two countries in the production of books, Nobel laureates, and professors. In the world of physics, there's Einstein's Relativity, Planck's constant, and the Heisenberg Uncertainty Principle. German inventions range from Gutenberg's printing press to Zeppelin's zeppelins to Roentgen's X-rays to Daimler's and Benz's cars to Geiger's counter. Musically, Germany dominated the scene for more than two centuries— Bach, Beethoven, Brahms, Handel, Pachelbel, Wagner, and more. Germans have a reputation as profound analytical thinkers, sprouting philosophers such as Kant, Hegel, Nietzsche, Marx, and Engels.

Germany is geographically big (compared to other European countries) but closely knit by transportation. Its autobahns—miles and miles of high-quality freeway—are famous (or notorious) for their no-speed-limit system (more fully

Germany Almanac

Official Name: Bundesrepublik Deutschland, or simply Deutschland.

Population: Germany's 82 million people (more than three times the population of Texas) are largely of Teutonic DNA (about 90 percent), plus a small but significant minority (2.4 percent) of Turkish-descent. A third of Germans are Catholic, and a third are Protestant. About 4 percent are Muslim; the rest are unaffiliated.

Latitude and Longitude: 51°N and 9°E. The latitude is similar to Alberta, Canada.

Area: At 138,000 square miles, Germany is about half the size of Texas. It's bordered by nine countries.

Geography: The terrain gradually rises—from flat land in the north to the rugged Alps in the south, culminating in the 9,700-foot Zugspitze mountain. The climate is temperate.

Biggest Cities: The capital city of Berlin has 3.4 million people, followed by Hamburg's 1.8 million and Munich's 1.3 million.

Economy: With a GDP of $3.5 trillion—similar to America's Midwest states combined—Germany is Europe's largest economy. Still, the GDP per capita is approximately $40,600, or about 12 percent less than America's. Germany's strength is in technology and manufacturing—exporting machinery and other high-quality items that developing countries (including China) want to buy. It's one of the world's most advanced economies, producing steel, cars, chemicals, pharmaceuticals, consumer electronics, and more. Germany also has around 1,300 breweries (Bavaria boasts about half), but much of the production is consumed domestically. Germany trades almost equally with a half-dozen

neighboring countries and the United States.

Since the 1990 reunification, Germany's economy has been burdened by the cost (about $80 billion a year) of integrating the former East Germany into the modern West. Germany's expensive social security system gets even costlier as the population ages. Thanks to powerful trade unions, workers get good benefits. Unemployment reached a post-reunification low of just 6.7 percent in 2010.

Government: In the 2005 elections, Angela Merkel became Germany's first woman chancellor. In 2009, the conservative Merkel became the head of a big-business-friendly coalition government that leans slightly to the right. A powerful minority party, the Greens, presses a pro-environment agenda. Germany's chancellor, similar to a prime minister, is not elected by the people but is the head of the lead party in parliament. The less-powerful president (currently Christian Wulff) is elected by parliament. The legislative branch includes the Bundestag (622 seats, elected by both direct and proportional representation) and Bundesrat (69 votes by officials of Germany's 16 states).

Flag: Deutschland's flag is composed of three horizontal bands of (from top to bottom) black, red, and gold.

The Average *Deutscher:* The average German is 44 years old—7 years older than the average American—has 1.4 kids, and will live to be 79. He or she lives in a household with two other people, may either own or rent their house (only about half prefer to own), watches 2.5 hours of TV a day, and spends 20 minutes reading the newspaper. The average German drinks a pint of beer every 32 hours—slightly less than the average Irish or Czech.

explained on page 837). InterCityExpress (ICE) trains zip by at up to 200 miles per hour, linking major cities quickly and efficiently.

As a nation, Germany is less than 150 years old ("born" in 1871), quite young compared to most of its European neighbors. In medieval times, there were 300 "countries" in what is now Germany, each with its own weights, measures, coinage, king, and lottery. By 1850, the number had dropped to a still formidable 35 countries. Today's Germany is a federation of 16 states, each with its own cultural identity and customs.

Traditionally—and in some ways even today—German culture divides at a sort of North-South Mason-Dixon Line. Northern Germany was barbarian, is predominantly

Protestant, and tackles life aggressively, while southern Germany (Bavaria) was Roman, is largely Catholic, and enjoys a more relaxed tempo. The romantic American image of Germany is beer-and-pretzel Bavaria (probably because that was "our" sector after the war). This historic North-South division is growing less pronounced as Germany becomes a more mobile society.

Germany's roots run deep. Thoughtful travelers can easily trace the country's history in their sightseeing. Find Germany's Roman roots at the impressive Porta Nigra Gate and Basilica of scenic Trier. When Rome fell, German lands fragmented into hundreds of small feudal kingdoms, each with its own castle—many of which still dot the German countryside today. Magnificent Gothic cathedrals, like the one in Köln, attest to the faith of medieval people. As

Germany's economy recovered, it became an important European hub for trade and transportation. Prosperous cities sprung up along the Romantic Road—today's prime tourist trail.

It was from Germany that a humble monk named Martin Luther rocked Europe with religious reform, and you'll see monuments, cities, and churches associated with him. Meanwhile, German Catholics lavishly decorated their churches (including the glorious Wieskirche) and palaces (in Munich and Würzburg) in the ornate Baroque/Rococo style, giving a glimpse of the heaven that awaited the faithful. Germany became a Europe-wide battleground for Protestants and Catholics in the Thirty Years' War that was duked out in towns such as Rothenburg (which today is besieged by tourists).

In the 1800s, Germany unified politically, and it became a cultural powerhouse. European nobles flocked to Baden-Baden's casino and thermal baths, while composer Richard Wagner spun operatic tales about German folk legends at the castle of Neuschwanstein with his friend "Mad" King Ludwig II.

Germany's prosperity ended in the humiliating defeat of World War I. You can see the rising specter of Hitler and Nazism at the Nürnberg Rally Grounds (where huge propaganda events were staged, now home to an excellent museum documenting the Nazis' rise to power), at Berlin's Reichstag (whose destruction helped the Nazis take control), and the sobering concentration camp museum at Dachau (one of many places where the Nazis snuffed out millions of lives). Germany's utter destruction in World War II is evident in the skylines of today's cities. Some, like Munich and Dresden, were rebuilt in a faux-Baroque style, while Frankfurt sprouted skyscrapers.

At war's end, Germany was divided East-West between the victorious Allies, and the Cold War set in (1945-1990). In Berlin, you can see a few surviving stretches of the Wall that divided the country, and the famous Checkpoint Charlie that controlled the East-West flow. Even today, Eastern cities such as Dresden and Görlitz bear the scars and stunted growth of Soviet occupation. Some friction still exists between the residents of the former East Germany ("Ossies" in impolite slang) and those from West Germany ("Wessies"). Two decades after reunification, and despite billions of dollars of economic aid, the East lags behind the West, with a higher unemployment rate (about  double the West's), lower income, and a few old-timers who miss the Red old days.

Many visitors can't help but associate Germany with its dark Nazi past. But while a small neo-Nazi skinhead element still survives in the back alleys of German society, for the most

part the nation has evolved into a surprisingly progressive, almost touchy-feely place. A genuine sense of responsibility for
World War II and the Holocaust pervades much of German
society. If you visit a concentration camp memorial, you'll
likely see several field-trip groups of German teens visiting
there to learn the lessons of the past.

Germany was a founding member of the European Union
and continues to lead the way in creating a healthy Europe for
the future—with peace, unity, tolerance (e.g., legalized gay
marriage), and human rights as its central motivations. It's the
world's second-biggest foreign-aid donor, after the US. Even
to a skeptical visitor, it's clear that most Germans are trying to
make up for the ugliness their ancestors subjected Europe to
not so long ago.

How does a country achieve such robust economic and
social success, despite losing two world wars? This is a country of "Type A" personalities. Bold, brassy Germans typically
aren't shy to speak their minds. Their directness (some might
say "bluntness") is refreshing to some, and startling to others.
At least you'll know where you stand. People who enjoy trains
that run on time are perfectly suited for travel in everything-
has-its-place Germany. Those who like to play it fast and loose
might find that improvisation has its limits here.

Paradoxically, the ultra-efficient Germans also have a weak spot for Hummel-esque quaintness and a sentimentality for their own history. They love nature. They love to go a-wandering along a mountain path with their hiking sticks, rucksacks, and state-of-the-art outdoor gear. Dramatic cable cars whisk visitors to sweeping cut-glass panoramas. Learn the word *schön*—"beautiful"—because you'll hear it often, from little old ladies and grown men alike as they survey beautiful vistas of their homeland. They're also prone to get misty-eyed when, after a glass or two of white wine, they and their mates start singing a traditional song from their youth. Cutesy traditions are respected and celebrated—especially in  Bavaria, where people wear dirndls and lederhosen on holidays, erect maypoles in spring, host exuberant Christmas markets in winter, and frequent Oktoberfest-type beer halls year-round.

Germans love to travel, throughout their own country and beyond. They're cosmopolitan and outward-looking. Two-thirds speak at least one other language (mostly English), and they enjoy watching TV and movies beamed in from other countries. Watch out—they may know American politics and history better than you do. They're products of high-quality schools that put kids on either fast or slow tracks, depending on ability and desire. To move on to college, they must pass a major SAT-like test. Once there, the university system is top-quality...and tuition, if there is any at all, is only a few hundred dollars a semester.

Germans aren't all work and no play. All Europeans love watching sports—but Germans actually play them. More

than six million are registered to play *Fussball* (soccer) every year in the official league. There's a big following for pro soccer Bundesliga, and Germany is always a strong contender for the World Cup and Euro Cup championship tournaments.

Motorsports are big time, especially Formula One—

the European answer to NASCAR—where racing legend Michael Schumacher is one of the world's highest-paid athletes. In the Olympics (winter and summer), Germany is consistently one of the world's top medal-finishers. Just try to keep up with them on one of their summer luge courses *(Sommerrodelbahn)* that allow amateur thrill-seekers to scream down a mountain at top speed.

As Germany speeds into the future, it's faced with a number of challenges—none bigger than immigration. After World War II, Germany needed cheap blue-collar laborers to help rebuild, and they welcomed many Turkish people as *Gastarbeiters* (guest workers). While many earned money and went home, many others married, had kids, and stayed. Today, more than 8 million immigrants (roughly 10 percent of Germany's population) live within its borders—more than every country but the US and Russia. Of these, almost 3 million are Turks, most of whom are Muslims—not always the easiest fit within a traditionally Christian nation.

Germany today is trying to stay competitive in the global marketplace while maintaining generous social services. It has taken a tough stance on bailing out other EU nations that have been less fiscally responsible. Neo-Nazism is a festering sore, and there's a declining birthrate (one of the world's lowest). And its enormous appetite for energy is increasingly at odds with its love for the environment (the government has strong incentives for sustainable energy in place, and in 2011, Chancellor Merkel announced plans to phase out nuclear power by 2022).

After the end of World War II, as the US evolved from an occupying force to a close ally, the two countries gradually built a strong relationship. Today more than 100,000 Americans live in Germany (many of them at US military bases, such as Ramstein near the Rhine). Americans generally find Germany to be one of Europe's most accessible nations. It's efficient, the people are almost aggressively welcoming, the language barrier is minimal...and the German roots that pervade America's melting pot don't hurt matters, either. (More

than 15 percent of Americans have some German ancestry—more than any other background.)

Germany today is reunited, a nation of cutting-edge industry, medieval castles, speedy autobahns, old-time beer halls, modern skyscrapers, and the best wurst. This young country with a long past continues to make history.

INTRODUCTION

This book focuses on Germany's top big-city, small-town, and rural destinations. It gives you all the information and opinions necessary to wring the maximum value out of your limited time and money. If you plan a month or less in Germany and have a normal appetite for information, this book is all you need. If you're a travel-info fiend, this book sorts through all the superlatives and provides a handy rack upon which to hang your supplemental information.

Experiencing Europe's culture, people, and natural wonders economically and hassle-free has been my goal through three decades of traveling, tour guiding, and travel writing. With this new edition, I pass on to you the lessons I've learned, updated for your trip in 2012.

The German destinations covered in this book are balanced to include a comfortable mix of cities and villages, mountaintop hikes and forgotten Roman ruins, sleepy river cruises and sky-high gondola rides. I've also included a taste of neighboring Austria, with side-trips into Tirol and Salzburg. While you'll find the predictable biggies (such as Rhine castles and chunks of the Berlin Wall), I've also mixed in a healthy dose of Back Door intimacy (a soak in a Black Forest mineral spa, a beer with Bavarian monks, and a thrilling mountain luge). I've been selective, including only the most exciting sights. For example, of the many castles in the Mosel Valley, I guide you to the best: Burg Eltz.

The best is, of course, only my opinion. But after spending half my adult life exploring and researching Europe, I've developed a sixth sense for what travelers enjoy. The places featured in this book will make anyone want to yodel.

Map Legend

⅃ʑ	Viewpoint	✈	Airport	)━━(	Tunnel
▲	Entry Arrow	Ⓣ	Taxi Stand	━━━	Pedestrian Zone
❶	Tourist Info	Ⓣ	Tram Stop	--✗-✗--	Railway
WC	Restroom	Ⓑ	Bus Stop	··············	Ferry/Boat Route
♜	Castle	Ⓟ	Parking	⊢━┿━┤	Tram
⛪	Church	)(	Mtn. Pass	▥▥▥▥	Stairs
▪	Statue/Point of Interest	⸾⸾⸾	Park	·· ·· ··	Walk/Tour Route
				-- -- --	Trail

Use this legend to help you navigate the maps in this book.

About This Book

Rick Steves' Germany 2012 is your friendly Franconian, your German in a jam, a tour guide in your pocket. The book is organized by destinations. Each destination is a mini-vacation on its own—filled with exciting sights, strollable neighborhoods, homey and affordable places to stay, and memorable places to eat. In the following chapters, you'll find these sections:

Planning Your Time suggests a schedule for how to best use your limited time.

Orientation includes specifics on public transportation, helpful hints, local tour options, easy-to-read maps, and tourist information.

Sights describes the top attractions and includes their cost and hours.

Self-Guided Walks take you through interesting neighborhoods, with a personal tour guide in hand.

Sleeping describes my favorite hotels, from good-value deals to cushy splurges.

Eating serves up a range of options, from inexpensive eateries to fancy restaurants.

Connections outlines your options for traveling to destinations by train, bus, and plane, plus route tips for drivers.

The **German History** chapter introduces you to some of the key people and events in this nation's complicated past, making your sightseeing that much more meaningful.

The **appendix** is a traveler's tool kit, with telephone tips, useful phone numbers, transportation basics (on trains, buses, car rentals, driving, and flights), recommended books and films, a festival list, a climate chart, a handy packing checklist, a hotel reservation form, and German survival phrases.

Browse through this book, choose your favorite destinations, and link them up. Then have a *wunderbar* trip! Traveling like a

Key to This Book

Updates

This book is updated every year, but things change. For the latest, visit www.ricksteves.com/update. For a valuable list of reports and experiences—good and bad—from fellow travelers, check www.ricksteves.com/feedback.

Abbreviations and Times

I use the following symbols and abbreviations in this book:

Sights are rated:

▲▲▲	**Don't miss**
▲▲	**Try hard to see**
▲	**Worthwhile if you can make it**
No rating	**Worth knowing about**

Tourist information offices are abbreviated as **TI,** and bathrooms are **WCs.** To categorize accommodations, I use a **Sleep Code** (described on page 21).

Like Europe, this book uses the **24-hour clock.** It's the same through 12:00 noon, then keep going: 13:00, 14:00, and so on. For anything over 12, subtract 12 and add p.m. (14:00 is 2:00 p.m.).

When giving **opening times,** I include both peak season and off-season hours if they differ. So, if a museum is listed as "May-Oct daily 9:00-16:00," it should be open from 9:00 a.m. until 4:00 p.m. from the first day of May until the last day of October (but expect exceptions).

For **transit** or **tour departures,** I first list the frequency, then the duration. So, a train connection listed as "2/hour, 1.5 hours" departs twice each hour, and the journey lasts an hour and a half.

temporary local, you'll get the absolute most out of every mile, minute, and dollar. As you visit places I know and love, I'm happy that you'll be meeting some of my favorite German people.

Planning

This section will help you get started on planning your trip—with advice on trip costs, when to go, and what you should know before you take off.

Travel Smart

Your trip to Germany is like a complex play—easier to follow and to really appreciate on a second viewing. While no one does the same trip twice to gain that advantage, reading this book in its entirety before your trip accomplishes much the same thing.

Design an itinerary that enables you to visit sights at the best possible times. Note festivals and holidays (see page 846), specifics on sights, and days when sights are closed. If you're traveling by public transportation or by rental car, read up on my tips in the appendix for taking trains and buses and for driving. A smart trip is a puzzle—a fun, doable, and worthwhile challenge.

Be sure to mix intense and relaxed periods in your itinerary. To maximize rootedness, minimize one-night stands. It's worth a long drive after dinner to be settled into a town for two nights. Hotels are more likely to give a better price to someone staying more than one night. Every trip—and every traveler—needs slack time (for laundry, picnics, people-watching, and so on). Pace yourself. Assume you will return.

Reread this book as you travel, and visit local TIs. Upon arrival in a new town, lay the groundwork for a smooth departure; write down (or print out from an online source) the schedule for the train or bus you'll take when you depart. Drivers can study the best route to their next destination.

Get online at Internet cafés or at your hotel, and buy a phone card or carry a mobile phone: You can find tourist information, learn the latest on sights (special events, English tour schedules, etc.), book tickets and tours, make reservations, reconfirm hotels, research transportation connections, check weather, and keep in touch with your loved ones.

Enjoy the friendliness of the German people. Connect with the culture. Set up your own quest for the best beer-and-bratwurst, castle, cathedral, or whatever. Slow down and be open to unexpected experiences. Ask questions—most locals are eager to point you in their idea of the right direction. Keep a notepad in your pocket for confirming prices, noting directions, and organizing your thoughts. Wear your money belt, learn the currency, and figure out how to estimate prices in dollars. Those who expect to travel smart, do.

Trip Costs

Five components make up your total trip cost: airfare, surface transportation, room and board, sightseeing and entertainment, and shopping and miscellany.

Airfare: A basic round-trip flight from the US to Frankfurt can cost $850-1,200—depending on where you fly from and when (cheaper in winter). Consider saving time and money in Europe by flying into one city and out of another; for instance, into Frankfurt and out of Berlin.

Surface Transportation: For a three-week whirlwind trip of all my recommended German destinations, allow $400 per person for public transportation (trains and buses) or $900 per person (based on two people sharing) for a three-week car rental, parking, tolls, gas, and insurance. Leasing is worth considering for trips of two and a half weeks or more. Car rentals and leases are cheapest when reserved from the US. Train passes are normally sold only outside of Europe, though you may save money by simply buying tickets as you go. For more on public transportation and car rental, see "Transportation" in the appendix.

Room and Board: You can thrive in Germany in 2012 on $110 a day per person for room and board (more in big cities). A $110-a-day budget allows an average of $15 for lunch, $20 for dinner, $5 for beer and *Eis* (ice cream), and $70 for lodging (based on two people splitting a $140 double room that includes breakfast). Students and tightwads can enjoy Germany for as little as $50 a day ($30 for a bed in a hostel, $20 for cheap meals and picnics).

Sightseeing and Entertainment: In big cities, figure about $10-18 per major sight (Munich's Deutsches Museum-$12, Berlin's Museum of The Wall-$17), $5-7 for minor ones, and $25-50 for splurge experiences (such as concert tickets, alpine lifts, and conducting the beer-hall band). An overall average of $30 a day works for most people. Don't skimp here. After all, this category is the driving force behind your trip—you came to sightsee, enjoy, and experience Germany.

Shopping and Miscellany: Figure roughly $3 per postcard, coffee, beer, and ice-cream cone. Shopping can vary in cost from nearly nothing to a small fortune. Good budget travelers find that this category has little to do with assembling a trip full of lifelong and wonderful memories.

Sightseeing Priorities
Depending on the length of your trip, and taking geographic proximity into account, here are my recommended priorities:

3 days:	Munich, Bavarian castles
5 days, add:	Rhine Valley, Rothenburg
7 days, add:	More of Bavaria and Tirol, side-trip to Salzburg
10 days, add:	Berlin
14 days, add:	Baden-Baden, Black Forest, Dresden
17 days, add:	Nürnberg, Mosel Valley, Trier
21 days, add:	Würzburg, and slow down
More time:	Choose among Frankfurt, Köln, Hamburg, Leipzig, the Martin Luther towns (Erfurt and Wittenburg), and Görlitz. (The itinerary and map on pages 10 and 11 include everything on the 21-day list.)

When to Go
The "tourist season" runs roughly from May through September. Summer has its advantages: the best weather, snow-free alpine

Germany at a Glance

▲▲▲**Munich** Lively city with a traffic-free center, excellent museums, Baroque palaces, stately churches, rowdy beer halls, convivial beer gardens, and beautiful parks (such as the English Garden)—plus the sobering concentration camp memorial at nearby Dachau.

▲▲▲**Bavaria and Tirol** Pair of Alps-straddling regions (one in Germany, the other in Austria) boasting the fairy-tale castles of Neuschwanstein, Hohenschwangau, and Linderhof; inviting villages such as the handy home base Füssen, Austrian retreat Reutte, and adorable Oberammergau; the towering Zugspitze and its high-altitude lifts; and hiking, luge, and other mountain activities.

▲▲▲**Salzburg and Berchtesgaden** Austrian musical mecca for fans of Mozart and *The Sound of Music,* offering a dramatic castle, concerts, Baroque churches, and an old town full of winding lanes; plus nearby Berchtesgaden, soaked in alpine scenery and Nazi history.

▲**Baden-Baden and the Black Forest** High-class resort/spa town of Baden-Baden, with decadent bath experiences, a peaceful riverside stroll, and a grand casino; lively university city of Freiburg and cozy village of Staufen; and a thickly forested countryside rife with healthy hikes, folk museums, cute hamlets, and cream cakes.

▲▲**Rothenburg and the Romantic Road** Well-preserved medieval city full of half-timbered buildings and cobbled lanes surrounded by intact and walkable medieval walls; jumping-off point for the "Romantic Road" scenic route through lovely countryside and time-passed towns, including Dinkelsbühl and Nördlingen.

▲**Würzburg** Residenz complex (with a palace, manicured gardens, and dazzling Rococo chapel) and lively wine bars and restaurants.

▲**Frankfurt** Europe's bustling banking center, offering a stunning skyscraper skyline and a look at today's Germany.

▲▲**Rhine Valley** Mighty river steeped in legend, where storybook half-timbered villages (including charming home-base towns Bacharach and St. Goar) cluster under imposing castles, such as Rheinfels and Marksburg.

▲▲**Mosel Valley** Peaceful meandering river lined with tiny wine-loving cobbled towns, such as handy Cochem and quaint Beilstein, plus my favorite European castle, Burg Eltz.

▲**Trier** Germany's oldest city, with a lively pedestrian zone and imposing Roman monuments, including the Porta Nigra gate.

▲**Köln** Spectacular Gothic cathedral looming above a busy, museum-packed riverside city.

▲▲**Nürnberg** City with old-fashioned sandstone core and great museums, along with reminders of the Nazi past thoughtfully presented on the outskirts of town.

▲**Lutherland** Charming university town of Erfurt, where Martin Luther spent his youth; Wartburg Castle, where he hid out from the pope's goons; and Wittenberg, where he taught, preached, and revolutionized Christianity.

▲**Leipzig** Formerly derelict "second city" of East Germany, now rejuvenated (if architecturally dull) with excellent Bach and Cold War sights, and a funky nightlife district.

▲▲**Dresden** Art-filled city offering exquisite museums, Baroque palaces, a delightful riverside promenade, and hard memories of a notorious WWII firebombing.

Görlitz Undiscovered town on the Polish border, filled with architectural gems.

▲▲▲**Berlin** Germany's vibrant and now-reunited capital, featuring world-class museums, gleaming modern architecture, and trendy nightlife, along with evocative monuments and memories of The Wall that once divided the city and country.

▲**Hamburg** Big port city with emigration, World War II, and Beatles history.

trails, very long days (light until after 21:00), and the busiest schedule of tourist fun.

Travel during "shoulder season" (May, June, Sept, and early Oct) is easier and can be a bit less expensive. Shoulder-season travelers usually enjoy smaller crowds, decent weather, the full range of sights and tourist fun spots, and the ability to grab a room almost whenever and wherever they like—often at a flexible price. Also, in fall, fun harvest and wine festivals enliven many towns and villages, while forests and vineyards display beautiful fiery colors.

Winter travelers find concert seasons in full swing, with absolutely no crowds, but some accommodations and sights are either closed or run on a limited schedule. Confirm your sightseeing plans locally, especially when traveling off-season. The weather can be cold and dreary, and nightfall draws the shades on sightseeing well before dinnertime. But dustings of snow turn German towns and landscapes into a wonderland, and December offers the chance to wander through Germany's famous Christmas markets. (For more information, see the climate chart in the appendix.)

Know Before You Go

Your trip is more likely to go smoothly if you plan ahead. Check this list of things to arrange while you're still at home.

You need a **passport**—but no visa or shots—to travel in Germany. You may be denied entry into certain European countries if your passport is due to expire within three to six months of your ticketed date of return. Get it renewed if you'll be cutting it close. It can take up to six weeks to get or renew a passport (for more on passports, see www.travel.state.gov). Pack a photocopy of your passport in your luggage in case the original is lost or stolen.

Book your rooms well in advance if you'll be traveling during peak season or any major **holidays or festivals,** such as Oktoberfest in Munich (see list on page 846). Try to schedule visits to **Frankfurt** and **Köln** outside of convention season to keep your hotel costs down.

To avoid peak-season lines at **Neuschwanstein Castle,** reserve tickets ahead on their website, by email, or by phone; see page 136 for tips.

For a **Munich BMW factory tour,** sign up online or phone far in advance (see page 92).

To visit the **Reichstag dome in Berlin,** reserve a free entry slot online a week or two in advance (see page 667).

To see **Dresden's Historic Green Vault,** book your tickets online, by email, or by phone at least a week or two before your visit. Or take your chances and line up early for same-day tickets (see page 606).

Tickets for the music-packed **Salzburg Festival** (late July

Top Destinations in Germany

HAMBURG

GERMANY

NEAR BERLIN

BERLIN

KÖLN

LUTHERLAND

GÖRLITZ

RHINE VALLEY

LEIPZIG

DRESDEN

MOSEL VALLEY

FRANKFURT

WÜRZBURG

TRIER

NÜRNBERG

ROTHENBURG & ROMANTIC ROAD

BADEN-BADEN & BLACK FOREST

MUNICH

BAVARIA & TIROL

SALZBURG (AUSTRIA) & BERCHTESGADEN

through August) can go fast. Consider buying tickets ahead if there's a specific event you want to see; for details, see page 204.

Call your **debit- and credit-card companies** to let them know the countries you'll be visiting, to ask about fees, and more (see page 14).

Do your homework if you want to buy **travel insurance.** Compare the cost of the insurance to the likelihood of your using it and your potential loss if something goes wrong. For details, see www.ricksteves.com/insurance.

If you're bringing a mobile device, you can download free information from **Rick Steves Audio Europe,** featuring hours of travel interviews and other audio content on Germany (via www .ricksteves.com/audioeurope, iTunes, or the Rick Steves Audio Europe free smartphone app; for details, see page 842).

If you're planning on **renting a car** in Germany, you'll need to bring your driver's license. Many German cities—including Munich, Freiburg, Frankfurt, Köln, Dresden, and Berlin—require drivers to buy a **special sticker** *(Umweltplakette)* to drive in the

Germany's Best Three-Week Trip by Car

Day	Plan	Sleep in
1	Fly into Frankfurt, pick up car, to Rhine	Bacharach
2	Rhine Valley	Bacharach
3	To Mosel Valley	Beilstein or Trier
4	Mosel Valley and/or Trier	Beilstein or Trier
5	To Baden-Baden	Baden-Baden
6	Relax and soak in Baden-Baden	Baden-Baden
7	Drive through the Black Forest	Staufen or Freiburg
8	To Bavaria and Tirol	Füssen or Reutte
9	Bavaria/Tirol and castles	Füssen or Reutte
10	More Bavaria/Tirol, then to Munich	Munich
11	Munich	Munich
12	More Munich, or side-trip to Salzburg	Munich
13	To Dachau, then follow Romantic Road to Rothenburg	Rothenburg
14	Rothenburg	Rothenburg
15	To Würzburg, drop off car*, then train to Nürnberg	Nürnberg or Würzburg
16	Nürnberg	Nürnberg
17	Train to Dresden	Dresden
18	Train to Berlin	Berlin
19	Berlin	Berlin
20	Berlin	Berlin
21	Fly home	

*After Day 15, you're visiting well-connected cities, making a car unnecessary. Drop the car in Würzburg to save several days of car-rental costs and parking fees.

Smaller Towns vs. Bigger Towns: This itinerary (especially the first half) is heavy on half-timbered villages—a German specialty. But for some, a little cuteness goes a long way. Depending on your preference, you can plan your overnights either to maximize or reduce quaintness. For example, for Days 3-4, 7, and 15, you can opt for smaller towns (Beilstein, Staufen, and mid-size Würzburg) or for bigger cities (Trier, Freiburg, and Nürnberg).

With Less Time: This trip can be pared down to two weeks by making the following changes: Skip the Mosel (a sleepier version of the Rhine), and go directly from the Rhine to Baden-Baden. From Baden-Baden, head straight for Füssen/Reutte instead of overnighting in Staufen/Freiburg. Skip the Salzburg side-trip; choose between Würzburg and Nürnberg, and stay just one night there; and reduce the stay in Berlin to two nights.

OVERNIGHTS
OTHER STOPS

200 Miles
200 Kilometer

GERMANY

Hamburg

Berlin

POLAND

Wittenberg

Görlitz

Leipzig

Dresden

RHINE
VALLEY
Bacharach

Erfurt

MOSEL
VALLEY

Frankfurt

Prague

Beilstein

Würzburg

LUX.

Trier

Nürnberg

CZECH.
REP.

Rothenburg

Baden-
Baden

BAVARIA

FRANCE

Freiburg

Dachau

Munich

Staufen

DCH

Zürich

Reutte

Füssen

TIROL

Salzburg

Berchtesgaden

SWITZ.

AUSTRIA

With More Time: Berlin and Salzburg are each easily worth another day. Depending on your interests, you could stay a day in Frankfurt (upon arrival); add another day for the Rhine to visit Köln from Bacharach; and see the town of Görlitz as a side-trip from Dresden (or as a detour en route to Berlin). The Martin Luther towns (Erfurt and Wittenburg) and Leipzig fit well between towns to the west and south (Frankfurt, Nürnberg) and those in the north and east (Berlin, Dresden). Hamburg isn't on the way to anything, but it's a worthwhile detour for those interested in its history.

By Train: This itinerary is designed to be done by car, but could be done by train with some modifications: Skip the southern Black Forest and take the train from Baden-Baden to Munich, which works well as a home base for visiting Bavaria and Salzburg. Then take the train or bus to Rothenburg; from there, Würzburg, Nürnberg, and Dresden are all on the way to Berlin. Or, for the best of both worlds, consider using trains to connect major cities, and then renting a car strategically to explore worthwhile countryside regions (such as Bavaria/Tirol).

city center (see page 840).

Consider buying a **railpass** after researching your options (see page 828 and www.ricksteves.com/rail for all the specifics).

Because **airline carry-on restrictions** are always changing, visit the Transportation Security Administration's website (www .tsa.gov/travelers) for an up-to-date list of what you can bring on the plane with you...and what you must check.

Practicalities

Emergency and Medical Help: In Germany, dial 112 for police help or a medical emergency. If you get sick, do as the Germans do and go to a pharmacist for advice. Or ask at your hotel for help—they'll know the nearest medical and emergency services.

Theft or Loss: To replace a passport, you'll need to go in person to your embassy (see page 823). If your credit and debit cards disappear, cancel and replace them (see "Damage Control for Lost Cards" on page 16). File a police report, either on the spot or within a day or two; it's required to submit an insurance claim for lost or stolen railpasses or travel gear, and can help with replacing your passport or credit and debit cards. For more information, see www.ricksteves.com/help. Precautionary measures can minimize the effects of loss: Back up photos and other files frequently, and use passwords to protect any sensitive data on your electronic devices.

Time Zones: Germany, like most of continental Europe, is generally six/nine hours ahead of the East/West Coasts of the US. The exceptions are the beginning and end of Daylight Saving Time: Europe "springs forward" the last Sunday in March (two weeks after most of North America) and "falls back" the last Sunday in October (one week before North America). For a handy online time converter, see www.timeanddate.com/worldclock.

Business Hours: In Germany, most shops are open from about 9:00 until 18:00-20:00 on weekdays, but close early on Saturday (generally between 12:00 and 17:00, depending on whether you're in a town or a big city). Sundays have the same pros and cons as they do for travelers in the US (special events, limited hours for sights, banks and many shops closed, no rush hours, less frequent public transportation). By law, stores must close by 22:00, but very few stay open that late. The law makes an exception for shops in train stations, which often have grocery stores that are open long hours. Bank hours vary depending on where you are: They generally open Monday-Friday around 9:00, and close anywhere between 15:00 and 19:00. Some branches close for an hour or two at lunchtime. Catholic regions, including Bavaria, shut down during religious holidays (see page 846). Turkish-owned shops are often open later than other stores. Many museums and sights are closed on Monday.

Watt's Up? Europe's electrical system is 220 volts, instead of North America's 110 volts. Most newer electronics (such as laptops, battery chargers, and hair dryers) convert automatically, so you won't need a converter plug, but you will need an adapter plug with two round prongs, sold inexpensively at travel stores in the US. Avoid bringing older appliances that don't automatically convert voltage; instead, buy a cheap replacement in Europe.

Discounts: Discounts are not listed in this book. However, seniors (age 60 and over), youths under 18, and students and teachers with proper identification cards (www.isic.org) can get discounts at many sights. Always ask. Some discounts are available only for EU citizens.

News: Americans keep in touch via the *International Herald Tribune* (published almost daily throughout Europe and online at www.iht.com). Another informative site is http://news.bbc.co.uk. Every Tuesday, the European editions of *Time* and *Newsweek* hit the stands with articles of particular interest to travelers in Europe. Sports addicts can get their daily fix online or from *USA Today*. Many hotels have CNN or BBC News television channels.

Money

This section offers advice on how to pay for purchases on your trip (including getting cash from ATMs and paying with plastic), dealing with lost or stolen cards, VAT (sales tax) refunds, and tipping.

What to Bring

Bring both a credit card and a debit card. You'll use the debit card at cash machines (ATMs) to withdraw euros for most purchases, and the credit card to pay for larger items. Some travelers carry a third card, in case one gets demagnetized or eaten by a temperamental machine.

For an emergency reserve, bring several hundred dollars in hard cash in easy-to-exchange $20 bills. Avoid using currency exchange booths (lousy rates and/or outrageous fees); if you have foreign currency to exchange, take it to a bank. Don't use traveler's checks—they're not worth the fees or long waits at slow banks.

Cash

Expect to use cash for most purchases. Small businesses (hotels, restaurants, and shops) prefer that you pay your bills with cash. Some vendors will charge you extra for using a credit card, and many won't take credit cards at all. Cash is the best—and sometimes only—way to pay for bus fare, taxis, and local guides.

Exchange Rate

1 euro (€) = about $1.40

To convert prices in euros to dollars, add about 40 percent: €20 = about $28, €50 = about $70. (Check www.oanda.com for the latest exchange rates.) Just like the dollar, one euro (€) is broken down into 100 cents. Coins range from €0.01 to €2, and bills from €5 to €500.

Throughout Europe, ATMs are the standard way for travelers to get cash. Most ATMs in Germany are located outside of a bank. Try to use the ATM when the branch is open; if your card is munched by a machine, you can immediately go inside for help.

To withdraw money from an ATM (known as a *Geldautomat* in Germany; *Bankomat* in Austria), you'll need a debit card (ideally with a Visa or MasterCard logo for maximum usability), plus a PIN code. Know your PIN code in numbers, because there are only numbers—no letters—on European keypads. For security, it's best to shield the keypad when entering your PIN at the ATM. Although you can use a credit card for ATM transactions, it's generally more expensive (because it's considered a "cash advance" rather than a "withdrawal").

When using an ATM, taking out large sums of money can reduce the number of per-transaction bank fees you'll pay. If the machine refuses your request, try again and select a smaller amount (some cash machines limit the amount you can withdraw—don't take it personally). If that doesn't work, try a different machine.

It's easier to pay for purchases with smaller bills; if the ATM gives you big bills, try to break them at major museums or larger stores.

To keep your cash safe, use a money belt—a pouch with a strap that you buckle around your waist like a belt and wear under your clothes. Pickpockets target tourists. A money belt provides peace of mind, allowing you to carry lots of cash safely. Don't waste time every few days tracking down a cash machine—withdraw a week's worth of money, stuff it in your money belt, and travel!

Credit and Debit Cards

Many shops and restaurants in Germany don't accept plastic (except for the local "EC" debit cards). Larger hotels, restaurants, and shops that take US cards more commonly accept Visa and MasterCard than American Express. I typically use my debit card to withdraw cash to pay for most purchases. I use my credit card only in a few specific situations: to book hotel reservations by phone, to cover major expenses (such as car rentals, plane tickets, and long hotel stays), and to pay for things near the end of my trip (to avoid another visit to the ATM). While you could use a debit card to make most large purchases, using a credit card offers a greater degree of fraud protection (because debit cards draw funds directly from your account).

Ask Your Credit- or Debit-Card Company: Before your trip, contact the company that issued your debit or credit cards.

• Confirm your card will work overseas, and alert them that you'll be using it in Europe; otherwise, they may deny transactions if they perceive unusual spending patterns.

• Ask for the specifics on transaction **fees.** When you use your credit or debit card—either for purchases or ATM withdrawals—you'll often be charged additional "international transaction" fees of up to 3 percent (1 percent is normal) plus $5 per transaction. If your card's fees are too high, consider getting a card just for your trip: Capital One (credit cards only, www.capitalone.com) and most credit unions have low-to-no international fees.

• If you plan to withdraw cash from ATMs, confirm your daily **withdrawal limit** (€300 is usually the maximum). Some travelers prefer a high limit that allows them to take out more cash at each ATM stop, while others prefer to set a lower limit in case their card is stolen.

• Ask for your credit card's **PIN** code in case you encounter Europe's "chip-and-PIN" system; since they're unlikely to tell you your PIN over the phone, allow time for the bank to mail it to you.

Chip and PIN: If your card is declined for a purchase in Europe, it may be because of chip and PIN, which requires card-holders to punch in a PIN instead of signing a receipt. While chip and PIN is not yet common in Germany, much of Europe is adopting it. Some merchants rely on it exclusively. If, when you're using your card, you're prompted to enter your PIN but don't know it, ask if the cashier can swipe your card and print a receipt for you to sign instead; if not, just pay cash. You're most likely to encounter chip and PIN at automated payment machines—such as those at train and subway stations, toll roads, parking garages, luggage lockers, bike-rental kiosks, and self-serve pumps at gas stations. If a machine won't take your card, look for a cashier nearby who can make your card work, or see if one of the machines takes cash.

You can avoid potential hassles by getting your own chip-and-PIN card just for your trip, but so far your options are limited. Chase offers a Visa credit card with a chip, called J. P. Morgan Select, but it comes with a hefty annual fee and requires a stellar credit rating. Travelex has a chip-and-PIN cash card called "Cash Passport" that's preloaded with euros and sold at many airports;

however, it comes with exorbitant exchange rates and only works at places that accept MasterCard. While handy, these cards are probably not worth it unless you're staying for several weeks in a country that's converted to chip-and-PIN cards, and you're willing to pay for the convenience.

Dynamic Currency Conversion: If merchants offer to convert your purchase price into dollars (called dynamic currency conversion, or DCC), refuse this "service." You'll pay even more in fees for the expensive convenience of seeing your charge in dollars.

Damage Control for Lost Cards

If you lose your credit, debit, or ATM card, you can stop people from using it by reporting the loss immediately to the respective global customer-assistance centers. Call these 24-hour US numbers collect: Visa (410/581-9994), MasterCard (636/722-7111), and American Express (623/492-8427).

At a minimum, you'll need to know the name of the financial institution that issued you the card, along with the type of card (classic, platinum, or whatever). Providing the following information will allow for a quicker cancellation of your missing card: full card number, whether you are the primary or secondary cardholder, the cardholder's name exactly as printed on the card, billing address, home phone number, circumstances of the loss or theft, and identification verification (your birth date, your mother's maiden name, or your Social Security number—memorize this, don't carry a copy). If you are the secondary cardholder, you'll also need to provide the primary cardholder's identification-verification details. You can generally receive a temporary card within two or three business days in Europe (see www.ricksteves.com/help).

If you promptly report your card lost or stolen, you typically won't be responsible for any unauthorized transactions on your account, although many banks charge a liability fee of $50.

Tipping

Tipping in Germany isn't as automatic and generous as it is in the US, but for special service, tips are appreciated, if not expected. As in the US, the proper amount depends on your resources, tipping philosophy, and the circumstance, but some general guidelines apply.

Restaurants: Tipping is an issue only at restaurants that have table service. If you order your food at a counter, don't tip. At German restaurants that have a wait staff, a service charge is generally included in the bill, although it's common to round up after a good meal (usually 5-10 percent; so, for an €18.50 meal, pay €20). Give the tip directly to your server. Rather than leaving coins, Germans usually pay with paper, saying how much they'd like the bill to be. For example, for an €8.10 meal, you can hand over a €20 bill and say *"Neun Euro"*—"Nine euros"—to include a €0.90 tip and get €11 change.

Taxis: To tip the cabbie, round up. For a typical ride, round up about 5-10 percent (for instance, to pay a €4.50 fare, give €5; for a €28 fare, give €30). If the cabbie hauls your bags and zips you to the airport to help you catch your flight, you might want to toss in a little more. But if you feel like you're being driven in circles or otherwise ripped off, skip the tip.

Special Services: It's thoughtful to tip a euro to someone who shows you a special sight and who is paid in no other way. Tour guides at public sights sometimes hold out their hands for tips after they give their spiel. If I've already paid for the tour, I don't tip extra unless they've really impressed me. At hotels, if you let porters carry your luggage, it's polite to give them a euro per bag (another reason to pack light). If you like to tip maids, leave a euro per overnight at the end of your stay.

In general, if someone in the service industry does a super job for you, a small tip (the equivalent of a euro or two) is appropriate...but not required.

When in doubt, ask. If you're not sure whether (or how much) to tip for a service, ask your hotelier or the TI; they'll fill you in on how it's done on their turf.

Getting a VAT Refund

Wrapped into the purchase price of your German souvenirs is a Value-Added Tax (VAT) of about 19 percent. You're entitled to get most of that tax back if you purchase more than €25 (about $35) worth of goods at a store that participates in the VAT-refund scheme. Typically, you must ring up the minimum at a single retailer—you can't add up your purchases from various shops to reach the required amount.

Getting your refund is usually straightforward and, if you buy a substantial amount of souvenirs, well worth the hassle. If you're lucky, the merchant will subtract the tax when you make your purchase. (This is more likely to occur if the store ships the goods to your home.) Otherwise, you'll need to:

Get the paperwork. Have the merchant completely fill out the necessary refund document, called a "Tax-Free Shopping Cheque." You'll need to present your passport at the store. Be sure to retain your original sales receipt.

Get your stamp at the border or airport. Process your VAT document at your last stop in the EU (e.g., at the airport) with the customs agent who deals with VAT refunds. Before checking in for your flight, find the local customs office, and be prepared to stand in line. It's best to keep your purchases in your carry-on for viewing, but if they're too large or dangerous to carry on (such as knives), have your purchases easily accessible in the bag you're about to check, ready to show the customs agent. You're not supposed to use your purchased goods before you leave. If you show up at customs wearing your new lederhosen, officials might look the other way—or deny you a refund.

Collect your refund. You'll need to return your stamped document to the retailer or its representative. Many merchants work with a service, such as Global Blue (www.global-blue.com) or Premier Tax Free (www.premiertaxfree.com), which have offices at major airports, ports, or border crossings (after check-in and security, probably strategically located near a duty-free shop). These services, which extract a 4 percent fee, can refund your money immediately in cash or credit your card (within two billing cycles). If the retailer handles VAT refunds directly, it's up to you to contact the merchant for your refund. You can mail the documents from home or, more quickly, from your point of departure (using a stamped, self-addressed envelope you've prepared or one that's been provided by the merchant). You'll then have to wait—it could take months.

Customs for American Shoppers

You are allowed to take home $800 worth of items per person duty-free, once every 30 days. You can also bring in duty-free a liter of alcohol. As for food, you can take home many processed and packaged foods: vacuum-packed cheeses, dried herbs, jams, chocolate, oil, vinegar, and honey. Fresh fruits and vegetables and most meats are not allowed. Any liquid-containing foods must be packed in checked luggage, a potential recipe for disaster. To check customs rules and duty rates, visit www.cbp.gov.

Sightseeing

Sightseeing can be hard work. Use these tips to make your visits to Germany's finest sights meaningful, fun, efficient, and painless.

Plan Ahead

Set up an itinerary that allows you to fit in all your must-see sights. For a one-stop look at opening hours, see the "At a Glance" sidebars for Munich, Salzburg, Berlin, and Hamburg. Most sights keep stable hours, but you can easily confirm the latest by checking with the TI or visiting museums' websites.

Don't put off visiting a must-see sight—you never know when a place will close unexpectedly for a strike or restoration. On holidays or during festivals (see list on page 846), expect reduced hours or closures. Off-season, many museums have shorter hours.

When possible, visit major sights in the morning (when your energy is best), and save other activities for the afternoon. At sights, hit the highlights first, then go back to other things if you have the time and stamina.

Going at the right time helps avoid crowds. This book offers tips on specific sights, such as Neuschwanstein Castle. Make reservations when possible, or try visiting popular sights very early, at lunch, or very late. Evening visits are usually peaceful, with fewer crowds.

Study up. To get the most out of the self-guided walks and sight descriptions in this book, read them before you visit.

At Sights

Here's what you can typically expect:

Some important sights may have metal detectors or conduct bag searches that will slow your entry, while others may require you to check daypacks and coats. They'll be kept safely. If you have something you can't bear to part with, stash it in a pocket or purse. To avoid checking a small backpack, carry it under your arm like a purse as you enter. From a guard's point of view, a backpack is generally a problem, while a purse is not.

Flash photography is often banned, but taking photos without a flash is usually allowed. Look for signs or ask. Flashes damage oil paintings and distract others in the room. Even without a flash, a handheld camera will take a decent picture (or you can buy postcards or posters at the museum bookstore). If photos are permitted, video cameras are generally OK, too.

Museums may have special exhibits in addition to their permanent collection. Some exhibits are included in the entry price; others come at an extra cost (which you may have to pay even if you don't want to see the exhibit).

Expect changes—artwork can be on tour, on loan, out sick, or shifted at the whim of the curator. To adapt, pick up any available free floor plans as you enter, and ask museum staff if you can't find a particular item.

Many sights rent audioguides, which generally offer useful recorded descriptions in English (about $4.50; often included with admission). If you bring along your own pair of headphones and a Y-jack, you can sometimes share one audioguide with your travel partner and save money.

Guided tours in English are most likely to be available during peak season (they can be included with your admission or cost up to $10, and range wildly in quality). If sights offer short films featuring their highlights and history, they're generally well worth your time. I make it standard operating procedure to ask when I arrive at a sight if there is a film in English.

Important sights often have an on-site café or cafeteria (usually a good place to rest and have a snack or light meal). The WCs at many sights are free and generally clean (it's smart to carry tissues in case a WC runs out of TP).

Many places sell postcards that highlight their attractions. Before you leave a sight, scan the postcards and thumb through the biggest guidebook (or skim its index) to be sure you haven't overlooked something that you'd like to see.

Most sights stop admitting people 30-60 minutes before closing time, and some rooms close early (often about 45 minutes before the actual closing time). Guards usher people out, so don't save the best for last.

Every sight or museum offers more than what is covered in this book. Use the information in this book as an introduction—not the final word.

Sightseeing Passes

In some cities, you can buy a combo-ticket for discounted entry to two or more sights. I've noted these in this book. If you'll be visiting several castles in Bavaria—including two of "Mad" King Ludwig's castles, and those in Munich, Würzburg, Nürnberg, and more—look into the **Bavarian Castles Pass,** which can save you a lot of money (€24/1 person, €40/2 adults plus children, valid 14 days; described on page 122).

Sleeping

Good-value accommodations in Germany are generally easy to find, comfortable, and include a hearty breakfast (typically an all-you-can-eat buffet). Choose from hotels; smaller, cheaper hotels and bed-and-breakfasts (called *Gasthof, Gasthaus,* or *Pension*); rooms in private homes (advertised as *Zimmer Frei*); self-catering apartments rented by the week *(Ferienwohnung);* and hostels *(Jugendherberge).*

Book your accommodations well in advance if you'll be traveling during busy times. See page 846 for a list of major holidays and festivals in Germany; for tips on making reservations, see page 24.

I favor hotels and restaurants that are handy to your sightseeing activities. Rather than list hotels scattered throughout a city, I choose two or three favorite neighborhoods and recommend the best accommodations values in each, from dorm beds to fancy doubles with all the comforts.

A major feature of this book is its extensive listing of good-value rooms. I like places that are clean, central, relatively quiet at night, reasonably priced, friendly, English-speaking, small

Sleep Code

(€1 = about $1.40, country code: 49)

To help you sort easily through my listings, I've divided the accommodations into three categories based on the price for a double room with bath during high season:

$$$	**Higher Priced**
$$	**Moderately Priced**
$	**Lower Priced**

I always rate hostels as $, whether or not they have double rooms, because they have the cheapest beds in town. Prices can change without notice; verify the hotel's current rates online or by email. For other updates, see www.rick steves.com/update.

Abbreviations

To pack maximum information into minimum space, I use the following code to describe accommodations in this book. Prices listed are per room, not per person. When a price range is given for a type of room (such as double rooms listing for €100-150), it means the price fluctuates with the season, day of week, size of room, or length of stay; expect to pay the upper end for peak-season stays.

S = Single room (or price for one person in a double).

D = Double or twin room. "Double beds" can be two twins sheeted together and are usually big enough for nonromantic couples.

T = Triple (generally a double bed with a single).

Q = Quad (usually two double beds; adding an extra child's bed to a T is usually cheaper).

b = Private bathroom with toilet and shower or tub.

s = Private shower or tub only (the toilet is down the hall).

According to this code, a couple staying at a "Db-€100" hotel would pay a total of €100 (about $140) for a double room with a private bathroom. Unless otherwise noted, breakfast is included, hotel staff speak basic English, and credit cards are accepted.

If I mention "Internet access" in a listing, there's a public terminal in the lobby for guests to use. If I say there's "Wi-Fi" or "cable Internet," you can generally access it in public areas and often (though not always) in your room, but only if you have your own laptop or other Wi-Fi device.

enough to have a hands-on owner and stable staff, run with a respect for German traditions, and not listed in other guidebooks. (In Germany, for me, six out of these nine criteria mean it's a keeper.) I'm more impressed by a convenient location and a fun-loving philosophy than flat-screen TVs and shoeshine machines.

At some establishments, singles are actually double rooms used by one person—so they cost about the same as a double. Single travelers get the best value at other places (usually smaller ones) where the price of a single is only a little more than half that of a double. This includes hostels, which always charge per person. In contrast, groups of four adults can often snare a four-bed room (with its own bath) in a hotel or B&B for about the same price a hostel would charge.

I've noted family-friendly hotels in the listings. Families do well to send an email with the ages of all those traveling and let the staff suggest a good-value configuration. Most hotels give families with smaller children a discounted triple or quad room, and a few let children as old as 12 stay free.

Especially in vacation areas and in private homes, where the boss changes the sheets, people staying several nights are most desirable. Some hotels phrase this as a discount for longer stays, while others call it a surcharge for one-nighters. At some resort towns such as Baden-Baden, visitors have to pay a small spa tax (per person and per night) that's added to their bill.

Air-conditioning is rare (and rarely needed). If you're here during a heat spell, ask to borrow a fan. Learn how the windows work: You'll often find the windows tipped open from the top to air out the room, with the window handle pointing up. To close the window, push it in and rotate the handle so it points down. The third handle position is horizontal, which lets you swing the entire window open.

In Germany, as elsewhere in northern Europe, beds don't come with a top sheet or blankets, but only with a comforter. A double bed comes with two comforters—rather than one bigger one. What's more, a double bed, even one intended for married couples, typically has two separate mattresses and sometimes two separate (but adjacent) frames. (A "real" double bed with a single mattress is called a *Französisches Bett*—a French bed.) Rooms with truly separate twin beds are less common in German hotels. When Americans request separate beds, German hotels often give them normal doubles with complete sincerity—reasoning that the mattresses, though adjacent, are separate.

Most hostels and some hotels and B&Bs offer half-board *(Halbpension)*, which means that dinner is included in the room price. This is often a good deal and gets you a hassle-free value-priced three-course meal, but limits your choices. A few hotels (including the Ibis chain) give you the option of skipping breakfast and paying less. Although German hotel breakfasts are usually excellent, you can buy breakfast easily and cheaply at a bakery or supermarket—the savings adds up, especially for families.

Because the train system in Germany is convenient and popular, both locals and foreigners have discovered that staying near the station saves hauling your luggage by foot or taxi. The concept of the train station hotel, which went out of favor during the 20th century, is making a big comeback in Germany. Frankfurt, Würzburg, Füssen, Munich, Köln, Dresden, Nürnberg, and Baden-Baden are among the destinations in this book that have good-value lodgings within steps of the train station.

Travel Review Websites: TripAdvisor (www.tripadvisor.com) and similar review websites are popular tools for finding hotels, but have drawbacks. To write a review, people need only an email address—making it easy to hide their true identity. If a hotel is well reviewed in a guidebook or two, and also gets good ratings on TripAdvisor, it's probably a safe bet—but I wouldn't stay at a hotel based solely on a TripAdvisor recommendation.

Rates and Deals

I've described my recommended accommodations using a Sleep Code (see the sidebar). Prices listed are for one-night stays in peak season, most include breakfast and assume you're booking directly (not through a TI or online hotel-booking engine). Book direct. Using an online booking service costs the hotel about 20 percent and logically closes the door on special deals.

Given the economic downturn, hoteliers are willing and eager to make a deal. I'd suggest emailing several hotels to ask for their best price. Comparison-shop and make your choice.

In general, prices can soften if you do any of the following: offer to pay cash, stay at least three nights, or mention this book. You can also try asking for a cheaper room or a discount, or offer to skip breakfast.

As you look over the listings, you'll notice that some accommodations promise special prices to my readers who book direct (without using a room-finding service or hotel-booking website, which take a commission). To get these rates, you must mention this book when you reserve, and then show the book upon arrival. Some readers with ebooks have reported difficulty getting a Rick Steves discount. If this happens to you, please show this to the hotelier: Rick Steves discounts apply to readers with ebooks as well as printed books.

Making Reservations

Given the good value of the accommodations I've found for this book, I recommend that you reserve your rooms in advance, particularly if you'll be traveling during peak season. Book several weeks ahead, or as soon as you've pinned down your travel dates. Note that some holidays and festivals jam things up and merit your making reservations far in advance (see page 846).

Phoning: To call Germany from the US or Canada, dial 011-49, then the area code (drop the initial 0), then the local number. (The 011 is our international access code, and 49 is Germany's country code.) If you're calling Germany from another European country, dial 00-49, the area code (without the initial 0), then the local number. (The 00 is Europe's international access code.) To make calls within Germany, dial just the local number if you're calling within the same area code. If you're calling long distance, dial the area code (which starts with a 0), then the local number. For more tips on calling, see page 816.

Requesting a Reservation: To make a reservation, contact hotels directly by email, phone, or fax. Email is the clearest and most economical way to make a reservation, or you can go straight to the hotel website. Many have secure online reservation forms and can instantly inform you of availability and any special deals. But be sure you use the hotel's official site and not a booking agency's site; otherwise you may pay higher rates than you should. If phoning from the US, be mindful of time zones (see page 12). Most recommended hotels are accustomed to guests who speak only English.

The hotelier wants to know these key pieces of information (also included in the sample request form in the appendix):

- number and type of rooms
- number of nights
- date of arrival
- date of departure
- any special needs (e.g., bathroom in the room or down the hall, twin beds vs. double bed, air-conditioning, quiet, view, ground floor, etc.)

When you request a room, use the European style for writing dates: day/month/year. For example, for a two-night stay in July, I would request "1 double room for 2 nights, arrive 16/07/12, depart 18/07/12." Consider carefully how long you'll stay; don't assume you can tack on extra days once you arrive. Make sure you mention any discounts—for Rick Steves readers or otherwise—when you make the reservation.

Confirming a Reservation: If the hotel's response includes its room availability and rates, it's not a confirmation. You must tell them that you want that room at the given rate. Most hoteliers will request your credit-card number to hold the room. While you can email your credit-card information (I do), it's safer to share that confidential info via phone call, fax, split between two emails, or via a secure online reservation form (if the hotel has one on its website).

Canceling a Reservation: If you must cancel your reservation, it's courteous to do so with as much advance notice as possible. Simply make a quick phone call or send an email. Family-run hotels lose money if they turn away customers while holding a room for someone who doesn't show up. Understandably, many hotels bill no-shows for one night.

Cancellation policies can be strict: For example, you might lose a deposit if you cancel within two weeks of your reserved stay, or you might be billed for the entire visit if you leave early. Internet deals may require prepayment, with no refunds for cancellations. Ask about cancellation policies before you book.

If canceling via email, request confirmation that your cancellation was received to avoid being accidentally billed.

Reconfirming Your Reservation: Always call to reconfirm your room reservation a day or two in advance from the road. (Don't have a TI call for you; they may take a commission.) Smaller hotels and pensions appreciate knowing your estimated time of arrival. If you'll be arriving late (after 17:00), let them know. On the small chance that a hotel loses track of your reservation, bring along a hard copy of their emailed or faxed confirmation.

Reserving Rooms as You Travel: You can make reservations as you travel, calling hotels a few days to a week before your arrival. If everything's full, don't despair. Call a day or two in advance and fill in a cancellation. If you'd rather travel without any reservations at all, you'll have greater success snaring rooms if you arrive at your destination early in the day. When you anticipate crowds (weekends are worst), call hotels at about 9:00 or 10:00 on the day you plan to arrive, when the hotel clerk knows who'll be checking out and just which rooms will be available. If you encounter a language barrier, ask the fluent receptionist at your current hotel to call for you.

Types of Accommodations
Hotels

In this book, the price for a double room in a hotel ranges from €45 (very simple, toilet and shower down the hall) to €200-plus (maximum plumbing and the works). In small towns such as Bacharach or Rothenburg, you can find a good double with a private bath for under €60; in more expensive cities like Munich or Trier, you'll usually pay at least €85.

Room prices depend on the season and the day of the week, but peak times vary from one town to the next. Low season in Rothenburg is January-March, in Füssen it's October-May, and in Nürnberg it's July and August. While weekends are cheaper in Frankfurt and Nürnberg, weekdays are cheaper in Trier, Dresden, and Füssen. Munich hotels keep the same prices all week.

Hotel lobbies, halls, and breakfast rooms are off-limits to smokers, though they can light up in their rooms. Most hotels have non-smoking rooms or floors—let them know your preference when you book. Some hotels have gone completely non-smoking.

Bigger hotels commonly have elevators. When you're inside an elevator, press "E" if you want to descend to the "ground floor" (Erdgeschoss).

If you're arriving early in the morning, your room probably won't be ready. You should be able to safely check your bag at the hotel and dive right into sightseeing.

Hoteliers can be a great help and source of advice. Most know their city well, and can assist you with everything from public transit and airport connections to finding a good restaurant, the nearest launderette, or an Internet café. But even at the best places, mechanical breakdowns occur: Air-conditioning malfunctions, sinks leak, hot water turns cold, and toilets gurgle and smell. Report your concerns clearly and calmly at the front desk. For more complicated problems, don't expect instant results.

If you suspect night noise will be a problem (if, for instance, your room is over a nightclub), ask for a quiet room in the back or on an upper floor. To guard against theft in your room, keep valuables out of sight. Some rooms come with a safe, and other hotels have safes at the front desk. Use them if you're concerned.

Checkout can pose problems if surprise charges pop up on your bill. If you settle your bill the night before you leave, you'll have time to discuss and address any points of contention (before 19:00, when the night shift usually arrives).

Above all, don't expect things to be the same as back home. Keep a positive attitude. Remember, you're on vacation. If your hotel is a disappointment, spend more time out enjoying the city you came to see.

INTRODUCTION

Smaller B&Bs (Pensions)

Compared to hotels, bed-and-breakfast places *(Pensions, Gast-häuser, or Gasthöfe)* give you double the cultural intimacy for half the price. While you may lose some of the conveniences of a hotel—such as in-room phones, frequent bed-sheet changes, and the ease of paying with a credit card—I happily make the trade-off for the lower rates and personal touches. If you have a reasonable but limited budget, skip hotels and look for smaller, family-run places.

The smallest establishments consist of private homes with rooms *(Zimmer)* rented out to travelers. Look for *Zimmer Frei* or *Privatzimmer* signs. These are inexpensive—as little as €20 per person with a hearty breakfast—and very common in areas popular with travelers (such as Germany's Rhine, the Romantic Road region, and southern Bavaria, and Austria's Tirol and Salzburg). Signs indicate whether they have available rooms (*Zimmer frei*, green) or not (*Zimmer belegt*, orange). TIs often have a list of private rooms; use the list to book rooms yourself to avoid having the TI take a cut from you and your host.

You'll get your own key to a private room that's clean, comfortable, and simple, though usually homey. Germans, especially in the south, are enthusiastic builders who like showing off their carpentry and decorating skills. Some private rooms are like mini-guesthouses, with a separate entrance and several rooms, each with a private bath. Others are family homes with spare bedrooms (the rooms sometimes lack sinks, but you have free access to the bathroom and shower in the home).

Germans depend heavily on expensive imported fuel and are very aware of their energy use. In any smaller establishment, you'll endear yourself to your hosts if you turn off lights when you leave and avoid excessively long showers.

Hostels

You'll pay about €20 per bed to stay at a *Jugendherberge*. Travelers of any age are welcome if they don't mind dorm-style accommodations and meeting other travelers. Accommodations are usually gender-segregated and dorm-style, in rooms of 4-8 beds. Most hostels offer Internet access, Wi-Fi, a self-service laundry, kitchen facilities, and sometimes cheap meals. Bring a sleeping sheet, or you can rent one at most hostels. Family and private rooms may be available on request.

Independent hostels tend to be easygoing, colorful, and informal (no membership required); see www.hostelz.com, www.hostelseurope.com, www.hostels.com, and www.hostelworld.com. **Official hostels** are part of Hostelling International and adhere to various rules (such as a 17:00 check-in, lockout during the day, a curfew at night); they require that you either have a membership card or pay extra per night (www.hihostels.com).

Vacation Rentals (Ferienwohnungen)

Throughout Germany, you can find reasonably priced rental apartments ideal for families and small groups who want to explore a region. This kind of arrangement is very popular with German travelers on vacation in rural areas.

You usually get a suite of two or three rooms with a kitchen. The owners discourage short stays and usually require a minimum five-day rental, plus a deposit. Hotels and pensions, including those in this book, often have an apartment or two (breakfast is not included, because you have a kitchen). If you'll be in one place for a while, the rate per night usually works out cheaper than in a normal hotel or guesthouse room.

Eating

Germanic cuisine is heavy, hearty, and—by European standards—inexpensive. Though it's tasty, it can get monotonous unless you

look beyond the schnitzel and wurst. Be adventurous. Each region has its specialties, which are often good values. Order house specials whenever possible.

Most German hotels and pensions include breakfast in the room price and pride themselves on laying out an attractive buffet spread. Expect fresh-baked bread and rolls, cereal, yogurt, cold cuts, cheese, fruit, and pastries. Even if you're not a big breakfast eater, take advantage of the buffet to fortify yourself for a day of sightseeing.

When restaurant-hunting, choose a spot filled with locals, not the place with the big neon signs boasting, "We Speak English and Accept Credit Cards." Venturing even a block or two off the main drag leads to higher-quality food for less than half the price of the tourist-oriented places. Locals eat better at lower-rent locales.

Traditional restaurants go by many names. For basic, stick-to-the-ribs meals—and plenty of beer—look for a beer hall *(Bräuhaus)* or beer garden *(Biergarten)*. *Gasthaus, Gasthof, Gaststätte,* and *Gaststube* all loosely describe an informal, inn-type eatery. A *Kneipe* is a bar, and a *Keller* (or *Ratskeller*) is a restaurant or tavern located in a cellar. A *Weinstube* serves wine and usually traditional food as well.

Germans are health-conscious and quite passionate about choosing organic *(Bio)* products: *Bio* fruits and vegetables, and even *Bio* bread, ice cream, and schnitzel. You'll often see footnotes on restaurant menus marking which dishes have artificial ingredients. However, despite Germans' healthy ways, many starchy, high-fat, high-calorie traditional foods remain staples of the German diet.

Most eateries have menus tacked onto their front doors, with an English menu inside. If you see a *Stammtisch* sign hanging over a table at a restaurant or pub, it means that it's reserved for regulars—don't sit here unless invited. Once you're seated, take your time—only a rude waiter will rush you. Good service is relaxed (slow to an American).

To wish others "Happy eating!" offer a cheery *"Guten Appetit!"* When you want the bill, say, *"Zahlen* (TSAH-lehn), *bitte* (please)." For information on tipping, see page 16.

Budget Tips

It's easy to eat a meal for €10 or less in Germany. At lunchtime, locals grab a sandwich (around €2-2.50) and perhaps a pastry (€1-1.50) from one of the ubiquitous bakeries, which often have tables to sit at (but not table service). If there aren't any sandwiches on display at the bakery counter, ask to have one made for you.

Department-store cafeterias (usually on the top floor) are common and handy, and they bridge the language barrier by letting you see your options. A *Schnell Imbiss* is a small fast-food takeaway stand where you can grab a bratwurst or other grilled sausage (usually less than €2, including a roll).

Most restaurants offer inexpensive €6-9 hot-lunch specials that aren't listed on the regular menu (look for the *Tageskarte* or *Tagesangebot*, or just ask—sometimes available at dinner, too). For smaller portions, order from the *kleine Hunger* (small hunger) section of the menu. Simple dishes of wurst with sauerkraut and bread tend to run €5-8. All schnitzeled out? See "Ethnic Food," on the page 31.

Traditional Fare

The classic dish is sausage—hundreds of varieties of *Bratwurst*, *Weisswurst*, and other types of *Wurst* are served with sauerkraut as an excuse for a vegetable (see sidebar next page).

Another ubiquitous meat dish is schnitzel. It's traditionally made with veal, but you'll also find pork schnitzel, which is cheaper. If a dish ends in *-braten*, it means it has been roasted. *Sauerbraten* is a marinated and roasted cut of beef (sometimes pork), typically served with red cabbage and potato dumplings. *Geschnetzeltes* isn't schnitzel, but rather meat that's been diced and cooked in a cream sauce. Many traditional eateries serve some kind of meat on the

Best of the Wurst

Sausage *(Wurst)* is a staple of the Germanic diet. You can get it at restaurants, but it's more traditionally eaten at take-out fast-food stands and counters. Sausage is fast, tasty, very local—and even a chance for culinary adventure, as your options go far beyond the hometown hot dog. Some sausages are boiled *(gekocht),* and some are grilled *(gegrillt).* Most are pork-based. Generally, the darker the weenie, the spicier it is.

The generic term *Bratwurst* simply means "grilled sausage," as opposed to boiled *Brühwurst.* Regional variations of both abound. While some types of *Wurst* can be found all over, others are unique to a particular area (as noted below). Here are some key words:

Frankfurter: A boiled sausage, like our hot dog (also called *Wiener Würstchen*).

Burenwurst: Pork sausage similar to what we'd call "kielbasa."

Beinwurst: Made of smoked pork, herbs, and wine.

Bockwurst: Thick pork sausage (white).

Weisswurst: Boiled white sausage (typically Bavarian; peel off the casing before you eat it), served with sweet mustard and a pretzel.

Currywurst: Grilled red sausage, often chopped into small pieces, with ketchup/curry sauce, served *mit* or *ohne Darm* (with or without skin—with skin tastes smokier; Berlin and eastern Germany).

Nürnberger: Short and spicy grilled pork sausage (Nürnberg and Bavaria).

Thüringer: Long, skinny, peppery, and wedged into a much shorter roll.

Blutwurst, Blunzn: Made from congealed blood.

Käsekrainer: Boiled, with melted cheese inside (Austrian).

Debreziner: Boiled, thin, and spicy, with paprika (Austrian).

Bosna: With onions and sometimes curry (Austrian).

Waldviertler: Smoked sausage (Austrian).

Sauces and sides include *Senf* (mustard; ask for *süss*—sweet; or *scharf*—sharp), *Ketchup, Curry-Ketchup* (a tasty curry-infused ketchup), *Kraut* (sauerkraut), and sometimes horseradish (called *Meerrettich* in the north, *Kren* in the south and Austria).

At sausage stands, you'll most commonly get a roll with your *Wurst* (which won't resemble an American hot-dog bun). Sometimes the sausage is inside the roll; sometimes you get it on a plate with a fork and the roll to the side. You might be given the choice of a slice of bread *(Brot),* a pretzel *(Breze),* or (in restaurants) potato salad instead of a roll. Traditionally, if the wurst is *frisch* (fresh), you're supposed to "eat it before the noon bell tolls."

bone, such as pork knuckle *(Schweinshaxe)* or shoulder, which has been roasted tender and goes down well with a big mug of beer. The fish and venison here are also good.

Besides bread and potatoes (boiled, fried, or grilled), typical starches include *Spätzle* (little noodles made from egg dough scraped through a wide-holed sieve; often served with melted cheese and fried onions as a meal in itself called *Käsespätzle*); various kinds of *Knödel* (baseball-sized dumplings, usually made from potatoes but also from bread); *Schupfnudeln* (stubby, diamond-shaped potato noodles); and *Kartoffelsalat* (potato salad).

Germans make excellent salads, and most menus feature big, varied, dinner-size salad plates. *Spargel* (giant white asparagus) is a must in early summer. If you're visiting in May or June, look for special asparagus menus, created to ensure the nation eats up the yearly crop.

A good dish to try is the southwestern specialty *Maultaschen* ("mouth pockets"), a Swabian version of ravioli with ground meat smuggled inside a big piece of pasta. Some say it was invented by Catholics as a culinary trick to eat meat when it wasn't allowed. The German answer to pizza is *Flammkuchen*, made with a thin, yeastless dough.

Ethnic Food

Ethnic restaurants provide a welcome break from Germanic fare. Italian, Turkish, Greek, and Asian food are generally good values, and Asian restaurants tend to serve inexpensive lunches. An Asian rice or noodle dish, a freshly baked pizza, or a Turkish sandwich will cost you only €3.50-7, and can be packed up to enjoy on a park bench or back in your room.

Originally from Turkey, *Döner Kebab* (sliced meat and vegetables served in pita bread) has become a classic take-out meal for Germans of all stripes (€3-3.50 at any time of day). Turkish cafés abound, even in small towns. Take a moment to study the menu; beyond the basic *Döner,* you can get a *Döner Teller* (on a plate instead of in bread), a *Döner Dürüm* (in a thin, tortilla-like flatbread wrap, also called *Dürüm Kebab* or *Yufka*), falafel (chick-pea croquettes), "Turkish pizzas," and much more.

Snacks and Sweets

Make sure to visit a bakery to browse the selection of fresh pastries and cakes. Pretzels (*Breze* or *Brez'n*), either plain or buttered, make for an inexpensive snack (the brown crust comes from dunking them in water boiled with baking soda or lye). Gummi Bears are local gumdrops with a cult following (look for the Haribo brand). Ice-cream stores, often run by Italian immigrants, abound. While you can always get a cone to go (ask for a *Kugel,* scoop—literally "ball"), many Germans sit down to enjoy their ice cream, ordering fancy sundaes in big glass bowls.

Beverages

Germany has excellent wine and beer. Sampling some helps create fond memories of your trip. The best-known white wines are from the Rhine and Mosel, and there are some good reds, especially from the south. You can order wine by the glass or sometimes by the *Viertel* (quarter-liter, or 8 oz.). Just ask for *"Ein Viertel Weisswein* (white wine) or *Rotwein* (red wine), *bitte."* Order your *Weisswein süss* (sweet), *halb trocken* (medium), or *trocken* (dry). Many hotels serve the inexpensive *Sekt,* or German champagne, at breakfast. *Weinschorle* is a spritzer—white wine pepped up with a little sparkling water.

The average German drinks 40 gallons of beer a year and has a tremendous variety to choose from. *Dunkles* is dark, *helles* or *Lager* is light, *Flaschenbier* is bottled, and *vom Fass* is on tap. *Pils* is barley-based; *Weizen, Hefeweizen,* or *Weissbier* is yeasty and wheat-based; and *Bock* (traditionally brewed by monks) has a higher alcohol content. When you order beer, ask for *eine Halbe* (a half-liter, not always available), or *eine Mass* (a whole liter, or about a quart). *Radler* is half beer and half lemon soda (specify *helles* or *dunkles Radler,* depending on whether you prefer light or dark beer); *Colaweizen* is a mixture of Coke and wheat-based beer.

Teetotalers—or anyone who wants a refreshing beer at lunch without being tipsy all afternoon—find a world of enticing non-alcoholic beer options. Look for *"ohne Alkohol"* or *"alkoholfrei."* While virtually all non-alcoholic brews in the US are watery, bitter lagers, Germany produces some excellent non-alcoholic white beers *(Weisses),* which have a somewhat sweeter flavor—very smooth drinking on a hot day. Better yet, look for the non-alcoholic drink called *Malztrunk* (or *Malzbier*)—the sweet, malted soft drink that children learn with.

Waiters aren't exactly eager to bring you *Leitungswasser* (tap water), preferring that you buy *Mineralwasser* (*mit/ohne Gas,* with/without carbonation). Popular soft drinks include *Apfelschorle* (half apple juice, half sparkling water) and *Spezi* (cola and orange soda). Menus list drink sizes by the tenth of a liter, or deciliter (dl): 0.2 liters is a small glass, and 0.4 or 0.5 is a larger one.

If you buy bottled drinks from a store, you'll have to pay a deposit *(Pfand,* often €0.15), which gets refunded if you return the bottle. The deposit amount is listed in small print on the shelf's price label. While I appreciate Germany's efforts to be green, they make it hard on the tourist, who winds up carrying around empty bottles looking for a place to reclaim their *Pfand.* While legally any place that sells *Pfand* bottles must also buy bottles of

How Was Your Trip?

Were your travels fun, smooth, and meaningful? If you'd like to share your tips, concerns, and discoveries, please fill out the survey at www.ricksteves.com/feedback. I value your feedback. Thanks in advance—it helps a lot.

those same brands, many shops flat-out refuse to accept bottles that they didn't actually sell you. Some supermarkets have vending machine-like bottle-return stations (marked *Flaschenrückgabe* or *Flaschenannahme*); when you're done feeding bottles in, the machine issues a coupon that you can redeem when you pay for your groceries. Easier still, just give returnable bottles to your hotel.

Traveling as a Temporary Local

We travel all the way to Germany to enjoy differences—to become temporary locals. You'll experience frustrations. Certain truths that we find "God-given" or "self-evident," such as cold beer, ice in drinks, bottomless cups of coffee, hot showers, and bigger being better, are suddenly not so true. One of the benefits of travel is the eye-opening realization that there are logical, civil, and even better alternatives. A willingness to go local ensures that you'll enjoy a full dose of German hospitality.

Germans generally like Americans. But if there is a negative aspect to their image of Americans, it's that we are big, loud, aggressive, impolite, rich, superficially friendly, and a bit naive.

While Germans look bemusedly at some of our Yankee excesses—and worriedly at others—they nearly always afford us individual travelers all the warmth we deserve.

Judging from all the happy feedback I receive from travelers who have used this book, it's safe to assume you'll enjoy a great, affordable vacation—with the finesse of an independent, experienced traveler.

Thanks, and *gute Reise!*

Back Door Travel Philosophy
From *Rick Steves' Europe Through the Back Door*

Travel is intensified living—maximum thrills per minute and one of the last great sources of legal adventure. Travel is freedom. It's recess, and we need it.

Experiencing the real Europe requires catching it by surprise, going casual..."Through the Back Door."

Affording travel is a matter of priorities. (Make do with the old car.) You can eat and sleep—simply, safely, and enjoyably—anywhere in Europe for $120 a day plus transportation costs (allow more for bigger cities). In many ways, spending more money only builds a thicker wall between you and what you traveled so far to see. Europe is a cultural carnival, and time after time, you'll find that its best acts are free and the best seats are the cheap ones.

A tight budget forces you to travel close to the ground, meeting and communicating with the people. Never sacrifice sleep, nutrition, safety, or cleanliness to save money. Simply enjoy the local-style alternatives to expensive hotels and restaurants.

Connecting with people carbonates your experience. Extroverts have more fun. If your trip is low on magic moments, kick yourself and make things happen. If you don't enjoy a place, maybe you don't know enough about it. Seek the truth. Recognize tourist traps. Give a culture the benefit of your open mind. See things as different, but not better or worse. Any culture has plenty to share.

Of course, travel, like the world, is a series of hills and valleys. Be fanatically positive and militantly optimistic. If something's not to your liking, change your liking.

Travel can make you a happier American, as well as a citizen of the world. Our Earth is home to seven billion equally precious people. It's humbling to travel and find that other people don't have the "American Dream"—they have their own dreams. Europeans like us, but with all due respect, they wouldn't trade passports.

Thoughtful travel engages us with the world. In tough economic times, it reminds us what is truly important. By broadening perspectives, travel teaches new ways to measure quality of life.

Globetrotting destroys ethnocentricity, helping us understand and appreciate other cultures. Rather than fear the diversity on this planet, celebrate it. Among your most prized souvenirs will be the strands of different cultures you choose to knit into your own character. The world is a cultural yarn shop, and Back Door travelers are weaving the ultimate tapestry. Join in!

MUNICH

München

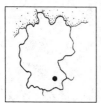

Munich, often called Germany's most livable city, is also one of its most historic, artistic, and entertaining. It's big and growing, with a population of 1.5 million. Until 1871, it was the capital of an independent Bavaria. Its imperial palaces, jewels, and grand boulevards constantly remind visitors that Munich has long been a political and cultural powerhouse. Meanwhile, the concentration camp in nearby Dachau reminds us that 80 years ago, it provided a springboard for Nazism.

Orient yourself in Munich's old center, with its colorful pedestrian zones. Immerse yourself in the city's art and history—crown jewels, Baroque theater, Wittelsbach palaces, great paintings, and beautiful parks. Spend your Munich evenings in a frothy beer hall or outdoor *Biergarten,* prying big pretzels from buxom, no-nonsense beer maids amidst an oompah, bunny-hopping, and belching Bavarian atmosphere.

Planning Your Time

Munich is worth two days, including a half-day side-trip to Dachau. But if all you have for Munich is one day, follow the self-guided walk laid out in this chapter (visiting museums along the way), tour the Residenz museum and treasury, and drink in the beer-hall culture for your evening's entertainment. With a second day, choose from the following: Tour the Dachau Concentration Camp Memorial, rent a bike to enjoy the English Garden, head out to the BMW-Welt and Museum, exhaust yourself at the Deutsches Museum, or—if you're into art—tour your choice of the city's many fine art galleries (especially the Alte Pinakothek). With all these blockbuster sights and activities, the city could

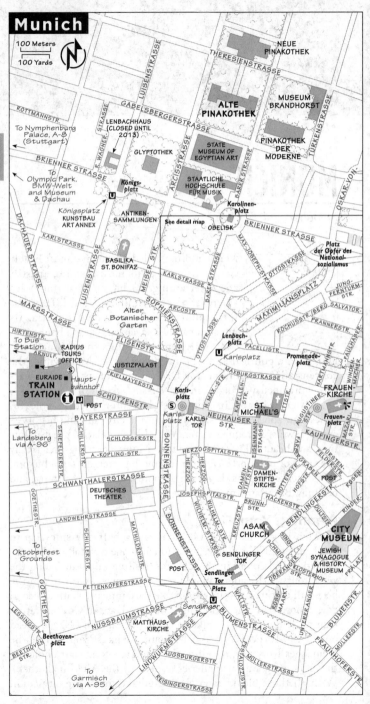

MUNICH

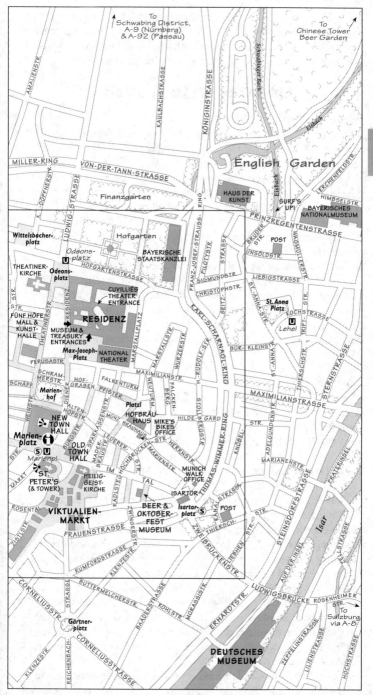

easily fill three days. And remember, many visitors spend an entire day side-tripping south to "Mad" King Ludwig's Castles (covered in the Bavaria and Tirol chapter). Austria's Salzburg (1.5-2 hours one-way by train) is also within day-tripping distance.

Orientation to Munich

(area code: 089)

The tourist's Munich is circled by a ring road (site of the old town wall) marked by four old gates: Karlstor (near the main train station—the Hauptbahnhof), Sendlinger Tor, Isartor (near the river), and Odeonsplatz (no surviving gate, near the palace). Marienplatz marks the city's center. A great pedestrian-only zone (Kaufingerstrasse and Neuhauser Strasse) cuts this circle in half, running neatly from the Karlstor and the train station through Marienplatz to the Isartor. Orient yourself along this east-west axis. Ninety percent of the sights and hotels I recommend are within a 20-minute walk of Marienplatz and each other.

Despite its large population, Munich feels small. This big-city elegance is possible because of its determination to be pedestrian- and bike-friendly, and because of a law that no building can be taller than the church spires. Despite ongoing debate about changing this policy, there are still no skyscrapers in downtown Munich.

Tourist Information

Munich has two helpful city-run TIs (www.muenchen.de). One is in front of the **main train station** (with your back to the tracks, walk through the central hall, step outside, and turn right; Mon-Sat 9:00-20:00, Sun 10:00-18:00, hotel reservations tel. 089/2339-6500—no info at this number). The other TI is on Munich's main square, **Marienplatz,** below the glockenspiel (Mon-Fri 10:00-19:00, Sat 10:00-17:00, Sun 10:00-14:00).

At either TI, pick up brochures and a city map (€0.40, better than the free map in hotel lobbies—especially for anyone using public transit), and confirm your sightseeing plans. Consider the *Monatsprogramm* (€2, German-language list of sights and events calendar) and the free, twice-monthly magazine *In München* (in German, lists all movies and entertainment in town). The TI can book you a room (you'll pay about 10 percent here, then pay the rest at the hotel), but you'll get a better value by contacting my recommended hotels directly. If you're interested in a Gray Line tour of the city or to nearby castles, don't buy your ticket at the TI; instead, you can get discounted tickets for these same tours at EurAide (see next page).

The **City Tour Card,** which covers public transportation and gives stingy discounts at minor sights, is a bad deal (€10/1 day, €19/3 days, sold at TIs). Two or more people traveling on a Munich "partner" all-day transit pass blow this deal out of the water (for details, see "Getting Around Munich," later).

The 14-day **Bavarian Castles Pass** covers admission to Munich's Residenz and Nymphenburg Palace Complex, as well as other castles and palaces in Bavaria (for a partial list, see page 122; €24, €40 family/partner pass, annual pass also available, not sold at TI—purchase at participating sights, www.schloesser.bayern .de). For avid castle-goers, this is a deal: Two people will save €5 with a family/partner pass even if only visiting the two Munich sights.

EurAide

At counter #1 in the train station's main *Reisezentrum* (travel center), the hardworking, eager-to-help EurAide desk is a godsend

for Eurailers and budget travelers. Alan Wissenberg and his EurAide staff can answer your train-travel and accommodations questions in clear American English. Paid by the German rail company to help you design your train travels, EurAide makes reservations and sells tickets, *couchettes*, and sleepers for the train at the same price you'd pay at the other counters (open April-Oct Mon-Fri 10:00-19:00, closed Sat-

Sun and Nov-March). EurAide sells a €0.50 city map and offers a free, information-packed newsletter, *The Inside Track* (described on page 41, always available in a rack at their door; also see www .euraide.com). As EurAide helps about 500 visitors per day in the summer, a line can build up; do your homework and have a list of questions ready. Chances are that your questions are already answered in *The Inside Track* newsletter—grab it and scan it first.

EurAide also sells tickets for Munich Walk city walking tours and Gray Line city bus tours, as well as for Gray Line tours to Neuschwanstein and Linderhof castles (all described later, under "Tours in Munich"). They offer a discount on these tickets to travelers with this book.

Arrival in Munich

By Train: Munich's main train station (München Hauptbahnhof) is a sight in itself—one of those places that can turn a homebody into a fancy-free vagabond.

Clean, high-tech **public toilets** are downstairs near track 26

(€1, showers-€7). For a quick rest stop, Burger King's toilets (upstairs) are as pleasant and accessible as its hamburgers.

Check out the bright and modern **food court** opposite track 14. For sandwiches and prepared meals to bring on board, I shop at **Yorma's** (two branches: one by track 26, another outside the station, next to the TI).

You'll find a city-run **TI** (out front of station and to the right) and **lockers** (€3-5, opposite track 26). **Car-rental agencies** are up the steps opposite track 21. A quiet, non-smoking **waiting room** *(Warteraum)* is open to anybody (across from track 23 and up the escalator), but the nearby, plush **DB Lounge** is only for those with a first-class ticket issued by DeutscheBahn (railpasses don't get you in). The **k presse + buch** shop (across from track 23) is great for English-language books, newspapers, and magazines. **Radius Tours** (at track 32) rents bikes and organizes tours.

Subway lines, trams, and buses connect the station to the rest of the city (though many of my recommended hotels are within walking distance of the station). If you get lost in the underground maze of subway corridors while you're simply trying to get to the train station, follow the signs for *DB* (DeutscheBahn) to surface successfully. Watch out for the hallways with blue ticket-stamping machines in the middle—these lead to the subway, where you could be fined if nabbed without a validated ticket.

By Bus: Munich's central bus station, called the **ZOB**, is by the Hackerbrücke S-Bahn station (from the train station, it's one S-Bahn stop, two stops on the #16/#17 tram, or a 10-15 minute walk; www.muenchen-zob.de). The Romantic Road bus leaves from here, as do many buses to Eastern Europe and the Balkans.

By Plane: For airport information, see "Munich Connections" at the end of this chapter.

Helpful Hints

Museum Hours: Sights closed on Monday include the Alte Pinakothek, Munich City Museum, Jewish Museum, Pinakothek der Moderne, Museum Brandhorst, Glyptothek, Bavarian National Museum, Beer and Oktoberfest Museum, Dachau Concentration Camp, and BMW-Welt and Museum. The Neue Pinakothek closes Tuesday. The art galleries are generally open late one night a week. On Sunday, the Pinakotheks, Glyptothek, Museum Brandhorst, and Bavarian National Museum cost just €1 apiece, but you'll pay extra for the usually free audioguides.

Internet Access: Hole-in-the-wall call centers near the train station and all over town have Internet terminals. **Internet Cafe München,** underneath the train station, feels wholesome and has long hours and low prices (€2.40/hour; go down stairs by track 26, then pass the WC and go left after the Rischart bakery, or find Arnulfsstrasse 10 and go down the stairway with the S-Bahn sign between #10 and #12; Mon-Fri 8:00-23:00, Sat-Sun 12:00-23:00, tel. 089/5161-7995).

Bookstore: The German bookstore chain **Hugendubel** runs a good English-language store at Salvatorplatz 2, between Marienplatz and Odeonsplatz (Mon-Sat 10:00-19:00, closed Sun, tel. 01801/484-484).

Need a Toilet? Munich had outdoor urinals until the 1972 Olympics and then decided to beautify the city by doing away with them. What about the people's needs? By law, any place serving beer must admit the public (whether or not they're customers) to use the toilets.

Pharmacy: Go out the front door of the train station, turn left, and walk a block to the corner of Elisenstrasse and Luisenstrasse (Mon-Fri 8:00-19:00, Sat 9:00-14:00, closed Sun, Elisenstrasse 5, tel. 089/595-444); another one is just below Marienplatz at Im Tal 13 (Mon-Fri 8:30-19:30, Sat 8:30-18:00, closed Sun, tel. 089/292-760).

Laundry: A handy self-service **Waschcenter** is a 10-minute walk from the train station (€7/load, €12 for larger machines, drop-off service €12/load, daily 7:00-23:00, English instructions, Paul-Heyse-Strasse 21, near intersection with Landwehrstrasse—see map on page 104). Taking the U-4 or U-5 to Theresienwiese actually brings you a little closer to the laundry than getting off at the train station.

Bikes and Pedestrians: Signs painted on the sidewalk or blue-and-white street signs show which part of the sidewalk is designated for pedestrians and which is for cyclists. The strip of pathway closest to the street is usually reserved for bikes. Pedestrians wandering into the bike path may hear the cheery ding-ding of a cyclist's bell just before being knocked unconscious.

Taxi: Call 089/21610 for a taxi.

Private Driver: Johann Fayoumi is reliable and speaks English (€60/hour, mobile 0174-183-8473, www.firstclasslimousines .de, johannfayoumi@gmail.com).

Car Rental: Several car-rental agencies are located upstairs at the train station, opposite track 21 (open daily, hours vary).

***The Inside Track* Train Travelers' Newsletter:** Anyone traveling by train should pick up this wonk-ish yet brilliant quarterly newsletter published by Alan Wissenberg at EurAide (free, always available at the EurAide counter in the train station—described earlier, under "Tourist Information"). You'll find all the tedious but important details on getting to Neuschwanstein, Dachau, Nymphenburg, and Prague; the ins and outs of supplements and reservations necessary for railpass-holders; a daily schedule of various tours in Munich; and (of course) plenty of tips on how to take advantage of EurAide's services.

Great City Views: Downtown Munich's three best city viewpoints (all described in this chapter) are from the towers of St. Peter's Church (stairs only), Frauenkirche (stairs plus elevator), and New Town Hall (elevator).

What's with Monaco? People walking around with guidebooks to Monaco aren't lost. "Monaco di Baviera" means "Munich" in *Italiano*.

Getting Around Munich

Much of Munich is walkable. To reach sights away from the city center, use the efficient tram, bus, and subway systems. Taxis are honest and professional, but expensive and generally unnecessary.

By Public Transit

Subways are called U-Bahns and S-Bahns (S-Bahns are actually commuter railways that run underground through the city). The U-Bahn lines mainly run north-south, while the S-Bahn lines are generally east-west. All S-Bahn lines converge on the central axis running from the Hauptbahnhof to Marienplatz. Subway lines are numbered (for example, S-3 or U-5). Eurailpasses are good on the S-Bahn (but not the U-Bahn), but if you use a flexipass, it activates the use of a travel day. Trams are more convenient than subways for some destinations (such as Nymphenburg Palace); one bus (#100) is useful for getting to the Alte Pinakothek and other major museums.

The entire transit system (subway/bus/tram) works on the same tickets, sold at TIs, at booths in the subway, and at easy-to-use ticket machines marked *MVV* (which take coins and €5 and €10 bills). There are four concentric zones—white, green, yellow, and orange. Almost everything described in this chapter is within the white/inner zone, except for Dachau (green zone) and the airport (orange zone).

A one-zone **regular ticket** *(Einzelfahrkarte)* costs €2.50 and is good for three hours in one direction, including changes and stops. For short rides (four stops max, only two of which can be on the subway lines), buy the €1.20 *Kurzstrecke* ("short stretch") ticket. The €5.40 **all-day pass** *(Single-Tageskarte)* for the white/inner zone

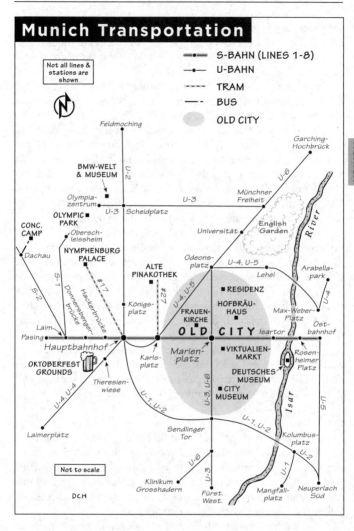

Munich Transportation

Not all lines &
stations are
shown

- ●══● **S-BAHN (LINES 1-8)**
- —●— **U-BAHN**
- ┄┄┄ **TRAM**
- — - **BUS**
- **OLD CITY**

Feldmoching

Garching-Hochbrück

BMW-WELT
& MUSEUM *U-2*

U-6

Olympia-
zentrum

Münchner
Freiheit

U-3

OLYMPIC
PARK ■

U-3 Scheidplatz

English
Garden

Oberschleissheim

Universität

River

CONC.
CAMP

Dachau

NYMPHENBURG
PALACE

ALTE
PINAKOTHEK ■

Odeonsplatz

U-4, U-5

Lehel

Arabellapark

■ RESIDENZ

U-4

S-1

#17

#27

HOFBRÄU-
HAUS ■

Max-Weber-
Platz

S-2

Donnersbergerbrücke

Hackerbrücke

Königsplatz

FRAUEN-
KIRCHE

U-4, U-5

Ostbahnhof

Laim

O L D   C I T Y

Isartor

Pasing

Hauptbahnhof

Karlsplatz

Marienplatz

■ VIKTUALIEN-
MARKT

Rosenheimer
Platz

OKTOBERFEST
GROUNDS 🍺

Theresienwiese

U-4, U-5

DEUTSCHES
MUSEUM

Isar

U-5

U-1, U-2

U-3, U-6

■ CITY
MUSEUM

U-1, U-2

Laimerplatz

Sendlinger
Tor

Kolumbusplatz

Not to scale

U-6

U-3

U-1

U-2

Klinikum
Grosshadern

Fürst.
West.

Mangfallplatz

Neuperlach
Süd

DCH

is a great deal for a single traveler. If you're going to Dachau, buy
the *XXL* version of the *Single-Tageskarte,* which also includes the
green zone (€7.30); the ***Gesamtnetz*** version of the pass covers all
four zones and gets you to the airport (€10.80).

All-day small-group passes *(Partner-Tageskarte)* are an even
better deal—they cover all public transportation for up to five
adults and a dog (two kids count as one adult, so two adults, six
kids, and a dog can travel with this ticket). A *Partner-Tageskarte*
for the white/inner zone costs €9.40. The *XXL* version, which
includes Dachau, costs €12.30; and the ***Gesamtnetz*** version,
including the airport, costs €19.60. These partner tickets—while

seemingly impossibly cheap—are for real. Read it again and do the arithmetic. Even two people traveling together save money, and for groups, it's a real steal. The only catch is that you've got to stay together.

For longer stays, consider a **three-day ticket** (€13.30/person, €22.80/partner ticket for the gang, white/inner zone only, does not include transportation to Dachau).

Maps of the transit system, available everywhere, help you navigate. To find the right platform, look for the name of the last station in the direction you want to travel. The name of this end-station is posted on trains and signs using the word *Richtung* ("direction"). Know where you're going relative to Marienplatz, the Hauptbahnhof, and Ostbahnhof, as these are so important to navigation that they are often referred to as end points.

In Munich, you must stamp all tickets with the date and time prior to using them (for an all-day or multi-day pass, you only have to stamp it the first time you use it). For the subway, punch your ticket in the blue machine *before* going down to the platform. For buses and trams, stamp your ticket once on board. Plainclothes ticket-checkers enforce this honor system, rewarding freeloaders with stiff €40 fines. All-day and multi-day passes are valid until 6:00 the following morning.

There's a transit customer-service center underground at Marienplatz (Mon-Fri 9:00-20:00, Sat 9:00-16:00, closed Sun, go down stairs by Beck's department store). For more transit info, call 01803/442-266 or visit www.mvv-muenchen.de.

By Bike

Level, compact, and with plenty of bike paths, Munich feels made for those on two wheels. When biking in Munich, follow these simple rules: You must walk your bike through pedestrian zones; you can take your bike on the subway, but not during rush hour and only if you have an extra ticket; and cyclists are expected to follow the rules of the road, just like drivers.

You can **rent bikes** quickly and easily from three great places: Radius Tours (in the train station), Mike's Bikes (near Marienplatz), and Munich Walk (at the Isartor). All have an extensive selection of bikes; provide helmets, maps, and route advice; and offer bike tours. Radius and Munich Walk give a 10 percent discount with this book in 2012.

Radius Tours (*Rad* means "bike" in German) is in the train station in front of track 32 (3- to 7-speed city bikes-€3/hour, €14.50/day, €17/24 hours, €25/48 hours, fancier bikes cost more, €50 cash or credit-card deposit, April-Oct Mon-Fri 9:00-18:00, Sat-Sun 9:00-20:00, closed Nov-March, tel. 089/543-487-7730, www.radiustours.com).

Mike's Bikes is between Marienplatz and the Hofbräuhaus (€9/3 hours, €15/24 hours, daily mid-April-early Oct 10:00-20:00, March-mid-April and early Oct-mid-Nov 10:30-13:00 & 16:30-17:30, closed mid-Nov-Feb, Bräuhausstrasse 10—enter around corner on Hochbrückenstrasse, tel. 089/2554-3987, www.mikes biketours.com).

Munich Walk is at the other end of the tourist zone from the train station, right by the Isartor (€4/hour, €18/24 hours, €12 from 14:30 until the next morning, 2-hour minimum, open daily 10:00-23:00, Thomas-Wimmer-Ring 1, storefront says *Tourist info*, tel. 089/2423-1767, www.munichwalktours.de).

For a great city ride, consider this day on a bike: From the station (where you rent your bike), take the bike path on Arnulfstrasse, pedaling along the canal out to Nymphenburg Palace. Ride around the palace grounds, then head to Olympic Park and BMW-Welt, and finish at the English Garden (for the late-afternoon or early-evening scene) before returning to the center. Or go for the Isar River bike ride described on page 92.

Tours in Munich

Munich's two largest conventional tour companies, Radius Tours and Munich Walk, both run bike tours (described earlier), walking tours, and day trips to Dachau Concentration Camp Memorial, Neuschwanstein Castle, and other places. Radius and Munich Walk compete directly with each other, and in my experience, they're comparable. **Radius Tours** has a convenient office and meeting point in the main train station, in front of track 32 (see map on page 104, tel. 089/543-487-7720, www.radiustours.com, run by Gabi Holder). **Munich Walk** has their office near the Isartor at Thomas-Wimmer-Ring 1, and uses Marienplatz as their meeting point (see map on page 50, tel. 089/2423-1767, www.munichwalk tours.de, tours@munichwalktours.de, Ralph Lünstroth). Both companies offer €2 off their walking tours with this book—don't forget to show this book and request your discount. There's also **Gray Line,** which runs sightseeing buses around town and on day trips (tel. 089/5490-7560, sightseeing-munich.com), and a couple of bike tour companies: Mike's Bikes and Lenny's (see later). You can buy discounted tickets for Gray Line and Munich Walk tours at EurAide.

"Free" Tours: You'll encounter brochures advertising "free" walking and biking tours. These tours aren't really free—tipping is expected, and the guides actually have to pay the company a cut for each person who takes the tour—so unless you tip at least a few euros per person, they don't make a penny. The tours tend to be light on history, and the guides work hard to promote their company's other tours (which are not free). Unless you're a poor backpacker, my advice is to favor the more established companies' tours, where you pay for a hardworking guide who can make the city's history come alive—and who is paid by the tour company.

Within Munich

Walking Tours—**Munich Walk** offers two daytime tours (€2 Rick Steves discount on each tour): a "City Walk" (€12, daily year-round at 10:45, May-mid-Oct also daily at 14:45, 2.25 hours) and "Hitler's Munich" (€12, daily at 10:15, 2.5 hours, extended €22 five-hour version Mon and Sat only). Their "Beer and Brewery" tour is more mature than your typical hard-partying pub crawl. You visit Paulaner, Munich's oldest brewery, to learn, eat, and drink in the city that made beer famous. The price includes three different beers in the brewery; afterward, the tour ends at the Hofbräuhaus (€20, May-mid-Sept daily at 18:15, fewer tours off-season, 3.5 hours). They also offer a Bavarian food-tasting tour, where you visit the Viktualienmarkt for lunch (€22 includes food), and a €14 Haunted Munich evening tour (check their website for schedules). All Munich Walk tours depart from under the glockenspiel on Marienplatz. You don't need to reserve—just show up.

Radius Tours runs two city walking tours, both with reliably good guides: "Priceless Munich" (no up-front charge but tip for guide requested, daily at 10:10, 2 hours) and "Birthplace of the Third Reich" (€12, €2 Rick Steves discount, April-mid-Oct daily at 15:00; mid-Oct-March Mon, Tue, Fri, and Sun at 11:30; 2.5 hours). They also offer an educational "Bavarian Beer and Food" tour that includes a visit to the Beer and Oktoberfest Museum (see page 63), samples of four varieties of beer, and regional food (€27, €2 Rick Steves discount; Tue, Thu, and Sat at 18:00; also Wed and Fri at 18:00 April-mid-Oct; no tours during Oktoberfest; 3 hours). All tours depart from the Radius office (in front of track 32 at the train station). No need to reserve—just show up.

Local Guides—A guide can be a great value—especially if you assemble a small group. Six people splitting the cost can make the luxury of a private guide affordable. I've had great days with two good guides, each charging the same price (€130/3 hours): **Georg Reichlmayr** (tel. 08131/86800, mobile 0170-341-6384, program explained on his website, www.muenchen-stadtfuehrung .de, info@muenchen-stadtfuehrung.de) and **Monika Hank** (tel. 089/311-4819, mobile 0175-923-2339, monika.hank@web.de). They've helped me with much of the historical information in this chapter.

Bike Tours—Munich lends itself to bike touring, and four outfits fit the bill. You don't need to reserve for any of these—just show up—but do confirm times in advance online or by phone.

Munich Walk offers 3.5-hour bike tours around Munich (€20, €2 Rick Steves discount, April-Oct only, daily at 10:45, depart from under the glockenspiel on Marienplatz). They also have a four-hour mountain bike tour out into the countryside along the Isar River, including a lunch stop at a beer garden (€29, €2 Rick Steves discount, Sat at 10:00, May-Oct only; departing from their Isartor office). Confirm times at www.munichwalktours.de.

Radius Tours has similar 3.5-hour bike tours on Tuesdays, Thursdays, and Sundays (€19.50, €1.50 Rick Steves discount, May-mid-Oct only at 10:30). Tours leave from the Radius office at track 32 in the train station (confirm times at www.radiustours.com).

Mike's Bike Tours, popular with the college crowd, are four hours of entertainment on wheels. The tours are high-energy, if a bit clunky with pacing, and the guides are better comedians than historians. Still, you get a great ride through the English Garden (€29, 1-hour break in Chinese Tower beer garden, daily mid-April-Aug at 11:30 and 16:00, March-mid-April and Sept-mid-Nov at 12:30, meet under tower of Old Town Hall on Marienplatz; tel. 089/2554-3987, mobile 0172-852-0660, www.mikesbiketours.com).

Lenny's Bike Tours has a €10 tour (with a request for tips at the end) that is generally led by young Brits (3.5 hours with an hour at the Chinese Tower beer garden, in English only, starts at the fish fountain in Marienplatz, daily mid-April-Aug at 11:30 and 16:00, March-mid-April and Sept-mid-Nov at 12:30, tel. 089/4202-4505, mobile 0176-8114-3062, www.discovermunichnow.com).

Quickie Orientation City Bus Tour—Gray Line Tours has hop-on, hop-off bus tours that leave from in front of the Karstadt department store at Bahnhofplatz, directly across from the train station. Choose from a basic, one-hour "Express Circle" that heads past the Pinakotheks, Marienplatz, and Karlsplatz (3/hour, 9:00-17:30); or the more extensive "Grand Circle" that lasts 2.5 hours and also includes the Nymphenburg Palace and BMW-Welt/Museum (1/hour, 9:00-16:00). If you plan on visiting Nymphenburg and the BMW center, this is a very efficient way to see both—just plan your visits to these sights around the tour schedule (bus generally leaves from Nymphenburg at :30 past the hour, and from BMW at :55 past). This tour is actually well worthwhile—sitting upstairs on the topless double-decker bus, you'll see lots of things missed by the typical visitor wandering around the center. It comple-ments the information in this book, though the live narration (in German and English) is delivered as stiffly as a tape recording. Just show up and pay the driver (cash only), or get a €1-2 discount by buying your ticket in advance at EurAide (€13 Express tour, €19 Grand tour, daily in season, tel. 089/5490-7560, www.sightseeing-munich.com).

Beyond Munich

While you can do all these day trips from Munich on your own by train, going as part of an organized group can be convenient—especially to Neuschwanstein.

"Mad" King Ludwig's Castle at Neuschwanstein—Choose between an escorted tour to Neuschwanstein by train and local bus, or guided private bus tours that include extras such as Linderhof Castle. Though they're a little more expensive, I prefer the bus tours—you're guaranteed a seat (public transport to Neuschwanstein is routinely standing-room only in summer), and you get to see more. All these tours can sell out, especially in summer, so it's wise to buy your ticket a day ahead (for information on visiting the castle on your own, see the next chapter).

Gray Line Tours offers rushed all-day bus tours of Neuschwanstein that also include Ludwig's Linderhof Castle and 30 minutes in Oberammergau (€49, €7 Rick Steves discount if you buy your ticket at EurAide—cash only, two castle admissions-€17 extra, daily April-Oct, no tours Mon Nov-March, www.sight seeing-munich.com). Tours meet at 8:10 and depart at 8:30 from the Karstadt department store (across from the station). While tours are designed to be in both English and German, if groups are large they may split them up and you'll get only English. **Munich Walk** advertises a tour that sounds similar—because they're simply selling tickets for this Gray Line trip.

Mike's Bike Tours runs a similar private bus tour with an outdoor theme—a bike ride and short hike near Neuschwanstein are included (€49, or €39 without bike ride; Neuschwanstein admission-€9 extra; June-mid-Sept at least Mon, Thu, and Sat at 8:35, during Oktoberfest at 9:35 but without bike ride, meet at Mike's Bike office, Bräuhausstrasse 10—enter around corner on Hochbrückenstrasse, tel. 089/2554-3987, mobile 0172-852-0660, www.mikesbiketours.com).

Radius Tours runs all-day tours to Neuschwanstein Castle using public transportation. Your guide will escort you onto the train to Füssen and then the bus from there to the castle, give you some general information, and help you into the castle for the standard tour that's included with any admission ticket (€32 with this book, €25 with railpass, castle admission-€9 extra; daily mid-April-Sept at 9:30, back by 19:00; Oct-mid-April tours run Mon, Wed, Fri, Sat, and Sun at 9:30; smart to reconfirm times, departs from the Radius office near track 32 in the train station, www .radiustours.com).

Dachau Concentration Camp—While several companies do Dachau tours, only Radius Tours and Munich Walk are allowed to actually guide inside the camp. The camp is easy to see on your own (see page 93). But if you'd prefer a guided visit, these tours are a great value, considering how good and passionate their guides are—and that you're only paying about €10 for the guiding, once you factor in transportation costs. Allow about five hours total, and keep in mind that Dachau is closed on Mondays. Both companies charge the same price (€21, includes the €7 cost of public transportation, €3 Rick Steves discount). It's smart to reserve the day before, especially for the morning tours. Choose between **Radius** (April-mid-Oct Tue-Sun at 9:15 and 12:30; mid-Oct-March Tue-Sun at 10:00) and **Munich Walk** (April-Oct Tue-Sun at 10:15 and 13:15; Nov-March Tue-Sun at 10:15).

Nürnberg—Just an hour away by fast train, this makes a great day trip from Munich. Do it on your own using this book (see Nürnberg chapter), or take the **Radius Tours** all-day excursion (see their website for details—www.radiustours.com).

Other Day Tours—Radius Tours also offers all-day trips to Salzburg, Augsburg, and the castles at Herrenchiemsee (details at radiustours.com). Munich Walk does Salzburg tours (www.munichwalktours.com). These trips cost around €35-40 and include public transport there and back.

Self-Guided Walk

Munich City Walk

I've laced the top sights in the old town center into a ▲▲▲ walk, starting at Marienplatz and ending at the Hofgarten. You can do these sights in any order and take a break from the walk to tour the museums (details about visiting sights are included later, under "Sights in Munich"), but if you want to cover the center in a logical way, this is a great template. I've included basic walking directions linking the sights, and you can also follow along on the map on page 50.

• *Begin your walk at the heart of the old city, with a stroll through...*

▲▲Marienplatz

Riding the escalator out of the subway into sunlit Marienplatz ("Mary's Square") gives you a fine first look at the glory of Munich: great buildings bombed flat and rebuilt, outdoor cafés, and people bustling and lingering like the birds and breeze with which they share this square. Take in the ornate facades of the gray, pointy Old Town Hall and the Neo-Gothic New Town Hall, with its beloved glockenspiel.

MUNICH

MUNICH

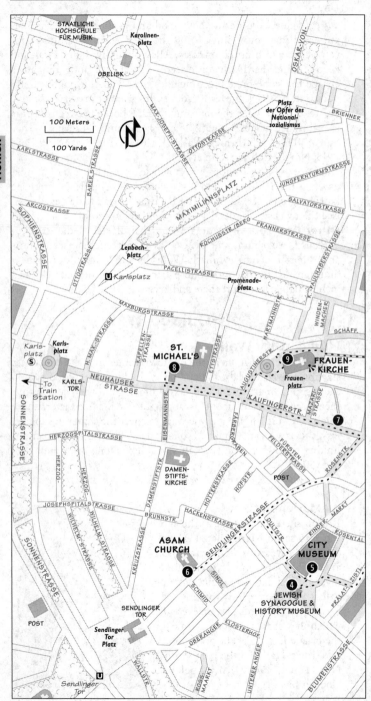

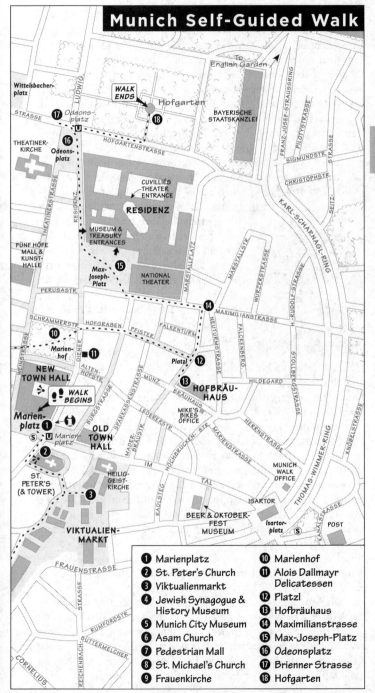

Munich Self-Guided Walk

1 Marienplatz
2 St. Peter's Church
3 Viktualienmarkt
4 Jewish Synagogue & History Museum
5 Munich City Museum
6 Asam Church
7 Pedestrian Mall
8 St. Michael's Church
9 Frauenkirche
10 Marienhof
11 Alois Dallmayr Delicatessen
12 Platzl
13 Hofbräuhaus
14 Maximilianstrasse
15 Max-Joseph-Platz
16 Odeonsplatz
17 Brienner Strasse
18 Hofgarten

The **New Town Hall** (Neues Rathaus), built from 1867 until 1908, dominates Marienplatz. This very Neo-Gothic structure is a fine example of the same Historicism (mixing-and-matching of historical styles) that you see in nearby Neuschwanstein, London's Houses of Parliament, Budapest's Parliament, and other buildings of that era. Notice the politics of the statuary: The 40 statues—though sculpted only in 1900—decorate the New Town Hall not with civic leaders, but with royals and blue-blooded nobility. Because this building survived the bombs and had a central location, it served as the US military headquarters in 1945.

The New Town Hall is famous for its **glockenspiel**—dating from 1908—which "jousts" daily at 11:00 and 12:00 all year (also at 17:00 May-Oct). The *Spiel* re-creates a royal wedding from the 16th century: The duke and his bride watch the action as the groom's Bavarian family (in Bavarian white and blue) joyfully jousts with the bride's French family (in red and white). Below, the barrel-makers—famous for being the first to dance in the streets after a deadly plague lifted—do their popular jig.

At the very top of the New Town Hall is a statue of a child with outstretched arms, dressed in monk's garb and holding a book in its left hand. This is the **Münchner Kindl,** the symbol of Munich (the city's name comes from *Kloster von Mönchen*—"cloister of monks"). You'll spot this mini-monk all over town, on everything from posters to tram cars (often holding other objects, like a bundle of radishes or a giant beer). Over the centuries, the monk has gone through several transformations. He started as a grown man, wearing a gold-lined black cloak and red shoes. Artists later represented him as a young boy, then a gender-neutral child, and, more recently, a young girl. Every year, a young woman dressed as the *Kindl* kicks off Oktoberfest by leading the opening parade on horseback, and then serves as the mascot throughout the festivities.

The New Town Hall tower offers **views** of the city (€2.50, elevator from under glockenspiel; May-Oct daily 10:00-19:00; Nov-April Mon-Fri 10:00-17:00, closed Sat-Sun).

Marienplatz is marked by a statue of the square's namesake, the **Virgin Mary,** moved here in 1638 from its original location in the Frauenkirche in thanks that the Swedes didn't sack the town during their occupation. It was also a rallying point for the struggle against the Protestants. The cherubs are fighting the four great biblical enemies of civilization: the dragon of war, the lion of hunger, the rooster-headed monster of plague and disease, and the serpent of heresy (Protestantism). The serpent that's being stepped upon represents the "wrong faith," a.k.a. Martin Luther.

The **Old Town Hall** (Altes Rathaus; at the right side of the square as you face New Town Hall) was completely destroyed by WWII bombs and later rebuilt. Ludwig IV, an early Wittelsbach who was Holy Roman Emperor back in the 14th century, stands in the center of the facade. He donated this great square to the people. On the bell tower, find the city seal with its monk/*Kindl* and towers. Munich flourished because, in its early days, all salt trade had to stop here on Marienplatz.

• *Just beyond the southeast corner of Marienplatz, with its steeple poking up above a row of buildings, is...*

St. Peter's Church

The oldest church in town, St. Peter's overlooks Marienplatz from its perch near the Viktualienmarkt. It's built on the hill where

Munich's original monastic inhabitants probably settled. (Founded in 1158, the city celebrated its 850th birthday in 2008.) Outside, notice the old tombstones plastered onto the wall—a reminder that in the Napoleonic age, the cemeteries surrounding most city churches were (for hygienic and practical space reasons) dug up and moved.

St. Peter's was badly damaged in World War II. Inside, photos show the bomb damage (near the entrance). As part of the soul of the city (according to a popular song, "Munich is not Munich without St. Peter's"), the church was lovingly rebuilt—half with Augustiner beer money, the rest with private donations—and the altar and ceiling frescoes were marvelously restored (possible with the help of Nazi catalog photos—see "The History of Munich: Part 2," on page 60).

Apostles line the nave, leading up to St. Peter above the altar. On the ceiling, you'll see Peter crucified upside-down. The finely crafted gray iron chapel fences were donated after World War II by the local blacksmiths of the national railway. The precious and fragile sandstone Gothic chapel altar (front left) survived the war

The History of Munich: Part 1
Monastic Beginnings to the Age of Kings

Born from Salt (1100-1500)

Munich began in the 12th century, when Henry the Lion (Heinrich der Löwe) muscled in on the lucrative salt trade, burning a rival's bridge over the Isar River and building his own near a monastery of "monks"—München. (The town's coat of arms features the Münchner Kindl, a child in monk's robes, see page 52.) Henry built walls and towers and opened a market, and peasants flocked in from the countryside. Marienplatz was the center of town and the crossroads of the Salzstrasse (Salt Road) from Salzburg to Augsburg. After Henry's death, the town was taken over by an ambitious merchant family, the Wittelsbachs (1240), and became the capital of the region (1255). Munich-born Louis IV (1282-1347) was elected king of Germany and Holy Roman Emperor, temporarily making Munich a major European capital.

By the 1400s, Munich's maypole-studded market bustled with trade. Besides salt, Munich gained a reputation for beer. More than 30 breweries pumped out the golden liquid that lubricated both trade and traders. The Bavarian Beer Purity Law assured quality control. Wealthy townspeople erected the twin-domed Frauenkirche and the Altes Rathaus on Marienplatz, and the Wittelsbachs built a stout castle that would eventually become the cushy Residenz. When the various regions of Bavaria united in 1506, Munich (pop. 14,000) was the natural capital.

Religious Wars, Plagues, Decline (1500-1800)

While Martin Luther and the Protestant Reformation raged in northern Germany, Munich became the ultra-Catholic heart of the Counter-Reformation. The devout citizens poured enormous funds into building the massive St. Michael's Church (1583) as a home for the Jesuits, and into the Residenz (early 1600s) as home of the Wittelsbachs. Both were showpieces of conservative power and the Baroque and Rococo styles.

During the Thirty Years' War, the Catholic city was surrounded by Protestants (1632). The Wittelsbachs surrendered quickly and paid a ransom, sparing the city from pillage, but it was soon hit by the bubonic plague. After that passed, the leaders erected the Virgin's column on Marienplatz to thank God for killing only 7,000 citizens. (Munich's many plagues are also remembered today when the glockenspiel's barrel-makers do their daily dance to ward off the plague.)

The double whammy of invasion and disease left Munich bankrupt and powerless, overshadowed by the more powerful Habsburgs of Austria. The Wittelsbachs took their cultural cues from France (Nymphenburg Palace is a mini-Versailles), England (the English Garden), and Italy (the Pitti Palace-inspired Residenz). While the rest of Europe modernized and headed toward democracy, Munich remained conservative and backward.

The Kings (1806-1918): Max I, Ludwig I, Max II, Ludwig II, Ludwig III

When Napoleon's army surrounded the city (1800), the Wittelsbachs again surrendered hospitably. Napoleon rewarded the Wittelsbach "duke" with more territory and a royal title: "king." Maximilian I (r. 1806-1825, see page 65), a.k.a. Max Joseph, now ruled the Kingdom of Bavaria, a nation bigger than Switzerland, with a constitution and parliament. When Max's popular son Ludwig married (Sept 1810), it touched off a two-week celebration that became an annual event: Oktoberfest.

As king, Ludwig I (r. 1825-1848) set about rebuilding the capital in the Neoclassical style we see today. Medieval walls and ramshackle houses were replaced with grand buildings of columns and arches (including the Residenz and Alte Pinakothek). Connecting these were broad boulevards and plazas for horse carriages and promenading citizens (Ludwigstrasse and Königsplatz). Ludwig established the university and built the first railway line, turning Munich (pop. 90,000) into a major transportation hub, budding industrial city, and fitting capital.

In 1846, the skirt-chasing King Ludwig (see Nymphenburg's Gallery of Beauties, page 89) was beguiled by a notorious Irish dancer named Lola Montez. She became his mistress, and he fawned over her in public, scandalizing Munich. The Münchners resented her spending their tax money and dominating their king (supposedly inspiring the phrase "Whatever Lola wants, Lola gets"). In 1848, as Europe was swept by a tide of revolution, the citizens rose up and forced Ludwig to abdicate. His son Maximilian II (r. 1848-1864) continued Ludwig's enlightened program of modernizing, while studiously avoiding dancers from Ireland.

In 1864, 18-year-old Ludwig II (r. 1864-1886) became king. He invited the composer Richard Wagner to Munich, planning a lavish new opera house to stage Wagner's operas. Munich didn't like the idea, and Ludwig didn't like Munich. For most of his reign, Ludwig avoided the Residenz and Nymphenburg, instead building castles in the Bavarian countryside at the expense of Munich taxpayers. (For more on the king, see page 139.)

In 1871, Bavaria became part of the newly united Germany, and overnight, Berlin overtook Munich as Germany's power center. But turn-of-the-century Munich was culturally rich, giving birth to the abstract art of Wassily Kandinsky, Paul Klee, and the Blue Rider group. But this artistic flourishing didn't last long. World War I devastated Munich. Poor, hungry, disillusioned, unemployed Münchners roamed the streets. Extremists from the left and right battled for power. In 1918, a huge mob marched to the gates of the Residenz and drove the forgettable King Ludwig III (r. 1913-1918)—the last Bavarian king—out of the city, ending nearly 700 years of continuous Wittelsbach rule.

For "The History of Munich: Part 2," see page 60.

only because it was buried in sandbags.

Munich has more relics than any city outside of Rome. For more than a hundred years, it was the pope's bastion against the rising tide of Protestantism in northern Europe during the Reformation. Favors done in the defense of Catholicism earned the Wittelsbachs neat relic treats. For instance, check out the tomb of Munditia (second side chapel on left as you enter). She's a third-century martyr (note the ancient Roman tombstone with red lettering), whose remains were given to Munich by Rome in thanks and as a vivid reminder that those who die for the cause of the Roman Church go directly to heaven without waiting for Judgment Day.

It's a long climb to the top of the **spire** (306 steps, no elevator)—much of it with two-way traffic on a one-lane stair-case—but the view is dynamite (€1.50, Mon-Fri 9:00-18:30, Sat-Sun 10:00-18:30, off-season until 17:30, last exit 30 minutes after closing). Try to be two flights from the top when the bells ring at the top of the hour. Then, when your friends back home ask you about your trip, you'll say, "What?"

• *Just behind and beyond (downhill from) St. Peter's, join the busy commotion of the...*

▲▲Viktualienmarkt

Early in the morning, you can still feel small-town Munich here, long a favorite with locals for fresh produce and good service (open Mon-Sat, food stalls open late, closed Sun).  The most expensive real estate in town could never really support such a market, but Munich charges only a percentage of the gross income, enabling these old-time shops to carry on (and keeping out fast-food chains).

The huge **maypole** is a tradition. Fifteenth-century town market squares posted a maypole as a practical information post—decorated with various symbols to explain which crafts and merchants were doing business in the market. Munich's maypole shows the city's six great brews, and the crafts and festivities associated with brewing. (You can't have a kegger without coopers—find the merry barrel-makers.) For more on maypoles, see page 328.

Notice the **beer counter.** Munich's breweries take turns here. Changing every day or two, a sign *(Heute im Ausschank)* announces which of the six brews is being served today. Here, under the standard beer-garden chestnut trees, you can order just half a liter—

unlike at other *Biergarten*s (handy for shoppers who want to have a quick sip and then keep on going). The Viktualienmarkt is ideal for a light meal (see page 109).

• *Leave the Viktualienmarkt from the far side, then walk two blocks (ask anyone: "Synagogue?") to find the...*

Jewish Synagogue and History Museum (Jüdisches Museum München)

Thanks to Germany's acceptance of religious refugees from former Soviet states, Munich's Jewish population has now reached

its pre-Nazi size—10,000 people. The city's new synagogue and Jewish History Museum anchor a revitalized Jewish quarter, which includes a kindergarten and day school, children's playground, fine kosher restaurant (at #18), and bookstore.

While the **synagogue** is shut tight to non-worshippers, its architecture is striking from the outside. Lower stones of travertine evoke the Wailing Wall in Jerusalem, while an upper section represents the tent that held important religious wares during the 40 years of wandering through the desert until the Temple of Solomon was built, ending the Exodus. The synagogue's door features the first 10 letters of the Hebrew alphabet, symbolizing the Ten Commandments.

The cube-shaped **museum** (behind the cube-shaped synagogue) is stark, windowless, and as inviting as a bomb shelter. Its small permanent exhibit in the basement is disappointing. The two floors of temporary exhibits might justify the entry fee.

Cost and Hours: Museum-€6, discount with Munich City Museum, Tue-Sun 10:00-18:00, closed Mon, St.-Jakobs-Platz 16, tel. 089/2339-6096, www.juedisches-museum-muenchen.de.

• *Facing the synagogue, on the same square, is the...*

▲▲Munich City Museum (Münchner Stadtmuseum)

Five floors of exhibits in this recently renovated museum tell the story of life in Munich through the centuries, including the history of "monk culture," the development of National Socialism (i.e., Nazism), and World War II—illustrated with paintings, photos, and models. Their good permanent exhibit, called "Typically Munich!", examines the various stereotypes—both positive and negative—that people around the world associate with this city.

Cost and Hours: €4, discount with Jewish History Museum, open Tue-Sun 10:00-18:00, closed Mon, English descriptions in loaner booklets, €3 audioguide, no crowds, bored and playful guards, St.-Jakobs-Platz 1, tel. 089/2332-2370, www.stadtmuseum-online.de.

Eating: The museum's Stadt Café is handy for a good meal (listed under "Eating in Munich," later).

• *Continue another three blocks away from the market—one block to Sendlinger Strasse, then two blocks south (left)—where you'll encounter the...*

Asam Church (Asamkirche)

The private church of the Asam brothers is a gooey, drippy Baroque-concentrate masterpiece by Bavaria's top two Rococonuts. Just 30 feet wide, it was built in 1740 to fit within this row of homes. While it was built as a private initiative by these two brother-architects to show off their work (on their own land, next to their home and business headquarters—to the left), it's also recognized by the Church as a legitimate place of worship.

The church served as a promotional brochure to woo clients, packed with every architectural trick in the books. Imagine approaching the church not as a worshipper, but as a shopper representing your church's building committee. First stand outside: Hmmm, the look of those foundation stones really packs a punch. And the legs hanging over the portico...nice effect. Those starbursts on the door would be a hit back home, too.

Then step inside: I'll take a set of those over-the-top golden capitals, please. We'd also like to order the gilded garlands draping the church in jubilation, and the twin cupids capping the confessional. Check out the illusion of a dome on the flat ceiling—that'll save us lots of money. The yellow glass above the altar has the effect of the thin-sliced alabaster at St. Peter's in Rome, but it's within our budget! And, tapping the "marble" pilasters to determine that they are just painted fakes, we decide to take that, too... Visiting the Asam Church, you can see why the Asam brothers were so prolific and successful.

Cost and Hours: Free, Sat-Thu 9:15-18:00, closed Fri.

• *Leaving the church, turn left and walk straight up Sendlinger Strasse, and then Rosenstrasse, until you hit Marienplatz and the big, busy...*

Pedestrian Mall

This car-free area (on Kaufingerstrasse and Neuhauser Strasse) leads you through a great shopping district, past carnivals of street entertainers and good old-fashioned slicers and dicers. As one of Europe's first pedestrian zones, the mall enraged shop-keepers when it was built in 1972 for the Olympics. Today, it is Munich's living room. Nearly 9,000 shoppers pass through it each hour. The shopkeepers are happy...and merchants nearby are beg-ging for their streets to become traffic-free. Imagine this street in Hometown, USA.

• *Stroll a few blocks away from Marienplatz toward the Karlstor, until you arrive at the big church on the right.*

St. Michael's Church

While one of the first great Renaissance buildings north of the Alps, this church has a brilliantly Baroque interior. Inspired by the Gesù (the Jesuits' main church in Rome), it was built in the late 1500s as a home to Bavaria's Jesuits (and rebuilt after WWII bombing—see photos in the back). The statue of Michael fighting a Protestant demon (on the front facade) is a reminder that this leader of heaven's army invited the Jesuits to literally counter the Reformation from here. The interior is striking for its barrel vault, the largest of its day. The crypt contains 40 stark royal tombs, including the resting place of King Ludwig II. Judging by all the flowers, romantics are still mad about their "mad" king.

Cost and Hours: Church entry free, daily 9:00-19:00, Thu until 20:45, Sun until 22:00; crypt-€2, Mon-Fri 9:30-16:30, Sat 9:30-14:30, closed Sun, less off-season; frequent concerts—check the schedule outside; www.st-michael-muenchen.de.

• *Backtrack a couple blocks on the pedestrian mall, then turn left at Augustinerstrasse to find Munich's towering, twin-domed cathedral.*

Frauenkirche

These twin onion domes are the sym-bol of the city. Some say Crusaders, inspired by the Dome of the Rock in Jerusalem, brought home the idea. Others say these domes are the inspi-ration for the characteristic domed church spires marking villages throughout Bavaria.

Cost and Hours: Free, Sat-Wed 7:00-19:00, Thu 7:00-20:30, Fri 7:00-18:00, www.muenchner-dom.de.

Touring the Church: Go inside. While much of the church was destroyed during World War II (see photos just inside the entrance, on the right), the towers survived, and the rest has been gloriously restored.

Built in Gothic style in the late 1400s, the Frauenkirche

The History of Munich: Part 2 Troubled 20th Century and Today's Revitalization

This picks up where "Part 1" leaves off (see page 54).

Nazis, World War II, and Munich Bombed (1918-1945)

Germany after World War I was in chaos. In quick succession, the prime minister was gunned down, Communists took power, and the army restored the old government. In the hubbub, one fringe group emerged—the Nazi party, headed by the charismatic war veteran Adolf Hitler.

Hitler—an Austrian who'd settled in Munich—made stirring speeches in Munich's beer halls (including the Hofbräuhaus) and galvanized the city's disaffected. On November 8-9, 1923, the Nazis launched a coup d'état known as the Beer Hall Putsch. They kidnapped the mayor, and Hitler led a mob to overthrow the German government in Berlin. The march got as far as Odeonsplatz before Hitler was arrested and sent to prison in nearby Landsberg. Though the Nazis eventually gained power in Berlin, they remembered their roots, dubbing Munich "Capital of the Movement." The Nazi headquarters stood near today's obelisk on Brienner Strasse, Dachau was chosen as the regime's first concentration camp, and Odeonsplatz was designated as a place where all who passed by were required to perform the Nazi salute.

As World War II drew to a close, it was clear that Munich would be destroyed. Hitler did not allow the evacuation of much of the town's portable art treasures and heritage—a mass empty-ing of churches and civil buildings would have caused hysteria and been a statement of no confidence in his leadership. While museums were closed (and could be systematically emptied over the war years), public buildings were not. Rather than save the treasures, the Nazis photographed everything.

Munich was indeed pummeled mercilessly by air raids, level-ing nearly half the city. What the bombs didn't get was destroyed by 10 years of rain and freezing winters.

(Church of Our Lady) has been the city's cathedral since 1821. Construction was funded with the sale of indulgences, but money problems meant the domes weren't added until Renaissance times. Late-Gothic buildings in Munich were generally built of brick—easy to make locally and cheaper and faster to build than stone. This church was constructed in a remarkable 20 years. It's located on the grave of Ludwig IV (who died in 1347). His big, black, ornate, tomb-like monument (now in the back) was originally in front at the high altar. Standing in the back of the nave, notice

Munich Rebuilds (1945-Present)

After the war, with generous American aid, Münchners set to reconstructing their city. During this time, many German cities established commissions to debate their rebuilding strategy: They could restore the old towns, or bulldoze and go modern. While Frankfurt decided to start from scratch (hence its Manhattan-like feel today), Munich voted—by a close margin—to rebuild its old town.

Münchners took care to preserve the original street plan and re-create the medieval steeples, Neo-Gothic facades, and Neoclassical buildings. They blocked off the city center to cars, built the people-friendly U-Bahn system, and opened up Europe's first pedestrian-only zone (Kaufingerstrasse and Neuhauser Strasse). Only now, nearly 65 years after the last bombs fell, are the restorations—based on those Nazi photographs—finally being wrapped up. And those postwar decisions still shape the city: Buildings cannot exceed the height of the church spires.

The 1972 Olympic Games, featuring a futuristic stadium and a squeaky-clean city, were to be Munich's postwar statement that it had arrived. However, the Games turned tragic when a Palestinian terrorist group stormed a dormitory and kidnapped (and eventually killed) 11 Israeli athletes. In 1989, when Germany reunited, Berlin once again became the focal point of the country, relegating Munich to the role of sleepy Second City.

These days, Munich seems to be comfortable just being itself rather than trying to keep up with Berlin. In fact, the city seems to be on a natural high, especially since the ascension of Joseph Ratzinger (the local archbishop) to the papacy in 2005, his wildly successful homecoming visit in 2006, and Munich hosting the World Cup soccer tournament that same year.

Today's Munich is rich—home to BMW and Siemens, and a producer of software, books, movies, and the latest fashions. It's consistently voted one of Germany's most livable cities—safe, clean, cultured, a university town, built on a people scale, and close to the beauties of nature. Though it's the capital of Bavaria and a major metropolis, Munich's low-key atmosphere has led Germans to dub it *Millionendorf*—the "village of a million people."

how your eyes go right to the altar...Christ...and (until recently) Ludwig. Those Wittelsbachs—always trying to be associated with God. In fact, this alliance was instilled in people through the prayers they were forced to recite: "Virgin Mary, mother of our duke, please protect us." A plaque over the last pew on the left recalls the life story of Joseph Ratzinger, who occupied the archbishop's seat in this very church from 1977 until 1982, when he moved into Pope John Paul II's inner circle in the Vatican, and ultimately became Pope Benedict XVI in 2005.

Other Church Sights: You can ascend the **tower** for the city's highest public viewpoint, at 280 feet (€3, 86 steps to elevator, April-Oct Mon-Sat 10:00-17:00, closed Sun and Nov-March). On many Wednesday evenings in summer, you can catch an **organ concert** here (€10, 19:00, tickets available at München Ticket office inside Marienplatz TI).

• *From here, we'll walk along back streets and squares, eventually ending up at the Hofgarten, the royal gardens. First walk two blocks directly behind the Frauenkirche to find the big, grassy square called...*

Marienhof

This square, tucked behind the New Town Hall, was left as a green island after the 1945 bombings. The square will be dug up for years while Munich builds a new subway tunnel here. With virtually the entire underground system converging on nearby Marienplatz, this new tunnel will provide a huge relief to the city's congested subterranean infrastructure.

• *On the far side of Marienhof is the most aristocratic grocery store in all of Germany...*

Alois Dallmayr Delicatessen

When the king called out for dinner, he called Alois Dallmayr. This place became famous for its exotic and luxurious food items: tropical fruits, seafood, chocolates, fine wines, and coffee (there are meat and cheese counters, too). As you enter, read the black plaque with the royal seal by the door: *Königlich Bayerischer Hof-Lieferant* ("Deliverer for the King of Bavaria and his Court"). Catering to royal and aristocratic tastes (and budgets), it's still the choice of Munich's old rich. Today, it's most famous for its sweets, chocolates, and coffee—dispensed from fine hand-painted Nymphenburg porcelain jugs.

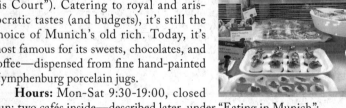

Hours: Mon-Sat 9:30-19:00, closed Sun; two cafés inside—described later, under "Eating in Munich"; Dienerstrasse 13-15, down the street to the right of New Town Hall, www.dallmayr.de.

• *From Marienhof, Hofgraben (which becomes Pfisterstrasse) leads three blocks east, directly to Platzl—"small square." (If you get turned around, just ask any local to point you toward the Hofbräuhaus.)*

Platzl

As you stand here, recall that everything around you was flattened in 1945, and appreciate the facades. Imagine the work that went

Oktoberfest

The 1810 marriage reception of King Ludwig I was such a success that it turned into an annual bash. These days, the

Oktoberfest lasts just over two weeks (Sept 22-Oct 7 in 2012), starting on the third Saturday in September and usually ending on the first Sunday in October (but never before Oct 3—the day Germany celebrates its recent reunification).

Oktoberfest kicks things off with an opening parade of more than 6,000 participants. Every night, it fills eight huge beer tents with about 6,000 people each. A million gallons of beer later, they roast the last ox.

It's best to reserve a room early, but if you arrive in the morning (except Fri or Sat) and haven't called ahead, the TI can usually help. The Theresienwiese fairground (south of the main train station), known as the "Wies'n" (VEE-zehn), erupts in a frenzy of rides, dancing, and strangers strolling arm-in-arm down rows of picnic tables while the beer god stirs tons of brew, pretzels, and wurst in a bubbling cauldron of fire. The triple-loop roller coaster must be the wildest on earth (best before the beer-drinking). During the fair, the city functions even better than normal. It's a good time to sightsee, even if beer-hall rowdiness isn't your cup of tea. For details, see www.oktoberfest.de.

If you're not visiting while the party's on, don't worry: You can still dance to oompah bands, munch huge pretzels, and show off your stein-hoisting skills any time of year at Munich's classic beer halls, including the venerable Hofbräuhaus (for descriptions of my favorite beer halls, see page 108).

Also in the city center, check out the humble **Beer and Oktoberfest Museum** (Bier- und Oktoberfestmuseum), which offers a low-tech and underwhelming take on history. Exhibits and artifacts outline the centuries-old quest for the perfect beer (apparently achieved in Munich) and the origins of the city's Oktoberfest celebration. The oldest house in the city center, the museum's home is noteworthy in itself (€4, Tue-Sat 13:00-17:00, closed Sun-Mon, between the Isartor and Viktualienmarkt at Sterneckerstrasse 2, tel. 089/2423-1607, www.bier-und-oktoberfestmuseum.de).

into rebuilding Munich after World War II. The reconstruction happened in stages: From 1945 to 1950, they removed 12 million tons of bricks and replaced roofs to make buildings weather tight. From 1950 to 1972, they redid the exteriors. From 1972 to 2000, they refurbished the interiors. Today, Platzl hosts a lively mix of places to eat and drink—pop-culture chains like Starbucks and Hard Rock Café alongside top-end restaurants like Schuhbecks.

• *A the bottom of the square (#6), you can experience the venerable...*

▲▲Hofbräuhaus

Whether or not you slide your lederhosen on its polished benches, it's a great experience just to walk through the world's most famous beer hall in all its rowdy glory.

Cost and Hours: Free to enter, daily 9:00-23:30, live oompah music during lunch and dinner; a five-minute walk northeast of Marienplatz at Platzl 6, www.hofbraeuhaus.de.

Touring the Hofbräuhaus: As you wander the Hofbräuhaus (HOAF-broy-howze), look for the various *Stammtisch* signs (mean-

ing "reserved" for regulars), hanging above tables where different clubs meet regularly; don't sit here unless you're specifically invited. Racks of locked steins, made of pottery and metal, are for regulars. You'll see locals stuffed into lederhosen and dirndls; giant gingerbread cookies that sport romantic messages; and postcards of the German (and apparently beer-drinking) pope.

After being bombed in World War II, this palace of beer was quickly rebuilt (reflecting the durability of traditional German priorities) and back in business within a few years. Notice the quirky 1950s-style painted ceiling, with Bavarian colors, grapes, chestnuts, and fun "eat, drink, and be merry" themes. A slogan on the ceiling above the band reads, *Durst ist schlimmer als Heimweh* ("Thirst is worse than homesickness"). For details on eating—and drinking—at the Hofbräuhaus, see page 109.

A bouncer at the door once told me he nabs 20-50 people (mostly Italians, he says) each day trying to steal mugs as souvenirs. The staircase to the left of the entrance displays historic old Hofbräuhaus photos and prints; there's a more extensive historical display on the second floor (daily 9:00-17:00).

• *Leaving the Hofbräuhaus, turn right and walk two blocks up to the street called...*

Maximilianstrasse

This boulevard is known as the home of Munich's most exclusive shops. Ludwig I made the grand but very impersonal Ludwigstrasse. In the 1850s, as a reaction to the unpopularity of that street and its namesake king, his son Maximilian II (father of "Mad" King Ludwig) built a street designed for the people and for shopping. It leads from the National Theater, over the Isar River, to the Bavarian parliament (which you can see from the theater end).

• *Walk left on Maximilianstrasse to the big square facing both the Residenz and the National Theater.*

Max-Joseph-Platz

The giant building wrapping around the square is the **Residenz,** the palace of the Wittelsbach royal family. Munich's best palace interior to tour, it features a museum (including some of the complex's most sumptuous staterooms), an impressive treasury, and the fine Cuvilliés Theater (all described on page 69).

The centerpiece of the square is a grand statue of King Maximilian I, a.k.a. **Max Joseph,** who was installed as Bavaria's king in 1806 by Napoleon. Because Napoleon was desperate to establish his family as royal, Max Joseph was crowned on one condition: that his daughter marry Napoleon's stepson.

Later, with the Holy Roman Empire gone and Napoleon history, modern 19th-century kings had little choice but to embrace constitutions that limited their power. (Remember that the country of Germany was only created in 1871. Until then, Bavaria was an independent and middle-sized power.) Max Joseph liberalized his realm with a constitution, emancipated Protestants and Jews, and established the Viktualienmarkt. He was a particularly popular king, and both his reign and his son's reign were full of grand

building projects designed to show that Bavaria was an enlightened state, Munich was a worthy capital, and the king was an equal with Europe's other royalty. The **National Theater** (fronting this square), which opened in 1818, celebrated Bavaria's strong culture, roots, and legitimacy. The Roman numerals MCMLXIII (1963) mark the year the theater reopened after WWII bombing restoration.

• *Leave Max-Joseph-Platz at the top corner, walking alongside the Residenz on Residenzstrasse to the next grand square.*

Munich at a Glance

In the Center

▲▲**Marienplatz** Munich's main square, at the heart of a lively pedestrian zone, watched over by New Town Hall (and its glockenspiel show). **Hours:** Always open; glockenspiel jousts daily at 11:00 and 12:00, plus 17:00 May-Oct; New Town Hall tower elevator runs May-Oct daily 10:00-19:00; Nov-April Mon-Fri 10:00-17:00, closed Sat-Sun. See page 49.

▲▲**Viktualienmarkt** Munich's "small-town" open-air market, perfect for a quick snack or meal. **Hours:** Mon-Sat, *Biergarten* open until late, closed Sun. See page 56.

▲▲**Munich City Museum** The city's history in five floors. **Hours:** Tue-Sun 10:00-18:00, closed Mon. See page 57.

▲▲**Hofbräuhaus** World-famous beer hall, worth a visit even if you're not chugging. **Hours:** Daily 9:00-23:30. See page 64.

▲▲**The Residenz** The elegant family palace of the Wittelsbachs, awash with Bavarian opulence. Complex includes the Residenz Museum (private apartments), Residenz Treasury (housing Wittelsbach family crowns and royal knickknacks), and the impressive, just-restored Cuvilliés Theater. **Hours:** Museum and treasury—daily April-mid-Oct 9:00-18:00, mid-Oct-March 10:00-17:00; theater—April-mid-Sept daily 9:00-18:00; mid-Sept-March Mon-Sat 14:00-17:00, Sun 10:00-17:00. See page 69.

▲▲**Alte Pinakothek** Bavaria's best painting gallery, with a wonderful collection of European masters from the 14th through the 19th centuries. **Hours:** Wed-Sun 10:00-18:00, Tue 10:00-20:00, closed Mon. See page 76.

▲▲**Deutsches Museum** Germany's version of our Smithsonian Institution, with 10 miles of science and technology exhibits. **Hours:** Daily 9:00-17:00. See page 84.

▲**Neue Pinakothek** The Alte's twin sister, with paintings from 1800 to 1920. **Hours:** Thu-Mon 10:00-18:00, Wed 10:00-20:00, closed Tue. See page 80.

▲**Pinakothek der Moderne** Hip contemporary-art museum near the Alte and Neue Pinakotheks—housed in a building that's as interesting as the art. **Hours:** Tue-Sun 10:00-18:00, Thu until 20:00, closed Mon. See page 80.

▲**Museum Brandhorst** Munich's newest art museum, with collections from the turn of the 21st century. **Hours:** Tue-Sun 10:00-

18:00, Thu until 20:00, closed Mon. See page 81.

▲**English Garden** The largest city park on the Continent, packed with locals, tourists, surfers, and nude sunbathers. (On a bike, I'd rate this ▲▲.) **Hours:** Always open. See page 82.

St. Peter's Church Munich's oldest church, packed with relics. **Hours:** Church—long hours daily; spire climb—Mon-Fri 9:00-18:30, Sat-Sun 10:00-18:30, off-season until 17:30. See page 53.

St. Michael's Church Renaissance church housing Baroque decor and a crypt of 40 Wittelsbachs. **Hours:** Church—daily 9:00-19:00, Thu until 20:45, Sun until 22:00; crypt—Mon-Fri 9:30-16:30, Sat 9:30-14:30, closed Sun, less off-season. See page 59.

Frauenkirche Huge, distinctive twin-domed church looming over the city center. **Hours:** Church—Sat-Wed 7:00-19:00, Thu 7:00-20:30, Fri 7:00-18:00; tower climb—April-Oct Mon-Sat 10:00-17:00, closed Sun and Nov-March. See page 59.

Away from the Center
▲▲**Nymphenburg Palace** The Wittelsbachs' impressive summer palace, featuring a hunting lodge, coach museum, fine royal porcelain collection, and vast park. **Hours:** Daily April-mid-Oct 9:00-18:00, mid-Oct-March 10:00-16:00. See page 87.

▲▲**BMW-Welt and Museum** The carmaker's futuristic museum and floating-cloud showroom shows you BMW past, present, and future in some unforgettable architecture. **Hours:** BMW-Welt—building open 9:00-24:00, exhibits open 9:00-18:00; museum—Tue-Sun 10:00-18:00, closed Mon. See page 91.

▲▲**Dachau Concentration Camp** Notorious Nazi camp on the outskirts of Munich, now a powerful museum and memorial. **Hours:** Tue-Sun 9:00-17:00, closed Mon. See page 93.

▲**Museum of Transportation** Deutsches Museum's cross-town annex devoted to travel. **Hours:** Daily 9:00-17:00. See page 85.

▲**Andechs Monastery** Baroque church, hearty food, and Bavaria's best brew, in the nearby countryside. **Hours:** *Biergarten* daily 10:00-20:00, church open until 18:00. See page 99.

Olympic Park Munich's 1972 Olympic stadium, now a lush park with a view tower and pool. **Hours:** Grounds always open; tower daily 9:00-24:00, pool daily 7:00-23:00. See page 92.

Odeonsplatz

This square is a part of the royal family's grand imperial Munich vision. The church on Odeonsplatz (Theatinerkirche) contains about half of the Wittelsbach tombs. The loggia on Odeonsplatz (honoring Bavarian generals) is modeled after the famous Renaissance-style loggia in Florence. And two grand boulevards, Ludwigstrasse and Brienner Strasse, lead away from there.

Ludwigstrasse leads to a Roman-type triumphal arch that hovers in the distance. Though Max Joseph was himself a busy and visionary leader, it was his son and successor, the builder-king Ludwig I, who made Munich into a grand capital. His street, Ludwigstrasse, remains an impressive boulevard, with 60-foot-tall buildings stretching a mile from Odeonsplatz to the Arch of Victory, capped with a figure of Bavaria riding a lion-drawn chariot. (And it was this Ludwig's wedding festival in 1810 that became an annual bash, giving Munich perhaps its greatest claim to fame: Oktoberfest.)

• *From Odeonsplatz, face west, and look (or wander) down the grand...*

Brienner Strasse

This street gives you a taste of the Wittelsbachs' ambitious city planning. In the distance, on Karolinenplatz, the black obelisk commemorates the 30,000 Bavarians who marched with Napoleon to Moscow and never returned. Beyond that is the grand Königsplatz, or "King's Square," with its stern Neoclassicism, evocative of ancient Greece (and home to Munich's cluster of art museums, described on page 75).

Between here and the obelisk, Brienner Strasse goes through a square called **Platz der Opfer des Nationalsozialismus** ("Square of the Victims of Nazism"). It's the site of Himmler's Gestapo headquarters for the entire Third Reich, now entirely gone. If you went farther along, past the obelisk toward Konigsplatz, you'd find two former Nazi administration buildings; one, with recognizably fascist architecture, was Hitler's main residence while in Munich (it's now the music academy; a plaque in the street explains the buildings' history).

• *Backtrack to Odeonsplatz, then finish your walk just beyond Ludwigstrasse in the royal gardens or the genteel café at the...*

Hofgarten

The elegant court garden *(Hofgarten)* is a delight on a sunny afternoon. The "Renaissance" temple centerpiece has great acoustics (and usually a musician performing for tips from

listeners). The lane leads to a building that houses the government of Bavaria and the Bavarian war memorial, which honors
the fallen *heroes* of World War I, but only the *fallen* of World War
II. The venerable old **Café Tambosi,** with an Italian-influenced
menu, Viennese elegance inside, and a relaxing garden setting outside, is a good antidote to all the beer halls (daily 8:00-24:00, €10
lunch specials, Odeonsplatz 18, tel. 089/298-322). Just beyond is a
lazy gravel *boules* court.

• *With this city walk completed, you've seen the essential Munich. From
here, you can walk a couple of blocks to the museum quarter (up Brienner
Strasse); head through the Hofgarten to the vast English Garden (best
on a bike); backtrack a block to tour the museum and treasury at the
Residenz (facing Max-Joseph-Platz); or descend into the U-Bahn from
the Odeonsplatz stop for points elsewhere. These—and many other—
sights are described in the next section.*

*If you're ready to eat, you have several choices. Café Tambosi and
the elegant Spatenhaus are nearby, and there are more options if you
backtrack toward Marienplatz (see "Eating in Munich," later).*

Sights in Munich

Most of the top sights in the city center are covered on the self-
guided walk, above. But there's much more to see in this city.

The Residenz

For a long hike through corridors of gilded imperial Bavarian
grandeur, tour the Wittelsbachs' family palace. The sprawling
Residenz, with a facade modeled after the Medici's Pitti Palace
in Florence, evolved from the 14th through the 19th centuries—as
you'll see on the charts near the entrance—and was largely rebuilt
after World War II.

If you're torn between visiting Munich's top two palaces, I'd
say the Residenz interior is best, while Nymphenburg (described
on page 87) has the finest garden.

Orientation: Within the Residenz complex are four sights:
the 90-room Residenz Museum, the eight-room Treasury, the
Halls of the Nibelungen (currently closed for renovation), and
the Cuvilliés Theater. To reach the first three, enter the complex
from the main entrance on Max-Joseph-Platz (at the corner of
the palace nearest Marienplatz); there's also a side entrance on
Residenzstrasse. Inside the main entrance, past the Halls of the
Nibelungen, you'll find the ticket office and the entrances to the
Museum and Treasury. The separate entrance to the Cuvilliés
Theater is a little ways up Residenzstrasse—ask staff to help if you
can't find it.

Cost and Hours: €7 each to visit the Residenz Museum

(palace apartments) and the Treasury, including audioguides; €11 combo-ticket covers both; €13 version also covers Cuvilliés Theater—see page 75; covered by Bavarian Castles Pass. The Halls of the Nibelungen are closed for renovation until at least 2013. All parts of the palace are open daily April-mid-Oct 9:00-18:00, mid-Oct-March 10:00-17:00, last entry one hour before closing. The complex is located three blocks north of Marienplatz. Tel. 089/290-671, www.residenz-muenchen.de.

Halls of the Nibelungen (Nibelungensäle)

The mythological scenes in these halls—currently closed for renovation—were the basis of Wagner's *Der Ring des Nibelungen*. Wagner and "Mad" King Ludwig were friends and spent time hanging out here (c. 1864). The images in this hall could well have inspired Wagner to write his *Ring* and Ludwig to build his "fairy-tale castle," Neuschwanstein.

▲▲Residenz Museum (Residenzmuzeum)

Though called a "museum," what's really on display here are the best parts of the Residenz itself: the palace's spectacular banquet and reception halls, and the Wittelsbachs' lavish private apartments. It's the best place to get a glimpse of the opulent lifestyle of Bavaria's late, great royal family. (Whatever happened to the Wittelsbachs, the longest continuously ruling family in European history? They're still around, but they're no longer royalty, so most of them have real jobs now—you may well have just passed one on the street.)

◑ Self-Guided Tour: Leave the ticket office and pick up the free audioguide; later, if you visit the Treasury, you'll need to stop by the desk again to have the guide switched over. Ask for a map of the museum (in English, often stacked up in the museum's first room or two).

You're about to walk through a 90-room residence, including three private chapels and several still-in-use banquet halls. Follow the red arrows along a one-way route made meaningful by the fine—if ponderous—audioguide and the English descriptions in each room. The rooms are numbered (in black on the bilingual information boards; these numbers are on the map too), and you'll also see red signs with numbers that you can punch into the audioguide. This tour just covers the highlights of the route, in the order you'll see them—use the audioguide to learn more about the rooms you find most compelling. Mercifully, you'll find chairs and benches in many rooms, as well as two WCs along the way.

• *One of the first rooms you'll come to is the...*

Shell Grotto (Room 6, actually outside, facing a courtyard, ground floor): The whole wall in front of you is made from Bavarian freshwater shells. This artificial grotto was an exercise in man controlling nature—a celebration of humanism. Renaissance humanism was a big deal when this was built in the 1550s. Imagine the ambience here during that time, with Mercury—the pre-Christian god of trade and business—overseeing the action, and red wine spurting from the mermaid's breasts and dripping from Medusa's head in the court-

yard. Like the rest of the palace, the grotto was destroyed by Allied bombs. After World War II, Germans had no money to contribute to the reconstruction—but they could gather shells. All the shells you see here were donated by small-town Bavarians, as the grotto was rebuilt according to Nazi photos (see "The History of Munich: Part 2" sidebar). To the right of the shells, the door marked *OO* leads to handy WCs.

• *The next room is the...*

Antiquarium (Room 7, ground floor): In the mid-16th century, Europe's royal families (such as the Wittelsbachs) collected and displayed busts of emperors—implying a connection between

themselves and the ancient Roman rulers. Given the huge demand for these Classical statues in the courts of Europe, many of the "ancient busts" are fakes cranked out by crooked Romans. Still, a third of the statuary you see here is original. This was, and still is, a festival banquet hall. Two hundred dignitaries can dine here, surrounded by

allegories of the goodness of just rule on the ceiling. Check out the small paintings around the room—these survived the bombs because they were painted in arches. Of great historic interest, these paintings show 120 Bavarian villages as they looked in 1550. Even today, when a Bavarian historian wants a record of how his village once looked, he comes here. Notice the town of Dachau in 1550 (above the door on the left as you enter).

• *Keep going through a few more rooms, then up a stairway to the upper floor. Now the tour winds through a couple dozen small rooms on either side of a large courtyard—many of them the private apartments of the prince and his consort. In Room 32, detour to the right to see the...*

All Saints' Chapel (Room 32, upper floor): This early-19th-century chapel, commissioned by King Ludwig I, was severely damaged in World War II—and didn't reopen until 2003. It still hasn't been fully decorated and outfitted; photos by the entrance show how it used to look.

• *Keep going along the other side of the courtyard until you come to Room 45, where you'll have a choice between "short" and "long" routes. Unless you're in a real hurry and want to skip some of the best parts of the palace, choose the long route and turn right. You'll wind around through the large Imperial Hall (Room 111) and then through several small rooms, where the centerpiece painting on the ceiling is just blank black, as no copy of the original survived World War II. A little farther on, peek into the...*

Reliquary Room (Room 95, upper floor): This room harbors a collection of gruesome Christian relics (bones, skulls, and even several mummified hands) in ornate golden cases.

• *A few more steps brings you to the balcony of the...*

Chapel (Hofkapelle; the balcony is Room 96, and the chapel itself is Room 89): Dedicated to Mary, this late-Renaissance/

early-Baroque gem was the site of "Mad" King Ludwig's funeral after his mysterious murder—or suicide—in 1886. (He's buried in St. Michael's Church, described on page 59.) Though Ludwig II was not popular in political circles, he was beloved by his people, and his funeral drew huge crowds. About 75 years earlier, his grandfather and namesake (Ludwig I) was married here, in 1810. After the wedding ceremony, carriages rolled his guests to a rollicking reception, which turned out to be such a hit that it became an annual tradition—Oktoberfest.

• *A couple rooms ahead is the...*

Private Chapel of Maximilian I (Room 98, upper floor): Duke Maximilian I, the dominant Bavarian figure in the Thirty Years' War, built one of the most precious rooms in the palace. The miniature pipe organ (from about 1600) still works. The room is sumptuous, from the gold leaf and the fancy hinges to the miniature dome and the walls made of stucco marble. (Stucco marble is fake marble—a special mix of stucco, applied and polished. Designers liked it because it was less expensive than real marble and the color could be controlled.) Note the post-Renaissance perspective tricks decorating the walls; they were popular in the 17th century. The case (on the right wall as you enter) supposedly contains skeletons of three babies from the Massacre of the Innocents in Bethlehem (where Herod, in an attempt to murder the baby

Jesus, ordered all sons of a certain age killed).

• Now you'll enter a set of rooms (#55-62) known as the Ornate Rooms (Reiche Zimmer), which were used for official business. The Wittelsbachs were always trying to keep up with the Habsburgs, and this long string of ceremonial rooms was all for show. The decor and furniture are Rococo—over-the-top Baroque. The family art collection, now in the Alte Pinakothek, once decorated these walls. The most lavish of these rooms is the...

Red Room (Room 62, upper floor): The ultimate room is at the end of the corridor—the coral red room from 1740. (Coral red

was *the* most royal of colors in Germany.) Imagine visiting the duke and having him take you here to ogle miniature copies of the most famous paintings of the day, composed with one-haired brushes. Notice the fun effect of the mirrors around you—the corner mirrors make things go forever and ever.

• From the Red Room, you'll circle around to a stairway that brings you back down to the ground floor, where you'll soon reach the long Ancestral Gallery (Room #4). Before walking down it, detour to the right, into the...

Porcelain Cabinet (Room 5, ground floor): In the 18th century, the royal family bolstered their status with an in-house porcelain works (just like the one the Wettins, the ruling family of Saxony, had at Meissen, near Dresden). The Wittelsbach family had their own Nymphenburg porcelain made for the palace. See how the mirrors and porcelain vases give the effect of infinite pedestals. If this inspires you to own some pieces of your own, head to the Nymphenburg Porcelain Store at Odeonsplatz (see "Shopping in Munich," later).

• Now go back into the...

Ancestral Gallery of the Wittelsbach Family (Room 4, ground floor): This room is from the 1740s (about 200 years younger than the Antiquarium). All official guests had to pass through here to meet the duke (and his 100 Wittelsbach relatives). The family tree in the center is labeled "genealogy of an imperial family." Notice how the tree is shown being actually planted by Hercules, to boost their royal street cred. The big Wittelsbach/ Habsburg rivalry was worked out through 500 years of marriages and battles—when they failed to sort out a problem through strategic weddings, they had a war. Opposite the tree are portraits of Charlemagne and Ludwig IV, each a Holy Roman Emperor and each wearing the same crown (now in Vienna). Ludwig IV was the first Wittelsbach HRE—an honor used for hundreds of years to substantiate the family's claim to power. You are surrounded by a scrapbook covering centuries of Wittelsbach family history.

Allied bombs took their toll on this hall. Above, the central ceiling painting has been restored, but since there were no photos of the other two ceiling paintings, those spots remain empty. Looking at the walls, you can see how each painting was hastily cut out of its frame. Museums were closed in 1939, then gradually evacuated in anticipation of bombings. But public buildings like this palace, which remained open to instill confidence in local people, could not prepare for the worst. It wasn't until 1944, when bombs were imminent, that the last-minute order was given to slice all portraits out of their frames and hide them away.

• *The doorway at the end of the hall deposits you back at the museum entrance. If you're also visiting the Treasury, go to the audioguide desk to have them reset your guide.*

▲▲Residenz Treasury (Schatzkammer)

The Treasury, next door to the Residenz Museum, shows off a thousand years of Wittelsbach crowns and knickknacks. Vienna's jewels are better, but this is the best treasury in Bavaria, with fine 13th- and 14th-century crowns and delicately carved ivory and glass (for cost and hours, see page 69).

◑ **Self-Guided Tour:** A clockwise circle through the eight rooms takes you chronologically through a thousand years of royal treasure. (You can't get lost, as there aren't any side rooms.) You'll see little signs with a headphone icon and black-and-white numbers—punch these into your audioguide for full explanations.

The oldest jewels in the first room are 200 years older than Munich itself. Many of these came from various prince-bishop collections when they were secularized (and their realms came under the rule of the Bavarian king from Munich) in the Napoleonic Era (c. 1800). The tiny mobile altar allowed a Carolingian king (from Charlemagne's family of kings) to pack light in 890—and still have a little Mass while on the road.

In Room 3, study the reliquary with St. George killing the dragon—sparkling with more than 2,000 precious stones. Get up close (it's OK to walk around the rope posts)...you can almost hear the dragon hissing. It was made to contain the relics of St. George, who never existed (Pope John Paul II declared him nothing more than a legend). If you could lift the miniscule visor, you'd see that the carved ivory face of St. George is actually the Wittelsbach duke (the dragon represents the "evil" forces of Protestantism).

In the next room (#4), notice the vividly carved ivory crucifixes from 1630 (#157 and #158, on the right). These incredibly realistic sculptures were done by local artist Georg Petel, a friend of Peter Paul Rubens (whose painting of Christ on the cross—which you'll see across town in the Alte Pinakothek—is Petel's obvious inspiration). Look at the flesh of Jesus' wrist pulling around the nails.

Continue into Room 5. The freestanding glass case (#245) holds the never-used royal crowns of Bavaria. Napoleon ended the Holy Roman Empire and let the Wittelsbach family rule as kings of Bavaria. As a sign of friendship, this royal coronation gear was made in Paris by the same shop that crafted Napoleon's crown. But before the actual coronation, Bavaria joined in an all-Europe anti-Napoleon alliance, and suddenly these were too French to be used.

Cuvilliés Theater

The exquisite Cuvilliés Theater is in a northern wing of the Residenz complex, best entered from Residenzstrasse. Your visit

consists of just one small but plush theater hall. It's so heavily restored, you can almost smell the paint. In 1751, this was Germany's ultimate Rococo theater. Mozart conducted here several times. Designed by the same brilliant dwarf architect who did the Amalienburg Palace (see page 89), this theater is dazzling enough to send you back to the days of divine monarchs.

Cost and Hours: €3.50, €11 combo-ticket with Museum and Treasury, covered by Bavarian Castles Pass; April-mid-Sept daily 9:00-18:00; mid-Sept-March Mon-Sat 14:00-17:00, Sun 10:00-17:00; last entry one hour before closing, no English information provided.

Munich's Cluster of Art Museums

This cluster of blockbuster museums (the Alte, Neue, and Moderne Pinakotheks, the Museum Brandhorst, the currently closed Lenbachhaus, and the Glyptothek) displays art spanning from the 14th century to the 21st. The Glyptothek and Lenbachhaus are right by the Königsplatz stop on the U-2 subway line. The three

Pinakothek museums and the Brandhorst are just to the northeast. Handy tram #27 whisks you right to the Pinakothek stop from Karlsplatz (between the train station and Marienplatz). You can also take bus #100 from the train station, or walk 10 minutes from the Theresienstrasse or Königsplatz stops on the U-2 line.

A €12 combo-ticket covers the three Pinakotheks and the Brandhorst, and pays for itself if you visit two museums. On Sundays, these museums and the Glyptothek let you in for just a token €1, but charge for the useful audioguides (normally included).

▲▲Alte Pinakothek

Bavaria's best painting gallery (the "Old Art Gallery," pronounced ALL-tuh pee-nah-koh-TAYK) shows off a world-class collec-

tion of European master-pieces from the 14th to 19th centuries, starring the two tumultuous centuries (1450-1650) when Europe went from medieval to modern. See paintings from the Italian Renaissance (Raphael, Leonardo, Botti-celli, Titian) and the German Renaissance it inspired (Albrecht Dürer). The Reformation of Martin Luther eventually split Europe into two subcultures—Protestants and Catholics—with their two distinct art styles (exemplified by Rembrandt and Rubens, respectively).

Cost and Hours: €7, €1 on Sun, covered by €12 combo-ticket, open Wed-Sun 10:00-18:00, Tue 10:00-20:00, closed Mon, last entry 30 minutes before closing, free and excellent audioguide (€4.50 on Sun), obligatory lockers with refundable €2 deposit, no flash photos; U-2: Theresienstrasse, tram #27, or bus #100; Barer Strasse 27, tel. 089/2380-5216, www.pinakothek.de/alte -pinakothek.

☉ Self-Guided Tour: From the ticket counter, head toward the back wall and walk up the stairway to the left. All the paint-ings we'll see are on the upper floor, which is laid out like a barbell. Start at one fat end and work your way through the "handle" to the other end. Along the way you'll find the following paintings, roughly in this order.

German Renaissance—Room II: Albrecht Altdorfer's *The Battle of Issus (Schlacht bei Issus)* shows a world at war. Masses of soldiers are swept along in the currents and tides of a battle com-pletely beyond their control, their confused motion reflected in

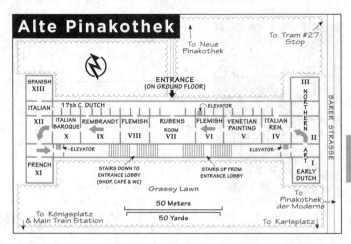

Alte Pinakothek

To Neue Pinakothek

To Tram #27 Stop

ENTRANCE (ON GROUND FLOOR)

SPANISH XIII

ITALIAN | 17th C. DUTCH

XII | ITALIAN BAROQUE X | REMBRANDT IX | FLEMISH VIII | RUBENS ROOM VII | FLEMISH VI | VENETIAN PAINTING V | ITALIAN REN. IV

ELEVATOR

ELEVATOR

FRENCH XI

STAIRS DOWN TO ENTRANCE LOBBY (SHOP, CAFÉ & WC)

STAIRS UP FROM ENTRANCE LOBBY

III

N O R T H E R N

A R T

II

I EARLY DUTCH

BARER STRASSE

Grassy Lawn

50 Meters

50 Yards

To Königsplatz & Main Train Station

To Pinakothek der Moderne

To Karlsplatz

MUNICH

the swirling sky. We see the battle from a great height, giving us a godlike perspective. Though the painting depicts Alexander the Great's victory over the Persians (find the Persian king Darius turning and fleeing), it could as easily have been Germany in the 1520s. Christians were fighting Muslims, peasants battled masters, and Catholics and Protestants were squaring off for a century of conflict. The armies melt into a huge landscape, leaving the impression that the battle goes on forever.

Albrecht Dürer's larger-than-life *Four Apostles* (*Johannes und Petrus* and *Paulus und Marcus*) are saints of a radical new religion:

Martin Luther's Protestantism. Just as Luther challenged Church authority, Dürer—a friend of Luther's—strips these saints of any rich clothes, halos, or trappings of power and gives them down-to-earth human features: receding hairlines, wrinkles, and suspicious eyes. The inscription warns German rulers to follow the Bible rather than Catholic Church leaders. The figure of Mark—a Bible in one hand and a sword in the other—is a fitting symbol of the dangerous times.

Dürer's *Self-Portrait in Fur Coat* (*Selbstbildnis im Pelzrock*)

MUNICH

looks like Jesus Christ but is actually 28-year-old Dürer himself, gazing out, with his right hand solemnly giving a blessing. This is the ultimate image of humanism: the artist as an instrument of God's continued creation. Get close and enjoy the intricately braided hair, the skin texture, and the fur collar. To the left of the head is Dürer's famous monogram—"A.D." in the form of a pyramid.

Italian Renaissance—Room IV: With the Italian Renaissance—the "rebirth" of interest in the art and learning of ancient Greece and Rome—artists captured the realism, three-dimensionality, and symmetry found in classical statues. Leonardo da Vinci's *Virgin and Child (Maria mit dem Kind)* need no halos—they radiate purity. Mary is a solid pyramid of maternal love, flanked by Renaissance-arch windows that look out on the hazy distance. Baby Jesus reaches out to play innocently with a carnation, the blood-colored symbol of his eventual death.

Raphael's *Holy Family at the Canigiani House (Die hl. Familie aus dem Hause Canigiani)* takes Leonardo's

pyramid form and runs with it. Father Joseph forms the peak, with his staff as the strong central axis. Mary and Jesus (on the right) form a pyramid-within-the-pyramid, as do Elizabeth and baby John the Baptist on the left. They all exchange meaningful contact, safe within the bounds of the stable family structure.

In Botticelli's *Lamentation over Christ (Die Beweinung Christi)*, the Renaissance "pyramid" implodes, as the weight of the dead Christ drags everyone down, and the tomb grins darkly behind them.

Venetian Painting—Room V: In Titian's *Christ Crowned with Thorns (Die Dornenkronung)*, a powerfully built Christ sits silently enduring torture by prison guards. The painting is by Venice's greatest Renaissance painter, but there's no symmetry, no pyramid form, and the brushwork is intentionally messy and Impressionistic. By the way, this is the first painting we've seen done on canvas rather than wood, as artists experimented with vegetable oil-based paints.

Rubens and Baroque—Room VII: Europe's religious wars split the Continent in two—Protestants in the northern countries, Catholics in the south. (Germany itself was divided, with Bavaria remaining Catholic.) The Baroque style, popular in Catholic countries, featured large canvases, bright colors, lots of flesh, rippling motion, wild emotions, grand themes...and pudgy winged babies, the sure sign of Baroque. This room holds several canvases by the great Flemish painter Peter Paul Rubens.

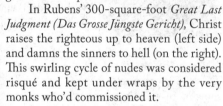

In Rubens' 300-square-foot *Great Last Judgment (Das Grosse Jüngste Gericht)*, Christ raises the righteous up to heaven (left side) and damns the sinners to hell (on the right). This swirling cycle of nudes was considered risqué and kept under wraps by the very monks who'd commissioned it.

Rubens and Isabella Brant shows the artist with his first wife, both of them the very picture of health, wealth, and success. They lean together unconsciously, as people in love will do, with their hands clasped in mutual affection. When his first wife died, 53-year-old Rubens found a replacement—16-year-old Hélène Fourment, shown in an adjacent painting (just to the left) in her wedding dress. You may recognize Hélène's face in other Rubens paintings.

The Rape of the Daughters of Leucippus (Der Raub der Tochter des Leukippos) has many of Rubens' most typical elements—fleshy, emotional, rippling motion; bright colors; and a classical subject. The legendary twins Castor and Pollux crash a wedding and steal the brides as their own. The chaos of flailing limbs and rearing horses is all held together in a subtle X-shaped composition. Like the weaving counterpoint in a Baroque fugue, Rubens

balances opposites.

Notice that Rubens' canvases were—to a great extent—cranked out by his students and assistants from small "cartoons" the master himself made (displayed in the next room).

Rembrandt and Dutch—Room IX: From Holland, Rembrandt van Rijn's *Six Paintings from the Life of Christ* are a down-to-earth look at supernatural events. The *Adoration (Die Anbetung der Hirten)* of Baby Jesus takes place in a 17th-century

Dutch barn with ordinary folk as models. The canvases are dark brown, lit by strong light. The *Adoration*'s light source is the Baby Jesus himself—literally the "light of the world." In the *Deposition (Kreuzabnahme)*, the light bounces off Christ's pale body onto his mother Mary, showing how his death also hurts her. The drama is underplayed, with subdued emotions. Looking on is a man dressed in blue—a self-portrait of Rembrandt.

▲Neue Pinakothek

The Alte Pinakothek's sister is a twin building across the street, showing off paintings from 1800 to 1920: Romanticism, Realism, Impressionism, *Jugendstil*, Claude Monet, Pierre-Auguste Renoir, Vincent van Gogh, Francisco Goya, and Franz von Stuck—Munich's answer to Gustav Klimt.

Cost and Hours: €7, €1 on Sun, covered by €12 combo-ticket, open Thu-Mon 10:00-18:00, Wed 10:00-20:00, closed Tue, well-done audioguide is usually free but €4.50 on Sun, classy Café Hunsinger in basement spills into park; U-2: Theresienstrasse, tram #27, or bus #100; Barer Strasse 29 but enter on Theresienstrasse, tel. 089/2380-5195, www.pinakothek.de/neue-pinakothek.

▲Pinakothek der Moderne

This museum picks up where the other two leave off, covering the 20th century. Four perma-nent displays (graphics, design, architecture, and paintings) are layered within the striking minimalist architecture. You'll find works by Pablo Picasso, Salvador Dalí, Joan Miró, René Magritte, Max Beckmann, Max Ernst, and abstract artists. The big, white, high-ceilinged build-

ing itself is worth a look. Even if you don't pay to visit the exhibits, step into the free entrance hall to see the sky-high atrium and the colorful blob-column descending the staircase.

Cost and Hours: €10, €1 on Sun, covered by €12 combo-ticket, open Tue-Sun 10:00-18:00, Thu until 20:00, closed Mon; U-2: Theresienstrasse, tram #27, or bus #100; Barer Strasse 40, tel. 089/2380-5360, www.pinakothek.de/pinakothek-der-moderne. This far-out collection offers little information in English—and there's no English audioguide.

▲Museum Brandhorst

Museum Brandhorst covers the end of the 20th century and the beginning of the 21st, with full English captions. You can't miss

the building—thousands of colored cylinders line the outside. The top floor (of three) is devoted to American artist Cy Twombly. A highlight is an ensemble of 12 Twombly paintings called *Lepanto*, after a 1571 battle in which Venice defeated the Ottoman fleet; six huge canvases of roses fill another room. On the lower floor, I liked the giant medicine cabinet full of multicolored pills by Damien Hirst, and the sizable Andy Warhol collection.

Cost and Hours: €7, €1 on Sun, covered by €12 combo-ticket, audioguide usually free but €4.50 on Sun, open Tue-Sun 10:00-18:00, Thu until 20:00, closed Mon, small café; U-2: Theresienstrasse, tram #27, or bus #100; Theresienstrasse 35a, tel. 089/2380-52286, www.museum-brandhorst.de.

▲Lenbachhaus

Closed for renovation until sometime in 2013, this museum is housed in a beautiful late 19th-century Tuscan-style villa (once owned by painter Franz von Lenbach). It features the most complete collection of the early Modernist movement known as Blaue Reiter (Blue Rider), a branch of Expressionism that flourished from 1911 to 1914. When Wassily Kandinsky, Paul Klee, Franz Marc, Gabriele Münter, and some of their art-school cronies got fed up with being told how and what to paint, they formed the Blaue Reiter around a common ideology: to strive for new forms that expressed spiritual truth. Already controversial in their own day, their work was later targeted by the Nazis as *entartete Kunst* ("degenerate art"). The collection allows visitors to trace Kandinsky's progression from his earlier, more realistic works to the complete abstraction he's best known for. Münter, Kandinsky's lover and a great painter in her own right, donated her entire private collection (90 paintings and 330 other works) to Lenbachhaus in 1957, putting this little museum on the world art map.

Cost and Hours: Closed for renovation; when it reopens: likely €5-10 depending on exhibits, Tue-Sun 10:00-18:00, closed Mon, worthwhile €3 audioguide, €8 guidebook is a nice souvenir but otherwise unnecessary, small café, U-2: Königsplatz, Luisenstrasse 33, tel. 089/2333-2000, www.lenbachhaus.de.

Glyptothek

A collection of Greek and Roman sculpture started by King Ludwig I, the Glyptothek includes the famous *Barberini Faun*,

statues from the Greek Classical period, funerary monuments of wealthy Athenian families, and pediments of the Temple of Aegina. For a Who's Who of ancient celebrities, visit the Room of Ancient Portraits, where you'll come face-to-face with Alexander the Great and other luminaries from ancient political and philosophical spheres.

Cost and Hours: €3.50, €1 on Sun, not much in English so invest in the worthwhile €1 guidebook, Tue-Sun 10:00-17:00, Thu until 20:00, closed Mon, U-2: Königsplatz, on Königsplatz, tel. 089/286-100, www.antike-am-koenigsplatz.mwn.de/glyptothek.

The English Garden and Nearby

▲**English Garden (Englischer Garten)**—Munich's "Central Park," the largest one on the Continent, was laid out in 1789 by

an American. More than 100,000 locals commune with nature here on sunny summer days. The park stretches three miles from the center, past the university to the trendy and bohemian Schwabing quarter. For the best quick visit, follow the river from the surfers (under the bridge just past Haus der Kunst) downstream into the garden. Just beyond the hilltop temple (walk up for a postcard view of the city), you'll find the big Chinese Tower beer garden and other places to enjoy a drink or a meal (described later, under "Eating in Munich"). A rewarding respite from the city, the park is especially fun—and worth ▲▲—on a bike under the summer

Green Munich

Although the capital of a very conservative part of Germany, Munich has long been a liberal stronghold. For nearly two decades, the city council has been controlled by a Social Democrat/Green Party coalition. The city policies are pedestrian-friendly—you'll find much of the town center closed to normal traffic, with plenty of bike lanes and green spaces. As you talk softly and hear birds rather than motors, it's easy to forget you're in the center of a big city. On summer Mondays, the peace and quiet make way for "blade Monday"—when streets in the center are closed to cars and as many as 30,000 inline skaters swarm around town in a giant rolling party.

sun and on warm evenings (unfortunately, there are no bike-rental agencies in or near the park; to rent some wheels, see page 44). Caution: While local law requires sun-worshippers to wear clothes on the tram, the park is sprinkled with buck-naked sunbathers—quite a shock to prudish Americans (they're the ones riding their bikes into the river and trees).

Haus der Kunst—Built by Hitler as a temple of Nazi art, this bold and fascist building—a rare surviving example of a purpose-built Nazi structure—is now an impressive shell for various temporary art exhibits. Ironically, the art now displayed in Hitler's "house of art" is the kind that annoyed the Führer most—modern. Its cellar, which served as a nightclub for GIs in 1945, is now the P-1 nightclub.

Cost and Hours: €5-10 per exhibit, combo-tickets save money if seeing at least two exhibits, daily 10:00-20:00, Thu until 22:00, little information in English but some exhibits may have English handouts, at south end of English Garden, tram #17 or bus #100 from station to Nationalmuseum/Haus der Kunst, Prinzregentenstrasse 1, tel. 089/211-270, www.hausderkunst.de.

Nearby: Just beyond the Haus der Kunst, where Prinzregentenstrasse crosses the Eisbach canal, you can watch adventure-seekers surfing in the rapids created as the small river tumbles underground.

Bavarian National Museum (Bayerisches National-museum)—This tired but interesting collection features Tilman Riemenschneider woodcarvings, manger scenes, traditional living rooms, and old Bavarian houses.

Cost and Hours: €5, €1 on Sun, open Tue-Sun 10:00-17:00, Thu until 20:00, closed Mon, tram #17 or bus #100 from station to Nationalmuseum/Haus der Kunst, Prinzregentenstrasse 3, tel. 089/211-2401, www.bayerisches-nationalmuseum.de.

Deutsches Museum

Germany's answer to our Smithsonian National Air and Space Museum, the Deutsches Museum traces the evolution of science and technology. The main branch of the Deutsches Museum is centrally located. The two other branches—the Museum of Transportation and the Flight Museum—are situated outside the city center, but are worth the effort for enthusiasts. You can pay separately for each museum, or buy one €15 combo-ticket, which covers all three. Since this ticket has no time limit, you can spread out your visits to the various branches over your entire stay.

▲▲Deutsches Museum (Main Branch)

Enjoy wandering through well-described rooms of historic airplanes, spaceships, mining, the harnessing of wind and water power, hydraulics, musical instruments, printing, chemistry, computers, astronomy, and nanotechnology...it's the Louvre of technical know-how. The museum is designed to be hands-on; if you see a button, push it. But with 11 acres of floor space and 10 miles of exhibits, from astronomy to zymurgy, even those on roller skates will need to be selective. While the museum was a big deal a generation ago, today it feels to many a bit dated, dusty, and overrated. It's far too vast and varied to cover completely. The key is to study the floor plan that shows all the departments and simply visit the ones that interest you. Many sections of the museum are well-described in English. The much-vaunted high-voltage demonstrations (3/day, 15 minutes, all in German) show the noisy creation of a five-foot bolt of lightning.

Cost and Hours: €8.50, €15 combo-ticket includes Museum of Transportation and Flight Museum, daily 9:00-17:00, worthwhile €4 English guidebook, self-service cafeteria, tel. 089/21791, www.deutsches-museum.de.

Getting There: Take the S-Bahn to Isartor, then walk 300 yards over the river, following signs.

◑ Self-Guided Tour: If you don't mind a very long, winding, one-way route that feels like a subterranean hike, start off in the **mines** (mines closed during daily German-language tours at 9:45 and 13:45). This exhibit traces the history of mining since prehistoric times. Enter just past the coat-check desk (just keep on going—there's only one way) through a vacant mine shaft with lots of old mining gear. While descriptions are only in German, the reconstructions of coal, potash, and salt mines are still impressive. When you emerge from the mines, skip the mineral oil and natural gas section *(Erdöl und Erdgas)* and follow the signs for *Ausgang* (exit).

The fascinating, compact exhibit on **marine navigation** (on the ground floor) has models of sail, steam, and diesel vessels, from early canoes to grand sailing ships. Take the staircase down into the galley, below the main floor, to check out how life on passenger ships has changed—and don't miss the bisected U1 submarine. This first German submarine, dating from 1906, has been in the museum since 1921.

Flying high above the masts of the marine navigation exhibit is the section on **aeronautics** (first floor). Displays cover the most basic airborne flights (flying insects and seed pods), Otto Lilienthal's successful efforts in 1891 to imitate bird flight, and the development of hot-air balloons and gas-powered zeppelins. Many of the planes here are original, including the Wright brothers' Type A (1909), fighters and cargo ships from the two World Wars, and the first functioning helicopter, made in 1936. Climb into the planes whenever permitted, and try out the flight simulator.

The **astronautics** exhibit is located on the second floor. Back in the 1920s, Germany was working on rocket-propelled cars and sleds. Germany's research provided the US and Soviet space teams with much of their technical know-how. Here, you can peer at models of the V-2 (one of the first remote-controlled rockets/weapons, from World War II), motors from the American Saturn rockets, and various space capsules, including Spacelab. The main focus is the walk on the moon, the Apollo missions, and the dogs-in-space program (monkeys, too)...but if you've ever been curious about how space underwear works, you'll find your answer here.

The third floor traces the **history of measurement,** including time (from a 16th-century sundial and an 18th-century clock to a scary Black Forest wall clock complete with grim reaper), weights, geodesy (surveying and mapping), and computing (from 18th-century calculators to antiquated computers from the 1940s and 1950s).

On your way to the state-of-the-art **planetarium** (worth a visit if open, requires €2 extra ticket, lecture in German), poke your head out into the **sundial garden** located above the third floor. Even if you're not interested in sundials, this is a great place for a view of the surrounding landscape. On a clear day, you can see the Alps.

▲Museum of Transportation (Verkehrszentrum)

You don't need to be an engineer or race-car driver to get a kick out of this fun museum. In 2003, the Deutsches Museum celebrated its centennial by opening this annex across town that shows off all aspects of transport, from old big-wheeled bikes to Benz's first car (a three-wheeler from the 1880s) to sleek ICE super-trains. It's housed in three giant hangar-like exhibition halls near the Oktoberfest grounds, a.k.a. Theresienwiese. All the exhibits are in both English and German.

Cost and Hours: €6, €15 combo-ticket includes Deutsches Museum and Flight Museum, daily 9:00-17:00, Theresienhöhe 14a, tel. 089/5008-06762, www.deutsches-museum.de.

Getting There: Take the U-4 or U-5 to Schwanthalerhöhe and follow signs for *Deutsches Museum* from the platform. The museum is just a few steps from the station exit.

Tours: The free tours daily at 13:30, 14:00, and 14:30 (each focusing on one of the museum's three halls) are primarily in German, but worth tagging along on for a chance to climb into the old carriage in Hall 2 (only allowed as part of the tour). The metal track simulates what it would have felt like to travel in the 18th century over different terrain (grass and cobblestones—pretty uncomfortable).

⊘ Self-Guided Tour: True to the Deutsches Museum's interactive spirit, the Museum of Transportation is totally hands-on, and comes with plentiful English explanations. The museum asks what our lives would be like without transportation, and the exhibits show how modes of transportation developed from Neolithic "bone" skates (predecessors to today's inline skates) to 19th-century Lapland skis, to today's snowboards and fast cars.

Hall 1 focuses on urban transport, with special attention to Munich. Climb into the original 1967 U-Bahn car, marvel at a cross-section of the intricate and multi-layered subway system, learn about the history of the bicycle, and admire the vintage cars arrayed into mock traffic jams. Once a day (usually at 11:30; confirm times to be sure) they fire up an S-Bahn simulator and let visitors pretend to drive the train.

Hall 2 gives you a look at the development of long-distance overland travel. The focus here is on trains and coach travel (serious train buffs, however, will be more excited by the Deutsche Bahn Museum in Nürnberg, described in that chapter). Don't miss the Maffei S3/6, a.k.a. "The Pride of Bavaria" (in its heyday the fastest steam engine, at nearly 80 miles per hour); climb aboard the clever old postal train car (complete with a mail slot on the side); and check out the 1950s panorama bus that shuttled eager tourists to fashionable destinations such as Italy.

Hall 3 is all about fun: motorcycles, bicycles, skis, and race cars. Famous prewar models include the deluxe Mercedes-Benz 370 (1930s) and the Auto Union Type C "Grand Prix" race car. Other tiny racers—which resemble metal pickles to the uninitiated—include the 1950s Mercedes-Benz 300 SLR and the famous Messerschmitt 200. You'll also find early 18th-century bicycles based on Leonardo da Vinci's drawings. Before the invention of the pedal crank, bikes were just silly-looking scooters for adults.

Flight Museum (Flugwerft Schleissheim)

Fans of all things winged will enjoy the Deutsches Museum's Flight Museum, with more than 50 planes, helicopters, gliders, and an original Europa rocket housed in a historical aerodrome on a former military airfield. Inside the museum is the glass-walled workshop, where visitors can watch as antique planes are restored.

Cost and Hours: €6, €15 combo-ticket includes Deutsches Museum and Museum of Transportation, daily 9:00-17:00; 20-minute S-Bahn trip from Marienplatz, take S-1 direction: Freising Flughafen and get off at Oberschleissheim, trip covered by Munich XXL day pass, Effnerstrasse 18, tel. 089/315-7140, www.deutsches-museum.de.

Sights Outside the City Center

Greater Munich

The following destinations are in Munich, but on the outskirts of town.

Nymphenburg Palace Complex

Nymphenburg Palace and the surrounding one-square-mile park are good for a royal stroll or bike ride. Here you'll find a pair of palaces, the Royal Stables Museum, and playful extras such as a bathhouse, pagoda, and artificial ruins.

Cost and Hours: €6 for just the palace, €11.50 for the palace plus outlying sights, covered by Bavarian Castles Pass. All sights are open daily April-mid-Oct 9:00-18:00, mid-Oct-March 10:00-16:00, except for Amalienburg Palace, which is closed in the winter. The park is open daily 6:30-dusk. Tel. 089/179-080, www.schloss-nymphenburg.de.

Getting There: The palace is three miles northwest of central Munich. From the center, take tram #17 from the Karlstor or the train station (15 minutes to palace), getting off at the Schloss Nymphenburg stop. From the bridge by the tram stop, you'll see the palace—a 10-minute walk away. A pleasant bike path follows Arnulfstrasse from the train station all the way to Nymphenburg (a 30-minute pedal).

▲▲**Nymphenburg Palace**—In 1662, after 10 years of trying, the Bavarian ruler Ferdinand Maria and his wife, Henriette Adelaide of Savoy, finally had a son, Max Emanuel. In gratitude for a male heir, Ferdinand gave this land to his Italian wife, who proceeded to build an Italian-style Baroque palace. Their son expanded the palace to today's size. For 200 years, this was the Wittelsbach family's summer escape from Munich. (They still refer to themselves as princes and live in one wing of the palace.)

MUNICH

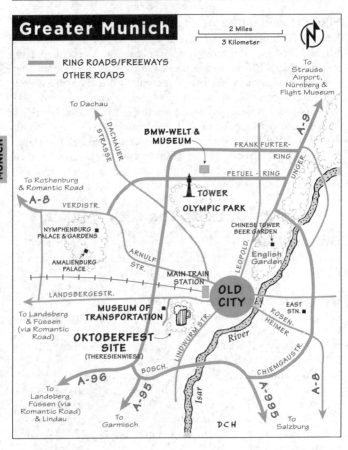

Greater Munich

2 Miles
3 Kilometer

RING ROADS/FREEWAYS
OTHER ROADS

To Strauss Airport, Nürnberg & Flight Museum

To Dachau

DACHAUER STRASSE

BMW-WELT & MUSEUM

FRANKFURTER-RING

PETUEL-RING

UNGER.

A-9

TOWER

OLYMPIC PARK

To Rothenburg & Romantic Road

A-8

VERDISTR.

NYMPHENBURG PALACE & GARDENS

AMALIENBURG PALACE

ARNULF STR.

CHINESE TOWER BEER GARDEN

LEOPOLD.

English Garden

MAIN TRAIN STATION

OLD CITY

LANDSBERGESTR.

To Landsberg & Füssen (via Romantic Road)

MUSEUM OF TRANSPORTATION

OKTOBERFEST SITE (THERESIENWIESE)

LINDWURM STR.

River

EAST STN.

ROSEN-HEIMER

BOSCH.

A-96

A-95

Isar

CHIEMGAUSTR.

A-8

A-995

To Landsberg, Füssen (via Romantic Road) & Lindau

To Garmisch

DCH

To Salzburg

Your visit is limited to 16 main rooms on one floor: the Great Hall (where you start), the King's Wing (to the right as you approach the palace), and the Queen's Wing (to the left). The place is stingy on information—not even providing a map without charging—and the rooms only have meaning if you invest in the €3.50 audioguide.

◉ Self-Guided Tour: The **Great Hall** in the middle was the dining hall, site of big Wittelsbach family festivals. One of the grandest Rococo rooms in Bavaria, it was decorated by Johann Baptist Zimmermann (of Wieskirche fame) and François de Cuvilliés in about 1760. The painting on the ceiling shows a pagan heavenly host of Olympian gods, a scene designed to help legitimize the supposedly divine rule of the Wittelsbachs. The windows connect you with the lavish gardens.

From here, the two wings (the King's and the Queen's) are mirror images of one another: antechamber, audience chamber, bedchamber, and private living quarters.

The **King's Wing** (north, right of entrance) has walls filled with Wittelsbach portraits and stories. In the second room straight ahead, notice the painting showing the huge palace grounds, with Munich (and the twin onion domes of the Frauenkirche) three miles in the distance. Imagine the logistics when the royal family—with their entourage of 200—decided to move out to the summer palace. The Wittelsbachs were high rollers; from 1624 until 1806, one of the seven electors of the Holy Roman Emperor was a Wittelsbach. In 1806, Napoleon ended that institution and made the Wittelsbachs kings. (Note: For simplicity, I often refer to the Wittelsbachs as kings and queens, even though before 1806, these rulers were technically dukes, duchesses, and electors—and some were even Holy Roman Emperors.)

In the **Queen's Wing** (south, left of entrance), head down the long hall. Near the end, you'll come to **King Ludwig I's Gallery of Beauties.** The gallery is decorated with portraits of 36 beautiful women—all of them painted by Joseph Stieler from 1827 to 1850. King Ludwig I was a consummate girl-watcher who prided himself on the ability to appreciate beauty regardless of social rank. He would pick the prettiest women from the general public and, with one of the most effective pickup lines of all time, invite them to the palace for a portrait. Who could refuse? He may not have been picky about status—the women range from royal princesses to a humble cobbler's daughter—but Ludwig sure seemed to prefer brunettes. (Find the cobbler's daughter, Helene Sedlmayr, in a dress way beyond her budget. She married the king's valet, had 10 kids, and lived until 1898.) The portraits reflect the modest Biedermeier style, as opposed to the more flamboyant Romanticism of the same period. If only these creaking floors could talk. Something about the place feels highly sexed, in a Prince Charles kind of way.

The next rooms are decorated in the Neoclassical style of the Napoleonic Era. At the rope, see the room where Ludwig II was born (August 25, 1845). Royal births were carefully witnessed, and the mirror allowed for a better view. While Ludwig's death was shrouded in mystery (see page 139), his birth was well-documented.

Amalienburg Palace—Three hundred yards from the Nymphenburg Palace, hiding in the park (head into the sculpted garden and veer to the left, following signs), you'll find a fine little Rococo hunting palace. In 1734, Elector Karl Albrecht had this hunting lodge built for his wife, Maria Amalia. It was designed by François de Cuvilliés and decorated by Johann Baptist Zimmermann.

Touring the Palace: As you approach, notice its facade. Above the pink-and-white grand entryway, Diana, goddess of the chase, is surrounded by themes of the hunt and flanked by busts of satyrs. The queen would shoot from the perch atop the roof. Behind a wall in the garden, dogs would scare non-flying pheasants. When they jumped up in the air above the wall, the sporting queen—as if shooting skeet—would pick the birds off.

Tourists enter this tiny getaway through the back door. The first room has doghouses under gun cupboards. Next, in the fine yellow-and-silver bedroom, the bed is flanked by portraits of Karl Albrecht and Maria Amalia—decked out in hunting attire. She liked her dogs. The door under the portrait leads to stairs to the rooftop pheasant-shooting perch. The relief in the door shows Vulcan forging arrows for amorous cupids.

The mini-Hall of Mirrors is a blue-and-silver commotion of Rococo nymphs designed by Cuvilliés. In the next room, paintings depict court festivities, formal hunting parties, and no-contest kills (where the animal is put at an impossible disadvantage—like shooting fish in a barrel). Finally, the kitchen is decorated with Chinese picnics on blue Dutch tiles.

Royal Stables Museum (Marstallmuseum)—This huge garage is lined with gilded Cinderella coaches. The highlight is just inside the entrance: the 1742 Karl Albrecht coronation coach. When the Elector Karl Albrecht was chosen as Emperor, he rode in this coach, drawn by eight horses. Kings got only six.

Touring the Museum: Wandering through the collection, you can trace the evolution of 300 years of coaches—getting lighter and with better suspension as they were harnessed to faster horses. The carousel for the royal kids made development of dexterity fun—lopping off noses and heads and tossing balls through the snake. The glass case is filled with accessories.

In the room after the carousel, find the painting on the right of "Mad" King Ludwig on his sleigh at night. In his later years, Ludwig was a Howard Hughes-type recluse who stayed away from the public eye and only went out at night. (At his nearby Linderhof Palace, he actually had a hydraulic-powered dining table that would rise from the kitchen below, completely set for the meal—so he wouldn't be seen by his servants.) In the next room, you'll find Ludwig's actual sleighs. Ludwig's over-the-top coaches were Baroque. But this was 1870. The coaches, like the king, were in the wrong century. Notice the photos (c. 1865, in the glass case) of Ludwig and the Romantic composer Richard Wagner. Ludwig cried on the day Wagner was married. Hmmm.

Across the passage from the museum entrance, the second hall is filled with more practical coaches for everyday use. At the end of that hall, head upstairs to see a collection of **Nymphenburg porcelain** (described by an English loaner booklet at the entrance). Historically, royal families such as the Wittelsbachs liked to have their own porcelain plants to make fit-for-a-king plates, vases, and so on. The Nymphenburg Palace porcelain works is still in operation. Ludwig ordered the masterpieces of his royal collection (now at the Alte Pinakothek) to be copied in porcelain for safekeeping into the distant future. Take a close look—these are exquisite.

▲▲BMW-Welt and Museum

A brand with a rich heritage, an impressive display of futuristic architecture, and an enthusiastic welcome to the public combine to

make the headquarters of BMW ("bay-em-VAY" to Germans) one of the top sights in Munich. This vast complex—built on the site of Munich's first airstrip and home to the BMW factory since 1920—has four components: the headquarters (in the building nicknamed "the Four Cylinders"—not open to the public), the factory (tourable with advance reservations), the showroom (called BMW-Welt—"BMW World"), and the new BMW Museum.

The **BMW-Welt** building itself—a cloud-shaped, glass-and-steel architectural masterpiece—is reason enough to visit. It's free and filled with exhibits designed to enthuse car lovers so they'll find a way to afford a Bimmer. While the adjacent museum reviews the BMW past, BMW-Welt shows you the present and gives you a breathtaking look at the future. With interactive stations, high-powered videos, an inviting cafeteria, and lots of horsepower, this is where customers come to pick up their new Bimmers, and where hopeful customers-to-be come to nurture their automotive dreams.

In the futuristic **BMW Museum**, a bowl-shaped building encloses a world of floating walkways linking exhibits highlighting BMW motorcycle and car design and technology through the years. Employing seven themes and great English descriptions, the museum traces the Bavarian Motor Works' history since 1917, when the company began making airplane engines. Motorcycles came next, followed by the first BMW sedan in 1929. You'll see how design was celebrated here from the start. Exhibits showcase motorsports, roadsters, and luxury cars. Stand on an *E* for English to hear the chief designer talk about his favorite cars in the "treasure trove." The Info Bar lets you review 90 years of history with the touch of a finger. And the 1956 BMW 507 is enough to rev almost anyone's engine.

Cost and Hours: BMW-Welt is free and open daily (building open 9:00-24:00, exhibits open 9:00-18:00, www.bmw-welt.com). The museum costs €12 (Tue-Sun 10:00-18:00, closed Mon, www .bmw-museum.de). English tours are offered of both the Welt (€7, daily at 14:00, 80 minutes) and the museum (€3, 1.5 hours, call ahead for times). Factory tours are booked long in advance (€8, 2.5 hours, register online or call, tel. 0180-211-8822, www.bmw -werk-muenchen.de; ask at the BMW-Welt building about cancellations—released to the public a half-hour before each tour).

Getting There: It's very easy: Ride U-3 to Olympia-Zentrum; the stop faces the BMW-Welt entry. To reach the museum, walk through BMW-Welt and over the swoopy bridge.

Olympic Park (Olympiapark München)

Munich's great 1972 Olympic stadium and sports complex is now a lush park. You can get a good look at the center's striking

"cobweb" style of architecture while enjoying the park's picnic potential. In addition, there are several activities on offer at the park, including a tower (Olympiaturm) with a commanding but so-high-it's-boring view from 820 feet and an excellent swimming pool, the Olympia-Schwimmhalle. With the construction of Munich's Allianz Arena for the 2006 World Cup, Olympic Park has been left in the past, and has melted into the neighborhood as simply a fine park and swimming pool.

Cost and Hours: Tower—€4.50, daily 9:00-24:00, last trip 23:30, tel. 089/30670, www.olympiapark.de. Pool—€4, daily 7:00-23:00, last entry 22:00, tel. 01801-796-223, www.swm.de. The U-3 runs from Marienplatz directly to the Olympia-Zentrum stop.

▲Isar River Bike Ride

Munich's river, lined by a gorgeous park, leads bikers into the pristine countryside in just a few minutes. From downtown (easy access from the English Garden or Deutsches Museum), follow

the riverside bike path south (upstream) along the east (left) bank. You can't get lost. Just stay on the lovely bike path. It crosses the river after a while, passing tempting little *Biergartens* and lots of Bavarians having their brand of fun—including gangs enjoying Munich's famous river party rafts. Go as far as you like, then retrace your route to get home. The closest bike rental is at Munich Walk, near the Isartor, which also offers a guided bike tour along this route (see page 45).

Near Munich
The following sights are a short train or bus ride away from Munich.

▲▲Dachau Concentration Camp Memorial (KZ-Gedenkstätte Dachau)
Dachau was the first Nazi concentration camp (1933). Today, it's

an easily accessible camp for travelers and an effective voice from our recent but grisly past, pleading "Never again." A visit here is a valuable experience and, when approached thoughtfully, well worth the trouble. After this powerful sightseeing experience, many people gain more respect for history and the dangers of mixing fear, blind patriotism, and an evil government. You'll likely see lots of students here, as all Bavarian schoolchildren are required to visit a concentration camp. It's interesting to think that little more than a couple of generations ago, people greeted each other with a robust *"Sieg Heil!"* Today, almost no Germans know the lyrics of their national anthem, and German flags are a rarity outside of major soccer matches.

Cost and Hours: Free, Tue-Sun 9:00-17:00, closed Mon except holidays, last entry 30 minutes before closing. Though the museum shuts down at 17:00, the grounds are unofficially open until about 17:30 or 18:00 (as it takes a while for people to walk back to the entrance). The museum discourages parents from bringing children under age 12.

Planning Your Time: Allow yourself about five hours here (four at a minimum), including your round-trip from central Munich. Giving yourself at least two and a half hours at the camp itself lets you see it at a comfortable pace (with just two hours, it's doable but rushed, and you'll have to skip the movie).

Getting There: The camp is a 45-minute trip from downtown Munich. Take the S-2 subway (direction: Petershausen) from any of the central S-Bahn stops in Munich to Dachau (3/hour, 20-minute trip from Hauptbahnhof). Then, at the Dachau station, go down the stairs and out to the bus platforms; find the one marked *KZ-Gedenkstätte*. Here, catch bus #726 and ride it seven minutes to the KZ-Gedenkstätte stop (3/hour; on Sundays, you can also take bus #724). The Munich XXL day pass covers the entire trip, both ways (€7.30/person, €12.80/partner ticket for up to 5 adults). If you've already invested in a three-day Munich transport pass (which covers only the white/inner zone), you can save a couple euros by buying and stamping single tickets (€2.50/person each way) to cover the part of the trip that's in the green zone. You can also take a guided tour from Munich (described on page 48).

Drivers follow Dachauer Strasse from downtown Munich to Dachau-Ost, then follow *KZ-Gedenkstätte* signs.

The Town: The town of Dachau is more pleasant than its unfortunate association with the camp on its outskirts, and tries hard to encourage you to visit its old town and castle (www.dachau.de). With 40,000 residents and quick access to downtown Munich, Dachau is now a high-priced and in-demand place to live.

Visitors Center: Coming from the bus stop or parking lot, you'll first see the visitors center, outside the camp wall. It doesn't have any exhibits, but does have some useful services: a café serving simple lunches (sandwiches and €5-6 pasta dishes), a bookstore with a modest selection of English-language books on Holocaust themes, and a small WC (there are larger ones in the

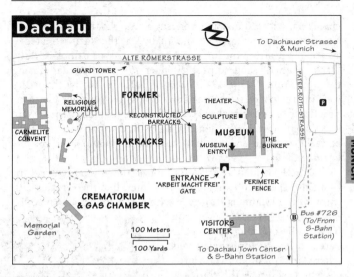

Dachau

ALTE RÖMERSTRASSE

To Dachauer Strasse & Munich

GUARD TOWER

FORMER

RELIGIOUS MEMORIALS

RECONSTRUCTED BARRACKS

CARMELITE CONVENT

BARRACKS

THEATER

SCULPTURE

MUSEUM

MUSEUM ENTRY

"THE BUNKER"

ENTRANCE "ARBEIT MACHT FREI" GATE

PERIMETER FENCE

CREMATORIUM & GAS CHAMBER

Memorial Garden

100 Meters
100 Yards

VISITORS CENTER

To Dachau Town Center & S-Bahn Station

Bus #726 (To/From S-Bahn Station)

PATER-ROTH-STRASSE

MUNICH

museum inside the camp). At the information desk, you can rent an audioguide or sign up for tours.

Tours: The €3.50 **audioguide** is informative and gives you a few extras (mainly short reminiscences by two camp survivors and three members of the Allied forces who liberated the camp), but isn't essential, since the camp is fully labeled in English. Two different free **guided walks** in English are offered, starting from the visitors center (daily at 11:00 and 13:00; limited to 30 people, so show up early, especially in summer; call or visit website to confirm times, tel. 08131/669-970, www.kz-gedenkstaette -dachau.de).

Background: While a relatively few 32,000 inmates died in Dachau between 1933 and 1945 (in comparison, more than a million were killed at Auschwitz in Poland), the camp is notorious because it was the Nazis' first. It was originally established to house political prisoners and opponents of the Nazi regime, and only later played a role in World War II. In the 1930s, the camp was located outside built-up areas, and was surrounded by a mile-wide restricted area. It was a work camp, where inmates were used for slave labor, including constructing the buildings that you see. A huge training center stood next to the camp. The people who ran the entire concentration-camp system during the war were trained here, and it was former Dachau officials who went on to manage the death camps farther east, mostly in Nazi-occupied Poland. For example, the first commandant at Auschwitz, Rudolf Höss, worked at Dachau from 1934 to 1938.

After war broke out, the regime found more purposes for Dachau: a departure point for people shipped east to the gas chambers, a special prison for priests, a center for barbaric medical experimentation on inmates, and finally—as the Nazis retreated—a transfer destination for prisoners from other camps. Oddly, Dachau actually housed people longer *after* the war than during the war. From 1945 to 1948, Nazi officials arrested by the Allies were interned here. After that (from 1948 to 1964), ethnic Germans expelled from Eastern Europe lived in the barracks, which were like a small town, with a cinema, shops, and so on. The last of the barracks was torn down in 1964, and the museum opened the following year.

◑ Self-Guided Tour: Walking past the visitors center, turn right into the main compound. You enter, like the inmates did, through the infamous **iron gate** with the taunting slogan *Arbeit macht frei* ("Work makes you

free"). The building around the gate, called the Jourhaus, was where new prisoners were processed. Inside are the four key experiences of the memorial: the museum, the bunker behind the museum, the restored barracks, and a pensive walk across the huge but now-empty camp to the shrines and crematorium at the far end.

Museum: The large camp maintenance building to your right has been converted into a gripping museum. Walk toward the

forecourt of the building and you'll see the museum entrance. Just inside is a small bookshop that funds a nonprofit organization (founded by former prisoners) that researches and preserves the camp's history. Here you can pick

up a €0.50 information sheet, or buy the excellent 200-page book with a CD (€15) that contains the same text and images that you'll see in the museum.

The museum is organized chronologically, focusing on three stages in the history of the camp: before the war (1933-1938), early in the war (1939-1942), and late in the war (1942-1945). Exhibits are thoughtfully and completely described in English, and computer touch-screens let you watch early newsreels.

In its first years, the camp was basically a political prison designed for opponents of the Nazi regime, and it could hold just under 3,000 inmates. Aside from political activists, these prisoners included homosexuals, Jehovah's Witnesses, Gypsies, so-called career criminals, and Germans who had been deported back home after trying to emigrate. As Nazi extremism increased, the camp operated with less and less regard for the rule of law, and after the Nazis whipped up domestic anti-Semitism, a number of German Jews were also sent to Dachau.

Prisoners had a regimented life, with lights out at 21:00, a wake-up call at 4:00 in the morning, and an 11-hour workday, plus standing for roll call at 5:15 and 19:00. In 1937 and 1938, the camp was expanded and the building that now houses the museum was built, as well as barracks intended to hold 6,000 prisoners.

Once Germany invaded Poland in 1939, fewer local detainees arrived at the camp, replaced by more and more prisoners from Poland and Czechoslovakia. Dachau was also the place of detention for almost 2,000 Polish Catholic clergymen and for former fighters in the Spanish Civil War. During these years, Dachau prisoners were used as convenient guinea pigs for war-related medical experiments of human tolerance for air pressure, hypothermia, and biological agents like malaria; the photos of these victims may be the most painful in the museum. After the Nazis put their plans for exterminating Europe's Jews in motion, Jewish prisoners at Dachau were typically sent east to the extermination camps in Poland and killed.

Once the tide of war started to turn in 1942 and 1943, both Nazi measures and camp conditions became more and more desperate. Inmates were now seen as a source of slave labor for the German war machine. Many were put to work in sub-camps (in nearby towns) making armaments. As the Allies closed in on both fronts, prisoners from concentration camps in France, the Low Countries, and Eastern Europe were transferred to Dachau, and the number of Jewish internees rose again. Disease broke out, and food ran short in the winter of 1944-1945. With coal for the crematorium running low, the corpses of those who died were buried in mass graves outside the camp site. Though the Nazis moved some camp inmates to the mountains of the Tirol in spring 1945, more than 30,000 people were jammed into Dachau's 34 barracks when the Allies arrived on April 29. Two thousand of them were so weak or sick that they died in the weeks after liberation.

In the middle of the museum building is a **theater,** which shows a powerful 22-minute documentary movie dating from the 1960s. Check the schedule for the next English-language showing.

• *Consider using the WC before leaving the museum building (there aren't any bathrooms elsewhere within the camp walls). Find the side door, at the end of the exhibition, which leads out to the long, low bunker behind the museum building.*

MUNICH

Bunker: This was a cellblock for prominent "special prisoners," such as failed Hitler assassins, German religious leaders, and politicians who challenged Nazism. Most of the 136 cells are empty, but exhibits in a few of them (near the entrance) profile the inmates and the SS guards who worked at Dachau, and allow you to listen to some inmates' testimonies. Look into cell #65, which was divided by partitions (now gone) into "standing cells,"

with less than three square feet of floor space. Inmates were tortured here by being forced to stay on their feet for days at a time.

• *Exit the bunker the way you came, and walk around past the* Arbeit macht frei *gate to the big square between the museum and the reconstructed barracks, which was used for roll call. Cross the square to the farther of the two reconstructed...*

Barracks: Take a quick look inside to get an idea of what sleeping and living conditions were like in the camp. There were

34 barracks, each measuring about 10 yards by 100 yards. When the camp was at its fullest, there was only about one square yard of living space per inmate.

• *Now walk between the two reconstructed barracks and down the tree-lined walk past the foundations of the other barracks. At the end of the camp, in space that once housed the camp vegetable garden, rabbit farm, and brothel, there are now three places of meditation and worship (Jewish to your right, Catholic straight ahead, and Protestant to your left). Beyond them, just outside the camp, is a Carmelite convent. Turn left toward the corner of the camp and find the small bridge leading to the...*

Camp Crematorium: A memorial garden surrounds the two camp crematorium buildings, which were used to burn the bodies of prisoners who had died or been killed. The newer, larger, concrete crematorium was built to replace the smaller wooden one. One of its rooms is a **gas chamber,** which worked on the same

principles as the much larger one at Auschwitz, and was originally disguised as a shower room (the fittings are gone now). It was never put to use at Dachau for mass murder, but some historians suspect that a few people were killed in it experimentally. In the garden near the buildings is a Russian Orthodox shrine.

To end your visit, retrace your steps back to the visitors center and bus stop.

▲Andechs Monastery

This monastery crouches quietly with a big smile between two lakes just south of Munich. For a fine Baroque church in a rural Bavarian setting at a monastery that serves hearty cafeteria-quality food and perhaps the best beer in Germany, consider a short side-trip here. The cafeteria terrace offers first-class views and second-class prices. Don't miss the stroll up to the church, where you can sit peacefully and ponder the striking contrasts a trip through Germany offers.

Hours: *Biergarten* open daily 10:00-20:00, church open until 18:00, tel. 08152/3760, www.andechs.de.

Getting There: Reaching Andechs from Munich without a car is doable with a little planning. Bus #951 stops at the monastery on its run between Herrsching (at the end of the S-8 subway line) and Starnberg Nord (on the S-6 line). Use the online train schedule at www.bahn.com to find a convenient connection (put in Kloster Andechs as your destination, about an 80-minute trip, buy Munich *Gesamtnetz* day ticket for €10.80 single or €19.60 for up to 5 people). You can also take the S-8 train to Herrsching, then hike, bike, or catch a taxi for the 3 miles to the monastery.

More Day Trips from Munich

For day trips to many Bavarian destinations, including the first four listed here, consider traveling by train with the **Bayern-Ticket.** It covers up to five people from Munich to anywhere in Bavaria (plus Salzburg) and back for only €29 (€21 for one person, not valid before 9:00 Mon-Fri, valid only on slower "regional" trains—most of them labeled on schedules as either "RB," "RE," or "IRE"). The ticket is explained in *The Inside Track* newsletter and sold at EurAide (see page 41).

▲▲▲**"Mad" King Ludwig's Castles**—The spectacular Neuschwanstein and Linderhof castles make a great day trip. Your easiest option is to take a tour (see "Tours in Munich," earlier). Without a tour, only Neuschwanstein is easy (2 hours by train to Füssen, then 10-minute bus ride to the castle). Or spend the night there. For all the details, see the next chapter.

▲▲**Nürnberg**—A handy but expensive ICE express train zips you to Nürnberg in about an hour (departures several times an hour), making this very historic city a viable day trip from Munich. Cheaper RE trains, covered by the Bayern-Ticket, take a little longer. For information, see the Nürnberg chapter.

▲▲▲**Salzburg**—This Austrian city is an easy day trip and offers some exciting sightseeing (hourly trains from Munich get you there in less than 2 hours). For details, see the Salzburg and Berchtesgaden chapter.

▲**Berchtesgaden**—This resort, near Hitler's Eagle's Nest getaway, is easier as a side-trip from Salzburg (just 12 miles from there). For more, see page 224.

MUNICH

Shopping in Munich

While the whole city is great for shopping, the most glamorous area is around Marienplatz. It's fun to window-shop, even if you have no plans to buy. Here are a few stores and streets to consider.

Department Stores: You'll see lots of modern department stores. Locals rate them this way: **C&A** (which sells only clothing) is considered cheap yet respected, **Kaufhof** (which sells everything) is mid-range, and **Karstadt** is upmarket. **Beck's,** an even more upscale department store at Marienplatz, has been a local institution since 1861. With six floors of expensive designer clothing (plus some music, stationery, and cosmetics), this is the place to go for a €200 pair of jeans. Beck's has long been to fabrics what Alois Dallmayr is to fine food (see page 62)—too expensive to actually buy anything in, but fun to browse (Mon-Sat 10:00-20:00, closed Sun).

Also on Marienplatz is the big **Hugendubel bookstore.** Their English selection is paltry—you'll find more at their English-language store on Salvatorplatz, behind Fünf Höfe (see "Helpful Hints," page 41).

Weinstrasse/Theatinerstrasse: Shoppers will want to stroll from Marienplatz down the pedestrianized Weinstrasse (it begins to the left as you face New Town Hall). After a few short blocks, the street name changes to Theatinerstrasse; look for **Fünf Höfe** on your left, a delightful mall filled with Germany's top shops (open until 20:00, www.fuenfhoefe.de). Named for its five courtyards, this is where tradition meets modern. Note how its Swiss architects (who also designed Munich's grand Allianz soccer stadium for the 2006 World Cup) play with light and color. Even if you're not a shopper, wander through the **Kunsthalle** to appreciate the architecture, the elegant window displays, and the sight of Bavarians living very well.

For fine-quality (and very expensive) traditional clothing, detour a block west along Maffeistrasse to **Loden-Frey Verkaufshaus.** The third floor of this fine department store is dedicated to classic Bavarian wear for men and women (Mon-Sat 10:00-20:00, closed Sun, Maffeistrasse 7, tel. 089/210-390, www.loden-frey.com).

Theatinerstrasse spills out onto Odeonsplatz, where you'll find the **Nymphenburg Porcelain Store** (Mon-Fri 10:00-18:30, Sat 10:00-18:00, closed Sun, Odeonsplatz 1, tel. 089/282-428, www.nymphenburg.com).

Maximilianstrasse: Built by Maximilian II in the 1850s, this street was designed for shoppers. Today it's home to Munich's most exclusive shops.

Lowbrow Tips: For that beer stein you promised to take home to your uncle, try the shops on the pedestrian zone by St. Michael's Church and the gift shops that surround the Hofbräuhaus. If you're looking for a used cell phone or exotic groceries, the area south of the train station is a lot of fun.

Sleeping in Munich

Unless you hit Munich during a fair, convention, or big holiday, you can sleep reasonably here. Lots of student hotels around the station house anyone who's young at heart for €20, and it's easy to find a fine double with breakfast in a good basic hotel for €80. I've listed accommodations in two neighborhoods: within a few blocks of the central train station (Hauptbahnhof), and in the old center, between Marienplatz and Sendlinger Tor. Many of these places have complicated, slippery pricing schemes. I've listed the normal non-convention, non-festival prices. There are major conventions about 30 nights a year—prices increase from 20 percent to as much as 300 percent during Oktoberfest (Sept 22-Oct 7 in 2012; reserve well in advance). On the other hand, during slow times, you may be able to do better than the rates listed here—always ask. Sunday is very slow and usually comes with a huge discount if you ask.

Near the Train Station

Good budget hotels cluster in the multicultural area immediately south of the station. It feels seedy after dark (erotic cinemas and men with moustaches loitering in the shadows), but it's dangerous only for those in search of trouble. Still, hotels in the old center (listed later) might feel more comfortable to some.

$$ Hotel Royal is perhaps the best value in its price range (as long as you can look past the strip joints flanking the entry). While a bit institutional, it's clean, entirely non-smoking, and plenty comfortable. Most importantly, it's energetically run by Pasha and Changiz. Each of its 40 rooms is fresh and bright (Sb-€54-69, Db-€74-89, Tb-€94-109, Qb-€99-129, lower prices generally Nov-March, book direct for a 10 percent discount off the prevailing

Sleep Code

(€1 = about $1.40, country code: 49, area code: 089)
S = Single, **D** = Double/Twin, **T** = Triple, **Q** = Quad, **b** = bathroom,
s = shower only. Unless otherwise noted, credit cards are
accepted, a buffet breakfast is included, there is an elevator
but no air-conditioning, and English is spoken.

To help you sort easily through these listings, I've divided
the accommodations into three categories based on the price
for a standard double room with bath:

$$$ Higher Priced—Most rooms €100 or more.
$$ Moderately Priced—Most rooms between €70-100.
$ Lower Priced—Most rooms €70 or less.

Prices can change without notice; verify the hotel's
current rates online or by email. For other updates, see www
.ricksteves.com/update.

price with this book, ask for a room on the quiet side—especially
in summer when you'll want the window open, free Internet access
and Wi-Fi, Schillerstrasse 11a, tel. 089/5998-8160, fax 089/5998-
81616, www.hotel-royal.de, info@hotel-royal.de).

$$ Hotel Uhland is a stately mansion that rents 29 delight-
ful rooms in a safe-feeling, less-seedy residential neighborhood a
slightly longer walk from the station than the others in this sec-
tion (toward the Theresienwiese Oktoberfest grounds). It's been in
the Hauzenberger family for 50 years (Sb-€75-80, small Db-€88,
big Db-€98-108, Tb-€123-130, price depends on room size, great
family rooms, online deals, non-smoking floor, free Wi-Fi, lim-
ited free parking; from station, take bus #58 to Georg-Hirth-
Platz, or walk 15 minutes: go up Goethestrasse and turn right on
Pettenkoferstrasse, cross Georg-Hirth-Platz to Uhlandstrasse and
find #1; tel. 089/543-350, fax 089/5433-5250, www.hotel-uhland
.de, info@hotel-uhland.de).

$$ Hotel Monaco is a delightful and welcoming little
hideaway, tucked inside the fifth floor of a giant nondescript
building two blocks from the station. Emerging from the elevator, you're warmly welcomed by Christine and her staff into a
flowery, cherub-filled oasis. It's homey, with 24 clean and fresh
rooms (S-€53, Sb-€73, D-€75, Db-€91-96, Tb-€134, €8/person
less without breakfast, free Wi-Fi, Schillerstrasse 9, entrance on
Adolf-Kolping-Strasse, tel. 089/545-9940, fax 089/550-3709, www
.hotel-monaco.de, info@hotel-monaco.de).

$$ Hotel Eckelmann has 65 sunny rooms in a practical,
concrete shell (Sb-€62, Db-€91, Tb-€120, €9/person less without

breakfast, parking-€13, non-smoking rooms, free Wi-Fi, Adolf-Kolping-Strasse 11, tel. 089/5999-3902, fax 089/5999-3994, www.hotel-eckelmann.de, info@hotel-eckelmann.de).

$$ Hotel Bristol has 57 comfortable, business-class rooms. While a longer walk from the station, it's bright, efficient, and pleasantly located just across the street from the Sendlinger Tor U-Bahn stop, one stop from the train station on the U-1 or U-2 (Sb-€89, Db-€99, non-smoking rooms, free Internet access and Wi-Fi, air-con in lobby, Pettenkoferstrasse 2, tel. 089/5434-8880, fax 089/5434-888111, www.bristol-munich.de, info@bristol-munich.de).

$$ Litty's Hotel is a basic hotel with 37 small rooms run by Verena and Bernd Litty (S-€46, Sb-€58, D-€66, Ds-€74, Db-€82, T-€84, free Wi-Fi at reception reaches lower floors, near Schillerstrasse at Landwehrstrasse 32c, tel. 089/5434-4211, fax 089/5434-4212, www.littyshotel.de, info@littyshotel.de).

$$ Hotel Deutsches Theater is a brass-and-marble-filled place with 27 tight, modern three-star rooms. The back rooms face the courtyard of a neighboring theater—when there's a show, there can be some street noise (Sb-€68, Db-€97, Tb-€136, pricier suites, €9/person less without breakfast, non-smoking floors, free Wi-Fi, Landwehrstrasse 18, tel. 089/5999-3903, fax 089/5999-3995, www.hoteldeutschestheater.de, info@hoteldeutschestheater.de).

$$ Hotel Europäischer Hof, across from the station, is a huge, impersonal business hotel with 150 decent rooms. Official rates are sky-high, but actual rates are usually lower (close to S-€50, Sb-€85, smaller "tourist class" D with head-to-toe twin beds-€57, Db-€92; 10 percent discount on prevailing rate with this book and advance reservation, *or* if you pay cash—no double discounts; no discounts during conventions, major events, and Oktoberfest weekends; check website for other discounts, non-smoking rooms, family rooms, free Internet access, expensive Wi-Fi and cable Internet, Bayerstrasse 31, tel. 089/551-510, fax 089/5515-11444, www.heh.de, info@heh.de). They also run **$$ Hotel Mark** around the corner, with a large lobby, dim hallways, 92 fine rooms, and a similar institutional 1970s ambience (Sb-€75, basic Db-€82, ask for 10 percent discount described above, free Internet access, expensive Wi-Fi and cable Internet, Senefelderstrasse 12, tel. 089/559-820, fax 089/5598-22444, www.hotel-mark.de, mark@heh.de).

$ The **CVJM (YMCA),** open to all ages, rents 85 beds in clean, slightly worn rooms with sinks in the rooms and showers and toilets down the hall. Doubles are head-to-head; triples are like doubles with a bunk over one of the beds (S-€36, D-€61, T-€83, €28/bed in a shared triple, guests over 26 pay €3/person more, cheaper for 3 nights or more and in winter, only €10/night per person more during Oktoberfest—reserve at least a year ahead;

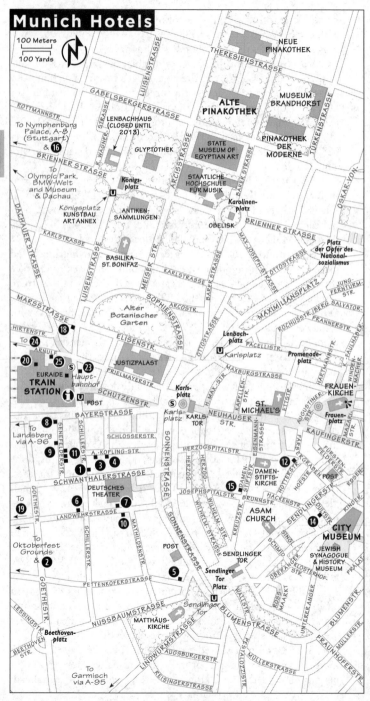

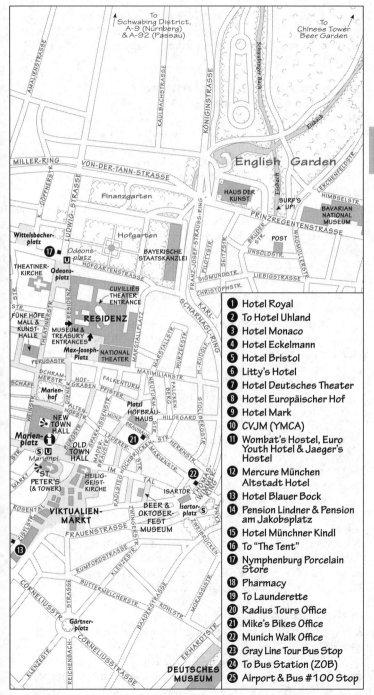

MUNICH

English Garden

1. Hotel Royal
2. To Hotel Uhland
3. Hotel Monaco
4. Hotel Eckelmann
5. Hotel Bristol
6. Litty's Hotel
7. Hotel Deutsches Theater
8. Hotel Europäischer Hof
9. Hotel Mark
10. CVJM (YMCA)
11. Wombat's Hostel, Euro Youth Hotel & Jaeger's Hostel
12. Mercure München Altstadt Hotel
13. Hotel Blauer Bock
14. Pension Lindner & Pension am Jakobsplatz
15. Hotel Münchner Kindl
16. To "The Tent"
17. Nymphenburg Porcelain Store
18. Pharmacy
19. To Launderette
20. Radius Tours Office
21. Mike's Bikes Office
22. Munich Walk Office
23. Gray Line Tour Bus Stop
24. To Bus Station (ZOB)
25. Airport & Bus #100 Stop

includes sheets, breakfast, and Internet access, but no lockers; pay Wi-Fi by reception, Landwehrstrasse 13, tel. 089/552-1410, fax 089/550-4282, www.cvjm-muenchen.org/hotel, hotel@cvjm -muenchen.org).

"Hostel Row" on Senefelderstrasse, a Block from the Station

All three of the following hostels are casual and well-run, with friendly and creative management, and all cater expertly to the needs of young beer-drinking backpackers enjoying Munich on a shoestring. With 900 cheap dorm beds, this is a spirited street. There's no curfew at any of these places, and each one has a lively bar that rages until the wee hours (Euro Youth's is open the latest—until 4:00 in the morning), along with staff who speak English as the primary language. All have 24-hour receptions, pay Internet access, free Wi-Fi laundry facilities, lockers, and included linens; none has a kitchen, but each offers a buffet breakfast for €4-5. Sleep cheap in big dorms, or spend a little more for a two-, three-, or four-bed room. Prices vary with demand, and can range a little higher than the rates listed here in summer—and quite a bit lower in the off-season.

$ **Wombat's Hostel,** perhaps the most hip and colorful, rents cheap doubles and six- to eight-bed dorms with lockers. Each bedroom is fresh and modern, with its own bathroom, and there's a relaxing and peaceful winter garden (300 beds, 8-bed dorms-€20/bed, 6-bed dorms-€25/bed, Db-€76, Senefelderstrasse 1, tel. 089/5998-9180, www.wombats-hostels.eu, office@wombats -munich.de).

$ **Euro Youth Hotel** fills a classy and rare pre-WWII building (200 beds, 10- to 12-bed dorms-€19/bed, 3- to 5-bed dorms-€25/bed; D-€59, Db-€70, breakfast included for private rooms; bike rental-€10/day, Senefelderstrasse 5, tel. 089/5990-8811, www .euro-youth-hotel.de, info@euro-youth-hotel.de, run by Alfio).

$ **Jaeger's Hostel** rounds out this trio, with 300 cheap beds and all the fun and efficiency you'd hope for in a hostel—plus the only air-conditioning on the street. If you're not looking to party, this is your hostel—it seems to be the quietest (40-bed dorm-€19/bed, 8-bed dorm-€23/bed, 3- to 6-bed rooms-€27/bed, hotel-quality Db-€78, towel-€1/day, Senefelderstrasse 3, tel. 089/555-281, fax 089/592-598, www.jaegershostel.de, info@jaegershostel.de).

In the Old Center

A few good deals remain in the area south of Marienplatz, going toward the Sendlinger Tor.

$$$ **Mercure München Altstadt Hotel** is a huge, impersonal, basic business-class hotel with all the modern comforts on

a boring street very close to the Marienplatz action. If you want an American-style hotel room buried deep in Munich for a decent price, this place has 75 of them (typically Sb-€114, Db-€156, better rates sometimes available online, parking-€17, non-smoking floors, air-con, inexpensive Wi-Fi, a block south of the pedestrian zone at Hotterstrasse 4, tel. 089/232-590, fax 089/2325-9127, www.mercure.com, h3709@accor.com).

$$$ **Hotel Blauer Bock,** formerly a dormitory for Benedictine monks, has been on the same corner near the Munich City Museum since 1841. Recently remodeled, it's a little spartan for the price, but offers 69 clean, decent rooms, a straightforward pricing system (the same rates every day, except during fairs and Oktoberfest), and a great location (S-€55, Sb-€75-99, D-€90, Db-€119, fancy premium Db-€153, extra bed-€40, €10 more if paying with credit card, free Wi-Fi with this book, parking-€19, Sebastiansplatz 9, tel. 089/231-780, fax 089/2317-8200, www.hotelblauerbock.de, info@hotelblauerbock.de).

$$ **Pension Lindner** is clean and quiet, with nine pleasant pastel-bouquet rooms off a bare stairway (S-€39, D-€60, Ds-€70, Db-€80, these prices with this book and cash payment, tiny elevator, free Wi-Fi, Dultstrasse 1, tel. 089/263-413, fax 089/268-760, www.pension-lindner.com, info@pension-lindner.com, Marion Sinzinger).

$$ **Pension am Jakobsplatz,** downstairs from Pension Lindner, has four basic but pleasant rooms. Two have fully private facilities, and the other two have a sink and shower but share a toilet. Showers here are in-room (Ss-€60-80, Sb-€70-90, Ds-€70-90, Db-€80-100, non-smoking, free Internet access and Wi-Fi, Dultstrasse 1, tel. 089/2323-1556, mobile 0173-973-4598, fax 089/2323-1564, www.pension-jakobsplatz.de, info@pension-jakobsplatz.de).

$$ **Hotel Münchner Kindl** is a no-frills place with 22 decent rooms above a friendly neighborhood bar (S-€50, D-€75, Db-€92, Tb-€115, Qb-€130, €8/person less without breakfast, lower rates possible in summer—ask, no elevator, pay Wi-Fi, night noises travel up central courtyard, no air circulation in courtyard-facing rooms so they can get hot in summer—request a fan, Damenstiftstrasse 16, tel. 089/264-349, fax 089/264-526, www.hotel-muenchner-kindl.de, reservierung@hotel-muenchner-kindl.de, Gunter and Renate).

Away from the Center

$ **The Tent**—a venerable Munich institution officially known as the International Youth Camp Kapuzinerhölzl—offers 400 spots in three huge circus tents near Nymphenburg Palace. It never fills up, though you are encouraged to reserve online. Choose a mattress on a wooden floor (€7.50) or a bunk bed (€10.50), or pitch your own tent (€5.50/tent plus €5.50/person). Blankets, hot showers, lockers (bring or buy a lock), a kitchen, and Wi-Fi are all included; breakfast is a few euros extra. It can be a fun but noisy experience—kind of a cross between a slumber party and Woodstock. It feels quite wholesome, but I wouldn't bring kids—it's really for young adults. There's a cool table-tennis-and-Frisbee atmosphere through-  out the day, nightly campfires, and no curfew, though silence is requested after 1:00 (open early June-mid-Oct only, prices a little higher during Oktoberfest, cash only, pay Internet access, self-service laundry, bikes-€9/day, catch tram #17 from train station for 18 minutes to Botanischer Garten, direction Amalienburgstrasse, then go right down Franz-Schrank-Strasse—it's behind the trees at the end of the street, tel. 089/141-4300, www.the-tent.com, cu @the-tent.com).

Eating in Munich

Munich cuisine is traditionally seasoned with beer. In beer halls, beer gardens, or at the Viktualienmarkt, try the most typical meal in town: *Weisswurst* (white-colored veal sausage—peel off the skin before eating, often available only until noon) with *süsser Senf* (sweet mustard), a salty *Brezel* (pretzel), and *Weissbier* ("white" wheat beer). Another traditional favorite is *Obatzda* (a.k.a. *Obatzter*), a mix of soft cheeses and butter with paprika and raw onions that's spread on bread. *Brotzeit*, literally "bread time," gets you a wooden platter of cold cuts, cheese, and pickles and is a good option for a light dinner. Also unique and memorable is a *Steckerlfisch*—fish on a stick (great with a pretzel and a big beer).

I'm here for the beer-hall and beer-garden fun (my first several listings). But when the *Wurst und Kraut* get to be too much for you, Munich has plenty of good alternatives; I've listed my favorites later in this section.

Bavarian restaurants are now smoke-free. The only ashtrays you'll see throughout Bavaria are outside.

Beer Halls, Beer Gardens, and Bavarian Food

For a boisterous cliché of the beer hall, nothing beats the Hofbräuhaus (the only place in town where you'll find oompah music). Locals prefer their innumerable beer gardens. On a warm day, when you're looking for the authentic outdoor beer-garden experience, your best options are the Augustiner (near the train station), the small beer garden at the Viktualienmarkt (near Marienplatz), or the thousands of tables in the Englischer Garten.

Near Marienplatz

The **Hofbräuhaus** (HOAF-broy-howze) is the world's most famous beer hall. While it's grotesquely touristy and filled with sloppy backpackers and tour groups, it's still a lot of fun—a Munich must. Even if you don't eat here, check it out to see 200 Japanese people drinking beer in a German beer hall...across from a Hard Rock Café. Germans go for the entertainment—to sing "Country Roads," see how Texas girls party, and watch tourists try to chug beer. You can drop by anytime for a large or light meal (my favorite: €7 for *Schweinswurst mit Kraut*—pork sausages with sauerkraut), or for just a drink. Except for Weissbier, they only sell beer by the *Mass* (one-liter mug, €7.30)—and they claim to sell 10,000 of these liters every day. The Hofbräuhaus is the only beer hall in town offering regular live oompah music. This music-every-night atmosphere is thick, and the fat, shiny-leather bands even get church mice to stand up and conduct three-quarter time with breadsticks (daily 9:00-23:30, music during lunch and dinner, 5-minute walk from Marienplatz at Platzl 6, tel. 089/2901-3610, www.hofbraeuhaus.de). For more on this Munich institution, see page 64.

The small beer garden at the center of the **Viktualienmarkt** taps you into about the best budget eating in town just steps from Marienplatz (closed Sun, see page 56). There's table service wherever you see a tablecloth; to picnic, choose a table without one. Buy your drinks from the counter. Countless stalls surround the beer garden and sell wurst, sandwiches, produce, and so on. This B.Y.O.F. tradition goes back to the days when monastery beer gardens served beer but not food. This is a good spot to grab a typical Munich *Weisswurst*—and some beer.

Jodlerwirt ("Yodeling Innkeeper") is a tiny, cramped, and smart-alecky pub. The food is great, and the ambience is as Bavarian as you'll find. Avoid the basic ground-floor bar and climb the stairs into the action. Even if it's just you and the accordionist, it's fun. Good food and lots of belly laughs...completely incomprehensible to the average tourist (€8-16 main courses, Tue-Sat 19:00-3:00 in the morning, food until 23:00, closed Mon except Sept-Dec, always closed Sun, accordion act nightly 20:00-2:00 in the morning, between Hofbräuhaus and Marienplatz at Altenhofstrasse 4, tel. 089/221-249).

The trendy **Andechser am Dom,** at the rear of the twin-domed Frauenkirche on a breezy square, serves Andechs beer and great food to appreciative regulars. Münchners favor the dark beer

Munich's Beer Scene

In Munich's beer halls *(Brauhäuser)* and beer gardens *(Biergartens),* meals are inexpensive, white radishes are salted and cut in delicate spirals, and surly beer maids pull mustard packets from their cleavage. Unlike with wine, spending more money on beer doesn't get you a better drink. Beer is truly a people's drink, and you'll get the very best here in Munich. The big question among connoisseurs (local and foreign) is, "Which brew today?"

Beer gardens go back to the days when monks brewed their beer and were allowed to sell it directly to the thirsty public. They stored their beer in cellars under courtyards kept cool by the shade of bushy chestnut trees. Eventually, tables were set up, and these convivial eateries evolved. The tradition (complete with chestnut trees) survives, and any real beer garden will keep a few tables (those without tablecloths) available for customers who buy only beer and bring their own food.

Huge liter beers (called *ein Mass* in German, or *"ein* pitcher" in English) cost about €7. You can order your beer *helles* (light but not "lite"—which is what you'll get if you say *"ein* beer"), *dunkles* (dark), or *Radler* (half lemon soda, half beer). Most beer gardens have a deposit *(Pfand)* system for their big glass steins: You pay €1 extra, and when you're finished, you can take the mug to the return man *(Pfandrückgabe)* for your refund, or leave it on the table and lose your money. (Men's rooms come with vomitoriums.)

Many beer halls have a cafeteria system. Eating outside is made more pleasant by the *Föhn* (warm winds that come over the Alps from Italy), which gives this part of Germany 30 more days of sunshine than the North—and sometimes even an Italian ambience. (Many natives attribute the city's huge increase in outdoor dining to global warming.)

Beer halls take care of their regular customers. You'll notice many tables marked *Stammtisch* (reserved for regulars and small groups, such as the "Happy Saturday Club"). These have a long tradition of being launch pads for grassroots action. In the days before radio and television, aspiring leaders used beer halls to connect with the public. Hitler hosted numerous political rallies in beer halls, and the Hofbräuhaus was the first place he talked to a big crowd.

(ask for *dunkles*), but I love the light *(helles)*. The €11.50 *Gourmetteller* is a great sampler of their specialties, and the *Rostbratwurst* with kraut (€6.90) gives you the virtual *Nürnberger* bratwurst experience (see next) with the better Andechs beer (€7-15 main courses, daily 10:00-24:00, Weinstrasse 7a, reserve during peak times, tel. 089/298-481).

Nürnberger Bratwurst Glöckl am Dom, just across from Andechser am Dom, is popular with tourists and offers a classier, fiercely Bavarian evening. Dine outside under the trees or in the dark, medieval, cozy interior—patrolled by wenches and spiked with antlers. I come here to enjoy the tasty little *Nürnberger* sausages with kraut (€8-19 main courses, Mon-Sat 10:00-24:00, Sun 11:00-23:00, Frauenplatz 9, tel. 089/291-9450).

Altes Hackerhaus is popular with locals for its traditional *Bayerisch* (Bavarian) fare served with a slightly fancier feel in one of the oldest buildings in town. It offers a small courtyard and a fun forest of characteristic nooks festooned with old-time paintings, ads, and posters. This place is much-appreciated for its Hacker-Pschorr beer (€7-10 wurst dishes, €9-25 main courses, daily 10:00-24:00, Sendlinger Strasse 14, tel. 089/260-5026).

Der Pschorr, an upscale beer hall occupying a former slaughterhouse, has a terrace overlooking the Viktualienmarkt and serves a special premium version of what many consider Munich's finest beer. With organic "slow food" and chilled glasses, this place mixes modern concepts—no candles, industrial-strength conviviality—with traditional, quality, classic dishes. They tap classic wooden kegs every few minutes with gusto. The sound of the hammer lets patrons know they're getting it good and fresh (€11-23 main courses, €8-9 lunch specials, daily 10:00-24:00, Viktualienmarkt 15, at end of Schrannenhalle, tel. 089/5181-8500).

Spatenhaus is the opera-goers' beer hall, serving more elegant food in a woodsy, traditional setting since 1896—maybe it's not even right to call it a "beer hall." You can also eat outside, on the square facing the opera and palace. It's pricey, but you won't find better-quality Bavarian cuisine (€13-25 main courses, daily 9:30-24:00, on Max-Joseph-Platz opposite opera, Residenzstrasse 12, tel. 089/290-7050, www.kuffler.de).

Heilig-Geist-Stüberl ("Holy Ghost Pub") is a funky, retro little hole-in-the-wall where you are sure to meet locals (the German cousins of those who go to Reno because it's cheaper than Vegas, and who consider karaoke high culture). The interior, a 1980s time warp, makes you feel like you're stepping into an alcoholic cuckoo clock. There's no food—just drink here (daily 9:00-22:00, just off the Viktualienmarkt at Heiliggeiststrasse 1, tel. 089/297-233).

MUNICH

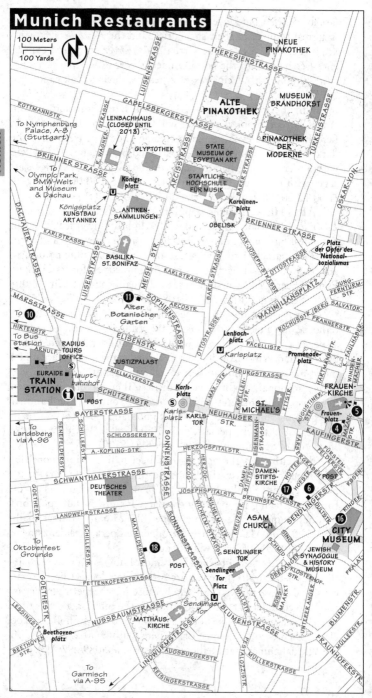

MUNICH

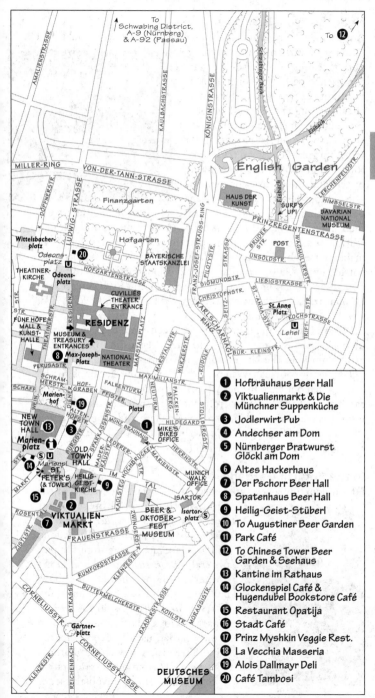

1. Hofbräuhaus Beer Hall
2. Viktualienmarkt & Die Münchner Suppenküche
3. Jodlerwirt Pub
4. Andechser am Dom
5. Nürnberger Bratwurst Glöckl am Dom
6. Altes Hackerhaus
7. Der Pschorr Beer Hall
8. Spatenhaus Beer Hall
9. Heilig-Geist-Stüberl
10. To Augustiner Beer Garden
11. Park Café
12. To Chinese Tower Beer Garden & Seehaus
13. Kantine im Rathaus
14. Glockenspiel Café & Hugendubel Bookstore Café
15. Restaurant Opatija
16. Stadt Café
17. Prinz Myshkin Veggie Rest.
18. La Vecchia Masseria
19. Alois Dallmayr Deli
20. Café Tambosi

Near the Train Station

Augustiner Beer Garden is a sprawling haven for well-established local beer-lovers on a balmy evening.

For a true under-the-leaves beer garden packed with Münchners, this is a delight. In fact, most Münchners consider Augustiner the best beer garden in town. There's no music, it's away from the tourist hordes, and it serves up great beer, good traditional food, huge portions, reasonable prices, and the perfect conviviality. The outdoor self-service ambience is best, making this place ideal on a nice summer evening (figure €12 for a main course and a drink). There's also indoor and outdoor seating at a more expensive restaurant with table service (€11-18 main courses) by the entrance (daily 10:00-23:00, self-service food outside until 22:00, Arnulfstrasse 52, 3 loooong blocks from station going away from the center—or take tram #16/#17 one stop to Hopfenstrasse, taxis always waiting at the gate, tel. 089/594-393, www.augustinerkeller.de).

Park Café, though in a park, is much more than a café. The indoor section is big and bold, with clean yet rustic ambience, DJs or live music in the late evening, few tourists, and quality food (€9-15 main courses). When it's hot, everyone decamps to the beer garden out back in the Alter Botanischer Garden, where you can order off the menu or from the self-service counters. Don't forget to reclaim the deposit for your plate and mug when you leave (daily 10:00-24:00, a short walk north of the train station at Sophienstrasse 7, tel. 089/5161-7980).

In the English Garden

For outdoor ambience and a cheap meal, spend an evening at the

English Garden's **Chinese Tower Beer Garden** *(Chinesischer Turm Biergarten)*. You're welcome to B.Y.O. food and grab a table, or buy from the picnic stall *(Brotzeit)* right there. Don't bother to phone ahead—they have 6,000 seats. This is a fine opportunity to try a *Steckerlfisch,* sold for €9 at a separate kiosk (daily, long hours in good weather, usually live music, tel. 089/383-8730, www.chinaturm.de; take tram #17 from main train station or Sendlinger Tor to Tivolistrasse, or

U-3 or U-6 to Universität).

Seehaus im Englischen Garten is famous among Münchners for its idyllic lakeside setting and excellent Mediterranean and traditional cooking. It's dressy and a bit snobbish, and understandably filled with locals who fit the same description. Choose from classy indoor or lakeside seating (€20-25 main courses, daily 10:00-late, a pleasant 15-minute hike into the English Garden—located on all the city maps—or take tram #44 or a taxi to the doorstep, Kleinhesselohe 3, tel. 089/381-6130).

Seehaus Beer Garden, adjacent to the fancy Seehaus restaurant, is a less expensive, more casual beer garden with all the normal wurst, kraut, pretzels, and fine beer at typical prices. What makes this spot special: You're buried in the English Garden, enjoying the fine lakeside setting (daily, long hours from 11:00 when the weather's fine).

Non-Beer Hall Restaurants
Man does not live by beer alone. Well, maybe some do. But for the rest of us, I recommend the following alternatives to the beer-and-wurst circuit.

On Marienplatz
Kantine im Rathaus is your solid, fast, economical, and no-nonsense standby in the center. The entrance is just behind the New Town Hall tower—go through the arch under the tower into the courtyard and look for the sign on the right. There's seating in the courtyard or inside (€5-10 main courses, Mon-Fri 11:00-18:30, Sat 12:00-16:00, closed Sun).

Glockenspiel Café is good for a coffee or a meal with a bird's-eye view down on the Marienplatz action—I'd come for the view more than the food. Locals like the sunroof, but regardless of the weather, I grab a seat overlooking Marienplatz (Mon-Sat 10:00-24:00, Sun 10:00-19:00, ride elevator from Rosenstrasse entrance, opposite glockenspiel at Marienplatz 28, tel. 089/264-256).

The **Hugendubel bookstore** has a Starbucks-style café on the top floor. It's quicker and less crowded than the Glockenspiel Café, and comes with the same great view (self-serve, take the glass elevator, Mon-Sat 9:30-20:00, closed Sun).

Around the Viktualienmarkt
The area south of Marienplatz—especially **Sebastiansplatz,** a long, pedestrianized square between the synagogue and Viktualienmarkt—is becoming a kind of SoHo, with lots of fun shops, wine bars, and bistros handy for a healthy and quick lunch. The options range from French to Italian, Asian to vegetarian, and all serve €10 plates on the busy cobbled square or inside. You can

just survey the scene and choose; I've listed a few reliable options below.

Restaurant Opatija, in the Viktualienmarktpassage a few steps from Marienplatz, brings the Adriatic to Munich with a big, eclectic Italian and Balkan menu, plus traditional German favorites. Choose between the comfortable indoor section and the outdoor seating in a quiet, narrow courtyard. Prices are low, it's family-friendly, and they do takeout (€7 pizzas, €7-10 pastas, €9 salad plates, €9-12 main courses, daily 11:30-22:30, kitchen closes at 21:30, enter the passage at Viktualienmarkt 6 or Rindermarkt 2, tel. 089/2323-1995).

Die Münchner Suppenküche ("Munich Soup Kitchen"), a self-service soup joint at the Viktualienmarkt, is fine for a small, cozy sit-down lunch at picnic tables under a closed-in awning (€4-6 soup meals, Mon-Fri 10:00-18:00, Sat 9:00-18:00, closed Sun, near corner of Reichenbachstrasse and Frauenstrasse, tel. 089/260-9599).

Stadt Café is a lively café serving healthy fare, with great daily specials (€7-10) and an inventive menu of Italian, German, salads, and vegetarian dishes. This informal, no-frills restaurant draws newspaper-readers, stroller moms, and tourists, too. Dine in the quiet cobbled courtyard, inside, or outside facing the new synagogue (blackboard has today's specials, daily 10:00-24:00, in Munich City Museum, St.-Jakobs-Platz 1, tel. 089/266-949).

Prinz Myshkin Vegetarian Restaurant is everybody's favorite upscale vegetarian eatery in the old center. The menu is totally meatless and dictated by the season. You'll find a clever, appetizing selection of €10-15 main courses. The decor is modern, the arched ceilings are cool, the outside seating is on a quiet street, and the clientele is entirely local. Don't miss the enticing appetizer selection on display as you enter (they do a fine €11 mixed-appetizer plate). They also have vegetarian sushi, pastas, Indian dishes, and their own baker, so they're proud of their sweets (€6 lunch specials, daily 11:30-23:00, Hackenstrasse 2, tel. 089/265-596).

Near the Train Station

La Vecchia Masseria, between Sendlinger Tor and the train station hotels, serves simple Italian food inside amid a cozy Tuscan farmhouse decor, or outside in a beautiful flowery courtyard. Try the €24 tasting *menu* (€6-8 pizza or pasta, €15 main courses, daily 11:30-23:30, reservations smart, Mathildenstrasse 3—see map on page 112, tel. 089/550-9090).

Picnics

For a truly elegant picnic, **Alois Dallmayr's** is the place to shop. The crown in their emblem reflects that no less than the royal family assembled its picnics at this historic and expensive delicatessen. Pretend you're a Bavarian aristocrat—King Ludwig himself, even—and put together a royal spread to munch in the nearby Hofgarten. Or visit the classy but pricey cafés that serve light meals on the ground floor and first floor (Mon-Sat 9:30-19:00, closed Sun, behind New Town Hall, Dienerstrasse 13-15). For more information, see page 62.

A Budget Picnic: To save money, browse at Dallmayr's but buy in the **supermarkets** that hide in the basements of department stores: the **Kaufhof** stores at Marienplatz and Karlsplatz (Mon-Sat 9:30-20:00, closed Sun), the more upmarket **Karstadt** across from the train station (same hours), or the **REWE** at Fünf Höfe (Mon-Sat 7:00-20:00, closed Sun, entrance is in Viscardihof).

Munich Connections

Munich is a super transportation hub (one reason it was the target of so many WWII bombs), with easy train and bus connections to most Bavarian destinations, as well as international trains.

Trains

For quick help at the main train station, stop by the service counter in front of track 18. For better English and more patience, drop by the EurAide desk at counter #1 in the *Reisezentrum* (see page 39). Train info: tel. 0180-599-6633, www.bahn.com.

From Munich by Train to: Füssen (hourly, 2 hours, some direct but most with easy transfer in Buchloe; for a Neuschwanstein Castle day trip, leave as early as possible and no later than 9:00), **Reutte,** Austria (every 2 hours, 2.5 hours, change in Garmisch), **Oberammergau** (nearly hourly, 1.75 hours, change in Murnau), **Salzburg,** Austria (2/hour, 1.5-2 hours), **Berchtesgaden** (at least hourly, 2.5-3 hours, change in Freilassing), **Nürnberg** (2-3/hour, 1-1.25 hours), **Köln** (2/hour, 4.5 hours, some with 1 change), **Würzburg** (1-2/hour, 2 hours), **Rothenburg** (hourly, 2.5-3.5 hours, 2-3 changes), **Frankfurt** (hourly, 3.25 hours), **Frankfurt Airport** (1-2/hour, 3.5 hours), **Leipzig** (every 2 hours direct, 5.5 hours; also every 2 hours with change in Nürnberg or Naumburg, 4.75-5 hours), **Erfurt** (about 2/hour, 4.5-4.75 hours, change in Würzburg or Fulda), **Dresden** (every 2 hours, 6 hours, change in Nürnberg), **Hamburg** (hourly, 6-6.5 hours), **Berlin** (1-2/hour, 6-6.75 hours, every 2 hours direct, otherwise a change in Göttingen), **Vienna** (direct trains every 2 hours, 4.25 hours), **Venice** (every 2 hours, 7-7.5 hours, change in Verona, 1 direct night train, 9.5 hours), **Paris** (4/day, 6 hours, usually with 1 change), **Prague** (2/day direct, 6.25 hours; 6 more/day with change in Nürnberg then express bus, 5.25 hours; no night trains), **Zürich** (4/day direct, 4.25 hours). Trains run nightly to Berlin, Vienna, Venice, Florence, Rome, Paris, Amsterdam, Budapest, and Copenhagen (at least 6 hours to each city). To use a railpass for a night train to Italy, your pass must include all countries on the train route (i.e., Austria or Switzerland), or you'll have to buy the segment that's not included.

Buses

For information on Munich's Central Bus Station (ZOB), see page 40.

Romantic Road Bus: The **Romantic Road bus** (mid-April-late Oct only) connects Munich's Central Bus Station to Füssen, Dinkelsbühl, Rothenburg, Würzburg, Frankfurt, and other destinations en route. This slower but more scenic alternative to the train allows a glimpse of towns such as Augsburg, Nördlingen, and Dinkelsbühl (no advance reservations needed, northbound bus departs Munich at 10:50, arrives Rothenburg at 15:50; southbound bus departs Munich at 17:50, arrives Füssen at 19:55). For more information on the bus, run by Deutsche Touring, see page 329.

Munich Airport

Munich's airport (code: MUC) is an easy 40-minute ride on the S-1 or S-8 **subway,** each of which runs every 20 minutes (starting at 4:00 in the morning and continuing until almost 2:00 in the morning) between the airport and Marienplatz and the train station. While you can buy a single ticket for €10, the €10.80 Munich *Gesamtnetz* day pass, which covers public transportation all day, is worth getting if you'll be making just one more public transport journey that same day. Groups of two or more should buy the €19.60 Munich *Gesamtnetz* partner day pass, which gives up to five adults the run of the system for the day (for more info on Munich transport passes, see page 42). The trip is also free with a validated and dated railpass. The S-8 is a bit quicker and easier, as the S-1 line has two branches and some trains split—if on the S-1 to the airport, be certain your train is going to the *Flughafen.* Another alternative is the Lufthansa **airport bus,** which links the airport with the main train station (€10.50, €17 round-trip, 3/hour, 45 minutes, buses depart train station 5:10-19:50, buy tickets on bus; from inside the station, exit near track 26 and look for yellow *Airport Bus* signs; www.autobusoberbayern.de). If you're traveling alone, going round-trip, and not using other public transport the same day, the bus saves a few euros. Avoid taking a **taxi** from the airport, as it's a long, expensive drive; it's better to take public transport and then switch to a taxi if needed. Airport info: tel. 089/97500, www.munich-airport.de.

BAVARIA and TIROL

Füssen • King's Castles • Wieskirche • Oberammergau • Linderhof Castle • Ettal Monastery • Zugspitze • Reutte, Austria

Two hours south of Munich, in Germany's Bavaria and Austria's Tirol, is a timeless land of fairy-tale castles, painted buildings shared by cows and farmers, and locals who still yodel when they're happy.

In Germany's Bavaria, tour "Mad" King Ludwig II's ornate Neuschwanstein Castle, Europe's most spectacular. Stop by the Wieskirche, a textbook example of Bavarian Rococo bursting with curlicues, and browse through Oberammergau, Germany's woodcarving capital and home of the famous Passion Play (next performed in 2020). Then, just over the border in Austria's Tirol, explore the ruined Ehrenberg Castle and scream down the mountain on an oversized skateboard.

In this chapter, I'll cover Bavaria first, then Tirol. My favorite home base for exploring Bavaria's castles is actually in Austria, in the Tirolean town of Reutte. Reutte's hotels offer better value to those with a car. Füssen, in Germany, is more touristy, but a handier home base for train travelers.

Planning Your Time and Getting Around Bavaria

While Germans and Austrians vacation here for a week or two at a time, the typical speedy American traveler will find two days' worth of sightseeing. With a car and more time, you could enjoy three or four days, but the basic visit ranges anywhere from a long day trip from Munich to a three-night, two-day stay. If the weather's good and you're not going to Switzerland on your trip, be sure to ride a lift to an alpine peak.

By Car

This region is best by car, and all the sights are within an easy 60-mile loop from Reutte or Füssen. Even if you're doing the rest of your trip by train, consider renting a car for your time here.

Here's a good one-day circular drive from Reutte (or from Füssen, starting half an hour later):

7:00	Breakfast
7:30	Depart hotel
8:00	Arrive at Neuschwanstein to pick up tickets for the two castles (Neuschwanstein and Hohenschwangau)
9:00	Tour Hohenschwangau
11:00	Tour Neuschwanstein
13:00	Drive to Oberammergau, and spend an hour there browsing the carving shops
15:00	Drive to Ettal Monastery for a half-hour stop (if you're not otherwise seeing the Wieskirche), then on to Linderhof Castle
16:00	Tour Linderhof
18:00	Drive along scenic Plansee lake back into Austria (or return to Füssen)
19:00	Back at hotel
20:00	Dinner at hotel

Off-season (Oct-March), start your day an hour later, since Neuschwanstein and Hohenschwangau don't open until 10:00; and skip Linderhof, as it closes an hour early.

The next morning, you could stroll through Reutte, hike to the Ehrenberg ruins, and ride the luge on your way to Munich, Innsbruck, Switzerland, Venice, or wherever.

By Public Transportation

Where you stay determines which sights you can see most easily. Train travelers use **Füssen** as a base, and bus or bike the three miles to Neuschwanstein and the Tegelberg luge or gondola. Staying in **Oberammergau** gives you easy access to Linderhof and Ettal Monastery, and you can day-trip to the top of the Zugspitze via Garmisch. Although **Reutte** is the least convenient base if you're carless, travelers staying there can easily bike or hike to the Ehrenberg ruins, and can reach Neuschwanstein by bus (via Füssen), bike (1.5 hours), or taxi (€35 one-way); if you stay at the recommended Gutshof zum Schluxen hotel (between Reutte and Füssen, in Pinswang, Austria) it's a one-hour hike through the

woods to Neuschwanstein.

Visiting sights farther from your home base is not impossible by local bus, but requires planning. The German Railway website (www.bahn.com) does a great job of finding bus connections that work, on both sides of the border. (Schedules for each route are available at www.rvo-bus.de, but only in German.) Those staying in **Füssen** can day-trip by bus to Reutte and the Ehrenberg ruins, to the Wieskirche, or, with some effort, to Linderhof via Oberammergau. From **Oberammergau,** you can reach Neuschwanstein and Füssen by bus. From **Reutte,** you can take the train to Ehrwald to reach the Zugspitze from the Austrian side, but side-trips from Reutte to Oberammergau and Linderhof are impractical. More transport details are provided later, under each individual destination.

Hitchhiking, though always risky, is a slow-but-possible way to connect the public-transportation gaps. For example, even reluctant hitchhikers can catch a ride from Linderhof back to Oberammergau, as virtually everyone leaving there is a tourist like you and heading that way.

Bavarian Craftsmanship

The scenes you'll see painted on the sides of houses in Bavaria are called *Lüftlmalerei*. The term came from the name of the house ("Zum Lüftl") owned by a man from Oberammergau who pioneered the practice in the 18th century. As the paintings became popular during the Counter-Reformation Baroque age, themes tended to involve Christian symbols, saints, and stories (such as scenes from the life of Jesus), to reinforce the Catholic Church's authority in the region. Some scenes also depicted an important historical event that took place in that house or town.

Especially in the northern part of this region, you'll see *Fachwerkhäuser*—half-timbered houses. *Fachwerk* means "craftsmanship," as this type of home required a highly skilled master craftsman to create. They are most often found inside fortified cities (such as Rothenberg, Nürnberg, and Dinkelsbühl) that were once strong and semi-independent.

Staying overnight in this region is magical, but travelers in a hurry can make it a day trip from **Munich.** If you can postpone leaving Munich until after 9:00 on weekday mornings, the **Bayern-Ticket** is a great deal for getting to Füssen or Oberammergau (covers buses and slower regional trains throughout Bavaria for €21/day, or €29/day for up to 5 people; for more information, see page 99 in the Munich chapter). If you're interested only in Ludwig's castles, consider an all-day organized bus tour of the Bavarian biggies as a side-trip from Munich (see page 48 in the Munich chapter).

By Bike
This is great biking country. Many hotels loan bikes to guests, and shops in Reutte and at the Füssen train station rent bikes for €8-15 per day. The ride from Reutte to Neuschwanstein and the Tegelberg luge (1.5 hours) is a natural.

Helpful Hints
Sightseeing Pass: The Bavarian Palace Department offers a 14-day **Bavarian Castles Pass** that covers admission to Neuschwanstein (but not Hohenschwangau) and Linderhof; the Residenz, Nymphenburg Palace, and Amalienburg Palace in Munich; the Imperial Palace in Nürnberg; the Residenz and Marienberg Fortress in Würzburg; and many other castles and palaces not mentioned in this book. The one-person pass costs €24, and the family/partner version (up to two adults plus children) costs €40. If you are planning to visit at least three of these sights within a two-week period, the pass will

likely pay for itself. (For longer stays, there's also an annual pass available—€45/single, €65/family.) The pass is sold at all covered castles and online. For more information, see www .schloesser.bayern.de.

Local Guest Tax: Hotels and B&Bs in the region are usually required to collect a local tax (called a *Kurtax*) of about €1.50 per person per night, which is not included in the rates listed here and will be added to your bill.

Visiting Churches: At any type of church, if you'd like to attend a service, look for the *Gottesdienst* schedule. In every small German town in the very Catholic south, when you pass the big town church, look for a sign that says *Heilige Messe*. This is the schedule for holy Mass, usually on Saturday *(Sa.)* or Sunday *(So.)*.

Füssen

Dramatically situated under a renovated castle on the lively Lech River, Füssen (FEW-sehn) is a handy home base for exploring the

region. This town has been a strategic stop since ancient times. Its main street sits on the Via Claudia Augusta, which crossed the Alps (over the Brenner Pass) in Roman times. Going north, early traders could follow the Lech River downstream to the Danube, and then cross over to the Main and Rhine valleys— a route now known to modern travelers as the "Romantic Road." Today, while Füssen is overrun by tourists in the summer, few venture to the back streets...which is where you'll find the real charm. Apart from my self-guided walk and the Füssen Heritage Museum, there's little to do here. It's just a pleasant small town with a big history and lots of hardworking people in the tourist business.

Halfway between Füssen and the border (as you drive, or a woodsy walk from the town) is the **Lechfall**, a thunderous waterfall (with a handy WC).

Orientation to Füssen

(area code: 08362)
Füssen's train station is a few blocks from the TI, the town center (a cobbled shopping mall), and all my hotel listings.

Tourist Information

The TI is in the center of town (July-mid-Sept Mon-Fri 9:00-18:00, Sat 10:00-14:00, Sun 10:00-12:00; mid-Sept-June Mon-Fri 9:00-17:00, Sat 10:00-14:00, closed Sun; one free Internet terminal, 3 blocks down Bahnhofstrasse from station at Kaiser-Maximilian-Platz 1, tel. 08362/93850, www.fuessen.de). If necessary, the TI can help you find a room. After hours, the little self-service info pavilion near the front of the TI features an automated room-finding service with a phone to call hotels.

Arrival in Füssen

From the train station (lockers available, €2-3), exit to the left and walk a few blocks to reach the center of town and the TI. Buses to Neuschwanstein, Reutte, and elsewhere leave from a parking lot next to the station.

Helpful Hints

Internet Access: Beans & Bytes is the best place to get online, with fast terminals and good drink service (€2/2 hours, Wi-Fi, Skype, disc-burning, Mon-Sat 10:00-20:00, closed Sun except July-Aug, down the pedestrian alley off the main drag at Reichenstrasse 33, tel. 08362/926-8960).

Bike Rental: Bike Station, sitting right where the train tracks end, outfits sightseers with good bikes and tips on two-wheeled fun in the area (€8-10/24 hours, March-Oct Mon-Fri 9:00-12:00 & 14:00-18:00, Sat 9:00-13:00, Sun in good weather 9:00-12:00, closed Nov-Feb, tel. 08362/983-651, mobile 0176-2205-3080, www.ski-sport-luggi.de). For a strenuous but enjoyable 20-mile loop trip, see page 142.

Car Rental: Peter Schlichtling, in the town center, rents cars for reasonable prices (€62/day, includes insurance, Mon-Fri 8:00-18:00, Sat 9:00-12:00, closed Sun, Kemptener Strasse 26, tel. 08362/922-122, www.schlichtling.de). **Auto Osterried/ Europcar** rents at similar prices, but is an €8 taxi ride away from the train station. Their cheapest car goes for about €59 per day (daily 8:00-19:00, past waterfall on road to Austria, Tiroler Strasse 65, tel. 08362/6381).

Local Guide: Silvia Beyer speaks English, knows the region very well, and can even drive you to sights that are hard to reach by train (€30/hour, silliby@web.de, mobile 0160-901-13431).

Self-Guided Walk

Welcome to Füssen

For most, Füssen is just a home base for visiting Ludwig's famous castles. But the town has a rich history and hides some evocative corners, as you'll see when you follow this short orientation walk. Throughout the town, "City Tour" information plaques explain points of interest in English. Use them to supplement the information I've provided.

· *Begin at the square in front of the TI, three blocks from the train station.*

❶ Kaiser-Maximilian-Platz: The entertaining "Seven Stones" fountain on this square, by sculptor Christian Tobin, was built in 1995 to celebrate Füssen's 700th birthday. The stones symbolize community, groups of people gathering, conviviality...each is different, with "heads" nodding and talking. It's granite on granite. The moving heads are not connected, and nod only with water-power. While frozen in winter, it's a popular and splashy play zone for kids on hot summer days.

BAVARIA AND TIROL

· *Just half a block down the busy street stands...*

❷ Hotel Hirsch and Medieval Towers: Recent renovations have restored some of the original Art Nouveau flavor to Hotel Hirsch, which opened in 1904. In those

days, aristocratic tourists came here to appreciate the castles and natural wonders of the Alps. Across the busy street stands one of two surviving towers from Füssen's medieval town wall (c. 1515), and next to it is a passageway into the old town.

· *Walk 50 yards farther down the street to another tower. Just before it, you'll see an information plaque and an archway where a small street called Klosterstrasse emerges through a surviving piece of the old town wall. Step through the smaller pedestrian archway, walk along Klosterstrasse for a few yards, and turn left through the gate into the...*

❸ Historic Cemetery of St. Sebastian (Alter Friedhof): This peaceful oasis of Füssen history, established in the 16th century, fills a corner between the town wall and the Franciscan monastery. It's technically full, and only members of great and venerable Füssen families (who already own plots here) can join those who are buried (free, daily April-Sept 7:30-19:00, Oct-March 8:00-17:00).

Just inside the gate (on the right) is the tomb of Dominic Quaglio, who painted the Romantic scenes decorating the walls

BAVARIA AND TIROL

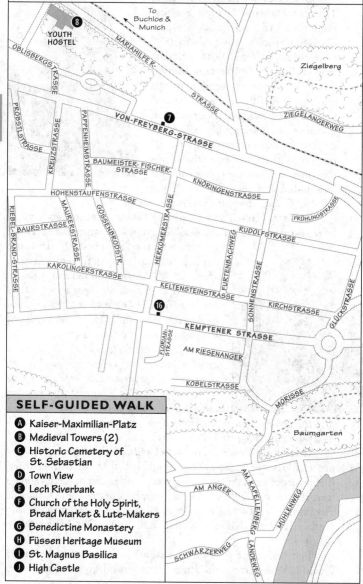

1 Hotel/Rest. Schlosskrone
2 Hotel Hirsch
3 Hotel Sonne
4 Altstadthotel zum Hechten & Rest. Ritterstub'n
5 Gästehaus Schöberl
6 Mein Lieber Schwan Apartments
7 House LA (2)
8 Youth Hostel
9 Gasthof Krone
10 Restaurant Aquila
11 Markthalle Food Court
12 Hohes Schloss Italian Ice Cream
13 Asian Eateries & Internet Café
14 Supermarket
15 Bike Rental
16 Car Rentals (2)

SELF-GUIDED WALK

A Kaiser-Maximilian-Platz
B Medieval Towers (2)
C Historic Cemetery of St. Sebastian
D Town View
E Lech Riverbank
F Church of the Holy Spirit, Bread Market & Lute-Makers
G Benedictine Monastery
H Füssen Heritage Museum
I St. Magnus Basilica
J High Castle

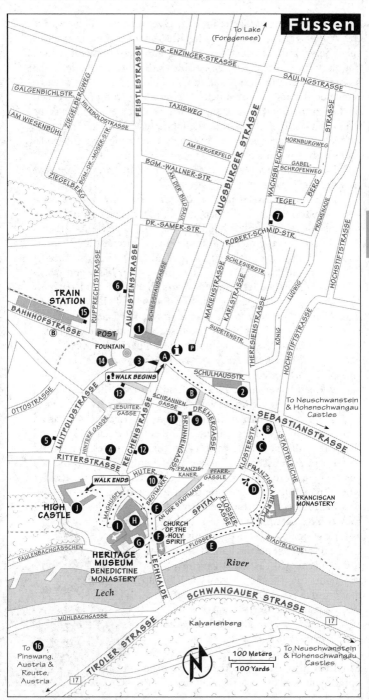

Füssen

of Hohenschwangau Castle in 1835. Over on the old city wall is the World War I memorial, listing all the names of men from this small town killed in that devastating conflict (along with each one's rank and place of death). A bit to the right, also along the old wall, is a statue of the hand of God holding a fetus—a place to remember babies who died before being born. And in the corner, farther to the right, are the simple wooden crosses of Franciscans who lived just over the wall in the monastery. Note the fine tomb art from many ages collected here, and the loving care this community gives its cemetery.

• *Exit on the far side, just past the dead Franciscans, and continue toward the big church.*

❶ Town View from Franciscan Monastery (Franziskanerkloster): From the Franciscan Monastery (which still has big responsibilities, but only a handful of monks in residence), there's a fine view over the medieval town. The Church of St. Magnus and the High Castle (the summer residence of the Bishops of Augsburg) break the horizon. The chimney (c. 1886) and workers' housing on the left are reminders that when Ludwig built Neuschwanstein, the textile industry (linen and flax) was very big here. Walk all the way to the far end of the monastery chapel and peek around the corner, where you'll see a gate that proclaims the *Ende der romantischen Strasse* (end of the Romantic Road).

• *Now go down the stairway and turn left, through the medieval "Bleachers' Gate," to the riverbank.*

❷ Lech Riverbank: This low end of town, the flood zone, was the home of those whose work depended on the river—bleachers, rafters, and fishermen. In its heyday, the Lech River was an expressway to Augsburg (about 70 miles to the north). Around the year 1500, the rafters established the first professional guild in Füssen. As Füssen was on the Via Claudia, cargo from Italy passed here en route to big German cities farther north. Rafters would assemble rafts and pile them high with goods—or with people needing a lift. If the water was high, they could float all the way to Augsburg in as little as one day. There they'd disassemble their raft and sell off the lumber along with the goods they'd carried, then make their way home to raft again. Today you'll see no modern-day rafters here, as there's a hydroelectric plant just downstream.

• *Walk upstream a bit, and head inland immediately after crossing under the bridge.*

❸ Church of the Holy Spirit, Bread Market, and Lute-Makers: Climbing uphill, you pass the colorful Church of the

Holy Spirit (Heilig-Geist-Spitalkirche) on the right. As this was the church of the rafters, their patron, St. Christopher, is prominent on the facade. Today it's the church of Füssen's old folks' home (it's adjacent—notice the easy-access skyway).

Farther up the hill on the right (almost opposite an archway into a big courtyard) is Bread Market Square (Brotmarkt), with a fountain honoring the famous 16th-century lute-making family, the Tieffenbruckers. In its day, Füssen was a huge center of violin- and lute-making, with about 200 workshops. Today only two survive.

• *Backtrack and go through the archway into the courtyard of the former...*

➏ Benedictine Monastery (Kloster St. Mang): From 1717 until secularization in 1802, this was the powerful center of town. Today the courtyard is popular for concerts, and the building houses the City Hall and Füssen Heritage Museum (and a public WC).

➐ Füssen Heritage Museum: This is Füssen's one mustsee sight (€6, €7 combo-ticket includes painting gallery and castle tower; April-Oct Tue-Sun 11:00-17:00, closed Mon; Nov-March Fri-Sun 13:00-16:00, closed Mon-Thu; tel. 08362/903-146, www .fuessen.de). Pick up the loaner English translations and follow the one-way route. In the St. Anna Chapel, you'll see the famous *Dance of Death*. This was painted shortly after a plague devastated the community in 1590. It shows 20 social classes, each dancing with the Grim Reaper—starting with the pope and

the emperor. The words above say, essentially, "You can say yes or you can say no, but you must ultimately dance with death."

Leaving the chapel, you walk over the metal lid of the crypt. Upstairs, exhibits illustrate the rafting trade and violin- and lutemaking (with a complete workshop). The museum also includes an exquisite *Festsaal* (main festival hall), an old library, an exhibition on textile production, and a King Ludwig-style "castle dream room."

• *Leaving the courtyard, hook left around the old monastery and go uphill. The square tower marks...*

➑ St. Magnus Basilica (Basilika St. Mang): St. Mang (or Magnus) is Füssen's favorite saint. In the eighth century, he worked miracles all over the area with his holy rod. For centuries, pilgrims came from far and wide to enjoy art depicting the great works of St. Magnus. Above the altar dangles a glass cross containing his relics (including that holy stick). Just inside the door is a chapel remembering a much more modern saint—Franz Seelos (1819-1867), the local boy who went to America (Pittsburgh and New Orleans) and lived such a righteous life that in 2000 he was beatified by Pope John Paul II. If you're in need of a miracle, fill out a request card next to the candles.

• *From the church, a lane leads high above, into the courtyard of the...*

❶ **High Castle (Hohes Schloss):** This castle, long the summer residence of the Bishop of Augsburg, houses a painting gallery (the upper floor is labeled in English) and a tower with a view over the town and lake (included in the €7 Füssen Heritage Museum combo-ticket, otherwise €6, same hours as museum). Its courtyard is interesting for the striking perspective tricks painted onto its flat walls. From below the castle, the city's main drag (once the Roman Via

Claudia, and now Reichenstrasse) leads from a grand statue of St. Magnus past lots of shops, cafés, and strolling people to Kaiser-Maximilian-Platz and the TI...where you began.

Sleeping in Füssen

(country code: 49, area code: 08362)
Though I prefer sleeping in Reutte, convenient Füssen is just three miles from Ludwig's castles and offers a cobbled, riverside retreat. It's fairly touristy, but it has plenty of rooms, and is the region's best base for those traveling by train. All recommended accommodations are within a few handy blocks of the train station and the town center. Parking is easy at the station, and some hotels also have their own lot or garage. Prices listed are for one-night stays; most hotels give about 5-10 percent off for two-night stays—always request this discount. Competition is fierce, and off-season prices are soft. High season is mid-June-September. Rooms are generally 10-15 percent less in shoulder season and much cheaper in off-season.

Big, Fancy Hotels in the Center of Town

$$$ Hotel Schlosskrone, with 62 rooms and all the amenities, is just a block from the station. It also runs a fine pastry shop—you'll notice at breakfast—and restaurant (Sb-€99-109, standard Db-€119-139, bigger Db-€129-165, Tb-€145-165, Qb-€159-179, 4-person suite-€199-255, lower prices are for Oct-April, you'll likely

Sleep Code

(€1 = about $1.40, Germany country code: 49, Austria country code: 43)

S = Single, **D** = Double/Twin, **T** = Triple, **Q** = Quad, **b** = bathroom, **s** = shower only. Unless otherwise noted, credit cards are accepted, English is spoken, and breakfast is included.

To help you sort easily through these listings, I've divided the accommodations into three categories, based on the price for a standard double room with bath:

$$$ Higher Priced—Most rooms €100 or more.
$$ Moderately Priced—Most rooms between €60-100.
$ Lower Priced—Most rooms €60 or less.

Prices can change without notice; verify the hotel's current rates online or by email. For other updates, see www.ricksteves.com/update.

save money by booking via their website, air-con in some rooms, elevator, free Wi-Fi and cable Internet, free sauna and fitness center, parking-€9/day, Prinzregentenplatz 2-4, tel. 08362/930-180, fax 08362/930-1850, www.schlosskrone.com, info@schlosskrone .com, Norbert Schöll and family).

$$$ Hotel Hirsch is a romantic, well-maintained, 53-room, old-style hotel on the main street two blocks from the station. Their standard rooms are fine, and their rooms with historical and landscape themes are a fun splurge (Sb-€70-95, standard Db-€120-140, theme Db-€150-180, lower prices are for Nov-March and during slow times, family rooms, elevator, expensive Internet access, free Wi-Fi, free parking, Kaiser-Maximilian-Platz 7, tel. 08362/93980, fax 08362/939-877, www.hotelfuessen.de, info@hotelhirsch.de).

$$$ Hotel Sonne, in the heart of town, has a modern lobby and takes pride in decorating (some would say over-decorating) its 50 stylish rooms (Sb-€89-111, Db-€111-129, bigger Db-€149-165, Tb-€139-149, bigger Tb-€169-193, Qb-€189-205, lower prices are for Nov-March, 5 percent discount if you book on their website, elevator, free Internet access and Wi-Fi, free sauna and fitness center, parking-€5-7, kitty-corner from TI at Prinzregentenplatz 1, tel. 08362/9080, fax 08362/908-100, www.hotel-sonne.de, info @hotel-sonne.de).

Smaller, Mid-Priced Hotels and Pensions

$$ Altstadthotel zum Hechten offers 35 modern rooms in a friendly, traditional building right under Füssen Castle in the old-town pedestrian zone (Sb-€59-69, Db-€94-108, Tb-€125,

Qb-€156, ask when you reserve for 5 percent off these prices with this book, also mention if you're very tall as most beds can be short, non-smoking, lots of stairs, free Internet access in lounge, free Wi-Fi, and parking-€3, laundry-€10-15/load, fun miniature bowling alley in basement, electrobike rental-€20/day; from TI, walk down pedestrian street and take second right to Ritterstrasse 6; tel. 08362/91600, fax 08362/916-099, www.hotel-hechten.com, info@hotel-hechten.com, Pfeiffer and Tramp families).

$$ Gästehaus Schöberl, run by the head cook at Altstadthotel zum Hechten, rents six attentively furnished, modern rooms a five-minute walk from the train station. One room is in the owners' house, and the rest are in the building next door (Sb-€40-50, Db-€65-75, Tb-€85-95, Qb-€100-120, lower prices are for Jan-Feb and Nov or for longer stays, cash only, free Wi-Fi, free parking, Luitpoldstrasse 14-16, tel. 08362/922-411, www.schoeberl-fuessen .de, info@schoeberl-fuessen.de, Pia and Georg Schöberl).

$$ Mein Lieber Schwan, a block from the train station, is a former private house with four superbly outfitted apartments, each with a double bed, sofa bed, and kitchen. The catch is the three-night minimum stay (Sb-€68-79, Db-€78-89, Tb-€88-99, Qb-€98-109, price depends on apartment size, slightly cheaper off-season, cash or PayPal only, no breakfast, free Wi-Fi, free parking, laundry facilities, garden, from station turn left at traffic circle to Augustenstrasse 3, tel. 08362/509-980, fax 08362/509-914, www.meinlieberschwan.de, fewo@meinlieberschwan.de, Herr Bletschacher).

Budget Beds

$ House LA, run by energetic mason Lahdo Algül and hardworking Agata, has two branches. The backpacker house has 11 basic, clean four-bed dorm rooms at rock-bottom prices about a 10-minute walk from the station (€18/bed, D-€42, breakfast-€2.50, free Internet access and Wi-Fi, free parking, Wachsbleiche 2). A second building has five family apartments with kitchen and bath, each sleeping 4-6 people (apartment-€60-90, breakfast-€2.50, free Wi-Fi, free parking, 6-minute walk back along tracks from station to von Freybergstrasse 26; contact info for both: tel. 08362/607-366, mobile 0170-624-8610, fax 08362/925-1909, www.housela .de, info@housela.de). Both branches rent bikes (€8/day) and have laundry facilities (€7/load).

$ Füssen Youth Hostel occupies a pleasant modern building in a grassy setting an easy walk from the center. There are ping-pong tables and a basketball net out front (bed in 2- to 6-bed dorm rooms-€21, D-€50, €3 more for nonmembers, includes breakfast and sheets, guests over age 26 without kids in tow pay €4 penalty for being so old, laundry-€3.20/load, dinner-€5, office open

7:00-12:00 & 17:00-23:00, Nov-March until 22:00, free Wi-Fi, free parking, from station backtrack 10 minutes along tracks, Mariahilfer Strasse 5, tel. 08362/7754, fax 08362/2770, www .fuessen.jugendherberge.de, jhfuessen@djh-bayern.de).

$ Gasthof Krone, a rare bit of pre-glitz Füssen in the pedestrian zone, has dumpy halls and stairs and 12 big, worn, time-warp rooms—left unrenovated by the building's owner. Still, the location makes it worth considering as an alternative to the youth hostel (S-€26, D-€46, T-€69, €3 less per person for 2-night stays, no breakfast but bakeries across the street, closed Nov-early June; from TI, head down pedestrian street and take first left to Schrannengasse 17; tel. 08362/7824, fax 08362/37505, www.krone -fuessen.de, info@krone-fuessen.de).

Eating in Füssen

Restaurant Aquila serves modern international dishes in a simple, traditional *Gasthaus* setting with great seating outside on the delightful little Brotmarkt Square (€10-16 main courses, serious €9-10 salads, Wed-Mon 11:30-14:30 & 17:30-22:00, closed Tue, Brotmarkt 9, tel. 08362/6253).

Restaurant Ritterstub'n offers delicious, reasonably priced fish, salads, veggie plates, and a fun kids' menu. They have three eating zones: modern decor in front, traditional Bavarian in back, and a courtyard. Demure Gabi serves while her husband cooks standard Bavarian fare (€8-15 main courses, €5.50 lunch specials, €19 three-course fixed-price dinners, Tue-Sun 11:30-14:30 & 17:30-23:00, closed Mon, Ritterstrasse 4, tel. 08362/7759).

Schenke & Wirtshaus (inside the recommended Altstadthotel zum Hechten) dishes up hearty, traditional Bavarian fare. They specialize in pike *(Hecht)* pulled from the Lech River, served with a tasty fresh-herb sauce (€8-14 main courses, salad bar, cafeteria ambience, daily 10:00-22:00, Ritterstrasse 6, tel. 0836/91600).

Hotel Schlosskrone's fine restaurant, right on Füssen's main traffic circle, has good weekly specials and live Bavarian zither music most Fridays and Saturdays during dinner. Choose between a traditional dining room and a pastel winter garden. If your pension doesn't offer breakfast, consider their €10 "American-style" breakfast or huge €14.50 Sunday spread (open daily 7:30-10:30 & 11:30-14:30 & 18:00-22:00, Prinzregentenplatz 2-4, tel. 08362/930-180).

The **Markthalle,** just across the street from Gasthof Krone, is a fun food court offering a wide selection of reasonably priced, wurst-free food. Located in an old warehouse from 1483, it's now home to a fishmonger, deli counters, a fruit stand, a bakery, and a wine bar. Buy your food from one of the vendors, park yourself at any one of the tables, then look up and admire the Renaissance ceiling (Mon-Fri 7:30-18:30, Sat 7:30-14:30, closed Sun, corner of Schrannengasse and Brunnengasse).

Gelato: **Hohes Schloss Italian Ice Cream** is a good *gelateria* on the main drag and has an inviting people-watching perch for coffee or dessert (Reichenstrasse 14).

Asian Food: You'll find inexpensive Thai, Indian, and Chinese restaurants in the Luitpold-Passage at Reichenstrasse 33.

Picnic Supplies: Bakeries and *Metzgers* (butcher shops) abound and frequently have ready-made sandwiches. For groceries, try the underground **Netto** supermarket at Prinzregentenplatz, the roundabout on your way into town from the train station (Mon-Sat 7:00-20:00, closed Sun).

Füssen Connections

From Füssen to: **Neuschwanstein** (bus #73 or #78, departs from train station, most continue to Tegelberg lift station after castles, 1-2/hour, 10 minutes, €1.90 one-way, €3.80 round-trip; taxis cost €10 one-way); **Oberammergau** (bus #73 to Echelsbacher Brücke, change there to bus #9622—often marked *Garmisch,* confirm with driver that bus will stop in Oberammergau; in summer 4-6/day Mon-Sat, 2/day Sun, 1.5 hours total, bus continues to **Garmisch/ Zugspitze**)—from Oberammergau, you can connect to **Linderhof Castle** or **Ettal Monastery; Reutte** (bus #74, Mon-Fri almost hourly, last bus 19:00, Sat-Sun every 2 hours, last bus 18:00, 45 minutes, €3.90 one-way; taxis cost €35 one-way); **Wieskirche** (4-5/day, 40-50 minutes each way, more frequently with a transfer in Steingaden; or take Romantic Road bus—see next); **Munich** (hourly trains, 2 hours, some change in Buchloe); **Innsbruck** (take bus #74 to Reutte, then train from Reutte to Innsbruck via Garmisch, 5/day, 3.5 hours); **Salzburg** (hourly via Munich, 4 hours, 1-2 changes); **Rothenburg ob der Tauber** (hourly, 5 hours, look for connections with only 2-3 changes—often in Augsburg, Treuchtlingen, and Steinach); **Frankfurt** (hourly, 5-6 hours, 1-2 changes). Train info: tel. 0180-599-6633, www.bahn.com.

Romantic Road Buses: The northbound Romantic Road bus departs Füssen at 8:00; the southbound bus arrives in Füssen at 19:55 (daily, mid-April-late Oct only, bus stop is at train station, www.romanticroadcoach.de). A railpass gets you a 20 percent discount on the Romantic Road bus (without using up a day of a flexipass). The northbound bus arrives in Munich at 10:50 and in Rothenburg at 15:50. The bus is much slower than the train, especially to Rothenburg; the only reason to take the bus is that it gives you the briefest glimpse of the Wieskirche, Ettal, Oberammergau, and other sights along the way, and requires no changes. Note that the northbound bus stops at the **Wieskirche** for 20 minutes, but the southbound bus stops there for just 10 minutes after the church is closed. For more details on the bus, see page 329 in the Rothenburg chapter.

The Best of Bavaria

Within a short drive of Füssen and Reutte, you'll find some of the most enjoyable—and most tourist-filled—sights in Germany. The otherworldly "King's Castles" of Neuschwanstein and Hohenschwangau capture romantics' imaginations, the ornately decorated Wieskirche puts the faithful in a heavenly mood, and the little town of Oberammergau overwhelms visitors with cuteness. Yet another impressive castle (Linderhof), another fancy church (Ettal), and a sky-high viewpoint (the Zugspitze) round out Bavaria's top attractions.

The King's Castles: Neuschwanstein and Hohenschwangau

The most popular tourist destinations in Bavaria are the "King's Castles" (Königsschlösser). The older Hohenschwangau, King Ludwig's boyhood home, is less touristy but more historic. The more dramatic Neuschwanstein, which inspired Walt Disney, is the one everyone visits. I'd recommend visiting both, and planning some time to hike above Neuschwanstein to Mary's Bridge—and, if you enjoy romantic hikes, down through the gorge below. Reservations are a magic wand to smooth out your visit. With fairy-tale turrets in a fairy-tale alpine setting built by a fairy-tale king, these castles are understandably a huge hit.

Getting There

If arriving by **car,** note that road signs in the region refer to the sight as *Königsschlösser,* not Neuschwanstein. There's plenty of parking (all lots-€5). The first lots require more walking. Drive right through Touristville and past the ticket center, and park in lot #4 by the lake for the same price.

From **Füssen,** those without cars can catch **bus** #73 or #78 (1-2/hour, €1.90 one-way, €3.80 round-trip, 10 minutes, catch bus at train station, extra buses often run when crowded), take a **taxi** (€10 one-way), or ride a rental **bike** (two level miles). The bus drops you at the tourist office; it's a one-minute walk from there to the ticket office.

From **Reutte,** take bus #74 to the Füssen train station, then hop on bus #73 or #78 to the castles. Or pay €35 for a taxi right to the castles.

Orientation to the King's Castles

Cost: Neuschwanstein costs €12, Hohenschwangau costs €10.50, a *Königsticket* for both castles costs €21.50, and children under 18 (accompanied by an adult) are admitted free. Neuschwanstein, but not Hohenschwangau, is covered by the Bavarian Castles Pass—see page 122. If you have the pass, note this in the "message" field when making an online reservation.

Hours: The ticket center, located at street level between the two castles, is open daily April-Sept 8:00-17:00, Oct-March 9:00-15:00. The first and last castle tours of the day depart an hour after the ticket office opens and closes: April-Sept at 9:00 and 18:00, Oct-March at 10:00 and 16:00.

Getting Tickets for the Castles: Every tour bus in Bavaria converges on Neuschwanstein, and tourists flush in each morning from Munich. A handy reservation system sorts out the chaos for smart travelers. Tickets, whether reserved in advance or bought on the spot, come with admission times. If you miss your appointed tour time, you can't get in. To tour both castles, you must do Hohenschwangau first (logical, since this gives a better introduction to Ludwig's short life). You'll get two tour times: Hohenschwangau and then, two hours later, Neuschwanstein.

Arrival: Make the **ticket center** your first stop. If you have a reservation, there's a short line for picking up tickets. If you don't have a reservation...welcome to the very long line. Arrive by 8:00 in summer, and you'll likely be touring at 9:00. During August, the busiest month, tickets for English tours usually run out between 16:00 and 17:00.

Reservations: It's smart to reserve in peak season (June-early Oct, especially July-Aug). Reservations cost €1.80 per person per castle, and must be made no later than 17:00 on the previous day, ideally online (www.ticket-center-hohenschwangau .de); it's also possible to reserve by phone (tel. 08362/930-830) or email (info@ticket-center-hohenschwangau.de). You must pick up reserved tickets an hour before the appointed entry time, as it takes a while to walk up to the castles. (It doesn't usually take an hour, though—so this might be a good time to pull out a sandwich or a snack.) Show up late and they may have given your slot to someone else (but then they'll likely help you make another reservation). Better yet, if you know a couple of hours in advance that you're running late and can call the office, they'll normally rebook you at no charge.

Tips for Day-Tripping from Munich: If coming by train, make a castle tour reservation and take a train leaving at least four hours before your reserved castle entry. (The train to Füssen takes over two hours, getting from Füssen to the castle ticket office by bus takes another half-hour, and you must be there an hour before your tour.) Trains from Munich leave hourly at :51 past the hour. So, if you take the 9:51 train, you can make a 14:00 castle tour. If you reserve a castle tour for 11:00, you'll need to pack breakfast and take the 6:51 train.

Getting Up to the Castles: From the ticket booth, Hohenschwangau is an easy 10-minute climb, while Neuschwanstein is a steep 30-minute hike in the other direction. To minimize hiking to Neuschwanstein, you can take a shuttle bus (leaves every few minutes from in front of Hotel Lisl, just above ticket office and to the left) or a horse-drawn carriage (in front of Hotel Müller, just above ticket office and to the right), but neither gets you to the castle doorstep. The shuttle bus drops you off near Mary's Bridge (Marienbrücke), leaving you a steep, 10-minute downhill walk to the castle—so be sure to see the view from Mary's Bridge *before* hiking down (€1.80 one-way, the €2.60 round-trip is not worth it since you have to hike uphill to the bus stop for your return trip). Carriages (€6 up, €3 down) are slower than walking and stop below Neuschwanstein, leaving you a five-minute uphill hike. Here's the most economic and least strenuous plan: Ride the bus to Mary's Bridge for the view, hike down to Neuschwanstein, and then catch the horse carriage from the castle back down to the parking lot. Carriages also run to Hohenschwangau (€4 up, €2 down).

Entry Procedure: For each castle, tourists jumble at the entry, waiting for their ticket number to light up on the board. When it does, power through the mob (most waiting there are holding higher numbers) and go to the turnstile. Warning: You must use your ticket while your number is still on the board. If you space out while waiting for a polite welcome, you'll miss your entry window and never get in.

Services: A helpful TI, bus stop, ATM, WC (€0.50), and telephones cluster around the main intersection a couple hundred yards before you get to the ticket office (TI open daily April-Sept 10:00-18:00, Oct-March 11:00-17:00, tel. 08362/81980, www.schwangau.de).

Eating: Bring a packed lunch. The park by the Alpsee (the nearby lake) is ideal for a picnic, although you're not allowed to sit on the grass—only on the benches (you could also eat out on the lake in one of the old-fashioned rowboats, rented by

BAVARIA AND TIROL

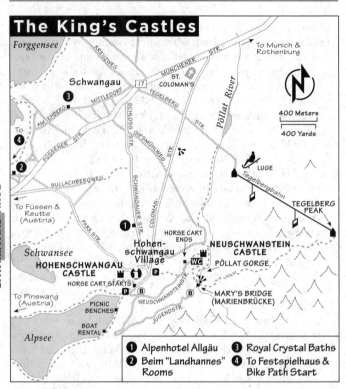

The King's Castles

Forggensee

To Munich & Rothenburg

KREUZWEG

MÜNCHENER STR.

ST. COLOMAN'S

Schwangau

17

TEGELBERG STR.

MITTLEDORF

❸

AM EHBERG

SCHLOSS /STR.

GIPSMÜHLWEG

Pöllat River

400 Meters

400 Yards

FÜSSENER STR.

To ❹

❷

BULLACHBERGWEG

LUGE

Tegelbergbahn

To Füssen & Reutte (Austria)

PARK STR.

SCHWANGAUER STR.

COLOMAN

TEGELBERG PEAK

❶

HORSE CART ENDS

Schwansee

Hohen-schwangau Village

NEUSCHWANSTEIN CASTLE

HOHENSCHWANGAU CASTLE

❶

P

WC

PÖLLAT GORGE

HORSE CART STARTS

To Pinswang (Austria)

P

B

NEUSCHWANSTEINSTR.

B

MARY'S BRIDGE (MARIENBRÜCKE)

PICNIC BENCHES

JUGENDSTR.

BOAT RENTAL

Alpsee

❶ Alpenhotel Allgäu
❷ Beim "Landhannes" Rooms
❸ Royal Crystal Baths
❹ To Festspielhaus & Bike Path Start

BAVARIA AND TIROL

the hour in summer). There are no grocery shops by the castles, but you can buy sandwiches and hot dogs across from the TI and at the Hotel Alpenstuben. The restaurants in the "village" at the foot of Europe's Disney castle are mediocre, feeding off the endless droves of hungry, shop-happy tourists. The **Bräustüberl cafeteria** serves the cheapest grub, but isn't likely to be a highlight of your visit (€6-7 gut-bomb grill meals, often with live folk music, daily 10:00-18:00, close to end of road and lake).

Sights at the King's Castles

▲▲▲Hohenschwangau Castle

Standing quietly below Neuschwanstein, the big, yellow Hohenschwangau Castle was Ludwig's boyhood home. Originally built in the 12th century, it was ruined by Napoleon. Ludwig's father, King Maximilian II, rebuilt it in 1830. Hohenschwangau (hoh-en-SHVAHN-gow, loosely translated as "High Swanland") was used by the royal family as a summer hunting lodge until 1912.

"Mad" King Ludwig
(1845-1886)

A tragic figure, Ludwig II (a.k.a. "Mad" King Ludwig) ruled Bavaria for 22 years until his death in 1886 at the age of 40. Bavaria was weak. Politically, Ludwig's reality was to "rule" either as a pawn of Prussia or a pawn of Austria. Rather than deal with politics in Bavaria's capital, Munich, Ludwig frittered away most of his time at his family's hunting palace, Hohenschwangau. He spent much of his adult life constructing his fanciful Neuschwanstein Castle—like a kid builds a tree house—on a neighboring hill upon the scant ruins of a medieval castle. Although Ludwig spent 17 years building Neuschwanstein, he lived in it only 172 days.

Ludwig was a true romantic living in a Romantic age. His best friends were artists, poets, and composers such as Richard Wagner. His palaces are wallpapered with misty medieval themes—especially those from Wagnerian operas. Eventually he was declared mentally unfit to rule Bavaria and taken away from Neuschwanstein. Two days after this eviction, Ludwig was found dead in a lake. To this day, people debate whether the king was murdered or committed suicide.

The interior decor is harmonious, cohesive, and original—all done in 1835, with paintings inspired by Romantic themes. The Wittelsbach family (which ruled Bavaria for nearly seven centuries) still owns the place (and lived in the annex—today's shop—until the 1970s). As you tour the castle, imagine how the paintings must have inspired young Ludwig. For 17 years, he lived here at his dad's place and followed the construction of his dream castle across the way—you'll see the telescope still set up and directed at Neuschwanstein.

The excellent 30-minute tours give a better glimpse of Ludwig's life than the more-visited and famous Neuschwanstein Castle tour. Tours here are smaller (35 people rather than 60) and more relaxed.

▲▲▲Neuschwanstein Castle

Imagine "Mad" King Ludwig as a boy, climbing the hills above his dad's castle, Hohenschwangau, dreaming up the ultimate fairy-tale castle. Inheriting the throne at the young age of 18, he had the power to make his dream concrete and stucco. Neuschwanstein (noy-SHVAHN-shtine, roughly "New Swanstone") was designed first by a theater-set designer...then by an architect. It looks medieval, but it's modern iron-and-brick construction with a sandstone veneer—only about as old as the Eiffel Tower. It feels like something you'd see at a home show for 19th-century royalty. Built from 1869 to 1886, it's the epitome of the Romanticism popular in 19th-century Europe. Construction stopped with Ludwig's death (only a third of the interior was finished), and within six weeks, tourists were paying to go through it.

During WWII, the castle took on a sinister role. The Nazis used Neuschwanstein as one of their primary secret storehouses for stolen art. After the war, Allied authorities spent a year sorting through and redistributing the art, which filled 49 rail cars from this one location alone. It was the only time the unfinished rooms were put to use.

Today, guides herd groups of 60 through the castle, giving an interesting—if rushed—30-minute tour. You'll go up and down more than 300 steps, through lavish rooms based on Wagnerian opera themes, the king's gilded-lily bedroom, and his extravagant throne room. You'll visit 15 rooms with their original furnishings and fanciful wall paintings. After the tour, before you descend to the king's kitchen, see the 20-minute video about the king's life and passions accompanied by Wagner's music (next to the café, alternates between English and German, schedule board at the entry says what's playing and what's on deck). After the kitchen (state of the art for this high-tech king in its day), you'll see a room lined with fascinating drawings (described in English) of the castle plans, construction, and drawings from 1883 of Falkenstein—a whimsical, over-the-top, never-built castle that makes Neuschwanstein look stubby. Falkenstein occupied Ludwig's fantasies the year he died.

Near the Castles

Mary's Bridge (Marienbrücke)—Before or after the Neuschwanstein tour, climb up to Mary's Bridge to marvel at Ludwig's castle, just as Ludwig did. This bridge was quite an engineering accomplishment 100 years ago. From the bridge, the frisky can hike even higher to the *Beware—Danger of Death* signs and an even more glorious castle view. (Access to the bridge is closed in bad winter weather, but many travelers walk around the barriers to get there—at their own risk, of course.) The most scenic way to descend from Neuschwanstein is to walk up to Mary's Bridge and then follow the signs down the Pöllat Gorge to the TI *(Pöllatschlucht,* 15 minutes longer than walking down the road but worth it, especially with new steel walkways and railings that make this slippery area safer).

▲**Tegelberg Gondola**—Just north of Neuschwanstein is a fun play zone around the mighty Tegelberg Gondola, a scenic ride to the mountain's 5,500-foot summit. On a clear day, you get great views of the Alps and Bavaria and the vicarious thrill of watching hang gliders and paragliders leap into airborne ecstasy. Weather permitting, scores of adventur-

ous Germans line up and leap from the launch ramp at the top of the lift. With someone leaving every two or three minutes, it's great for spectators. Thrill-seekers with exceptional social skills may talk themselves into a tandem ride with a paraglider. From the top of Tegelberg, it's a steep and demanding 2.5-hour hike down to Ludwig's castle. (Avoid the treacherous trail directly below the gondola.) At the base of the gondola, you'll find a playground, a cheery eatery, the stubby remains of an ancient Roman villa, and a luge ride.

Cost and Hours: €17.50 round-trip, €11 one-way, daily 9:00-17:00, closed Nov, 4/hour, last ride at 16:30, in bad weather call first to confirm, tel. 08362/98360, www.tegelbergbahn.de. Most buses #73 and #78 from Füssen continue from the castles to Tegelberg.

▲**Tegelberg Luge**—Next to the Tegelberg Gondola is a luge course. A luge is like a bobsled on wheels (for more details, see "Luge Lesson" on page 163). This stainless-steel track is heated, so it's often dry and open even when drizzly weather shuts down the concrete luges. A funky cable system pulls riders (in their sleds) to the top without a ski lift. It's not as long, fast, or scenic as Austria's Biberwier luge (described on page 164), but it's handy, harder to get hurt on, and half the price.

Cost and Hours: €3/ride, 6-ride shareable card-€11, July-Sept daily 10:00-18:00, otherwise same hours as gondola, in winter sometimes opens late due to wet track, in bad weather call first to confirm, waits can be long in good weather, no children under 3, ages 3-8 may ride with an adult, tel. 08362/98360, www.tegelberg bahn.de.

▲**Royal Crystal Baths (Königliche Kristall-Therme)**—This pool/sauna complex just outside Füssen is the perfect way to relax on a rainy day, or to cool off on a hot one. The downstairs contains two heated indoor pools and a café; outside you'll find a shallow kiddie pool, a lap pool, a heated *Kristallbad* with massage jets and a whirlpool, and a salty mineral bath. The extensive saunas upstairs are well worth the few extra euros, as long as you're OK with nudity. (Swimsuits are required in the downstairs pools, but *verboten* in the upstairs saunas.) You'll see pool and sauna rules in German all over, but don't worry—just follow the locals' lead.

To enter the baths, first choose the length of your visit and your focus (big outdoor pool only, all ground-floor pools but not the saunas, or the whole enchilada—a flier explains all the prices in English). You'll get a wristband and a credit-card-sized ticket with a bar code. Insert that ticket into the entry gate, and keep it—you'll need it to get out. Enter through the yellow changing stalls—where you'll change into your bathing suit—then choose a storage locker (€1 coin deposit). When it's time to leave, reinsert your ticket in the gate—if you've gone over the time limit, feed extra euros into the machine.

Cost and Hours: €9.90/2 hours, €14.20/4 hours, €17.80/day, saunas-€5, towel rental-€2.50, bathing suit rental-€3, Sun-Thu 9:00-22:00, Fri-Sat until 23:00, nude swimming everywhere Tue and Fri after 19:00; from Füssen, drive, bike, or walk across the river, turn left toward Schwangau, and then, about a mile later, turn left at signs for *Kristall-Therme*, Am Ehberg 16; tel. 08362/819-630, www.kristalltherme-schwangau.de.

Bike Ride Around the Forggensee—On a beautiful day, nothing beats a bike ride around the bright turquoise Forggensee, a nearby lake. This 20-mile ride is almost exclusively on bike paths, with just a few stretches on country roads. Locals swear that going clockwise is less work, but either way has a couple of strenuous uphill parts. Still, the amazing views of the surrounding Alps will distract you from your churning legs—so this is still a great way to spend the afternoon. Rent a bike, pack a picnic lunch, and figure about a three-hour round-trip. From Füssen, follow *Festspielhaus* signs; once you reach the theater, follow *Forggensee Rundweg* signs.

From the theater, you can also take a **boat ride** on the Forggensee (€8/50-minute cruise, 6/day; €11/2-hour cruise, 3/day; or buy a one-way ticket and bike back, fewer departures Oct-May, tel. 08362/921-363, www.schifffahrt.fuessen.de).

Sleeping near the King's Castles

(€1 = about $1.40, country code: 49, area code: 08362)
Inexpensive farmhouse B&Bs abound in the Bavarian countryside
around Neuschwanstein, offering drivers a decent value. Look for
Zimmer Frei signs ("room free"/vacancy). The going rate is about
€50-65 for a double, including breakfast. Though a bit inconve-
nient for those without a car, my listings here are a quick taxi ride
from the Füssen train station and also close to local bus stops.

$$ Alpenhotel Allgäu is a small, family-run hotel with 18
rooms in a bucolic setting. It's a 15-minute walk from the castle
ticket office, not far beyond the humongous parking lot (small Sb
without balcony-€48, Sb-€58, perfectly fine older Db-€80, newer
Db-€88, Tb-€120, these are book-direct prices, ask about discount
with cash and this book, all rooms except one single have porches
or balconies—some with castle views, family rooms, free Wi-Fi,
elevator, free parking, just before tennis courts at Schwangauer
Strasse 37 in the town of Schwangau—don't let your GPS take
you to Schwangauer Strasse 37 in Füssen, tel. 08362/81152, fax
08362/987-028, www.alpenhotel-allgaeu.de, info@alpenhotel-all-
gaeu.de, Frau Reiss).

$ Beim "Landhannes," a 200-year-old working dairy farm
run by Conny Schön, rents three creaky but sunny rooms, and
keeps flowers on the balconies, big bells and antlers in the halls,
and cows in the yard (Sb-€30, Db-€60, €5 less per person for 3
or more nights, also rents apartments with kitchen with a 5-night
minimum, cash only, free Wi-Fi, nearby bike rental, poorly signed
in the village of Horn on the Füssen side of Schwangau, look for
the farm down a tiny lane through the grass 100 yards in front
of Hotel Kleiner König, Am Lechrain 22, tel. 08362/8349, www
.landhannes.de, info@landhannes.de).

Wieskirche

Germany's greatest Rococo-style church, this recently restored
"Church in the Meadow"—worth ▲▲—looks as brilliant as the

day it floated down from
heaven. Overripe with deco-
ration but bright and burst-
ing with beauty, this church
is a divine droplet, a curly
curlicue, the final flowering
of the Baroque movement.

Cost and Hours: Dona-
tion requested, daily April-Oct 8:00-19:00, Nov-March 8:00-
17:00, tel. 08862/932-930, www.wieskirche.de.

BAVARIA AND TIROL

Getting There: The Wieskirche is a 30-minute drive north of Neuschwanstein. The Romantic Road bus tour stops here for 20 minutes on the northbound route to Frankfurt. Southbound buses stop here for 10 minutes, but it's after the church has closed for the day. For information on taking the bus from Füssen to the Wieskirche, see page 134. By car, head north from Füssen, turn right at Steingaden, and follow the signs. Take a commune-with-nature-and-smell-the-farm detour back through the meadow to the parking lot (€1/hour).

○ **Self-Guided Tour:** This pilgrimage church is built around the much-venerated statue of a scourged (or whipped) Christ, which supposedly wept in 1738. The carving—too graphic to be accepted by that generation's Church—was the focus of worship in a peasant's barn. Miraculously, it shed tears—empathizing with all those who suffer. Pilgrims came from all around. A tiny and humble chapel was built to house the statue in 1739. (You can see it where the lane to the church leaves the parking lot.) Bigger and bigger crowds came. Two of Bavaria's top Rococo architects, the Zimmermann brothers (Johann Baptist and Dominikus), were commissioned to build the Wieskirche that stands here today.

Follow the theological sweep from the altar to the ceiling: Jesus whipped, chained, and then killed (notice the pelican above the altar—recalling a pre-Christian story of a bird that opened its breast to feed its young with its own blood); the painting of a baby Jesus posed as if on the cross; the sacrificial lamb; and finally, high on the ceiling, the resurrected Christ before the Last Judgment. This is the most positive depiction of the Last Judgment around. Jesus, rather than sitting on the throne to judge, rides high on a rainbow—a symbol of forgiveness—giving any sinner the feeling that there is still time to repent, with plenty of mercy on hand. In the back, above

the pipe organ, notice the empty throne—waiting for Judgment Day—and the closed door to paradise.

Above the entrances to both side aisles are murky glass cases with 18th-century handkerchiefs. People wept, came here, were healed, and no longer needed their hankies. Walk up either aisle flanking the high altar to see votives—requests and thanks to God (for happy, healthy babies, and so on). Notice how the kneelers are positioned so that worshippers can meditate on scenes of biblical miracles painted high on the ceiling and visible through the ornate tunnel frames. A priest here once told me that faith, architecture, light, and music all combine to create the harmony of the Wieskirche.

Two paintings flank the door at the rear of the church. One shows the ceremonial parade in 1749 when the white-clad monks of Steingaden carried the carved statue of Christ from the tiny church to its new big one. The second painting, from 1757, is a votive from one of the Zimmermann brothers, the artists and architects who built this church. He is giving thanks for the successful construction of the new church.

If you can't visit the Wieskirche, visit one of the other churches that came out of the same heavenly spray can: Oberammergau's church, Munich's Asamkirche, Würzburg's Hofkirche Chapel (at the Residenz), the splendid Ettal Monastery (free and near Oberammergau), and, on a lesser scale, Füssen's basilica.

Route Tips for Drivers: If you're driving from Wieskirche to Oberammergau, you'll cross the **Echelsbacher Bridge,** which arches 230 feet over the Pöllat Gorge. Thoughtful drivers let their passengers walk across to enjoy the views, then meet them at the other side. Any kayakers? Notice the painting of the traditional village woodcarver (who used to walk from town to town with his art on his back) on the first big house on the Oberammergau side. It holds the Almdorf Ammertal shop, with a huge selection of overpriced carvings and commission-hungry tour guides.

Oberammergau

The Shirley Temple of Bavarian villages, and exploited to the hilt by the tourist trade, Oberammergau wears way too much makeup. During its famous Passion Play (every 10 years, next in 2020), the

crush is unbearable—and the prices at the hotels and restaurants can be as well. The village has about 1,200 beds for the 5,000 playgoers coming daily. If you're passing through, Oberammergau is a ▲ sight—worth a wander among the half-timbered *Lüftlmalerei* houses frescoed with biblical scenes and famous fairy-tale characters. It's also a relatively convenient home base for visiting Linderhof Castle, Ettal Monastery, and the Zugspitze (via Garmisch). A day trip to Neuschwanstein from Oberammergau is manageable if you have a car, but train travelers do better to stay in Füssen.

Tourist Information: The TI is at Eugen-Papst-Strasse 9A (Mon-Fri 9:00-18:00, Sat 10:00-14:00, closed Sun, tel. 08822/922-740, www.ammergauer-alpen.de).

Oberammergau

1. Gasthof zur Rose & Gästehaus Magold
2. Hotel Garni Fux
3. Pension Anton Zwink
4. Youth Hostel
5. Hotel Maximilian (Beer Garden)
6. To Sommerrodelbahn Steckenberg

Getting There

Trains run from Munich to Oberammergau (nearly hourly, 1.75 hours, change in Murnau). From Füssen to Oberammergau, **buses** run daily (in summer 4-6/day Mon-Sat, 2/day Sun, 1.5 hours, most change at Echelsbacher Brücke). **Drivers** entering the town from the north should cross the bridge, take the second right, and park in the free lot a block beyond the TI. Leaving town (to Linderhof or Reutte), head out past the church and turn toward Ettal on Road 23. You're 20 miles from Reutte via the scenic Plansee. If heading to Munich, Road 23 takes you to the autobahn, which gets you there in less than an hour.

Sights in Oberammergau

Oberammergau Church—Visit the town church, which is typically Bavarian Baroque—but a poor cousin of the one at Wies. Being in a woodcarving center, it's only logical that all the statues are made of wood, and then stuccoed and gilded to look like marble or gold. Saints Peter and Paul flank the altar, where the central painting can be raised to reveal a small stage decorated to celebrate special times during the church calendar. In the central dome, a touching painting shows Peter and Paul bidding each other fare-

---

Woodcarving in Oberammergau

The Ammergau region is relatively poor, with no appreciable industry and no agriculture, save for some dairy farming. What they *do* have is wood. Carving religious and secular themes became a lucrative way for the locals to make some money, especially when confined to the house during the long, cold winter. Carvers from Oberammergau peddled their wares across Europe, carrying them on their backs as far away as Rome. Today, the Oberammergau Carving School is a famous institution that takes only 20 students per year out of 450 applicants. Their graduates do important restoration work throughout Europe. For example, much of the work on Dresden's Frauenkirche (see page 602) was done by these artists.

well (with the city of Rome as a backdrop) on the day of their execution—the same day, in the year A.D. 67. On the left, Peter is crucified upside-down. On the right, Paul is beheaded with a sword. (A fine little €3 booklet explains it all.) Wander through the lovingly maintained graveyard. A stone WWI and WWII memorial at the gate reads, "We honor and remember the victims of the violence that our land gave the world."

Local Arts and Crafts—The town's best sights are its woodcarving shops. Browse through these small art galleries filled with very expensive whittled works. The beautifully frescoed **Pilatus House** at Ludwig-Thoma-Strasse 10 has an open workshop where you can watch woodcarvers and painters at work (free; mid-May-mid-Oct Tue-Sat 13:00-18:00, closed Sun-Mon; open two weeks after Christmas 11:00-17:00; closed rest of year, tel. 08822/949-511).

Oberammergau Museum—The museum's main branch at Dorfstrasse 8 showcases local woodcarving. A museum ticket also lets you into the lobby of the Passion Play theater, which houses a modest exhibition on the history of the performances, and into a small gallery of "reverse glass" paintings in the Pilatus House. The museum also organizes guided tours of the theater (see next).

Cost and Hours: €6; museum and theater lobby open April-Oct and Dec-mid-Jan Tue-Sun 10:00-17:00; Pilatus House exhibit open same days 15:00-17:00; all three closed Mon, in Nov and mid-Jan-March; tel. 08822/94136, www.oberammergaumuseum.de.

Passion Play—Back in 1633, in the midst of the bloody Thirty Years' War and with horrifying plagues devastating entire cities, the people of Oberammergau promised God that if they were spared from extinction, they'd "perform a play depicting the suffering, death, and resurrection of our Lord Jesus Christ" every decade thereafter. The town survived, and, heading into its 41st decade, the people of Oberammergau are still making good on the deal. For 100 days every 10 years (most recently in 2010), about half of the town's population (a cast of 2,000) are involved in the production of this extravagant five-hour Passion Play—telling the story of Jesus' entry into Jerusalem, Crucifixion, and Resurrection.

Until the next show in 2020, you'll have to settle for reading the book, seeing Nicodemus tool around town in his VW, or taking a quick look at the **Passion Play theater**, a block from the center of town. The only way to see the theater hall itself is on a twice-weekly 45-minute guided tour organized by the Oberammergau Museum (€6, April-Oct Wed and Sat at 14:00, in German and—on request—English, no tours off-season, tel. 08822/94136, www.oberammergaumuseum.de).

Sommerrodelbahn Steckenberg—This stainless-steel luge track (near Oberammergau) is faster than the Tegelberg luge, but not quite as wicked as the one in Biberwier.

Cost and Hours: €2.50/ride, €11/6 rides, May-Oct daily 8:30-17:00, closed when wet, Liftweg 1 in Unterammergau, clearly marked and easy 2.5-mile bike ride to Unterammergau along Bahnhofstrasse/Rottenbucherstrasse, take the first left when entering Unterammergau, tel. 08822/4027, www.steckenberg.de.

Sleeping in Oberammergau

(€1 = about $1.40, country code: 49, area code: 08822)
$$ Gasthof zur Rose is a big, central, classic, family-run place with 21 straightforward rooms. At the reception desk, look at the several decades of photos showing the family performing in the Passion Play (Sb-€50, Db-€80, Tb-€90, Qb-€100, free Internet access and Wi-Fi, Dedlerstrasse 9, tel. 08822/4706, fax 08822/6753, www.rose-oberammergau.de, info@rose-oberammergau.de, Frank family).

$$ Hotel Garni Fux, quiet and romantic and a little fancier than the Rose, rents eight large rooms and six apartments decorated in the Bavarian *Landhaus* style (Sb-€65, Db-€84; apartment prices without breakfast: Sb-€68, Db-€78, larger apartments-€89-120; cheaper Nov-April, free Internet access and Wi-Fi, Mannagasse 2a, tel. 08822/93093, www.firmafux.de, info@firmafux.de).

$ Pension Anton Zwink offers 10 small, quiet, no-frills rooms in a neighborhood adjacent to the town center (Sb-€33,

Db-€56, cash only, free Wi-Fi, behind Gasthof zur Rose at Daisenbergerstrasse 10, tel. 08822/6334, www.pension-zwink.de, info@pension-zwink.de).

$ **Gästehaus Magold** is a homey, grandmotherly place with three bright and spacious rooms—twice as nice as the cheap hotel rooms in town, and for much less money (Db-€50, cash only, non-smoking, free cable Internet, also has two family apartments, immediately behind Gasthof zur Rose at Kleppergasse 1, tel. 08822/4340, www.gaestehaus-magold.de, info@gaestehaus -magold.de, Christine).

$ **Oberammergau Youth Hostel,** on the river, is a short walk from the center (€17/bed, includes breakfast and sheets, €3 extra for nonmembers, €4 extra if over 26, closed mid-Nov-Dec, Malensteinweg 10, tel. 08822/4114, fax 08822/1695, www.ober ammergau.jugendherberge.de, oberammergau@jugendherberge.de).

Eating in Oberammergau

Locals won't be caught dead inside the chic, five-star **Hotel Maximilian.** But they fill its serene beer garden to enjoy the hotel's home-brewed beer and summertime grill, which cooks up delicious chicken, sausage, and spareribs. On summer Wednesdays after 18:00, they offer all-you-can-eat from the grill for €17.50 (daily 11:00-23:00, right behind the church, Ettaler Strasse 5, tel. 08822/948-740).

Oberammergau Connections

From Oberammergau to: Linderhof Castle (bus #9622, 6/day Mon-Fri, 4/day Sat-Sun, 30 minutes; many of these also stop at **Ettal Monastery**), **Füssen** (in summer 4-6 buses/day Mon-Sat, 2/day Sun, most transfer at Echelsbacher Brücke and stop also at **Hohenschwangau** for Neuschwanstein, 1.5 hours total), **Garmisch** (nearly hourly buses, 40 minutes; also possible by train with a transfer in Murnau, 1.5 hours; from Garmisch, you can ascend the **Zugspitze**), **Munich** (nearly hourly trains, 1.75 hours, change in Murnau). Train info: tel. 0180-599-6633, www.bahn.com.

Linderhof Castle

This homiest of "Mad" King Ludwig's castles is small and comfortably exquisite—good enough for a minor god, and worth ▲▲. Set in the woods 15 minutes from Oberammergau and surrounded by fountains and sculpted, Italian-style gardens, it's the only palace I've toured that actually had me feeling envious.

Ludwig was king for 22 of his 40 years. He lived much of

his last 8 years here—the only one of his castles that was finished in his lifetime. Frustrated by the limits of being a "constitutional monarch," he retreated to Linderhof, inhabiting a private fantasy world where extravagant castles glorified his otherwise weakened kingship. He lived here as a royal hermit; his dinner table—pre-set with dishes and food—rose from the kitchen below into his dining room, so he could eat alone.

Beyond the palace is Ludwig's **grotto.** Inspired by Wagner's *Tannhäuser* opera, this performance space is 300 feet long and 70 feet tall. Its rocky walls are actually made of cement poured over an iron frame. The grotto provided a private theater for the reclusive king to enjoy his beloved Wagnerian operas—he was usually the sole member of the audience. The grotto features a waterfall, fake stalactites, and a swan boat floating on an artificial lake (which could be heated for swimming). The first electricity in Bavaria was generated here, to change the colors of the stage lights and to power Ludwig's fountain and wave machine.

Cost and Hours: €8.50, covered by Bavarian Castles Pass—see page 122, €3.50 for grotto only, daily April-mid-Oct 9:00-18:00, mid-Oct-March 10:00-16:00, last tour 30 minutes before closing, fountains often erupt on the half-hour, tel. 08822/92030, www.linderhof.de.

Getting There: Without a car, getting to (and back from) Linderhof is a royal headache, unless you're staying in Oberammergau. Buses from Oberammergau take 30 minutes (6/day Mon-Fri, 4/day Sat-Sun). If you're driving, park near the ticket office (obligatory €2.50). Driving from Reutte, take the scenic Plansee route.

Visiting the Castle: The complex sits isolated in natural splendor. Plan for lots of walking and a two-hour stop to fully enjoy this royal park. Bring raingear in iffy weather. Your ticket comes with an entry time to tour the palace, which is a five-minute hike from the ticket office. At the palace entrance, wait in line at the turnstile listed on your ticket (A through D) to take the required 30-minute English tour. Afterwards, hike 10 minutes uphill to the grotto (take the brief but interesting free tour in English, no reservations necessary). Then see the other royal buildings dotting the king's playground if you like. You can eat lunch at a café across from the ticket office.

Crowd-Beating Tips: July and August crowds can mean an hour's wait between when you buy your ticket and when you start your tour. During this period, you're wise to arrive after 15:00. Any other time of year, you should get your palace tour time shortly after you arrive. Unlike Neuschwanstein, Linderhof doesn't take advance reservations online.

Ettal Monastery and Pilgrimage Church

In 1328, the Holy Roman Emperor was returning from Rome with what was considered a miraculous statue of Mary and Jesus. He

was in political and financial trouble, so to please God, he founded a monastery with this statue as its centerpiece. The monastery was located here because it was suitably off the beaten path, but today Ettal is on one of the most-traveled tourist routes in Bavaria. Stopping here (free and easy for drivers) offers a convenient peek

at a splendid Baroque church. Restaurants across the road serve lunch.

BAVARIA AND TIROL

Cost and Hours: Free, daily 8:00-19:45 in summer, until 18:00 off-season, tel. 08822/740, www.kloster-ettal.de. If you're moved to make a donation, there are self-serve credit-card machines for doing so to the right as you enter.

Getting There: The Ettal Monastery is a few minutes' **drive** (or a delightful **bike** ride) from Oberammergau. Just park for free and wander in. Some Oberammergau-to-Linderhof **buses** stop here (see "Oberammergau Connections," earlier).

◑ Self-Guided Tour: As you enter the more than 1,000-square-foot **courtyard,** imagine the 14th-century Bene-

dictine abbey, an independent religious community. It produced everything it needed right here. In the late Middle Ages, abbeys like this had jurisdiction over the legal system, administration, and taxation of their district. Since then, the monastery has had its ups and downs.

Secularized during the French Revolution and Napoleonic age, the Benedictines' property was confiscated by the state and sold. Religious life returned a century later. Today the abbey survives, with 50 or 60 monks. It remains a self-contained community, with living quarters for the monks, workshops, and guests' quarters. Along with their religious responsibilities, the brothers make their

20 + C + M + B + 12

All over Germany (and much of Catholic Europe), you'll likely see written on doorways a mysterious message: "20 + C + M + B + 12." This is marked in chalk on Epiphany (Jan 6), the Christian holiday celebrating the arrival of the Magi to adore the newborn Baby Jesus. In addition to being the initials of the three wise men (Caspar, Melchior, and Balthazar), the letters also stand for the Latin phrase *Christus mansionem benedicat*—"May Christ bless the house." The little crosses separating the letters remind all who enter that the house has been blessed in this year (20+12). Epiphany is a bigger deal in Catholic Europe than in the US. The holiday includes gift-giving, feasting, and caroling door to door—often collecting for a charity organization. Those who donate get their doors chalked up in thanks, and these marks are left on the door through the year.

famous liqueur, brew beer, run a hotel, and educate 380 students in their private high school. The monks' wares are for sale at two shops (look for the *Klosterladen* by the courtyard or the *Kloster-Markt* across the street).

At the front of the church, you pass a **tympanum** over the door dating from 1350. It shows the founding couple, Emperor Louis the Bavarian and his wife Margaret, directing our attention to the crucified Lord and inviting us to enter the church contemplatively.

Stepping inside, the light draws our eyes to the **dome** (it's a double-shell design 230 feet high) rather than to the high altar. Illusions—with the dome opening right to the sky—merge heaven and earth. The dome fresco shows hundreds of Benedictines worshipping the Holy Trinity...the glory of the Benedictine Order. This is classic "south-German Baroque."

Statues of the **saints** on the altars are either engaged in a holy conversation with each other or singing the praises of God. Broken shell-style patterns seem to create constant movement, with cherubs adding to the energy. Side altars and confessionals seem to grow out of the architectural structure; its decorations and furnishings become part of an organic whole. Imagine how 18th-century farmers and woodcutters, who never traveled, would step in here on Sunday and be inspired to praise their God.

The origin of the monastery is shown over the **choir arch:** An angel wearing the robe of a Benedictine monk presents the emperor with a marble Madonna and commissions him to found this monastery. (In reality, the statue was made in Pisa, circa 1300, and given to the emperor in Italy.)

Dwarfed by all the magnificence and framed by a monumental tabernacle is that tiny, most precious statue of the abbey—the miraculous **statue of Mary and the Baby Jesus.**

Zugspitze

The tallest point in Germany, worth ▲▲, is also a border crossing. Lifts from both Austria and Germany meet at the 9,700-foot summit of the Zugspitze (TSOOG-

shpit-seh). You can straddle the border between two great nations while enjoying an incredible view. Restaurants, shops, and telescopes await you at the summit.

German Approach: First, head to Garmisch (for details on getting there from Füssen, see

page 134; from Oberammergau, see page 149). From Garmisch, there are two ways to ascend the Zugspitze: the whole way by cogwheel train (1.25 hours one-way), or a faster cogwheel train-plus-cable car option (about 45 minutes one-way). Both cost the same (€48 round-trip). Although the train ride takes longer, many travelers enjoy the more involved cog-railway experience. The train departs from Garmisch, stops at Eibsee for the cable-car connection, and then continues up—and through—the mountain (hourly departures daily 8:15-14:15). The cable car simply zips you to the top in five minutes from the Eibsee station. Cable cars go up daily 8:00-14:15. The last cable car down departs at about 16:15 (tel. 08821/7970, www.zugspitze.de). Allow plenty of time for afternoon descents: If bad weather hits in the late afternoon, cable cars can be delayed at the summit, causing tourists to miss their train connection from Eibsee back to Garmisch.

Drivers can park for €3 at the cable-car station at Eibsee. Hikers can enjoy the easy six-mile walk around the lovely Eibsee (start 5 minutes downhill from cable-car station).

Austrian Approach: The Tiroler Zugspitzbahn ascent is less crowded and cheaper. Departing from above the village of Ehrwald (a 30-minute train trip from Reutte, runs almost hourly), the lift zips you to the

BAVARIA AND TIROL

top in 10 minutes (€35.50 round-trip, departures in each direction at :00, :20, and :40 past the hour, daily 8:40-16:40 except closed late April-mid-May and most of Nov, last ascent at 16:00, drivers follow signs for *Tiroler Zugspitzbahn*, free parking, Austrian tel. 05673/2309, www.zugspitze.at). While the German ascent from Garmisch is easier for those without a car, buses connect the Ehrwald train station and the Austrian lift nearly every hour (or pay €8 for the 5-minute taxi ride from Ehrwald train station).

○ Self-Guided Tour: Whether you ascended from the Austrian or German side, you're high enough now to enjoy a little tour of the summit. The two terraces—Bavarian and Tirolean—are connected by a narrow walkway, which was the border station before Germany and Austria opened their borders. The Austrian (Tirolean) side was higher until the Germans blew its top off in World War II to make a flak tower, so let's start there.

Tirolean Terrace: Before you stretches the Zugspitzplatt glacier. Each summer, a 65,000-square-foot reflector is spread over the ice to try to slow the shrinking. Since metal ski lift towers collect heat, they, too, are wrapped to try to save the glacier. Many ski lifts fan out here, as if reaching for a ridge that defines the border between Germany and Austria. The circular metal building is the top of the cog-railway line that the Germans cut through the mountains in 1931. Just above that, find a small square building—the wedding chapel (Hochzeitskapelle) consecrated in 1981 by Cardinal Joseph Ratzinger (now Pope Benedict XVI).

Both Germany and Austria use this rocky pinnacle for communication purposes. The square box on the Tirolean Terrace provides the Innsbruck airport with air-traffic control, and a tower nearby is for the German *Kathastrophenfunk* (civil defense network).

This highest point in Germany (there are many higher points in Austria) was first climbed in 1820. The Austrians built a cable car that nearly reached the summit in 1926. (You can see it just over the ridge on the Austrian side—look for the ghostly, abandoned concrete station.) In 1964, the final leg, a new lift, was built connecting that 1926 station to the actual summit, where you stand now. Before then, people needed to hike the last 650 feet to the top. Today's lift dates from 1980, but was renovated after a 2003 fire. The Austrian station, which is much nicer than the German station, has a fine little museum—free with Austrian ticket, €2.50 if you came up from Germany—that shows three interesting videos (6-minute 3-D mountain show, 30-minute making-of-the-lift documentary, and 45-minute look at the nature, sport, and culture of the region).

Looking up the valley from the Tirolean Terrace, you can see the towns of Ehrwald and Lermoos in the distance, and the valley that leads to Reutte. Looking farther clockwise, you'll see the Eibsee lake below. Hell's Valley, stretching to the right of Eibsee, seems to merit its name.

Bavarian Terrace: The narrow passage connecting the two terraces used to be a big deal—you'd show your passport here at the little blue house and shift from Austrian shillings to German marks. Notice the regional pride here: no German or Austrian banners, but regional ones instead—*Freistaat Bayern* (Bavaria) and *Land Tirol*.

The German side features a golden cross marking the summit...the highest point in Germany. A priest and his friends hauled it up in 1851. The historic original was shot up by American soldiers using it for target practice in the late 1940s, so what you see today is a modern replacement. In the summer, it's easy to "summit" the Zugspitze, as there are steps and handholds all the way to the top. Or you can just stay behind and feed the birds. The yellow-beaked ravens get chummy with those who share a little pretzel or bread.

The oldest building up here is the rustic tin-and-wood weather tower, erected in 1900 by the *Deutscher Wetterdienst* (German weather service). The first mountaineers' hut, built in 1897, didn't last. The existing one—entwined with mighty cables that cinch it down—dates from 1914. In 1985, observers clocked 200-mph winds up here—those cables were necessary. Step inside the restaurant to enjoy museum-like photos and paintings on the wall (including a look at the team who hiked up with the golden cross in 1851).

Reutte, Austria

Reutte (ROY-teh, with a rolled *r*), a relaxed Austrian town of 5,700, is located 20 minutes across the border from Füssen. While overlooked by the international tourist crowd, it's popular with Germans and Austrians for its climate. Doctors recommend its "grade 1" air. I like Reutte for the opportunity to simply be in a real community. As an example of how the town is committed to its character, real estate can be sold only to those using it as a primary residence. (Many formerly vibrant alpine towns made a pile of money but lost their sense of community by becoming resorts. They allowed wealthy foreigners—who just drop in for a week or two a year—to buy up all the land, and are now shuttered up and dead most of the time.)

Reutte has one claim to fame among Americans: As Nazi Germany was falling in 1945, Hitler's top rocket scientist, Werner von Braun, joined the Americans (rather than the Russians) in

Reutte. You could say that the American space program began here.

Reutte isn't featured in any other American guidebook. While its generous sidewalks are filled with smart boutiques and lazy coffeehouses, its charms are subtle. It was never rich or important. Its castle is ruined, its buildings have painted-on "carvings," its churches are full, its men yodel for each other on birthdays, and its energy is spent soaking its Austrian and German guests in *Gemütlichkeit*. Most guests stay for a week, so the town's attractions are more time-consuming than thrilling.

Orientation to Reutte

(country code: 43, area code: 05672)
Remember, Reutte is in a different country. While Austrians use the same euro currency the Germans do, postage stamps and phone cards only work in the country where you buy them.

To **telephone** from Germany to Austria, dial 00-43 and then the number listed in this section (omitting the initial zero). To call from Austria to Germany, dial 00-49 and then the number (again, omitting the initial zero).

Tourist Information

Reutte's TI is a block in front of the train station (Mon-Fri 8:00-12:00 & 14:00-17:00, no midday break July-Aug, Sat 8:30-12:00, closed Sun, Untermarkt 34, tel. 05672/62336, www.reutte.com). Go over your sightseeing plans, ask about a folk evening, pick up city and biking maps and the *Sommerprogramm* events schedule (in German only), and ask about discounts with the hotel guest cards. Their free informational booklet has a good self-guided town walk.

Ask your hotel to give you an **Aktiv-Card,** which gives free travel on local buses (including the Reutte-Füssen route) as well as small discounts on sights and activities.

Arrival in Reutte

If you're coming by car from Germany, skip the north *(Nord)* exit and take the south *(Süd)* exit into town. For parking in town, blue lines denote pay-and-display spots. There is a free lot (P-1) near the train station on Muhlerstrasse.

While Austria requires a **toll sticker** *(Vignette)* for driving on its expressways (€8/10 days, buy at the border, gas stations, car-rental agencies, or *Tabak* shops), those just dipping into Tirol from Bavaria do not need one—even on the expressway-like bypass around Reutte.

Helpful Hints

Internet Access: Café Alte Post has one expensive terminal in a back room (€7.20/hour, Mon-Fri 7:00-19:00, Sat-Sun 9:00-18:00, Untermarkt 15).

Laundry: There isn't an actual launderette in town, but the recommended Hotel Maximilian lets non-guests use its laundry service (wash, dry, and fold-€16/load).

Bike Rental: Try **Intersport** (€15/day, Mon-Fri 9:00-18:00, Sat 9:00-17:00, closed Sun, Lindenstrasse 25, tel. 05672/62352), or check at the recommended Hotel Maximilian.

Taxi: STM Shuttle Service promises 24-hour service (mobile tel. 0664-113-3277).

Car Rental: Autoreisen Köck rents cars at Mühlerstrasse 12 (tel. 05672/62233, www.koeck-tours.com, koeck@koeck-tours .com).

"Nightlife": Reutte is pretty quiet. For any action at all, there's a strip of bars, dance clubs, and Italian restaurants on Lindenstrasse.

BAVARIA AND TIROL

Sights in and near Reutte

▲▲Ehrenberg Castle Ensemble (Festungsensemble Ehrenberg)

If Neuschwanstein was the medieval castle dream, Ehrenburg is the medieval castle reality. Once the largest fortification in Tirol,

its brooding ruins lie about two miles outside Reutte. Ehrenburg is actually an "ensemble" of four castles, built to defend against the Bavarians and to bottle up the strategic Via Claudia trade route, which cut through the Alps as it connected Italy and Germany. Today, these castles have become a European "castle museum," showing off 500 years of military architecture in one swoop. The European Union is helping fund the project (paying a third of its €9 million cost) because it promotes the heritage of a multinational region—Tirol—rather than a country.

The four parts of the complex are the fortified Klause toll booth on the valley floor, the oldest castle on the first hill above (Ehrenberg), a mighty and more modern castle high above

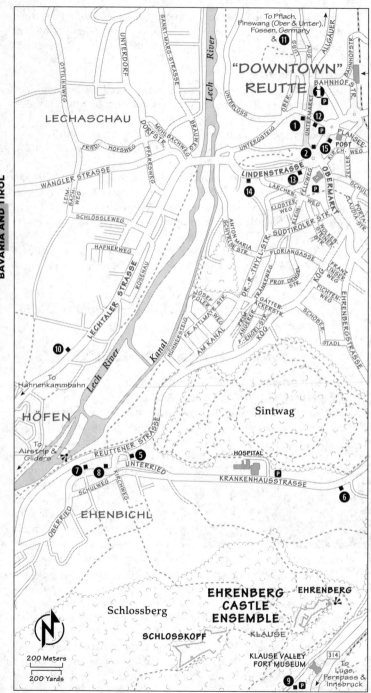

BAVARIA AND TIROL

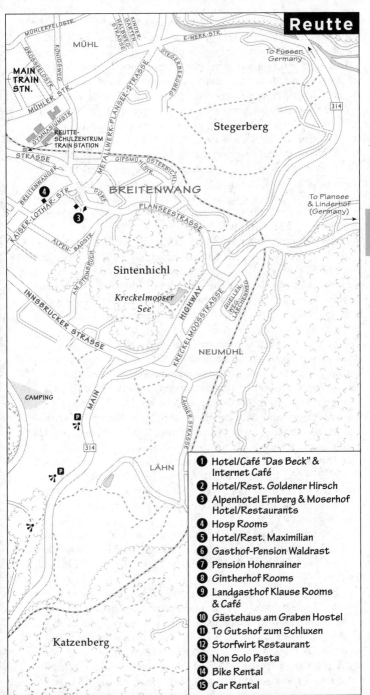

Reutte

BAVARIA AND TIROL

① Hotel/Café "Das Beck" & Internet Café
② Hotel/Rest. Goldener Hirsch
③ Alpenhotel Ernberg & Moserhof Hotel/Restaurants
④ Hosp Rooms
⑤ Hotel/Rest. Maximilian
⑥ Gasthof-Pension Waldrast
⑦ Pension Hohenrainer
⑧ Gintherhof Rooms
⑨ Landgasthof Klause Rooms & Café
⑩ Gästehaus am Graben Hostel
⑪ To Gutshof zum Schluxen
⑫ Storfwirt Restaurant
⑬ Non Solo Pasta
⑭ Bike Rental
⑮ Car Rental

(Schlosskopf, built in the age when cannon positioned there made the original castle vulnerable), and a smaller fourth castle across the valley (Fort Claudia, an hour's hike away). All four were once a single complex connected by walls. Signs posted throughout the site help visitors find their way and explain some background on the region's history, geology, geography, culture, flora, and fauna. (While the castles are free and open all the time, the museum and multimedia show at the fort's parking lot charge admission.)

Getting to the Castle Ensemble: The Klause, Ehrenberg, and Schlosskopf castles are on the road to Lermoos and Innsbruck. These are a pleasant 30- to 45-minute walk or a short bike ride from Reutte; bikers can use the *Radwanderweg* along the Lech River (the TI has a good map). Local buses run from Reutte to Ehrenberg several times a day (see www.vvt.at for schedules—the stop name is "Ehrenberger Klause").

▲**Klause Valley Fort Museum**—Historians estimate that about 10,000 tons of precious salt passed through this valley (along the route of Rome's Via Claudia) each year in medieval times, so it's no wonder the locals built this complex of fortresses and castles. Beginning in the 14th century, the fort controlled traffic and levied tolls on all who passed. Today, these scant remains hold a museum and a theater with a multimedia show.

While there are no real artifacts here (other than the sword used in A.D. 2008 to make me the honorary First Knight of Ehrenberg), the clever, kid-friendly **museum** takes one 14th-century decade (1360-1370) and attempts to bring it to life. It's a hands-on experience, well-described in English. You can try on a set of armor (and then weigh yourself), see the limited vision knights had to put up with when wearing their helmet, empathize with victims of the plague, and join a Crusade.

The **multimedia show** takes you on a 30-minute spin through the 2,000-year history of this valley's fortresses, with images projected on the old stone walls and modern screens (50-minute English version at 13:00 with a minimum of 5 people, or sometimes by request).

Cost and Hours: €7.50 for museum, €10.50 combo-ticket also includes multimedia show, €17.80 family pass for 2 adults and any number of kids, daily 10:00-17:00, closed Nov-mid-Dec, tel. 05672/62007, www.ehrenberg.at.

Eating: Next to the museum, the **Landgasthof Klause** serves typical Tirolean meals (€9-15 main courses, officially Tue-Sun 10:00-18:00 but likely longer hours in summer, closed Mon, closed Nov and Jan-Feb, tel. 05672/62213). They also rent a few rooms if you'd like to stay right at Ehrenberg (see page 168).

▲▲**Ehrenberg Ruins**—Ehrenberg, a 13th-century rock pile, provides a super opportunity to let your imagination off its leash.

Hike up 30 minutes from the parking lot of the Klause Valley Fort Museum for a great view from your own private ruins. Ehrenberg (which means "Mountain of Honor") was the first castle here, built in 1296. Thirteenth-century castles were designed to stand boastfully tall. With the advent of gunpowder, castles dug in. (Notice the 18th-century **ramparts** around you.)

Approaching Ehrenberg Castle, look for the small **door** to the left. It's the night entrance (tight and awkward, and therefore safer against a surprise attack). Entering this castle, you go through two doors. Castles allowed step-by-step retreat, giving defenders time to regroup and fight back against invading forces.

Before climbing to the top of the castle, follow the path around to the right to a big, grassy courtyard with commanding views and a fat, newly restored **turret.** This stored gunpowder and held a big cannon that enjoyed a clear view of the valley below. In medieval times, all the trees approaching the castle were cleared to keep an unobstructed view.

Look out over the valley. The pointy spire marks **Breitenwang,** which was a stop on the ancient Via Claudia. In A.D. 46, there was a Roman camp there. In 1489, after the Reutte bridge crossed the Lech River, Reutte (marked by the onion-domed church) was made a market town and eclipsed Breitenwang in importance. Any gliders circling? They launch from just over the river in Höfen.

For centuries, this castle was the seat of government—ruling an area called the "judgment of Ehrenberg" (roughly the same as today's "district of Reutte"). When the emperor came by, he stayed here. In 1604, the ruler moved downtown into more comfortable quarters, and the castle was no longer a palace.

Now climb to the top of Ehrenberg Castle. Take the high ground. There was no water supply here—just kegs of wine, beer, and a cistern to collect rain.

Ehrenberg repelled 16,000 Swedish soldiers in the defense of Catholicism in 1632. Ehrenberg saw three or four other battles, but its end was not glorious. In the 1780s, a local businessman bought the castle in order to sell off its parts. Later, in the late 19th century, when vagabonds moved in, the roof was removed to make squatting miserable. With the roof gone, deterioration quickened, leaving only this evocative shell and a whiff of history.

▲**Schlosskopf**—From Ehrenberg, you can hike up another 30 minutes to the mighty Schlosskopf ("Castle Head"). When the Bavarians captured Ehrenberg in 1703, the Tiroleans climbed up to the bluff above it to rain cannonballs down on their former fortress. In 1740, a mighty new castle—designed to defend against modern artillery—was built on this sky-high strategic location. By the end of the 20th century, the castle was completely overgrown with trees—you literally couldn't see it from Reutte. But today the trees are shaved away, and the castle has been excavated. In 2008, the Castle Ensemble project, led by local architect Armin Walch, opened the site with English descriptions and view platforms. One spot gives spectacular views of the strategic valley. The other looks down on the older Ehrenberg Castle ruins, illustrating the strategic problems presented with the advent of cannon.

In the Town

Reutte Museum (Museum Grünes Haus)—Reutte's cute city museum, offering a quick look at the local folk culture and the story of the castles, was recently redone. There are exhibits on Ehrenberg and the Via Claudia, local painters, and more—ask to borrow the English translations.

Cost and Hours: €3; May-Oct Tue-Sat 13:00-17:00, closed Sun-Mon; early Dec-Easter Wed-Sat 14:00-17:00, closed Sun-Tue; closed Easter-April and Nov-early Dec; in the bright-green building at Untermarkt 25, around corner from Hotel Goldener Hirsch, tel. 05672/72304, www.museum-reutte.at.

▲▲**Tirolean Folk Evening**—Ask the TI or your hotel if there's a Tirolean folk evening scheduled. During the summer (July-Aug), nearby towns (such as Höfen on Tuesdays) occasionally put on an evening of yodeling, slap dancing, and Tirolean frolic. These are generally free and worth the short drive. Off-season, you'll have to do your own yodeling. There are also weekly folk concerts featuring the local choir or brass band in Reutte's Zeiller Platz (free, July-Aug only, ask at TI). For listings of these and other local events, pick up a copy of the German-only *Sommerprogramm* schedule at the TI.

▲**Flying**—For a major thrill on a sunny day, drop by the tiny airport in Höfen (across the river from downtown) and fly. You have two options: prop planes and gliders. Small single-prop planes, which take three passengers, can buzz the Zugspitze and Ludwig's castles and give you a bird's-eye peek at Reutte's Ehrenberg ruins.

Cost and Hours: €110/30 minutes, €220/1 hour, ask at Fliegerklause café, tel. 05672/63207, www.flugsportverein-reutte .at. The phone is rarely answered (and then not in English), so your best bet is to show up at the Höfen airport on good-weather afternoons.

▲**Gliding**—To try something more angelic, how about gliding (*Segelfliegen*)? For a relatively modest price, you and a pilot get 30 minutes in a two-seat glider. Just watching the towrope launch the graceful glider like a giant slow-motion rubber-band gun is

Luge Lesson

Taking a wild ride on a luge (pronounced "loozh") is a quintessential alpine experience. It's also called a *Sommerrodelbahn,* or "summer toboggan run."
To try one of Europe's great accessible thrills (€3-7), take the lift up to the top of a mountain, grab a wheeled sled-like go-cart, and scream back down the mountainside on a banked course. Then take the lift back up and start all over again.

Luge courses are highly weather-dependent, and can close at the slightest hint of rain. If the weather's questionable, call ahead to confirm that your preferred luge is open. Stainless-steel courses are more likely than concrete ones to stay open in drizzly weather.

Operating the sled is simple: Push the stick forward to go faster, pull back to apply brakes. Even a novice can go very, very fast. Most are cautious on their first run, speed demons on their second...and bruised and bloody on their third. A woman once showed me her travel journal illustrated with her husband's dried five-inch-long luge scab. He had disobeyed the only essential rule of luging: Keep both hands on your stick. To avoid getting into a bumper-to-bumper traffic jam, let the person in front of you get way ahead before you start. You'll emerge from the course with a windblown hairdo and a smile-creased face.

Here are a few key luge terms:

Lenkstange	lever
drücken / schneller fahren	push / go faster
ziehen / bremsen	pull / brake
Schürfwunde	scrape
Schorf	scab

exhilarating.

Cost and Hours: €40/30 minutes, €65/1 hour, May-mid-Sept 12:00-19:00 in good but breezy weather only, find someone in the know at the airport's "Thermik Ranch" café, English not always spoken, tel. 05672/64010, mobile 0676-945-1288, www.segelflug verein-ausserfern.at.

Hahnenkammbahn—This mountain lift swoops you high above the tree line to an attractive restaurant and starting point for several hikes. In the alpine flower park, special paths lead you past countless varieties of local flora. Unique to this lift is a barefoot hiking trail *(Barfusswanderweg)*, designed to be walked without shoes—no joke.

Cost and Hours: €10 one-way, €14.50 round-trip, flowers best in late July, runs mid-June-Sept daily 9:00-16:30, also in good weather late May-mid-June and through late Oct, base station across the river in Höfen, tel. 05672/62420, www.reuttener -seilbahnen.at.

Near Reutte

Bird Lookout Tower—Between Reutte and Füssen is a pristine (once you get past the small local industrial park) nature preserve with an impressive wooden tower from which to appreciate the vibrant bird life in the wetlands along the Lech River. Look for *Vogel-Erlebnispfad* signs as you're driving through the village of Pflach (on the road between Reutte and Füssen). The EU gave half the money needed to enjoy the nature preserve—home to 110 different species of birds that nest here. The best action is early in the day. Be quiet, as eggs are being laid.

▲▲Biberwier Luge Course—Near Lermoos, on the road toward Innsbruck, you'll find the Biberwier *Sommerrodelbahn*. At 4,250 feet, it's the longest luge in Tirol. The only drawbacks are its brief season, short hours, and a proclivity for shutting down sporadically—even at the slightest bit of rain. But if you don't have a car, this is not worth the trouble; consider the luge near Neuschwanstein instead (see "Tegelberg Luge" on page 141). The ugly cube-shaped building marring the countryside near the luge course is a hotel for outdoor adventure enthusiasts. You can ride your mountain bike right into your room, or skip the elevator by using its indoor climbing wall.

Cost and Hours: €7.20/ride, less for 3-, 5-, and 10-ride tickets, June-early Oct daily 9:00-16:30, closed early Oct-May, tel. 05673/2323, www.bergbahnen-langes.at. It's 20 minutes from Reutte on the main road toward Innsbruck; Biberwier is the first exit after a long tunnel.

▲Fallerschein—Easy for drivers and a special treat for those who may have been Kit Carson in a previous life, this extremely remote log-cabin village is a 4,000-foot-high flower-speckled world of serene slopes and cowbells. Thunderstorms roll down the valley like it's God's bowling alley, but the pint-size church on the high ground, blissfully simple in a land of Baroque, seems to promise that this huddle of houses will survive, and the river and breeze will just keep flowing. The couples sitting on benches are mostly Austrian vacationers who've rented cabins here. Some of them, appreciating the remoteness of Fallerschein, are having affairs.

Getting to Fallerschein: From Reutte, it's a 45-minute drive. Take road 198 to Stanzach (passing Weisenbach am Loch, then Forchach), then turn left toward Namlos. Follow the L-21 Berwang road for about five miles to a parking lot. From there, it's a two-mile walk down a drivable but technically closed one-lane road. Those driving in do so at their own risk.

Sleeping in Fallerschein: $ Michl's **Fallerscheiner Stube** is a family-friendly mountain-hut restaurant with a low-ceilinged attic space that has basic beds for up to 17 sleepy hikers. The accommodations aren't fancy, but if you're looking for remote, this is it (dorm bed-€19, €11 cheaper without breakfast, dinner-€11, sheets-€4, open May-Oct only, wildlife viewing deck, mobile 0676-727-9681, www.alpe-fallerschein.at, michaelknitel@mountainmichl.at, Knitel family).

Sleeping in and near Reutte

(€1 = about $1.40, country code: 43, area code: 05672)

Reutte is a mellow Füssen with fewer crowds and easygoing locals with a contagious love of life. Come here for a good dose of Austrian ambience and lower prices. While it's not impossible by public transport, staying here makes most sense for those with a car. Reutte is popular with Austrians and Germans, who come here year after year for one- or two-week vacations. The hotels are big, elegant, and full of comfy carved furnishings and creative ways to spend lots of time in one spot. They take great pride in their restaurants, and the owners send their children away to hotel-management schools. All include a great breakfast, but few accept credit cards. Most hotels give a small discount for stays of two nights or longer.

The Reutte TI has a list of 50 private homes that rent out generally good rooms *(Zimmer)* with facilities down the hall, pleasant communal living rooms, and breakfast. Most charge €20 per person per night, and the owners speak little or no English. As these are family-run places, it is especially important to cancel in advance if your plans change. I've listed a few favorites in this section, but the TI can always find you a room when you arrive.

Reutte is surrounded by several distinct "villages" that basically feel like suburbs—many of them, such as Breitenwang, within easy walking distance of the Reutte town center. If you want to hike through the woods to Neuschwanstein Castle, stay at Gutshof zum Schluxen. To locate these accommodations, see the Reutte map. Remember, to call Reutte from Germany, dial 00-43- and then the number (minus the initial zero).

In Central Reutte

These two hotels are the most practical if you're traveling by train or bus.

$$ Hotel "Das Beck" offers 17 clean, sunny rooms (many with balconies) filling a modern building in the heart of town close to the train station. It's a great value, and guests are personally taken care of by Hans, Inge, Tamara, and Pipi. Their small café offers tasty snacks and specializes in Austrian and Italian wines. Expect good conversation overseen by Hans (Sb-€46, Db-€70, Tb suite-€95, Qb suite-€112, these prices with this book in 2012, all rooms non-smoking, Internet access and Wi-Fi free for Rick Steves readers, free parking, Untermarkt 11, tel. 05672/62522, fax 05672/625-2235, www.hotel-das-beck.at, info@hotel-das-beck.at).

$$ Hotel Goldener Hirsch, also in the center of Reutte just two blocks from the station, is a grand old hotel with 56 rooms and one lonely set of antlers (Sb-€58-62, Db-€88-98, Tb-€135, Qb-€148, less for 2 nights, elevator, free Wi-Fi, restaurant, Mühlerstrasse 1, tel. 05672/62508, fax 05672/625-087, www.goldener-hirsch.at, info@goldener-hirsch.at; Monika, Helmut, and daughters Vanessa and Nina).

In Breitenwang

Now basically a part of Reutte, the older and quieter village of Breitenwang has good *Zimmer* and a fine bakery. It's a 20-minute walk from the Reutte train station: From the post office, follow Planseestrasse past the onion-dome church to the pointy straight-dome church near the two hotels. The Hosps—as well as other B&Bs—are along Kaiser-Lothar-Strasse, the first right past this church. If your train stops at the tiny Reutte-Schulzentrum station, hop out here—you're just a five-minute walk from Breitenwang.

$$ Alpenhotel Ernberg's 26 fresh rooms are run with great care by friendly Hermann, who combines Old World elegance with modern touches. Nestle in for some serious coziness among the carved-wood eating nooks, tiled stoves, and family-friendly backyard (Sb-€55, Db-€90, less for 2 nights, free Wi-Fi, popular restaurant, swimming complex nearby, Planseestrasse 50, tel. 05672/71912, fax 05672/719-1240, www.ernberg.at, info@ernberg.at).

$$ Moserhof Hotel has 40 new-feeling rooms plus an elegant dining room (Sb-€53, Db-€92, larger Db-€100, these special rates promised in 2012 if you ask for the Rick Steves discount when you reserve, extra bed-€35, most rooms have balconies, elevator, free Wi-Fi, restaurant, sauna and whirlpool, free parking, Planseestrasse 44, tel. 05672/62020, fax 05672/620-2040, www.hotel-moserhof.at, info@hotel-moserhof.at, Hosp family).

$ Walter and Emilie Hosp rent three rooms in a comfortable, quiet, and modern house two blocks from the Breitenwang church steeple. You'll feel like you're staying at Grandma's (S-€25, D-€40, T-€60, Q-€80, cash only, Kaiser-Lothar-Strasse 29, tel. 05672/65377).

In Ehenbichl, near the Ehrenberg Ruins

The next listings are a bit farther from central Reutte, a couple of miles upriver in the village of Ehenbichl (under the Ehrenberg ruins). From central Reutte, go south on Obermarkt and turn right on Kög, which becomes Reuttenerstrasse, following signs to Ehenbichl. These listings are best for car travelers—you'll need to take a taxi if you arrive by train.

$$ Hotel Maximilian offers 30 rooms at a great value. It includes table tennis, play areas for children (indoors and out), a pool table, and the friendly service of Gabi, Monika, and the rest of the Koch family. They host many special events, and their hotel has lots of wonderful extras such as a sauna and a piano (Sb-€50-57, Db-€80-90, ask for these special Rick Steves prices when you reserve, family deals, elevator, free Internet access and Wi-Fi in common areas, pay Wi-Fi in rooms, laundry service-€12/ load, good restaurant, Reuttenerstrasse 1, tel. 05672/62585, fax 05672/625-8554, www.maxihotel.com, info@hotelmaximilian .at). They rent cars to guests only (€0.72/km, book in advance) and bikes to anyone (€5/half-day, €8/day, higher if you're not a guest, those staying at the hotel have free use of older bikes).

$$ Gasthof-Pension Waldrast, separating a forest and a meadow, is run by the farming Huter family and their dog, Picasso. The place feels hauntingly quiet and has no restaurant, but it's inexpensive and offers 10 nice rooms with generous sitting areas and castle-view balconies (Sb-€39, Db-€66, Tb-€82, Qb-€99; discounts with this book in 2012: 5 percent off second night, 10 percent off third night; cash only, non-smoking, free Wi-Fi, free parking; about a mile from Reutte, just off main drag toward Innsbruck, past campground and under castle ruins on Ehrenbergstrasse; tel. & fax 05672/62443, www.waldrasttirol.com, info@waldrasttirol.com, Gerd).

$$ Pension Hohenrainer, a big, quiet, no-frills place, is a good value with 12 modern rooms and some castle-view balconies (Sb-€30-32, Db-€60-64, €1.50/per person less for 2 nights, €3/person less for 3 nights, lower prices are for April-June and Sept-Oct, cash only, family rooms, non-smoking rooms, free Internet access and Wi-Fi, restaurant and reception in Gasthof Schlosswirt across the street, follow signs up the road behind Hotel Maximilian into village of Ehenbichl, Unterried 3, tel. 05672/62544 or 05672/63262, fax 05672/62052, www.hohenrainer.at, hohenrainer @aon.at).

$$ Gintherhof is a working farm that provides its guests with fresh milk, butter, and bacon. Annelies Paulweber offers geranium-covered balconies, six nice rooms with carved-wood ceilings, and a Madonna in every corner (Db-€62, Db suite-€64, €3/person less for third night, cash only, free Wi-Fi, Unterried 7, just up the road behind Hotel Maximilian, tel. 05672/67697, www.gintherhof.com, gintherhof@aon.at).

At the Ehrenberg Ruins

$$ Landgasthof Klause café, just below the Ehrenberg ruins and next to the castle museum, rents six non-smoking rooms with balconies on its upper floor. The downside is that you may have to go out for dinner (the café officially closes at 18:00), and you'll need a car to get anywhere besides Ehrenberg (Sb-€37, Db-€74, Tb-€111, ask for Rick Steves discount when you book, discount for 2 or more nights, free Wi-Fi, apartments available, closed Nov and Jan, tel. 05672/62007, fax 05672/620-0777, www.gasthof-klause.com, gasthof-klause@gmx.at).

A Hostel Across the River

The homey **$ Gästehaus am Graben hostel** has 4-6 beds per room and includes breakfast and sheets. It's lovingly run by the Reyman family—Frau Reyman, Rudi, and Gabi keep the 50-bed place traditional, clean, and friendly. This is a super value less than two miles from Reutte, and the castle views are fantastic. If you've never hosteled and are curious (and have a car or don't mind a bus ride), try it. If traveling with kids, this is a great choice. The double rooms are hotel-grade, and they accept nonmembers of any age (dorm bed-€25, hotel-style Db-€68, cash only, non-smoking, expensive Internet access and Wi-Fi, laundry service-€9, no curfew, closed April and Nov-mid-Dec; from downtown Reutte, cross bridge and follow main road left along river, or take the bus— hourly until 19:30, ask for Graben stop; Graben 1, tel. 05672/626-440, fax 05672/626-444, www.hoefen.at, info@hoefen.at).

In Pinswang

The village of Pinswang is closer to Füssen (and Ludwig's castles), but still in Austria.

$$ Gutshof zum Schluxen gets the "Remote Old Hotel in an Idyllic Setting" award. This family-friendly farm offers rustic elegance draped in goose down and pastels. Its picturesque meadow setting will turn you into a dandelion-picker, and its proximity to Neuschwanstein will turn you into a hiker—the castle is just an hour's hike away (Sb-€49-51, Db-€88-96, extra person-€29, these prices with this book in 2012, about 5-10 percent cheaper Nov-March, 5 percent discount for stays of three or more nights, free Wi-Fi in common areas, laundry-€9, mountain-bike rental-€10/ day or €5/half-day, restaurant, fun bar, between Reutte and Füssen in village of Pinswang, free pickup from Reutte or Füssen but call 24 hours ahead if you'll arrive after 18:00, tel. 05677/89030, fax 05677/890-323, www.schluxen.com, info@schluxen.at).

To reach Neuschwanstein by foot or bike, follow the dirt road up the hill behind the hotel. When the road forks at the top of the hill, go right (downhill), cross the Austria-Germany border (marked by a sign and deserted hut), and follow the narrow paved road to the castles. It's a 1- to 1.5-hour hike or a great circular bike trip (allow 30 minutes; cyclists can return to Schluxen from the castles on a different 30-minute bike route via Füssen).

Eating in Reutte

The hotels here take great pride in serving local cuisine at reasonable prices to their guests and the public. Rather than go to a cheap restaurant, eat at one of the Reutte hotels recommended earlier (**Alpenhotel Ernberg, Moserhof Hotel, Hotel Maximilian,** and **Hotel Goldener Hirsch**). Hotels typically serve €10-15 dinners from 18:00 to 21:00 and are closed one night a week.

Storfwirt is *the* place for a quick and cheap weekday lunch. You can get the usual sausages here, as well as baked potatoes and salads (€5.50-9 daily specials, salad bar, always something for vegetarians, Mon-Fri 9:00-14:30, closed Sat-Sun, Schrettergasse 15, tel. 05672/62640).

Non Solo Pasta, just off the traffic circle, is a local favorite for Italian food (€7-9 pizzas and pastas, €8-12 main courses, Mon-Fri 11:30-14:00 & 18:00-23:00, Sat 18:00-23:00, closed Sun, Lindenstrasse 1, tel. 05672/72714).

Across the street from the Hotel Goldener Hirsch on Mühlerstrasse is a **Bauernladen** (farmer's shop) with rustic sandwiches and meals prepared from local ingredients (Wed-Fri 9:00-18:00, Sat 9:00-12:00, closed Sun-Tue, mobile 0676-575-4588).

Picnic Supplies: **Billa** supermarket has everything you'll need (across from TI, Mon-Fri 7:15-19:30, Sat 7:15-18:00, closed Sun).

Reutte Connections

From Reutte by Train to: Ehrwald (at base of Zugspitze lift, every 2 hours, 30 minutes), **Garmisch** (every 2 hours, 1 hour), **Innsbruck** (every 2 hours, 2.5 hours, change in Garmisch), **Munich** (every 2 hours, 2.5 hours, change in Garmisch), **Salzburg** (every 2 hours, 4.5-5.5 hours, quickest with changes in Garmisch and Munich). Train info: tel. 0180-599-6633, www.bahn.com.

By Bus to: Füssen (Mon-Fri almost hourly, Sat-Sun every 2 hours, 45 minutes, €3.90 one-way, buses depart from train station, pay driver).

Taxis cost about €35 one-way to Füssen or the King's Castles.

SALZBURG (AUSTRIA) and BERCHTESGADEN

Salzburg, just over the Austrian border, makes a fun day trip from Munich (1.5-2 hours by direct train). Thanks to its charmingly preserved old town, splendid gardens, Baroque churches, and Europe's largest intact medieval fortress, Salzburg feels made for tourism. As a musical mecca, the city puts on a huge annual festival, as well as constant concerts, and its residents—or at least its tourism industry—are forever smiling to the tunes of Mozart and *The Sound of Music*. It's a city with class. Vagabonds wish they had nicer clothes.

In the mountains just outside Salzburg is Berchtesgaden, a German alpine town that was once a favorite of Adolf Hitler's, but thrills a better class of nature-lovers today.

Planning Your Time

While Salzburg's sights are, frankly, mediocre, the town itself is a Baroque museum of cobbled streets and elegant buildings—simply a touristy stroller's delight. Even if your time is short, consider allowing half a day for the *Sound of Music* tour. The *S.O.M.* tour kills a nest of sightseeing birds with one ticket (city overview, *S.O.M.* sights, and a fine drive by the lakes).

You'd probably enjoy at least two nights in Salzburg—nights are important for swilling beer in atmospheric local gardens and attending concerts in Baroque halls and chapels. Seriously consider one of Salzburg's many evening musical events (a few are free, some are as cheap as €12, and most average €30-40).

To get away from it all, bike down the river or hike across the Mönchsberg cliffs that rise directly from the middle of town.

Or consider swinging by Berchtesgaden, just 15 miles away in Germany. A direct bus gets you there from Salzburg in 45 minutes.

Salzburg

Even without Mozart and the von Trapps, Salzburg is steeped in history. In about A.D. 700, Bavaria gave Salzburg to Bishop Rupert in return for his promise to Christianize the area. Salzburg remained an independent city (belonging to no state) until Napoleon came in the early 1800s. Thanks in part to its formidable fortress, Salzburg managed to avoid the ravages of war for 1,200 years...until World War II. Much of the city was destroyed by WWII bombs (mostly around the train station), but the historic old town survived.

Eight million tourists crawl its cobbles each year. That's a lot of Mozart balls—and all that popularity has led to a glut of businesses hoping to catch the tourist dollar. Still, Salzburg is both a must and a joy.

Orientation to Salzburg

(country code: 43, area code: 0662)
Salzburg, a city of 150,000 (Austria's fourth-largest), is divided into old and new. The old town, sitting between the Salzach River and its mini-mountain (Mönchsberg), holds nearly all the charm and most of the tourists. The new town, across the river, has its own share of sights and museums, plus some good accommodations.

Welcome to Austria: Austria uses the same euro currency as Germany, but postage stamps and phone cards only work in the country where you buy them.

To **telephone** from Germany to Austria, dial 00-43 and then the number listed in this section (omitting the initial zero). To call from Austria to Germany, dial 00-49 and then the number (again, omitting the initial zero).

Note that **Berchtesgaden**—also covered in this chapter—is in Germany, not Austria.

Tourist Information

Salzburg has three helpful TIs (main tel. 0662/889-870, www
.salzburg.info): at the **train station** (daily June-Aug 8:15-19:30,
Sept-May 8:45-18:00, tel. 0662/
8898-7340); on **Mozartplatz** in
the old center (daily 9:00-18:00,
July-mid-Sept until 19:00, closed
Sun mid-Jan-Easter and Oct-
mid-Nov, tel. 0662/889-870);
and at the **Salzburg Süd park-
and-ride** (generally open daily
July-Aug 10:00-16:30 but some-

times longer hours, May-June Thu-Sat 10:00-16:30, Sept Mon-Sat
10:00-16:30, closed in winter, tel. 0662/8898-7360).

At any TI, you can pick up a free city-center map (the €0.70
map has a broader coverage and more information on sights, but
probably isn't necessary), the Salzburg Card brochure (listing sights
with current hours and prices), and a bimonthly events guide. Book
a concert upon arrival. The TIs also book rooms (€2.20 fee and 10
percent deposit).

Salzburg Card: The TIs sell the Salzburg Card, which covers
all your public transportation (including the Mönchsberg elevator
and funicular to the fortress) and admission to all the city sights
(including Hellbrunn Castle and a river cruise). The card is pricey,
but if you'd like to pop into all the sights, it can save money and
enhance your experience (€25/24 hours, €34/48 hours, €40/72
hours, cheaper Nov-April). To analyze your potential savings,
here are the major sights and what you'd pay without the card:
Hohensalzburg Fortress and funicular-€10.50; Mozart's Birthplace
and Residence-€12; Hellbrunn Castle-€9.50; Salzburg Panorama
1829-€2; Salzach River cruise-€13; 24-hour transit pass-€4.20.
Busy sightseers can save plenty. Get this card, feel the financial
pain once, and the city will be all yours.

Arrival in Salzburg

By Train: The Salzburg station is undergoing a huge renovation,
so for the next several years its services will be operating out of

temporary structures in the
parking lot. Still, you'll find
it all here: train information,
tourist information, luggage
lockers, and so on.

Getting downtown
couldn't be easier, as immediately in front of the station
a bus stop labeled *Zentrum-*

Altstadt has **buses** lined up and leaving every two minutes. Buses #1, #3, #5, #6, and #25 all do the same route into the city center before diverging at the far end of town. For most sights and city-center hotels, get off just after the bridge. For my recommended hotels in the new town, get off at Makartplatz, just before the bridge. (Buses to and from the airport use the *Flughafen* stop in front of the train station.) **Taxis** charge about €8 (plus €1/bag) to take you to your hotel.

To **walk** downtown (15 minutes), turn left as you leave the station, and walk straight down Rainerstrasse, which leads under the tracks past Mirabellplatz, turning into Dreifaltigkeitsgasse. From here, you can turn left onto Linzergasse for many of my recommended hotels, or cross the Staatsbrücke bridge for the old town (and more hotels). For a slightly longer but more dramatic approach, leave the station the same way but follow the tracks to the river, turn left, and walk the riverside path toward the fortress.

By Car: Coming on A-8 from Munich, cross the border into Austria. Take A-10 toward Hallein, and then take the next exit (Salzburg Süd) in the direction of Anif. First, you'll pass Hellbrunn Castle (and zoo), then the Salzburg Süd TI and a park-and-ride lot—a smart place to park while visiting Salzburg. Park your car (€5/24 hours), get sightseeing information and transit tickets from the TI, and catch the shuttle bus into town (€1.90 single-ride ticket, covered by €4.20 *Tageskarte* day pass, both sold at the TI, more expensive if you buy tickets on board, every 5 minutes; bus #3, #8, or #28). If traveling with more than one other person, take advantage of a park-and-ride combo-ticket: For €13 (€10 July-Aug), you get 24 hours of parking and a round-trip on the shuttle bus for up to five people.

Mozart never drove in the old town, and neither should you. But if you don't believe in park-and-rides, the easiest, cheapest, most central parking lot is the 1,500-car Altstadt lot in the tunnel under the Mönchsberg (€14/day, note your slot number and which of the twin lots you're in, tel. 0662/846-434). Your hotel may provide discounted parking passes.

Helpful Hints

Recommendations Skewed by Kickbacks: Salzburg is addicted to the tourist dollar, and it can never get enough. Virtually all hotels are on the take when it comes to concert and tour recommendations, influenced more by their potential kickback than by what's best for you. Take any advice with a grain of salt.

Music Festival: The Salzburg Festival (Salzburger Festspiele) runs each year from late July to the end of August (see page 204).

Internet Access: Two Internet cafés at the bottom of the cliff,

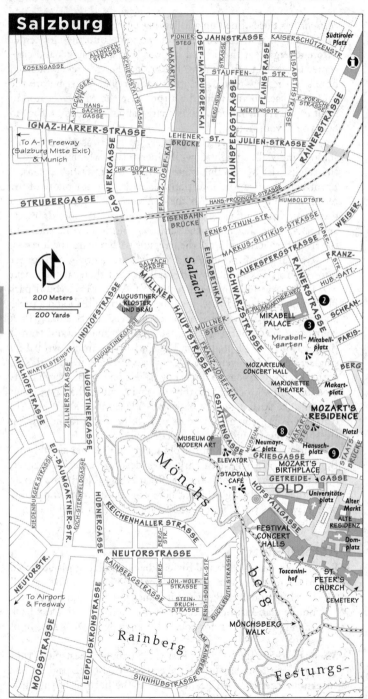

SALZBURG

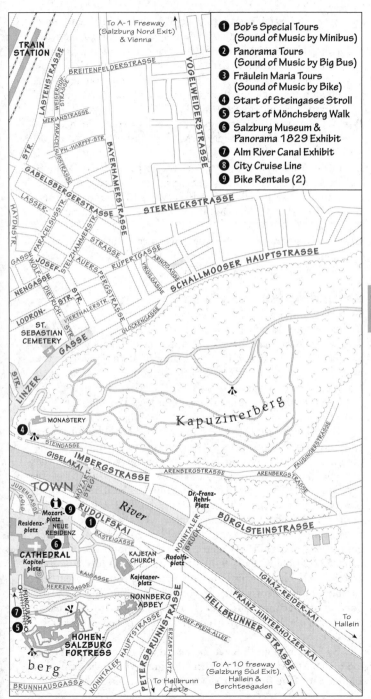

1. Bob's Special Tours (Sound of Music by Minibus)
2. Panorama Tours (Sound of Music by Big Bus)
3. Fräulein Maria Tours (Sound of Music by Bike)
4. Start of Steingasse Stroll
5. Start of Mönchsberg Walk
6. Salzburg Museum & Panorama 1829 Exhibit
7. Alm River Canal Exhibit
8. City Cruise Line
9. Bike Rentals (2)

SALZBURG

between Getreidegasse and the Mönchsberg lift, have good prices and long hours (€2/hour, daily 10:00-22:00). Across the river, there's a big, handy Internet café on Theatergasse (near Mozart's Residence, €2/hour, daily 9:00-23:00). Travelers with this book can get online free for a few minutes (long enough to check email) at the Panorama Tours terminal on Mirabellplatz (daily 8:00-18:00).

Post Office: A full-service post office is located in the heart of town, in the New Residenz (Mon-Fri 8:00-18:00, Sat 9:00-12:00, closed Sun).

Laundry: A handy launderette is at the corner of Paris-Lodron-Strasse and Wolf-Dietrich-Strasse, near my recommended Linzergasse hotels (€10 self-service, €15 same-day full-service, Mon-Fri 7:30-18:00, Sat 8:00-12:00, closed Sun, tel. 0662/876-381).

Cinema: Das Kino is an art-house movie theater that plays films in their original language (a block off the river and Linzergasse on Steingasse, tel. 0662/873-100).

Getting Around Salzburg

By Bus: Single-ride tickets for central Salzburg *(Einzelkarte-Kernzone)* are sold on the bus for €2.10. At machines and *Tabak/Trafik* shops, you can buy €1.90 single-ride tickets or a €4.20 day pass *(Tageskarte,* good for 24 hours; €5 if you buy it on the bus). To get from the old town to the station, catch bus #1 from Hanuschplatz; or, from the other side of the river, catch #1, #3, #5, or #6 at Theatergasse, near Mirabell Gardens. Bus info: tel. 800-660-660.

By Bike: Salzburg is great fun for cyclists. The following two bike-rental shops offer 20 percent off to anyone with this book—ask for it. **Top Bike** rents bikes on the river next to the Staatsbrücke (€6/2 hours, €10/4 hours, €15/24 hours, usually daily April-June and Sept-Oct 10:00-17:00, July-Aug 9:00-19:00, closed Nov-March, free helmets with this book, tel. 06272/4656, mobile 0676-476-7259, www.topbike.at, Sabine). **A'Velo Radladen** rents bikes in the old town, just outside the TI on Mozartplatz (€4.50/1 hour, €10/2 hours, €16/24 hours; electric or mountain bike-€6/hour, €22/24 hours; daily 9:00-18:00, until 19:00 July-Aug, but hours unreliable, shorter hours off-season and in bad weather, passport number for security deposit, mobile 0676-435-5950). Some of my recommended hotels and pensions also rent bikes, and several of the B&Bs on Moosstrasse have free loaner bikes for guests.

By Funicular and Elevator: The old town is connected to the top of the Mönchsberg mountain (and great views) via funicular and elevator. The **funicular** *(Festungsbahn)* whisks you up to the imposing Hohensalzburg Fortress (included in castle admission, goes every few minutes—for details, see page 194). The **elevator** *(MönchsbergAufzug)* on the east side of the old town propels you to the recommended Gasthaus Stadtalm café and hostel, the Museum of Modern Art, wooded paths, and more great views (€2 one-way, €3.20 round-trip, daily 8:30-19:00, Wed until 21:00, July-Aug daily until 1:00 in the morning, May-Sept starts running at 8:00).

By Taxi: Meters start at about €3 (from train station to your hotel, allow about €8). Small groups can taxi for about the same price as riding the bus.

By Buggy: The horse buggies *(Fiaker)* that congregate at Residenzplatz charge €36 for a 25-minute trot around the old town (www.fiaker-salzburg.at).

Tours in Salzburg

Walking Tours—On any day of the week, you can take a two-language, one-hour guided walk of the old town without a reservation—just show up at the TI on Mozartplatz and pay the guide. The tours are informative, but you'll likely be listening to everything in both German and English (€9, daily at 12:15 and 14:00, tours split into two single-language groups when turnout is sufficiently high, tel. 0662/8898-7330). To save money (and avoid all that German), you can easily do it on your own using this chapter's self-guided walk.

Local Guides—Salzburg is home to over a hundred licensed guides. I recommend two hardworking young guides in particular. **Christiana Schneeweiss** ("Snow White") has been instrumental in both my guidebook research and my TV production in Salzburg (€135/2 hours, €150/3 hours, tel. 0664/340-1757, www.kultur -tourismus.com, info@kultur-tourismus.com); check her website for bike tours, private minibus tours, and more. **Sabine Rath** also knows her city well, and is a joy to learn from (€140/2 hours, €180/4 hours, €270/8 hours, tel. 0664/201-6492, www.tourguide -salzburg.com, info@tourguide-salzburg.com). Salzburg has many other good guides (to book, call 0662/840-406).

Boat Tours—**City Cruise Line** (a.k.a. Stadt Schiff-Fahrt) runs a basic 40-minute round-trip river cruise with recorded commentary (€13, 9/day July-Aug, 7/day May-June, fewer Sept-Oct and April, no boats Nov-March). For a longer cruise, ride to Hellbrunn and return by bus (€16, 1-2/day April-Oct). Boats leave from the old-town side of the river just downstream of the Makartsteg bridge (tel. 0662/825-858, www.salzburgschifffahrt.at). While views can be cramped, passengers are treated to a fun finale just before docking, when the captain twirls a fun "waltz."

SALZBURG

Salzburg at a Glance

▲▲▲**Salzburg's Old Town Walk** Old Town's best sights in handy orientation walk. **Hours:** Always open. See page 181.

▲▲**Salzburg Cathedral** Glorious, harmonious Baroque main church of Salzburg. **Hours:** Easter-Oct Mon-Sat 9:00-18:00, Sun 13:00-18:00; Nov-Easter Mon-Sat 10:00-17:00, Sun 13:00-17:00. See page 184.

▲▲**Getreidegasse** Picturesque old shopping lane with characteristic wrought-iron signs. **Hours:** Always open. See page 189.

▲▲**Hohensalzburg Fortress** Imposing castle capping the mountain overlooking town, with tourable grounds, several mini-museums, commanding views, and good evening concerts. **Hours:** Daily May-Sept 9:00-19:00, Oct-April 9:30-17:00. Concerts nearly nightly. See page 194.

▲▲**Mozart's Residence** Restored house where the composer lived, with the best Mozart exhibit in town. **Hours:** Daily 9:00-17:30, July-Aug until 20:00. See page 199.

▲▲**Salzburg Museum** Best place to learn more about the city's history. **Hours:** Tue-Sun 9:00-17:00, Thu until 20:00, closed Mon. See page 191.

▲▲*The Sound of Music* Tour Cheesy but fun tour through the S.O.M. sights of Salzburg and the surrounding Salzkammergut Lake District, by minibus, big bus, or bike. **Hours:** Various options daily at 9:00, 9:30, 14:00, and 16:30. See page 178.

▲**Old Residenz** Prince archbishop Wolf Dietrich's palace, with ornate rooms and good included audioguide. **Hours:** Daily 10:00-17:00. See page 184.

▲**Salzburg Panorama 1829** A vivid peek at the city in 1829. **Hours:** Daily 9:00-17:00, Thu until 20:00. See page 191.

▲▲*The Sound of Music* **Tour**—I took this tour skeptically (as part of my research)—and liked it. It includes a quick but good general city tour, hits the *S.O.M.* spots (including the stately home used in the movie, flirtatious gazebo, and grand wedding church), and shows you a lovely stretch of the Salzkammergut Lake District. This is worthwhile for *S.O.M.* fans and those who won't otherwise be going into the Salzkammergut. Warning: Many think rolling through the Austrian countryside with 30 Americans singing "Doe, a deer..." is pretty schmaltzy. Local Austrians don't

▲**Mozart's Birthplace** House where Mozart was born in 1756, featuring his instruments and other exhibits. **Hours:** Daily 9:00-17:30, July-Aug until 20:00. See page 192.

▲**Mönchsberg Walk** "The hills are alive" stroll you can enjoy right in downtown Salzburg. **Hours:** Doable anytime during daylight hours. See page 196.

▲**Mirabell Gardens and Palace** Beautiful palace complex with fine views, Salzburg's best concert venue, and *Sound of Music* memories. **Hours:** Gardens—always open; concerts—free in the park May-Aug Sun at 10:30 and Wed at 20:30, in the palace nearly nightly. See page 198.

▲**Steingasse** Historic cobbled lane with trendy pubs—a tranquil, tourist-free section of old Salzburg. **Hours:** Always open. See page 199.

▲**St. Sebastian Cemetery** Baroque cemetery with graves of Mozart's wife and father, and other Salzburg VIPs. **Hours:** Daily April-Oct 9:00-18:30, Nov-March 9:00-16:00. See page 201.

▲**Hellbrunn Castle** Palace on the outskirts of town featuring gardens with trick fountains. **Hours:** Daily May-Sept 9:00-17:30, July-Aug until 21:00, mid-March-April and Oct 9:00-16:30, closed Nov-mid-March. See page 201.

St. Peter's Cemetery Atmospheric old cemetery with mini-gardens overlooked by cliff face with monks' caves. **Hours:** Cemetery—daily April-Sept 6:30-19:00, Oct-March 6:30-18:00; caves—May-Sept Tue-Sun 10:30-17:00, closed Mon, shorter hours Oct-April. See page 187.

St. Peter's Church Romanesque church with Rococo decor. **Hours:** Open long hours daily. See page 187.

understand all the commotion, and the audience is mostly native English speakers. For more on *S.O.M.*, see the sidebar on page 206.

Of the many companies doing the tour, consider Bob's Special Tours (usually uses a minibus) and Panorama Tours (more typical and professional, big 50-seat bus). Each one provides essentially the same tour (in English with a live guide, 4 hours) for essentially the same price: €37 for Panorama, €45 for Bob's. You'll get a €5 discount from either if you book direct, mention Rick Steves, pay cash, and bring this book along (you'll need to show them this book to get the deal). Getting a spot is simple—just call and make a reservation (calling Bob's a week or two in advance is smart). Note: Your hotel will be eager to call to reserve for you—to get their commission—but if you let them do it, you won't get the discount I've negotiated.

Minibus Option: Most of **Bob's Special Tours** use an eight-seat minibus (and occasionally a 20-seat bus) and therefore have good access to old-town sights, promote a more casual feel, and spend less time waiting to load and unload. Calling well in advance increases your chances of getting a seat (€45 for adults, €5 discount with this book if you pay cash and book direct, €40 for kids and students with ID, €35 for kids in car seats, daily at 9:00 and 14:00 year-round, they'll pick you up at your hotel for the morning tour, afternoon tours leave from Bob's office along the river just east of Mozartplatz at Rudolfskai 38, tel. 0662/849-511, mobile 0664-541-7492, www.bobstours.com). Nearly all of Bob's tours stop for a fun luge ride when the weather is dry (mountain bobsled-€4.30 extra, generally April-Oct, confirm beforehand). Some travelers looking for Bob's tours at Mozartplatz have been hijacked by other companies...have Bob's pick you up at your hotel (morning only), or meet the bus at their office. If you're unable to book with Bob's, and still want a minibus tour, try **Kultur Tourismus** (€45, tel. 0664/340-1757, www.kultur-tourismus.com, info@kultur-tourismus.com).

Big-Bus Option: Panorama Tours depart from their smart kiosk at Mirabellplatz daily at 9:30 and 14:00 year-round (€37, €5 discount with this book if you book direct and pay cash, book by calling 0662/874-029 or 0662/883-2110, or online at www.panoramatours.com). Many travelers appreciate their more businesslike feel, roomier buses, and slightly higher vantage point.

Bike Option: For some exercise with your tour, you can meet **Fräulein Maria** at the Mirabell Gardens (at Mirabellplatz 4, 50 yards to the left of palace entry) for a *S.O.M.* bike tour. The main attractions that you'll pass during the seven-mile pedal include the Mirabell Gardens, the horse pond, St. Peter's Cemetery, Nonnberg Abbey, Leopoldskron Palace, and, of course, the gazebo (€24 includes bike, €2 discount with this book, €15 for kids 6-15, €10 for kids under 6, daily May-Sept at 9:30, June-Aug also at 16:30, allow 3.5 hours, family-friendly, reservations required only for afternoon tours, tel. 0650/342-6297, www.mariasbicycletours.com). For €8 extra, you're welcome to keep the bike all day.

Beyond Salzburg

Both Bob's and Panorama Tours also offer an extensive array of other day trips from Salzburg (e.g., Berchtesgaden/Eagle's Nest, salt mines, and Salzkammergut lakes and mountains).

Bob's Special Tours offers two particularly well-designed day tours (both depart daily at 9:00; either one costs €90 with a €10 discount if you show this book and book direct, does not include entrance fees). Their *Sound of Music/*Hallstatt Tour first covers everything in the standard four-hour *Sound of Music* tour, then continues for a four-hour look at the scenic, lake-speckled Salzkammergut (with free time to explore charming Hallstatt). Bob's **Bavarian Mountain Tour** covers the main things you'd want to do in and around Berchtesgaden (Königssee cruise, Hitler's mountaintop Eagle's Nest, salt mine tour). Although you can do all the top Berchtesgaden sights on your own with the information I've provided later in this chapter, Bob's tour makes it easy for those without a car to see these sights in one busy day.

Self-Guided Walk

▲▲▲Salzburg's Old Town

I've linked the best sights in the old town into this handy self-guided orientation walk.

• *Begin in the heart of town, just up from the river, near the TI on...*

❶ Mozartplatz

All the happy tourists around you probably wouldn't be here if not for the man honored by this statue—Wolfgang Amadeus Mozart (erected in 1842; locals consider the statue a terrible likeness). Mozart spent much of his first 25 years (1756-1777) in Salzburg, the greatest Baroque city north of the Alps. But the city itself is much older: The Mozart statue sits on bits of Roman Salzburg, and the pink Church of St. Michael that overlooks the square dates from A.D. 800. The first Salzburgers settled right around here. Near you is the TI (with a concert box office), and just around the downhill corner is a pedestrian bridge leading over the Salzach River to the quiet and most medieval street in town, Steingasse (described on page 199).

• *Walk toward the cathedral and into the big square with the huge fountain.*

❷ Residenzplatz

Important buildings have long ringed this square. Salzburg's energetic prince archbishop Wolf Dietrich von Raitenau (who ruled 1587-1612) was raised in Rome, was a cousin of the influential Florentine Medici family, and had grandiose Italian ambitions for

SALZBURG

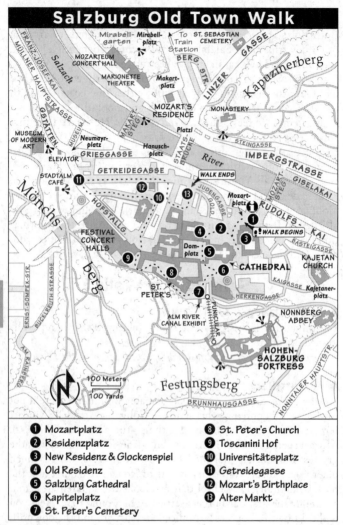

Salzburg Old Town Walk

1. Mozartplatz
2. Residenzplatz
3. New Residenz & Glockenspiel
4. Old Residenz
5. Salzburg Cathedral
6. Kapitelplatz
7. St. Peter's Cemetery
8. St. Peter's Church
9. Toscanini Hof
10. Universitätsplatz
11. Getreidegasse
12. Mozart's Birthplace
13. Alter Markt

Salzburg. After a convenient fire destroyed the town's cathedral, Wolf Dietrich set about building the "Rome of the North." This square, with his new cathedral and palace, was the centerpiece of his Baroque dream city. A series of interconnecting squares—like you'll see nowhere else—make a grand processional way, leading from here through the old town. As we enjoy this heart and soul of historic Salzburg, notice how easily we slip from noisy commercial streets to peaceful, reflective courtyards. Also notice the two dominant kinds of stone around town: a creamy red marble and a chunky conglomerate, both quarried nearby.

For centuries, Salzburg's leaders were both important church officials *and* princes of the Holy Roman Empire, hence the title "prince archbishop"—mixing sacred and secular authority. But Wolf Dietrich misplayed his hand, losing power and spending his last five years imprisoned in the Hohensalzburg Fortress. (It's a complicated story—basically, the pope counted on Salzburg to hold the line against the Protestants for several generations following the Reformation. Wolf Dietrich was a good Catholic, as were most Salzburgers. But the town's important businessmen and the region's salt miners were Protestant, and for Salzburg's financial good, Wolf Dietrich dealt with them in a tolerant and pragmatic way. So the pope—who couldn't allow any tolerance for Protestants in those heady Counter-Reformation days—had Wolf Dietrich locked up and replaced.)

The fountain is as Italian as can be, with a Triton matching Bernini's famous Triton Fountain in Rome. Situated on a busy trade route to the south, Salzburg was well aware of the exciting things going on in Italy. Things Italian were respected (as in colonial America, when a bumpkin would "stick a feather in his cap and call it macaroni"). Local artists even Italianized their names in order to raise their rates.

• *Along the left side of Residenzplatz (as you face the cathedral) is the...*

❸ New (Neue) Residenz & Glockenspiel

This former palace, long a government administration building, now houses the central post office, the **Heimatwerk** (a fine shop showing off all the best local handicrafts, Mon-Fri 9:00-18:00, Sat 9:00-17:00, closed Sun), and two worthwhile sights: the fascinating **Salzburg Panorama 1829** exhibit (definitely worth the entry fee); and the **Salzburg Museum,** which offers the best peek at the history of this one-of-a-kind city (both sights described on page 191).

The famous **glockenspiel** rings atop the New Residenz. This bell tower has a carillon of 35 17th-century bells (cast in Antwerp) that chimes throughout the day and plays tunes (appropriate to the month) at 7:00, 11:00, and 18:00. A big barrel with adjustable tabs turns like a giant music-box mechanism, pulling the right bells in the appropriate rhythm. Notice the ornamental top: an upside-down heart in flames surrounding the solar system (symbolizing that God loves all of creation). Seasonal twice-weekly tours let you get up close to watch the glockenspiel action (€3, April-Oct Thu at 17:30 and Fri at 10:30, no tours Nov-March, meet in Salzburg Panorama 1829, just show up).

Look back, past Mozart's statue, to the 4,220-foot-high **Gaisberg**—the forested hill with the television tower. A road leads to the top for a commanding view. Its summit is a favorite

destination for local nature-lovers and strong bikers.
• *Head to the opposite end of the square. This building is the...*

❹ Old (Alte) Residenz

Across from the New Residenz is Wolf Dietrich's palace, the Old Residenz, which is connected to the cathedral by a skyway. Its series of ornately decorated rooms is well-described in an included audioguide, which gives you a good feel for the wealth and power of the prince archbishop. Walking through 15 fancy state rooms (all on one floor), you'll see Renaissance, Baroque, and Classicist styles—200 years of let-them-eat-cake splendor.

Cost and Hours: €8.50, daily 10:00-17:00, tel. 0662/8042-2690.
• *Walk under the prince archbishop's skyway and step into Domplatz (Cathedral Square), where you'll find...*

❺ Salzburg Cathedral (Salzburger Dom)

This cathedral, rated ▲▲, was one of the first Baroque buildings north of the Alps. It was consecrated in 1628, during the Thirty Years' War. (Pitting Roman Catholics against Protestants, this war devastated much of Europe and brought most grand construction projects to a halt.) Experts differ on what motivated the builders: to emphasize Salzburg's commitment to the Roman Catholic cause and the power of the Church here, or to show that there could be a peaceful alternative to the religious strife that was racking Europe at the time. Salzburg's archbishop was technically the top papal official north of the Alps, but the city managed to steer

clear of the war. With its rich salt production, it had enough money to stay out of the conflict and carefully maintain its independence from the warring sides, earning it the nickname "Fortified Island of Peace."

Domplatz is surrounded by the prince archbishop's secular administration buildings. The **statue of Mary** (1771) is looking away from the church, welcoming visitors. If you stand in the rear of the square, immediately under the middle arch, you'll see that she's positioned to be crowned by the two angels on the church facade.

The dates on the iron gates refer to milestones in the church's history: In 774, the previous church (long since destroyed) was founded by St. Virgil, to be replaced in 1628 by the church you see today. In 1959, a partial reconstruction was completed, made necessary by a WWII bomb that had blown through the dome.

Cost and Hours: Free, but donation requested; Easter-Oct Mon-Sat 9:00-18:00, Sun 13:00-18:00; Nov-Easter Mon-Sat 10:00-17:00, Sun 13:00-17:00.

Touring the Cathedral: Enter the cathedral as if part of a festival procession—drawn toward the resurrected Christ by the

brightly lit area under the dome, and cheered on by ceiling paintings of the Passion.

Built in just 14 years (1614-1628), the church boasts harmonious architecture. When Pope John Paul II visited in 1998, some 5,000 people filled the cathedral (330 feet long and 230 feet tall). The baptismal font (dark bronze, left of the entry) is from the previous cathedral (basin from about 1320, although the lid is modern). Mozart was baptized here (Amadeus means "beloved by God"). Concert and Mass schedules are posted at the entrance; the Sunday Mass at 10:00 is famous for its music.

The **paintings** lining the nave, showing events leading up to Christ's death, are relatively dark. But the Old Testament themes that foreshadow Jesus' resurrection, and the Resurrection scene painted at the altar, are well-lit. The church has never had stained glass—just clear windows to let light power the message.

The stucco, by a Milanese artist, is exceptional. Sit under the **dome**—surrounded by the tombs of 10 archbishops from the 17th century—and imagine all four organs playing, each balcony filled with musicians...glorious surround-sound. Mozart, who was the organist here for two years, would advise you that the acoustics are best in pews immediately under the dome. Study the symbolism of the decor all around you—intellectual, complex, and cohesive. Think of the altar in Baroque terms, as the center of a stage, with sunrays as spotlights in this dramatic and sacred theater.

In the left transept, stairs lead down into the **crypt** *(Krypta)*, where you can see foundations of the earlier church, more tombs, and a tourist-free chapel (reserved for prayer) directly under the dome.

Other Cathedral Sights: The **Cathedral Excavations Museum** (outside the church on Residenzplatz and down the stairs) offers a chance to see the foundations of the medieval church, some Roman engineering, and a few Roman mosaics from Roman street level. It has the charm of an old basement garage; unless you've never seen anything Roman, I'd skip it (€2.50, July-Aug daily 9:00-17:00, closed Sept-June).

The **Cathedral Museum** (Dom Museum) has a rich collection of church art (entry at portico, €6, mid-May-Oct Mon-Sat 10:00-17:00, Sun 11:00-18:00, closed Nov-mid-May except during Advent, tel. 0662/8047-1870).

• *From the cathedral, exit left and walk toward the fortress into the next square.*

❻ Kapitelplatz

Head past the underground public WCs (€0.50) to the giant **chessboard.** It's just under the golden orb topped by a man gazing up at the castle, trying to decide whether to walk up or shell out €10.50 for the funicular. Every year since 2002, a foundation has commissioned a different artist to create a new work of public art somewhere in the city; this is the piece from 2007. A small road leads uphill to the fortress (and fortress funicular; see arrow pointing to the *Stieglkeller*).

Keep going across the square to the pond. This was a **horse bath,** the 18th-century equivalent of a car wash. Notice the puzzle above it—the artist wove the date of the structure into a phrase. It says, "Leopold the Prince Built Me," using the letters LLDVICMXVXI, which total 1732 (add it up...it works)—the year it was built. With your back to the cathedral, leave the square through a gate in the right corner that reads *zum Peterskeller.* It leads to a waterfall and St. Peter's Cemetery (described later).

The **waterwheel** is part of a clever canal system that has brought water into Salzburg from Berchtesgaden, 15 miles away, since the 13th century. Climb uphill a few steps to feel the medieval water power. The stream was divided into smaller canals and channeled through town to provide fire protection, to flush out the streets (Thursday morning was flood-the-streets day), and to power factories (there were more than 100 watermill-powered firms as late as the 19th century). Because of its water-powered hygiene (relatively good for the standards of the time), Salzburg never suffered from a plague—it's probably the only Austrian town you'll see with no plague monument. For more on the canal system, check out the **Alm River Canal exhibit** (at the exit of the funicular, described on page 196).

Before leaving, drop into the fragrant and traditional **bakery** at the waterfall, which sells various fresh rolls—both sweet and not, explained on the wall, for less than €1 (Thu-Tue 7:00-17:30, Sat until 13:00, closed Wed). There's a good view of the funicular climbing up to the castle from here.

• *Now find the* Katakomben *sign and step into...*

❼ St. Peter's Cemetery

This collection of lovingly tended mini-gardens abuts the Mönchberg's rock wall. Walk in about 50 yards to the intersection of lanes at the base of the cliff marked by a stone ball. You're surrounded by three churches, each founded in the early Middle Ages atop a pagan Celtic holy site. St. Peter's Church is closest to the stone ball. Notice the fine Romanesque stonework on the apse of the chapel nearest you, and the rich guys' fancy Renaissance-style tombs decorating its walls.

Wealthy as those guys were, they ran out of caring relatives. The graves surrounding you are tended by descendants of the deceased. In Austria, gravesites are rented, not owned. Rent bills are sent out every 10 years. If no one cares enough to make the payment, your tombstone is removed.

While the cemetery where the von Trapp family hid out in *The Sound of Music* was a Hollywood set, it was inspired by this one.

Look up the cliff. Legendary medieval hermit monks are said to have lived in the hillside—but "catacombs" they're not. You can climb lots of steps to see a few old caves, a chapel, and some fine views.

Cost and Hours: Cemetery—free, silence is requested, daily April-Sept 6:30-19:00, Oct-March 6:30-18:00; caves—€1, May-Sept Tue-Sun 10:30-17:00, closed Mon, shorter hours Oct-April.

Nearby: To enjoy a peaceful side-trip, stroll past the stark Gothic funeral chapel (c. 1491) to the uphill corner of the cemetery, and return along the high lane to see the finer tombs in the arcade. Tomb #XXXI belongs to the cathedral's architect—forever facing his creation. Tomb #LIV, at the catacomb entry, is a chapel carved into the hillside, holding the tombs of Mozart's sister and Joseph Haydn's younger brother Michael, also a composer of great note.

• *Continue downhill through the cemetery and out the opposite end. Just outside, hook right and drop into...*

❽ St. Peter's Church

Just inside, enjoy a carved Romanesque welcome. Over the inner doorway, a fine tympanum shows Jesus on a rainbow flanked by Peter and Paul over a stylized Tree of Life and under a Latin inscription reading, "I am the door to life, and only through me can you find eternal life." Enter the nave and notice how the once purely Romanesque vaulting has since been iced with a sugary Rococo finish. Salzburg's only Rococo interior feels Bavarian (because it is—the fancy stucco work was done by Bavarian artists). Up the right side aisle is the tomb of St. Rupert, with a painting showing Salzburg in 1750 (one bridge, salt ships sailing the river, and angels hoisting barrels of salt to heaven as St. Rupert prays for his city). If you're here during the town's Ruperti-Kirtag festival in late September, you'll see candles and fresh flowers, honoring the city's not-forgotten saint. On pillars farther up the aisle are faded bits of 13th-century Romanesque frescoes. Similar frescoes hide under Rococo whitewash throughout the church.

Cost and Hours: Free, long hours daily.

• *Leaving the church, notice on the left the recommended **Stiftskeller St. Peter** restaurant—known for its Mozart Dinner Concert. Charlemagne ate here in A.D. 803, allowing locals to claim that it's the oldest restaurant in Europe. Opposite where you entered the square (look through the arch), you'll see St. Rupert waving you into the next square. Once there, you're surrounded by early 20th-century Bauhaus-style dorms for student monks. Notice the modern crucifix (1926) painted on the far wall. Here's a good place to see the two locally quarried stones (marble and conglomerate) so prevalent in all the town's buildings.*

Walk through the archway under the crucifix into...

❾ Toscanini Hof

This square faces the 1925 **Festival Hall**. The hall's three theaters seat 5,000. This is where Captain von Trapp nervously waited before walking onstage (in the movie, he sang "Edelweiss"), just before he escaped with his family. On the left is the city's 1,500-space, inside-the-mountain parking lot; ahead, behind the *Felsenkeller* sign, is a tunnel (generally closed) leading to the actual concert hall; and to the right is the backstage of a smaller hall where carpenters are often building stage sets (door open on hot days). The stairway leads a few flights up to a picnic perch with a fine view, and then up to the top of the cliff and the recommended Stadtalm Café and hostel.

Walk downhill to **Max-Reinhardt-Platz.** Pause here to survey the line of Salzburg Festival concert halls. As the festival was started in the austere 1920s, the city remodeled existing buildings (e.g., the prince archbishop's stables and riding school) for venues.

• *Continue straight—passing the big church on your left, along with lots of popular wurst stands and a public WC—into...*

❿ Universitätsplatz

This square hosts an **open-air produce market**—Salzburg's liveliest (mornings Mon-Sat, best on Sat). Salzburgers are happy to pay more here for the reliably fresh and top-quality produce. (These days, half of Austria's produce is grown organically.) The market really bustles on Saturday mornings, when the farmers are in

town. Public marketplaces have fountains for washing fruit and vegetables. The fountain here—a part of the medieval water system—plummets down a hole and to the river. The sundial (over the water hole) is accurate (except for the daylight savings hour) and two-dimensional, showing both the time (obvious) and the date (less obvious). The fanciest facade overlooking the square (the yellow one) is the backside of Mozart's Birthplace (we'll see the front soon).

• *Continue past the fountain to the end of the square, passing several characteristic and nicely arcaded medieval tunnels (on right) that connect the square to Getreidegasse (described next). Just for fun, weave between this street and Getreidegasse several times, following these "through houses" as you work your way toward the cliff face. For a look at the giant horse troughs, adjacent to the prince's stables, cross the big road (looking left at the string of Salzburg Festival halls again). Paintings show the various breeds and temperaments of horses in his stable. Like Vienna, Salzburg had a passion for the equestrian arts.*

Turn right (passing a courtyard on your left that once housed a hospital for the poor, and now houses a toy museum and a museum of historic musical instruments), and then right again, which brings you to the start of a long and colorful pedestrian street.

⓫ Getreidegasse

This street, rated ▲▲, was old Salzburg's busy, colorful main drag. It's been a center of trade since Roman times (third century). It's lined with *Schmuck* (jewelry) shops and other businesses. This is the burgher's (businessman's) Salzburg. The buildings, most of which date from the 15th century, are tall for that age, and narrow, and densely packed. Space was tight here because such little land was available between the natural fortifications provided by the mountain and the river, and much of what was available was used up by the Church. Famous for its old wrought-iron signs (best viewed from this end), the architecture on the

street still looks much as it did in Mozart's day—though its former elegance is now mostly gone, replaced by chain outlets.

As you walk away from the cliffs, look up and enjoy the

traditional signs indicating what each shop made or sold: Watch for spirits, bookmakers, a horn (indicating a place for the postal coach), brewery (the star for the name of the beer, Sternbräu— "Star Brew"), glazier (window-maker), locksmith, hamburgers, pastries, tailor, baker (the pretzel), pharmacy, and a hatter.

On the right at #39, **Sporer** serves up homemade spirits (€1.50/shot, open 8:30-17:00). This has been a family-run show for a century—fun-loving, proud, and English-speaking. *Nuss* is nut, *Marille* is apricot (typical of this region), the *Kletzen* cocktail is like a super-thick Baileys with pear, and *Edle Brande* are the stronger schnapps. The many homemade firewaters are in jugs at the end of the bar.

Continue down Getreidegasse, noticing the old doorbells— one per floor. At #40, **Eisgrotte** serves good ice cream. Across from Eisgrotte, a tunnel leads to the recommended **Balkan Grill** (signed as *Bosna Grill*), the local choice for the very best wurst in town. At #28, Herr Wieber, the iron- and locksmith, welcomes the curious. Farther along, you'll pass McDonald's (required to keep its arches Baroque and low-key).

The knot of excited tourists and salesmen hawking goofy gimmicks marks the home of Salzburg's most famous resident. **Mozart's Birthplace** (*Geburtshaus*, ⓬ on map)—the house where Mozart was born, and where he composed many of his early works—is worth a visit for his true fans (described on page 192). But for most, his **Residence,** across the river, is more interesting (described on page 199).

At #3, dip into the passage and walk under a whalebone, likely once used to advertise the wares of an exotic import shop. Look up at the arcaded interior. On the right, at the venerable **Schatz Konditorei,** you can enjoy coffee under the vaults with your choice of top-end cakes and pastries (Mon-Fri 8:30-18:30, Sat 8:00-17:00, closed Sun).

Leaving the pastry shop, go straight ahead through the passage to Sigmund-Haffner-Gasse. Before heading right, look left to see the tower of the old City Hall at the end. The blue-and-white ball halfway up is an 18th-century moon clock. It still tells the phase of the moon.

• *Go right, then take your first left to....*

⓭ Alter Markt

Here in Salzburg's old marketplace, you'll find a sausage stand, the recommended **Café Tomaselli,** a fun **candy shop** at #7, and, next door, the beautifully old-fashioned **Alte F.E. Hofapotheke** pharmacy—duck in discreetly to peek at the Baroque shelves and containers (be polite—the people in line are here for medicine, no photography).

• *Our walk is finished. From here, you can circle back to some of the old town sights (such as those in the New Residenz, described next); head up to the Hohensalzburg Fortress on the cliffs over the old town (see next page); or continue to some of the sights across the river. To reach those sights, head for the river, jog left (past the fast-food fish restaurant and free WCs), climb to the top of the Makartsteg pedestrian bridge, and turn to page 197.*

Sights in Salzburg

In the Old Town

In the New (Neue) Residenz

▲▲**Salzburg Museum**—This two-floor exhibit is the best in town for history. The included audioguide wonderfully describes the great artifacts in the lavish prince archbishop's residence.

The Salzburg Personalities exhibit fills the first floor with a charming look at Salzburg's greatest historic characters—mostly artists, scientists, musicians, and writers who would otherwise be forgotten. And upstairs is the real reason to come: lavish ceremonial rooms filled with an exhibit called The Salzburg Myth, which traces the city's proud history, art, and culture since early modern times. The focus is on its quirky absolutist prince archbishop and its long-standing reputation as a fairy-tale "Alpine Arcadia." The *Kunsthalle* in the basement shows off special exhibits.

From the Salzburg Museum, the Panorama Passage (clearly marked from the entry) leads underground to the Salzburg Panorama (described next). This passage is lined with archaeological finds (Roman and early medieval), helping you trace the development of Salzburg from its Roman roots until today.

Cost and Hours: €7, €8 combo-ticket with Salzburg Panorama, includes audioguide, Tue-Sun 9:00-17:00, Thu until 20:00, closed Mon, tel. 0662/620-8080, www.smca.at.

▲**Salzburg Panorama 1829**—In the early 19th century, before the advent of photography, 360-degree "panorama" paintings of great cities or events were popular. These creations were even taken on extended road trips. When this one was created, the 1815 Treaty of Vienna had just divvied up post-Napoleonic Europe, and Salzburg had become part of the Habsburg realm. This photo-realistic painting served as a town portrait done at the emperor's request. The circular view, painted by Johann Michael Sattler, shows the city as seen from the top of its castle. When complete, it spent 10 years touring the great cities of Europe, showing off Salzburg's breathtaking setting.

Today, the exquisitely restored painting offers a fascinating look at the city in 1829. The river was slower and had beaches. The old town looks essentially as it does today, and Moosstrasse still

SALZBURG

leads into idyllic farm country. Paintings from that era of other great cities around the world are hung around the outside wall with numbers but without labels, as a kind of quiz game. A flier gives the cities' names on one side, and keys them to the numbers. See how many 19th-century cities you can identify.

Cost and Hours: €2, €8 combo-ticket with Salzburg Museum, open daily 9:00-17:00, Thu until 20:00, Residenzplatz 9.

▲Mozart's Birthplace (Geburtshaus)

Mozart was born here in 1756. It was in this building that he composed most of his boy-genius works. Today it's the most popular Mozart sight in town—for fans, it's almost a pilgrimage. American artist Robert Wilson was hired to spiff up the exhibit, to make it feel more conceptual and less like a museum. Even so, I was unimpressed. If you're tackling just one Mozart sight, skip this one. Instead, walk 10 minutes from here to Mozart's Residence

(described later), which provides a more informative visit. But if you want to max out on Mozart, a visit here is worthwhile.

Shuffling through with all the crowds, you'll peruse three floors of rooms with old-school exhibits displaying paintings, letters, personal items, and lots of facsimiles, all attempting to bring life to the Mozart story (and all explained in English). A period living room shows what Wolfgang's world likely looked like, and portraits introduce you to the family. A particular highlight is an old clavichord he supposedly composed on. (A predecessor of the more complicated piano, the clavichord's keys hit the strings with a simple teeter-totter motion that allowed you to play very softly—ideal for composers living in tight apartment quarters.) At the end, there's a room of dioramas dedicated to Mozart's operas.

Cost and Hours: €7, €12 for combo-ticket includes Mozart's Residence, daily 9:00-17:30, July-Aug until 20:00, last entry 30 minutes before closing, only the shop has air-con, Getreidegasse 9, tel. 0662/844-313.

Atop the Cliffs Above the Old Town

The main "sight" above town is the Hohensalzburg Fortress. But if you just want to enjoy the sweeping views over Salzburg, you have a couple of cheap options: Head up to the castle grounds on foot, take the elevator up the cliffs of Mönchsberg (explained in "Getting Around Salzburg" on page 176), or visit the castle in the evening on a night when they're hosting a concert (about 300

Battlefield Salzburg: Popes vs. Emperors

Salzburg is so architecturally impressive today to a great degree because of the Roman Catholic Church. This town was on the frontline of a centuries-long power struggle between Church and emperor. The town's mighty Hohensalzburg Fortress—a symbol of the Church's determination to assert its power here—was built around 1100, just as the conflict was heating up.

The medieval church-state argument, called the "Lay Investiture Controversy," was a classic tug-of-war between a series of popes and Holy Roman Emperors. The prize: the right to appoint (or "invest") church officials in the Holy Roman Emperor's domain. (Although called "Holy," the empire was headed not by priests, but by secular—or "lay"—rulers.)

The Church impinged on the power of secular leaders in several ways: Their subjects' generous tithes went to Rome, leaving less for the emperor to tax. In many areas, the Church was the biggest landowner (people willed their land to the Church in return for prayers for their salvation). And the pope's appointees weren't subject to secular local laws. Holy Roman Emperors were plenty powerful, but not as powerful as the Church.

In 1075, Emperor Henry IV bucked the system, appointing his own set of church officials and boldly renouncing Gregory VII as pope. In retaliation, Gregory excommunicated both Henry and the bishops he'd appointed. One of Henry's chief detractors was Salzburg's pope-appointed archbishop, Gebhard, who started construction of Hohensalzburg Fortress in a face-off with the defiant emperor.

The German nobility seized on the conflict as an opportunity to rebel, seizing royal property and threatening to elect a new emperor. To placate the nobles, Henry sought to regain the Church's favor. In January of 1077, Henry traveled south to Italy—supposedly crossing the Alps barefoot and in a monk's hair-shirt—to Canossa, where the pope was holed up. The emperor knelt in the snow outside the castle gate for three days, begging the pope's forgiveness. (To this day, the phrase "go to Canossa" is used to refer to any act of humility.)

But the German princes continued their revolt, electing their own king (Henry's brother-in-law, Rudolf of Rheinfelden). Henry's reconciliation with the Church was brief: In short order he named an antipope (Clement III), killed Rudolf in battle, and invaded Rome. Archbishop Gebhard was forced out of Salzburg and spent a decade in exile, raising forces against Henry in an attempt to reclaim the Salzburg archdiocese.

The back-and-forth continued until 1122, when a power-sharing accord was finally reached between Henry's son, Emperor Henry V, and Pope Calistus II.

nights a year). This is the only time you can buy a funicular ticket without paying for the castle entrance—since the castle museums are closed, but the funicular still runs to bring up concert-goers.

▲▲Hohensalzburg Fortress (Festung)

Construction of Hohensalzburg Fortress was begun by Archbishop Gebhard of Salzburg as a show of the Catholic Church's power (see

sidebar). Built on a rock (called Festungsberg) 400 feet above the Salzach River, this fortress was never really used. That's the idea. It was a good investment—so foreboding, nobody attacked the town for 1,000 years. The city was never taken by force, but when Napoleon stopped by, Salzburg wisely surrendered. After a stint as a military barracks, the fortress was opened to the public in the 1860s by Habsburg Emperor Franz Josef. Today, it remains one of Europe's mightiest castles, dominating Salzburg's skyline and offering incredible views.

Cost: Your daytime funicular ticket includes admission to the fortress grounds and all the museums inside—whether you want to see them or not (€10.50, €24.30 family ticket). Save a few euros by walking up—the climb is much easier than it looks, and the views are fantastic. At the top, you'll pay €7.40 to enter (includes grounds and museums). If you'd rather take the funicular but want to skip the museums, head up the hill in the evening: Within one hour of the museums' closing time, the funicular and entry to the castle grounds cost €6.20 one-way/€7.60 round-trip; on concert nights and in summer, after the museums have closed, the funicular is just €3.80 round-trip.

Hours: The complex is open daily year-round (May-Sept 9:00-19:00, Oct-April 9:30-17:00, last entry 30 minutes before closing, tel. 0662/8424-3011). On nights when there's a concert, and nightly in July and August, the castle grounds are free and open from after the museums close until 22:00.

Concerts: The fortress also serves as a venue for evening concerts (Festungs-konzerte). For details, see "Music in Salzburg" on page 204.

Café: The café between the funicular station and the castle entry is a great place to nibble on apple strudel while taking in the jaw-dropping view.

Orientation: The fortress visit has three parts: a relatively dull courtyard with some fine views from its various ramparts; the fortress itself (with a required and escorted 45-minute audio tour); and the palace museum (by far the best exhibit of the lot). At the bottom of the funicular, you'll pass through an interesting little exhibit on the town's canal system (free).

◑ Self-Guided Tour: From the top of the funicular, head to your right and down the stairs to bask in the **view,** either from the café or the view terrace a little farther along.

Once you're done snapping photos, walk through to the castle grounds and go left, following the path up and around to reach the inner courtyard (labeled *Inneres Schloß*). Immediately inside, circling to the right (clockwise), you'll encounter cannons (still poised to defend Salzburg against an Ottoman invasion), a marionette exhibit, the palace museum, the Kuenburg Bastion, scant ruins of a Romanesque church, the courtyard (with path down for those walking), toilets, shops, a restaurant, and the fortress tour.

• *Begin at the...*

Marionette Exhibit: Several fun rooms show off this local tradition, with three videos playing continuously: two with peeks at Salzburg's ever-enchanting Marionette Theater performances of Mozart classics (described under "Music in Salzburg," later) and one with a behind-the-scenes look at the action. Give the hands-on marionette a whirl.

• *Hiking through the former palace, you'll find the best exhibits at the...*

Palace Museum (Festungsmuseum Carolino Augusteum): The second floor has exhibits on castle life, from music to torture. The top floor shows off fancy royal apartments, a sneak preview of the room used for the nightly fortress concerts, and the Rainier military museum, dedicated to the Salzburg regiments that fought in both world wars.

Castle Courtyard: The courtyard was the main square for the castle's 1,000-some medieval residents, who could be self-sufficient when necessary. The square was ringed by the shops of craftsmen, blacksmiths, bakers, and so on. The well dipped into a rain-fed cistern. The church is dedicated to St. George, the protector of horses (logical for an army church) and decorated by fine red marble reliefs (c. 1502). Behind the church is the top of the old lift that helped supply the fortress. (From near here, steps lead back into the city, or to the mountaintop "Mönchsberg Walk," described later.) You'll also see the remains of a Romanesque chapel, which are well-described.

• *Near the chapel, turn left into the Kuenburg Bastion (once a garden) for fine city and castle views.*

Kuenburg Bastion: Notice how the castle has three parts: the original castle inside the courtyard, the vast whitewashed walls (built when the castle was a residence), and the lower, beefed-up fortifications (added for extra defense against the expected Ottoman invasion). Survey Salzburg from here and think about fortifying an important city by using  nature. Mönchsberg (the cliffs to the left) and Festungsberg (the little mountain you're on) naturally cradle the old town, with just a small gate between the ridge and the river needed to bottle up the place. The new town across the river needed a bit of a wall arcing from the river to its hill. Back then, only one bridge crossed the Salzach into town, and it had a fortified gate.

• *Back inside the castle courtyard, continue your circle. The Round Tower (1497) helps you visualize the inner original castle.*

Fortress Interior: Tourists are allowed in this part of the fortified palace only with an escort. (They say that's for security, though while touring it, you wonder what they're protecting.) A crowd assembles at the turnstile, and every quarter-hour 40 people are issued their audioguides and let in for the escorted walk. You'll go one room at a time, listening to a 45-minute commentary. While the interior furnishings are mostly gone—taken by Napoleon—the rooms survived as well as they did because no one wanted to live here after 1500, so the building was never modernized. Your tour includes a room dedicated to the art of "excruciating questioning" ("softening up" prisoners, in American military jargon)—filled with tools of that gruesome trade. The highlight is the commanding city view from the top of a tower.

• *After seeing the fortress, consider hiking down to the old town, or along the top of Mönchsberg (see "Mönchsberg Walk," below). If you take the funicular down, don't miss (at the bottom of the lift) the...*

Alm River Canal Exhibit: At the base of the funicular, below the castle, is this fine little exhibit on how the river was broken into five smaller streams—powering the city until steam took up the energy-supply baton. Pretend it's the year 1200 and follow (by video) the flow of the water from the river through the canals, into the mills, and as it's finally dumped into the Salzach River. (The exhibit technically requires a funicular ticket—but you can see it by slipping through the exit at the back of the amber shop, just uphill from the funicular terminal.)

Mönchsberg Sights

▲**Mönchsberg Walk**—For a great 30-minute hike, exit the fortress by taking the steep lane down from the castle courtyard. At the first intersection, right leads into the old town, and left leads across the Mönchsberg. The lane leads 20 minutes through the woods high above the city (stick to the high lanes, or you'll end up back in town), taking you to the recommended Gasthaus Stadtalm café (light meals, cheap beds). From the Stadtalm, pass under the medieval wall and walk left along the wall to a tableau showing how it once looked. Take the switchback to the right and follow the lane downhill to the Museum of Modern Art (described next), where the *MönchsbergAufzug* elevator zips you back into town (€2 one-way, €3.20 round-trip, daily 8:00-19:00, Wed and July-Aug until 21:00). If you stay on the lane past the elevator, you eventually pass the Augustine church that marks the rollicking Augustiner Bräustübl beer garden (see page 221).

In 1669, a huge Mönchsberg landslide killed more than 200 townspeople. Since then the cliffs have been carefully checked each spring and fall. Even today, you might see crews on the cliff, monitoring its stability.

Museum of Modern Art on Mönchsberg—The modern-art museum on top of Mönchsberg was built in 2004. While the collection is not worth climbing a mountain for, the M32 restaurant has some of the best views in town.

Cost and Hours: €8, €9.70 including elevator ticket, Tue-Sun 10:00-18:00, Wed until 20:00, closed Mon except during festival; restaurant open Tue-Sat 9:00-24:00, closed Mon except during festival; at top of Mönchsberg elevator, tel. 0662/842-220-403, www.museumdermoderne.at.

In the New Town, North of the River

The following sights are across the river from the old town. I've connected them with walking instructions.

• *Begin at the Makartsteg pedestrian bridge, where you can survey the...*

Salzach River

Salzburg's river is called "salt river" not because it's salty, but because of the precious cargo it once carried—the salt mines of Hallein are just nine miles upstream. Salt could be transported from here all the way to the Danube, and on to the Mediterranean via the Black Sea. The riverbanks and roads were built when the river was regulated in the 1850s. Before that, the Salzach was much wider and slower moving. Houses opposite the old town fronted the river with docks and "garages" for boats. The grand buildings just past the bridge (with their elegant promenades and cafés) were built on reclaimed land in the late 19th century.

Scan the cityscape. Notice all the churches. Salzburg, nick-named the "Rome of the North," has 38 Catholic churches (plus two Protestant churches and a synagogue). Find the five streams gushing into the river. These date from the 13th century, when the river was split into five canals running through the town to power its mills. The Stein Hotel (upstream, just left of next bridge) has a popular roof-terrace café (see page 200). Downstream, notice the Museum of Modern Art atop Mönchsberg, with a view restaurant and a faux castle (actually a water reservoir). The Romanesque bell tower with the green copper dome in the distance is the Augustine church, site of the best beer hall in town (the recommended Augustiner Bräustübl).

• *Cross the bridge, pass the recommended Café Bazar (a fine place for a drink), walk two blocks inland, and take a left past the heroic statues into...*

▲Mirabell Gardens and Palace (Schloss)

The bubbly gardens laid out in 1730 for the prince archbishop have been open to the public since 1850 (thanks to Emperor Franz Josef,

who was rattled by the popular revolutions of 1848). The gardens are free and open until dusk. The palace is open only as a concert venue (explained later). The statues and the arbor (far left) were featured in *The Sound of Music*. Walk through the gardens to the palace. Look back, enjoy the garden/cathedral/castle view, and imagine how the prince archbishop must have reveled in a vista that reminded him of all his secular and religious power. Then go around to the river side of the palace and find the horse.

The rearing **Pegasus statue** (rare and very well-balanced) is the site of a famous *Sound of Music* scene where the kids all danced before lining up on the stairs (with Maria 30 yards farther along). The steps lead to a small mound in the park (made of rubble from a former theater, and today a rendezvous point for Salzburg's gay community).

Nearest the horse, stairs lead between two lions to a pair of tough dwarfs (early volleyball players with spiked mittens) welcoming you to Salzburg's **Dwarf Park.** Cross the elevated walk (noticing the city's fortified walls) to meet statues of a dozen dwarfs who served the prince archbishop—modeled after real people with real fashions in about 1600. This was Mannerist art, from the hyper-realistic age that followed the Renaissance.

There's plenty of **music** here, both in the park and in the palace. A brass band plays free park concerts (May-Aug Sun at 10:30 and Wed with lighted fountains at 20:30, unless it's raining). To properly enjoy the lavish Mirabell Palace—once the prince arch-bishop's summer palace and now the seat of the mayor—get a ticket to a Schlosskonzerte (my favorite venue for a classical concert—see page 204).

• *To visit Salzburg's best Mozart sight, go a long block southeast to Makartplatz, where, opposite the big and bright Hotel Bristol, you'll find...*

▲▲Mozart's Residence (Wohnhaus)

This reconstruction of Mozart's second home (his family moved here when he was 17) is the most informative Mozart sight in town. The English-language audioguide provides fascinating insight into Mozart's life and music, with the usual scores, old pianos, and an interesting 30-minute film (#17 on your audioguide for soundtrack) that runs continuously.

In the main hall—used by the Mozarts to entertain Salzburg's high society—you can hear original instruments from Mozart's time. Mozart was proud to be the first in his family to compose a duet. Notice the family portrait (c. 1780) on the wall, showing Mozart with his sister Nannerl, their father, and their mother—who'd died two years earlier in Paris. Mozart also had silly crude bull's-eyes made for the pop-gun game popular at the time (licking an "arse," Wolfgang showed his disdain for the rigors of high society). Later rooms feature real artifacts that explore his loves, his intellectual pursuits, his travels, and more.

Cost and Hours: €7, includes 1.5-hour audioguide, €12 combo-ticket includes Mozart's Birthplace in the old town, daily 9:00-17:30, July-Aug until 20:00, last entry 30 minutes before closing, allow at least one hour for visit, Makartplatz 8, tel. 0662/8742-2740.

• *From here, you can walk a few blocks back to the main bridge (Staatsbrücke), where you'll find the Platzl, a square once used as a hay market. Pause to enjoy the kid-pleasing little fountain. Near the fountain (with your back to the river), Steingasse leads darkly to the right.*

▲Steingasse Stroll

This street, a block in from the river, was part of the only road in the Middle Ages going south over the Alps to Venice (this was the first stop north of the Alps). Today, it's wonderfully tranquil and free of Salzburg's touristy crush. Inviting cocktail bars along here come alive at night (see "Steingasse Pub Crawl" on page 223).

At #9, a plaque (of questionable veracity) shows where Joseph Mohr, who wrote the words to "Silent Night," was born—poor and illegitimate—in 1792. There is no doubt, however, that the popular Christmas carol was composed and first sung in the village of Oberndorf, just outside of Salzburg, in 1818. Stairs lead from near here up to a 17th-century Capuchin monastery.

On the next corner, the wall is gouged out. This scar was left even after the building was restored, to serve as a reminder of the American GI who tried to get a tank down this road during a visit to the town brothel—two blocks farther up Steingasse.

At #19, find the carvings on the old door. Some say these are notices from beggars to the begging community (more numerous after post-Reformation religious wars, which forced many people out of their homes and towns)—a kind of "hobo code" indicating whether the residents would give or not. Trace the wires of the old-fashioned doorbells to the highest floors.

Farther on, you'll find a commanding Salzburg view across the river. Notice the red dome marking the oldest nunnery in the German-speaking world (established in 712) under the fortress and to the left. The real Maria, who inspired *The Sound of Music*, taught in this nunnery's school. In 1927, she and Captain von Trapp were married in the church you see here (not the church filmed in the movie). He was 47. She was 22. Hmmmm.

From here look back, above the arch you just passed through, at part of the town's medieval fortification. The coat of arms on the arch is of the prince archbishop who paid Bavaria a huge ransom to stay out of the Thirty Years' War (smart move). He then built this fortification (in 1634) in anticipation of rampaging armies from both sides.

Today, this street is for making love, not war. The Maison de Plaisir (a few doors down, at #24) has for centuries been a Salzburg brothel. But the climax of this walk is more touristic.

• *For a grand view, head back to the Platzl and the bridge, enter the Stein Hotel (left corner, overlooking the river), and ride the elevator to...*

Stein Terrasse

This café offers perhaps the best views in town (aside from the castle). Hidden from the tourist crush, it's a trendy, professional, local scene. You can discreetly peek at the view, or enjoy a drink or light meal (small snacks, indoor/outdoor seating, Sun-Thu 9:00-24:00, Fri-Sat 9:00-1:00 in the morning).

• *Back at the Platzl and the bridge, you can head straight up Linzergasse (away from the river) into a neighborhood packed with recommended accommodations, as well as our final new-town sight, the...*

▲St. Sebastian Cemetery

Wander through this quiet oasis. Mozart is buried in Vienna, his mom's in Paris, and his sister is in Salzburg's old town (St. Peter's)—but Wolfgang's wife Constanze ("Constantia") and his father Leopold are buried here (from the black iron gate entrance on Linzergasse, walk 17 paces and look left). When prince archbishop Wolf Dietrich had the cemetery moved from around the cathedral and put here, across the river, people didn't like it. To help popularize it, he had his own mausoleum built as its centerpiece. Continue straight past the Mozart tomb to this circular building (English description at door). In the corner to the left of the entrance is the tomb of

the Renaissance scientist and physician Paracelsus, best known for developing laudanum as a pain-killer.

Cost and Hours: Free, daily April-Oct 9:00-18:30, Nov-March 9:00-16:00, entry at Linzergasse 43 in summer; in winter go around the corner to the right, through the arch at #37, and around the building to the doorway under the blue seal.

Near Salzburg

▲**Hellbrunn Castle**—About the year 1610, prince archbishop Sittikus (after meditating on stewardship and Christ-like val-

ues) decided he needed a lavish palace with a vast and ornate garden purely for pleasure. He built this and just loved inviting his VIP guests out for fun with his trick fountains. Today, the visit is worthwhile for the Baroque garden, one of the oldest in Europe. More notably, it's full of clever fountains...and tour guides getting sadistic joy from soaking tourists. (Hint: When you see a wet place, cover your camera.) After buying your ticket, you must wait for the English tour and laugh and scramble through the entertaining 40-minute trick-water-toy tour, and are then free to tour the forgettable palace with an included audioguide.

While it can be fun—especially on a hot day or with kids—for many, it's a lot of trouble for a few water tricks. *Sound of Music* fans not taking an *S.O.M.* tour, however, may want to visit just to see the "Sixteen Going on Seventeen" gazebo, now located in the gardens.

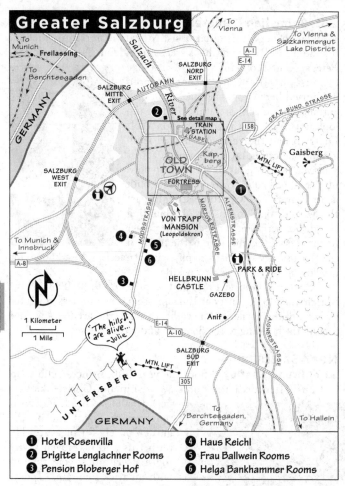

Greater Salzburg

1 Hotel Rosenvilla
2 Brigitte Lenglachner Rooms
3 Pension Bloberger Hof
4 Haus Reichl
5 Frau Ballwein Rooms
6 Helga Bankhammer Rooms

Cost and Hours: €9.50, daily May-Sept 9:00-17:30, July-Aug until 21:00—but tours from 18:00 on don't include the castle, mid-March-April and Oct 9:00-16:30, these are last tour times, closed Nov-mid-March, tel. 0662/820-3720, www.hellbrunn.at.

Getting There: Hellbrunn is nearly four miles south of Salzburg (bus #25 from station or from Staatsbrücke bridge, 2-3/hour, 20 minutes). In good weather, it makes a pleasant 30-minute bike excursion along the riverbank from Salzburg (described next).

▲▲**Riverside or Meadow Bike Ride**—The Salzach River has smooth, flat, and scenic bike lanes along each side (thanks to medieval tow paths—cargo boats would float downstream and be dragged back up by horses). On a sunny day, I can think of no more shout-worthy escape from the city. The nearly four-mile path upstream to Hellbrunn Castle is easy, with a worthy destination (leave Salzburg on castle side). For a nine-mile ride, continue on to Hallein (where you can tour a salt mine—see next listing; the north, or new-town, side of river is most scenic). Perhaps the most pristine, meadow-filled farm-country route is the four-mile Hellbrunner Allee from Akademiestrasse. Even a quickie ride across town is a great Salzburg experience. In the evening, the riverbanks are a world of floodlit spires.

▲**Hallein Bad Dürrnberg Salt Mine (Salzbergwerke)**—You'll be pitched plenty of different salt-mine excursions from Salzburg, all of which cost substantial time and money. One's plenty. This

salt-mine tour (above the town of Hallein, 9 miles from Salzburg) is a good choice. Wearing white overalls and sliding down the sleek wooden chutes, you'll cross underground from Austria into Germany while learning about the old-time salt-mining process. The tour entails lots of time on your feet as you walk from cavern to cavern, learning the history of the mine by watching a series of video skits with an actor channeling prince archbishop Wolf Dietrich. The visit also includes a "Celtic Village" open-air museum.

Cost and Hours: €18, allow 2.5 hours for the visit, daily April-Oct 9:00-17:00, Nov-March 10:00-15:00—these are last tour times, English-speaking guides—but let your linguistic needs be known loud and clear, tel. 06132/200-8511, www.salzwelten.at.

Getting There: The convenient *Salz Erlebnis* ticket from Salzburg's train station covers admission, train, and shuttle bus tickets, all in one money-saving round-trip ticket (€42, buy ticket at train station, no discount with railpass; 40-minute trip with hourly departures in each direction at about :15 after the hour, with synchronized train-bus connection in Hallein—schedule posted in flier).

▲▲**Hallstatt and Berchtesgaden**—Rustic Hallstatt, crammed like a swallow's nest into the narrow shore between a lake and a steep mountainside, is a 2.5-hour train ride from Salzburg, and my favorite town in the scenic Salzkammergut Lake District. Berchtesgaden (covered later in this chapter) is equally scenic, and home to Hitler's Eagle's Nest and other interesting sights. Both of these towns make for busy but worthwhile side-trips from Salzburg, and both are easy enough to do on your own. But if you're on a quick schedule, taking an all-day bus tour to these places can be a good use of your time and money (for details, see page 181).

Music in Salzburg

▲▲Salzburg Festival (Salzburger Festspiele)

Each summer, from late July to the end of August, Salzburg hosts its famous Salzburg Festival, founded in 1920 to employ Vienna's musicians in the summer. This fun and festive time is crowded, but there are usually plenty of beds (except for a few August weekends). Events take place primarily in three big halls: the Opera and Orchestra venues in the Festival House, and the Landes Theater, where German-language plays are performed. Tickets for the big festival events are generally expensive (€50-600) and sell out well in advance (bookable from January). Most tourists think they're "going to the Salzburg Festival" by seeing smaller non-festival events that go on during the festival weeks. For these lesser events, same-day tickets are normally available (the ticket office on Mozartplatz, in the TI, prints a daily list of concerts and charges a 30 percent fee to book them). For specifics on this year's festival schedule and tickets, visit www.salzburg festival.at, or contact the Austrian National Tourist Office in the United States (tel. 212/944-6880, fax 212/730-4568, www.austria .info, travel@austria.info).

▲▲Musical Events Year-Round

Salzburg is busy throughout the year, with 2,000 classical performances in its palaces and churches annually. Pick up the events calendar at the TI (free, bimonthly). I've never planned in advance, and I've enjoyed great concerts with every visit. Whenever you visit, you'll have a number of concerts (generally small chamber groups) to choose from. Here are some of the more accessible events:

Concerts at Hohensalzburg Fortress (Festungskonzerte)— Nearly nightly concerts—Mozart's greatest hits for beginners—are held atop Festungsberg, in the "prince's chamber" of the fortress, featuring small chamber groups (open seating after the first six more expensive rows, €31 or €38 plus €3.80 for the funicular; at 19:30, 20:00, or 20:30; doors open 30 minutes early, tel. 0662/825-858 to reserve, pick up tickets at the door). The medieval-feeling chamber has windows overlooking the city, and the concert gives you a chance to enjoy the grand city view and a stroll through the castle courtyard. (The funicular ticket costs €3.80 within an hour of the show—ideal for people who just want to ascend for the view.) For €51, you can combine the concert with a four-course dinner (starts 2 hours before concert).

Concerts at the Mirabell Palace (Schlosskonzerte)—The nearly nightly chamber music concerts at the Mirabell Palace are performed in a lavish Baroque setting. They come with more sophisticated programs and better musicians than the fortress concerts. Baroque music flying around a Baroque hall is a happy bird in the right cage (open seating after the first five pricier rows, €29-35, usually at 20:00—but check flier for times, doors open one hour ahead, tel. 0662/848-586, www.salzburger-schlosskonzerte.at).

"Five O'Clock Concerts" (5-Uhr-Konzerte)—These concerts—next to St. Peter's in the old town—are cheaper, since they feature young artists. While the series is formally named after the brother of Joseph Haydn, it offers music from various masters (€12-15, July-Sept Tue and Thu at 17:00, no concerts Oct-June, 45-60 minutes, tel. 0662/8445-7619, www.5-uhr-konzerte.com).

Mozart Piano Sonatas—St. Peter's Abbey hosts these concerts each weekend. This short (45-minute) and inexpensive concert is ideal for families (€18, €9 for children, €45 for a family of four, Fri and Sat at 19:00 year-round, in the abbey's Romanesque Hall—a.k.a. Romanischer Saal, tel. 0664/423-5645).

Marionette Theater—Salzburg's much-loved marionette theater offers operas with spellbinding marionettes and recorded music. Adults and kids alike are mesmerized by the little people on stage (€18-35, June-Sept nearly nightly at 17:00 or 19:30, none on Sun, also 3-4/week in May, some 14:00 matinees, box office open Mon-Sat 9:00-13:00 and 2 hours before shows, near the Mirabell Gardens and Mozart's Residence at Schwarzstrasse 24, tel. 0662/872-406, www.marionetten.at). For a sneak preview, check out the videos playing at the marionette exhibit up in the fortress.

Mozart Dinner Concert—For those who'd like some classical music but would rather not sit through a concert, the recommended Stiftskeller St. Peter restaurant offers a traditional candlelit meal with Mozart's greatest hits performed by a string quartet and singers in historic costumes gavotting among the tables. In this elegant Baroque setting, tourists clap between movements and get three courses of food (from Mozart-era recipes) mixed with three 20-minute courses of crowd-pleasing music (€51, Mozart-lovers with this guidebook pay €42 when booking direct, almost nightly at 20:00, dress is "smart casual," call to reserve at 0662/828-695, www.mozartdinnerconcert.com).

Sound of Salzburg Dinner Show—The show at the recommended Sternbräu Inn is Broadway in a dirndl with tired food. But it's a fun show, and *Sound of Music* fans leave with hands red from clapping. A piano player and a hardworking quartet of singers wearing historical costumes perform an entertaining mix of *S.O.M.* hits and traditional folk songs (€46 for dinner, begins at 19:30). You can also come by at 20:30, pay €32, skip the dinner, and get the show and a drink. Those who book direct (not through a hotel) and pay cash get a 10 percent discount with this

The Sound of Music Debunked

Rather than visit the real-life sights from the life of Maria von Trapp and family, most tourists want to see the places where Hollywood chose to film this fanciful story. Local guides are happy not to burst any *S.O.M.* pilgrim's bubble, but keep these points in mind:

- "Edelweiss" is not a cherished Austrian folk tune or national anthem. Like all the "Austrian" music in *The S.O.M.*, it was composed for Broadway by Rodgers and Hammerstein. It was, however, the last composition that the famed team wrote together, as Hammerstein died in 1960—nine months after the musical opened.

- *The S.O.M.* implies that Maria was devoutly religious throughout her life, but Maria's foster parents raised her as a socialist and atheist. Maria discovered her religious calling while studying to be a teacher. After completing school, she joined the convent not as a nun, but as a novitiate (that is, she hadn't taken her vows yet).

- Maria's position was not as governess to all the children, as portrayed in the musical, but specifically as governess and teacher for the Captain's second-oldest daughter, also called Maria, who was bedridden with rheumatic fever.

- The Captain didn't run a tight domestic ship. In fact, his seven children were as unruly as most. But he did use a whistle to call them—each kid was trained to respond to a certain pitch.

- Though the von Trapp family did have seven children, the show changed all their names and even their genders. Rupert, the eldest child, responded to the often-asked question, "Which one are you?" with a simple, "I'm Liesl!"

- The family didn't escape by hiking to Switzerland (which is a five-hour drive away). Rather, they pretended to go on one of their frequent mountain hikes. With only the possessions in their backpacks, they "hiked" all the way to the train station

book (nightly mid-May–mid-Oct, Griesgasse 23, tel. 0662/826-617, www.soundofsalzburgshow.com).

Music at Mass—Each Sunday morning, three great churches offer a Mass, generally with glorious music. The Salzburg Cathedral is likely your best bet for fine music to worship by (10:00). The Franciscan church—the locals' choice—is enthusiastic about its musical Masses (at 9:00). St. Peter's Church also has music (10:30). See the Salzburg events guide (available at TIs) for details.

Free Brass Band Concert—A traditional brass band plays in the Mirabell Gardens (May–Aug Sun at 10:30 and Wed with lighted fountains at 20:30).

(it was at the edge of their estate) and took a train to Italy. The movie scene showing them climbing into Switzerland was actually filmed near Berchtesgaden, Germany...home to Hitler's Eagle's Nest, and certainly not a smart place to flee to.

- The actual von Trapp family house exists...but it's not the one in the film. The mansion in the movie is actually two different buildings—one used for the front, the other for the back. The interiors were all filmed on Hollywood sets.

- For the film, Boris Levin designed a reproduction of the Nonnberg Abbey courtyard so faithful to the original (down to its cobblestones and stained-glass windows) that many still believe the cloister scenes were really shot at the abbey. And no matter what you hear in Salzburg, the graveyard scene (in which the von Trapps hide from the Nazis) was also filmed on the Fox lot.

- In 1956, a German film producer offered Maria $10,000 for the rights to her book. She asked for royalties, too, and a share of the profits. The agent claimed that German law forbids film companies from paying royalties to foreigners (Maria had by then become a US citizen). She agreed to the contract and unknowingly signed away all film rights to her story. Only a few weeks later, he offered to pay immediately if she would accept $9,000 in cash. Because it was more money than the family had seen in all of their years of singing, she accepted the deal. Later, she discovered the agent had swindled them—no such law existed.

    Rodgers, Hammerstein, and other producers gave the von Trapps a percentage of the royalties, even though they weren't required to—but it was a fraction of what they otherwise would have earned. But Maria wasn't bitter. "The great good the film and the play are doing to individual lives is far beyond money," she said.

Sleeping in Salzburg

Finding a room in Salzburg, even during its music festival (mid-July-Aug), is usually easy. Rates rise significantly (20-30 percent) during the music festival, and sometimes around Easter and Christmas; these higher prices do not appear in the ranges I've listed. Many places charge 10 percent extra for a one-night stay. Remember, to call

Sleep Code

(€1 = about $1.40, country code: 43, area code: 0662)
S = Single, **D** = Double/Twin, **T** = Triple, **Q** = Quad, **b** = bathroom, **s** = shower only. Unless otherwise noted, credit cards are accepted and breakfast is included. All of these places speak English.

To help you sort easily through these listings, I've divided the accommodations into three categories, based on the price for a standard double room with bath:

$$$ Higher Priced—Most rooms €90 or more.
 $$ Moderately Priced—Most rooms between €60-90.
  $ Lower Priced—Most rooms €60 or less.

Prices can change without notice; verify the hotel's current rates online or by email. For other updates, see www .ricksteves.com/update.

Salzburg from Germany, dial 00-43 and then the number (minus the initial zero).

In the New Town, North of the River

These listings, clustering around Linzergasse, are in a pleasant neighborhood (with easy parking) a 15-minute walk from the train station (for directions, see "Arrival in Salzburg," earlier) and a 10-minute walk to the old town. If you're coming from the old town, simply cross the main bridge (Staatsbrücke) to the mostly traffic-free Linzergasse. If driving, exit the highway at Salzburg-Nord, follow Vogelweiderstrasse straight to its end, and turn right.

$$$ Altstadthotel Wolf-Dietrich, around the corner from Linzergasse on pedestrians-only Wolf-Dietrich-Strasse, is well-located (half its rooms overlook St. Sebastian Cemetery). With 27 tastefully plush rooms, it's a good value for a big, stylish hotel (Sb-€80, Db-€120, price depends on size, family deals, €20-40 more during festival, complex pricing but readers of this book get a 10 percent discount on prevailing price—insist on this discount deducted from whatever price is offered that day, elevator, free Internet access and Wi-Fi, pool with loaner swimsuits, sauna, free DVD library, Wolf-Dietrich-Strasse 7, tel. 0662/871-275, fax 0662/871-2759, www.salzburg-hotel.at, office@salzburg-hotel.at). Their annex across the street has 14 equally comfortable rooms (€20 less, no elevator).

$$$ Hotel Trumer Stube, well-located three blocks from the river just off Linzergasse, has 20 clean rooms and is warmly run by the Hirschbichler family (official rates: Sb-€65, Db-€105, Tb-€128, Qb-€147—email and ask for the best Rick Steves cash-only rate; buffet breakfast extra, non-smoking, elevator, free Wi-Fi, easy parking, Bergstrasse 6, tel. 0662/874-776, fax 0662/874-326, www.trumer-stube.at, info@trumer-stube.at; the mom and daughter, both named Marianne, may charm you into extending your Salzburg stay).

$$$ Hotel Goldene Krone, about five blocks from the river, is plain and basic, with 20 big, quiet, creaky, and well-kept rooms. Stay a while in their pleasant cliffside garden (Sb-€69, Db-€119, Tb-€159, Qb-€189, claim your 15 percent discount off these prices with this book, dim lights, elevator, free Wi-Fi, parking-€12/day, Linzergasse 48, tel. 0662/872-300, fax 0662/8723-0066, www.hotel-goldenekrone.com, office@hotel-goldenekrone.com, Günther Hausknost). Günther offers tours (€10/person, 2 hours, 5 people minimum) and a "Rick Steves Two Nights in Salzburg" deal, which covers your room, a 24-hour Salzburg Card, a concert in Mirabell Palace, and a tour with Günther (Sb-€171, Db-€304, Tb-€429, Qb-€532; book on the hotel's website).

$$ Hotel Schwarzes Rössl is a university dorm that becomes a student-run hotel each July, August, and September. The location couldn't be handier. It looks like a normal hotel from the outside, and its 50 rooms, while a bit spartan, are as comfortable as a hotel on the inside (S-€50, Sb-€60, D-€80, Db-€100, Tb-€132, good breakfast, Internet access and Wi-Fi, no rooms rented Oct-June, just off Linzergasse at Priesterhausgasse 6, tel. 0662/874-426, www.academiahotels.at, schwarzes.roessl@academiahotels.at).

$$ Institute St. Sebastian is in a somewhat sterile but very clean historic building next to St. Sebastian Cemetery. From October through June, the institute houses female students from various Salzburg colleges and also rents 40 beds for travelers (men and women). From July through September, the students are gone, and they rent all 100 beds (including 20 twin rooms) to travelers. The building has spacious public areas, a roof garden, a piano that guests are welcome to play, and some of the best rooms and dorm beds in town for the money. The immaculate doubles come with modern baths and head-to-toe twin beds (S-€36, Sb-€44, D-€55, Db-€70, Tb-€84, Qb-€98, includes simple breakfast, elevator, self-service laundry-€4/load; reception open daily July-Sept 7:30-12:00 & 13:00-21:30, Oct-June 8:00-12:00 & 16:00-21:00; Linzergasse 41, enter through arch at #37, tel. 0662/871-386, fax 0662/8713-8685, www.st-sebastian-salzburg.at, office@st-sebastian-salzburg.at). Students like the €21 bunks in 4- to 10-bed dorms (€2 less if you have sheets, no lockout, free lockers, free showers). You'll find self-service kitchens on each floor (fridge space is free; request a key). If you need parking, request it well in advance.

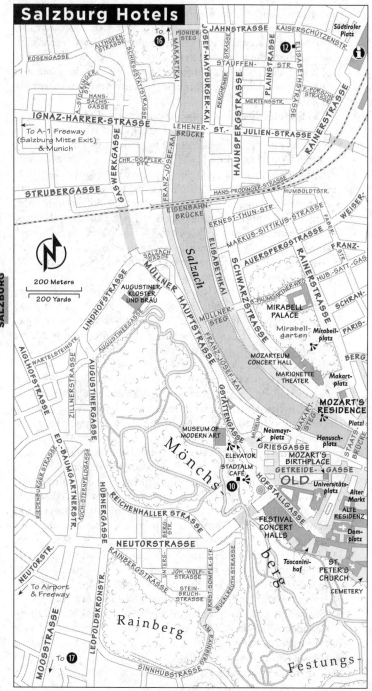

Salzburg Hotels

SALZBURG

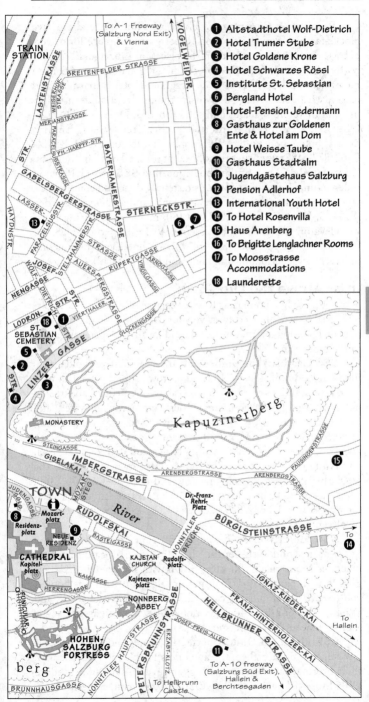

1. Altstadthotel Wolf-Dietrich
2. Hotel Trumer Stube
3. Hotel Goldene Krone
4. Hotel Schwarzes Rössl
5. Institute St. Sebastian
6. Bergland Hotel
7. Hotel-Pension Jedermann
8. Gasthaus zur Goldenen Ente & Hotel am Dom
9. Hotel Weisse Taube
10. Gasthaus Stadtalm
11. Jugendgästehaus Salzburg
12. Pension Adlerhof
13. International Youth Hotel
14. To Hotel Rosenvilla
15. Haus Arenberg
16. To Brigitte Lenglachner Rooms
17. To Moosstrasse Accommodations
18. Launderette

SALZBURG

Pensions on Rupertgasse: These two hotels are about five blocks farther from the river on Rupertgasse, a breeze for drivers but with more street noise than the places on Linzergasse. They're both modern and well-run—good values if you don't mind being a bit away from the old town. **$$$ Bergland Hotel** is charming and classy, with comfortable neo-rustic rooms. It's a modern building and therefore spacious and solid (Sb-€65, Db-€100, Tb-€125, Qb-€155, elevator, pay Internet access, free Wi-Fi, English library, bike rental-€6/day, Rupertgasse 15, tel. 0662/872-318, fax 0662/872-3188, www.berglandhotel.at, office@berglandhotel.at, Kuhn family). The similar, boutique-like **$$$ Hotel-Pension Jedermann,** a few doors down, is tastefully done and comfortable, with an artsy painted-concrete ambience and a backyard garden (Sb-€65, Db-€95, Tb-€120, Qb-€160, much more during festival, elevator, free Internet access and Wi-Fi, Rupertgasse 25, tel. 0662/873-2410, fax 0662/873-2419, www.hotel-jedermann.com, office@hotel-jedermann.com, Herr und Frau Gmachl).

In or Above the Old Town

Most of these hotels are near Residenzplatz. While this area is car-restricted, you're allowed to drive your car in to unload, pick up a map and parking instructions, and head for the €14-per-day garage in the mountain.

$$$ Gasthaus zur Goldenen Ente is in a 600-year-old building with medieval stone arches and narrow stairs. Located above a good restaurant, it's as central as you can be on a pedestrian street in old Salzburg. The 22 rooms are modern and newly renovated, and include classy amenities. While the advertised rates are too high, travelers with this book get 10 percent off (except in July-Aug), and prices may dip lower according to demand. Ulrike, Franziska, and Anita run a tight ship for the absentee owners (most of the year: Sb-€85, Db-€125; late July-Aug and Dec: Sb-€95, Db-€160; extra person-€40, firm mattresses, elevator, free Internet access, Goldgasse 10, tel. 0662/845-622, fax 0662/845-6229, www.ente.at, hotel@ente.at).

$$$ Hotel Weisse Taube has 30 comfortable rooms in a quiet dark-wood 14th-century building, well-located about a block off Mozartplatz (Sb-€69-88, Db with shower-€98-139, bigger Db with bath-€119-172, 10 percent discount with this book if you reserve direct and pay cash, elevator, pay Internet access and Wi-Fi, tel. 0662/842-404, fax 0662/841-783, Kaigasse 9, www.weissetaube.at, hotel@weissetaube.at).

$$$ Hotel am Dom is perfectly located—on Goldgasse a few steps from the cathedral—and offers 15 chic rooms, some with their original wood-beam ceilings (twin Db-€90-160, standard Db-€130-240, "superior" Db-€150-290, air-con, non-smoking, free Internet access and Wi-Fi, Goldgasse 17, tel. 0662/842-765, fax 0662/8427-6555, www.hotelamdom.at, office@hotelamdom.at).

Hostels

For another hostel (on the other side of the river), see "International Youth Hotel," on the next page.

   $ Gasthaus Stadtalm (a.k.a. the *Naturfreundehaus*) is a local version of a mountaineer's hut and a great budget alternative. Snuggled in a forest on the remains of a 15th-century castle wall atop the little mountain overlooking Salzburg, it has magnificent town and mountain views. While the 22 beds are designed-for-backpackers basic, the price and view are the best in town—with the right attitude, it's a fine experience (€18.50/person in 4- and 6-bed dorms, same price for room with double bed; includes breakfast, sheets, and shower; lockers, 2 minutes from top of €2 Mönchsberg elevator, Mönchsberg 19C, tel. & fax 0662/841-729, www.diestadtalm.com, info@diestadtalm.com, Peter). Once you've dropped your bags here, it's a five-minute walk down the cliffside stairs into Toscanini Hof, in the middle of the old town (path always lit).

   $ Jugendgästehaus Salzburg, just steps from the old town center, is nevertheless removed from the bustle. While its dorm rooms are the standard crammed-with-beds variety—and the hallways will bring back high-school memories—the doubles and family rooms are modern, roomy, and bright, and the public spaces are quite pleasant (bed in 8-person dorm-€23; Db, Tb, and Qb available at much higher prices; includes breakfast and sheets, pay Internet access, free Wi-Fi, *The Sound of Music* plays daily, bike rental-€10/day or €6/half-day, free parking, just around the east side of the castle hill at Josef-Preis-Allee 18; from train station, take bus #5 or #25 to the Justizgebäude stop, then head left one block along the bushy wall, cross Petersbrunnstrasse, find shady Josefs-Preis-Alle, and walk a few minutes to the end—the hostel is the big orange/green building on the right; tel. 0662/842-670, fax 0662/841-101, www.jufa.at/salzburg, salzburg@jufa.at). The hotel at the back of the hostel isn't as cheap, but does offer more standard hotel amenities, such as TVs (Db-€110 depending on season, includes breakfast).

Near the Train Station

$$ Pension Adlerhof, a plain and decent old pension, is two blocks in front of the train station (left off Kaiserschutzenstrasse), but a 15-minute walk from the sightseeing action. It has a quirky staff, a boring location, and 30 stodgy-but-spacious rooms (Sb-€56, Db-€80, Tb-€115, Qb-€130, price varies a bit with the season and size of room, cash only, elevator, pay Internet access and free

Wi-Fi, limited free parking, Elisabethstrasse 25, tel. 0662/875-236, fax 0662/873-663, www.gosalzburg.com, adlerhof@pension-adlerhof.at).

$ International Youth Hotel, a.k.a. the "Yo-Ho," is the most lively, handy, and American of Salzburg's hostels. This backpacker haven is a youthful and easygoing place that speaks English first; has cheap meals, 186 beds, lockers, tour discounts, and no curfew; plays *The Sound of Music* free daily at 10:30; runs a lively bar; and welcomes anyone of any age. The noisy atmosphere and lack of a curfew can make it hard to sleep (€18-19/person in 4- to 8-bed dorms, €21-22 in dorms with bathrooms, D-€55, Ds-€65, Q-€72, Qs-€81, includes sheets, cheap breakfast, pay Internet access, free Wi-Fi, laundry-€4 wash and dry, 6 blocks from station toward Linzergasse and 6 blocks from river at Paracelsusstrasse 9, tel. 0662/879-649, fax 0662/878-810, www.yoho.at, office@yoho.at).

Four-Star Hotels in Residential Neighborhoods away from the Center

If you want plush furnishings, spacious public spaces, generous balconies, gardens, and free parking, consider the following places. These two modern hotels in nondescript residential neighborhoods are a fine value if you don't mind the 15-minute walk from the old town. While not ideal for train travelers, drivers in need of no-stress comfort for a home base should consider these (see map on page 210).

$$$ Hotel Rosenvilla, close to the river, offers 16 rooms with bright furnishings, surrounded by a leafy garden (Sb-€79-108, Db-€135-165, bigger Db-€145-199, Db suite-€168-255, at least €30 more during festival, free Wi-Fi, Höfelgasse 4, tel. 0662/621-765, fax 0662/625-2308, www.rosenvilla.com, hotel@rosenvilla.com).

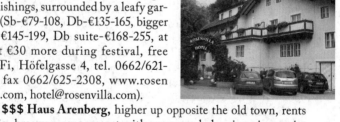

$$$ Haus Arenberg, higher up opposite the old town, rents 17 big, breezy rooms—most with generous balconies—in a quiet garden setting (Sb-€85-105, Db-€129-165, Tb-€149-176, Qb-€158-185, higher prices are during festival, Blumensteinstrasse 8, tel. 0662/640-097, fax 0662/640-0973, www.arenberg-salzburg.at, info@arenberg-salzburg.at, family Leobacher).

Private Rooms (Privatzimmer)

These are generally roomy and comfortable, and come with a good breakfast, easy parking, and tourist information. Off-season, competition softens prices. While they are a bus ride from town, with a €4.20 transit day pass *(Tageskarte)* and the frequent service, this shouldn't keep you away (see map on page 202). In fact, most homeowners will happily pick you up at the train station if you simply telephone them and ask. Most will also do laundry for a small fee for those staying at least two nights. I've listed prices for two nights or more—if staying only one night, expect a 10 percent surcharge. Most push tours and concerts to make money on the side. As they are earning a commission, if you go through them, you'll probably lose the discount I've negotiated for my readers who go direct.

Beyond the Train Station

$ Brigitte Lenglachner rents eight basic, well-cared-for rooms in her home in a quiet suburban-feeling neighborhood that's a 25-minute walk, 10-minute bike ride, or easy bus ride away from the center. Frau Lenglachner serves breakfast in the garden (in good weather) and happily provides plenty of local information and advice (S-€25, D-€40, Db-€49, Tb-€68, Qb-€96, 5b-€113; apartment with kitchen—Db-€56, Tb-€95, Qb-€110; apartment requires minimum 3-night stay, easy and free parking, Scheibenweg 8, tel. & fax 0662/438-044, www.bei-brigitte.at, bedandbreakfast 4u@yahoo.de). It's a 10-minute walk from the station: Head for the river, cross the pedestrian Pioneer Bridge (Pioniersteg), turn right, and walk along the river to the third street (Scheibenweg). Turn left, and it's halfway down on the right.

On Moosstrasse

The busy street called Moosstrasse, which runs southwest of Mönchsberg (behind the mountain and away from the old town center), is lined with farmhouses offering rooms. Handy bus #21 connects Moosstrasse to the center frequently (Mon-Fri 4/hour until 19:00, Sat 4/hour until 17:00, evenings and Sun 2/hour, 20 minutes). To get to these pensions from the train station, take bus #1, #5, #6, or #25 to Makartplatz, where you'll change to #21. If you're coming from the old town, catch bus #21 from Hanuschplatz, just downstream of the Staatsbrücke bridge near the *Tabak* kiosk. Buy a €1.90 *Einzelkarte-Kernzone* ticket (for one trip) or a €4.20 *Tageskarte* (day pass, good for 24 hours) from the street-side machine and punch it when you board the bus. The bus stop you use for each place is included in the following listings. If you're driving from the center, go through the tunnel, continue straight on Neutorstrasse, and take the fourth left onto Moosstrasse. Drivers exit the autobahn at *Süd* and then head in the direction of *Grodig*. Each place can recommend a favorite Moosstrasse eatery (Reiterhof, at #151, is particularly popular).

 $$ Pension Bloberger Hof, while more a hotel than a pension, is comfortable and friendly, with a peaceful, rural location and 20 farmer-plush, good-value rooms. It's the farthest out, but reached by the same bus #21 from the center. Inge and her daughter Sylvia offer a 10 percent discount to those who have this book, reserve direct, and pay cash (Sb-€55-70, Db-€75-80, big new Db with balcony-€95-100, Db suite-€120, extra bed-€20, 10 percent extra for one-night stays, family apartment with kitchen, non-smoking, free Internet access and Wi-Fi, restaurant for guests, free loaner bikes, free station pickup if staying 3 nights, Hammerauer Strasse 4, bus stop: Hammerauer Strasse, tel. 0662/830-227, fax 0662/827-061, www.blobergerhof.at, office@blobergerhof.at).

$$ Haus Reichl, with three good rooms at the end of a long lane, feels the most remote. Franziska offers free loaner bikes for guests (20-minute pedal to the center) and bakes fresh cakes most days (Sb-€36-45, Db-€58-64, Tb-€75-84, Qb-€92-104, cash preferred, doubles and triples have balcony and view, all have in-room tea/coffee, non-smoking, between Ballwein and Bankhammer B&Bs, 200 yards down Reiterweg to #52, bus stop: Gsengerweg, tel. & fax 0662/826-248, www.privatzimmer.at/haus-reichl, haus.reichl@telering.at).

$ Frau Ballwein offers four cozy, charming, and fresh rooms in two buildings, some with intoxicating-view balconies (Sb-€35-45, Db-€53-64, Tb-€75-85, Qb-€80-95, 2-bedroom apartment for up to 5 people-€95-110, prices depend on season, family deals, cash only, farm-fresh breakfasts amid her hanging teapot collection, non-smoking, small pool, 2 free loaner bikes, free parking, Moosstrasse 69-A, bus stop: Gsengerweg, tel. & fax 0662/824-029, www.haus-ballwein.at, haus.ballwein@gmx.net).

$ Helga Bankhammer rents four nondescript rooms in a farmhouse, with a real dairy farm out back (D-€44, Db-€55, no surcharge for one-night stays, family deals, non-smoking, laundry about €6/load, Moosstrasse 77, bus stop: Marienbad, tel. & fax 0662/830-067, www.privatzimmer.at/helga.bankhammer, bankhammer@aon.at).

Eating in Salzburg

In the Old Town

Salzburg boasts many inexpensive, fun, and atmospheric eateries. Most of these restaurants are centrally located in the old town, famous with visitors but also enjoyed by locals.

Gasthaus zum Wilden Mann is *the* place if the weather's bad and you're in the mood for *Hofbräu* atmosphere and a hearty, cheap meal at a shared table in one small, smoky, well-antlered room. Notice the 1899 flood photo on the wall. For a quick lunch, get the *Bauernschmaus*, a mountain of dumplings, kraut, and peasant's meats (€11.50). While they have a few outdoor tables, the atmosphere is all indoors, and the menu is not great for hot-weather food. Owner Robert—who runs the restaurant with Schwarzenegger-like energy—enjoys fostering a convivial ambience (you'll share tables with strangers) and serving fresh traditional cuisine at great prices. I simply love this place (€8.50 two-course lunch specials, €10-12 daily specials posted on the wall, kitchen open Mon-Sat 11:00-21:00, closed Sun, 2 minutes from Mozart's Birthplace, enter from Getreidegasse 22 or Griesgasse 17, tel. 0662/841-787).

Stiftskeller St. Peter has been in business for more than 1,000 years—it was mentioned in the biography of Charlemagne. It's classy and high-end touristy, serving uninspired traditional Austrian cuisine. Through the centuries, they've learned to charge for each piece of bread and don't serve free tap water (€10-27 meals, daily 11:30-22:30, indoor/outdoor seating, next to St. Peter's Church at foot of Mönchsberg, restaurant tel. 0662/841-268). They host the Mozart Dinner Concert described on page 205.

St. Paul's Stub'n Beer Garden is tucked secretly away under the castle with a decidedly untouristy atmosphere. The food is better than a beer hall, and a young, bohemian-chic clientele fills its two troll-like rooms and its idyllic tree-shaded garden. *Kasnock'n* is a tasty mountaineers' pasta with cheese served in an iron pan with a side salad for €9—it's enough for two (€6-12 daily specials, €7-15 plates, Mon-Sat 17:00-22:30, open later for drinks only, closed Sun, Herrengasse 16, tel. 0662/843-220).

Zirkelwirt serves modern Mediterranean, Italian, and Austrian dishes, a daily fish special, and always a good vegetarian option. It's an old *Gasthaus* dining room with a medieval tiki-hut terrace a block off Mozartplatz, yet a world away from the tourism of the old town. While the waitstaff, music, and vibe feel young, it attracts Salzburgers of all ages (€9-15 plates, cheese dumplings and daily fish special, nightly 17:00-24:00, Pfeifergasse 14, tel. 0662/843-472).

Fisch Krieg Restaurant, on the river where the fishermen used to sell their catch, is a great value. They serve fast, fresh, and inexpensive fish in a casual dining room—where trees grow through the ceiling—as well as great riverside seating (€2 fish-wiches to go, self-serve €7 meals, salad bar, Mon-Fri 8:30-18:30, Sat 8:30-13:00, closed Sun, Hanuschplatz 4, tel. 0662/843-732).

Sternbräu Inn, a sloppy, touristy Austrian food circus, is a sprawling complex of popular eateries (traditional, Italian, self-serve, and vegetarian) in a cheery garden setting. Explore both courtyards before choosing a seat (Bürgerstube is classic, most restaurants open daily 9:00-24:00 with food served until 23:00, enter from Getreidegasse 34, tel. 0662/842-140). One fancy, air-conditioned room hosts the Sound of Salzburg dinner show

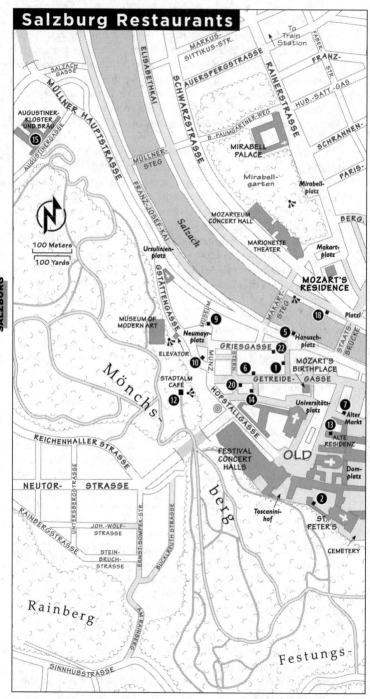

Salzburg Restaurants

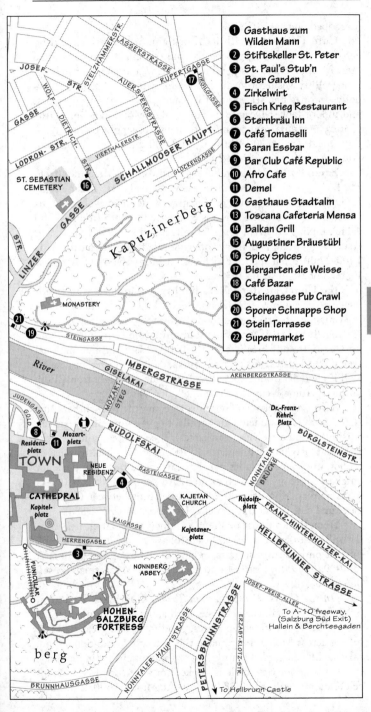

1. Gasthaus zum Wilden Mann
2. Stiftskeller St. Peter
3. St. Paul's Stub'n Beer Garden
4. Zirkelwirt
5. Fisch Krieg Restaurant
6. Sternbräu Inn
7. Café Tomaselli
8. Saran Essbar
9. Bar Club Café Republic
10. Afro Cafe
11. Demel
12. Gasthaus Stadtalm
13. Toscana Cafeteria Mensa
14. Balkan Grill
15. Augustiner Bräustübl
16. Spicy Spices
17. Biergarten die Weisse
18. Café Bazar
19. Steingasse Pub Crawl
20. Sporer Schnapps Shop
21. Stein Terrasse
22. Supermarket

SALZBURG

(described on page 205).

Café Tomaselli (with its Kiosk annex and terrace seating across the way) has long been Salzburg's top place to see and be seen. While pricey, it is good for lingering and people-watching. Tomaselli serves light meals and lots of drinks, keeps long hours daily, and has fine seating on the square, a view terrace upstairs, and indoor tables. Despite its fancy inlaid wood paneling, 19th-century portraits, and chandeliers, it's surprisingly low-key (€3-7 light meals, daily 7:00-21:00, until 24:00 during music festival, Alter Markt 9, tel. 0662/844-488).

Saran Essbar is the product of hardworking Mr. Saran (from the Punjab), who cooks and serves with his heart. This delightful little eatery casts a rich orange glow under medieval vaults. Its fun menu is small (Mr. Saran is committed to both freshness and value), mixing Austrian (great schnitzel and strudel), Italian, and Asian vegetarian, and always offering salads (€10-15 meals, daily 11:00-22:00, often open later, a block off Mozartplatz at Judengasse 10, tel. 0662/846-628).

Bar Club Café Republic, a hip hangout for local young people near the end of Getreidegasse, feels like a theater lobby during intermission. It serves good food with smoky indoor and outdoor seating. It's ideal if you want something mod, untouristy, and un-wursty (trendy breakfasts 8:00-18:00, Asian and international menu, €9-15 plates, lots of hard drinks, daily until late, music with a DJ Fri and Sat from 23:00, salsa dance club Tue night from 21:00, no cover, Anton Neumayr Platz 2, tel. 0662/841-613).

Afro Cafe, between Getreidegasse and the Mönchsberg lift, is a hit with local students. Its agenda: to put a fun spin on African cuisine (adapted to European tastes). It serves tea, coffee, cocktails, and tasty food with a dose of '70s funk and a healthy sense of humor. The menu includes pan-African specialties—try the spicy chicken couscous—as well as standard soups and salads (€9-13 main courses, Mon-Fri 9:00-24:00, closed Sun, between Getreidegasse and cliff face at Bürgerspitalplatz 5, tel. 0662/844-888).

Demel, an outpost of Vienna's famed chocolatier, is a wonderland of desserts that are as beautiful as they are delectable. Sink into the pink couches upstairs, or have them box up a treat for later (daily 9:00-19:00, near TI and cathedral at Mozartplatz 2, tel. 0662/840-358).

On the Cliffs Above the Old Town: **Gasthaus Stadtalm,** Salzburg's mountaineers' hut, sits high above the old town on the edge of the cliff with cheap prices, good food, and great views. If hiking across Mönchsberg, make this your goal (traditional food, salads, cliffside garden seating or cozy-mountain-hut indoor seating—one indoor view table is booked for a decade of New Year's celebrations, daily 10:00-18:00, July-Aug until 23:00, 2 minutes from top of €3.20 round-trip Mönchsberg elevator, also reachable by stairs from Toscanini Hof, Mönchsberg 19C, tel. 0662/841-729, Peter). For the location, see map on page 218.

Eating Cheaply in the Old Town

Toscana Cafeteria Mensa is the students' lunch canteen, fast and cheap—with indoor seating and a great courtyard for sitting outside with students and teachers instead of tourists. They serve a daily soup-and-main course special for €5 (Mon-Fri 8:30-18:00, hot meals served 11:00-13:30 only, closed Sat-Sun, behind the Old Residenz, in the courtyard opposite Sigmund-Haffner-Gasse 16).

Sausage stands *(Würstelstände)* serve the town's favorite "fast food." The best stands (like those on Universitätsplatz) use the same boiling water all day, which gives the weenies more flavor. The Salzburgers' favorite spicy sausage is sold at the 60-year-old **Balkan Grill,** run by chatty Frau Ebner (€3; survey the five spicy options—described in English—and choose a number; takeaway only, steady and sturdy local crowd, daily 11:00-19:00, hours vary with demand, hiding down the tunnel at Getreidegasse 33 across from Eisgrotte).

Picnickers will appreciate the bustling morning **produce market** (daily except Sun) on Universitätsplatz behind Mozart's Birthplace, as well as the well-stocked **Billa supermarket** (Mon-Fri 7:15-19:30, Sat 7:15-18:00, closed Sun), just across the street from the recommended Fisch Krieg Restaurant on Griesgasse.

Away from the Center

Augustiner Bräustübl, a huge 1,000-seat beer garden within a monk-run brewery in the Kloster Mülln, is rustic and raw. On busy nights, it's like a Munich beer hall with no music but the

volume turned up. When it's cool outside, you'll enjoy a historic setting inside beer-sloshed and smoke-stained halls. On balmy evenings, it's like a Renoir painting—but with beer breath—under chestnut trees. Local students mix with tourists eating hearty slabs of schnitzel with their fingers or cold meals from the self-serve picnic counter, while children frolic on the playground kegs. For your beer: Pick up a half-liter or full-liter mug, pay the lady (*schank* means self-serve price, *bedienung* is the price with waiter service), wash your mug, give Mr. Keg your receipt and empty mug, and you will be made happy. Waiters only bring beer; they don't bring food—instead, go up the stairs, survey the hallway of deli counters, and assemble your own meal (or, as long as you buy a drink, you can bring in a picnic). Classic pretzels from the bakery and spiraled, salty radishes make great beer even better. For dessert—after a visit to the strudel kiosk—enjoy the incomparable floodlit view of old Salzburg from the nearby Müllnersteg pedestrian bridge and a riverside stroll home (open daily 15:00-23:00, Augustinergasse 4, tel. 0662/431-246).

Getting There: It's about a 15-minute walk along the river (with the river on your right) from the Staatsbrücke bridge. After passing the pedestrian Müllnersteg bridge, just after Café am Kai, follow the stairs up to a busy street, and cross it. From here, either continue up more stairs into the trees and around the small church (for a scenic approach to the monastery), or stick to the sidewalk as it curves around to Augustinergasse. Either way, your goal is the huge yellow building. Don't be fooled by second-rate gardens serving the same beer nearby.

North of the River, near Recommended Linzergasse Hotels

Spicy Spices is a trippy vegetarian-Indian restaurant where Suresh Syal (a.k.a. "Mr. Spicy") serves tasty curry and rice, samosas, organic salads, vegan soups, and fresh juices. It's a *namaste* kind of place, where everything's proudly organic (€6.50 specials, Mon-Fri 10:30-21:30, Sat-Sun 12:00-21:30, takeout available, Wolf-Dietrich-Strasse 1, tel. 0662/870-712).

Biergarten die Weisse, close to the hotels on Rupertgasse and away from the tourists, is a longtime hit with the natives. If a beer hall can be happening, this one—modern yet with antlers—is it. Their famously good beer is made right there; favorites include their fizzy wheat beer *(Weisse)* and their seasonal beers (on request). Enjoy the beer with their good, cheap traditional food in the great garden seating, or in the wide variety of indoor rooms—sports bar, young and noisy, or older and more elegant (daily specials, Mon-Sat 10:00-24:00, closed Sun, Rupertgasse 10, east of Bayerhamerstrasse, tel. 0662/872-246).

Café Bazar, overlooking the river between Mirabell Gardens and the Staatsbrücke bridge, is as close as you'll get to a Vienna coffee house in Salzburg. It's *the* venerable spot for a classy drink with an old-town-and-castle view (light meals, Mon-Sat 7:30-23:00, Sun 9:00-18:00, Schwarzstrasse 3, tel. 0662/874-278).

Steingasse Pub Crawl

For a fun post-concert activity, crawl through medieval Steingasse's trendy pubs (all open until the wee hours). This is a local and hip scene, but accessible to older tourists: dark bars filled with well-dressed Salzburgers lazily smoking cigarettes and talking philosophy as avant-garde Euro-pop throbs on the soundtrack. Most of the pubs are in cellar-like caves...extremely atmospheric. (For more on Steingasse, see page 199.) These four pubs are all within about 100 yards of each other. Start at the Linzergasse end of Steingasse. As they are quite different, survey all before choosing your spot.

Pepe Cocktail Bar, with Mexican decor and Latin music, serves Mexican snacks *con* cocktails (nightly 19:00-3:00 in the morning, live DJs Fri-Sat from 19:00, Steingasse 3, tel. 0662/873-662).

Shrimps Bar-Restaurant, next door and less claustrophobic, is more a restaurant than a bar, serving creative international dishes (spicy shrimp sandwiches and salads, Mon-Sat 17:30-24:00, closed Sun, Steingasse 5, tel. 0662/874-484).

Saiten Sprung wins the "Best Atmosphere" award. The door is kept closed to keep out the crude and rowdy. Ring the bell and enter its hellish interior—lots of stone and red decor, with mountains of melted wax beneath age-old candlesticks and a classic soul music ambience. Stelios, who speaks English with Greek charm, serves cocktails, fine wine, and wine-friendly Italian antipasti (nightly 21:00-4:00 in the morning, Steingasse 11, tel. 0662/881-377).

Fridrich, just next door, is an intimate little place under an 11th-century vault, with lots of mirrors and a silver ceiling fan. Bernd Fridrich is famous for his martinis and passionate about Austrian wines, and has a tattered collection of vinyl that seems to keep the 1970s alive. He serves little dishes to complement the focus, which is socializing and drinking (€5-12 small dishes, Thu-Mon from 18:00 in summer, from 17:00 in winter, closed Tue-Wed, Steingasse 15, tel. 0662/876-218).

Salzburg Connections

By train, Salzburg is the first stop over the German-Austrian border. This means that if Salzburg is your only stop in Austria, and you're using a railpass that covers Germany (including the Bayern-Ticket) but not Austria, you don't have to pay extra or add Austria to your pass to get here.

From Salzburg by Train to: Berchtesgaden (hourly, 45-60 minutes; bus #840 is easier—hourly, 45 minutes, buses leave across from Salzburg train station and also stop in Mirabellplatz and near Mozartplatz), **Munich** (2/hour, 1.5-2 hours), **Füssen**

(roughly hourly, 4 hours, 1-2 changes), **Reutte,** Austria (hourly, 5 hours, change either in Munich and Kempten, or in Innsbruck and Garmisch), **Nürnberg** (hourly with change in Munich, 3 hours), **Hallstatt,** Austria (hourly, 50 minutes to Attnang Puchheim, 20-minute wait, then 1.5 hours to Hallstatt), **Innsbruck,** Austria (direct every 2 hours, 2 hours), **Vienna,** Austria (2/hour, 2.5-3 hours), **Ljubljana,** Slovenia (every 2 hours, 4.25-5 hours, some with change in Villach), **Prague,** Czech Republic (7/day, 6.5-7.5 hours, via Linz and České Budějovice, no decent overnight connection), **Interlaken,** Switzerland (7/day, 7.5-8 hours, 2-3 changes), **Florence,** Italy (4/day, 8-8.5 hours, 2 changes, 1 overnight option via Villach). Austrian train info: Austrian tel. 051-717 (to get an operator, dial 2, then 2), from Germany call 00-43-51-717, www .oebb.at. German train info: tel. 0180-599-6633, from Austria call 00-49-180-599-6633, www.bahn.com.

Berchtesgaden

This alpine ski town, just across the border from Salzburg in a finger of German territory that pokes south into Austria, is famous for its fjord-like lake and its mountaintop Nazi retreat. Long before its association with Hitler, Berchtesgaden (BERKH-tehsgah-dehn) was one of the classic Romantic corners of Germany. In fact, Hitler's propagandists capitalized on the Führer's love of this region to establish the notion that the native Austrian was truly German at heart. Today visitors cruise up the romantic Königssee to get in touch with the soul of Bavarian Romanticism; ride a bus up to Hitler's mountain retreat (5,500 feet); see the remains of the Nazis' elaborate last-ditch bunkers; and ride an old miners' train into the mountain to learn all about salt mining in the region.

Getting There

Berchtesgaden is only 15 miles from Salzburg. The quickest way there **from Salzburg** is by bus #840 from the Salzburg train station (runs almost hourly Mon-Fri, 6/day Sat-Sun, usually at :15 past the hour, 45 minutes, buy tickets from driver, €9.60 *Tageskarte* day pass covers your round-trip plus most local buses in Berchtesgaden—except bus #849 up to the Eagle's Nest, last bus back leaves Berchtesgaden at 18:15, check schedules at www.albus.at and click "Linienverkehr"). While the Salzburg station is undergoing renovation, buses aren't necessarily leaving from the main bus platforms out front—ask around (on my last visit, bus #840 left from stall 6/Forum, beyond the bike racks and across the street). You can also catch bus #840 from the middle of Salzburg—after leaving the station, it stops a few minutes later on Mirabellplatz, and then in Salzburg's old town (on Rudolfskai, near Mozartplatz).

Coming **from Munich,** it's simplest to reach Berchtesgaden by train (almost hourly, 3 hours, change in Freilassing). You can also get to Berchtesgaden from Salzburg by train via Freilassing, but it takes twice as long as the bus and is less scenic.

Planning Your Time

The Nazi and Hitler-related sites outside Berchtesgaden are the town's main draw. Berchtesgaden also has salt mines (similar to the Hallein salt mine tour—see page 203) and a romantic, pristine lake called Königssee (extremely popular with less-adventurous Germans). Plan on a full day from Salzburg, including the drive or bus ride there and back. Drivers and those taking bus tours from Salzburg can do everything in one busy day trip; otherwise I'd skip the salt mines and possibly the lake trip. If you're visiting Berchtesgaden on your way between Salzburg and points in Germany, you can leave luggage in lockers at the Berchtesgaden train station during your visit.

Remote little Berchtesgaden (pop. 7,500) can be inundated with Germans during peak season, when you may find yourself in a traffic jam of tourists desperately trying to turn their money into fun.

Orientation to Berchtesgaden

Buses from Salzburg to Berchtesgaden stop in front of the town's train station, which—though sorely dilapidated—is worth a stop for its luggage lockers (along the train platform), WC (free, also near platform), and history (specifically, its vintage 1937 Nazi architecture and the murals in the main hall). The oversized station was built to accommodate (and intimidate) the hordes of Hitler fans, who flocked here in hopes of seeing the Führer. The building next to the station, just beyond the round tower, was Hitler's own V.I.P. reception area.

Tourist Information

The TI is across from the train station, in the yellow building with green shutters (mid-June-Sept Mon-Fri 8:30-18:00, Sat 9:00-17:00, Sun 9:00-15:00; Oct-mid-June Mon-Fri 8:30-17:00, Sat 9:00-12:00, closed Sun; German tel. 08652/9670, from Austria call 00-49-8652-9670, www.berchtesgadener-land.info). Pick up a local map, and consider the 30-page local-bus schedule *(Fahrplan)* if you'll be hopping more than one bus.

Getting Around Berchtesgaden

None of the sights I list are within easy walking distance from the station, but they're all connected by convenient local buses, which use the station as a hub (all these buses—except the shuttle between the Obersalzberg Documentation Center and the Eagle's Nest chalet—are free with the €9.60 *Tageskarte* day pass from Salzburg; timetables at www.rvo-bus.de, or call 08652/94480). You'll want to note departure times and frequencies while still at the station, or pick up a schedule at the TI.

From the train station, buses #840 (the same line as the bus from Salzburg) and #837 go to the salt mines (a 20-minute walk otherwise). Bus #838 goes to the Nazi Documentation Center, and bus #841 goes to the Königssee.

Tours in Berchtesgaden

Eagle's Nest Historical Tours—For 20 years, David and Christine Harper—who rightly consider this visit more an educational opportunity than simple sightseeing—have organized thoughtful tours of the Hitler-related sites near Berchtesgaden. Their bus tours, always led by native English speakers, depart from the TI, opposite the Berchtesgaden train station. Tours start by driving through the remains of the Nazis' Obersalzberg complex, then visit the bunkers underneath the Documentation Center, and end with a guided visit to the Eagle's Nest (€50/ person, €1 discount with this book, English only, daily at 13:15 mid-May-late Oct, 4 hours, 25 people maximum, reservations strongly recommended, German tel. 08652/64971, from Austria call 00-49-8652-64971, www.eagles-nest-tours.com). While the price is €50, your actual cost for the guiding is only about €23, as the tour takes care of your transport and admissions, not to mention relieving you of having to figure out the local buses up to Obersalzberg. Coming from Salzburg, you can take the 10:15 or 11:15 bus to Berchtesgaden, eat a picnic lunch, take the tour, then return on the 18:15 bus from Berchtesgaden, which gets you back to Salzburg at 19:00. If you're visiting near the beginning or end of the season, be aware that tours will be cancelled if it's snowing at the Eagle's Nest (as that makes the twisty, precipitous mountain roads too dangerous to drive). David and Christine also arrange off-season tours, though the Eagle's Nest isn't open for visitors in winter (€100/up to 4 people; see website for details).

Bus Tours from Salzburg—**Bob's Special Tours,** based in Salzburg, make it easy to see all the sights described here on one busy day trip in a cheerful minibus, and offers a €10 discount with this book. **Panorama Tours,** which usually runs larger buses, also offers excursions to Berchtesgaden (€5 discount with this book). For more information on both of these, see page 181.

Sights in Berchtesgaden

▲▲▲Nazi Sites near Berchtesgaden

Early in his career as a wannabe tyrant, Adolf Hitler had a radical friend who liked to vacation in Berchtesgaden, and through him

 Hitler came to know and love this dramatic corner of Bavaria. Berchtesgaden's part-Bavarian, part-Austrian character held a special appeal to the Austrian-German Hitler. In the 1920s, just out of prison, he checked into an alpine hotel in Obersalzberg, three miles uphill from Berchtesgaden, to finish work on his memoir and Nazi primer, *Mein Kampf.* Because it was here that he claimed to be inspired and laid out his vision, some call Obersalzberg the "cradle of the Third Reich."

In the 1930s, after becoming the German Chancellor, Hitler chose Obersalzberg to build his mountain retreat, a supersized alpine farmhouse called the Berghof. His handlers crafted Hitler's image here—surrounded by nature, gently receiving alpine flowers from adoring little children, lounging around with farmers in lederhosen...no modern arms industry, no big-time industrialists, no ugly extermination camps. In reality, Obersalzberg was home to much more than Hitler's alpine chalet. It was a huge compound of 80 buildings—built largely by forced labor and fenced off from the public after 1936—where the major decisions leading up to World War II were hatched. Hitler himself spent about a third of his time at the Berghof, hosted world leaders in the compound, and later had it prepared for his last stand.

Some mistakenly call the entire area "Hitler's Eagle's Nest." But that name actually belongs only to the Kehlsteinhaus, a small mountaintop chalet on a 6,000-foot peak that juts up two miles south of Obersalzberg. (A visiting diplomat humorously dubbed it the "Eagle's Nest," and the name stuck.) In 1939, it was given to the Führer for his 50th birthday. While a fortune was spent building this perch and the road up to it, Hitler, who was afraid of heights, visited only 14 times. Hitler's mistress, Eva Braun, though, liked to hike up to the Eagle's Nest to sunbathe.

In April of 1945, Britain's Royal Air Force bombed the Obersalzberg compound nearly flat, but missed the difficult-to-target Eagle's Nest entirely. Almost all of what survived the bombing at Obersalzberg was blown up in 1952 by the Allies, who wanted

Near Berchtesgaden

to leave nothing as a magnet for future neo-Nazi pilgrims before turning the site over to the German government. The most extensive surviving remains are of the Nazis' bunker system, intended to serve as a last resort for the regime as the Allies closed in. In the 1990s, a museum, the Obersalzberg Documentation Center, was built on top of one of the bunkers. The museum and bunker, plus the never-destroyed Eagle's Nest, are the two Nazi sites worth seeing near Berchtesgaden.

Obersalzberg Documentation Center and Bunker—To reach the most interesting part of this site, walk through the museum and down the stairs into the vast and complex bunker system. Construction began in 1943, after the Battle of Stalingrad ended the Nazi aura of invincibility. This is a professionally engineered underground town, which held meeting rooms, offices, archives for the government, and lavish living quarters for Hitler—all con-

nected by four miles of tunnels cut through solid rock by
slave labor. You can't visit all
of it, and what you can see was
stripped and looted bare after
the war. But enough is left
that you can wander among
the concrete and marvel at
megalomania gone mad.

The museum above,
which has almost no actual artifacts, is designed primarily for
German students and others who want to learn and understand
their still-recent history. There's little English, but you can rent the
€2 English audioguide.

Cost and Hours: €3 covers both museum and bunker; April-
Oct daily 9:00-17:00; Nov-March Tue-Sun 10:00-15:00, closed
Mon; last entry one hour before closing, allow 1.5 hours for visit,
German tel. 08652/947-960, from Austria tel. 00-49-8652-947-
960, www.obersalzberg.de.

Getting There: Reach the Documentation Center on bus
#838 from Berchtesgaden's train station (Mon-Fri almost hourly,
Sat-Sun 4/day, 12 minutes, 5-minute walk from Obersalzberg
stop).

Eagle's Nest (Kehlsteinhaus)—Today, the chalet that Hitler
ignored is basically a three-room, reasonably priced restaurant

with a scenic terrace, 100 yards
below the summit of a mountain. You could say it's like any
alpine hiking hut, just more
massively built. On a nice day,
the views are magnificent. If
it's fogged in (which it often is),
most people won't find it worth
coming up here (except on David
and Christine Harper's tours—described earlier—which can make
the building come to life even without a view). Bring a jacket, and
prepare for crowds in summer (less crowded if you go early or late
in the day).

From the upper bus stop, a finely crafted tunnel (which will
have you humming the *Get Smart* TV theme song) leads to the
original polished brass elevator, which takes you the last 400 feet
up to the Eagle's Nest. Wander into the fancy back dining room
(the best-preserved from Hitler's time), where you can see the
once-sleek marble fireplace chipped up by souvenir-seeking troops
in 1945.

Cost and Hours: Free, generally open mid-May-late Oct,

snowfall sometimes forces a later opening or earlier closing.

Getting There: The only way to reach the Eagle's Nest—even if you have your own car—is by specially equipped bus #849, which leaves from the Documentation Center and climbs steeply up the one-way, private road—Germany's highest (every 25 minutes, 15 minutes, €15.50 round-trip, *Tageskarte* day passes not valid, buy ticket from windows, last bus up 16:00, last bus down 16:50, free parking at Documentation Center).

▲Salt Mines

At the Berchtesgaden salt mines, you put on traditional miners' outfits, get on funny little trains, and zip deep into the mountain. For two hours (which includes time to get into and back out of your miner's gear), you'll cruise subterranean lakes; slide speedily down two long, slick, wooden banisters; and learn how they mined salt so long ago. Call for crowd-avoidance advice. When the weather gets bad, this place is mobbed. You can buy a ticket early and browse through the town until your appointed tour time. Tours are in German, while English-speakers get audioguides.

Cost and Hours: €15, daily May-Oct 9:00-17:00, Nov-April 11:30-15:00—these are last-entry times, German tel. 08652/600220, from Austria dial 00-49-8652-600220, www.salzzeitreise.de.

Getting There: The mines are a 20-minute walk or quick bus ride (#837 or #840) from the Berchtesgaden station; ask the driver to let you off at the Salzbergwerk stop. (Since buses coming from Salzburg pass here on the way into Berchtesgaden, you can also simply hop off at the mines before getting into town, instead of backtracking from the station.)

▲Königssee

Three miles south of Berchtesgaden, the idyllic Königssee stretches like a fjord through pristine mountain scenery to the dramatically situated Church of St. Bartholomä and beyond. To get to the lake from Berchtesgaden, hop on bus #841 (about hourly from train station to boat dock), or take the scenically woodsy, reasonably flat 1.25-hour walk (well-signed). Drivers pay €3 to park.

Most visitors simply glide scenically for 35 minutes on the silent, electronically propelled **boat** to the church, enjoy that peaceful setting, then glide back. Boats, going at a sedate Bavarian speed and filled with Germans chuckling at the captain's commentary, leave with demand—generally 2-4 per hour (€13 round-trip, German tel. 08652/96360, from Austria dial 00-49-8652-96360, www.seenschifffahrt.de). At a rock cliff midway through the journey, your captain stops, and the first mate pulls out a trumpet to demonstrate the fine echo.

The remote, red-onion-domed **Church of St. Bartholomä** (once home of a monastery, then a hunting lodge of the Bavarian royal family) is surrounded by a fine beer garden, rustic fishermen's pub, and inviting lakeside trails. The family next to St. Bartholomä's lives in the middle of this national park and has a license to fish—so very fresh trout is the lunchtime favorite.

BADEN-BADEN and the BLACK FOREST

Baden-Baden • Freiburg • Staufen • Best of the Black Forest

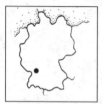

Combine Edenism and hedonism as you explore this most romantic of German regions and dip into its mineral spas. The Black Forest ("Schwarzwald" in German) is a range of hills stretching along the French border 100 miles from Switzerland north to Karlsruhe (its highest peak is the 4,900-foot Feldberg). Because this region's thick forests allowed little light in, people called it black.

Until the last century, the Schwarzwald was cut off from the German mainstream. The poor farmland drove medieval locals to become foresters, glassblowers, and clockmakers. Today, the Black Forest offers clean air, cuckoo clocks, cheery villages, and countless hiking possibilities. This is where Germans come to recuperate from their hectic workaday lives, as well as from medical ailments—often compliments of Germany's generous public health system. Key words you'll see everywhere are *Bad* (or *Baden*), meaning "bath"; and *Kur*, loosely, "cure." Either term is synonymous with "spa" and directs you to a place to relax, soak, and recover. The region is also known for its favorite dessert, *Schwarzwälder Kirschtorte*—Black Forest cherry cake, a mouthwatering concoction with alternating layers of schnapps-soaked chocolate cake, cherries, and whipped cream. Ahhhhh!

Germans use the term Schwarzwald to refer to the entire southwestern corner of Germany rather than just its forested parts. The region's two major (and very different) towns are Baden-Baden in the north and Freiburg in the south. Neither feels particularly woodsy—instead, their proximity to France lends both cities a sunny elegance. Baden-Baden is Germany's grandest 19th-century spa resort. Stroll through its elegant streets and casino. Soak in its

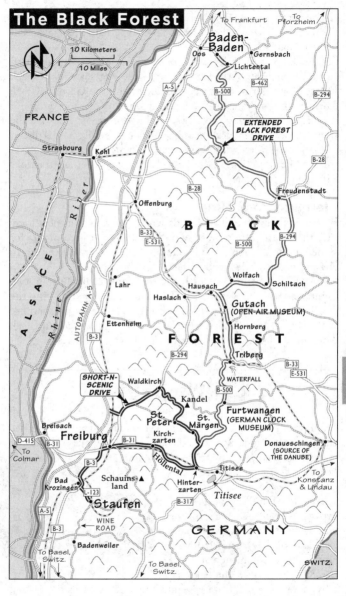

The Black Forest

To Frankfurt
To Pforzheim

Baden-Baden
Oos
Gernsbach
Lichtental

A-5
B-500
B-462
B-294

FRANCE

**EXTENDED
BLACK FOREST
DRIVE**

Strasbourg
Kehl

B-28

B-28

Freudenstadt

Offenburg

B L A C K

B-33
E-531

B-500
B-294

Wolfach
Schiltach

Lahr
Hausach

Haslach

Gutach
(OPEN-AIR MUSEUM)

Ettenheim

Hornberg

B-3

F O R E S T

B-294

Triberg

B-33
E-531

WATERFALL

**SHORT-N-
SCENIC
DRIVE**
Waldkirch
B-500

Kandel

Furtwangen
(GERMAN CLOCK
MUSEUM)

St.
Peter
St.
Märgen

Breisach
Kirch-
zarten

Freiburg
B-31

B-3

Höllental

Donaueschingen
(SOURCE OF
THE DANUBE)

Titisee

To
Konstanz
& Lindau

D-415
B-31

To
Colmar

Bad
Krozingen
L-123

Schauins-
land

Hinter-
zarten

Titisee

Staufen
A-5

G E R M A N Y

B-317

B-3

WINE
ROAD

Badenweiler

To Basel,
Switz.

To Basel,
Switz.

SWITZ.

10 Kilometers
10 Miles

N

ALSACE

Rhine River

AUTOBAHN A-5

BADEN-BADEN

famous baths. Freiburg is the Black Forest's de facto capital and main university town. For a small-town experience, hang your hat in cozy Staufen.

Back up in the hills, a pair of worthwhile museums show off two different sides of the local culture—the Vogtsbauernhof Black Forest Open-Air Museum near Gutach, and the German Clock Museum in Furtwangen. You'll also find plenty of opportunity for lazy drives and hikes. The area's two biggest tourist traps are the tiny Titisee (a lake not quite as big as its parking lot) and Triberg, a small town filled with cuckoo-clock shops and a sprinkling of worthwhile attractions. Skip these places in favor of the attractions listed in this chapter.

Planning Your Time

By **train,** Freiburg and Baden-Baden are easy, as is a short foray into the forest from either town. Save a day and two nights for Baden-Baden. Tour Freiburg by day, but consider sleeping in charming and overlooked Staufen.

With more time and a **car,** do the whole cuckoo thing: two nights and a relaxing day in Baden-Baden, a busy day doing the small-town forest medley south (with stops at the Vogtsbauernhof Black Forest Open-Air Museum and Furtwangen's German Clock Museum), a quick visit to Freiburg, and a night in Staufen.

Baden-Baden

Of all the high-class resort towns I've seen, Baden-Baden is the easiest to enjoy in jeans with a picnic. The town makes a great first stop in Germany (1.5 hours from Frankfurt's airport, direct trains every 2 hours).

Baden-Baden was the playground of Europe's high-rolling elite around 150 years ago. Royalty and aristocracy came from all corners of the continent to take the *Kur*—a soak in the (supposedly) curative mineral waters—and enjoy the world's top casino. Wrought-iron balconies on handsome 19th-century apartment buildings give Baden-Baden an elegant, almost Parisian feel. The town acquired its hyphenated double name—short for "Baden in Baden" (that is, Baden in the state of Baden)—in 1931, to distinguish it from other places named Baden (German for "baths").

The town remains popular today. How popular? Hoteliers in

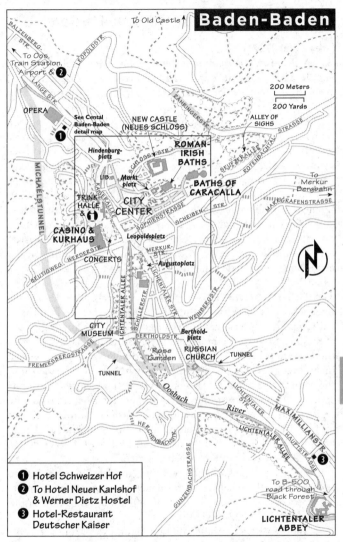

Baden-Baden

To Old Castle

To Oos,
Train Station,
Airport & **2**

BALZENBERG STR.

LEOPOLDSTR.

LANGE STR.

OPERA

1

See Cental
Baden-Baden
detail map

NEW CASTLE
(NEUES SCHLOSS)

ZÄHRINGERSTR.

ALLEY OF
SIGHS

SEUFFERALLEE

ROTENBACHTAL STRASSE

MICHAELSTUNNEL

Hindenburg-
platz

SCHLOSS-STR.

ROMAN-
IRISH
BATHS

LIB

Markt
platz

BATHS OF
CARACALLA

TRINK-
HALLE
&

CITY
CENTER

SOPHIENSTRASSE

SCHEIBEN-
STR.

MARKGRAFENSTRASSE

To
Merkur
Bergbahn

CASINO &
KURHAUS

Leopoldsplatz

MERKUR-
STR.

REUTIGWEG

WERDERSTR.

CONCERTS

Augustaplatz

N

LICHTENTALER ALLEE

LICHTENTALER STR.

WEINBERGSTR.

CITY
MUSEUM

SCHILLERSTR.

BERTHOLDSTR.

Berthold-
platz

FREMERSBERGSTRASSE

Rose
Garden

RUSSIAN
CHURCH

TUNNEL

TUNNEL

HERCHENBACHSTR.

Oosbach

River

GUNZENBACHSTRASSE

LICHTENTALER STR.

MAXIMILIANSTR.

LICHTENTALER ALLEE

HAUPTSTRASSE

3

To B-500
road through
Black Forest

LICHTENTALER
ABBEY

200 Meters

200 Yards

1 Hotel Schweizer Hof
2 To Hotel Neuer Karlshof
& Werner Dietz Hostel
3 Hotel-Restaurant
Deutscher Kaiser

typical convention towns expect that 85 percent of their guests will need single rooms and 15 percent will need doubles. As spouses insist on coming to conventions held in Baden-Baden, hoteliers here flip-flop those figures, anticipating that 85 percent of the demand will be for doubles.

Along with conventioneers, this lush resort town attracts a middle-class crowd consisting of tourists in search of a slower pulse, and Germans enjoying the fruits of their generous health-care system.

Orientation to Baden-Baden

(area code: 07221)

Baden-Baden, with 50,000 residents, is made for strolling with a poodle. Except for the train station and a few accommodations, everything that matters is clustered within a 10-minute walk between the baths and the casino.

Although you'll barely notice if you just stick around the center, Baden-Baden is actually a long, skinny town, strung over several miles along the narrow valley of the Oosbach River (conveniently accessed by bus #201—see "Getting Around Baden-Baden," later). The train station is at the lower (northern) end of the valley, in a suburb called Baden-Oos, three miles from downtown; the Lichtentaler Abbey marks the upper end of the valley. The casino and town center are about halfway between, at the point where a small side valley joins the Oosbach valley. The church, castle, baths, and oldest sections of town are a few blocks uphill on the north slope of this side valley.

Tourist Information

Baden-Baden's understaffed main TI is in the ornate Trinkhalle building. The TI has enough recommended walks and organized excursions to keep the most energetic vacationer happy. Pick up the free monthly events program, *Baden-Baden Aktuell*, which includes a good, fine-print, fold-out map. If you're headed into the countryside, consider two other maps: the accessible cartoon-style €1 *Outline Map*, which helps you get your bearings for the region; and the €1.50 *Panoramaweg* map, which has better details for hikers (but is in German only). They also sell a €6 Black Forest guidebook (Mon-Sat 10:00-17:00, Sun 14:00-17:00, WC-€0.50, tel. 07221/275-200, www.baden-baden.de).

The main TI shares space with a genteel-feeling café and an agency that sells tickets to performances in town (theater, opera, orchestra, and musicals; Tue-Sat 10:00-18:00, Sun 14:00-17:00, closed Mon, tel. 07221/932-700).

Another TI is at the B-500 autobahn exit (Mon-Sat 9:00-18:00, Sun 9:00-13:00, Schwarzwaldstrasse 52).

Arrival in Baden-Baden

By Train: Walk out of the train station (lockers at platform 1, €2-4) and catch bus #201 in front of the kiosks on your right (€2.20 single ticket; see "Getting Around Baden-Baden," later). Get off in about 15 minutes at the 11th stop, Leopoldsplatz, usually also announced as *Stadtmitte* (town center). Allow about €16 for a taxi from the train station to the center.

By Car: Because most traffic goes underneath Baden-Baden (through long underground tunnels), finding your way to your hotel can be counterintuitive. Most hotels I recommend are in the town center; to reach them, first follow the blue *Therme* signs to the baths neighborhood, then look for green signs directing you to each individual hotel. Ask your hotelier for parking tips (you'll likely wind up at one of the big garages in the town center). For outlying accommodations, I've listed specific driving directions (see each listing under "Sleeping in Baden-Baden," later).

By Plane: Baden-Baden's airport is served by Ryanair from London, Air Berlin from Berlin, and a few smaller airlines (www.badenairpark.de). Bus #205 connects the airport with Baden-Baden's city center (Mon-Fri hourly, less frequent on weekends, 45 minutes, tel. 07221/277-650).

Helpful Hints

Shopping: The big **Wagener Galerie** shopping mall at Lange Strasse 44 has just about everything, including a modern supermarket on the top floor (Mon-Sat 9:00-19:00, closed Sun) and a post office on the ground floor (Mon-Fri 9:00-19:00, Sat 9:00-14:00, closed Sun).

Horse Races: Book well in advance if you'll be visiting Baden-Baden during its three annual horse races (May 12-20, Aug 25-Sept 2, and probably Oct 13-14 in 2012; races are held in nearby town of Iffezheim, www.baden-racing.com).

Internet Access: Two good 10-terminal places sit at opposite ends of downtown—**Internet and Callshop** in the north (€2/hour, Mon-Sat 10:00-22:00, Sun 11:00-22:00, Lange Strasse 54, tel. 07221/398-400) and **Medialounge** in the south (€2.40/hour, Mon-Fri 10:00-20:00, Sat 10:00-18:00, closed Sun, in passage at Kreuzstrasse 3, tel. 07221/22522).

Laundry: Klara Ross Wäscherei is a dry-cleaning shop in the town center that also does laundry (full service, same-day or next morning turnaround). Friendly Klara speaks Russian, but no English (€10/load; Mon-Tue and Thu-Fri 8:00-12:00 & 14:00-18:00, Wed and Sat 8:00-12:00, closed Sun; Eichstrasse 14, tel. 07221/22676).

Bike Rental: You can rent cheap bikes at the parking-garage office under the casino (€1/2 hours, €2.50/6 hours, €5/12 hours, show ID and leave €20 as deposit, half-price with *Kurkarte* discount card you'll get from your hotel, rental daily 8:00-18:00, return until 20:00; first-come, first-served—no reservations; enter garage and find section A, space 52—easiest way down is from stairs off Kaiserallee marked *Kasse/Garage*; tel. 07221/277-203).

Train Info: The **Derpart** travel agency, between Leopoldsplatz and the casino, posts a train schedule outside. They'll charge you a

€5 fee to answer your train questions and/or sell you a ticket—which is pricey, but saves you a trip to the station (Mon-Fri 9:00-18:00, Sat 10:00-14:00, closed Sun, Sophienstrasse 1B, tel. 07221/21050).

Getting Around Baden-Baden

Within town, only one bus really matters: **Bus #201** runs straight through Baden-Baden, connecting the train station in Oos, the town center (Leopoldsplatz is the most central stop), and the Lichtentaler Abbey at the southeast end of town (every 10 minutes until 20:00, then about every 20 minutes until around midnight; buy tickets from machines at stops or from driver: €2.20/person, 24-hour Citysolo pass for 1 adult-€4.90, 24-hour Cityplus pass for up to 5 adults-€7.70, bus info at www.kvv.de). Tickets are sold without a date-stamp and must be validated in the machine on board. Single tickets are valid for 90 minutes in one direction. With bus #201, you don't need to mess with downtown parking.

Bus #208, though infrequent, can serve as a fun sightseeing bus. Hop on at Leopoldsplatz, and you'll take a big scenic drive (actually a kind of figure-eight with three loops) through Baden-Baden, returning to the center 55 minutes later (leaves Leopoldsplatz Mon-Fri at 9:07, 10:07, 13:07, 16:07, and 17:07; Sat at 9:07 and 12:07; no buses run Sun). **Buses #204** and **#205** go to the recommended Merkur funicular.

Self-Guided Walk

Welcome to Baden-Baden

• *This walk starts at the casino, loops through the Old Town to both of the famous baths, and ends back at the river where you can stroll up to the abbey. In other words, it covers everything. Start on the steps of the...*

Casino: The impressive building called the Kurhaus is wrapped around a grand casino. Built in the 1850s in wannabe-French style, it was declared "the most beautiful casino" by Marlene Dietrich. You can tour it in the morning, and gamble away the afternoon and evening.

To get a visual overview of the town from the casino, stand on the steps between the second and third big white columns from the entrance, and survey the surroundings from left to right: Find the ruined castle near the top of the hill, then the rock-climbing cliffs, the new

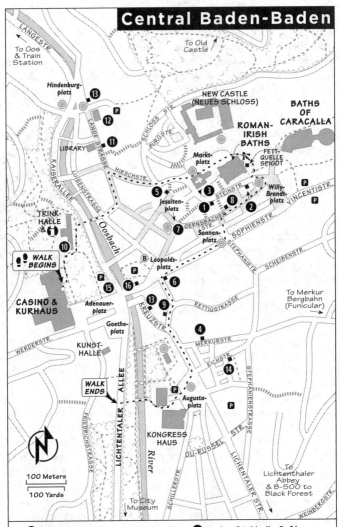

Central Baden-Baden

1. Hotel/Rest. Rathausglöckel
2. Hotel/Café Beek
3. Hotel am Markt
4. Hotel Etol
5. Weinstube im Baldreit
6. Peter's am Leo Café
7. Gasthaus Löwenbräu
8. Lotus Restaurant
9. Café König
10. In der Trinkhalle Café
11. Böckeler Café
12. Wagener Galerie Shopping Mall (Grocery)
13. Internet Access (2)
14. Laundry
15. Bike Rental
16. Derpart Travel Agency

castle (top of town) next to the salmon-colored spire of the Catholic Church (the famous baths are just behind that), the Merkur peak (marked by a TV tower, 2,000 feet above sea level, easy to reach by bus and funicular), and the bandstand in the Kurhaus garden. The Baden-Baden orchestra plays here on most good-weather days in summer (sometimes also weekends in spring and fall, free, usually at 16:00).

• *Now walk about 100 yards to your left, to the...*

Trinkhalle: Beyond the colonnade is the old Trinkhalle—a long entrance hall decorated with nymphs and romantic legends (explained in the book *Trinkhalle Baden-Baden: Its Tales and Legends*, sold inside for €10). It's now home to the main TI, a recommended café, and a ticket agency. Wander around its fancy portico, studying the romantic paintings that spa-goers a century

ago could easily relate to. For a sample of the warm spring water, go inside and look for the tap by the TI desk (cups available in café for €0.20).

• *From the Trinkhalle, walk down the steps, tip your hat to Kaiser Wilhelm (no moustache jokes now), and cross the river. Walk one block inland, then go left on the pedestrian Lange Strasse. After a block, take a hard right, and climb up Hirschstrasse (under the "Bad" Hotel zum Hirsch skybridge) until you hit a big church.*

Catholic Church and Marktplatz: Baden-Baden's Catholic Church looks over the marketplace that has marked the center of town since Roman times. You're standing upon the "emperor's spa." Though it's not open to the public, every year city workers don oxygen masks and descend, through the square metal hatch in the cobbles, to clean its sumptuous marble.

Enter the Catholic Church (the door on the left side is usually open). Because it sits atop the spa, the church is muggy and warm all year. There are no heaters inside; the floor stones are designed to transmit the natural spa heat in the winter. Notice a musty smell? The air in the nave is at a steady 85 percent humidity level. That means the wooden pews have to be replaced every 50 years, and all the art consists of copies (originals are stored safely in the regional museum).

Back outside, you can see the edge of the "new castle" towering above the square. It's owned by a Kuwaiti woman who hopes to turn it into a fabulous five-star hotel at a cost of €500 million (if she can clear the hurdles that come with renovating a historic building).

• *Now we'll explore the area around Baden-Baden's namesake and claim to fame...*

The Baths Area: Walk to the back of the church, under a modern art installation holding jugs three stories high (reminders of the Roman spa that once stood here), and down the cobbled lane behind the Roman-Irish Bath complex. Because the soil is spa-warmed, the vegetation is lush—Mediterranean pines and orange trees. At the end (top of stairs), enjoy the **viewpoint;** Baden-Baden's high-rent district—nicknamed "Paradise"—climbs the hills opposite.

Take the steps down to the water spigot that taps the underground spring called the **Fettquelle** ("rich water source"). It's 105 degrees—very hot—as hot as a spa open to the public can legally be. Bring a cup if you want a taste. Until recently, this was a practical source of hot water for Baden-Baden residents. Older locals remember being sent here to fetch hot water for their father's shave.

Find the handless **statue** on the lawn 50 yards farther. She's got her rear to the modern fun baths (Baths of Caracalla) and is eyeing the luxurious old-school Roman-Irish Bath (both described later).

• *Return halfway to the Fettquelle spigot and take the stairs down into the parking level (signposted* Römische Badruinen*) to the small...*

Ancient Spa Museum: This spa, now in ruins, was built for Roman soldiers to use. It's just one room—most of which you can see through the big windows—and worth the admission only if you want to use the included audioguide to learn the story of the ancient spa, including how it was engineered. As it was only for soldiers, this spa is just a simple terra-cotta structure with hollow walls and elevated floors to let the heat circulate (€2.50, mid-March-mid-Nov daily 11:00-12:00 & 15:00-16:00, closed mid-Nov-mid-March).

• *Leaving the museum, jog left, then right, and head down...*

Gernsbacher Strasse: Walking down Gernsbacher Strasse, consider the 2,000-year heritage of guests who have been housed, fed, and watered here at the spa. Fyodor Dostoyevsky, Mark Twain, Johannes Brahms, and Russian princes all called this neighborhood home in its 19th-century heyday. Germany's oldest tennis and golf clubs were created here (for the English community) in the 19th century.

The late 20th-century German health-care system was very, very good for Baden-Baden—the government provided lavishly for spa treatment for its tired citizens. Times have changed, and now doctors must make the case to insurance companies that their patients are more than tired...they must actually be sick to have their visit subsidized. And the insurance company then dictates where they'll go. The government will still pay for up to three weeks of recreation at a spa like this, but patients must go to the spa that is recommended and sleep in its clinic. If they want to sleep in a hotel, the jig is up—and they lose their government funding.

• *After two blocks, you hit Sonnenplatz. Jog left, and at the corner, continue right down Sophienstrasse, where a signpost directs you toward* Lichtentaler Allee.

Sophienstrasse: This street enjoys the reliable shade of a long row of tall chestnut trees. In the 1870s, when it was lined exclusively by hotels, this was the town's aristocratic promenade. Back then there were 15,000 bedrooms for rent in Baden-Baden (triple what the city has today).

• *Sophienstrasse leads into...*

Leopoldsplatz: Until 1985, this square was a main traffic hub, with 30,000 cars muscling through it each day. Now a 1.5-mile-long tunnel takes the east-west traffic under the city, and the peace and quiet you'd expect in a spa town has returned. Actually, Baden-Baden had to get rid of the noise and pollution caused by the traffic in order to maintain its top rating as a spa resort—lose that, and Baden-Baden would lose half its business. The main city bus stop is just off the square, on Luisenstrasse. The modern art decorating Leopoldsplatz (and streets and squares throughout the city) changes on a regular basis, as many artists want the exposure that an open-air exhibit in Baden-Baden brings.

• *From Leopoldsplatz, head left on Lichtentaler Strasse. You'll pass the venerable and recommended Café König (on right), antiques shops (on left), and fine little malls. Head for the big fountain in the distance, which marks Augustaplatz. At the fountain, go right, through the park, and over the petite bridge, where you'll come to a sweet riverside path called Lichtentaler Allee (described under "Sights in Baden-Baden," next). From here the casino is to your right. A stroll to the left—down Lichtentaler Allee—takes you to the rose garden, City Museum (an elegant old mansion with a humble but well-displayed collection of artifacts and etchings showing the history of the spa town), and out to Lichtentaler Abbey. You choose which way to go. My walk is done.*

Sights in Baden-Baden

▲▲**Casino and Kurhaus**—Baden-Baden's grand casino occupies a classy building called the Kurhaus. Built in the 1850s, it was inspired by the Palace of Versailles and is filled with rooms honoring French royalty who never actually set foot in the place. But many other French people did. Gambling was illegal in 19th-century France...just over the border. The casino is licensed on the condition that it pays 92 percent of its earnings to the state. The

amount of revenue it generates to help the state fund social services is a secret, but insiders estimate that it's more than $30 million a year. The staff of 150 is paid by tips from happy gamblers.

You can visit the casino on a guided tour in the mornings, when it's closed to gamblers, but it is most interesting to see in action, after 14:00. You can gamble if you want, but a third of the visitors come only to people-watch under the chandeliers. The scene is more subdued than at an American casino; anyone showing emotion is more likely a tourist than a serious gambler. Lean against a gilded statue and listen to the graceful reshuffling of personal fortunes. Do some imaginary gambling or buy a few chips at the window near the entrance (an ATM is nearby).

Cost and Hours: €5 entry, €2 minimum bet, €14,000 maximum bet; open daily 14:00-2:00 in the morning, Fri-Sat until 3:00 in the morning, livelier after dinner and liveliest after 22:00; no athletic shoes, tie and coat and collared shirt required for men—can be rented for €11 with an €11 deposit, nice jeans OK; passport required—driver's license isn't enough, under 21 not admitted, no photos, pick up game rules as you enter, tel. 07221/30240, www .casino-baden-baden.de).

Lower rollers and budget travelers can try their luck downstairs at the casino's slot machines, called *Automatenspiel* (€1 entry or included in €5 casino admission, opens at 12:00—otherwise same hours and age restrictions, passport required, no dress code).

Tours: The casino gives 30-minute German tours every morning (€5; departures every half-hour from 9:30 to 11:30, no 9:30 tour Nov-March; some guides speak English, or call ahead and pay €15 extra per group for an English tour—tel. 07221/30240, or just pick up the paltry English brochure). Even camera-toting peasants in T-shirts, shorts, and sandals with their kids in tow are welcome on tours.

▲▲**Strolling Lichtentaler Allee**—Imagine yourself in top hat and tails as you promenade down the famous Lichtentaler Allee, a pleasant, picnic-perfect 1.5-mile-long lane. You'll stroll through a park along the babbling brick-lined Oosbach River, past old mansions and under hardy oaks and exotic trees (street-lit all night). By the elitist tennis courts, make sure to cross the footbridge into the free Art Nouveau rose garden (Gönneranlage, 400 labeled kinds of roses bloom May-Oct—best in early summer, great lounge chairs). If you wish, continue all the way to the historic Lichtentaler Abbey, a Cistercian convent founded in 1245. Either walk round-trip, or take city bus #201 one-way (runs along the main street, parallel to the promenade, on the other side of the river). Many bridges cross the river, making it easy to shortcut to bus #201 anytime. Biking is another option (see "Bike Rental" under "Helpful Hints," earlier), but you'll have to stay on the road in the bike lane, since the footpath is only for pedestrians.

Russian Baden-Baden—The town's Russian link dates back to 1793, when the future Czar Alexander I took Louise, Princess of Baden, as his wife. Later, many Russians, including Dostoyevsky and Tolstoy, flocked here after gambling was banned in their motherland. Some lost their fortunes, borrowed a pistol, and did themselves in on the "Alley of Sighs" (Seufzerallee, near the Caracalla baths). You'll find a **Russian Orthodox church** just south of the center—step in (€1 donation requested, daily April-Oct 10:00-18:00, Nov-March 10:00-17:00, services normally Sat 17:00-20:00 and Sun 9:40-11:30, near Gönneranlage rose garden across river from Lichtentaler Allee, or take bus #201 to Bertholdplatz stop).

While the church dates from about 1900 and was quiet for generations, a current boom in the Russian population here makes the church livelier than ever. Even the Soviet period did little to dim the allure of this spa town in the Russian imagination. In the 1990s, Russians of German ethnic origin were allowed to emigrate to Germany, and many decided to settle in Baden-Baden. More recently, ultra-wealthy Russians seeking safe property investments have poured their rubles into Baden-Baden: Many of the town's top hotels are now Russian-owned, and direct flights from Moscow land at Baden-Baden's airport. While more Americans visit Baden-Baden each year, Russian tourists stay longer and account for more overnights. You'll see Russian on multilingual signs around town.

▲Funicular to the Summit of Merkur—This delightful trip to a hilltop overlooking Baden-Baden is easy, quick, and a good reason to buy a 24-hour bus card rather than single tickets. Catch bus #204 or #205 from the city center (departing 2/hour from Leopoldsplatz) and ride 11 minutes through the ritzy "Paradise" neighborhood to the end of the line at the base of the Merkur Bergbahn. Take the funicular to the 2,000-foot summit.

At the top, you can enjoy a meal or drink (restaurant open same hours), and, if the weather's good (with winds from the south or west), you can watch the paragliders leap into ecstasy. Take the funicular back down, or follow an easy paved lane back to the base of the funicular (2.5 miles, signposted *Merkurbahn Talstation*); hiking enthusiasts can follow many other trails from here (buy maps at bookstores in town). From the bottom of the funicular, buses depart back to Baden-Baden twice hourly.

Cost and Hours: €2 each way, funicular departs every 6 minutes, daily mid-May–mid-Sept 10:00–22:00, mid-Sept–mid-May 10:00–18:00.

Mini-Black Forest Walks—Baden-Baden is at the northern end of the Black Forest. If you're not going south, but want a taste of Germany's favorite woods, consider one of several hikes from town. The TI has details and can suggest routes. If you're serious about hiking, invest in the TI's good (but German-only) €1.50 *Panoramaweg* map, which outlines a 30-mile trail leading all the way around Baden-Baden's perimeter and the nearby Geroldsau valley (it's easy to do just part of the trail, since you're never far from the town center).

Experiences in Baden-Baden

The Baths

Baden-Baden's two much-loved but very different baths stand side by side in a park at the top of the Old Town. The Roman-Irish Bath is traditional, stately, indoors, contemplative, and extremely relaxing...just you, the past, and your body. The perky, fun, and modern Baths of Caracalla are half the price, both indoor and outdoor, and more social. Caracalla is better in the sunshine; the Roman-Irish is fine anytime. Some hotels sell discounted tickets (10-15 percent off) to one or both of the baths—ask at your hotel.

At either bath, you'll get an electronic wristband, which you'll need when you're ready to leave. If you overstay your allotted time, you pay extra. You can relax while your valuables are stowed in very secure lockers. The baths share a huge underground Bäder-Garage, which is free for the first two hours (then €1/hour) if you validate your parking ticket before leaving either bath (garage entrance on Rotenbachtalstrasse).

Most years, one bath (but never both) closes for two weeks of maintenance in June or July; this is announced prominently at www.carasana.de.

▲▲▲Roman-Irish Bath (Friedrichsbad)

The highlight of most visits to Baden-Baden is a sober 17-step

ritual called the Roman-Irish Bath. This bathhouse pampered the rich and famous in its elegant surroundings when it opened in 1877. Today, this steamy world of marble, brass columns, tropical tiles, herons, lily pads, and graceful nudity welcomes gawky tourists as well as locals.

Cost and Hours: €21/3 hours,

€10 more gets you a soap-and-brush massage and another half-hour, another €10 for final crème massage; daily 9:00-22:00; last entry 3 hours before closing if you're getting a massage, 2 hours before otherwise; kids under 14 not allowed, Römerplatz 1, tel. 07221/275-920, www.carasana.de. It's possible to speed through the bath in less than an hour, but you'll probably want to slow down and enjoy the experience.

Dress Code: Everyone in these baths is always nude. On Mondays, Thursdays, and Saturdays, men and women use separate and nearly identical facilities—but the sexes can mingle briefly in the pool under the grand dome in the center of the complex (yes, everyone's nude there, too). Shy bathers should avoid Tuesdays, Wednesdays, Fridays, Sundays, and holidays, when all of the rooms are mixed—including the steam and massage rooms. If you're concerned, you needn't be; there's no ogling going on. It's a very classy and respectful ritual, and a shame to miss just because you're intimidated by nudity.

Procedure: Read this carefully before stepping out naked: In your changing cabin, load all your possessions onto the fancy hanger. Then hang it in the locker across the way, and close the locker by pressing on the button with your wristband. As you enter (in the "body crème" room), check your weight on the digital scale. Do this again as you leave to see how much you sweated off—you'll lose about a kilo...all in sweat. The complex routine is written (in English) on the walls with recommended times—simply follow the room numbers from 1 to 17. Instructions are repeated everywhere. For the first couple of stops only, you will use plastic slippers (marked with European sizes, see page 849 for conversions) and a towel (given to you by the attendant for the hot-room lounges) for hygienic reasons and because the slats are too hot to sit on without the towel.

Start by taking a shower. Grab a towel and put on plastic slippers before hitting the warm-air bath for 15 minutes and the hot-air bath for 5 minutes. Shower again. If you paid extra, take the rough and slippery soap-brush massage—which may finish off with a good Teutonic spank. Play Gumby in the shower; lounge under sunbeams in one of several thermal steam baths; and glide like a swan under a divine dome in the mixed-gender royal pool. Don't skip the invigorating cold plunge. Dry in more warmed towels and lie on a bed for 30 minutes, thinking prenatal thoughts, in the mellow, yellow silent room. At the end, there's a room with tea, chaise lounges, and magazines. You don't appreciate how clean you are after this experience until you put your dirty socks back on. Ewwww (bring a clean pair).

All you need is money. You'll get an electronic wristband, locker, and towel; hair dryers are available. If you wear glasses, consider leaving them in your locker (it's more relaxing without them). Otherwise, you'll find trays throughout for you to park your specs.

Afterward, before going downstairs, browse through the Roman artifacts upstairs in the Renaissance Hall (also accessible to non-bathers), sip just a little of the terrible but "magic" hot water *(Thermalwasser)* from the elegant fountain, and stroll down the broad royal stairway, feeling, as they say, five years younger—or, at least, 2.2 pounds (a kilo) lighter.

▲▲Baths of Caracalla (Caracalla Therme)

For a more modern experience, spend a few hours at the Baths of Caracalla, a huge palace of water, steam, and relaxed people. More

like a mini-water park, and with everyone clothed most of the time, this is a fun and accessible experience, and is recommended for those intimidated by nudity.

Cost and Hours: €14/2 hours, €17/3 hours, €20/4 hours, €122 for 10 2-hour entries for multiple visits or to split among your group; massages—€28/25 minutes, €54/50 minutes; daily 8:00-22:00, last entry at 20:00, no kids under age 7, kids aged 7-14 must be with parents (it's not really a splashing and sliding kind of pool). Tel. 07221/275-920, www.carasana.de.

Procedure: At this bath, you need to bring a towel (or rent one for €5 plus a €10 deposit) and a swimsuit (shorts are OK for men).

Find a locker, change clothes, strap the band around your wrist, and go play. Your wristband gets you into another poolside locker if you want to lock up your glasses. If you buy something to drink, you'll pay on exit (it's recorded on your wristband). Bring your towel to the pool (there are plenty of places to stow it). The baths are an indoor/outdoor wonderland of steamy pools, waterfalls, neck showers, Jacuzzis, hot springs, cold pools, lounge chairs, saunas, a cafeteria, and a bar. After taking a few laps around the fake river, you can join some kinky Germans for water spankings (you may have to wait a few minutes to grab a vacant waterfall). Then join the gang in the central cauldron. The steamy "inhalation" room seems like purgatory's waiting room, with a misty minimum of visibility, filled with strange, silently aging bodies.

Nudity is limited to one zone upstairs. The grand spiral staircase leads to a naked world of saunas, tanning lights, cold plunges, and sunbathing outside on lounge chairs. At the top of the stairs everyone stows their suit in a cubbyhole and wanders around with their towel (some are modest and wrapped; others just run around buck naked). There are three eucalyptus-scented saunas of varying temperatures (80, 90, and 95 degrees) and two saunas in outdoor log cabins (with mesmerizing robotic steam-makers). Follow the instructions on the wall. Towels are required, not for modesty but to separate your body from the wood benches. The highlight is the arctic bucket in the shower room. Pull the chain. Only rarely will you feel so good. And you can do it over and over.

Sleeping in Baden-Baden

(area code: 07221)

While Baden-Baden has some grand hotels, my recommended places are mostly small (20-30 rooms), family-run, and more budget-friendly (though all accommodations are pricey in this posh town). Hotel am Markt is a particularly great value and worth reserving in advance. Note that most hotels here don't have 24-hour reception desks; most close for the night at 21:00 or 23:00, though they can wait up for you if they know you're arriving later. It's wise to call ahead with your specific arrival details if you'll be coming after 17:00.

While weekends and summer are generally more expensive, demand—and prices—change from day to day based on conventions, theater performances, and other events.

All hotels and pensions are required to extract an additional €3.20 per person, per night "spa tax," so don't get upset when this is added to the bill. This comes with a "guest card" *(Kurkarte),* offering small discounts on tourist admissions around town (including casino entry and bike rental). If you're coming into town by car or foot, look for the helpful green signs that direct you to each hotel by name.

In the Center, near the Baths

These well-located options stick you right in the heart of Baden-Baden, in a pleasant, stepped pedestrian zone a short saunter from the baths.

$$$ Hotel Rathausglöckel is a 16th-century guest house that recently underwent a tasteful 21st-century renovation. Oliver (a German-American) and his Ukrainian wife Zoia have turned this classic little place into one of the town's most inviting hotels. Steep stairs lead to 15 antique-furnished rooms (plus a few grand suites) and an inviting rooftop deck (Sb-€80-100, Db-€110-130, junior suite-€130-170, multi-room suite-€160-200, higher prices are for weekends and events, 10 percent discount for Rick Steves readers if you book direct, free Internet access and Wi-Fi, church bells every 15 minutes 6:15-22:00, parking-€10/day, Steinstrasse

Sleep Code

(€1 = about $1.40, country code: 49)
S = Single, **D** = Double/Twin, **T** = Triple, **Q** = Quad, **b** = bathroom, **s** = shower only. Unless otherwise noted, credit cards are accepted, English is spoken, and breakfast is included.

To help you sort easily through these listings, I've divided the accommodations into three categories based on the price for a standard double room with bath:

$$$ Higher Priced—Most rooms €100 or more.
$$ Moderately Priced—Most rooms between €80-100.
$ Lower Priced—Most rooms €80 or less.

Prices can change without notice; verify the hotel's current rates online or by email. For other updates, see www.ricksteves.com/update.

7-9, tel. 07221/90610, fax 07221/906-161, www.rathausgloeckel.de, info@rathausgloeckel.de).

$$$ Hotel Beek rents 15 attractive and comfortable rooms, run from a delectable pastry shop/café on the ground floor. It's wonderfully situated, facing the baths on a little square in a pedestrian zone. The reception (in the café) closes at 20:00, so be sure to call ahead if you'll be arriving later (Sb-€85, Db-€109, balcony-€10 extra, Db suite-€165, extra bed-€30, elevator, free Wi-Fi, parking-€11/day, on Römerplatz at Gernsbacher Strasse 44, tel. 07221/36760, fax 07221/367-610, www.hotel-beek.de, info@hotel-beek.de).

$$ Hotel am Markt is Baden-Baden's best little hotel. Family-run, with 25 rooms, it offers all the comforts a commoner could want in a peaceful, central, nearly traffic-free location, two cobbled blocks from the baths. For romantics, the church bells blast charmingly through each room every quarter-hour from 6:15 until 22:00; for others, they are a nuisance. Otherwise, quiet rules. The ambience and the clientele make it a joy to have breakfast or just kill time on the small terrace (S-€33-36, Sb-€45-48, D-€66-70, Db-€84-88, Tb-€105-120, extra bed-€20, elevator, free Internet access, free Wi-Fi in lounge; first-come, first-served parking-€4/day; Marktplatz 18, tel. 07221/27040, fax 07221/270-444, www.hotel-am-markt-baden.de, info@hotel-am-markt-baden.de, run by sisters Frau Bogner-Schindler and Frau Jung).

In the Modern Town

$$$ Hotel Etol is in the quiet courtyard of a renovated industrial complex, which celebrates its history as a tile and bathtub factory from around the year 1900. You'll climb the stairs to reach most of the 18 rooms, but natural light, tasteful design, friendly staff (well-run by Saraya), and a central location make this a winning choice (Sb-€78-85, Db-€105-130, book direct and mention Rick Steves for a discount off these prices—except during events, non-smoking, family rooms, free Wi-Fi with this book, parking-€5/day, Merkurstrasse 7, 2-minute walk from Augustaplatz stop of bus #201, tel. 07221/973-470, fax 07221/9734-7111, www.hotel-etol.de, info@hotel-etol-badenbaden.de).

$$$ Hotel Schweizer Hof's 34 rooms mix classic style and modern comfort. It's about a five-minute walk north of the pedestrian district, on a little square next to the opera building (Sb-€72-87, Db-€102-115, suite-€135, extra bed-€35, higher prices are during opera events, elevator, free Wi-Fi and Internet access, Lange Strasse 71-73—for location see map on page 235, bus #201 stop: Alter Bahnhof/Festspielhaus—then walk 50 yards ahead, drivers follow *Festspielhaus/Casino* signs and find it right next to the opera, tel. 07221/30460, fax 07221/304-646, www.schweizer hof.de, mail@schweizerhof.de).

Outside the Center

The following listings are a few stops from the center on bus #201 (for locations, see the map on page 235).

$ Hotel Neuer Karlshof is in the Baden-Baden train station building, up a flight of stairs from the Coffee Fellows café (where you'll check in). Four of the nine new and attractive rooms are trackside and have a little train noise—despite multi-paned windows— light sleepers beware. Otherwise, it's a great deal for a short stay (Sb-€60, Db-€79, Db suite-€99, extra bed-€25, non-smoking, free Wi-Fi, free parking, Ooser Bahnhofstrasse 4, tel. 07221/971-5695, fax 07221/971-5696, www.hotel-neuer-karlshof .de, info@hotel-neuer-karlshof.de).

$ Hotel-Restaurant Deutscher Kaiser, a good choice for those looking to spend less, is a traditional guest house with 22 simple, spacious, dated-but-clean rooms, run by no-nonsense Frau Peter. Herr Peter cooks fine local-style dinners for guests (€8-17 main courses, Wed-Sun 18:00-20:00, closed Mon-Tue). It's right at the Eckerlestrasse bus stop (bus #201, 6/hour, 10 minutes from center, 20 minutes from train station) or a 25-minute stroll from the city center down polite Lichtentaler Allee—cross the river at the green *Restaurant Deutscher Kaiser* sign, then turn right (S-€35, Sb-€47-51, D-€46-49, Db-€63-72, family rooms, check website for discounts, mostly non-smoking rooms, free Internet access and Wi-Fi, free and easy parking, Hauptstrasse 35, tel. 07221/72152, fax 07221/72154, www.hoteldk.de, info@hoteldk.de). Drivers: From the autobahn, skip the town center by following *Congress* signs into Michaelstunnel. Take the tunnel's first exit, then another right at the end of the exit (direction: Lichtental). Outside, the hotel is about a half-mile down on the left. From the Black Forest, follow *Zentrum* signs. Just 10 yards after the Aral gas station, turn left down the small road to Hauptstrasse.

$ Werner Dietz Hostel, between the station and the center, is big, modern, and has the cheapest beds in town (€21.30/bed in 4- to 6-bed dorm, €3.10 less for 2 nights or more, €4 more if you're over 26, nonmembers pay €3.10 extra, single- or double-room surcharge-€10, includes sheets and breakfast, 23:30 curfew, Internet access, outdoor swimming pool next door, Hardbergstrasse 34, tel. 07221/52223, www.jugendherberge-baden-baden.de, info @jugendherberge-baden-baden.de). To reach the hostel from the train station or downtown, take bus #201 to Grosse Dollenstrasse (also announced as *Jugendherberge*), six stops from the station or five from downtown; it's a steep, well-marked 10-minute climb from there. Drivers should call the hostel for careful directions.

Eating in Baden-Baden

Dining with Elegance and Atmosphere

Weinstube im Baldreit, with both a cozy cellar and a leafy back courtyard, is ideal on a hot evening. Dining here, I feel like a pampered salamander in a Monet terrarium. While her French husband Philippe cooks wonderful regional dishes, Nicole is happy to translate the daily specials chalked in German on the board. The priority here is near-gourmet food at great prices. Reservations are smart (€8-19 main courses, Mon-Sat 17:00-22:00, closed Sun; from Lange Strasse 10, walk up the narrow alley called Küferstrasse, look for *Weinstube* signs, and enter under archway, Küferstrasse 3, tel. 07221/23136).

Hotel Rathausglöckel's homey, air-conditioned restaurant features traditional cuisine in a dining room with understated Old World elegance. Reservations are smart, especially for the limited outdoor seating upstairs (€9-19 main courses, Mon-Tue and Thu-Fri 18:00-23:00, Sat-Sun 11:30-14:00 & 18:00-23:00, closed Wed, reservations smart, Steinstrasse 7-9, tel. 07221/90610).

Quick and Simple Meals near Leopoldsplatz

Peter's am Leo Café is a fun self-service café offering big breakfasts, sandwiches, lunch specials, pastries, and views over Baden-Baden's central square. (Try to snare one of the outdoor tables.) This is where commoners pile their plates high (€5-7 lunch specials, Mon-Sat 6:30-19:00, Sun 8:00-19:00, on Leopoldsplatz at Sophienstrasse 10, tel. 07221/392-817).

On Jesuitenplatz: This thriving people zone, between Leopoldsplatz and the baths (at the bottom of Gernsbacher

Strasse), has several options. The square is dominated by **Gasthaus Löwenbräu,** a sloppy, rude Bavarian-style *Biergarten* slinging good beer and basic schnitzel fare under a vine-covered trellis (€6-10 grill and wurst plates, €13-22 main courses, daily 10:00-24:00). Across the street, several decent restaurants offer curbside tables—great for people-watching. Two blocks up Gernsbacher Strasse from here (at #17), **Lotus Restaurant** serves big, cheap portions of Chinese and some Thai specialties, and has a few outdoor tables (€6-8 meals, daily 11:00-23:00).

Prime People-Watching Cafés

Baden-Baden's many cafés are variations on a genteel theme. They serve chocolates, coffee, cakes (including the famous *Schwarzwälder Kirschtorte*—Black Forest cake), and light meals. Figure around €5-6 to savor a slice of cake and cup of coffee, or €5-8 for light food (such as sandwiches and salads). Most cafés are closed for dinner. While you have no shortage of options in this town, I like these four.

Café König is *the* place to bring your poodle and spend too much for an elegant cup of coffee and a slice of Black Forest cake (€3.40, €2.80 "to go"). Look for the sign with the squiggly script (daily 8:30-18:30, counter opens Mon-Sat at 9:30 and Sun at 10:30, fine shady patio, between Leopoldsplatz and Augustaplatz at Lichtentaler Strasse 12, tel. 07221/23573).

In der Trinkhalle, a café that shares the handsome Trinkhalle building with the TI, has comfy leather sofas, international newspapers and magazines, and a casino-view terrace (Sun-Wed 10:00-19:00, Thu-Sat 10:00-24:00, Kaiserallee 3, tel. 07221/302-905).

Café Beek fills a delightful tree-shaded square just in front of the baths with relaxing café tables (daily 6:30-20:00, Gernsbacher Strasse 44-46 at Römerplatz, tel. 07221/36760). They also rent rooms (see "Sleeping in Baden-Baden," earlier).

Böckeler Café, a good but less fancy option, is a bit cheaper, and has a praline counter, an ice-cream sundae menu, light meals, a modern interior, and outdoor tables along a lively pedestrian street (Mon-Fri 8:00-18:30, Sat 8:00-18:00, Sun 9:30-18:00, Lange Strasse 40-42, tel. 07221/949-594).

Baden-Baden Connections

From Baden-Baden by Train to: Freiburg (direct fast trains every 1-2 hours, 45 minutes; cheaper regional trains take 1.5 hours with change in Offenburg), **Triberg** (hourly, 1.25 hours), **Munich**

(hourly, 4 hours, change in Mannheim or Karlsruhe), **Frankfurt** (hourly, 1.5 hours, direct or with a change in Karlsruhe), **Frankfurt Airport** (hourly, 1.5 hours, mostly with a change in Mannheim or Karlsruhe), **Bacharach** (hourly, 3 hours, 1-3 changes), **Strasbourg,** France (every 1-2 hours, usually 1.25 hours with a change in Appenweier), **Bern** or **Zürich,** Switzerland (every 1-2 hours, 3 hours, change in Basel). Train info: tel. 0180-599-6633, www .bahn.com.

Freiburg

Freiburg (FRY-boorg) is the capital of the Schwarzwald. This "sunniest town in Germany," with 30,000 students, lacks must-see

attractions but offers the pleasures of a university town: small shops, cozy cafés, fine food, and fewer tourists than Baden-Baden. Exuding an "I could live here" appeal, Freiburg is surrounded by lush forests and filled with creative and environmentally aware people. Bikers and hikers seem to outnumber cars, the town center is laced with cute miniature canals, and silent, efficient trams run everywhere. The city merits a visit, if only to appreciate its thriv-
ing center and very human scale. Freiburg's striking red-sandstone cathedral is worth a peek, and its own little mountain offers sunset views over the rooftops.

Orientation to Freiburg

(area code: 0761)

With about 210,000 people, Freiburg is a happening mid-sized city. Most points of interest to visitors are concentrated in the compact Old Town (Altstadt), bounded to the west by the train station and to the east by Freiburg's mountain, Schlossberg, and circled by a ring road. You can walk from one end of this zone to the other in about 20 minutes. The town's centerpiece, always in view, is the spiny spire of its cathedral.

Tourist Information

Freiburg's helpful TI, on Rathausplatz, has free city maps and sells better maps for €1, as well as various city and regional guidebooks.

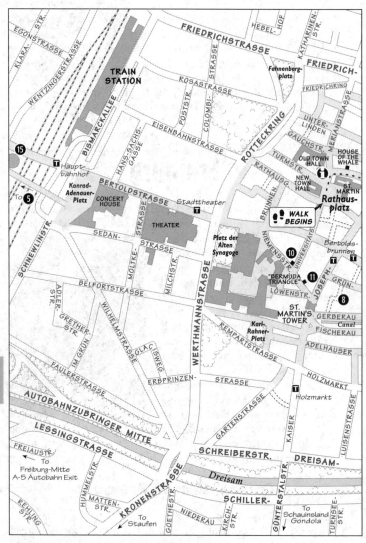

The TI also offers a room-booking service for Freiburg and the Black Forest area (€3/booking plus deposit), weekly walking tours in English (€8, 1.5 hours, May-Oct Sat at 11:30, off-season only in German), and lots of information on the Black Forest region (TI open June-Sept Mon-Fri 8:00-20:00, Sat 9:30-17:00, Sun 10:00-12:00; Oct-May Mon-Fri 8:00-18:00, Sat 9:30-14:30, Sun 10:00-12:00; tel. 0761/388-1880, www.freiburg.de).

Freiburg

200 Meters
200 Yards

Karlsplatz

Schlossberg

LOOKOUT TOWER

Münsterplatz

CATHEDRAL

CITY HISTORY MUSEUM

HIST. MERCH. HOUSE

Oberlinden

AUGUSTINER MUSEUM

Augustinerplatz

WALK ENDS

SWABIAN GATE

ELEVATOR

Kanonenplatz

PLATEAU BASTION

Canal

To ⑥

KARTÄUSER-

GRANATGÄSSLE

LEO-WOHLEB-STR.

River

To St. Märgen & St. Peter via B-31

① Hotel Oberkirch
② Schwarzwälder Hof
③ Hotel Alleehaus
④ Hotel/Restaurant zur Sichelschmiede
⑤ To Hotel Schemmer
⑥ To Black Forest & Freiburg Youth Hostels
⑦ Hausbrauerei Feierling
⑧ Markthalle & Osteria
⑨ Tacheles & Chang Thai
⑩ UC/Uni-Café
⑪ Incontro Gelato
⑫ Greiffenegg Schlössle & Biergarten Kastaniengarten
⑬ Karstadt Dep't Store (Migros Grocery)
⑭ Alte Wache Wine Bar
⑮ Bike Rental
⑯ Launderette

FREIBURG

Arrival in Freiburg

The bustling train station has lockers (€2-4 old-fashioned ones by sector B of track 1, or €4 high-tech versions in the station hall), a WC (€0.80), and a helpful *Reisezentrum* that dispenses rail info and sells tickets (Mon-Fri 7:00-20:00, Sat 8:30-19:00, Sun 8:30-20:00). The bus station is next door (to the right as you exit).

To access city **trams** from the train platform, take the escalators up to the tram stop on the bridge above the tracks. To reach the city center by **foot** (about 15 minutes), walk straight out of the train station, cross the street, and continue ahead up the tree-lined boulevard called Eisenbahnstrasse (passing the post office). Within three blocks, you'll cross the busy ring road, then continue straight (on Rathausgasse) to Rathausplatz. This is where you'll find the TI (in the bright-red building), and where my self-guided walk begins. Most of my recommended accommodations are within a 10-minute walk of here.

Helpful Hints

Laundry: There's a small self-service **launderette** at Adelhauser Strasse 24 (Mon-Fri 7:00-20:00, Sat 7:00-17:00, closed Sun, in passageway behind hair salon at corner with Marienstrasse, tel. 0761/35656).

Supermarket: Pick up picnic supplies at **Migros** (Mon-Fri 9:30-20:00, Sat 9:00-20:00, closed Sun, in basement of Karstadt department store on Kaiser-Joseph-Strasse, near the cathedral).

Bike Rental: Mobile Fahrradstation, across the tracks from the train station, rents bikes and has free route maps (€8/4 hours, €15/24 hours, subsequent days-€5, show ID and leave €50 cash deposit per bike, daily 10:00-18:00; from station, cross tram bridge over train tracks to round building on left and go downstairs; Wentzingerstrasse 15, tel. 0761/292-7998, www.car-sharing-freiburg.de—German only).

Local Guide: Iris Bürklin leads good tours around Freiburg (€99/2 hours; book through Freiburg Kultour and request Iris: tel. 0761/290-7447, info@freiburg-kultour.com; Iris' mobile 0162-595-6876).

Getting Around Freiburg and Surroundings

The city center (which includes all my recommended hotels) is completely walkable, though you might want to use a taxi or a tram to haul luggage from the station. Trams are also useful to reach outlying sights, such as the Schauinsland lift (€2.10/ride, €5.30/24-hour pass, €9/24-hour pass for 2-5 people, buy tickets from machines at stops or inside cars). For local transport info in English, see www.vag-freiburg.de.

To visit **Staufen, St. Peter,** or **St. Märgen** by regional train and bus, you'll need a two-zone ticket (€3.60 each way) or a 24-hour regional pass (€10.60 for 1 adult, €18 for 2-5 adults, available from ticket machines). If you're staying in one of those towns, your hotel tax includes a KONUS card, giving you free access to all public transit in the region (see page 276); unfortunately, this does not apply if you're sleeping in Freiburg.

Self-Guided Walk

Welcome to Freiburg

This orientation walk, starting at Rathausplatz (and the TI), leads you through the top sights in the old center of Freiburg in about an hour.

• *Begin on the square in front of the Town Hall buildings.*

Rathausplatz: The relaxing square with the fountain used to be an enclosed courtyard—the cloister of the neighboring Franciscan Church of St. Martin. Today it's fronted by twin city administration buildings: the bright-red Old Town Hall (on the right, with the TI inside) and the white-and-pink New Town Hall (on the left).

Embedded in the cobbles in front of both of the Town Hall buildings, you'll see mosaic coats of arms representing each of Freiburg's **sister cities.** Many of them—including Padua (Italy), Madison (Wisconsin), and Isfahan (Iran) are university towns, like Freiburg. The town has been a university center since the mid-15th century, and the prestigious university is still the town's biggest employer.

• *Curl around the far side of St. Martin's Church and head up Franziskanerstrasse. As you walk, you'll notice the first of many small canals lining the street.*

Bächle: These tiny streams, running down nearly every street in the pedestrianized core since the 13th century, are Freiburg's trademark. Originally they were designed to keep fires from spreading (in case of fire, the canals could be quickly dammed to flood the street). It worked—Freiburg had no major fires after it introduced its *Bächle.* The canals also provided a constantly replenishing source of water for people and cattle. These days, the canals are just fun: A sunny day turns any kid-at-heart into a puddle-jumper. Toddlers like to dangle their feet in the water to cool off when it's hot. Freiburg still employs two *Bächleputzer* to scrub the canals clean each day with steel

FREIBURG

brooms. Local lore says that if you fall into a *Bächle*, you are destined to marry a Freiburger.

At the end of the church, look at the facade of the red building

ing on the left, the **House of the Whale,** featuring the first of many whimsical little statues that decorate Freiburg. Look closely at the right-hand gargoyle on the facade. The veiny growth hanging from her neck is a goiter (a result of iodine deficiency). These were so common in the Middle Ages that the local folk costume includes a tightly fitting band around the neck to disguise a goiter.

• *Continue ahead one block, until you reach the wide cross-street called...*

Kaiser-Joseph-Strasse: Since the Middle Ages, this has been the center of commerce in Freiburg, lined with its biggest department stores and malls.

Look before crossing the street: Virtually silent trams glide along here constantly. With some 220 miles of tram and bus lines, Freiburg is very proud of its reputation as a "green" city. Only 40 percent of trips taken in Freiburg are by car, and the percentage of locals who own bikes rivals that

of pedal-happy Amsterdam. The city is home to a large solar-panel factory, and it started the annual Intersolar trade fair (which has since outgrown the town and moved to California).

Looking down the street to the right, you can see one of the two surviving towers of Freiburg's former town wall, **St. Martin's Tower** (or as some call it, McDonald's Tower—thanks to the

not-subtle-enough golden arches that try to fit into its facade). If you were to head in that direction, then cut up the street to the right just before you reached the tower, you'd wind up in the colorful student quarter called the "Bermuda Triangle" that visitors of any age enjoy exploring (described later, under "Eating in Freiburg"). The tower is dedicated to the beloved saint who famously offered half of his cape to a beggar; he's celebrated with children's parades all over Germany every November 11th. The top of the tower once held the town prison; so those who went to jail were euphemistically said to have "put on St. Martin's cape."

• *Jog a half-block to the right and continue straight to the...*

Münsterplatz and Market: This main square of Freiburg hosts a bustling outdoor produce and crafts market six mornings a week (Mon-Sat 7:30-13:00, biggest on Wed and Sat, no market on Sun). On the north side of the cathedral (to the left), vendors sell local produce; in front of the cathedral's door, flowers and herbs; and to the south (right), imported produce. Around the left side, you'll also find stands selling Freiburg's distinctive type of bratwurst—long, red, and skinny, called a *lange Rote*. If you order one, they'll ask you *Mit oder ohne?*—"with or without" onions.

The market goes way back. On the giant pillar to the left of the cathedral's main door, look for the **engravings** with different years (e.g., ADMCCLXX—that's A.D. 1270) next to oval and circular shapes. These were the officially decreed sizes for a loaf of bread; customers could bring their purchases here to be sure they weren't being cheated. Notice that the size of the loaf shrunk between 1270 and 1317. The price stayed the same, but the bread got smaller...medieval inflation.

In the alcove in front of the cathedral entrance are more official measures. For example, to the left, you'll see the standard measures for a basket (the circle plus the line), an "elbow" (the line), and a barrel (the square with a diagonal line). On the right are even more measures, dictating home-construction supplies (the proper size of bricks, roof tiles, floor tiles, and beams). Nearby, the inscription boasts that since the 16th century, Freiburg has enjoyed the right to hold a large-scale market twice a year (a rare privilege in the Holy Roman Empire).

• *Now's a good time to visit the **cathedral** (for details, see my self-guided cathedral tour on page 262). When you're done, exit the cathedral out the side door (around the right side of the building) to continue this walk.*

Münsterplatz, Side View: For many visitors, the most memorable part of the cathedral is its many **gargoyles.** Find the "mooning" gargoyle (facing the entrance, walk around the right and look at the second butt-ress)...and wait for rain.

The **Historical Merchant House** (Historisches Kaufhaus, from 1532) was the trading and customs center in the 16th century, and briefly housed the state parliament after the war. You'll notice lots of red buildings in town. During the Middle Ages around here, a red paint job on a building indicated it was a place where you'd be required to pay a tax or fee.

To the left as you face the Merchant House, you'll see the gray building that houses the **City History Museum** (with a pair of interesting models in the cellar—see page 264), then the yellow building marked *Alte Wache*. A former police station, this was recently turned into a wine bar and is a fine place to sample local wines, either indoors or out on the square (€2-4.50 glasses, Mon-Fri 10:00-19:00, Sat 10:00-16:00, may stay open later in good weather, closed Sun, Münsterplatz 38, tel. 0761/202-870). Most of the wine made here uses grape varieties that originated in Burgundy. This corner of Germany enjoys some of the country's balmiest weather, thanks to the so-called "Burgundy Gate"—a gap between the Vosges and Jura mountains, which channels in warm Mediterranean air from the south of France. Winds coming through the "gate" also carry with them Burgundian sediments, enriching the German soil.

· *Go up the narrow lane (called Buttergasse) to the left of the Merchant House. Then turn left and head up...*

Schusterstrasse: This pleasant street is typical of old Freiburg, lined with a *Bächle*, with historic labels on many of the houses and mosaic seals (made of Rhine River stones) in front of most doors. For example, the building at #35 (on the left) is labeled *Haus zur kleinen Meise* (House of the Little Titmouse), with a knife mosaic out front. While the house labels date from the Middle Ages, the mosaics are typically more modern, paid for by today's merchants to match the purpose of the building. This one is a knife shop. The mosaics are portable, so if the vendor moves shop, he can just lift his up and take it with him.

· *Cross Herrenstrasse and continue up the narrow lane called Münzgasse. When it dead-ends, turn right along...*

Konviktstrasse: Named not for a convict but for a convent, this is another typical Freiburg street (see photo). Chain stores and chain restaurants are forbidden along here, and in the springtime, the street is draped with fragrant purple wisteria.

· *Konviktstrasse plops you onto a major street right in front of the...*

Swabian Gate (Schwabentor): This second of Freiburg's surviving gates is named for the Swabians, the historical rivals of the Freiburgers (the gate leads to where you'd head to meet them). Just below the big painting, at the apex of the arch, look for the little figure pulling a thorn out of his foot. This is the last thing Freiburgers would see before leaving town, to remind them to stay on the right path and avoid the "thorns" of sinful living.

• *Freiburg's little mountain, Schlossberg, is nearby. It's best at sunset, but if you want to head up now, simply climb the stairs at the Schwabentor, use the pedestrian overpass to cross the busy road, and take the free elevator on up (see page 264).*

Or, for some back-street experiences, stick with me for a few more minutes. Facing the Schwabentor, turn right, then veer right again onto the downhill road, toward the little river.

Riverside Freiburg: This is the main branch of the much bigger river that splits into all those little canals at the top of town. Walking down this incline, you can see how the street level of town was actually raised to create a steeper incline to power the canals. While this was once the smelly tanners' and millers' quarter, now it's a delightfully low-key neighborhood. Follow the pleasant river for a while, and soon you'll reach two recommended eateries: Across the canal (on the left) is the picturesque Sichelschmiede; a few more steps up on the left is the modern-inside, rollicking-outside Hausbrauerei Feierling microbrewery, with an inviting beer garden across the street (on the right). If you keep on past these two, you'll end up at the broad square called Augustinerplatz, with the entrance (uphill and to the right) to the **Augustiner Museum.** Continuing along the little street called Grünwälderstrasse (directly across from the Augustiner Museum entrance) brings you to even more eateries, including the wonderful Markthalle food circus on the left (all described later, under "Eating in Freiburg").

• *Our Freiburg walk is finished. Now go splash in those canals.*

Sights in Freiburg

▲▲Cathedral (Münster)

The lacy spire rocketing up from Freiburg's skyline marks its impressive main church. While Germany has bigger and better cathedrals, Freiburg's has some interesting details that make it

FREIBURG

worth a visit.

Cost and Hours: Cathedral interior—
free, usually Mon-Fri 10:00-12:00 & 12:30-
17:00, Sat 10:00-11:30 & 12:30-17:00, Sun
13:00-19:30; tower—€1.50, Mon-Sat 9:30-
17:00, Sun 13:00-17:00, enter from outside
church and pay at top; choir—free, Mon-
Fri 10:00-11:45 & 13:00-16:00, Sat 10:00-
11:15 & 13:00-15:30, Sun 13:00-16:00.

◐ Self-Guided Tour: Begin out front.
The exterior **scaffolding** is a semi-per-
manent feature of the church. The cathedral's distinctive pink color comes from a
soft local sandstone that's easy to work, but also extremely fragile.
Decorations need to be replaced every 30 to 60 years. Keeping the
church from falling apart is a never-ending task—elderly locals
who've lived here their entire lives report having never seen the
church without at least some scaffolding.

The frilly **tower** *(Münsterturm)* is as tall as the church is long
(127 yards)...but not worth the 329-step ascent. Up in the tower
are 16 different bells, each one with a different name and purpose.
Traditionally, Catholics could not eat meat on Fridays, so instead
they'd eat *Spätzle* (German egg noodles)—giving the oldest bell,
rung just before lunchtime on Fridays, its nickname, the "*Spätzle*
Bell." Other bells include one that tolls each night at 20:00 (originally to remind townspeople that the city gates were closing), and
a "Tax Bell" that rings twice weekly in November and December,
when taxes traditionally came due.

Before heading inside, spend a few minutes looking around
the ornately decorated **entryway** (outside the door itself, but inside
the gated area). The 418 colorfully painted statues (recently restored
and now protected with netting from destructive pigeons) ooze
with medieval church symbolism. Each has an identifying symbol.

As you look back out to the square, the
first figure on the right is St. Catherine,
holding a wheel (her bones were broken
on a wheel).

Two particularly memorable characters have become mascots of Freiburg.
First is the so-called **"praying devil."** In
the tympanum (over the door), look for
Jesus on the cross. Just below him and
a bit to the right is a pot-bellied devil,
greedily rubbing his hands together
as he watches the Archangel Michael
weigh the goodness of a person's soul

(while two other devils try to fix the results). Then, along the left wall, notice the strange little character under the third statue from the right—playing his nose like a trumpet.

Now go **inside.** Go left and look along the back wall, where you'll find photos of Freiburg after it was devastated by WWII bombs. The city made it through most of the war virtually unscathed—until November 27, 1944, when, in a space of just 20 minutes, about 80 percent of Freiburg's buildings were destroyed by an Allied bombing run. Miraculously, the cathedral was one of the few structures that survived. Some credit divine intervention, while others claim the bombers intentionally avoided it; either way, the steeple's lattice-work top and underground lead anchors probably saved it, since shockwaves from explosions all around it would have leveled a solid, less-supported tower.

The **stained-glass windows** are originals, from the 13th and 14th centuries, which were hidden away and protected during World War II. Each one is marked with the seal of a local merchant who sponsored it (go on a scavenger hunt to find the pretzel, from the baker; the barrel, from the cooper; the scissors, from the tailor; and the hammer, tongs, and snake—representing fire— from the blacksmith).

Now stroll down the **nave** toward the altar. After its thriving market and Black Forest silver mine made Freiburg rich, this cathedral was built on the site of an earlier church. Begun in about 1200, most of the structure was finished relatively quickly (it has the only Gothic steeple in Germany that was actually completed during Gothic times, in 1330), but it still demonstrates various styles. The earliest part of the church, at the **transept,** is Romanesque (notice the rounded tops to the windows); but as Gothic engineering swept neighboring France, Freiburg's cathedral builders began to incorporate that style (see the telltale pointed arches elsewhere in the church).

Many churches from this era have 12 **pillars** lining the nave, each one with the statue of an apostle. But after the primary construction on this cathedral was finished, a large choir was added beyond the altar, so two more pillars were built—bringing the total to 14. Judas was given the heave-ho, and pillars were granted to Paul, Matthias, and Jesus himself. Look at the statues on the two pillars flanking the altar: On the right is Jesus, and on the left is Thomas—pointing two fingers because of his insistence on touching Jesus before he'd believe in the Resurrection. Thomas' privileged position in this church is based on the philosophy that non-believers should be closest to Christ.

You can take a quick spin around the **choir** to see some ornately decorated chapels, the crypt, and a closer look at the painting over the altar (enter to the right of the altar). When you're finished, head outside using the side door (right transept), and you'll be back out on Münsterplatz.

Other Sights

Augustiner Museum—Freiburg's top museum displays local fine art and medieval artifacts around the reconstructed shell of an Augustinian church. The highlights are close-up looks at some of the cathedral's original 13th-century medieval statuary (first floor) and 16th-19th-century stained glass (second floor). The top floor shows off regional 19th-century paintings; a second wing is scheduled to open in a few years.

Cost and Hours: €6, ticket serves as day pass to all city museums, Tue-Sun 10:00-17:00, closed Mon, entrance on Augustinerplatz, tel. 0761/201-2521, www.freiburg.de/museen.

Nearby: The area around Augustinerplatz is the heart of the **Gerberau district,** popular with locals. It's quieter and filled with little galleries and restaurants that are less expensive than on Münsterplatz (several are recommended later, under "Eating in Freiburg").

City History Museum—Telling the story of Freiburg, this museum is worthwhile if only to see the two town models in the cellar. One shows medieval Freiburg circa 1590, with the city wall and all five city gates intact. Notice the little wall around the cathedral (today's Münsterplatz). This was the town cemetery, and the little house huddled next to the grand church was the *Beinhaus* (charnel house, where exhumed remains were stored). The other model, from the early 1700s, shows how the French King Louis XIV turned the city into a gigantic fortress—one of Europe's largest at the time (see next listing). Upstairs you'll find another model—this one of the cathedral while it was under construction—along with Freiburg-manufactured player pianos and other exhibits and artifacts documenting town history.

Cost and Hours: €3, covered by €6 city museum day pass, Tue-Sun 10:00-17:00, closed Mon, Münsterplatz 30, tel. 0761/201-2515.

Schlossberg (Castle Hill)—Schlossberg towers over the east end of Freiburg's Old Town. A monstrous 18th-century fort once stood here on "Castle Hill," built by the French to control the citizens of Freiburg during a period of French occupation. The giant fortress garrisoned as many as 150,000 soldiers at once. (The debate about where the border between France and Germany should be was only put to rest

after World War II.) The French destroyed the fortress when they retreated, leaving behind virtually no traces of the fort, except for a few stony walls. Today Schlossberg is Freiburg's playground, popular for its views over the city. A modern lookout tower (100 feet high) stands where the French Fort d'Aigle (eagle tower) once stood.

To get to the top of Schlossberg, you can either hike or (easier) take a free elevator up. From Schwabentor, the half-timbered tower at the east end of the Old Town, look for the pedestrian walkway over the busy ring road. Once across, if you want to walk, bear left and hike up the steep switchbacks for 10 minutes. Or, to take the elevator *(Aufzug)*, continue straight through the cave-like tunnel to access it. At the top of the elevator and trail, you'll come to the pricey Greiffenegg Schlössle restaurant, and (in good weather) an affordable beer garden just above; both have knockout sunset views (and are described later, under "Eating in Freiburg").

For even better views, keep hiking to higher and higher perches. About a seven-minute hike above the restaurant is a broad, flat plateau with benches overlooking the town's rooftops. From there, you can hike about five more minutes up to a stubby stone bastion; or, for the highest vantage point, trek about 20 minutes up to the modern lookout tower. You can loop up to the tower and back on different paths. For the most straightforward approach to the tower, begin at the plateau with your back to the benches, walk the level path to the left, then veer right uphill at the big white cross (follow small silver signs with a picture of the tower).

Schauinsland—Freiburg's own mountain, little more than an oversized hill, is nine miles southeast of the center. The viewpoint at its 4,000-foot summit, which won't wow anyone from Colorado, offers the handiest panorama view of the Schwarzwald for those without wheels. The gondola system that takes you up—one of Germany's oldest—was designed for Freiburgers relying on public transportation. At the top, you'll find a view restaurant, pleasant circular walks, and the Schniederli Hof, a 1592 farmhouse museum. A tower on a nearby peak offers an even more commanding Black Forest view.

Cost and Hours: €12 round-trip for gondola, €25.50 family ticket includes 2 adults and up to 4 kids, daily July-Sept 9:00-18:00, Oct-June 9:00-17:00; catch tram #2—direction: Günterstal—from town center to the end, then take bus #21 seven stops to Talstation stop for gondola; city center to gondola takes 25 minutes, gondola ride lasts 20 minutes; tel. 0761/451-1777, www.bergwelt-schauinsland.de.

Hikes—If you want to hike, consider the St. Peter-St. Märgen trail described on page 280, which is cheaper and quicker to reach from Freiburg than the Schauinsland.

Sleeping in Freiburg

(€1 = about $1.40, country code: 49, area code: 0761)

Though I prefer nights in sleepy Staufen (where you'll get better value for your money—see page 276), Freiburg is livelier and easier for non-drivers. If you have a car, hotels can get €9/day deals in city parking garages (normally €23/day). All my listings are in or near Freiburg's Old Town. In this university town, May, June, September, and October are the busiest months, with the highest rates.

$$$ Hotel Oberkirch is pricey but ideally situated. Nine of its 26 rooms sit right on the main square (facing the cathedral and above a restaurant); the rest are in a nearby building on Schusterstrasse, a pleasant pedestrian street. Each of the Old World rooms is different; some are a bit dated, but all are clean and comfortable (Schusterstrasse rooms: Sb-€99-121, Db-€149-155; main-square rooms: Sb-€121-169, Db-€165-192; up to €20 extra during busy times, elevator, free Wi-Fi at reception, free cable Internet in rooms, reception and most rooms at Schusterstrasse 11, main-square rooms at Münsterplatz 22, tel. 0761/202-6868, fax 0761/202-6869, www.hotel-oberkirch.de, info@hotel-oberkirch.de).

$$$ Schwarzwälder Hof, just a block behind the cathedral, has 43 straightforward rooms over a reasonably priced restaurant. Guests get a free regional transport card (Regiokarte), valid as far as St. Peter and Staufen—a deal worth about €10/person per day (Sb-€65-75, Db-€95-125, Tb-€125-150, prices depend on room size and amenities; elevator, free Internet access and Wi-Fi, Herrenstrasse 43, from station take tram #1 in direction: Littenweiler three stops to Oberlinden, tel. 0761/38030, fax 0761/380-3135, www.shof.de, info@schwarzwaelder-hof.eu, Engler family).

$$ Hotel Alleehaus has 19 comfy, creaky-floored rooms at the south edge of the Old Town. While close to the action, it's on a quiet, leafy street in a big, old house—think Art Nouveau with a hint of ramshackle. It feels like home and is warmly run by Bernd and his team (S-€50, Sb-€65-75, small Db-€85, twin Db-€98, larger Db-€104, Tb-€139, Qb-€159, reception closed 20:00-6:00, call by 18:00 if arriving later than 20:00, free Wi-Fi, Marienstrasse 7, tel. 0761/387-600, fax 0761/387-6099, www.hotel-alleehaus.de, wohlfuehlen@hotel-alleehaus.de). From the station, walk 20 minutes or take tram #3 (direction: Vauban) or #5 (direction: Rieselfeld) three stops to Holzmarkt; then walk along Holzmarkt, which becomes Wallstrasse, and turn right on Marienstrasse.

$$ Hotel zur Sichelschmiede rents six small rooms with attractive, traditional decor above a recommended restaurant in the cutest part of town, overlooking a canal (Sb-€65, Db-€85, may be cheaper in winter, Insel 1, tel. 0761/35037, fax 0761/31250, www.sichelschmiede.de, info@sichelschmiede-freiburg.de, Gerdi Stark and family).

$ **Hotel Schemmer,** though literally on the wrong side of the tracks, is close to public transport and a workable option if you're on a tight budget. It has 16 basic rooms on five floors (no elevator). Rooms with a private bath, which face the back, are quieter than shared-bath rooms, which front a busy street (S-€45, Sb-€55, D-€58, Db-€71, Tb-€90, Qb-€100, free Wi-Fi, Eschholzstrasse 63; 10-minute walk from station or take tram #1, #3, or #5 one stop to Eschholzstrasse and walk a block; tel. 0761/207-490, fax 0761/207-4950, www.hotel-schemmer.de, kontakt@hotel-schemmer.de).

Hostels

$ **Black Forest Hostel** has 105 of the cheapest beds in Freiburg. Run by friendly Tania, with a young, bohemian attitude, it's bare-bones simple (€14-17/bed in 10- to 21-bed rooms, €18-23/bed in 3- to 8-bed rooms, S-€30, D-€50, sheets-€4, sleeping bags OK, cash only, no curfew, no smoking in rooms, lockers, pay Internet access, self-service kitchen, laundry-€5, Kartäuser Strasse 33—look for anchor sign and go down driveway; 20-minute walk from station or take tram #1—direction: Littenweiler—to Oberlinden stop, then walk 5 more minutes; tel. 0761/881-7870, fax 0761/881-7895, www.blackforest-hostel.de, backpacker@blackforest-hostel.de). If full, they might direct you to the much larger, more distant $ **Freiburg Youth Hostel** at Kartäuser Strasse 151 (tel. 0761/67656, www.jugend herberge-freiburg.de, info@jugendherberge-freiburg.de).

Eating in Freiburg

Many of Freiburg's best eateries are conveniently concentrated within a block or two of the square called Augustinerplatz. Browse your options here and choose your favorite. Or consider a picnic at the Schlossberg viewpoint (buy supplies at the Migros supermarket—see "Helpful Hints," earlier).

In the Gerberau District

These two places are just downhill from Augustinerplatz, along the town creek.

Hausbrauerei Feierling is a rollicking microbrewery that also serves good meals. On warm summer evenings, their *Biergarten* across the street offers cool, leafy shade and a bustling atmosphere. If you're dining inside, try the cozy upstairs seating, looking down over the big copper vats (€5-13 main courses, daily 11:00-24:00, indoor section closed in afternoons when weather is hot, Gerberau 46, tel. 0761/243-480).

Sichelschmiede is a good option rain or shine. Its timbered alcoves and cluttered interior give it a cozy living-room feel, and its creekside seating can't be beat. Come here for easygoing seasonal regional cuisine, good value, and a family-friendly ambience (€8-16 main courses, daily 12:00-24:00, Insel 1, tel. 0761/35037; also rents rooms—see "Sleeping in Freiburg"). Don't confuse it with a neighboring, lesser-value restaurant that shares the outdoor terrace—notice the color-coded tables.

Along Grünwälderstrasse

This street, connecting Augustinerplatz to the shopping and university zone, is lined with tempting choices.

Markthalle is a wonderful food court where you can peruse cuisines from around the world—German, French, Swiss, Italian, Indian, Brazilian, Chinese, Arabic, and more (most meals around €5-10, eat at stand-up tables or find scarce stools, Mon-Thu 8:00-20:00, Fri-Sat 8:00-24:00, closed Sun, live music on weekends after 20:00—no cover, Grünwälderstrasse 4). At the front of the complex is a restaurant called **Osteria.** You can bring food from the other vendors in here to sit and enjoy—but only before 17:00 and only if you order a drink. They also serve their own food (Mon-Sat 9:00-24:00, closed Sun, Grünwälderstrasse 2, tel. 0761/32054).

Tacheles appeals to student-size appetites (big) and budgets (small). Who knew that schnitzel could be prepared in literally a dozen different ways? Here at the self-proclaimed *"Schnitzel Paradies,"* they serve up big schnitzels (€1.20 extra for *Pute*—turkey—instead of the usual pork), a salad, and your choice of a side dish (french fries, *Spätzle*, and so on) for a mere €6.50 before 18:00 on weekdays (€7.50 evenings and weekends). Non-schnitzel lunch specials (Mon-Fri only) cost €6.50. The pub downstairs, a favorite hangout, can be crowded and smoky; instead, opt for the quiet courtyard seating upstairs (daily 11:30-24:00 or later, also vegetarian options, occasional live *Fussball* broadcasts, Grünwälderstrasse 17, tel. 0761/319-6669). There's a disco in the cellar on Friday and Saturday nights between 23:00 and 5:00 in the morning (with DJ, free entry).

Chang Thai, two doors down from Tacheles, is where students satisfy their Asian-food cravings (€5-7 lunches, €7-10 main courses, Mon-Sat 12:00-23:00, Sun 13:00-22:30, Grünwälderstrasse 21).

In the "Bermuda Triangle" Neighborhood

Night owls flock around St. Martin's Tower (Martinstor), in the area affectionately called Freiburg's "Bermuda Triangle." Take the street to your right just before going through the gate, and get sucked in. Look at the Burger King ahead of you; mischievous Puck does a little dance and plays the pan pipes. He's a fitting mascot for a district known for its fun, colorful bars.

At **UC/Uni-Café,** join the cerebral grad-student crowd for cheap salads, breakfasts, crêpes, *Flammkuchen,* and light meals. Have a cappuccino outside on the square, or pop inside to drink beer and watch a *Fussball* match on the flat-screen TV (€4-8 salads and sandwiches, Mon-Sat 8:00-24:00, Sun 9:00-24:00, Niemensstrasse 7, at Universitätsstrasse, tel. 0761/383-355).

Gelato: Drop by **Incontro,** where you'll be greeted with a robust *"Buona sera!"* before choosing your favorite flavor (€0.90/ scoop, daily 10:00-23:00, on Niemensstrasse).

On Freiburg's Schlossberg

For directions on getting to these scenic eateries, see page 264.

Greiffenegg Schlössle offers rooftop views over Freiburg, but the meals are expensive, and worth it only if you can get a table on the terrace in good weather (€9 soups, €15 starters, €17-29 main courses, Mon-Sat 11:00-24:00, Sun 10:00-24:00, reservations smart, tel. 0761/32728). Consider instead their self-service open-air **Biergarten Kastaniengarten,** just above the restaurant (€6-9 main courses, open April-Oct in good weather, same hours). If the weather is iffy, before ascending look for the *Biergarten geöffnet* ("beer garden open") sign near the base of the elevator.

Freiburg Connections

The full name of the town—and the station—is Freiburg im Breisgau, often abbreviated as "Freiburg (Brsg)" on schedules.

By Train to: Staufen (hourly until about 19:00, 30 minutes, most require transfer at Bad Krozingen; for details, see "Staufen Connections" later in this chapter), **Baden-Baden** (direct fast trains every 1-2 hours, 45 minutes; cheaper regional trains take 1.5 hours with change in Offenburg), **Munich** (hourly, 4.5 hours, 1 change), **Basel,** Switzerland (hourly, 40 minutes; 55 minutes on cheaper regional train), **Bern,** Switzerland (hourly, 2 hours, some transfer in Basel), **Frankfurt** (hourly, 2 hours, most direct), **Frankfurt Airport** (hourly, 2 hours, most with 1 change). Train info: tel. 0180-599-6633, www.bahn.com.

Staufen

Hemmed in by vineyards and watched over by the ruins of a protective castle, Staufen (SHTOW-fehn, rhymes with "now then") is

small and off the beaten path—except on weekends, when it's a popular destination for Germans, who fill hotels and parking spots. Staufen's quiet pedestrian zone of colorful old buildings is bounded by a happy creek that actually babbles. The hotels in Staufen make a peaceful and delightful home base for your exploration of Freiburg and the southern trunk of the Black Forest. You can also make Staufen a half-day outing from Freiburg (better for lunch than for dinner, as the last

public transport back from Staufen leaves around 19:00).

Orientation to Staufen

Staufen (pop. 7,500) is simple to master. The main square is an easy 10-minute walk from the train station, and everything I list is along the way (or just off it). Though Staufen feels small, its high school, courthouse, and shopping district serve all the villages in the Münstertal valley. Staufen hosts a modest annual music festival, the Staufener Musikwoche, at the beginning of August (July 28-August 4 in 2012; check TI website below for information).

Tourist Information

Staufen's helpful TI, on the main square in the Rathaus, has Internet access for €4 per hour (April-Oct Mon-Fri 9:00-12:30 & 14:00-17:30, Sat 10:00-12:00, closed Sun; Nov-March Mon-Fri 9:00-12:00 plus Mon, Wed, and Fri 14:00-16:30, closed Sat-Sun; tel. 07633/80536, www.muenstertal-staufen.de).

Local Guide: Marianne Pfadt, a German who speaks English with a charming Scottish brogue, enjoys taking visitors on a casual but insightful tour around the back streets of her hometown (€50 for 1.5-hour walk, tel. 07633/982-529, siegfried.pfadt@t-online.de).

Arrival in Staufen

There are no lockers at the often-unstaffed **train station,** but try Bahnhof Hotel (see "Sleeping in Staufen," later). To get to town, exit the station with your back to the pond and angle right up Bahnhofstrasse. Turn right onto Hauptstrasse, which leads through the town center to the Rathaus and TI.

If you're arriving by **car,** follow signs for *Stadtmitte* to find the town center. If your hotel is in the pedestrian zone, it's OK to drive there to park. If you're day-tripping, you'll find a handy parking lot right at the entrance to the center (and at the start of my self-guided walk).

Self-Guided Walk

Welcome to Staufen

Few small German towns are as enjoyable to explore as Staufen. It's tourist-friendly without being a tourist trap—a real town with

real shops and residents, but still accessible to visitors. This walk will help you get your bearings. It begins at the start of the cobbled pedestrian zone, near the parking lot; if you're coming from the train station, this is the first part of the old center you'll reach.

• *Begin at the Wine Cooperative building, near the big tree, fountain, and giant wine press.*

Wine Co-op Square

As you can see from the vineyards blanketing its little castle hill, this is a wine-growing region. Wine production (along with taxes levied on silver that was mined deeper in the Black Forest) once brought Staufen wealth...and it still helps out. People "taking the cure" at the rehab centers in nearby Bad Krozingen come to this square to take a break from their treatment and sip local wines. The building labeled *Winzergenossenschaft* is Staufen's **bottling cooperative,** where several local vintners produce and sell their wines. They offer free tastes and sell affordable bottles (most bottles €4-8, Mon-Fri 9:00-18:00, Sat 9:00-14:00, Sun 10:00-15:00 except closed Sun Jan-Feb, Auf dem Rempart 2, tel. 07633/5510, www.wg-staufen.de). Or, if you'd just like a glass of wine in the summer, you can sit out front at the little **wine garden** (€2-3/glass, Mon-Fri 14:00-22:00, Sat-Sun 11:00-22:00). The Gutedel grape, also known as Chasselas, is common in this area.

At the benches between the fountain and the gigantic wine press, look for the photo of a red-sandstone courthouse that once stood here. That building, like much of Staufen, was devastated by an Allied bombing late in World War II (February 8, 1945)—you'll see other photos of the damage scattered around town.

• *Now walk up Staufen's main street called...*

Hauptstrasse

Like its big sister Freiburg, Staufen has little canals called *Bächle* running along its main street (originally made for fire protection and now enjoyed for their own sake). The charm of this colorful drag is governed by strict building codes: Only certain colors can be used, and the shutters are uniform. But locals grumble that sometimes the rules go too far. Notice the rain gutters that empty out onto the cobbles. These used to run underground, but were brought aboveground to be more authentically medieval—and now the streets turn into an ice rink in cold weather.

But the careful restrictions aren't just for the tourists. You'll notice that most of the shops even along this main street aren't trinket boutiques, but real services. Staufen's downtown is thriving, and you'll see bakers, butchers, pharmacies (such as the old-time *Apotheke* on the right, at #52), and other everyday shops. In fact, some Freiburgers like to come to Staufen on Saturday mornings, to shop where the stores are smaller and the owner-clerks are friendlier.

Just before you reach the main square, on the left (at #47), look for the red **Gasthaus zum Löwen.** In the early 16th century, a popular and successful doctor/scientist/fortune teller/alchemist named Johann Georg Faust was brought to Staufen to produce gold for the town. He lived and worked in this very house, experimenting with chemical processes until an accidental explosion killed him around the year 1540. This being the Middle Ages, the townspeople assumed that the devil must have had a hand in his death, and legends began to swirl. Over time, these stories grabbed the attention of various writers, including Johann Wolfgang von Goethe (sometimes regarded as the "German Shakespeare"). In Goethe's seminal work *Faust,* the title character makes a pact with a demon named Mephistopheles, who then breaks Faust's neck—a scene depicted on the side of the building. You might see a costumed Mephistopheles leading tours through the streets of Staufen (in German only). The building is now run as a guest house, and believe it or not, you can sleep in Faust's very room—it's a double with a private bath (€105; tel. 07633/908-9390, www.fauststube -im-loewen.de).

Across the street, at #56 (marked *Stubenhaus Stadtmuseum*), you can duck into one of Staufen's oldest **courtyards.** Go down the half-timbered passage (and past the cheesy Restaurant Käsestube) to get inside. Historically, the building overlooking this courtyard was used by the local guilds to host special events...and it can still be rented out today. The courtyard itself is filled with occasional concerts (usually advertised by posters nearby).

• *Continue out to Staufen's main square.*

Marktplatz (Market Square)

Looking around the square, notice the accidentally clever design: Four streets converge, but are offset, so as you approach you see not other streets—but buildings. This makes the square feel especially cozy.

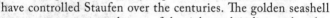

The soldier atop the **fountain** holds the shield of Staufen, with its symbol: three golden goblets on a red field. The medieval word *Stuff* meant "goblet"; Staufen was named for its castle hill, which resembles an upside-down goblet.

Dominating the square is the **Town Hall** *(Rathaus).* The left part (Gothic) is older than the right part (Renaissance), but the whole thing was restored in 2007. The coats of arms represent the various powers that have controlled Staufen over the centuries. The golden seashell at the top of the right peak indicates that this was a stop along the Camino de Santiago, the medieval pilgrimage route that leads all the way to the northwest corner of Spain. Inside the Town Hall are the TI and a very humble town **museum** (Stadtmuseum, upstairs, a few town artifacts, German only, free Mon-Fri, €1 Sat-Sun, open Mon 8:00-12:00 & 14:00-18:00, Tue-Fri 8:00-12:00, Sat-Sun 14:00-17:00).

The Town Hall restoration left the building looking beautiful...but is also threatening to destroy Staufen. Notice the troubling **cracks** running along the building facade adjoining the Town Hall (you'll see similar cracks all over town). The restoration included the installation of a heat pump—an environmentally friendly solution intended to set a good example for townsfolk. Engineers drilled deep into the ground behind the Town Hall, built heat exchangers, and for a few weeks everything worked perfectly. But then cracks began to appear. Apparently, the drilling punctured a layer of anhydrite, a mineral that soaks up groundwater and turns into a bigger-moleculed mineral called gypsum—and the ground beneath Staufen is rising at rates of up to a centimeter each month. While experts scramble to stop it (if they can), more and more precious old buildings show still-growing cracks—250 homes in all have been damaged so far. The costs are huge, and it's not clear who will pay them.

• *Before moving on, put your back to the Town Hall and look out toward the busy street in the distance. The yellow building on the right with the*

STAUFEN

big CAFE *sign is the recommended* **Café Decker,** *the best place in town for cakes and chocolates. Five minutes' walk beyond that is Staufen's fascinating little cemetery (explained later).*

But first, if you'd like to see a side of Staufen most tourists miss, walk through...

Staufen's Back Streets (Hinterstädtle)

Leave Marktplatz on the little lane (called Freihofgasse) between the Kornhaus and the Volksbank. Stick with this lane as it curls around to the left (passing a butcher shop on the right) and goes through a residential neighborhood. Then continue moseying straight along Spitalstrasse, the oldest quarter of town. Until a few decades ago, this was a poor neighborhood; wealthier folk (including well-heeled retirees)  lived in villas on the hillside above. But in the 1980s, gentrification began to turn many of the once-humble cottages in this area into fancy town houses. Today it's a hodgepodge of spiffed-up yuppie homes and ramshackle older ones. As you stroll, you'll enjoy the constant sound of running water from little fountains (most marked *Kein Trinkwasser*—"not drinking water"). After passing a few art galleries, look for the former town wall (on the right). Where the street does a little jog and hits a bigger road, the big building on the left (marked *Renoviert A.D. 1978* on the upper window, and *Re: 1830* above the door) was a hospice *(Spital)*, which wealthy townspeople financed to house people who were ill and too poor to care for themselves.

Turn left and head for the church. This area has some fun boutique shops: Around the right side of the church is a local **coffee roaster** (Coffee & More Kaffeerösterei, buy a bag of coffee to go or sip a cup here on the square, Mon-Fri 9:30-18:00, Sat 9:30-14:00, Sun 14:00-17:30 except closed Sun Nov-Feb, St. Johannesgasse 14, tel. 07633/981-824), and around the left side is a **chocolatier** who trained under the experts at the recommended Café Decker (Chocolaterie Axel Sixt, €4.80/100 grams—mix and match, Mon-Tue and Thu-Fri 9:00-12:30 & 15:00-18:00, Sat 9:00-14:00, closed Sun and Wed, Kirchstrasse 11, tel. 07633/801-255). Choose your poison. The church itself is big and empty-feeling.

You could follow the paved street right back to Marktplatz. Or, to savor residential Staufen, face the church, look left, and notice the big doorway at #9, marked *Jägergasse.* Go into the passage and continue through local neighborhoods. Watch kids having fun at the playground or peek over fences into somebody's garden patch. You can turn left at Meiergasse, or keep going straight as the path narrows—both options lead you right back to the cobbled pedestrian zone...you've come full-circle.

• *If you still have time and energy, consider poking around Staufen's evocative cemetery, just across the river, or hiking up to its hilltop castle (both described next).*

To reach the cemetery, leave Market Square toward Café Decker, Staufen's largest chocolate shop. Cross the big bridge next to the shop, turn right, and walk a short distance between the river and the busy road. When you reach the small footbridge on your right, turn left, cross the busy road, and walk down Wettelbrunner Strasse. A few steps down the street on the left, a small onion-domed chapel marks Staufen's...

Cemetery (Friedhof)—Staufen has one of the more atmospheric and unexpectedly pleasant little cemeteries I've seen. It's a good

place for a contemplative walk, and to ponder German burial customs. Ornate headstones stand in a garden of trees and plants, giving it a comforting feel. As in much of Europe, plots in the cemetery are not purchased, only leased. When your lease is up, someone else moves in. Notice that some headstones have several added-on plaques identifying the remains of many generations of tenants. You may see people here lovingly tending to the graves, tidying the ivy and planting flowers: Tenants' survivors are responsible for maintenance. Some graves have huge trees growing right up out of them, like towering headstones reminding visitors that mortality is nothing new.

Nearby: On your way back to Market Square, you'll see Staufen's **pottery museum,** in the building labeled Keramik-Museum (€2.50, Wed-Sat 14:00-17:00, Sun 11:00-13:00 & 14:00-17:00, closed Mon-Tue and Dec-Jan, Wettelbrunner Strasse 3, tel. 07633/6721, www.landesmuseum.de).

For another detour, go down the street on the right side of the Hotel Kreuz-Post, where you'll find the Schladerer **liquor distillery** and its outlet shop (look for the *Verkauf* sign).

Castle—Staufen's own little vineyard-covered mountain is topped by the remains of a castle (once the residence of the Lords of Staufen) that was destroyed by Swedish troops in 1632. The most direct route to visit these ruins is to charge right on up, but you can also take one of the less-steep roundabout trails.

Sleeping in Staufen

(€1 = about $1.40, country code: 49, area code: 07633)

Unless otherwise noted, your hotel will add a local tax of €1.40 per person per night to the rates below (€1 in Nov-March). In Staufen—as in other small Black Forest towns—this comes with a big return for those relying on public transportation: the KONUS card *(KONUS Gästekarte)*, which covers all transit for the entire Black Forest region (south to Switzerland, west to France, and north to Baden-Baden). This includes unlimited use of all buses, regional trains, and local transit (such as buses or trams in Freiburg or Baden-Baden), but doesn't cover express ICE or IC trains. (Unfortunately, hotel guests in Freiburg or Baden-Baden don't get the KONUS card.) For more details, see www.konus-schwarz wald.info.

All of the following listings have free parking.

$$$ Hotel-Gasthof Kreuz-Post, in the pedestrian zone directly ahead of the Town Hall (on the left), is the town splurge. It rents 12 colorful, tidy rooms over a well-regarded but pricey restaurant (Sb-€85-90, Db-€98-135, price depends on room size, non-smoking, pay Wi-Fi, Hauptstrasse 65, tel. 07633/95320, fax 07633/953232, www.kreuz-post-staufen.de, kreuz-post-staufen @t-online.de).

$$ Gasthaus Krone, the town's top value, sits in the middle of Staufen's main pedestrian drag like it owns it. Charming, friendly, and with nine comfortable rooms, it's a winner. Try here first (Sb-€70, Db-€90, Tb-€120, some rooms with balconies, non-smoking, free Wi-Fi, Hauptstrasse 30, tel. 07633/5840, fax 07633/82903, www.die-krone.de, info@die-krone.de, Lahn family—father Kurt reminds me of Dan Rather).

$$ Zum Hirschen, also family-run and with a storybook location on the main pedestrian street, has 15 dated rooms, a roof deck, and a traditional restaurant on the ground floor (Sb-€65, Db-€85, Tb-€110, some rooms with balconies, elevator, Hauptstrasse 19, tel. 07633/5297, fax 07633/5295, www.hirschen-staufen.de, info @hirschen-staufen.de, Dieter and Isabelle). Their top floor is a two-bedroom suite with room for up to six people (€168 for 4 people).

$ Gästehaus Kaltenbach is a great deal in a rural-feeling location. It's a 10-minute, moderately uphill walk from the station or town center; they'll pick you up if you arrive by train with luggage. English teacher Gabriele Kaltenbach and her police-man-turned-farmer husband Günter rent six rooms in a huge farmhouse with horses out back. They have maps of local hiking trails (Sb-€32, Db-€64, cheaper with 4-night stay, free Internet access and Wi-Fi, laundry facilities, free loaner bikes, yard with swing set; Bötzenstrasse 37, tel. 07633/95310, fax 07633/953-123, www.gaestehaus-kaltenbach.de, info@gaestehaus-kaltenbach.de). From the station, walk toward town and after a block look for the Bacchus statue at the corner of Bahnhofstrasse and Hauptstrasse. Head up Sixtgasse behind the statue, with the vineyards on your left, continue straight through the barrier along Im Rondell, then turn left at the T-intersection onto Bötzenstrasse.

$ Bahnhof Hotel is the closest thing Staufen has to a hostel. Its seven basic-but-cozy rooms (which share two bathrooms) are the cheapest in town. The rooms are situated over an antique restaurant/bar that delicately mingles budget travelers and grizzled locals. Packed full of old furniture, this place makes you feel like you're staying with an eccentric great-aunt. There's a dynamite castle view from the upstairs terrace, a self-service kitchen, and a tiny washing machine for guests (S-€21, D-€41, no breakfast, across from the train station, Bahnhofstrasse 6, tel. 07633/6190, no English spoken).

Eating in Staufen

Many of the hotels listed earlier also have their own good restaurants. For fine dining, head for **Gasthaus Krone** (€19-28 main courses, €22 four-course vegetarian fixed-price meal, €27 three-course fixed-price lunch includes one drink and coffee, closed Fri lunch and all day Sat, Hauptstrasse 30, tel. 07633/5840). For a mid-range option, try **Gasthaus zum Löwen** (tables right on the main square next to Town Hall, or eat in the comfy interior, €9-13 lunch specials, €14-24 main courses, fixed-price meals around €30, daily 10:00-22:00, Rathausgasse 8, tel. 07633/908-9390). Across the square, the informal **Kornhaus** is a less expensive, family-friendly option (€9-15 main courses, daily 11:00-23:00, Am Marktplatz, tel. 07633/5401). To dine very cheaply, drop by **Bahnhof Hotel**, where you can eat on the tree-shaded patio or in the antler-filled restaurant. If you want to chomp red meat under a tree at a table made out of a wine barrel, this is the place. It can get raucous (€7.50 dinners, daily, across from train station, Bahnhofstrasse 6, tel. 07633/6190).

Dessert: Every sweet-tooth in Staufen adores **Café Decker** for its 50 different types of chocolates (€5.60/100 grams) and long display case showing off a wide array of cakes (around €2.60/slice to go, or €3.70 to eat there). The dining room is genteel, but don't miss the inviting rooftop terrace, with views over Staufen's babbling brook (also €4-9 full breakfasts and €8-11 light lunch specials including dessert, Mon-Sat 6:30-18:00, Sun 13:30-18:00, Hauptstrasse 70, tel. 07633/5316).

STAUFEN

Staufen Connections

By Train: Staufen is on a tiny branch line (called the Münstertalbahn) that connects to the main line at Bad Krozingen, a few stops south of Freiburg by slow milk-run train. Train info: tel. 0180-599-6633, www.bahn.com. From Freiburg, it's a 30-minute ride to Staufen (hourly, covered by a single €3.60 two-zone local transport ticket, available from ticket machines; if you're staying in Staufen, the trip is covered by your KONUS Card). Three times every weekday, a handy direct train connects Freiburg straight to Staufen. Otherwise, you'll transfer to another train in Bad Krozingen. Occasionally—especially late in the day—you might have to take bus #113 from Bad Krozingen to Staufen instead of the train (same ticket valid, bus stop is next to train station). Plan ahead by checking schedules online (www.vag-freiburg .de), asking at the Freiburg train or bus station (pick up a printed schedule), calling the bus station at 0761/368-0388 during business hours, or by using the regional schedule helpline (tel. 0180-577-9966, recording in German).

If you're staying in Staufen, be aware of the last through connection from Freiburg (leaves Mon-Fri at 20:15, Sat-Sun at 19:15). If you're visiting Staufen but sleeping elsewhere, note that the last through connection back to Freiburg leaves Staufen around 19:00 daily. If you really need to stay later in Staufen, a shared, subsidized taxi leaves from Staufen station for Bad Krozingen station at appointed times, but only when riders reserve a seat at least 30 minutes in advance by calling 07633/5386 (service called *Anrufsammeltaxi* or AST, regular ticket required, taxi also charges small "comfort supplement"). You can also call a regular taxi (same number).

The Best of the Black Forest

Baden-Baden, Freiburg, and Staufen are appealing towns and fine places to stay overnight. But to let the Black Forest live up to its name, spend a few daytime hours delving into the countryside in this land of cuckoo clocks and healthy hikes. Using public transport, you can day-trip from Freiburg to the small towns of St. Märgen and St.

Peter, and enjoy the two-hour hike between them. Drivers can choose between a short excursion out and back from Freiburg or, with a day to connect Baden-Baden and Freiburg, a longer drive that takes in some fun museums and activities. Everything that can be done from Freiburg can also be done from Staufen (just add another 30 minutes or so each way). Fair warning: The Black Forest is what I'd call "gently scenic." Do it before you delve into the bigger, better Alps in Switzerland or Bavaria; otherwise, you might be underwhelmed.

St. Märgen and St. Peter Day Trip

This pleasant train-and-bus excursion focuses on a pair of charming upland towns nestled in the idyllic Black Forest landscape: St. Märgen and St. Peter. You can connect the two towns by bus, or hike the five miles between St. Märgen and St. Peter in about two hours without stops; the walk requires no more than average fitness and offers lots of picnic benches. The trail runs partly (but not entirely) through woods, so you may want to bring along a hat, water, and sunscreen. Both towns have restaurants, and each has modest sights worth about a half-hour of your time.

Planning Your Time: Here's a relaxed plan: 9:40—Train leaves Freiburg; 10:30—Arrive St. Märgen, see museum if open; 11:30—Start hike to St. Peter, with leisurely picnic lunch along the way; 14:00—Arrive St. Peter, take a quick look at the abbey church; 15:00—Bus leaves for the 45-minute ride back to Freiburg.

Before you start, buy two €3.60 two-zone local transport tickets or a 24-hour regional pass (€10.60 for 1 adult, €18 for 2-5 adults, available from ticket machines). These cover your transport from Freiburg to St. Märgen, and from St. Peter back to Freiburg. Though not absolutely necessary, it's not a bad idea to pick up the *Hochtouren/St. Märgen* 1:25,000 hiking map, which shows the route in detail; buy it from bookstores in Freiburg or at the St. Märgen TI.

From Freiburg to St. Märgen

Trains run regularly from Freiburg to Kirchzarten (13 minutes, leaves Freiburg at :40 past the hour). At Kirchzarten, you'll wait about five minutes to change to bus #7216, which winds 25 minutes up to St. Peter and then another 10 minutes to St. Märgen (confirm times in advance at www.bahn.com or at the Freiburg train station). In St. Märgen, the bus drops you in the village center, near the Rathaus, abbey, supermarket, and bakery—a last chance to picnic-shop (shops closed Sat afternoon and all day Sun).

St. Märgen

St. Märgen (pop. 1,900) is a pleasant, sleepy town dominated by its Augustinian abbey (nice, but less impressive than the abbey in St. Peter). The St. Märgen **TI** is in the back of the *Rathaus* (open July-Sept Mon-Fri 9:00-12:00 & 14:00-17:00, Sat 10:00-12:00, closed Sun; Oct-June Mon-Fri 9:00-12:00, closed Sat-Sun; tel. 07652/1206-8390; www.hochschwarzwald.de).

The only real sightseeing in town is the **Kloster Museum St. Märgen,** attached to (and named for) the Augustinian cloister. This small but delightful collection is worth a peek if it's open. While there's not a word of English, the highlights include Black Forest clocks (from ancient clocks using stones as counterweights, to more familiar cuckoo clocks, all displayed chronologically) and the *Reise ins Uhrenland* exhibit, which describes how Black Forest clock vendors spread far and wide around the world to sell these affordable timepieces. You'll see Black Forest clocks decorated for customers in many different countries. If you're not going to Furtwangen's German Clock Museum, this is a decent substitute. Rounding out the collection are landscape paintings, local history exhibits, and ecclesiastical art, including folk pieces and paintings on glass (€3.50, €25 English tour possible; May-Oct Wed-Thu 10:00-13:00 & 14:00-17:00, closed Fri-Sat and Mon-Tue; Sun 10:00-13:00 year-round; Rathausplatz 1, tel. 07669/911-817, www.kloster-museum.de).

Hiking from St. Märgen to St. Peter

From the St. Märgen bus stop, follow the signposts marked *St. Peter (Höhenweg)*. The first 40 minutes of the walk go gently uphill, with a height gain of about 500 feet. Walk through the village, and by the Hotel Hirsch, make a left turn up a small paved road. (When the trail branches left and changes to dirt, you can detour right 100 yards to the Rankmühle, a picturesque old house.) Eventually you'll reach a small chapel, the Kapfenkapelle.

The trail is level for the next half hour, with views down into the valley. At a clearing in the woods, you'll find another chapel, the Vogesenkapelle. This chapel was built in 1938 by a local man who had fought during World War I in France's Vosges mountains (*Vogesen* in German, just across the Rhine valley from the Schwarzwald). On a clear winter evening at sunset in the Vosges, the man was able to see all the way to the Black Forest—and could even make out his own farm. He vowed then to build a chapel near his home if the Black Forest was spared the horrors of the war.

From the Vogesenkapelle, the path leads down about 45 minutes through farms and residential neighborhoods on the outskirts of St. Peter, and deposits you just below the abbey at the main St. Peter bus stop. Explore the town (described next), or hop on bus #7216 back to Kirchzarten (1-2/hour) where you can catch a train to Freiburg.

Although you can also do this hike in reverse—from St. Peter to St. Märgen—it's more strenuous (as St. Märgen is 500 feet higher than St. Peter) and a little harder to follow.

St. Peter

St. Peter (pop. 2,500) is one of those healthy, go-take-a-walk-in-the-clean-air places that doctors actually prescribe for people from all over Germany. The well-organized little **TI**, under the archway across from the Benedictine Abbey, can give you details on the region or recommend a countryside walk (TI open May-Oct Mon-Fri 9:00-12:00 & 15:00-17:00, Sat 10:00-12:00, closed Sun; Nov-April Mon-Fri 9:00-12:00, closed Sat-Sun; Klosterhof 11, tel. 07660/910-224). To find a public WC and reasonably priced eating options, go through the archway to the square.

The town of St. Peter is dominated by its giant namesake

Benedictine abbey—red sandstone outside, with an interior dripping with white Rococo curlicues. Duck into the church, finished in 1727, for a glimpse at a classic Rococo interior. While it's not the finest in Germany— you'll see bigger and better in Bavaria—it's the best in the Black Forest. The most interesting feature, the attached library, can be entered only with a German-language tour (church—free, daily 8:00-19:00; library tour—€6; runs Tue at 11:00, Thu at 14:30, Sun at 11:30; enter at Geistliches Zentrum next door to church, tel. 07660/91010).

BLACK FOREST

Returning to Freiburg

Just below St. Peter's abbey is the town's main bus stop, called Zähringer Eck, where you can catch bus #7216 back to Kirchzarten (1-2/hour); from there, catch the train to Freiburg.

Sleeping in St. Märgen and St. Peter

(€1 = about $1.40, country code: 49, area codes: 07669 and 07660)
Accommodations in both towns come with the same KONUS card public-transit deal as Staufen (see page 276)—you could easily stay up here and day-trip down into the valley.

In St. Märgen: $ Gasthaus Pension Rössle is centrally located with 19 rooms (Sb-€34, Db-€66, less for 3 nights or more, Wagensteigstrasse 7, tel. 07669/213, fax 07669/1352, www.roessle -st-maergen.de, roessle-st-maergen@t-online.de).

In St. Peter: $ Gasthof Hirschen is a traditional, old 18-room guest house conveniently situated on the main square (Sb-€39-44, Db-€66-82, Tb-€87-99, Qb-€120, pay Wi-Fi, Bertholdsplatz 1, tel. 07660/204, fax 07660/1557, www.gasthof-hirschen.de, info @gasthof-hirschen.de). **$ Pension Kandelblick,** your budget option, has five basic rooms a 10-minute walk from the abbey and main square (D/Ds-€50-60, cash only, Seelgutweg 5, a block off the main drag at the St. Märgen end of town, tel. 07660/1259).

Short-and-Scenic Black Forest Drive from Freiburg

This pleasant loop takes you through the most representative chunk of the area, including the towns of St. Märgen and St. Peter. This basically passes through much the same scenery as my "St. Märgen and St. Peter Day Trip," earlier, but by car.

Leave Freiburg on Schwarzwaldstrasse (signs to *Donau-eschingen*), which becomes scenic road B-31 down the dark Höllental ("Hell's Valley"). Here the cliffs on either side begin to close in. Just before you enter the narrowest part of the canyon, you'll pass an area known as Himmelreich ("heaven"). This valley was made to order for bandits—those surviving the Höllental felt like they'd reached heaven when they reached this point.

As you enter the narrowest part of the valley, watch for the *Hirschensprung* sign, then look up to the top of the cliff on the right to see a bronze statue of a deer *(Hirsch)* preparing to leap *(Sprung)* over the chasm to escape a hunter, a feat memorialized in a local legend.

After the moody, narrow stretch of the valley, you'll hit a straightaway, and then the road begins a series of switchbacks up and out of the canyon. En route, you're sure to see signs to over-rated, overcrowded Titisee. This famous lake, with a giggle-induc-ing name, is improbably popular among Germans. One glance and you'll be wondering why they even bothered to develop this dull spot into a tourist attraction—and yet it's a huge hit. Don't let morbid curiosity take you to Titisee...or you'll squander valuable Black Forest time. (After all, you can't spell "tourist trap" without "T. T.")

Instead, at Hinterzarten (just before Titisee), turn onto B-500 toward Furtwangen and St. Märgen. Soon you'll come to a fork in the road, where you can choose between heading straight to

BLACK FOREST

Furtwangen (and its German Clock Museum—a detour from this route but worth a visit if you have a car and plenty of time, described on page 288); or turning off for St. Märgen, then St. Peter (both described earlier).

At St. Märgen, visit the museum in the Augustinian cloister—if it's open—and in St. Peter, check out the Rococo church in the former Benedictine abbey. If you have at least three hours, you could park in St. Märgen, do the walk from St. Märgen to St. Peter, and then take the bus back from St. Peter to St. Märgen.

After passing through St. Peter, stick with the main B-31 road (toward Kirchzarten) to head back down to Freiburg. Or, for a longer drive, continue up about 15 minutes from St. Peter through idyllic Black Forest scenery to the pass over Mount Kandel (head for Glottertal; just outside St. Peter, turn right at Elmehof to follow brown signs to *Kandel*). At the summit is the Berghotel Kandel, with parking and fine views on either side of the ridge. For even better views, take a short hike to the 4,000-foot peak (Kandelgipfel), where on a nice day, you can watch paragliders psych themselves up and take off.

On the other side of the pass, the road winds steeply down through a dense forest to Waldkirch, where a fast road takes you down to the Freiburg Nord autobahn entrance. From here you can return to Freiburg, or drive on to Baden-Baden.

Extended Black Forest Drive Between Baden-Baden and Freiburg

For a more thorough (and more interesting) look at the Black Forest, try this drive. Some of these sights are accessible to a point by public transportation, as noted, but can't be done as efficiently as by car. The two major museums of this area—both worth visiting—focus on different characteristics of the Black Forest: farming (the Vogtsbauernhof Black Forest Open-Air Museum) and clockmaking (Furtwangen's German Clock Museum).

Getting Around

Here are the directions for taking in all of the attractions listed here, whether you're heading from Baden-Baden to Freiburg, or vice versa.

By Car from Baden-Baden to Freiburg: Head south from Baden-Baden on B-500, a.k.a. the Schwarzwald-Hochstrasse, which takes you along a ridge through 30 miles of pine forests (and becomes B-28—take it east, signs to Freudenstadt). Eventually you'll reach Freudenstadt, the workaday capital of the northern Black Forest. Wind your way through the sprawl of Freudenstadt, and hop on B-294 southbound toward Triberg. Just after Wolfach and before Hausach, turn south onto B-33/E-531 to Gutach, where you'll visit the Vogtsbauernhof Black Forest Open-Air Museum. Next, continue south on B-33/E-531, turning off to visit Triberg. Leaving Triberg, head south on B-500 to Furtwangen and its impressive German Clock Museum. From Furtwangen, continue south on B-500. From this road, you have two options for joining up with different scenic areas (both described earlier, under "Short and Scenic Black Forest Drive from Freiburg"): Turn off for St. Märgen, then St. Peter. From here, you could take the slower and higher-altitude route to Freiburg via Mount Kandel and Waldkirch. For a more direct, but still scenic approach, continue a bit farther south on B-500 to Hinterzarten, where you can turn right onto B-31 and follow the claustrophobic Höllental ("Hell's Valley"). Either option brings you to Freiburg's backyard.

By Car from Freiburg to Baden-Baden: Begin by following the "Short- and-Scenic Black Forest Drive from Freiburg," described earlier, but continue north on B-500 to Furtwangen for a visit to its German Clock Museum, then Triberg. From Triberg, head north on B-33/E-531 (toward Hausach) to the open-air museum in Gutach, then continue north and pick up B-294 to Freudenstadt, and on to the Schwarzwald-Hochstrasse (B-28, then B-500), which dumps you right on Baden-Baden's back porch.

Sights Between Baden-Baden and Freiburg

▲Vogtsbauernhof Black Forest Open-Air Museum

This museum, the Schwarzwälder Freilichtmuseum Vogts-bauernhof, offers the best look at this region's traditional folk architecture. Built around one grand old farmhouse, the museum is a collection of several old farm buildings, some of which house exhibits on the local dress and lifestyles. While English information is sparse, the place gives you a good sense of traditional rural life in the Black Forest.

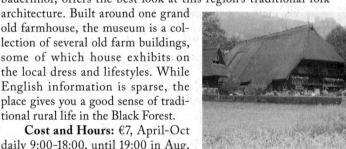

Cost and Hours: €7, April-Oct daily 9:00-18:00, until 19:00 in Aug, last entry one hour before closing, closed Nov-March, €8 guidebook, just outside the town of Gutach, tel. 07831/93560, www.vogtsbauernhof.org.

Getting There: Drivers will find it just south of the town of Hausach (not to be confused with nearby Halsach) on B-33/E-531;

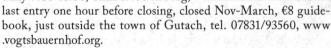

while technically in Gutach, the museum is actually in the countryside. Parking costs €4 (first 45 minutes free), or just €1 if you're visiting the museum (if so, take your parking ticket to the museum entrance rather than paying at the machine, and get it validated when you buy your museum ticket).

Without a car, take the **train** to Hausach (reached via a branch line from Offenburg, on the main Baden-Baden-to-Freiburg line). From the Hausach station, take bus #7150 to the museum (5 minutes) or walk 35 minutes; the whole trip takes 1.5-2 hours from Freiburg or 1-1.5 hours from Baden-Baden.

Demonstrations and Tours: In July and August, you might see costumed docents posted at certain parts of the museum. At other times, it can be pretty sleepy, but occasional live presentations give it some zip; look for a schedule of today's demonstrations on the chalkboard at the entry hall, or ask when you buy your ticket. There are no regularly scheduled English tours; if you'd like to arrange one, you'll pay €35 and must call well in advance.

❍ Self-Guided Tour: From the parking lot, it's a five-minute walk past eateries (described later) and under the railroad tracks to reach the ticket windows and main building. Pick up the map of the complex when you buy your ticket. The various buildings are identified out front (find English on the spinning language board), but the explanations inside are in German only. The following light commentary will bring some meaning to your visit.

The museum is named for its biggest building, the *Vogts-bauernhof,* or "farmhouse of the district governor"—the first, and only original, building on the premises, around which the rest of the complex grew. (As with all open-air folk museums, the other structures were moved here from around the region and then reconstructed.) Built in 1612 and occupied until 1965, this giant farmhouse has distinctive Black Forest features that you'll also see (on a smaller scale) in the surrounding buildings. The characteristic "semi-hipped" roof is wider than the frame of the house, which creates ample dry storage space under the eaves all around the perimeter of the building. In case of a storm, the farmer and livestock could rush in quickly for shelter.

The house is built into the side of a hill, allowing easy ramp access to any of its levels—including the vast "attic." From here, hay would be unloaded into the middle level, and then could easily be dropped down as needed to where the livestock lived below.

People and animals lived under one roof. Explore the people's quarters. In that age of poor nutrition, people didn't grow as tall—you'll see short beds and short doorways made for short people. The kitchen occupied the center of the building, where its stove radiated heat to the surrounding living areas. Notice the lack of a

BLACK FOREST

chimney, and the blackened walls in the kitchen—the stove was open to the roof to allow smoke to flow through the house, dry out the air (which was otherwise made uncomfortably humid by the animals), and sift out through the thatch. The two-story kitchen allowed farmers to smoke meat above while they cooked meals below. The soot also helped to coat and preserve the wood frame. Windows were a sure sign of wealth and status—the bigger the windows, the more prosperous the family.

Surrounding the main *Vogtsbauernhof* building are several smaller ones to explore. The **farm mill** is popular during its live grain-grinding demonstrations, when water power sets the giant gears in motion (daily at 11:15, 12:15, and 14:15, in German only). The **day laborer's cottage** once housed a family with 14 kids; two brothers lived here right up until 1993. Even though it has electricity, it's undeniably simple. The **bakery and distillery** has a communal oven where families from the community baked their bread all at once—an efficient use of limited resources. The "knock-and-drop" **saw mill,** which runs only sporadically (on special request for groups), systematically—little by little—saws planks of wood from huge trunks.

Eating: The shops and restaurants scattered between the parking lot and museum entrance are awfully touristy, but are a fair source for local specialties. Skip the indoor restaurants and instead try your *Frikadelle* (a spiced pork-and-beef patty) or *Schupfnudeln* (potato-based noodles, served fried up with sauerkraut) at the outdoor stands. Don't be shy to try a little of everything; the friendly ladies ladling the portions will fill up your plate with whatever you point to and charge about €7. Be sure to indulge in a creamy slice of *Schwarzwälder Kirschtorte* (€2.50). Closer to the museum, in the main building, is the pricey but convenient Hofengel ("House Angel") restaurant (€5-10 salads, €7-9 light dishes, €12-15 main courses).

Triberg

Deep in the Black Forest, Triberg is a mid-size town that exploits its cuckoo-clock heritage to the hilt. Despite the kitsch, it's a pleasant place to stretch your legs under giant cuckoo-clock facades. Convenient eateries cluster around the lowest reaches of the town's waterfall, near the two main attractions (described on the next page). Touristy as Triberg is, it offers an easy way for travelers without cars to enjoy the Black Forest. The **TI** is located in the Black Forest Museum (tel. 07722/866-490, www.triberg.de).

Getting to Triberg: Drivers on B-500 will go right through the center of town. By **train,** it's a scenic trip from **Freiburg** (hourly, 1.5-1.75 hours, change in Offenburg) or **Baden-Baden** (hourly, 1.25 hours).

▲**Black Forest Museum (Schwarzwaldmuseum)**—Don't confuse this museum with the nearby Vogtsbauernhof Black Forest

Open-Air Museum. Triberg's
Black Forest Museum gives a
fine look at the local culture. It's
well-explained; as you explore its
three floors, you'll find insightful exhibits on various aspects of
Black Forest cultural heritage,
with a special emphasis on engineering (clockmaking, railways,
locally built SABA radios) and crafts (woodcarving, glassmaking).

The main hall contains dozens of dolls wearing traditional
dress from the region, including the distinctive maidens' hats,
piled with gigantic cranberries (married women's hats have black
puffballs). Player pianos, barrel organs, orchestrions ("orchestras-
in-a-box"), and other music-making machines—which were built
here alongside cuckoo clocks—were extremely popular in the days
before radio or record players, when it was the only cheap way to
listen to music. Rounding out the museum are exhibits on farming (a replica of a farmer's traditional quarters), mineral mining,
winter sports, and creepy masks used to celebrate Germanic Mardi
Gras, called Fasnacht.

Cost and Hours: €5, pick up the free one-page English
"Short Tour" at the entrance, a few additional posted explanations in English, daily May-Sept 10:00-18:00, Oct-April 10:00-
17:00, Wallfahrtsstrasse 4, tel. 07722/4434, www.schwarzwald
museum.de.

Triberg Waterfall (Triberger Wasserfall)—Triberg's other
claim to fame is Germany's highest waterfall, where the Gutach
River tumbles 500 feet in several
bounces. Although it seems odd to pay to
see a waterfall, this one really is impressive—especially if you have time to walk
through its steep, misty gorge. Three
entrances lead to the waterfall, at different altitudes (scattered along the twisty
main road toward Furtwangen). While
the lowest entrance—"Haupteingang,"
in the town center, across from the
Black Forest Museum—is most convenient, drivers might want to stop by
the middle entrance ("Scheffelplatz," a

5-minute downhill walk to the middle of the falls). If you're traveling in a group, it's handy to drop the gang off at Scheffelplatz to
hike down, while the driver loops down into town to meet them at

the lower entrance. If you don't want to pay, you can get a partial glimpse of the falls through the trees near the lower entrance.

Cost and Hours: €3.50, less in winter, daily May-Sept 9:00-19:00, Oct-April 10:00-18:00, free entry at other times.

▲▲Furtwangen's German Clock Museum (Deutsches Uhrenmuseum)

The unremarkable town of Furtwangen hosts the most interesting museum in the Black Forest: the excellent German Clock Museum. More than a chorus of cuckoo clocks, this museum is practically evangelical in tracing the development of clocks from the Dark Ages to the Space Age. Because it's modern and well-presented in English, this exhibit makes the history of timekeeping more fascinating than it has any right to be.

Cost and Hours: €4, €10 family ticket, daily April-Oct 9:00-18:00, Nov-March 10:00-17:00, Robert-Gerwig-Platz 1, tel. 07723/920-2800, www.deutsches-uhrenmuseum.de.

Getting There: It's hiding out in the town center of Furtwangen; as you approach the town, closely track the low-profile signs to *Deutsches Uhrenmuseum* or simply *Uhrenmuseum*. It's related—and attached—to the local technical university.

Tours: Tours run daily at 11:00 and cost €2; ask to hear it in English as well as German. In the afternoon, if it's quiet, someone might be able to demonstrate one or two of the interactive pieces for you.

➋ **Self-Guided Tour:** As you enter, borrow the thorough English translations of the descriptions, then match them to the pictures on the posted information to find the right text. Appropriately enough, the collection is displayed chronologically, starting on the first floor (upstairs), then working its way down through the split-level building—follow the *Rundgang* (tour) signs.

Floor 1: Starting with Stonehenge (speculated to be a celestial calendar) and early sundials, the exhibit takes in the full breadth of timepiece history. In the display case of celestial clocks, find the highly detailed **astronomical-geographical clock** from 1787, which used just 24 gears to tell not only the time, but also the position of the stars in the night sky, which saint's day it was, and the phase of the moon.

Black Forest clockmakers achieved a breakthrough when they simplified the timekeeping mechanism so that it could be built almost entirely of wood, allowing the clocks to be sold at a much lower price (leading to a worldwide boom in clock sales). In this collection, you can watch **Black Forest clocks** evolve from rough-hewn wood to delicately painted white lacquer faces. You'll see that locals also figured out how to make musical clocks with

The Black Forest Clockmaker Diaspora

Black Forest clockmakers specialized in affordable, everyday timepieces. Because they could be produced and sold cheaply, Black Forest clocks became popular around the world. Between 1800 and 1850 alone, 15 million Black Forest clocks were sold worldwide. This demand—combined with a need for steady employment among a growing population—persuaded many Black Forest natives to leave home and sell clocks in foreign lands.

From the 1770s through the early 1900s, roving Black Forest clockmakers (called *Uhrenhändler*) traveled far. They'd load their wares onto a wood-frame rucksack and cry, *Ins Uhrenland!*—"To clock country!"...that is, wherever people were buying clocks. Once they found a good market abroad, they'd settle in, set up shop, and create a lucrative little business. Many clockmakers were away from home for months, or even years—and quite a few married into their adopted local communities. (Emigrants from this part of Germany likely started out as clock-sellers.)

Most of these *Uhrenhändler* sold simple "shield clocks" (*Schilduhr*), with a simple face that hid the mechanical workings. The face of the clock could be painted to match the local tastes of the buyer, whether in England, France, Italy, Spain, Russia, Turkey, China, Australia...or the US. But no matter how far from home the clockmakers wandered, and no matter how different the clocks looked, they were still Black Forest at heart.

wooden flutes and bellows—much more affordable than bells or other metal instruments.

The vast collection of **cuckoo clocks** (*Kuckucksuhren* in German) explains the evolution of the Black Forest's most iconic product. The cuckoo clock as we know it was created for a contest in 1850 by Friedrich Eisenlohr, a railway architect who modeled his *Bahnhäusleuhr* clock after a railroad house. While the clocks strike us as quaint and kitschy now, consider how Eisenlohr's idea of shaping a clock like a little house revolutionized the cuckoo-clock-making industry. Cuckoo clocks became very popular—especially among tourists during the late 19th-century heyday of the romantic "Grand Tour" era—and were eventually copied by clockmakers in Switzerland. (If you even hint that cuckoo clocks are Swiss, proud Black Forest natives will quickly set you straight.)

On the way downstairs, ogle the gigantic **"Astronomical**

World Clock" by August Noll. In addition to the giant clock dial, notice the smaller dials to show different time zones—a new concept in the slow-travel era when this was created. The clock has many details to examine—and even more if its mechanical gears are whirring. If a tour is going on, you might get to see this giant

clock in action, with Jesus blessing the 12 apostles as they shuffle past. (If it's not too busy, you can try asking the front desk to turn it on for you.) Next, head downstairs to...

Floor -1: Now in the 20th century, the exhibit shows off pocket watches with precious details (including, at #19, a French watch with decimalized time—one branch of the metric system that never took off). Wristwatches became popular first among women, who didn't have pockets, but were later adopted by men in World War I for easy access while using a rifle. The exhibit on Black Forest clockmaking in the 20th century demonstrates that, even as technology advanced, local clockmakers specialized in straightforward, affordable, everyday timepieces. Quartz technology allowed for far greater accuracy at a much lower price, which made clocks cheap and effectively crippled the industry. Furtwangen no longer makes clocks today, but it's still a respected industrial town.

Ponder this: If Germany is known for its engineering prowess, you can thank clocks. As technology evolved, technical know-how came to be applied to more and more complicated machines. And so, in a way, precision BMWs are the direct descendant of the rough wooden cuckoo clocks that have been made in the Black Forest for centuries.

Floor -2: The bottom level brings the story up to the modern day, from punch-clocks to atomic clocks that strive for ever more precise timekeeping. One fascinating exhibit explains how faster and faster transportation in the late 19th century brought about the need for standardized time across locales. In the past, each town used its own, local solar time. As the railroad advanced, this made a wreck of train schedules and connections (since different towns and countries were a few minutes off from each other). The innovation of the telegraph sealed it: The world's clocks needed to be in sync. Only in the 1870s did scientists begin to pursue standardization, leading in 1884 to the creation of the prime meridian (to use as a starting point for calculating world time zones). Germany didn't adopt a standardized time zone until 1893.

The grand finale is an upbeat combo of mechanical musical instruments, from player pianos to giant wind-up carnival organs.

Notice it's in a soundproof room; to hear some of the thunderous music, you can ask at the desk for someone to turn one on for you. Hearing the amazing variety of sounds, it's fun to imagine how the simple "cuck-oo" of a clock with a little wooden bird evolved into a self-playing musical band in a box.

BLACK FOREST

ROTHENBURG
and the ROMANTIC ROAD

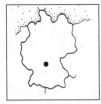

The Romantic Road takes you through Bavaria's medieval heartland, a route strewn with picturesque villages, farmhouses, onion-domed churches, Baroque palaces, and walled cities. The route, which runs from Würzburg to Füssen, is the most scenic way to connect Frankfurt with Munich. No trains run along the full length of the Romantic Road, but Rothenburg (ROH-tehn-burg), the most interesting town along the route, is easy to reach by rail. Drivers can either zero in on Rothenburg or take some extra time to meander from town to town en route. For non-drivers, a tour bus travels the Romantic Road once daily in each direction.

Countless travelers have searched for the elusive "untouristy Rothenburg." There are many contenders (such as Michelstadt, Miltenberg, Bamberg, Bad Windsheim, and Dinkelsbühl), but none holds a candle to the king of medieval German cuteness. Even with crowds, overpriced souvenirs, Japanese-speaking night watchmen, and, yes, even *Schneeballen*, Rothenburg is best. Save time and mileage and be satisfied with the winner.

Rothenburg ob der Tauber

In the Middle Ages, when Frankfurt and Munich were just wide spots on the road, Rothenburg ob der Tauber was a "free imperial city" beholden only to the Holy Roman Emperor. With a whopping population of 6,000, it was one of Germany's largest. Today, it's the country's best-preserved medieval walled town, enjoying tremendous tourist popularity without losing its charm.

During Rothenburg's heyday, from 1150 to 1400, it was a strategic stop on the trade routes between northern and southern Europe. Today, the great trade is tourism: Two-thirds of the townspeople are employed to serve you. While 2.5 million people visit each year, a mere 500,000 spend the night. Rothenburg is yours after dark, when the groups vacate and the town's floodlit cobbles wring some romance out of any travel partner.

Too often, Rothenburg brings out the shopper in visitors before they've had a chance to see the historic town. True, this is a fine place to do your German shopping, but appreciate Rothenburg's great history and sights, too.

Planning Your Time

If time is short, you can make just a two- to three-hour midday stop in Rothenburg, but the town is really best appreciated after the day-trippers have gone home. Spend at least one night in Rothenburg (hotels are cheap and good). With two nights and a day, you'll be able to see more than the essentials and actually relax a little.

Rothenburg in one day is easy, with four essential experiences: the Medieval Crime and Punishment Museum, Tilman Riemenschneider's wood carving in St. Jakob's Church, a walk along the city wall, and the entertaining Night Watchman's Tour. With more time, you could visit several mediocre but entertaining museums, take some scenic hikes and bike rides in the nearby countryside, and enjoy the town's plentiful cafés and shops.

Rothenburg is very busy through the summer and in the Christmas Market month of December. Spring and fall are a joy, but it's pretty bleak from January through March—when most locals are hibernating or on vacation. Many shops stay open on Sundays during the tourist season, but close on Sundays in November and from Christmas to Easter.

There are several Rothenburgs in Germany, so make sure you are going to **Rothenburg ob der Tauber** (not "ob der" any other river); people really do sometimes drive or ride the train to other, nondescript Rothenburgs by accident.

Orientation to Rothenburg

(area code: 09861)
To orient yourself in Rothenburg, think of the town map as a human head. Its nose—the castle garden—sticks out to the left, and the skinny lower part forms a wide-open mouth, with the youth hostel and a recommended hotel in the chin. The town is a delight on foot. No sights or hotels are more than a 15-minute walk from the train station or each other.

Most of the buildings you'll see were in place by 1400. The city was born around its long-gone castle—built in 1142, destroyed

in 1356—which was located where the castle garden is now. You can see the shadow of the first town wall, which defines the oldest part of Rothenburg, in its contemporary street plan. A few gates (called *Tors*—such as the Rödertor or the Spitaltor) from this wall still survive. The richest and biggest houses were in this central part. The commoners built higgledy-piggledy (read: picturesque) houses farther from the center, but still inside the present walls. Rothenburg's classic street scene is the Plönlein ("Little Square"), a picture-perfect tableau of a yellow house wedged between two towers at a diverging road (3 blocks due south of Market Square).

Although Rothenburg is technically in Bavaria, the region around the town is called by its medieval name, *Franken* (Franconia).

Tourist Information

The TI is on Market Square (May-Oct and Dec Mon-Fri 9:00-18:00, Sat-Sun 10:00-17:00; Nov and Jan-April Mon-Fri 9:00-17:00, Sat 10:00-13:00, closed Sun; Marktplatz 2, tel. 09861/404800, www.rothenburg.de). If there's a long line, just raid the rack where they keep all the free pamphlets. The free *Map & Guide* comes with a walking guide to the town. The free *RoTour* monthly magazine lists all the events and entertainment (mostly in German; also look for current concert listing posters here and

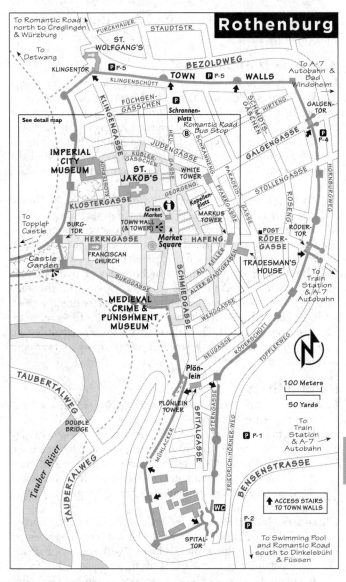

at your hotel). Ask about the daily English walking tour at 14:00 (€7, April-Oct and Dec; see "Tours in Rothenburg," later). The TI has one free Internet terminal (15-minute maximum). Visitors who arrive after closing can check the handy map highlighting which hotels have rooms available, with a free direct phone connection to them; it's just outside the door. A pictorial town map is available free with this book at the Friese shop, two doors west from the TI (toward St. Jakob's Church; see "Shopping in Rothenburg," later).

Arrival in Rothenburg

By Train: It's a 10-minute walk from the station to Rothenburg's Market Square (following the brown *Altstadt* signs, exit left from station, turn right on Ansbacher Strasse, and head straight into the Middle Ages). Day-trippers can leave luggage in station lockers (€1-2, on platform) or at a local shop (try the Friese shop on Market Square, listed on page 310). Free WCs are behind the snack bar next door to the station. Taxis wait at the station (€5-6 to any hotel).

By Car: For tips on getting here from Frankfurt, see "Route Tips for Drivers" on page 322. While much of the town is closed to traffic, anyone with a hotel reservation can drive through pedestrian zones to get to their hotel. The easiest way to enter and leave Rothenburg is generally via Spitalgasse and the Spitaltor (south end). But driving in town can be a nightmare, with many narrow, one-way streets. If you're packing light, just park outside the walls and walk five minutes to the center. Parking lots line the town walls: P1 costs €5 per day; P5 and the south half of P4 are sometimes free on weekends. Only those with a hotel reservation can park within the walls after hours (but no one may park overnight during festivals).

Helpful Hints

Festivals: For one weekend each spring, *Biergartens* spill out into the street and Rothenburgers dress up in medieval costumes to celebrate Mayor Nusch's Meistertrunk victory (May 25-28 in 2012; the story of the draught that saved the town is described under "Meistertrunk Show" on page 299, more info at www.meistertrunk.de). The Reichsstadt festival every September celebrates Rothenburg's history (September 7-9 in 2012).

Christmas Market: Rothenburg is dead in November, January, and February, but December is its busiest month—the entire town cranks up the medieval cuteness with concerts and costumes, shops with schnapps, stalls filling squares, hot spiced wine, giddy nutcrackers, and mobs of earmuffed Germans. Christmas markets are big all over Germany, and Rothenburg's is considered one of the best. The market takes place each year during Advent (Nov 30-Dec 23 in 2012). Virtually all sights listed in this chapter are open longer hours during these four weeks. Try to avoid Saturdays and Sundays, when big-city day-trippers really clog the grog.

Internet Access: Most hotels have Internet access. If yours doesn't, head to the **Nuschhaus Café,** just below Market Square, which has terminals (€3/hour) and Wi-Fi (€2/hour, Mon-Thu 10:00-18:30, Fri-Sun 10:00-20:00, across the street from the Medieval Crime and Punishment Museum at Obere Schmiedgasse 23, tel. 09861/976-838). The **TI** has one free terminal for brief use (maximum 15 minutes).

Laundry: A handy launderette is near the station, off Ansbacher Strasse (€5.50/load, includes soap, English instructions, owner isn't always around to make change so it's smart to bring coins, opens at 8:00, last load Mon-Fri at 18:00, Sat at 14:00, closed Sun, Johannitergasse 9, tel. 09861/2775).

Bike Rental: Consider renting a bike to enjoy the nearby countryside; you can follow the route described on page 309. **Fahrradhaus Krauss** is a big, cheap, reliable bike shop a 10- to 15-minute walk from the old town that rents eight-gear bikes. From the old town, head toward the train station, then continue along Ansbacher Strasse, bearing right over the train tracks (€5/6 hours, €10/24 hours, €15/all weekend, no helmets, Mon-Fri 9:00-18:00, Sat 9:00-13:00, closed Sun but ask about arranging return, Ansbacher Strasse 85, tel. 09861/3495, www.fahrradhaus-krauss.de). Another rental shop—more expensive but closer to town—is **Rad & Tat** (€9/6 hours, €12/24 hours, Mon-Fri 9:00-18:00, Sat 9:00-13:00, closed Sun, Bensenstrasse 17, tel. 09861/87984, www.mietraeder.de).

Taxi: For a taxi, call 09861/2000 or 09861/7227.

Haircuts: At **Salon Wack** (pronounced "vack," not "wack"), Horst and his team speak English and welcome both men and women (wash and cut: €20 for men, €29-34 for women; Tue-Fri 8:00-12:00 & 13:30-18:00, Sat 8:30-14:00, closed Sun-Mon, in the old center just off Wenggasse at Goldene Ringgasse 8, tel. 09861/7834).

Swimming: Rothenburg has a fine swimming complex, with a heated outdoor pool *(Freibad)* from mid-May to mid-September, and an indoor pool and sauna the rest of the year. It's about a 15-minute walk south of the Spitaltor along the main road toward Dinkelsbühl (adults-€3.50, kids-€2, swimsuit rental-€2, towel rental-€2.50; outdoor pool Fri-Tue 9:00-20:00, Wed 6:30-20:00, Thu 10:00-20:00; indoor pool Mon 14:00-21:00, Tue-Thu 9:00-21:00, Fri-Sun 9:00-18:00; Nördlinger Strasse 20, tel. 09861/4565).

Tours in Rothenburg

▲▲**Night Watchman's Tour**—This tour is flat-out the most entertaining hour of medieval wonder anywhere in Germany. The Night Watchman (a.k.a. Hans-Georg Baumgartner) jokes like a

ROTHENBURG

medieval Jerry Seinfeld as he lights his lamp and takes tourists on his rounds, telling slice-of-gritty-life tales of medieval Rothenburg (€7, Easter-Dec nightly at 20:00, in English, meet at Market Square, www.nightwatchman.de). This is the best evening activity in town. Night Watchman fans can also visit his store (see page 310).

Executioner's Tour—Georg Lehle leads a macabre one-hour tour as a 14th-century executioner (€7, April-Dec nightly at 19:00, in English, meet at Market Square).

Old Town Historic Walk—The TI offers 1.5-hour guided walking tours in English (€7, April-Oct and Dec daily at 14:00, no English tours in Nov or Jan-March, departs from Market Square). Take this tour for the serious side of Rothenburg's history, and to make sense of the town's architecture; you won't get as much of that on the fun—and completely different—Night Watchman's Tour. It would be a shame not to take advantage of this informative tour just because you took the other.

Local Guides—A local historian can really bring the ramparts alive. Prices are standardized (€62/1.5 hours, €80/2 hours). Reserve a guide by emailing the TI (info@rothenburg.de; more info under "Guided Tours" at www.rothenburg.de). I've had good experiences with **Martin Kamphans,** who also works as a potter (tel. 09861/7941, www.stadtfuehrungen-rothenburg.de, post@stadtfuehrungen-rothenburg.de).

Self-Guided Walk

Welcome to Rothenburg

This one-hour circular walk weaves Rothenburg's top sights together.

• *Start the walk on Market Square.*

Market Square Spin-Tour

Stand at the bottom of Market Square (10 feet below the wooden post on the corner) and spin 360 degrees clockwise, starting with the Town Hall tower. Now do it again, this time more slowly, following these notes:

Town Hall and Tower: Rothenburg's tallest spire is the Town Hall tower (Rathausturm). At 200 feet, it stands atop the old Town Hall, a white, Gothic, 13th-century building. Notice the tourists enjoying the best view in town from the black top of the tower (€2 and a rigorous but interesting climb, 214 steps, narrow

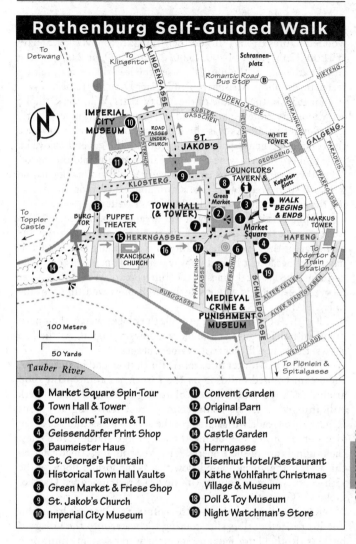

Rothenburg Self-Guided Walk

1. Market Square Spin-Tour
2. Town Hall & Tower
3. Councilors' Tavern & TI
4. Geissendörfer Print Shop
5. Baumeister Haus
6. St. George's Fountain
7. Historical Town Hall Vaults
8. Green Market & Friese Shop
9. St. Jakob's Church
10. Imperial City Museum
11. Convent Garden
12. Original Barn
13. Town Wall
14. Castle Garden
15. Herrngasse
16. Eisenhut Hotel/Restaurant
17. Käthe Wohlfahrt Christmas Village & Museum
18. Doll & Toy Museum
19. Night Watchman's Store

ROTHENBURG

and steep near the top—watch your head, April-Oct daily 9:30-12:30 & 13:00-17:00, closed Nov-March, enter on Market Square through middle arch of new Town Hall). After a fire burned down part of the original building, a new Town Hall was built alongside what survived of the old one (fronting the square). This half of the rebuilt complex is in the Renaissance style from 1570.

Meistertrunk Show: At the top of Market Square stands the proud Councilors' Tavern (clock tower from 1466). In its day, the city council—the rich guys who ran the town government—drank here. Today, it's the TI and the focus of most tourists' attention when the little doors on either side of the clock flip open and the wooden figures (from 1910) do their thing. Be on Market Square at 11:00, 12:00, 13:00, 14:00, 15:00, 20:00, 21:00, or 22:00 for the ritual gathering of the tourists to see the less-than-breathtaking reenactment of the Meistertrunk ("Master Draught") story:

In 1631, in the middle of the Thirty Years' War, the Catholic army took the Protestant town and was about to do its rape, pillage, and plunder thing. As was the etiquette, the mayor had to give the conquering general a welcoming drink. The general enjoyed a huge tankard of local wine. Feeling really good, he told the mayor, "Hey, if you can drink this entire three-liter tankard of wine in one gulp, I'll spare your town." The mayor amazed everyone by drinking the entire thing, and Rothenburg was saved.

While this is a nice story, it was dreamed up in the late 1800s for a theatrical play designed (effectively) to promote a romantic image of the town. In actuality, if Rothenburg was spared, it happened because it bribed its way out of a jam. It was occupied and ransacked several times in the Thirty Years' War, and it never recovered—which is why it's such a well-preserved time capsule today.

For the best show, don't watch the clock; watch the open-mouthed tourists gasp as the old windows flip open. At the late shows, the square flickers with camera flashes.

Bottom of Market Square: At the bottom end of the square, the cream-colored building on the corner has a fine **print shop** around back (described under "Shopping in Rothenburg," later). Adjoining that is the **Baumeister Haus,** featuring a famous Renaissance facade with statues of the seven virtues and the seven vices—the former supporting the latter. The statues are copies; the originals are in the Imperial City Museum (described later on this walk). The green house below that is the former home of the 15th-century Mayor Toppler (it's now the recommended Gasthof Goldener Greifen).

Keep circling to the big 17th-century **St. George's fountain.** The long metal gutters slid, routing the water into the villagers' buckets. Rothenburg had an ingenious water system. Built on a rock, it had one real source above the town, which was plumbed to serve a series of fountains; water flowed from high to low through Rothenburg. Its many fountains had practical functions beyond providing drinking water (some were stocked with fish on market days and during times of siege). Water was used for fighting fires, and because of its plentiful water supply—and its policy of requiring relatively wide lanes as fire breaks—the town never burned entirely, as so many neighboring villages did.

Two fine buildings behind the fountain show the old-time lofts with warehouse doors and pulleys on top for hoisting. All over town, lofts were filled with grain and corn. A year's supply was required by the city so they could survive any siege. The building behind the fountain is an art gallery showing off work by members of the local artists' association (free, Tue-Sun 14:00-18:00, closed Mon). To the right is Marien Apotheke, an old-time pharmacy mixing old and new in typical Rothenburg style.

The broad street running under the Town Hall tower is **Herrngasse.** The town originated with its castle (built in 1142 but now long gone; only the castle garden remains). Herrngasse connected the castle to Market Square. The last leg of this circular walking tour will take you from the castle garden up Herrngasse to where you now stand. For now, walk a few steps down Herrngasse and stand by the arch under the Town Hall tower (between the new and old town halls). On the left wall are the town's measuring rods—a reminder that medieval Germany was made of 300 independent little countries, each with its own weights and measures. Merchants and shoppers knew that these were the local standards: the rod (4.3 yards), the *Schuh* ("shoe," roughly a foot), and the *Ell* (from elbow to fingertip—four inches longer than mine...try it). Notice the protruding cornerstone. These are all over town—originally to protect buildings from reckless horse carts (and vice versa).

• *Under the arch, you'll find the...*

▲Historical Town Hall Vaults (Historiengewölbe)

This grade-schoolish little museum gives a waxy but interesting look at Rothenburg during the Catholics-vs.-Protestants Thirty Years' War. With helpful English descriptions, it offers a look at "the fateful year 1631," a replica of the mythical Meistertrunk tankard, and a dungeon complete with three dank cells and some torture lore.

Cost and Hours: €2.50, daily May-Oct 9:30-17:30, shorter hours April and Dec, closed Nov and Jan-March, tel. 09861/86751.

• *Leaving the museum, turn left (past a much-sketched-and-photographed venerable door), and walk through the courtyard to a square called...*

Green Market (Grüner Markt)

Once a produce market, this is now a parking lot that fills with Christmas shops during December. Notice the clay-tile roofs. These "beaver tail" tiles became standard after thatched roofs were outlawed to prevent fires. Today, all of the town's roofs are made of these. The little fences keep the snow from falling, and catch tiles that blow off during storms. The free public WC is on your left, the recommended Friese shop is on your right, and straight ahead is St. Jakob's Church.

Outside the church, you'll see 14th-century statues (mostly original) showing Jesus praying at Gethsemane, a common feature of Gothic churches. The artist is anonymous, because in the Gothic age (pre-Albrecht Dürer), artists were just nameless craftspeople working only for the glory of God. Five yards to the left (on the wall), notice the nub of a sandstone statue—a rare original, looking pretty bad after 500 years of weather and, more recently, pollution. Most original statues are now in the city museum. The better-preserved statues you see on the church are copies.

• *If it's your wedding day, take the first entrance. Otherwise, use the second (downhill) door to enter...*

▲▲St. Jakob's Church (St. Jakobskirche)

Rothenburg's main church is home to Tilman Riemenschneider's breathtaking, wood-carved *Altar of the Holy Blood.*

Cost and Hours: €2, worthwhile 45-minute audioguide-€2, daily April-Oct 9:00-17:15, Dec 10:00-16:45, Nov and Christmas-March 10:00-12:00 & 14:00-16:00, on Sun wait to enter until services end at 10:45, free helpful English info sheet, concerts and tour schedule posted on the door. There are guided tours in English for no extra charge on Saturdays at 15:00.

Touring the Church: Built in the 14th century, this church has been Lutheran since 1544. The **interior** was "purified" by Romantics in the 19th century—cleaned of everything Baroque or not original and refitted in the Neo-Gothic style. (For example, the baptismal font and the pulpit above the second pew *look* Gothic, but are actually Neo-Gothic.) The stained-glass windows behind the altar, which are most colorful in the morning light, are originals from the 1330s.

At the back of the church, take the stairs that lead up behind the pipe organ. In the loft, you'll find the artistic highlight of Rothenburg and perhaps the most wonderful wood carving in all of Germany: the glorious 500-year-old, 35-foot-high *Altar of the Holy Blood.* Tilman Riemenschneider, the Michelangelo of German woodcarvers, carved this from 1499 to 1504 to hold a precious rock-crystal capsule (set in a cross) that contains a scrap of tablecloth miraculously stained in the shape of a cross by a drop of communion wine. The altar is a realistic commotion, showing that Riemenschneider—while a High Gothic artist—was ahead of his time. Below, in the scene of the Last Supper, Jesus gives Judas a piece of bread, marking him as the traitor, while John lays his head on Christ's lap. Everything is portrayed exactly as described in the Bible. On the left: Jesus enters a walled city. (Historians dispute whether it's Jerusalem, in keeping with the altar's Holy Week theme, or Jericho—notice the man in the tree, who could

ROTHENBURG

be Jericho's shy tax collector Zacchaeus.) Notice the fun attention to detail—down to the nails on the horseshoe. On the right: Jesus prays in the Garden of Gethsemane. Judas, with his big bag of cash, could be removed from the scene—illustrated by photos on the wall nearby—as was the tradition for the four days leading up to Easter.

Head back down the stairs to the church's main hall. Go up front to take a close look at the **main altar** (from 1466, by Friedrich Herlin). Below Christ are statues of six saints. St. James (Jakob in German) is the one with the shell. He's the saint of pilgrims, and this church was a stop on the medieval pilgrimage route to Santiago ("St. James" in Spanish) de Compostela in Spain. Study the painted panels—ever see Peter with spectacles? Around the back of the altarpiece (upper left) is a painting of Rothenburg's Market Square in the 15th century—looking much like it does today, with the exception of the full-Gothic Town Hall (as it was before the big fire of 1501). Notice Christ's face on the veil of Veronica (center of back side). It follows you as you walk from side to side—this must have given the faithful the religious heebie-jeebies four centuries ago.

The **small altar** to the left is also worth a look. It's a century older than the main altar. Notice the unusual Trinity: the Father and Son are literally bridged by a dove, which represents the Holy Spirit. Stepping back, you can see that Jesus is standing on a skull—clearly "overcoming death."

Before leaving the front of the church, notice the old **medallions** above the carved choir stalls. They feature the coats of arms of Rothenburg's leading families and portraits of city and church leaders.

• *Leave the church and, from its outside steps, walk around the corner to the right and under the chapel (built over the road). Go two blocks down Klingengasse and stop at the corner of the street called Klosterhof. Looking down Klingengasse, you see the...*

Klingentor

This cliff tower was Rothenburg's water reservoir. From 1595 until 1910, a copper tank high in the tower provided clean spring water (pumped up by river power) to the privileged. To the right of the Klingentor is a good stretch of wall rampart to walk. To the left, the wall is low and simple, lacking a rampart because it guards only a cliff. Now find the shell decorating a building on the street corner next to you. That's the symbol of St. James (pilgrims commemorated their visit to Santiago de Compostela with a shell),

indicating that this building is associated with the church.
• *Turn left down Klosterhof, passing the shell and, on your right, the colorful, recommended Altfränkische Weinstube am Klosterhof pub, to reach the...*

▲▲Imperial City Museum (Reichsstadt-Museum)

You'll get a scholarly sweep through Rothenburg's history at this museum, housed in the former Dominican convent. Cloistered nuns used the lazy Susan embedded in the wall (to the right of the museum door) to give food to the poor without being seen.

Just follow the *Rundgang/Tour* signs. Highlights include *The Rothenburg Passion*, a 12-panel series of paintings from 1492 showing scenes leading up to Christ's crucifixion (in the *Konventsaal*); an exhibit of Jewish culture in Rothenburg through the ages *(Judaika);* a 14th-century convent kitchen *(Klosterküche)* with a working model of the lazy Susan and a massive chimney; romantic paintings of the town *(Gemäldegalerie);* the fine Baumann collection of weapons and armor; and sandstone statues from the church and Baumeister Haus (the seven vices and seven virtues).

Cost and Hours: €4, daily April-Oct 9:30-17:30, Nov-March 13:00-16:00, English info sheet and descriptions, Klosterhof 5, tel. 09861/939-043, www.reichsstadtmuseum.info.

• *Leaving the museum, go around to the right and into the Convent Garden (when locked at night, continue straight to the T-intersection and see the barn three doors to the right).*

Convent Garden

This spot is a peaceful place to work on your tan...or mix a poisoned potion. Monks and nuns, who were responsible for concocting herbal cures in the olden days, often tended herb gardens. Smell (but don't pick) the *Pfefferminze, Juniper* (gin), *Chamomilla* (disinfectant), and *Origanum*. Don't smell the plants in the poison corner (potency indicated by the number of crosses...like spiciness stars in a restaurant).

Cost and Hours: Free, daily April-Oct 9:00-18:00, Nov-March 13:00-16:00.

• *Exit opposite from where you entered, angling left through the nuns' garden (site of the now-gone Dominican church), eventually leaving via an arch at the far end. Looking to your left, you'll see the back end of an...*

Original Barn

This is the back side of a complex that fronts Herrngasse. Medieval Germans often lived in large structures like this that were like small villages in themselves, with a grouping of buildings and open spaces. The typical design included a house, a courtyard, a stable, a garden, and, finally, a barn. Notice how the bulging wall is corseted by a brace with iron washers. Crank on its nuts and the building will stand up straight.

• *Now go downhill to the...*

Town Wall

This part of the wall (view through bars, look to far right) takes advantage of the natural fortification provided by the cliff, and is therefore much smaller than the ramparts. Angle left along the wall to the big street (Herrngasse), then right under the Burgtor tower. Notice the tiny "eye of the needle" door cut into the big door. If trying to get into town after curfew, you could bribe the guard to let you through this door (which was small enough to keep out any fully armed attackers).

• *Step through the gate and outside the wall. Look around and imagine being locked out in the year 1400. This was a wooden drawbridge (see the chain slits above). Notice the "pitch nose" mask—designed to pour boiling Nutella on anyone attacking. High above is the town coat of arms: a red castle* (roten Burg).

Castle Garden (Burggarten)

The garden before you was once that red castle (destroyed in the 14th century). Today, it's a picnic-friendly park. The chapel (50 yards into the park on the left) is the only bit of the original castle to survive. It's now a memorial to local Jews killed in a 1298 slaughter. A few steps beyond that is a grapevine trellis that provides a fine picnic spot. If you walk all the way out to the garden's far end, you'll find a great viewpoint (well past the tourists, and considered the best place to kiss by romantic local teenagers). But the views of the lush Tauber River Valley below are just as good from the top end of the park. Facing the town, on the left, a path leads down to the village of Detwang (you can see the church spire below)—a town even older than Rothenburg (for a walk to Detwang, see "A Walk in the Countryside," page 308). To the right is a fine view of the fortified Rothenburg and the "Tauber Riviera" below.

• *Return to the tower, cross carefully under the pitch nose, and hike back up Herrngasse to your starting point.*

Herrngasse

Many towns have a Herrngasse, where the richest patricians and merchants (the *Herren*) lived. Predictably, it's your best chance to see the town's finest old mansions. Strolling back to Market Square, you'll pass the old-time puppet theater (German only, on left) and the Franciscan church (from 1285, oldest in town, on right). The house at #18 is the biggest patrician house on the street. The family, which has lived here for three centuries, disconnected the four old-time doorbells. Their door—big enough to allow a carriage in (with a human-sized door cut into it)—is typical of the age. To see the traditional house-courtyard-stables-garden-barn layout, pop into either #14 (now an apartment block) or—if that's closed—the shop across the street, at #11. The Eisenhut Hotel, with its recommended restaurant, is Rothenburg's fanciest and worth a peek inside. The Käthe Wohlfahrt Christmas shops (at Herrngasse 1 and 2; described later, under "Shopping in Rothenburg") are your last, and perhaps greatest, temptations before reaching your starting and ending point: Market Square.

Sights in Rothenburg

Museums Within a Block of Market Square

▲▲Medieval Crime and Punishment Museum (Mittelalterliches Kriminalmuseum)—This museum is the best of its kind, specializing in everything connected to medieval criminal justice. Learn about medieval police, medieval criminal law, and above all, instruments of punishment and torture—even a special cage complete with a metal gag for nags. The museum is more eclectic than its name, and includes exhibits on general history, superstition, biblical art, and temporary displays in a second building.

Follow the yellow arrows—the one-way traffic system makes it hard to double back. Exhibits are tenderly described in English.

Cost and Hours: €4, daily May-Oct 10:00-18:00, Nov and Jan-Feb 14:00-16:00, Dec and March 13:00-16:00, April 11:00-17:00, last entry 45 minutes before closing, fun cards and posters, Burggasse 3-5, tel. 09861/5359, www.kriminalmuseum.rothen burg.de.

Nearby: If you insist on trying a *Schneeball*, the museum café (located in the next building down Burggasse) sells mini-*Schneeballen* for €0.40 (open May-Oct Tue-Thu and Sat-Sun, closed Mon and Fri and Nov-April, no museum admission required for café after 13:00).

▲Doll and Toy Museum (Puppen- und Spielzeugmuseum)— These two floors of historic *Kinder* cuteness are a hit with many little kids. Pick up the free English binder (just past the entry curtain) for an extensive description of the exhibits.

Cost and Hours: €4, family ticket-€10, daily March-Dec 9:30-18:00, Jan-Feb 11:00-17:00, just off Market Square, downhill from the fountain at Hofbronnengasse 11-13, tel. 09861/7330, www.spielzeugmuseum.rothenburg.de.

▲**German Christmas Museum (Deutsches Weihnachts- museum)**—This excellent museum, upstairs in the giant Käthe Wohlfahrt Christmas Village shop, tells the history of Christmas decorations. There's a unique and thoughtfully described collection of Christmas-tree stands, mini-trees sent in boxes to WWI soldiers at the front, early Advent calendars, old-time Christmas cards, and a look at tree decorations through the ages—including the Nazi era and when you were a kid. The museum is not just a ploy to get shoppers to spend more money, but a serious collection managed by professional curator Felicitas Höptner.

Cost and Hours: €4, April-Dec daily 10:00-18:00, Jan-March Sat-Sun 10:00-18:00 and irregularly on weekdays, last entry at 17:00, Herrngasse 1, tel. 09861/409-365, www.germanchristmas museum.com. You can visit the museum at the €2.50 student rate with this book in 2012—if you promise to learn something.

More Sights in Rothenburg

▲▲**Walk the Wall**—Just longer than a mile and a half around, providing great views and a good orientation, this walk can be done

by those under six feet tall in less than an hour (unless your camera can't stop snapping). The hike requires no special sense of balance. This walk is covered and is a great option in the rain. Photographers will stay very busy, especially before breakfast or at sunset, when the lighting is best and the crowds are fewest. You can enter or exit the ramparts at nearly every tower. The best fortifications are in the Spitaltor (south end). Climb the Rödertor en route (described next). The names you see along the way belong to people who donated money to rebuild the wall after World War II, and those who've more recently donated €1,000 per meter for the maintenance of Rothenburg's heritage.

▲**Rödertor**—The 13th-century wall tower nearest the train station is the only one you can climb. It's worth the 135 steps for the view and a short but fascinating rundown on the bombing of Rothenburg in the last weeks of World War II, when the east part of the city was destroyed. If you climb this, you can skip the more claustrophobic Town Hall tower climb.

Cost and Hours: €1.50, pay at top, unreliable hours, usually open daily April-Oct 10:00-16:00, closed Nov-March, WWII photos have English translations.

▲▲**The Allergic-to-Tourists Wall and Moat Walk**—For a quiet and scenic break from the tourist crowds and a chance to

ROTHENBURG

appreciate the marvelous fortifications of Rothenburg, consider this hike: From the Castle Garden, go right and walk outside the wall to the Klingentor. At the Klingentor, climb up to the ramparts and walk on the wall past the Galgentor to the Rödertor. Then descend, leave the old town, and hike through the park (once the moat) down to the Spitaltor. Explore the fortifications here before hiking a block up Spitalgasse, turning left to pass the youth hostel, popping back outside the wall, and heading along the upper scenic reaches of the river valley and above the vineyards back to the Castle Garden.

▲**Tradesman's House (Alt-Rothenburger Handwerkerhaus)**—See the everyday life of a Rothenburger in the town's heyday in this restored 700-year-old home.

Cost and Hours: €2.50; Easter-Oct Mon-Fri 11:00-17:00, Sat-Sun 10:00-17:00; Dec daily 14:00-16:00; closed Nov and Jan-Easter; near Markus Tower at Alter Stadtgraben 26, tel. 09861/5810.

St. Wolfgang's Church—This fortified Gothic church is built into the medieval wall at the Klingentor. Its dungeon-like passages and shepherd's-dance exhibit are pretty lame.

Cost and Hours: €1.50, Wed-Mon April-Sept 10:00-13:00 & 14:30-17:00, Oct 10:00-16:00, closed Tue and Nov-March.

Near Rothenburg

▲**A Walk in the Countryside**—From the *Burggarten* (castle garden), head into the Tauber Valley. With your back to town, go down the hill, exiting the castle garden on your left. Once outside the wall, walk around, keeping the castle and town on your right. The trail becomes really steep, taking you down to the wooden covered bridge on the valley floor. Across the bridge, the road goes left to Toppler Castle and right (downstream, with a pleasant parallel footpath) to Detwang.

Toppler Castle (Topplerschlösschen) is cute, skinny, sky-blue, and 600 years old. It was the castle/summer home of the medieval

Mayor Toppler. The tower's top looks like a house—a sort of tree fort for grownups. It's in a farmer's garden, and it's open whenever he's around and willing to let you in (€1.50, normally Fri-Sun 13:00-16:00, closed Mon-Thu and Nov, one mile from town center at Taubertalweg 100, tel. 09861/7358). People say the mayor had this valley-floor escape built to get people to relax about leaving the fortified town...or to hide a mistress.

To extend your stroll, walk back

to the bridge and follow the river downstream (passing the recommended Unter den Linden beer garden) to the peaceful village of **Detwang.** One of the oldest villages in Franconia (one of Germany's medieval dukedoms), Detwang dates from 968. Like Rothenburg, it has a Riemenschneider altarpiece in its church.

Franconian Bike Ride—To get a fun, breezy look at the countryside around Rothenburg, rent a bike from Fahrradhaus Krauss (see "Helpful Hints" on page 297). For a pleasant half-day pedal, escape the old town through the Rödertor, bike along Topplerweg to the Spitaltor, and follow the curvy road down into the river valley. Turn right at the yellow *Leutzenbronn* sign to cross the double-arcaded bridge. From here a peaceful road follows the river downstream to **Detwang,** passing the cute Toppler Castle (described earlier). From Detwang, follow the main road to the old mill, and turn left to follow the *Liebliches Taubertal* bike path signs as far up the Tauber River (direction: Bettwar) as you like. After 2.5 miles, you'll arrive in the sleepy farming town of **Bettwar,** where you can claim a spot among the chickens and the apple trees for a picnic or have a drink at one of the two restaurants in town.

Franconian Open-Air Museum (Fränkisches Freilandmuseum)—A 20-minute drive from Rothenburg—in the undiscovered "Rothenburgy" town of Bad Windsheim—is an open-air folk museum that, compared with others in Europe, is a bit humble. But it tries very hard and gives you the best look around at traditional rural Franconia.

Cost and Hours: €6, daily mid-March-Sept 9:00-18:00, Oct-mid-Dec 10:00-16:00, closed mid-Dec-mid-March, last entry one hour before closing, tel. 09841/66800, www.freilandmuseum.de.

Shopping in Rothenburg

Be warned...Rothenburg is one of Germany's best shopping towns. Do it here and be done with it. Lovely prints, carvings, wine glasses, Christmas-tree ornaments, and beer steins are popular. Rödergasse is the old town's everyday shopping street. There's also a modern shopping center across the street from the train station.

Christmas Souvenirs

Rothenburg is the headquarters of the **Käthe Wohlfahrt** Christmas trinkets empire, which is spreading across the half-timbered reaches of Europe. In Rothenburg, tourists flock to two Käthe Wohlfahrt stores (at Herrngasse 1 and 2, just off Market Square). Start with the **Christmas Village** (Weihnachtsdorf) at Herrngasse 1. This Christmas wonderland is filled with enough twinkling lights (196,000—mostly LEDs) to require a special electrical hookup. You're greeted by instant Christmas mood music (best appreciated on a hot day in July) and American and Japanese tourists hungrily filling little woven shopping baskets with €5-8 goodies to hang on their trees. (OK, I admit it, my Christmas tree sports a few KW ornaments.) Let the spinning flocked tree whisk you in, but pause at the wall of Steiffs, jerking uncontrollably and mesmerizing little kids. The **Christmas Museum** upstairs is described earlier, under "Sights in Rothenburg." The smaller **Christmas Market** (Weihnachtsmarkt), across the street at Herrngasse 2, specializes in finely crafted wooden ornaments. A third, much smaller store is at Untere Schmiedgasse 19. Käthe started the business in Stuttgart in 1964, and it's now run by her son Harald Wohlfahrt, who lives in Rothenburg (all stores open Mon-Sat 9:00-18:00, May-Dec also most Sun 10:00-17:00, Jan-April closed Sun but museum and museum shop open, 10 percent discount on official KW products with this book in 2012, tel. 09861/409-150, www.wohlfahrt.com or www.bestofchristmas.com).

Traditional German Souvenirs

The **Friese shop** has been welcoming my readers for more than 30 years (on the smaller square just off Market Square, west of TI, on corner across from free public WC). Cuckoo with friendliness, trinkets, and souvenirs, they give shoppers with this book tremendous service: a 10 percent discount and a free pictorial map (normally €1.50). Anneliese Friese, who runs the place with her son Bernie (ask him about the plaque on the town wall), charges only her cost for shipping and lets tired travelers leave their bags in her back room for free (Mon-Sat 9:00-17:00, Sun 10:00-16:00, Grüner Markt 8, tel. 09861/7166, fax 09861/936-619, anneliese-friese@gmx.de).

The **Night Watchman's Store** (Nachtwächterladen), run by the watchman's wife, gives Night Watchman fans a chance to try on the Night Watchman's hat, blow through a drinking horn, or browse medieval clothing (April-Dec daily 10:00-18:00; Jan-March open only Sat 11:00-17:00; just below Market Square at Untere Schmiedgasse 7, tel. 09861/938633). See page 297 for details on the Night Watchman's entertaining tour.

Romantic Prints: The Ernst Geissendörfer print shop has sold fine prints, etchings, and paintings on the corner of Market Square since 1908. To find the shop, walk a few steps down Hafengasse (it's on your right, just before the Bosporus Café). If you're interested in more expensive prints and etchings than those on display, ask Frau Geissendörfer to take you upstairs—she'll offer you a free shot of German brandy while you browse. In 2012, show this book for a 10 percent discount off marked prices on all cash purchases, or minimum €50 credit-card purchases (May-Dec daily 11:00-18:00; March-April Mon-Sat 11:00-18:00, closed Sun;

closed Jan-Feb; Obere Schmiedgasse 1 at corner of Hafengasse, tel. 09861/2005, www.geissendoerfer.de).

Wine Stuff: You'll recognize local Franconian wines by the shape of the bottle—short, stubby, and round. For characteristic wine glasses, winemaking gear, and the real thing from the town's oldest winemakers, drop by the **Glocke Weinladen am Plönlein** (daily 10:00-18:00, Untere Schmiedgasse 27—see page 320 for info on wine-tasting).

Books: A good bookstore is **Rothenburger Büchermarkt** at Rödergasse 3, on the corner of Alter Stadtgraben (Mon-Sat 9:00-18:30, Sun 10:30-18:00, Jan-April closed Sun).

Mailing Your Goodies Home: You can get handy yellow €2.50 boxes at the old town **post office** (Mon-Fri 9:00-13:00 & 14:00-17:30, Sat 9:00-12:00, closed Sun, inside photo shop at Rödergasse 11). The main post office is in the shopping center across from the train station.

Pastries: Those who prefer to eat their souvenirs browse the *Bäckereien* (bakeries). Their succulent pastries, pies, and cakes are

pleasantly distracting...but skip the bad-tasting *Rothenburger Schneeballen*. Unworthy of the heavy promotion they receive, *Schneeballen* are bland pie crusts crumpled into a ball and dusted with powdered sugar or frosted with sticky-sweet glop. There's little reason to waste your appetite on a *Schneeball* when you can enjoy a curvy *Mandelhörnchen* (almond crescent), a triangular *Nussecke* ("nut corner"), a round *Florentiner* cookie, a couple of fresh *Krapfen* (like jelly doughnuts), or even just a soft, warm German pretzel.

Sleeping in Rothenburg

Rothenburg is crowded with visitors, but most are day-trippers. Except for the rare Saturday night and during festivals (see page 296), finding a room is easy throughout the year. Competition keeps quality high. If you want to splurge, you'll snare the best value by paying extra for the biggest and best rooms at the hotels I recommend.

Train travelers save steps by staying in the area toward the Rödertor (east end of town). Hotels and guest houses will sometimes pick up tired heavy-packers at the station. If you're driving and unable to find where you're sleeping, stop and give them a call. They will likely come rescue you.

Keep your key when out late. Rothenburg's hotels are small,

Sleep Code

(€1 = about $1.40, country code: 49, area code: 09861)
S = Single, **D** = Double/Twin, **T** = Triple, **Q** = Quad, **b** = bathroom,
s = shower only. Unless otherwise noted, credit cards are
accepted, English is spoken, and breakfast is included.

To help you sort easily through these listings, I've divided
the accommodations into three categories, based on the price
for a standard double room with bath:

$$$ Higher Priced—Most rooms €80 or more.
$$ Moderately Priced—Most rooms between €60-80.
$ Lower Priced—Most rooms €60 or less.

Prices can change without notice; verify the hotel's
current rates online or by email. For other updates, see www
.ricksteves.com/update.

and they often lock the front entrance at about 22:00, asking you
to let yourself in through a side door.

In the Old Town

$$$ Hotel Kloster-Stüble, deep in the old town near the cas-
tle garden, is my classiest listing. Rudolf does the cooking, while
Erika—his fun and energetic first mate—welcomes guests.
Twenty-one rooms fill two medieval buildings, connected by
a modern atrium. The hotel is just off Herrngasse on a tiny side
street (Sb-€58-78, traditional Db-€88-108, bigger and more mod-
ern Db-€108-128, Tb-€108-146, see website for suites and fam-
ily rooms, kids 5 and under free, free Internet access, free Wi-Fi
in most rooms, Heringsbronnengasse 5, tel. 09861/938-890, fax
09861/938-829, www.klosterstueble.de, hotel@klosterstueble.de).

$$$ Hotel Spitzweg is a rustic-yet-elegant 1536 mansion
(never bombed or burned) with 10 big rooms, open beams, and
endearing hand-painted antique furniture. It's run by gentle Herr
Hocher, whom I suspect is the former Wizard of Oz—now retired
and in a very good mood (Sb-€65, Db-€85-95, Tb-€115, Qb apart-
ment-€150, non-smoking, elegant breakfast room, free parking, pay Internet access and Wi-Fi at son-in-law's nearby hotel,
Paradeisgasse 2, tel. 09861/94290, fax 09861/1412, www.hotel
-spitzweg.de, info@hotel-spitzweg.de).

$$$ Hotel Gerberhaus is warmly run by Inge and Kurt and
daughter Deborah, who mix modern comforts into 20 bright and
airy rooms while maintaining a sense of half-timbered elegance.
Enjoy the pleasant garden in back (Sb-€65-75, Db-€79-120,
Tb-€139-150, Qb-€145-165, prices depend on room size; 2-room

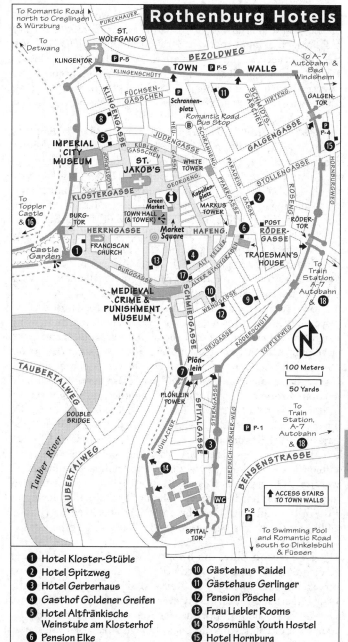

Rothenburg Hotels

- ➊ Hotel Kloster-Stüble
- ➋ Hotel Spitzweg
- ➌ Hotel Gerberhaus
- ➍ Gasthof Goldener Greifen
- ➎ Hotel Altfränkische Weinstube am Klosterhof
- ➏ Pension Elke
- ➐ Hotel Café Uhl
- ➑ Gästehaus Flemming
- ➒ Kreuzerhof Hotel
- ➓ Gästehaus Raidel
- ⓫ Gästehaus Gerlinger
- ⓬ Pension Pöschel
- ⓭ Frau Liebler Rooms
- ⓮ Rossmühle Youth Hostel
- ⓯ Hotel Hornburg
- ⓰ To Pension Fuchsmühle
- ⓱ Internet Café
- ⓲ To Bike Rentals (2)

ROTHENBURG

suite in separate building-€130/2 people, €180/4 people; 10 percent off the second and subsequent nights and a free *Schneeball* if you pay cash, non-smoking, 4 rooms have canopied 4-poster *Himmel* beds, free Internet access, free Wi-Fi with this book, laundry-€7, close to P1 parking lot, Spitalgasse 25, tel. 09861/94900, fax 09861/86555, www.gerberhaus.rothenburg.de, gerberhaus@romanticroad.com). The downstairs café and *Biergarten* serve good soups, salads, and light lunches.

$$$ Gasthof Goldener Greifen, once Mayor Toppler's home, is a big, traditional, 600-year-old place with 14 spacious rooms and all the comforts. It's run by a helpful family staff and creaks with rustic splendor (Sb-€48, small Db-€65, big Db-€85-90, Tb-€105-125, Qb-€125-145, 10 percent less for 3-night stays, non-smoking, Wi-Fi-€2 per stay, full-service laundry-€8, free and easy parking, half a block downhill from Market Square at Obere Schmiedgasse 5, tel. 09861/2281, fax 09861/86374, www.gasthof-greifen-rothenburg.de, info@gasthof-greifen-rothenburg.de, Brigitte and Klingler family). The family also has a couple of loaner bikes free for guests, and runs a good restaurant, serving meals in the back garden or dining room.

$$ Hotel Altfränkische Weinstube am Klosterhof is *the* place for well-heeled bohemians. Mario, Hanne, and their lovely daughter Viktoria rent six cozy rooms above their dark and evocative pub in a 600-year-old building. It's an upscale *Lord of the Rings* atmosphere, with TVs, modern showers, open-beam ceilings, and canopied four-poster beds. They also have two similarly decorated rooms of equal quality in another building a couple of doors away (Sb-€59, Db-€65, bigger Db-€74, Db suite-€82, Tb-€89, cash preferred, kid- and dog-friendly, free Wi-Fi, free parking, off Klingengasse at Klosterhof 7, tel. 09861/6404, fax 09861/6410, www.romanticroad.com/altfraenkische-weinstube, info on second building at www.am-klosterhof.de, email through website). Their pub is a candlelit classic—and a favorite with locals, serving hot food to Hobbits until 22:30, and closing at 1:00 in the morning. Drop by on Wednesday evening (19:00-24:00) for the English Conversation Club (see "Meet the Locals" on page 321).

$$ Pension Elke, run by spry Erich Endress and his son Klaus, rents 12 modern and comfy rooms above the family grocery store. Guests who jog are welcome to join Klaus on his half-hour run around the city every evening at 19:30 (S-€30, Sb-€40, D-€42-48, Db-€60-65, price depends on room size, extra bed-€18, 10 percent discount with this book through 2012 when you stay at least 2 nights, cash only, free Internet access and Wi-Fi; reception in grocery store until 19:00, otherwise go around corner to back of building and ring bell at top of stairs; near Markus Tower at

Rödergasse 6, tel. 09861/2331, fax 09861/935-355, www.pension -elke-rothenburg.de, info@pension-elke-rothenburg.de).

$$ Hotel Café Uhl offers 12 fine rooms over a pastry shop (Sb-€35-58, Db-€59-79, Tb-€82-105, Qb-€98-125, price depends on room size, 10 percent discount with this book and cash in 2012, reception in café, pay Internet access, free Wi-Fi, parking-€6, closed Jan, Plönlein 8, tel. 09861/4895, fax 09861/92820, www .hotel-uhl.de, info@hotel-uhl.de, Paul and Robert the baker).

$$ Gästehaus Flemming has seven tastefully modern, fresh, and comfortable rooms and a peaceful terrace and garden behind St. Jakob's Church (Sb-€49, Db-€62, Tb-€84, cash only, non-smoking, no Internet access, Klingengasse 21, tel. 09861/92380, fax 09861/976-384, www.gaestehaus-flemming.de, gaestehaus -flemming@t-online.de, Regina).

$$ Kreuzerhof Hotel offers nine pleasant rooms surrounding a courtyard on a quiet side street near the Rödertor (Sb-€45, Db-€64-69, Tb-€84-92, Qb-€99-109, 6-bed room-€135-149, family deals, non-smoking, free Internet access and Wi-Fi, laundry-€6/load, parking in courtyard-€3, Millergasse 2-6, tel. 09861/3424, fax 09861/936-730, www.kreuzerhof.eu, info @kreuzerhof.eu, Heike and Walter Maltz).

$ Gästehaus Raidel rents eight rooms in a 500-year-old house filled with beds and furniture, all handmade by friendly Norry Raidel himself. The ramshackle ambience makes me want to sing

the *Addams Family* theme song—but the place has a rare, time-passed family charm. Norry, who plays in a Dixieland band, has invented a fascinating hybrid saxophone/trombone called the Norryphone... and loves to jam (Sb-€45, Db-€69, Tb-€90, Qb suite-€120, cash only, free Wi-Fi, Wenggasse 3, tel. 09861/ 3115, Norry asks you to use the reservations form at www.romantic road.com/raidel).

$ Gästehaus Gerlinger, a fine value, has four comfortable rooms in a pretty 16th-century house with a small terrace for guests (Db-€55, or €53/night with 2-night stay; Tb-€68, cash only, non-smoking, Wi-Fi, easy parking, Schlegeleinsweth 10, tel. 09861/87979, mobile 0171-690-0752, www.pension-gerlinger.de, info@pension-gerlinger.de, Hermann).

$ Pension Pöschel is simple and friendly, with six plain rooms in a concrete but pleasant building, and an inviting garden out back. Only one room has a private shower and toilet (S-€25, D-€45, Db-€50, T-€60, Tb-€65, small kids free, cash only, non-smoking, free Wi-Fi, Wenggasse 22, tel. 09861/3430, mobile

ROTHENBURG

01707-007-041, www.pensionpoeschel.de, pension.poeschel@t -online.de, Bettina).

$ Frau Liebler rents two large modern ground-floor rooms with kitchenettes. They're great for those looking for real privacy— you'll have your own room fronting a quiet cobbled lane just below Market Square. On the top floor is an attractive two-bedroom apartment (Db-€44, apartment-€44, extra bed-€12, 10 percent discount for 2 or more nights with this book in 2012, breakfast-€6, cash only, non-smoking, pay Internet access, free Wi-Fi, laundry-€5, behind Christmas shop at Pfäffleinsgässchen 10, tel. 09861/709-215, fax 09861/709-216, www.gaestehaus-liebler.de).

$ Rossmühle Youth Hostel, run since 1981 by Eduard Schmitz, rents 186 beds in two buildings. While it's mostly four- to six-bed dorms, this charming hostel also has 15 doubles. Reception is in the droopy-eyed building—formerly a horse mill, it was used when the old town was under siege and the river-powered mill was inaccessible (dorm bed-€23, bunk-bed Db-€53-55, guests over 26 pay €4 extra unless traveling with a family, nonmembers pay €3 extra, includes breakfast and sheets, all-you-can-eat dinner-€5.50, pay Wi-Fi, self-serve laundry including soap-€5, close to P1 parking lot, entrance on Rossmühlgasse, tel. 09861/94160, fax 09861/941-620, www.rothenburg.jugendherberge.de, rothenburg @jugendherberge.de).

Outside the Wall

$$$ Hotel Hornburg, a grand 1903 mansion, is close to the train station, a two-minute walk outside the wall. With groomed grounds, gracious sitting areas, and 10 spacious, tastefully decorated rooms, it's a super value (Sb-€58-78, Db-€78-108, Tb-€100-130, ground-floor rooms, non-smoking, family-friendly, dogs welcome—ask for pet-free room if you're allergic, free Internet access and Wi-Fi; if walking, exit station and go straight on Ludwig-Siebert-Strasse, then turn left on Mannstrasse until you're 100 yards from town wall; if driving, the hotel is across from parking lot P4; Hornburgweg 28, at intersection with Mannstrasse, tel. 09861/8480, fax 09861/5570, www.hotel-hornburg.de, info@hotel -hornburg.de, Gabriele and Martin).

$$ Pension Fuchsmühle is a guest house in a renovated old mill on the river below the castle end of Rothenburg, across from the Toppler Castle. It feels rural, but is a pleasant (though steep) 15-minute hike to Market Square, and a €10 taxi ride from the train station. Alex and Heidi Molitor, a young couple with kids, run a book-lined café on summer weekends and offer eight bright, modern light-wood rooms. The building's electric power comes from the millwheel by the entrance, with excess sold to the grid (Sb-€45, Db-€68, Tb-€90, Qb-€120 3-room suite-€150/5 people or €180/6 people, extra bed-€25, less if you stay at least 5 days, includes healthy farm-fresh breakfasts—or €9 less per person if you don't want breakfast, non-smoking, free Wi-Fi, free parking, flashlights provided for your walk back after dark, Taubertalweg 103, tel. 09861/92633, fax 09861/933895, www.fuchsmuehle.de, fuchsmuehle@t-online.de).

Eating in Rothenburg

Many restaurants take a mid-afternoon break, and stop serving lunch at 14:00 and dinner as early as 20:00. My recommendations are all within a five-minute walk of Market Square. While all survive on tourism, many still feel like local hangouts. Your choices are typical German or ethnic. Any bakery will sell you a sandwich for a couple of euros.

Traditional German Restaurants

Gasthof Goldener Greifen is in a historic building just off the main square. The Klingler family serves quality Franconian food at a good price...and with a smile. The wood is ancient and polished from generations of happy use, and the ambience is practical rather than posh—and that's just fine with me (€8-15 main courses, €12 three-course daily specials, €10 one-plate specials include a drink, super-cheap kids' meals, Mon-Sat 11:30-21:00, may open Sun 11:30-14:00, Obere Schmiedgasse 5, tel. 09861/2281).

Hotel Restaurant Kloster-Stüble, on a small street off Herrngasse near the castle garden, is a classy place for delicious and beautifully presented traditional cuisine, including homemade *Maultaschen* (similar to ravioli). Chef Rudy's food is better than his English, so head waitress Erika makes sure communication goes smoothly. The shady terrace is nice on a warm summer evening. I prefer their traditional dining room to the stony, sleek, modern room (€10-16 main courses, Thu-Tue 11:00-14:00 & 18:00-21:00, closed Wed, Heringsbronnengasse 5, tel. 09861/938-890).

Bürgerkeller is a typical European cellar restaurant with a quiet, calming atmosphere, medieval murals, pointy pikes, and a few sidewalk tables for good weather. Without a burger in sight (*Bürger* means "townsman"), English-speaking Harry Terian and his family pride themselves on quality local cuisine, offering a small but inviting menu and reasonable prices. Harry likes oldies, and you're welcome to look over his impressive playlist and request your favorite music (€7-13 main courses, cash only, Thu-Tue 12:00-14:00 & 17:30-21:00, closed Wed, near bottom of Herrngasse at #24, tel. 09861/2126).

Altfränkische Weinstube am Klosterhof seems designed for gnomes to celebrate their anniversaries. At this very dark pub,

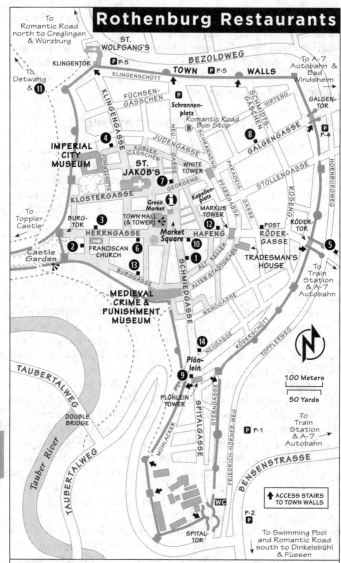

Rothenburg Restaurants

1. Gasthof Goldener Greifen
2. Hotel Restaurant Kloster-Stüble
3. Bürgerkeller
4. Altfränkische Weinstube am Klosterhof
5. Gasthof Rödertor & Beer Garden
6. Eisenhut Restaurant & Beer Garden
7. Reichs-Küchenmeister
8. Pizzeria Roma
9. China-Restaurant Peking
10. Bosporus Café
11. To Unter den Linden Beer Garden
12. Eis Café D' Isep
13. Trinkstube zur Hölle
14. Restaurant Glocke

ROTHENBURG

classically candlelit in a 600-year-old building, Mario whips up gourmet pub grub (€7-14 main courses, hot food served 18:00-22:30, closes at 1:00 in the morning, off Klingengasse at Klosterhof 7, tel. 09861/6404). If you'd like dinner company, drop by on Wednesday evening, when the English Conversation Club has a big table reserved from 19:00 on (see "Meet the Locals," page 321). You'll eat well and with new friends—both travelers and locals.

Gasthof Rödertor, just outside the wall through the Rödertor, is a lively place where Rothenburgers go for a hearty meal at a good price. Their passion is potatoes—the menu is dedicated to spud cuisine. Try a €7 plate of *Schupfnudeln,* potato noodles with sauerkraut and bacon (€6-12 main courses, daily 11:30-14:00 & 17:30-22:00, Sun until 21:00, Ansbacher Strasse 7, tel. 09861/2022). They also run a popular *Biergarten* (described later).

Eisenhut Restaurant, in Hotel Eisenhut, is a fine place for a dress-up splurge with surprisingly reasonable prices. You'll enjoy elegantly presented dishes, both traditional and international, with formal service. Sit in their royal dining room or on their garden sun terrace (€17-25 main courses, fixed-price meals from €28, daily 12:00-14:30 & 18:30-21:30, Herrngasse 3, tel. 09861/7050).

Reichs-Küchenmeister is a forgettable big-hotel restaurant, but on a balmy evening, its pleasant tree-shaded terrace overlooking St. Jakob's Church is hard to beat. Their €13 *Vesperbrett* plate is a fine selection of cold cuts (€8-20 main courses, daily 11:00-23:00, Kirchplatz 8, tel. 09861/9700).

Breaks from Pork and Potatoes

Pizzeria Roma is the locals' favorite for €5-7 pizza and pastas, with good Italian wine. The Magrini family moved here from Tuscany in 1970 (many Italians immigrated to Germany in those years), and they've been cooking pasta for Rothenburg ever since (Thu-Tue 11:00-24:00, closed Wed and mid-Aug-mid-Sept, Galgengasse 19, tel. 09861/4540, Ricardo).

China-Restaurant Peking, on the picturesque Plönlein square, has two-course lunch specials (€5-7, Mon-Sat only), and its noisy streetside tables have a fine tower view (open daily 11:00-15:00 & 17:00-23:00, Plönlein 4, tel. 09861/938-738).

The **Bosporus Café** at Hafengasse 2, just off Market Square, serves cheap and tasty Turkish food to go or eat in. Their *Döner Kebabs* must be the best €3.50 hot meal in Rothenburg (daily 9:00-19:00, sometimes closes earlier in winter).

Picnic Goodies: A small **grocery store** is in the center of town at Rödergasse 6 (Mon-Fri 7:30-19:00, Sat 7:30-18:00, April-Dec also Sun 10:00-18:00, closed Sun Jan-March). **Supermarkets** are outside the wall: Exit the town through the Rödertor, turn left through the cobbled gate, and cross the parking lot to reach the

ROTHENBURG

Edeka supermarket (Mon-Fri 8:00-20:00, Sat 7:00-20:00, closed Sun); or head to the even bigger Kaufland in the shopping center across from the train station (Mon-Sat 7:00-20:00, closed Sun).

Beer Gardens (Biergartens)

Rothenburg's *Biergarten*s can be great fun, but they're open only when the weather is balmy.

Unter den Linden, a family-friendly (with sandbox and swing), slightly bohemian *Biergarten* in the valley along the river, is worth the 20-minute hike on a pleasant evening (daily 10:00-21:00 in season with decent weather, sometimes later, self-service food and good beer, Sunday breakfast buffet until noon-€11, call first to confirm it's open, Kurze Steige 7, tel. 09861/5909, Helmut Dürrer). As it's in the valley on the river, it's cooler than Rothenburg; bring a sweater. Take a right outside the Burgtor, then a left on the footpath toward Detwang; it's at the bottom of the hill on the left.

Gasthof Rödertor, just outside the wall through the Rödertor, runs a backyard *Biergarten* that's great for a rowdy crowd, cheap food, and good beer (May-Sept daily 17:00-24:00 in good weather, look for wooden gate, tel. 09861/2022). If the *Biergarten* is closed, their indoor restaurant (described earlier) is a good value.

Eisenhut Restaurant (described earlier), behind the fancy hotel of the same name on Herrngasse, is a good bet for gentle and casual *Biergarten* ambience within the old center.

Dessert

Eis Café D'Isep, with a pleasant "Venetian minimalist" interior, is the town's ice-cream parlor, serving up cakes, drinks, fresh-fruit ice cream, and fancy sundaes. Their sidewalk tables are great for lazy people-watching (daily 9:30-22:30, closed early Oct-mid-Feb, one block off Market Square at Hafengasse 17, run by Paolo and Paola D'Isep).

Wine-Drinking in the Old Center

Trinkstube zur Hölle ("Hell") is dark and foreboding, offering a thick wine-drinking atmosphere, pub food, and a few main courses (€11-17). It's small and can get painfully touristy in summer (daily 17:00-24:00, closed Sun Jan-March, a block past Medieval Crime and Punishment Museum on Burggasse, with the devil hanging out front, tel. 09861/4229).

Mario's **Altfränkische Weinstube am Klosterhof** (listed earlier) is the liveliest place, and a clear favorite with locals for an atmospheric drink or late meal. When every other place is asleep, you're likely to find good food, drink, and energy here.

Restaurant Glocke, a *Weinstube* (wine bar) popular with locals, is run by Rothenburg's oldest winemakers, the Thürauf family. The menu, which has a very extensive wine list, is in German only because the friendly staff wants to explain your options in person. Their €4.40 deal, which lets you sample five Franconian wines, is popular (€8-18 main courses, Mon-Sat 11:00-23:00, Sun 11:00-14:00, Plönlein 1, tel. 09861/958-990).

Meet the Locals—English Conversation Club

For a rare chance to mix it up with locals who aren't selling anything, bring your favorite slang and tongue twisters to the English Conversation Club at Mario's Altfränkische Weinstube am Klosterhof (Wed 19:00-24:00; see restaurant listing earlier, under "Traditional German Restaurants"). This group of intrepid linguists has met more than 1,000 times. Hermann the German and his sidekick Wolfgang are regulars. Consider arriving early for dinner, or after 21:00, when the beer starts to sink in, the crowd grows, and everyone seems to speak that second language a bit more easily.

Rothenburg Connections

Reaching Rothenburg ob der Tauber by Train: A tiny branch train line connects Rothenburg to the outside world via **Steinach** in 14 minutes (generally 1/hour from Rothenburg at :07 and from Steinach at :34). Train connections in Steinach are usually quick and efficient (trains to and from Rothenburg generally use track 5).

If you plan to arrive in Rothenburg in the evening, note that the last train from Steinach to Rothenburg departs at about 22:30. All is not lost if you arrive in Steinach after the last train—there's a subsidized taxi service to Rothenburg (cheaper for the government than running an almost-empty train). To use this handy service, called AST *(Anrufsammeltaxi),* make an appointment with a participating taxi service (call 09861/2000 or 09861/7227) at least an hour in advance (2 hours ahead is better), and they'll drive you from Steinach to Rothenburg for the train fare (€4/person) rather than the regular €25 taxi fare.

The Rothenburg station has a touch-screen terminal for fare and schedule information and ticket sales. If you need extra help, visit the combined ticket office and travel agency in the station building (€1-4 surcharge for most tickets, €0.50 charge for questions without ticket purchase, Mon-Fri 9:00-18:00, Sat 9:00-13:00, closed Sun, tel. 09861/7711). The station at Steinach is entirely unstaffed, but also has touch-screen ticket machines. As a last resort, call for train info at tel. 0180-599-6633, or visit www.bahn.com.

From Rothenburg by Train to: Würzburg (hourly, 70 minutes), **Nürnberg** (hourly, 1.25 hours, change in Ansbach), **Munich**

(hourly, 2.5-3.5 hours, 2-3 changes), **Füssen** (hourly, 5 hours, often with changes in Treuchtlingen and Augsburg), **Frankfurt** (hourly, 2.5-3 hours, change in Würzburg), **Frankfurt Airport** (hourly, 3-3.25 hours, change in Würzburg), **Berlin** (hourly, 5-6 hours, often via Würzburg and Göttingen). Remember, all destinations also require a change in Steinach.

From Rothenburg by Bus: The Romantic Road bus stops in Rothenburg once a day (mid-April-late Oct) on its way from Frankfurt to Munich and Füssen (and vice versa). The bus stop is at Schrannenplatz, a short walk north of Market Square. See the schedule and tour description at the end of this chapter.

Route Tips for Drivers

From Frankfurt Airport (and Other Points North) to Rothenburg: The three-hour autobahn drive from Frankfurt Airport to Rothenburg is something even a jet-lagged zombie can handle. It's a 75-mile straight shot to Würzburg on the A-3 autobahn; just follow the blue autobahn signs toward *Würzburg*. Then turn south on A-7 and take the *Rothenburg o.d.T.* exit (#108).

The Romantic Road

The countryside between Frankfurt and Munich is Germany's medieval heartland. Walls and towers ring half-timbered towns, and flowers spill over the windowsills of well-kept houses. Glockenspiels dance from town halls by day, while night watchmen still call the hours after dark. Many travelers bypass these small towns by fast train or autobahn. But consider an extra day or two to take in the slow pace of small-town German life. With a car,

you can wander through quaint hills and rolling villages, and stop wherever the cows look friendly or a town fountain beckons.

In the 1950s, towns in this region joined together to work out a scenic driving route for visitors that they called the Romantic Road (Romantische Strasse, www.romanticroad.de). Because local train service was poor, they also organized a bus along the route for tourists, from Würzburg in the north to Füssen in the south.

The Romantic Road is the oldest and most famous of Germany's two dozen signposted scenic routes. Others celebrate toys, porcelain, architecture (Swabian Baroque or brick Gothic),

The Romantic Road

Romantic Road
Bus Route

- - - Other Buses

NOTE: Not all rail lines shown

clocks, and baths—and there are even two separate *Spargelstrassen* (asparagus roads). The "Castle Road" that runs between Rothenburg and Mannheim sounds intriguing, but it's nowhere near as interesting.

Now that the A-7 autobahn parallels the old two-lane route, the Romantic Road itself has become less important, but its destinations are still worthwhile. For drivers, the Romantic Road is basically a set of scenic stepping stones to Rothenburg, which is the most exciting town along the way. You can make a day out of the drive between Würzburg (or Frankfurt) and Rothenburg, stopping in the small towns along the Tauber River Valley. If linking Rothenburg and Munich, stop in Dinkelsbühl or Nördlingen. The drive from Rothenburg to Füssen on two-lane roads makes for a full day, but it's possible to squeeze in a quick visit to Dinkelsbühl, Nördlingen, the Wieskirche, or Landsberg am Lech, hopping on the autobahn to speed up parts of the trip. If you're driving with limited time, just zero in on Rothenburg by autobahn.

For those without a car, the tour bus that still runs along the Romantic Road route once a day during the summer is a way to connect Rothenburg with Frankfurt, Würzburg, and Munich, or to go between Munich and Füssen, while seeing more scenery than you'd get on the train.

Sights Along the Romantic Road

I've divided the Romantic Road into three sections. The stretch from Würzburg (or Frankfurt) to Rothenburg runs up the Tauber River Valley, offering views that are pleasant, though not dramatic. Rothenburg to Augsburg is fairly flat and dull. From Augsburg south to Füssen, the route follows the Lech River up to where the Alps begin, and the scenery gets more exciting at every turn. To help you find your way, I've included some driving directions. While I've listed public-transit connections for major stops, most of these out-of-the-way destinations aren't worth the hassle if you lack a car. The Romantic Road bus is an option, but can be disappointing (see end of chapter).

From Würzburg (or Frankfurt) to Rothenburg

To take this scenic back-road approach from Frankfurt, take A-3, then turn south on A-81, get off at the Tauberbischofsheim exit, and follow signs for *Bad Mergentheim*. Or stay on A-3 to the Heidingsfeld-Würzburg exit and follow *Stuttgart/Ulm/Road 19* signs south to Bad Mergentheim. From Würzburg, follow *Ulm/ Road 19* signs to Bad Mergentheim.

Bad Mergentheim—In 1525, when the Teutonic Knights lost their lands in East Prussia and the Baltic states, the order's leadership retreated to their castle at Bad Mergentheim, which became their headquarters for the next three centuries. The order's properties were dissolved in 1806, but European history fans will enjoy the castle, which houses an extensive museum on the history of the order that was key in Christianizing northeastern Europe (Deutschordensmuseum, €5; April-Oct Tue-Sun 10:30-17:00, closed Mon; Nov-March Tue-Sat 14:00-17:00, Sun 10:30-17:00, closed Mon;

tel. 07931/52212, www.deutschordensmuseum.de). The castle park has benches for your picnic, and cafés line the street by the castle entrance and the old town square. Don't try to park in the old town; follow the *Altstadt/Schloss* parking signs to the inexpensive covered garage, then the signs and painted footprints to the castle.

Leaving Bad Mergentheim, continue east. Turn into Weikersheim off the main road, following *Stadtmitte* and *Schloss* signs, then bear right to park in the large free lot. From there it's a couple minutes' walk to the town square.

Weikersheim—The town's **palace** (Schloss Weikersheim), right on the picturesque town square, has an orangerie and fine Baroque

gardens that make for a luxurious picnic spot. Admission to the gardens and a few museum exhibits is €2.50, while another €3 gets you a one-hour guided tour of the palace itself (German only—ask for English text, hourly tours, daily April-Oct 9:00-18:00, Nov-March 10:00-12:00 & 13:00-17:00, tel. 07934/992-950, www.schloss-weikersheim.de). The castle rose garden, to the right before you enter, is free; a gate off the rose garden leads to a spooky "alchemy garden" with plants used by medieval witches. The city park (Stadtpark, enter off town square) is also a fine and free picnic spot, and from it you can peer over the hedge into the palace gardens.

▲**Creglingen**—While Creglingen itself isn't worth much fuss (TI tel. 07933/631, www.creglingen.de), two quick and rewarding sights sit across the road from each other a mile south of town.

The peaceful 14th-century **Herrgottskirche** church is graced with Tilman Riemenschneider's greatest carved altarpiece, completed sometime between 1505 and 1510. The impressive altar is nearly 30 feet high, and you can get right up close to it (€2; Easter-Oct daily 9:15-18:00; Nov-Dec and Feb-Easter Tue-Sun 13:00-16:00, closed Mon; closed Jan; tel. 07933/338, www.herrgotts kirche.de).

The **Fingerhut Museum** shows off thimbles—literally, "finger hats"—with descriptions in German. It's actually interesting to look at the collection, which numbers about 4,000 (but still fits in a single room) and comes from all over the world; some are centuries old. Owner Thorvald Greif got a head start from his father, who owned a thimble factory (€2, Tue-Sun April-Oct 10:00-12:30 & 14:00-17:00, Nov-March 13:00-16:00, closed Mon, tel. 07933/370, www.fingerhut museum.de).

From Rothenburg to Augsburg

Dinkelsbühl and Nördlingen are the main attractions between Rothenburg and Augsburg. The A-7 and A-8 autobahns, which parallel the Romantic Road here, can speed up your trip.

▲Dinkelsbühl—Rothenburg's little sister is cute enough to merit a short stop. A moat, towers, gates, and beautifully preserved medieval wall surround this town. Dinkelsbühl is pretty, and less touristy than Rothenburg, but also less exciting.

Park at the free lots outside the town walls (there's a one-hour limit inside). To orient yourself, head for the tower of St. Georg's Church, at the center of town. This 15th-century church has fine carved altarpieces and a surprisingly light, airy interior. Follow the signs around the corner (first into Ledermarkt, then Altrathausplatz) to the TI, which sells a "Tour of the Town" brochure with a map and short walking tour; they can also help find rooms (May-Oct Mon-Fri 9:00-18:00, Sat-Sun 10:00-17:00; Nov-April daily 10:00-17:00; tel. 09851/9020, www.dinkelsbuehl .de). In the TI, take a minute to watch the TV monitor showing the stork nest on top of the old Town Hall (also visible at www .storch24.de).

The TI doubles as the ticket office for the fine **City History Museum** (Haus der Geschichte) in the same building (€4, ask for English audioguide, same hours as TI, kids' play area). This shiny, up-to-date museum shows how Dinkelsbühl sat along important north-south travel routes in early times, and explains how the tug-of-war between Catholics and Protestants ended in a power-sharing agreement and the loss of the town's medieval prosperity. On the top floor is a self-service movie theater showing short film clips about Dinkelsbühl (in English, plus old silent clips).

You can accompany Dinkelsbühl's **Night Watchman** on his one-hour rounds every evening at 21:00 (in German only, free, April-Oct daily, Nov-March Sat only, meet at St. Georg's Church, not as fun as Night Watchman Tour in Rothenburg). The Kinderzeche children's festival turns Dinkelsbühl wonderfully on end for a week at the end of July, celebrating the success of the local children who pleaded with the Swedish army during the Thirty Years' War, convincing them to spare the town (www .kinderzeche.de).

Sleeping in Dinkelsbühl: Dinkelsbühl has a good selection of hotels. Its **$ youth hostel** is in a handsome medieval building (€19/ bed in 6- to 8-bed dorms, nonmembers pay €3 extra, guests over 26 and without kids pay €4 extra, closed Nov-Feb, no Internet access, Koppengasse 10, tel. 09851/9509, www.dinkelsbuehl.jugendher berge.de). The hostel is just steps from the Schweinemarkt, where Romantic Road buses stop once a day in each direction.

No trains run to Dinkelsbühl, so you'll have to switch to a bus to get there (in Crailsheim, Ellwangen, or Nördlingen) or take the once-a-day Romantic Road bus.

Nördlingen—Though less cute than Dinkelsbühl, Nördlingen nevertheless merits a short stop if you're interested in city walls

or meteorites. The town's almost perfectly circular wall is better preserved than Rothenburg's or Dinkelsbühl's, and you can walk the whole way around. For centuries, Nördlingen's residents puzzled over the local terrain, a flattish plain called the Ries, which rises to a low circular ridge that surrounds the town in the distance. In the 1960s, geologists figured out that Nördlingen lies in the middle of an impact crater blasted out 15 million years ago by a meteor, which hit Earth with the force of 250,000 Hiroshima bombs.

Weekday (all day) and Saturday morning parking at the entrances to the old town (and inside) is limited to 1.5 hours, which isn't really enough time to see the town. Unless visiting on Saturday afternoon or Sunday, drivers should use the big, free lots at the Delninger Tor and the Baldinger Tor or the free parking garage at the Berger Tor.

After parking, head through one of the gates in the wall and into the center of town by zeroing in on the tower of **St. Georg's Church** (yes, the same saint as in Dinkelsbühl). The rickety 350-step climb up the church tower (which locals call "the Daniel") rewards you with the very best view of the city walls and the rim of the meteorite crater (open daily year-round, €2.50). The small square next to the church is called Marktplatz, and just behind the step-gabled Rathaus (Town Hall) is the **TI**, which gives out free town maps (Easter-Oct Mon-Thu 9:30-18:00, Fri 9:30-16:30, Sat 10:00-14:00, May-Sept Sun 10:00-14:00 but otherwise closed Sun, shorter hours Nov-Easter, Marktplatz 2, tel. 09081/84116, www .noerdlingen.de).

Maypoles

Along the Romantic Road and throughout Bavaria, you'll see colorfully ornamented maypoles *(Maibaum)* decorating town squares. Many are painted in Bavaria's colors, white and blue. The decorations that line each side of the pole symbolize the craftspeople and businesses of that community (similar to the Chamber of Commerce billboards that greet visitors to small American towns today). Originally these allowed passing traders to quickly determine whether their services were needed in that town. The decorations are festively replaced each May Day (May 1). Traditionally, rival communities try to steal each other's maypole. Locals guard their new pole night and day as May Day approaches. Stolen poles are ransomed only with lots of beer for the clever thieves.

Now walk out the bottom of Marktplatz and down Baldinger Strasse. At the traffic light, turn right and then left, past the Stadtmuseum, to the **Ries Crater Museum** (Rieskrater-Museum). Ask them to play the two 10-minute English films, which explain meteors and the formation of the solar system. The exhibits themselves are only described in German, but for €3 they'll let you borrow a dry and detailed English guide (€4, Tue-Sun 10:00-12:00 & 13:30-16:30, closed Mon, Eugene-Shoemaker-Platz 1, tel. 09081/273-8220, www.rieskrater-museum.de).

Circle back to Baldinger Strasse and continue to the Baldinger Tor (tower). Climb the stairs to the walkway along the **town wall,** which you can follow back to the lot where your car is parked. The city started building the wall in 1327 and financed it with a tax on wine and beer; it's more than a mile and a half long, has 16 towers and five gates, and offers great views of backyards and garden furniture.

For those with extra time, there's a **City Wall Museum** (Stadtmauermuseum) in the Löpsinger Tor, which lets you climb up to the tower's top level (closed Mon, no English descriptions). If you have energy for only one climb, the view from the church tower is better.

Sleeping in Nördlingen: Several small hotels surrounding St. Georg's Church vie for your business with mediocre but reasonably priced rooms. Of these, try **$$ Hotel Altreuter,** over an inviting bakery/café (Sb-€36-50, Db-€58-75, prices depend on room size, non-smoking, lots of stairs, Marktplatz 11, tel. 09081/4319, fax 09081/9797, www.hotel-altreuter.de, mail@hotel-altreuter.de).

Nördlingen is reachable by train (change in Donauwörth).

Augsburg—Founded more than 2,000 years ago by Emperor Augustus, Augsburg enjoyed its heyday in the 15th and 16th centuries. Today, it's Bavaria's third-largest city (population 264,000). It lacks must-see sights, but the old town is pleasant, especially the small streets below the main square, where streams diverted from the River Lech run alongside pedestrians (www.augsburg.de).

From Augsburg to Füssen

From Augsburg, you can either continue south to Füssen on the two-lane road, or you can hop on A-8, which brings you quickly into Munich (in about an hour).

Landsberg am Lech—Like many towns in this area, Landsberg (on the River Lech) has its roots in the salt trade. Every four years, the town returns to its medieval roots and hosts the Ruethenfest. The town was shaped by the architect Dominikus Zimmerman (of Wieskirche fame). Adolf Hitler wrote *Mein Kampf* while serving his prison sentence here after the Beer Hall Putsch of 1923 (when Hitler and his followers unsuccessfully attempted to take over the government of Bavaria).

Rottenbuch—This nondescript village, near the Wieskirche, has an impressive church in a lovely setting.

▲▲Wieskirche—This is Germany's most glorious Baroque-Rococo church, beautifully restored and set in a sweet meadow. Heavenly! Romantic Road buses (described next) stop here for 20 minutes—but only on the northbound Munich-to-Frankfurt run. Southbound buses stop here only after the church is closed. (See the full Wieskirche description on page 143 of the Bavaria and Tirol chapter, which also covers Füssen.)

The Romantic Road Bus

From mid-April to late October, the Deutsche Touring company runs daily tour buses that roughly follow the Romantic Road. One bus per day goes from Frankfurt to Munich to Füssen, and another goes from Füssen to Munich to Frankfurt (tel. 069/719-126-268, www.romanticroadcoach.de). While this bus tour used to be a traveler's dream, it has become less special in recent years—with higher prices, just one daily departure, and fewer (and shorter) sightseeing stops than before. Even so, the bus is still worthwhile if you have no car but want to catch a fleeting glimpse of the towns along the Romantic Road, or if you're planning an overnight stay in a town that's poorly served by train (such as Dinkelsbühl). The bus also offers the convenience of a direct connection between towns

Romantic Road Bus Schedule

The Romantic Road bus runs daily from mid-April to late October. Every day, one bus goes north to south (Frankfurt to Munich to Füssen), and another follows the same route south to north (Füssen to Munich to Frankfurt). Only the northbound bus stops at the Wieskirche during opening hours. You can begin or end your journey

at any of these stops. The following times include only the main stops, based on the 2011 schedule. In Munich, the bus stops at the bus station (ZOB), not the train station (southbound bus only stops on request). The bus also stops in other towns, including Bad Mergentheim, Weikersheim, Creglingen, Nördlingen, Augsburg, Oberammergau, the Wieskirche, and Hohenschwangau. Check the full schedule at www.romantic roadcoach.de for any changes.

North to South
Depart Frankfurt	8:00
Arrive Würzburg	9:40
Depart Würzburg	9:45
Arrive Rothenburg	12:30
Depart Rothenburg	13:15
Arrive Dinkelsbühl	14:00
Depart Dinkelsbühl	14:35
Arrive Munich	17:50
Depart Munich	17:50
Arrive Füssen	19:55

South to North
Depart Füssen	8:00
Arrive Wieskirche	8:30
Depart Wieskirche	8:50
Arrive Munich	10:50
Depart Munich	10:50
Arrive Dinkelsbühl	14:25
Depart Dinkelsbühl	14:50
Arrive Rothenburg	15:50
Depart Rothenburg	16:30
Arrive Würzburg	18:00
Depart Würzburg	18:00
Arrive Frankfurt	19:35

ROMANTIC ROAD

where you'd have to transfer if traveling by train, such as between Rothenburg and the cities of Munich and Frankfurt. But the trip is slow, and there's just one bus a day, while there are hourly train connections on these same routes.

The Frankfurt-Rothenburg leg passes through the small towns in the Tauber River Valley (Bad Mergentheim, Weikersheim, and Creglingen), but only stops to pick up and drop off passengers. The Rothenburg-Munich leg includes half-hour stops in Dinkelsbühl and Augsburg—just enough for a glimpse of each. The north-bound buses (Füssen-Munich) make a 20-minute rest stop at the Wieskirche during opening hours—just long enough to peek into the church. Be warned that in case of delays, these stops can be shortened or skipped altogether.

Frankfurt to Rothenburg costs €42, Rothenburg to Munich is €36, and Munich to Füssen is €26 (each about the same as the train). The entire ride (Frankfurt to Füssen) costs €104. Pay by cash or credit card on the bus. Students and seniors—without a rail-pass—get a 10 percent discount. You can get a 20 percent discount on your bus ticket if you have a German railpass, Eurail Global Pass, or Eurail Selectpass (if Germany is one of your selected countries). You don't have to activate the use of a travel day of a flexipass to get this discount; if bus drivers say it takes a travel day, set them straight.

Bus reservations are almost never necessary. But they are free and easy, and, technically, without one you can lose your seat to someone who has one (reserve online at www.romanticroadcoach .de or call 069/719-126-268). The only ticket office is in Frankfurt (see page 371).

Bus stops are not well-signed, but their location in each town is listed on the bus brochure and website. Look for a small *Touring* or *Romantische Strasse* sign.

ROMANTIC ROAD

WÜRZBURG

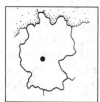

A historic city—though freshly rebuilt since World War II—Würzburg (VEWRTS-boorg) is worth a stop to see its impressive prince-bishop's Residenz and the palace's sculpted gardens. Surrounded by vineyards and filled with atmospheric *Weinstuben* (wine bars), this tourist-friendly town is easy to navigate by foot or streetcar. Today, 25,000 of its 130,000 residents are students—making the town feel young and very alive.

Planning Your Time

Würzburg has a few hours' worth of sightseeing. Begin at the Residenz (prince bishop's palace), then take my self-guided walk through town to the Old Main Bridge. With more time, hike up to the hilltop Marienberg Fortress across the bridge.

Orientation to Würzburg

(area code: 0931)

Tourist Information

Würzburg's helpful TI is in the Rococo-style Falken Haus on Market Square (May-Oct Mon-Fri 10:00-18:00, Sat-Sun 10:00-14:00; April and Nov-Dec same hours but closed Sun; Jan-March Mon-Fri 10:00-16:00, Sat 10:00-14:00, closed Sun; Market Square, tel. 0931/372-398, www.wuerzburg.de). The TI gives out a free

---

Würzburg's Beginnings

The city was born centuries before Christ at an easy-to-ford part of the Main River under an easy-to-defend hill. A Celtic fort stood where the fortress stands today. Later, three Irish missionary monks came here to Christianize the local barbarians. In A.D. 686, they were beheaded, and their relics put Würzburg on the pilgrimage map. About 500 years later, when the town was the seat of a bishop, Holy Roman Emperor Frederick Barbarossa came here to get the bishop's OK to divorce his wife. The bishop said, "No problem," and the emperor thanked him by giving him secular rule of the entire region of Franconia. From then on, the bishop was also a prince, and the prince-bishop of Würzburg answered only to the Holy Roman Emperor.

---

city map, books rooms for free, and sells detailed maps for biking through the local wine country. If you're continuing on the Romantic Road (see previous chapter), the TI has a *Romantische Strasse* brochure and a list of car-rental options.

Tours: The TI rents audioguides (€7.50/3 hours) that give a self-guided tour of the old town. The audio tour is also available as a free MP3 download from the TI's website (www.wuerzburg .de) or by calling a special number from your mobile phone (ask for details). The TI also offers a traditional 1.5-hour walking tour in English (€6, Sat at 11:00, April-Oct only).

Sightseeing Passes: The TI sells the **Würzburg Welcome Card,** offering minimal discounts on a few sights and restaurants (€3/7 days). Würzburg's Residenz and Marienberg Fortress are covered by the **Bavarian Castles Pass** (€24, family/partner version-€40 for two adults plus children, valid for 14 days, sold at all participating sights; see details on page 122).

Arrival in Würzburg

By Train: Würzburg's train station is user-friendly and filled with handy services (€2-4 lockers, WCs between main hall and tunnel to platforms). Walk out of the train station to the small square in front. A big **city map** board provides a quick orientation (on small building to the right). Farther right is the **post office** and the **Romantic Road bus stop** (track 13, curb closest and parallel to station building, look for *Touring* sign and schedule).

From the cul-de-sac in front of the station, **tram** #1, #2, #3, or #5 will take you one stop to the Juliuspromenade stop, near my recommended hotels. Another stop (to Dom or Ulmer Hof) brings you close to Market Square and the TI. By **foot,** cross over the busy Röntgenring and head up the shop-lined Kaiserstrasse. To reach the **Residenz,** it's simplest to walk (15 minutes), but you can get part of the way by taking tram #1, #3, or #5 to the Dom stop.

By Car: Drivers entering Würzburg can keep it simple by following signs to the *Residenz* and parking in the vast cobbled square that faces the palace.

Helpful Hints

Festivals: Würzburg—always clever when it comes to trade—schedules its three annual festivals (wine, Mozart, and the Kiliani-Volksfest) in rapid succession, and keeps things busy from the beginning of June through late July.

Internet Access: Log Inn Internet Café is near Market Square, down the street behind the Marienkapelle (€3/hour, Mon-Sat 9:00-23:00, Sun 12:00-23:00, Häfnergasse 5).

Supermarket: Kupsch, at Domstrasse 10, is just a few doors from City Hall (Mon-Sat 7:00-20:00, closed Sun). Another branch is on Kaiserstrasse, near the station and recommended hotels.

Bike Rental: Fahrrad Körner rents bikes right in the old town, a five-minute walk north of Market Square (€10/24 hours, Mon-Fri 9:00-18:00, Sat 9:00-14:00, closed Sun, Bronnbachergasse 3, tel. 0931/52340).

Local Guide: Maureen Aldenhoff, who grew up in Liverpool but has been married to a German for 30 years, gives good private walking tours (€90/2 hours, €130/3 hours, €190/day, tel. 0931/52135, maureen.aldenhoff@web.de).

Getting Around Würzburg

You can easily walk to everything but the hilltop Marienberg Fortress. For public transit, the same tickets work on all city bus and tram lines (including the bus up to the fortress). Your options include a single ticket (*Einzelfahrschein*-€2.20, good for 1.5 hours in one direction with transfers) or a day pass (*Tageskarte Solo*-€4.45 for one person; or *Tageskarte Familie*-€8.90 for two adults and kids under age 15; both valid Sun also if purchased on Sat). You can buy either type of ticket from the bus driver or at a streetside machine (marked *Fahrausweise*). Single tickets are only valid if you stamp them, using the little box inside the tram or bus (day passes come pre-stamped). For transit info, call tel. 0931/362-320.

Sights in Würzburg

Würzburg's Residenz

Würzburg's opulent palace and its associated sights—the chapel (Hofkirche) and garden—are the town's main attraction. The chapel, which has been closed for restoration, should reopen to visitors in mid-2012.

Getting There: Don't confuse the Residenz (a 15-minute walk southeast of the train station) with Marienberg Fortress (on the hilltop across the river). The Residenz is the far more important sight to visit. Easy parking is available in front of the Residenz (€1.50/hour for first 2 hours, €1/each additional hour, pay at the machine marked *Kasse* before you drive out of the lot).

▲▲**Residenz Palace**—This Franconian Versailles features grand rooms, 3-D art, and a massive (and recently restored) fresco by

 Giovanni Battista Tiepolo. Your entry ticket lets you circle through some of the most impressive rooms in the North Wing of the palace on your own. To see the South Wing, you'll need to join a tour.

Cost and Hours: €7.50, covered by Bavarian Castles Pass, includes optional guided tour, daily April-Oct 9:00-18:00, Nov-March 10:00-16:30, last entry 30 minutes before closing, no photos, tel. 0931/355-170 or 0931/355-1712, www.residenz-wuerzburg.de.

Information: The €5 English guidebook is dry and lengthy. Few English descriptions are provided in the Residenz; follow my self-guided tour for an overview.

Tours: English tours, offered daily year-round at 11:00 and 15:00, include the otherwise inaccessible South Wing, which has some notable rooms (45 minutes, call ahead or tell the cashier you want to join the English tour, covered in entry price, but tips are welcome if the guide is good). The only other way to see the South Wing is to be trapped on a German tour (at least 3/hour).

Services: On the right as you exit the ticket office, you'll find free WCs and storage lockers (€1 deposit is returned).

❷ **Self-Guided Tour:** The following self-guided tour gives you the basics to appreciate this fine palace.

• *Begin at the entrance.*

Vestibule: This area functioned as a grand circular driveway—just right for six-horse carriages to drop off their guests at the base of the stairs. The elegant stairway comes with low steps, enabling high-class ladies to glide up gracefully, heads tilted back to enjoy Europe's largest and grandest fresco opening up above them. Hold your lady's hand high and get into the ascending rhythm. Enjoy the climb.

• *Ascend the stairs and look up at the...*

Tiepolo Fresco: In 1752, the Venetian master Giovanni Battista Tiepolo was instructed to make a grand fresco illustrating the greatness of Europe, Würzburg, and the prince-bishop. And he did—in only 13 months. Find the four continents, each

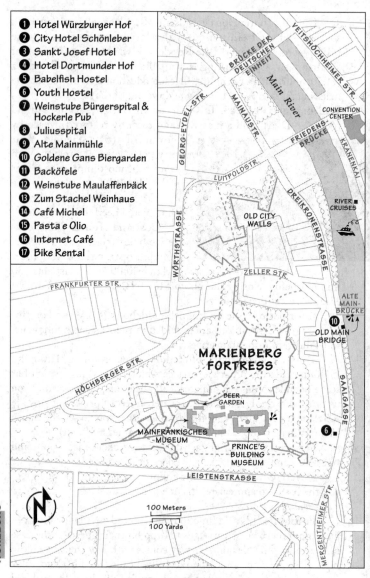

1 Hotel Würzburger Hof
2 City Hotel Schönleber
3 Sankt Josef Hotel
4 Hotel Dortmunder Hof
5 Babelfish Hostel
6 Youth Hostel
7 Weinstube Bürgerspital & Hockerle Pub
8 Juliusspital
9 Alte Mainmühle
10 Goldene Gans Biergarden
11 Backöfele
12 Weinstube Maulaffenbäck
13 Zum Stachel Weinhaus
14 Café Michel
15 Pasta e Olio
16 Internet Café
17 Bike Rental

WÜRZBURG

symbolized by a woman on an animal and pointing to the prince-bishop in the medallion above Europe. America—desperately uncivilized—sits naked with feathers in her hair on an alligator among severed heads. She's being served hot chocolate, a favorite import and nearly a drug for Europeans back then. Africa sits on a camel in a land of trade and fantasy animals (based on secondhand reports, and therefore inaccurate). Asia rides her elephant (with the

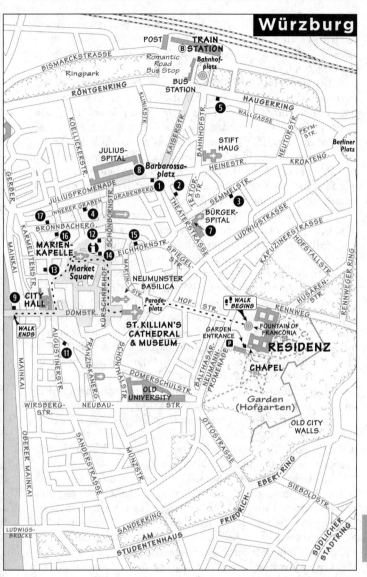

Würzburg

backward ear) in the birthplace of Christianity and the alphabet. And Europe is shown as the center of high culture—Lady Culture points her brush not at Rome, but at Würzburg. The prince-bishop had a healthy ego. The ceiling features Apollo and a host of Greek gods, all paying homage to the PB.

The White Hall: This hall, actually gray, was kept plain to punctuate the colorful rooms on either side. It's a Rococo-stucco fantasy. (The word "Rococo" comes from the Portuguese word for the frilly rocaille shell.)

• *Straight ahead is the palace gift shop. Continue to your left, following signs for* Rundgang.

The Imperial Hall: This glorious hall—which was smartly restored—is the ultimate example of Baroque: harmony, symmetry, illusion, and the bizarre; lots of light and mirrors facing windows; and all with a foundation of absolutism (a divine monarch, inspired by Louis XIV). Take a moment to marvel at all the 3-D tricks in the ceiling. Here's another trick: As you enter the room, look left and check out the dog in the fresco. When you get to the window, have another look...notice that he has gotten older and fatter while you were crossing the hall.

The room features three scenes: On the ceiling, find Father Main (the local river) amusing himself with a nymph. The two walls tell more history. On one, the bishop presides over the marriage of a happy Barbarossa (whose bride was actually 12 years old, unlike the woman in the painting, who looks considerably older; for more on Barbarossa, see the "Würzburg's Beginnings" sidebar, earlier). The bishop's power is demonstrated through his oversized fingers (giving the benediction) and through the details of his miter, which—unlike his face—is not shown in profile to allow you to see his coat of arms. Opposite that is the pay-off: Barbarossa, now the Holy Roman Emperor, gives the bishop Franconia and the secular title of prince. From this point onward, the prince-bishop rules. Also in the Imperial Hall, the balcony offers a great vantage point for surveying the Italian section of the garden (explained later).

The North Wing: This wing is a string of lavish rooms—evolving from fancy Baroque to fancier Rococo—used for the prince-bishop's VIP guests. It's a straight shot, with short English descriptions in each room, to the Green Room in the corner.

The Green Lacquer Room: This room is named for its silver-leaf walls, painted green. The Escher-esque inlaid floor was painstakingly restored after WWII bombings. Have fun multiplying in the mirrors before leaving. The little four-foot-tall doors were used by tiny servants who stoked the stoves, unseen from this hallway.

• *Keep going through a few more small rooms to the...*

Opera Theater: In the 1700s, half of this oval room was set up as a stage for Italian opera performances, with amphitheater-like seating for the audience in the other half.

Photos of Restoration Work: As you leave, you'll see photos of the building's destruction in the 1945 firebombing of Würzburg, and its subsequent restoration. A temporary roof saved the palace from total ruin, but it was not until the late 1970s that it was returned to more or less its original condition.

Prince-Bishop Portraits: Just before returning to the stairway, dip into the Fürstensaal (on the left, by the black stove), which shows portraits of the eight prince-bishops who ruled Würzburg from 1684 to 1779.

▲▲Chapel (Hofkirche)—This sumptuous chapel is scheduled to reopen after extensive restoration in mid-2012. If you visit before

then, you can still walk in the main door and down a short, enclosed passage that displays photos of the chapel's artwork. Windows allow a glimpse of the work in progress.

The chapel was for the exclusive use of the prince-bishop (private altar upstairs with direct entrance to his residence) and his court (ground floor). The decor and design are textbook Baroque. Architect Johann Balthasar Neumann was stuck with the existing walls. His challenge was to bring in light and create symmetry—

essential to any Baroque work. He did it with mirrors and hidden windows. All the gold is real—if paper-thin—gold leaf. The columns are "manufactured marble," which isn't marble at all but marbled plaster. This method was popular because it was uniform, economical, and the color could be controlled. Pigment was mixed into plaster, which was rolled onto the stone or timber core of the column. This half-inch veneer was then polished. You can tell if a "marble" column is real or fake by resting your hand on it. If it warms up, it's not marble. The faded painting high above the altar shows three guys in gold robes losing their heads (for more on these martyred Irish monks, see the "Würzburg's Beginnings" sidebar). The two side paintings are by the great fresco artist Tiepolo. Since the plaster wouldn't dry in the winter, Tiepolo spent his downtime painting with oil.

Cost and Hours: Free, likely daily April-Oct 9:00-18:00, Nov-March 10:00-16:30, closed during Sun 10:00 Mass and on Catholic holidays; facing the palace, use separate entrance at far right just before garden entrance.

Residenz Garden—One of Germany's finest Baroque gardens is a delightful park. By definition, Baroque gardens have three sections: English, French, and Italian. The French section, just inside the gate, features statues of Greek gods (with lots of kidnapping action), carefully trimmed 18th-century yew trees, and an orangerie. The English section (to the right) is like a rough park. The Italian section, directly behind the palace around to the left, is grand—à la Versailles—but uses terraces to create the illusion of spaciousness (since it was originally hemmed in by the town wall). Behind the orangerie is the replanted palace kitchen garden. A modern feature has been added to the garden: WCs (to the right as you come in the main entrance, next to the orangerie).

Cost and Hours: Free, open daily until dusk—20:00 at the latest, enter through gate at right of Residenz building.

Self-Guided Walk

Welcome to Würzburg

This brief walk gets you from the Residenz, which you may want to tour first (described earlier), to the Old Main Bridge (Alte Mainbrücke) via the key old-town sights.

• *Begin at the fountain in front of the Residenz palace.*

Fountain of Franconia: In 1814, the prince-bishop got the boot, and the region of Franconia was secularized and given to the Bavarian Wittelsbach dynasty. Technically, Franconia is a part of Bavaria, but that status is like Scotland being part of Great Britain. (Never call a Franconian a Bavarian.) This statue—a gift from the townspeople to their then-new royal family—turns its back to the palace and faces the town. It celebrates the artistic and intellectual genius of Franconia with statues of three great hometown boys (a medieval bard, the woodcarver Tilman Riemenschneider, and the Renaissance painter Matthias Grünewald).

• *If Franconia hopped down and ran 300 yards ahead down Hofstrasse, she'd hit the twin-spired cathedral. Meet her there.*

St. Kilian's Cathedral (Dom): This building's core is Romanesque (1040-1188), with Gothic spires and Baroque additions to the transepts. Destroyed in World War II, the cathedral was rebuilt in the 1960s. (Before 1945, the entire church was slathered in Baroque stucco decor.) Restoration work on the interior will keep the church closed until 2013.

• *Turn left, and go into the next-door museum.*

Cathedral Museum (Museum am Dom): This museum features a poignant combination of old and new religious art. It pairs 11th- to 18th-century works with modern interpretations, sprinkles it all with a Christian theme, and wraps it in a shiny modern building (€3.50, €4.50 combo-ticket includes Cathedral Treasury, Tue-Sun April-Oct 10:00-18:00, Nov-March 10:00-17:00, closed Mon year-round, tel. 0931/3866-5600, www.museum-am -dom.de).

• *Upon leaving, hook right through a tunnel, which emerges on a delight-ful urban scene. Domstrasse leads down to the spire of the City Hall and* the Old Main Bridge (where this walk will end). On your left you'll see a sign for the **Cathedral Treasury** (Domschatz, €2, €4.50 combo-ticket includes Cathedral Museum, Tue-Sun 14:00-17:00, closed Mon, tel. 0931/3866-5600). But we're looping right. Go a block up Kurschner Hof. On your right, you'll pass the entrance to the...

Neumünster Basilica: Like the cathedral, this church has a Romanesque body with a Baroque face. Go up the stairs to take a look inside, then continue up the street, noticing the vineyards in the distance. Appreciate this quiet pedestrian zone. Locals wouldn't have it any other way—electric trolleys, bikes, and pedestrians.

• Enter the square on the left with the lacy, two-tone church.

Market Square (Marktplatz): Imagine this square during the wine fest in June, with 75 vintners showing off their best wines, or during the Christmas market, when the square is full of quaint stalls selling holiday goodies. The fancy yellow-and-white Rococo-designed Falken Haus (House of the Falcon) once had three different facades. To fix it, the landlady gave a wandering band of stucco artists a chance to show their stuff...and ended up with this (inside are the TI and a prizewinning library with Internet access).

• Set your eyes on the church.

Marienkapelle: The two-tone late-Gothic church was the merchants' answer to the prince-bishop's cathedral. Since Rome didn't bankroll the place, it's ringed with "swallow shops" (like swallows' nests cuddled up against a house)—enabling the church to run little businesses. The sandstone statues (replicas of Riemenschneider originals) depict the 12 apostles and Jesus. Walk downhill along the church to the lower marketplace, where the city's produce market bustles daily except Sunday (May-Oct 8:00-16:00). The famous Adam and Eve statues (flanking the side entrance to the church) show off Riemenschneider's mastery of the human body. Continue around the church to the west portal, where the carved Last Judgment (above the main doors) shows kings, ladies, and bishops—some going to heaven, others making up the chain gang bound for hell, via the monster's mouth. (This was commissioned by those feisty town merchants tired of snooty bluebloods.) Continue around to the next entry to see the Annunciation, with a cute angel Gabriel telling Mary (who is a virgin, symbolized by the lilies) the good news. Notice how God whispers through a speaking tube as baby Jesus slips down and into her ear.

• Go back around to the lower market (Adam-and-Eve side) and leave—passing the obelisk—in the direction of the yellow building. Follow Schustergasse, a pedestrian lane lined with shops that leads back to Domstrasse. The cathedral is on your left, while the City Hall and bridge are to the right. Head right to the City Hall's tower.

City Hall (Rathaus): Würzburg's City Hall is relatively humble because of the power of the prince-bishop. A side room (facing the building, around the left side, free, always open) holds the *Gedenkraum 16 März 1945*. This commemorates the 20-minute Allied bombing raid on March 16, 1945, and the resulting firestorm that destroyed (and demoralized) Würzburg six weeks before the end of World War II. The damage was almost as bad as in Dresden: Almost every downtown building was reduced to a shell, with roofs, floors, and windows gone. Most residents survived in bomb shelters, but 5,000 died—largely women and children. Check out the sobering model, and ponder the names (lining the ceiling) of those killed. As you leave, notice the horizontal lines cut into the archway on your right. These mark the floodwaters *(Hochstand des Maines)* of the years 1342, 1682, and 1784.

• *Now, find the bridge.*

Old Main Bridge (Alte Mainbrücke): This isn't the town's "main" (as in primary) bridge; rather, it spans the Main (pronounced "mine") River, which also flows through Frankfurt.

The bridge, from 1133, is the second-oldest in Germany. The 12 statues lining the bridge are Würzburg saints and prince-bishops. Walk to the St. Kilian statue (with the golden sword)—one of the three monks who are shown being beheaded in the Residenz Palace's chapel. Stand so that you can't see the white power-plant tower and enjoy the best view in town. Marienberg Fortress caps the hill. Squint up at Kilian pointing to God...with his head on.

The hillside is blanketed with grapevines destined to become the fine Stein Franconian wine. Johann Wolfgang von Goethe, the great German author often compared to Shakespeare, ordered 900 liters of this vintage annually. A friend once asked Goethe what he thought were the three most important things in life. He said, "Wine, women, and song." The friend then asked, "If you had to give one up, which would it be?" Without hesitating, Goethe answered "Song." Then, when asked what he would choose if he had to give up a second, Goethe paused and said, "It depends on the vintage."

• *Your walking tour is over. From here, consider paying a visit to the fortress on the hill above you (described next), or have lunch at the recommended Alte Mainmühle restaurant, with a terrace overlooking the bridge.*

Marienberg Fortress (Festung Marienberg)

This 13th-century fortified retreat was the original residence of Würzburg's prince-bishops. After being stormed by the Swedish army during the 17th-century Thirty Years' War, the fortress was rebuilt in Baroque style. The **fortress grounds** (free) provide fine city views and a good place for a picnic. There's a restaurant inside

(weekends only in the winter) and a summer *Biergarten* by the entrance (both described later). For the best views, go through the archway off the inner courtyard into the **Prince's Garden**—look for the *Fürstengarten* sign (free, April-Oct Mon 9:00-16:00, Tue-Sun 9:00-17:45, closed Nov-March).

The fortress houses two museums (both covered by a €6 combo-ticket): The **Prince's Building Museum** (Fürstenbaumuseum) is in the inner courtyard. One floor shows off relics of the prince-bishops, and the other focuses on the history of Würzburg (€4.50, covered by Bavarian Castles Pass; Tue-Sun mid-March-Oct, first floor open 9:00-18:00, second floor open 10:00-17:00; closed Mon and Nov-mid-March; tel. 0931/355-170, www.schloesser.bayern .de). The **Mainfränkisches Museum,** which highlights the work of Riemenschneider, Germany's top woodcarver and onetime mayor of Würzburg, is in the red-and-white building at the back of the fortress, near the bus stop (€4, few English explanations, useful €3 audioguide; Tue-Sun April-Oct 10:00-17:00, Nov-March 10:00-16:00, closed Mon year-round, tel. 0931/205-940, www.mainfraenkisches-museum.de). Riemenschneider fans will also find his work throughout Würzburg's many churches.

A 45-minute English-language **tour** brings the fortress to life from mid-March to October (€3, Sat-Sun at 15:00, no tours off-season, meet at ticket desk of Prince's Building Museum). The €2.90 *Marienberg Castle* **booklet,** available at either sight, is well-written and has basic information on both museums.

Eating at Marienberg Fortress: If you're up here at lunchtime, the **Burggaststätte,** in the inner courtyard next to the Prince's Building Museum, is forgettable but handy (€7-12 meals; May-Sept daily 10:00-19:00; Oct-April Sat-Sun only 10:00-18:00; tel. 0931/47012). There's also a self-service **beer garden** next to the Mainfränkisches Museum by the fortress entrance, with typical sausage-and-pretzel fare and a great vineyard view (weather permitting).

Getting There: Take bus #9 (direction: Festung) to the last stop (Schönborntor) and walk through the tunnel to enter the fortress (€2.20 one-way, runs daily 10:00-18:00 every 45 minutes, departs from Residenzplatz and Juliuspromenade). To walk there, cross the Old Main Bridge and follow small *Festung Marienberg* signs to the right uphill for a heart-thumping 20 minutes (signs pointing left indicate a longer, more gradual 40-minute path through vineyards).

Sleeping in Würzburg

Würzburg's hotels and hostels are a stress-free option for a first or last night when flying into or out of Frankfurt. Trains run at least hourly between Würzburg and Frankfurt's airport; the journey takes 1.5 hours.

The following hotel listings are less than a 10-minute walk from the train station. To reach the Hotel Würzburger Hof, head from the station up Kaiserstrasse—the hotel is directly across Barbarossaplatz. For the Hotel Dortmunder Hof, continue to Grabenberg and turn left. For the City Hotel Schönleber, angle left at the circular awning at Barbarossaplatz, toward KFC, for Theaterstrasse; and for the Sankt Josef Hotel, follow Theaterstrasse and take your first left onto Semmelstrasse. In these hotels, quieter rooms are in back, front rooms have street noise, and all rooms are entertained by church bells.

$$$ Hotel Würzburger Hof has 30 large, Baroque rooms and friendly staff (Sb-€70-100, Db-€120-150, Tb-€170, elevator, free Internet access, pay Wi-Fi, Barbarossaplatz 2, tel. 0931/53814, fax 0931/58324, www.hotel-wuerzburgerhof.de, info@hotel-wuerz burgerhof.de).

$$ City Hotel Schönleber has 33 simple, up-to-date rooms (S-€45, Sb-€69, D-€66, small twin Db-€72, Db-€89-99 depending on size, Tb-€118, elevator, pay Internet access and Wi-Fi, parking-€8/day, Theaterstrasse 5, tel. 0931/304-8900, fax 0931/3048-9030, www.cityhotel-schoenleber.de, reservierung @cityhotel-schoenleber.de, Ulrich Kölbel).

$$ Sankt Josef Hotel's 33 rooms are small but sufficient (Sb-€55-60, Db-€80-100, price depends on room size and season—cheaper Nov-April and Aug, non-smoking rooms, no elevator, free Wi-Fi, reserve ahead for parking-€8/day, reception on second floor, Semmelstrasse 28-30, tel. 0931/308-680, fax 0931/308-6860, www.hotel-st-josef.de, hotel.st.josef@t-online.de, Herr and Frau Casagrande speak some English). The hotel restaurant serves dinner only (€8-14 main courses, Thu-Tue from 17:00, closed Wed).

$ Hotel Dortmunder Hof has 13 simple and bright rooms in a quiet downtown location. Mellow jazz tunes play in the cozy restaurant and wine bar (Sb-€42-65, Db-€76-100, Tb-€117, free Wi-Fi, reception in the bar to the right of the entrance, Innerer Graben 22, tel. 0931/56163, fax 0931/571825, www.dortmunder -hof.de, info@dortmunder-hof.de).

Hostels: **$ Babelfish Hostel,** across the street from the station, welcomes travelers of all ages. This laid-back place is clean, modern, and feels safe (dorm beds-€17-23, Sb-€45, Db-€62—some with kitchenettes, includes sheets, breakfast-€5, free Internet access and Wi-Fi, laundry-€4.90, free lockers, kitchen, roof deck,

Sleep Code

(€1 = about $1.40, country code: 49, area code: 0931)
S = Single, **D** = Double/Twin, **T** = Triple, **Q** = Quad, **b** = bathroom,
s = shower only. Credit cards are accepted, English is spoken,
and breakfast is included.

To help you sort easily through these listings, I've divided
the accommodations into two categories, based on the price
for a standard double room with bath:

$$$ **Higher Priced**—Most rooms €120 or more.
$$ **Moderately Priced**—Most rooms between €80-120.
$ **Lower Priced**—Most rooms less than €80.

Prices can change without notice; verify the hotel's
current rates online or by email. For other updates, see www
.ricksteves.com/update.

wheelchair-accessible, reception on second floor, Haugering 2,
tel. 0931/304-0430, fax 0931/304-3632, www.babelfish-hostel
.de, info@babelfish-hostel.de). **$** Würzburg's official **youth hostel**
(Jugendherberge), across the river in a former prison, has 238 beds
(€22-25/bed in 4- to 8-bed rooms, a few S-€28-31, Sb-€30-
37, D-€50-56, Db-€52-62, includes sheets and breakfast, non-
members-€3.10 extra, over 26 years old-€4 extra, slightly cheaper
mid-Nov-Feb, family rooms, coin-op Internet access, pay Wi-Fi,
no curfew—get night code, frequent musical/theatrical performances in attached courtyard—the "Kulturgarten"—in summer; 20-minute walk from station: cross Old Main Bridge and
turn left on Saalgasse to Fred-Joseph-Platz 2; or take tram #3 or
#5 to Löwenbrücke stop, then follow *Jugendherberge* signs; tel.
0931/42590, www.wuerzburg.jugendherberge.de, jhwuerzburg
@djh-bayern.de).

Eating in Würzburg

Restaurants and Wine Bars
That Support the Needy

In medieval times, rich Würzburgers founded charitable foundations to support the city's elderly and poor. They began making
and selling wine to fund their charity work, and this tradition
continues today. Still occupying grand Baroque complexes, the
foundations have restaurants, wine shops (selling wine in the area's
distinctive, bulbous *Bocksbeutel* bottles), and extensive wine cellars
(for serious buyers only).

WÜRZBURG

The oldest and best-known of these foundations is the **Bürgerspital,** which now cares for about a hundred local seniors. Its characteristic restaurant, pub, and wine store are right downtown, near recommended hotels. The restaurant, **Weinstube Bürgerspital,** is candlelit but informal, with a cloistered feel and gorgeous courtyard seating (€6-18 main courses, daily 10:00-24:00, Theaterstrasse 19, tel. 0931/352-880). The funky little **Hockerle** pub, adjacent to the wine store, is a time warp, filled with locals munching B.Y.O. sandwiches while sipping wine sold by the glass—as explained on its blackboard (both pub and store open Mon-Fri 9:00-18:00, Sat 9:00-15:00, closed Sun, corner of Theaterstrasse and Semmelstrasse at Theaterstrasse 19, tel. 0931/350-3403).

Nearby, the **Juliusspital** has updated its traditional *Weinstube* with a slightly modern, Mediterranean feel. Its courtyard is especially popular (€7-9 wurst plates, €10-21 main courses, daily 10:00-24:00, kitchen closes at 22:00, Juliuspromenade 19 at Barbarossaplatz, tel. 0931/54080).

More Restaurants in the Center

Alte Mainmühle, on the bridge in a converted mill, is a great place to end your walking tour. On a warm day, nothing beats a cold beer on their deck, which overlooks the river and the fortress—choose from their sunny top-floor terrace or the shade below. They have fresh fish specials (try their *Forelle* or *Zanderfilet*) and traditional fare with a Franconian twist. Their homemade sourdough bread *(Natursauerteigbrot)* is a delicious nod to their milling history (€7-8 wurst plates, €8-21 main courses, daily 10:00-24:00, kitchen open 11:00-22:30, Mainkai 1, tel. 0931/16777).

Goldene Gans Biergarden offers a simple, riverside beer garden setting, with wooden benches and shady views of the Old Main Bridge (€5-9 main courses, daily 11:00-24:00; coming from the town center, it's just to the left as you cross the Old Main Bridge, Burkarderstrasse 2-4; tel. 0931/2919-0817).

Backöfele is a fun hole-in-the-wall (literally). Named "The Oven" for its entryway, this place is a hit with Germans, offering a rustic menu full of local meat and fish dishes (€7-19 main courses, daily 12:00-24:00, reservations smart; with your back to the City Hall, go straight on Augustinerstrasse, take the first left onto Wolfhartsgasse, then the first right to Ursulinergasse 2; tel. 0931/59059).

Weinstube Maulaffenbäck, tucked away in an alley near Market Square and the cathedral with a few outdoor tables, is a characteristic place for cheap Franconian meals and good wine. If you order wine, you're welcome to bring your own food—they'll provide the plate and fork. This is an old tradition unique to Würzburg. If you choose to follow this custom, consider stopping at the butcher shop next door (conveniently owned by the same family; Mon-Fri 7:30-18:00, Sat 8:00-14:00, closed Sun) to pick up great cold cuts before finding a table (€5-10 main courses, Mon-Thu 10:00-22:00, Fri-Sat 10:00-23:00, closed Sun, Maulhardgasse 9, tel. 0931/52351).

Zum Stachel, Würzburg's oldest *Weinhaus,* originated as the town's tithe barn—where people deposited 10 percent of their produce as tax. In 1413, it began preparing the produce and selling wine. Today, it's a worthy splurge, serving gourmet Franconian meals in an elegant stone-and-ivy courtyard and woody dining room. The ceiling depicts a medieval *Stachel* (mace) in deadly action (€19-24 main courses, €31 three-course fixed-price meals, Mon-Sat 11:00-24:00, closed Sun, reservations smart for this dressy place; from Market Square head toward river, turn right on Gressengasse to intersection with Marktgasse, Gressengasse 1; tel. 0931/52770).

Café Michel, right on Market Square and next to the TI, is a family-oriented bakery and tea house with quiet indoor seating and tables on the square. The selection of cakes and strudels is outstanding, even for Germany. It serves soups, small sandwiches, cakes, tea, coffee, and—until 16:00—inexpensive egg breakfasts. This place has been around since 1911 (€5-7 light meals, Mon-Sat 9:00-18:00, Sun 10:00-18:00, Marktplatz 11, tel. 0931/53776).

Pasta e Olio, a couple of blocks east of Market Square, is a fun and popular stand-up pasta lunch counter. Because Signora Aucone makes pasta fresh daily, the menu is limited, but usually includes a pasta dish, lasagna, a vegetarian option, and mixed antipasti. Place your order, then eat standing at one of the tables (€4.50-5 plates, Mon-Fri 11:00-17:00, Sat 11:00-15:00, closed Sun, no WC, Eichhornstrasse 6, tel. 0931/16699).

Würzburg Connections

From Würzburg by Train to: Rothenburg (hourly, 70 minutes, transfer in Steinach; 45 minutes to Steinach, then 15 minutes to Rothenburg; tiny Steinach-Rothenburg train leaves usually from track 5 shortly after the Würzburg train arrives), **Frankfurt Airport** (1-2/hour, 1.5 hours), **Frankfurt** (1-2/hour, 70 minutes, or 2 hours on cheaper RE trains), **Nürnberg** (2-3/hour, 1-1.25 hours), **Munich** (1-2/hour, 2 hours), **Köln** (hourly, 2.5 hours, some with change in Frankfurt), **Leipzig** (about every 2 hours, 3.25-4 hours, transfer in Fulda or Bamberg), **Berlin** (hourly, 4 hours, change in Göttingen). Train info: tel. 0180-599-6633, www.bahn.com.

FRANKFURT

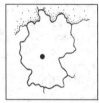

Frankfurt, while low on Old World charm, offers a good look at today's no-nonsense, modern Germany. There's so much more to this country than castles and old cobbled squares. Cosmopolitan Frankfurt is a business hub of the united Europe and home to the European Central Bank. Especially in the area around the train station, you'll notice the fascinating multiethnic flavor of the city. A third of its 650,000 residents carry foreign passports. Though it's often avoided as a sterile business and transportation hub, Frankfurt's modern energy makes it worth a look.

Planning Your Time

You might fly into or out of Frankfurt am Main, or at least pass through—this glossy city links the best wine-and-castles stretch of the Rhine to the north with the fairy-tale Romantic Road to the south. Even two or three hours in Frankfurt leaves you with some powerful impressions. The city's main sights are a 20-minute walk from its train station, which is a 12-minute train ride from its airport. At a minimum, head up to the top of the Main Tower for commanding city views and wander through the pedestrian zone to the old town area (Römerberg). My self-guided walk provides a framework for your explorations. With more time or an overnight, Frankfurt has plenty of museums and other attractions to choose from.

Orientation to Frankfurt

(area code: 069)

Frankfurt, with its forest of skyscrapers perched on the banks of the Main (pronounced "mine") River, has been dubbed Germany's

"Mainhattan." The city is Germany's trade and banking capital, leading the country in high-rises (mostly bank headquarters)...and yet, a third of Frankfurt is green space.

The convention center *(Messe)* and the red light district are near the train station. Just to the east is the skyscraper banking district and the shopping and pedestrian area around the Hauptwache. Beyond that is what remains of Frankfurt's old town, around Römerberg, the city's central market square. A short walk across the river takes you to a different part of town: Frankfurt's top museums line the south bank of the Main, and nearby is Sachsenhausen, a residential neighborhood and schmaltzy restaurant zone.

Tourist Information

Frankfurt has several TIs. The handiest (though it's small) is inside the **train station**'s main entrance, offering an abundance of brochures and a free hotel-booking service (Mon-Fri 8:00-21:00, Sat-Sun 9:00-18:00, tel. 069/2123-8800, www.frankfurt-tourismus .de). Another TI is on **Römerberg square** (Mon-Fri 9:30-17:30, Sat-Sun 10:00-16:00); there's also one at the **airport.** At any TI, buy the city/subway map (the basic €0.50 version is fine—skip the detailed €1 map). The train station and Römerberg TIs rent iPods loaded with an audiovisual city tour (€7.50/4 hours, €10/day, leave photo ID as deposit; you can download it to your own MP3 player from iTunes for €3.99). The TI also offers city bus tours and weekend walking tours (see "Tours in Frankfurt," later).

Discount Deals: Two discount passes compete for your attention, both sold at local TIs. The **Museum Ticket** gets you free entry into 34 museums (€15, valid 2 days). The **Frankfurt Card** gives you a transit pass (including connections to and from the airport), 50 percent off all major museums, and 25 percent off the city bus tour, which virtually pays for the pass (1 person: €8.90/1 day, €12.90/2 days; 2-5 people: €18/1 day, €26/2 days). These are both potentially good deals and worth considering if you'll be taking public transportation and visiting several sights.

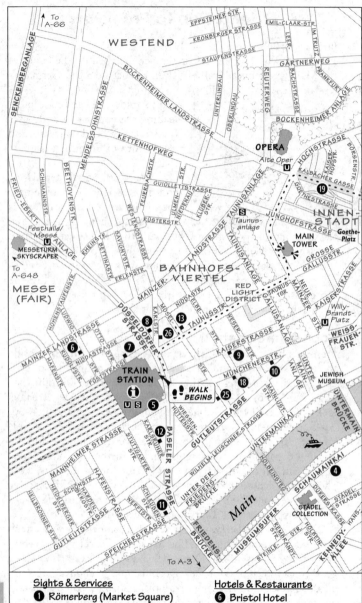

FRANKFURT

Sights & Services

1. Römerberg (Market Square)
2. St. Bartholomew's Cathedral
3. Schirn Art Center
4. Museum Embankment
5. Romantic Road Bus Stop

Hotels & Restaurants

6. Bristol Hotel
7. Hotel Hamburger Hof
8. Manhattan Hotel
9. Victoria Hotel
10. Memphis Hotel
11. Ibis Hotel Frankfurt Friedensbrücke

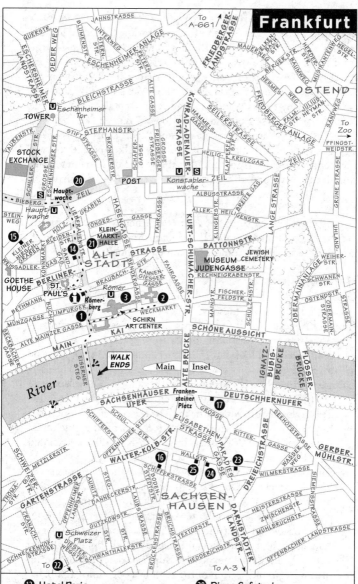

12 Hotel Paris
13 Five Elements Hostel
14 Hotel Neue Kräme
15 Hotel Zentrum
16 Maingau Hotel
17 Haus der Jugend Hostel
18 Merkez Kebap Haus
19 Fressgass' ("Feeding St.")

20 Dinea Cafeteria
21 Kleinmarkthalle Eateries
22 To Zum Gemalten Haus & Adolf Wagner Restaurants
23 Klaane Sachsehäuser
24 Fichtekränzi Restaurant
25 Launderettes (2)
26 Supermarket

Arrival in Frankfurt

By Train: The Frankfurt main train station (Hauptbahnhof) bustles with travelers. The TI is in the main hall just inside the front door. There are three sets of lockers; the least expensive are along track 24. The post office is across from track 24 (Mon-Fri 7:00-19:00, Sat 9:00-16:00, closed Sun). WCs (€0.70) are down the stairway by tracks 9 and 10. Inquire about train tickets in the *Reisezentrum* across from track 9 (Mon-Fri 6:00-22:00, Sat-Sun 7:00-22:00). Pick up a snack at the good food court across from tracks 4 and 5. The station is a five-minute walk from the convention center *(Messe)*, a three-minute subway ride or 20-minute walk from Römerberg, and a 12-minute shuttle train from the airport.

By Plane: See "Frankfurt Connections," at the end of this chapter.

By Car: Follow signs for *Frankfurt,* then *Messe,* and finally *Hauptbahnhof* (train station). The Hauptbahnhof garage (€27/day) is under the station, near most recommended hotels.

Helpful Hints

Closed Day: Most museums are closed Monday. Many are open until 20:00 on Wednesday.

Internet Access: You'll find terminals underneath the train station—take the escalators down from track 19 to the shopping level, and look left (€2/hour, daily 5:30-24:00, must be over 18).

Laundry: Miele Wash World is near the station and feels a little worn, with instructions in broken English (Mon-Sat 6:00-23:00, closed Sun, Moselstrasse 17, by the corner of Münchener Strasse). In Sachsenhausen, by the recommended Fichtekränzi restaurant, is an **SB-Waschsalon** (Mon-Sat 6:00-23:00, closed Sun, Wallstrasse 8, instructions in German only).

Supermarket: The **REWE** supermarket, near the station, is small but well-stocked (Mon-Fri 7:00-22:00, Sat 7:00-22:00, closed Sun, Karlstrasse 4, use Kaiserstrasse exit from underground passageway). There are larger supermarkets in the center of town, near the Hauptwache, in the basements of the Galeria Kaufhof department store and the MyZeil shopping mall. On Sundays, the smaller, expensive **Supermarket im Bahnhof** in the underground section of the station is open until 22:00.

Getting Around Frankfurt

By Public Transportation: Frankfurt's subway (U-Bahn) and suburban train (S-Bahn) network is easy to use, but trams are more convenient and give you a better look at the city. For all forms of public transit, buy your tickets *(Fahrkarten)* from an RMV machine. Tickets are issued with a validating stamp already on them, and are valid only immediately after they're bought. Find your destination on the chart, key in the number, choose your ticket type, then pay. Choose *Einzelfahrt* for a regular single ticket (€2.40), *Kurzstrecke* for a short ride (€1.50—valid destinations listed on machines), *Tageskarte Frankfurt* for an all-day pass (€6.20 without the airport, €9.50 with), or *Gruppentageskarte* for an all-day group ticket for up to five adults (€9.50 without the airport, €14.70 with). If you'll be going to or from the airport, note that the Frankfurt Card is cheaper than the all-day pass, and also includes sightseeing discounts (described earlier, under "Tourist Information"). An individual one-way ticket to the airport costs €3.90 (no group rate for airport-only trips). Some hotels sell guests a two-day *Tageskarte* that includes the airport for €12.90—a good deal. For more information in English, see www.rmv.de.

By Taxi: A taxi stand is just outside the main entrance of the train station to your left. A typical ride, such as to Römerberg square, should cost you €7 (up to €10 in slow traffic).

Tours in Frankfurt

City Bus Tour—The basic city bus tour gives a 2.5-hour orientation to Frankfurt, including Römerberg and a visit to either the Goethe House or (summer only) the observation deck of the Main Tower (€26, 25 percent discount with Frankfurt Card, recorded narration; April-Oct daily at 10:00 and 14:00; Nov-March daily at 14:00, Sat-Sun also at 10:00). The bus picks up at the scheduled times at the Römerberg TI, then stops 15 minutes later at the Frankfurt train station TI.

Hop-on, Hop-off Bus Tour—Double-decker hop-on, hop-off buses follow essentially the same route as the city bus tour, pausing at 16 stops in a one-hour loop. Buy tickets at the TI or on the bus (€18/one-day pass, €15 for one time around with no hop-on/hop-off privileges, daily 10:00-17:00, departs every 30 minutes from near St. Paul's Church). The one-day pass also covers a second, extended hop-on, hop-off route (focuses on city architecture, 5/day).

Walking Tours—Frankfurt on Foot/Insider Tour's three-hour walks, led by Ohioan Jodean Ator and her husband David, hit the major sights and explain Frankfurt's history (€12, €1 discount with this book, basic walk leaves daily at 10:30, walks depart from Römer/Paulskirche tram stop next to Römerberg TI—just show up, mobile 01520-846-4200, www.frankfurtonfoot.com, info @frankfurtonfoot.com). Their flexible **"Frankfurt Layover Tour"** is ideal for those with long layovers at the Frankfurt Airport (€75/3 hours, €25/each additional hour, includes pickup and drop-off at the airport).

On weekends, the **TI** organizes two-hour themed walks in English (topics vary from history and architecture to banking and apple wine—check ahead on www.infofrankfurt.de), which leave from the Römerberg TI (€12, 20 percent discount with Frankfurt Card, April-Oct Sat-Sun at 13:30, Nov Sat only at 13:30, no tours Dec-March).

Local Guide—**Elisabeth Lücke** loves her city and shares it very well (€60/hour, cash only, reserve in advance, tel. 06196/45787, mobile 0173-913-3157, www.elisabeth-luecke.de, elisabeth.luecke @t-online.de).

Self-Guided Walk

Welcome to Frankfurt

This sightseeing walk, worth ▲▲, shows you both the new Frankfurt and the old—starting at its train station, taking you past junkies and brothels, up the Main Tower, through the modern shopping and eating districts, into the lively square at the center of the old town, and finishing on a bridge overlooking the city and its river.

Train Station

Frankfurt has Germany's busiest train station: 350,000 travelers make their way to 24 platforms to catch 1,800 trains every day.

Hop a train and you can be in either Paris or Berlin in less than four hours. While it was big news when it opened in the 1890s, it's a dead-end terminus station, which, with today's high-speed trains, makes it outdated. Complaining that it takes an extra 20 minutes to stop here, railway officials threatened to have the speedy ICE trains bypass Frankfurt altogether

unless it dug a tunnel to allow for a faster pass-through stop. But this proved too expensive, and—while some trains stop only at the pass-through airport station—most fast trains begrudgingly serve downtown Frankfurt.

Leaving through the station's front door, walk directly away from the station to the traffic island facing the pedestrian Kaiserstrasse, and turn to look back at the building's Neo-Renaissance facade—a style popular with Industrial Revolution-era architects. This classic late 19th-century glass-and-iron construction survived World War II. High above, a statue of Apollo carries the world—but only with some heavy-duty help: Green copper figures representing steam power and electricity pitch in. The 1890s were a confident age, when people believed that technology would solve the world's problems.

• *With your back to the station, look down...*

Kaiserstrasse

This grand 19th-century boulevard features appropriately elegant facades that were designed to dress up the approach to what was a

fine new station. Towering above and beyond the 100-year-old buildings are the skyscrapers of Frankfurt's banking district. But look at street level and notice the human riffraff and cheap eateries lining this once-genteel street. As we'll see on this walk, Frankfurt is a city of contrasts.

Warning: This walk now goes into a neighborhood of hard-drug users and prostitutes. It can be creepy any time of day. If you use common sense, it's not dangerous, but it unnerves many. If you'd rather go directly to the Main Tower, walk straight down Kaiserstrasse four blocks to the park and skip ahead to "Frankfurt's Banking District" on page 356.

• *OK, if you're game, jog left (note the pyramid-topped skyscraper in the distance marking the huge Frankfurt Trade Center) one block to the corner of Taunusstrasse. Turn right and walk a block to the corner of Taunusstrasse and Moselstrasse. Ahead of you, Taunusstrasse is lined half with brothels and half with bank towers. Cross the street and look left.*

▲▲Brothels and Junkies

A half-block down Moselstrasse, on the left, you'll probably see a gang congregating in front of Café Fix (at #47), one of several such **"junkie cafés"** in Frankfurt. In 1992, Frankfurt began offering "pump rooms" to its hard-drug users. These centers provide clean needles and a safe and caring place for addicts to go to maintain their habit and get counseling and medical help. Two decades later, locals consider the program a success, and are accustomed to wasted people congregating in neighborhoods like this one. While unsightly, the compassionate "harm reduction" approach much of Europe uses to deal with this problem saves lives.

Walk a block farther down Taunusstrasse to Elbestrasse. Look or turn left down Elbestrasse, where you'll find a row of high-rise brothels, or **"eros towers."** There are about 20 of these five-story brothels within a block of here—each filled with prostitutes (charging around €25). These women rent their rooms and essentially run their own little businesses. Since they are legal and

pay taxes, they successfully lobbied to get the same benefits that other taxed workers receive. Climbing through a few of these towers may be one of the more memorable experiences of your European trip. While hiking through the towers feels safe, the aggressive women at the neighboring strip shows can be unsettling.

Ever since the Middle Ages, Frankfurt's thriving prostitution industry has gone hand-in-hand with its trade fairs. Today, prostitution thrives with the *Messe* (convention center). Both hotels and prostitutes double their prices during big trade fairs. Prostitutes note that business varies with the theme of the trade show—while the auto show is boom time, they complain that Frankfurt's massive book fair is a bust.

On the other side of Taunusstrasse, at Elbestrasse 31, is a strip joint called **Pik-Dame.** Old-timers are nostalgic about this lone remnant from "the good old days" just after World War II, when 30,000 US soldiers stationed in Frankfurt provided a stimulus for this neighborhood's economy. Later, the troops left and the Russian mob moved in, replacing any old-time gentility with a criminal and thuggish edge.

• *Continue down Taunusstrasse out of the red light district and into the banking district. Look up and see why this city is nicknamed "Mainhattan." Cross the street to the park and go to the statue of the poet Schiller (a Romantic poet and friend of Goethe), on your left.*

▲Frankfurt's Banking District

This park is part of a circular greenbelt that circles the old center and marks the site of Frankfurt's medieval fortifications. These walls (along with many castles on the Rhine) were destroyed by the French in 1806. Napoleon was on his way to Russia, and, since he had the upper hand, he figured it was wise to preemptively destroy any German fortifications that might haunt him if the Germans turned against France in the future.

The park is the center of Frankfurt's banking district. The post-WWII Marshall Plan was administered from here—requiring fancy money-handling. And the mighty Deutsche Mark was born in a 1930s-era building facing this square (in the low Art Deco building on the left of the square as you entered, behind the greenery from where you now stand). After World War II, Germany's economy was in chaos. In 1948, the US gave it a complete currency transfer—like a blood transfusion, literally printing up the new Deutsche Marks and shipping them across the Atlantic to inject them from here directly into the German economy. As if catching water from a fountain, banks naturally grew up around this square.

But Frankfurt was "Bankfurt" long before World War II. This was the Rothschilds' hometown. Born in Frankfurt's Jewish ghetto in 1744, Mayer Rothschild went from being a pauper to the richest banker in the world in one lifetime. His five sons set up business in Rome, London, Paris, and Vienna, and in two generations the Rothschild banking dynasty was established. (Their former palace now houses Frankfurt's Jewish Museum, described on page 363.) Today, locals call Frankfurt's legion of bankers "penguins," as they all dress the same. Tour guides here talk of banks as part of the cultural soil (the way French Riviera guides talk of the big yachts).

Beyond the statue of Schiller stand the twin towers of the Deutsche Bank (not to be confused with the DB—DeutscheBahn—tower to your left). This country's #1 bank, its assets are greater than the annual budget of the German government. If money makes the world go round, decisions that spin Germany are made in Frankfurt. But, with the recent economic crisis, a third of these skyscraper offices are empty. No one knows what the future holds for this European money capital.

• *Find the skyscraper with the red-and-white candy cane on top. That's your destination—the Main Tower. To reach it, continue straight along Taunustor a block, then turn left on Neue Mainzer Strasse and look for the tower symbol on the door on the right.*

▲▲Main Tower

Finished in 2000, this tower houses the Helaba Bank and offers the best (and only public) viewpoint from the top of a Frankfurt skyscraper. A 55-second, ear-popping elevator ride to the 54th floor (watch the meter on the wall as you ascend) and then 50 stairs take you to the rooftop, 650 feet above the city.

Cost and Hours: €5; April-Sept Sun-Thu 10:00-21:00, Fri-Sat 10:00-23:00; Oct-March Sun-Thu 10:00-19:00, Fri-Sat 10:00-21:00; last entry 30 minutes before closing, enter at Neue Mainzer Strasse 52, between Taunustor and Junghofstrasse, tel. 069/3650-4740, www.maintower.de.

⊙ Self-Guided Spin-Tour: Here, from Frankfurt's ultimate viewpoint, survey the city circling clockwise, starting with the biggest skyscraper (with the yellow emblem).

Commerzbank Building: Designed by Norman Foster (of

Berlin Reichstag and London City Hall fame), the Commerzbank building was finished in 1997. It's 985 feet high, with nine winter gardens spiraling up its core and windows that actually open. It's considered the first ecological skyscraper...radically "green" in its day. Just to the left is Römerberg—the old town center (the half-timbered houses huddled around the red-and-white church; we'll visit there soon).

European Central Bank: The blue-and-gold euro symbol (€) decorates the front yard of the Euro Tower, home of the European Central Bank (a.k.a. "City of the Euro"). The all-Europe currency is administered from here. Typical of skyscrapers from the 1970s, it's slim—to allow maximum natural light into all workplaces inside. The euro symbol in the park was unveiled on January 1, 2002, the day the euro went into circulation in the first 12 Eurozone countries. Today 17 countries officially use the euro, and the euro club continues to grow.

The **Museum Embankment** (see page 364) lines Schaumainkai on the far side of the Main River, just beyond the Euro Tower.

Airport: The Rhine-Main airport, off in the distance in the forest, is the largest employment complex in Germany (62,000 workers). Frankfurt's massive train station dominates the foreground. From the station, the grand Kaiserstrasse cuts through the city to Römerberg.

Messe: The Frankfurt fair *(Messe)*, marked by the skyscraper with the pointy top, is a huge convention center—the size of 40 soccer fields. It sprawls behind the skyscraper that looks like a classical column sporting a visor-like capital. (The protruding lip of the capital is heated so that icicles don't form, break off, and impale people on the street below.) Frankfurt's fair originated in 1240, when the emperor promised all participating merchants safe passage. The black twin towers of the Deutsche Bank in the foreground are typical of mid-1980s mirrored architecture.

The West End: With vast green spaces and the telecommunications tower, this is Frankfurt's priciest residential quarter. The city's most enjoyable zone cuts from the West End to the right. Stretching from the classic-looking Opera House below are broad and people-filled boulevards made to order for eating and shopping. Find the "Beach Club" filling the rooftop of a parking garage with white tents and two pools. This is a popular family zone by day, and a chic club after dark.

Take a moment from this vantage point to trace the rest of this walk: from the Opera House, along the tree-lined eating and shopping boulevards to St. Paul's Church and Römerberg. After a short side-trip from Römerberg to the cathedral, we'll finish on Eiserner Steg, the iron pedestrian bridge over the Main River.

As you leave the Main Tower, step into the Helaba Bank lobby

(20 yards from base of elevator). A mosaic flanking the elevator shows cultural superstars of 20th-century Frankfurt, from composer Paul Hindemith to industrialist and humanitarian Oskar Schindler.

• *Leave the Main Tower and continue walking along Neue Mainzer Strasse (crossing Junghofsstrasse) for a couple of blocks, to where you see a large square open to your left. Across the square is the Opera House.*

Frankfurt's Good-Living People Zone

Opera House (Alte Oper): Finished in 1880, Frankfurt's opera house celebrated German high culture and the newly created nation. Mozart and Goethe flank the entrance, reminders that this is a house of both music and theater. The original opera house was destroyed in World War II. Over the objections of a mayor nicknamed "Dynamite Rudi," the city rebuilt it in the original style. Underneath is a U-Bahn station (Alte Oper).

• *Facing the Opera, turn right down Frankfurt's famous...*

Fressgass': The official names for this pedestrian street are Grosse Bockenheimer Strasse and Kalbächer Gasse...but everyone in Frankfurt calls it the Fressgass', roughly "Feeding Street."

Herds of bank employees come here on their lunch breaks to fill their bellies before returning for another few hours of cud-chewing at their computers. It's packed gable-to-gable with eateries and shoulder-to-shoulder with workers wolfing €2 sandwiches, plates of Asian food, and, yes, burgers from McDonald's. Join in if you're hungry—or wait for more eating options in a couple blocks.

• *Fressgass' leads to a square called Rathenauplatz. Cross the square and continue straight—the pedestrian street is now called Biebergasse— another block to the...*

Hauptwache: The small, red-and-white building—which has given its name to the square (and the subway station below it)— was built in 1730 to house the Frankfurt city militia. Now it's a café. The square, entirely closed to traffic, is one of the city's hubs.

• *To the right, at the south side of the square, is the Protestant Katharinenkirche, which was destroyed in the bombing raids of March 1944 and rebuilt after the war. Straight ahead of you is a boulevard called the...*

Zeil: This tree-lined pedestrian drag is Frankfurt's main shopping street. Crowds swirl through the Galeria Kaufhof department store, the Zeil Galerie, and the MyZeil shopping center along the left side of the street. For lunch or just good views, the Galeria Kaufhof has a recommended rooftop cafeteria, the Dinea (overlook open to non-guests). MyZeil has a cool atrium with a really long escalator that leads straight to the top-floor food court. There are supermarkets in the basements of both buildings; the one in the MyZeil shopping center has a bakery with seating.

• *Instead of walking all the way down the Zeil, turn right (across from the last Galeria Kaufhof entrance doorway and the column of porthole-like windows) down Liebfraustrasse, another pedestrian street. A block down, you'll come to Liebfrauberg, a square with a brown stone fountain. To reach the recommended **Kleinmarkthalle**—an indoor produce market with both stand-up and sit-down lunch options—cross the square, then head to the left and down the stairs. A block farther down Liebfraustrasse, cross Berliner Strasse and come to Paulsplatz.*

▲St. Paul's Church (Paulskirche)

To your right, the former church dominating the square is known as the "cradle of German democracy." It was here, during the political upheaval of 1848, that the first freely elected National Assembly met and the first German Constitution was drafted, paving the way for a united Germany in 1871. Following its destruction by Allied bombs in 1944, the church became the first historic building in the city to be rebuilt. This was a symbolic statement from the German people that they wanted to be free (as they had demonstrated here in 1848), democratic...and no longer fascist. Around the outside of the building, you'll see reliefs honoring people who contributed to the German nation, including Theodor Heuss, the first president, and John F. Kennedy, who spoke here on June 25, 1963.

Step inside. Displays described in English tell the story of 1848. Check out the circular mural, from the 1980s. Called *The March of Members of Parliament*, it was controversial when unveiled. Commissioned to honor the political heroes of 1848, the portraits are cartoonish figures with faces of contemporary politicians. Political leaders seem to sneer at the working class, and two naked men who look like they're having sex represent forces of democracy and monarchy fighting within Germany. Upstairs is a 900-seat assembly hall with no decor except the flags of the 16 states of the Federal Republic of Germany.

Cost and Hours: Free, daily 10:00-17:00.

• *Crossing the street on the far side of the square brings you into what's left of...*

Frankfurt's Old Town

Römerberg: Frankfurt's market square, worth ▲, was the birthplace of the city. This is where the first trade fairs were held in

the 12th century. The Town Hall *(Römer)* houses the *Kaisersaal,* or Imperial Hall, where Holy Roman Emperors celebrated their coronations. Today, the *Römer* houses the city council and mayor's office. The cute row of half-timbered homes (rebuilt in 1983) opposite the *Römer* is typical of Frankfurt's quaint old center before the square was completely destroyed in World War II. Hosting everything from Christmas markets to violent demonstrations, this square is the beating heart of Frankfurt.

• *Facing the Town Hall, the river and the bridge where this walk ends are just two blocks to the left. But first, we'll take a short detour. Circle around the red-and-white church (heading left from the skippable History Museum) to Saalgasse.*

Saalgasse and Roman Ruins: Literally "Hall Street," Saalgasse is lined by postmodern buildings echoing the higgledy-piggledy houses that stood here until World War II. In the 1990s,

famous architects from around the world were each given a ruined house of the same width and told to design a new structure to reflect the one that stood there before the war. As you continue down the street, guess which one is an upside-down half-timbered house with the stars down below. (Hint: Animals are on the "ground floor.")

Saalgasse leads to some ancient Roman ruins in front of St. Bartholomew's Cathedral (turn left when you first see the cathedral). The grid of stubs was the subfloor of a Roman bath (allowing the floor to be heated). Romans had settled Frankfurt by A.D.

100, although the town wasn't mentioned in records until 794, when Charlemagne (king of the Franks and the first Holy Roman Emperor) held a meeting here with the local bishop. In the center is a small model of the church that stood upon this Roman site in the early Middle Ages. All around you is the architectural hodgepodge of postwar Frankfurt. The skyscraper with the yellow emblem in the distance is the Commerzbank building, the tallest office block in Western Europe (985 feet). The shorter, glassy building next to it, also with a red-and-white antenna, is the Main Tower we visited earlier.

• *Behind the Roman ruins is...*

St. Bartholomew's Cathedral (Kaiserdom): Walk around the front of the church and enter on the side opposite the river. Rebuilt in the 1950s, the church—still bright and airy like the original—is made of modern concrete with paint to imitate mortar and medieval bricks. Holy Roman Emperors were elected here starting in 1152, and crowned here between 1562 and 1792. The cathedral was destroyed by fire in 1867 and had to be rebuilt. It was seriously damaged in World War II (as the photos in the entranceway testify), but repaired and reopened in 1953. Frescoes from the 13th century survive (flanking the high altar and ringing the choir). They show 27 scenes from the life of St. Bartholomew. Everything of value that could be moved was taken out of the church before the WWII bombs came. The delightful red-sandstone chapel of Sleeping Mary (to the left of the high altar), carved and painted in the 15th century, was too big to move—so it was fortified with sandbags. The altarpiece and fine stained glass next to it survived the bombing. The Dom Museum (enter from church vestibule) is not particularly interesting (Cathedral-free, Dom Museum-€3, daily 9:00-12:00 & 14:30-18:00).

• *Retrace your steps back to Römerberg. Finish this tour by walking down to the river and out onto the fine old iron Eiserner Bridge. From the middle of the bridge, survey the skyline and enjoy the lively scene along the riverbanks of Frankfurt.*

For a quick ride back to your starting point, take the U-Bahn or, from the stop across the street from the square, hop either tram #11 or #12, and get off at the Hauptbahnhof stop.

Sights in Frankfurt

In or near the Old Town (Römerberg)

▲**Goethe House (Goethehaus)**—Johann Wolfgang von Goethe (1749-1832), a scientist, minister, poet, lawyer, politician, and playwright, was a towering figure in the early Romantic Age. His birthplace, now a fine museum, is a five-minute walk northwest of Römerberg. It's furnished as it was in the mid-18th century, when the boy destined to become the "German Shakespeare" grew up here.

Borrow a laminated card at the bottom of the stairs for a refreshingly brief commentary on each of the 16 rooms. Since nothing's roped off and there are no posted signs, it's easy to picture real people living here. Goethe's father dedicated his life and wealth to cultural pursuits, and his mother told young Johann Wolfgang fairy tales every night, stopping just before the ending so that the boy could exercise his own creativity. Goethe's family gave him all the money he needed to travel and learn. His collection of 2,000 books was sold off in 1795. In recent decades, more than half of these have been located and repurchased by the museum (you'll see them in the library). This building honors the man who inspired the Goethe-Institut, dedicated to keeping the German language strong.

Cost and Hours: €5, €3 high-tech but easy-to-use and informative audioguide, €1.50 English booklet has same info as free laminated cards—worthwhile only as a souvenir, Mon-Sat 10:00-18:00, Sun 10:00-17:30; 15-minute walk from Hauptbahnhof up Kaiserstrasse, turn right on Am Salzhaus to Grosser Hirschgraben 23; tel. 069/138-800, www.goethehaus-frankfurt.de.

Schirn Art Center (Schirn Kunsthalle)—Opened in 1986, this facility has quickly become one of Europe's most respected homes of modern and contemporary art. Rotating exhibits pay homage to everything and everyone from Kandinsky and Kahlo to contemporary artists, movements, and topics.

Cost and Hours: €6-9 depending on exhibits, Tue and Fri-Sun 10:00-19:00, Wed-Thu until 22:00, closed Mon, Römerberg, tel. 069/299-8820, www.schirn.de.

Jewish Sights—Housed in the former Rothschild Palace (of the famous banking family), the worthwhile **Jewish Museum** (Jüdisches Museum) traces the history of Frankfurt's Jews since the 12th century. Rather than simply presenting artifacts, it tries to engage visitors in a dialogue about culture and society as a whole. The €7.80 English guidebook is unnecessary, since detailed English handouts are available on each floor (€4, €5 combo-ticket with Museum Judengasse—described next; Tue-Sun 10:00-17:00, Wed until 20:00, closed Mon, Untermainkai 14/15, tel. 069/2123-5000, www.juedischesmuseum.de). The museum is along the river between Römerberg and the train station, just across the road from the lovely riverside promenade—a perfect place to rest your feet and watch people and planes go by.

The museum also runs the smaller and less interesting **Museum Judengasse,** centering on the foundations of the buildings (built in 1462) in the old Jewish ghetto (€2, €5 combo-ticket with Jewish Museum, same hours and website as Jewish Museum, Kurt-Schumacher-Strasse 10 at corner of Battonstrasse, a few blocks or one tram stop east of Römerberg, tel. 069/297-7419).

Behind the Museum Judengasse and more worth seeing is Frankfurt's old **Jewish cemetery.** You can look through the locked gate into the cemetery grounds—only a few gravestones survive. But the real draw is the cemetery wall, where 11,000 tiny metal memorials bear the names of Frankfurt Jews killed in the Holocaust, including Anne Frank (who was born in Frankfurt in 1929, though her family later moved to Amsterdam).

Across the River, on the South Bank

Schaumainkai and Frankfurt's Museum Embankment (Museumsufer)—The Schaumainkai riverside promenade (across the river from Römerberg over the Eiserner Steg pedestrian bridge, and then to the right) is great for an evening stroll or people-watching on any sunny day. Keep your eyes peeled for nude sunbathers. Every other Saturday, the museum strip street is closed off for a sprawling flea market.

Nine museums in striking buildings line the Main River along Schaumainkai. In the 1980s, Frankfurt decided that it wanted to buck its "Bankfurt" and "Krankfurt" (*krank* means "sick") image. It went on a culture kick and devoted 11 percent of the city budget to the arts and culture. The result: Frankfurt has become a city of art. These nine museums (covering areas such as architecture, film, world cultures, and great European masters—the Städel Collection) and a dozen others are all well-described in the TI's *Museumsufer* brochure.

Cost and Hours: All museums here are covered by the 2-day €15 Museum Ticket sold at TIs and participating museums—see page 349; most museums open Tue-Sun 10:00-17:00, Wed until 20:00, closed Mon; www.kultur-frankfurt.de.

Sleeping in Frankfurt

Planning to sleep in Frankfurt is a gamble, since the city's numerous trade fairs *(Messe)* send hotel prices skyrocketing—a €70 double can suddenly shoot up to €300. Visit www.messefrankfurt.com (and select "The Company," then "Our Publications," then "Calendar of Trade Fairs") for an exact schedule. During these trade fairs, skip Frankfurt altogether and stay in Würzburg, Bacharach, or St. Goar.

When trade fairs aren't in town, room prices in most Frankfurt hotels fluctuate €20 or more with the day of the week. If you'll be staying overnight in Frankfurt during a non-convention summer weekend, you can land a great place relatively cheaply. Frankfurt hotels are business-oriented, so many are empty and desperate for guests from Friday night to Monday morning. The lower prices listed here are for weekends, and the higher prices for weekdays. Although the ranges listed here are typical, varying demand may skew them higher or lower.

Keep overnights in Frankfurt to a minimum: Pleasant Rhine

Sleep Code

(€1 = about $1.40, country code: 49, area code: 069)
S = Single, **D** = Double/Twin, **T** = Triple, **Q** = Quad, **b** = bathroom, **s** = shower only. Unless otherwise noted, credit cards are accepted, English is spoken, and breakfast is included. All listed hotels have non-smoking rooms.

To help you sort easily through these listings, I've divided the accommodations into three categories, based on the price for a standard double room with bath:

$$$ Higher Priced—Most rooms €100 or more.
$$ Moderately Priced—Most rooms between €75-100.
$ Lower Priced—Most rooms €75 or less.

Prices can change without notice; verify the hotel's current rates online or by email. For other updates, see www .ricksteves.com/update.

and Romantic Road towns are just a quick drive or train ride away, offering a mom-and-pop welcome that you won't find here in the big city.

Near the Train Station

The following places are within a few blocks of the train station and its fast and handy train to the airport (to sleep even closer to the airport, see "Sleeping at or near Frankfurt Airport," page 372). The first three hotels are on the north (and most sedate) side of the station. The Victoria and the Memphis are in a more middlebrow, Turkish, and multiethnic neighborhood to the east of the station. The Paris and Ibis are south of the station, where there are many Eastern European shops and services.

All these listings are well-run and feel safe and respectable. I like staying in this colorful and convenient neighborhood (which gets more gentrified every year). But the red light district is close by, with gritty clubs and drug users. Don't wander into seedy-feeling streets, and use care and common sense after dark.

For a rough idea of directions to hotels, using an imaginary clock as a compass, stand with your back to the main entrance of the station: Manhattan Hotel is across the street at 10 o'clock, Five Elements at 11 o'clock, Victoria Hotel at 1 o'clock, Memphis Hotel at 2 o'clock, Hotel Paris at 5 o'clock, and Bristol Hotel and Hotel Hamburger Hof at 7 o'clock. Ibis Hotel is on a nicer street two blocks beyond Hotel Paris.

$$$ Bristol Hotel is a swanky 145-room place, part of a new generation of train-station hotels. It serves up style and flair, from its nod to Pacific Rim architecture to its teak-furnished breakfast room and patio café. Although it's just two blocks from the station, it enjoys quiet and respectable surroundings. If you're looking to splurge on your first or last night in Europe, this is the place (Sb-€60-95, larger Sb-€70-120, Db-€85-120, larger Db-€100-140, huge breakfast buffet, elevator, free Internet access and Wi-Fi, Ludwigstrasse 15, tel. 069/242-390, fax 069/251-539, www.bristol -hotel.de, info@bristol-hotel.de). Exit the station by track 24, cross the street, turn left, then right on Ottostrasse, then left on Niddastrasse to Ludwigstrasse.

$$ Hotel Hamburger Hof, right next to the train station but in a quiet and safe-feeling location, has a classy, shiny lobby and 66 elegant rooms. The side facing the station is cheerfully sunny, while rooms on the other side are quieter (Sb-€60-85, Db-€80-110, Tb-€100-130, air-con, non-smoking floors, elevator, free Internet access, expensive Wi-Fi, Poststrasse 10-12, tel. 069/2713-9690, fax 069/235-802, www.hamburgerhof.com, info@hamburgerhof.com). Exit the station by track 24, cross the street, turn left, and walk to the end of the block.

$$ Manhattan Hotel, with 54 fine, recently renovated rooms, is a straightforward option that fronts a high-traffic street a few doors from the station (Sb-€55-99, Db-€65-125, mention this book when reserving to get a 10 percent discount during non-convention times in 2012, one child under 12 free, elevator, free Internet access and Wi-Fi, Düsseldorfer Strasse 10, tel. 069/269-5970, fax 069/2695-97777, www.manhattan-hotel.com, manhattan-hotel @t-online.de). Exit the station by track 24, cross the street, and go right until you see the hotel; to cross Düsseldorfer Strasse safely, walk up to the tram stop.

$$ Victoria Hotel, midway between the station and Römerberg on the grand Kaiserstrasse, has 73 smartly redone rooms (with lots of pillows), and feels a world apart from the red light district a block away (Sb-€55-75, Db-€75-100, Db suite-€105-140, air-con, elevator, free Internet access and cable Internet, expensive Wi-Fi, Kaiserstrasse 59, entrance on Elbestrasse, tel. 069/273-060, fax 069/2730-6100, www.victoriahotel.de, victoria-hotel@t-online.de). To reach the hotel, go down the escalators to the underground passageway below the station and follow the *Kaiserstrasse* signs.

$$ Memphis Hotel, three long blocks or one tram stop from the station on a colorful street in the Turkish district, has 42 modern rooms and is another stylish business hotel that's affordable when there's no convention in town (Sb-€55-85, Db-€70-95, prices soft—call for exact rates, ask for a room on the quiet side— *ruhige Seite*, free Internet access, pay Wi-Fi, Münchener Strasse 15, tel. 069/242-6090, fax 069/2426-0999, www.memphis-hotel.de, memphis-hotel@t-online.de). To get here, use the same directions as for the Victoria Hotel, then cut one street right to the parallel Münchener Strasse.

$$ Ibis Hotel Frankfurt Friedensbrücke, a reliable chain hotel, is a good value, with 233 rooms on a quiet riverside street away from the station (Sb/Db-€59-79, Tb-€109, breakfast-€10/person, elevator, free Internet access, expensive Wi-Fi, parking-€10/day; exit station by track 1 and follow busy Baseler Strasse three blocks, turn right before river on Speicherstrasse to #4, across the street from the green office tower; tel. 069/273-030, fax 069/2730-3300, www.ibishotel.com, h1445@accor.com).

$ Hotel Paris, a short block from the station on a street with Eastern European restaurants, has 20 small but fine rooms and a nice staff (Sb-€40-60, Db-€50-80, Tb-€60-95, four floors and no elevator, free Internet access and Wi-Fi, Karlsruher Strasse 8, tel. 069/273-9963, fax 069/2739-9651, www.hotelparis.de, info@hotel paris.de). Exit the station by track 1, cross the street, turn right and go one block, and then turn left on Karlsruher Strasse. They also run the attached—and much pricier—Hotel Villa Oriental.

Hostel: **$ Five Elements** has 150 beds a block from the train station. It's clean and modern and feels very safe. But because it's smack in the middle of the red light district, families might feel more comfortable elsewhere. It's best to reserve by email (€20/bed in 6- and 8-bed dorms, €24 in 4-bed dorms, S-€45, Sb-€50, D-€55, Db-€60, breakfast-€4; includes sheets and lockers, free Internet access and Wi-Fi, elevator, non-smoking, laundry-€4.50, Moselstrasse 40, tel. 069/2400-5885, fax 069/2424-6955, www .5elementshostel.de, welcome@5elementshostel.de). From the station, exit the underground hall onto Taunusstrasse and go one block to the corner of Moselstrasse; the hostel is across the intersection to your left.

Away from the Station

If you're in Frankfurt for one night, stay near the station—but if you're in town for a few days and want to feel like you belong, choose one of the following listings. Hotel Neue Kräme and Hotel Zentrum are near Römerberg, and the Maingau Hotel and the hostel are in the Sachsenhausen district (see "Eating in Frankfurt," later).

$$ Hotel Neue Kräme is a quiet little 21-room oasis tucked away above the center of Frankfurt's downtown action, just steps from Römerberg. Friendly Georg welcomes guests in this bright and cheerful little blue-and-white place (Sb-€69-75, Db-€79, mention this book when reserving to get these prices, elevator, expensive Wi-Fi, Neue Kräme 23, tel. 069/284-046, fax 069/296-288, www.hotel-neuekraeme.de, info@hotel-neuekraeme.de).

$$ Hotel Zentrum, on the upper floors of a downtown building, has good rooms in a great location across the street from the

FRANKFURT

Hauptwache (Sb-€66-77, Db-€77-88, Tb-€99-110, Qb-€140-170, mention this book when reserving to get these prices, elevator, free Internet access and Wi-Fi, Rossmarkt 7, tel. 069/5050-0190, fax 069/5050-01977, www.hotel-zentrum.de, info@hotel-zentrum.de).

$$ Maingau Hotel, located across the river in the Sachsen-hausen district, is on a quiet, residential street facing a neighbor-hood park. The 84 rooms are simple and bright. If you're looking for a little tranquility in an authentic residential setting, stay here (Sb-€62-78, Db-€72-108, Sunday nights even cheaper, prices soft, elevator, expensive Wi-Fi, parking-€15/day, fancy dinners and €33-70 fixed-price meals at adjacent restaurant, Schifferstrasse 38-40, tel. 069/609-140, fax 069/620-790, www.maingau.de, info@maingau.de).

Hostel: The **$ Haus der Jugend** hostel, with 434 beds, is right along the river (€18/bed in 8- and 10-bed dorms, €21 in 3- to 4-bed dorms, Sb-€36.50, Db-€63; €4.50 more for guests age 27 or older, families excepted; nonmembers-€3.10/day extra, includes sheets and breakfast, elevator, pay Internet access and Wi-Fi, lunch or dinner-€5, laundry-€2, 2:00 curfew, Deutschherrnufer 12, tel. 069/610-0150, fax 069/6100-1599, www.jugendherberge -frankfurt.de, info@hellofrankfurt.de). To reach the hostel from the station, exit by track 1 and take bus #46 (3/hour, direction: Mühlberg) to the Frankensteiner Platz stop, which is one door from the hostel.

Eating in Frankfurt

Near the Station and Downtown

Expect to eat ethnic around Frankfurt's train station—there are dozens of hole-in-the-wall Asian and Turkish restaurants on Kaiserstrasse, Münchener Strasse, and surrounding streets.

Merkez Kebap Haus, two blocks from the station at the cor-ner of Elbestrasse and Münchener Strasse, is an informal Turkish restaurant that's a cut above the usual *Döner Kebab* shop. Their *Döners* cost only a euro more (€4), and there's table service, WCs, and a large selection of main dishes, salads, and desserts—most on view at the counter (€6-15 main courses, daily 8:00-24:00, Münchener Strasse 33, tel. 069/233-995).

Downtown, your options include the café-lined **Fressgass'**, the top-floor **Dinea** cafeteria in the Galeria Kaufhof depart-ment store near the Hauptwache (view terrace, Mon-Sat 9:30-20:30, closed Sun), and the stand-up and sit-down lunches in the **Kleinmarkthalle** indoor market at Liebfrauberg (Mon-Fri 8:00-18:00, Sat 8:00-16:00, closed Sun). All of these are mentioned on my self-guided "Welcome to Frankfurt" walk, earlier). Try to steer clear of the few, somewhat overpriced and touristy restaurants right around Römerberg.

Apple-Wine Pubs in the Sachsenhausen District

Instead of beer-garden ambience, Frankfurt entices visitors and locals to its apple-wine pub district. The cobbled and cozy Sachsenhausen neighborhood is both a well-heeled residential area and a traditional eating-and-drinking zone. There are more than a hundred characteristic apple-wine pubs here (and plenty of other options). *Apfelwein*, drunk around here since Charlemagne's time 1,200 years ago, became more popular in the 16th century, when local grapes were diseased. It enjoyed another boost two centuries later, when a climate change made grape-growing harder. Apple wine is about the strength of beer (5.5 percent alcohol) and is served spiced and warm in winter, cold in summer. To complement your traditional drink with a traditional meal, order Frankfurt sausage or pork chops and kraut.

All the places I've listed have both indoor and outdoor seating in a woodsy, rustic setting. Not just for tourists, these characteristic places are truly popular with Frankfurters, too. If you are craving *Leiterchen* ("mini-ladders," or spare ribs—surprisingly meaty and salty), these are your best bet. Two more widely available local specialties for the adventurous to try are boiled eggs (or beef) and potatoes topped with a green sauce of seven herbs, called *Grüne Sosse;* and an aged, cylindrical ricotta-like cheese served with onions and vinegar, called *Handkäse mit Musik* ("hand cheese with music").

In West Sachsenhausen, near Schweizer Strasse

These are in the handsome residential neighborhood along Schweizer Strasse, in the west of Sachsenhausen. To get there from Römerberg, cross the river on the pedestrian-only Eiserner Steg and walk right. From the train station, take tram #16 (direction: Offenbach) to the Schwantalerstrasse stop, or take the U-Bahn (changing at Willy-Brandt-Platz) to Schweizer Platz.

Zum Gemalten Haus, named for the wall murals that adorn its facade, serves German cuisine and is deceptively mellow—it's rumored to get a little wild on the weekends (€5-12 main courses, Tue-Sun 10:00-24:00, closed Mon, Schweizer Strasse 67, tel. 069/614-559).

Adolf Wagner, two buildings away, is a traditional joint where the fourth generation of Wagners serves pork knuckles and ribs, as well as less meaty fare, to a local constituency (€7-13 main courses, daily 11:00-24:00, Schweizer Strasse 71, tel. 069/612-565).

In East Sachsenhausen

These listings are in the core of the apple-wine area in the east of Sachsenhausen. To get here from Römerberg, cross the river on the pedestrian-only Eiserner Steg or the Alte Brücke, and walk left. From the train station, take tram #16 (direction: Offenbach) to the Textorstrasse stop and walk left up Darmstädter Landstrasse, or take bus #46 (direction: Mühlberg) to Frankensteiner Platz.

Klaane Sachsehäuser, owned by the same family for five generations, is popular with German tour groups and locals alike, and prides itself on its *Leiterchen* (€8-16 main courses, €5-8 wurst plates, Mon-Sat 16:00-24:00, closed Sun, Neuer Wall 11, tel. 069/615-983).

Fichtekränzi offers the typical specialties (and some lighter fare), both in its cozy, bench-filled beer hall and outside under the trees. The staff is friendly and the atmosphere relaxed—expect to share a table and make some new friends (€8-14 main courses, daily from 17:00, Wall Strasse 5, tel. 069/612-778).

Pub Crawl: Irish pubs and salsa bars clutter the pedestrian zone around Rittergasse and Klappergasse, close to Frankensteiner Platz. The cobblestone streets and medieval buildings feel like Epcot Center, rather than historic Frankfurt. But if you're looking for a place to do a pub crawl, this is it.

Frankfurt Connections

By Train

From Frankfurt am Main by Train to German Destinations: Rothenburg (hourly, 2.5-3 hours, changes in Würzburg and Steinach; the tiny Steinach-Rothenburg train often leaves from track 5, shortly after the Würzburg train arrives), **Würzburg** (1-2/hour, 70 minutes, or 2 hours on cheaper RE trains), **Nürnberg** (1-2/hour, 2 hours), **Munich** (hourly, 3.25 hours), **Baden-Baden** (hourly, 1.5 hours, direct or transfer in Karlsruhe), **Bacharach** (hourly, 1.25-1.75 hours, change in Mainz or Bingen), **Freiburg** (hourly, 2-2.5 hours), **Cochem** (1-2/hour, 2.5 hours, change in Koblenz), **Köln** (direct ICE trains hourly, 1-1.5 hours; cheaper, less frequent IC trains take 2.5 hours and show you more of the Rhine), **Leipzig** (every 2 hours direct on ICE, 3.5 hours; a few additional on IC, 4 hours), **Berlin** (hourly, 4 hours), **Hamburg** (hourly, 4 hours). Train info: tel. 0180-599-6633, www.bahn.com.

By Train to International Destinations: Amsterdam (2/day direct, 4.75 hours; more with changes, 5.75-7 hours), **Bern** (hourly, 4 hours, some with change in Basel), **Zürich** (hourly, 4 hours, most change in Basel), **Brussels** (every 2 hours, 3-5 hours, most change in Köln), **Copenhagen** (3/day, 9 hours, change in Hamburg), **Paris** (every 1-2 hours, 4-6 hours, most with 1 change), **Vienna**

(6/day direct, 7 hours), **Prague** (5/day, 6 hours, change to bus in Nürnberg; 1 direct night train, 10 hours). In 2013, the German Railway plans to start running high-speed trains from Frankfurt to **London** (via Köln and Brussels).

By Romantic Road Bus

The bus departs promptly at 8:00 (early May-late Oct) from the Deutsche Touring bus stop on the south side of the Frankfurt train station. Exit the station by track 1; the bus stop is to the right under the white canopy marked with a turquoise *Touring* sign (the Deutsche Touring/Eurolines office is across the street). You can either pay cash when you board, or buy your ticket at the Deutsche Touring office (Mon-Fri 7:00-19:00, Sat 7:00-14:00, Sun 7:00-13:00; entrance at Mannheimer Strasse 15—tel. 069/719-126-268, www.romanticroadcoach.de). It's free to book a seat in advance by phone or on their website. Frankfurt to Rothenburg costs €42, to Munich is €79, and all the way to Füssen is €104. For more information, see page 329.

By Plane

Frankfurt Airport

Frankfurt's airport *(Flughafen)*, just a few stops by S-Bahn from the city center, has its own long-distance train station, which makes it a snap to connect from a flight to other German cities. For flight information in English, visit www.frankfurt-airport.com, call 01805-372-4636, or contact your airline.

There are two separate terminals (know your terminal—check your ticket or the airport website). **Terminal 1,** a multi-level maze of check-in counters and shops, is linked to the train station. **Terminal 2** is small and quiet, with few services. A Skytrain and buses connect the two terminals. Pick up the free brochure *Your Airport Guide* for a map and detailed information (available at the airport and at most Frankfurt hotels).

Services: The airport has three **baggage-storage** desks (*Gepäckausbewahrung*, €5/day per bag; the branch in Terminal 1A, Level 1 is open 24 hours, others daily 6:00-22:00). There is a **post office** (in Terminal 1B, Level 2, daily 7:00-22:00), a **pharmacy** (in Terminal 1B, Level 2, and also in Terminal 2, daily 7:00-22:00), a 24-hour **medical clinic** (Terminal 1C, Level 1), public **showers** (Terminal 1B, Level 2, near the pharmacy, €6, shampoo and towel included, open 24 hours), and expensive **Wi-Fi.** A good-sized, fairly priced **supermarket** is handy for last-minute shopping for European treats (Terminal 1C, Level 0, daily 6:00-22:00; tricky to find: Go down the escalators from the underpass on Level 1 between Terminals 1B and 1C, or up the escalators from train platforms 1-3). Take advantage of the **luggage carts,** ingeniously designed to ride on the airport's escalators (and even all the way up to, but not into, the Skytrain). But heed the instructions on the carts and at the escalator entrances. If you're meeting someone, note that each terminal has a hard-to-miss **"meeting point"** near where those arriving pop out. There are **customs desks** in both terminals for VAT refunds (daily 7:00-21:00; after hours, ask the information desk to page a customs officer for you). There's even McBeer at three McDonald's, one allegedly Europe's largest. McWelcome to Germany.

Frankfurt Airport Train Station

The airport's train station has two parts, both reachable from Terminal 1. Regional S-Bahn trains to downtown Frankfurt and nearby towns and suburbs depart from platforms 1-3. Long-distance trains to other German cities leave from the slightly more distant *Fernbahnhof*, platforms 4-7.

Getting Between the Airport and Downtown Frankfurt: The airport is a 12-minute train ride on the **S-Bahn** from Frankfurt's main train station, or Hauptbahnhof (€3.90, 4/hour, ride included in €8.90 Frankfurt Card and €9.50 individual/€14.70 group version of all-day *Tageskarte Frankfurt* transit pass, but not in €6.20 individual/€9.50 group version of *Tageskarte Frankfurt*). Figure about €25 for a **taxi** from the airport to any of my recommended hotels.

From Frankfurt Airport by Long-Distance Train: Train travelers can validate railpasses or buy tickets at the counters on the level above the long-distance train platforms. Destinations include **Rothenburg** (hourly, 3-3.25 hours, change in Würzburg and Steinach), **Würzburg** (1-2/hour, 1.5 hours), **Nürnberg** (1-2/hour, 2.5 hours), **Munich** (1-2/hour, 3.5 hours), **Baden-Baden** (roughly hourly, 1.5 hours, change in Karlsruhe and/or Mannheim), **Köln** (1-2/hour, 1 hour; trains along Rhine go less often and take 2.25 hours), **Bacharach** (hourly, 1-1.5 hours, most change in Mainz, some depart from regional platforms), **Berlin** (1-2/hour, 4.5-5 hours, most with 1 change). There are also many **international connections** from here (such as Paris, London, Brussels, Amsterdam, Zürich, Bern, and Prague).

Sleeping at or near Frankfurt Airport

Because train connections to Frankfurt Airport are so good, if your flight doesn't leave too early, you can sleep in another city and still make it to the airport for your flight. If you wake up in Köln, Baden-Baden, Würzburg, or Bacharach, you can still catch a late-morning or midday flight; you can often make it from Nürnberg, Rothenburg, Freiburg, the Mosel, and even Munich for an early-afternoon flight. But plan ahead and leave room for delays; don't take the last possible connection.

Because of these easy connections—and since downtown Frankfurt is just 12 minutes away by frequent train—it makes little sense for train travelers to sleep at the airport. Drivers who want to stay near the airport the night before returning a rental car can try two hotels in Kelsterbach, just across the expressway from the airport: **$$ Airport Hotel Tanne** (Db-€89-94, Tannenstrasse 2, tel. 06107/9340, www.airporthoteltanne.de, Laun family) or **$$ Ibis Frankfurt Airport Hotel** (Sb/Db without breakfast-€59-79, Langer Kornweg 9a-11, tel. 06107/9870, www.ibishotel.com). If you're desperate, **$$$ Sheraton Frankfurt** is conveniently connected to Terminal 1 and has 1,008 international business-class rooms (Db-about €200-250, check website or the hotel desk in the airport for lower rates, tel. 069/69770, www.sheraton.com /frankfurt, salesfrankfurt@sheraton.com).

"Frankfurt" Hahn Airport
This smaller airport, misleadingly classified as a "Frankfurt" airport for marketing purposes, is actually almost two hours' drive away in the Mosel region. Regular buses connect Frankfurt Hahn Airport to Bullay (for trains to Cochem), Trier, Mainz, Köln, and Frankfurt (more info at www.hahn-airport.de). Hahn Airport is popular with low-cost carriers (such as Ryanair). To avoid any confusion, double-check the three-letter airport code on your ticket (FRA for Frankfurt Airport, HHN for Frankfurt Hahn).

RHINE VALLEY

Best of the Rhine • Bacharach • St. Goar

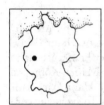

The Rhine Valley is storybook Germany, a fairy-tale world of legends and robber-baron castles. Cruise the most castle-studded stretch of the romantic Rhine as you listen for the song of the treacherous Loreley. For hands-on thrills, climb through the Rhineland's greatest castle, Rheinfels, above the town of St. Goar. Castle connoisseurs will also enjoy the fine interior of Marksburg Castle. Spend your nights in a castle-crowned village, either Bacharach or St. Goar.

Planning Your Time

The Rhineland is magical, but doesn't take much time to see. Both Bacharach and St. Goar are an easy 1- to 1.5-hour train ride (€15) or drive from Frankfurt Airport, and they make a good first or last stop for travelers flying in or out.

The blitziest tour of the area is an hour looking at the castles from your train window—use the narration in this chapter to give it meaning. The non-stop express runs every hour, connecting Koblenz and Mainz in 50 scenic minutes. (The super-express ICE trains between Köln and Frankfurt bypass the Rhine entirely.) For a better look, cruise in, tour a castle or two, sleep in a medieval town, and take the train out.

Ideally, if you have two nights to spend here, sleep in Bacharach, cruise the best hour of the river (from Bacharach to St. Goar), and tour Rheinfels Castle. If rushed, focus on Rheinfels Castle and cruise less. With more time, ride the riverside bike path. With another day, mosey through the neighboring Mosel Valley or day-trip to Köln (both covered in different chapters).

There are countless castles in this region, so you'll need to be selective in your castle-going. Aside from Rheinfels Castle, my favorites are Burg Eltz (see page 428 in next chapter; well-preserved with medieval interior, set evocatively in a romantic forest the next valley over), Marksburg Castle (page 386; rebuilt medieval interior, with commanding Rhine perch), and Rheinstein Castle (page 391; 19th-century duke's hunting palace overlooking the Rhine). Of these, Marksburg is the easiest to reach by train. Though only in German, www.burgen-am-rhein.de is a handy website with photos and opening times of the main Rhine castles.

The Best of the Rhine

Ever since Roman times, when this was the empire's northern boundary, the Rhine has been one of the world's busiest shipping rivers. You'll see a steady flow of barges with 1,000- to 2,000-ton loads. Tourist-packed buses, hot train tracks, and highways line both banks.

Many of the castles were "robber-baron" castles, put there by petty rulers (there were 300 independent little countries in medieval Germany, a region about the size of Montana) to levy tolls on passing river traffic. A robber baron would put his castle on, or even in, the river. Then, often with the help of chains and a tower on the opposite bank, he'd stop each ship and get his toll. There were 10 customs stops in the 60-mile stretch between Mainz and Koblenz alone (no wonder merchants were early proponents of the creation of larger nation-states).

Some castles were built to control and protect settlements, and others were the residences of kings. As times changed, so did the lifestyles of the rich and feudal. Many castles were abandoned for more comfortable mansions in the towns.

Most Rhine castles date from the 11th, 12th, and 13th centuries. When the pope successfully asserted his power over the German emperor in 1076, local princes ran wild over the rule of their emperor. The castles saw military action in the 1300s and 1400s, as emperors began reasserting their control over Germany's many silly kingdoms.

The castles were also involved in the Reformation wars, in which Europe's Catholic and Protestant dynasties fought it out using a fragmented Germany as their battleground. The Thirty Years' War (1618-1648) devastated Germany. The outcome: Each ruler got the freedom to decide if his people would be Catholic or Protestant, and one-third of Germany was dead. (Production of Gummi Bears ceased entirely.)

The French—who feared a strong Germany and felt the Rhine

Rhine Overview

Düsseldorf
Rhine
Köln
Bruhl
Aachen
Bonn
Bad Godesberg
Remagen
UNROMANTIC RHINE
BEST OF THE RHINE
See detail map
GERMANY
BELG.
BURG ELTZ
Koblenz
Cochem
Beilstein
Mosel R.
HAHN
St. Goar
Bacharach
Frankfurt
Wies-Baden
Main R.
FRANK-FURT
Mainz
LUX.
Trier
Lux. City
GERMANY
Neckar R.
Heidelberg
Rhine
FRANCE

30 Miles
50 Kilometers

was the logical border between them and Germany—destroyed most of the castles prophylactically (Louis XIV in the 1680s, the Revolutionary army in the 1790s, and Napoleon in 1806). Many were rebuilt in Neo-Gothic style in the Romantic Age—the late 1800s—and today are enjoyed as restaurants, hotels, hostels, and museums.

Getting Around the Rhine

The Rhine flows north from Switzerland to Holland, but the scenic stretch from Mainz to Koblenz hoards all the touristic charm. Studded with the crenellated cream of Germany's castles, it bustles with boats, trains, and highway traffic. Have fun exploring with a mix of big steamers, tiny ferries *(Fähre)*, trains, and bikes.

By Boat: While some travelers do the whole Mainz-Koblenz trip by boat (5.5 hours downstream, 8.5 hours up), I'd just focus on the most scenic hour—from St. Goar to Bacharach. Sit on the boat's top deck with your handy Rhine map-guide (or the kilometer-keyed tour in this chapter) and enjoy the parade of castles, towns, boats, and vineyards.

K-D Line Rhine Cruise Schedule

Boats run May through September and on a reduced schedule for parts of April and October; no boats run November through March. These times are based on the 2011 schedule. Check www.k-d.com for the latest.

Koblenz	Boppard	St. Goar	Bacharach
—	9:00	10:20	11:30
*9:00	*11:00	*12:20	*13:30
11:00	13:00	14:20	15:30
—	14:00	15:20	16:30
14:00	16:00	17:20	18:30
13:10	11:50	10:55	10:15
14:10	12:50	11:55	11:15
—	13:50	12:55	12:15
18:10	16:50	15:55	15:15
*20:10	*18:50	*17:55	*17:15

These sailings are on the 1913 paddle-wheeler Goethe.

Two boat companies take travelers along this stretch of the Rhine. Boats run daily in both directions from early April through October, with no boats off-season.

Most travelers sail on the bigger, more expensive, and romantic **Köln-Düsseldorfer (K-D) Line** (free with German railpass or any Eurailpass that covers Germany, but starts the use of a day of any flexipass; recommended Bacharach-St. Goar trip: €11 one-way, €13.20 round-trip, bikes-€2.50, €2 extra if paying with credit card; discounts: Mon and Fri—half-price for seniors over 60; Tue and Thu—2 bicyclists travel for the price of 1; tel. 06741/1634 in St. Goar, tel. 06743/1322 in Bacharach, www.k-d.com). You'll see K-D's abridged schedule above. Complete, up-to-date schedules are posted at any Rhineland station, hotel, TI, and www.k-d.com. Purchase tickets at the dock up to five minutes before departure. (Confirm times at your hotel the night before.) The boat is never full. Romantics will enjoy the old-time paddle-wheeler *Goethe*, which sails each direction once a day (noted on schedule, confirm time locally).

The smaller **Bingen-Rüdesheimer Line** is slightly cheaper than the K-D, isn't covered by railpasses, and makes three trips in each direction daily (St. Goar to Bacharach: €10.50 one-way, €12.50 round-trip, buy tickets on boat; departs St. Goar at 11:00,

14:10, and 16:10; departs Bacharach at 10:10, 12:00, and 15:00; no morning departures last two weeks of Oct; tel. 06721/14140, www .bingen-ruedesheimer.de).

By Car: Drivers have these options: 1) skip the boat; 2) take a round-trip cruise from St. Goar or Bacharach; 3) draw pretzels and let the loser drive, prepare the picnic, and meet the boat; 4) rent a bike, bring it on the boat for free, and bike back; or 5) take the boat one-way and return by train. When exploring by car, don't hesitate to pop onto one of the many little ferries that shuttle across the bridgeless-around-here river.

By Ferry: While there are no bridges between Koblenz and Mainz, you'll see car-and-passenger ferries (usually family-run for generations) about every three miles. Bingen-Rüdesheim, Lorch-Niederheimbach, Engelsburg-Kaub, and St. Goar-St. Goarshausen are some of the most useful routes (times vary; St. Goar-St. Goarshausen ferry departs each side every 15-20 minutes, Mon-Sat 6:00-21:00, Sun 8:00-21:00, May-Sept until 23:00; one-way fares: adult-€1.30, car and driver-€3.50, pay on the boat; www.faehre-loreley.de). For a fun little jaunt, take a quick round-trip with some time to explore the other side.

By Bike: You can bike on either side of the Rhine, but for a designated bike path, stay on the west side, where a 35-mile path runs between Koblenz and Bingen. The six-mile stretch between St. Goar and Bacharach is smooth and scenic, but mostly along the highway. The bit from Bacharach to Bingen hugs the riverside and is road-free. Either way, biking is a great way to explore the valley. Many hotels provide free or cheap bikes to guests; in Bacharach, anyone can rent bikes at Hotel Hillen (see page 400, €12/day for non-guests).

Consider biking one-way and taking the bike back on the riverboat, or designing a circular trip using the fun and frequent shuttle ferries. A good target might be Kaub (where a tiny boat shuttles sightseers to the better-from-a-distance castle on the island) or Rheinstein Castle.

By Train: Hourly milk-run trains hit every town along the Rhine (St. Goar-Bacharach, 10 minutes, €3.20; Bacharach-Mainz, 1 hour; Mainz-Koblenz, 1.5 hours). Express trains speed past the small towns, taking only 50 minutes non-stop between Mainz and Koblenz. Some train schedules list St. Goar but not Bacharach as a stop, but any schedule listing St. Goar also stops at Bacharach. Tiny stations are not staffed—buy tickets at the platform machines (user-friendly, take paper money, may not accept US credit cards).

The **Rheinland-Pfalz-Ticket** day pass covers travel on milk-run trains to anywhere in this chapter—plus the Mosel and Trier chapters (and also Remagen, but not Frankfurt, Köln, or Bonn). It can save heaps of money, particularly on longer day trips or if there's more than one in your party (1 person-€21, 2-5 people-€33, buy from station ticket machines, good after 9:00 Mon-Fri and all day Sat-Sun, valid on trains labeled *RB, RE,* and *MRB*). For a day trip between Bacharach and Burg Eltz (normally €28 round-trip; Burg Eltz described in next chapter), even one person saves with a Rheinland-Pfalz-Ticket, and a group of five adults saves more than €100—look for travel partners at breakfast.

Self-Guided Tour

▲▲▲Rhine Blitz Tour by Train or Boat

One of Europe's great train thrills is zipping along the Rhine enjoying this blitz tour. Or, even better, do it relaxing on the deck of a Rhine steamer, surrounded by the wonders of this romantic and historic gorge. This quick and easy tour (you can cut in anywhere) skips most of the syrupy myths filling normal Rhine guides. You can follow along on a train, boat, bike, or car. By train or boat, sit on the left (river) side going south from Koblenz. While nearly all the castles listed are viewed from this side, train travelers need to clear a path to the right window for the times I yell, "Cross over!"

You'll notice large black-and-white kilometer markers along the riverbank. I erected these years ago to make this tour easier to follow. They tell the distance from the Rhinefalls, where the Rhine leaves Switzerland and becomes navigable. (Today, river-barge pilots also use these markers to navigate.) We're tackling just 36 miles (58 km) of the 820-mile-long (1,320-km) Rhine. Your Rhine Blitz Tour starts at Koblenz and heads upstream to Bingen. If you're going the other direction, it still works. Just hold the book upside-down.

Km 590—Koblenz: This Rhine blitz starts with Romantic Rhine thrills—at Koblenz. Koblenz is not a nice city (it was hit hard in World War II), but its place as the historic *Deutsche Eck* (German corner)—the tip of land where the Mosel joins the Rhine—gives it a certain charm. Koblenz, from the Latin for "confluence," has Roman origins. If you stop here, take a walk through the park, noticing the reconstructed memorial to the *Kaiser.* Across the river, the yellow Ehrenbreitstein Castle now houses a hostel. It's a 30-minute hike from the station to the Koblenz boat dock.

Km 586—Lahneck Castle (Burg Lahneck): Above the modern autobahn bridge over the Lahn River, this castle *(Burg)* was built in 1240 to defend local silver mines; the castle was ruined by the French in 1688 and rebuilt in the 1850s in Neo-Gothic style. Burg Lahneck faces another Romantic rebuild, the yellow Schloss Stolzenfels (out of view above the train, a 10-minute climb from tiny parking lot, open for touring, closed Mon). Note that a *Burg* is

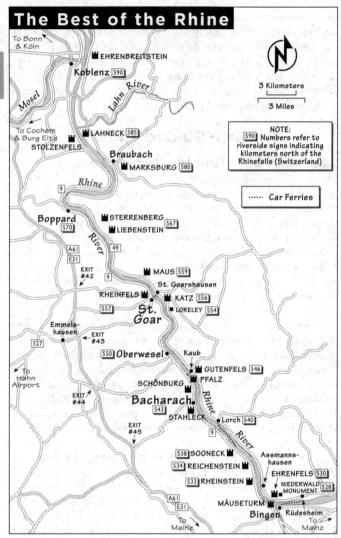

The Best of the Rhine

To Bonn & Köln

EHRENBREITSTEIN

Koblenz 590

Lahn River

Mosel

3 Kilometers

3 Miles

To Cochem & Burg Eltz

LAHNECK 585

STOLZENFELS

Braubach

MARKSBURG 580

NOTE:
590 Numbers refer to riverside signs indicating kilometers north of the Rhinefalls (Switzerland)

Rhine

9

•••••• Car Ferries

Boppard 570

River

STERRENBERG
LIEBENSTEIN 567

A61
E31

49

9

EXIT #42

MAUS 559

St. Goarshausen

RHEINFELS

KATZ 556

557

St. Goar

LORELEY 554

Emmels-hausen

EXIT #43

327

550 **Oberwesel**

Kaub

To Hahn Airport

GUTENFELS 546

PFALZ

SCHÖNBURG

EXIT #44

Bacharach 543

Rhine

STAHLECK

Lorch 540

EXIT #45

9

River

538 SOONECK

534 REICHENSTEIN

Assmanns-hausen

533 RHEINSTEIN

EHRENFELS 530

NIEDERWALD MONUMENT 528

A61
E31

MÄUSETURM

Bingen

Rüdesheim

To Mainz

To Mainz

a defensive fortress, while a *Schloss* is mainly a showy palace.

Km 580—Marksburg Castle: This castle (bold and white, with the three modern chimneys behind it, just before the town of Spay) is the best-looking of all the Rhine castles and the only surviving medieval castle on the Rhine. Because of its commanding position, it was never attacked in the Middle Ages (though it was captured by the US Army in March of 1945). It's now open as a museum with a medieval interior second only to the Mosel's Burg Eltz. (A self-guided tour for Marksburg appears on page 386; Burg

Eltz is covered in the next chapter.) The three modern smokestacks vent Europe's biggest car-battery recycling plant just up the valley.

If you haven't read the sidebar on river traffic (later in this chapter), now's a good time.

Km 570—Boppard: Once a Roman town, Boppard has some impressive remains of fourth-century walls. Notice the Roman towers and the substantial chunk of Roman wall near the train station, just above the main square. You'll notice that a church is a big part of each townscape. Many small towns have two towering churches—the Rhine is the dividing line between Catholic and Protestant Europe. Four centuries ago, after enduring a horrific war, each prince or king decided which faith his subjects would follow (generally Protestants north of the Rhine and Catholics to the south). While church attendance in Germany is way down, the towns here, like Germany as a whole, are still divided between Catholic and Protestant church-goers.

If you visit Boppard, head to the fascinating Church of St. Severus below the main square. Find the carved Romanesque crazies at the doorway. Inside, to the right of the entrance, you'll see Christian symbols from Roman times. Also notice the painted arches and vaults (originally, most Romanesque churches were painted this way). Down by the river, look for the high-water *(Hochwasser)* marks on the arches from various flood years. (You'll find these flood marks throughout the Rhine and Mosel valleys.)

Km 567—Sterrenberg Castle and Liebenstein Castle: These are the "Hostile Brothers" castles across from Bad Salzig. Take the wall between the castles (actually designed to improve the defenses of both castles), add two greedy and jealous brothers and a fair maiden, and create your own legend. Burg Liebenstein is now a fun, friendly, and affordable family-run hotel (9 rooms, Db-€130, suite-€155, giant king-and-the-family room-€230, easy parking, tel. 06773/308 or 06773/251, www.castle-liebenstein.com, hotel -burg-liebenstein@rhinecastles.com, Nickenig family).

Km 560: While you can see nothing from here, a 19th-century lead mine functioned on both sides of the river, with a shaft actually tunneling completely under the Rhine.

Km 559—Maus Castle (Burg Maus): The Maus (mouse) got its name because the next castle was owned by the Katzenelnbogen family. (*Katz* means "cat.") In the 1300s, it was considered a state-of-the-art fortification...until Napoleon had it blown up in 1806 with state-of-the-art explosives. It was rebuilt true to its original plans in about 1900. Today, the castle is open only for concerts and weddings, with occasional guided tours (20-minute walk up, tel. 06771/7669 or tel. 06771/9100, www.burg-maus.de).

Km 557—St. Goar and Rheinfels Castle: Cross to the other side of the train. The pleasant town of St. Goar was named for a

Rhine River Trade and Barge-Watching

The Rhine is great for barge-watching. There's a constant parade of action, and each boat is different. Since ancient times, this has been a highway for trade. Today, Europe's biggest port (Rotterdam) waits at the mouth of the river.

Barge workers are almost a subculture. Many own their own ships. The captain lives in the stern, with his family. The family car is often parked on the stern. Workers live in the bow.

In the Rhine town of Kaub, there was once a boarding school for the children of the Rhine merchant marine—but today it's closed, since most captains are Dutch, Belgian, or Swiss. The flag of the boat's home country flies in the stern (Dutch—horizontal red, white, and blue; Belgian: vertical black, yellow, and red; Swiss—white cross on a red field; German—horizontal black, red, and yellow; French—vertical red, white, and blue). Logically, imports go upstream (Japanese cars, coal, and oil) and exports go downstream (German cars, chemicals, and pharmaceuticals). A clever captain manages to ship goods in each direction. Recently, giant Dutch container ships (which transport five times the cargo) have been driving many of the traditional barges out of business, presenting the German economy with another challenge.

Going downstream, tugs can push a floating train of up to five barges at once, but upstream, as the slope gets steeper (and the stream gradient gets higher), they can push only one at a time. Before modern shipping, horses dragged boats upstream (the faint remains of towpaths survive at points along the river). From 1873 to 1900, workers laid a chain from Bonn to Bingen, and boats with cogwheels and steam engines hoisted themselves

sixth-century hometown monk. It originated in Celtic times (really old) as a place where sailors would stop, catch their breath, send home a postcard, and give thanks after surviving the seductive and treacherous Loreley crossing. St. Goar is worth a stop to explore its mighty Rheinfels Castle. (For information, a self-guided castle tour, and accommodations, see page 404.)

Km 556—Katz Castle (Burg Katz): Burg Katz (Katzeneln-bogen) faces St. Goar from across the river. Together, Burg Katz (built in 1371) and Rheinfels Castle had a clear view up and down the river, effectively controlling traffic (there was absolutely no duty-free shopping on the medieval Rhine). Katz got Napoleoned in 1806 and rebuilt in about 1900.

Today, the castle is shrouded by intrigue and controversy. In 1995, a wealthy and eccentric Japanese man bought it for about $4 million. His vision: to make the castle—so close to the Loreley that Japanese tourists are wild about—an exotic escape for his countrymen. But the town wouldn't allow his planned renova-

upstream. Today, 265 million tons travel each year along the 530 miles from Basel on the German-Swiss border to the Dutch city of Rotterdam on the Atlantic.

Riverside navigational aids are of vital interest to captains who don't wish to meet the Loreley (see next page). Boats pass

on the right unless they clearly signal otherwise with a large blue sign. Since ships heading downstream can't stop or maneuver as freely, boats heading upstream are expected to do the tricky do-si-do work. Cameras monitor traffic all along and relay warnings of oncoming ships by posting large triangular signals before narrow and troublesome bends in the river.

There may be two or three triangles per signpost, depending upon how many "sectors," or segments, of the river are covered. The lowest triangle indicates the nearest stretch of river. Each triangle tells whether there's a ship in that sector. When the bottom side of a triangle is lit, that sector is empty. When the left side is lit, an oncoming ship is in that sector.

The **Signal and River Pilots Museum** (Wahrschauer- und Lotsenmuseum), located at the signal triangles at the upstream edge of St. Goar, explains how barges are safer, cleaner, and more fuel-efficient than trains or trucks (free, May-Sept Wed and Sat 14:00-17:00, outdoor exhibits always open).

tion of the historic (and therefore protected) building. Stymied, the frustrated investor abandoned his plans. Today, Burg Katz sits empty...the Japanese ghost castle.

Below the castle, notice the derelict grape terraces—worked since the eighth century, but abandoned in the last generation. The Rhine wine is particularly good because the local slate absorbs the heat of the sun and stays warm all night, resulting in sweeter grapes. Wine from the flat fields above the Rhine gorge is cheaper, and good only as table wine. Wine from the steep side of the Rhine gorge—where grapes are harder to grow and harvest—is tastier and more expensive.

About Km 555: A statue of the Loreley, the beautiful-but-deadly nymph (see next listing for legend), combs her hair at the end of a long spit—built to give barges protection from vicious ice floes that until recent years raged down the river in the winter. The actual Loreley, a cliff (marked by the flags), is just ahead.

Km 554—The Loreley: Steep a big slate rock in centuries of legend and it becomes a tourist attraction—the ultimate Rhine-stone. The Loreley (flags and visitors center on top, name painted near shoreline), rising 450 feet over the narrowest and deepest point of the Rhine, has long been important. It was a holy site in pre-Roman days. The fine echoes here—thought to be ghostly voices—fertilized legend-tellers' imaginations.

Because of the reefs just upstream (at km 552), many ships never made it to St. Goar. Sailors (after days on the river) blamed their misfortune on a *wunderbares Fräulein,* whose long, blond hair almost covered her body. Heinrich Heine's *Song of Loreley* (the CliffsNotes version is on local postcards) tells the story of a count sending his men to kill or capture this siren after she distracted his horny son, who forgot to watch where he was sailing and drowned. When the soldiers cornered the nymph in her cave, she called her father (Father Rhine) for help. Huge waves, the likes of which you'll never see today, rose from the river and carried Loreley to safety. And she has never been seen since.

But alas, when the moon shines brightly and the tour buses are parked, a soft, playful Rhine whine can still be heard from the Loreley. As you pass, listen carefully ("Sailors...sailors...over my bounding mane").

Km 552—The Seven Maidens: Killer reefs, marked by red-and-green buoys, are called the "Seven Maidens." Okay, one more goofy legend: The prince of Schönburg Castle (*über* Oberwesel—described next) had seven spoiled daughters who always dumped men because of their shortcomings. Fed up, he invited seven of his knights to the castle and demanded that his daughters each choose one to marry. But they complained that each man had too big a nose, was too fat, too stupid, and so on. The rude and teasing girls escaped into a riverboat. Just downstream, God turned them into the seven rocks that form this reef. While this story probably isn't entirely true, there was a lesson in it for medieval children: Don't be hard-hearted.

Km 550—Oberwesel: Cross to the other side of the train. Oberwesel was a Celtic town in 400 B.C., then a Roman military station. It now boasts some of the best Roman-wall and medieval-tower remains on the Rhine, and the commanding Schönburg Castle (now a posh hotel). Notice how many of the train tunnels have entrances designed like medieval turrets—they were actually built in the Romantic 19th century. OK, back to the river side.

Km 546—Gutenfels Castle and Pfalz Castle, the Classic Rhine View: Burg Gutenfels (now a privately owned hotel) and the shipshape Pfalz Castle (built in the river in the 1300s) worked very effectively to tax medieval river traffic. The town of Kaub grew rich as Pfalz raised its chains when boats came, and lowered them only when the merchants had paid their duty. Those

RHINE VALLEY

who didn't pay spent time touring its prison, on a raft at the bottom of its well. In 1504, a pope called for the destruction of Pfalz, but the locals withstood a six-week siege, and the castle still stands. Notice the overhanging outhouse (tiny white room between two wooden ones). Pfalz (also known as Pfalzgrafenstein) is tourable but bare and dull (€3 ferry from Kaub, €3 entry, March-Oct Tue-Sun 10:00-18:00, closed Mon, shorter hours off-season, closed Dec, last entry one hour before closing, mobile 0172-262-2800).

In Kaub, on the riverfront directly below the castles, a green statue (near the waving flags) honors the German general Gebhard von Blücher. He was Napoleon's nemesis. In 1813, as Napoleon fought his way back to Paris after his disastrous Russian campaign, he stopped at Mainz—hoping to fend off the Germans and Russians pursuing him by controlling that strategic bridge. Blücher tricked Napoleon. By building the first major pontoon bridge of its kind here at the Pfalz Castle, he crossed the Rhine and outflanked the French. Two years later, Blücher and Wellington teamed up to defeat Napoleon once and for all at Waterloo.

Immediately opposite Kaub (where the ferry lands, marked by blue roadside flags) is a gaping hole in the mountainside. This marks the last working slate mine on the Rhine.

Km 544—"The Raft Busters": Just before Bacharach, at the top of the island, buoys mark a gang of rocks notorious for busting up rafts. The Black Forest, upstream from here, was once poor, and wood was its best export. Black Foresters would ride log booms down the Rhine to the Ruhr (where their timber fortified coal-mine shafts) or to Holland (where logs were sold to shipbuilders). If they could navigate the sweeping bend just before Bacharach and then survive these "raft busters," they'd come home reckless and horny—the German folkloric equivalent of American cowboys after payday.

Km 543—Bacharach and Stahleck Castle (Burg Stahleck): Cross to the other side of the train. The town of Bacharach is a great stop (described on page 391). Some of the Rhine's best wine is from this town, whose name likely derives from "altar to Bacchus." Local vintners brag that the medieval Pope Pius II ordered Bacharach wine by the cartload. Perched above the town, the 13th-century Burg Stahleck is now a hostel.

Km 541—Lorch: This pathetic stub of a castle is barely visible from the road. Check out the hillside vineyards. These vineyards once blanketed four times as much land as they do today, but modern economics have driven most of them out of business. The vineyards that do survive require government subsidies. Notice the small car ferry, one of several along the bridgeless stretch between Mainz and Koblenz.

Km 538—Sooneck Castle: Cross back to the other side of the train. Built in the 11th century, this castle was twice destroyed by people sick and tired of robber barons.

Km 534—Reichenstein Castle and **Km 533—Rheinstein Castle:** Stay on the other side of the train to see two of the first castles to be rebuilt in the Romantic era. Both are privately owned, tourable, and connected by a pleasant trail. See my listing for Rheinstein Castle on page 391.

Km 530—Ehrenfels Castle: Opposite Bingerbrück and the Bingen station, you'll see the ghostly Ehrenfels Castle (clobbered by the Swedes in 1636 and by the French in 1689). Since it had no view of the river traffic to the north, the owner built the cute little *Mäuseturm* (mouse tower) on an island (the yellow tower you'll see near the train station today). Rebuilt in the 1800s in Neo-Gothic style, it's now used as a Rhine navigation signal station.

Km 528—Niederwald Monument: Across from the Bingen station on a hilltop is the 120-foot-high Niederwald monument, a memorial built with 32 tons of bronze in 1877 to commemorate "the re-establishment of the German Empire." A lift takes tourists to this statue from the famous and extremely touristy wine town of Rüdesheim.

From here, the Romantic Rhine becomes the industrial Rhine, and our tour is over.

Sights Along the Rhine

The following sights—Marksburg Castle, the Loreley Visitors Center, and Rheinstein Castle—are listed in the order you'd see them on the Rhine Blitz Tour, described earlier.

▲▲Marksburg Castle

Medieval invaders decided to give Marksburg a miss thanks to its formidable defenses. This best-preserved castle on the Rhine can be toured only with a guide. In summer, tours in English normally run daily at 12:00 and 16:00. Otherwise, you can join a German tour (4/hour in summer, hourly in winter) that's almost as good—there are no explanations in English in the castle itself, but your ticket includes an

English handout. It's an awesome castle, and between the handout and my self-guided tour, you'll feel fully informed, so don't worry about being on time for the English tours.

Cost and Hours: €6, family card-€13, daily Easter-Oct 10:00-18:00, Nov-Easter 11:00-17:00, last tour departs one hour before closing, tel. 02627/206, www.marksburg.de.

Getting There: Marksburg caps a hill above the village of Braubach, on the east bank of the Rhine. By **train**, it's a 10-minute trip from Koblenz to Braubach (1-2/hour); from Bacharach or St. Goar, it takes 1-2 hours, depending on the length of the layover in Koblenz (€10.50 one-way). The train is quicker than the **boat** (downstream from Bacharach to Braubach-2.25 hours, upstream return-3.5 hours; €20.80 one-way, €26.80 round-trip). Consider taking the downstream boat to Braubach, and the train back. If traveling with luggage, store it in the convenient lockers in the underground passage at the Koblenz train station (Braubach has no enclosed station—just platforms—and no lockers).

Once you reach Braubach, **walk** into the old town (follow *Altstadt* signs—coming out of tunnel from train platforms, it's to your right); then follow the *Zur Burg* signs to the path up to the castle. Allow 20 to 30 minutes for the climb up. Scarce **taxis** charge about €10 from the train platforms to the castle. A green **tourist train** circles up to the castle, but there's no fixed schedule, so don't count on it (Easter-Oct Tue-Sun, no trains Mon or off-season, €2.50 one-way, €4.50 round-trip, leaves from Barbarastrasse, tel. 06773/587, www.ruckes-reisen.de). Even if you take the tourist train, you'll still have to climb the last five minutes up to the castle from its parking lot (cars-€2).

❿ Self-Guided Tour: The tour starts inside the castle's first gate.

Inside the First Gate: While the dramatic castles lining the Rhine are generally Romantic rebuilds, Marksburg is the real McCoy—nearly all original construction. It's littered with bits of its medieval past, like the big stone ball that was swung on a rope to be used as a battering ram. Ahead, notice how the inner gate—originally tall enough for knights on horseback to gallop through—was made smaller, and therefore safer from enemies on horseback. Climb the Knights' Stairway carved out of slate and pass under the murder hole—handy for pouring boiling pitch on invaders. (Germans still say someone with bad luck "has pitch on his head.")

Coats of Arms: Colorful coats of arms line the wall just inside the gate. These are from the noble families who have owned the castle since 1283. In that year, financial troubles drove the first family to sell to the powerful and wealthy Katzenelnbogen family (who made the castle into what you see today). When Napoleon took this region in 1803, an Austrian family who sided with the French got the keys. When Prussia took the region in 1866, control passed to a friend of the Prussians who had a passion for medieval things—typical of this Romantic period. Then it was sold to the German Castles Association in 1900. Its offices are in the main palace at the top of the stairs.

Romanesque Palace: White outlines mark where the larger original windows were located, before they were replaced by easier-to-defend smaller ones. On the far right, a bit of the original plaster survives. Slate, which is vulnerable to the elements, needs to be covered—in this case, by plaster. Because this is a protected historic building, restorers can use only the traditional plaster methods...but no one knows how to make plaster that works as well as the 800-year-old surviving bits.

Cannons: The oldest cannon here—from 1500—was backloaded. This was advantageous because many cartridges could be pre-loaded. But since the seal was leaky, it wasn't very powerful. The bigger, more modern cannons—from 1640—were one piece and therefore airtight, but had to be front-loaded. They could easily hit targets across the river from here. Stone balls were rough, so they let the explosive force leak out. The best cannonballs were stones covered in smooth lead—airtight and therefore more powerful and more accurate.

Gothic Garden: Walking along an outer wall, you'll see 160 plants from the Middle Ages—used for cooking, medicine, and witchcraft. *Schierling* (hemlock, in the first corner) is the same poison that killed Socrates.

Inland Rampart: This most vulnerable part of the castle had a triangular construction to better deflect attacks. Notice the factory in the valley. In the 14th century, this was a lead, copper, and silver mine. Today's factory—Europe's largest car-battery recycling plant—uses the old mine shafts as vents (see the three modern smokestacks).

Wine Cellar: Since Roman times, wine has been the traditional Rhineland drink. Because castle water was impure, wine—less alcoholic than today's beer—was the way knights got their fluids. The pitchers on the wall were their daily allotment. The bellows were part of the barrel's filtering system. Stairs lead to the...

Gothic Hall: This hall is set up as a kitchen, with an oven designed to roast an ox whole. The arms holding the pots have notches to control the heat. To this day, when Germans want someone to hurry up, they say, "give it one tooth more." Medieval windows were made of thin sheets of translucent alabaster or animal skins. A nearby wall is peeled away to show the wattle-and-daub construction (sticks, straw, clay, mud, then plaster) of a castle's inner walls. The iron plate to the left of the next door enabled servants to stoke the heater without being seen by the noble family.

Bedroom: This was the only heated room in the castle. The canopy kept in heat and kept out critters. In medieval times, it was impolite for a lady to argue with her lord in public. She would wait for him in bed to give him what Germans still call "a curtain lecture." The deep window seat caught maximum light for needlework and reading. Women would sit here and chat (or "spin a yarn") while working the spinning wheel.

Hall of the Knights: This was the dining hall. The long table is an unattached plank. After each course, servants could replace it with another pre-set plank. Even today, when a meal is over and Germans are ready for the action to begin, they say, "Let's lift up the table." The action back then consisted of traveling minstrels who sang and told of news gleaned from their travels.

Notice the outhouse—made of wood—hanging over thin air. When not in use, its door was locked from the outside (the castle side) to prevent any invaders from entering this weak point in the castle's defenses.

Chapel: This chapel is still painted in Gothic style with the castle's namesake, St. Mark, and his lion. Even the chapel was designed with defense in mind. The small doorway kept out heavily armed attackers. The staircase spirals clockwise, favoring the sword-wielding defender (assuming he was right-handed).

Linen Room: About the year 1800, the castle—with diminished military value—housed disabled soldiers. They'd earn a little extra money working raw flax into linen.

Two Thousand Years of Armor: Follow the evolution of armor since Celtic times. Because helmets covered the entire head, soldiers identified themselves as friendly by tipping their visor up with their right hand. This evolved into the military salute that is still used around the world today. Armor and the close-range weapons along the back were made obsolete by the invention of the rifle. Armor was replaced with breastplates—pointed (like the castle itself) to deflect enemy fire. This design was used as late as the start of World War I. A medieval lady's armor hangs over the door. While popular fiction has men locking up their women before heading off to battle, chastity belts were actually used by women as protection against rape when traveling.

The Keep: This served as an observation tower, a dungeon (with a 22-square-foot cell in the bottom), and a place of last refuge. When all was nearly lost, the defenders would bundle into the keep and burn the wooden bridge, hoping to outwait their enemies.

Horse Stable: The stable shows off bits of medieval crime and punishment. Cheaters were attached to stones or pillories. Shame

RHINE VALLEY

masks punished gossipmongers. A mask with a heavy ball had its victim crawling around with his nose in the mud. The handcuffs with a neck hole were for the transport of prisoners. The pictures on the wall show various medieval capital punishments. Many times the accused was simply taken into a torture dungeon to see all these tools, and, guilty or not, confessions spilled out of him. On that cheery note, your tour is over.

The Loreley Visitors Center (Besucherzentrum Loreley)

Easily reached from St. Goar, this lightweight exhibit reflects a little on Loreley, but focuses mainly on the landscape, culture, and people of the Rhine Valley. Though English explanations accompany most of the geological and cultural displays, the information about the famous mythical *Mädchen* is given in German only—making this place not worth its admission price. The 3-D movie is essentially a tourist brochure for the region, with scenes of the grape harvest over Bacharach that are as beautiful as the sword-fighting is lame.

Far more exciting than the exhibit is the view from the cliffs themselves. A five-minute walk from the bus stop and visitors center takes you to the impressive viewpoint overlooking the Rhine Valley from atop the famous rock.

Cost and Hours: €2.50; March daily 10:00-17:00; April-Oct daily 10:00-18:00; Nov-Feb Sat-Sun 11:00-16:00, closed Mon-Fri; café and shops, tel. 06771/599-093, www.loreley-besucher zentrum.de.

Getting There: For a good hour's **hike,** catch the ferry from St. Goar across to the village of St. Goarshausen (€1.30 round-trip, every 15-20 minutes, daily 6:00-21:00, May-Sept until 23:00). Then follow green *Burg Katz* (Katz Castle) signs up Burgstrasse under the train tracks to find steps on right *(Loreley über Burg Katz)* leading to the Katz Castle (privately owned) and beyond. Traverse the hillside, always bearing right toward the river. You'll pass through a residential area, hike down a 50-yard path through trees, then cross a wheat field until you reach the Loreley Visitors Center and rock-capping viewpoint. If you're not up for a hike, you can catch **bus #595** from St. Goarshausen up to the visitors center. From the St. Goarshausen ferry ramp, walk to your left along the river about 40 yards to the K-D dock to get the bus (€1.65 each way, departs almost hourly, daily 10:15-17:15, www.vrminfo.de).

To return to St. Goarshausen and the St. Goar ferry, you can take the bus (last departure 17:25), retrace your steps along the Burg Katz trail, or hike a steep 15 minutes directly down to the river, where the riverfront road takes you back to St. Goarshausen.

▲▲Rheinstein Castle
(Schloss Burg Rheinstein)

This castle seems to rule its chunk of the Rhine from a commanding position. While its 13th-century exterior is medieval as can

be, the interior is mostly a 19th-century duke's hunting palace. Visitors wander freely (with an English flier) among trophies, armor, and Romantic Age decor.

Cost and Hours: €4.30; mid-March-mid-Nov daily 9:30-18:00; mid-Nov-mid-Dec and Feb-mid-March Sat-Sun only 10:00-17:00; last admission 30

minutes before closing, closed mid-Dec-Jan, tel. 06721/6348, www .burg-rheinstein.de.

Getting There: This castle (at km 533 marker, 2 km upstream from Trechtingshausen on the main B-9 highway) is easy by **car** (small, free parking lot on B-9, steep 5-minute hike from there), or **bike** (35 minutes upstream from Bacharach, stick to the great riverside path, after km 534 marker look for small *Burg Rheinstein* sign and Rösler-Linie dock). It's less convenient by **boat** (no K-D stop nearby) or **train** (nearest stop in Trechtingshausen, 30-minute walk away).

Bacharach

Once prosperous from the wine and wood trade, charming Bacharach (BAHKH-ah-rahkh, with a guttural *kh* sound) is now

just a pleasant half-timbered village of a thousand people working hard to keep its tourists happy. Businesses that have been "in the family" for eons are dealing with succession challenges, as the allure of big-city jobs and a more cosmopolitan life lure away the town's younger generation. But for now, Bacharach retains its time-capsule quaintness.

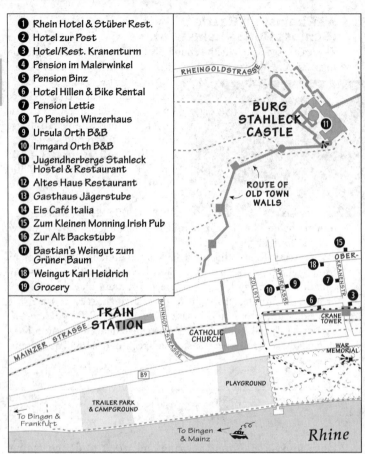

1. Rhein Hotel & Stüber Rest.
2. Hotel zur Post
3. Hotel/Rest. Kranenturm
4. Pension im Malerwinkel
5. Pension Binz
6. Hotel Hillen & Bike Rental
7. Pension Lettie
8. To Pension Winzerhaus
9. Ursula Orth B&B
10. Irmgard Orth B&B
11. Jugendherberge Stahleck Hostel & Restaurant
12. Altes Haus Restaurant
13. Gasthaus Jägerstube
14. Eis Café Italia
15. Zum Kleinen Monning Irish Pub
16. Zur Alt Backstubb
17. Bastian's Weingut zum Grüner Baum
18. Weingut Karl Heidrich
19. Grocery

Orientation to Bacharach

Tourist Information

The TI, on the main street in the Posthof courtyard next to the church, will store bags for day-trippers (April-Oct Mon-Fri 9:00-17:00, Sat-Sun 10:00-15:00; Nov-March Mon-Fri 9:00-13:00, closed Sat-Sun; from train station turn right and walk 5 blocks down main street with castle high on your left, Oberstrasse 45; tel. 06743/919-303, www.bacharach.de or www.rhein-nahe-touristik.de, Herr Kuhn and his team).

Helpful Hints

Shopping: The **Jost** German gift store, across the main square from the church, carries most everything a souvenir-shopper could want—from beer steins to cuckoo clocks—and

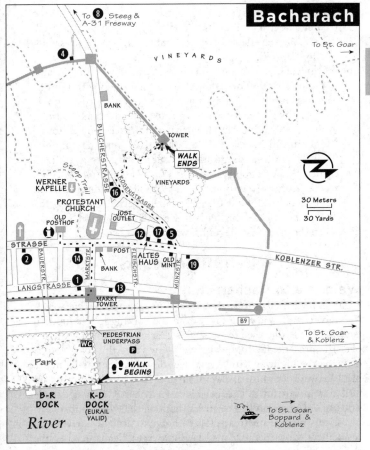

can ship purchases to the US. This family shop is celebrating its centennial (see a photo of their great-grandfather on the wall). The Josts offer discounts to my readers: 10 percent if paying with cash, 5 percent with credit card (March-Oct Mon-Fri 8:30-18:00, Sat 8:30-17:00, possibly Sun 10:00-16:00; Nov-Feb shorter hours and closed Sun; Blücherstrasse 4, tel. 06743/1224, phil.jost@t-online.de).

Internet Access: The **TI** has a coin-op terminal (€0.50/15 minutes).

Post Office: It's inside a news agents' shop, across from the church and Altes Haus, at Oberstrasse 56.

Grocery Store: Pick up picnic supplies at **Nahkauf,** a basic grocery store (Mon-Fri 8:00-12:30 & 14:00-18:30, Sat 8:30-14:00, closed Sun, Koblenzer Strasse 2).

Bike Rental: While many hotels loan bikes to guests, the only real bike-rental business in the town center is run by Erich at the recommended **Hotel Hillen** (non-guests-€12/day, guests-€7/day, 35 bikes available, daily 9:00 until dark, Langstrasse 18, tel. 06743/1287).

Local Guides: Get acquainted with Bacharach by taking a walking tour. These guides enjoy sharing their town with visitors: **Thomas Gundlach** is a charming local who's licensed as a guide and happily gives 1.5-hour town walks to individuals or small groups for €25. He can also drive up to three people around the region in his car (€70/6 hours, €120/long day, mobile 0179-353-6004, tomgund@web.de or thomas_gundlach @gmx.de). Also good are **Birgit Wessels** (tel. 06743/937-514, wessels.birgit@t-online.de) and Aussie **Joanne Augustin** (€30/1.5 hours, mobile 0179-231-1389, jopetit90@yahoo.com). The TI books 1.5-hour tours in English (€70/group). Or take one or both of my self-guided walks, below.

Self-Guided Walks

Welcome to Bacharach

• *Start at the Köln-Düsseldorfer ferry dock (next to a fine picnic park).*

Riverfront: View the town from the parking lot—a modern landfill. The Rhine used to lap against Bacharach's town wall, just over the present-day highway. Every few years the river floods, covering the highway with several feet of water. The **castle** on the hill is now a youth hostel. Two of the town's original 16 towers are visible from here (up to five if you look really hard). The huge roadside keg declares that this town was built on the wine trade.

Reefs farther upstream forced boats to unload upriver and reload here. Consequently, in the Middle Ages, Bacharach became the biggest wine-trading town on the Rhine. A riverfront crane hoisted huge kegs of prestigious "Bacharach" wine (which, in practice, was from anywhere in the region). The tour buses next to the dock and the flags of the biggest spenders along the highway remind you that today's economy is basically founded on tourism.

• *Before entering the town, walk upstream through the...*

Riverside Park: This park was laid out in 1910 in the English style: Notice how the trees were planted to frame fine town views, highlighting the most picturesque bits of architecture. The dark, sad-looking monument—its "eternal" flame long snuffed out—is a **war memorial.** The German psyche is permanently scarred by war memories. Today, many Germans would rather avoid monuments like this, which revisit the dark periods before Germany became a nation of pacifists. Take a close look at the monument. Each panel honors sons of Bacharach who died for the Kaiser: in 1864 against Denmark, in 1866 against Austria, in 1870 against France, in 1914 during World War I. The military Maltese cross—flanked by classic German helmets—has a W at its center, for Kaiser Wilhelm.

• *Look (but don't go) upstream from here to see the...*

Trailer Park and Campground: In Germany, trailer vacationers and campers are two distinct subcultures. Folks who travel in trailers, like many retirees in the US, are a nomadic bunch, cruising around the countryside in their motor homes and paying a few euros a night to park. Campers, on the other hand, tend to set up camp in one place—complete with comfortable lounge chairs and TVs—and stay put for weeks, even months. They often come back to the same spot year after year, treating it like their own private estate. These camping devotees have made a science out of relaxing.

• *Continue to where the park meets the playground, and then cross the highway to the fortified riverside wall of the Catholic church, decorated with...*

High-Water Marks: These recall various floods. Twenty yards to the left is a metal ring on the medieval slate wall. Before the 1910 reclamation project, the river extended out to here, and boats would use the ring to tie up.

• *From the church, go under the 1858 train tracks and hook right past the yellow floodwater yardstick and up the stairs onto the town wall. Atop the wall, turn left and walk under the long arcade. After 30 meters, on your left, notice a...*

Well: Rebuilt as it appeared in the 17th century, this is one of 40 such wells that provided water to the townsfolk until 1900. Walk 50 yards past the well along the wall to an alcove in the medieval tower with a view of the war memorial in the park. You're under the crane tower *(Kranenturm)*. After barrels of wine were moved overland from Bingen past dangerous stretches of river, the precious cargo could be lowered by cranes from here into ships to continue more safely down the river. The Rhine has long been a major shipping route through Germany. In modern times, it's a bottleneck in Germany's train system. The train company gives hotels and residents along the tracks money for soundproof windows (hotels along here routinely have quadruple-pane windows... and earplugs on the nightstand).

• *Continue walking along the town wall. Pass the recommended Rhein Hotel (hotel is before the Markt tower, which marks one of the town's 15 original 14th-century gates), descend, pass another well, and follow Marktstrasse away from the river toward the town center, the two-tone church, and the town's...*

Main Intersection: From here, Bacharach's main street (Oberstrasse) goes right to the half-timbered red-and-white Altes Haus (from 1368, the oldest house in town) and left 400 yards to the train station. Spin around to enjoy the higgledy-piggledy building styles.

• *To the left (south) of the church, a golden horn hangs over the old...*

Posthof: The postal horn symbolizes the postal service throughout Europe. In olden days, when the postman blew this, traffic stopped and the mail sped through. This post station (now home to the TI) dates from 1724, when stagecoaches ran from Köln to Frankfurt and would change horses here, Pony Express-style.

Step past the old oak doors into the courtyard—once a carriage house and inn that accommodated Bacharach's first VIP visitors. Notice the fascist eagle (from 1936, on the left as you enter; a swastika once filled its center) and the fine view of the church and a ruined chapel above.

Two hundred years ago, Bacharach's main drag was the only road along the Rhine. Napoleon widened it to fit his cannon wagons. The steps alongside the church lead to the castle.

• *Return to the church, passing the recommended Italian ice-cream café (Eis Café Italia), where friendly Mimo serves his special invention: Riesling wine-flavored gelato.*

Protestant Church: Inside the church (daily 10:00-18:00, English info on table near door), you'll find Grotesque capitals, brightly painted in medieval style, and a mix of round Romanesque and pointed Gothic arches. The church was fancier before the Reformation wars, when it (and the region) was Catholic. Bacharach lies on the religious border of Germany and, like the country as a whole, is split between Catholics and Protestants. To the left of the altar, some medieval frescoes survive where an older Romanesque arch was cut by a pointed Gothic one.

• *Continue down Oberstrasse to the...*

Altes Haus: Notice the 14th-century building style—the first floor is made of stone, while upper floors are half-timbered (in the ornate style common in the Rhine Valley). Some of its windows still look medieval, with small, flattened circles as panes (small because that's all that glass-blowing technology of the time would allow), pieced together with molten lead (like medieval stained glass in churches). Frau Weber welcomes visitors to enjoy the fascinating ground floor of the recommended Altes Haus restaurant, with its evocative old photos and etchings (consider eating here later).

• *Keep going down Oberstrasse to the...*

Old Mint (Münze): The old mint is marked by a crude coin in its sign. Across from the mint, the recommended **Bastian** family's wine garden is a lively place after dark. Above you in the vineyards stands a lonely white-and-red tower—your final destination.

• *At the next street, look right and see the mint tower, painted in the medieval style, and then turn left. Wander 30 yards up Rosenstrasse to the **well**. Notice the sundial and the wall painting of 1632 Bacharach* *with its walls intact. Climb the tiny-stepped lane behind the well up into the vineyard and to the...*

Tall Tower: The slate steps lead to a small path through the vineyard that deposits you at a viewpoint atop the stubby remains of the old town wall. If the tower's open, hike to its top floor for the best view.

Romantic Rhine View: A grand medieval town spreads before you. For 300 years (1300-1600), Bacharach was big (popu-

lation 4,000), rich, and politically powerful.

From this perch, you can see the chapel ruins and six surviving **city towers.** Visually trace the wall to the castle. The castle was actually the capital of Germany for a couple of years in the 1200s. When Holy Roman Emperor Frederick Barbarossa went away to fight the Crusades, he left his brother (who lived here) in charge of his vast realm. Bacharach was home of one of seven electors who voted for the Holy Roman Emperor in 1275. To protect their own power, these prince electors did their best to choose the weakest guy on the ballot. The elector from Bacharach helped select a two-bit prince named Rudolf von Habsburg (from a no-name castle in Switzerland). However, the underestimated Rudolf brutally silenced the robber barons along the Rhine and established the mightiest dynasty in European history. His family line, the Habsburgs, ruled much of Central and Eastern Europe from Vienna until 1918.

Plagues, fires, and the Thirty Years' War (1618-1648) finally did in Bacharach. The town, with a population of about a thousand, has slumbered for several centuries. Today, the castle houses commoners—40,000 overnights annually by youth hostelers.

In the mid-19th century, painters such as J. M. W. Turner and writers such as Victor Hugo were charmed by the Rhineland's romantic mix of past glory, present poverty, and rich legend. They put this part of the Rhine on the old Grand Tour map as the "Romantic Rhine." Victor Hugo pondered the ruined 15th-century chapel that you see under the castle. In his 1842 travel book, *Excursions Along the Banks of Rhine,* he wrote, "No doors, no roof or windows, a magnificent skeleton puts its silhouette against the sky. Above it, the ivy-covered castle ruins provide a fitting crown. This is Bacharach, land of fairy tales, covered with legends and sagas." If you're enjoying the Romantic Rhine, thank Victor Hugo and company.

• *To get back into town, take the level path away from the river that leads along the once-mighty wall up the valley past the next tower. Then cross the street into the parking lot. Pass Pension im Malerwinkel on your right, being careful not to damage the old arch with your head. Follow the creek past a delightful little series of half-timbered homes and cheery gardens known as "Painters' Corner" (Malerwinkel). Resist looking into some pervert's peep show (on the right) and continue downhill back to the village center. Nice work.*

Walk Along the Old Town Walls

A well-maintained and clearly marked walking path follows the remains of Bacharach's old town walls and makes for a good hour's workout. The TI has maps that show the entire route. The path starts near the train station, then climbs up to the youth hostel, descends into the side valley, and then continues up the other side to the tower in the vineyards before returning to town. To start the walk at the train station, find the house at Oberstrasse 2 and climb up the stairway to its left. Then follow the *Stadtmauer-Rundweg* signs. Good bilingual signposts tell the history of each of the towers along the wall—some are intact, one is a private residence, and others are now only stubs.

Sleeping in Bacharach

(area code: 06743)

Parking in Bacharach is simple along the highway next to the tracks (3-hour daytime limit is generally not enforced) or, better, in the big lot by the boat dock. For locations, see the map on page 392.

$$$ Rhein Hotel, overlooking the river with 14 spacious and comfortable rooms, is classy, well-run, and decorated with modern flair. Since it's right on the train tracks, its river- and train-side rooms come with quadruple-paned windows and air-conditioning. This place has been in the Stüber family for six generations (Sb-€55, Db-€90, Tb-€120, Qb-€140, these prices good with this book and direct reservation in 2012, cheaper for longer stays and off-season, €17/person half-board includes big three-course dinner, non-smoking, free loaner bikes, pay Wi-Fi, directly inland from the K-D boat dock at Langstrasse 50, tel. 06743/1243, fax 06743/1413, www.rhein-hotel-bacharach.de, info@rhein-hotel -bacharach.de). Their recommended Stüber restaurant is considered the best in town.

$$ Hotel zur Post, refreshingly clean and quiet, is conveniently located right in the town center with no train noise. It comes with a focus on solid comfort rather than old-fashioned character, and rents good rooms for a good price (Db-€66-70, Oberstrasse 38, tel. 06743/1277, www.hotel-zur-post-bacharach.de,

---

Sleep Code

(€1 = about $1.40, country code: 49)

S = Single, **D** = Double/Twin, **T** = Triple, **Q** = Quad, **b** = bathroom, **s** = shower only. Staff at all hotels speak at least some English. Breakfast is included, and credit cards are accepted unless otherwise noted.

To help you sort easily through these listings, I've divided the accommodations into three categories, based on the price for a standard double room with bath:

$$$ **Higher Priced**—Most rooms €80 or more.
  $$ **Moderately Priced**—Most rooms between €55-80.
   $ **Lower Priced**—Most rooms €55 or less.

The Rhine is an easy place for cheap sleeps. B&Bs and *Gasthäuser* with €25-30 beds abound (and normally discount their prices for longer stays). Rhine-area hostels offer €20 beds to travelers of any age. Each town's TI is eager to set you up, and finding a room should be easy any time of year (except for Sept-Oct winefest weekends). Bacharach and St. Goar, the best towns for an overnight stop, are 10 miles apart, connected by milk-run trains, riverboats, and a riverside bike path. Bacharach is a much more interesting town, but St. Goar has the famous castle (for St. Goar recommendations, see that section).

---

h.zurpost@t-online.de, Precoma family).

$$ Hotel Kranenturm, offering castle ambience without the climb, combines hotel comfort with *Privatzimmer* funkiness

right downtown. Run by hardworking Kurt Engel and his intense but friendly wife, Fatima, this 17-room hotel is part of the medieval town wall. The rooms in its former *Kranenturm* (crane tower) have the best views. When the riverbank was higher, cranes on this tower loaded barrels of wine onto Rhine boats. While just 15 feet from the train tracks, a combination of medieval sturdiness, triple-paned windows, and included earplugs makes the riverside rooms sleepable (Sb-€40-46, small Db-€57-62, regular Db-€59-65, Db in huge tower rooms with castle and river views-€73-80, Tb-€85-95, Qb great for families with small kids-€100-110, lower prices are for 3-night stay, family deals, cash preferred, €2 extra if paying with credit card, Rhine views come with train noise, back rooms are quiet, non-smoking, showers can be temperamental, kid-friendly, good breakfast, free Internet access and Wi-Fi in lobby, laundry service-€13, Langstrasse 30, tel. 06743/1308, www.kranenturm.com, hotel-kranenturm@t-online.de). Kurt, a good cook, serves €10-14 dinners in their recommended restaurant.

$$ Pension im Malerwinkel sits like a grand gingerbread house that straddles the town wall in a quiet little neighborhood so charming it's called "Painters' Corner" *(Malerwinkel)*. The Vollmer family's 20-room place is super-quiet and comes with a sunny garden on a brook, views of the vineyards, and easy parking (Sb-€40; Db-€65 for one-night stay, €59/night for 2 nights, €56/night for 3 nights or more; family rooms, cash only, no train noise, non-smoking, free Wi-Fi, bike rental-€6/day; from Oberstrasse, turn left at the church, and stay to the left of the babbling brook until you reach Blücherstrasse 41-45; tel. 06743/1239, www.im-malerwinkel.de, info@im-malerwinkel.de, Armin and Daniela).

$$ Pension Binz offers four large, bright, plainly furnished rooms in a good location with no train noise (Sb-€37, Db-€60, Tb-€78, slightly more for one-night stays, Koblenzer Strasse 1, tel. 06743/1604, fax 06743/937-9916, http://pensionbinz.funpic.de, pension.binz@freenet.de, Carla speaks a little English).

$ Hotel Hillen, a block south of Hotel Kranenturm, has less charm and similar train noise (with the same ultra-thick windows). It offers spacious rooms and friendly owners (S-€30, Sb-€35, D-€40, Ds-€45, Db-€50, Tb-€65, Qb-€80, these prices when you reserve direct with this book in 2012, 10 percent discount for 2-night stay, closed mid-Nov-mid-March, family rooms, Langstrasse 18, tel. 06743/1287, fax 06743/1037, hotel-hillen@web.de, kind Iris speaks some English). The hotel also rents bikes (see page 393).

$ Pension Lettie, run by effervescent and eager-to-please Lettie, rents four bright rooms. Lettie speaks English (she worked for the US Army before they withdrew) and does laundry for €12/load (Sb-€38, Db-€55, Tb-€75, Qb-€90, Quint/b-€105, these prices with this book in 2012 when you reserve direct, €5 discount for 2-night stay, 10 percent more if paying with credit card, non-smoking, buffet breakfast with waffles and eggs, no train noise, free Wi-Fi, inland from Hotel Kranenturm, Kranenstrasse 6, tel. 06743/2115, pension.lettie@t-online.de).

$ Pension Winzerhaus, a 10-room place run by friendly Sybille and Stefan, is outside the town walls, 200 yards up the side-valley road from the town gate, directly under the vineyards. The rooms are simple, clean, and modern, and parking is easy (Sb-€33, Db-€49, Tb-€69, Qb-€75, 10 percent off in 2012 when you show this book at check-in, cash only, non-smoking, free Wi-Fi, free loaner bikes for guests, Blücherstrasse 60, tel. 06743/1294, www.pension-winzerhaus.de, winzerhaus@gmx.de).

$ Ursula Orth B&B rents five basic rooms. Ursula speaks a smidge of English and is proud of her homemade jam, and daughter Karin helps run things (Sb-€22, Db-€38, Tb-€48, cash only, non-smoking, Spurgasse 3, tel. 06743/1557, k.w.68@hotmail.de). From the station, walk down Oberstrasse, turn right on Spurgasse, and look for the *Orth* sign. Be careful not to confuse Ursula at #3 with Irmgard at #2 (listed next). While across the street from each other and related, they are two different businesses.

$ Irmgard Orth B&B rents three fresh rooms, two of which share a bathroom on the hall. Irmgard speaks almost no English, but is exuberantly cheery and serves homemade honey with breakfast (S-€22, D-€36, Db-€38, 5 percent more for one-night stay, cash only, non-smoking, Spurgasse 2, look for *Honig* signs with picture of a beehive, tel. 06743/1553, speak slowly).

$ Jugendherberge Stahleck hostel is a 12th-century castle on the hilltop—350 steps above Bacharach—with a royal Rhine view. Open to travelers of any age, this is a gem with 168 beds and a private modern shower and WC in most rooms. The hostel offers hearty €7.50 all-you-can-eat buffet dinners, and its pub serves cheap local wine and snacks until midnight. If you're arriving at the train station with luggage, it's an €8.50 taxi ride to the hostel—call 06743/1653 (€20 dorm beds with breakfast and sheets, non-members-€3.10 extra, couples can share one of five €51 Db, no smoking in rooms, pay Internet access and Wi-Fi,  laundry-€6; reception open 7:30-20:00, after that check in at bar until 21:30; curfew at 22:00, tel. 06743/1266, www.diejugendher bergen.de, zentrale@diejugendherbergen.de). If driving, don't go in the driveway; park on the street and walk 200 yards.

Eating in Bacharach

Restaurants

Bacharach has no shortage of reasonably priced, atmospheric restaurants offering fine indoor and outdoor dining. Two of my recommended hotels—Rhein and Kranenturm—have good restaurants.

Non-German options on the main street include a pizzeria and *Döner Kebab* joint (open daily until late) and an Irish pub.

The Rhein Hotel's **Stüber Restaurant** is Bacharach's best top-end choice. Chef Andreas Stüber, his family's sixth-generation chef, prepares regional, seasonal plates, served at river- and track-side seating or indoors with a spacious wood-and-white-tablecloth elegance. Consider his €15 William Turner pâté sampler plate, named after the British painter who liked Bacharach (€12-19 main courses, €27-35 fixed-price meals, always a good vegetarian option, open Wed-Mon 11:30-14:15 & 17:30-21:15, closed Tue and mid-Dec-Feb, call to reserve on weekends or for an outdoor table, facing the K-D boat dock below town center, Langstrasse 50, tel. 06743/1243).

Hotel Kranenturm is another good value, with hearty dinners (Kurt prides himself on his *Sauerbraten*—marinated beef with potato dumplings and red cabbage) and good main-course salads. If you're a trainspotter, sit on their trackside terrace and trade travel stories with new friends over dinner, letting screaming trains punctuate your conversation. If you prefer charming old German decor, sit inside (€9-15 main courses, open 6 days a week 17:00-21:00—closed day varies, restaurant closed Dec-Feb). Kurt and Fatima are your hosts.

Altes Haus, the oldest building in town (see page 396), serves food with Bacharach's most romantic atmosphere. Find the cozy little dining room with photos of the opera singer who sang about Bacharach, adding to its fame (€9-15 main courses, Thu-Tue 12:00-15:30 & 18:00-23:00, closed Wed and off-season, dead center by the Protestant Church, tel. 06743/1209).

Gasthaus Jägerstube is every local's non-touristy, good-value hangout. It's a no-frills place with no outdoor seating, run by a former East German family determined to keep Bacharach's working class well-fed and watered. Next to the WC is a rare "party cash box." Regulars drop in bits of money throughout the year, Frau Tischmeier banks it, and by year's end...there's plenty in the little savings account for a community party (€10-12 daily specials, daily 11:00-21:30, Marktstrasse 3, tel. 06743/1492, Tischmeier family).

Bacharacher Kebap Haus is the town favorite for €4 *Döner Kebabs,* cheap pizzas, and salads (daily 10:00-23:00, on the main drag in the town center).

Eis Café Italia, on the main street, is run by friendly Mimo Calabrese, who brought gelato to town in 1976. He's known for his refreshing, not-too-sweet Riesling-flavored gelato. Notice the big sundae bowls on the shelves. To enjoy your *Eis* German-style, sit down and order ice cream off the menu, or just stop by for a cone "to go" for your evening stroll (€0.80/scoop, no tastes offered, April-mid-Oct daily 10:00-22:00, closed off-season, Oberstrasse 48).

Jugendherberge Stahleck—Bacharach's youth hostel—welcomes anyone hungry or thirsty enough to hike 20 minutes up to its romantic perch above the Rhine. The hostel offers hearty €7.50 all-you-can-eat buffet dinners, while the pub serves cheap local wine and snacks until midnight (see listing under "Sleeping in Bacharach," earlier).

RHINE VALLEY

Pubs

Zum Kleinen Monning Irish Pub, with international beers on tap, provides the liveliest after-dinner scene in town. Bacharach's 1,000 residents hail from 26 different nations, and you'll meet many of them here enjoying the convivial atmosphere created by Martina and Marcus (light meals too, Oberstrasse 35).

If the Zum Kleinen Monning is dead, the other late-night spot for drinks (and pizza) is **Zur Alt Backstubb** (seating inside and out, €7 pastas and pizzas, nightly until late, Blücherstrasse 16).

Wine-Tasting

Bacharach is proud of its wine. Two places in town—Bastian's rowdy and rustic Grüner Baum, and the more sophisticated Weingut Karl Heidrich—offer visitors an inexpensive tasting memory. Each creates carousels of local wines that small groups of travelers (who don't mind sharing a glass) can sample and compare. Both places offer light plates of food if you'd like a rustic meal.

At **Bastian's Weingut zum Grüner Baum,** groups of 2-6 people pay €19.50 for a wine carousel of 15 glasses—14 different white wines and one lonely rosé—and a basket of bread. Your mission: Team up with others who have this book to rendezvous here after dinner. Spin the Lazy Susan, share a common cup, and discuss the taste. Doris Bastian insists: "After each wine, you must talk to each other" (Mon-Wed and Fri from 13:00, Sat-Sun from 12:00, closed Thu and Feb-mid-March, just past Altes Haus, tel. 06743/1208). To make a meal of a carousel, consider the €8 *Käseteller* (seven different cheeses—including *Spundekäse,* the local soft cheese—with bread and butter).

Weingut Karl Heidrich is a fun family-run wine shop and *Stube* in the town center (at Oberstrasse 16), where Markus and daughter Magdalena proudly share their family's centuries-old wine tradition, explaining its fine points to travelers. They offer a variety of carousels with English descriptions, six wines, and bread (€11.50), which are ideal for the more sophisticated wine taster (Thu-Tue 11:00-22:00, closed Wed and Nov-Easter, will ship to the US, tel. 06743/93060).

RHINE VALLEY

Bacharach Connections

Train Connections from the Rhine

Milk-run trains stop at Rhine towns each hour starting as early as 6:00, connecting at Mainz and Koblenz to trains farther afield. Trains between St. Goar and Bacharach depart at about :20 after the hour in each direction (€3.20, buy tickets from the machine in the unstaffed stations). The ride times listed below are calculated from Bacharach; for St. Goar, the difference is only 10 minutes. Train info: tel. 0180-599-6633, www.bahn.com.

From Bacharach by Train to: St. Goar (hourly, 10 minutes), **Moselkern** near Burg Eltz (hourly, 1.75 hours, change in Koblenz), **Cochem** (hourly, 1.5 hours, change in Koblenz), **Trier** (hourly, 2.5 hours, change in Koblenz), **Köln** (hourly, 1.75 hours with change in Koblenz, 2.5 hours direct), **Frankfurt Airport** (hourly, 1-1.5 hours, change in Mainz or Bingen), **Frankfurt** (hourly, 1.25-1.75 hours, change in Mainz or Bingen), **Rothenburg ob der Tauber** (every 2 hours, 4.25 hours, 3-4 changes), **Munich** (hourly, 5 hours, 2 changes), **Berlin** (hourly, 6.5-7.5 hours, 1-3 changes), **Amsterdam** (hourly, 7 hours, change in Köln, sometimes 1-2 more changes).

Route Tips for Drivers

This area is a logical first (or last) stop in Germany. If you're using Frankfurt Airport, here are some tips.

Frankfurt Airport to the Rhine: Driving from Frankfurt to the Rhine or Mosel takes 1.5 hours (follow blue autobahn signs from airport, major cities are signposted).

The Rhine to Frankfurt: From St. Goar or Bacharach, follow the river to Bingen, then autobahn signs to *Mainz,* then *Frankfurt.* From there, head for the airport *(Flughafen)* or downtown (signs to *Messe,* then *Hauptbahnhof,* to find the parking under Frankfurt's main train station—see "Arrival in Frankfurt—By Car," page 352).

St. Goar

St. Goar (sahnkt gwahr) is a classic Rhine tourist town. Its hulk of a castle overlooks a half-timbered shopping street and leafy riverside park, busy with sightseeing ships and contented strollers. Rheinfels Castle, once the mightiest on the Rhine, is the single best Rhineland ruin to explore. From the riverboat docks, the main drag—a dull pedestrian mall without history—cuts through town before ending at the road up to the castle. Explore beyond the shops: Thoughtful little placards scattered around town explain factoids (in English) about each street, lane, and square.

While the town of St. Goar itself isn't much more than a few hotels and restaurants—and is less interesting than Bacharach—it  still makes a good base for hiking or biking the region. A tiny car ferry will shuttle you back and forth across the busy Rhine from here. (If you run out of things to see, a great pastime in St. Goar is simply chatting with friendly Heike at the K-D boat kiosk.) For train connections, see "Bacharach Connections," earlier.

RHINE VALLEY

Orientation to St. Goar

Tourist Information

The helpful St. Goar TI, which books rooms and stores bags for free, is on the pedestrian street, three blocks from the K-D boat dock and train station (May-Sept Mon-Fri 9:00-12:30 & 13:30-18:00, Sat 10:00-12:00, closed Sun; April and Oct Mon-Fri until 17:00, closed Sat-Sun; Nov-March Mon-Thu until 17:00, Fri 9:00-14:00, closed Sat-Sun; from train station, go downhill around church and turn left, Heerstrasse 86, tel. 06741/383, www.st-goar.de).

Helpful Hints

Picnics: St. Goar's waterfront park is hungry for picnickers. You can buy picnic fixings at the tiny **St. Goarer Stadtladen** grocery store on the pedestrian street (Mon-Fri 8:00-18:00, Sat 8:00-13:00, closed Sun, Heerstrasse 106).

Shopping: The Montag family runs two shops (one specializes in steins and the other in cuckoo clocks), all at the base of the castle hill road. The stein shop under the hotel has Rhine guides and fine steins. The other shop boasts "the largest free-hanging cuckoo clock in the world" (both open daily 8:30-18:00). A couple of other souvenir shops are across from the K-D boat dock. Shops offer 10 percent off any of their souvenirs (including Hummels) for travelers with this book. They'll ship your purchase home—or give you a VAT form to claim your tax refund at the airport if you're carrying your items with you.

Internet Access: The **TI** is your best bet (€0.50/10 minutes), but if it's crowded or closed, the backup option is the expensive coin-op access (€6/hour, 6 terminals) or Wi-Fi (€5/hour) at **Hotel Montag** (Heerstrasse 128).

Bike Rental: Goar Bike, run by Richard and Gabriele Langhans,

RHINE VALLEY

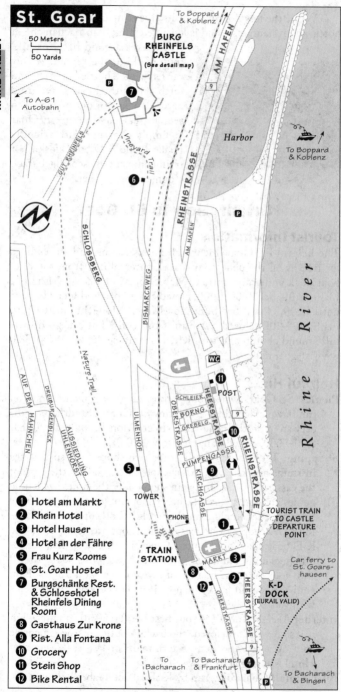

St. Goar

50 Meters
50 Yards

To Boppard & Koblenz

BURG RHEINFELS CASTLE
(See detail map)

To A-61 Autobahn

AM HAFEN

Harbor

To Boppard & Koblenz

RHEINSTRASSE

SCHLOSSBERG

GUT RHEINFELS

Vineyard Trail

6

7

P

9

P

AM HAFEN

Nature Trail

BISMARCKWEG

AUF DEM HAHNCHEN

DREIBURGENBLICK

AUSSIEDLUNG UHLENHORST

ULMENHOF

R h i n e   R i v e r

WC

11

POST

SCHLEIER

OBERSTRASSE

BORNG

GREBELG

HEERSTRASSE

9

10

PUMPENGASSE

9

i

5

KIRCHGASSE

TOWER

PHONE

TRAIN STATION

1

TOURIST TRAIN TO CASTLE DEPARTURE POINT

MARKT

3

8

Car ferry to St. Goars-hausen

12

2

OBERSTRASSE

HEERSTRASSE

K-D DOCK
(EURAIL VALID)

To Bacharach

To Bacharach & Frankfurt

4

9

To Bacharach & Bingen

1 Hotel am Markt
2 Rhein Hotel
3 Hotel Hauser
4 Hotel an der Fähre
5 Frau Kurz Rooms
6 St. Goar Hostel
7 Burgschänke Rest. & Schlosshotel Rheinfels Dining Room
8 Gasthaus Zur Krone
9 Rist. Alla Fontana
10 Grocery
11 Stein Shop
12 Bike Rental

is near the train station (€7/6 hours, €10/day, must show ID and leave €50 deposit, April-Oct Tue-Sun 9:00-13:00 & 15:00-19:00, closed Mon and Nov-March, go right as you exit station, Oberstrasse 44, tel. 06741/1735, goarbike@web .de). Richard, who speaks English, has maps and can suggest routes (or ask at the TI).

Parking: A free lot is at the downstream end of town. On-street parking by the K-D boat dock and recommended hotels costs about €4/day.

Sights in St. Goar

▲▲▲Rheinfels Castle

Sitting like a dead pit bull above St. Goar, this mightiest of Rhine castles rumbles with ghosts from its hard-fought past. This hollow but interesting shell offers your single best hands-on ruined-castle experience on the river.

Cost and Hours: €4, family card-€10; mid-March-Oct daily 9:00-18:00, last entry at 17:00; Nov-mid-March Sat-Sun only 11:00-17:00, last entry at 16:00—weather permitting. Managed by Gaby Loch, tel. 06741/7753, in winter 06741/383, www.st-goar.de.

Tours and Information: Follow my self-guided tour on page 409. The castle map is helpful, but the €2 English booklet is of no real value. English tours (€30/group) can be booked in advance. If it's damp, be careful of slippery stones.

Services: A handy WC is immediately across from the ticket booth (check out the guillotine urinals—stand back when you pull to flush).

Let There Be Light: If planning to explore the mine tunnels, bring a flashlight, or do it by candlelight (museum sells candles with matches, €0.50).

Getting to the Castle: A **taxi** up from town costs €5 (tel. 06741/7011). Or take the kitschy "tschu-tschu" **tourist train** (€2 one-way, €3 round-trip, 8 minutes to the top, hours vary but generally April-Oct daily 10:00-17:30, 2/hour, complete with lusty music, mobile 0171-496-3762). The train waits between the train station and the K-D dock. To avoid feeling silly as you sit on the train waiting for Ralph (the "conductor") to decide it's time to go, browse the shopping street and hop on as he goes by (just wave him down, then pay at the top). The train returns to town from the castle at about the top and bottom of each hour.

To **hike** up to the castle, you can simply follow the main road up through the railroad underpass at the top end of the pedestrian street. But it's more fun to take the nature trail: Start at the St. Goar train station. Take the underpass under the tracks at the north end of the station, climb the steep stairs uphill, and turn

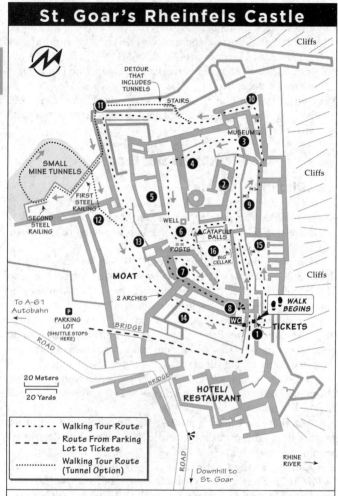

St. Goar's Rheinfels Castle

1. Ticket Office & Entry
2. Darmstädter Bau
3. Museum & Castle Model
4. Inner Courtyard
5. Stables
6. Well
7. High Battery
8. Clock Tower Lookout
9. Stairs to Defense Galleries
10. Corner of Castle & Crossbow Slits
11. Foxhole & Mine Tunnel
12. Halsgraben ("Neck Ditch")
13. Gunsmiths' Tower
14. Prison
15. Slaughterhouse
16. Big Cellar

right (following *Burg Rheinfels* signs) along the path just above the old city wall, which takes you to the castle in 10 minutes.

Background: Burg Rheinfels *was* huge—for five centuries, it was the biggest castle on the Rhine. Built in 1245 to guard a

toll station, it soon earned the nickname "the unconquerable fortress." In the 1400s, the castle was thickened to withstand cannon fire. Rheinfels became a thriving cultural center and, in the 1520s, was visited by the artist Albrecht Dürer and the religious reformer Ulrich Zwingli. It saw lots of action in the Thirty Years' War

(1618-1648), and later became the strongest and most modern fortress in the Holy Roman Empire. It withstood a siege of 28,000 French troops in 1692. But eventually the castle surrendered to the French without a fight, and in 1797, the French Revolutionary army destroyed it. For years, the ruined castle was used as a source of building stone, and today—while still mighty—it's only a small fraction of its original size.

❸ Self-Guided Tour: Rather than wander aimlessly, visit the castle by following this tour. We'll start at the museum, then circulate through the courtyards, up to the highest lookout point, and down around through the fortified ramparts, with an option to go into the dark tunnels. We'll finish in the prison and big cellar. The basic route below can be done without a flashlight or any daring acts of chivalry. (To go through the tunnels, bring a light or buy candles at the castle museum.)

Pick up the free map and use its commentary to navigate from red signpost to signpost through the castle. My self-guided tour route is similar to the one marked on the castle map. That map, the one in this book, and this tour all use the same numbering system. (You'll notice that I've skipped a few stops—just walk on by signs for ❷ *Darmstädter Bau*, ❺ *stables*, and ❽ *Gunsmiths' Tower.*)

• *The ticket office is under the castle's clock tower, labeled* ❶ *Uhrturm. Walk through the entranceway and continue straight, passing several points of interest (which we'll visit later), until you get to the* ❸ *museum.*

Museum and Castle Model: The pleasant museum, located in the only finished room of the castle, has good English descriptions and comes with Romantic Age etchings that give a sense of the place in the 19th century (daily 10:00-12:30 & 13:00-17:30).

The seven-foot-tall carved stone immediately inside the door (marked *Flammensäule*)—a tombstone from a nearby Celtic grave—is from 400 years before Christ. There were people here long before the Romans...and this castle.

The sweeping castle history exhibit in the center of the room is well-described in English. The massive fortification was the only Rhineland castle to withstand Louis XIV's assault during the 17th century. At the far end of the room is a model reconstruction of the castle showing how much bigger it was before French Revolutionary troops destroyed it in the 18th century. Study this. Find where you are. (Hint: Look for the tall tower.) This was the living quarters of the original castle, which was only the smallest ring of buildings around the tiny central courtyard (13th century). The ramparts were added in the 14th century. By 1650, the fortress was largely complete. Since its destruction by the French in the late 18th century, it's had no military value. While no WWII bombs were wasted on this ruin, it served St. Goar as a stone quarry for generations. The basement of the museum shows the castle pharmacy and an exhibit of Rhine-region odds and ends, including tools, an 1830 loom, and photos of icebreaking on the Rhine. While once routine, icebreaking hasn't been necessary here since 1963.

• *Exit the museum and walk 30 yards directly out, slightly uphill into the castle courtyard, where you'll see a sign for the inner courtyard (❹ Innenhof).*

Medieval Castle Courtyard: Five hundred years ago, the entire castle encircled this courtyard. The place was self-sufficient

and ready for a siege, with a bakery, pharmacy, herb garden, brewery, well (top of yard), and livestock. During peacetime, 300-600 people lived here; during a siege, there would be as many as 4,000. The walls were plastered and painted white. Bits of the original 13th-century plaster survive.

• *Continue through the courtyard under the Erste Schildmauer (first shield wall) sign, turn left, and walk straight to the two old wooden upright posts. Find the pyramid of stone catapult balls on your left.*

Castle Garden: Catapult balls like these were too expensive not to recycle—they'd be retrieved after any battle. Across from the balls is a well (❻ *Brunnen*)—essential for any castle during the age of sieges. Look in. Thirsty? The old posts are for the ceremonial baptizing of new members of the local trading league. While this guild goes back centuries, it's now a social club that fills this court with a huge wine party the third weekend of each September.

• *Climb uphill to the castle's highest point by walking along the cobbled path up past the high battery (❼ Hohe Batterie) to the castle's best viewpoint—up where the German flag waves (signed ❽ Uhrturm).*

Highest Castle Tower Lookout: Enjoy a great view of the river, the castle, and the forest. Remember, the fortress once covered five times the land it does today. Notice how the other castles (across the river) don't poke above the top of the Rhine canyon. That would make them easy for invading armies to see.

From this perch, survey the Rhine Valley, cut out of slate over millions of years by the river. The slate absorbs the heat of the sun, making the grapes grown here well-suited for wine. Today the slate is mined to provide roofing. Imagine St. Goar settling here 1,500 years ago, establishing a place where sailors—thankful to have survived the treacherous Loreley—would stop and pray. Imagine the frozen river of years past, when the ice would break up and boats would huddle in manmade harbors like the one below for protection. Consider the history of trade on this busy river—from the days when castles levied tolls on ships, to the days when boats would be hauled upstream with the help of riverside towpaths, to the 21st century when 300 ships a day move their cargo past St. Goar. And imagine this castle before the French destroyed it... when it was the mightiest structure on the river, filled with people and inspiring awe among all who passed.

• *Return to the catapult balls, walk downhill past the well and through the tunnel, veer left through the arch marked* ❾ zu den Wehrgängen *("to the defense galleries"), and go down two flights of stairs. Turn left and step into the dark, covered passageway. From here, we'll begin a rectangular walk taking us completely around (counterclockwise) the perimeter of the castle.*

Covered Defense Galleries with "Minutemen" Holes: Soldiers—the castle's "minutemen"—had a short commute: defensive positions on the outside, home in the holes below on the left. Even though these living quarters were padded with straw, life was unpleasant.

• *Continue straight through the dark gallery, up the stairs, and to the corner of the castle, where you'll see a white painted arrow at eye level and a red signpost with the number* ❿. *Stand with your back to the arrow on the wall.*

Corner of Castle: Gape up. A three-story, half-timbered building originally rose beyond the highest stone fortification. The two stone tongues near the top just around the corner (to the right) supported the toilet. (Insert your own joke here.) Turn around and face the wall. The crossbow slits below the white arrow were once steeper. The bigger hole on the riverside was for hot pitch.

• *Follow that white arrow along the outside to the next corner. At the corner, turn left.*

Thoop...You're Dead: Look ahead at the smartly placed crossbow slit. While you're lying there, notice the stonework. The little round holes were for scaffolds used as they built up. They indicate this stonework is original. Notice also the fine stonework on the chutes. More boiling pitch...now you're toast, too.

• *Continue along the castle wall around the corner. Notice the stairs on the right, which lead down to the Small Mine Tunnels—if you'd like to visit them, see the "Optional Detour" on page 413. You'll rejoin this tour at the Prison.*

Otherwise, at the gray railing, look up the valley and uphill where the sprawling fort stretched. Below, just outside the wall, is land where attackers would gather. The mine tunnels are under there, waiting to blow up any attackers.

Keep going along the perimeter, jog left, go down five steps and into an open field, and walk toward the wooden bridge. The "old" wooden bridge is actually modern.

Dark Tunnel Detour: For a short detour through a castle tunnel, turn your back to the main castle (with the modern bridge to your left) and face the stone structure labeled ⓬ *Halsgraben.* (You'll exit in a few minutes at the high railing above the red *#12* sign.) Go 20 yards to the right, and enter the tunnel at the bottom, following the red *Grosser Minengang* sign. At the end of the short, big tunnel, take two steps up and walk eight level steps, turn left, and follow the long uphill ramp (this is where it's pitch-black). At the end, a spiral staircase takes you up to the high-railing opening you saw earlier, and then back to the courtyard.

• *When ready to leave this courtyard, angle left (under the red* zum Verliess *sign, before the bridge) through two arches and through the rough entry to the* ⓮ Verliess *(prison) on the left.*

Prison: This is one of six dungeons. You just walked through an entrance prisoners only dreamed of 400 years ago. They came and went through the little square hole in the ceiling. The holes in the walls supported timbers that thoughtfully gave as many as 15 residents something to sit on to keep them out of the filthy slop that gathered on the floor. Twice a day, they were given bread and water. Some prisoners actually survived longer than two years in here. While the town could torture and execute, the castle had permission only to imprison criminals in these dungeons. Consider this: According to town records, the two men who spent the most time down here—2.5 years each—died within three weeks of regaining their freedom. Perhaps after a diet of bread and water, feasting on meat and wine was simply too much.

• *Continue through the next arch, under the white arrow, then turn left and walk 30 yards to the* ⓯ Schlachthaus.

Slaughterhouse: Any proper castle was prepared to survive a six-month siege. With 4,000 people, that's a lot of provisions. The cattle that lived within the walls were slaughtered in this room. The castle's mortar was congealed here (by packing all the organic waste from the kitchen into kegs and sealing it). Notice the drainage gutters. "Running water" came through from drains built into the walls (to keep the mortar dry and therefore strong...and less smelly).

• *Back outside, climb the modern stairs to the left (look for the* zum Ausgang *sign). A skinny, dark passage leads you into the...*

Big Cellar: This ⑯ *Grosser Keller* was a big pantry. When the castle was smaller, this was the original moat—you can see the rough lower parts of the wall. The original floor was 13 feet deeper. The drawbridge rested upon the stone nubs on the left. When the castle expanded, the moat became this cellar. Halfway up the walls on the entrance side of the room, square holes mark spots where timbers made a storage loft, perhaps filled with grain. In the back, an arch leads to the wine cellar (sometimes blocked off) where finer wine was kept. Part of a soldier's pay was wine... table wine. This wine was kept in a single 180,000-liter stone barrel (that's 47,550 gallons), which generally lasted about 18 months.

The count owned the surrounding farmland. Farmers got to keep 20 percent of their production. Later, in more liberal feudal times, the nobility let them keep 40 percent. Today, the German government leaves the workers with 60 percent...and provides a few more services.

• *You're free. Climb out, turn right, and leave. For coffee on a terrace with a great view, visit Schlosshotel Rheinfels, opposite the entrance.*

Optional Detour—Into the Small Mine Tunnels: Tall people might want to skip this foray into low, cramped tunnels (some only three feet high). In about 1600, to protect their castle, the Rheinfellers cleverly booby-trapped the land just outside their walls by building tunnels topped with thin slate roofs and packed with explosives. By detonating the explosives when under attack, they could kill hundreds of invaders. In 1626, a handful of underground Protestant Germans blew 300 Catholic Spaniards to—they figured—hell. You're welcome to wander through a set of never-blown-up tunnels. But be warned: It's 600 feet long, assuming you make no wrong turns; it's pitch-dark, muddy, and claustrophobic, with confusing dead-ends; and you'll never get higher than a deep crouch. It cannot be done without a light (candles available at entrance). Be sure to bring the castle map, which shows the tunnels in detail.

To tour the Small Mine Tunnels, start at the red ⑩ signpost at the crossbow slits (described earlier). Follow the modern stairs on the right leading down to the mine (*zu den Minengängen* sign on upper left). The ⑪ *Fuchsloch* (foxhole) sign welcomes you to a covered passageway. Walk level (take no stairs) past the first black-steel railing (where you hope to emerge later) and around a few bends to the second steel railing. Climb down.

The "highway" in this foxhole is three feet high. The ceiling may be painted with a white line indicating the correct path. Don't venture into the narrower side aisles. These were once filled with the gunpowder. After a small decline, take the second right. At the T-intersection, go right (uphill). After about 10 feet, go left. Take the next right and look for a light at the end of the tunnel. Head up a rocky incline under the narrowest part of the tunnel, and you'll emerge at that first steel railing. The stairs on the right lead to freedom. Cross the field, walk under the bigger archway, and continue uphill toward the old wooden bridge. Angle left through two arches (before the bridge) and through the rough entry to the ⓮ *Verlies* (prison) on the left, where you can rejoin the self-guided tour.

Sleeping in St. Goar

(€1 = about $1.40, country code: 49, area code: 06741)
Parking in St. Goar is tight; ask at your hotel.

$$ Hotel am Markt, run by Herr and Frau Marx and their friendly staff, is rustic and a good deal, with all the modern comforts. It features a hint of antler with a pastel flair, 17 bright rooms, and a good restaurant. It's a good value and a stone's throw from the boat dock and train station (S-€40, Sb-€50, standard Db-€65, bigger riverview Db-€80, cheaper March-mid-April and Oct, closed Nov-Feb, free Internet access and Wi-Fi, parking-€4, Markt 1, tel. 06741/1689, fax 06741/1721, www.hotel-am-markt-sankt-goar.de, info@hotel-am-markt-sankt-goar.de).

$$ Rhein Hotel, two doors down from Hotel am Markt and run with enthusiasm by energetic Gil Velich, has 10 quality rooms in a spacious building and its own restaurant (Sb-€50, quiet viewless Db-€65, river-view balcony Db-€85-95, non-smoking, free Wi-Fi, laundry-€12/load, closed mid-Nov-Feb, Heerstrasse 71, tel. 06741/981-240, www.rheinhotel-st-goar.de, info@rheinhotel-st -goar.de).

$ Hotel Hauser, across the square from Hotel am Markt, is a very basic place with ramshackle halls and 12 tidy rooms (S-€23, D-€46, Db-€54, Db with Rhine-view balconies-€58, these prices with this book and cash through 2012, flexible à la carte half-pension-€14, free Wi-Fi, Heerstrasse 77, tel. 06741/333, fax 06741/1464, www.hotelhauser.de, info@hotelhauser.de).

$ Hotel an der Fähre is a simple, well-run place on the busy road at the end of town, immediately across from the ferry dock. It rents 12 cheap but decent rooms (D-€40, Db-€50, extra bed-€20, cash only, street noise but double-glazed windows, free Internet access, closed Nov-Feb, Heerstrasse 47, tel. 06741/980-577, www .hotel-stgoar.de, anderfaehre@t-online.de, Armin and Svetla Stecher).

$ Frau Kurz has been housing my readers since 1988. With the help of her daughter, Jeanette, she offers St. Goar's best B&B,

 renting three delightful rooms (sharing 2.5 bathrooms) with bathrobes, a breakfast terrace, garden, fine three-castle views, and homemade marmalade (S-€30, D-€52, 2-night minimum, D-€48 if you stay at least 4 nights, cash only, non-smoking, free and easy parking, ask about apartment with kitchen if staying at least 5 days, Ulmenhof 11, tel. 06741/459, www.gaestehaus-kurz.de, jeanette.kurz@super kabel.de). It's a steep five-minute hike from the train station: Exit left from the station, take an immediate left at the yellow phone booth, pass under the tracks, go up the stairs, and follow the zig-zag path, turning right through an archway onto Ulmenhof; #11 is just past the tower.

$ St. Goar Hostel, the big beige building down the hill from the castle, rents 126 beds, mostly in 4- to 10-bed dorms but also in 18 doubles. The facilities hark back to an earlier age of hosteling, with shared baths down the hall (hence the low price), but it has Rhine views, a nice terrace, and hearty €6 dinners (dorm beds-€15, D-€36, includes breakfast, nonmembers-€3.10 extra, non-smoking, open all day, curfew 22:30—but you can borrow the key, reconfirm reservation by phone the day before, Bismarckweg 17, tel. 06741/388, fax 06741/2869, www.diejugendherbergen.de, st-goar@diejugendherbergen.de). It's a fairly level 10-minute walk from the train station, following the red *Jugendherberge* signs.

Eating in St. Goar

Hotel am Markt serves tasty traditional meals with plenty of game and fish (specialties include marinated roast beef and homemade cheesecake) at fair prices with good atmosphere and service. Choose cozy indoor seating, or dine outside with a river view (€9-15 main courses, March-Oct daily 8:00-21:00, closed Nov-Feb, Markt 1, tel. 06741/1689).

Burgschänke, on the ground floor of Schlosshotel Rheinfels (the hotel across from the castle ticket office—enter through the souvenir shop) offers the only reasonably priced lunches up at Rheinfels Castle. It's family-friendly and has a Rhine view from its fabulous outdoor terrace (€9-13 main courses, Sun-Thu 11:00-18:00, Fri-Sat 11:00-21:00, tel. 06741/802-806).

The **Schlosshotel Rheinfels** dining room is your Rhine splurge, with an incredible indoor view terrace in an elegant, dressy setting (€19-24 main courses, €32-36 three-course fixed-price meals, daily 7:00-11:00 & 12:00-14:15 & 18:30-21:15, call to reserve a window table, tel. 06741/8020).

Gasthaus Zur Krone is the local choice for traditional German food in a restaurant that has no river view and isn't part of a hotel (€7-10 main courses, Thu-Tue 18:00-21:00, closed Wed, next to the train station and church at Oberstrasse 38, tel. 06741/1515).

Ristorante Alla Fontana, tucked away on a back lane and busy with locals, serves the best Italian food in town at great prices in a lovely dining room (€7 pizza and pasta, Tue-Sun 11:30-14:00 & 17:30-22:00, closed Mon, reservations smart, Pumpengasse 5, 06741/96117).

Picnics: The grocery store (see "Helpful Hints," earlier) has plenty of goodies. You can assemble a picnic to enjoy at the riverside park or up at the castle.

MOSEL VALLEY

Cochem • Burg Eltz • Beilstein

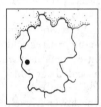

The misty Mosel is what some visitors hope the Rhine will be—peaceful, sleepy, romantic villages slipped between impossibly steep vineyards and the river; fine wine; a sprinkling of castles (Burg Eltz is tops); and lots of friendly small pensions. Boat, train, and car traffic here is a trickle compared to the roaring Rhine. While the swan-speckled Mosel (MOH-zehl in German; Moselle/moh-ZEHL in French) moseys 300 miles from France's Vosges mountain range to Koblenz (where it dumps into the Rhine), the most scenic piece of the valley lies between the towns of Bernkastel-Kues and Cochem. I'd savor only this section. Cochem and Trier (see next chapter) are easy day trips from each other (45-60 minutes by train, 55 miles by car). Cochem is the handiest home base, unless you have a car and want the peace of Beilstein.

Getting Around the Mosel Valley

By Train and Bus: Fast trains zip you between Koblenz, Cochem, Bullay, and Trier in a snap. Other destinations require changing to a slow train or bus. Beilstein is a 20-minute ride on bus #716 from Cochem (almost hourly Mon-Fri, 3-4/day on weekends, last bus leaves between 18:30 and 19:00, €3.15). Burg Eltz is a scenic 1.5-hour hike or €20 taxi ride from the tiny Moselkern train station (or about a €55 taxi ride from Cochem). For bus times, pick up printed schedules at train stations and TIs, or check

the regional transit website (www.vrminfo.de) or Germany's train timetable (www.bahn.com).

By Boat: Thanks to its many locks, Mosel cruises feel more like a canal-boat ride than the cruises on the mighty Rhine. The Kolb Line has the most frequent departures and cruises the most scenic stretch of the Mosel (tel. 06512/6666, www.moselfahrplan .de). A simple and fun outing is the one-hour cruise between **Cochem** and **Beilstein,** passing through the Fankel lock (4-5/day in each direction May-Oct, weekends only in April, no boats off-season, first departure from Cochem at about 10:30, last departure from Beilstein at about 17:30, €11 one-way, €14 round-trip). Another option is the boat in the other direction (downstream) from **Cochem** to **Karden** (3/day, runs mid-July-Aug daily; May-mid-July and Sept-Oct Wed and Sat-Sun only; no boats off-season; 45 minutes, €9 one-way, €11 round-trip). From Karden, you can get to Burg Eltz via a long hike (2 hours, steep in places), train-and-hike combination, weekend bus (May-Oct only), or taxi ride—though it's generally easier to reach Burg Eltz from the Moselkern train station. Kolb also runs one-hour **sightseeing cruises** and two-hour **dancing cruises** from Cochem (€9 sightseeing cruises 5/day April-Oct; €15 dancing cruises with live music daily at 20:15 mid-July-Aug, Tue and Sat only May-mid-July and Sept-Oct).

The KD (Köln-Düsseldorfer) line sails the lower Mosel, between **Cochem** and **Koblenz**—but not every day, and only once a day in each direction (€26.60 one-way, Wed-Mon only mid-June-Sept, Fri-Mon only May-mid-June, none in winter, Koblenz to Cochem 9:45-15:00, Cochem to Koblenz 15:40-20:00; free with a German railpass or any Eurailpass that covers Germany, but begins the use of a flexipass day; tel. in Cochem 02671/980-023, www.k-d.com).

Each year in early to mid-June (dates vary), the Mosel locks close for 10 days of annual maintenance, and none of the boats listed here run.

By Car: Two-lane roads run along both riverbanks. While these riverside roads are a delight, the river valley is very windy. Shortcuts overland can "cut the corners" and save you serious time—especially between Burg Eltz and Beilstein (see page 433) and if you're driving between the Mosel and the Rhine (note the Brodenbach-Boppard shortcut). Both Koblenz and Trier have car-rental agencies. A mile-long, 500-foot-high, €270 million express-way bridge (called Hochmoselbrücke) is being built near the town of Ürzig, just southwest/upstream of Cochem and Beilstein.

By Bike: Biking along the Mosel is the rage among Dutch and German tourists. You can rent bikes in most Mosel towns (I've listed options in both Cochem and Beilstein). A fine bike path follows the river from Koblenz to Zell (with some bits sharing the

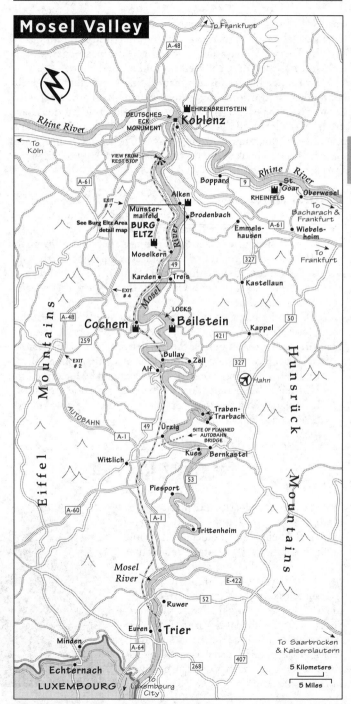

Mosel Valley

A-48

To Frankfurt

Rhine River

To Köln

A-61

EXIT #7

DEUTSCHES ECK MONUMENT

EHRENBREITSTEIN

Koblenz

VIEW FROM REST STOP

Boppard

9

Rhine River

St. Goar

RHEINFELS

Oberwesel

To Bacharach & Frankfurt

Wiebelsheim

A-61

To Frankfurt

Alken

Munster-maifeld

BURG ELTZ

See Burg Eltz Area detail map

Brodenbach

Emmels-hausen

327

Moselkern

49

Karden

Treis

Kastellaun

EXIT #4

LOCKS

Cochem

A-48

259

EXIT #2

Beilstein

Kappel

50

421

Bullay

Alf

Zell

327

Hahn

AUTOBAHN

A-1

49

Ürzig

Traben-Trarbach

SITE OF PLANNED AUTOBAHN BRIDGE

Wittlich

Kues

Bernkastel

53

Piesport

A-60

A-1

Trittenheim

Mosel River

E-422

Ruwer

52

Euren

Trier

To Saarbrücken & Kaiserslautern

Minden

A-64

Echternach

LUXEMBOURG

To Luxembourg City

268

407

5 Kilometers

5 Miles

Eiffel Mountains

Hunsrück Mountains

Mosel River

road with cars). Allow one hour between Cochem and Beilstein. Many pedal one-way, then relax on a return cruise or train ride.

By Ferry: About a dozen small car-and-passenger ferries *(Fähre)* cross the Mosel between Koblenz and Trier.

By Plane: The confusingly named Frankfurt Hahn Airport, a popular hub for low-fare airlines such as Ryanair, is actually located near the Mosel (www.hahn-airport.de). You can ride a bus from the airport to Bullay (€6.80, runs every 2 hours, 50 minutes; then 10-minute train ride from Bullay to Cochem). Groups of five or more need to book ahead for this bus (tel. 01805-066-735, www .airportshuttle-mosel.de).

Helpful Hints

Wine Festivals: Throughout the Mosel region on summer weekends and during the fall harvest, wine festivals with oompah bands, dancing, and colorful costumes are powered by good food and wine. You'll find a wine festival in some nearby village any weekend, June through September. The tourist season lasts from April through October. Things close down tight through the winter.

Carry Cash: Be prepared to pay cash for nearly everything in the Mosel Valley, including food, hotels, and transportation.

Helpful Guidebook: Look for the booklet *The Castles of the Moselle* (€3.80, at local TIs), with information on castles from Koblenz to Trier (including Burg Eltz, Cochem, and Metternich in Beilstein). The booklet not only has historical and structural information, but also some drawings of what the now-ruined castles once looked like.

Cochem

With a majestic castle and picturesque medieval streets, Cochem (KOHKH-ehm) is the hub of the middle Mosel. With 6,000 inhabitants, it's a larger, more bustling town than Beilstein, Bacharach, or St. Goar. Duck into a damp wine cellar to sample the local white wine (*Weinprobe* means "wine-tasting"). Stroll pleasant paths along the idyllic riverbank, play life-size chess, or just grab a bench and watch Germany at play. River-cruise passengers clog the old town during the day, but evenings are peaceful.

Orientation to Cochem

(area code: 02671)

Tourist Information

The information-packed TI is by the bridge at the main bus stop. Most of the pamphlets (free map with town walk, town history flier) are kept behind the desk—ask. Their thorough 24-hour room listing in the window comes with a free phone connection. The TI also has information on special events, wine-tastings held by local vintners, public transportation to Burg Eltz, and area hikes. You can also pick up the informative, six-foot-long, €3 *Mosellauf* poster/brochure here (mid-July-Oct Mon-Sat 9:00-17:00, Sun 11:00-16:00; May-mid-July Mon-Fri 9:00-17:00, Sat 9:00-15:00, closed Sun; Nov-April Mon-Fri 9:00-13:00 & 14:00-17:00, closed Sat-Sun; Endertplatz 1, tel. 02671/60040, www.ferienland-cochem.de).

Arrival in Cochem

By Train: Cochem's train station is often unstaffed and has no lockers, but you can leave your bags at the Gleis 9 café off the station hall (€2/bag, Mon-Fri 7:00-19:00, Sat-Sun 10:00-19:00). Make a hard right out of the station and walk about 10 minutes along cobbled Ravenéstrasse to the TI and bus station (both on your left, before the bridge). To get to the main square (Markt) and colorful medieval town center, continue under the bridge (€0.50 WC), then angle right and follow Bernstrasse.

By Car: Drivers can park in the multistory garage just up Endertstrasse from the bridge, or in a lot behind the train station (€2/day, reach it by circling around on Ravenéstrasse and Pinnerstrasse).

Helpful Hints

Festival: Cochem's biggest wine festival is held the last weekend in August (Aug 23-27 in 2012). High season for wine aficionados lasts from August through October.

Internet Access: The very pleasant **Espresso I-O** café has two terminals (€1/15 minutes, €3.50/hour, also has Wi-Fi, Mon-Fri 8:00-18:00, Sat-Sun 11:00-18:00, between TI and train station at Ravenéstrasse 18-20).

Bike Rental: Consider taking a bike on the boat or train, and pedaling back. **Radsport Schrauth** is run by serious cyclists (€5/half-day, €8/day, €10/day for mountain bikes, Mon-Fri 9:30-18:00, Sat 9:00-13:00, Sun only May-Oct 10:00-12:00, arrange weekend drop-off time, Sehler Anlagen 10, tel. 02671/7974). **Radverleih Schaltwerk,** between the station

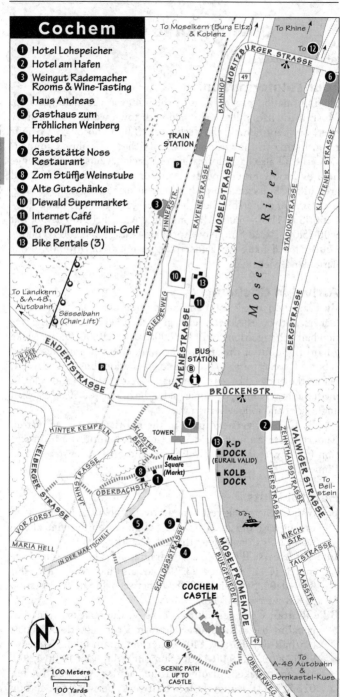

Cochem

1. Hotel Lohspeicher
2. Hotel am Hafen
3. Weingut Rademacher Rooms & Wine-Tasting
4. Haus Andreas
5. Gasthaus zum Fröhlichen Weinberg
6. Hostel
7. Gaststätte Noss Restaurant
8. Zom Stüffje Weinstube
9. Alte Gutschänke
10. Diewald Supermarket
11. Internet Café
12. To Pool/Tennis/Mini-Golf
13. Bike Rentals (3)

MOSEL VALLEY

To Moselkern (Burg Eltz) & Koblenz
To Rhine
To 12

MORITZBURGER STRASSE
BAHNHOF
6
KLOTTENER STRASSE
TRAIN STATION
P
PINNERSTR.
RAVENÉSTRASSE
MOSELSTRASSE
STADIONSTRASSE
Mosel River
10
13
BRIEDERWEG
11
BERGSTRASSE
To Landkern & A-48 Autobahn
Sesselbahn (Chair Lift)
ENDERTSTRASSE
IN DER PLAN
P
RAVENÉSTRASSE
BUS STATION
B
1
BRÜCKENSTR.
HINTER KEMPELN
KLOSTERBERG
TOWER
7
2
ZEHNTHAUSSTRASSE
VALWIGER STRASSE
KELBERGER STRASSE
JAHNSTRASSE
8
1
OBERBACHSTR.
Main Square (Markt)
13 K-D DOCK (EURAIL VALID)
KOLB DOCK
UFERSTRASSE
To Beilstein
VOR FORST
5
9
MARIA HELL
IN DER MARTSCHELT
SCHLOSSSTRASSE
4
MOSELPROMENADE
BURGFRIEDEN
KIRCH-STR.
TALSTRASSE
KAASSTR.
COCHEM CASTLE
B
SCENIC PATH UP TO CASTLE
OBERERWEG
49
To A-48 Autobahn & Bernkastel-Kues

N

100 Meters
100 Yards

and TI, offers helmets with rentals (€8/day, €10/day for mountain bikes, Mon-Fri 9:00-18:00, Sat 9:00-13:00, Sun only April-Oct 10:00-13:00, weekend drop-off possible until 18:00, tel. Ravenéstrasse 18-20, tel. 02671/603-500, www.schaltwerk-bikes.de). The ticket office at the **K-D boat dock** also rents bikes (€8/day, May-Sept daily 9:30-18:00, tel. 02671/980-023).

Sights in Cochem

Cochem Castle (Reichsburg Cochem)—This pretty, pointy castle on a hill above town is the work of overly imaginative 19th-

century restorers. Like many castles along the Rhine and Mosel, Cochem's was blown up by French troops in 1689. For almost two hundred years it stood in ruins—much like Beilstein's—until it caught the attention of Louis Ravené, a rich Berliner who'd made a fortune in the steel industry. He bought the castle dirt-cheap in 1868 and spared no expense in turning it into a luxurious private residence furnished with tasteful antiques. Today, the castle can only be visited on a 40-minute tour (these run frequently throughout the day and are in German only, but guides pass out a helpful English info sheet that makes the visit worthwhile). You'll see seven beautiful rooms, complete with antlers on the wall and hidden doors leading to secret passages. The other 43 rooms are empty, as Ravené's descendants took most of their stuff in 1942 when they were forced to sell the castle to the Nazi government (which then used it as a training center for lawyers). The castle is now owned by the town of Cochem.

Cost and Hours: €5, daily mid-March-mid-Nov, first tour at 9:00, last tour at 17:00, closed mid-Nov-mid-March, café serves lunches, tel. 02671/255, www.reichsburg-cochem.de.

Falcon Show: Below the entrance, the resident falconer frequently shows off his flock—check the notice at the gate to see if the birds are in fine feather (€3.50, 40-minute show, Tue-Sun at 11:00, 13:00, 14:30, and 16:00, no shows Mon, look for *Falknerei* sign, mobile 0160-9912-7380, www.falknerei-reichsburg-cochem.de).

Getting There: *Zur Burg* signs point the way up. From the old town's main square (Markt), with your back to the tower, the quickest way is to **walk** a block straight ahead on Herrenstrasse and then turn right up Schlossstrasse (10- to 15-minute huff and puff). A 25-minute scenic route is to continue along Herrenstrasse, which changes its name to Burgfriedenstrasse and then turns into a path winding up to the castle from behind. Even if you ride up to the castle (explained next), this trail is the best way to walk back down (look for the *Zur Mosel* sign below the castle). If you've already *probed* a little *Wein* and would rather ride up, consider the **shuttle bus** that runs to the castle from the bus station (next to the TI)—though you still have to walk the last five minutes uphill (€2.50 one-way, €4 round-trip, 1-3/hour, May-Oct only, first bus up at 10:30, last bus down at 18:18, look for *Reichsburg Shuttle-Bus* sign at bus station, tel. 02671/7647).

Chairlift and Hikes—For great views, ride the *Sesselbahn* (chairlift), which ascends the hill on the opposite side of town from the castle (€4.30 one-way, €5.80 round-trip, late March-mid-Nov 10:00-18:00, closed off-season, tel. 02671/989-065, www .cochemer-sesselbahn.de). There's a reasonably priced restaurant at the top, along with a short, rocky path that leads to the Pinnerkreuz overlook. Instead of riding to the top, you can scramble up the narrow path under the lift for 20 minutes of heart-pounding, aerobic excitement. Or take the trail up to the same point from behind the train station (find trailhead behind station parking lot). For the best of all worlds, ride the lift up, take in the view from the restaurant, then follow the path to the station *(Bahnhof)*, then down through the forest and then the vineyards to a wine-tasting at Weingut Rademacher.

Wine-Tasting—At **Weingut Rademacher,** behind the train station, you can taste four local wines for €2.90. There's no charge for tasting if you buy at least three bottles or are staying in their rooms (usually open May-Sept Mon and Wed-Sat 10:00-19:30, Tue and Sun 10:00-13:30, different hours during festivals, call ahead to confirm, open by arrangement Oct-April, Pinnerstrasse 10, tel. 02671/4164, www.weingut-rademacher.de; they also rent rooms—see "Sleeping in Cochem," later). Other wine cellars in town also offer tastings. For a unique treat, look for the Roter-Weinbergs-Pfirsich Likör—a local cordial made from the small, tart "red peaches" that are unique to the Mosel Valley.

If you have a car, consider going upriver to the town of **Zell,** famous for its Schwarze Katze ("Black Cat") wine. English-speaking Peter Weis runs **F. J. Weis** winery and gives a clever, entertaining, and free tour of his 40,000-bottle-per-year wine cellar. The tour usually runs daily at 17:00, but it's important to call ahead to reserve a spot. Buying a bottle or two helps keep this fine tour going (open April-mid-Nov daily 10:30-18:00, closed mid-Nov-March except with advance notice, tel. 06542/41398, mobile 0172-780-7153, www.weingut-fjweis.de, f.j.weis@t-online.de). A blue flag marks his *Weinkeller,* south of the town of Zell. It's 200 yards past the bridge toward Bernkastel, riverside at Notenau 30. Peter also rents two luxurious apartments with kitchen facilities (Db-€65, less for 2 or more nights, extra person-€12, breakfast-€7.50).

Swimming, Tennis, and Golf—Cochem's Moselbad and Freizeit Zentrum offers an array of family-friendly activities: an indoor wave pool, an outdoor pool, a sauna, tennis courts, and mini-golf. The downside: It's 30 minutes on foot from the center of town.

Cost and Hours: Indoor pool-€7.70/3 hours, Tue-Fri 10:00-22:00, Sat-Sun 10:00-19:00, closed Mon; other activities have different hours and prices; 10 minutes beyond youth hostel at Moritzburger Strasse 1, tel. 02671/97990, www.moselbad.de.

Cruise—The Kolb Line offers one-hour sightseeing cruises and schmaltzy two-hour "Tanz Party" dancing cruises with live music (see "Getting Around the Mosel Valley—By Boat," page 418).

Sightseeing Train—A little yellow tourist train leaves from under the bridge at the TI and does a 25-minute sightseeing loop through town. Since the commentary is only in German (ask for English flier), and Cochem is such a pedestrian-friendly town anyway, this is worth it only if you're bored and lazy.

Cost and Hours: €5, includes a glass of wine, 1-2/hour, May-Oct daily 10:00-17:00, doesn't run Nov-April.

Sleeping in Cochem

(area code: 02671)

Cochem is a good base for train travelers. Weingut Rademacher is a five-minute walk from the train station; all the other listings are within a 10- to 15-minute walk or a €6 taxi ride. August is very tight on rooms, with various festivals and generally inflated prices. Cochem has no launderette.

$$$ Hotel Lohspeicher, an upscale-rustic hotel just off the main square on a street with tiny steps, is for those willing to pay a bit extra for quality lodgings in the thick of things. Its nine high-ceilinged rooms have modern comforts, and the owner is a gourmet chef (Sb-€65, Db-€90-120, prices depend on room size, includes big breakfast in a fine stone-and-timber room, elevator, free Wi-Fi, fancy restaurant, parking-€8, closed Feb, Obergasse 1, tel. 02671/3976, fax 02671/1772, www.lohspeicher.de, service @lohspeicher.de, Ingo and Birgit).

$$$ Hotel am Hafen, across the bridge from the TI, offers views over the river to Cochem amidst a mellow atmosphere. Some of the 20 rooms have balconies (Sb-€70-85, Db-€85, slightly nicer Db-€108, deluxe Db-€120, €10 less Nov-June or for 2 nights, free Internet access and Wi-Fi, free parking, Uferstrasse 3, tel. 02671/97720, fax 02671/977-227, www.hotel-am-hafen.de,

MOSEL VALLEY

Sleep Code

(€1 = about $1.40, country code: 49)
S = Single, **D** = Double/Twin, **T** = Triple, **Q** = Quad, **b** = bathroom,
s = shower only. Unless otherwise noted, credit cards are accepted, English is spoken, and breakfast is included.

To help you sort easily through these listings, I've divided the accommodations into three categories based on the price for a standard double room with bath:

$$$ Higher Priced—Most rooms €80 or more.
$$ Moderately Priced—Most rooms between €50-80.
$ Lower Priced—Most rooms €50 or less.

Prices can change without notice; verify the hotel's current rates online or by email. For other updates, see www.ricksteves.com/update.

---

hotel-am-hafen.cochem@t-online.de).

$$ Weingut Rademacher rents six ground-floor rooms that share a TV room with a fridge and a microwave. Wedged between vineyards and train tracks, with a pleasant garden, it's a good value. Andrea and her husband Hermann own the vineyards behind the house, and guests are welcome to a free tasting (Sb-€36, Db on train side-€63, Db on quieter vineyard side-€69, cheaper for 3 nights, family deals, non-smoking, no Internet access, free parking; exit station at rear and walk diagonally across the municipal parking lot to Pinnerstrasse 10—see map on website; tel. 02671/4164, fax 02671/91341, www.weingut-rademacher.de, info@weingut-rademacher.de). This place also offers wine-tastings to non-guests (described earlier, under "Sights in Cochem").

$ Haus Andreas has 10 clean rooms at fair prices in the old town (Sb-€25-30, Db-€46-50, Tb-€69-75, lower prices are for at least 2 nights, cash only, no Internet access, free parking, Schlossstrasse 9, reception is often across the street in shop at #16, tel. 02671/1370 or 02671/5155, fax 02671/603-808, www.haus andreas.de, reserve by phone or fax, kind Frau Pellny speaks a little English). From the main square, take Herrenstrasse (go straight if coming from the station); after a block, angle right up the steep hill on Schlossstrasse.

$ Gasthaus zum Fröhlichen Weinberg, also in the old town, is a relaxed jumble of eight inexpensive rooms, some with low ceilings and tiny bathrooms, topped by a fun roof garden with a view over town. It's run by a mother-and-daughter team (Sb-€23.50, Db-€47-51, ask about family rooms, lower prices for longer stays, cash only, on-street parking, lots of stairs, Schlaufstrasse 11, tel.

02671/4193, fax 02671/917-559, www.zum-froehlichen-weinberg
.de, info@zum-froehlichen-weinberg.de). From the main square,
go up Oberbachstrasse (in the far-right corner if coming from the
station) and then left up tiny Schlaufstrasse.

Hostel: Cochem's **$ hostel** is a huge, family-friendly com-
plex just across the river from the train station, with 148 beds,
picnic tables, grill pit, playground, game room, bar, restaurant,
and a sundeck over the Mosel (dorm bed in 4- to 6-bed rooms-
€20, Db-€51, more for nonmembers, includes sheets and breakfast, dinner-€7.50, pay Internet access and Wi-Fi, fills up—reserve
in advance, Klottener Strasse 9, tel. 02671/8633, fax 02671/8568,
www.diejugendherbergen.de/cochem, cochem@diejugendher
bergen.de). From the train station, walk straight down to the river,
turn left, and use the stairway to cross the modern bridge to the
hostel.

Eating in Cochem

Gaststätte Noss is one of several restaurants along the riverside
promenade. It's open later than most and supplies meat from its
own butcher shop—a plus in Germany. Don't confuse it with the
hotel of the same name (€10-14 main courses, cheaper daily specials; Easter-Oct Fri-Wed 10:00-21:30, also open Thu Aug-Sept
only; Nov-Easter Fri-Wed 10:00-15:00 & 17:30-21:30, closed Thu;
Moselpromenade 4, tel. 02671/7067).

Zom Stüffje, in the old town, is a traditional half-timbered
Weinstube with €11-18 main courses and €9 veggie options (Wed-
Mon 11:30-14:30 & 17:30-22:30, closed Tue, Oberbachstrasse 14,
enter on side street, tel. 02671/7260).

Alte Gutschänke, better known as "Arthur's place," is where
locals go for a glass of wine in a cozy cellar. Seating is at long,
wooden, get-to-know-your-neighbor tables (extensive wine list and
very basic pub food, Easter-Oct Tue-Fri from 18:00, Sat-Sun from
14:00, closed Mon and in winter, just uphill from the old town's
Markt square at Schlossstrasse 6, tel. 02671/8950).

Picnics: The **Diewald supermarket** is at Ravenéstrasse 33,
between the train station and TI; enter from the side lane (Mon-
Fri 7:30-20:00, Sat 8:00-18:00, closed Sun).

Cochem Connections

From Cochem by Train to: Moselkern (for hike to Burg Eltz;
hourly, 16 minutes), **Trier** (2/hour, 45-60 minutes), **Frankfurt
Airport** (hourly, 2-2.5 hours, change in Koblenz and sometimes
Mainz), **Köln** (1-2/hour, 1.75-2.25 hours, most change in Koblenz),
Bacharach (hourly, 1.5 hours, change in Koblenz), **Rothenburg**

(every 2 hours, 5 hours, 3-4 changes), **Berlin** (roughly hourly, 7-8 hours, 1-2 changes), **Paris** (best routings roughly every 2 hours, 4-5 hours, with one transfer in Saarbrücken or Luxembourg).

Train info: tel. 0180-599-6633, www.bahn.com. Bus info: tel. 02671/8976, www.vrminfo.de.

Burg Eltz

My favorite castle in all of Europe—worth ▲▲▲—lurks in a mysterious forest. It's been left intact for 700 years and is deco-

rated and furnished throughout much as it was 500 years ago. Thanks to smart diplomacy, clever marriages, and lots of luck, Burg Eltz (pronounced "boorg elts") was never destroyed (it survived one five-year siege). It's been in the Eltz family for 850 years. The scenic 1.5-hour walk up the Elz Valley to the castle makes a great half-day outing if you're staying anywhere along the Mosel—and a worthwhile day trip if you're staying on the Rhine.

Elz is the name of a stream that runs past the castle through a deep valley before emptying into the Mosel. The first record of a *Burg* (castle) on the Elz is from 1157. By about 1490, the castle looked like it does today, with the homes of three big landlord families gathered around a tiny courtyard within one formidable fortification. Today, the excellent 45-minute tour winds you through two of those homes, while the third is still the residence of the castellan (the man who maintains the castle). This is where members of the Eltz family stay when they're not at one of their other feudal holdings. The elderly countess of Eltz—whose family goes back 33 generations here (you'll see a photo of her family)—enjoys flowers. Each week for 40 years, she's had grand arrangements adorn the public castle rooms.

It was a comfortable castle for its day: 80 rooms made cozy by 40 fireplaces and wall-hanging tapestries. Many of its 20 toilets were automatically flushed by a rain drain. The delightful **chapel** is on a lower floor. Even though "no one should live above God," this chapel's placement was acceptable because it filled a bay window, which flooded the delicate Gothic space with light. The three families met—working out common problems as if sharing a condo complex—in the large "conference room." A carved jester and a rose look down on the big table, reminding those who gathered

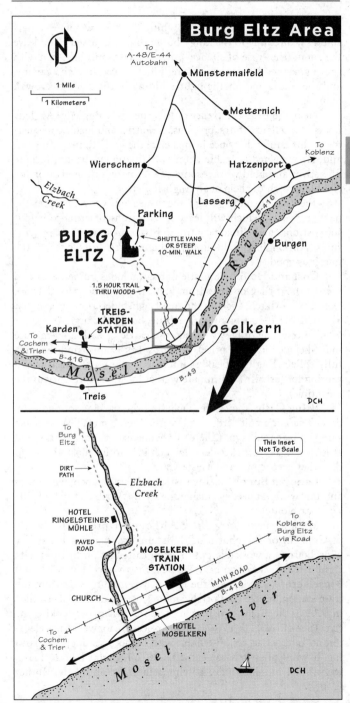

that they were free to discuss anything ("fool's freedom"—jesters could say anything to the king), but nothing discussed could leave the room (the "rose of silence"). In the **bedroom,** have fun with the suggestive decor: the jousting relief carved into the canopy, and the fertile and phallic figures hiding in the lusty green wall paintings.

Near the exit, the **treasury** fills the four higgledy-piggledy floors of a cellar with the precious, eccentric, and historic mementos of this family that once helped elect the Holy Roman Emperor and, later, owned a sizable chunk of Croatia (Habsburg favors). The silver and gold work—some of Germany's best—is worth a close look with the help of an English flier.

The castle is undergoing a much-needed renovation over the next few years, which will leave it with iron corseting to help it stand strong, and climate control to better preserve its many treasures. Although scaffolding mars the majesty of its exterior, the tour is as good as ever.

Cost and Hours: €8 castle entry (includes guided tour and treasury), April-Oct daily from 9:30, last tour departs at 17:30, closed Nov-March. Pick up the free English descriptions at entry. Tel. 02672/950-500, www.burg-eltz.de, burg@eltz.org.

Tours: The only way to see the castle is with a 45-minute tour (included in entry price). Guides speak English and thoughtfully collect English speakers into their own tours—well worth waiting for (usually a 30-minute wait at most; visit treasury in the meantime).

Bring Cash: The castle (including the parking lot and café) doesn't accept credit cards—only cash. There's no ATM, so make sure you bring enough. (There's only one exception: If you spend at least €50 at the ticket desk—which is hard for most visitors to do—they accept Visa and MasterCard.)

Eating at Burg Eltz: The **castle café** serves lunch, with soups and bratwurst-and-fries cuisine for €4-6 (April-Oct daily 9:30-17:30, cash only).

Sleeping near Burg Eltz: Although I prefer the bustle of Cochem or the charm of Beilstein, staying in tiny, sleepy Moselkern is a workable option. You can start off to Burg Eltz right after breakfast to beat the heat on a warm day. **$$ Hotel Moselkern**, set alongside the river a five-minute walk from the train station, has 26 comfortable rooms in a solid, 1970s-era building. All of the rooms have balconies, most of them overlooking the river (Sb-€40-43, Db-€70-76, higher prices are for weekends, elevator, no Internet access, restaurant with outdoor seating, free parking, bowling alley in basement, tel. 02672/1303, fax 02672/913310, www.hotel-moselkern.de, hotelmoselkern@t-online.de, Rother family).

Getting to Burg Eltz

The castle is a pleasant 1.5-hour **walk** from the nearest train station, in the little village of Moselkern—the walk is not only easy, it's the most fun and scenic way to visit the castle.

Alternatively, if the weather is bad, or you prefer not to walk, you can take a **taxi** (or, on summer weekends only, the **bus**) to the castle from the village of Karden (see "By Bus from the Treis-Karden Station," later).

Cars (and taxis) park in a lot near, but not quite at, Burg Eltz. From the lot, hike 10 minutes downhill to the castle or wait (10 minutes at most) for the red castle shuttle bus (€1.50 each way).

Each of your options is explained below.

Hiking from Moselkern

The hike between the Moselkern train station and Burg Eltz runs through a magical pine forest, where sparrows carry crossbows,

and maidens, disguised as falling leaves, whisper "watch out." You can do the hike in 70 minutes at a steady clip, but allow an extra 20 minutes or so to enjoy the scenery. The trail is mostly gentle, except for a few uneven parts that are slippery when wet and the steep flight of stairs leading up to the castle at the end. But the overall rise from the river to the castle is less than 400 feet.

Getting to Moselkern: To start the hike, take the slow milk-run train (hourly) to Moselkern from Cochem (16 minutes, €4.05). If you're returning to Cochem, buy an €8.10 round-trip ticket; groups of at least three can get a €16.40 *Minigruppenkarte* (covers round-trips for up to 5 people, not valid before 9:00 on weekdays). You can also reach Moselkern from towns on the Rhine (including Köln and Bacharach) with a change at Koblenz.

Storing Luggage: The Moselkern train station is unstaffed and has no lockers, phones, or taxis. If you need to store luggage, you can leave it at the Hotel Moselkern, on the river a five-minute walk from the station (see "Sleeping near Burg Eltz," earlier). While there's no charge, consider thanking them by eating at their reasonably priced restaurant (food served Mon-Fri 17:00-22:00, Sat-Sun 11:00-22:00) or buying a drink at the hotel bar.

The Hike: The path up to the castle begins at the other end of Moselkern village from the station. Turn right from the station along Oberstrasse, cross the intersection with Weinbergsstrasse, and continue straight along narrow Oberstrasse. In about five minutes, you'll pass the village church. Keep going straight a few houses past the church; then, as the street ends, turn right through the underpass. On your left is the Elzbach stream that you'll follow all the way up to the castle. Follow the road straight along the stream through a mostly residential neighborhood. Where the road crosses the stream on a stone bridge, take either the footpath (stay right) or the bridge—they join up again later.

After about a 30-minute walk from the train station, the road ends at the parking lot of the Hotel Ringelsteiner Mühle. Stay to the right of the hotel and continue upstream along the easy-to-follow trail, which starts out paved but soon changes to dirt—from here, it's another 45 minutes through the forest to the castle.

Hiking from Karden (with Optional Boat Trip)

If you don't mind a longer hike, consider a boat ride to the village of Karden, then walk to Burg Eltz from there. (Karden is also on the train line between Cochem and Moselkern.) This two-hour hike is steep in places, and harder to follow and less shady than the hike from Moselkern.

Getting to Karden: Kolb Line riverboat cruises run between Cochem and Karden three times a day in midsummer and less frequently in spring and fall (described on page 418). Make sure to get off the boat in Karden (not in Treis, across the river). If you come by train, get off at the Treis-Karden stop, which is in Karden but serves both villages.

Storing Luggage: If you need to store luggage before the hike, the elegant Schloss-Hotel Petry, across from the Treis-Karden station, is happy to guard your bags if you eat at their restaurant (€10-22 main courses, lunch daily 11:30-14:15, St. Castorstrasse 80, tel. 02672/9340, www.schloss-hotel-petry.de).

The Hike: The path from Karden to Burg Eltz starts at the far end of Karden village, beyond the white-towered St. Castor's church (follow *Burg Eltz* signs). Get a trail map (available locally), and be prepared for full sun when the hike travels through open fields.

Shortcuts: To ride the boat but avoid the lengthy hike to Burg Eltz, you can either hop the hourly train from Treis-Karden to Moselkern and take the shorter 1.5-hour hike from there (described earlier); take the bus from the Treis-Karden station straight up to Burg Eltz on weekends (May-Oct only, described next); or take a taxi from Karden to the castle (see later).

By Bus from the Treis-Karden Station

From May through October on Saturdays and Sundays only, bus #330 runs to Burg Eltz from the Treis-Karden railway station (4/day, 35 minutes; leaves Treis-Karden station at 9:15, 11:15, 14:50, and 16:50; returns from Burg Eltz at 10:27, 12:27, 16:07, and 18:07; confirm times at Cochem TI, with bus operator at tel. 02671/8976, or at www.rhein-mosel-bus.de).

By Taxi

You can taxi to the castle from **Cochem** (30 minutes, about €55 one-way for up to 4 people, Cochem taxi tel. 02671/8080), **Moselkern** (€20 one-way, taxi tel. 02672/1407), or **Karden** (€30 one-way, taxi tel. 02672/1407). Remember: Even with a taxi, you'll still have a 10-minute walk from the parking lot to the castle. If you're planning to taxi from Moselkern, call ahead and ask the taxi to meet your train at Moselkern station. Consider taxiing up to Burg Eltz and then enjoying the hike downhill back to the train station in Moselkern.

By Car

Be Careful: Signs direct drivers to two different "Burg Eltz" parking lots—some deceptively take drivers far from the castle, while others get you right there. From Koblenz, leave the river at Hatzenport, following the white *Burg Eltz* signs through the towns of Münstermaifeld and Wierschem. From Cochem, follow the *Münstermaifeld* signs from Moselkern. The castle parking lot (€1.50/day, daily 9:00-18:30) is just over a mile past Wierschem. (Note that the *Eltz* signs at Moselkern lead to Hotel Ringelsteiner Mühle and the trailhead for the hike to the castle—see next. To drive directly to the castle, ignore the *Eltz* signs until you reach Münstermaifeld.)

Drive/Hike Combo: If you're traveling by car but would enjoy walking part of the path from Moselkern up to the castle, drive to Moselkern, follow the *Burg Eltz* signs up the Elz Valley, park at the Hotel Ringelsteiner Mühle (€2, buy ticket from machine), and hike about 45 minutes up the trail to the castle (full hike described earlier).

Shortcut to Beilstein: If driving from Burg Eltz to Beilstein, you'll save 30 minutes with this shortcut: Cross the river at Treis-Karden, go through town, and bear right at the swimming pool (direction: Bruttig-Fankel). This overland route deposits you in Bruttig, a scenic three-mile riverside drive from Beilstein.

Beilstein

Just upstream from Cochem is the quaintest of all Mosel towns. Cozy Beilstein (BILE-shtine) is Cinderella-land—touristy but tranquil, except for its territorial swans. Beilstein has zero food shops, zero ATMs (make sure to bring cash), one bus stop, one mailbox, and 180 residents who run about 30 guest houses and eateries. It's nicknamed the "Sleeping Beauty of the Mosel" because until about 1900, it was inaccessible except by boat. Beilstein has  no TI, but there is an information board by the bus stop, and cafés and guest houses can give you town info.

Planning Your Time

Car travelers use Beilstein as a base, day-tripping from here to Cochem, Trier, Burg Eltz, and the Rhine. If you're staying in Cochem and using public transportation, you can day-trip to Beilstein: Take the bus to Beilstein, follow my self-guided walk up to the castle, have lunch, and then return by boat. While the town is peaceful and a delight in the evening, midday crowds in peak season can trample all its charm and turn it into a human traffic jam. But in the winter (mid-Nov until Easter), Beilstein is dead as a doornail.

Getting to Beilstein

Beilstein has no train station, but it's easy to reach from Cochem— either by **bus** (#716, almost hourly Mon-Fri, 3-4/day on weekends, last buses in both directions leave between 18:30 and 19:00, 20 minutes, €3.15, www.vrminfo.de), by **taxi** (€25), or by one-hour **river cruise** (4-5/day in each direction May-Oct, weekends only in April, no boats off-season, first departure from Cochem at about 10:30, last departure from Beilstein at about 17:30, €11 one-way, €14 round-trip). If **driving,** you can park for free in any space you find along the riverside road.

Self-Guided Walk

Welcome to Beilstein

Explore the narrow lanes, ancient wine cellar, resident swans, and ruined castle by following this short walk.

• *Stand where the village hits the river.*

Beilstein's Riverfront: In 1963, the big road and the Mosel locks were built, making the river peaceful today. Before then, access to Beilstein was limited to a tiny one-way lane and the small ferry. The cables that tether the ferry once allowed the motorless craft to go back and forth, powered only by the current and an angled rudder. Since the river was tamed by locks, it has no current, and the ferry needs its motor. Today, the funky little ferry shuttles people (€1.30), bikes, and cars constantly (Easter-Oct daily 9:00-12:00 & 13:00-18:00, no ferries off-season).

The campground across the river is typical of German campgrounds—nearly all of its residents set up their trailers and tents at Easter and use them as summer homes until October, when the regular floods chase them away for the winter. If you stood where you are now through the winter, you'd have cold water up to your crotch five times.

Look inland. The town was given market rights in 1310 and was essentially an independent city-state for centuries (back when there were 300 such petty kingdoms and dukedoms in what we now call "Germany"). The Earl of Beilstein ruled from his castle above town. He built the Altes Zollhaus in 1634 to levy tolls from river traffic. Today, the castle is a ruin, the last monk at the once-mighty monastery (see the big church high on the left) retired in 2009, and the town's economy is based only on wine and tourists.

Beilstein is so well-preserved because it was essentially inaccessible by road until about 1900. And its tranquility is a result of Germany's WWI loss, which cost the country the regions of Alsace and Lorraine (now part of France, these provinces have flip-flopped between the two nations since the Thirty Years' War). Before World War I, the Koblenz-Trier train line—which connects Lorraine to Germany—was the busiest in the country, tunneling through the grape-laden hill across the river in what was the longest train tunnel in Germany. The construction of a supplemental line designed to follow the riverbank (like the lines that crank up the volume on the Rhine) was stopped in 1914, and since Alsace and Lorraine went to France in 1918, the new line no longer made any sense, and the plans were scuttled.

• *Follow Bachstrasse into town. You'll notice blue plaques on the left marking the high-water* (Hochwasser) *points of historic floods. At the first corner (Weingasse), detour left to a picturesque corner.*

Town Center: In 1840, a quarter of the town's 300 inhabitants were Jewish. The **synagogue** (which dates from 1310) and the adjacent rabbi's home were at #13. The medallion above the door shows the Star of David embedded in the double-headed eagle of the Holy Roman Emperor, indicating that the Jews would be protected by the emperor. This was perhaps of some comfort, but not reliable. Of the town's many Jews, a majority left for the US in the late 1800s. By 1933, only one Jewish family was left in Beilstein to deal with the Nazis. There are no practicing Jews in town today.

• *Continue on this lane uphill, heading right, and then right again, with the church high above. You'll reach a long flight of stairs (marked* Klostertreppe) *that leads to the monastery.*

Although the last Carmelite monk just retired, Rome maintains a handsome but oversized-for-this-little-town **Catholic church** that runs a restaurant with a great view. It's a screwy situation that seems to make locals uncomfortable when you ask them about it.

Continue back to the main street. **Bachstrasse** ("Creek Street") continues straight inland through Beilstein, covering up the brook that once flowed through town, providing a handy disposal service 24/7. Today, Bachstrasse is lined with wine cellars. The only way for a small local vintner to make any decent money these days is to sell his wine directly to customers in inviting little places like these.

• *On the other side of Bachstrasse is the...*

Market Square (Marktplatz): For centuries, neighboring farmers sold their goods on Marktplatz. The *Zehnthaus* (tithe house) was the village IRS, where locals would pay one-tenth *(Zehnte)* of their produce to their landlord (either the Church or the earl). Pop into the **Zehnthauskeller.** Stuffed with peasants' offerings 400 years ago, it's now packed with vaulted medieval ambience. It's fun at night for candlelit wine-tasting, soup and cold cuts, and schmaltzy music (often live Fri and Sat). The adjacent **Bürgerhaus** (above the fountain) had nothing to do with medieval fast food. First the village church, then the residence of the *Bürger* (like a mayor), and later the communal oven and the village grade school, today it's *the* place for a town party or wedding (upstairs) and a venue for local craftspeople to show their goodies (below). **Haus Lipmann** (on the riverside, now a recommended hotel and restaurant) dates from 1727. It was built by the earl's family as a residence after the French destroyed his castle. Haus Lipmann's main dining hall was once the knights' hall.

• *The stepped lane leads uphill (past the Zehnthaus, follow signs for* Burgruine Metternich) *to...*

Beilstein's Castle: Beilstein once rivaled Cochem as the most powerful town on this part of the Mosel. Like so much around here, it was destroyed by the French in 1688. Its castle (officially named Burg Metternich) is a sorry ruin today, but those who make the steep 10-minute climb are rewarded with a postcard Mosel view and a chance to hike even higher to the top of its lone surviving tower (€2.50, Easter-Oct daily 9:00-18:00, last entry 30 minutes before closing, closed Nov-Easter, view café/restaurant, tel. 02673/93639, www.burgmetternich.de).

For more exercise and an even better **viewpoint,** exit through the turnstile at the rear of the castle and continue uphill 100

yards, where you'll find the ultimate "castle/river bend/carpets of vineyards" photo op. The derelict roadside vineyard is a sign of recent times—the younger generation is abandoning the family plots, opting out of all that hard winemaking work.

From this viewpoint, a surprising sight is 200 yards farther up the road: a small but evocative **Jewish cemetery** *(Jüdische Friedhof).* The Jewish community in Koblenz maintains this lovely burial ground.

To reach the viewpoint and the cemetery without going through the castle, continue up the road past the castle entrance, then follow the signs for *Jüdische Friedhof.*

• *From here, you can return to the castle gate, ring the bell* (Klingel), *and show your ticket to get back in and retrace your steps; or continue on the road, which curves and leads downhill (a gravel path at the next bend on the left leads back into town).*

Activities in Beilstein

Biking and Boating—Boats come and go all day for extremely relaxing river trips (for details, see page 418). While scenic, these rides can take longer than you'd like because of the locks. I prefer a riverside bike ride (perhaps combined with a boat trip). Biking is very popular along the Mosel, and roads are accompanied by smooth and perfectly flat bike lanes. The lanes are separate from the car traffic, letting you really relax as you pedal through gorgeous riverside scenery. To rent a quality bike in Beilstein, visit **Herr Nahlen** (€7/day, April-Oct daily 9:00-12:00, return bikes between 16:00 and 19:00, no rentals Nov-March, reservations smart for groups, Bachstrasse 47, tel. 02673/1840, www.fahrrad verleih-in-beilstein.de).

Five-Hour Trip to Zell and Back: You could rent a bike in Beilstein, catch the 9:30 boat to Zell (2.5-hour ride), enjoy that pretty town, and cycle 15 miles back to Beilstein along the sleepy and windy riverside bike path.

Hour-and-a-Half Loop: For a shorter bike trip, ride the little ferry across the river from Beilstein, explore the campground, continue left past Poltersdorf, cycle under vineyards to Senhals, cross the bridge to Senheim, and return to Beilstein on the other side of the river. At the edge of Mesenich, leave the road and take the peaceful bike lane along the river, explore another campground, and head for Beilstein, with its castle in the distance encouraging you home.

Sleeping in Beilstein

(€1 = about $1.40, country code: 49, area code: 02673)
Many of Beilstein's hotels shut down from mid-November until Easter; the Gasthaus Winzerschenke an der Klostertreppe is the only one of my listings that stays open during the winter (and then only on weekends).

$$$ Hotel Haus Lipmann is your chance to live in a medieval mansion with hot showers and TVs. A prizewinner for atmosphere, it's been in the Lipmann family for 200 years. The creaky wooden staircase and the elegant dining hall, with long wooden tables surrounded by antlers, chandeliers, and feudal weapons, will get you in the mood for your castle sightseeing, but the riverside terrace may mace your momentum. There are six guest rooms in the main building and six larger rooms in an equally old building next door. The entire family—Marion (née Lipmann) and her husband Jonas Thölén, their hardworking son David, and his wife Anja—hustle for their guests (Db-€100-120, usually €20 higher Fri-Sat, higher prices are for Mosel views, discount for 2 or more nights, extra bed-€30, family deals, cash only, €15 half-board—sensible here, free Internet access and Wi-Fi, closed Nov-April, Marktplatz 3, tel. 02673/1573, fax 02673/1521, www.hotel-haus-lipmann.com, hotel.haus.lipmann@t-online.de).

$$$ Hotel Lipmann Am Klosterberg, run by Marion's brother Joachim and his wife Marlene, is a big, modern place with 17 comfortable rooms at the extremely quiet top of town (Sb-€55, Db-€75-95, closed mid-Nov-Easter, elevator, free Wi-Fi, free parking, Auf dem Teich 8, up the main street 200 yards inland, tel. 02673/1850, fax 02673/1287, www.hotel-lipmann.de, lipmann@t-online.de).

$$$ Hotel Lipmann Altes Zollhaus, run by Joachim Lipmann's daughter Julia, packs all the comforts into eight tight, bright riverfront rooms (same prices and contact details as Hotel Lipmann Am Klosterberg, free Wi-Fi, free on-street parking). The adjoining Alte Stadtmauer restaurant is run by Joachim's daughter Kristina (Wed-Mon 11:00-23:00, closed Tue and mid-Nov-Easter).

The welcoming **$$ Gasthaus Winzerschenke an der Klostertreppe** is a great value, with five rooms right in the tiny heart of town at the bottom of the stairs to the cloister (Db-€55, bigger Db-€65, cash only, discount for 4-night stays, open weekends only Nov-Easter, free Internet access, go up main street and take second left onto Fürst-Metternich-Strasse, reception in restaurant, tel. 02673/1354, fax 02673/962-371, www.winzerschenke-beilstein.de, winzerschenke-beilstein@t-online.de, young and eager Stefanie and Christian Sausen).

$$ Hotel Gute Quelle offers half-timbers, a good restaurant, and 13 inviting rooms, plus 7 more in an annex across the street (Sb-€42, Db-€72, less if staying 4 nights, closed Dec-March, free Wi-Fi, Marktplatz 34, tel. 02673/1437, fax 02673/1399, www.hotel -gute-quelle.de, info@hotel-gute-quelle.de, helpful Susan speaks Irish).

Eating in Beilstein

You'll have no problem in Beilstein finding a characteristic dining room or a relaxing riverview terrace.

Restaurant Haus Lipmann serves good, fresh food with daily specials on a glorious, leafy riverside terrace. For a wonderful trip memory, enjoy a slow meal here while watching the lazy riverside action and the changing light on the distant vineyards (€8-19 main courses, May-Oct daily 10:00-23:00, last meal order at 20:00, closed Nov-April).

The **Zehnthauskeller** on the Marktplatz is *the* place for wine-tasting, a light meal, and lively *Schlager* music (kitschy German folk-pop). Hang with old locals on holiday, sitting under a dark medieval vault (soup, *Flammkuchen*—German version of white pizza, €9-11 cold plates, Easter-Oct Tue-Sun 11:00-23:00, closed Mon and Nov-Easter, run by Joachim Lipmann's daughter Sabine).

The recommended **Hotel Gute Quelle** runs a popular restaurant (€11-17 main courses, €9-10 daily specials, daily 11:00-21:00, closed Dec-March, Marktplatz 34).

TRIER

Germany's oldest city lies at the head of the scenic Mosel Valley, near the border with Luxembourg. An ancient Roman capital, Trier brags that it was inhabited by Celts for 1,300 years before Rome even existed. Today, Trier is thriving and feels very young. A short stop here offers you a look at Germany's oldest Christian church, one of its most enjoyable market squares, and its best Roman ruins.

Founded by Augustus in 16 B.C., Trier (pronounced "treer") was a Roman town called Augusta Treverorum for 400 years. When Emperor Diocletian (who ruled A.D. 285-305) divided his overextended Roman Empire into four sectors, he made Trier the capital of the west: roughly modern-day Germany, France, Spain, and England. For most of the fourth century, this city of 80,000—with a four-mile wall, four great gates, and 47 round towers—was a favored residence of Roman emperors. Emperor Constantine lived here, spending lavishly on urban projects. As a military town in a godforsaken corner of the empire, Trier received lots of perks from Rome to make it livable for those assigned here. But when the last emperor checked out in A.D. 395, the money pretty much dried up, and that was the end of Trier's ancient glory days. In the late 400s, when Rome fell to the barbarians, so did Trier.

Roman Trier was much bigger than medieval Trier. The pedestrian center of town—containing nearly all of your sightseeing and browsing—is defined by the medieval wall (which encloses only half the area the Roman wall did). Trier's Roman sights include the huge city gate (Porta Nigra), basilica, baths, and amphitheater.

Trier's main draw is the chance to experience Germany's

Roman and early Christian history. If you're more interested in wine-tasting and scenery, stay elsewhere on the Mosel River (see previous chapter).

Orientation to Trier

(area code: 0651)

Tourist Information

Trier's cramped and busy TI is just through the Porta Nigra. The TI sells an easily readable map for €1.50, but cheapskates can squint at the free and sufficient small-print map. The TI also sells a useful little guide to the city called *Trier: History and Monuments* (€4). Also consider the booklet *Walking Tours Through Trier* (€3), which has little information on sights but a great map and proposed walking routes (Roman, medieval, Jewish, rainy day). The TI also offers tours (see "Tours in Trier," later) and a free room-booking service (May-Oct Mon-Sat 9:00-18:00, Sun 10:00-17:00; Nov-Dec and March-April Mon-Sat 9:00-18:00, Sun 10:00-15:00; Jan-Feb Mon-Sat 9:00-17:00, Sun 10:00-13:00; tel. 0651/978-080, www.trier-info.de).

Discount Deals: The **Antique Card** can save you a few euros. The €9 version covers the Archaeological Museum (otherwise €6) and any two of Trier's four Roman sights (Porta Nigra, Imperial Baths, Viehmarkt Baths, and amphitheater—otherwise €3 each). The €14 version covers the museum and all four Roman sights (available at TI and participating sights). The **Trier Card** allows free use of city buses and roughly 25 percent discounts on city tours, museums, and Roman sights, but isn't worth it if you're staying in the center of this small, walkable town (€9, family-€19, valid 3 days, sold at TI).

Arrival in Trier

By Train: The *Reisezentrum* at the train station can answer your train-schedule questions and book tickets (Mon-Fri 6:50-19:15, Sat 8:30-17:15, Sun 10:30-18:15). The station also has lockers (€1.50-2.50), a WC (€0.50, coins only), and bike rental (see "Helpful Hints," later). To reach the town center from the train station, walk 10 boring minutes and four blocks up Theodor-Heuss-Allee to the big black Roman gate (Porta Nigra), and turn left under the gate to

Trier

TRIER

To Luxembourg & Köln

To Koblenz & Saarbrücken

BOAT DOCK

1. Hotel/Rest. zum Christophel
2. Hotel Römischer Kaiser
3. Astoria Hotel
4. Warsberger Hof Hostel/ Restaurant & Eateries
5. Hotel Vinum
6. Hotel Pieper
7. Hotel Petrisberg Trier
8. Zum Domstein Restaurant
9. Zeitsprung Café
10. Krim Restaurant
11. Launderette
12. Internet Café
13. Karstadt Supermarket

SELF-GUIDED WALK

A. Porta Nigra
B. House of the Three Magi
C. Market Square
D. Cathedral
E. Bishop's Museum
F. Basilica/Imperial Throne Room
G. Archaeological Museum
H. Imperial Baths
I. Amphitheater

Mosel River

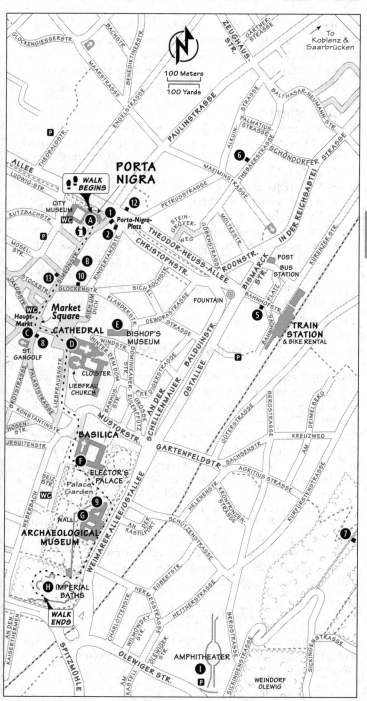

find the TI. From here, the main pedestrian mall (Simeonstrasse) leads right to the sights: Market Square and the cathedral (a five-minute walk), and the basilica (five more minutes).

By Car: Drivers get off at Trier Verteilerkreis and follow signs to *Zentrum.* There's parking near the gate and TI.

Helpful Hints

Internet Access: Arcor/ITS-Trier, across the busy intersection from the Porta Nigra, charges a low hourly rate (€1/hour, Mon-Fri 10:00-22:00, Sat-Sun 12:00-22:00, Porta Nigra Platz 4).

Laundry: A well-maintained self-service launderette is just beyond Karl Marx's House (€7.50/load, daily 8:00-22:00, instructions in English, Brückenstrasse 19).

Bike Rental: A local citizens' group called **Bürgerservice** rents bikes for reasonable daily rates. Find them just off track 10 at the train station (€10/24 hours, spiffy 27-gear bikes-€2 extra, show ID and leave €30 as deposit; mid-April-Oct daily 9:00-13:00 & 15:00-18:00; Nov-mid-April Mon-Fri 10:00-13:00 & 15:00-18:00, closed Sat-Sun; tel. 0651/148-856, www.bues -trier.de).

Tours in Trier

Walking Tours—The TI offers a €7.50 two-hour walking tour in English on Saturdays at 13:30 (May-Oct only) and can put you in touch with local guides who do private tours (€80/2 hours, tel. 0651/978-0821).

Bus Tours—For a live guide and a big air-conditioned bus, take the one-hour tour offered by the TI (€7.50, May-Oct daily at 13:00 in English, at 11:00 and 12:00 in German, no tours Nov-April).

Tourist Train—If you're tired and want a city overview, consider riding the hokey little red-and-yellow tourist train, the Römer-Express, for its 35-minute loop of Trier's major old-town sights (€7, daily April-Oct 2/hour 10:00-18:00, daily March and Nov-Dec hourly 10:00-17:00, Jan-Feb may run Sat-Sun hourly 11:00-16:00—weather permitting, recorded narration in English, departs from TI, buy tickets from driver or at TI, tel. 0651/9935-9525, www.roemer-express.de).

Sights in Trier

I've laced together the historic city's top sights on this fascinating walk, offering a taste of Trier old, new, and in-between.

• *Start at the...*

▲Porta Nigra

Roman Trier was built as a capital. Its architecture mirrored the grandeur of the empire. Of the four-mile town wall's four huge

gates, only this northern gate survives. This is the most impressive Roman fortification in Germany, and it was built without mortar—only iron pegs hold the sandstone blocks together. While the other three gates were destroyed by medieval metal and stone scavengers, this "black gate" (originally lighter sandstone, but darkened by time) survived because it became a church. St. Simeon—a pious Greek recluse—lived inside the gate for seven years. After his death in 1035, the St. Simeon monastery was established, and the Roman gate was made into a two-story church—lay church on the bottom, monastery church on top. The 12th-century Romanesque apse—the round part at the east end—survives. You can climb around inside the gate, but there's little to see other than a fine town view. You can enter through the adjacent City Museum (described below). As you go in, look for pictures of how the gate looked during various eras, including its church phase.

Cost and Hours: €3, €6 for both Porta Nigra and City Museum, daily April-Sept 9:00-18:00, March and Oct 9:00-17:00, Nov-Feb 9:00-16:00, last entry 30 minutes before closing, www.trier-info.de.

Nearby: The remaining arcaded courtyard and buildings of the monastery of St. Simeon, next to the Porta Nigra, are now home to the TI and a **City Museum** (Stadtmuseum Simeonstift). The museum's collection seems to be largely made up of anything old that turned up in townspeople's basements, and most of the items on display are only mildly interesting. The third level, however, holds a fascinating model—painstakingly constructed over 19 years—of Trier as it looked in 1800 (€5, includes audioguide, €6 combo-ticket with Porta Nigra, Tue-Sun 10:00-18:00, closed Mon, tel. 0651/718-1459, www.museum-trier.de).

The busy road beyond the Porta Nigra follows what was a dry moat outside the Roman wall. In the 19th century, Trier's wealthy built their mansions along this belle époque promenade. Today, it's a people's park lined with fine old buildings, interrupted by newer construction where WWII bombs hit.

• *Trier's main pedestrian drag, which leads from the gate into the town center, is named for St. Simeon. As you walk to Market Square, you'll follow the main north-south axis of the grid-planned Roman town. The small pink house (on the left, at #8, next to pharmacy) was where Karl*

Marx lived for 17 years—nearly his entire childhood. (Marx enthusiasts can visit a museum in the house where he was born, described on page 455.) Farther down Simeonstrasse, on your left at #19, is the...

House of the Three Magi (Dreikönigenhaus)

Now a restaurant, this colorful Venetian-style building was constructed in the 13th century as a keep. Before the age of safe banking, rich men hoarded their gold and silver inside their homes... and everyone knew it. Understandably paranoid, they needed fortified houses like this one. Look for the floating door a story above the present-day entrance. A wooden staircase to this door—once the only way in or out—could be pulled up when necessary.

• *Continue down the pedestrian street. As you walk, ignore street-level storefronts—instead, look up to appreciate the variety and richness of the town's architecture. Eventually you'll reach the...*

▲▲Market Square (Hauptmarkt)

Trier's Hauptmarkt is a people-filled swirl of fruit stands, flowers, painted facades, and fountains (plus stairs down to a handy public WC). This is one of Germany's most in-love-with-life market squares.

For an orientation to the sights, go to the square's centerpiece, a market cross, and stand on the side of the cross closest to the big gray-stone **cathedral** a block away. This cathedral (described later in more detail) was the seat of the archbishop. In medieval times, the cathedral was its own walled city, and the archbishop of Trier was one of the seven German electors who chose the Holy Roman Emperor. This gave the archbishop tremendous political, as well as spiritual, power.

The pink-and-white building (now an H&M clothing store) on the corner of the lane leading to the cathedral was a **palace** for the archbishop. Notice the seal above the door: a crown flanked by a crosier (representing the bishop's ecclesiastical power) and a sword (demonstrating his political might). This did not sit well with the townspeople of Trier. The square you're standing in was the symbolic battlefield of a centuries-long conflict between Trier's citizens and its archbishop.

The stone market **cross** (a replica of the A.D. 958 original, now in the City Museum) was the archbishop's way of bragging about the trading rights granted to him by King Otto the Great. This was a slap in the face to Trier's townspeople. They'd wanted Trier to be designated a "free imperial city," with full trading rights and beholden only to the Holy Roman Emperor, not a local prince or archbishop.

Look across the square. Facing the cathedral is the 15th-century **Town Hall** (Steipe). The people of Trier wanted a town hall, but the archbishop wouldn't allow it—so they built this "assembly hall" instead, with a knight on each second-story corner. The knight on the left, facing Market Square, has his mask up, watching over his people. The other knight, facing the cathedral and the archbishop, has his mask down and his hand on his sword, ready for battle.

Just below the knights are four brightly painted 16th-century statues of Christian figures nestled between the arches (right to left): St. Paul, with his sword, was patron saint of Trier's university in the 15th century. St. Peter, with his bushy beard and key, is the patron saint of Trier. St. Helena, Emperor Constantine's mom and a devout Christian, lived in Trier and brought many super relics here from the Holy Land, giving the town lasting importance. And St. James, with his staff and scallop shell, is the patron saint of pilgrims—a reminder that Trier was the staging point for northern European pilgrims heading south on the spiritual trek to Santiago de Compostela (in northwest Spain).

Elsewhere on the square are more indications of tension between the archbishop and the townsfolk. Look to the left, at the tall white steeple with yellow trim. This is the Gothic tower of the **Church of St. Gangolf,** the medieval townspeople's church and fire watchman's post. (From medieval times until the present day, a bell has rung nightly at 22:00, reminding drunks to go home. When the automatic bell-ringer broke a few years back, concerned locals flooded the mayor with calls.) In 1507, Trier's mayor built this new Gothic tower to make the people's church higher than the cathedral. A Bible verse in Latin adorns the top in gold letters: "Stay awake and pray." In retaliation, the archbishop raised one tower of his cathedral (all he could afford). He topped it with a threatening message of his own, continuing the Town Hall's verse: "For you never know the hour when the Lord will come."

Look farther to the left, to the Renaissance **St. Peter's Fountain** (1595). This fountain symbolizes thoughtful city government, with allegorical statues of justice (sword and scale), fortitude (broken column), temperance (wine and water), and prudence (a snake and, formerly, a mirror—but since the mirror was stolen long ago, she's now empty-handed). The ladies represent idealized cardinal virtues—but notice the rude monkeys hiding on the column behind them, showing the naughty way things are really done. The recommended **Zum Domstein** restaurant is next to the fountain (described later, under "Eating in Trier").

The rest of the square is a textbook of architectural styles.

Look for the Art Deco hotel that now houses a McDonald's (forced to keep its presence low-key). The half-timbered houses at the north end of the square (toward the Porta Nigra) mark Trier's 14th-century Jewish ghetto. Judengasse ("Jews' Alley") led under these facades into a gated ghetto where 60 families earned enough from moneylending to buy protection from the arch-bishop. But the protection only went so far—in 1418 Trier's Jews were expelled. (They tried to collect interest owed them by the prince, but rather than pay up, he sent them packing.) The build-ings lining Judengasse today, while quaint, date only from the 18th century.

• *When you're finished on the square, head down Sternstrasse to the...*

▲▲Cathedral (Dom)

This is the oldest Christian church in Germany. After Emperor Constantine legalized Christianity in the Roman Empire in A.D. 312, his mother, Helena (now a saint), allowed part of her pal-ace in Trier to be used as the first church on this spot. In A.D. 326, to celebrate the 20th anniversary of his reign, Constantine began the construction of two great churches: St. Peter's in Rome and this huge cathedral in Trier—also called St. Peter's.

Cost and Hours: Cathedral—free, daily April-Oct 6:30-18:00, Nov-March 6:30-17:30. Treasury—€1.50, April-Oct and Dec Mon-Sat 10:00-17:00, Sun 12:30-17:00; Nov and Jan-March Mon-Sat 11:00-16:00, Sun 12:30-16:00.

Information: The Dom Information Office (on the square facing the church) runs a gift shop, has a handy WC (€0.50), and provides services for Santiago de Compostela-bound pilgrims (April-Oct and Dec Mon-Sat 9:30-17:30, Sun 12:00-17:30; Nov and Jan-March Mon-Fri 9:30-17:30, Sat 9:30-14:00, closed Sun; tel. 0651/979-0790, www.trierer-dom.de).

❷ **Self-Guided Tour:** Begin your visit in the cathedral's large front **courtyard.** As you face the cathedral, look in the cor-ner behind you and to your left (near the pink palace); you'll see a large patch of light-colored bricks in an L shape in the ground. The original Roman cathedral was more than four times its present size; these light-colored bricks mark one corner of this massive "double cathedral." (The opposite corner was at the back of the smaller Liebfrau church, waaay across the courtyard.) The plaque by the corner shows the floor plan of the original Roman cathedral (from A.D. 380).

The cathedral's mighty **facade** is 12th-century Romanesque. To the right is the more delicate 13th-century Gothic facade of the Liebfrau church (which dates from 1235 and claims to be the oldest Gothic church in Germany).

As you walk toward the cathedral entrance, you'll pass an evocative bit of Roman scrap stone (just outside the door on the left). This was part of a 60-ton ancient granite column quarried near Frankfurt—one of four columns used in the fourth-century Roman church.

Enter the cathedral (€0.50 English info brochure in racks on right). The many **altars** lining the nave are dedicated not to saints, but to bishops. These ornate funeral altars were a fashionable way for the powerful archbishop-electors to memorialize themselves. Even the elaborate black-and-white altar at the back of the church (above where you entered) is not a religious shrine, but a memorial for a single rich archbishop. (His black 1354 tomb dominates the center of that chapel.)

The "pilgrim's walk" (the stairway to the right of the altar) leads to the chapel at the far east end of the church that holds the cathedral's most important relic: the supposed **Holy Robe of Christ,** thought to have been found by St. Helena on a pilgrimage to Jerusalem (rarely on view, but you can see its reliquary; look for photos of the robe itself as you approach, after the first flight of stairs).

Midway along the "pilgrim's walk," you'll find the entrance to the **treasury** *(Schatzkammer),* displaying huge bishops' rings, medieval Bibles, St. Andrew's sandal (in a box topped with a golden foot), and a holy nail supposedly from the Crucifixion. At the base of the steps below the treasury, pause and look back up at the statues of St. Helena and Emperor Constantine.

Down the stairs, the door on your immediate left marked *Kreuzgang* leads to the peaceful 12th-century Domkreuzgang cloister between the Dom and the Liebfrau church.

A door from inside the cathedral leads to the adjoining **Liebfrau Church,** which claims to be the oldest Gothic church in Germany (it dates from 1235). This church was built when Gothic was in vogue, so French architects were brought in—and paid with money borrowed from the bishop of Köln when funds ran dry. The church was recently renovated and is filled with colorful, modern stained glass.

When you're ready to leave the cathedral, head back toward the main door, where you'll see two controversially modern (1972) paintings at the back of the church, representing the Alpha (Paradise/Creation, to the left) and the Omega (the Last Judgment, to the right). The archbishop pushed this artwork through, arguing that a living church needs contemporary art, and overriding objections from the congregation's conservative old guard.

Once outside the cathedral, go right, then turn down the first street on your right (Windstrasse). As you walk with the cathedral on your right, you'll be able to see the different **eras of its construction.** The big red cube that makes up the back half of the present-day cathedral is all that remains of the enormous, original fourth-century Roman construction (at one time twice as tall as what you see here). Arched bricks in the facade show the original position of Roman windows and doors. Around this Roman nucleus, chunks were grafted on over a millennium and a half of architectural styles: the front half of the cathedral facing the big courtyard, added in the 11th century; the choir on the back, from the 12th century; and the transept and round Baroque shrine on the far back, from the 18th century.

If you look at the original Roman construction squarely, you'll see that it's not perfectly vertical. Locks were built along the Mosel River in the 1960s, depleting groundwater—which was the only thing preserving the church's original wooden foundation. When dry, the foundation disintegrated, and the walls began to settle. Architects competed to find a way to prevent the cathedral from collapsing. The winning solution: a huge steel bracket above the main nave, holding the walls up with cables.

• *Just past the cathedral on Windstrasse (to the left) is the...*

▲Bishop's Museum (Bischöfliches Diözesanmuseum)

This museum focuses on the history of the cathedral. Its highlight is the pieced-together remains of exquisite ceiling frescoes from St. Helena's palace. The vivid reds, greens, and blues of the restored works depict frolicking cupids, bejeweled women, and a philosopher clutching his scroll. The 15 panels are displayed in such a way that you feel mysteriously transported back to when they were made, in A.D. 320. The frescoes were discovered in 50,000 pieces while cleaning up from WWII bombs. Incredibly, with the help of computers (and using patterns from the wattle-and-daub work on the back sides of the pieces), the jigsaw puzzle was put back together. There are no English descriptions, but you can—and should—borrow the book in English that explains the frescoes and their restoration (also on sale for €3.60). Elsewhere in this small, modern museum, you'll see an interesting model of the original Roman church, stone capitals, gold chalices, vestments, and icons.

Cost and Hours: €3.50; June-March Tue-Sat 9:00-17:00, Sun 13:00-17:00; April-May Tue-Sat 10:00-17:00, Sun 13:00-

17:00; Windstrasse 6, tel. 0651/710-5255, www.museum.bistum
-trier.de.

• *Return to the front of the cathedral and head two blocks south (passing the Liebfrau Church, under an arch capped by a crucifixion scene—
indicating that you're leaving the archbishop's walled ecclesiastical city).
Bear left on An der Meerkatz, to the 200-foot-by-100-foot...*

▲▲Basilica/Imperial Throne Room (Konstantin Basilica)

This building is the largest intact Roman structure outside of

Rome. It's best known as a basilica, but
it actually started out as a throne room.
The last emperor moved out in A.D. 395,
and petty kings set up camp in the building throughout the Middle Ages. By the
12th century, the archbishops had taken
it over, using the nave as a courtyard
and converting the apse into a five-story
palace. The building became a Lutheran
church in 1856, and it remains the leading
Protestant church in Trier. It was badly
damaged by WWII bombs (as illustrated by photographs at the
cashier's desk), and later restored.

Cost and Hours: Free, €2.50 *Basilica of Trier* English booklet brings the near-empty shell to life; April-Oct Mon-Sat 10:00-
18:00, Sun 12:00-18:00; Nov-March Tue-Sat 11:00-12:00 &
15:00-16:00, Sun 12:00-13:00, closed Mon; tel. 0651/209-0040,
www.konstantin-basilika.de.

Touring the Basilica: Standing inside the vast structure, you
see the genius of Roman engineering. Notice the 65-foot-wide
round arch over the apse. The small rectangular holes between the
windows were chimneys, which vented the hot air that circulated
below the floor, heating the place. It's a huge expanse to span without columns. Each of the squares in the ceiling above you measures 10 feet by 10 feet—as big as your hotel room. While today's
roof cheats, using concrete girders, the Roman original was all
wood, relying on triangular trusses above the flat ceiling. Today's
windows match the Roman originals—small frosted panes held in
place by a wooden frame. The place is enormous. (A little model in
the back near the entry shows the Porta Nigra fitting comfortably
inside this building.)

Picture this throne room in ancient times, decorated with
golden mosaics, rich marble, colorful stucco, and busts of
Constantine and his family filling the seven niches. The emperor
sat in majesty under a canopy on his altar-like throne. The windows in the apse around him were smaller than the ones along the

TRIER

side walls, making his throne seem even bigger.

Posters along the far wall (with English text) give a full run-down on the building's history, including artist reconstructions that help you envision how the basilica was used through the ages.

Nearby: A pink Rococo wing, the Elector's Palace, was added to the basilica in the 18th century to house the archbishop-elector; today, it houses local government offices (closed to the public).

• *The Rococo wing faces a fragrant, picnic-riffic garden. Beyond the garden are three more sights: the Archaeological Museum (with a handy cafe for lunch—see "Eating in Trier," later), the remains of a Roman bath, and a 16,000-seat Roman amphitheater. Cut across the garden toward Weimarer Strasse (the main street in the distance) and veer right, passing through the medieval city wall to the entrance of the...*

▲▲Archaeological Museum (Rheinisches Landesmuseum)

This is clearly Trier's top museum, with arguably the best collection of Roman art in Germany. The museum tells the town's story from prehistoric times to today. The best pieces are all from the Roman period, including funeral art, mosaics, coins, and a fine model of Roman Trier.

Cost and Hours: €6, Tue-Sun 10:00-17:00, closed Mon, tel. 0651/97740, www.landesmuseum-trier.de. Get a map as you enter, and pick up the free English audioguide in the museum shop. Brief English overviews are posted in each room.

❯ Self-Guided Tour: *Rundgang* signs guide you through the museum's 19 exhibition rooms in a logical order. I'll focus just on the museum's most important collections.

Start by walking down the round staircase and out to the gaudy copy of a **Roman funerary monument** in the courtyard. (The original still stands in a nearby Mosel River Valley village.) You'll see more funerary monuments like this in a minute. For pagan Roman big shots, the closest thing to eternal life was to be remembered after they died. Consequently, those who could afford it erected big memorials to their own lives and accomplishments along the road leading into Trier. When Roman Trier went Christian in A.D. 320, these pagan ideals were no longer respected. The memorials were scavenged for their stones, which were then used as a foundation for a nearby fortress and forgotten. In 1890, a resident of the modern village sitting on the ruins of that Roman fortress dug up one of these stones, the museum paid a handsome price for it, and everyone in the village went wild digging up old Roman stones to cash in.

From here, go down to basement level and through three rooms of displays on prehistoric Trier, then back up and through two rooms on the Romanization of the area's Celtic population.

In Room 6, a big room at the back of the courtyard, find the rich collection of **funerary art;** originally these were all painted like the courtyard replica. Browse around, finding glimpses of everyday Roman life: the tax collector at work, the boys with their Latin teacher, a woman visiting a beauty salon, and a ship laden with barrels of Mosel wine. Behind the wine ship, a wall painting shows how the mausoleum-lined road into Roman Trier might have looked. Archeologists have learned a lot about life in this corner of the Roman Empire by studying these artifacts.

The **Roman mosaics** in Room 8 (just beyond the wine ship) are another highlight. On one wall is a mosaic of four horses surrounding the superstar charioteer Polydus, discovered intact at the Imperial Baths. Mosaic floors were the *Sports Illustrated* covers of the Roman world.

Room 11 displays a **map** showing Trier's position in the Roman Empire. You can see how Gaul (roughly modern France) was divided into three parts, with Trier in the northern ("Belgian") section. Roads led from Trier south toward Rome via modern-day Lyon and Marseille.

Upstairs, in Room 12, don't miss the huge **model** of Roman Trier—a thriving city of 80,000. Notice the grid street plan, and pick out the sights you're visiting today: Porta Nigra, the cathedral, basilica, baths, and amphitheater.

Back down a flight, in the small, darkened Room 13, is an exhibit of **coins** through the centuries of Roman rule. In 1993, some Trier construction workers dug up a bag holding 2,600 golden Roman coins; the coins are in the central display case. Experts used the emperor's face on each coin to date the finds. Look closely and you can follow the steady progression of emperors and their coins from Nero (54 B.C.) to Septimius Severus (A.D. 211). It's impressive that 250 years of coinage were in circulation when this bag was lost.

Finally, Rooms 15-16 show how medieval Trier was built on the ruins of the Roman town. A model lets you see how the Porta Nigra looked as a church.

• *Exit the Archaeological Museum, walk right (paralleling the main Weimarer Strasse through the trees), then follow the* Tourist Route *signs through the archway in the wall to the modern, red-brick entry arcade of the...*

Imperial Baths (Kaiserthermen)

Built by Constantine, these were destined to be the biggest of Trier's three Roman baths and the most intricate baths of the Roman world. Trier's cold northern climate, the size of the complex, and the enormity of Constantine's ego meant that these Imperial Baths required a two-story subterranean complex of pipes, furnaces, and slave galleys to keep the water at a perfect 47 degrees Celsius (120 degrees Fahrenheit). But the grandiose vision was never finished. When Constantine left Trier in A.D. 316, the huge and already costly project was scuttled. Later the site was used as a military barracks. The giant courtyard—originally

for exercising and lounging—became a parade ground for the Praetorian Guard.

Stepping into the unfinished building section, you can imagine the intended pools (cold, tepid, and hot) and the heated floor. Thirty years of construction left nearly a mile of underground tunnels and foundation work, which are fun to explore. Imagine the engineering, slave labor, and wood that would have been necessary to make all this work, if it had ever been completed. A literal river of water was planned to flow into the baths via an aqueduct. And the surrounding land would ultimately have been deforested as it supplied enough wood to keep the ovens going to heat the water.

Cost and Hours: €3, daily April-Sept 9:00-18:00, March and Oct 9:00-17:00, Nov-Feb 9:00-16:00, good €2.50 English booklet, tel. 0651/436-2550, www.trier-info.de.

• *To finish your tour of Trier's Roman sights, hike from the baths about 10 minutes farther to the amphitheater. If you're beat, you can skip it (just look at amphitheater photos in shop postcard racks), head back to Market Square, and enjoy the town.*

To reach the amphitheater, follow the signs through the pedestrian underpass, then follow Hermesstrasse as it curves up the hill, and then turn left on Olewigerstrasse.

Amphitheater

Roman Trier's amphitheater, built around A.D. 200, seated at least 16,000. The city was largely inhabited by Celts who learned Latin and wanted to adopt the Roman lifestyle. And any self-respecting Roman town needed an amphitheater. While Trier's amphitheater had some gore, the scene here wasn't Roman degenerates egging on gladiators—it was more often used for less-bloody spectacles, assemblies, and religious festivals.

You'll enter where grand processions did. To tour the site, follow the crude little map you'll get with your ticket, which sends you left up the hill to a handy illustrated diagram of ancient Trier that helps put the amphitheater into context with the city. After enjoying this best high vantage point, walk away from the amphitheater around back, circling down and left. Enter the amphitheater through one of its grand entries (called vomitoria, these were named for the way crowds could spew out quickly after events). Then descend a staircase in the center of the amphitheater into the cellar, where gear for the spectacles was kept (and which is below the water table—so it's always wet). After Rome fell, the amphitheater was used as a refuge from barbarian attacks, a quarry, and a vineyard.

Cost and Hours: €3, daily April-Sept 9:00-18:00, March and Oct 9:00-17:00, Nov-Feb 9:00-16:00, tel. 0651/73010, www.trier-info.de.

More Sights in Trier

Karl Marx's House—Communists can lick their wounds at Karl Marx's birthplace, a 1727 house with two floors of exhibits in

German. While the influential economist/philosopher is a fascinating and important figure, this place has almost no historic artifacts. Visiting this "museum" is like reading a book in a foreign language, while standing up. The included English audioguide gives more meaning to the displays, but even that is pretty tedious.

Cost and Hours: €3, includes audioguide and free brochure; April-Oct daily 10:00-18:00; Nov-March Tue-Sun 11:00-17:00, Mon 14:00-17:00; from Market Square follow signs for 10 minutes to Brückenstrasse 10, tel. 0651/970-680, www.fes.de/Karl-Marx-Haus.

Viehmarkt Baths Museum—A beautiful modern glass building covers the ruins of a Roman bath, mixed with stone monastery foundations and medieval waste-wells. It's certainly historic, but almost meaningless unless you have a good guide and a freakish interest in Roman stones. You can see nearly everything without paying just by looking in from the entry and through the many windows. The best thing about going here is walking down Fahrstrasse to the museum—a block away, you'll pass a cool fountain showing Trier craftsmen at work.

Cost and Hours: €3, Tue-Sun 9:00-17:00, closed Mon, Viehmarktplatz, tel. 0651/994-1057, www.trier-info.de.

Sleeping in Trier

I've listed prices for high season; rates drop from November through February or March. All hotels in Trier charge a city tax of €1.07 per person per day, which normally isn't included in quoted rates.

Sleep Code

(€1 = about $1.40, country code: 49, area code: 0651)

S = Single, **D** = Double/Twin, **T** = Triple, **Q** = Quad, **b** = bathroom, **s** = shower only. Unless otherwise noted, credit cards are accepted, English is spoken, and breakfast is included.

To help you sort easily through these listings, I've divided the accommodations into three categories, based on the price for a standard double room with bath:

$$$ Higher Priced—Most rooms €90 or more.
 $$ Moderately Priced—Most rooms between €55-90.
  $ Lower Priced—Most rooms €55 or less.

Prices can change without notice; verify the hotel's current rates online or by email. For other updates, see www.ricksteves.com/update.

Near the Porta Nigra

$$$ Hotel zum Christophel offers top comfort in its 11 classy rooms next to the Porta Nigra, above a fine restaurant and with a kind owner. It's an easy roll from the train station with your luggage (Sb-€60-75, Db-€85-99; price varies with room size, season, and day of week; elevator, free Wi-Fi, parking-€5/day, Am Porta Nigra Platz 1, tel. 0651/979-4200, fax 0651/840-8410, www.zumchristophel.de, info@zumchristophel.de).

$$$ Hotel Römischer Kaiser, next door, is also nice, but a lesser value—charging more for a polished lobby and 43 comparable rooms (Sb-€72-82, Db-€98-108, Tb-€130; price varies with season—most expensive in May, Sept-Oct, and during festivals; family rooms, elevator, free Wi-Fi, free parking, Am Porta Nigra Platz 6, tel. 0651/977-0100, fax 0651/9770-1999, www.friedrich-hotels.de, rezeption@friedrich-hotels.de).

$$ Astoria Hotel, three blocks beyond the Porta Nigra when coming from the train station, is a 15-room family-run place. Rooms are colorfully decorated, and there's a rosy terrace outside the breakfast room (Sb-€58-62, Db-€79-88, lower prices are for weekdays, cheaper Nov-March, no elevator, free Wi-Fi, parking-€5/day, Bruchhausenstrasse 4, tel. 0651/978-350, fax 0651/41121, www.astoria-hotel.de, info@astoria-hotel.de, American-born Paula and her husband Sudhir like to offer guests a welcome drink).

Near Market Square

$ Warsberger Hof, run by a local Catholic citizens' league, is a clean, simple hostel and budget hotel two blocks from Market

Square, with 168 beds and an inexpensive restaurant. This is your best value for cheap sleeps in town (€21.50/bed in 3- to 6-bed dorms, includes sheets, S-€26-28, D-€47-51, T-€71, Q-€86-94, showers down the hall, breakfast-€5.80, pay Internet access, limited free parking in courtyard, Dietrichstrasse 42, tel. 0651/975-250, fax 0651/975-2540, www.warsberger-hof.de, info@warsberger -hof.de).

Near the Train Station

$$$ Hotel Vinum, with 29 rooms directly across from the train station, is owned and run by the Lutheran Church and has a wine theme (all guests get a free bottle). It's slightly overpriced, but freshly remodeled and convenient, if you can look past the gambling and strip clubs around the square (Sb-€54-64, Db-€85-105, price depends on room size, non-smoking, elevator, free Wi-Fi, parking-€7.50/day, Bahnhofsplatz 7, tel. 0651/994-740, fax 0651/9947-4222, www.hotelvinum.de, info@hotelvinum.de).

$$ Hotel Pieper, a good value, is run by the friendly Becker family (he cooks and she keeps the books). They rent 20 comfortable rooms furnished with dark wood over a pleasant neighborhood restaurant (Sb-€48, Db-€78, Tb-€115, free Wi-Fi, free garage parking; 8-minute walk from station, 2 blocks off main drag at Thebäerstrasse 39; tel. 0651/23008, fax 0651/12839, www.hotel -pieper-trier.de, info@hotel-pieper-trier.de). From the station, follow Theodor-Heuss-Allee (toward Porta Nigra) to the second big intersection, angle right onto Göbenstrasse, and continue as the road curves and becomes Thebäerstrasse.

Outside the Center

$$$ Hotel Petrisberg Trier, up a steep road behind the amphitheater, is top-quality, reasonably priced, and ideal if you have a car. It's on a hillside overlooking the city, exuding old-school elegance without being stuffy. The Pantenburg family takes great care to spoil all their guests; Helmut whips up tasty egg breakfasts, while his niece Christina—the 2001 Trier Wine Queen—works reception. A pleasant footpath brings you downhill to the cathedral in 20 minutes (35 rooms, Sb-€75, Db-€105, family rooms, non-smoking, free Internet access and Wi-Fi, free parking, taxi from train station-€8, Sickingenstrasse 11-13, tel. 0651/4640, fax 0651/46450, www.hotel-petrisberg.de, info@hotel-petrisberg.de).

Eating in Trier

Zum Domstein, right on Market Square, serves standard German fare at decent prices and also has a special, pricier menu of dishes based on ancient Roman recipes. The Roman menu was inspired during renovations, when the owner discovered a Roman column in her cellar. (In Trier, you can't put a rec room in your basement without tripping over Roman ruins.) The finished cellar dining room incorporates the column, plus a mini-museum of Roman crockery (€10-20 main courses, €10-12 lunch specials, daily 8:30-24:00, last orders at 22:30, Roman dishes served in cellar 18:00-21:00, Am Hauptmarkt 5, tel. 0651/74490).

Zeitsprung Café, at the rear of the Archaeological Museum building, has good-value lunches and salads in a pretty setting overlooking the Elector's Palace and fountain (€7-10 main courses and daily specials, April-Sept Tue-Sun 9:30-19:00, Oct-March Tue-Sun 9:30-18:00 except closed first 2 weeks of Jan, closed Mon year-round, outdoor seating, Weimarer Allee 1, tel. 0651/994-5820).

At **Krim,** just off Market Square, young locals enjoy trendy Mediterranean cuisine (€10-17 main courses, €6-8 lunch specials, Mon-Sat 9:00-24:00, Sun 10:00-24:00, Glockenstrasse 7, tel. 0651/73943).

The recommended **Warsberger Hof hostel** runs three inexpensive eateries in the big yellow pastel building a few doors down Dietrichstrasse from Market Square: the Leonardy pub and café (Mon-Sat 11:30-15:00 & 17:00-24:00, closed Sun); the Rautenstrauch restaurant (€12-17 main courses, Mon-Sat 11:30-14:00 & 18:00-22:00, Sun 11:30-14:00, nice enclosed terrace, kid-friendly); and the **Kasino** self-service cafeteria, serving cheap lunches (Mon-Fri 11:30-14:15, closed Sat-Sun).

The recommended **Hotel zum Christophel** also has a reasonably priced restaurant with a view of the Porta Nigra (€11-18 main courses, daily 11:00-22:00, Am Porta Nigra Platz).

Picnics: One of several supermarkets in the center is in the basement of the Karstadt department store on Simeonstrasse (open Mon-Sat 9:00-20:00, closed Sun).

Trier Connections

From Trier by Train to: Cochem (2/hour, 45-60 minutes), **Köln** (at least hourly, 2.5-3 hours, some change in Koblenz), **St. Goar/Bacharach** (hourly, 2.5 hours, change in Koblenz), **Frankfurt Airport** (hourly, 3 hours, change in Koblenz and sometimes Mainz), **Paris** (roughly hourly, 3-3.5 hours, best with change in Saarbrücken or Luxembourg). Train info: tel. 0180-599-6633, www.bahn.com.

KÖLN
and the UNROMANTIC RHINE

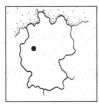

Romance isn't everything. Köln ("Cologne" in English) is an urban Jacuzzi that keeps the Rhine churning. It's home to Germany's greatest Gothic cathedral and its best collection of Roman artifacts, a world-class art museum, and a healthy dose of German urban playfulness.

Peaceful Bonn, which offers good people-watching and fun pedestrian streets, used to be the capital of West Germany. The small town of Remagen had a bridge that helped defeat Hitler in World War II, and unassuming Aachen, near the Belgian border, was once the capital of Europe.

Köln

Germany's fourth-largest city, Köln (pronounced "kurln") has a compact, lively center. The Rhine was the northern boundary of the Roman Empire, and, 1,700 years ago, Constantine—the first Christian emperor—made what was

then called "Colonia" the seat of a bishopric. (Five hundred years later, under Charlemagne, Köln became the seat of an archbishopric.) With 40,000 people within its walls, Köln was the largest German city and an important cultural and religious center throughout the Middle Ages. Today, the city is most famous for its toilet water: Eau de Cologne was first made here by an Italian chemist in 1709.

During World War II, bombs destroyed 95 percent of Köln—driving its population from 800,000 down to an estimated 30,000 at its lowest ebb. But with the end of the war, the city immediately began putting itself back together (the population rebounded to about 400,000 by Christmas of 1945). Today, it's a bustling commercial and cultural center that still respects its rich past.

Planning Your Time

Köln makes an ideal on-the-way stop; it's a major rail junction, and its top sights are clustered near the train station. With a couple of hours, you can toss your bag in a locker, take my self-guided town walk, zip through the cathedral, and make it back to the station for your train. If you're planning that short of a stop, make sure you'll be here when the whole church is open (in between its services—times are listed on page 467). More time (or an overnight) allows you to delve into a few of the city's fine museums and take in an old-time beer pub.

Orientation to Köln

(area code: 0221)

Köln's core was bombed out, then rebuilt in mostly modern styles with a sprinkling of quaint. The city has two areas that matter to visitors: One is the section right around the train station and cathedral. Here you'll find most sights, all my recommended hotels, plus the TI and plenty of eateries and services. Hohe Strasse, Köln's pedestrian shopping street, begins near the cathedral. The other area—called the "old town"—is between the river and the Alter Markt, a few blocks to the south. After the war, this section was chosen to be rebuilt in the old style, and today pubs and music clubs pack the restored buildings.

Tourist Information

Köln's energetic TI, opposite the cathedral entrance, has a basic €0.20 city map and can find you a room (Mon-Sat 9:00-20:00, Sun 10:00-17:00, Kardinal-Höffner-Platz 1, tel. 0221/2213-0400, www.koelntourismus.de).

Arrival in Köln

Köln couldn't be easier to visit—its three important sights cluster within two blocks of the TI and train station. This super pedestrian zone is a constant carnival of people.

By Train: Köln's busy train station has everything you need: drugstore, bookstore, food court, juice bar, grocery store, pricey

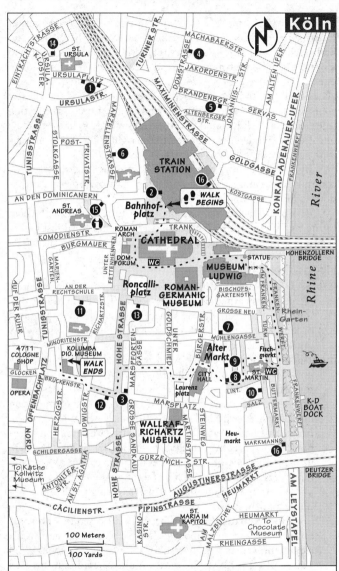

Köln

KÖLN

1. Classic Hotel Harmonie & Hotel Cristall
2. Hotel Ibis Köln am Dom
3. Hotel Engelbertz
4. Hotel Domstern
5. Hotel Müller
6. Station Hostel
7. Peters Brauhaus
8. Gaffel Haus Restaurant
9. Papa Joe's Klimperkasten Pub
10. Papa Joe's Jazzlokal
11. Holtmann's im MAK Café
12. Café Eigel
13. Früh am Dom Beer Hall
14. Schreckenskammer Beer Hall
15. Internet Café
16. Bike Rentals (2)

24-hour "McClean" WC (€1) with showers (€7), travel center (*Reisezentrum*, Mon-Fri 6:00-22:00, Sat-Sun 7:00-21:00), and high-tech lockers (€2.50/2 hours, €5/24 hours, accepts coins and €5 and €10 bills, put money in and wait 30 seconds for door to open, your luggage—up to four pieces—is transferred to storage via an underground conveyor belt and retrieved when you re-insert your ticket; next to *Reisezentrum*). Exiting the front of the station (the end near track 1), you'll find yourself smack-dab in the shadow of the cathedral. Up the steps and to the right is the main entrance to the cathedral (TI across street).

By Car: If you drive to Köln, follow signs to *Zentrum,* then continue to the huge Parkhaus am Dom pay lot under the cathedral (€1.80/hour, €18/day).

By Boat: If you're arriving on a K-D Line boat, exit the boat to the right, then walk along the waterside park until just before the train bridge, when the cathedral comes into view on the left.

Helpful Hints

Closed Day: Note that most museums are closed on Monday (though the cathedral remains open). The cathedral is off-limits to sightseers during services, which are more frequent on Sundays. For information on Köln's museums, visit www .museenkoeln.de.

Sightseeing Discount Cards: Köln has two different cards, only one of which is worth considering. The **MuseumCard** is valid for two consecutive days (or a Sunday and Tuesday, as museums close Monday). It covers all local public transportation on the first day and includes the Roman-Germanic Museum, Museum Ludwig, and Wallraf-Richartz Museum, plus several lesser museums (but not the cathedral sights). If you're visiting all three of these museums, this card will save you money (€15/person, or €28 for a family pass—includes 2 adults and 2 kids up to 18, available at participating museums, www .museenkoeln.de).

The **WelcomeCard,** offering small discounts on some museums, is a waste of money; though it covers the city's transit system, you can easily reach the top sights on foot (€9/24 hours, €16/2 cards, €23/3 cards; multiple cards can be used consecutively by individuals or concurrently by groups, www .koelntourismus.de).

Festivals: Though **Carnival** is celebrated all over Germany, Köln's celebration is famously exuberant. Join the locals as they dress up, feast, and exchange *Bützje*—innocent pursed-lip kisses. Festivities start on the Thursday before Ash Wednesday and culminate with a huge parade on the following Monday ("Rose Monday," or *Rosenmontag*, February 20 in 2012). The parade draws musicians from all over Germany, and families line the parade route to grab the thousands of pieces of candy tossed off the floats (www.koelnerkarneval.de). Köln's **Lichter Festival** lights up the sky in July with fireworks, music, and lots of boats on the river (July 14 in 2012, get details from TI or at www.koelner-lichter.de).

Internet Access: Consider **Via Phone Internet Café,** a block from the station at Marzellenstrasse 3-5 (€2.50/hour, also sells cheap phone cards, Mon-Sat 9:30-24:00, Sun 11:00-24:00, tel. 0221/1399-6200).

Bike Rental: Convenient rental is available at friendly **Radstation,** tucked under the train-track arcade (€5/3 hours, €10/day, Mon-Fri 5:30-22:30, Sat 6:30-20:00, Sun 8:00-20:00; from the station, exit out the back by track 11 to Breslauer Platz, turn right, and cross street; tel. 0221/139-7190, www.radstation koeln.de). You can also rent bikes from the riverside **Kölner Fahrradverleih,** a 10-minute walk from the station (€2/hour, €10/day, April-Oct daily 10:00-18:00, on Markmannsgasse, 100 yards upstream from K-D Line docks, mobile 0171-629-8796). Consider biking the path along the Rhine River up past the convention center *(Messe)* to the Rheinpark for a picnic. Or consider a guided bike tour (described under "Tours in Köln," next).

Tours in Köln

Walking Tours—An English-language walking tour leaves from the TI on Saturdays at 11:30 (€10, www.koelntourismus.de).

Bus Tours—The TI sells tickets and is the departure point for hop-on, hop-off city bus tours (€15) and standard 1.5-hour bus tours offered by three competing companies (€12, departures at least hourly in summer; most have recorded commentary in both German and English, but one company, Stadtrundfahrten, has live guides every 2 hours—see www.cityfahrten.de).

Bike Tours—Kölner Fahrradverleih (listed earlier, under "Bike Rental") offers German/English guided bike tours of the city (€15, 3-3.5 hours, daily April-Oct at 13:30, rain poncho provided just in case, about 10 people per guide, reservations recommended, mobile 0171-629-8796, www.koelnerfahrradverleih.de).

Self-Guided Walk

▲▲Welcome to Köln

Köln lends itself to a fine orientation walk. The old town, towering cathedral, and most of the sights cluster near the train station. Starting at the train station, this walk takes less than an hour and provides a good introduction.

Bahnhofsvorplatz: Stepping out of the train station, you're confronted with a modern hodgepodge of post-WWII architecture and the towering icon of Köln, its cathedral. The city feels rebuilt—because it was. The Allies bombed Köln hard in retaliation for Germany's bombing of London. Your gaze is grabbed by the cathedral. While it was built according to the original 13th-century plans, and the left (east) part was completed in the 13th century, the right half wasn't built until after German unification, in the 1880s.

• *Climb the steps and circle right, to the people-filled square facing the cathedral.*

Cathedral Plaza (Roncalli Platz): In centuries past, a clutter of half-timbered huts crowded around the cathedral. They were all

cleared out in the late 1800s so the great building would have a suitable approach.

This has been a busy commercial zone since ancient times. The Roman arch was discovered nearby and set up here as a reminder of the town's Roman roots. This north gate of the Roman city, from A.D. 50, marks the start of Köln's nearly 2,000-year-old main shopping street, Hohe Strasse.

Look for the life-size replica tip of a spire. The real thing is 515 feet above you. The cathedral facade, while finished in the 1880s, is exactly what was envisioned by the original church planners in 1280. (For more on the cathedral, see page 467.)

• *Continue around the right side of the church, passing modern buildings and public spaces. Step up to the window of the Roman-Germanic Museum to see a...*

Roman Mosaic: Through the Roman-Germanic Museum's generous window, you can get a free look at the museum's prize piece—a fine mosaic floor. Once the dining-room floor of a rich Roman merchant, this is actually in its original position (the museum was built around it). It shows scenes from the life of Dionysus...wine, women, and song, Roman-style. The mosaic is quite sexy, with several scenes showing a satyr seducing and ultimately disrobing a half-goddess, half-human maenad. First he offers her grapes, then he turns on the music. After further wining and dining—all with an agenda—the horny satyr finally scores. The cupid on a lion's back symbolizes the triumph of physical love.

The mosaic is at the original Roman street level. The tall

monument above and left of the mosaic is the mausoleum of a first-century Roman army officer. Directly across from you (at eye level, beyond the mosaic) are beautifully carved stone reliefs—an indication of what a fine city Roman Köln must have been. If you'd like to visit the Roman-Germanic Museum's good collection, see page 473.

• *Walk 20 steps beyond the mosaic farther along the cathedral and look down to see the...*

Cathedral Workshop: Any church of this size is a work in progress. There is constant renovation, repairs, and care. Sandstone blocks are stacked and waiting to be shaped and plugged in wherever needed. The buttresses above are the church's showiest, because they face the bishop's palace, city center, and original entrance (south transept). For 500 years, the church was left unfinished, simply capped off midway. You're facing the functional part of church, where services were held from the 1300s until the late 1800s.

• *From the cathedral, walk past the Museum Ludwig (described on page 473, and with a convenient WC in the lobby) and toward the river.*

Riverfront: The statue (to your left) honors Kaiser Wilhelm II, who paid for the Hohenzollernbrücke (named after his family)—the busiest railway bridge in the world (30 trains an hour all day long). A classic Industrial Age design from around 1900, the bridge was destroyed in World War II and rebuilt in its original style. Stairs lead down to a people-friendly riverside park. This is urban planning from the 1970s: Real and forward-looking. The riverside, once a noisy highway, is now a peaceful park. All that traffic still courses through the city, but flows unnoticed, below you in a tunnel. A bike-and-pedestrian path follows the riverside in each direction, and families let their children frolic in the fountain.

Turn right, walking away from the bridge, to a small square in front of the Romanesque church tower. (Köln's famous chocolate museum, described on page 474, is a five-minute walk farther downstream.) Notice a strip of sockets for a metal flood wall (on the inland side of the grassy stretch; an eight-foot-high structure can be erected here when needed). Locals see a definite change in climate here: They say that "floods of the century" now happen every decade, thunderstorms are 10 times more prevalent, and for the first time, this part of Europe has witnessed little tornadoes.

Fish Market Square and "Old Town": At the foot of Great St. Martin Church, this tiny square—once the fish market—faces the river. Fish Market Square is ringed by medieval-looking buildings from the 1930s. In the early 20th century, Köln's entire old town was a scruffy, half-timbered, prostitute-ridden slum. To the disgusted Nazis, prostitutes were human dirt. Their vision for old towns all over Germany: Clear out the clutter, boot the riffraff,

KÖLN

and rebuild in the clean, tidy, stone-and-stucco style you see here. After World War II, Köln decided to rebuild in a faux-medieval style to approximate what had once been. This square and the streets around the church are from that period.

• *From the church door, a passageway leads away from the river directly to Alter Markt (Old Market Square).*

Alter Markt and City Hall: The ornate City Hall tower symbolized civic spirit standing strong against the power of the bishops in the 15th century. (The square's a mess today because of subway construction.) Circle around the tower to see the City Hall's fine Renaissance porch—the only historic facade left standing after the 1945 bombings. Its carvings stress civic independence. The busts of emperors bring to mind Köln's strong Roman past; the lions symbolize the evil aspect of church authority. Above the door, the mayor kills the lion (thus establishing independence from church government for his city). This scene is flanked by Biblical parallels: the angel saving Daniel from the lions (on right), and Samson fighting lions (on left). Beware of flying rice—the City Hall is often busy with civil wedding parties (Mon-Sat).

• *From the City Hall, pass through Laurenzplatz and walk two blocks farther away from the river to Hohe Strasse.*

Shopping, Church Art, and Eau de Cologne: Jog left onto the town's busy pedestrian shopping street. **Hohe Strasse** thrived during the Middle Ages, when Köln was a major player in the heavyweight Hanseatic League of northern European merchant towns. The street was rebuilt after its complete destruction in World War II and was the first pedestrian shopping mall in Germany. Today it's a rather soulless string of chain stores—most interesting for its seas of shoppers (the big MediaMarkt electronics store, Germany's version of Best Buy, is ahead on the left).

Now take your first right on Brückenstrasse to the modern white building, set atop the ruins of a bombed-out Gothic church. This is the **Kolumba Diocesan Museum** (described on page 472). Inside, from the corner, you can grab a free peek at what was the church interior.

Across busy Tunisstrasse stands Köln's circa-1960s Opera House (a big deal in Germany when built). And across the street from that, on the right, is a historic building at **Glockengasse** 4. When Köln's houses were renumbered in a single series during the Napoleonic era in 1796, this building was given the number 4711—which the perfume-making firm based here later adopted as its trademark. There's a shop on the ground floor with Cologne water running in a fountain by the door—sample this year's new fragrances for free at the counter. Just up the stairs is a small, free exhibit (Mon-Fri 9:30-18:30, Sat 9:30-18:00, closed Sun, tel. 0221/2709-9910, www.glockengasse.de).

Sights in Köln

▲▲▲Köln's Cathedral (Dom)

The Gothic Dom—Germany's most exciting church—looms immediately up from the train station in one of Germany's starkest

juxtapositions of the modern and the medieval. The church is so big and so important that it has its own information office, the Domforum, in a separate building across the street (described on page 472, under "More Cathedral Sights").

Cost and Hours: Free, open daily May-Oct 6:00-21:00, Nov-April 6:00-19:30—but tourist visits are not permitted during services (generally Mon-Sat at 6:30, 7:15, 8:00, 9:00, 12:00, and 18:30; Sun at 7:00, 8:00, 9:00, 10:00, 12:00, 17:00, and 19:00; confirm times at Domforum office or www.koelner-dom.de).

Tours: The one-hour English-only tours are reliably excellent (€6, Mon-Sat at 10:30 and 14:30, Sun at 14:30, meet inside front door of Dom, tel. 0221/9258-4730). Your tour ticket also gives you free entry to the 20-minute English video in the Domforum directly following the tour.

➋ Self-Guided Tour: If you don't take the guided tour, follow this seven-stop walk (note that stops 3-7 are closed off during confession Sat 14:00-18:00, and any time services are under way).

➊ Cathedral Exterior: The cathedral—the most ambitious Gothic building project north of France in the 13th century—was stalled in the Middle Ages and not finished until 1880. Even though most of it was built in the 19th century, it's still technically a Gothic church (not "Neo-Gothic") because it was finished according to its original plans.

• *Step inside the church. Grab a pew in the center of the nave.*

➋ Nave: If you feel small, that's because you're supposed to. The 140-foot-tall ceiling reminds us of our place in the vast scheme of things. Lots of stained glass—enough to cover three football fields—fills the church with light, representing God.

The church was begun in 1248. The choir—the lofty area from the center altar to the far end ahead of you—was inaugurated in 1322. Later,

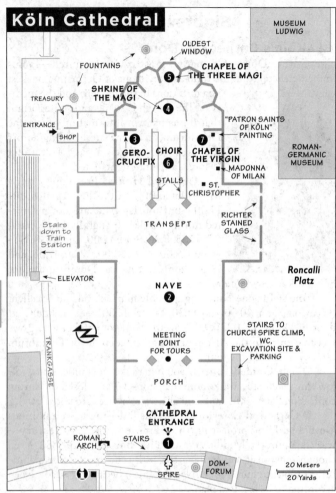

Köln Cathedral

during the tumultuous wars of religious reformation, Catholic pilgrims stopped coming. This dried up funds, and eventually construction stopped. For 300 years, the finished end of the church was walled off and functioned as a church, while the unfinished nave (where you now sit) waited. For centuries, the symbol of Köln's skyline was a huge crane that sat atop the unfinished west spire.

With the rise of German patriotism in the early 1800s, Köln became a symbol of German unity. And the Prussians—the movers and shakers behind German unity—mistakenly considered Gothic (which actually originated in France) a German style. They paid for the speedy completion of this gloriously Gothic German church. With nearly 700 workers going at full speed, the church was finished in just 38 years (1842-1880). The great train station was built in the shadow of the cathedral's towering spire.

The glass windows at the east end of the church (in the chapels and high above) are medieval. The glass surrounding you in

the nave is not as old, but it's precious nevertheless. The glass on the left is early Renaissance. Notice the many coats of arms, which depict the lineage of the donors. One of these windows would have cost as much as two large townhouses. The glass on the right—a gift from Ludwig I, grandfather of the "Mad" King Ludwig who built the fairy-tale castles—is 19th-century Bavarian. Compare both the colors and the realism of the faces between the windows to see how techniques advanced and tastes changed over the centuries.

While 95 percent of Köln was destroyed by WWII bombs, the cathedral held up fairly well. (It was hit by 15 bombs, but the skeletal Gothic structure flexed, and it remained standing.) In anticipation of the bombing, the glass and art treasures were taken to shelters and saved.

The "swallow's nest" organ above you was installed to celebrate the cathedral's 750th birthday in 1998. Attaching it to the wall would have compromised the cathedral's architectural integrity, so the organ is actually suspended from precarious-looking steel wires.

The guys in the red robes are cathedral cops, called *Schweizer* (after the Swiss guard at the Vatican); if a service is getting ready to start, they hustle tourists out (but you can stay for the service if you like).

• *Leave the nave by stepping through the gate on the left, into the oldest part of the church. As you enter, look down.*

This 19th-century mosaic shows a saint holding the Carolingian Cathedral, which stood on this spot for several centuries before this one was built.

❸ Gero-Crucifix: Ahead of you on the left, the Chapel of the Cross features the oldest surviving monumental crucifix from north of the Alps. Carved in the 970s with a sensitivity that was 300 years ahead of its time, it shows Jesus not suffering and not triumphant—but with eyes closed...dead. He paid

KÖLN

the price for our sins. It's quite a twofer: great art and powerful theology in one. The cathedral has three big pilgrim stops: this crucifix, the Shrine of the Magi, and the *Madonna of Milan*.

• *Continue to the front end of the church, stopping to look at the big golden reliquary in the glass case behind the high altar.*

❹ **Shrine of the Magi:** Relics were a big deal in the Middle Ages. Köln's acquisition of the bones of the Three Kings in the 12th century put it on the pilgrimage map and brought in enough money to justify the construction of this magnificent place. By some stretch of medieval Christian logic, these relics also justified the secular power of the German king. This reliquary, made in about 1200 of gilded silver, jewels, and enamel, is the biggest and most splendid I've seen. On the long sides, Old Testament prophets line the bottom, and 12 New Testament apostles—with a wingless angel in the center—line the top. The front looks like three stacked coffins, showing scenes of Christ's flagellation, Crucifixion, and Resurrection.

Inside sit the bones of the Magi...three skulls with golden crowns. So what's the big deal about these three kings (of Christmas-carol fame)? They were the first to recognize Jesus as the Savior and the first to come as pilgrims to worship him—inspiring medieval pilgrims and countless pilgrims since. For a thousand years, a theme of this cathedral has been that life is a pilgrimage...a search for God.

• *Opposite the shrine, at the far-east end of the church, is the...*

❺ **Chapel of the Three Magi:** The center chapel, at the church's far end, is the oldest. It also features the church's oldest window (center, from 1265). The design is typical: a strip of Old Testament scenes on the left with a theologically and visually parallel strip of New Testament scenes on the right (such as, on bottom panels: to the left, the birth of Eve; to the right, the birth of Mary with her mother Anne on the bed).

Later glass windows (which you saw lining the nave) were made from panes of clear glass that were painted and glazed. This medieval window, however, is actually colored glass, which is assembled like a mosaic. It was very expensive. The size was limited to what pilgrim donations could support. Notice the plain, budget design higher up.

• *Peek into the center zone between the high altar and the carved wooden central stalls. (You can't usually get inside, unless you take the tour.)*

❻ **Choir:** The choir is surrounded by 13th- and 14th-century art with carved oak stalls, frescoed walls, statues painted as they would have been, and original stained glass high above. Study the fanciful oak carvings. The woman cutting the man's hair is a Samson-and-Delilah warning to the sexist men of the early Church.

• *The nearby chapel holds one of the most precious paintings of the important Gothic School of Köln.*

❼ **Chapel of the Virgin:** *The Patron Saints of Köln* was painted around 1440, probably by Stefan Lochner. Notice the photo-graphic realism and believable

depth. There are literally doz-ens of identifiable herbs in the grassy foreground. During the 19th century, the city fought to move the painting to a museum. The Church went to court to keep it. The judge ruled that it could stay in the cathedral—as long as a Mass was said before it every day. For more than a hundred years, that happened at 18:30. Now, 21st-century comfort has trumped 19th-century law: In winter, services take place in the warmer Sacrament Chapel instead. (If you like this painting, you'll enjoy the many other fine works from the School of Köln at the Wallraf-Richartz Museum—see page 473.)

Overlooking the same chapel (between the windows), the delicate *Madonna of Milan* sculpture (1290), associated with mir-acles, was a focus of pilgrims for centuries. Its colors, scepter, and crown were likely added during a restoration in 1900. The reclining medieval knight in the cage at the back of the chapel (just before the gate) is a wealthy but childless patron who donated his entire county to the cathedral.

As you head for the exit, look into the transept on your left. The stained-glass windows above you are a random and abstract pattern of 80 colors, "sampled" from the church's more-historic windows. The local artist Gerhard Richter designed these win-dows to create a "harmony of colors" in 2007.

Before leaving, look above the tomb with the cage and find the statue of St. Christopher (with Jesus on his shoulder and the pilgrim's staff). He's facing the original south transept entry to the church. Since 1470, pilgrims and travelers have looked up at him and taken solace in the hope that their patron saint is looking out for them.

• *Go in peace.*

More Cathedral Sights

Church Spire Climb (Dom-Turm)—An exterior entry (to the right of the church as you face the west facade) takes you into a modern excavation site, where you can see an arch and the founda-tions from the cathedral's predecessor (free), and pay to climb the cathedral's dizzying south tower. For a workout of 509 steps, you can enjoy a fine city view. From the *Glockenstube* (only 400 steps up), you can see the Dom's nine huge bells, including *Dicke Peter* (24-ton Fat Peter), claimed to be the largest free-swinging church bell in the world.

Cost and Hours: €3, €6 combo-ticket also includes treasury, daily May-Sept 9:00-18:00, March-April and Oct until 17:00, Nov-Feb until 16:00.

Treasury—The treasury sits outside the cathedral's left transept (when you exit through the front door, turn right and continue right around the building to the gold pillar marked *Schatzkammer*). The six dim, hushed rooms are housed in the cathedral's 13th-century stone cellar vaults. Spotlights shine on black cases filled with gilded chalices and crosses, medieval reliquaries (bits of chain, bone, cross, and cloth in gold-crusted glass capsules), and plenty of fancy bishop garb: intricately embroidered miters and vestments, rings with fat gemstones, and six-foot gold crosiers. Displays come with brief English descriptions, but the little €4.50 *Cologne Cathedral* book sold inside the adjacent cathedral shop *(Domladen)* provides extra information.

Cost and Hours: €5, €6 combo-ticket also includes spire climb, daily 10:00-18:00, last entry 30 minutes before closing, lockers at entry with €1 coin deposit, tel. 0221/1794-0530.

Domforum—This helpful visitors center, across from the entrance of the cathedral, is a good place to support the Vatican Bank (notice the Pax Bank ATM just outside the entrance), or just to take a break.

Cost and Hours: Free, Mon-Fri 10:00-18:30, Sat 10:00-17:00, Sun 13:00-17:00, may close for special events, plenty of cathedral info, welcoming lounge with €1-2.50 coffee and juice, clean WC downstairs—€0.50, tel. 0221/9258-4720, www.domforum .de. They offer an English "multi-vision" video on the history of the church (Mon-Sat at 11:30 and 15:30, Sun at 15:30 only, starts slow but gets a little better, 20 minutes, €2 or included with church tour).

Kolumba Diocesan Museum—This museum contains some of the cathedral's finest art. A stop on my self-guided walk, it's on Kolumbastrasse, which runs between Minoritenstrasse and Brückenstrasse a few blocks southwest of the cathedral. Built around the Madonna in the Ruins church, the museum is conceived as a place of reflection. There are no tours or information or noise. It's just you and the art in a modern building built upon the rubble of war. The daring modernist rebuild is a statement: We lost the war. Just accept it.

Cost and Hours: €5, Wed-Mon 12:00-17:00, closed Tue, tel. 0221/933-1930, www.kolumba.de.

Near the Cathedral

▲▲**Roman-Germanic Museum (Römisch-Germanisches Museum)**—One of Germany's top Roman museums offers minimal English among its elegant and fascinating display of Roman artifacts: glassware, jewelry, and mosaics. All these pieces are evidence of Köln's status as an important site of civilization long before the cathedral was ever imagined. The permanent collection is downstairs and upstairs; temporary exhibits are on the ground floor. Upstairs, you'll see a reassembled arched original gate to the Roman city with the Roman initials for the town, CCAA, still legible, and incredible glassware that Roman Köln was famous for producing. The museum's main attraction, described near the start of my self-guided walk, is the in situ Roman-mosaic floor—which you can see from the street for free through the large window.

Cost and Hours: €6, Tue-Sun 10:00-17:00, closed Mon, Roncalliplatz 4, tel. 0221/2212-4590, www.museenkoeln.de/rgm. The gift shop sells a €20 *Roman-Germanic Cologne* book if you're serious about learning more about the collection.

▲▲**Museum Ludwig**—Next door and more enjoyable, this museum—in a slick and modern building—offers a stimulating trip through the art of the last century, including American Pop and post-WWII art. The ground floor shows special exhibits. Upstairs (on the right) is the Haubrich collection. Josef Haubrich managed to keep his impressive collection of German Expressionist art out of Nazi hands (they considered it "decadent art") and eventually gave it to the city. The collection includes works by the great German Expressionists Max Beckmann, Otto Dix, and Ernst Ludwig Kirchner. Their paintings capture the loss of idealism and innocence following World War I and helped take art into the no-holds-barred modern world. The first floor also has a fine Picasso collection. The top floor is mostly contemporary and abstract paintings.

Cost and Hours: €10, Tue-Sun 10:00-18:00, closed Mon, audioguide-€3, €0.50 lockers mandatory for big bags, free WC in entry hall, exhibits are fairly well-described in English, pricey cafeteria, Heinrich-Böll-Platz, tel. 0221/2212-6165, www.museum-ludwig.de.

Farther from the Cathedral

These museums are several blocks south of the cathedral.

▲▲**Wallraf-Richartz Museum**—Housed in a cinderblock of a building near the City Hall, this minimalist museum features a world-class collection of old masters, from medieval to northern Baroque and Impressionist. You'll see the best collection anywhere of Gothic School of Köln paintings (1300-1550), offering an intimate peek into those times. Also included are German, Dutch, Flemish, and French works by masters such as Albrecht Dürer, Peter Paul Rubens, Rembrandt, Frans Hals, Jan Steen, Vincent van Gogh, Pierre-Auguste Renoir, Claude Monet, Edvard Munch, and Paul Cézanne.

Cost and Hours: €7-10, price depends on special exhibitions, Tue-Fri 10:00-18:00, Thu until 22:00, Sat-Sun 11:00-18:00, closed Mon, on Obenmarspforten, tel. 0221/2212-1119, www.museen koeln.de/wrm.

▲Imhoff Chocolate Museum (Schokoladenmuseum)— Chocoholics love this place, cleverly billed as the "MMMuseum." Three levels of displays—well-described in English—follow the cocoa bean from its origin to the finished product. Local historians, noting the "dumbing-down" of this generation of tourists, complain that this museum gets more visitors than all of Köln's other museums combined. You'll see displays on the history, culture, and business of chocolate from the Aztecs onward, step into a hot and muggy greenhouse to watch the beans grow,  and follow sweet little treats as they trundle down the conveyor belt in the functioning chocolate factory, the museum's highlight. The top-floor exhibit of chocolate advertising is fun. Some find that the museum takes chocolate too seriously, and wish the free samples weren't so meager—you'll have to do your indulging in the fragrant, choc-full gift shop.

Cost and Hours: €7.50, Tue-Fri 10:00-18:00, Sat-Sun 11:00-19:00, closed Mon, last entry one hour before closing, Am Schokoladenmuseum 1a, tel. 0221/931-8880, www.schokoladen museum.de. The museum is a pleasant 10-minute walk south on the riverfront, between the Deutzer and Severins bridges.

Käthe Kollwitz Museum—This contains the largest collection of the artist's powerful Expressionist art, welling from her experiences living in Berlin during the tumultuous first half of the 20th century.

Cost and Hours: €3, Tue-Fri 10:00-18:00, Sat-Sun 11:00-18:00, closed Mon, Neumarkt 18-24, tel. 0221/227-2899, www .kollwitz.de.

Getting There: From Hohe Strasse, walk west on Schilder-gasse for about 10 minutes to Neumarkt; go past the Neumarkt Gallerie shopping center to Neumarkt Passage, enter Neumarkt Passage, and walk to the glass-domed center courtyard, where you'll take the glass elevator to the fifth floor.

Sleeping in Köln

Köln is *the* convention town in Germany. Consequently, hotels are either jam-packed, with their rooms going for €180-200, or empty and hungry for guests. Unless otherwise noted, prices listed are the non-convention weekday rates. Prices are soft, so ask the hotel for its best offer. During conventions, rates double or even triple. Outside of convention times, the TI can always get you a discounted room in a business-class hotel (free by phone or Internet, walk-ins pay a €3 booking fee).

An updated list of dates for conventions in 2012 is posted at www.koelnmesse.de (choose English, then click on "Trade fairs and events," then "Trade fairs in Cologne"). Unlisted smaller conventions can also lead to small price increases, and big conventions in nearby Düsseldorf can also fill rooms and raise rates in Köln.

All the options listed here are an easy roll from the train station with your luggage.

Classy Hotels on Ursulaplatz

Two good business-class splurge hotels stand side by side a five-minute walk northwest of the station (exit straight out the station near track 1, turn right on Marzellenstrasse, and go up to Ursulaplatz). These can be pricey, but are an excellent value on non-convention weekends.

$$$ Hotel Cristall is a modern "designer hotel" with 97 cleverly appointed rooms (enjoy the big easel paintings). The deeply hued breakfast room and lounge are so hip that German rock stars have photo shoots here (Sb-€69, Db-€99, nicer Db with

Sleep Code

(€1 = about $1.40, country code: 49, area code: 0221)
S = Single, **D** = Double/Twin, **T** = Triple, **Q** = Quad, **b** = bathroom, **s** = shower only. Unless otherwise noted, credit cards are accepted, English is spoken, and breakfast is included.

To help you sort easily through these listings, I've divided the accommodations into three categories, based on the price for a standard double room with bath:

$$$ Higher Priced—Most rooms €95 or more.
$$ Moderately Priced—Most rooms between €70-95.
$ Lower Priced—Most rooms €70 or less.

Prices can change without notice; verify the hotel's current rates online or by email. For other updates, see www.ricksteves.com/update.

air-con-€109, prices can drop—especially in summer, request quiet room to escape street and train noise, non-smoking rooms, elevator, free Wi-Fi, Ursulaplatz 9-11, tel. 0221/16300, fax 0221/163-0333, www.hotelcristall.de, info@hotelcristall.de).

$$$ Classic Hotel Harmonie's 72 rooms include some very small, good-priced singles as well as luxurious "superior" rooms, which have hardwoods and swanky bathrooms with heated floors. It's plenty pricey during conventions, but becomes affordable on weekends and is a downright steal when business is slow (Sb-€60-90, Db-€80-110, price depends on room category, non-smoking rooms, most doubles have air-con, elevator, pay Wi-Fi, Ursulaplatz 13-19, tel. 0221/16570, fax 0221/165-7200, www.classic-hotel -harmonie.de, harmonie@classic-hotels.com).

Other Hotels near the Station

The Ibis hotel is actually inside the station building, the Hotel Engelbertz is a short walk south in the pedestrian zone, and the Hotel Domstern and Hotel Müller are on the other side of the station in a quiet neighborhood. If the last two hotels are full, look among the other affordable, family-run hotels on Brandenburger Strasse and Domstrasse.

$$$ Hotel Ibis Köln am Dom, a 71-room chain hotel, offers predictability and tidiness, and you can't beat the location—but it lacks personality (Sb-€88, Db-€103; convention rates: Sb-€104-210, Db-€124-230; breakfast-€10, non-smoking rooms, air-con, elevator, free Internet access and Wi-Fi in lobby, expensive Wi-Fi in rooms, Bahnhofsvorplatz, entry across from station's *Reisezentrum,* tel. 0221/912-8580, fax 0221/9128-58199, www .ibishotel.com, h0739@accor.com).

$$ Hotel Engelbertz is a fine, family-run, 40-room enterprise. It's an eight-minute walk from the station and cathedral at the end of the pedestrian mall (non-convention-time specials in 2012 for readers with this book: last-minute Sb-€59 and Db-€85 if you reserve on same day or day before, Sb-€68 and Db-€95 with advance reservation; regular rate Sb-€79 and Db-€114, convention rates up to Db-€195, elevator, inexpensive Wi-Fi, parking-€12; just off Hohe Strasse at Obenmarspforten 1-3, coming from station turn left at Hohe Strasse 96; tel. 0221/257-8994, fax 0221/257-8924, www.hotel-engelbertz.de, info@hotel-engelbertz.de).

$$ Hotel Domstern is a 16-room boutique hotel with fresh, pleasant rooms above a colorful lobby, located in a fine townhouse just steps from the station (Sb-€55-69, Db-€75-89, lower prices are for slower times—typically Sun and July-Aug, non-smoking, elevator, free Wi-Fi, parking-€8/day; from the train station, take the Breslauer Platz exit by track 11 and walk two blocks up Domstrasse to #26; tel. 0221/168-0080, fax 0221/1680-0829, www.domstern

.de, info@domstern.de).

$$ Hotel Müller, run with great pride by enthusiastic Frau Müller, has 16 nicely renovated rooms on a quiet street and offers three-star quality at two-star prices (because there's no elevator). Enjoy the grotto-like basement breakfast room/bar and the court-yard terrace (Sb-€64, Db-€79, Tb-€110, €7 less per person without breakfast, book direct and pay cash for 8 percent Rick Steves discount, non-smoking, free Wi-Fi; exit station from the back by track 11 to Breslauer Platz, walk 2 short blocks up Johannisstrasse, then left on Brandenburger Strasse to #20; tel. 0221/912-8350, fax 0221/9128-3517, www.hotel-mueller.net, info@hotel-mueller.net).

Budget Rooms

$ Station Hostel, with 200 beds, is a five-minute walk from the train station and full of young travelers (dorm bed-€17-22, S-€32, Sb-€39, twin-bed D-€48, Db-€55, Tb-€75, includes sheets, towel-€1, key deposit-€1, does not include breakfast—café on premises, kitchen, no elevator, no curfew, free Internet access and Wi-Fi, laundry-€4, tel. 0221/912-5301, fax 0221/912-5303; exit station on cathedral side, walk straight 1 block, turn right on Marzellenstrasse to #44-56; www.hostel-cologne.de, station@hostel-cologne.de).

Eating in Köln

The city's distinct type of beer, called *Kölsch,* is pale, hoppy, and fermented in a way more typical of wheat-based beers than of pilsner, lending it a slight sweetness. Beer-hall menus tend to be similar, with the real defining feature which brand of beer they serve (usually Gaffel, Päffgen, Peters, or Früh). Beers come in delicate glasses (by Bavarian standards) and are shuttled around in small wreath-like trays *(Bierkränze).* Köln's waiters, called *Köbes,* have a reputation for grumpiness, and some beer halls have a sloppy, sticky-tabled feeling, but others have helpful and attentive service and attractive interiors. This is the place to satisfy your cravings for blood sausage *(Blutwurst)* and kidneys *(Nierchen)*...or, for something a little more mainstream, look for the tasty *Rheinischer Sauerbraten* with *Klössen* (dumplings) and applesauce. Pub after pub advertises yard-high beer glasses and yard-long bratwurst.

Near Alter Markt

The area around Alter Markt, a square a few blocks from the cathedral, is home to dozens of beer halls, most with both outdoor and indoor seating. Wander from Alter Markt through Heumarkt (an adjacent square) and down Salzgasse to Frankenwerft (along the river) to catch the flavor.

Peters Brauhaus, at the top of Alter Markt, is a reliable eating choice with an unusually nice interior and outdoor seating across the street (€11-14 main courses, kids' menu, daily 11:00-24:00, Mühlengasse 1, tel. 0221/257-3950).

In **Gaffel Haus,** at the bottom of the square, look for the wall filled with coats of arms of Köln's old guilds *(Gaffeln)*—see how many crafts you can guess by their pictures (€10-17 main courses, daily 11:00-24:00, near Lintgasse at Alter Markt 20-22, tel. 0221/257-7692).

If you're more interested in music and beer than in food, check out **Papa Joe's Klimperkasten,** a dark pub packed with memorabilia and live jazz daily (€5-10 pub meals, Gaffel on tap, daily 11:00-24:00, live piano jazz Sept-May Sun-Thu from 20:00, Alter Markt 50-52, tel. 0221/258-2132). A couple minutes' walk away is its rowdier sibling, **Papa Joe's Jazzlokal** (live bands nightly from 20:00, Buttermarkt 37, tel. 0221/257-7931, www.papajoes.de for jazz schedule—American jazz and Dixieland have a big following in Germany). The pubs on the Frankenwerft, along the river across from the K-D boat dock, tend to be a bit more expensive.

Near the Train Station and Cathedral

Holtmann's im MAK, a museum café with sophisticated locals enjoying light fare, is a good option for a non-*Brauhaus* lunch. If you eat here on a Sunday morning, be sure to sit outside and enjoy a free organ concert al fresco—the courtyard abuts a church (€9-11 main courses, Tue-Sun 11:00-17:00, closed Mon, on other side of Hohe Strasse from the cathedral in Museum of Applied Arts—Museum für Angewandte Kunst—at An der Rechtschule 1, inside front door and down the stairs, no museum ticket needed, tel. 0221/2779-8860).

Café Eigel, just off Hohe Strasse near the recommended Hotel Engelbertz, is a good option for *Kaffee und Küchen* (afternoon cake and coffee) or for a light lunch (including salads and omelets). It's been in the same location for 50 years, but was recently remodeled in a fresh, sleek, modern style. Enjoy delicious pastries in the airy atrium, and be sure to pick up some homemade chocolates (€7-10 main courses, €3-4 slices of cake, Mon-Fri 9:00-19:00, Sat 9:00-18:00, Sun 14:00-18:00, Brückenstrasse 1-3, tel. 0221/257-5858).

Früh am Dom, close to the cathedral, is the closest beer hall to the station, offering three floors of touristy, traditional German drinking and dining options. Head to the back wall to check out a painting of what the city looked like in 1534 (€10-15 main courses, daily 8:00-24:00, Am Hof 12-14, tel. 0221/261-3211).

Schreckenskammer is a down-home joint and might be the least touristy beer hall in central Köln. It's located just behind the St. Ursula church, near the recommended Harmonie and Cristall hotels and the Station Hostel. The sand on the floor, swept out and replaced each morning, buffs the hardwood and also keeps it clean. The *kammer* is small and cozy, so be prepared to share a table and make new friends over a *Kölsch* or two. Most meals (choose from the *Tageskarte,* or daily specials) start with a complimentary cup of *Brühe* (broth). Don't mistake this as an act of hospitality—it only serves to make you thirstier. This eatery is really popular, so arrive early or make a reservation (€8-15 main courses, Tue-Sat 11:00-13:45 & 16:30-22:30, closed Sun-Mon, Ursulagartenstrasse 11-15, tel. 0221/132-581).

Köln Connections

From Köln by Train to: Bonn (5/hour, 20-30 minutes), **Remagen** (2-3/hour, 30-50 minutes), **Aachen** (2/hour, 50-60 minutes), **Frankfurt** (direct ICE trains almost hourly, most leave from Köln-Messe station a 2-minute trip across river by S-Bahn, 1-1.5 hours; slower, cheaper, less frequent IC trains along Rhine are better for enjoying scenery, 2.5 hours), **Frankfurt Airport** (1-2/hour, 1 hour; trains along Rhine go less often and take 2.25 hours), **Bacharach/St. Goar** (hourly; 1.75 hours with change in Koblenz, 2.5 hours direct), **Cochem** (hourly, 1.75-2.25 hours; most change in Koblenz), **Trier** (at least hourly, 2.5-3 hours, some change in Koblenz), **Würzburg** (at least hourly, 2.5 hours, some with change in Frankfurt), **Hamburg** (hourly, 4 hours), **Munich** (2/hour, 4.5 hours, some with 1 change), **Berlin** (hourly, 4.75 hours), **Paris** (6/day direct, 3.25 hours, Thalys train—requires seat reservation), **Amsterdam** (7/day direct, 2.75 hours). Train info: tel. 0180-599-6633, www.bahn.com. In 2013, the German Railway plans to start running high-speed trains from Frankfurt to London (via Köln and Brussels).

The Unromantic Rhine

Highlights

▲**Bonn**—Bonn was chosen for its sleepy, cultured, and peaceful nature as a good place to plant West Germany's first post-Hitler government. Since the two Germanys became one again in 1989, Berlin has taken back its position as capital.

Today, Bonn is sleek, modern, and, by big-city standards, remarkably pleasant and easygoing. The pedestrian-only old town stretching out from the station will make you wonder why the US can't trade in its malls for real, people-friendly cities. The market square and Münsterplatz—filled with street musicians—are a joy. People-watching doesn't get much better, though the actual sights are disappointing.

The **TI** is a five-minute walk from the station (Mon-Fri 10:00-18:00, Sat 10:00-16:00, Sun 10:00-14:00, go straight on Windeckstrasse, next to Karstadt department store, tel. 0228/775-000, www.bonn.de).

If you're a classical-music fan, you can stop by **Beethoven's Birthplace,** with its sparse exhibits. Try to time your visit to catch the daily 14:30 tour (fami-

The Unromantic Rhine

Düsseldorf

Rhine

Köln

Bruhl • Bonn

•Aachen

Bad Godesberg

Remagen•

River

Koblenz

Mosel

30 Miles

50 Kilometers

BEST OF RHINE

lies-only tours on Sun and first Sat of month; entry-€5, includes tour; April-Oct Mon-Sat 10:00-18:00, Sun 11:00-18:00; Nov-March Mon-Sat 10:00-17:00, Sun 11:00-17:00; last entry 25 minutes before closing, free English brochure, Bonngasse 18-26, tel. 0228/981-7525, www.beethoven-haus-bonn.de).

▲**Remagen**—Midway between Koblenz and Köln are the scant remains of the Bridge at Remagen, of WWII (and movie) fame. But the memorial and the bridge stubs are enough to stir the emotions of Americans who remember when it was the only bridge that remained, allowing the Allies to cross the Rhine and race to Berlin in 1945. The bridge was built during World War I to help supply the German forces on the Western Front. (Ironically, one war later, Eisenhower said the bridge was worth its weight in gold for its service *against* Germany.) An American unit captured the bridge on March 7, 1945, just after two failed attempts to demolish it (Hitler executed four generals for this failure). Ten days after US forces arrived, the bridge did collapse, killing 28 American soldiers. Today you can pay your respects here and visit the **Peace Museum,** which tells the bridge's fascinating story in English (€3.50, early March-mid-Nov daily 10:00-17:00, May-Oct until 18:00, closed mid-Nov-early March; it's on the Rhine's west bank, south side of Remagen town, follow *Brücke von Remagen* signs; tel. 02642/42893, www.bruecke-remagen.de). Remagen **TI:** tel. 02642/20187.

▲**Aachen (Charlemagne's Capital)**—This city was the capital of Europe in A.D. 800, when Charles the Great (Charlemagne) called it Aix-la-Chapelle. The remains of his rule include an impressive Byzantine- and Ravenna-inspired church, with his sarcophagus and throne. Enjoy the town's charming historic pedestrian center and festive Christmas market. See the headliner newspaper museum and great fountains, including a clever arrange-'em-yourself version.

Lowlights

Heidelberg—This famous old university town attracts hordes of Americans. Any surviving charm is stained almost beyond recognition by commercialism. It doesn't make it into Germany's top three weeks.

Mainz, Wiesbaden, and Rüdesheim—These towns are all too big or too famous. They're not worth your time. Mainz's Gutenberg Museum is also a disappointment.

NÜRNBERG

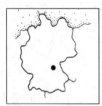

Nürnberg (sometimes spelled "Nuremberg" in English), Bavaria's second city, is known for its glorious medieval architecture, its important Germanic history museum, its haunting Nazi past, its famous Christmas market (Germany's biggest), and its little bratwurst (Germany's tiniest). Nürnberg (NEWRN-boorg) was one of Europe's leading cities in about 1500, and its large imperial castle marks it as a stronghold of the Holy Roman Empire. Today, though Nürnberg has a half-million residents, the charming Old Town—with its red-sandstone Gothic buildings—makes visitors feel like they are in a far smaller city.

Planning Your Time

Nürnberg is an easy add-on to any itinerary that includes Munich, Würzburg, or Rothenburg (each about an hour away by frequent trains), and a handy stop on the way to Frankfurt, Berlin, or Dresden.

If you are staying one night or day-tripping from elsewhere, visit the Nazi sites, stroll through the Old Town from the train station up to the castle (following my self-guided walk), and—on the way back to the station (or your hotel)—dip into the wonderful Germanic National Museum.

If you have two days (only worthwhile if you have a serious interest in Nazi history), spend one at Nazi sites and the other in the Old Town.

For the quickest visit to Nürnberg, toss your bag in a locker at the station and head directly to the former Nazi Rally Grounds.

Orientation to Nürnberg

(area code: 0911)

Nürnberg's Old Town is surrounded by a three-mile-long wall and moat, and, beyond that, a ring road. At the southeast corner of the ring is the train station; across the street, just inside the ring, is the medieval Frauentor gate. Sights cluster along Königstrasse downhill from the Frauentor to the small Pegnitz River, then back uphill through the main market square (Hauptmarkt) to the castle (Kaiserburg). The former Nazi Rally Grounds are southeast of the center (easily accessible by tram or bus).

Tourist Information

Nürnberg's handy and helpful TI is across the ring road from the station, in the modern building just opposite the Frauentor (Mon-Sat 9:00-19:00, Sun 10:00-16:00, Königstrasse 93, tel. 0911/233-6132, www.tourismus.nuernberg.de). Pick up the free city-guide booklet (with updated sight hours and prices) and get information about bus and walking tours. The TI also offers free Internet access (15-minute maximum), books rooms (no fee), and sells transit passes and the Nürnberg Card (see below). The TI has a small branch office at #18 on the Hauptmarkt (Mon-Sat 9:00-18:00, also open Sun May-Oct and during the Christmas market 10:00-16:00).

Discount Deals: When you buy a €5 ticket at any of Nürnberg's city-run museums—including the Nazi Documentation Center, Albrecht Dürer House, Toy Museum, and the City Museum—you can pay an additional €2.50 for a **day pass** that lets you visit all the others free of charge on the same day (see www.museen.nuernberg.de). Because this is such a great value, I'd skip the **Nürnberg Card** (€21/2 days, free for kids 11 and under, sold at the TI and most hotels, covers all local public transportation and admission to all Nürnberg's museums, plus small discounts off bus and walking tours, only available to those spending at least one night in Nürnberg).

Arrival in Nürnberg

By Train: Nürnberg's stately old Hauptbahnhof—with a shiny new interior—is conveniently located just outside the old city walls and ring road. The station has WCs, lockers, ATMs, and lots of shops. You can get train information and buy tickets at the *Reisezentrum* in the main hall (center of building, Mon-Fri 6:00-21:00, Sat 8:00-18:00, Sun 8:00-21:00).

To reach the **Frauentor** (the medieval city's southern gate)—which is near most recommended hotels and is also the starting point for exploring the Old Town—follow signs for *Ausgang/City* down the escalator, then signs to *Königstor/Frauentor* and *Altstadt* in the underpass. When you emerge, the TI is on your right and the Frauentor tower is on your left.

To go directly to the **former Nazi Rally Grounds** from the station, follow the pink *Tram* signs in the underpass to the stop in front of the Postbank Center, and catch tram #9 in the direction of Doku-Zentrum (leaves every 10 minutes).

Getting Around Nürnberg

Most of Nürnberg's sights are in the strollable Old Town, but the Nazi sites are far beyond walking distance. Nürnberg has the typical German lineup of trams, buses, U-Bahns (subways), and S-Bahns (faster suburban trains). All work on the same tickets, which you can buy at vending machines (marked *VAG Fahrausweise*) on the tram platform or before entering the U- or S-Bahns, or on board (buses only). A **single ticket** *(Einzelfahrkarte)* costs €2.10 (good for 90 minutes of travel in one direction, including transfers). A **day ticket** is €4.20 (*TagesTicket Solo*, good for one calendar day or both Sat and Sun; the €7 *TagesTicket Plus* covers 2 adults and up to 4 children; day tickets also sold at TI). Everything in this chapter is within zone *(Preisstufe)* 2. Vending machines time-stamp single and day tickets, so you don't need to validate them separately. For more information, see www.vgn.de.

Helpful Hints

Internet Access: While there are several Internet cafés in the city center (including two beneath the train station), save some euros and take advantage of free Internet access in the TI (15-minute time limit).

Laundry: A Schnell & Sauber coin launderette with instructions in English is at Pirckheimerstrasse 121, right at the Wurzelbauerstrasse stop of tram #9 (5 stops from train station, direction: Thon, same tram as Nazi Rally Grounds but in the other direction, daily 6:00-23:00).

Tours in Nürnberg

Walking Tours—Tours in English of Nürnberg's Old Town leave from the branch TI at Hauptmarkt 18 daily in season at 13:00 (May-Oct and Dec, €9 plus €2 for castle admission, kids under 14 free, 2.5 hrs, no reservation needed, buy ticket from TI or guide, www.nuernberg-tours.de). This is the only way to see the sights in the castle interior with an English-speaking guide.

Bus Tours—These tours, which include some walking, leave daily at 9:30 (May-Oct and Dec) from the Old Granary (Mauthalle) at Hallplatz, two blocks up from the Frauentor TI (€16, buy ticket on

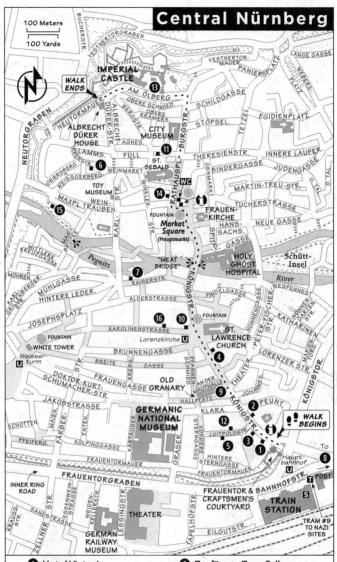

Central Nürnberg

100 Meters
100 Yards

WALK ENDS

IMPERIAL CASTLE ⑬

ALBRECHT DÜRER HOUSE

CITY MUSEUM

⑪ ST. SEBALD

TOY MUSEUM

⑭

⑮

WC

Market Square (Hauptmarkt)

FOUNTAIN

FRAUEN-KIRCHE

"MEAT BRIDGE"

⑦

HOLY GHOST HOSPITAL

Schütt-Insel

River

⑯ ⑩

FOUNTAIN

Lorenzkirche

ST. LAWRENCE CHURCH

④

WHITE TOWER

FOUNTAIN

Weisser-turm

OLD GRANARY

GERMANIC NATIONAL MUSEUM

⑨

⑫

⑤ ③ ①

② PEUNT

WALK BEGINS

⑧ To

Haupt-bahnhof

INNER RING ROAD

THEATER

FRAUENTOR & CRAFTSMEN'S COURTYARD

TRAIN STATION

POST

GERMAN RAILWAY MUSEUM

TRAM #9 TO NAZI SITES

① Hotel Victoria
② Hotel Drei Raben & Aldi Supermarket
③ Ibis Altstadt Hotel
④ City Hotel
⑤ Hotels Garni Probst & Keiml
⑥ Hotel Elch
⑦ Hotel/Café Lucas
⑧ To A&O Nürnberg Hauptbahnhof Hostel

⑨ Barfüsser Beer Cellar
⑩ Nassauer Keller Restaurant
⑪ Goldenes Posthorn Rest.
⑫ Literaturhaus Nürnberg Restaurant
⑬ Burgwächter Restaurant
⑭ Bratwursthäusle Rest.
⑮ Kettensteg Biergarten
⑯ Karstadt Supermarket

NÜRNBERG

bus or at TI, 2.5 hours, in German and English, tel. 0911/202-290, www.neukam.de).

Tourist Train—A goofy little tourist train makes the rounds in the Old Town (€7, 40 minutes, live narration in German only, written information in English, schedule posted at fountain, leaves Hauptmarkt about hourly 10:30-16:00, www.nuernberg-tourist.de).

Private Guide—For a good and charming local guide, call **Doris Ritter** (€95/3 hours, tel. 0911/518-1719, mobile 0176-2421-5863, ritter.doris@t-online.de). Guides can also be booked through the TI (tel. 0911/233-6123, fuehrung@ctz-nuernberg.de).

Self-Guided Walk

▲▲Nürnberg's Old Town

Nürnberg's best sights are conveniently clustered along a straightline thoroughfare connecting the train station (Hauptbahnhof) with the main market square (Hauptmarkt) and the castle (Kaiserburg). For a good orientation, take the following self-guided stroll. Plan on an hour, not including stops.

• *Begin at the Frauentor (where you emerge from the Hauptbahnhof underpass). Review the lay of the land on the 10-foot-tall city map posted in front of the tunnel (find the four towers). This walk will take you from the red dot at the bottom to the* Burg *(castle) at the top.*

Frauentor

This tower guards one of the four medieval entrances to Nürnberg's Old Town. Of the three miles of wall that once surrounded the city, 90 percent survives. Many Central European cities (such as Vienna) tore down their walls to make way for expansion in the 1800s, and Nürnberg nearly did the same. Now the city is glad it didn't: It's better for tourism.

• *Between the walls just next to the gate, you'll see the entrance to the...*

Craftsmen's Courtyard (Handwerkerhof)

This hokey collection of half-timbered houses was built in 1971 to celebrate craftsmanship and to honor the 500th birthday of Nürnberg's favorite son, Albrecht Dürer. Nürnberg didn't have abundant natural resources or a navigable waterway, so its citizens made their living through trade and crafts (such as making scientific instruments, weapons, and armor). Dürer, arguably Germany's best painter, was considered the ultimate craftsman. The proud

medieval tradition of craftsmanship continues today, as the city is home to some of Germany's top goldsmiths and glassblowers.

While a bit kitschy, this courtyard is good for picking up a medieval vibe as you enter the Old Town. It's packed with replicas of medieval shops, where artisans actually make—and, of course, sell—leather, pottery, and brass goods. In the Middle Ages, this area between the walls was not a medieval mall but a *Passkontrolle*—a customs and security checkpoint zone where all visitors had to register before they could enter the town.

At the back of the courtyard, step through the old gate and out onto a bridge over what was the moat. The bridge marks one of four entries into the medieval town. Look up at the mighty round Frauentor tower. It was originally square, but was made round after the development of better cannons (so balls would glance off rather than hit it head-on). Imagine cannons lined up under the eaves of the tower, set to defend the city. When local kids look at the mighty train station (across the street), they remember that the first train in Germany choo-chooed from here in 1835.

• *When you're finished poking around the courtyard, head into town (with the train station at your back) on...*

Königstrasse

Though it had always been one of the four primary entrances to Nürnberg, this street became the city's main drag only after the train station was built in the early 20th century. It's lined with key sights, several recommended hotels and restaurants, and some wonderful Gothic and Neo-Gothic architecture.

Nürnberg hit its peak in the 14th century. In 1356 Emperor Charles IV issued a decree from Nürnberg called the Golden Bull, which regularized many aspects of imperial government. From then throughout the Middle Ages, German emperors were elected in Frankfurt, crowned in Aachen, and were supposed to hold their first Imperial Diet (a gathering of German nobles and VIPs) right here in Nürnberg, though not all bothered to follow through on such democratic notions.

Nürnberg's low point came during World War II. By the end of the war, 90 percent of the Old Town was destroyed; it was the only German city hit worse than Dresden. Damaged buildings were repaired in the original Gothic style—check out the building with the Peschke Optik shop at Königstrasse 81. But some structures were completely destroyed. Instead of replicating these exactly as they were, or replacing them with modern-style buildings, postwar German architects compromised, creating styles that were at once modern and traditional. In Nürnberg, they often rebuilt in local sandstone. Look 50 yards down the street at #71. The design is mid-20th-century modern, but it replicates some Gothic lines and uses the same distinctive red stone as older buildings.

Ahead, on the left, is the small **Clara Church** (Klarakirche). In the Middle Ages, Nürnberg had nine monasteries like this one. When the Reformation hit, Nürnberg turned Lutheran, and most of the monasteries were torn down. As they fell, so did Nürnberg's importance; the city was now Lutheran, but the emperors were still Catholic. They moved the increasingly frequent Imperial Diet—once Nürnberg's claim to fame—to more Catholic-friendly Regensburg. (Today, this church is an "ecumenical free church"—meaning it's neither Lutheran nor Catholic and welcomes all stripes.)

Across the street from Clara Church, look for Mary on the second-story corner. Statues like this bless houses all over Nürnberg.

• *Continue down Königstrasse to Hallplatz and the Old Granary (where the pedestrian stretch begins). The minimalist metal arch (left) remembers the German refugees of World War II and the hospitality of the Bavarians who took them in.*

If you want to visit the excellent Germanic National Museum (described on page 496) now, detour left at Hallplatz and walk 200 yards. Otherwise, check out the...

Old Granary (Mauthalle)

Medieval Nürnberg had 11 of these huge granaries to ensure that residents would have enough food in case of famine or siege. The

grain was stored up above in the attic (behind all those little dormer windows). Today, the cellar is home to a lively and recommended beer hall, Barfüsser.

Go around the right side of the building and find the fun little **Vom Fass shop,** which sells liquor, wine, vinegar, and oils "from the tap" (as the name indicates). Bring or buy a container of any size, fill it with what you like (tastes allowed), and have the store write a gifty message right on the bottle (Mon-Fri 10:00-19:00, Sat 10:00-18:00, closed Sun, An der Mauthalle 2, Herr Eduard Stöber).

Continue down pedestrians-only Königstrasse. This drag used to have more cars and trams than any other street in town. But when the U-Bahn came in the 1970s, this part of the street became traffic-free.

• *After another two blocks, you'll see...*

▲▲St. Lawrence Church (Lorenzkirche)

This once-Catholic, now Protestant church is a massive house of worship. It was never a cathedral because Nürnberg never had a bishop (a fact locals were very proud of—a bishop would have threatened their prized independence). The name of Königstrasse ("King's Street")—where you've been walking—is misleading. When most royals came to town, they actually preferred to come through the west gate, so they could approach this masterful facade head-on.

Cost and Hours: €1 donation requested, €5 to take photos, Mon-Sat 9:00-17:00, Sun 13:00-16:00, www.lorenzkirche.de.

◐ Self-Guided Tour: Stand in front of the church's **main door.** Flip around and imagine the Holy Roman Emperor parading—right past Starbucks—toward this magnificent Oz-like church.

Study the 260-foot-tall **facade** (completed c. 1360). Adam and Eve flank the doors (looking for a sweater). In the first row above  the left door, you'll see two scenes: an intimate take on Jesus' birth on top, and the visit from the Magi on the bottom (with the starfish of Bethlehem shining from above). Over the right door, you'll see the slaughter of the innocents (with a baby skewered by a Roman sword—classic medieval subtlety), and below that the presentation of Jesus in the temple and the flight to Egypt. Above those scenes is the Passion story (from lowest to highest: trial, scourging, carrying the cross, Crucifixion, deposition, entombment, Resurrection, and people coming out of their graves for Judgment Day). The saved (Peter—with his huge key—and company) are on the left, and the sorry chain gang of the damned (including kings and bishops) is shuttled off literally into the jaws of hell on the right. Above it all stands the triumphant resurrected Christ, with the sun and moon at his feet, flanked by angels tooting alphorns.

Step inside (enter around right side). The **interior** wasn't completely furnished until more than a century after the church was built—just in time for the Reformation (so the Catholic decor adorned a now-Lutheran church). Most of the decorations inside were donated by wealthy Nürnbergers trying to cut down on their time in purgatory. Through the centuries, this art survived three separate threats: the iconoclasm of the Reformation, the whitewashing of the Baroque age, and the bombing of World War II. While Nürnberg was the first "free imperial city" to break with the Catholic Church and become Lutheran, locals didn't go wild (like

Swiss Protestants did) in tearing down the rich, Mary-oriented decor of their fine churches. Luther told the iconoclasts, "Tear the idols out of your heart, and you'll understand that these statues are only pieces of wood."

Suspended over the altar, the sculptural *Annunciation* is by a Nürnberg citizen and one of Central Europe's best woodcarvers, Veit Stoss. Carved in 1517, it shows the angel Gabriel telling Mary that she'll be giving birth to the Messiah. Startled, she drops her prayer book. This is quite Catholic (notice the rosary frame with beads, and a circle of roses—one for each Hail Mary, and with a medallion depicting the "Joys of Mary"). The dove sits on Mary's head, and God the Father—looking as powerful as a Holy Roman Emperor—looks down. The figures are carved from the wood of linden trees. The piece survived the Reformation covered in a sack, revealed only on special occasions. Around back, enjoy more details—Mary's cascading hair, and the sun and the moon. Nearby, the altar painting at the very front of the church (behind the altar) shows the city of Nürnberg in 1483 (before the city's square towers were made round).

To the left of the altar, the frilly **tabernacle** tower is the "house of sacraments" that stored the consecrated Communion wafer. After the Mass, leftovers needed a worthy—even heavenly—home, and this was it. The cupboard behind the gold grate was the appropriate receptacle for "the body of Christ." The theme of the carving is the Passion. The scenes ascend in chronological order: Last Supper, Judas' kiss, arrest, Crucifixion, and so on. Everything is carved of stone except for the risen Christ (way up high). He was living, and so was this—it's made of wood. The man holding the tabernacle on his shoulders is the artist who created it, Adam Kraft. In the Middle Ages, artists were faceless artisans, no more important than a blacksmith or a stonemason. But in the 1490s, when this was made, the Renaissance was in the air, and artists like Kraft began  putting themselves into their works. Kraft's contemporary, the painter Albrecht Dürer, actually signed his works—an incredible act in Germany at that time (for more on Dürer, see page 495). In anticipation of the Allied bombs of World War II, this precious work was encased in protective concrete except for the top 22 feet—which was the only part destroyed when the church was hit.

Adam Kraft is looking up at a **plaque** honoring American philanthropist brothers Samuel and Rush Kress, who donated nearly a million Deutschmarks in 1950 to help rebuild the church. The plaque is in English, but it's hard to read, as it's written in an old-style black-letter font. Though the church was devastated by WWII bombs, everything movable had been hidden away in bunkers, including the stained glass you see today. Back at the rear of the church, a silent **video** (with dates in the upper corner) shows the preparations in anticipation of WWII bombs, the destruction, and the reconstruction.

As you leave, notice that the church has many **side chapels**— employing an innovative trick of expanding the nave out so the buttresses are actually inside the church.

From St. Lawrence Church to the River: Back outside, find the castle-like building on the corner across from the church facade. This is the only remaining **tower house** in Nürnberg. When it was built, in 1200, there was no city wall, and locals had to defend their own homes. It's basically a one-family castle. (In the basement, you'll find a recommended, appropriately medieval restaurant—complete with suits of armor—called the Nassauer Keller.)

Continue downhill to the river. American moralists might shield their eyes from the kinky 16th-century **Fountain of the Seven Virtues** (Tugendbrunnen). Otherwise, play a game: Circle the sprightly fountain and try to identify the classic virtues by the symbolism: justice (on top), faith, love, hope (anchor), courage (lion), moderation, patience. Are any birds sipping?

• *Continue down the street. Caution: On your left, you'll pass Kaiserstrasse—the most expensive shopping street in town (with a little shop filled with insanely expensive Steiff teddy bears). When you get to the bridge, look to the right to see the...*

Holy Ghost Hospital (Heilig-Geist-Spital)

This river-spanning hospital was donated to Nürnberg in the 14th century by the city's richest resident, eager to do his part to help

the poor—and hopefully skip purgatory altogether. (A statue of this donor hangs out on the second-story corner of the Spital Apotheke, the first building after the bridge.) He funded this very scenic hospital to care for ill, disabled, and elderly Nürnbergers. The wing over the river dates from the 16th century. The dove beneath the middle window under the turret represents the Holy Ghost, the hospital's namesake.

If you look in the distance to the right—beyond the hospital and the next two bridges—you'll see a half-timbered fragment of the town wall. The big white building to the right of that is Germany's biggest multiplex cinema, with 21 screens (most underground).

Cross to the other side of the bridge, and look at the next bridge over (the Fleischbrücke—**"Meat Bridge"**). This is the narrowest point of the river, and flooding was a big concern. Since this bridge doesn't have any piers, there's less chance of a collapse. When it was built in 1596, this was considered the most high-tech bridge in Central Europe, an engineering feat inspired by Venice's single-span Rialto Bridge. The river once powered the town's medieval water mills.

Continue across the bridge and study the monument depicting characters from a 15th-century satire called *The Ship of Fools (Das Narrenschiff)*. It's adapted to follies that plague modern society: violence, technology, and apathy. Hey, how about the quiet, people-friendly ambience created by making this big city traffic-free in the center? Do a slow 360-degree spin and imagine this back home.

• *Now enter the...*

▲▲Market Square (Hauptmarkt)

When Nürnberg began booming in the 13th century, it consisted of two distinct walled towns separated by the river. As the towns grew, they merged and the middle wall came down. This square, built by Holy Roman Emperor Charles IV, became the center of the newly united city. Though Charles is more often associated with Prague (he's the namesake for the Charles Bridge and Charles University), he also loved Nürnberg—and visited 60 times during his reign.

The **Frauenkirche** church on the square is located on the site of a former synagogue (inside, there's a Star of David on the floor). When Nürnberg's towns were separate, Jewish residents were required to live in this swampy area close to the river and outside the walls. When the towns merged and the land occupied by the Jewish quarter became valuable, Charles IV allowed his subjects to force out the Jews. Six hundred were killed in the process—a somber reminder that anti-Semitism predated the Nazis. Charles IV, the most powerful man in Europe in his time, oversees the square from a perch high on the church facade. He's waiting for noon, when the electors dance around him.

Year-round, the Hauptmarkt is lively with fruit, flower, and souvenir stands. For a few weeks before Christmas, it hosts Germany's largest **Christmas market** (*Christkindlesmarkt*, more than 2 million visitors annually, starts the Friday before the first Sunday in Advent, www.christkindlesmarkt.de).

Walk across the square to the pointy gold **Beautiful Fountain** (Schöner Brunnen). Medieval tanneries, slaughterhouses, and the

hospital you just saw dumped their by-products into the river. So this fountain brought clean drinking water into the square. Of course, it's packed with allegorical meaning. Step up to the iron railing. The outermost figures ringing the bottom represent the arts (such as philosophy, music, and astronomy). On the pillars just above are the four church fathers and the four evangelists, showing that religion is higher than the arts. On the column itself, the lowest figures are the seven electors of the Holy Roman Emperor and nine heroes: three Christian (including King Arthur and Charlemagne); three Jewish (such as King David); and three heathen (such as Julius Caesar). At the very top are eight prophets, hovering above—but granting legitimacy to—worldly power. On the side of the fountain facing the McDonald's, you'll probably see tourists fussing over a gold ring. If you believe in such silly tour-guide tales, spinning this ring three times brings good luck...OK, go ahead and spin it. The black ring opposite (nearest the stork bearing a baby—look for the rice on the ground) brings fertility. Civic marriage ceremonies that take place at the adjacent City Hall often end up here for photos.

• *Leave the square straight uphill from the fountain, heading for the castle. Along the way, you'll pass St. Sebald (Sebaldkirche), Nürnberg's second great Gothic church. About 100 yards farther up the hill, you'll see the...*

City Museum (Stadtmuseum Fembohaus)

This museum is packed with fine artifacts, but you'll need the English audioguide to give them meaning (included in admission). Check out the top-floor model of Nürnberg. The museum's *Noricama Nürnberg Film* is a fascinating 50-minute video shown on the hour (in English with headphones) that gives a fun and thoughtful overview of the city, its history, and its great sights in a comfortable little theater.

Cost and Hours: Museum-€5 or covered by day pass—see "Discount Deals" on page 483, film-€4, €7 combo-ticket includes both, Tue-Fri 10:00-17:00, Sat-Sun 10:00-18:00, closed Mon, Burgstrasse 15, tel. 0911/231-2595, www.museen.nuernberg.de).

• *Now huff the rest of the way up to the Imperial Castle. The cobbled path forks at the castle's base. The right fork leads to the Castle Garden and youth hostel. The left fork leads to the castle courtyard (see big, round tower high above) and over the recommended Burgwächter restaurant. For now, take the left fork and visit the...*

▲Imperial Castle (Kaiserburg)

In the Middle Ages, Holy Roman Emperors stayed here when they were in town. This huge complex has 45 buildings. The part on the right, which housed the stables and stored grain, is now a youth hostel.

The castle interior and museum are standard fare. The most interesting bits are the so-called Deep Well (which, at 165 feet, is...well, deep) and the Romanesque double-decker chapel (higher nobility in the upper chapel, lower nobility down below, plus a special balcony for the emperor). The tower climb offers only a higher city view and lots of exercise.

The castle grounds are free, but unfortunately you can only see the interior sights with a German-language tour. There is one alternative: Go with the TI's English tour of the entire Old Town, which includes the castle (departs at 13:00; see "Tours in Nürnberg," earlier).

Visits to the **deep well** (about 4/hour), even with the German guide, are simple, quick, and fun: You'll see water poured way, waaay down—into an incredible hole dug in the 14th century. Then a small candle is lowered until it almost disappears into the water table.

Cost and Hours: €7 for one-hour tour of museum, palace, chapel, well—after which you can visit the museum and climb the tower on your own; €3.50 to visit just the well and then climb the tower on your own; covered by Bavarian Castles Pass—see page 122; tickets sold in office at top end of courtyard; daily April-Sept 9:00-18:00, Oct-March 10:00-16:00, tel. 0911/244-6590, www.schloesser.bayern.de.

• *Now you get to walk downhill again. The quick way down is to retrace your steps to the Burgwächter restaurant, then turn right and walk beneath the castle along Am Ölberg and Obere Schmiedgasse to Tiergärtnertorplatz (described later). The scenic route, which takes an extra 15 minutes, leads you around the back of the castle through the...*

Castle Garden (Burggarten)

Find the entrance to the castle garden. It's at the back of the hill, between the main complex and the youth hostel, and signposted

Burggarten, but a bit hidden (you may have to ask). The garden, wrapped around the back of the castle, offers great views of the town's 16th-century fortifications and former moat.

Cost and Hours: Free, April-Oct daily 8:00-20:00, closes at dusk if it comes first, closed Nov-March.

• *Follow the path around the castle. Either make a quick return through the first archway on your left, or continue another five minutes through landscaped gardens along the old city walls. Eventually you'll be spit out between two archways in front of a round tower (Neutor). Go through the archway on your left, then turn left, and walk two slightly uphill blocks along Neutormauer to the square with the giant rabbit statue. This is...*

Tiergärtnertorplatz

Near the top of the square, inspect the giant rabbit. While it looks like roadkill with mice gnawing at it, it's actually a modern interpretation of one of the best-known paintings by medieval Nürnberg artist Albrecht Dürer, *The Hare.* (The original painting is in Vienna.)

• *The rabbit faces a half-timbered building at the bottom of the square. That's the...*

▲Albrecht Dürer House (Albrecht-Dürer-Haus)

Nürnberg's most famous local lived in this house for the last 20 years of his life. Albrecht Dürer (1471-1528), a contemporary of

Michelangelo, studied in Venice and brought the Renaissance to stodgy medieval Germany. He did things that were unthinkable to other northern European artists of his time—such as signing his works, or painting things like hares simply for study (not on commission).

Nothing in the museum is original (all the paintings are replicas—the only Dürer originals in Nürnberg are in the Germanic National Museum, described later). But the museum does a fine job of capturing the way Dürer actually lived, and it includes a replica of the workshop, with a working printing press, where he printed his woodcuts. In one room, a 17-minute movie plays continuously (in English on your headphones). The top floor is a gallery with copies of Dürer's most famous paintings and wood-cuts. On Saturdays at 14:00, you can meet Dürer's wife, Agnes, who speaks English and takes you through their house.

Cost and Hours: €5 or covered by day pass—see "Discount Deals" on page 483, includes Agnes-led audioguide, live Agnes tour-€2.50 extra, €1.50 English brochure available, Tue-Wed and Fri 10:00-17:00, Thu 10:00-20:00, Sat-Sun 10:00-18:00, closed Mon except July-Sept and Dec 10:00-17:00, Albrecht-Dürer-Strasse 39, tel. 0911/231-2568, www.museen.nuernberg.de.

• *You've walked from the southern gate of Nürnberg to the northern gate, and your tour is over. If heading from here to the Nazi sites, bus #36 from Hauptmarkt or a taxi are your best bets. Or, for more sight-seeing on your way back to the Frauentor, three more Old Town muse-ums are listed in the next section.*

More Sights in Nürnberg

In and near the Old Town

Toy Museum (Spielzeugmuseum)—Nürnberg is famous for woodworking. You can see some examples of this local craft—and lots more—at this entertaining, interactive collection of toys from across the ages. The chronological display starts on the ground floor and heads up through four more floors. Highlights are: for history buffs—the section on the militarization of the 1930s and the rubble years through the 1950s; for Nebraskans—a miniature replica of the Omaha train station; and for kids—the top-floor play zone. Get an English audioguide (€1), or consider the good little €3 booklet.

Cost and Hours: €5 or covered by day pass—see "Discount Deals" on page 483, any number of children admitted for €0.50 each with a paying parent, Tue-Fri 10:00-17:00, Sat-Sun 10:00-18:00, closed Mon except during Christmas market, Karlstrasse 13-15, near Albrecht Dürer House, tel. 0911/231-3164, www .museen.nuernberg.de.

▲▲Germanic National Museum (Germanisches National-museum)—This sprawling, sweeping museum is dedicated to the cultural history of the German-speaking world. It occupies an interconnected maze of buildings, old and new, in the southern part of the Old Town, near the station and recommended hotels.

Cost and Hours: €6, Wed 10:00-21:00 (free after 18:00); open Tue-Sun 10:00-18:00 (upper floor closes at 17:00), Wed all floors until 21:00, closed Mon; €2 English tours every other Sun at 14:00, mandatory bag check (lockers with €1 refundable deposit), Kartäusergasse 1, 2 blocks west of Königstrasse (enter on far side of building), tel. 0911/13310, www.gnm.de.

Touring the Museum: Approaching the museum along Kartäusergasse, you walk along the "Way of Human Rights." Designed by an Israeli artist, its pillars trumpet each of the provisions of the United Nations' Universal Declaration of Human Rights.

As you enter the museum, you'll stand before a wall displaying a few street signs from East Germany, dating from the time when the Soviets had renamed the main drag in many towns *Strasse der Befreiung* ("Street of the Liberation"—from the Nazis and capitalism).

The museum's star attraction is its medieval German art collection. It includes works by Dürer (the only originals in town), Cranach, Rembrandt, and Tilman Riemenschneider. Other "must-sees" in the collection include an early globe (since it dates from 1492, the Americas are conspicuously missing) and the delicate wooden *Nürnberg Madonna* (1515). This intimate, anonymous carving of the favorite hometown girl was the symbol of the city during the 19th-century Romantic Age. All these works are collected together in a single exhibit just upstairs from the entrance hall, with good English descriptions. A free English audioguide is available at the ticket office (leave ID as deposit).

The rest of this huge museum covers a vast spectrum of German culture, from fine arts to prehistory to science to musical instruments. There are also regular temporary exhibits. Pick out a few things you are really interested in with the help of the bilingual "Floor Plan" brochure *(Orientierungsplan)*, which lists the different collections. Note the room numbers and the color codes of the wings you're headed for. In general, few labels or signposts are in English, but temporary exhibits may come with an audioguide or free English brochures in a rack by the entrance.

German Railway Museum (DB Museum)—Germany's first railway was built in Nürnberg in 1835, and the German Railway (DeutscheBahn) now runs a huge museum just outside the Old Town telling the story of German trains from 1835 to 1989. The "Serving Dictatorship" exhibit explains the role of the train system during the Nazi regime. A big, hands-on kids' section is full of games and model railroads, while the petting zoo of real engines and carriages appeals to all ages. Get the English audioguide (€1, must leave ID), or pick up the free English booklet as you enter.

Cost and Hours: €5, €4 with valid train or city transit ticket, Tue-Fri 9:00-17:00, Sat-Sun 10:00-18:00, closed Mon except in Dec, Lessingstrasse 6; from Germanic National Museum take the footbridge over the old moat, cross the ring road and walk a block down Lessingstrasse; tel. 0911/219-1233, www.dbmuseum.de.

Nazi Sites

Though the city tries to present itself as the "City of Human Rights," its reputation as Hitler's favorite place for a really big party is hard to shake. To understand Nürnberg's role in the Nazi movement, visit Hitler's vast Nazi Party Rally Grounds (Reichsparteitagsgelände) and the excellent museum—the Nazi Documentation Center—set amid the mute remains of the Third Reich.

Planning Your Time: World War II buffs might want to make this an all-day visit (a café in the museum serves lunch). With half a day, spend two hours in the museum and then another hour following the path around the lake. On a lightning visit, see the museum, peek into the courtyard of the Congress Hall, and if time allows, walk to Zeppelin Field and back. Only part of the outdoor circuit is shaded, so bring a hat and sunscreen on a hot day. Make sure to pick up the free map and the €1 English guidebook from the museum counter before doing the walk around the lake.

Getting to the Nazi Documentation Center and Rally Grounds: The sprawling complex is wrapped around a pond called Dutzendteich, southeast of the Old Town. Take handy tram #9, which leaves from the front of the Postbank Center at the train station (Hauptbahnhof) every 10 minutes (direction: Doku-Zentrum, 15-minute trip). Get off at the Doku-Zentrum stop (check return times before going to the sites). From the Hauptmarkt or Rathaus (City Hall), you can also hop on bus #36, which ends at the Doku-Zentrum stop. Both options cost the same (€2.10 one-way; it's better to purchase the €4.20 day ticket). As you get off the tram or bus, you'll see the Nazi Documentation Center.

▲▲▲Nazi Documentation Center (Dokumentationszentrum)

Visitors to Europe's Nazi and Holocaust sites inevitably ask the same haunting question: How could this happen? This superb museum does its best to provide an answer. It meticulously traces the evolution of the National Socialist (Nazi) movement, focusing on how it both energized and terrified the German people (the exhibit's title is "Fascination and Terror"). Special attention is paid to Nürnberg's role in the Nazi movement, including the construction and

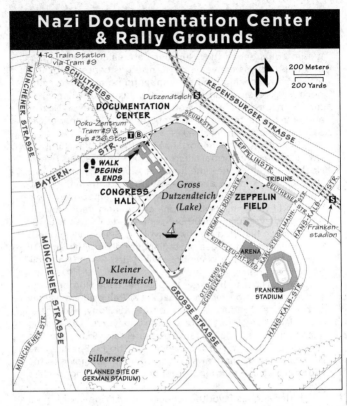

Nazi Documentation Center & Rally Grounds

(Map labels:)

To Train Station via Tram #9

200 Meters
200 Yards

SCHULTHEISS ALLEE

MÜNCHENER STRASSE

REGENSBURGER STRASSE

Dutzendteich S

DOCUMENTATION CENTER

Doku-Zentrum Tram #9 & Bus #36 Stop T B

SEUMESTR.

ZEPPELINSTR.

BAYERN- STR.

WALK BEGINS & ENDS

CONGRESS HALL

Gross Dutzendteich (Lake)

TRIBUNE

BEUTHENE

ZEPPELIN FIELD

HERMANN-BÖHM-STR.

KARL-STEGELMANN-STR.

HANS-KALB-STR.

Franken- stadion

S

Kleiner Dutzendteich

KURT-LEUCHT-WEG

ARENA

OTTO-ERNST-SCHWEIZER-STR.

GROSSE STRASSE

FRANKEN STADIUM

HANS-KALB-STR.

MÜNCHENER STRASSE

Silbersee
(PLANNED SITE OF GERMAN STADIUM)

NÜRNBERG

use of the Rally Grounds, where Hitler's largest demonstrations took place. This is not a World War II or Holocaust museum; those events are almost an afterthought. Instead, the center frankly analyzes the Nazi phenomenon, to understand how it happened—and to prevent it from happening again.

Cost and Hours: €5 or covered by day pass—see "Discount Deals" on page 483, includes audioguide, Mon-Fri 9:00-18:00, Sat-Sun 10:00-18:00, last entry at 17:00, Bayernstrasse 110, tel. 0911/231-5666, www.museen.nuernberg.de.

Touring the Documentation Center: The museum is housed in one small wing of Hitler's cavernous, unfinished Congress Hall—the largest surviving example of Nazi architecture. The building was planned to host the mammoth annual Nazi Party gatherings. Today, it's symbolically sliced open by its modern entryway to show the guts and brains of the Nazi movement.

The exhibit is a one-way walk. Allow two hours just for the fine videos you can see along the way. WWII history buffs should allow an extra hour for the two movies that play continuously in the *Kino* at the start of the exhibit, offering excellent insights

Nazis in Nürnberg

It's no coincidence that Nürnberg appealed to Hitler. For one thing, it was convenient: Nürnberg is centrally located in Germany, making it a handy meeting point for Nazi supporters. Hitler also had a friend here, Julius Streicher (a.k.a. the "Franconian Führer"), who fanned the flames of Nazism and anti-Semitism through his inflammatory newspaper *Der Stürmer (The Storm Trooper)*.

But of far greater importance was the fact that Nürnberg was steeped in German history. Long before the rise of Nazism, the city—one-time home of Albrecht Dürer and the Holy Roman Emperor, and packed with buildings in the quintessential German Gothic style—was nicknamed the "most German of German cities." As one of the most important cities of medieval Europe, Nürnberg appealed to Hitler as a way to legitimize his Third Reich by invoking Germany's glorious past. Hitler loved the idea of staging his rallies within sight of the Kaiserburg castle, a symbol of the "First Reich" (the Holy Roman Empire).

When Hitler took power in 1933, he made Nürnberg the site of his *Reichsparteitage*—**Nazi Party Rallies.** Increasingly elaborate celebrations of Nazi culture, ideology, and power took place here annually for the next six years. The chilling images from Leni Riefenstahl's documentary *Triumph of the Will* were filmed at the 1934 rallies. At the 1935 rallies, the Nazis devised the first laws—which came to be known as the **Nürnberg Laws**—that legally defined Jews as second-class citizens.

Hitler and his favorite architect, Albert Speer, designed staggeringly massive buildings (such as a stadium seating 400,000 spectators) to host the proceedings. Only a few of the plans were completed before World War II broke out in 1939, forcing the construction budget to be reassigned to the war effort. Today, it's possible to walk around the still-unfinished remains of Hitler's megalomaniacal super-structures. The Rally Grounds were the ultimate example of Hitler's preferred architecture style: stark, huge, and Neoclassical.

As the war drew to a close, the world puzzled over what to do with the Nazi officers who had overseen some of the most gruesome atrocities in the history of humankind. It was finally decided that they should be tried as war criminals by an international tribunal (spearheaded by the United States and based on the Anglo-American code of law). These trials took place right here, in the **Nürnberg Trials Courtroom** (see page 502). The Nürnberg Trials—the first-ever international war-crimes tribunal—brought about a new concept of international law, which continues today in The Hague, Netherlands.

into the mass hypnosis of the German nation (interviews and old footage with English subtitles). Exhibit captions are in German only, so the English audioguide is a must (turns on automatically at video presentations, you dial room numbers for overviews and specific numbers for details of displays—if rushed, listen to the overviews only). You'll see parts of Leni Riefenstahl's 1934 propaganda classic *Triumph of the Will* and, just before the end, footage of the Nürnberg Trials. The last stop (before the long ramp back to the start) is a catwalk giving you a look into the core of the Congress Hall (an artist's sketch of the hall filled with 50,000 cheering Nazis is on a nearby wall).

▲Rally Grounds (Reichsparteitagsgelände)

The Rally Grounds occupy four square miles behind the museum. Albert Speer, Hitler's favorite architect, designed this immense complex of buildings for the Nazi rallies. Not many of Hitler's ambitious plans were completed, but you can visit the courtyard of the Congress Hall, Zeppelin Field (where Hitler addressed his followers), and a few other remains. The easiest way to see them is to follow the circular route around the lake that's shown in the map on page 499 and on the museum's free bilingual area plan *(Geländeplan)*. The numbers on the plan correspond to the information pillars that you'll find on-site (this information also appears at www.reichsparteitagsgelaende.de).

Figure an hour round-trip from the Documentation Center for the full circuit. If you have less time, you can visit the courtyard of the Congress Hall, or walk to Zeppelin Field and back, without doing the full loop. If you're really short on time, remember that you'll get the best sense of the Rally Grounds simply from the exhibits inside the Documentation Center.

I've listed the main sites here in the order you reach them while circling the lake.

Congress Hall (Kongresshalle)—This huge building—big enough for an audience of 50,000—was originally intended to be topped with a roof and skylight. The Nazi Documentation

Center occupies part of the hall. To see the vast, Colosseum-like courtyard, turn right as you leave the Documentation Center, and walk along the side of the building. Dip through the archway into the courtyard to appreciate its dimensions. Part of the hall is now used by the Nürnberg symphony orchestra. Turn around and return to the main path. When you get to the end, turn right again and continue walking with the Congress Hall on your right. Continue past the end of the building, and then turn left (under the *Kommen Sie gut nach Hause* sign) onto the...

Great Road (Grosse Strasse)—At 200 feet wide, the Great Road was big enough to be used as a runway by the Allies after the war. Now it's a parking lot for trucks serving the nearby conference center. The road points toward Nürnberg's imperial palace, Kaiserburg—Hitler's symbolic connection to the Holy Roman Empire (the First Reich). The lights you see in the distance hover above the Franken Stadium (a soccer field before Hitler used it for Nazi rallies and, most recently, the site of the 2006 World Cup soccer tournament).

Ahead and to the right was to be the site of the **German Stadium (Deutsches Stadion)**—the biggest in the world (with 400,000 seats). They got as far as digging a foundation before funding was redirected to the war effort. Today, the site is a park surrounding the big lake, Silbersee—which was the hole for the never-built stadium's foundation. If you like, you can detour across the road to an information sign about the stadium. Otherwise, follow the Dutzenteich lakeshore to the left for about 15 minutes until you hit a parking lot. To your right is the huge...

Zeppelin Field (Zeppelinwiese)—This was the site of the Nazis' biggest rallies, including those famously filmed by Leni Riefenstahl. You can climb up on the grandstand and stand on the platform in front of the Zeppelin Tribune, where Hitler stood to survey the masses (up to 250,000 people at a time). The Tribune is based on the design of the ancient Greek Pergamon Altar (now in Berlin's Pergamon Museum); it was originally topped by a tower-

ing swastika, which was blown up by the Allies soon after the end of the war. Warning: Clowning around on the speaking platform with any Nazi gestures is illegal and taken seriously by the police.

From Zeppelin Field, continue the rest of the way around the lake back to the Documentation Center.

Nürnberg Trials Courtroom (Memorium Nürnberger Prozesse)

In 1945, in courtroom *(Saal)* #600 of Nürnberg's Palace of Justice (Justizgebäude), 21 Nazi war criminals stood trial before an international tribunal of judges appointed by the four victorious countries. After a year of trials and deliberations, 12 Nazis were sentenced to death by hanging, 3 were acquitted, and the rest were sent to prison. One of the death sentences was for Hitler's right-hand man, Hermann Göring. He wanted to be shot by firing squad—a proper military execution—but his request was denied. Instead, two hours before his scheduled hanging, Göring committed suicide with poison he had smuggled into his cell, infuriating many who thought that this death was too easy for him.

Visitors aren't guaranteed access to the courtroom itself, which is still in use (with proceedings about 100 days a year).

Cost and Hours: €5 or covered by day pass—see "Discount Deals" on page 483, includes audioguide, Wed-Mon 10:00-18:00, closed Tue, last entry at 17:00. The building is a four-stop subway ride from the Hauptbahnhof (Fürther Strasse 110, enter on Bärenschanzstrasse, take U-1 subway line to Bärenschanze, it's just behind *Pit Stop* sign, tel. 0911/321-79372, www.memorium -nuremberg.de.

Sleeping in Nürnberg

Prices spike during major conventions in the spring and fall, and in December—when the Christmas market brings visitors from around the world. Nürnberg gets a lot of business travelers, so some hotels drop their rates on weekends. July and August are generally low season and come with the lowest prices.

Near the Frauentor, on Königstrasse

These hotels clustered along Königstrasse, just inside the Frauentor and the city walls, are convenient to both the train station and city sightseeing. From the station, you can roll your luggage here in five minutes without a single stair.

$$$ Hotel Victoria offers friendly staff and 64 fresh, new-feeling rooms behind its historic 1896 facade just inside the Frauentor. The standard rooms are a better value than the slightly bigger business rooms (standard rooms: S-€50-60, Sb-€80-90, Db-€100-110; business rooms €10 extra, discounts on slow weekends, most rooms non-smoking, elevator, free cable Internet in business rooms, free Internet access, free Wi-Fi in lobby, pay Wi-Fi in rooms, parking garage-€11/day, Königstrasse 80, tel. 0911/24050, fax 0911/227-432, www.hotelvictoria.de, mail@hotelvictoria.de).

$$$ Hotel Drei Raben is an artsy and fun splurge, with a super-stylish lobby, 22 comfortable rooms, a huge breakfast buffet (ask for eggs or a cappuccino), and lots of elegant touches. In this "theme hotel" you might get the Dürer room, the soccer room, the toys room, or even the graffiti room (Sb/Db-€100, €120, or €150 depending on size; spacious suites with freestanding bathtubs: Db-€185; ask for special summer discounts—especially on weekends; non-smoking, air-con, elevator, free Internet access and Wi-Fi, valet parking-€15/day, Königstrasse 63, tel. 0911/274-380,

---

Sleep Code

(€1 = about $1.40, country code: 49, area code: 0911)
S = Single, **D** = Double/Twin, **T** = Triple, **Q** = Quad, **b** = bathroom, **s** = shower only. Unless otherwise noted, credit cards are accepted, English is spoken, and breakfast is included.

To help you sort easily through these listings, I've divided the accommodations into three categories, based on the price for a standard double room with bath:

$$$ Higher Priced—Most rooms €100 or more.
$$ Moderately Priced—Most rooms between €70-100.
$ Lower Priced—Most rooms €70 or less.

Prices can change without notice; verify the hotel's current rates online or by email. For other updates, see www.ricksteves.com/update.

---

fax 0911/232-611, www.hoteldreiraben.de, info@hoteldreiraben.de).

$ Ibis Altstadt Hotel, sandwiched between a bunch of fast-food joints, offers 61 good-value cookie-cutter rooms in a convenient location (normal rates: Sb/Db-€59-69; during Christmas market: Sb-€75, Db-€95; during conventions: Sb-€169, Db-€169; breakfast-€10, family deals, elevator, free Internet access in lobby, expensive Wi-Fi in rooms, Königstrasse 74, tel. 0911/232-000, fax 0911/209-684, www.ibishotel.com, h1069@accor.com).

$ City Hotel, with 20 old, very basic rooms, has decent prices for the location and amenities (Sb-€39, Db-€49, Tb-€65, breakfast-€5, elevator, reception on third floor, Königstrasse 25-27, tel. 0911/232-645, fax 0911/203-999, www.cityhotel-nuernberg.de, info@cityhotel-nuernberg.de, Widtmann family).

Near the Frauentor, on Luitpoldstrasse

These two affordable, family-run hotels are next door to each other, around the corner from the ones just described, set amidst a harmless sprinkling of strip clubs and sex shops. Either hotel will do if you're watching your budget, but some guests complain about noise, so ask for a room on the back side (especially if staying on Friday or Saturday night).

$$ Hotel Garni Probst has been run for 65 years by the hardworking Probst family. They rent 39 clean, cheap rooms on floors 2-4 of an older apartment building (Ss-€40, Sb-€56, Db-€67-75, Tb-€87-93, ask about lower prices in summer and on weekends, non-smoking rooms, elevator to third floor, pay Wi-Fi, Luitpoldstrasse 9, tel. 0911/203-433, fax 0911/205-9336, www.hotel-garni-probst.de, info@hotel-garni-probst.de).

$ Hotel Keiml is run by gracious Frau Keiml, who has been welcoming guests here since 1975. She rents 22 bright and homey rooms up several flights of stairs (no elevator) in another former apartment building (Sb-€45, Db-€65-70, these prices with this book and cash in 2012, non-smoking rooms, free Wi-Fi, Luitpoldstrasse 7, tel. 0911/226-240, fax 0911/241-760, www.hotel-keiml.de, info@hotel-keiml.de).

Closer to the Castle

These accommodations are closer to the castle at the far side of Old Town. Getting here is an €8 taxi ride or a long hike from the station. You can get partway by taking the U-Bahn (line #1) to Lorenzkirche and exiting toward Kaiserstrasse.

$$ Hotel Elch, the oldest hotel in town (with 500-year-old exposed beams adding to its classic elk-friendly woodiness), is buried deep in the Old Town near the castle. It rents 12 charming and well-equipped rooms and has a small restaurant (Tue-Sun 18:00-22:00, closed Mon) specializing in schnitzel (Sb-€59, Db-€70, extra bed free for kids under 14, non-smoking, free Wi-Fi, nearby parking garage-€10/day, near St. Sebald Church at Irrerstrasse 9, tel. 0911/249-2980, fax 0911/2492-9844, www.hotel-elch.com, info@hotel-elch.com).

$$ Hotel Lucas occupies three floors above a busy, similarly named café a short walk from the Hauptmarkt (market square). The 11 rooms and 7 river-view apartments next door are modern and cheerful, making this a great home base if you don't mind that there's no elevator (Sb-€50-65, Db-€75-90, extra person-€25, lower prices are for Fri-Sun; non-smoking, free Wi-Fi, Kaiserstrasse 22, tel. 0911/227-845, fax 0911/244-9158, www.hotel-lucas.de, info@hotel-lucas.de). Coming from the train station with luggage, I'd hop on the U-1 subway line for one stop to Lorenzkirche. Exit following the *Kaiserstrasse* signs to emerge a couple doors from the hotel.

Hostel: **$ A&O Nürnberg Hauptbahnhof Hostel** is brand new, with 380 beds and a fifth-floor sky bar overlooking the city center. Conveniently located near the main train station, the interiors are simple and modern, and the rooms bright and clean (bed in 4- to 6-bed dorm-€10-24, Sb-€38-54, Db-€45-68—but check the website as prices vary with demand, no membership required, breakfast-€4, sheets-€3, elevator, pay Internet access and Wi-Fi, Bahnhofstrasse 13-15, tel. 0911/309-168-4401, www.aohostels.com, reception@aohostels.com). From the train station, head into the underpass, then walk to the far left side, following signs for *Bahnhofstrasse/ZOB*. After emerging on the street, walk another 100 yards to the hostel.

Eating in Nürnberg

Nürnberg is famous for its pinkie-sized bratwurst (called, like local residents, *Nürnberger*). Nürnbergers—the people—insist that size doesn't matter; they maintain that *in der Kürze liegt die Würze* (in the shortness lies the tastiness). All over town, signs read *3 im Weckle,* meaning "three *Nürnberger* bratwurst in a little bun" (a good snack for about €2). Old-timers go for mustard, while children like ketchup. Restaurant menus often offer them in 6-, 8-, or 10-weenie servings with *Beilagen* (side dishes, generally potato salad and/or kraut). Nürnberg's butchers churn out 1.3 billion of the little buggers every year.

For convenience, I've listed restaurants that are on (or near) Königstrasse, the main drag connecting the station to the castle. Only the Kettensteg Biergarten is away from this tourist zone—buried in the west end of the Old Town, and known only to locals.

Barfüsser Beer Cellar serves its own popular microbrew and fills the basement of the old grain storehouse *(Mauthalle)* with jovial Germans munching meat-on-the-bone (from pork knuckle to duck) and swilling beer. This is good German fun. On hot nights, the cellar's empty and tables spill out onto Königstrasse. Locals love the *Schäufele,* oven-roasted pork shoulder in home-brewed dark beer sauce, and the *Frankenschmaus,* a "greatest hits" platter of sausages, pork shoulder, kraut, and dumplings (€7-13 meals, daily 11:00-24:00, Hallplatz 2, tel. 0911/204-242).

Nassauer Keller is a snug and classy 13th-century vaulted cellar filled with suits of armor and diners enjoying the romantic atmosphere and traditional food. A small door leads down steep steps (watch your head) into a dressy dining room—popular for roast shoulder of pork and venison dishes. It's a little pricey and worth the extra euros in wintertime—but avoid this place on hot days (€10-16 meals, Mon-Sat 12:00-15:00 & 18:00-24:00, kitchen closes at 14:00 and at 22:00, closed Sun, reservations smart, across from Lorenzkirche at Karolinenstrasse 2-4, tel. 0911/225-967).

Goldenes Posthorn is a venerable institution and—while no longer in its original historic location—was once Albrecht Dürer's favorite hangout. Come here to enjoy everything from Franconian specialties and bratwurst to daily fish and vegetarian plates, either in the light-wood chalet-chic interior or on the patio in the shadow of St. Sebald Church (€6-12 meals, daily 11:00-23:00, daily specials, cash only, Glöckleingasse 2, tel. 0911/225-153).

Literaturhaus Nürnberg is a Parisian-style café run by the local book club and popular for readings. It serves theme breakfasts (daily until 15:00) and creative international dishes for €8-14. Locals like to order several varied plates tapas-style, or just enjoy its bookish café ambience for drinks and desserts (Mon-Sat 9:00-24:00, Sun 9:00-22:00, 2 blocks from Frauentor just off Königstrasse at Luitpoldstrasse 6, tel. 0911/234-2658).

Burgwächter is just under the castle, and therefore both touristy and practical. It serves up German cuisine in its cozy restaurant and on a covered patio with big, rustic picnic tables (€7-13 main courses, good salads, daily 12:00-23:00, Jan-March may open only for dinner weekdays, Am Ölberg 10, tel. 0911/222-126).

Bratwursthäusle is a high-energy, woody-yet-mod place with a leafy terrace (and enjoyable people-watching). Its cozy interior feels like a big farmhouse with tables gathered around an open grill. The menu is very limited, with little more than bratwurst and some nasty pickled animal parts. You come here for the best bratwurst in town—all made in-house by the *Häusle*'s own butcher, and dished up with efficient service. Chat up the owner, friendly Herr Behringer, and he'll be happy to tell you about Bratwurst Saints (Mon-Sat 10:00-21:30, closed Sun, midway between Hauptmarkt and the castle on the main drag, Rathausplatz 1, tel. 0911/227-695). For bratwurst to go, head inside, pay €2 at the half-door on your right, take your receipt to the grill...and in seconds, you'll be on your way with Nürnberg's "Little Mac" (three *Nürnberger* in a fresh roll).

Cafe Lucas, a couple of blocks west of Königstrasse, has tables both indoors and out, some overlooking the river. There's a full, bratwurst-free menu of light German, Mediterranean, and Asian dishes for €8-13 and good salads for €7-10 (daily 8:00-24:00, Kaiserstrasse 22, tel. 0911/227-845).

Kettensteg Biergarten, the usual Bavarian jumble of picnic tables under trees, enjoys an above-average setting overlooking the city's river and medieval wall. It's named after, and is next to, Germany's first iron suspension bridge (built in 1824). Kettensteg's youthful energy and big flames give it a tribal vibe after dark. Though service can be curt, it's ideal on a balmy evening for leafy outdoor dining surrounded by happy locals and in-the-know foreign students (€8-13 meals, modern German cuisine and decent salads, daily 11:00-23:00, west of Hauptmarkt where the river hits the wall, Maxplatz 35, tel. 0911/221-081).

Cheap Eats: There are many inexpensive Asian and Middle Eastern restaurants in the block closest to the station.

Picnic: There's an Aldi discount **supermarket** near recommended hotels at Königstrasse 83 (limited selection, Mon-Sat 8:00-20:00, closed Sun) and a more upscale supermarket in the sub-basement of the Karstadt department store at the Lorenzkirche U-Bahn entrance (enter store at Karolinenstrasse 6 and take the escalators down two flights, Mon-Sat 9:30-20:00, closed Sun).

Nürnberg Connections

From Nürnberg by Train to: Rothenburg (hourly, 1.25 hours, change in Ansbach and Steinach), **Würzburg** (2-3/hour, 1-1.25 hours), **Munich** (2-3/hour, 1-1.25 hours), **Frankfurt** (1-2/hour, 2 hours), **Frankfurt Airport** (1-2/hour, 2.5 hours), **Dresden** (hourly, 4.5 hours, may change in Leipzig), **Leipzig** (every 2 hours direct, 3.5 hours; more with transfer in Naumburg), **Berlin** (hourly, 4.5 hours), **Salzburg** (hourly with change in Munich, 3 hours), **Prague** (3 slow trains/day, 5 hours; better to take express bus, 6/day, 3.75 hours, covered by railpasses). Train info: tel. 0180-599-6633, www.bahn.com.

LUTHERLAND

Erfurt • Wartburg Castle • Wittenberg

Martin Luther—pious monk, fiery orator, and religious whistle-blower—came from this humble, pastoral corner of Germany's heartland. In the charming university town of Erfurt, Luther was a student before casting his former life aside to become a monk. At Wartburg Castle, he hid out to translate the New Testament. And he eventually made his home in Wittenberg, where he worked as a university professor, nailed his 95 theses to the church door, and enjoyed married life with Katharina von Bora.

Located in the present-day states of Saxony and Thuringia, these three destinations—Erfurt, Wartburg Castle, and Wittenberg—mark the cradle of the Protestant Reformation. Luther's groundbreaking work here set into motion a chain of events that would split the Western Christian faith, plunge Europe into a century of warfare, cause empires to rise and fall, and inspire new schools of art and thought.

OK, I'll admit it—I'm a Lutheran. So of course I enjoy this area. But anyone with an appreciation for history could find it interesting. Erfurt is pleasant for a stroll. Wartburg Castle had a long heritage as a cultural center long before the Reformation. And Wittenberg's excellent sights—almost exclusively dedicated to Luther—make even an atheist appreciate the dramatic impact this dreamer had on European history. The city of Leipzig (with a few Luther ties itself) sits smack-dab in the center of this region; if you're connecting Luther towns, you'll almost certainly pass through Leipzig, which is worth a visit in its own right (see next chapter).

Throughout the region that I call (tongue-in-cheek) Lutherland, keep an eye out for the Luther rose, a symbol of the great Reformer: a black cross in a red heart (symbolizing the Crucifixion) inside a white rose (the peace and joy of faith), all within a golden ring that symbolizes the infinite nature of heaven.

Planning Your Time

Lutherland is easy to visit on the way between the Frankfurt/ Würzburg area to the west and the Berlin/Dresden area to the east. Luther pilgrims may want several days to linger at the historic sights. But if you're short on time and have a limited appetite for Luther lore, here's a concise two-day plan for splicing Lutherland into your itinerary:

Day 1: Ride the train to Eisenach, throw your bag in a locker, and visit Wartburg Castle. In the evening, continue by train 30 minutes to Erfurt, where you'll sleep.

Day 2: Spend the morning in Erfurt; at mid-day, head to Wittenberg, then take an evening train to Berlin. (If you'd also like to visit Leipzig, do it today and stay the night, then see Wittenberg on the morning of Day 3 en route to Berlin.)

Background

A basic understanding of Martin Luther's life and times is essential to fully appreciate this region. The following overview explains the most important events that shaped the man known as the great Reformer.

Martin Luther (1483-1546)

Martin Luther lived a turbulent life. In early adulthood, the newly ordained priest suffered a severe personal crisis of faith, before finally emerging "born again." In 1517, he openly protested against Church corruption and was later excommunicated. Defying both the pope and the emperor, he lived on the run as an outlaw, watching as his ideas sparked peasant riots. He still found time to translate the New Testament from Greek to modern German, write

hymns such as "A Mighty Fortress," and spar with fellow Reformer Ulrich Zwingli.

Early Life (Erfurt)

Martin Luther was born on November 10, 1483, in Eisleben, south of Berlin. His dad owned a copper smelter, affording Luther a middle-class upbringing—a rarity in the medieval hierarchy of nobles, clergy, and peasants.

Luther spent much of his childhood in the towns of Eisleben, Mansfeld, and Eisenach, and enrolled at the University of Erfurt in 1501. There Luther earned a liberal-arts degree, entered law school, and earned himself two nicknames—"the philosopher" for his wide-ranging mind, and "the king of hops" for his lifelong love affair with beer. In 1505, he received his master's degree (graduating second in his class) and appeared to have a very bright future ahead of him.

On July 2, 1505, while Luther was riding through the countryside, he was suddenly caught up in an intense thunderstorm, and a bolt of lightning knocked him to the ground. Luther cried out, "St. Anne, save me, and I will become a monk!" Surviving the storm,

ÆTHERNA IPSE SVÆ MENTIS SIMVLACHRA LVTHERVS
EXPRIMIT AT VVLTVS CERA LVCÆ OCCIDVOS
· M · D · XX ·

Luther was determined to make good on his promise. He returned to Erfurt, sold all of his possessions, and threw a dinner party for his friends, saying, "After this day, you will see me no more." The next morning, he knocked on the door of Erfurt's Augustinian Monastery and dedicated his life to Christ.

After spending several years in the monastery, Luther realized that being a simple, pious monk did not suit his inquisitive, intellectual nature. Encouraged by his supervisor, Luther returned to academic life. In 1507, he was ordained a priest in Erfurt's cathedral and was soon on the fast track to become a professor of theology. By 1508, he was teaching theology part-time at the university in nearby Wittenberg.

In 1509, Luther set out to travel on foot all the way to Rome. This pilgrimage would change him forever—but not in ways he expected. After a months-long walk, he finally arrived at the Eternal City. But instead of seeing poor, humble monks like himself, he was dismayed to find rich, corrupt priests and bishops selling "indulgences" that supposedly guaranteed entry to heaven to those able to pay the price. This was the Rome of Pope Julius II, who was in the midst of an expensive vanity project: an over-the-top remodel of Vatican City. At the time of Luther's visit, Michelangelo was lying on his back high in the air on scaffolding, executing painstakingly detailed frescoes on the Sistine Chapel ceiling, while Raphael was slathering nearby hallways with his own Renaissance masterpieces.

All of this clashed violently with Luther's own, deeply held ideas. Luther believed that people's faith, not their pocketbook, would determine the final destination of their souls. Indulgences were an insult to this worldview—and, to Luther, a betrayal of the Christian faith.

Professor and Preacher (Wittenberg)

After returning to Germany in 1512, Luther received his doctorate and got a permanent job teaching theology at the university in Wittenberg—the progressive city that would be his home for the rest of his life. Frederick the Wise, the prince elector of Saxony, had decided to make this (formerly backwater) town his royal seat, building a castle, a grand church, and a university, and inviting the region's best and brightest to populate his dynamic new burg. Here, Luther mingled with other great thinkers (including fellow professor Philipp Melanchthon) and artists (most notably Lucas Cranach the Elder).

During these early years in Wittenberg, Luther lived in a monastery and spent hours alone in his cell (living quarters). Consumed with the notion that he was a sinner, he devoured the Bible, looking for an answer and finding it in Paul's letter to the Romans. Luther concluded that God makes sinners righteous through their faith in Jesus Christ, not by earning it through good deeds. As this concept of grace took hold, Luther said, "I felt myself to have been born again."

Energized, he began a series of Bible lectures at Wittenberg's twin-towered St. Mary's City Church. The pews were packed as Luther quoted passages directly from the Bible. Speaker and audience alike began to see discrepancies between what the Bible said and what the Church was doing. Coincidentally, a representative of

Catholic and Protestant Differences

The differences between Protestant and Catholic doctrines have divided Christians for centuries. The Protestants' Reformation-era "protest" against Catholic corruption and rigidity is at the core of their spiritual identity. Both faiths see Jesus Christ as the central figure in bringing salvation, but they take different approaches.

Protestants emphasize the direct relationship between the individual and God. Bible study and personal prayer make this connection. With this as their core, they don't consider church rituals or doctrines essential. Protestant clergy are either lay people or pastors (who can marry) hired to facilitate worship.

Catholics use church rituals and an ordained clergy to help the individual make his or her connection to God. Catholics receive forgiveness for their sins through the act of Confession. They venerate saints and the Virgin Mary. They consider official pronouncements by the pope to be the word of God. Catholic priests must be celibate, and the Church recognizes organizations of monks and nuns.

the pope chose this moment to arrive in Wittenberg, selling letters of indulgence that promised "forgiveness for all thy sins, transgressions, and excesses, how enormous so ever they may be"...a bargain at twice the price. (The new pope—Leo X, a luxury-loving member of Florence's prominent Medici family—was raising funds to build an ambitious new Michelangelo-designed dome at St. Peter's Basilica in Rome.)

Luther was outraged at the idea that God's grace could be bought, and he thought the subject should be debated openly. On October 31, 1517, Luther approached Wittenberg's Castle Church and nailed his now-famous 95 theses—topics for discussion—to the door. The theses questioned indulgences and other Church practices and beliefs. Thesis #82 boldly asked: "If the pope redeems a number of souls for the sake of miserable money with which to buy a church, why doesn't he empty Purgatory for the sake of holy love?" Luther's propositions were printed on Lucas Cranach's new-fangled presses (some of Europe's first). It was the talk of Germany, and Luther became famous—or infamous—almost overnight.

Excommunication (Wartburg Castle)

Luther didn't set out to start a new church; he wanted to reform the existing one. He preached throughout the region, spreading his provocative ideas and publicly debating his positions in such venues as Leipzig's town hall. In 1520, a furious Pope Leo X sent the rebellious monk a papal bull threatening excommunication.

Luther burned the edict on the spot in Wittenberg reserved for disposing of dead animal carcasses (today marked by an oak tree). Soon after, Leo X formally excommunicated Luther.

Luther was branded a heretic and ordered to Rome to face charges, but he refused to go. Finally, the most powerful man in Europe, Emperor Charles V, stepped in to arbitrate, calling an Imperial Diet (congress) at Worms (1521). Luther made a triumphal entry into Worms, greeted by cheering crowds. The Diet convened, and Luther took his place in the center of the large hall, standing next to a stack of his writings. Inquisitors grilled him while the ultra-Catholic Charles looked on from his throne. Luther refused to disavow his beliefs. "Here I stand," he told the assembly, "I can do no other. So help me God. Amen."

The emperor retaliated by declaring Luther an outlaw, banning his writings, and putting a price on his head. But after leaving Worms, Luther disappeared. Rumor was that Luther had been kidnapped, but in fact he'd escaped (with the help of Frederick the Wise) to safety in Wartburg Castle. There Luther spent 10 months disguised as the bearded "Squire George" (Junker Jörg), fighting depression and translating the Bible's New Testament from the original Greek sources into German. This "September Testament" (the German precursor to the "King James Version") was revolutionary, bringing the Bible to the masses and shaping the modern German language.

Meanwhile, Luther's ideas caught on back home in Wittenberg, where they were used to justify armed uprisings and worse. When town officials asked him to return to quell the turmoil, Luther felt obligated to comply (in March of 1522). Back in Wittenberg, he gradually began preaching to his congregation anew, clashing with the more radically minded proto-Protestants who had moved in.

Later Life (Wittenberg)

In 1525, Luther's friend and follower Thomas Müntzer used a violent interpretation of Luther's writings to lead an uprising known as the Peasant Revolt. Poor farmers attacked their feudal masters with hoes and pitchforks, fighting for more food, political say-so, and respect. Some 5,000 peasants died in battle, and Müntzer was executed. Luther decried the violence, preaching that Church corruption did not justify outright societal rebellion: "Give to Caesar what is Caesar's..."

In April of 1523, Luther helped 12 nuns escape from a

Cistercian convent. Among them was a feisty young woman named Katharina von Bora, who came to Wittenberg to start a new life—and to find a husband. She was attracted to Luther. While he initially rebuffed her, Katharina gradually wore him down. In 1525, the 41-year-old ex-priest married the 26-year-old ex-nun, "to please my father and annoy the pope." (Their wedding set a precedent—still followed today—allowing Protestant clergy to marry.) They moved into the former Wittenberg monastery

where Luther had lived as a monk (today's Luther House), where they let out rooms to students. Luther turned his checkbook over to "my lord Katie," who also ran the family farm, raised their six children and 11 adopted orphans, and hosted Luther's circle of friends at loud, chatty dinner parties.

Though living in Wittenberg under the protection of prince elector John the Steadfast (Frederick the Wise's brother and successor), Luther traveled, spreading the Protestant message. In 1529, at Marburg Castle just north of Frankfurt, Luther attended a summit of leading Protestants to try and forge an alliance against Catholicism. They agreed on everything except a single theological point: whether Christ was present in the wine and bread of Communion in a physical sense (according to Luther) or symbolic sense (per the Swiss Reformer Ulrich Zwingli). The disagreement doomed the Protestant movement to splinter into dozens of sects.

Luther wasn't the first to speak out against Church corruption (the Czech priest and professor Jan Hus voiced similar criticisms a century earlier—and was burned at the stake). It's not insignificant that Luther's ideas found a receptive audience around the year 1500, as mass hysteria gripped Europe—a sort of "Y1.5K crisis" comparable to our own era's "Y2K" panic. Many were convinced that the Armageddon was nigh. This great fear and uncertainty provided Luther with fertile ground for his revolutionary ideas.

In 1534, Luther finished the first German translation of the complete Bible. Lucas Cranach illustrated it with woodcuts and published it on his printing presses. Luther also wrote a German Mass (based on the Catholic Latin Mass, but with important adjustments), catechisms, and several hymns including the still-beloved "A Mighty Fortress" ("A mighty fortress is our God, / A bulwark never failing; / Our helper He amid the flood / Of mortal ills prevailing").

In his 50s, Luther's health declined and he grew bitter, a fact made clear in such writings as "Against the Papacy at Rome

Founded by the Devil" and "Of the Jews and Their Lies." A general tone of anti-Semitism pollutes his later work. Tragically, these words were later invoked to justify hateful anti-Semitic speech and actions during the early days of Nazism.

Martin Luther died on February 18, 1546, and was buried in Wittenberg. To this day, pilgrims bring flowers. To read more about Luther's lasting legacy, see the sidebar on page 550.

Erfurt

A half-timbered, many-steepled medieval townscape with a shallow river gurgling through its middle, the place where Martin Luther spent his formative early years, and the capital of the region of Thuringia, Erfurt (AIR-foort) is an inviting destination. While its Luther sights aren't as exciting as the ones at Wartburg Castle or in Wittenberg, the town itself more than makes up for it. You can see the monastery where  Martin Luther became a monk and the cathedral where he became a priest, stroll across an atmospheric medieval bridge lined with characteristic shops, ogle an unearthed treasure-trove in one of Europe's oldest surviving synagogues, hike up to the citadel for views over town, or just bask in Erfurt's quaintness.

Sitting on an important medieval trade route, Erfurt boomed in the Middle Ages thanks largely to its production of woad, a blue dye made from local plants. In the 16th century, trade with India flooded the market with less-expensive, true indigo dyes, and Erfurt's fortunes tumbled, leaving it a well-preserved backwater for centuries. It enjoyed another boom with the creation of a united Germany in 1871, when Erfurt's central position in the new nation made it a strategic trading depot. Unlike the nearby cities of Berlin, Dresden, and Leipzig, Erfurt emerged from World War II relatively unscathed. This imbues Erfurt with a delightful time-capsule quality—rare for an eastern German city of its size.

These days, Erfurt is very popular among German tourists and Martin Luther pilgrims (including Pope Benedict XVI, who visited in September of 2011), but largely undiscovered by American visitors—English information is in maddeningly short supply. Erfurt provides a handy launch pad for visiting Wartburg Castle, where Luther hid out while translating the New Testament (just 30 minutes west by train).

LUTHERLAND

Planning Your Time

Erfurt deserves a day's visit, and possibly an overnight. You can get the gist of the town in a few hours: Take my self-guided walking tour, then drop into your choice of other sights—the twin churches are enjoyable, the citadel offers great views over town, Luther fans appreciate the Augustinian Monastery, and the truly old, Old Synagogue interests historians.

Orientation to Erfurt

(area code: 0361)

Although it has about 205,000 people, Erfurt feels smaller—particularly its downtown core, where you'll spend most of your time. Erfurt's Old Town, huddled picturesquely at a bend in the Gera River, is loosely bound by a ring road. The train station sits just beyond the southeastern edge of the ring, and the cathedral and citadel perch at the western edge. The Old Town core is about a 10- to 15-minute walk (or speedy tram ride) from the train station; once there, virtually all points of interest are within a 10-minute walk of each other.

Tourist Information

Erfurt's TI is right in the town center, between the Merchants' Bridge and Town Hall. It has piles of brochures and Erfurt souvenirs for sale. The basic free map is good enough for a short visit (April-Dec Mon-Fri 10:00-19:00, Sat 10:00-18:00, Sun 10:00-16:00; Jan-March Mon-Sat 10:00-18:00, Sun 10:00-16:00; Benediktplatz 1, tel. 0361/66400, www.erfurt-tourismus.de). The TI's website helps put visitors in touch with locals renting private rooms.

You'll see tour groups all over town, but there are no regularly scheduled English tours; instead, you can follow my self-guided walk, buy the TI's self-guided tour booklet (€1.70), or rent the iTour audioguide (€7.50/4 hours).

Arrival in Erfurt

The Erfurt Hauptbahnhof (main train station) has a few shops and eateries, and luggage lockers (below track 2, €1.50-3). There's no city TI at the station, but a regional (Thuringia) TI is directly across the square from the main door.

From the station, you can walk into the heart of town in about 10-15 minutes (a few minutes farther to Cathedral Square or the Augustinian Monastery), or you can hop a tram part of the way.

To **walk**, exit through the main door and bear left until you reach Bahnhofstrasse, with the tram tracks. Turn right and head five short blocks up Bahnhofstrasse. You'll pop out at the shopping

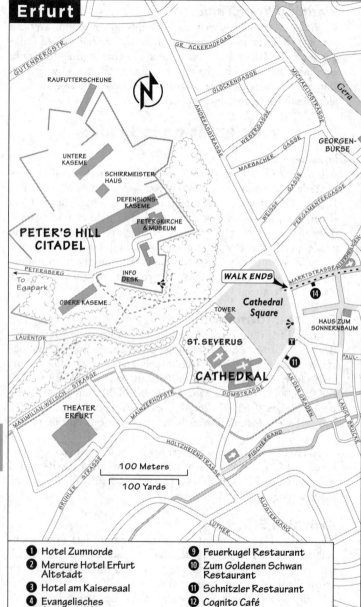

Erfurt

LUTHERLAND

1 Hotel Zumnorde
2 Mercure Hotel Erfurt Altstadt
3 Hotel am Kaisersaal
4 Evangelisches Augustinerkloster
5 Gästehaus Nikolai
6 Pension Rad-Hof
7 Ibis Hotel Erfurt Altstadt
8 Zum Güldenen Rade Restaurant
9 Feuerkugel Restaurant
10 Zum Goldenen Schwan Restaurant
11 Schnitzler Restaurant
12 Cognito Café
13 Faust Food
14 Eiscafé San Remo
15 Modern Masters Bar
16 Prager Bierstube & Übersee Bar

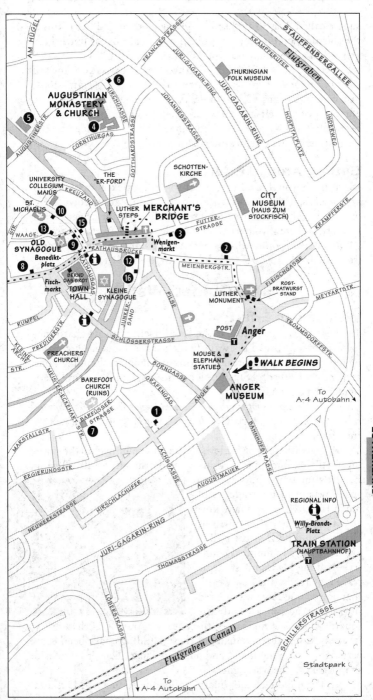

STAUFFENBERGALLEE

Flutgraben

KRAMPFERUFER

THURINGIAN
FOLK MUSEUM

JURI-GAGARIN-RING

FRANCKESTRASSE

HOSPITALPLATZ

LINDENWEG

AM HÜGEL

AUGUSTINERSTR.

KIRSCHGASSE

**AUGUSTINIAN
MONASTERY
& CHURCH**

⑤

④

⑥

CORNTHURGAS

GOTHARDSTRASSE

JOHANNESSTRASSE

SCHOTTEN-
KIRCHE

CITY
MUSEUM
(HAUS ZUM
STOCKFISCH)

KRÄMPFERSTR.

THE
"ER-FORD"

KREUZAND

UNIVERSITY
COLLEGIUM
MAIUS

ST.
MICHAELIS

⑩

LUTHER
STEPS

**MERCHANT'S
BRIDGE**

FUTTER-
STRASSE

⑬

WAAGE

STR.

**OLD
SYNAGOGUE**

⑮

⑨

RATHAUSBRÜCKE

*Wenigen-
markt*

③

②

FLEISCHGASSE

KRÄMPFERSTR.

MEYFARTSTR.

⑧

*Benedikt-
platz*

⑫

MEIENBERGSTR.

ROST-
BRATWURST
STAND

*Fisch-
markt*

BERND
DAS BROT

**TOWN
HALL**

⑯

**KLEINE
SYNAGOGUE**

PILSE

JUNKER-
SAND

**LUTHER
MONUMENT**

TROMMSDORFFSTR.

KÜMPEL

KLEINE
ARCHE

PREDIGERSTR.

SCHLÖSSERSTRASSE

POST

Anger

PREACHERS'
CHURCH

BORNGASSE

MOUSE &
ELEPHANT
STATUES

👣**WALK BEGINS**

MEISTER ECKEHART STR.

**BAREFOOT
CHURCH
(RUINS)**

BARFÜSSER-
STRASSE

⑦

GRAFENGASS E

ANGER

**ANGER
MUSEUM**

To
A-4 Autobahn →

①

MARSTALLSTR.

REGIERUNGSSTR.

NEUWERKSTRASSE

JURI-GAGARIN-RING

HIRSCHLACHUFER

LACHSGASSE

AUGUSTMAUER

BAHNHOFSTRASSE

REGIONAL INFO

*Willy-Brandt-
Platz*

**TRAIN STATION
(HAUPTBAHNHOF)**

THOMASSTRASSE

TÖBESTRASSE

SCHILLERSTRASSE

Flutgraben (Canal)

To
A-4 Autobahn →

Stadtpark

LUTHERLAND

square called Anger (marked by a glassy modern building). This is
the starting point for my self-guided walk; most of the hotels I list
are within a 10-minute walk of Anger.

Or, to take a **tram,** exit out the side of the station, toward
Ausgang Bahonhofstrasse; you'll run right into the tram stops.
You can take trams #3, #4, or #6 to Anger (main shopping zone
and start of my self-guided walk), then to Domplatz (Cathedral
Square); tram #1 goes first to Anger, then continues to the
Augustinerkloster (Augustinian Monastery).

Getting Around Erfurt

It's unlikely you'll need to use Erfurt's trams, except possibly to
spare yourself the short walk from the train station downtown,
or to reach the Egapark gardens. But the straightforward tram
network is there if you need it. One ride costs €1.70, and there are
automated coin-op machines both at the stops and on the trams
(select "CityTarif Efurt" for rides within town).

Self-Guided Walk

Welcome to Erfurt

The best "sight" in Erfurt is the town itself, with its charming,
half-timbered core. This walk (which takes about an hour, not
including sightseeing breaks) begins at the main shopping zone
and ends at Cathedral Square; along the way, it passes nearly every
sightseeing option in town.

• *Begin in the main shopping square, called Anger. To get here from the
train station, follow my walking directions, earlier. Or you can ride the
tram to the Anger stop.*

Anger: Literally "Meadow," this area's name evokes the graz-
ing land that once sprawled just outside the city walls. During
Erfurt's medieval heyday, this
space was used for trade. And
much later, when Germany unified for the first time in 1871,
Erfurt found itself at the bull's-
eye of the newly founded country—making it a highly strategic
trade crossroads. The new wealth
that flowed into town was poured
into construction around this
square. Study the fine late-19th-century and early-20th-century
facades. More recently, many of these buildings have been converted into shopping malls, and numbered (e.g., "Anger 1") to help
shoppers keep them straight.

In the middle of the square, notice the statues of Maus and

Elefant—two beloved characters from the Erfurt-based children's television network **KI.KA** (short for "Kinder Kanal"). When German families come here, their kids can't wait to pose with figures like these, which are scattered around town.

The palatial yellow building, across the tram tracks from the glassy, modern building, hosts the **Anger Museum** (described later, under "Sights in Erfurt"). No, this doesn't highlight the Germanic ill temper. This building was recently restored to showcase the city's marginally interesting collections of paintings, applied arts, and medieval artifacts.

• *Turn your back to the glassy shopping mall, turn left, and walk along the tram tracks with the red-and-white-striped post office on your left-hand side. You'll reach a small church with a statue in front, depicting...*

Martin Luther: Although he was born 60 miles north in Eisleben, Luther came to Erfurt in 1501 to enroll at the university. After graduating, the smart young student began to pursue a doctorate at the prestigious law faculty, but after a close call with a lightning storm, Luther had a change of heart and became a monk at Erfurt's Augustinian Monastery for several years. This walk passes a few blocks from the monastery.

• *To the right of the statue, notice the...*

Rostbratwurst Stand: Locals are extremely proud of what they stress is *"originale"* Thüringer bratwurst—a long, skinny, relatively low-fat pork sausage amply seasoned with pepper, marjoram, and other spices. When you buy one, grab a roll and hold it open, and they'll insert the wurst straight from the grill. While there's ketchup standing by, purists put only the locally made Born brand mustard *(Senf)* on their weenie.

• *As you munch, go around the left side of the church, then turn left up Meienbergstrasse, and walk for a couple of blocks—passing a row of* Döner Kebab *joints—to...*

Wenigemarkt: This "Little Market Square" is one of Erfurt's most charming, encircled with al fresco cafés and watched over by the fortified tower of the Methodist Church of St. Aegidius.

• *Head for that church tower, and go through the large gateway in the green building just to its right. Jog left with the covered lane, and you'll pop out at...*

The "Er-Ford": Notice the ramp that goes right down into the Gera River, out the other side, then continues through the far branch of the river. Like any German town with "-furt" in its name, Erfurt is named for a shallow point where ancient traders could ford a river. (The "Er" part comes from an old German word for "dirty"—the water was muddied when people would cross.) This ford was along the ancient

Via Regia, an important trading route that connected Paris and Frankfurt to the west to Leipzig and all the way to Kiev in the east.

Spanning the river on your left is the **Merchants' Bridge.** Notice that—unlike the famous Ponte Vecchio in Florence—people actually make their homes along this bridge (see the flower boxes on the lived-in balconies). As in ages past, the residents live upstairs and run shops downstairs.

Find the narrow staircase at the left end of the bridge. These are nicknamed the **"Luther steps"** (Luthertreppen) because he may have begged here. After he left his promising university career for the humble monastic life, Luther took a vow of poverty that forced him to beg for food. However, many historians doubt that city leaders would actually allow a university dropout to panhandle in the city limits—too embarrassing for the proud tradition of the U. of Erfurt. More likely, Luther did his begging in smaller villages outside the city limits.

• *From here, it's about a five-minute walk to the **Augustinian Monastery** where Luther first became a monk (described later, under "Sights in Erfurt"; to side-trip to the monastery, follow the river to the right, then jog inland).*

But for now, let's continue the walk. At the top of the Luther steps, turn right and begin exploring the...

Merchants' Bridge (Krämerbrücke): The bridge dates from 1325, but the shops that line it sprouted around the late 15th and early 16th centuries (about Martin Luther's time). A *Krämer* was an upscale merchant, who usually dealt in small portions of highly valuable items. And, to this day, lowbrow McDonald's still hasn't won out along this shopping thoroughfare—most of the shops remain small, good-quality, and local (if still tourist-friendly). Across from the

Luther steps is a shop dealing in Thuringian specialties, including wines, mustard, cheese, and sausage. Nearly across the street (on the right) is the **Goldhelm Schokolade shop,** selling chocolates and delicious ice cream (the chocolate flavor is tasty, but the caramel is *wunderbar*; daily 10:00-18:00, until 19:00 in summer).

Window-shop your way across the bridge. Near the end, on the right, don't miss the window marked **Theatrum Mundi.** This is the brilliant work of a local puppet-maker, Martin Gobsch. It's well worth popping in a €1 coin to see the evil queen pull back her arm to reveal an intricately detailed, fully articulated rendering of the Snow White story—it plays for a few minutes, just long enough to take in all the delightful details.

• *At the end of Merchants' Bridge, you emerge at...*

Benediktplatz: Originally Merchants' Bridge was guarded at either end by fortified churches; the one on this end—St.

Benedict's—was torn down by Napoleonic troops, but its name survives. The TI is at the bottom of this square. In the TI's window display down the side-street, look for a small exhibit about woad (*Waid* in German). This four-foot-tall plant with yellow flowers was converted into a highly valuable blue dye that buoyed Erfurt's economy in the Middle Ages. First the plant was mashed up and fermented with urine for two months. (How they worked out this procedure, I don't care to know.) After the mixture dried, it was ground into a fine powder that could be used to create a brilliant blue dye—literally worth its weight in gold.

• *Before continuing ahead, consider a detour up...*

Michaelisstrasse: Historically the core of the university district, today this drag hosts some of the town's most popular restaurants and bars. After a block, go down the first lane on the left, then look left to find the entrance to the **Old Synagogue**—one of Europe's earliest surviving synagogues, displaying a recently rediscovered treasure in its cellar (see "Sights in Erfurt," later).

Continuing another long block along Michaelisstrasse, you'll come to an intersection shared by a church and an old pink building—both related to the **University of Erfurt.** Founded in 1379, the university was the third in present-day Germany, and it remained prestigious for centuries—counting both Martin Luther and Johannes Gutenberg as alums. It closed its doors in 1816, but reopened in 1994 and is going strong today. The pink building, called the Collegium Maius, was the town's first university building (though it's mostly a reconstruction—the original was one of

Erfurt's few WWII casualties). Medieval students had a rough life: They had to get up at 4:00 in the morning to attend Mass, ate just two meals a day (breakfast at 10:00 and dinner at 16:00), and were required to bathe once per month. On the upside, students were rationed one liter of beer per meal (it was more pure than the water). Notice the modern stained-glass windows above the door depicting the four traditional areas of study: theology (cross and fish), law (weights), medicine (snake on staff), and philosophy (eye). The church, St. Michaelis, was once the university church (now independent).

• *Head back to Benediktplatz and the TI, and turn right (in the direction you were originally going) toward...*

Fischmarkt: You'll immediately see the back of the Town Hall on your left. Up near the corner of the building, look for another KI.KA character—a morose, SpongeBob-looking slice of bread named **Bernd das Brot.** In

what surely ranks among the most dramatic art heists in European history, this statue was stolen in 2009 by squatters protesting an eviction notice. They even put a tongue-in-cheek ransom video on YouTube. Several days later, Bernd was discovered by kids in an abandoned building and returned to his rightful home.

The square itself is dominated by the Town Hall building. The statue in the center of the square holds a flag and shield, both with the city symbol—a wheel in a circle. Erfurt, which was never a free city, spent much of its history as part of the Archbishop of Mainz's holdings, so this wheel is based on that city's symbol.

• *Stand with the Town Hall at your back, and walk straight ahead (along the tram tracks) up...*

Marktgasse: At the tall white steeple (after passing Werner's Head Shop on your left), look left down the street to see **Haus zum Sonnenbaum** (a yellow house with brown timbers and trim). At this popular venue for weddings, notice the intertwined golden

LUTHERLAND

rings on the grate over the window to the right of the door, and to the left, the cage (whose symbolism is obvious). Lovers are trying to start a new custom by locking padlocks inscribed with their initials on this cage.

• *A block farther on the left is the recommended* **Eiscafé San Remo,** *with Italian-style gelato. Soon after, you'll reach...*

Cathedral Square (Domplatz): This vast square is dominated by twin churches: the **cathedral** (on the left) and **St. Severus**

(right). While Erfurt's history is tied to religion, the atheistic East German government successfully smothered the local faith: These days, just 7 percent of Erfurters profess to be Catholic, 14 percent are Protestant, and the rest are unchurched. On the hill to the right, you can see the base of **Peter's Hill Citadel,** a gigantic fortress that's free to explore and offers sweeping views over Erfurt. (The churches and citadel are described later, under "Sights in Erfurt.")

The street leading away from Cathedral Square to the right, **Andreasstrasse,** was called "the longest street in Erfurt" during communist times. The bright-red building behind the wall to the right of the cathedral was a prison run by the Stasi, East Germany's secret police, reserved for those who were caught trying to escape to the West. Why was it the longest street? "It takes five minutes to go in, and five years to get out."

• *Our tour is finished. Visit the churches and citadel, then enjoy exploring the town. Or, if you're ready to head back to the train station, you can ride tram #3, #4, or #6 three stops to the Hauptbahnhof.*

Sights in Erfurt

Martin Luther Sights

▲**Augustinian Monastery and Church (Augustinerkloster und Augustinerkirche)**—On July 17, 1505, a young student knocked on the door of this monastery and declared that he wished to become a monk. Martin Luther lived here for several years—even after becoming a priest and a part-time professor—until he officially moved to Wittenberg in 1512. Inside the still-active complex, you can see the church, a small museum of Luther artifacts, and the cell where Monk Martin lived.

Cost and Hours: Church-free, cell/museum-€3.50, guided tour in German-€3.50, combo-ticket for tour and cell/museum-€5, photo permission-€2, cell/museum open Mon-Sat 10:00-16:00, Sun 11:00-13:00, church open longer hours, Augustinerstrasse 10, tel. 0361/576-600, www.augustinerkloster.de.

Touring the Monastery: Entering through the door, you emerge into a tranquil, park-like courtyard. On the left, the modern building (housing offices and a concert hall) marks the site of an earlier library, where 267 people suffocated while hiding in the cellar to escape WWII bombs. (A propagandistic communist-era plaque condemning this "Anglo-American terrorist attack" has been replaced by a more tasteful one simply listing the victims.) The new building is connected by an elevated walkway to the main part of the complex, with two major sights: the church and the Martin Luther museum and cell.

The **church,** dating from the late 13th century, is where Martin Luther worshipped as a monk. The stained-glass windows (c. 1330) include a motif of lions (symbolizing Jesus) flanking a rose (Mary). This window, which monks used as a focal point for meditation, must have made a deep impression on Luther—who later adopted a similar rose icon for his personal coat of arms. In front of the main altar, the tomb of a prominent priest was a place where monks (including Luther) would meditate overnight—lying on their backs, with their arms outstretched. The deeply introspective Luther struggled with all this meditation, which caused him a heavy angst that he eventually escaped by returning to academia.

To see the **museum and cell,** you have two options: Join a German-language tour (depart roughly at the top of each hour,

one-hour tour; also includes the peaceful cloister), or visit it on your own. Since the exhibits are explained in English—and the tour isn't—visiting on your own works well. You'll find exhibits about the history of the Bible and a room dedicated to Martin Luther that contains a few original artifacts, as well as replicas of his straw bed, gown, book, lute, and so on. The room is lined with small cells where monks would sleep and meditate. The lattice windows allowed others to look in on the monks to be sure they were behaving appropriately. The cell at the far corner (called the Lutherzelle) was Martin Luther's final home at the monastery. (When he was first here, he likely slept on the floor with other new recruits.) Inside the cell is a writing table, similar to the one Luther used for carrying out the monastic task of copying Bibles. In the chapter hall, monks would convene for meetings and to confess before each other; sinners could be punished, or even beaten.

Georgenburse—Luther pilgrims can drop by this old dorm where Luther lived as a student. It's basically one big room with information about university life and the U. of E.'s most famous alum, Luther.

Cost and Hours: €2.50; Mon, Wed, and Fri 9:00-14:00; Tue and Thu 13:00-17:00; closed Sat-Sun; Augustinerstrasse 27.

Other Churches—While the biggest churches in town (on Cathedral Square, described later) are Catholic, two Protestant churches are near the Luther sights. **Preachers' Church** (Predigerkirche) is the town's main Protestant church (free, Tue-Sat 11:00-16:00, Sun 12:00-16:00, closed Mon, Predigerstrasse 4). Nearby sit the ruins of the bombed-out **Barefoot Church** (Barfüsserkirche)—in Germanic countries, "barefoot" is synonymous with Franciscan, evocative of St. Francis' simple lifestyle. Peek in the gate to see the open space once occupied by the nave, now used as a concert venue.

Other Sights in the Town Center

▲▲**Old Synagogue (Alte Synagogue)**—One of the oldest surviving synagogues in Europe, this building was forgotten for

several centuries before its original identity was finally rediscovered in the 1980s. Today it has been restored to highlight its medieval heyday, while preserving its other layers of history. The good, modern exhibit inside explains the history of the building, examines the relationship between Jews and Christians in medieval Erfurt, and shows off a fantastic cache of coins and jewelry that was discovered nearby.

Cost and Hours: €5, includes audioguide, Tue-Sun 10:00-18:00, closed Mon, mandatory bag check, no photos, Waagegasse 8, tel. 0361/655-1608, www.juedisches-leben.erfurt.de.

Background: With sections dating all the way back to around 1100, this building was the religious center of Erfurt's bustling medieval Jewish community. Rather than being forced into a ghetto, Erfurt's Jews were allowed to mix freely with their Christian neighbors. In fact, the synagogue's location is one of the most desirable in town, situated near the main trading routes.

All of that changed during the Black Death plague pandemic of 1348-1349, when far more of Erfurt's Christians perished than Jews. Guess who got the blame. (In reality, the Jews likely survived at a higher rate because their faith emphasized cleanliness, reducing the spread of disease.) A major pogrom (anti-Semitic riot) devastated the Jewish community, with many expelled or killed.

Because the Archbishop of Mainz received "protection money" from the Jews, he insisted that Erfurt allow them back in

1350, but from that point on they were relegated to a ghetto. The synagogue building was taken over by the town and sold. Over the next several centuries, it was used first as a warehouse, then (in the late 19th century) as a restaurant, bowling alley, and dance hall. Finally, in the 1980s, historians realized that it had once been a synagogue, and it was restored.

Touring the Synagogue: On the **ground floor,** models illustrate how the original synagogue building grew over time. The rail high on the wall once held lamps. The octagon in the center of the room marks the location of the bima, a raised area for reading Jewish scripture (similar to a pulpit in Christian worship). A projection on the wall shows the niche where the Torah was kept. The map of medieval Erfurt shows where Jews (red) and Christians (blue) resided before the 1349 pogrom—notice how well-integrated Jews were into the community.

Now go **upstairs.** Nothing here is original—it looks more like the colorfully decorated dance hall that was here from 1876 through the 1930s. The balcony ringing the room was the so-called "dragon's watch," where mothers could keep an eye on their daughters dancing with would-be suitors. Imagine young Nazis waltzing here, oblivious to the fact that they were partying in a former synagogue. (Had they known, the Nazis would have torn the place down.) Among the replicas of parchment scrolls and important books is a copy of the biggest handwritten Hebrew Bible in the world (notice that the illustrations are made up of tiny Hebrew characters). The originals are in a Berlin museum. In display case #48, press the button to see an original document from the late 12th century (the Erfurt Jewish Oath), regulating interactions between Christians and Jews—one of the oldest surviving texts on this topic.

For the grand finale, head into the **cellar.** In 1998, a remarkable collection of gold, silver, and jewels—some 60 pounds—was discovered in the cellar of a nearby building. Called the "Erfurt Treasure," this almost certainly belonged to a wealthy local Jew who was killed in the 1349 pogrom. Display cases show off brooches, tableware, and golden decorations for a belt and other garments. The wheel-shaped necklace was used for perfume. (They've reformulated this original medieval perfume—you can ask to sniff it at the ticket desk upstairs.) Find the museum's prize piece, a finely detailed golden wedding ring from the early 14th century. On the ring's central pillar is the hard-to-see inscription *mazel tov,* indicating that this belonged to a Jewish woman. Nearby are mannequins dressed as a Jewish bride and groom from that period—wearing rich materials and draped in gold. The stacks of coins come from all over Europe, especially from France. The 50-pound bag with chunks of silver is marked with the seal of an Erfurt goldsmith.

Anger Museum—This modern, well-presented museum, almost completely lacking in English information, displays paintings, applied arts, and artifacts from the Middle Ages. The ground-floor medieval collection includes wood-carved statues, altarpieces, and a huge collection of shields. The Heckelarium is a small room slathered with frescoes by German Expressionist painter Erich Heckel (1883-1970). Part of the early-1900s art movement called Die Brücke, Heckel strove to create a bridge between two emotional, artistic styles: dramatic Romanticism and edgy Expressionism. The first floor features the good applied

arts collection (Kunsthandwerke, featuring historic room interiors with period furnishings, a treasury of precious items, and a collection of glass and porcelain) and a painting gallery (mostly Romantic canvases by largely unknown artists). Temporary exhibits fill the top floor.

Cost and Hours: €5, Tue-Sun 10:00-18:00, closed Mon, Anger 18, tel. 0361/655-1651, www.angermuseum.de.

Cathedral Square (Domplatz) and Nearby

Erfurt's grandest square is watched over by three giant structures: a pair of churches on the small hill called Domberg (the cathedral on the left, St. Severus on the right) and the citadel atop Peter's Hill (Petersburg).

Climb up the 70 steps to enter the two churches, whose entrances face each other. Both churches are Catholic and Gothic, dating from the 14th century and later expanded after a fire in the 15th century.

▲▲**Cathedral (Dom)**—The seat of a bishopric founded in the eighth century by St. Boniface, Erfurt's cathedral is the church where Martin Luther was ordained a priest. It sticks out from the hill on a massive substructure to level out the foundation. Inside you'll find a gorgeously carved choir and a few interesting pieces of ecclesiastical art.

Cost and Hours: Free, daily 10:00-18:00, until 17:00 in winter, tel. 0361/576-960, www.dom-erfurt.de.

Touring the Cathedral: Upon entering, turn left to reach the late-14th-century **choir**, with its intricately carved oak seats. This was built around the time of the 1349 pogrom, when anti-Semitic feelings were running high. To the left near

the entrance to the choir, find the carving depicting a duel between two knights—one on the horse, the other on a swine. The *Schweinereiter* ("Swine Knight") wears a Jewish helmet; this negative caricature both insults Jews (particularly because the Jewish faith considers pigs unclean) and emphasizes the triumph of

Christianity over Judaism. Look up to appreciate the stained-glass windows (c. 1370-1380), depicting Old and New Testament stories, and missionaries in the region of Thuringia.

Directly across from the main entrance, find the remarkably old (c. 1160) **Wolfram,** a bronze candelabra shaped like a man holding up a pair of candles, fighting off evil with light. Nearby, the light hanging from the ceiling was stolen from the Jewish synagogue during the 1349 pogrom.

Filling the wall to the right, the giant **fresco** shows St. Christopher using Erfurt's namesake ford to walk Christ to safety (notice this cathedral's steeples over his shoulder). This fresco helped make the saint's story real to the medieval congregation.

Below St. Christopher is a **tomb** relief panel showing the Duke of Gleichen flanked by two women. This gravestone gave

rise to a popular (but almost certainly made-up) fairy tale: Supposedly "the only man allowed to have two wives," this influential knight went to the Holy Land to fight in the Crusades, was captured and enslaved, and was forced to toil in the garden of the sultan. He married the sultan's daughter in exchange for her help escaping, then brought her back with him to Erfurt...where he introduced her to his first wife. (Awwk-waaard.) The new bride was accepted by the first one, the knight received special dispensation from the pope to be a bigamist, and the valley where the three of them lived in wedded bliss is still called Freudenthal ("Happy Valley").

▲**Church of St. Severus (Severikirche)**—This "hall church" has five parallel naves (notice the two narrow ones flanking the

main nave) and no perpendicular transept. To the left of the fine Baroque organ is a 14th-century sarcophagus containing the remains of the church's namesake. Originally "St. Paul's," this church was renamed in the ninth century, when some of the relics of St. Severus were brought here from Ravenna. On the sides of Severus' tomb, see the scenes of Severus' life (a poor craftsman being designated as the chosen one by a white dove over his head—representing the Holy Spirit—and then being "crowned" the bishop of Ravenna) and the Three Magi bringing gifts to the Baby Jesus.

Cost and Hours: Free, daily 10:00-18:00, until 17:00 in winter.

▲**Peter's Hill Citadel (Zitadelle Petersberg)**—This sprawling fortress complex, occupying the hill just above Cathedral Square, is

an enjoyable place to go for a stroll and enjoy views over the rooftops of Erfurt. Built from the 17th to the 19th centuries, this is one of the best-preserved citadels of its kind in Europe. While the grounds are extensive, you can have a satisfying quick

visit: Walk up the ramp from Cathedral Square, pausing at the gatehouse to visit the Military History Museum (a couple of rooms with mannequin soldiers and other displays, well-explained in English). As you continue up into the main courtyard of the castle complex, the glassy building on your right is a visitors center with a helpful info desk, a view café, and panoramic terrace offering sweeping views over Cathedral Square and the rest of Erfurt. The visitors center hands out a helpful, free map and mini-guide of the entire complex. Across the field from the center is a large church building with an exhibit of interesting "concrete art" (modern art with 3-D optical illusions). You can visit the underground tunnels only on a guided German tour (ask at info desk).

Cost and Hours: Free; grounds—always open; info desk and Military History Museum—daily April-Oct 11:00-18:30, Nov-March 11:00-16:00; church/art exhibit—Wed-Sun 10:00-18:00, closed Mon-Tue; tel. 0361/601-5384.

LUTHERLAND

On or near the Ring Road

Thuringian Folk Museum (Museum für Thüringer Volks-kunde)—This former hospital contains artifacts and old photos illustrating everyday folk life in the region of Thuringia. You'll climb up rickety stairs to see representations of various walks of life, including church, school, bars, farming, shops, kitchen, and home life. The top floor features clothing and dress-up dolls from the 19th through the early 20th centuries. While charming, the museum has not a word of English.

Cost and Hours: €5, Tue-Sun 10:00-18:00, closed Mon, Juri-Gagarin-Ring 140A, tel. 0361/655-5607, www.volkskundemuseum-erfurt.de.

City Museum (Stadtmuseum)—Filling the historic Haus zum Stockfisch town house, this old-fashioned collection shows off items relating to the history of Erfurt. You'll see a model of the town, dusty cases of artifacts, military uniforms, collections of guns and typewriters (both manufactured in Erfurt), and a film about the growth of Erfurt over time. Look for the wall of street signs from Erfurt's time as part of the former German Democratic Republic (DDR—communist East Germany). Under the communists, Erfurt's main drags were renamed Karl-Marx-Allee, Waffenbrüderschaft ("Brothers in Arms"—i.e., the Warsaw Pact), Völkerfreundschaft ("Peoples' Friendship"—a favorite buzzword of Stalin's), and October 7 Street (celebrating the date, in 1949, when the DDR was officially formed). In a display case, you can compare banknotes from West Germany and East Germany. A new permanent exhibit about Martin Luther is planned for 2012.

Cost and Hours: €5, Tue-Sun 10:00-18:00, closed Mon, Johannesstrasse 169, tel. 0361/655-5651, www.stadtmuseum-erfurt.de.

On the Outskirts of Town

Egapark—Garden-lovers flock to this sprawling green space at the western edge of town. You can stroll through various gardens (perennials, roses, dahlias, irises, sculptures, Japanese rock and water), visit the houses (for butterflies, tropical plants, and more), climb the observation tower, and tour the museum.

Cost and Hours: €6, €2 after 17:00, more during special events; daily May-mid-Sept 9:00-20:00, March-April and mid-Sept-Oct 9:00-18:00, Nov-Feb 10:00-16:00; Gothaer Strasse 38, ride tram #2 from the train station, tel. 0361/564-3737, www.egapark-erfurt.de.

LUTHERLAND

Sleeping in Erfurt

Like many other former-East German cities, Erfurt is short on characteristic little family-run inns; accommodations here gravitate toward sterile business-class hotels offering predictable comfort. All of my listings are in the Old Town core. Erfurt hoteliers enjoy grumbling about a hefty 5 percent "cultural tax" that is levied on all overnights in town; this tax is not included in the rates listed below.

$$$ Hotel Zumnorde, buried deep in the Anger shopping district, has 54 spacious, somewhat overpriced rooms (Sb-€95-130 but usually around €100, Db-€115-160 but usually around €125; rate depends on demand and room size; air-con in some rooms, elevator, free Wi-Fi, parking-€11, Anger 50-51 but enter on the side street at Weitergasse 26, tel. 0361/56800, www.hotel-zumnorde.de, info@hotel-zumnorde.de).

$$ Mercure Hotel Erfurt Altstadt, part of the Europe-wide business-class chain, has 142 rooms on a nondescript street between the Anger shopping district and the main sightseeing zone (Sb-€72-176 but usually around €95, Db-€77-216 but usually around €100, breakfast-€17, elevator, pay Wi-Fi, parking-€12, Meienbergstrasse 26-27, tel. 0361/59490, www.mercure.com, h5375@accor.com).

$$ Hotel am Kaisersaal offers 36 business-class rooms at good rates in an inviting location, just a few steps off the charming Wenigermarkt restaurant square (Sb-€84, Db-€94, Tb-€104, rates can flex with demand, breakfast-€5, elevator, free Wi-Fi, parking-€9, Futterstrasse 8, tel. 0361/658560, www.hotel-am-kaisersaal.de, info@hotel-am-kaisersaal.de).

Sleep Code

(€1 = about $1.40, country code: 49, area code: 0361)
S = Single, **D** = Double/Twin, **T** = Triple, **Q** = Quad, **b** = bathroom, **s** = shower only. All of these places speak English and accept credit cards. Unless otherwise noted, breakfast is included.

To help you sort easily through these listings, I've divided the accommodations into three categories, based on the price for a standard double room with bath:

$$$ Higher Priced—Most rooms €100 or more.
$$ Moderately Priced—Most rooms between €70-100.
$ Lower Priced—Most rooms €70 or less.

Prices can change without notice; verify the hotel's current rates online or by email. For other updates, see www.ricksteves.com/update.

$$ The **Evangelisches Augustinerkloster**—Martin Luther's monastery—rents 51 simple rooms with no Wi-Fi, phones, or TV (if Martin didn't need them, why do you?) right on the monastery grounds. Popular with traveling church groups, it offers monastic comfort and tranquility at reasonable prices (Sb-€49, Db-€78, all doubles are twins, Augustinerstrasse 10, tel. 0361/576-600, www.augustinerkloster.de, info@augustinerkloster.de). Just up the street along the river, **Gästehaus Nikolai**—also run by the monastery—is similarly old-fashioned, though more hotelesque: Its 17 rooms have TVs and phones (Sb-€64, Db-€88, tel. 0361/598-170, www.gaestehaus-nikolai.de, gaestehaus-nikolai@augustinerkloster.de).

$ **Pension Rad-Hof** is a wonderful oasis run with justifiable pride by bike aficionado Sigrid Odau and her family. Located next to the Augustinian Monastery, this characteristic B&B has six homey rooms (many decorated with musical instruments) overlooking a chirpy garden courtyard. While the lodgings aren't fancy, this place has more character than the rest of Erfurt's hotels combined (Sb-€30-50, Db-€60, Tb-€80, Qb-€100, €3/person more for one-night stays, free Wi-Fi, bike rental, Kirchgasse 1B, tel. 0361/602-7761, www.rad-hof.de, erfurt@rad-hof.de).

$ **Ibis Hotel Erfurt Altstadt** is a great value, offering 105 centrally located rooms (across the street from the ruined Barfüsserkirche) at rock-bottom prices with cookie-cutter comfort. Considering the dearth of characteristic hotels in town, if you're going to sleep in an Ibis, it might as well be here (Sb/Db-€61-69, Tb-€15 more, breakfast-€10, air-con, elevator, free Wi-Fi in lobby, pay Wi-Fi in rooms, parking garage-€6, Barfüsserstrasse 9, tel. 0361/66410, www.ibishotel.com, h1648@accor.com).

Eating in Erfurt

The Thuringian staple is the distinctive potato dumpling called *Klösse:* About the size of a tennis ball, these are soft and light, though generally drenched in gravy. Many Erfurt menus include several *Klösse* dishes. Thuringians are also proud of their own special type of peppery sausage (described on page 30).

Most of Erfurt's restaurants are quite plain-Jane—don't expect culinary variety here. Since little distinguishes one place from the next, the stakes are low—consider just looking for an ambience that appeals.

Zum Güldenen Rade ("At the Golden Wheel") has a pleasant enough beer hall, but the real draw is Erfurt's most appealing beer garden out back—under trees and surrounded by half-timbers (with both table service and self-service sections). Understandably touristy, it offers classic German and Thuringian cuisine (including a few vegetarian *Klösse* options; €5-10 starters, €10-15 main dishes, €2-3 bratwurst at self-service beer garden counter, daily 11:00-24:00, Marktstrasse 50, tel. 0361/561-3506).

Feuerkugel serves up good, traditional Thuringian cooking from "Oma Käthe" (Granny Katie). Its cozy, warm, woody interior is particularly inviting (€10 *Klösse* dishes, €8-13 meals, daily 11:00-24:00, Michaelisstrasse 3-4, tel. 0361/789-1256).

Zum Goldenen Schwan ("At the Golden Swan") is a brew-pub with several rooms, both new and old. Sit inside, near the big copper brewing vats, or head outside to the beer garden (€8-15 meals, daily 11:00-24:00, Michaelisstrasse 9, tel. 0361/262-3742).

Schnitzler, true to its name, serves schnitzel...and not much else. When I asked how many different versions of schnitzel were on the menu, they shrugged and said, "Enough." I lost count at around 30. It's right on Cathedral Square, with a nondescript interior and outdoor tables looking toward the cathedral and St. Severus (€8-12 schnitzel dishes, daily 11:00-23:00, Domplatz 23-33, tel. 0361/644-7557).

Cognito offers a fresh, healthy, self-service alternative right next to the Merchants' Bridge. This student-vibe place dishes up €5-10 soups, curries, and salads, as well as coffee drinks. You can get it to go, or enjoy the comfortable, hip lounge interior on two floors (daily 7:00-22:00, Hefengasse 1, tel. 0361/660-4666).

Fast Food: To grab a Thüringer bratwurst in a hurry, stop by **Faust Food,** which grills up sausages and other quick meaty options at low prices (less than €3). Get yours to go, or grab a table inside or out. It's on a forgotten lane in the middle of town—so near to all the tourists, yet so far away (Tue-Sat 11:00-23:00, Sun 11:00-19:00, closed Mon, Waagegasse 1, tel. 0361/786-9969).

Ice Cream: **Eiscafé San Remo,** on Marktstrasse just a block off Cathedral Square, has a loyal following for its Italian-style gelato (daily 10:00-22:00, Marktstrasse 21, tel. 0361/643-0449).

Late-Night Drinks: **Modern Masters** is the favorite in this student town for cocktails after dark in a sophisticated yet unsnooty atmosphere (no food—only drinks, Tue-Sat from 17:00, closed Sun-Mon, right at the start of Michaelisstrasse at #48). Two other bars have tables on terraces over the river, just upstream from the Merchants' Bridge; while both serve food, I'd come here first for the setting: **Prager Bierstube** is a Czech beer hall with Budvar and Staropramen on tap and a mixed trad-mod interior (€3-5 starters, €8-10 Czech meals, daily, Kürschnergasse 3, tel. 0361/6441-2380). **Übersee** (literally "Over the Water") is just that, with an eclectic international menu and tables that sprawl through two adjacent buildings—one new, one old—and out onto the best riverfront terraces in town (€8-13 meals, daily 9:00-24:00, Kürschnergasse 8, tel. 0361/644-7607).

Erfurt Connections

From Erfurt by Train to: Eisenach and **Wartburg Castle** (2/ hour, 30 minutes on IC or ICE train, 45 minutes on regional train), **Leipzig** (hourly, 1.25-1.75 hours), **Wittenberg** (every 2 hours, 1.75 hours, most transfer in Naumburg; also possible in 2.5 hours with additional changes), **Dresden** (nearly hourly direct, 2.5 hours; more possible with change in Leipzig, 3 hours), **Berlin** (hourly, 2.5-3 hours, transfer in Leipzig or Naumburg/Saale), **Frankfurt** (hourly, 2.25-2.5 hours), **Würzburg** (every 2 hours direct, 2.5 hours; more with transfer in Fulda), **Nürnberg** (at least hourly, 3-3.5 hours, most transfer in Fulda, a few in Lichtenfels or Würzburg), **Munich** (about 2/hour, 4.5-4.75 hours, transfer in Würzburg or Fulda). Train info: tel. 0180-599-6633, www.bahn.de.

Wartburg Castle

Just west of Erfurt is another important Martin Luther sight: Wartburg Castle (VART-boorg), perched over the town of Eisenach (EYE-zehn-nahkh).

When Luther spoke out against Church corruption, he made powerful enemies (including the pope and emperor) and put his life in jeopardy. Luther fled to this remote castle. Hidden away in a small room at Wartburg, he diligently translated the New Testament from the original Greek sources into the German vernacular, allowing everyday people to directly engage the scripture without the interference of a middleman Church. As this translation became the basis for official High German, it could be said that Wartburg was also the birthplace of the modern German language.

The castle was important long before and long after Luther, and in the late 19th century—with the spirit of German unity in the air—it was renovated and slathered with glittering golden mosaics and other over-the-top decorations as an important symbol of German cultural identity.

The town of **Eisenach,** squatting in the valley below Wartburg, is worth a quick visit for those with extra time. The TI is on the main square, called the Markt (Mon-Fri 10:00-18:00, Sat-Sun 10:00-17:00, Markt 24, tel. 03691/79230, www.eisenach.info). A house where Martin Luther lived as a child has been turned into

LUTHERLAND

a museum (Lutherhaus), as has the birthplace of Johann Sebastian Bach (Bachhaus).

Planning Your Time

Wartburg Castle works well either as a side-trip from Erfurt, or on the way between Erfurt and points west (such as Frankfurt or Würzburg). Try to time your visit around the castle's once-daily English tour (April-Oct only): Come to Eisenach on a train that arrives a few minutes before 13:00. Hop on the 13:00 bus up to the castle (or take a taxi) and make a beeline to the ticket office, just in time for the 13:30 tour. It's possible to visit the castle at other times, but the tours are in German only (with an English handout).

Getting There

First head for the town of Eisenach, which is about 30 minutes west of Erfurt on the main train line. The train station has automated lockers (€1.50/small bag, €3/large bag, exact change only). From the station, you can take the bus, catch a taxi, or hike up to Wartburg.

Bus #10 (€2.50) runs from the parking lot across the street from the station up to Wartburg at the top of each hour (Easter-Oct only, daily 9:00-17:00, 20-minute trip). From the Wartburg bus stop, it's a steep 10-minute walk up to the castle.

A **taxi** costs about €10 and takes you to a parking lot a five-minute uphill walk below the castle.

The steep, uphill **walk** from the train station all the way to Wartburg Castle takes from 45 to 60 minutes, and includes an elevation gain of about 650 feet. Exiting the station, turn right and walk about 10 minutes into the Eisenach town center; then hike up into the hills (following signs for *Wartburg*; get more detailed directions at TI).

Drivers can park in the lot just below the castle entrance (€5).

Orientation to Wartburg Castle

Dramatically stretching along a forested ridgeline high above Eisenach, Wartburg Castle is famous among Luther-lovers as a place that gave solace to an on-the-skids (and recently excommunicated) young scholar who was determined to translate the New Testament into a living language for the first time in a millennium.

LUTHERLAND

Pilgrims come here to see the room where Martin Luther carried out that important work, and to tour the museum dedicated to the fledgling days of the Reformation. Luther aside, Wartburg is a fine fortress in its own right, with opulent rooms that were lovingly redecorated during a surge of German pride in the late 1880s.

Cost and Hours: Museum only-€5, museum and guided tour-€9, photo permission-€5, daily April-Oct 8:30-20:00, Nov-March 9:00-17:00, tel. 03691/250-00, www.wartburg.de.

Tours: In the summer (April-Oct), an English tour departs every day at 13:30. One-hour tours in German run every 20 minutes, with a tiny-print and incomplete handout of dry English translations (April-Oct 8:30-17:00, Nov-March 9:00-15:30).

Background: Although it's a major site on the Martin Luther trail, Wartburg's history aside from its short tenure with the great Reformer is also impressive. In 1130, the castle became the seat of Thuringia's landgraves (counts who ruled the region on behalf of the Holy Roman Empire). Most of the castle's history was peaceful (read: dull), but it was an important cultural center—most notably as the site of a contest of minstrels in 1207, a story later famously dramatized by Richard Wagner in his opera *Tannhäuser*.

Around this same time, Wartburg became the home of St. Elisabeth (1207-1231). This daughter of the Hungarian king was sent to Germany for a politically expe-dient marriage, and became the sub-ject of an often-told legend: The pious, kindly Elisabeth was known to sneak scraps of food out of the house to give to poor people on the street. One eve-ning, her cruel confessor saw her leav-ing the house and stopped her. Seeing her full apron (which was loaded with bread for the poor), he demanded to know what she was carrying. "Roses,"

she replied. "Show me," he growled. Elisabeth opened her apron, the bread was gone, and rose petals miraculously cascaded out onto the floor. In her short life, Elisabeth went on to found hospitals and carry out other charitable acts, and she remains a popular symbol of charity not only in Germany, but also in her native Hungary.

In May of 1521, Luther came to the castle, disguised as a bearded man named "Squire George" (Junker Jörg). While it took him less than a year to secretly translate the New Testament into German, that short visit helped put Wartburg on the map.

In October of 1817, shortly after a victory of German-speaking armies against Napoleon, recently formed fraternal organizations from around the region came together at this castle to celebrate German unity. It was one of the first occasions when German-speakers began to band together and forge a common pride. In fact, the flag of one of those fraternities (from Jena) was later adopted as the flag of a united Germany, which still flies all over the country.

Touring the Castle: If your main interest is Luther, the guided tour is skippable—it barely mentions the Reformer and is only offered in English once daily. However, the tour is the only way to see some rooms that were gorgeously restored and redecorated in the late-19th-century Historicist style (which mixed and matched previous styles to dramatic effect).

The **museum** has a few non-Luther items—the chance to peek into a duke's bedroom, the "collection of historical

cutlery"—but the main feature is the good biographical exhibit about Luther's life. Several original portraits show Luther at various stages in his life—in the garb of an Augustinian monk, wearing the cap of a distinguished professor, in the bearded disguise of Squire George—as well as some of his notable contemporaries. The portraits of Luther's parents (by Luther friend Lucas Cranach) show the strength of their character, which they passed on to their boy.

After touring the exhibit, walk along the gallery with low timber arches to find the humble but important **Luther Room** (Lutherstube). This was the site of one of the greatest intellectual revolutions in human history: For 10 months, Luther hunkered down at the desk here and used original Greek sources to translate the New Testament directly into everyday German. For centuries Christian worship had been passed through the obscure Latin-speaking filter of the Roman Catholic Church. Luther's translation gave Germans, even peasants, direct access to the Word of God. Luther's work also helped to codify the

evolving German language—setting the foundation for the tongue still being spoken by the people around you.

The guided **tour** includes the castle's most historic, opulent rooms. Highlights include Elisabeth's Bower (with spectacular glittering Neo-Byzantine mosaics from the early 1900s); the Elisabeth Gallery (decorated with beautiful frescoes about the life of St. Elisabeth); the Hall of Minstrels (with walls decorated with

LUTHERLAND

the text of a poem about Wartburg's famous contest of minstrels—this room was the setting for part of Wagner's *Tannhäuser*); and the vast Banquet Hall (decorated in an exuberant Historicist style rivaling the creations of "Mad" King Ludwig, who had a replica of this room created at his Neuschwanstein Castle).

Leaving the Castle: The steep downhill hike back down into Eisenach is pleasant if you have strong knees. Exiting the castle, hike down the red-gravel paths (to avoid the traffic on the black-asphalt roads) until you reach the snack stand. From here, you can turn left to reach the **bus** stop (bus #10 departs at :25 past each hour, Easter-Oct 9:25-17:25, goes to the train station), or continue straight to **walk** about 20-25 minutes through the woods back into town—follow signs for *Markt* to reach the main square.

Eisenach Connections

From Eisenach by Train to: Erfurt (2/hour, 30 minutes on IC or ICE train, 45 minutes on regional train), **Leipzig** (hourly, 1.75-2.25 hours), **Wittenberg** (every 2 hours, 2.25 hours, most transfer in Naumburg; also possible in 3 hours with additional changes), **Frankfurt** (hourly, 1.75 hours), **Würzburg** (hourly, 1.75 hours, transfer in Fulda). Train info: tel. 0180-599-6633, www.bahn.de.

Wittenberg

You only need look at its official name—Lutherstadt Wittenberg—to know this town's claim to fame. The adopted hometown of Martin Luther, and the birthplace of his Protestant Reformation, little Wittenberg has a gigantic history that belies its straightforward townscape. With a pair of historic churches—the Town Church of St. Mary's where Luther preached, Castle Church where he famously hammered his 95 theses to the door—and an excellent museum about

Luther's life (Luther House), this town is intriguing even to those unfamiliar with the great Reformer. The notable painter Lucas Cranach, a contemporary and friend of Luther's who also lived and worked in Wittenberg, left behind a slew of fine paintings and woodcuts, as well as his former home.

Centuries of Germans have celebrated Wittenberg for its ties to Luther. In 1983, which marked Martin Luther's 500th birthday, Wittenberg was part of communist East Germany, whose atheistic regime was tearing down proud old churches elsewhere. But ignoring the Luther anniversary would have made the DDR government, already unpopular, seem woefully out of touch. (They also sensed an opportunity to attract Luther tourists flush with much-needed hard Western currency.) So the communists swallowed hard and rehabilitated the memory of Luther, tidying up the Luther sights.

This may be why Wittenberg emerged from communism in better shape than most East German towns. And, thanks partly to the steady stream of Luther pilgrims, the town has only gotten better since then. While pleasant and impressively manicured, the town of Wittenberg itself is relatively unexciting; its broad main street feels almost deserted. But the city conscientiously invests in its Luther sights, crafting museums that are unusually world-class for such a small town. Wittenberg is already gearing up for the banner year of 2017—the 500th anniversary of Martin Luther's 95 theses. Local authorities have secured EU funds to support the festivities, so you may find a lot of construction in your way.

Planning Your Time

Wittenberg's sights are easy to see quickly—you can have a satisfying visit in just four or five hours. This makes it an ideal day-trip from Berlin or Leipzig (it's about a half-hour train ride from either place) or an on-the-way destination (speedy ICE trains between Berlin and Leipzig—which has connections to Erfurt, Dresden, and beyond—stop a short walk from Wittenberg's town center).

Various festivals enliven Wittenberg's calendar, including a three-day celebration of the wedding of Luther and Katharina (second weekend in June), a pottery and craft market (last weekend in Sept), and special events for Reformation Day (Oct 31, when Luther nailed his 95 theses to the church door).

Orientation to Wittenberg

(area code: 03491)

Literally "White Hill," Wittenberg (Germans say VIT-tehn-behrk, pop. 49,000) sits atop a very gentle rise above the Elbe River, which attracts plenty of riverboat cruise groups heading from Hamburg

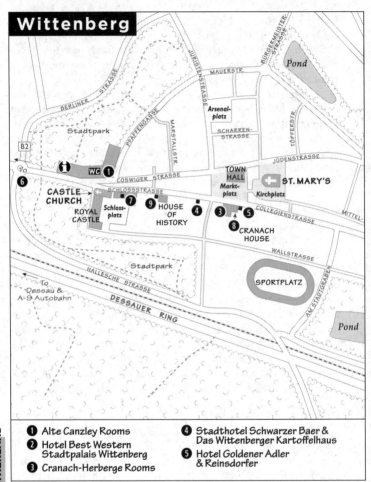

Wittenberg

1 Alte Canzley Rooms
2 Hotel Best Western Stadtpalais Wittenberg
3 Cranach-Herberge Rooms
4 Stadthotel Schwarzer Baer & Das Wittenberger Kartoffelhaus
5 Hotel Goldener Adler & Reinsdorfer

to Dresden and Prague. The tourists' Wittenberg is essentially a one-street town: Its main drag runs about three-quarters of a mile from Luther House (where the street is called Collegienstrasse) to Castle Church (where it's called Schlossstrasse). The rest of the Old Town consists only of a few side streets; the modern part of town sprawls mostly to the north and east.

Tourist Information

Wittenberg's TI is at the far end of town from the train station, across the street from Castle Church (April-Oct Mon-Fri 9:00-18:00, Sat-Sun 10:00-16:00; Nov-Dec daily 10:00-16:00; Jan-March Mon-Fri 10:00-16:00, closed Sat-Sun; tel. 0800-202-0114 or 03491/498-610, www.lutherstadt-wittenberg.de). You can watch

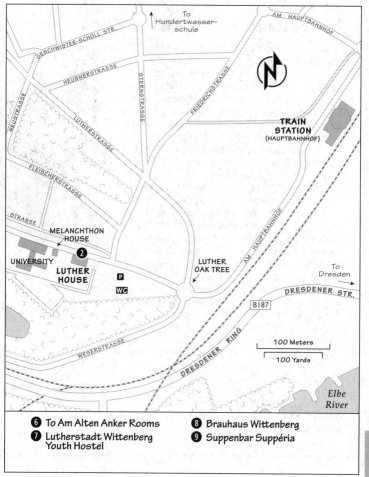

- ❻ To Am Alten Anker Rooms
- ❼ Lutherstadt Wittenberg Youth Hostel
- ❽ Brauhaus Wittenberg
- ❾ Suppenbar Suppéria

a 25-minute film about Martin Luther, or rent a town audioguide (€6/day, 1.5 hours of commentary).

Tours: Most local walking-tour options (you'll likely see costumed Martin Luthers and Katharina von Boras leading groups through town) are in German only—there's no regularly scheduled English tour. However, you can hire your own local guide—**Katja Köhler** does a great job telling Wittenberg's story (€75/2-hour tour, €120/4-hour tour, also does tours costumed as Katharina, mobile 0177-688-8218, katjakoehler@gmx.net).

Arrival in Wittenberg

Wittenberg has several train stations. You'll find the best connections (especially for Berlin and Leipzig) at the **main train station**

Wittenberg in the Early 1500s

As you explore Wittenberg, mentally time-travel to the days of Luther—the first few decades of the 16th century. The Renaissance was percolating to the south, in Italy (where Michelangelo and Raphael were hard at work redecorating the Vatican), and a spirit of new ideas was also beginning to take hold in Germany. The influential Frederick III "the Wise" (1463-1525), prince elector of Saxony, chose sleepy Wittenberg as his royal seat. He built a stout castle here in 1492, and began remaking the humble fishing village into a proper Renaissance town. (That explains Wittenberg's relatively intuitive grid of streets, compared to the twisty medieval muddle of many other German towns.) Frederick the Wise hired Lucas Cranach to be his official court painter. Cranach—along with his wife Barbara

and son Lucas Cranach the Younger—lived in a gigantic mansion on Market Square (today a museum; his statue—pictured above—is in the courtyard). Frederick also founded a university here (in 1502) and stocked it with some of the brightest minds of his time, including the promising young theologian Martin Luther and the brilliant classical languages specialist Philipp Melanchthon. Cranach, Luther, Melanchthon, and others were good friends who regularly socialized and swapped ideas.

Although he remained a devout Catholic until the end of his life, Frederick the Wise supported Luther and the Reformers in their darkest hour, likely saving them from obscurity or worse. If not for Luther, Wittenberg would not be famous—but, most likely, if not for Frederick the Wise, Luther would not be either.

(Lutherstadt Wittenberg Hauptbahnhof—Hbf), a dull 10-minute walk from the edge of the Old Town. Flanking the tracks are two areas with services: a white-tented area toward town with buses and taxis, and, on the opposite side, the main arrivals hall with lockers. A major reconstruction of the station is planned over the next year or two, so things may be different when you visit.

On the side toward town (follow signs to *Ausgang Historische Altstadt*), you'll find a small information kiosk, a taxi stand (figure €6-8 into town; if no taxis are waiting, call 03491/666-666), and a row of bus stops (bus #300 runs about 2/hour into the Markt at the center of the Old Town, generally leaves from stall B or C). From here, you can also walk into town (about 10 minutes to the near end of the Old Town at Luther House, then another 15 minutes to the far end and the TI): Exit to the left, walk beneath the overpass, and look for signs directing you to the city center.

On the side of the tracks away from town (follow signs for *Bahnhofshalle*) is the arrivals hall, with a Reisezentrum ticket office; lockers (€1-2) are outside the arrivals hall, along track 4.

A smaller train station (Lutherstadt Wittenberg Altstadt) is a bit closer to the Old Town (between the Markt and the river, about a five-minute walk), but serves only slower, regional trains.

Sights in Wittenberg

Martin Luther Sights

I've organized these sights roughly in order from the TI end of town (with Castle Church) to the Luther House end of town. If you're arriving at the train station, you'll come across these sights in reverse order.

Royal Castle (Schloss)—While today Wittenberg is synonymous with Martin Luther, it was first put on the map by prince elector Frederick the Wise, who chose the town as his capital (see sidebar). Although there's nothing to see inside Frederick's actual castle, you can view the surviving walls and towers attached to Castle Church (from the park just beyond the town gate). In the inner courtyard (enter through the small gateway just left of Castle Church), one wing of the castle is being rebuilt. The rest of this complex houses the kid-oriented City Museum (Stadtmuseum)—an oddball collection of bric-a-brac that's likely to move as this building is renovated.

▲▲Castle Church (Schlosskirche)—This Church of All Saints was the site of one of the most important moments in European his-

tory: Martin Luther nailing his 95 theses to the church door. That door—and most of the church itself from Luther's time—are long gone (destroyed in 1760, during the Seven Years' War). But in the late 19th century, as Germany was uniting as a nation for the first time, the church and the door were rebuilt in Romantic style as a temple of Luther and his fellow Reformers. While Luther rarely set foot inside this church (which was reserved for royals and admitted commoners to enter only on special occasions), it's worth a visit to pay respects at this shrine of Protestantism.

Cost and Hours: Free; Easter-Oct Mon-Sat 10:00-18:00, Sun 11:30-18:00; Nov-Easter Mon-Sat 10:00-16:00, Sun 11:30-16:00; Schlossplatz, tel. 03491/402-585, www.schlosskirche-wittenberg.de.

⊘ Self-Guided Tour: Before entering, take a close look at that famous **side door** (in the middle of the church, to the left of the present-day entrance). According to most accounts, on October 31, 1517, a frustrated Martin Luther nailed a handwritten copy of 95 theses—topics for discussion—to this wooden door. (Remember, this is a 19th-century bronze replica of the wooden original, engraved with the Latin theses.) The act wasn't quite as defiant as it sounds—the door served as a sort of community bulletin board. But the strong arguments Luther made about ending the practice of indulgences and other forms of Church corruption was revolutionary...as was his timing. The following day—All Saint's Day—was the one day each year that the church's interior was open to the public, who were invited to come inside, view Frederick the Wise's vast collection of relics, and purchase indulgences. Granted, historians quibble over the exact day Luther made his theses public and whether he actually nailed them to the door, but there's no doubt that his work spurred a nascent sentiment of reform and cemented his role as that movement's leader. Above the door is a glittering image of the crucified Christ flanked by Luther (on the left) and his fellow Reformer Philipp Melanchthon (on the right), with the skyline of Wittenberg behind them.

Go inside (the main entrance is to the right, near the back of the church). Walking down the **nave,** notice the colorful coats of arms on the upper stained-glass windows, which represent German cities that became Protestant when they joined Luther's Reformation. The carved coats of arms on the railing honor larger principalities that also adopted Protestantism. The lower stained-glass windows, with images of Reformers, were grudgingly added for Luther's 500th birthday, in 1983, by the notoriously atheistic East German government.

In the middle of the church, to the right (in front of the pulpit, with a raised plaque), you'll see the flower-bedecked **tomb of**

Martin Luther. On the wall behind it is a replica of the large bronze tomb marker that originally covered Luther's remains. While this wasn't his home church (that would be the Town Church of St. Mary's, just up the street and described later), this university church was traditionally where professors like Luther were entombed. On the left side of the nave is a similar raised plaque marking the grave of Luther's right-hand man and fellow professor, **Philipp Melanchthon.**

Proceed to the front of the church. In front of the high altar are large tomb markers for the **prince electors** who called Wittenberg home and provided safe harbor for

Philipp Melanchthon
(1497-1560)

While everyone who comes to Wittenberg has heard of Martin Luther, many are surprised to find another important figure celebrated here with almost equal reverence: Philipp Melanchthon. The Garfunkel to Luther's Simon, Melanchthon was a brilliant university professor who also played a critical role in the Protestant Reformation. But to call Melanchthon "the #2 Reformer" sells him short. Born Philipp Schwartzerdt in southern Germany, he later changed his name to its Greek translation, Melanchthon (same meaning: "black soil"). Although he was short, young, sickly, and notoriously unattractive, Melanchthon impressed everybody in Wittenberg with his keen intellect. In fact, when Melanchthon became disillusioned with Wittenberg and threatened to move away, Frederick the Wise persuaded him to stay by arranging a marriage for him (to the mayor's daughter, no less). While Luther was no intellectual slouch, Melanchthon was even more brilliant—he taught several topics (specializing in ancient languages, pedagogy, and theology) and encouraged women to pursue university study. Particularly gifted with languages, he provided Luther with invaluable assistance when translating the Bible into German from the original Greek texts.

Luther's provocative ideas. On the left is Frederick the Wise, and on his right is his younger brother, John the Steadfast. While Frederick remained devoutly Catholic throughout his life, his support for Luther, Melanchthon, and the early Protestant Reformers never wavered. Frederick's successor John converted to Protestantism—and, in a fit of iconoclasm, destroyed his brother's impressive collection of relics. Above these markers are larger plaques and statues (from the original church) that depict these important brothers.

You can pay €2 to climb up the **tower**—but in this largely flat town, the views aren't worth it.

▲**Market Square (Marktplatz)**—This wide square is much the same today as it was in Luther's time. An all-purpose space back then, it was used variously for a tournament of knights, a hunting ground for the prince elector, and a place of executions. The square is dominated by the Renaissance-style **Town Hall** (Rathaus). Notice the seven small doors at the left end of the building, which led to a shopping gallery back when the building's cellar hosted a little marketplace (today it houses a 20th-century Christian art collection).

In the middle of the square are newly restored, 19th-century **statues** of Martin Luther (on the right) and Philipp Melanchthon (left). While these statues were in Berlin for restoration, creative city officials filled this square with 800 three-foot-tall plastic replicas of Luther. When the originals returned, the replicas were sold off for €250 apiece; you'll see them in various hotels and restaurants around town.

The main street through town is lined by delightful gurgling **canals.** When Martin Luther first moved to Wittenberg, he was turned off by these, which carried both drinking water (on the way into town) and smelly sewage (on the way out). Years later, they were covered over by the modern street. But recently they were opened up to the air, to evoke the ambience of Luther's time.

Across Market Square from the Town Hall are several smaller sights. The small orange building was the first house of Lucas Cranach, and today it hosts workshops for female artists. The recommended Brauhaus Wittenberg serves good beer and food, and has a pleasant courtyard.

▲Cranach House (Cranachhaus)—This big yellow Renaissance home, circling a delightful and surprisingly large courtyard at Schlossstrasse 1, was the residence of the artist Lucas Cranach (whose statue you'll find sketching at the far end—see page 544). While there are no actual Cranach works on display, this sprawling, hundred-room complex is designed to evoke Cranach's lifestyle (and his wealth and prominence). As the

official court painter for Frederick the Wise, Cranach was one of the most esteemed men in town, but he was also an entrepreneur who dabbled in printing, running a pharmacy, and other business endeavors. Cranach and Luther were fast friends. Cranach was the only painter who had permission to do portraits of Luther and his family (Cranach and his school produced some 2,000 Luther

LUTHERLAND

portraits), and he was one of the first printers to print Luther's writings. This house is also where Luther's future bride, Katharina von Bora, lived when she first came to Wittenberg and befriended Cranach and his wife, Barbara. For decades, this space sat in ruins. But recently local authorities converted it into a kind of cultural center, hosting artists' studios, a small bar, a gift shop, comfortable hotel rooms, and—at the far end of the courtyard—an old-fashioned print shop. Operated by a quirky printer who speaks some English but enjoys explaining the importance of Luther's statement, "This is a German nation—the people speak German," the shop uses traditional methods to create postcards and replicas of Luther and Cranach works.

▲▲**Town Church of St. Mary's (Stadtkirche St. Marien)**— Peeking up over a row of buildings at the end of Market Square,

this is the oldest building in town and the most historic place to be surrounded by Luther lore. For most of his life, this was Luther's home church—where he was married, where his children were baptized, and where he preached over 2,000 times. Inside this church, what many consider to be the first-ever Protestant service took place, on Christmas Day in 1521 (although Martin Luther wasn't in attendance—he was hiding out at Wartburg Castle). The readings were in German, communion was taken by everyone, and hymns were sung by the congregation. It's also home to several engaging pieces of early Protestant artwork by Lucas Cranach and his son.

Cost and Hours: Free; Easter-Oct Mon-Sat 10:00-18:00, Sun 11:30-18:00; Nov-Easter Mon-Sat 10:00-16:00, Sun 11:30-16:00; Jüdenstrasse 36, tel. 03491/404-415, www.stadtkirchengemeinde -wittenberg.de.

❂ **Self-Guided Tour:** From the **outside,** notice that the tops of the twin towers don't quite match the rest of the building. Formerly pointy Gothic steeples, these were knocked down to fortify the towers with cannons during a 1546 battle. They were later rebuilt in the round Baroque style you see today.

Step inside. The focal point of the church is the colorful, engaging, almost whimsical **altar painting** by Lucas Cranach the Elder, the Younger, and their school

Luther's Legacy

It's difficult to overstate the impact Luther and the Protestant Reformation he led had on European history.

Even during Luther's lifetime, the Reformation raged across northern Europe. In Holland, Protestant extremists marched into Catholic churches, lopped off the heads of holy statues, stripped gold-leaf angels from the walls, and shattered stained-glass windows in a fit of anti-Catholic iconoclasm. Switzerland—with its deep roots in democracy and self-rule—was a haven for free thinkers, led by Ulrich Zwingli (1484-1531) and the exiled Frenchman John Calvin (1509-1564), who established a theocratic government and inspired French followers called Huguenots. When England's charismatic King Henry VIII (r. 1509-1547) was excommunicated for divorcing Catherine of Aragon so he could marry Anne Boleyn, Henry "divorced" England from the Catholic Church, established the Church of England (or "Anglican Church") and "dissolved" (destroyed) England's many country-side abbeys.

The Vatican responded to these Protestant revolutions with the Counter-Reformation, which was an attempt to put the universal Catholic Church back together using a carrot-and-stick approach. On the one hand, the Church worked diligently to eliminate corruption from within, reach out to alienated members, do missionary work, and inspire the faithful with attractive Church art. This "Counter-Reformation" art, Baroque and bubbly, was designed to appeal to worshippers by offering a glimpse of the heaven that awaited those who remained faithful. On the other

(completed in 1547). The gang's all here: All of the big-name early Protestants and their buddies have showed up to re-enact classic ecclesiastical scenes. True to the spirit of the Reformation, these aren't saints or royals—they're just people.

The bottom panel shows Martin Luther preaching from a pulpit as he points to the congregation—evocative of his mission to make worship more engaging for the people. The fluttering loincloth of Jesus helps to convey the message from preacher to parishioner. But notice that, true to life, some of those people aren't paying attention—they're chatting and looking around. The woman watching Luther most intently is his wife, Katharina.

The panel on the left shows Philipp Melanchthon (who was not a priest) baptizing a baby. The early Reformers believed that lay people—not exclusively priests—could perform baptisms. In the foreground, the extravagantly dressed woman with her back to us is Cranach's wife, Barbara. Supposedly, she grew frustrated that her husband was always painting Luther, Katharina, and others, but never her. "Fine," he said. "I'll include you in the altarpiece." (She was reportedly displeased.)

hand, when need be, the Church resorted to propaganda, intimidation, and outright force—doled out by the dreaded Inquisition.

As tensions rose, the Reformation spawned a century of Catholics-versus-Protestants wars. The Treaty of Augsburg (1555), which allowed each German prince to choose the religion of his territory, brought a lull in the fighting, but it didn't last long. The Thirty Years' War (1618-1648), which is often called the "first world war," pitted mercenary soldiers from just about every European country against each other. Protestants and Catholics alike were fueled by religious fervor, convinced that God was on their side and that the enemy was Satan himself.

When these wars finally ended, Europe was devastated, a third of Germany was dead, and Western civilization realized what it should have known from the start: Catholics and Protestants would have to live together. The Peace of Westphalia (1648) decreed that the leader of each country would decide the religion of his nation. Ultimately this divided Europe in half: the generally Protestant north (Scandinavia, the Low Countries, northern Germany, and England), and the predominantly Catholic south (Spain, Portugal, Italy, and southern Germany). Northern/Protestant Europe eventually became capitalist and prosperous, while southern/Catholic Europe lagged behind.

It's clear that Luther's legacy lives on. If you are a Lutheran, Presbyterian, Methodist, Baptist, Episcopalian—or any one of a number of other Christian faiths—you're the spiritual descendant of this German monk.

On the right panel, Johannes Bugenhagen (among Reformers, he ranks third after Luther and Melanchthon) is hearing confession from two very different people. Over the head of the obviously distraught and repentant man on the left, Bugenhagen holds the key of heaven—the sinner has done right by confessing and will reap ethereal rewards. The man on the right, however, is trying to buy his way into heaven—but his hands are tied and the key of heaven is behind him, indicating you can't purchase paradise (in its most literal form, indulgences).

The central panel features the Last Supper, with the Reformers standing in for the apostles. Notice the round table—in Protestantism, all are equal. People from all walks of life are actively engaging each other. It's easy to pick out Judas, who wears yellow (as evildoers often do in Cranach paintings). On the opposite side of the table, Martin Luther (clad in black, wearing the bearded disguise of Squire George) is being handed a chalice by Lucas Cranach the Younger. In contrast to Catholic worship at the time, Protestant services invited everybody to participate in communion.

LUTHERLAND

Now circle around **behind the altar** and look at the lower panel, which looks like it's been defaced by some rowdy students. It was...centuries ago. Around Luther's time, students of theology came here at the end of their studies and scratched their names or initials into the painting: on the left, in the river of knowledge, if they'd done well—or on the right, in hell, if they'd flunked. Looking carefully among the damned, you can find the name "Johannes Luther"—Martin's son. (Thankfully, he had more success after he switched to law.)

Back in front of the altar is a highly symbolic **baptismal font**

where Luther's own children were baptized. Notice the tube extending from the basin directly down toward the ground. This allowed water, after having washed away the sin, to be drained directly into what was a sandy floor, so it could be transmitted, unimpeded, to hell. Around the lower legs of the font, notice the many evil demons attempting to reach the baby being baptized up top—but their progress is blocked by the righteous saints.

Directly to the left of the altar is a modern sign marking the former location of the **pulpit** from which Martin Luther preached for many years (the original pulpit is now in Luther House).

In the back-right corner (behind and to the right of the main altar), find the smaller painting, *The Vineyard of the Lord*, by Lucas Cranach the Younger. This work's political

motives are almost painfully obvious: On the right, the Reformers tend to the garden of the Lord (that's Martin Luther raking and Philipp Melanchthon pulling water from the well—just as the Reformers went back to the original source to translate their Bible). On the left, the pope and his cronies (in their excessively opulent robes) trash all of their hard work. Subtle. In the lower-left corner, everyone lines up to receive their reward from Jesus. The pope (wearing yellow, again symbolizing evil) has already

received his, but keeps his hand outstretched, expecting more than his share. In the lower right, the Reformers (in their simple black robes) pray reverently.

Leaving the church, notice the grand **organ** over the main door. Dating from the communist period (1983), this booms out free organ concerts Fridays at 18:00.

Back outside the church, face the building and head around its right side. Go to the back corner of the church and look up at the bottom of the roofline to find the engraving of a pig, called the **Judensau** ("Jewish Sow"). This hateful bit of medieval anti-Semitic propaganda was designed to intimidate Wittenberg's Jews (who lived in the area just behind the church). Looking carefully at the pig—which is considered unclean in the Jewish faith—you'll see that Jewish kids are suckling from it, and a rabbi seems to be peering inquisitively into its rear end. When restoring the church, church authori-

ties asked the Jewish community in Berlin what they should do with this painful remnant of a less-enlightened time. Rather than cover it, they suggested leaving it here as a part of the town's heritage, and adding a modern monument: Look for the plaque in the cobbles directly below the pig. You'll see four paving stones being pried apart by something bubbling up from beneath. The message: You can't hide uncomfortable facts; they will find a way to see the light of day. The cedar tree nearby was donated by students in Tel Aviv.

And finally, if you go through the gap between the buildings near the pig, you'll stumble on one of Wittenberg's 16th-century **fountains**. Part of Frederick the Wise's improvements, this network of fountains (with wooden pipes) still works—but nobody knows how.

▲▲▲**Luther House (Lutherhaus)**—A must-see sight even for non-Lutherans, Luther's former home has been recently converted

into a state-of-the-art museum gorgeously displaying original paintings, manuscripts, and other Luther-era items. While enjoyable at any time, this museum provides an ideal grand finale for your Wittenberg visit—since you'll see actual artifacts related to all of the other sights in town, including the pulpit from which Luther preached, famous portraits of Luther and the other Reformers by Lucas Cranach, and Luther's original New Testament and Bible translations into High German.

Cost and Hours: €5, guidebook-€5.80; April-Oct daily 9:00-18:00; Nov-March Tue-Sun 10:00-17:00, closed Mon;

Collegienstrasse 54, tel. 03491/420-3118, www.martinluther.de.

→ **Self-Guided Tour:** From the street, step through the passage (at #59) into the inner courtyard to see the giant, turreted building. Not really a "house," this was originally a monastery. Luther lived here first as a monk and, later, when he was married

to Katharina von Bora (the building was a wedding gift from John the Steadfast). Katharina ran the facility as a business. She rented out rooms to students and kept them fed and watered by cultivating the garden, brewing beer, and even breeding cattle. In the middle of the courtyard is a **statue of Katharina** stepping through a doorway. Erected on her 500th birthday in 1999, the sculpture symbolizes her leaving her former life at a nunnery and beginning a new one with Martin Luther.

Head inside and buy your ticket. The museum fills three floors of this building, plus the cellar. The ground and first floors display a biographical exhibit about Martin Luther, with several actual artifacts.

From the ticket desk, go straight into the first room to see a town model of Wittenberg during Luther's time; paintings by Lucas Cranach (including a portrait of Frederick the Wise, the prince elector who supported Luther); and a woodcut of a knights' tournament at Market Square.

The next room juxtaposes several **historic items** to tell the whole complicated story of what Martin Luther did, why, and how the powers-that-be responded. Begin by facing the door you just came through. Flanking the door are an indulgence chest and an actual letter of indulgence, from 1492. Those who bought indulgences would supposedly be rescued from their sins...while generating substantial income for the Catholic Church. And that "sin tax" was applied directly to an ambitious building project at the Vatican: On the right,

see the engraving of St. Peter's Basilica, with its spectacular dome still under construction (and a knights' tournament taking place in the foreground). Archbishop Albrecht of Mainz and Pope Leo X (both pictured at right), stunningly influential and wealthy, were part of a finely tuned business model of selling salvation.

In contrast to the opulence of the Vatican, turn right to see Martin Luther's original linden-wood pulpit from the Town Church of St. Mary's. Befitting the preacher who fought against church extravagance, notice how humble it is—imagine him climbing up to the top, then sitting or kneeling while he preached. To the right, find the first printed version of Luther's 95 theses (printed in Basel, Switzerland, in 1517; later, Luther handwrote a version for his friend Cranach to print).

Continue into the **refectory,** where students would sit around a long table to dine. At the far end of this great hall is Cranach's wonderful painting, *The Ten Commandments* (1516). This was origi-

nally designed for the Town Hall so that anybody could see it; and today, as then, it's handy for a review of long-forgotten Sunday school lessons.

Quiz yourself to identify each of the 10 sins, which are illustrated by townspeople in everyday clothes (often yellow, Cranach's short-hand for evildoers). Look for the demon (with eerie glowing eyes) prodding each one of the sinners.

Head upstairs to the **first floor,** where you'll see original printings of four major Luther works, his robe, and a rare painting of a young Martin Luther by Cranach (1520). You'll also see the Cranach-printed 1522 first edition of Luther's German transla-tion of the New Testament, illustrated with Cranach woodcuts (which made the scripture accessible not only to those who could read German, but also to the illiterate). See the "community chest," the first systematized charity for poor people—Protestants began steering donations to the needy rather than into Church coffers. (Compare this to the Church's indulgence chest we saw earlier.) Other items illuminate the revolutionary changes brought about by Luther—such as the German hymn books and the shared chalice. (Before Luther's time, both singing and communion were practiced exclusively by priests.) The lecture hall is dominated by a fancy gilded lectern with portraits of great professors, flanked by prince electors in full Santa Claus regalia.

Then you'll pass into the actual private **residence** of the Luther family. Look for his-and-hers Cranach paintings of Martin and Katharina, three years after their wedding. Of about 2,000 portraits of Luther painted by Cranach and

LUTHERLAND

his school, this is one of the most famous. Imagine the lifestyle of these newlyweds—he a former monk and priest, she a former nun. While the idealistic Luther took little or no payment for preaching and writing, and got by mainly through the charity of wealthy local supporters, Katharina had the unenviable duty of balancing the books and keeping this huge household going. Look for the lockbox they used to protect their valuables. Katharina kept the key so Luther wouldn't give everything they owned to the poor. The centerpiece is the so-called **Lutherstube**—the long room with benches, a stove, and the table where Luther engaged in spirited conversations with his colleagues (later written down and published as Luther's *Table Talk*). Notice the names scratched into the ceiling, left behind by visiting VIPs (on the door, protected by glass, is the John Hancock of Russian Czar Peter the Great). Luther's adjoining study contains one of his collections of beer mugs (Luther loved his brew).

In the final room, see Luther's translation of the complete Bible from 1534 (both Old and New Testaments), printed by Cranach and illustrated by 266 Cranach woodcuts. Also look for the tiny hymnal from 1533. Luther, who believed that music should be an important part of worship, composed hymns that are still sung today ("A mighty fortress is our God...").

The top floor features an exhibit of various images of Luther (many of them by Lucas Cranach) and a small treasury. The cellar contains an exhibit about the everyday life of the Luther clan.

Luther Sights near Luther House—Several other Reformation sights cluster along Collegienstrasse, at the Luther House end of town.

First, from Luther House, turn right down Collegienstrasse and head out of town (toward the ring road). At the big roundabout (at the intersection of Collegienstrasse and Hauptbahnhofstrasse), at the edge of the park on the left, is the famous **"Luther Oak" tree** marking the spot where Luther burned his papal bull threatening excommunication.

About a block toward Market Square from Luther House are two other buildings of interest to Lutherans. At #60 (with the rounded gables) is the **Melanchthon House** (Melanchthonhaus), which was given to Philipp Melanchthon to convince him to stay in Wittenberg when he threatened to move elsewhere. The house—with a fine garden out back—is currently closed for an extensive renovation (likely through September of 2012).

At #62a, duck through the doorway into the **university courtyard.** This area is called Leucorea—the Greek translation of "White Mountain" (Wittenberg), a.k.a. "Mountain of Knowledge." These are some of the original buildings where Luther, Melanchthon, and their colleagues worked. Notice the plaques ringing the courtyard, celebrating famous professors and alums. Unfortunately, under Prussian rule in 1817, the University of Wittenberg was folded into the University of Halle, and today this complex houses only a few adjunct facilities. But a different Wittenberg University lives on across the Atlantic—in Springfield, Ohio, this town's sister city.

English Worship Services—Local Lutherans offer English-language services in historic Wittenberg churches during the summer (May-Oct Wed-Fri at 14:30 in small Corpus Christi chapel next to Town Church of St. Mary's, Sat at 17:00 in either Castle Church or Town Church of St. Mary's, www.wittenbergenglish ministry.com).

Non-Luther Sights

▲House of History (Haus der Geschichte)—Those intrigued by the communist chapter of Wittenberg's history will enjoy stroll-

ing through this museum's three floors of everyday items from DDR times. You'll either be escorted by a white-gloved guide (who speaks very broken English), pay to rent an audioguide, or borrow English explanations (basically the printed audioguide text). Climb to the top floor and work your way down, seeing kitchens, living rooms, bedrooms, as well as schoolrooms, shops, and bars, from the 1920s to the 1980s. The emphasis is on items from the communist period (1949-1989), when cheap, garish plastic items were in vogue. (Keep in mind that "our" Western styles weren't much better during those plastic-crazy days.) Since products were in short supply, "do-it-yourself" items and arts-and-crafts magazines were popular. Kitchen appliances and electronics (such as TVs, hi-fi systems, and even an early communist computer) were all made in the DDR or other Eastern Bloc countries. You'll also see a few Western items mixed in with the collection. These were available in the "hard Western currency" Intershopps for highly inflated West German Deutsche Mark prices (or at Exquisit and Delikat shops for even more inflated East German prices).

Cost and Hours: €5, audioguide-€2, photo permission-€2, Mon-Fri 10:00-18:00, Sat-Sun 11:00-18:00, Schlossstrasse 6, tel. 03491/409-004, www.pflug-ev.de.

Hundertwasserschule—This formerly drab DDR-era public school, on the northeast outskirts of town, was redecorated in 1993 with wildly colorful and imaginative flair by Austrian architect Friedensreich Hundertwasser. Most intriguing to architecture buffs, it's a long 25- to 30-minute walk from the city center (interior closed to the public but exterior viewable anytime, officially called "Martin-Luther-Gymnasium," Schillerstrasse 22a).

The Elbe River Valley: Cruises and Biking—While you can pay to take a brief cruise on the Elbe River, there's not much to see other than a panoramic view of town (for details, ask at the TI). The Elbe Valley also attracts many bicycle tourists, following the bike path called the Elberadweg. This route is especially popular among former West Germans, for whom this historic valley was off-limits through 1989.

Sleeping in Wittenberg

(€1 = about $1.40, country code: 49, area code: 03491)
Wittenberg has a wide range of charming hotels. All of my listings (except Am Alten Anker) are right in the heart of the Old Town. Air-conditioning and elevators are rare here.

$$$ Alte Canzley, right next to the TI and across from Castle Church, has eight comfortable, modern rooms in a building dating from 1391. Each room is a bit different, but all combine old-style furnishings and modern touches. The straightforward double rooms are more affordable (Sb-€70-95, Db-€85-115), while the five apartments have kitchens (Sb-€105-125, Db-€125-139; price depends on size, cheaper Nov-March, elevator, free cable Internet in rooms, Schlossplatz 3-5, tel. 03491/429-110, www.alte-canzley.com, info@alte-canzley.de). It's above a "mostly organic" restaurant (€5-10 starters, €14-24 main dishes, daily in summer, closed Mon in winter) that also offers cooking classes.

$$$ Hotel Best Western Stadtpalais Wittenberg is a professional-feeling place with 78 business-class rooms offering predictable comfort right on the main drag, near Luther House (Sb-€75-92, Db-€98-117, rate depends on demand, some rooms have air-con, free Wi-Fi, parking-€6.50, Collegienstrasse 56-57, tel. 03491/4250, www.stadtpalais.bestwestern.de, info@stadtpalais.bestwestern.de).

$$ Cranach-Herberge rents 25 rooms in the 16th-century former home of the artist Lucas Cranach. While it fills a very old space (you'll climb up an original stone spiral staircase to reach your room), the furniture is new and simple. A few of the rooms share bathrooms for the same price (Sb-€45, Db-€75, Tb-€99, Qb-€120; fancier "Cranach room" with a view of Market Square: Sb-€75, Db-€105; reception open daily 12:00-18:00—call ahead if coming at other times, free Wi-Fi, Schlossstrasse 1, tel. 03491/698-195, www.cranach-herberge-wittenberg.de, info@cranach-herberge-wittenberg.de). Scattered around the same courtyard are an inviting bar, a gift shop, and an old-fashioned printing press.

$$ Stadthotel Schwarzer Baer ("Black Bear") has 32 sleek, modern, comfortable rooms with hardwood floors right on Market Square (Sb-€60, Db-€75, elevator, free Wi-Fi, free parking, Schlossstrasse 2, tel. 03491/420-4344, www.stadthotel-wittenberg .de, info@stadthotel-wittenberg.de).

$ Hotel Goldener Adler is a traditional place with 17 straightforward but modern-enough rooms over a restaurant and antique shop (Sb-€46-52, small twin Db-€58, bigger Db-€68, Db with tub-€75, cash only, lots of stairs with no elevator, free Wi-Fi in some rooms, Markt 7, tel. 03491/404-137, www.goldeneradler -wittenberg.de, hotel@goldeneradler-wittenberg.de).

$ Am Alten Anker, above a restaurant in a drab area at the far end of town (about a 10- to 15-minute walk beyond the TI, or a 30-minute walk from the train station), has 21 basic but comfortable rooms at a reasonable price (Sb-€35, Db-€55, free Wi-Fi, Dessauer Strasse 286, tel. 03491/768-760, www.amaltenanker.de, steffi.wetzer@amaltenanker.de).

$ Lutherstadt Wittenberg Youth Hostel, an official HI hostel, has 152 beds in a sleek building just behind the castle (€18.60/bunk, S-€28.60, D-€35.10, nonmembers-€3.10 more, over age 26-€3 more, includes breakfast, sheets-€3.50, elevator, pay Wi-Fi, self-serve laundry-€5, tucked behind Castle Church at Schlossstrasse 14-15, tel. 03491/505-205, www.jugendherberge -wittenberg.de, jh-wittenberg@djh-sachsen-anhalt.de).

Eating in Wittenberg

Not much distinguishes restaurants in Wittenberg, but plenty of options offer stick-to-your-ribs German grub.

Brauhaus Wittenberg is the beer-lovers' choice, with a rollicking beer hall (decorated with big copper vats where they brew their own "Wittenberger Original" pilsner) and a wonderful beer garden in a classic old courtyard. The menu includes big portions of tasty German standards and Wittenberg specialties (€7-16 meals, most dishes €10-11, daily 11:00-23:00, Markt 6, tel. 03491/433-130).

Das Wittenberger Kartoffelhaus serves up hearty, heavy skillets piled high with potatoes, potatoes, potatoes, prepared a variety of ways. The interior is cozy and kitschy, and the outdoor seating is across the street from Market Square (€4-9 baked potatoes, €11-14 grilled or pan-fried dishes, €7-12 other meals, Schlossstrasse 2, daily 11:00-24:00, tel. 03491/411-200).

Suppenbar Suppéria is a great choice for a fast, central, light lunch. They dish up five or six soups (the selection changes regularly). Choose one (€3-5/bowl), or try the €5 three-bowl sampler to taste a variety (Mon-Fri 11:00-16:00, Sat 11:00-15:00, closed Sun, Schlossstrasse 9, tel. 03491/695-095).

Reinsdorfer offers a quick lunch on the go, with a bakery on one side and a butcher on the other, serving up €2-3 grilled sausages and prepared side dishes (order sausages and sides at the counter in back, Mon-Fri 8:00-18:00, Sat 8:00-12:00, closed Sun, Markt 6).

Wittenberg Connections

From Wittenberg by Train to: Berlin (hourly on ICE, 42 minutes; also every 2 hours on slower regional train, 1.25 hours), **Leipzig** (6/day on ICE, 30-40 minutes; also hourly on regional trains, 1 hour, some with transfer in Bitterfeld), **Erfurt** (every 2 hours, 1.75 hours, most transfer in Naumburg; also possible in 2.5 hours with additional changes), **Eisenach** and Wartburg Castle (every 2 hours, 2.25 hours, most transfer in Naumburg; also possible in 3 hours with additional changes), **Dresden** (1-2/hour, 2-3.5 hours, transfer in Leipzig and sometimes also Bitterfeld), **Frankfurt** (every 2 hours, 4 hours, transfer in Naumburg), **Hamburg** (nearly hourly direct on ICE, 2.5-2.75 hours; also possible about hourly with transfer in Berlin, 2.5-2.75 hours), **Nürnberg** (every 2 hours direct on ICE, 4.25 hours). Train info: tel. 0180-599-6633, www .bahn.de.

LEIPZIG

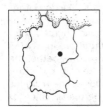

Leipzig has always been a capital of business and of culture. It's also a city of great history—Martin Luther, Johann Wolfgang von Goethe, Johann Sebastian Bach, Felix Mendelssohn, Richard Wagner, Angela Merkel, and many other German VIPs have spent time here. It also has some intriguing East German (called "DDR" here) sights and great cultural institutions, from the storied Gewandhaus Orchestra to the St. Thomas Boys' Choir. Leipzig's venerable university and always-thriving commercial engine—both of which helped put the city on the map—are still going strong today.

There are drawbacks—Leipzigers can be a bit stand-offish, and the city is one of the most architecturally drab destinations in this book. But for the sightseer, Leipzig (LYPE-tsikh) offers plenty. Those fascinated by Germany's communist chapter can tour the excellent Stasi Museum (documenting the atrocities of the DDR's secret police) and the Contemporary History Forum (with exhibits contrasting life in the East and West). Music-lovers make a pilgrimage to St. Thomas Church—where Bach was a choirmaster—and the excellent museum dedicated to him. Art-lovers enjoy exploring the Museum of Fine Arts, beer-lovers make a point to taste the Bayerischer Bahnhof's unique Gose brew, history buffs trek to the Napoleonic battle site and monument at the edge of town, and those turned on by hipster hangouts flock to the Südmeile district.

Planning Your Time

Conveniently located on the way between the former East Germany (Berlin, Dresden) and the former West (Frankfurt,

Leipzig History

Although it's the biggest city in Saxony, Leipzig has long been overshadowed by its glamour-girl sister, Dresden. While Dresden was the prettified capital of the rulers of Saxony, Leipzig was its down-and-dirty economic engine.

Leipzig first boomed in the 15th century. Its trade fairs attracted medieval vendors and businesspeople from throughout the region, and rich deposits of silver in the nearby Erzgebirge hills boosted the mining industry. While Dresden's glories were funded by princes who collected, then squandered, their subjects' wealth, Leipzig was imbued with a strong civic sensibility—its citizens took pride in voluntarily funding musicians and artists. Among the beneficiaries was an organist, choirmaster, and composer named Johann Sebastian Bach, who went largely unappreciated in his lifetime but whose works were later rediscovered and popularized by another Leipzig resident, Felix Mendelssohn.

Leipzig's university attracted great minds. Martin Luther came here to work with local printers and publishers to distribute his writings and to debate one of the Catholic Church's chief theologians (an event called the Leipzig Disputation) in what is today's New Town Hall. And Johann Wolfgang von Goethe, the "German Shakespeare"—who studied law at Leipzig U. before following his muse into literature—set a famous scene from his verse drama *Faust* at a cellar restaurant here. German Chancellor Angela Merkel is also an alum.

Leipzig's cityscape is a victim of its own success. In the late 19th century, the city boomed once again when it innovated the idea of a "sample fair." (Instead of toting along their full inventory, vendors would bring samples of their wares, allowing them to take orders and sell in much larger volumes.) Never architecturally oriented, the newly flush people of Leipzig tore down most of their characteristic medieval Old Town. The city center—defined by a busy ring road that marks the former course of the town wall—features large, hulking buildings that are shot through with fun-to-explore passages...but are visually dull.

After World War II, Leipzig became the second city, after

Nürnberg), Leipzig could easily fill a day or more, but it's equally satisfying in just a few hours. If your train comes through Leipzig, consider throwing your bag in a locker at the station and enjoying a short visit. With limited time, stay in the city center and tailor your visit to your interests—the best options are the Bach sights (St. Thomas Church and Bach Museum) and the Cold War sights (Augustusplatz, Stasi Museum, Contemporary History Forum, St. Nicholas Church). With more time, visit the City History Museum or the worthwhile outlying sights: the lively Südmeile restaurant and nightlife zone and the Monument to the Battle of the Nations.

East Berlin, of communist East Germany (DDR). The infamous Berlin Wall was built under DDR premier Walter Ulbricht, a Leipzig native who spoke with a thick Saxon accent. (To this day, many people in the former East Germany bristle at the sound of this accent.) But the city's size and historical importance didn't protect it from communist neglect. Damaged (but not destroyed) by WWII bombs, postwar Leipzig fell into abhorrent disrepair. Making matters worse, a coal mine at the edge of town (the primary source of heat during the austere DDR days) covered everything in soot. People who lived here in the 1980s say they could never wear white clothes outside, because they'd turn gray in minutes.

The people of Leipzig—as always, taking their civic responsibility with the utmost seriousness—were also at the forefront of the so-called "Peaceful Revolution" that toppled the communists. The famous scenes of Berliners joyfully partying atop the Wall were made possible by lesser-known protests that slowly began in Leipzig in 1982 and eventually came to a head in the series of civil-disobedience actions that caught the regime completely off-guard in 1989. Expecting an armed insurrection, DDR leaders were so flummoxed by the peaceful tone of the protests that they simply allowed them to continue. A month later, the Wall was history. (For more, see the sidebar on page 571.)

As Germany moved toward reunification, DDR television broadcast a provocative documentary asking: Can ragtag Leipzig be salvaged? (Their conclusion: No.) But salvaged it was—and then some. Pictures from just 20 years ago show a different city. The area within the ring road has been rejuvenated with shiny new shopping malls and university buildings. In other zones—such as the colorful stretch south of downtown called the Südmeile ("South Mile")—trendy young entrepreneurs have turned decrepit buildings into a world of funky, engaging bars and restaurants. Leipzig may lack half-timbered and lederhosen charm, but its welcome urban contrast and fascinating history earn it a place on many itineraries.

Orientation to Leipzig

(area code: 0341)

With 520,000 people, Leipzig sprawls over a large area. But the majority of its important sights are within or very near the ring road—called simply the Ring—that follows what once was the city wall. This compact downtown core is called Mitte—the "Middle"; you can walk from one end to the other in about 15 minutes. Market Square (Markt) represents the center of this bull's-eye; at the east end is the communist-style Augustusplatz, with the main university buildings and venues for the opera and orchestra. The gigantic main train station (Hauptbahnhof) looms at the north-eastern edge of the Ring.

In general, the shopping-mall-crazy central core lacks person-ality—the cobbled charm that pervades many German city centers is sorely missing. (One saving grace here are the many fine galler-ies burrowing through the middle of blocks.) For more local color, head for two other neighborhoods: Gottschedstrasse, easy to reach just west of the Ring, is lined with restaurants, bars, and cafés. But the most interesting zone is the Südmeile ("South Mile"), along Karl-Liebknecht-Strasse, a 20-minute walk or 5-minute tram ride due south from downtown. Other worthwhile attractions reachable by tram include the Monument to the Battle of the Nations, the Bayerischer Bahnhof brewpub, and the Spinnerei artists' complex.

Tourist Information

Leipzig's TI, next to the Museum of Fine Arts, hands out several good, free brochures and a free map; sells books and souvenirs; books rooms; and provides information about local tours (March-Oct Mon-Fri 9:30-18:00, Sat 9:30-16:00, Sun 9:30-15:00; Nov-Feb Mon-Fri 10:00-18:00, closed Sat-Sun; Katharinenstrasse 8, tel. 0341/710-4260).

The TI offers an English **guided tour** of the city that com-bines an hour of walking and a 1.5-hour bus ride (€15, March-Dec daily at 13:30, departs from TI, smart to reserve ahead on week-ends—call or visit the TI).

The skippable **Leipzig Card** covers local transit, free entrance into a few sights (including the City History Museum), and minor discounts at most others (€8.90/1 day, €18.50/3 days, valid until 4:00 in the morning, buy at TI or some transit offices).

Arrival in Leipzig

One of Europe's biggest train stations, **Leipzig Hauptbahnhof** can be intimidating. Twin arrivals halls flank the building, book-ending the tracks. (Until Hitler consolidated the sta-tion, it had separate, parallel terminals for Prussian and Saxon destinations.) With the tracks to your back, the Westhalle is to the right, and the Osthalle is to your left. Under your feet are two sto-ries of shops—a sprawling

shopping mall with hundreds of stores open until 22:00.

To reach most places in town, exit toward the Westhalle (at the right end of the long concourse). In the main hall of the Westhalle are lockers (tucked under the stairs) and the Reisezentrum (train tickets and reservations). Exit through the front door to find waiting taxis and the busy Ring, with cars and trams zipping in both directions. From here, **trams** fan out across the city (generally, the first set of tram stops is headed north, and the second set is going south—including Augustusplatz and the Südmeile; for specifics on reaching your hotel, see the listings under "Sleeping in Leipzig," later). To **walk** into the town center (about 10-15 minutes), continue across the Ring and past the tram tracks, pass the public-transit kiosk, and keep going straight on Nikolaistrasse. After one block, turn right onto Brühl (you'll see a colorful mural honoring the 1989 Peaceful Revolution up ahead). Walking a block along Brühl, you can't miss the giant glass box holding the Museum of Fine Arts; the TI is on the museum's far side, and the main Market Square is two blocks beyond that.

Getting Around Leipzig

Leipzig's tram system is easy to use and essential to get comfortable with for all but the shortest visit. Each ride costs €2 (or €1.50 for a *Kurzstrecke*—"short stretch"—of four stops or less). A day ticket costs €5. Tickets are available from automated machines at tram platforms. Local transit is also covered by the TI's Leipzig Card (described earlier).

The main train station (Hauptbahnhof) is the hub for the city's trams. A secondary hub is to the south, at Augustusplatz (most trams connect these two central stops). You're most likely to take the tram south from either the train station or Augustusplatz to the Südmeile restaurant and nightlife zone (handiest stop for a quick look is Südplatz), or to reach the Monument to the Battle of the Nations (stop: Leipzig Völkerschlachtdenkmal). Transit info: www.lvb.de.

The S-Bahn's new City Tunnel—due to be completed in 2013 or 2014—will efficiently connect the Hauptbahnhof to points south; it will be most useful for tourists who want to get from the main train station to the city-center Market Square quickly.

Sights in Leipzig

Within the Ring

The majority of sights in town are within the ring road. I've divided them into subneighborhoods for easier navigation.

Town Center (Mitte)

These sights are all in the heart of town, on or near Market Square (Markt), which hosts a lively farmer's market each Tuesday and Friday, and special events at other times.

Leipzig

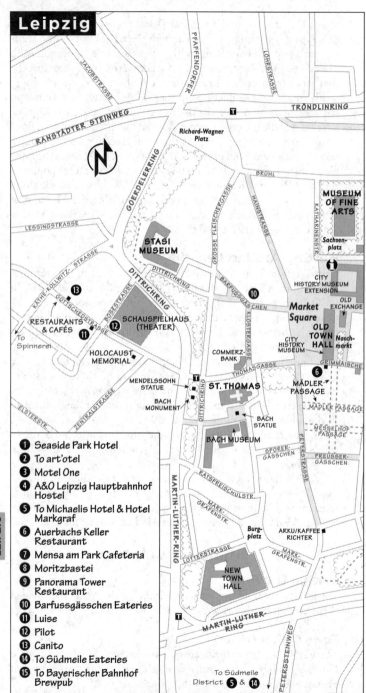

RANSTÄDTER STEINWEG

JACOBSTRASSE

PFAFFENDORFER

LÖHRSTRASSE

TRÖNDLINRING

Richard-Wagner Platz

GOERDELERRING

BRÜHL

KATHARINENSTR.

MUSEUM OF FINE ARTS

Sachsen-platz

LESSINGSTRASSE

DITTRICHRING

DITTRICHRING

HAINSTRASSE

GROSSE FLEISCHERGASSE

BARFUSSGÄSSCHEN

STASI MUSEUM

CITY HISTORY MUSEUM EXTENSION

BARFUSSGÄSSCHEN

KÄTHE-KOLLWITZ-STRASSE

GOTTSCHEDSTRASSE

BOSESTRASSE

⑬

RESTAURANTS & CAFÉS

⑪ ⑫

To Spinnerei

SCHAUSPIELHAUS (THEATER)

⑩

KLOSTERGASSE

Market Square

OLD EXCHANGE

CITY HISTORY MUSEUM

OLD TOWN HALL

Nasch-markt

HOLOCAUST MEMORIAL

COMMERZ-BANK

THOMASGASSE

GRIMMAISCHE

⑥

MÄDLER PASSAGE

MENDELSSOHN STATUE

BACH MONUMENT

DITTRICHRING

ST. THOMAS

MÄDLER PASSAGE

ELSTERSTR.

ZENTRALSTRASSE

BACH STATUE

BACH MUSEUM

PETERSTRASSE

MESSELHOF PASSAGE

PREUSSER-GÄSSCHEN

SPÖRER-GÄSSCHEN

RATSFREISCHULSTR.

MARTIN-LUTHER-RING

MARK-GRAFENSTR.

Burg-platz

ARKU/KAFFEE RICHTER

LOTTERSTRASSE

MARK-GRAFENSTR.

NEW TOWN HALL

MARTIN-LUTHER-RING

PETERSSTEINWEG

① Seaside Park Hotel
② To art'otel
③ Motel One
④ A&O Leipzig Hauptbahnhof Hostel
⑤ To Michaelis Hotel & Hotel Markgraf
⑥ Auerbachs Keller Restaurant
⑦ Mensa am Park Cafeteria
⑧ Moritzbastei
⑨ Panorama Tower Restaurant
⑩ Barfussgässchen Eateries
⑪ Luise
⑫ Pilot
⑬ Canito
⑭ To Südmeile Eateries
⑮ To Bayerischer Bahnhof Brewpub

To Südmeile District ⑤ & ⑭

LEIPZIG

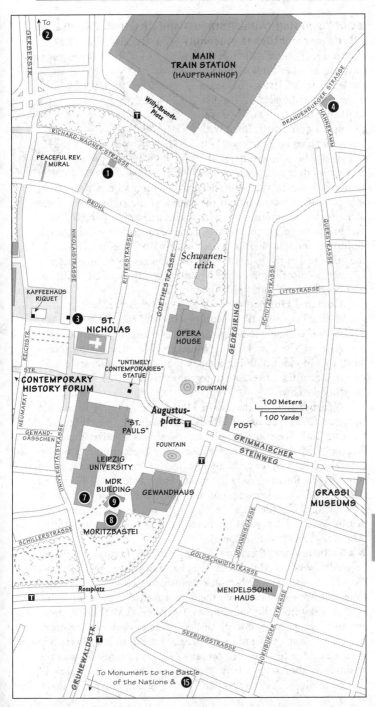

▲Old Town Hall (Altes Rathaus) and City History Museum (Stadtgeschichtliches Museum)—The Renaissance-style Old

Town Hall, overlooking the bustling Market Square, houses the good City History Museum upstairs (with condensed English explanations). You'll enter through a grand hall, lined with ornate benches and giant portraits of judges who presided here. The extremely detailed town model shows Leipzig in 1823. Smaller exhibit rooms branch off from this central hall. Exhibits in the rooms to the right as you enter include an old ceramic stove with big heated knobs (which people grabbed to warm up cold hands), antique furniture, and a famous, definitive portrait of Bach painted during his lifetime (1746). At the other end of the hall (left from the entrance) is a chronology of Leipzig from prehistory to the Middle Ages; the exhibit continues upstairs, from the Industrial Age to today.

Cost and Hours: €4, free first Wed of each month, audio-guide-€1, Tue-Sun 10:00-18:00, closed Mon, Markt 1, tel. 0341/965-1338, www.stadtgeschichtliches-museum-leipzig.de.

Annex: The City History Museum's **New Extension (Neubau),** in a modern building a block north, has temporary exhibits (separate €3 ticket, next to the Museum of Fine Arts at Böttchergässchen 3).

Nearby: Behind the Town Hall is the ornately decorated Baroque **Old Exchange (Alte Börse)** building, now used as a meeting hall. The statues in the top corners symbolize important facets of Leipzig life: on the left, Apollo, representing art; and on the right, Mercury, for trade and commerce. The statue standing in front depicts Johann Wolfgang von Goethe, who studied law here (1765-1768) before dropping out to become a writer. It worked out well for him. Goethe set a scene from *Faust* in a restaurant in the nearby Mädler Passage (at the far end of the long square from the Alte Börse, and explained next).

▲▲Galleries and Passages—Leipzig once had the higgledy-piggledy cobbles-and-red-rooftops charm of many other German cities. But in the late 19th century, prospering city leaders decided to modernize—tearing down the quaint medieval townscape and replacing it with bulky buildings. After some WWII bomb damage and decades of communist neglect, the city center was a wasteland, but in just a generation, Leipzigers have dramatically remade their city. One feature they preserved—and expanded—was the tradition of shopping galleries that burrow through the middle of many buildings. As you wander the city center, don't miss doorways that lead into these areas (usually lined with shops); some are nondescript, but many are more beautiful than what's on the outside. The TI has a free brochure to help you locate these galleries. Two in particular worth seeking out are Speck's Hof (between the Nicholas Church and Reichsstrasse) and Mädler Passage (enter roughly across the street from the end of the Town Hall).

Just inside **Mädler Passage,** statues in front of the recommended Auerbachs Keller restaurant enact a scene from *Faust* that Goethe set here: The brilliant thinker Faust (wearing a scholar's gown and floppy hat) has made a deal with Mephistopheles (gesturing skyward) to experience as much as possible of the world—but if anything so impresses Faust that he refuses to move on, the devil gets his soul. Mephistopheles brings Faust to Auerbachs Keller to show him the simple pleasures of revelry with friends ("Before all else, I bring thee hither/Where boon companions meet together,/To let thee see how smooth life runs away./ Here, for the folk, each day's a holiday"). Across the passage are drunken students who have been bewitched by Mephistopheles.

Cafés—Leipzig has some classic cafés with old-timey interiors that are worth a peek. Consider dropping by **Kaffeehaus Riquet** (decorated with elephants, daily 9:00-20:00, Schuhmachergässchen 1) and **arko** (a chain now occupying the elegant former home of Kaffee Richter, Petersstrasse 43).

Museum of Fine Arts (Museum der bildenden Künste)—
Located in a fancy glass house in the center of town, this museum displays Leipzig's eclectic collection of fine arts. Instead of being organized chronologically, the items are displayed thematically—juxtaposed by some clever curator to create a "dialogue" between otherwise unrelated works. While this treatment thrills a certain breed of museumgoer, it's sometimes alienating to lowbrows (like me). Worse, there's very little English (aside from the thick €12.80 catalog), and the €2 audioguide is only in German (though English may be coming soon—ask).

Within the vast, glassy building, the basement features temporary exhibits; the first floor displays excellent works by local sculptor Max Klinger, as well as other 20th-century and Leipzig art; the second floor has mostly Dutch and Flemish works from the 15th to 18th centuries; and the third floor shows predominantly Romanticism, 19th-century works, and contemporary pieces.

The museum's highlight is Leipzig artist **Max Klinger**'s (1857-1920) sculpture of Beethoven (1902, restored 2004). The marble and bronze sculpture—depicting the great composer pensively hunched over on a throne, nude, legs crossed, with Prometheus' eagle in clouds at his feet—took Klinger some 15 years to complete. Installed as the centerpiece of a 1902 Vienna Secession exhibit devoted to Beethoven, the sculpture was surrounded by Gustav Klimt's famous *Beethoven Frieze*. On the same floor, look for Expressionist works by another Leipzig artist, Max Beckmann, including *Portrait of a Carpet Dealer* (1946). The rest of the collection features minor works by major artists (such as Frans Hals' *The Mulatto* and Rembrandt's *Head of an Old Man*) and some genuinely interesting pieces from lesser-known artists. For example, Paul de la Roche's evocative *Napoleon at Fontainebleau* shows the pudgy, diminutive Frenchman dejected after learning that he's lost Paris.

Cost and Hours: €5, special exhibits extra—usually €8, €10 combo-ticket covers everything, Tue and Thu-Sun 10:00-18:00, Wed 12:00-20:00, closed Mon, a short block north of Market Square at Katharinenstrasse 10, tel. 0341/216-990, www.mdbk.de.

Cold War Sights

These attractions are scattered around the city center, but are all within about a 10-minute walk of each other. See also my spin tour of Augustusplatz (listed later), Leipzig's quintessential showcase of DDR architecture.

▲**St. Nicholas Church (Nikolaikirche)**—Leipzig's oldest church (1165) played a pivotal role in recent German history. In the

1980s, prayer meetings held here every Monday gradually became the forum for those deeply dissatisfied with the communist status quo to lick their wounds and compare notes. As anti-communist sentiment grew, the church was a major staging ground for the Peaceful Revolution that would ultimately topple the regime. During these protests, people would bravely go inside the church to meet—not knowing what would happen to them when they came back out.

The church sits in what was once a market square—appropriate, since its namesake, St. Nicholas, is the patron saint of traders. The unusual but dull interior belies the church's importance in recent history. In the 1780s, the church was redecorated in a very clean, bright Neoclassical style, with a pastel pink-and-green color scheme and fluted columns that sprout green fronds at the top. Above the door is the largest organ in Saxony, which booms out free organ concerts each Saturday at 17:00.

Outside and behind the church, find the single column with

The Peaceful Revolution

While the fall of the Berlin Wall got all the press, the end of communism in East Germany arguably began seven years

earlier and a hundred miles to the south...in Leipzig.

In 1982, parishioners at Leipzig's St. Nicholas Church began gathering on Monday evenings to pray for peace and a better world. This continued until 1989, when a series of events sparked citizens to action. That spring, the Tiananmen Square protests in China inspired East Germans who felt similarly oppressed. And that summer, Hungary opened its border to the West, offering an enticing glimmer of hope to East Germans that freedom might lie ahead.

By September of that year, the Monday prayer meetings at St. Nicholas started taking on an increasingly political bent; more people joined, regardless of religious belief, and the meetings turned into more of a protest movement than a prayer group. DDR government officials watched with concern; after the October 2 gathering, they stated that the use of deadly force would be authorized to put down any uprisings.

On October 7, Mikhail Gorbachev came to Berlin to celebrate the 40th anniversary of the founding of the DDR. He made a cryptic remark implying that the people of Eastern Europe had a right to bring about change. This partly inspired a huge demonstration in Leipzig on Monday, October 9. An estimated 100,000 protesters carried banners bellowing *Wir sind das Volk!* (We are the people!). The Stasi (secret police) embedded undercover agents in the crowds to stoke the protesters to violence—but it didn't work. One official said, "We were ready for anything...except candles and prayer." With no excuse for clamping down on the demonstration, DDR officials for the first time allowed a major protest to continue—a turning point in the struggle to topple the Berlin Wall.

On Monday, October 16, an estimated 320,000 people participated in demonstrations. Two days later, DDR premier Erich Honecker and several other top officials resigned. The government was in disarray, and within two and a half weeks, people were dancing on top of the Berlin Wall.

Today Leipzig remains fiercely proud of the crucial role it played in ousting the communists through nonviolent means. Around town, look for "89" plaques that explain sites relating to the Peaceful Revolution.

green leaves at the top. This column echoes the decoration inside the church, conveying the message that the anti-communist protests that began here gradually spread throughout the city. After dark, multicolored panels in the pavement outside the church light up, symbolizing the varying opinions about communism.

Cost and Hours: Free, daily 10:00-18:00, Nikolaikirchhof 3, tel. 0341/124-5380, www.nikolaikirche-leipzig.de.

▲**Contemporary History Forum (Zeitgeschichtliches Forum)**—Funded by the German government, this center exam-ines life in a divided Germany, focusing mainly on the East but dipping into the West to provide contrast. The statue out front represents Germany's two 20th-century dictatorships: the flat-palmed *Sieg Heil!* Nazi salute and the proletariat's raised communist fist.

The exhibit is modern and well-presented, but designed for Germans, making it challenging for foreigners to appreciate. There's no English audioguide, but you can ask to borrow the dif-ficult-to-follow English exhibit translations at the gift shop coun-ter where you enter. Ride the elevator (with patriotic DDR songs and voice clips piped in) up to the second floor, where the circu-lar permanent exhibit spins off from a central timeline. Displays include actual photographs, propaganda posters, a mock-up of a DDR-era apartment, film footage of DDR authorities destroying churches and Soviet tanks putting down a 1953 protest at Berlin's Brandenburg Gate, a van used by the secret police to transport prisoners, an original "You are leaving the American sector" sign from an East/West border crossing, a simple airplane used to escape to the West, heads from several Stalin statues, protest signs from the fall of 1989, and the long table where the East German politburo met to hash out their plans for the country. Temporary exhibits fill the third floor.

Cost and Hours: Free, Tue-Fri 9:00-18:00, Sat-Sun 10:00-18:00, closed Mon, Grimmaische Strasse 6, tel. 0341/22200.

▲▲**Stasi Museum in the "Runde Ecke"**—In the notorious so-called "Round Corner" building, the communist secret police (Stasi) imprisoned and interrogated those suspected of being trai-tors to the state. That same building—once the Stasi headquar-ters—now houses a ramshackle but intriguing exhibit about those harrowing times. A citizens' committee created the museum in 1990 as a temporary exhibit to document Stasi atrocities, with the goal of preventing such things from happening again. More than two decades later, the museum and its committee are still going strong. The museum is humble—basically one long hallway with a few rooms of dusty exhibits—but fascinating to those interested in this dark chapter of German history. And it's chilling to see all this while walking through the actual perpetrators' offices, which still boast the antiseptic smell they had back in the Red old days.

Cost and Hours: Free but €3 for essential audioguide, daily 10:00-18:00, Dittrichring 24, tel. 0341/961-2443, www.runde -ecke-leipzig.de.

Background: To keep their subjects in line, the DDR government formed the Ministerium für Staatssicherheit (MfS, "Ministry for State Security")—nicknamed the Stasi. Modeled after the Soviet Union's secret police, the Stasi actively recruited informants from every walk of life, often intimidating them into cooperating by threatening their employment, their children's education, or worse. The Stasi eventually gathered an army of some 600,000 "unofficial employees" *(inoffizielle Mitarbeiter)*, 189,000 of whom were still active when communism fell in 1989. These "employees" were coerced into reporting on the activities of their coworkers, friends, neighbors, and even their own immediate family members. Preoccupied with keeping track of "nonconformist" behavior, the Stasi collected whatever bits of evidence they could about suspects—including saliva, handwriting, odors, and voice recordings—and wound up with vast amounts of files. In late 1989, when it was becoming clear that communism was in its waning days, Stasi officials attempted to destroy their files—but barely had time to make a dent before government officials decreed that all documentation be preserved as evidence of their crimes. These days, German citizens can come here to read the files that were once kept on them. For a recent film that brilliantly captures the paranoid Stasi culture, see the 2006 Oscar-winner *The Lives of Others*.

Touring the Museum: As the museum exhibits are entirely in German, it's essential to rent an audioguide before you start: Go partway down the hall and ask in the office on your left. Then return to the entrance to view the permanent exhibit.

The exhibit's title, "Power and Banality," invokes scholar Hannah Arendt's notion of the "banality of evil"—the idea that if horrific acts are systematized and repeated, they become routine and therefore more acceptable to the perpetrator. The first section of the exhibit documents the pivotal protest of October 9, 1989 (see sidebar on page 571), with shields and batons, and photos of the candles that stymied riot police who were instead expecting Molotov cocktails. The **surveillance cameras** mounted overhead and a wall of monitors suggest just how closely the secret police observed the East German people. In the hallway, look for the copy of a 14-year-old student's essay questioning aspects of communist life. It's chilling to think that this innocent assignment could have barred this schoolboy from university and ruined his life; fortunately, he wrote it in 1989, just before the Wall fell.

The **former offices** contain several items and tools used by the Stasi, such as a camera that could easily be concealed in a briefcase, microphones that could be hidden just about anywhere, disguises

(including a fake beer belly with a hidden camera), and forged documents. One display case holds several jars with pale yellow cloths impregnated with "odor samples." Stasi agents would sit suspects on cloths to interrogate them, then save the sweat-drenched swatch for trained dogs to identify the scent. (For example, the dog would sniff an anti-DDR propaganda leaflet, then smell several odor samples and bark at the one that matched.) The police also used under-car mirrors to check for potential escapees at border crossings. The replica prison cell, with original fixtures, illustrates what life was like in a detention center. All mail and packages coming into the country were searched for contraband—inspectors would steam them open, read them, then reseal them. Stasi mail inspectors stole millions in West German Deutsche Marks (which people would send to their East German relatives) and also confiscated piles of cassette tapes containing Western pop music—which officials then re-used to record interrogation sessions.

Bach Sights

These sights cluster along the west side of the Ring.

▲**St. Thomas Church (Thomaskirche)**—At this historic church, Martin Luther introduced Leipzig to Protestantism, and Johann

Sebastian Bach conducted the boys' choir. The most famous boys' choir in Germany—the Thomanerchor—still performs here.

Cost and Hours: Free, daily 9:00-18:00, from 9:30 in winter, Thomaskirchhof 18, tel. 0341/222-240, www.thomaskirche.de.

Concerts: The St. Thomas boys' choir performs Fridays at 18:00 and Saturdays at 15:00, unless they are traveling (€2).

Touring the Church: Before entering the church, look (just outside the church door) for the **statue of Bach** standing in front of his favorite instrument, a pipe organ. Bach was the cantor (leader of the boys' choir) here from 1723 until 1750. While here, Bach was remarkably prolific—for a time, he even composed a new cantata every week. Examine the details of this portrait: He's holding a rolled-up sheet of music, which he used as a baton. Notice the button open on his vest—he could stick the "baton" into his shirt, if necessary, to free up his hands. And notice that his

jacket pocket is turned out. Bach was famously always scrounging for more money, not because he was greedy, but because he had a huge family to feed, including his own brood and the boys in the choir. His dedication to the arts led him to advocate tirelessly for the funding of local musicians.

Inside, the clean, white, stripped-down Neo-Gothic interior evokes the Protestant aesthetic of uncluttering the congregation's communion with God. On Pentecost in 1539, Martin Luther came here to perform Leipzig's first Protestant service. Look up at the 19th-century **stained-glass window** on the wall above the door through which you entered. In the panel to the left, Martin Luther is flanked by his supporter prince elector Frederick the Wise (on the left) and fellow reformer Philipp Melanchthon (on the right).

The **main altar** actually comes from a different historic church, St. Paul's on Augustusplatz, which was demolished by the atheistic communist regime in 1968 to make way for the expansion of university buildings. The university is building a new, modern version of that church (across town and explained on page 578); when that happens, this altar will move back there.

In front of the altar is the **tomb of Bach**...or is it? Largely

unappreciated in his own time and forgotten after his death, Bach was buried in a humble graveyard. But after he was rediscovered in the 19th century, aficionados tracked down what they thought were his remains. Three cadavers that could have been Bach were compared to portraits of the composer to determine which one was most likely to be the real Bach.

Facing the altar, look up and to the left to see the new **organ**, built in 2000 but designed to sound like a much older, Bach-era organ.

Nearby: On the Ring side of the church, look for the **statue of Felix Mendelssohn**

Johann Sebastian Bach
(1685-1750)

Johann Sebastian Bach was a man of many musical trades—composer, musical director, organist, organ-builder, and violinist.

Born in 1685, he lived immersed in music from the very beginning. His father was the director of the town musicians (because the family was so musically talented, people from Erfurt—where Bach senior was from— would use the word *Bache* to describe any musician). After his parents' early deaths, Bach lived with his older brother, Johann Christoph, who helped him develop the musical skill they had both inherited from their father.

In 1723, Bach was selected as the cantor of St. Thomas Church in Leipzig. He spent the last 27 years of his life in the city, working as the director of music for the city's four main churches and directing the St. Thomas boys' choir, the Thomanerchor. Responsible for providing Sunday music at the churches, in just five years Bach composed some 150 cantatas, two great Passions, and numerous other sacred pieces for his choir to perform.

In addition to shepherding the 50 boys in the choir, Bach had a number of his own children. He and his first wife, Maria Barbara, had seven children; after she passed away, he remarried and had another thirteen with his second wife, Anna Magdalena. Of the twenty, only nine survived into adulthood. And of those

(1809-1847). Mendelssohn came to Leipzig at age 26 to conduct the Gewandhaus Orchestra, which he led to great success, putting Leipzig on the world musical map. Mendelssohn is remembered today primarily as a composer, but perhaps his greatest contribution was to popularize the works of Bach, who had been all but forgotten after his death. If not for Mendelssohn, the name "Bach" would probably mean nothing to you today. Because he was Jewish, Mendelssohn's statue was torn down and used for scrap metal by the Nazis; this copy was re-erected here in 2008.

Go a bit farther along the park (with the Ring on your right) to find another, much older **monument to Bach.** Mendelssohn was so dedicated to honoring the genius of the Baroque composer

nine children, six had musical careers of their own.

While living in Leipzig, Bach began directing a group of university-student musicians, who were more interested in convivial entertainment than somber church music. Their crowd-pleasing performances of his secular compositions drew attention to the composer's work, elevating his status in Leipzig.

Later in life, Bach entered a more withdrawn and reflective period, composing complex, abstract Baroque pieces. He enjoyed entertaining guests with private concerts in his personal music room. But his eyesight began failing near the end of his life, and he died in 1750 after suffering a stroke. He was buried in an unmarked grave and soon forgotten.

In 1829, the musician and composer Felix Mendelssohn received from his grandmother a copy of Bach's manuscript for *St. Matthew Passion.* When Mendelssohn conducted and performed Bach's profoundly expressive music in Berlin, it was an instant hit. Mendelssohn's concert sparked a newfound appreciation for Bach's music that began in Germany, took over Europe, and soon spread around the world.

In the mid-1800s, several Bach fans and Leipzig scholars succeeded in rediscovering Bach's remains, which they moved to a grave in Leipzig's Johanneskirche. After that church was destroyed by WWII bombs, what was left of the composer's remains was rescued and laid to rest, for a third time, at St. Thomas Church—where appreciative pilgrims and Bach admirers still bring flowers to honor one of the greatest musical geniuses of all time.

that he funded the construction of this monument. At the top of the pillar, see Bach depicted as an organist, a good Christian, and a teacher (of the boys' choir).

Across the Ring and a block up Gottschedstrasse (which is also lined with some great restaurants—see "Eating in Leipzig," later), you'll find a **Holocaust memorial,** with 140 chairs on the site of the city's former main synagogue. The empty seats encourage people to "stand up" for what's right.

▲▲**Bach Museum**—Across the little square from St. Thomas is this small, pricey, but very well-presented museum about Leipzig's favorite composer. Its good interactive exhibits, all described in English, are displayed mostly upstairs in 12 rooms on one manageable floor.

At the entry is a replica of a famous portrait-bust of the great composer. The family tree makes it clear that he came from a very musical family. In the research laboratory, you can virtually "touch" archive items on a light table. In the listening studio, touch the organ pipes to hear music, or settle in at a station to listen to one of Bach's many compositions on headsets. You'll see the actual organ console where Bach played his favorite instrument, an iron chest that came from his household, and original manuscripts. The orchestra exhibit explains Baroque music by letting you press buttons to isolate the different instruments. The Leipzig room shows sites in town associated with the composer—including a model of the residence (in the boarding school for his 50 choirboys) where he lived with his huge family. Film clips show the many cinematic depictions of Bach.

Cost and Hours: €6, Tue-Sun 10:00-18:00, closed Mon, Thomaskirchhof 15-16, tel. 0341/913-70, www.bachmuseumleipzig .de.

▲Augustusplatz

This somewhat severe square is home to Leipzig's famous university and its two most respected musical institutions. During the DDR period, the square was renamed Karl-Marx-Platz and became a showcase for the communist aesthetic. In September of 1989, protesters against the communist regime gathered here— and were dispersed by the police. Today it's a busy people zone and a hub for trams around the city.

◉ Self-Guided Spin-Tour: Begin between the fountain with the obelisk and the tram stops, and face the tallest skyscraper.

The **MDR building** was erected in the 1970s as part of the university. Today it's privately owned and features the Panorama

Tower rooftop restaurant/view terrace with an affordable business lunch (€9/ three courses, available Mon-Fri 11:00-14:30; otherwise €9-11 starters and €12-25 main dishes). Hiding behind this building (not quite visible from here) is the **Moritzbastei.** This bastion is all that survives from Leipzig's former city wall, which was torn down in the early 19th century to build the ring road. Today it hosts a happening student pub.

Stretching to the right is a complex of glassy buildings housing **Leipzig University**—the second oldest in present-day Germany. Alums include Goethe and Chancellor Angela Merkel.

The pointed facade marks **"St. Paul's."** The 13th-century church that once stood here was demolished by the communists in 1968. To pay homage to the site's former purpose, the new building (still under construction, due to be completed in 2013) will resemble a church—complete with high vaulted ceiling—but will remain part of the university and be used for secular assemblies as well as religious services.

At either end of this square are two buildings from the communist period, housing Leipzig's two main cultural institutions: At the left end is the **Gewandhaus,** home to the city's world-

renowned orchestra. (If you step in the lobby, you'll see models of the three different buildings that have hosted this vaunted institution, including the original location in the clothmakers' guild hall—as the name *Gewandhaus* implies.) At the right end is the **Opera House.**

Facing the Opera House, the tall building on the left with the two bell-ringers is Leipzig's earliest "skyscraper." To the right, down the street in the far distance (red building with black spire), you can see the Grassi Museum complex (described next).

If you're intrigued by quirky public art, head a few steps up the pedestrianized shopping street, Grimmaische Strasse (to the left as you face the Opera House), and find the sculpture *Untimely Contemporaries* (a pun that works better in German),

with insulting, exaggerated caricatures of hypocritical DDR figures. For example, the teacher (on the right) clutches a mallet used to pound communist ideology into her students; the third guy over, with the too-big laurel wreath covering his

eyes, is detonating St. Paul's Church.

From this square, **trams** fan out to various sights in town. To visit the towering Monument to the Battle of the Nations, hop on tram #15 (going to the right as you face the opera); to reach the happening Südmeile restaurant zone, take tram #10 or #11; or to make the short trip to the train station, take just about any northbound tram.

Just East of the Ring

▲**Grassi Museums (Museen im Grassi)**—This trio of museums beautifully presents three different subjects: applied arts, anthropology, and musical instruments. For Germans, this would rank ▲▲▲ and could easily fill the better part of a day—but since there's virtually nothing here unique to Leipzig, foreigners may find it less interesting than other options in town.

The **Museum of Applied Arts** (Museum für Angewandte Kunst) features pieces—such as furniture and decorative items—from both European and Asian cultures. The excellent **Museum of Anthropology** (Völkerkundemuseum) displays an impressive range of artifacts gathered from around the world, arranged by geographical region. And the **Museum of Musical Instruments** (Museum für Musikinstrumente)

boasts a fine collection. Use the touch screens to hear the instruments in surround-sound. As the exhibits are almost entirely in German, invest €1 in the excellent English audioguide (with one hour of commentary on the Applied Arts collection, and three hours apiece on the others).

Cost and Hours: Applied Arts-€5, Anthropology-€6, Musical Instruments-€5, combo-ticket for everything-€12, Tue-Sun 10:00-18:00, closed Mon, Johannisplatz 5-11, tel. 0341/222-9100, www.grassimuseum.de.

South of the Town Center

▲▲The Südmeile

Literally the "South Mile," this funky zone of boutiques, cafés, restaurants, and nightclubs runs along Karl-Liebknecht-Strasse (a.k.a. "Karli"). Renamed "Adolf-Hitler-Strasse" during the Führer's

reign, today's Südmeile would make Hitler spin in his grave. This hipster squatter's haven is filled with run-down buildings housing lots of fun eateries and nonconformist hangout spots, all slathered with artistic graffiti. (Locals sometimes mash up its many different names, sarcastically calling the drag "Adolf-Südknecht-Strasse.") For more details, see the description under "Eating in Leipzig," later.

Getting There: Ride tram #10 or #11 about 5 minutes south from downtown (to Südplatz), or walk there in about 20 minutes.

▲Monument of the Battle of the Nations (Völkerschlachtdenkmal)

This gigantic, heavy-handed monument—Europe's biggest—commemorates a pivotal battle that involved forces from all over Europe. While it's on the outskirts of town and a bit anticlimactic (it looks like a giant pedestal missing a statue on top), this is worth an ogle for its sheer size and chillingly patriotic design, especially if you're a history buff.

Cost and Hours: €6 ticket covers both monument and museum, audioguide-€1, daily April-Oct 10:00-18:00, Nov-March 10:00-16:00, Strasse des 18 Oktober 100, tel. 0341/241-6870, www.voelkerschlachtdenkmal-leipzig.de.

Getting There: Ride tram #15 from the Hauptbahnhof or Augustusplatz to the Leipzig Völkerschlachtdenkmal stop, which is right next to the big park surrounding the monument.

Background: In October 1813, the Battle of the Nations (*Völkerschlacht,* also called the Battle of Leipzig) pitted Napoleon's army against a united force of Prussian, Austrian, Russian, and Swedish fighters. With more than a half-million involved and casualties approaching 100,000 men, it was the largest battle in European history until World War I. The Battle of the Nations marked the turning point in the fight against Napoleon, who was routed and forced to retreat to France. It was the ultimate victory of predominantly German forces against French invaders.

A century later—during a surge of nationalism following the unification of the modern nation of Germany—Leipzig city leaders built this 300-foot-tall memorial on the site of the bloodiest

warfare. Looming over a huge reflecting pool, the concrete monument has a granite facade and is decorated inside and out with gigantic, heroic (almost mythical) statues of faceless soldiers and other archetypes celebrating German might. Not surprisingly, it later became a favorite backdrop for Hitler's speeches. The Soviet puppet government of East Germany wasn't thrilled with its German nationalistic overtones, but decided to let it stand as a monument to German-Russian cooperation.

Touring the Monument: A visit here has several parts: viewing the massive monument (ideally from the far end of the reflecting pool); entering the atmospheric crypt; riding the elevator up to the viewing platform; and visiting the Forum 1813 museum. Note that the monument is currently being restored (so some sections may be covered for your visit) and is due to be completely spiffed up by its 100th birthday in 2013.

On the **exterior,** the Archangel Michael straddles the main door, flanked by flights of stairs topped with stylized heads of the 12th-century Holy Roman Emperor Barbarossa, the ultimate enlightened despot. Circling the rounded top of the monument, a

LEIPZIG

dozen stoic 40-foot-tall soldiers lean menacingly on their swords—which they will use, if necessary, to protect their nation.

Buy your ticket at the building to the left, and then head through the main door and ride the elevator up to floor 3 and the **crypt.** The atmospheric atrium is ringed by 16 soldiers with their heads respectfully bowed to honor the sacrifice of those lost in battle. Above them, four gigantic 30-foot-tall statues represent the

virtues of the German people during wartime: bravery (flexing muscles), faith (an idealistic child), power (a mother nursing two young children—more fodder for the battlefield), and sacrifice (holding out a piece of fruit). Rocketing up 225 feet from the crypt is a dome decorated with hundreds of cavalry triumphantly returning from battle. From here, continue up the elevator to the **viewing platform,** with sweeping (if distant) views over Leipzig.

Back on the ground, the Forum 1813 **museum,** in the smaller building to the right of the monument, narrates the story of the battle with paintings, models, uniforms, weapons, and a large diorama (all in German, but explained by the €1 English audioguide).

Spinnerei

Formerly Europe's largest cotton mill—in the 19th century, it was a self-contained community of both factories and homes—this industrial complex has been converted into a sprawling artistic venue with some 10 galleries and dozens of artists' studios. Many showcase the "New Leipzig" art movement (contemporary eastern German art from after reunification). Gallery-hoppers, or anyone interested in the gentrification of old industrial wastelands, may find this place (with the slogan "from cotton to culture") worth a visit.

Cost and Hours: Most galleries are free to enter, but hours are variable—most are open Mon-Fri from 11:00 or 12:00 until 17:00 or 18:00, Sat until 16:00, most closed Sun and many also on Mon, check schedules at www.spinnerei.de.

Getting There: It's about three miles southwest of the town center. Ride tram #8 or #15 from the Hauptbahnhof to the Lindenau Bushof stop. Exit the tram, turn left, walk to the corner, and turn right on Saalfelder Strasse. After crossing the bridge, turn right onto Spinnereistrasse.

Nightlife in Leipzig

Leipzig's city center is dead as a doornail after dark—most of the action is outside the Ring. Music-lovers can look into performances at the **Opera House** or **Gewandhaus,** home of the city's orchestra (both on Augustusplatz). Nearby, the **Moritzbastei** is a popular-with-students place for cultural events (described later, under "Eating in Leipzig"). Within the city, **Barfussgässchen** bustles with cafés and bars, but it's quite crowded and very touristy. For a more eclectic and interesting range of hangouts close to the city center, cross the Ring, stroll up **Gottschedstrasse,** and take your pick (details under "Eating in Leipzig," later).

But Leipzig's most happening nightlife zone is the **Südmeile,** loaded with cutting-edge restaurants, cafés, bars, and nightspots (see "Eating in Leipzig," later). Of the many live music venues along here, one of the best established is **die naTo,** a cultural center presenting theater, film, and music as well as a bar with drinks and food (events nightly from 18:30, Karl-Liebknecht-Strasse 48, tel. 0341/301-4397, www.nato-leipzig.de).

Sleeping in Leipzig

Thanks to the one-two punch of being both a convention town and a post-communist one, Leipzig lacks the characteristic, family-run little pensions I favor in other parts of Germany. Instead, I've listed functional, business-oriented hotels—anonymous and low on character, but offering predictable comfort. Rates skyrocket during conventions and fairs—usually about four to six weeks a year, concentrated during the months of April-June and Sept-Oct (for a schedule, see www.leipziger-messe.com). In general, rates fluctuate wildly but are typically highest on weeknights, middling on weekends, and lowest in July-Aug.

Within or near the Ring

$$ Seaside Park Hotel has an anonymous, business-class vibe but an extremely convenient location, just across the busy Ring from the train station and an easy walk to anywhere in the town center. With 288 rooms, and a lot of marble, mirrors, and brass in the lobby, it feels elegant for the price (Sb-€85, Db-€95, rates can vary with demand, breakfast-€16, air-con, elevator, Wi-Fi, restaurant, Richard-Wagner-Strasse 7, exit the station through the Westhalle's main door and cross the street, tel. 0341/98520, www.parkhotelleipzig.de, info@parkhotelleipzig.de).

$$ art'otel, part of a stylish European chain, has 40 comfortable, minimalist rooms, decorated with class and charm by area

Sleep Code

(€1 = about $1.40, country code: 49, area code: tel. 0341)
S = Single, **D** = Double/Twin, **T** = Triple, **Q** = Quad, **b** = bathroom,
s = shower only. All of these places speak English and accept
credit cards. Unless otherwise noted, breakfast is included.

To help you sort easily through these listings, I've divided
the accommodations into three categories, based on the price
for a standard double room with bath:

$$$ Higher Priced—Most rooms €120 or more.
 $$ Moderately Priced—Most rooms between €80-120.
  $ Lower Priced—Most rooms €80 or less.

Prices can change without notice; verify the hotel's
current rates online or by email. For other updates, see www
.ricksteves.com/update.

artist Anna Tessenow. It's in a dull urban neighborhood one tram
stop (or a 10-minute walk) north of the train station, but the prices
are reasonable for what you get (Sb-€75, Db-€85; bigger "art loft"
Sb-€95, Db-€105; breakfast-€14.50, air-con, elevator, free Wi-Fi;
from station ride tram #10, #11, or #16 one stop north to Wilhelm-
Liebknecht-Platz; Eutritzscher Strasse 15, tel. 0341/303-840,
www.artotel-leipzig.com, info@artotel-leipzig.com).

$ Motel One, part of a German chain, is the best deal in town
for well-located comfort. The most central hotel in Leipzig (facing St. Nicholas Church), its 194 rooms are cookie-cutter predictable, have spongy carpets, and lack some basic amenities (phones,
minibars)—but that's what keeps the prices low. Still, the rooms
are surprisingly stylish, and the staff is professional (Sb/Db-€59,
up to €79 during fairs, breakfast-€7.50, free Wi-Fi if you buy
breakfast—otherwise pay €5, walkable from train station but a bit
closer to Augustusplatz—one tram stop south—at Nikolaistrasse
23, tel. 0341/337-4370, www.motel-one.com, leipzig@motel-one
.com).

$ A&O Leipzig Hauptbahnhof Hostel fills the former post
office with 163 rooms, ranging from dorms to private rooms. Vast
and institutional, it caters to a wide range of travelers, from backpackers to families (dorm bunk-€10-16, Sb-€40-55, Db-€40-69,
ask about family specials, breakfast-€4, sheets-€3, towel-€1, pay
Internet access and Wi-Fi, bar and lounge in lobby, Brandenburger
Strasse 2, tel. 0341/2507-94900, www.aohostels.com, booking
@aohostels.com). From inside the train station, exit toward the
Osthalle (to the left with the tracks to your back) and turn left to

hook around the building; the hostel is across the street from the bus parking lot.

On the Südmeile (Karl-Liebknecht-Strasse/Karli)

This area has Leipzig's best bar and nightclub scene, and some of its most appealing restaurants. Staying here puts you close enough to the sightseeing while helping you escape the relatively characterless downtown for a funkier, more colorful people zone. These hotels sit about a block off the main drag, so night noise is minimal, though you may hear rowdy people and rumbling trams in the distance—ask for a quieter back room. To get here from the train station (or Augustusplatz), ride tram #10 or #11 south (see listings for specific stops).

$$$ Michaelis Hotel is a class act, with 62 rooms, sophisticated decor, and good service (Mon-Fri: Sb-€99, Db-€129; Sat-Sun: Sb-€89, Db-€119; even cheaper July-Aug and Jan-Feb: Sb-€79, Db-€99; free cable Internet in rooms, free Wi-Fi in lobby, parking-€6, tram stop: Hohe Strasse, Paul-Gruner-Strasse 44, tel. 0341/26780, www.michaelis-leipzig.de, info@michaelis-leipzig.de).

$ Hotel Markgraf is simple but professionally run, offering 51 straightforward rooms with sterile comfort at fair rates just a block from the handy Südplatz tram stop—close but not *too* close to the Südmeile action (Sb-€50-65, Db-€60-75, rates depend on demand, even cheaper in July-Aug, breakfast-€9.50, elevator, free Wi-Fi, tram stop: Südplatz, Körnerstrasse 36, tel. 0341/303-030, www.markgraf-hotel-leipzig.com, hotel@markgraf-leipzig.de).

Eating in Leipzig

Leipzig's restaurants are divided between traditional German eateries (specializing in hearty Saxon dishes) and more eclectic modern options—from well-executed international bar food to a rainbow of ethnic options. Since traditional German fare is easy to come by in most other towns, my listings focus on Leipzig's more creative choices.

Dining options within the sterile city center are mostly unimaginative chain restaurants or German tourist-traps. Because little distinguishes the places within the Ring, make an effort to walk or take a quick tram ride to some of Leipzig's more appealing neighborhoods, where you'll get more interesting options (and better value).

In the City Center (Mitte)

Auerbachs Keller appears in every Leipzig guidebook (they made me sign a contract before they let me off the train). The food—German and Saxon classics—is passable. But this place's claim to fame isn't culinary: Goethe set a pivotal scene of his masterwork *Faust* here, in what was a dive bar he frequented as a student at Leipzig U. You'll dine in a long, vaulted hall ("only" a hundred years old and not the one Goethe frequented—that's only for special events). If you want traditional fare downtown, you might as well do it here (€4-14 starters, €9-25 main dishes—most around €15, in the Mädler-Passage near Grimmaische Strasse 2-4, tel. 0341/216-100).

Student Grub near the University and Augustusplatz: Two popular student eateries sit behind the big MRD skyscraper, just off Augustusplatz. **Mensa am Park,** in the student center at the base of the tower, is a basic cafeteria offering filling meals at low prices (Mon-Fri 6:00-22:00, Sat 6:00-14:30, closed Sun, enter through courtyard). **Moritzbastei** is a maze of vaulted cellars that were once part of the city fortifications. After World War II, these passages were covered with dirt until a group of students—including, reportedly, Angela Merkel—organized to excavate them. Today the complex is filled mostly with students enjoying its indoor and outdoor seating, bars, basic €3-5 bar food and sandwiches (most popular at lunch), and live entertainment (Mon-Fri 10:00-24:00, Sat 12:00-24:00, Sun 9:00-24:00, Universitätsstrasse 9, tel. 0341/702-590, check events schedule at www.moritzbastei.de). Also consider an affordable business-like lunch with a view at the skyscraper-topping **Panorama Tower** (described on page 578).

Touristy "**Restaurantmeile**": **Barfussgässchen** ("Barefoot Lane"), a tight lane leading west from Market Square, has the highest concentration of bars and eateries within the Ring. While you have plenty of options, and the crowded sidewalk seating is enticing, the variety and value are far better just across the ring road along Gottschedstrasse (described next). Unless you're exhausted and ready to sit down at the first place you see, consider doing a lap down Gottschedstrasse (just another five minutes of walking) before settling down on Barfussgässchen.

On Gottschedstrasse, Just Outside the Ring

Leipzig's most user-friendly "restaurant row"—thanks to both its proximity to the town center and its dizzying array of fine options—is the obvious choice for a stroll at lunch or dinnertime. Each place is dramatically different from the last. Choose the cuisine and ambience you like best: Thai, tapas, Russian, Italian, Vietnamese, trendy lounge, and so on. Just about the only thing you won't find is a German beer hall.

These options are worth considering: **Luise** is a big, rollicking, red-and-yellow bar with happening outdoor seating (€4-6 starters, €6-9 main dishes, daily 8:00-24:00, at Gottschedstrasse and Bosestrasse at Bosestrasse 4, tel. 0341/961-1488). **Pilot**, attached to the Central Theater, is hip yet accessible, with eclectic German and international food in a relaxed setting with secondhand furniture (€7-9 salads, €5-12 main dishes, daily, at Gottschedstrasse and Bosestrasse at Bosestrasse 1, tel. 0341/126-8117). **Canito** is a classy wine bar serving light antipasti meals, with live piano music, a wall of wines, and a Mediterranean deli case in back (€5-15 dishes, Mon-Tue 11:00-19:00, Wed-Fri 10:00-24:00; open first weekend of each month—Sat 10:00-24:00 and Sun 10:00-25:00; Gottschedstrasse 13, tel. 0341/993-8011).

On the Südmeile (Karl-Liebknecht-Strasse/Karli)

While it takes a bit more effort to reach this area (hop on tram #10 or #11 at the train station or Augustusplatz), the payoff is substantial: a several-block stretch of artfully dilapidated, graffitoed buildings hosting both eccentric and upscale boutiques, bars, restaurants, and venues for concerts and other artistic happenings. Leipzig's avant-garde epicenter is accessible to visitors of any age. You can walk here from downtown (across the Ring, south of the New Town Hall), but it doesn't get interesting until the Südplatz tram stop—the best action is the four-block stretch between there and the Karl-Liebknecht-/Kurt-Eisner-Strasse stop.

Most eateries here are bars with decent food and indoor or outdoor seating. You'll find a favorite neighborhood hangout (**Volkshaus**, #30-32); a French brasserie (**Maître**, #62); a Czech beer hall (**U Fleku,** #72); an edgy Russian-themed bar (**Café Pushkin,** #74); a Caribbean place (**La Cosita**, #89); a tapas bar (**Pata Negra,** #75); and so on (all open daily). In good weather, food trucks gather under the "Mrs. Hippie" gateway, marking a courtyard with boutiques and occasional events.

Fela, more restaurant than bar, is a notch more upscale than the options mentioned above—but still trendy—with green marble, hardwood floors, and the slogan "Good food, good people" (€4-12 snacks, €10-12 starters, €15-24 main dishes, daily 9:00 until late, #92, tel. 0341/225-3509).

Cheap and Fast: **El-Amir,** a Moroccan-run fast-food joint, has good *Döner Kebabs* and *Dürüm Kebabs,* either to go or to eat at the few tables (€3-5, Mon-Fri from 11:00, Sat-Sun from 12:00, closes late, right by Südplatz tram stop at #59, tel. 0341/308-2568). **Holy Soup** features several types of vegetarian or vegan soups (€2-4, Mon-Fri 11:00-21:00, Sat 11:30-16:00, closed Sun, #85, tel. 0341/2465-9384).

Characteristic Leipzig Brauhaus

Bayerischer Bahnhof is the city's main draw for beer pilgrims eager to sample the local brew, Gose (GOH-zeh). Originating in the town of Goslar, this extremely acidic-tasting light brew (to which coriander is added in the final stage) became a Leipzig favorite. But through the tumultuous 20th century, the recipe was all but lost, and Gose was forgotten. In the 1980s, a Berlin brewer dusted off the recipe

and started making Gose once more. Its fizziness makes Gose especially refreshing on a hot day and also helps it mix well with various shots and flavors (you'll see a list on the menu; for example, the *Frauenfreundliche*—"women friendly"—has a shot of cherry syrup). Adding a shot isn't a bad idea, as first-timers sometimes find Gose sour and a bit salty. True to its name, the restaurant is actually inside one wing of the old Bayerische Bahnhof ("Bavarian train station," where trains from Bavaria first reached all the way north to Saxony). Built in 1842, this station is in the midst of an extensive renovation to become part of the city's S-Bahn system, allowing it to retain its title as the "world's oldest functioning train station." Besides beer, the restaurant also has a full menu of tasty beer-hall dishes. Choose between several brewpub seating sections—some with a view of the giant copper vats—or the delightful beer garden (daily 11:00-24:00, Bayerischer Platz 1, ride tram #16 from Hauptbahnhof or Augustusplatz a few minutes to Bayerischer Platz and head for the forlorn-looking train station, tel. 0341/124-5760).

Leipzig Connections

Leipzig is a major rail hub for eastern Germany; if you're traveling between towns in the western part of the country (Frankfurt, Würzburg, Nürnberg) and towns in the east (Berlin, Dresden), you'll likely pass through here.

From Leipzig by Train to: Berlin (hourly direct, 1.25-1.5 hours), **Dresden** (1-2/hour direct, 1.25-1.5 hours), **Erfurt** (hourly direct, 1.25-1.75 hours), **Eisenach** and Wartburg Castle (hourly direct, 1.75-2.25 hours), **Wittenberg** (6/day on ICE, 30-40 minutes; also hourly on regional trains, 1 hour, some with transfer in Bitterfeld), **Frankfurt** (every 2 hours direct on ICE, 3.5 hours; a few additional on IC, 4 hours), **Würzburg** (about every 2 hours, 3.25-4 hours, transfer in Fulda or Bamberg), **Hamburg** (hourly,

3-3.5 hours, some direct, others transfer in Berlin), **Nürnberg** (every 2 hours direct, 3.5 hours, a few more with a transfer in Naumburg), **Munich** (every 2 hours direct, 5.5 hours; also every 2 hours direct with transfer in Nürnberg or Naumburg, 4.75-5 hours), **Prague** (about every 2 hours, 3.5-4.5 hours, transfer in Dresden). Train info: tel. 0180-599-6633, www.bahn.com.

DRESDEN

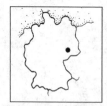

Dresden surprises visitors, with fanciful Baroque architecture in a delightful-to-stroll cityscape, a dynamic history that mingles tragedy with inspiration, and some of the best museum-going in Germany. Today's Dresden is a young and vibrant city, crawling with proud locals, cheery tourists, and happy-go-lucky students who barely remember communism. This intriguing and fun city winds up on far fewer American itineraries than it deserves to. Don't make that mistake.

At the peak of its power in the 18th century, this capital of Saxony ruled most of present-day Poland and eastern Germany from the banks of the Elbe River. Dresden's answer to Louis XIV was Augustus the Strong. As both prince elector of Saxony and king of Poland, he imported artists from all over Europe, peppering his city with stunning Baroque buildings and filling his treasury with lavish jewels and artwork. Dresden's grand architecture and dedication to the arts—along with the gently rolling hills surrounding the city—earned it the nickname "Florence on the Elbe."

Sadly, these days Dresden is better known for its destruction in World War II. American and British pilots firebombed the city on the night of February 13, 1945. More than 25,000 people were killed, and 75 percent of the historical center was destroyed. American Kurt Vonnegut, who was a POW in Dresden during the firebombing, later memorialized the event in his novel *Slaughterhouse-Five*. Today, you'll see circa-1946 photos displayed everywhere.

During the Cold War, Dresden was known as the "Valley of the Clueless," since it was one of the only spots in East Germany where you couldn't get Western television. Under the communists, Dresden patched up some of its damaged buildings, left many others in ruins, and replaced even more with huge, modern, ugly sprawl. But after the Berlin Wall fell, city leaders wasted no time in getting Dresden back on its feet, rebuilding virtually the entire city center. A devastating flood in August of 2002—which also swept through Prague—provided a setback, but most construction projects have since wrapped up. The transformation has been astonishing.

While bombs devastated the Old Town (most of the important and beautiful historic buildings have been restored), they missed the New Town, across the river. While well-worn, it retains its prewar character and has emerged as the city's fun and lively people zone. Most tourists never cross the bridge away from the famous Old Town museums...but a visit to Dresden isn't complete without a wander through the New Town.

Planning Your Time

Dresden, conveniently located about halfway between Prague and Berlin, is well worth even a quick stop. If you're short on time, Dresden's top sights can be seen in a midday break from your Berlin-Prague train ride (each one is less than a 2.5-hour ride away). Catch the early train, throw your bag in a locker at the main train station, follow my self-guided walk, and visit some museums before taking an evening train out. If possible, reserve far ahead to visit one of Dresden's top sights, the Historic Green Vault (for details, see page 606).

If you have more time, Dresden merits spending at least one night. The city is a handy home base for a quick bike ride to the "Blue Wonder" bridge, a paddleboat cruise along the Elbe, getting back to nature at Saxon Switzerland National Park, or side-tripping to the town of Görlitz for its intriguing mix of rich architecture and culture (see next chapter).

Orientation to Dresden

(area code: 0351)

Dresden is big, with half a million residents. Its city center hugs a curve on the Elbe River. Despite the city's size, most of its sights are within easy strolling distance along the south bank of the Elbe in the Old Town (Altstadt). South of the Old Town (a 5-minute tram ride or 15-minute walk away) is the main train station (Hauptbahnhof). North of the Old Town, across the river, you'll find the residential-feeling New Town (Neustadt). While the New Town boasts virtually no sights, it's lively, colorful, and fun to explore—especially after dark, when the funky, cutting-edge

Dresden

1. Hotel Kipping
2. Ibis Hotels Bastei, Königstein & Lilienstein
3. Hotel Bayerischer Hof Dresden
4. Hotel Martha Hospiz
5. AHA Hotel
6. Hostel Louise 20
7. Hostel Mondpalast Dresden
8. Marché Cafeteria
9. Augustus Garten Rest.
10. Wenzel Prager Bierstuben
11. Good Friends Restaurant
12. To Brauhaus am Waldschlösschen
13. To Ball und Brauhaus Watzke
14. Watzke Brauerei-ausschank am Goldenen Reiter
15. Feldschlösschen Stammhaus
16. Kunsthofpassage
17. Lebowski-Bar
18. Kneipe Raskolnikoff
19. To Carte Blanche & Zora Bars
20. Roll-On Bike Rental
21. Nightwalk Dresden Meeting Point & Launderette

DRESDEN

MESSERING
Alter Schlachtohof
PIESCHENER ALLEE
MAGDEBURGER STR.
FRIEDRICHSTR.
Kranken-haus Friedrich-stadt
Kongresszentrum
DEVRIENSTR
Weisseritz-str.
KÖNNERITZSTR.
OSTRA-ALLEE
BRAUER-GASSE
SEMINAR-STR.
WEISSERITZSTR.
WACHS-BLEICH-STR.
ALDERG.
Bahnhof Mitte
SCHIESSGASSE
Maxstr.
AM
Schäfer-strasse
SCHÜTZE
Am Zwingerteich
SCHWERINER
ALFRED-ALTHUS-STR.
Schweriner Str.
BAUHOFSTRASSE
EHRLICHSTR.
ERMISCHSTR.
FREIBERGER STR.
Alfred-Althus-Strasse
Haltepunkt Freiberger Strasse
MATERNI-STR.
ROSENSTR.
ANNENSTRASSE
JAKOBSG.
AM
PAPIER-MÜHLEN-GASSE
AMMONSTRASSE
JOSEPHINEN-STR.
LILIENGASSE
ROSENSTRASSE
POLIERSTR.
BUDAPESTER STR.
STRASSE
FELDGASSE
FREIBERGER STR.
Budapester Strasse
NOSSENER BRÜCKE
FELDSCHLÖSSCHEN-STR.
ZWICKAUER STR.
BUDAPESTER STR.
SCHWEIZER STR.
WIELANDSTR.
HOHE
MAIN STATION
BAYRISCHE STR.
BERGSTR.
WERD-AUER-STR.
LEUBNITZER STR.
KAITZER STR.

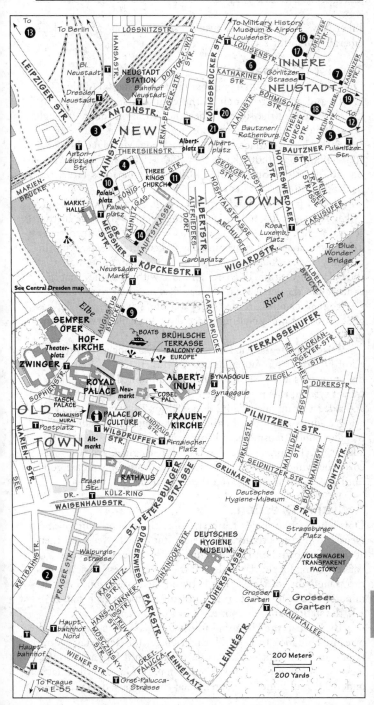

Inner New Town (Innere Neustadt) sets the tempo for Dresden's emerging nightlife scene.

Tourist Information

Dresden has a TI in its Hauptbahnhof train station (daily 9:00-19:00) and another branch in the communist-style Palace of Culture between the Royal Palace and Altmarkt square (though it's scheduled to move next door, to Wilsdruffer Strasse 16, in late 2012 during palace renovations; open May-Dec Mon-Fri 10:00-19:00, Sat 10:00-18:00, Sun 10:00-15:00; Jan-April Mon-Sat 10:00-18:00, Sun 10:00-14:00—or sometimes later; tel. 0351/5016-0160).

Both TIs stock a handy, free one-page city map with a listing of key sights, hours, and prices on the back. If you'll be hitting several sights, pick up the Dresden-City-Card (explained next). To find out about live entertainment and cultural events, skim the monthly *Theater Konzert Kunst* (free, in German only); note that the Palace of Culture TI shares an office with an agency that sells concert and theater tickets. You can also use their room-booking service (€3/person). Dresden's city website, www.dresden.de, has good information, including a free downloadable city guide and map.

Discount Deals: The **Dresden-City-Card** includes entry into all of Dresden's top museums (except the Historic Green Vault), discounts on some lesser museums, and unlimited use of the city's transit system; this pays for itself if you visit two major museums and ride the tram once (€24/2 days, €41 for 2-day family card covering 2 adults and up to 4 children). The one-day version (€9.50) includes public transit, but only offers discounts at sights—not free admission. The pricey five-day **Dresden-Regio-Card** (€75) also covers outlying areas. All cards are sold at both TIs and are good until 4:00 in the morning after the expiration date.

Arrival in Dresden

Dresden has two major train stations: the Hauptbahnhof and Neustadt. (Express trains from Berlin stop first at Neustadt, then at the Hauptbahnhof; from Prague, it's the other way around.) If you're coming for the day and want the easiest access to sights, use the Hauptbahnhof. Trains run between the two stations every 10 minutes (€1.90, 10-minute ride, most trains stop at each station—ask; the stations are also connected by slower tram #3).

By Train at the Hauptbahnhof: Dresden's main train station owes its chic look to Lord Norman Foster (of Reichstag Dome fame). In the bright, white arrivals hall, you'll find a TI kiosk, lockers (€4), Internet access (Point Shop To Go, described later under "Helpful Hints"), bike rental (at the baggage desk), a pleasantly airy, recommended cafeteria, and plenty of shops and other services.

To take a **tram** into the center, exit the station following signs for *Ausgang 1,* head straight out across the tram tracks, and hop on tram #8 to the historical center (Theaterplatz or Postplatz). The 20-minute **walk** to the Old Town offers an insightful glimpse of the communist era as you stroll down Prager Strasse (described on page 613). From the station, exit toward *Ausgang 2/City/Prager Strasse,* and continue straight through Wiener Platz, under and past the towering Mercure Hotel. You'll pop out at the top of Prager Strasse, which leads straight into the heart of town (the street changes names to Seestrasse just before reaching Altmarkt and the Old Town).

By Train at Neustadt: The Neustadt train station serves the New Town north of the river, near some recommended hotels. From this station, **tram** #11 runs to Am Zwingerteich, a park in the center of the Old Town right next to the sights.

Helpful Hints

Sightseeing Strategies: Note that many of Dresden's top museums are closed either Monday or Tuesday. The Historic Green Vault treasuries requires a reservation well in advance; if you don't get one, try to line up early to buy a same-day ticket, sold at 10:00 (for details, see page 606). Once you have your appointed Historic Green Vault visit time, plan the rest of your day around it (it's conveniently located right in the center of the Old Town). The Hofkirche hosts free pipe-organ concerts twice a week (Wed and Sat at 11:30, sometimes more—check schedule at door).

Internet Access: To get online in the Hauptbahnhof, find the Sidewalk Express computers in the **Point Shop To Go** (€2/ hour, one-hour minimum, open long hours daily).

Laundry: Eco-Express Waschsalon is a self-service launderette in the heart of the New Town (Mon-Sat 6:00-23:00, closed Sun, Königsbrücker Strasse 2, mobile 0241-8869-1565)

Local Guides: Liane Löwe enjoys sharing the story of her hometown with visitors (€80/2-hour tour, lianeloewe@gmx.de).

Getting Around Dresden

Dresden's efficient **trams** and **buses** work well for visitors. The tram network is so slick, you might just spend the hour joyriding. Buy tickets at the machines on the platforms or in the trams (€2 for a single *Einzelfahrkarte* ticket for rides up to 1 hour; €5 for a 4-pack of *Kurzstrecke* tickets for rides up to 4 stops in length; machines accept coins only). A day ticket (*Tageskarte,* €5 for one calendar day) works for sightseeing within the city. Validate your

ticket by date-stamping it in the little boxes on train platforms
and on board buses and trams (for the day ticket, stamp it only the
first time you ride). Free use of public transit is included with the
Dresden-City-Card (described earlier).

Taxis are reasonable, plentiful, and generally honest (€2.50 to
start, then €1.20/kilometer, tel. 0351/211-211).

Self-Guided Walk

▲▲▲Do-It-Yourself Dresden Baroque Blitz Tour

Dresden's major sights are conveniently clustered along a delightfully strollable promenade next to the Elbe River. Get to know
this sightseeing zone by taking this walk. Though the city has a
long and colorful history, we'll focus on the four eras that have
shaped it the most: Dresden's Golden Age in the mid-18th century
under Augustus the Strong; the city's destruction by firebombs in
World War II; the communist regime (1945-1989); and the current
"reconstruction after reunification" era.

The following walk laces together Dresden's top sights in
about an hour, not counting museum stops. It includes the three
major sights (Zwinger, Royal Palace with Historic Green Vault
treasuries, and Frauenkirche), each of which is described later in
the chapter. Incorporating these visits into the walk will fill your
day.

• Begin at Theaterplatz (a convenient drop-off point for tram #8 from
the Hauptbahnhof).

Theaterplatz

Face the equestrian statue (King John, an unimportant mid-19th-
century ruler) in the middle of the square. In front of you, behind
the statue, is the Saxon State Opera House—nicknamed the
Semperoper after its architect, Gottfried Semper (visits only with
a tour, see page 613).

As you face the Opera House, the smaller building on your
left is the Neoclassical guardhouse called the Schinkelwache
(housing the opera box office).
The big building behind it is
the vast Zwinger palace complex (your next stop). Across the
square from the Opera House is
the Hofkirche, with its distinctive green-copper steeple, and to
its right is the sprawling Royal
Palace (with shiny new clock; both
described later). All the build-

Central Dresden

- ❶ Theaterplatz
- ❷ Rampart Pavilion
- ❸ Crown Gate
- ❹ Glockenspielpavillon
- ❺ Semper Gallery
- ❻ Green Vault Entrance
- ❼ Palace of Culture
- ❽ Palace Square
- ❾ Watchman's Tower
- ❿ Parade of Nobles Mural
- ⓫ Neumarkt Square
- ⓬ Frauenkirche
- ⓭ Münzgasse
- ⓮ Goldene Reiter Statue
- ⓯ Academy of Fine Arts

ings you see here—Dresden's Baroque treasures—are thoroughly reconstructed. The originals were destroyed in a single night by American and British bombs. For more than 60 years, Dresden has been rebuilding.

Note the building along the river with a facade that looks a bit like a Florentine villa. It's a remnant from the time of Augustus the Strong, whose son set about building the Hofkirche to gain the pope's favor. Since Protestant locals refused to build the church, he had to import Catholic workers from Italy. Knowing that the workers wouldn't exactly be welcomed here, Frederick Augustus II built them their own lodgings, in the Italian Renaissance style. Today the Italienisches Dörfchen (Italian Hamlet) is overlooked by most visitors. Inside the main building is, no surprise, an Italian restaurant.

• *Walk up the path between the Semperoper and the Zwinger. Notice the small statue of composer Carl Maria von Weber to your left. Weber's Der Freischütz was the last opera performed in the building before its destruction in 1945—and the first opera performed when the building reopened in 1985.*

In the little corner by the café, go up the stairs and turn left up the path. As you turn the corner onto the upper balcony, you'll pass above a small courtyard (on the left) with a soothing, cooling fountain. Then head out to the railing and absorb the breathtaking view of the grand courtyard. As you stand on the balcony, imagine yourself as one of Dresden's 18th-century burghers, watching one of Augustus' wild parties in the courtyard below.

Walk down the stairs onto the Zwinger courtyard (either at the far end of the balcony, or via the pleasant fountain courtyard). Once you're down in the main courtyard, stand in the middle to survey all four wings.

▲▲The Zwinger

This palace complex is a Baroque masterpiece—once the pride and joy of the Wettin dynasty, and today filled with fine museums. The

Wettins ruled Saxony for more than 800 years, right up until the end of the First World War (like so many of Europe's royal families). Saxony wasn't ruled by a king, but by a prince elector—one of a handful of nobles who elected the Holy Roman Emperor. The prince elector of Saxony was one of Germany's most powerful people. In the 18th century, the larger-than-life Augustus the Strong—who was both prince elector of Saxony and king of Poland—kicked off Saxony's Golden Age.

"Zwinger" means the no-man's-land running along the city wall. This empty space gradually evolved into the complex of buildings you see today. By Augustus' time, the Zwinger was used for celebrations of Saxon royalty. Imagine an over-the-top royal wedding in this complex. The courtyard served as an open-air palace, complete with orange trees in huge Chinese porcelain pots.

Let's get oriented. Face the north wing (where you entered). You're looking at the **Rampart Pavilion** (Wallpavillon), the first wing of the palace—an orangerie capped with a sun pavilion built for Augustus' fruit trees and parties. Up top is Atlas (who happens to have Augustus' features) with the Earth on his back—a fitting symbol for Augustus the Strong. Stairs lead to a fine view from the terrace above. This wing of the Zwinger houses the fun

Mathematics-Physics Salon (described later, under "Sights in Dresden").

Turn to the left, facing the **Crown Gate** (Kronentor). The gate's golden crown is topped by four golden eagles supporting a smaller crown—symbolizing Polish royalty (since Augustus was also king of Poland).

Turn again to the left to see the **Glockenspielpavillon.** The glockenspiel near the top of the gate has 40 bells made of Meissen porcelain (bells chime every 15 minutes and play a sweet 3-minute melody at 10:15, 14:15,

and 17:15). This wing of the Zwinger also houses Augustus the Strong's **Porcelain Collection** (see listing, later).

Turn once more to the left (with the Crown Gate behind you) to see the **Semper Gallery.** This Zwinger wing was added to the original courtyard a hundred years later by Gottfried Semper (of Opera House fame). It houses Dresden's best painting collection, the **Old Masters Gallery,** as well as the **Royal Armory** (both described later).

Throughout the city, you'll see the local sandstone looking really sooty. It's not from pollution, but natural oxidation that turns the stone black in about 30 years. Once restored, the statues are given a silicon treatment that lets the stone breathe but keeps it from going black. Among Dreseners, this is a controversial approach. Many think that the resulting combination of black and white stone is odd, arguing that it departs from what Dresden "should" look like.

Take time to enjoy some of the Zwinger's excellent museums. Anticipating WWII bombs, Dresdeners preserved their town's art treasures by storing them in underground mines and cellars in the countryside. This saved these great works from Allied bombs... but not from the Russians. Nearly all of the city's artwork ended up in Moscow until after Stalin's death in 1953, when the art was returned by the communist regime to win over their East German subjects. Today, Russians invade only as tourists.

When you're finished with the museums, exit the Zwinger through the Glockenspielpavillon (south gate). Halfway through the corridor, look for the **timelines** telling the history of the Zwinger in German: to the right, its construction, and to the left, its destruction and reconstruction. Notice the Soviet spin: On February 13, 1945, gangs of Anglo-American bombers obliterated *(vernichteten)* the city. On May 8, 1945, the Soviet army liberated *(befreite)* Dresden from "fascist tyranny" *(faschistischen Tyrannei),*

Augustus the Strong
(1670-1733)

Friedrich Augustus I of the Wettin family exemplified royal excess, and made Dresden one of Europe's most important cities of culture. Legends paint Augustus as a macho, womanizing, powerful, ambitious, properly Baroque man—a real Saxon superstar. A hundred years after his death, historians dubbed Augustus "the Strong." Today, tour guides love to impart silly legends about Augustus, who supposedly fathered 365 children and could break a horseshoe in half with his bare hands.

As prince elector of Saxony, Augustus wheeled and dealed—and pragmatically converted from his Saxon Protestantism to a more Polish-friendly Catholicism—to become King Augustus II of Poland. Like most Wettins, Augustus the Strong was unlucky at war, but a clever diplomat and a lover of the arts.

The Polish people blame Augustus and his successors—who were far more concerned with wealth and opulence than with sensible governance—for Poland's precipitous decline after its own medieval Golden Age. According to Poles, the Saxon kings did nothing but "eat, drink, and loosen their belts" (it rhymes in Polish).

Whether you consider them the heroes of history, or the villains, Augustus and the rest of the Wettins—and the nobles who paid them taxes—are to thank for Dresden's rich architectural and artistic heritage.

and from 1945 to 1964, the Zwinger was rebuilt with the "power of the workers and peasants" *(Arbeiter- und Bauern-Macht)*.

• *As you exit the corridor, cross the street and the tram tracks and jog left, walking down the perpendicular street called Taschenberg, with the yellow Taschenberg Palace on your right (ruined until 1990, today the city's finest five-star hotel). The yellow-windowed sky bridge ahead connects the Taschenberg, which was the crown prince's palace, with the prince electors'* **Royal Palace.** *The gate on your left is one of several entrances to the* **Green Vault** *treasuries (described later, under "Sights in Dresden"; entrance is before crossing under the sky bridge, through fancy gate). But if your Historic Green Vault reservation is for later today, you can continue this walk for now.*

Exiting the Royal Palace, go under the sky bridge. Ahead of you and to the right, the blocky modern building is the...

Palace of Culture (Kulturpalast)

Built by the communist government in 1969, today this hall is still used for concerts (and houses Dresden's TI). Notice the mural depicting communist themes: workers, strong women, care for the elderly, teachers and students, and—of course—the red star and the seal of former East Germany. The bronze doors on the street side give a Marxist interpretation of the history of Dresden. Little of this propaganda, which once inundated the lives of locals, survives in post-communist Germany. The palace is scheduled to close in late 2012 for restoration work (to clean up damage sustained in the 2002 floods).

• *Now turn left (with the Palace of Culture behind you). Walk along the palace wall toward the two small copper domes, through a tunnel with (mostly Russian) musicians, until you emerge into **Palace Square**. Ahead of you and to the left is the **Katholische Hofkirche** (described later, under "Sights in Dresden"). Now turn around and face the gate you just came through. You're looking at the palace complex entry (with the **Watchman's Tower** above on the right—see listing, later). To the left, next to one of the palace's entrances, you'll see a long, yellow mural called the...*

▲▲Parade of Nobles (Fürstenzug)

This mural is painted on 24,000 tiles of Meissen porcelain. Longer than a football field, it illustrates 700 years of Saxon royalty. It

was built to commemorate Saxon history and heritage after Saxony became a part of Germany in 1871. The artist carefully studied armor and clothing through the ages, allowing you to accurately trace the evolution of weaponry and fashions for seven centuries. (This is great for couples—try this for a switch: As you stroll, men watch the fashions, women the weaponry.)

The very last figure (or the first one you see, coming from this direction) is the artist himself, Wilhelm Walther. In front of him are commoners (miners, farmers, carpenters, teachers, students, artists), and then the royals, with 35 names and dates marking more than 700 years of Wettin rule. Stop at 1694. That's August II (Augustus the Strong), the most important of the Saxon kings. His horse stomps on the rose (symbol of Martin Luther, the Protestant movement, and the Lutheran church today) to gain the Polish crown. The first Saxon royal is Konrad der Grosse ("the Great"). And waaay up at the very front of the parade, an announcer with a band and 12th-century cheerleaders excitedly herald the arrival of this wondrous procession. The porcelain tiles, originals from 1907, survived the bombing. When created, they were fired three times at 2,400 degrees Fahrenheit...and then fired again during the 1945 firestorm, at only 1,800 degrees.

• *When you're finished looking at the mural, dogleg right and walk into the big square. Find a statue of Martin Luther.*

Neumarkt

This "New Market Square" was once a town center ringed by rich merchants' homes. After many years of construction, it is once again a lively people-and-café center. The statue of Martin Luther holds not just any Bible, but the Word of God he translated into German so that regular people could get their minds on it without Church control—basically what the Reformation was all about. (For more on Luther—  who came from this part of Germany and spent most of his life in nearby Erfurt and Wittenberg—see page 511.) Toppled in 1945, Luther is cleaned up and back on his feet again.

• *The big church looming over the square is the...*

▲▲▲Frauenkirche (Church of Our Lady)

This church is the heart and soul of the city. The people of Dresden mobilized their Protestant pride to raise the money and built this impressive Lutheran church on the ruins of a much smaller Romanesque building. When completed in 1743, this was Germany's biggest Protestant church (310 feet high). Its unique central-stone-cupola design gave it the nickname "the stone bell." While it's a great church, this building garners the world's attention primarily because of its tragic history and phoenix-like resurrection: On the night of February 13, 1945, the firebombs came. When the smoke cleared the next morning, the Frauenkirche was smoldering but still standing. It burned for two days before finally collapsing. After the war, the Frauenkirche was kept in rubble as a peace monument. It was the site of many memorial vigils. After being completely and painstakingly rebuilt, it reopened to the public in 2005 (see listing later, under "Sights in Dresden").

A big hunk of the bombed **rubble** stands in the square (near door E, river side of church) as a memorial. Notice the small metal relief of the dome that shows where this piece came from.

• *From here, stroll downhill through a busy little restaurant-lined street, Münzgasse, and up the stairs to Dresden's grand river-view balcony. Find a bulge in the promenade 30 yards to the left. Belly up to that banister.*

▲▲Brühlsche Terrasse

This so-called "Balcony of Europe," a delightful promenade, was once Dresden's defensive rampart. Look along the side of the ter-

race facing the Elbe River to see openings for cannons. By Baroque times, fortresses were no longer necessary, and this became one of Europe's most charming promenades, with a leafy canopy of linden trees.

Dresden claims to have the world's largest and oldest fleet of historic paddleboat steamers: nine riverboats from the 19th century. The hills in the distance (to the left) are home to Saxon vineyards, producing some of Germany's northernmost wine. Because only a small amount of the land is suitable for vineyards, the area's respected, expensive wine (mostly white) is consumed almost entirely by Saxons.

Below you to the left is the **Augustus Bridge** (Augustusbrücke), connecting Dresden's old and new towns. During the massive

floods in August of 2002, the water reached two-thirds of the way up the arches. At the far end of the Augustus Bridge, you may be able to faintly see the golden equestrian statue, a symbol of Dresden. It's Augustus the Strong, the **Goldene Reiter** (Golden Rider), facing east to his kingdom of Poland.

The area across the bridge is the **New Town** (Neustadt). While three-quarters of Dresden's Old Town was decimated by Allied firebombs, much of the New Town survived. The 18th-century apartment buildings here were restored—giving the area a Baroque look instead of the blocky Soviet style predominant on the Old Town side of the river. Today, the New Town is a trendy district well worth exploring. The **Three Kings Church** (Dreikönigskirche, steeple visible above the Goldene Reiter) marks a neighborhood with some recommended restaurants.

To the far left, the interesting **mosque-shaped building** in the distance (marked *Yenidze*), originally a tobacco factory designed to advertise Turkish cigarettes, is now an office building with restaurants and nightclubs. A few steps to your left is the recommended **Radeberger Spezialausschank Café**—the best place for a drink or meal with a river view.

Behind you on the right, you'll see the glass domes of the **Academy of Fine Arts,** capped by a trumpeting gold angel. (Locals call the big dome on the right "the lemon juicer.") Around the far side of this building is another great museum, the **Albertinum,** which houses sculpture and modern art collections (see listing later).

• *Your tour is over. Stairs at the end of the promenade lead back to Palace Square; just beyond the Hofkirche is Theaterplatz, where you began.*

Sights in Dresden

Major Museums

Dresden's excellent museum scene focuses on three main locations: the Zwinger, the Royal Palace, and the Albertinum. Each location houses a number of collections, generally covered by a single ticket. Tickets are valid all day, so you can come and go as you please. All are covered by the Dresden-City-Card—see page 594—except the Historic Green Vault, which is not included in any special deal and must be reserved in advance (see page 606).

The Zwinger Museums

Four museums are located off the Zwinger palace courtyard: the Old Masters Gallery, Royal Armory, Mathematics-Physics Salon, and Porcelain Collection.

Cost and Hours: €10 ticket covers entrance to all of the museums; museums share the same hours: Tue-Sun 10:00-18:00, closed Mon—except Old Masters Gallery may be open Mon late June-Sept; tel. 0351/4914-2000, www.skd.museum.

▲▲▲**Old Masters Gallery (Gemäldegalerie Alte Meister)**— Dresden's best museum, in the Zwinger's Semper Gallery, features works by Raphael, Titian, Rembrandt, Peter Paul Rubens, Jan Vermeer, and more. While it hangs 750 paintings at a time, it feels particularly enjoyable for its "quality, not quantity" approach to showing off great art. Locals remember the Old Masters Gallery as the first big public building reopened after the war, in 1956.

Information: The dry €3 audioguide covers 55 paintings. Consider the good €15 English guidebook.

Touring the Museum: The ground floor features temporary exhibits. To see the permanent collection, make your way up the stairs to the main gallery. You'll pass a small room with portraits of the Wettin kings who patronized the arts and founded this collection. The next room shows five cityscapes of Dresden, painted by **Canaletto** during the city's Golden Age. These paintings of mid-18th-century Dresden—showing the Hofkirche (still under construction) and the newly completed Frauenkirche—offer a great study of the city. Next, you enter a world of **Rubens** and Belgian Baroque. This high-powered Catholic art is followed by the humbler, quieter Protestant art of the Dutch Masters, including a fine collection of **Rembrandts** (don't miss his jaunty self-portrait—with Saskia on his lap and a glass of ale held aloft) and a pristine **Vermeer** *(Girl at a Window Reading a Letter)*.

Take a detour down the stairs to find the German late-Gothic/early-Renaissance rooms, with exquisite canvases by **Lucas Cranach** and **Albrecht Dürer.** Farther on, the Venetian masters include a sumptuous *Sleeping Venus* by **Giorgione** (1510). He died while still working on this, so Titian stepped in to finish it. Giorgione's idealized Venus sleeps soundly, at peace with the plush nature.

The collection's highlight: **Raphael**'s masterful *Sistine Madonna.* The portrait features the Madonna and Child, two early Christian martyrs (Saints Sixtus and Barbara), and wispy angel faces in the clouds. Mary is in motion, offering the Savior to a needy world. Note the look of worry and despair on Mary's face, making this piece different from most *Madonna* paintings, which show her smiling and filled with joy. That's because this *Madonna* was originally part of a larger altarpiece, and Mary's mournful gaze was directed at another painting—one of the Crucifixion. These days, the gaze of most visitors is directed at the pair of whimsical angels in the foreground—which Raphael added after the painting was completed, just to fill the empty space. These lovable tykes—of T-shirt and poster fame—are bored...just hanging out, oblivious to the exciting arrival of the Messiah just behind them. They connect the heavenly world of the painting with you and me.

Royal Armory (Rüstkammer)—One big room packed with swords and suits of armor, the armory is especially interesting for its tiny children's armor and the jousting exhibit in the back. The Armory is located across the entry passage from the Old Masters Gallery.

Mathematics-Physics Salon (Mathematisch-Physikalischer Salon)—After extensive renovations, this fun collection should be open in time for your visit. It features globes, lenses, and clocks from the 16th to the 19th centuries (north end of Zwinger courtyard).

▲Porcelain Collection (Porzellansammlung)—In the early 18th century, porcelain was considered "white gold"—an incredibly valuable material that could only be produced in faraway China and transported to Europe at great expense. Augustus the Strong commissioned an alchemist named Johann Friedrich Böttger to derive a method for creating his own porcelain. Böttger was reluctant—he'd already failed at creating actual gold—but Augustus persuaded him by locking him up until he complied. Eventually Böttger succeeded, and the Saxon prince electors became pioneers in European porcelain production. Every self-respecting European king had a porcelain works, and the Wettins had the most famous: Meissen. They inspired other royal courts to get into the art form. They also collected other types—from France to Japan and China. Augustus the Strong was obsessed with the precious stuff...he liked to say he had "porcelain sickness." Here you can enjoy some of his symptoms, under chandeliers in elegant galleries. Peruse the menagerie of delicate white-porcelain animals, the long halls of vases, the small collection of Asian porcelain, and the large collection of locally produced goods (fine English descriptions, south end of Zwinger courtyard).

Royal Palace (Residenzschloss)

This Renaissance palace was once the residence of the Saxon prince elector. Formerly one of the finest Renaissance buildings in Germany, it's been rebuilt since its destruction in World War II. The grand state rooms of Augustus the Strong are closed for the foreseeable future. Until they reopen, the prince's treasures are the big draw here: The New Green Vault is quite remarkable, while the Historic Green Vault (reservation required) is one of the more impressive treasury collections in Europe.

Cost and Hours: €10 includes New Green Vault, Turkish Vault, Watchman's Tower, and special exhibitions; Historic Green Vault requires a separate ticket (€10 on the same day, €2 surcharge to book in advance, €1.50 to book at the TI); hours for the entire complex: Wed-Mon 10:00-18:00, Historic Green Vault until 19:00, closed Tue. The palace has four entrances, each leading to a glass-domed inner courtyard, where you'll find the ticket windows and restrooms. Tel. 0351/4914-2000, www.skd.museum.

▲▲**Historic Green Vault (Historisches Grünes Gewölbe)**— The famed, glittering Baroque treasury collection was begun by Augustus the Strong in the early 1700s. It evolved into the royal family's extravagant treasure trove of ivory, silver, and gold knick-knacks, displayed in rooms as opulent as the collection itself.

Reservations: To protect these priceless items and the extravagant rooms in which they're displayed, the number of visitors each day is carefully controlled. It makes sense to book your required reservation well in advance—at least a week ahead in May, June, or September, and two or three weeks ahead on Saturdays in those months. At other times, you should be able to book just a few days out. You'll be given a 15-minute entry window for your visit (once inside, you can stay as long as you like). You can book online and print your own ticket (www.skd.museum); or you can book by phone or email and either pick up your ticket at the ticket office or receive an e-ticket via email (tel. 0351/4919-2000, besucher service@skd.museum). If your preferred dates are listed as sold out, keep checking back, since tour groups often cancel on short notice. If you don't have a reservation, try showing up by 10:00 for a same-day ticket (the line forms at 9:00, but your chances for an afternoon slot are still decent at 10:00); the number of spots still available— *Freie Plätze*—is indicated at the ticket desk. To avoid the line, get your ticket at the TI (for an extra €1.50 service charge).

Touring the Historic Green Vault: Your visit is designed to wow you in a typically Baroque style—starting easy and crescen-doing to a climax, taking a quick break, and finishing again with a flurry. You'll enter through a "dust sluice," which protects the vault's delicate collection by cleaning any irritants off visitors— a good feeling. Following the included (but torturously dry) audioguide, you'll spend about an hour progressing through nine rooms.

The **Amber Cabinet** serves as a reminder of just how many different things you can do with fossilized tree sap (in a surprising range of colors), and the **Ivory Room** does the same for elephant tusks, with some strikingly delicate hand-carved sculptures. The **White Silver Room,** painted its original vermillion color, holds a chalice carved from a rhino horn, and the **Silver-Gilt Room** dis-plays tableware and gold-ruby glass.

The wide variety of items in the largest room—the aptly named **Hall of Precious Objects**—includes mother-of-pearl sculptures, along with a model of the Hill of Calvary atop a pile of pearls and polished seashells. The oak cupboards that line the **Heraldry Room** are emblazoned with copper-and-gold coats-of-arms boasting of the various territories in Augustus the Strong's domain.

The vault's high-water mark is the grandly decorated **Jewel Room.** The incredible pieces in here (especially the Obeliscus Augustalis) are fine examples of *Gesamtkunstwerk*—a symphony of artistic creations, though obnoxiously gaudy by today's tastes. The *Moor with Emerald Tier*—a "Moor" (actually a Native American) clad in jewels and gold—was designed to carry a chunk of rock embedded with large gems. Nearby, an overly decorated obelisk trumpets the greatness of Augustus the Strong.

The exhibit concludes in the relatively subdued **Bronze Room,** with its eight-foot-tall equestrian statue of Augustus the Strong (designed to compete with similar depictions of his rival, Louis XIV), as well as a statue of Apollo surrounded by six women. Your audioguide also describes treasures in the "pre-vault" (where you pick up and drop off the audioguide). In this room, don't miss photos of vaults before the war and Luther's signature ring.

▲**New Green Vault (Neues Grünes Gewölbe)**—This collection shows off more of the treasure in a modern setting. Don't miss the 6.2-carat one-of-a-kind green diamond that "mysteriously" appeared here from India. The included audioguide describes the best 65 objects in 1.5 hours.

▲**Turkish Vault (Türkisches Cammer)**—In the 16th through 19th centuries, Western European elites were crazy about all things Turkish, and Augustus the Strong was no exception. Augustus collected Ottoman art with a passion, even dressing up as a sultan in his own court. This fascinating collection of Ottoman art is the result of centuries of collecting, diplomatic gifts, trades, and shopping trips to Constantinople. Although the collection consists largely of ornamental swords and longbows (one dating back to 1586), the real reason to visit is to see the 20-yard-long, three-poled ornamented silk tent—the only complete three-masted Ottoman tent on display in Europe.

Watchman's Tower (Hausmannsturm)—This palace tower is completely rebuilt (and feels entirely modern). You can climb past an underwhelming coin collection, see the rebuilt medieval clock mechanism from behind, peruse an extensive series of dome-damage photos, and earn a good city view after a long climb. In bad weather, the view terrace is closed, and you'll peer through small windows—a big disappointment. If climbing the Frauenkirche dome (which affords the best view in town but costs €8), skip this.

▲▲The Albertinum

The Elbe floods of 2002 severely damaged this historic arsenal building at the end of the Brühlsche Terrasse. The reconstructed complex is a fascinating architectural mix—an old building with an ultramodern interior and minimalist white central atrium. The museum's excellent collections feature artwork from the Romantic period (late 18th and early 19th centuries) to the present. The included audioguide does

a beautiful job of explaining the artwork.

Cost and Hours: €8, Tue-Sun 10:00-18:00, closed Mon, entrance on the Brühlsche Terrasse and on Georg-Treu-Platz, tel. 0351/4914-2000, www.skd.museum.

Touring the Museum: The collections are arranged on three floors: Most of the Sculpture Collection is on the ground floor; the first floor up has contemporary art (with temporary exhibits), turn-of-the-century art, more sculptures, and display cases crammed with odds and ends; and the New Masters Gallery is on the top floor.

Sculpture Collection (Skulpturensammlung): Gathered in one huge *Skulpturhalle*, this easy-on-the-eyes collection looks at the last 5,000 years of Western sculpture, with a special focus on the last 200 years. Look for Edgar Degas' *Little Dancer Aged Fourteen* (one of 29 bronze casts from the wax original) and several plaster casts by Auguste Rodin, including a *Thinker*. At the contemporary end of the spectrum is Tony Cragg's *Ever After* (2010), a 10-foot-tall wooden sculpture that appears to be melting; look closely to see profiles of human faces emerge on the left side.

Mosaiksaal, Klingerhalle, and Other Collections: On the first floor up, the Mosaiksaal features sculpture from the Classicist era on up to Ernst Rietschel's mid-19th-century depictions of his-

torically important Germans.

The Klingerhalle takes on the next chronological era, with slinky *fin de siècle* paintings and sculptures. Look for Gustav Klimt's atmospheric *Buchenwald*, a tranquil beech forest that shimmers with color, achieving startling depth. In Ferdinand Hodler's portrait of *Madame de R.*, the subject regards us with a steely gaze.

Connecting the Klingerhalle and Mosaiksaal to the other side of the building is a pair of *Schaudepot*s—display storerooms jammed full of items that didn't find a permanent home in the public exhibits, giving a glimpse into the vastness of the Albertinum's collection. Running along the other side of this floor is the contemporary art hall, with ever-changing exhibits.

New Masters Gallery (Galerie Neue Meister): On the top floor, take a counterclockwise walk around this chronologically organized collection, showcasing paintings from German Romanticism to 20th-century Modernism. In Caspar-David Friedrich's landscapes, notice that people are small and blend into the background, reminding us that German Romanticism is all about the exploration of man's place as a part of nature—not as its dominating force. Friedrich's Norwegian counterpart and friend, Johan Christian Dahl—who moved to Dresden later in life—captures his adopted hometown in his *View of Dresden at Full Moon*, which seems not so different from today's reconstructed city.

Take a breather with Ludwig Richter's bucolic scenes of the Italian countryside, then move into the top-notch Modernist wing, with works by Paul Gauguin (Polynesian women), Vincent van Gogh *(Still Life with Quinces)*, Max Liebermann (insightful portraits), Oskar Kokoschka (vibrantly colored, almost garish portraits), Claude Monet, Edouard Manet, and more. Some of the lesser-known works are also worth a good look, such as Max Slevogt's evocative paintings of North Africa.

Don't miss Otto Dix's haunting, frank images—particularly his stirring triptych *War*, rooted in his firsthand experience fighting in the trenches of France and Flanders during World War I. This vision, modeled after a medieval altarpiece, has a circular composition that's kept moving by the grotesque pointing skeleton. In this fetid wasteland, corpses are decomposing, and helmets and gas masks make even the intact bodies seem inhuman. Dix painted this in the 1930s, when Adolf Hitler was building a case for war (ostensibly to reclaim territory Germany lost after WWI). The Führer didn't care for Dix's pacifist message, dismissing the artist from his teaching job at Dresden's art academy and adding Dix's works to his collection of "degenerate art."

The collection wraps up with works by Paul Klee, Pablo Picasso, some harrowing Expressionistic works, and Gerhard Richter's recent acrylics under glass.

Major Churches
▲▲▲Frauenkirche (Church of Our Lady)

This landmark church was originally built by local donations—Protestant people-pride. Destroyed by the Allied firebombing in World War II, the church sat in ruins for decades. Finally, in 1992, reconstruction of the church began, following carefully considered guidelines: Rebuild true to the original design; use as much of the original material as possible; avoid using any concrete or rebar; maximize modern technology; and make it a lively venue for 21st-century-style worship. The church was fitted together like a giant jigsaw puzzle, with about a third made of the darker original stones—all placed lovingly in their original spots. The reconstruction cost more than €100 million, 90 percent of which came from donors around the world.

Cost and Hours: Free but donation requested, 45-minute audioguide-€2.50, Mon-Fri 10:00-12:00 & 13:00-18:00, open between services and concerts on Sat-Sun, enter through door D, www.frauenkirche-dresden.de.

Climbing the Dome: Get a great view over the city by hiking to the top of the dome. After an elevator takes you a third of the way, you still have a long climb up many stairs (€8—consider it a donation to the church, Mon-Sat 10:00-18:00, Sun 12:30-18:00, enter through door G, follow signs to *Kuppelaufstieg*).

Gift Shop: Located behind the Albertinum, the church's shop has all of your tasteful-refrigerator-magnet needs covered. Interesting books, videos, and jewelry help fund the work and upkeep of the church (Mon-Sat 10:00-18:00, Sun 11:00-17:00, Georg-Treu-Platz 3, tel. 0351/656-0683).

Touring the Church: The Frauenkirche is as worthwhile for its glorious **interior** as for its tragic, then uplifting, recent history. Stepping inside, you're struck by the shape—not so wide (150 feet) but very tall (inner dome 120 feet, under a 225-foot main dome). The color scheme is pastel, in an effort to underline the joy of faith and enhance the festive ambience of the services and ceremonies held here. The curves help create a feeling of community. The seven entrances are perfectly equal (as people are, in the eyes of God). When the congregation exits, the seven exits point to all quarters—a reminder to "go ye," the Great Commission to spread the Word everywhere.

The Baroque sandstone **altar** shows Jesus praying in the Garden of Gethsemane the night before his crucifixion. Soldiers,

led by Judas, are on their way, but Christ is firmly in the presence of God and his angels. Eighty percent of today's altar is from original material—in the form of 2,000 individual fragments that were salvaged and pieced back together by restorers.

The **Cross of Nails** at the high altar is from Coventry, England—Dresden's sister city. Two fire-blackened nails found in the smoldering rubble of Coventry's bombed church are used as a symbol of peace and reconciliation. Coventry was bombed as thoroughly as Dresden (so thoroughly, it

gave the giddy Luftwaffe a new word for "bomb to smithereens"—to "coventrate"). From the destroyed town of Coventry was born the Community of the Cross of Nails, a worldwide network promoting peace and reconciliation through international understanding.

Near the exit stands the church's **twisted old cross,** which fell 300 feet and burned in the rubble. Lost until restorers uncovered it from the pile of stones in 1993, it stands exactly on the place it was found, still relatively intact. A copy—a gift from the British people in 2000 on the 55th anniversary of the bombing—crowns the new church. It was crafted by an English coppersmith whose father had dropped bombs on the church on that fateful night. Visitors are invited to light a candle before this cross and enter a wish for peace in the guest book.

Go downstairs to the **cellar** to see a modern-feeling, very stark chapel under vaulted ceilings. Look for the old grave markers, from when the crypt was here in prewar times. In each stairwell, plaques list the names of the donors who helped resurrect this church from the rubble. In a separate room (first up, then down some stairs) is a modest exhibit about the history of the building.

▲Katholiche Hofkirche (Catholic Church of the Royal Court)

Why does Dresden, a stronghold of local boy Martin Luther's Protestant Reformation, boast such a beautiful Catholic cathedral? When Augustus the Strong died, his son wanted to continue as king of Poland, like his father. The pope would allow it only if Augustus Junior built a Catholic church in Dresden. Now, thanks to Junior's historical kissing-up, the mere 5 percent of locals who are Catholic get to enjoy this fine church. The elevated passageway connecting the church with the palace allowed the royal family to avoid walking in the street with commoners.

Cost and Hours: Free, Mon-Thu 9:00-17:00, Fri 13:00-17:00, Sat 10:00-18:00, Sun 12:00-16:00, enter through side door facing palace, tel. 0351/484-4712, www.kathedrale-dresden.de.

Touring the Church: Inside the cathedral, on the right side of the main nave, is the fine Baroque **pulpit,** carved from linden wood and hidden in the countryside during World War II.

The glorious 3,000-pipe **organ** filling the back of the nave is played for the public for free on Wednesdays and Saturdays at 11:30 (and occasionally at other times as well).

The **Memorial Chapel** (as you face the rear of the church, it's on the left) is dedicated to those who died in the WWII firebombing and to all victims of violence. Its evocative *pietà* altarpiece was constructed in 1976 of Meissen porcelain. Mary offers the faithful the crown of thorns made from Dresden's rubble, as if to remind us that Jesus—on her lap, head hanging lifeless on the left—died to save humankind. Jesus' open heart shows us his love, offers us atonement for our sins, and proves that reconciliation is more powerful than hatred. The altar (freestanding, in front) shows five flaming heads. It seems to symbolize how Dresdeners suffered...in the presence of their suffering savior. The dates on the high altar (30-1-33 and 13-2-45) mark the dark period between Hitler's rise to power and the night Dresden was destroyed.

The basement houses the **royal crypt,** including the heart of the still-virile Augustus the Strong—which, according to legend, still beats when a pretty woman comes near (crypt open only for one or two 45-minute German tours each day).

More Sights in Dresden

▲**Semperoper**—This elegant opera house watches over Theaterplatz in the heart of town. Three opera houses have stood in this

spot: The first was destroyed by a fire in 1869, the second by firebombs in 1945. The rebuilt Semperoper continues to be a world-class venue, and tickets for the Saxon State Orchestra (the world's oldest) are hard to come by (on sale a year in advance, you can book in advance online or by phone and pick up tickets at the box office in Schinkelwache across the square, Mon-Fri 10:00-17:00, Sat-Sun 10:00-16:00, tel. 0351/491-1705, www.semperoper.de).

The opulent interior can only be visited with a tour. German-language tours (with an English handout) go regularly throughout the day. There is one daily English tour at 15:00.

Cost and Hours: €8, €2 extra to take photos, 1 hour, tour schedule depends on rehearsal schedule, enter on right side, tel. 0351/796-6305.

Prager Strasse—This communist-built pedestrian mall, connecting the train station and the historic center, was in ruins until the 1960s. Even today, "Prague Street" reflects Soviet ideals: big, blocky, functional buildings without extraneous ornamentation. As you stroll down Prager Strasse, imagine these buildings without much color or advertising (which were unnecessary back in the no-choices days of communism). Today, the street is filled with corporate logos, shoppers with lots of choices, and a fun summertime food circus. The street has developed into exactly what the communists envisioned for it, but never quite achieved: a pedestrian-friendly shopping area where people could stroll and relax, combined with residential space above.

Deutsches Hygiene Museum—This museum, a highly conceptual compilation of vaguely health-related exhibits, is well-suited for the legions of Germans fanatical about hygiene and public health. Visitors with strong stomachs get a kick out of this highly interactive museum, but those easily disturbed should stay away—or at least plan meal times accordingly.

The building has the dubious honor of once serving as the headquarters of the Nazi eugenics and "racial studies" administration, and the exterior fresco—by German Expressionist Otto Dix—sets the tone for the unsettling interior. Since its founding in 1911, the museum has produced and collected models—some more than 500 years old. The exhibit is divided into weirdly themed sections (Life and Death, Disease, Physiology, Reproduction, and Grooming). Check out the little wooden anatomical figures with removable parts (complete with strategically placed fig leaves), X-ray machines from the 1930s, and graphic wax models of venereal diseases.

The museum offers some English explanations and an included audioguide, but most of the exhibits speak (or shriek) for themselves. Perhaps as a reflection of many Germans' pragmatic approach to sexuality, this place is usually filled with school groups and families with young kids.

Cost and Hours: €7, Tue-Sun 10:00-18:00, closed Mon; Lingnerplatz 1, take tram #1, #2, #4, or #12 from Postplatz to the Deutsches Hygiene Museum stop; tel. 0351/484-6400, www .dhmd.de.

Volkswagen Transparent Factory (Gläserne Manufaktur)— Car buffs will want to make a pilgrimage to the recently built VW factory on the southeastern edge of town. Two floors of this fascinating, transparent building are open to visitors interested in the assembly of one of VW's *luxus-schlitten* (luxury sleds). You don't have to custom-order a high-end Phaeton to see how they're manufactured. (But if you do buy a car, you can bring a folding chair, park yourself on the platform, and follow it through every moment of the 36-hour "birth" process.) The parts are delivered to the logistics plant on the edge of town, then transported to this manufacturing plant by "cargo trams" (instead of trucks, to keep traffic congestion down).

While a visit here can feel like a VW ad, the automotively inclined will find it worthwhile for the chance to see the wild building, peek at the assembly line, and play with the informative, high-tech English touch-screen displays.

Cost and Hours: €5 for 1.5-hour guided tour—call ahead to ask about English tour times, daily 8:00-20:00, tel. 01805-896-268, www.glaesernemanufaktur.de.

Getting There: Take tram #1, #2, or #4 from Theaterplatz or Prager Strasse, or tram #10 from the Hauptbahnhof, to Strassburgerplatz. From there it's a 100-yard walk to Lennestrasse 1.

▲**New Town (Neustadt)**—A big sign across the river from the old center declares, "Dresden continues here"—directed at tourists who visit the city without ever crossing the river into the New Town. Don't be one of them: While there are no famous sights in this district, it's the only part of Dresden that looks as it did before World War II. Today, it's thriving with cafés, shops, clubs, and—most importantly—actual Dresdeners. (For hotel and restaurant recommendations in the neighborhood, see "Sleeping in Dresden" and "Eating in Dresden," later.)

Military History Museum (Militärhistorisches Museum der Bundeswehr)—This recently renovated museum covers over 800 years of German military history and focuses on the causes and consequences of war and violence. At over 180,000 square feet, it's the largest museum in Germany. The museum is housed in Dresden's Neoclassical former arsenal building, forcefully severed by a Daniel Libeskind-designed wedge of glass and steel (signalling the break from Germany's militaristic past and its hope for a transparent government and peaceful future).

Cost and Hours: Likely €5, includes audioguide; Mon 10:00-21:00, Tue and Thu-Sun 10:00-18:00, closed Wed; Olbrichtplatz 2, tel. 0351/823-2803, www.mhmbundeswehr.de.

Near Dresden

Dresden is the starting point for two pleasant excursions—a peaceful half-day's walk or bike ride up the Elbe River, and a day of hiking in dramatic "Saxon Switzerland."

Elbe River Valley to the Blue Wonder Bridge

The Elbe River Valley makes for a wonderful excursion from Dresden. For a great slice-of-life glimpse at Germans at play, walk or bike along the 3.5-mile path that hugs the banks of the Elbe River all the way from central Dresden to the Blue Wonder bridge. If the weather's warm, pack a swimsuit.

The path starts underneath and to the right of the Brühlsche Terrasse, and makes its scenic way—past several tempting beer gardens—to the **Blue Wonder** (a.k.a. Loschwitz Bridge), a canti-

lever truss bridge that connects the Dresden suburbs of Loschwitz and Blasewitz. When the bridge was completed in 1893, Blasewitz and Loschwitz were the most expensive pieces of real estate in Europe—note the ultra-posh villas near the bridge. The bridge is indeed a wonder in that it survived World War II completely untouched, and it is, in fact, blue—but its name is a pun on the German expression, "to witness a blue wonder" *(ein Blaues Wunder erleben)*—to experience a nasty surprise. The real surprise is how relaxing the whole trip is, as the closer you get to the bridge the more opportunities you'll find for swimming and boating (several places rent kayaks, Jet Skis, and so on).

Underneath the bridge, a delightful beer garden awaits: **Schiller Garten,** a vast, 300-year-old complex of gastronomic delights and cold suds. The garden area serves good grilled food, has a self-service buffet (in the building marked *Lichtspiel*), and pours an unfiltered *Zwickel* beer brewed specially for this garden by Feldschlösschen (Dresden's best brewery). The garden includes a playground and a digital departure board for the nearby Schillerplatz tram stop (€3-6 plates and snacks, daily 11:00-24:00). If you're looking for something fancier, try the sit-down restaurant in the half-timbered house, which serves excellent pheasant (€8-15 plates, daily 11:00-22:00). Both the garden and restaurant have been supplied by their own butcher and pastry kitchen since 1764 (tel. 0351/811-990, www.schillergarten.de).

Getting to the Blue Wonder: If you have enough time and sunny weather, slow down and do this outing on foot (about one hour each way) or by bike (about 30 minutes each way). **Roll-On** rents bikes for €9-10 per day and will gladly deliver and pick up the bike at your hotel for €0.25 per kilometer extra (Mon-Fri 10:00-13:00 & 16:00-19:00, Sat 10:00-13:00, closed Sun; in the New Town, near Albertplatz at Königsbrücker Strasse 4a, tel. 0152/2267-3460, reserve by email at info@rollondresden.de). You can also rent bikes through the German Railway at Dresden's Hauptbahnhof. They charge less for bikes than Roll-On does, but have a smaller selection, and the staff speaks little English (€7/day, daily 6:15-11:30 & 12:00-18:00 & 18:30-21:30, tel. 0351/461-3232).

You can also make the trip by boat or tram: The **Saxon Steamboat Service** (Sächsische Dampfschifffahrt) runs steam-powered paddle boats along the Elbe (€5 one-way, about hourly in summer, 40 minutes, board at Brühlsche Terrasse, get off at Blasewitz dock; to return to Dresden, board at Loschwitz; check schedule in advance—low water levels on the Elbe can limit traffic). **Tram #12** from Postplatz takes you to Schillerplatz, about 50 yards from the Blue Wonder. The tram ride is particularly interesting, as it starts in beautiful downtown Dresden and travels a path of destruction through communist prefabricated housing, then to post-unification strip-mall urban sprawl, before taking you to a delightful collection of villas and large single-family 19th-century dwellings. On the way, keep your eyes peeled at the Trinitatis Platz stop for a beautiful bombed church, which sits amid a sea of dreary prefab architecture. You can take your bike on the tram for €1.40 (choose the *Einzelfahrt-Ermäßigt* button for your bike fare).

Saxon Switzerland National Park

Consider a break from big-city sightseeing to spend a half-day taking a *wunderbar* hike through this scenic national park.

Twenty miles southeast of Dresden (an easy 45-minute S-Bahn ride away), the Elbe River cuts a scenic swath through the beech forests and steep cliffs of Saxon Switzerland (Sächsische Schweiz) National Park. You'll share the trails with serious rock climbers and equally serious Saxon grandmothers. Allow five hours (including lunch) to enjoy this day trip.

Take the S-Bahn line 1 from either the Hauptbahnhof or Neustadt Station (direction Bad Schandau, 2/hour, 45 minutes; round-trip day tickets: single-€7.70, family-€15, group of up to 5 adults-€23). Get off at the Kurort Rathen stop, follow the road downhill five minutes through town to the dock, and take the ferry across the Elbe (€1.50 round-trip, pay on board, crossing takes 2 minutes, runs continuously). When the ferry docks on the far (north) side of the river, turn your back on the river and walk 100 yards through town, with the little creek on your right. Turn left after the **Sonniges Eck Restaurant** (tasty lunch option, check out the 2002 flood photos in their front dining room) and walk up the lane. The trail begins with stairs on your left just past Hotel Amselgrundschlösschen (follow *Bastei* signs).

A 45-minute walk uphill through the woods leads you to the **Bastei Bridge** and stunning views of gray sandstone sentries rising

several hundred feet above forest ridges. Elbe Valley sandstone was used to build Dresden's finest buildings (including the Frauenkirche and Zwinger), as well as Berlin's famous Brandenburg Gate. The multiple-arch bridge looks straight out of Oz—built in 1851 specifically for Romantic Age tourists, and scenic enough to be the subject of the first landscape photos ever taken in Germany. Take the time to explore the short 50-yard spur trails that reward you with classic views down on the Elbe 900 feet below. Watch the slow-motion paddleboat steamers leave V-shaped wakes as they chug upstream toward the Czech Republic, just around the next river bend. If you're not afraid of heights, explore the maze of catwalks through the scant remains of the **Felsenberg Neurathen,** a 13th-century Saxon fort perched precariously on the bald stony spires (€1.50, entrance 50 yards before Bastei Bridge).

DRESDEN

Just a five-minute uphill hike beyond the bridge is the **Berg Hotel Panorama Bastei,** with a fine restaurant, a snack bar, and memorable views. Return to the Elbe ferry down the same trail.

Nightlife in Dresden

Innere Neustadt

To really connect with Dresden as it unfolds, you need to go to the Innere Neustadt ("Inner New Town," a 10-minute walk from Neustadt train station). This area was not bombed in World War II, and after 1989 it sprouted the first entrepreneurial cafés and bistros. While eateries are open long hours, the action picks up after 22:00. The clientele is young, hip, pierced, and tattooed.

Rather than seek out particular places in this continuously evolving scene, I'd just get to the epicenter—at the corner of Görlitzer Strasse and Louisenstrasse—and wander. You'll find unconventional *Biergartens* (not your grandfather's oompah bands) with young adults hanging out on the curb, nursing beer bottles. Here are a few places worth checking out:

Kunsthofpassage is a Hundertwasser-type apartment block with a series of fanciful, imaginatively decorated courtyards surrounded by boutiques. This is a delightful fantasy world, tucked improbably between grimy urban streets (just as interesting by day; enter at Görlitzer Strasse 21, 23, or 25, or at Alaunstrasse 70; www.kunsthof-dresden.de).

Lebowski-Bar, with a tight interior and screens showing the Coen Brothers' masterpiece on a continuous loop, is an inviting spot for fans of The Dude to sip a White Russian (Görlitzer Strasse 5).

The Russian-flavored **Kneipe Raskolnikoff** has an imported beach, giving it a Moscow/Maui ambience (Böhmische Strasse 34, a half-block off Lutherplatz).

Carte Blanche Transvestite Bar is a hoot for some (€25 burlesque show, most nights from 20:00, Priessnitzstrasse 10, tel. 0351/204-720, www.carte-blanche-dresden.de). Across the courtyard is the inviting **Zora Cocktail Bar,** a great place to enjoy a drink before or after the show.

For a fun tour around the Neustadt neighborhood, call **Nightwalk Dresden.** Their nightly tour is much more than just a pub crawl; it's a journey through the unique culture of a virtually undiscovered part of the city—that just happens to include some free drinks. This is a great option for travelers looking for company or who hesitate to visit a new area after dark. Tours visit some great pubs and run in English and German simultaneously (€13, daily at 21:00, 3 hours; starts in Neustadt on the north end of Albertplatz, between the artesian well and a building called the Nudelturm; tel. 0172/781-5007, www.nightwalk-dresden.de).

Near the Innere Neustadt: For more sedate entertainment, stroll along the New Town's riverbank after dark for fine floodlit views of the Old Town—a scene famous among Germans as the *Dresden-Blick* (Dresden view).

Sleeping in Dresden

Dresden is packed with big conference-style hotels. Characteristic, family-run places are harder to come by. (The communists didn't do "quaint" very well.) Peak season for big business-class hotels is May, June, September, and October. Peak season for hostels is July and August (especially weekends).

In or near the Old Town

$$$ Aparthotels an der Frauenkirche rents 104 new units in four beautifully restored houses (many with views) in the heart of the Old Town. Designed for longer stays but also welcoming two-nighters (minimum), these modern, comfortable apartments come with kitchens and the lived-in works. Two buildings ("Neumarkt" and "Altes Dresden") overlook the pleasant Neumarkt square in front of the Frauenkirche, another is just above the restaurant action on Münzgasse, and the fourth is a bit closer to the Hauptbahnhof on Altmarkt square (rates for up to 2 people: studio-€95-155, 2-room apartment-€125-195, 3-room apartment-€135-180, €25-30/extra person, rates depend on unit size and amenities, cheaper off-season—roughly Nov-March, breakfast-€12 at nearby café, cheaper for longer stays and off-season, free Wi-Fi, parking at nearby garage-€15, reception for Neumarkt and Altmarkt units is

---

Sleep Code

(€1 = about $1.40, country code: 49, area code: 0351)
S = Single, **D** = Double/Twin, **T** = Triple, **Q** = Quad, **b** = bathroom, **s** = shower only. All of these places speak English and accept credit cards. Unless otherwise noted, breakfast is included.

To help you sort easily through these listings, I've divided the accommodations into three categories, based on the price for a standard double room with bath:

$$$ Higher Priced—Most rooms €120 or more.
$$ Moderately Priced—Most rooms between €80-120.
$ Lower Priced—Most rooms €80 or less.

Prices can change without notice; verify the hotel's current rates online or by email. For other updates, see www.ricksteves.com/update.

DRESDEN

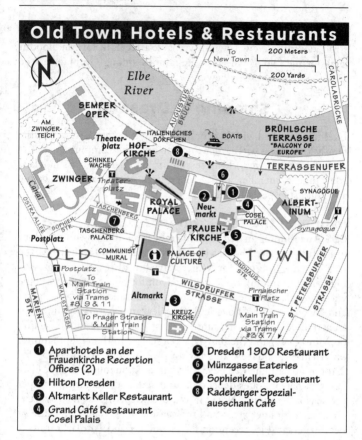

Old Town Hotels & Restaurants

- **1** Aparthotels an der Frauenkirche Reception Offices (2)
- **2** Hilton Dresden
- **3** Altmarkt Keller Restaurant
- **4** Grand Café Restaurant Cosel Palais
- **5** Dresden 1900 Restaurant
- **6** Münzgasse Eateries
- **7** Sophienkeller Restaurant
- **8** Radeberger Spezialausschank Café

in gift shop at An der Frauenkirche 20, reception for Münzgasse apartments is at Münzgasse 10, tel. 0351/438-1111, www.aparthotels -frauenkirche.de, info@aparthotels-frauenkirche.de, Drescher family).

$$$ Hilton Dresden has 333 luxurious rooms (some with views of the Frauenkirche) in the center of the Old Town, one block from the river. Complete with porters, fitness club, pool, and a dozen restaurants, it's everything you'd expect from a soulless four-star chain hotel (standard Sb/Db-€105-195, €25 more for "deluxe" rate that includes more amenities and view, check online for specific rates, breakfast-€15 or €22, air-con, elevator, pay Internet access and Wi-Fi, parking-€20, An der Frauenkirche 5, tel. 0351/86420, fax 0351/864-2725, www.hilton.de, info.dresden @hilton.com).

$$ Hotel Kipping, with 20 tidy rooms 100 yards behind the Hauptbahnhof, is professionally run by the friendly and proper Kipping brothers (Rainer and Peter). The building was one of few in this area to survive the firebombing—in fact, people took shelter here during the attack (Sb-€65-105, Db-€80-120; suite: Sb-€115-130, Db-€130-145; child's bed-€25—or free under age 6; higher prices are for weekends, May-June, and Sept-Oct; elevator, free Internet access and Wi-Fi, free parking; exit the station following signs for *Bayerische Strasse* near track 6, it's at Winckelmannstrasse 6, from here tram #8 whisks you to the Old Town; tel. 0351/478-500, fax 0351/478-5090, www.hotel-kipping .de, reception@hotel-kipping.de). Their restaurant serves international cuisine and Saxon specialties (€9-12 main courses, Mon-Sat 18:00-22:00, closed Sun).

$ Hotels Bastei, Königstein, and **Lilienstein** are cookie-cutter members of the Ibis chain, goose-stepping single-file up

Prager Strasse (listed in order from the station to the center). There are more than 300 rooms total, and each place is practically identical. Though utterly lacking in charm, they are a good value in a convenient location between the Hauptbahnhof and the Old Town (Sb-€55-95, Db-€55-105, €15 more for larger Db that can be used as a Tb, €25 more for apartment for a family of 4, prices vary with demand—book online for best deal, breakfast-€10, elevator, pay Wi-Fi, parking-€6, reservations for all: tel. 0351/4856-2000; individual receptions: tel. 0351/4856-5445, tel. 0351/4856-6445, and tel. 0351/4856-7445, respectively; www.ibis-dresden.de).

In the New Town

The first two hotels are fancy splurges in a tidy residential neighborhood surrounding the Neustadt train station. The rest are cheap and funky, buried in the trendy, happening Innere Neustadt zone (see "Nightlife in Dresden," earlier).

$$$ Hotel Bayerischer Hof Dresden, 100 yards toward the river from the Neustadt train station, offers 50 rooms and elegant, inviting public spaces in a grand old building. Ask for a room facing the courtyard (Sb-€95, Db-€132, suite-€160, non-smoking rooms, elevator, free Internet access, pay Wi-Fi, free parking, Antonstrasse 33-35, yellow building across from station, tel. 0351/829-370, fax 0351/801-4860, www.bayerischer-hof-dresden .de, info@bayerischer-hof-dresden.de).

$$ Hotel Martha Hospiz, with 50 rooms near the recommended restaurants on Königstrasse, is bright and cheery. The two old buildings that make up the hotel have been smartly renovated and connected in back with a glassed-in winter garden and an outdoor breakfast terrace. It's a 10-minute walk to the historical center and a 5-minute walk to Neustadt Station (S-€55, Sb-€79-86, Db-€113, "superior" Db-€121, extra bed-€27, elevator, free Internet access and Wi-Fi; leaving Neustadt Station, turn right on Hainstrasse, left on Theresenstrasse, then right on Nieritzstrasse to #11; tel. 0351/81760, fax 0351/8176-222, www.hotel-martha -hospiz.de, rezeption@marthahospiz-dresden.com).

$$ AHA Hotel may have an unassuming facade on a big, noisy street, but inside you'll find a homey and welcoming ambience. The 30 simple-but-neat apartments all come with kitchens; most have balconies. It's a bit farther from the center—10 minutes by foot east of Albertplatz, a 20-minute walk or a quick ride on tram #11 from the Old Town—but its friendliness, coziness, and good value make it a winner (Sb-€58-63, Db-€83-93, breakfast-€9, request quieter back side, non-smoking rooms, elevator, free Internet access, pay Wi-Fi, Bautzner Strasse 53, tel. 0351/800-850, fax 0351/8008-5114, www.ahahotel-dresden.de, kontakt@aha hotel-dresden.de).

$ Hostel Louise 20 rents 83 beds in the middle of the Innere Neustadt action. Though located in the wild-and-edgy nightlife district, it feels safe, solid, clean, and comfy. The recently furnished rooms, guests' kitchen, cozy common room, and friendly staff make it a good place for cheap beds (S-€30-35, D-€38-46, small dorm-€14-17/bed, sheets-€2.50, breakfast-€5.50, laundry, generally booked on summer weekends, down the courtyard at Louisenstrasse 20, tel. 0351/889-4894, www.louise20.de, info @louise20.de).

$ Hostel Mondpalast Dresden is young and hip, in the heart of the Innere Neustadt above a trendy bar. Its super-groovy vibe makes it one of the coolest hostels in Europe—it's good for backpackers with little money and an appetite for late-night fun. Fortunately, breakfast is served until 14:00 (S-€34, Sb-€44, D-€44, Db-€52, dorm bed-€14-20, sheets-€2, breakfast-€6, free Wi-Fi, pay Internet access, lockers, kitchen, lots of facilities, bike rental-€7/day, near Kamenzer Strasse at Louisenstrasse 77, tram #7 from Hauptbahnhof or #11 from Neustadt Station, tel. 0351/563-4050, fax 0351/563-4055, www.mondpalast.de, info@mond palast.de).

Eating in Dresden

Nearly every restaurant seems bright, shiny, and modern. While Old Town restaurants are touristy, the prices are reasonable, and it's easy to eat for €10-15 just about anywhere. For cheaper prices and authentic local character, leave the famous center, cross the river, and wander through the New Town.

The special local dessert sold all over town is *Dresdner Eier-schecke,* an eggy cheesecake with vanilla pudding, raisins, and almond shavings.

In the Old Town

Altmarkt Keller (a.k.a. Sächsische-Böhmische Bierhaus), a few blocks from the river on Altmarkt square, is a festive beer cellar that serves nicely presented Saxon and Bohemian food (from separate menus) and has good Czech beer on tap. The lively crowd, cheesy music (live Sat only), and jolly murals add to the fun. While the on-square seating is fine, the vast-but-stout air-conditioned cellar offers the most memorable seating. The giant mural inside the entryway portrays the friendship between Dresden and Prague, proclaiming that "the sunshine of life is drinking and being merry" (€8-15 meals, daily 11:00-24:00, Altmarkt 4, to the right of McDonald's, tel. 0351/481-8130).

Grand Café Restaurant Cosel Palais serves Saxon and French cuisine in the shadow of the newly rebuilt Frauenkirche. This is a Baroque chandeliered dining experience with fine, if touristy, courtyard seating—great for an elegant meal or tea and pastries (€9-20 meals, daily specials, daily 10:00-24:00, An der Frauenkirche 12, tel. 0351/496-2444).

Dresden 1900, a streetcar-themed eatery, can't be beat for a good lunch right in the midst of the action. Sure, it's touristy and tacky, but most of the main courses are under €10, their apple strudel is some of the finest in town, and the service is friendly and efficient. Try to get a seat inside the 1899-era streetcar (daily 9:00-24:00, An der Frauenkirche 20, tel. 0351/4820-5858).

Dresden's "Restaurant Row": **Münzgasse,** the busy and touristy lane that connects the Brühlsche Terrasse promenade and the Frauen-kirche, is the liveliest street in the Old Town, with a fun selection of restaurants. Choose from tapas, Aussie, goulash, crêpes, and even antiques (Kunst Café Antik scatters its tables among a royal estate sale of fancy furniture and objets d'art— around the corner, riverside). Service is a necessary evil, the clientele is  international, and the action spills out onto the cobbled pedestrian lane on balmy evenings.

Medieval Theme Restaurants: All the rage among Dresdeners (and German tourists in Dresden) is *Erlebnisgastronomie* ("Experience Gastronomy"). Elaborately decorated theme restaurants have sprouted next to the biggest-name sights around town, with over-the-top theme-park decor and historically costumed waitstaff. These can offer a fun change of pace and aren't the bad value you might expect. The best is **Sophienkeller,** which does its best to take you to the 18th century and the world of Augustus the Strong. The king himself, along with his countess, musicians, and magicians, stroll and entertain, while court maidens serve traditional Saxon food from ye olde menu. Read their colorful brochure to better understand the place. It's big (470 seats), and it even has a rotating carousel table with suspended swing-chairs that you sit in while you eat. Before choosing a seat, survey the two big and distinct zones—one bright and wide open, the other more intimate and cellar-like (€9-18 main courses, daily 11:00-24:00, under the five-star Taschenberg Palace Hotel at Taschenberg 3, tel. 0351/497-260).

With a River View: Radeberger Spezialausschank Café is dramatically situated on the Brühlsche Terrasse promenade, with a rampart-hanging view terrace and three levels taking you down to the river. For river views from the "Balcony of Europe," this is your spot. The inviting-yet-simple menu includes daily Saxon specials and cheap wurst and kraut. This is the only place in town that serves Radeberger's unfiltered beer, and the cool river-level bar comes with big copper brewery vats (€7-15 meals, daily 11:00-24:00, reservations smart for view terrace, Terrassenufer 1, tel. 0351/484-8660).

In the Main Train Station: For a quick bite at the Hauptbahnhof, the healthy market-style **Marché Cafeteria** is fast and reasonable (daily 8:00-21:00).

In the New Town

Venture to these eateries—across Augustus Bridge from the Old Town—for lower prices and a more local scene. I've listed them nearest to farthest from the Old Town.

Just Across Augustus Bridge

Augustus Garten is a lazy, crude-yet-inviting beer garden with super-cheap self-service food (pork knuckle, kraut, cheap beer, and lots of mustard). You'll eat among big bellies—and no tourists—with a fun city-skyline-over-the-river view. While enjoyable in balmy weather, this place is dead when it's cool out (€5-10 main courses, €2-5 beers, €2 refundable deposit on beer glasses, daily 11:00-24:00, closed in bad weather, Wiesentorstrasse 2, tel. 0351/404-5531). As you walk across the bridge from the Old Town, it's on your immediate right.

On Königstrasse

For trendy elegance without tourists, have dinner on Königstrasse.

After crossing the Augustus Bridge, hike five minutes up Hauptstrasse, the communist-built main drag of the New Town, then turn left to find this charming Baroque street. As this is a fast-changing area, you might survey the other options on and near Königstrasse (be sure to tuck into a few courtyards) before settling down.

Wenzel Prager Bierstuben serves country Bohemian cuisine in a woodsy bar that spills out into an airy, glassed-in gallery—made doubly big by its vast mirror. Stepping inside, the interior immediately wins you over. They offer a fun Bohemian menu with three varieties of the great Czech Staropramen beer on tap (€9-10 dinner-with-beer specials on Tue-Thu, €8-14 main courses, daily 11:00-24:00, Königstrasse 1, tel. 0351/804-2010).

Good Friends is a favorite for Thai and Vietnamese food, and a welcome relief from pork and potatoes (€8-14 main courses, daily 11:30-15:00 & 17:30-23:00, Sat-Sun from 12:00, An der Dreikönigskirche 8, tel. 0351/646-5814). Walk down Königstrasse to the towering Three Kings Church. It's under the steeple.

Beer Halls

All of Dresden's famous beer halls were destroyed in the war, and the communists refused to rebuild them. But after unification, ambitious Dresdeners began re-creating this tradition. Beer halls usually serve their own brew and hearty Saxon cuisine. Saxons love to eat and talk, so a beer hall is a great place to meet locals and get a taste of life outside of tourist areas. All of these places are far from the city center but easily reached by public transportation.

Brauhaus am Waldschlösschen is fun and lively, with nightly music that really gets going after 21:00. The restaurant serves traditional Saxon cuisine with some fine salads. The view of Dresden's Old Town can't be beat—it's worth the extra effort it takes to reach this self-service beer garden (snacks under €6.50, €9 daily specials include a large beer, €10-14 main courses, daily 11:00-24:00, Am Brauhaus 8b, tram #11 to Waldschlösschen, tel. 0351/652-3900). Their *Hefeweizen* tastes like bananas.

Ball und Brauhaus Watzke, the oldest of the beer halls, started life as a ballroom (it still holds public balls once a month). It sits pleasantly on the banks of the Elbe, with nice views of the Old Town. Watzke serves traditional beer-hall food in huge portions and features €10 dinner-with-beer specials on some nights (€5-10 main courses, daily 11:00-24:00, Kötzschenbroderstrasse 1, tram #4 or #9 to Altpieschen, tel. 0351/852-920). The brewery also operates the **Watzke Brauereiausschank am Goldenen Reiter** pub in the New Town. It has the same beer and menu, with a good view of the Frauenkirche and an open atmosphere—but lacks the original's ambience (daily 11:00-24:00, Hauptstrasse 1—in front

DRESDEN

of the Golden Rider statue, tel. 0351/810-6820). Their *Hefeweizen* tastes like pineapple.

Feldschlösschen Stammhaus was the original brewery and hops warehouse for Feldschlösschen beer, but the company moved to another part of Dresden in the 1970s. Although significantly farther afield than the other beer halls, Stammhaus is worth the trek—it's a cozy, energy-filled spot in a sea of East German prefab apartments. Traditional fare dominates the menu, but Stammhaus sneaks in large portions of fresh vegetables and fresh homemade bread (€8-12 main courses, €5-8 lunch and dinner specials with a beer, daily 11:00-24:00, Budapester Strasse 32, bus #62 from the Prager Strasse Transit Center to the Arbeitsamt stop—yes, there is a beer hall next to the unemployment office, tel. 0351/471-8855). Sadly, they don't brew *Hefeweizen* here.

Dresden Connections

From Dresden by Train to: Görlitz (hourly, 1.25-1.75 hours), **Bautzen** (about hourly, 30-45 minutes; Bautzen-bound trains continue on to Görlitz), **Zittau** (better from Neustadt, hourly, 1.5-2 hours), **Leipzig** (1-2/hour direct, 1.25-1.5 hours), **Berlin** (every 2 hours, more with transfer in Leipzig, 2.25 hours), **Erfurt** (nearly hourly direct, 2.5 hours; more possible with change in Leipzig, 3 hours), **Wittenberg** (1-2/hour, 2-3.5 hours, transfer in Leipzig and sometimes also Bitterfeld), **Prague** (every 2 hours, 2.25-2.5 hours), **Hamburg** (4/day direct, 4.5 hours; otherwise about hourly with change in Leipzig or Berlin, 4-4.5 hours), **Frankfurt** (hourly, 4.75 hours), **Nürnberg** (hourly, 4.5 hours, may change in Leipzig), **Munich** (every 2 hours, 6 hours, transfer in Nürnberg), **Vienna** (2/day direct, 7 hours; plus 1 night train/day, 9 hours), **Budapest** (1/day plus 1 night train, 9 hours). There are overnight trains from Dresden to Zürich, the Rhineland, and Munich. Train info: tel. 0180-599-6633, www.bahn.com.

GÖRLITZ

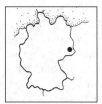

Tucked away in Germany's easternmost corner, the surprisingly beautiful town of Görlitz is a treasure trove of architecture and one of this country's best-kept secrets.

During the Middle Ages, Görlitz (GUR-lits) was a major European crossroads, at the intersection of trade routes from Moscow to Barcelona and from the Baltic Sea to Venice. Trade in cloth and beer made the city flourish. Görlitz's rich cultural tapestry was gradually enhanced as the centuries passed, leaving it a delightful collage of architectural styles. The town escaped most of World War II's bombs, but soon after was split down the middle along its river—with half of the town in Germany, the other half in Poland. Görlitz's historic buildings were preserved by the East German government, saving it from the unsightly communist-era blemishes that mark most former East German towns.

Since the Wall fell, Görlitz has sprung back to life and is busily polishing its gorgeous facades. The town offers a unique opportunity to venture to the eastern fringes of Germany, sample Silesian culture and cuisine, and appreciate some breathtaking architecture and stay-a-while squares. Best of all, although German tourists fill Görlitz on weekends during the summer, it's still virtually undiscovered by foreign tourists—making it a real Back Door experience.

Planning Your Time

Although Görlitz is an ideal day trip from Dresden (hourly trains, 1.5 hours), the city's subtle charm warrants an overnight stay. Görlitz opens up on long summer nights, as pubs and cafés spill out into the cobbles. Get lost and wander the back streets and alleys.

Orientation to Görlitz

(area code: 03581)

With a population of about 56,000, Görlitz is the largest city in what's left of German Silesia. While Görlitz lost a third of its population to Poland in 1945, the historic center and most sights of interest to travelers remain in Germany. The compact Old Town (Altstadt), containing almost everything to see and do, is an easy stroll, roughly between Marienplatz and the western bank of the Neisse River. The focal point of the Old Town is its twin market squares, Upper (Obermarkt) and Lower (Untermarkt).

Tourist Information

The TI, called Görlitzinformation, has free, but very basic, maps (their website has more detailed maps available as free downloads) and can book you a room for free. Information in English is sparse, but a few English guidebooks are available, and people seem genuinely helpful and welcoming (Mon-Fri 9:00-19:00, Sat-Sun 9:00-18:00, between Obermarkt and Untermarkt at Obermarkt 32, tel. 03581/47570, www.goerlitz.de). Pick up the €6.90 *Görlitz Town Guide,* a small but informative do-it-yourself walking tour, but skip the €3 map. The *Architectural Guide Through the Old Town of Görlitz* (€10) is overkill for most visitors but indispensable for architecture buffs, describing almost every building in the Old Town in a convenient flip-out format.

To arrange a guided **tour** in English, call 03581/475-713.

Arrival in Görlitz

Görlitz's train station, about a half-mile southwest of the city center, is a sight in itself. Built in 1901, the main hall is a pearl of Prussian *Jugendstil* (Art Nouveau), while the building itself is Neoclassical. Its opening hours are shorter than those at larger stations, and it's virtually deserted after 21:00. Lockers are in the passage between the tracks and the main hall (€2.50-3.50). You'll also find handy WCs (€0.50, deposit coin, then wait for buzzer and pull on door) and a *Reisezentrum* for train information and tickets (Mon-Fri 7:30-17:30 except Wed closed 13:00-13:45, Sat 8:00-13:00, closed Sun).

To get into town (a 15-minute **walk**), exit straight through the front entrance and follow Berliner Strasse. At the first large square *(Postplatz),* the road veers left, and you'll see the former Hertie department store building (marking Marienplatz and the start of my self-guided walk). You can also take **tram** #2 or #3 to

GÖRLITZ

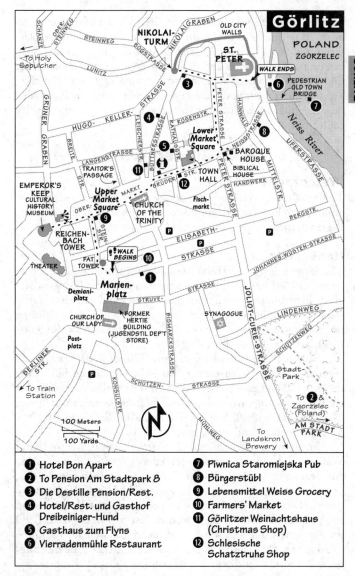

1. Hotel Bon Apart
2. To Pension Am Stadtpark 8
3. Die Destille Pension/Rest.
4. Hotel/Rest. und Gasthof Dreibeiniger-Hund
5. Gasthaus zum Flyns
6. Vierradenmühle Restaurant
7. Piwnica Staromiejska Pub
8. Bürgerstübl
9. Lebensmittel Weiss Grocery
10. Farmers' Market
11. Görlitzer Weinachtshaus (Christmas Shop)
12. Schlesische Schatztruhe Shop

Demianiplatz (departs from the platform on your right as you exit the station; €1.20, 5 minutes).

Getting Around Görlitz

The communists left little Görlitz with a highly developed and efficient public-transportation system (€1.20/ride, *Einzelfahrt Normal;* €3 day pass, *Tageskarte Normal;* €6.50 pass for up to 5 people, *Kleingruppenkarte*). Tickets are valid on both trams and buses. Buy tickets from bus drivers or the machines on the platforms and trams (coins only), and validate tickets in the little blue box on board. All buses and trams converge at Demianiplatz. The Old Town is compact, so unless you're planning to visit the Holy Sepulcher or go out to the Landeskrone mountain, you'll probably only use public transit to get from the train station into the city center.

Self-Guided Walk

Welcome to Görlitz

The joy of Görlitz is simply wandering the Old Town and appreciating the architecture. Begin this orientation walk at Marienplatz, the small square right outside the former city walls.

Marienplatz

The unique *Jugendstil* **Hertie department store** building (completed in 1911) has a richly decorated facade concealing an ornate glass-domed interior with intricate staircases and galleries. Hertie went bankrupt in 2009, but you can still peek inside the building by visiting the perfume store on the ground floor (Mon-Fri 9:00-18:30, Sat 9:00-16:00, closed Sun).

Behind the building is the **Church of Our Lady** (Frauenkirche), a 15th-century late-Gothic church built near the hospital and poorhouse outside the city walls. Although this church seems unremarkable, take a moment to step inside (free, Mon-Sat 10:00-18:00, Sun 11:00-18:00; Mon-Fri try to catch the *Mittagsrast* prayer and organ music at 12:00).

Imagine being here in the fall of 1989, shortly before the Berlin Wall came down. This church served as a forum for discussions and peace prayers *(Friedensgebete)*. A poster announcing the first prayer meeting was placed in the glass cabinet on the front of the church. Soon, like-minded shopkeepers began to follow suit, and 580 people attended the first meeting. Just two weeks later, 1,300 people showed up, and subsequent meetings swelled to 5,000—so large that they spilled over into other churches. The meetings became a forum for discussing impending political changes, civil rights, and environmental issues. As each participant came forward and voiced his or her concerns, a candle was blown out until the church was dark. Then, as those who had a hopeful or positive experience came forward, a candle was lit until the church was illuminated once again.

The East German secret police, the Stasi, stationed plain-clothes police in the buildings across the street to document who was participating in these "acts of civil disobedience." Many people

Görlitz: A Silesian Brew

Görlitz is a city with an identity crisis, much like the entire region of Silesia. Silesia, which has never been a "nation" of its own, encompasses parts of Germany (where it's called "Schlesien"), Poland ("Śląsk"), and the Czech Republic ("Slezsko"). Silesians are proud of this diversity and of their pragmatic ability to work and live peacefully with each other despite the borders that separate them. Just like the Silesians themselves, their cuisine, folk art, and customs are a mish-mash of German, Polish, and Czech.

After Slavic Sorbs founded Gorelec in 1071, the village—renamed Görlitz—came under the German sphere of cultural influence in the 12th century and has been predominantly German ever since. For most of its early existence, the city technically belonged to Bohemia but was ceded to Saxony after the Peace of Prague in 1635. In 1815, Görlitz fell into Prussian hands at the Congress of Vienna and became the largest city in the province of Lower Silesia.

The city's unusual experience in World War II made it the unique place it is today: While Görlitz almost miraculously escaped destruction (only its Old Town Bridge was bombed), it was split in two by the Potsdam Agreement in 1945. This treaty determined the Neisse River—which runs through the center of Görlitz—to be the border between Germany and Poland. The following year, Poland expelled all Germans from its country, which included booting them out of Silesia and, therefore, out of the Polish side of Görlitz.

This expulsion created two ethnically distinct halves: the German town of Görlitz on the west side of the river and the Polish town of Zgorzelec, which is still part of Poland on the east. Although most German Silesians have long since abandoned any hope of re-establishing their lost homeland, they have gone to great efforts to stress the unity between Silesians of all ethnic backgrounds—Germans, Poles, and Czechs—by re-establishing cultural connections across the rivers and mountains. Czechs and Poles are strong partici-pants at all city festivals. After German, Polish and Czech are the most common languages you'll hear spoken in the streets and see on signs in Görlitz.

In 2004, German Görlitz and Polish Zgorzelec completed the reconstruction of a new pedestrians-only Old Town Bridge (Altstadtbrücke) across the Neisse. Locals like to think this largely symbolic gesture makes Görlitz the most European city in Europe. And now that Poland has joined the open-borders Schengen Agreement, anyone can freely cross the bridge without even having to flash a passport.

lost their jobs or were punished. But the hope for democracy and self-determination had already caught on, and today, this church stands as a symbol of peace and solidarity.

To the north, the **Fat Tower** (Dicker Turm) is the second-oldest tower in the city's defensive network. Although the tower itself is Gothic (from 1270), it's topped by a copper Renaissance cupola. The tower was attached to the so-called Women's Gate (Frauen Tor) in 1477. It's decorated with a sandstone relief of the Görlitz city coat of arms, featuring a Bohemian lion and a Silesian black eagle—representing Görlitz as an independent and free city.
• *Walk down the street to the left of the tower (Steinstrasse) and onto the...*

Upper Market Square (Obermarkt)

This 13th-century square is lined with mainly Baroque houses, with the **Reichenbach Tower** dominating its western end. The

tower formed part of the western city wall and dates from the 13th century, although the cylindrical portion was added in 1485 and is topped with a Baroque cupola from 1782. The tower housed city guards and watchmen—who among other things kept a lookout for fires— until the last "tower family" moved out in 1904. Inside is an impressive collection of armaments, early 20th-century photographs, and an interesting exhibit on the daily lives of the tower's occupants (€3, May-Oct Tue-Sun 10:00-17:00, closed Mon and Nov-April, Platz des 17 Juni, tel. 03581/671-355). The view from the top is worth the 165 steps.

In 1490, Görlitz strengthened its city fortifications by building a circular bastion outside Reichenbach Tower. The structure came to be known as the **Emperor's Keep** (Kaisertruz) when the Swedish troops made their last stand against the Imperial Saxon army during the Thirty Years' War. Since then, the Emperor's Keep has been used as an archive, and today it houses the Cultural History Museum (closed for renovation until mid-2012; when open: May-Oct Tue-Sun 10:00-17:00, closed Mon and Nov-April).
• *The tall tower on Obermarkt belongs to the...*

Church of the Trinity (Dreifaltigkeitskirche)

In 1245, Franciscan monks consecrated this church, at the southeast side of Obermarkt. Although originally a Romanesque structure, renovations in 1380 gave the church its current late-Gothic appearance. When the Reformation took hold in Silesia in 1563, the monks surrendered the keys to the church and monastery—with the condition that the monastery be used as a school. A school operates in the former monastery to this day.

Cost and Hours: Free, daily 10:00-18:00, tel. 03581/643-460.

Touring the Church: Go inside the church. The interior seems austere, but upon careful inspection it reveals delightful little details. As you enter, go immediately to your left. This is the oldest part of the church. Pillars from the original 13th-century Romanesque chapel are integrated into the walls. The fancy balcony is where the nobility sat. If you've been to Dresden, the high altar will look familiar. Built by artists brought from Dresden, it resembles the crown gate of the Zwinger. The swirly clouds identify this as Rococo. The missing crucifix on the left wall (now in Warsaw) is a reminder of the artifacts that were pillaged from this church during various wars, but the choir stalls, carved in the 1430s, are original. As you follow signs to the *Marienaltar,* look up at the vaulted ceiling and notice how complex it gets as you walk into newer parts of the church.

The church's trophy is the beautiful 15th-century carved triptych, the ***Marienaltar.*** The simple

side was used on regular worship days, while the gilded side—containing an almost life-size carving of the Virgin Mary—was reserved for high feast days. Today, you can usually see it open, and can admire the closed panels via the display on the bench to the right of the altar. (If the altar is closed, ask one of the guides to open it for you.) It's an eyeful—rich with action and symbolism. The symmetry and order of the checked tablecloth is replaced in the other panels by lots of action and purposefully conflicting lines that create energy and tension. Notice the symbolism—there's a turban-wearing Ottoman (archenemy of the time) and Jesus wearing a Franciscan frock (a nod to the church's Franciscan heritage).

Behind you, an exhausted **Jesus,** reminiscent of Auguste Rodin's *Thinker,* ponders the fate of man. This statue, from 1910, used to sit on the grass outside of the Holy Sepulcher (described under "More Sights in Görlitz," later)—notice the rotting wood at the base.

Görlitz Architecture

Although no bombs fell on Görlitz itself during World War II (only on its bridge), the city has experienced its share of destruction, from the Thirty Years' War to the ravages of three great city fires. Each wave of devastation allowed Görlitz to rebuild in the architectural style of the time. The results are an astonishing collection of exemplary buildings from every architectural era: Gothic, Renaissance, Baroque, *Gründerzeit* (late 19th century), and *Jugendstil*. In the late 20th  century, the East German government placed the entire city under a protection order, rescuing it from the bleak communist aesthetic of the time. More than 3,700 buildings are registered historical monuments.

Even now, energetic reconstruction efforts continue, partly thanks to the city's secret admirer: Every year since 1993, an unnamed benefactor has donated the equivalent of one million Deutsch Marks (about $665,000) to renovation projects. Nobody knows who this person is, and anyone who attempts to find out is dealt a swift warning from a high-priced Munich lawyer. All of these factors have contributed to making Görlitz the gem that it is today.

The church's **tower** is unusually thin—the locals call it the *Mönch* ("Monk"). The clock doesn't keep very good time, thanks to one in a series of Cloth-Maker Rebellions. In the Middle Ages, Görlitz was run by the powerful guilds of the cloth trade and the brewers, who neglected the rights of their workers and forbade nonmembers from practicing their trades. Finally, in the early 16th century, the workers rose up against the corrupt city council, which allowed the guilds to continue their unfair practices. The rebels ended their meetings punctually at midnight to avoid the night watchmen, who would be on the other side of town at that hour. But the city council was one step ahead: They ordered the church bell to chime seven minutes before midnight to fool the conspirators out onto the street and into the waiting arms of the guard. Fourteen of the conspirators were executed, and 25 more banished from the city. To this day, the bell chimes seven minutes early.

Across the square is the **Traitor's Passage** (Verrätergasse), a dark, sinister passageway used by the instigators of the rebellion to sneak in and out of the main marketplace. Walk about halfway

down and you'll see the letters *DVRT 1527* carved into the stone next to a gate. This was the house where the traitors met and stored their weapons. "DVRT" stands for *"die verräterische Rotte Tor,"* or "The Gate of the Traitorous Gang"—it's a warning.

• *To leave Obermarkt, walk down...*

Brüderstrasse

This street, connecting Obermarkt and Untermarkt, is home to a fine collection of Renaissance houses. These houses were the single-family dwellings of Görlitz's rich tradesmen, who lived on the upper floors and stored their goods on the street level. The orange-and-gray house at the end of Brüderstrasse (#8) claims to be Germany's oldest Renaissance civic building (from 1526) and now houses the **Silesian Museum of Görlitz** (Schlesisches Museum zu Görlitz), a state museum featuring Silesian culture (€5, Tue-Sun 10:00-17:00, closed Mon, Brüderstrasse 8, tel. 03581/87910, www .schlesisches-museum.de).

As you pass Schwarzestrasse, look left. The street's flying buttresses are typical of Görlitz's Old Town—these two are remnants of a series of brick barriers used to keep insurgents out of the inner city during the Cloth-Maker Rebellions.

• *At the end of Brüderstrasse, you'll reach...*

Lower Market Square (Untermarkt)

The remarkably well-preserved Untermarkt is typical of Central European squares: It's built up in the middle to make maximum use of this prime real estate. The square shows just how prosperous the cloth trade made Görlitz.

Ignoring the tall tower (we'll get to it later), take a look around the square. The building at #14 (east end of the square) housed the city **scales** and was one of the most important commercial buildings because, at its peak, more than 1,000 wagons per day entered Görlitz. Everything had to be weighed and duties paid here. The late-Gothic ground floor, which housed the scales, is topped off with three Renaissance levels. The column-topping busts are a virtual Who's Who of the town's masons and scale-masters.

Around the corner from the scales, on the northern edge of the square, the city established a **commodity exchange** at the beginning of the 18th century. The building was also a kind of department store used to drive simple street vendors away from the financial center. With the rabble banished, the Baroque building with its adorning portal was a favored place for merchants to meet and deal.

• *Untermarkt is dominated by the tall Gothic tower of the...*

Town Hall

Görlitz had no Town Hall until 1350, when the city purchased this building from a prominent citizen. The tower was extended to 195 feet in 1368. A lightning strike blew the top off the tower on July 9, 1742, prompting the addition of the current Baroque turret. The tower houses two clocks: The upper clock measures the day, month, and phase of the moon, while the lower clock tells the time. The warrior's head used to stick out his tongue every hour, but now he just seems to open his mouth. The date inscribed on the  clock, 1584, commemorates the year when Bartholomäus Sculteus, an astronomer and mathematician, first divided the clock into 12 points. Sculteus also helped develop the Gregorian calendar. The city honored Sculteus, a Görlitz native, by being the first city in Germany to adopt both the new calendar and the clock. The Town Hall stairs represent the height of Görlitz Renaissance sculpture and lead from the street level to the building's then-main entrance. Local officials used the balcony to make public announcements and decrees. Look closely at the statue of Justice (1591): She's not blindfolded—in other words, the city is the highest authority.

• *For evidence that Görlitz is definitely a Protestant town, head down Neissstrasse to #29. There you'll find the...*

Biblical House

As the Catholic Church had banned religious depictions on secular buildings, the carvings on the Biblical House made it clear that the Reformation was here to stay. The houses in the Neissstrasse had all burned to the ground in 1526. Hanz Heinz, a cloth trader, purchased this house and rebuilt it completely in the Renaissance style. The house is named after the sandstone reliefs decorating the facade between the first- and second-floor parapets. The top level represents the New Testament, with (from left to right) the Annunciation, birth of Jesus, Jesus' baptism, the Last Supper, and the Crucifixion. The bottom row depicts the creation of Eve, the Fall of Man, Isaac's sacrifice, Moses receiving the Ten Commandments, and Moses banishing serpents.

• *Next door, step into the...*

Baroque House (Barockhaus)

This museum offers a peek at life in the 17th and 18th centuries.

There's also an exhibit honoring another of Görlitz's favorite sons (the philosopher Jacob Böhme, who lived here from 1575-1624), and a fascinating library, which is accessible only with an escort (request a viewing when you buy your ticket). This amazing library is still functioning today—for a €12 annual fee, you can have access to any of the books three days a week...anyone interested in tax records from 1475? The rest of the exhibit includes elaborately painted farm furniture, formal 18th-century apartments, a glass exhibit, and a unique lab of electrophysical instruments that belonged to a local contemporary of scientist (and "volt" namesake) Alessandro Volta. The natural sciences library holds geological samples, topographic models, and a first edition of a book by Benjamin Franklin.

Cost and Hours: €5, Tue-Sun 10:00-17:00, closed Mon, little English information but ask for the free explanatory fliers, tel. 03581/671-351, www.museum-goerlitz.de.

• *Backtrack to Untermarkt and hang a right onto...*

Peterstrasse

On the corner of Peterstrasse is the **City Apothecary** (Ratsapotheke). The owner attempted to transform a Gothic building into a Renaissance masterpiece, but ended up only combining the two styles. The two sundials on the southern facade were added in 1550. The left dial (Solarium) displays the time using the Arabic, local, Roman, and Babylonian clocks. The dial on the right (*Arachne*, "spider" in Greek) displays the position of the planets and the signs of the zodiac. The City Apothecary houses one of the city's best cafés, Kretschmer Ratscafé.

Peterstrasse is yet another impressive street. Look inside #14—the staircase seems to hang in mid-air. The house at #6 is a perfect example of renovations gone wrong: The building is Renaissance, with Gothic doors and windows, Ionic columns, and Baroque decorations—the combination doesn't really work, does it?

At the end of Peterstrasse, you can turn either right or left. Left leads to the **Nikolaiturm** (open to the public only on rare occasions), the oldest of Görlitz's towers, which marks the site of the original village of Gorelec. The Nikolaiturm, like all of the city-wall towers, got a facelift in the 18th century that replaced its pointy top with its current round dome. The city walls and gates were destroyed in 1848, and the stones were used to build the Jägerkaserne, a barracks off in the

distance to the left of the Nikolaiturm. The only remaining section of the city wall is now a pleasant park that curves around from the base of the Nikolaiturm to the back of the Church of St. Peter. Alternatively, to the right of the park entrance, a small alleyway (Karpfengurnd) snakes its way back to Peterstrasse.

• *If you turn right at the end of Peterstrasse, you'll reach the...*

Church of St. Peter (Peterskirche)

The church was completed—after many setbacks, landslides, and Hussite invasions—in 1457, and renovated after fire destroyed the interior in 1691. The spires were added in 1890. The facade looks like a thousand other Gothic churches, but it's what's inside that counts: The Silesian-Italian Eugenio Casparini's **Sun Organ** (Sonnenorgel) is a spectacular, one-of-a-kind musical instrument and the center of Görlitz's musical life since 1701. The organ gets its name not from the golden sun at the center (which spins when air is pushed through the pipe), but for the circularly arranged pipes that shoot out like the sun's rays. Take in a free concert Thursday or Sunday at noon (Nov-March Sun only). The colorful baptistery, from 1617, is also worth a look.

• *Your walk is finished. Consider visiting some of Görlitz's other sights, or relax with a local Landskron beer.*

More Sights in Görlitz

▲**Holy Sepulcher (Heiliges Grab)**—One of Görlitz's most unusual and interesting sights, this is the only complete and rel-

atively accurate replica of the garden of Gethsemane and the holy places in Jerusalem, as they appeared in the 15th century. It takes a bit longer to visit than other sights in Görlitz, but pilgrims find it well worth ▲▲▲.

After making a pilgrimage to Jerusalem, Georg Emmerich commissioned this site as an offering to those who could not make such a journey themselves (built 1480-1503). The first building is the two-story Chapel of the Holy Cross. Reflecting the traditional belief that Christ was crucified on the site of Adam's grave, the crypt represents the tomb of Adam with the Golgotha Chapel above. Next door is the Salbhaus, a tiny chapel with a statue of Mary anointing Jesus' dead body. The Church of the Holy Sepulcher itself is a much smaller version of the original, but nonetheless is an interesting fusion of Middle Eastern and European architecture. This version actually predates the restored Jerusalem site, which was damaged by fire in the 16th century. Medieval pilgrims to this site purchased a *Görlitzer Scheckel*—gold, silver, or pewter, according to their means—as payment to the church and a symbol of their pilgrimage.

Cost and Hours: €1.50; April-Sept Mon-Sat 10:00-18:00, Sun 11:00-18:00; Oct-March daily 10:00-16:00; English handout, Heilige-Grab-Strasse 79, tram #2 or #3 to Heilige Grab, www.heiligesgrab-goerlitz.de.

▲**Landskron Brewery**—Beer has been brewed in Görlitz since the 12th century. The last remaining (and best) brewery is Landskron, which brews 12 different beers, including the best *Hefeweizen* (wheat beer) in Germany. It's also one of the last breweries to use open fermentation. The brewery offers tours in German, but the staff tries to be accommodating to English speakers. In the end, it's all about the taste samples anyway.

Cost and Hours: €6.50 for the ".33l Tour" (1.5 hours) or €9.50 for the ".5l Tour" (2.5 hours), contact the brewery in advance to check the tour schedule and reserve (although it's usually possible to sneak into an already scheduled tour, if you ask Frau Prescher nicely), An der Landskronbrauerei 116, tel. 03581/465-100, www.landskron.de, info@landskron.de. In the summer, the brewery hosts concerts and other events.

▲**Landeskrone**—On the outskirts of the city is a dormant volcano that stretches 1,376 feet above sea level. The city of Görlitz purchased the Landeskrone from the aristocracy and incorporated it into the city in 1440. The mountainside provided wood for building (especially for rebuilding the town after fires) and basalt for cobblestones, and gave the city a commanding view into three countries at once—helping to defend itself against marauding robber-barons. The observation tower on top, built on the ruins of a Bohemian fort, came in the 18th century, and was followed by a small restaurant and hotel in 1844 (the current version was rebuilt in 1951). The entire area is a park, ideal for short hikes. To get here, take tram #2 to the Biesnitz/Landeskrone stop. It's about a 40-minute hike from the tram stop to the top.

Near Görlitz

Three Silesian towns near Görlitz offer an interesting and diverse glimpse into this unique cultural crossroads.

▲**Zgorzelec**—When everything east of the Neisse River (and, farther north, the Oder River) became a part of Poland, Görlitz lost its eastern suburb. By 1946, Poles transplanted from Belarus and Ukraine eliminated all traces of the German past and created the city of Zgorzelec. On both sides of the river, government and citizenry are making great strides to glue the city back together (at least culturally) in a united Europe. And since Germany and

Poland opened their borders in late 2007, you can stroll freely between the two countries. A walk into Poland is an interesting experience and offers a stark contrast to wonderfully restored Görlitz. Zgorzelec is obviously the less wealthy part of the city but offers a fine collection of patrician and burgher houses (along ulica Warszawska). Some have been lovingly renovated, but others are in desperate need of repair.

The main part of Zgorzelec is across the Pope John Paul II Bridge (Neissebrücke), south of the Old Town. Once across the bridge, turn to the right and go up the hill to reach the Upper Lusatian Memorial Hall (nowadays the Dom Kultury, or Civic House of Culture), a memorial to Kaiser Wilhelm I. Wander north through Poland, then cross back into Germany at the pedestrian Old Town Bridge, behind the Church of St. Peter.

Zittau and Oybin Castle (Burg Oybin)—Although Zittau is a splendid city in its own right, with pretty squares and a Town Hall by Karl Friedrich Schinkel, the real reason to come here is to take the narrow-gauge steam railroad to the top of Oybin Mountain to see the castle ruins. Bohemian Emperor Charles IV built the fortress and monastery Burg Oybin in the 14th century. The structure fell into disuse by the 16th century and was repeatedly struck by lightning in the 18th and 19th centuries. Nineteenth-century painters such as Caspar David Friedrich made the castle famous again. The ruins are huge and fun to poke around, and the views of the unique geological formations of the Zittau Mountains are grand.

Cost and Hours: Castle entry-€4, daily April-Oct 9:00-18:00, Nov-March 10:00-16:00, www.burgundkloster-oybin.de.

Getting There: Zittau is an easy train ride from Gorlitz. Once in Zittau, to find the steam railroad (Zittauer Schmalspurbahn), exit the train station at the front, walk across the square with the bus stops, and turn left. If you're lucky, one of the steam trains will be puffing away, waiting for you. Trains generally leave Zittau for Oybin Castle every two hours, and may run more frequently on the weekends (€13 round-trip, or covered by Lausitz Tageskarte with "historical train supplement"—see "Görlitz Connections," later, tel. 03583/540540, www.soeg-zittau.de.)

Bautzen/Budyšin—This town, about halfway between Dresden and Görlitz, is the cultural capital of the Sorbs (or Wends, as they are known in the US). The Sorbs—not to be confused with the Serbs of the former Yugoslavia, much farther south—are of Slavic descent, and still speak a distinct language that's a hybrid of Polish and Czech. About 20,000 Sorbs live in Germany, making up the country's only indigenous ethnic minority.

Bautzen's dual-language signs and slightly Mediterranean feel of spacious squares and public fountains, combined with intact city walls and a tower that's more off-center than Pisa's, make this town a perfect stopover between Dresden and Görlitz. Bautzen is also home to Germany's only Simultaneous Church, a house of worship shared by Catholics on one side and Protestants on the other. Germany's best spicy mustard comes from Bautzen. For lunch, try **Restaurant Wjelbik,** which serves wonderful Sorbian food (Kornstrasse 7). For more information on the town, see www .bautzen.de.

Shopping in Görlitz

Görlitzer Weinachtshaus celebrates Christmas all year long. Stop here for good deals on traditional crafts such as nutcrackers, incense burners shaped like smoking men, and Nativity scenes. Big draws are traditional paper stars from Herrnhut, hand-blown Sorbian glass eggs, and Thuringian glass (Mon-Fri 10:00-17:00, Sat 10:00-16:00, Sun 11:00-15:00 in summer only, otherwise closed Sun, Fleischerstrasse 19, just off Obermarkt—look for the huge nutcracker out front, tel. 03581/649-205).

Schlesische Schatztruhe is one-stop shopping for all your Silesian souvenir needs: books, posters, maps, cookbooks, and more. This is the first place to stop for Silesian ceramics and "Polish pottery" from Bolesławiec (Bunzlau in German). Unfortunately, they don't ship pottery to the US—you'll have to send or carry it yourself. Their *Streuselkuchen* pastry seems to stay fresh forever (Mon-Sat 9:00-19:00, Sun 10:00-18:00, Brüderstrasse 13, tel. 03581/410-956, www.schlesien-heute.de).

Sleeping in Görlitz

$$ Hotel Bon Apart is a comfortable hotel with an eclectic interior design that can only be described as "Gothic meets Baroque." It's a great value, with the best breakfast buffet in town. The rooms and suites have kitchens, and they brew their own beer (Sb-€80-90, Db-€95-130, 1-person suite-€130, 2-person suite-€150, family suites-€170-220, Elisabethstrasse 41, tel. 03581/48080, fax 03581/480-811, www.bon-apart.de, hotel@bon -apart.de). Owner François also owns the slightly cheaper **Pension Am Stadtpark 8,** a pension with renovated rooms in a gorgeous old building on the edge of the city park, a little farther from the center overlooking the former border crossing (same

Sleep Code

(€1 = about $1.40, country code: 49, area code: 03581)
S = Single, **D** = Double/Twin, **T** = Triple, **Q** = Quad, **b** = bathroom,
s = shower only. Unless otherwise noted, credit cards are accepted, English is spoken, and breakfast is included.

To help you sort easily through these listings, I've divided the accommodations into two categories, based on the price for a standard double room with bath:

$$ Higher Priced—Most rooms €85 or more.
$ Lower Priced—Most rooms less than €85.

Prices can change without notice; verify the hotel's current rates online or by email. For other updates, see www.ricksteves.com/update.

contact info as Hotel Bon Apart, Am Stadtpark 8).

$ Die Destille ("The Distillery") is a clean, friendly, family-run pension with well-apportioned rooms near the Nikolaiturm. A good breakfast is served in the recommended ground-floor restaurant. During renovation of the building in the 1990s, workers discovered a *mikveh* (ritual Jewish bath) in the basement (Sb-€50, Db-€68, cash only, Nikolaistrasse 6, tel. & fax 03581/405-302, www.destille-goerlitz.de).

$ Hotel und Gasthof Dreibeiniger-Hund ("Three-Legged Dog"), down the street from Die Destille, is a small, meticulously restored pension offering 13 cozy and romantic rooms in a 14th-century shell (Sb-€60, Db-€73-83, cash only, book ahead in summer, recommended restaurant, Büttnerstrasse 13, tel. 03581/423-980, www.dreibeinigerhund.de).

Eating in Görlitz

Silesians are a hearty people, and their cooking combines German, Polish, and Czech elements into one of Germany's most interesting regional cuisines. *The* Silesian specialty is *Schlesisches Himmelreich* ("Silesian Heaven"), a mix of pork roast and ham with stewed fruit in a white sauce served with dumplings. For dessert, try Silesian *Streuselkuchen*, a yummy crumb cake available everywhere. Landskron, Görlitz's ubiquitous brew, is one of the best pilsners in Germany. The first two places listed here also rent rooms (described earlier).

Die Destille, literally in the shadow of the Nikolaiturm, is a delightful restaurant oozing comfortable country elegance, with a friendly staff to boot. They excel at extremely traditional Silesian dishes, including the best *Schlesisches Himmelreich* in town. It's small, so come early or be prepared to share a table (€8-15 plates, daily 12:00-22:00, Nikolaistrasse 6, tel. 03581/405-302).

Gasthof Dreibeiniger-Hund has a personal and homey restaurant. Regional cuisine with fresh seasonal specialties makes the "Dog" a must. In summer, sit outside under the sprawling oak tree (€6-12 plates, daily 11:00-23:00, Büttnerstrasse 13, tel. 03581/423-980).

Gasthaus zum Flyns is a small place located behind Town Hall. Named for the Sorbian lion idol that adorns its doorway, the restaurant serves traditional Silesian dishes and solid German cuisine. The highlight is the eponymous Flyns Steak—a grilled pork chop with roasted banana-curry cream sauce (€6-12 plates, Thu-Tue 11:30-14:00 & 18:00-23:00, closed Wed, Langenstrasse 1, tel. 03581/400-697).

Vierradenmühle, Germany's easternmost restaurant, is the perfect place to ponder the division and reunification of Europe. The restaurant sits on top of a water-filtration station and former power plant (with museum) in the Neisse River, so the eastern foundation wall is actually the German-Polish border. The two sides of the border are marked by wooden poles on either side in the colors of their respective countries: white and red for Poland, and black, red, and yellow for Germany. The food is mediocre and overpriced, but the location is great—making it the ideal spot to enjoy a cold beer (daily 11:00-24:00, at the end of Neissstrasse at Hotherstrasse 20, tel. 03581/406-661).

In Poland: **Piwnica Staromiejska** ("Old Town Pub"), in a former grain mill on the Polish side of the Old Town Bridge, serves traditional eastern Polish specialties. The lively, largely Polish crowd welcomes visitors from both sides of the city, and the friendly and helpful staff will explain the menu. Don't worry about paying with Polish *złoty*—the restaurant accepts euros and won't cheat you on the exchange (€3-12 plates, *pelmeni* dumplings and a Żywiec beer-€5.50, lavish salads, daily 12:00-22:00, ulica Wrocławska 1, Zgorzelec, from Germany dial 00-48-75-775-2692).

Along Peterstrasse and Neissstrasse: Good eateries abound near the Untermarkt. The best are on Peterstrasse, between the market and the Church of St. Peter; and on Neissstrasse, stretching from Untermarkt to the river. Almost every building on Neissstrasse was once a brewery. The pick of the litter is the **Bürgerstübl,** which was recently renovated with the help of the Landskron brewery and has a secret *Biergarten* in the back (€8-14 plates, open daily from 17:30, Sat-Sun also 12:00-14:00, Neissstrasse 27, tel. 03581/879-579).

Picnic Supplies: The only grocery store in the city center is **Lebensmittel Weiss,** at the corner of Steinstrasse and Obermarkt (Mon-Fri 8:00-18:30, Sat 8:00-16:00, closed Sun). For fresh fruit and produce, try the **Farmer's Market,** on Elisabethstrasse across from Hotel Bon Apart (Mon-Fri 6:00-18:00, Sat 6:00-12:00, closed Sun).

Görlitz Connections

From Görlitz by Train to: Bautzen (about hourly, 30-45 minutes; Bautzen-bound trains continue on to Dresden), **Dresden** (hourly, 1.25-1.75 hours), **Berlin** (every two hours, 2.5 hours, transfer in Cottbus to the green-and-yellow ODEG train).

If you're day-tripping from Gorlitz to **Zittau** (hourly, 45 minutes) to take the Oybin steam train, you'll save money with the Lausitz Tageskarte day pass (€14), which covers the steam train if you also buy the "historical train supplement" (€4). If Zittau is a stop on a trip into the Czech Republic or Poland, your best bet is the Euro-Neisse Tageskarte day pass (valid for travel as far as Liberec in the Czech Republic and Bolesławiec in Poland): At the ticket machine, choose *Euro-Neisse Tageskarte,* then *1* (€10); for groups of up to five adults, choose *Euro-Neisse Kleingruppenkarte,* then *1* (€20).

Train info: tel. 0180-599-6633, www.bahn.com.

BERLIN

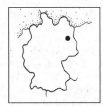

No tour of Germany is complete without a look at its historic and reunited capital. Over the last two decades, Berlin has been a construction zone. Standing on ripped-up tracks and under a canopy of cranes, visitors witnessed the rebirth of a great European capital. Although construction continues, today the once-divided city is thoroughly woven back together. Berlin has emerged as one of Europe's top destinations: captivating, lively, fun-loving, all-around enjoyable—and easy on the budget.

As we enjoy the thrill of walking over what was the Wall and through the well-patched Brandenburg Gate, it's clear that history is not contained in some book, but is an exciting story of which we are a part. In Berlin, the fine line between history and current events is excitingly blurry. But even for non-historians, Berlin is a city of fine experiences. Explore the fun and funky neighborhoods emerging in the former East, packed with creative hipster eateries and boutiques trying to one-up each other. Go for a pedal or a cruise along the delightful Spree riverfront. In the city's world-class museums, stroll up the steps of a classical Greek temple amid rough-and-tumble ancient statuary, and peruse canvases by Dürer, Rembrandt, and Vermeer. Nurse a stein of brew in a rollicking beer hall, or dive into a cheap *Currywurst* (arguably the most beloved food ever to come out of Berlin). On the outskirts of town, at Potsdam, glide like a swan through the opulent halls of an imperial palace, and ponder the darkest chapter of this nation's history at the Sachsenhausen Concentration Camp Memorial (both covered in the next chapter).

Of course, Berlin is still largely defined by its tumultuous

The History of Berlin

Berlin was a humble, marshy burg—its name perhaps derived from an old Slavic word for "swamp"—until prince electors from the Hohenzollern dynasty made it their capital in the mid-15th century. Gradually their territory spread and strengthened, becoming the powerful Kingdom of Prussia in 1701. As the leading city of Prussia, Berlin dominated the northern Germanic world—both militarily and culturally—long before there was a united "Germany."

The only Hohenzollern ruler worth remembering was Frederick the Great (1712-1786). The ultimate enlightened despot, he was both a ruthless military tactician (he consolidated his kingdom's holdings, successfully invading Silesia and biting off a chunk of Poland) and a cultured lover of the arts (he actively invited artists, architects, and other thinkers to his lands). "Old Fritz," as he was called, played the flute, spoke six languages, and counted Voltaire among his friends. Practical and cosmopolitan, Frederick cleverly invited groups to Prussia who were being persecuted for their Protestantism elsewhere in Europe—including the French Huguenots and Dutch traders. Prussia became the beneficiary of these groups' substantial wealth and know-how. Frederick the Great left Berlin—and Prussia—a far more modern and enlightened place than he found it. Thanks largely to Frederick, Prussia was well-positioned to become a magnet of sorts for the German unification movement in the 19th century.

When Germany first unified, in 1871, Berlin (as the main city of its most powerful constituent state, Prussia) was its natural capital. After Germany lost World War I, although the country was in disarray, Berlin thrived as an anything-goes, cabaret-crazy cultural capital of the Roaring '20s. The city was Hitler's headquarters—and the place where the Führer drew his final breath—during World War II. When the Soviet Army reached Berlin, the

20th century. The city was Hitler's capital during World War II, and in the postwar years, Berlin became the front line of a new global war—one between Soviet-style communism and American-style capitalism. The East-West division was set in stone in 1961, when the East German government boxed in West Berlin with the Berlin Wall. The Wall stood for 28 years. In 1990, less than a year after the Wall fell, the two Germanys—and the two Berlins—officially became one. When the dust settled, Berliners from both sides of the once-divided city faced the monumental challenge of reunification.

Berliners joke that they don't need to go anywhere because their city's always changing. Spin a postcard rack to see what's new. A 10-year-old guidebook on Berlin covers a different city.

protracted fighting (and vengeful postwar destruction) left the city in ruins.

In the years following World War II, Berlin was divided by the victorious Allied powers: The American, British, and French sectors became West Berlin, and the Soviet sector, East Berlin. In 1948 and 1949, the Soviet Union tried to starve the Western half (with approximately 2.2 million people) into submission in an almost medieval-style siege, blockading all roads into and out. But the siege was foiled by the Western Allies' Berlin Airlift, which flew in supplies from Frankfurt 24 hours a day for 10 months. With the overnight construction of the Berlin Wall—which completely surrounded West Berlin—in 1961, an Iron (or, at least, concrete) Curtain literally fell through the middle of the city. For details, see "The Berlin Wall (and Its Fall)" on page 706.

While the wild night when the Wall came down was inspiring, Berlin still faced a long and fitful transition to reunification. Two cities—and countries—became one at a staggering pace. Reunification had its negative side, and locals say, "The Wall survives in the minds of some people." Some "Ossies" (impolite slang for Easterners) miss their security. Some "Wessies" miss their easy ride (military deferrals, subsidized rent, and tax breaks offered to West Germans willing to live in an isolated city surrounded by the communist world). For free spirits, walled-in West Berlin was a citadel of freedom within the East.

But in recent years, the old East-West division has faded more and more into the background. Ossi-Wessi conflicts no longer dominate the city's political discourse. The city government has been eager to charge forward, with little nostalgia for anything that was associated with the East. Big corporations and the national government have moved in, and the dreary swath of land that was the Wall and its notorious "death strip" has been transformed. Berlin is a whole new city—ready to welcome visitors.

City planners have seized on the city's reunification and the return of the national government to make Berlin a great capital once again. When the Wall fell, the East was a decrepit wasteland and the West was a paragon of commerce and materialism. More than 20 years later, the roles are reversed: It is the East that feels the vibrant pulse of the city, while the West seems like yesterday's news.

Today, Berlin is like the nuclear fuel rod of a great nation. It's so vibrant with youth, energy, and an anything-goes-and-anything's-possible buzz that Munich feels spent in comparison. Berlin is both extremely popular and surprisingly affordable. As a booming tourist attraction, Berlin welcomes more visitors than Rome.

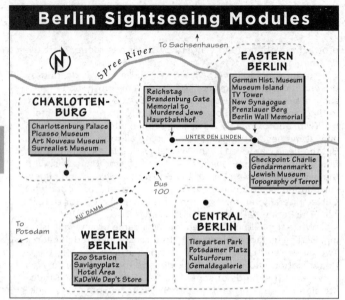

Berlin Sightseeing Modules

To Sachsenhausen

Spree River

N

EASTERN BERLIN

German Hist. Museum
Museum Island
TV Tower
New Synagogue
Prenzlauer Berg
Berlin Wall Memorial

CHARLOTTEN-BURG

Charlottenburg Palace
Picasso Museum
Art Nouveau Museum
Surrealist Museum

Reichstag
Brandenburg Gate
Memorial to
Murdered Jews
Hauptbahnhof

UNTER DEN LINDEN

Checkpoint Charlie
Gendarmenmarkt
Jewish Museum
Topography of Terror

Bus 100

KU' DAMM

To Potsdam

WESTERN BERLIN

Zoo Station
Savignyplatz
Hotel Area
KaDeWe Dep't Store

CENTRAL BERLIN

Tiergarten Park
Potsdamer Platz
Kulturforum
Gemaldegalerie

Planning Your Time

On a three-week trip through Germany, I'd give Berlin three nights and at least two full days, and spend them this way:

Day 1: Begin your day getting oriented to this huge city. For a quick and relaxing once-over-lightly tour, jump on one of the many hop-on, hop-off buses that make a two-hour narrated orientation loop through the city. Use the bus as you like, to hop off and on at places of interest (such as Potsdamer Platz). Then walk from the Reichstag (reservations required), under the Brandenburg Gate, and down Unter den Linden. Tour the German History Museum, and cap your sightseeing day by catching the one-hour Spree River boat tour (or pedaling a rented bike) along the parklike banks of the Spree River from Museum Island to the Chancellery.

Day 2: Spend your morning touring the great museums on Museum Island (Pergamon Museum and the Egyptian collection at the Neues Museum—timed-entry tickets required for both, and Romantic German art in the Old National Gallery). Dedicate your afternoon to sights of the Third Reich and Holocaust: After lunch, hike via Potsdamer Platz to the Topography of Terror exhibit and along the surviving Zimmerstrasse stretch of the Wall to the Museum of the Wall at Checkpoint Charlie. You could also head up to the Berlin Wall Memorial for a more in-depth survey of that infamous barrier, or swing by the Jewish Museum. Finish your day in the lively East—ideally in the once glum, then edgy, now fun-loving and trendy Prenzlauer Berg district.

Berlin merits additional time if you have it. There's much more in the city (such as the wonderful Gemäldegalerie). And nearby are some very worthwhile side-trips: the concentration camp memorial at Sachsenhausen, the palaces at Potsdam (both covered in the next chapter), and the historic town of Wittenberg (see the Lutherland chapter).

Orientation to Berlin

(area code: 030)

Berlin is huge, with 3.4 million people. The city is spread out and its sights numerous, so you'll need to be well-organized to experience the city smartly. The tourist's Berlin can be broken into three main digestible chunks:

1. Eastern Berlin has the highest concentration of notable sights and colorful neighborhoods. Near the landmark Brandenburg Gate, you'll find the Reichstag building, Pariser Platz, and the Memorial to the Murdered Jews of Europe. From Brandenburg Gate, the famous Unter den Linden boulevard runs eastward through former East Berlin, passing the German History Museum (a history lover's favorite) and Museum Island (Pergamon Museum, Neues Museum, and Berlin Cathedral) on the way to Alexanderplatz (TV Tower). The intersection of Unter den Linden and Friedrichstrasse has reclaimed its place as the center of the city. South of Unter den Linden, you'll find the delightful Gendarmenmarkt square, most Nazi sites (including the Topography of Terror), some good Wall-related sights (Museum of the Wall at Checkpoint Charlie and East Side Gallery), the Jewish Museum, and the colorful Turkish neighborhood of Kreuzberg. North of Unter den Linden are these worth-a-wander neighborhoods: Oranienburger Strasse (Jewish Quarter and New Synagogue), Hackescher Markt, and Prenzlauer Berg (several recommended hotels and a very lively restaurant/nightlife zone). Just west of Prenzlauer Berg is the Berlin Wall Memorial (with an intact surviving section of the Wall). Eastern Berlin's pedestrian-friendly Spree riverbank is also worth a stroll (or a river cruise).

2. Central Berlin is dominated by the giant Tiergarten park. South of the park are Potsdamer Platz and the Kulturforum museum cluster (including the Gemäldegalerie, New National Gallery, Musical Instruments Museum, and Philharmonic Concert Hall). To the north, the huge Hauptbahnhof (main train station) straddles the former Wall in what was central Berlin's no-man's-land.

3. Western Berlin centers on the Bahnhof Zoo (Zoo train station, often marked "Zoologischer Garten" on transit maps) and the grand Kurfürstendamm boulevard, nicknamed "Ku'damm"

Berlin

- - - - **Course of Former Wall**
+●+ **Elevated S-Bahn Line & Station**

½ Mile
1 Kilometers

CHARLOTTENBURG PALACE

Spree River

VICTORY COLUMN

CHARLOTTENBURG

Ernst-Reuter-Platz

STRASSE DES

17

BISMARCKSTR.

Tiergarten

BAHNHOF ZOO

Savigny-Platz

HARD.

KANTSTR.

ZOO

KULTUR FORUM

EUROPA CENTER

Witt.-platz

GERMAN RESISTANCE MUSEUM

KU' DAMM

MEMORIAL CHURCH

KUFÜRSTENSTR

LIETZEN-STR.

KaDeWe STORE

KLEISTRTR.

KOLLWITZ MUSEUM

DCH

(transportation hub, tours, information, shopping, and recommended hotels). The East is all the rage. But the West, while staid in comparison, is bouncing back—with big-name stores and destination restaurants that keep the area buzzing. During the Cold War, this "Western Sector" was the hub for Western visitors. Capitalists visited the West, with a nervous side-trip beyond the Wall into the grim and foreboding East. (Cubans, Russians, Poles, and Angolans stayed behind the Wall and did their sightseeing in the East.) Remnants of this Iron Curtain-era Western focus have left today's visitors with a stronger focus on the Ku'damm and Bahnhof Zoo than the district deserves.

Tourist Information

With any luck, you won't have to use Berlin's TIs—they're for-profit agencies working for the city's big hotels, which colors the information they provide. TI branches, appropriately called "info-stores," are unlikely to have the information you need (tel. 030/250-025, www.visitberlin.de). You'll find them at the **Hauptbahnhof** train station (daily 8:00-22:00, by main entrance on Europaplatz), **Ku'damm** (Kurfürstendamm 22, in the glass-and-steel Neues Kranzler Eck building, daily 9:30-20:00), and the **Brandenburg**

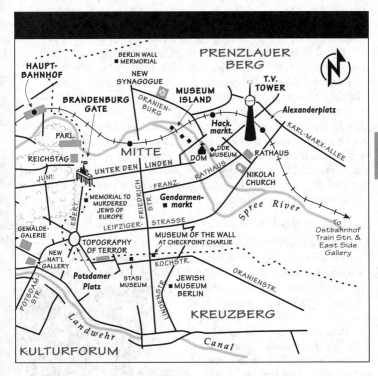

BERLIN

Gate (daily 9:30-19:00, until 18:30 Nov-March).

Skip the TI's €1 map, and instead pick up any of the walking tour companies' brochures—they include nearly-as-good maps for free (most hotels also provide free city maps). While the TI does sell the three-day Museumspass (described next), it's also available at major museums. If you take a walking tour, your guide is likely a better source of nightlife or shopping tips than the TI.

Museum Passes: The three-day, €19 **Museumspass** is a great value. It gets you into more than 50 museums, including the national museums and most of the recommended biggies, on three consecutive days. As you'll routinely spend €6-10 per admission, this pays for itself in a hurry. And you'll enjoy the ease of popping in and out of museums that you might not otherwise want to pay for. Buy it at the TI or any participating museum. The pass generally lets you skip the line and go directly into the museum (though occasionally you may have to wait in line to get a printed free ticket). The €16 **Museum Island Pass** (Bereichskarte Museumsinsel, price can change with special exhibits) covers all the museums on Museum Island (otherwise €8-12 each) and is a fine value—but for just €3 more, the three-day Museumspass gives you triple the days and many more entries. TIs also sell the **WelcomeCard,** a transportation pass that also includes some museum discounts (described later, under "Getting Around Berlin").

Local Publications: Various magazines can help make your time in Berlin more productive (available at the TI and/or many newsstands). *Berlin Programm* is a comprehensive German-language monthly, especially strong in high culture, that lists upcoming events and museum hours (€2, www.berlin-programm .de). *Exberliner Magazine,* the only English monthly (published mostly by expat Brits who love to poke fun at expat Americans), is very helpful for curious travelers. It has an edgy, somewhat pretentious, youthful focus and gives a fascinating insider's look at this fast-changing city (€2.50 but often given away at theaters or on the street, www.exberliner.com).

Arrival in Berlin

By Train at Berlin Hauptbahnhof

Berlin's newest and grandest train station is Berlin Hauptbahnhof (main train station, a.k.a. simply "der Bahnhof", abbreviated Hbf).

All long-distance trains arrive here, at Europe's biggest, mostly underground train station. This is a "transfer station"—unique for its major lines coming in at right angles—where the national train system meets the city's train system (S-Bahn).

The gigantic station can be intimidating on arrival, but it's laid out logically on five floors (which, confusingly, can be marked in different ways). Escalators and elevators connect the **main floor** (*Erdgeschoss,* EG, a.k.a level 0); the two **lower levels** (*Untergeschoss,* UG1 and UG2, a.k.a. levels -1 and -2); and the two **upper levels** (*Obersgeschoss,* OG1 and OG2, a.k.a. levels +1 and +2). Tracks 1-8 are in the lowest underground level (UG2), while tracks 11-16 (along with the S-Bahn) are on the top floor (OG2). Shops and services are concentrated on the three middle levels (EG, OG1, and UG1). The south entrance (toward the Reichstag and downtown, with a taxi stand and the stop for bus #TXL to Tegel Airport) is marked *Washingtonplatz,* while the north entrance is marked *Europaplatz.*

Services: You can store your **luggage** at the Gepäck Center, an efficient and secure deposit service (€5/day per bag, daily 6:00-22:00, on upper level OG1 directly under track 14). Luggage lockers (€4) are difficult to find since they're in the parking garage (levels P-1, P-2, and P-3; look for the garage entrance near Kaisers supermarket on the underground shopping level UG1). The **TI** is on the main floor (EG)—facing the north/*Europaplatz* entrance, look left; a 24-hour **pharmacy** is across the hall on the right (one floor above you, on OG1). The **WC Center** (public pay toilets) is on the main floor (EG) near the Burger King and food court.

Train Information and Tickets: The station has two DeutscheBahn *Reisezentrum* information counters: one on the upper level (OG1/+1, daily 6:00-22:00), and the other on the lower level (UG1/-1, daily 8:00-22:00; this branch also has the EurAide counter described next). If you're staying in western Berlin, keep in mind that the info center at the Bahnhof Zoo station is just as good and much less crowded.

EurAide is an English-speaking information desk with answers to your questions about train travel around Europe. It operates from a single counter in the underground shopping level *Reisezentrum* (follow signs to tracks 5-6 and *Reisezentrum –1*). It's American-run, so communication is simple. This is an especially good place to make fast-train and *couchette* reservations for later in your trip (May-July Mon-Fri 10:00-20:00, Sun 14:00-20:00, closed Sat; Aug Mon-Fri 11:00-20:00, Sun 14:00-20:00, closed Sat; Sept-April Mon-Fri 11:00-19:00, closed Sat-Sun; www.euraide.com).

Shopping: In addition to all those trains, the Hauptbahnhof is also the home of 80 shops with long hours—some locals call the station a "shopping mall with trains" (daily 8:00-22:00, only stores selling travel provisions are open Sun). The Kaisers supermarket (on underground shopping level UG1, follow signs for tracks 1-2) is handy for assembling a picnic for your train ride.

Getting into Town: Taxis and buses wait outside the station, but the S-Bahn is probably the best means of connecting to your destination within Berlin. The cross-town express S-Bahn line connects the station with my recommended hotels in a few minutes. It's simple: All S-Bahn trains are on tracks 15 and 16 at the top of the station (level OG2/+2). All trains on track 15 go east, stopping at Friedrichstrasse, Hackescher Markt (with connections to Prenzlauer Berg), Alexanderplatz, and Ostbahnhof; trains on track 16 go west, toward Bahnhof Zoo and Savignyplatz. Your train ticket or railpass into the station covers your connecting S-Bahn ride into town (and your ticket out includes the transfer via S-Bahn to the Hauptbahnhof). U-Bahn rides are not covered by tickets or railpasses.

If you're sleeping at one of my recommended hotels in eastern Berlin's Prenzlauer Berg neighborhood, take any train on track 15 two stops to Hackescher Markt, then catch tram #M1 north (see map on page 740).

If you're sleeping at one of my recommended hotels in western Berlin, catch any train on track 16 to Savignyplatz, and you're a five-minute walk from your hotel (see map on page 746). Savignyplatz is one stop after **Bahnhof Zoo** (rhymes with "toe";

a.k.a. Bahnhof Zoologischer Garten), the once-grand train hub now eclipsed by the Hauptbahnhof. Nowadays Bahnhof Zoo is useful mainly for its shops, uncrowded train-information desk, and BVG transit office (outside the entrance, amid the traffic).

The Berlin Hauptbahnhof is not well-connected to the city's U-Bahn (subway) system—yet. The station's sole U-Bahn line—U55—goes only two stops, to the Brandenburger Tor station, and doesn't really connect to the rest of the system. It's part of a planned extension of the U5 line to Alexanderplatz that's far from completion. But for transit junkies, it is an interesting ride on Europe's newest and shortest subway line.

By Plane
For information on reaching the city center from Berlin's airports, see "Berlin Connections" at the end of this chapter.

Helpful Hints
Medical Help: "**Call a doc**" is a nonprofit referral service designed for tourists (tel. 01805-321-303, phone answered 24 hours a day, www.calladoc.com). Payment is arranged between you and the doctor, and is likely far more affordable than similar care in the US. The US Embassy also has a list of local English-speaking doctors (tel. 030/83050, www.usembassy.de).

Museum Tips: Some major Berlin museums are closed on Monday—if you're in town on that day, review hours carefully before making plans. If you plan to see several museums, you'll save money with the €19 Museumspass, which covers nearly all the city sights for three days—including everything covered by the one-day €16 Museum Island Pass (see "Tourist Information—Museum Passes," earlier).

Addresses: Many Berlin streets are numbered with odd and even numbers on the same side of the street, often with no connection to the other side (for example, Ku'damm #212 can be across the street from #14). To save steps, check the white street signs on curb corners; many list the street numbers covered on that side of the block.

Cold War Terminology: Cold War history is important here, so it's helpful to learn a few key terms. What Americans called "East Germany" was technically the German Democratic Republic—known here by its German name, the Deutsche Demokratische Republik. The

initials **DDR** (day-day-AIR) are the shorthand you'll still see around what was once East Germany. The formal name for "West Germany" was the Federal Republic of Germany—the Bundesrepublik Deutschland (BRD)—and is the name now shared by all of reunited Germany.

Internet Access: You'll find Internet access in most hotels and hostels, as well as at small Internet cafés all over the city. Near Savignyplatz, **Internet-Terminal** is at Kantstrasse 38. In eastern Berlin, try **Hotdog World** in Prenzlauer Berg (Weinbergsweg 4, just a few steps from U8: Rosenthaler Platz toward Kastanienallee), or **Surf Inn** at Alexanderplatz 9. Bahnhof Zoo, Friedrichstrasse, and Hauptbahnhof train stations have coin-operated Internet terminals (though these unmanned machines can come with greater security risks).

Bookstore: Berlin Story, a big, cluttered, fun bookshop, has a knowledgeable staff and the best selection anywhere in town of English-language books on Berlin. They also stock an amusing mix of knickknacks and East Berlin nostalgia souvenirs (daily 10:00-20:00, Unter den Linden 40, tel. 030/2045-3842, www.berlinstory.de). I'd skip the overpriced little museum in back.

Other Berlin Souvenirs: If you're taken with the city's unofficial mascot, the *Ampelmännchen* (traffic-light man), you'll find a world of souvenirs slathered with his iconic red and green image at **Ampelmann Shops** (various locations, including near Gendarmenmarkt at Markgrafenstrasse 37, near Museum Island inside the DomAquarée mall, in the Hackeschen Höfe, and at Potsdamer Platz).

Laundry: Berlin has several self-service launderettes with long hours (wash and dry-€4-9/load). Near my recommended hotels in Prenzlauer Berg, try **Waschsalon 115** (daily 6:00-23:00, exact change required, free Wi-Fi, Torstrasse 115, around the corner from the recommended Circus hostel) or **Eco-Express Waschsalon** (daily 6:00-23:00, handy pizzeria next door, Danziger Strasse 7). The **Schnell & Sauber Waschcenter** chain has a location in Prenzlauer Berg (daily 6:00-23:00, exact change required, Oderberger Strasse 1).

Getting Around Berlin

Berlin's sights spread far and wide. Right from the start, commit yourself to the city's fine public-transit system.

By Public Transit: Subway, Train, Tram, and Bus

Berlin's many modes of transportation are consolidated into one system that uses the same ticket: U-Bahn (*Untergrund-Bahn*, Berlin's subway), S-Bahn (*Stadtschnellbahn*, or "fast urban train," mostly aboveground and with fewer stops), *Strassenbahn* (street-cars, called "trams" by locals), and buses. For all types of transit, there are three lettered zones (A, B, and C). Most of your sightseeing will be in zones A and B (the city proper)—but you'll need to buy a ticket that also covers zone C if you're going to Potsdam, Sachsenhausen, Schönefeld Airport (a.k.a. Brandenburg/Willy Brandt Airport), or other outlying areas. Get and use the excellent *Discover Berlin by Train and Bus* map-guide published by the public transit operator BVG (at subway ticket windows).

Ticket Options: You have several options for tickets.

• The €2.30 **basic** ticket *(Einzelfahrschein)* covers two hours of travel in one direction on buses or subways. It's easy to make this ticket stretch to cover several rides...as long as they're all in the same direction.

• The €1.40 **short-ride** ticket *(Kurzstrecke)* covers a single ride of six bus stops or three subway stations (one transfer allowed).

• The €8.20 **four-trip** ticket *(4-Fahrten-Karte)* is the same as four basic tickets at a small discount.

• The **day pass** *(Tageskarte)* is good until 3:00 the morning after it expires (€6.30 for zones AB, €6.80 for zones ABC). For longer stays, consider a seven-day pass *(Sieben-Tage-Karte;* €27.20 for zones AB, €33.50 for zones ABC), or the WelcomeCard (described below), which is good for up to five days and also includes sightseeing discounts. The *Kleingruppenkarte* lets groups of up to five travel all day (€15 for zones AB, €15.50 for zones ABC).

• If you've already bought a ticket for zones A and B, and later decide that you also want to go to zone C, you can buy an **"extension ticket"** *(Anschlussfahrschein)* for €1.50 per ride in that zone.

• If you plan to cover a lot of ground using public transportation during a two- or three-day visit, the **WelcomeCard** (available at TIs) is usually the best deal. For longer stays, there's even a five-day option. It covers all public transportation and gives you up to 50 percent discounts on lots of minor and a few major museums (including Checkpoint Charlie), sightseeing tours (including 25 percent off the recommended Original Berlin Walks), and music and theater events (www.visitberlin.de/welcomecard). If you plan to stay inside the city, the Berlin-only option works best (covers transit zones AB, €16.90/48 hours, €22.90/72 hours). For trips beyond the city center, you might want to get the Berlin-with-Potsdam option (zones ABC, €18.90/48 hours, €24.90/72 hours). If you're a museum junkie, consider the **WelcomeCard+Museumsinsel** (€34/72 hours), which combines travel in zones A and B with unlimited access to the five museums on Museum Island. Families get an extra price break: The ABC versions (€36/72 hours) are valid for one adult and up to three kids younger than 15.

Buying Tickets: You can buy U- and S-Bahn tickets from machines at stations. (They are also sold at BVG pavilions at train stations, airports, and the TI, and on board trams and buses—drivers give change.) *Erwachsener* means "adult"—anyone 14 or older. Don't be afraid of the automated machines: First select the type of ticket you want, then load the coins or paper bills. As you board the bus or tram, or enter the subway system, punch your ticket in a red or yellow clock machine to validate it (or risk a €40 fine; for an all-day or multiday pass, stamp it only the first time you ride). Be sure to travel with a valid ticket. Tickets are checked frequently, often by plainclothes inspectors. Within Berlin, Eurailpasses are good only on S-Bahn connections from the train station when you arrive and to the station when you depart.

BERLIN

Transit Tips: The S-Bahn crosstown express is a river of public transit through the heart of the city, in which many lines converge on one basic highway. Get used to this, and you'll leap within a few minutes between key locations: Savignyplatz (hotels), Bahnhof Zoo (Ku'damm, bus #100), Hauptbahnhof (all major trains in and out of Berlin), Friedrichstrasse (a short walk north of the heart of Unter den Linden), Hackescher Markt (Museum Island, restaurants, nightlife, connection to Prenzlauer Berg hotels and eateries), and Alexanderplatz (eastern end of Unter den Linden).

Sections of the U- or S-Bahn sometimes close temporarily for repairs. In this situation, a bus route often replaces the train (*Ersatzverkehr*, or "replacement transportation"; *zwischen* means "between").

Berlin's public transit is operated by BVG (except the S-Bahn, run by DeutscheBahn). Schedules, including bus timetables, are available on the helpful BVG website (www.bvg.de).

By Taxi

Taxis are easy to flag down, and taxi stands are common. A typical ride within town costs €8-10, and a crosstown trip (for example, Bahnhof Zoo to Alexanderplatz) will run about €15. Tariff 1 is for a *Kurzstrecke* (see below). All other rides are tariff 2 (€3.20 drop plus €1.60/kilometer). If possible, use cash—paying with a credit card comes with a hefty surcharge (about €4, regardless of the fare).

Money-Saving Taxi Tip: For any ride of less than two kilometers (about a mile), you can save several euros if you take advantage of the **Kurzstrecke** (short-stretch) rate. To get this rate, it's important that you flag the cab down on the street—not at or even near a taxi stand. Also, you must ask for the *Kurzstrecke* rate as soon as you hop in: Confidently say *"Kurzstrecke, bitte"* (KOORTS-shtreh-keh, BIT-teh), and your driver will grumble and flip the meter to a fixed €4 rate (for a ride that would otherwise cost €7).

By Bike

Flat Berlin is a very bike-friendly city, but be careful—Berlin's motorists don't brake for bicyclists (and bicyclists don't brake for pedestrians). Fortunately, some roads and sidewalks have special red-painted bike lanes. Don't ride on the regular sidewalk—it's *verboten*. Better yet, to get out of the city on two wheels, rent a bike, take it on the subway (requires extra €1.50 ticket) to the pleasant Potsdam/Wannsee parkland area west of town, then ride through forests and along skinny lakes to the vast Grünewald park, then back into the city. (Back during the Cold War, Grünewald was the Wessies' playground, while Ossies communed with nature at the Müggelsee east of town.) Good bike shops can suggest a specific route.

Fat Tire Bikes rents good bikes at two handy locations— East (at the base of the TV Tower near Alexanderplatz—facing the entrance to the tower, go around to the right) and West (at Bahnhof Zoo—leaving the station onto Hardenbergplatz, turn left and walk 100 yards to the big bike sign). Both locations have the same hours and rates (€7/4 hours, €12/day, daily May-Sept 9:30-20:00, March-April and Oct-Nov 9:30-18:00, shorter hours or by appointment only Dec-Feb, leave ID, tel. 030/2404-7991, www.berlinbikerental.com).

In eastern Berlin, **Take a Bike** near the Friedrichstrasse S-Bahn station is owned by a lovely Dutch-German couple who know a lot about bikes and have a huge inventory. They can help you find the perfect fit (3-gear bikes: €12.50/day, €19/2 days; more for better bikes, slightly cheaper for longer rentals; electric bikes-€29/ day, helmets, daily 9:30-19:00, Neustädtische Kirchstrasse 8, tel. 030/2065-4730, info@takeabike.de). To find it, leave the S-Bahn station via the Friedrichstrasse exit, turn right, go through a triangle-shaped square, and hang a left on Neustädtische Kirchstrasse.

Tours in Berlin

▲▲▲Hop-on, Hop-off Bus Tours

Several companies offer the same routine: a €15 circuit of the city with unlimited hop-on, hop-off privileges all day (about 14 stops at the city's major sights) on buses with cursory narration in English and German by a live (but tired) guide or a boring recorded commentary in whatever language you want to dial up. In season, each company has buses running four times per hour. They are cheap and great for photography—and Berlin really lends itself to this kind of bus-tour orientation. You can hop off at any major tourist spot (Potsdamer Platz, Museum Island, Brandenburg Gate, the Kaiser Wilhelm Memorial Church, and so on). Go with a live guide rather than the recorded spiel (so you get a few current asides). When choosing seats, check the sun/shade situation—some buses are entirely topless, and others are entirely covered. My favorites are topless with a shaded covered section in the back (April-Oct daily 10:00-18:00, last bus leaves all stops at 16:00, 2-hour loop; for specifics, look for brochures in your hotel lobby or at the TI). Keep your ticket so you can hop off and on (with the same company) all day. In winter (Nov-March), buses come only twice an hour, and the last departure is at 15:00. Brochures explain extras offered by each company.

Other Bus Tours
City Bus #100—For do-it-yourselfers, Berlin's city bus #100 is a great alternative to the commercial hop-on, hop-off bus tours—and you can follow along with my self-guided bus tour on page 664.

Full-Blown Bus Tours—**Severin & Kühn** offers a long list of bus tours (not hop-on, hop-off) in and around Berlin; their three-hour "Berlin Classic Live" tour is a good introduction (€19, daily at 10:00, Fri-Sun also at 14:00, live guides in two languages, interesting historical photos displayed on bus monitors, departs from Ku'damm 216, buy ticket at bus, tel. 030/880-4190, www.berliner stadtrundfahrten.de).

▲▲▲Walking Tours
Berlin, with a fascinating recent history that can be challenging to appreciate on your own, is an ideal place to explore with a walking tour. The city is a battle zone of extremely competitive and creative walking-tour companies. Unlike many other European countries, Germany has no regulations controlling who can give city tours. This can make guide quality hit-or-miss, ranging from brilliant history buffs who've lived in Berlin for years while pursuing their PhDs, to new arrivals who memorize a script and start leading tours after being in town for just a couple of weeks. A good Berlin tour guide is equal parts historian and entertainer; the best tours make the city's dynamic story come to life. While upstart companies abound, in general you have the best odds of landing a great guide by using one of the more established companies I recommend in this section.

Most outfits offer walks that are variations on the same themes: general **introductory** walk, **Third Reich** (Hitler and Nazi sites), and day trips to **Potsdam** and the **Sachsenhausen Concentration Camp Memorial**. Most tours cost about €12-15 and last about three to four hours (longer for the side-trips to Potsdam and Sachsenhausen—for details, see the next chapter); public-transit tickets and entrances to sights are extra. I've included some basic descriptions for each company, but for details—including prices

Berlin at a Glance

▲▲▲**German History Museum** The ultimate swing through Germany's tumultuous story. **Hours:** Daily 10:00-18:00. See page 684.

▲▲▲**Pergamon Museum** World-class museum of classical antiquities on Museum Island, featuring the fantastic second-century B.C. Greek Pergamon Altar and frieze. **Hours:** Daily 10:00-18:00, Thu until 22:00. See page 688.

▲▲**Reichstag** Germany's historic parliament building, topped with a striking modern dome you can climb (reservations required). **Hours:** Daily 8:00-24:00, last entry at 23:00. See page 666.

▲▲**Brandenburg Gate** One of Berlin's most famous landmarks, a massive columned gateway, at the former border of East and West. **Hours:** Always open. See page 673.

▲▲**Memorial to the Murdered Jews of Europe** Holocaust memorial with almost 3,000 symbolic pillars, plus an exhibition about Hitler's Jewish victims. **Hours:** Memorial always open; information center open Tue-Sun 10:00-20:00, Oct-March until 19:00, closed Mon. See page 675.

▲▲**Unter den Linden** Leafy boulevard through the heart of former East Berlin, lined with some of the city's top sights. **Hours:** Always open. See page 677.

▲▲**Neues Museum and Egyptian Collection** Proud home (on Museum Island) of the exquisite 3,000-year-old bust of Queen Nefertiti. **Hours:** Daily 10:00-18:00, Thu-Sat until 20:00. See page 691.

▲▲**Gendarmenmarkt** Inviting square bounded by twin churches (one with a fine German history exhibit), a chocolate shop, and a concert hall. **Hours:** Always open. See page 699.

▲▲**Topography of Terror** Chilling exhibit documenting the Nazi perpetrators, built on the site of the former Gestapo/SS headquarters. **Hours:** Daily 10:00-20:00. See page 701.

▲▲**Museum of the Wall at Checkpoint Charlie** Kitschy but moving museum with stories of brave Cold War escapes, near the former site of the famous East-West border checkpoint; the surrounding street scene is almost as interesting. **Hours:** Daily 9:00-22:00. See page 708.

▲▲Jewish Museum Berlin Engaging, accessible museum celebrating Jewish culture, in a highly conceptual building. **Hours:** Daily 10:00-20:00, Mon until 22:00. See page 709.

▲▲Gemäldegalerie Germany's top collection of 13th- through 18th-century European paintings, featuring Holbein, Dürer, Cranach, Van der Weyden, Rubens, Hals, Rembrandt, Vermeer, Velázquez, Raphael, and more. **Hours:** Tue-Sun 10:00-18:00, Thu until 22:00, closed Mon. See page 725.

▲Old National Gallery German paintings, mostly from the Romantic Age. **Hours:** Tue-Sun 10:00-18:00, Thu until 22:00, closed Mon. See page 693.

▲DDR Museum Quirky collection of communist-era artifacts. **Hours:** Daily 10:00-20:00, Sat until 22:00. See page 696.

▲New Synagogue Largest prewar synagogue in Berlin, damaged in World War II, with a rebuilt facade and modest museum. **Hours:** March-Oct Sun-Mon 10:00-20:00, Tue-Thu 10:00-18:00, Fri 10:00-17:00—until 14:00 Oct and March-May, closed Sat; Nov-Feb Sun-Thu 10:00-18:00, Fri 10:00-14:00, closed Sat. See page 713.

▲Berlin Wall Memorial A "docu-center" with videos and displays, several outdoor exhibits, and lone surviving stretch of an intact Wall section. **Hours:** Visitor Center Tue-Sun 9:30-19:00, Nov-March until 18:00, closed Mon; outdoor areas open 24 hours daily. See page 716.

▲Potsdamer Platz The "Times Square" of old Berlin, long a postwar wasteland, now rebuilt with huge glass skyscrapers, an underground train station, and—covered with a huge canopy—the Sony Center mall. **Hours:** Always open. See page 722.

▲Deutsche Kinemathek Film and TV Museum An entertaining look at German film and TV, from *Metropolis* to Dietrich to Nazi propaganda to the present day. **Hours:** Tue-Sun 10:00-18:00, Thu until 20:00, closed Mon. See page 723.

▲Kaiser Wilhelm Memorial Church Evocative destroyed church in the heart of the former West Berlin, with a modern annex. **Hours:** Church—daily 9:00-19:00; Memorial Hall in the bombed tower—Mon-Sat 10:00-18:00, shorter hours Sun. See page 731.

▲Käthe Kollwitz Museum The black-and-white art of the Berlin artist who conveyed the suffering of her city's stormiest century. **Hours:** Daily 11:00-18:00. See page 732.

and specific schedules—see the various websites or look for brochures in town (widely available at TIs, hotel reception desks, and many cafés and shops).

Original Berlin Walks—This well-established operation offers tours aimed at a clientele that's curious about the city's history. Their flagship introductory walk, Discover Berlin, offers a good overview in four hours (daily year-round, meet at 10:00 at Bahnhof Zoo, April-Oct also daily at 13:30). They offer a Third Reich walking tour (4/week in summer), tours to Potsdam and Sachsenhausen (see page 659), and themed Jewish Life in Berlin and Nest of Spies walks (both 1/week April-Oct only). Readers of this book get a €1 discount per tour in 2012. You can buy tickets in advance at any S-Bahn service center, or just show up and buy a ticket from the guide. All tours meet at the taxi stand in front of the Bahnhof Zoo train station; the Discover Berlin, Jewish Life, and Sachsenhausen tours also have a second departure point opposite East Berlin's Hackescher Markt S-Bahn station, outside the Weihenstephaner restaurant (tour info: tel. 030/301-9194, www.berlinwalks.de, office@berlinwalks.de).

Vive Berlin—This "guiding collective" was formed by some of the city's most experienced guides. They offer the usual lineup, with an introductory walk (Essential Berlin—Mon, Wed, and Fri-Sat at 10:00; Sun at 13:00), plus Third Reich, Potsdam, and Sachsenhausen itineraries, and a walk through East Berlin. All tours meet at Potsdamer Platz 10, in front of Balzac Coffee (U2/S-Bahn: Potsdamer Platz, use Stresemannstrasse exit; tel. 0157/845-46696, www.viveberlintours.de).

Insider Tour—This well-regarded company runs the full gamut of itineraries: introductory walk (daily), Third Reich, Cold War, Jewish Berlin, Sachsenhausen, and Potsdam, as well as bike tours, pub crawls, and a day trip to Dresden. Their tours have two meeting points (some tours convene at both, others at just one—check the schedule): in the West at the McDonald's across from Bahnhof Zoo, and in the East at AMT Coffee at the Hackescher Markt S-Bahn station (www.insidertour.com, tel. 030/692-3149).

Brewer's Berlin Tours—Specializing in longer, more in-depth walks, this company was started by Terry Brewer, who retired from the British diplomatic service in East Berlin. Today Terry's guides lead exhaustive—or, for some, exhausting—tours through the city (their Best of Berlin introductory tour, billed at 6 hours, can last 8 hours or more; daily at 10:30). Terry himself (who can be a bit gruff) leads a "six-hour" tour to some off-the-beaten-path hidden gems of Berlin twice weekly. They also do all-day Potsdam tours. Their tours depart from Bandy Brooks ice cream shop at the Friedrichstrasse S-Bahn station (tel. 030/2248-7435, mobile 0177-388-1537, www.brewersberlintours.com).

Sandeman's New Europe Berlin "Free" Tours—You'll see this company advertising supposedly "free" introductory tours, plus paid itineraries similar to those offered by competitors. But Sandeman's tours aren't really free—just misleading. Guides for the "free" tours pay the company a cut of €3 per person, so they hustle for tips. They expect to be "tipped in paper" (i.e., €5 minimum tip per person). This business model leads to high guide turnover, meaning that the guides are, overall, less experienced (though some are quite entertaining). They offer the standard Berlin itineraries, but target a younger crowd. Basic introductory city walks leave daily at 11:00, 13:00, and 16:00 from outside the Deutsche Bank near Bahnhof Zoo. Paid tours include a wildly popular €12 pub crawl (nightly; for more info, see page 737) and an excellent Alternative Berlin tour, which explores Berlin's gritty counterculture, squats, and urban life (€12, daily at 14:00; tel. 030/5105-0030, www.newberlintours.com).

Berlin Underground Association (Berliner Unterwelten Verein)—Much of Berlin's history lies beneath the surface, and this group has an exclusive agreement with the city to explore and research what is hidden underground. Their one-of-a-kind **Dark Worlds** tour of a WWII air-raid bunker features a chilling explanation of the air war over Berlin (Wed-Mon at 11:00, also Mon at 13:00). The **From Flak Towers to Mountains of Debris** tour enters the Humboldthain air defense tower (April-Oct Thu, Sat, and Sun at 16:00). The **Subways, Bunkers, Cold War** tour visits a completely stocked and fully functional nuclear emergency bunker in former West Berlin (Tue-Sun at 13:00, also Tue at 11:00; each tour costs €10; meet in the hall of the Gesundbrunnen U-Bahn/S-Bahn station, follow signs to *Humboldthain/Brunnenstrasse* exit and walk up the stairs to their office, tel. 030/4991-0517, www .berliner-unterwelten.de).

Local Guides—Both **Nick Jackson** (from the Berlin Underground Association, mobile 0176-633-64975, nick.jackson@berlin .de) and **Lee Evans** (my longtime helper in Berlin, mobile 0177-423-5307, lee.evans@berlin.de) enjoy sharing the story of their adopted hometown with visitors. If they are busy, try **Jennifer DeShirley** at Berlin and Beyond—this company has a crew of excellent, professional guides with an academic bent (tel. 030/8733-0584, mobile 0176-633-55565, info@berlinandbeyond.de).

Bike Tours

Fat Tire Bike Tours—Choose among three different four-hour, six-mile tours (€22 each): City Tour (March-Nov daily at 11:00, May-Sept also daily at 16:00, Dec-Feb Wed and Sat at 11:00), Berlin Wall Tour (April-Oct Mon, Thu, and Sat at 10:30), and Third Reich Tour (April-Oct Wed, Fri, and Sun at 10:30). For any tour, meet at the TV Tower at Alexanderplatz—but don't get distracted by the Russians pretending to be Fat Tire (reserve ahead for the Wall or Third Reich tours, no reservations necessary for City Tour, tel. 030/2404-7991, www.fattirebiketours.com, berlin @fattirebiketours.com).

Boat Tours

Spree River Cruises—Several boat companies offer one-hour, €10 trips up and down the river. A relaxing hour on one of these boats can be time and money well-spent. You'll listen to excellent English audioguides, see lots of wonderful new government-commissioned architecture, and enjoy the lively park action fronting the river. Boats leave from various docks that cluster near the bridge at the Berlin Cathedral

(just off Unter den Linden). I enjoyed the Historical Sightseeing Cruise from **Stern und Kreisschiffahrt** (mid-March-Nov daily 10:30-18:30, leaves from Nikolaiviertel Dock—cross bridge from Berlin Cathedral toward Alexanderplatz and look right, tel. 030/536-3600, www.sternundkreis.de). Confirm that the boat you choose comes with English commentary.

Self-Guided Bus Tour

Bus #100 from Bahnhof Zoo to Alexanderplatz

While hop-on, hop-off bus tours are a great value, Berlin's city bus #100 laces together the major sights in a kind of poor man's bus tour. Bus #100 stops at Bahnhof Zoo, the Berlin Zoo, Victory Column, Reichstag, Unter den Linden, Brandenburg Gate, Pergamon Museum, and Alexanderplatz. A reader board inside the bus displays the upcoming stop. A basic €2.10 bus ticket is good for two hours of travel in one direction, and buses leave every few minutes.

Starting in the West from Bahnhof Zoo, here's a quick review of what you'll see: Leaving the train station, on your left and straight ahead, you'll spot the bombed-out hulk of the **Kaiser Wilhelm Memorial Church,** with its postwar sister church (described on page 731). Then, on the left, the elephant gates mark the entrance to the venerable and much-loved **Berlin Zoo** (see page 733) and its aquarium. After a left turn, you cross the canal and pass Berlin's **embassy row.** The first interesting embassy is Mexico's, with columns that seem to move when you're driving by (how do they do that?). The big turquoise wall marks the communal home of all five Nordic embassies. This building is very "green," run entirely on solar power.

The bus then enters the 400-acre **Tiergarten** park, packed with cycling paths, joggers, and—on hot days—nude sunbathers. Straight ahead, the **Victory Column** (Siegessäule; with the gilded angel—see page 720), towers above this vast city park that was once a royal hunting grounds. A block beyond the Victory Column (on the left) is the 18th-century late-Rococo **Bellevue Palace.** Formerly the official residence of the Prussian (and later German) crown prince, and at one time a Nazi VIP guest house, it's now the residence of the federal president (whose power is mostly ceremonial—the chancellor wields the real clout). If the flag's out, he's in.

Driving along the Spree River (on the left), you'll see buildings of the **national government.** The huge brick "brown snake" complex (across the river) was built to house government workers—but it didn't sell, so now its apartments are available to anyone. A metal Henry Moore sculpture titled *Butterfly* (a.k.a. "The Drinker's Liver") floats in front of the slope-roofed House of World Cultures (Berliners have nicknamed this building "the pregnant oyster" and "Jimmy Carter's smile"). The modern tower (next, on the left) is a carillon with 68 bells (from 1987). Through the trees on the left you'll see Germany's **Chancellery**—essentially Germany's White House. The big open space is the **Platz der Republik,** where the Victory Column (which you passed earlier) stood until Hitler moved it. The Hauptbahnhof (Berlin's vast main train station, marked by its tall tower with the *DB* sign) is across the field between the Chancellery and the **Reichstag** (Germany's parliament—the old building with the new dome, described on next page).

If you get off here, the "Sights in Eastern Berlin" descriptions starting on the next page cover the next string of attractions, which are best seen on foot. If you stay on the bus, you'll zip by them in this order:

Unter den Linden, the main east-west thoroughfare, stretches from the **Brandenburg Gate** (behind you) through Berlin's historic core (ahead) to the TV Tower in the distance (Alexanderplatz, where this bus finishes). You'll pass the **Russian Embassy** and the Aeroflot airline office (right). Crossing **Friedrichstrasse,** look right for a Fifth Avenue-style conga line of big, glitzy department stores. Later, on the left, are the **German History Museum, Museum Island** (with the **Pergamon Museum**), and the **Berlin Cathedral;** across from these (on the right) is the construction site of the new **Humboldt-Forum** (with the Humboldt-Box visitors center). Then you'll rumble to a final stop at what was the center of East Berlin in communist times: **Alexanderplatz.**

Sights in Eastern Berlin

The following sights are arranged roughly west to east, from the Reichstag down Unter den Linden to Alexanderplatz. It's possible to link these sights as a convenient self-guided orientation walk (I've included walking directions for this purpose)—allow about 1.5 hours without stops for sightseeing. Adding tours of several sights can easily fill a whole day. Remember that reservations are required for the Reichstag dome, and you'll need timed-entry tickets for the Pergamon and Neues museums.

Also described here are sights to the south and north of Unter den Linden.

▲▲Reichstag

The parliament building—the heart of German democracy—has a short but complicated and emotional history. When it was

inaugurated in the 1890s, the last emperor, Kaiser Wilhelm II, disdainfully called it the "chatting home for monkeys" *(Reichs-saffenhaus)*. It was placed outside of the city's old walls—far from the center of real power, the imperial palace. But it was from the Reichstag that the German Republic was proclaimed in 1918.

In 1933, this symbol of democracy nearly burned down. The Nazis—whose influence on the German political scene was on the rise—blamed a communist plot. A Dutch communist, Marinus van der Lubbe, was eventually convicted and guillotined for the crime. Others believed that Hitler himself planned the fire, using it as a handy excuse to frame the communists and grab power. Even though Van der Lubbe was posthumously pardoned by the German government in 2008, most modern historians concede that he most likely was guilty and acted alone—the Nazis were just incredibly lucky to have his deed advance their cause.

The Reichstag was hardly used from 1933 to 1999. Despite the fact that the building had lost its symbolic value, Stalin ordered his troops to take the Reichstag from the Nazis by May 1, 1945 (the date of the workers' May Day parade in Moscow). More than 1,500 Nazi soldiers made their last stand here—extending World War II by two days. On April 30, after fierce fighting on this rooftop, the Reichstag fell to the Red Army.

For the building's 101st birthday in 1995, the Bulgarian-American artist Christo wrapped it in silvery gold cloth. It was then wrapped again—in scaffolding—and rebuilt by British architect Lord Norman Foster into the new parliamentary home of the Bundestag (Germany's lower house, similar to the US House of Representatives). To many Germans, the proud resurrection of the Reichstag symbolizes the end of a terrible chapter in their country's history.

The **glass cupola** rises 155 feet above the ground. Its two sloped ramps spiral 755 feet to the top for a grand view. Inside the dome, a cone of 360 mirrors reflects natural light into the legislative chamber below. Lit from inside at night, this gives Berlin a memorable nightlight. The environmentally friendly cone—with an opening at the top—also helps with air circulation, drawing stale air out of the legislative chamber (no joke) and pulling in cool air from below.

Because of a terrorist plot discovered and thwarted in 2010, the building has tight security: Getting in now requires a reservation.

Cost and Hours: Free but reservations required—see below, daily 8:00-24:00, last entry at 23:00, metal detectors, no big luggage allowed, Platz der Republik 1; S- or U-Bahn: Friedrichstrasse, Brandenburger Tor, or Bundestag; tel. 030/2273-2152, www.bundestag.de.

Reservations: As of this book's publication in late 2011, a visit to the dome was possible only with a (free) advance reservation. Spots book up several days in advance.

You can only reserve **online.** The website is user-friendly, if (not surprisingly) a bit bureaucratic. Go to www.bundestag.de, click "English" at the top of the screen, and—under the "Visit the Bundestag" menu—select "Online registration." On this page, select "Visit the dome." Fill in the number of people in your party, ignore the "Comments" field, and click "Next." After entering the scrambled code (captcha), you can select your preferred visit date and time (you can request up to three different time slots) and fill in your contact information. Once you complete the form and agree to their privacy policy, you'll be sent a confirmation email with a link to a website where you'll enter the name and birthdate for each person in your party and confirm your request. After completing this form, you'll receive a confirmation of your request (not a confirmation of your visit) by email. But you still have to wait for yet another email confirming your visit. If the English page isn't working, you can try using the German version: Go to https://www.bundestag.de/besuche/besucherdienst/index.jsp and call up a German-speaking friend to help you out. Or, if you use the Google Chrome browser—which you can download free at www.google.com/chrome—simply click the "Translate" button to see the steps in English.

While they claim it's possible to **email** a reservation request

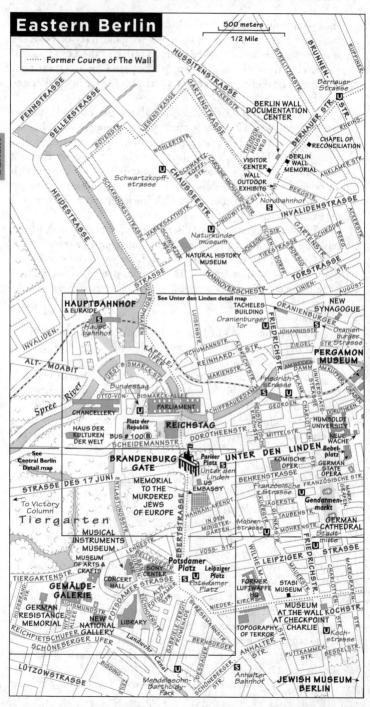

Eastern Berlin

500 meters
1/2 Mile

...... Former Course of The Wall

BERLIN WALL
DOCUMENTATION
CENTER

CHAPEL OF
RECONCILIATION

VISITOR
CENTER

BERLIN
WALL
MEMORIAL

WALL
OUTDOOR
EXHIBITS

Bernauer
Strasse

Schwartzkopf-
strasse

Nordbahnstrasse

Naturkunde
museum

NATURAL HISTORY
MUSEUM

See Unter den Linden detail map

TACHELES
BUILDING

Oranienburger
Tor

NEW
SYNAGOGUE

PERGAMON
MUSEUM

HAUPTBAHNHOF
& EURAIDE

Haupt-
bahnhof

Friedrich-
strasse

Bundestag

CHANCELLERY

PARLIAMENT

HAUS DER
KULTUREN
DER WELT

Platz der
Republik

REICHSTAG

HUMBOLDT
UNIVERSITY

NEUE
WACHE

Spree River

BUS #100

See
Central Berlin
Detail map

BRANDENBURG
GATE

Pariser
Platz

UNTER DEN LINDEN

KOMISCHE
OPER

Bebel-
platz

GERMAN
STATE
OPERA

Unter den
Linden US
EMBASSY

MEMORIAL
TO THE
MURDERED
JEWS OF
EUROPE

STRASSE DES 17 JUNI

To Victory
Column

Tiergarten

Gendarmen-
markt

GERMAN
CATHEDRAL

Stadt-
mitte

MUSICAL
INSTRUMENTS
MUSEUM

MUSEUM
OF ARTS &
CRAFTS

SONY
CENTER

Concert
Hall

Potsdamer
Platz

Leipziger
Platz

LEIPZIGER STRASSE

FORMER
LUFTWAFFE
HQ

STASI
MUSEUM

GEMÄLDE-
GALERIE

GERMAN
RESISTANCE
MEMORIAL

NEW
NATIONAL
GALLERY

LIBRARY

Potsdamer
Platz

MUSEUM
AT THE WALL
AT CHECKPOINT
CHARLIE

KOCHSTR.

TOPOGRAPHY
OF TERROR

Koch-
strasse

Landwehr Canal

Mendelssohn-
Bartholdy-
Park

Anhalter
Bahnhof

JEWISH MUSEUM
BERLIN

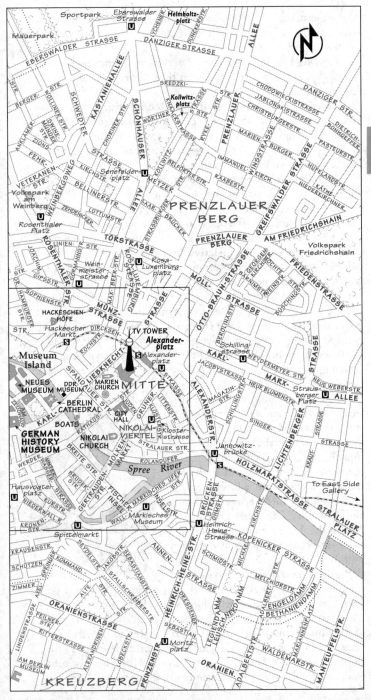

(kuppelbesuch@bundestag.de), you won't receive a confirmation until the day before your visit—which can be stressful. Use the website instead.

Getting In: Once you have a reservation, simply report to the security checkpoint at the appointed time. Give your name to the attendant, and you'll be let right in.

Tours: Pick up the English **"Outlooks" flier** just after the security checkpoint. The free GPS-driven **audioguide** explains the building and narrates the view as you wind up the spiral ramp to the top of the dome; the commentary starts automatically as you step onto the bottom of the ramp.

◉ Self-Guided Tour: As you approach the building, look above the door, surrounded by stone patches from WWII bomb damage, to see the motto and promise: *Dem Deutschen Volke* ("To the German People"). The open, airy lobby towers 100 feet high, with 65-foot-tall colors of the German flag. See-through glass doors show the **central legislative chamber.** The message: There will be no secrets in this government. Look inside. Spreading his wings behind the podium is the *Bundestagsadler* (a.k.a. "the fat hen"), a stylized German eagle representing the Bundestag (each branch of government has its own symbolic eagle). Notice the doors marked *Ja* (Yes), *Nein* (No), and *Enthalten* (Abstain)...an homage to the Bundestag's traditional "sheep jump" way of counting votes by exiting the chamber through the corresponding door (although for critical issues, all 669 members vote with electronic cards).

Ride the elevator to the base of the glass **dome.** Pick up the free audioguide and take some time to study the photos and read the circle of captions—around the base of the central funnel—for an excellent exhibit telling the Reichstag story. Then study the surrounding architecture: a broken collage of new on old, torn between antiquity and modernity, like Germany's history. Notice the dome's giant and unobtrusive sunscreen that moves as necessary with the sun. Peer down through the skylight to look over the shoulders of  the elected representatives at work. For Germans, the best view from here is down—keeping a close eye on their government.

Start at the ramp nearest the elevator and wind up to the top of the **double ramp.** Take a 360-degree survey of the city as you hike: The big park is the **Tiergarten,** the "green lungs of Berlin." Beyond that is the **Teufelsberg,** or "Devil's Hill" (built of rubble from the destroyed city in the late 1940s, it was famous during the

Cold War as a powerful ear of the West—notice the telecommunications tower on top). Knowing the bombed-out and bulldozed story of their city, locals say, "You have to be suspicious when you see the nice, green park." Find the **Victory Column** (Siegessäule), glimmering in the middle of the park. This was moved by Hitler in the 1930s from in front of the Reichstag to its present position in the Tiergarten, as the first step in creating a grandiose axis he envisioned for postwar Berlin. Next, scenes of the new Berlin spiral into your view—**Potsdamer Platz,** marked by the conical glass tower that houses Sony's European headquarters. Continue circling left, and find the green chariot atop the **Brandenburg Gate.** The **Memorial to the Murdered Jews of Europe** stretches south of the Brandenburg Gate. Next, you'll see **former East Berlin** and the city's next huge construction zone, with a forest of 300-foot-tall skyscrapers in the works. Notice the TV Tower, the Berlin Cathedral's massive dome, and the golden dome of the New Synagogue.

Follow the train tracks in the distance to the left toward Berlin's huge main train station, the **Hauptbahnhof.** Complete your spin-tour with the blocky **Chancellery,** nicknamed by Berliners "the washing machine." It may look like a pharaoh's tomb, but it's the office and home of Germany's most powerful person, the chancellor (currently Angela Merkel). To remind the chancellor who he or she works for, the Reichstag, at about 130 feet, is about six feet taller than the Chancellery.

Continue spiraling up. You'll pass all the same sights again, twice, from a higher vantage point.

Near the Reichstag

Memorial to Politicians Who Opposed Hitler—Near the road in front of the Reichstag, enmeshed in all the security appara-

tus, is a memorial of slate stones embedded in the ground. This row of slate slabs (which looks like a fancy slate bicycle rack) is a memorial to the 96 members of the Reichstag (the equivalent of our members of Congress) who were persecuted and murdered because their politics didn't agree with Chancellor Hitler's. They were part of the Weimar Republic, the weak and ill-fated attempt at post-WWI democracy in Germany. These were the people who could have stopped Hitler...so they became his first victims. Each slate slab remembers one man—his name, party (mostly KPD—Communists, and SPD—Social Democrats), and the date and location of his death—generally in concentration camps. (*KZ* stands for "concentration camp.") They are honored here, in front of the building in which they worked.

• *Facing the Reichstag, you can take a short side-trip to the river by circling around to the left of the building.*

Spree Riverfront—Admire the wonderful architecture incorporating the Spree River into the people's world. It's a poignant spot because this river was once a symbol of division—the East German regime put nets underwater to stymie those desperate enough for freedom to swim to the West. When kings ruled Prussia, government buildings went right up to the water. But today, the city is incorporating

the river thoughtfully into a people-friendly cityscape. From the Reichstag, a delightful riverside path leads around the curve, past "beach cafés," to the Chancellery. For a slow, low-impact glide past this zone, consider a river cruise (see page 664; we'll pass the starting point—on Museum Island—later on this walk). The fine bridges symbolize the connection of East and West.

• *Leaving the Reichstag, return to the busy road, and cross the street at your first opportunity, to the big park. Walk (with the park on your right) to the corner. Along the railing at the corner of Scheidemannstrasse and Ebertstrasse is a small memorial of white crosses. This is the...*

Berlin Wall Victims Memorial—This monument—now largely usurped by business promos and impromptu wacko book stalls—

commemorates some of the East Berliners who died trying to cross the Wall. Of these people, many perished within months of the wall's construction on August 13, 1961. Most died trying to swim the river to freedom. The monument used to stand right on the Berlin Wall behind the Reichstag. Notice that the last person killed while trying to escape was 20-year-old Chris Gueffroy, who died nine months before the Wall fell. (He was shot through the heart in no-man's-land.) For more on the Wall, see "The Berlin Wall (and Its Fall)" sidebar on page 706.

In the park just behind the monument, another memorial is planned. It will remember the Roma (Gypsy) victims of the Holocaust. The Roma, as persecuted by the Nazis as the Jews were, lost the same percentage of their population to Hitler.

The Brandenburg Gate, Arch of Peace

Two hundred years ago, the Brandenburg Gate was designed as an arch of peace, crowned by the Goddess of Peace and showing Mars sheathing his sword. The Nazis misused it as a gate of triumph and aggression. Today a Room of Silence, built into the gate, is dedicated to the peaceful message of the original Brandenburg Gate (daily 11:00-18:00). As you consider the history of Berlin in this room—which is carefully not dedicated to any particular religion—you may be inspired to read the prayer of the United Nations:

"Oh Lord, our planet Earth is only a small star in space. It is our duty to transform it into a planet whose creatures are no longer tormented by war, hunger, and fear, no longer senselessly divided by race, color, and ideology. Give us courage and strength to begin this task today so that our children and our children's children shall one day carry the name of man with pride."

Unfortunately, the project is stalled for lack of a well-funded individual or group to finance it.

• *From here, head to the Brandenburg Gate. Stay on the park side of the street for a better view of the gate ahead. As you cross at the light, notice the double row of* **cobblestones**—*it goes around the city, marking where the Wall used to stand.*

Brandenburg Gate and Nearby

▲▲**Brandenburg Gate (Brandenburger Tor)**—The historic Brandenburg Gate (1791) was the grandest—and is the last survi-

vor—of 14 gates in Berlin's old city wall (this one led to the neighboring city of Brandenburg). The gate was the symbol of Prussian Berlin—and later the symbol of a divided Berlin. It's crowned by a majestic four-horse chariot with the Goddess of Peace at the reins. Napoleon took this statue to the Louvre in Paris in 1806. After the Prussians defeated Napoleon and got it back (1813), she was renamed the Goddess of Victory.

The gate sat unused, part of a sad circle dance called the Wall, for more than 25 years. Now postcards all over town show the ecstatic day—November 9, 1989—when the world enjoyed the sight of happy Berliners jamming the gate like flowers on a parade float. Pause a minute and think about struggles for freedom—past and present. (There's actually a special room built into the gate for this purpose—see the sidebar.) Around the gate, look at the information boards with pictures of how this area changed throughout the 20th century. There's a TI within the gate (daily 9:30-19:00, until 18:30 Nov-March, S-Bahn: Brandenburger Tor).

The Brandenburg Gate, the center of old Berlin, sits on a major boulevard running east to west through Berlin. The western segment, called Strasse des 17 Juni (named for a workers' uprising against the DDR government on June 17, 1953), stretches for four miles from the Brandenburg Gate and Victory Column to the Olympic Stadium. But we'll follow this city axis in the opposite direction, east, walking along a stretch called Unter den Linden—into the core of old imperial Berlin and past what was once the palace of the Hohenzollern family who ruled Prussia and then Germany. The palace—the reason for just about all you'll see—is a phantom sight, long gone. Alexanderplatz, which marks the end of this walk, is near the base of the giant TV Tower hovering in the distance.

• Cross through the gate into...

▲Pariser Platz—"Parisian Square," so named after the Prussians defeated Napoleon in 1813, was once filled with important government buildings—all bombed to smithereens in World War II. For decades, it was an unrecognizable, deserted no-man's-land—cut off from both East and West by the Wall. But now it's rebuilt, and the banks, hotels, and embassies that were here before the bombing have reclaimed their original places—with a few additions: a palace of coffee (Starbucks) and the small Kennedys Museum (described later). The winners of World War II enjoy this prime real estate: The American, French, British, and Soviet (now Russian) embassies are all on or near this square.

Face the gate and look to your left. The **US Embassy** reopened in its historic location in 2008. The building has been controversial: For safety's sake, Uncle Sam wanted more of a security zone around the building, but the Germans wanted to keep Pariser Platz a welcoming people zone. (Throughout the world, American embassies are the most fortified buildings in town.) The compromise: The extra security the US wanted is built into the structure. Easy-on-the-eyes barriers keep potential car bombs at a distance, and its front door is on the side farthest from the Brandenburg Gate.

Just to the left, the **DZ Bank building** is by Frank Gehry, the unconventional American architect famous for Bilbao's organic Guggenheim Museum, Prague's Dancing House, Seattle's Experience Music Project, Chicago's Millennium Park, and Los Angeles' Walt Disney Concert Hall. Gehry fans might be surprised at the DZ Bank building's low profile. Structures on Pariser

Platz are designed to be bland so as not to draw attention away from the Brandenburg Gate. (The glassy facade of the Academy of Arts, next to Gehry's building, is controversial for drawing attention to itself.) For your fix of the good old Gehry, step into the lobby and check out its undulating interior. It's a fish—and you feel like you're both inside and outside of it. The architect's vision is explained on a nearby plaque. The best view of Gehry's creation is from the Reichstag dome.

• *Next door to Gehry's building is the **Academy of Arts** (Akademie der Kunst), with its notorious glass facade. Its doors lead to a lobby (with a small food counter, daily 10:00-22:00), which leads directly to the vast...*

▲▲Memorial to the Murdered Jews of Europe (Denkmal für die Ermordeten Juden Europas)

—This Holocaust memorial, consisting of 2,711 gravestone-like pillars (called "stelae") and

completed in 2005, is an essential stop for any visit to Berlin. It was the first formal, German government-sponsored Holocaust memorial. Jewish American architect Peter Eisenman won the competition for the commission (and built it on time and on budget—€27 million). It's been criticized for focusing on just one of the groups targeted by the Nazis, but the German government has promised to erect memorials to other victims.

Cost and Hours: Free, memorial always open; information center open Tue-Sun 10:00-20:00, Oct-March until 19:00, closed Mon year-round; last entry 45 minutes before closing, S-Bahn: Brandenburger Tor or Potsdamer Platz, tel. 030/2639-4336, www.stiftung-denkmal.de. The €4 audioguide augments the experience.

Touring the Memorial: The pillars are made of hollow concrete, each chemically coated for easy removal of graffiti. (Ironically, the chemical coating was developed by a subsidiary of the former IG Farben group—the company infamous for supplying the Zyklon B gas used in Nazi death camps.) The number of pillars, symbolic of nothing, is simply how many fit on the provided land.

Once you enter the memorial, notice that people seem to appear and disappear between the columns, and that no matter where you are, the exit always seems to be up. Is it a labyrinth...a symbolic cemetery...and intentionally disorienting? It's entirely up to the visitor to derive the meaning, while pondering this horrible chapter in human history.

The pondering takes place under the sky. For the learning, go under the field of concrete pillars to the state-of-the-art **information center** (there may be a short line because visitors must go through a security check). Inside, a thought-provoking exhibit (well-explained in English) studies the Nazi system of extermination and humanizes the victims, while also

providing space for silent reflection. In the Starting Hall, exhibits trace the historical context of the Nazi and WWII era, while six portraits—representing the six million Jewish victims—look out on the visitors. The Room of Dimensions has glowing boxes in the floor containing diaries, letters, and final farewells penned by Holocaust victims. The Room of Families presents case-studies of 15 Jewish families from around Europe, to more fully convey the European Jewish experience. Remember: Behind these 15 stories are millions more tales of despair, tragedy, and survival. In the Room of Names, a continually running soundtrack lists the names and brief biographical sketches of Holocaust victims; reading the names of all those murdered would take more than six and a half years. The Room of Sites documents some 220 different places of genocide. You'll also find exhibits about other Holocaust monuments and memorials, a searchable database of victims, and a video archive of interviews with survivors.

The memorial's location—where the Wall once stood—is coincidental. Nazi propagandist Joseph Goebbels' bunker was discovered during the work and left buried under the northeast corner of the memorial. Hitler's bunker is just 200 yards away, under a nondescript parking lot. Such Nazi sites are intentionally left hidden to discourage neo-Nazi elements from creating shrines.

• *Now backtrack to Pariser Platz (through the yellow building). Across the square (next to Starbucks), consider dropping into...*

The Kennedys Museum—This crisp private enterprise facing the Brandenburg Gate recalls John F. Kennedy's Germany trip in 1963, with great photos and video clips as well as a photographic shrine to the Kennedy clan in America. It's a small, overpriced, yet delightful experience with interesting mementos—such as old campaign buttons and posters, and JFK's notes with the phonetic "Ish bin ein Bearleener." Jacqueline Kennedy commented on how strange it was that this—not even in his native language—was her husband's most quotable quote. Most of the exhibit consists of photographs that, if nothing else, spark a nostalgic longing for the days of Camelot.

Cost and Hours: €7, includes special exhibits, reduced to €3.50 for a broad array of visitors—dream up a discount and ask

Imagining Hitler in the 21st Century

More than six decades after the end of World War II, the bunker where Hitler killed himself lies hidden underneath a Berlin parking lot. While the Churchill War Rooms are a major sight in London, no one wants to turn Hitler's final stronghold into a tourist attraction.

Germans tread lightly on their past. It took 65 years for the Germany History Museum to organize its first exhibit on the life of Hitler. Even then, the exhibit was careful not to give neo-Nazis any excuse to celebrate—even the size of the Hitler portraits was kept to a minimum.

The image of Hitler has been changing in Germany. No longer is he exclusively an evil mass murderer—sometimes he is portrayed as a nervous wreck, such as in the 2004 film *Downfall*, or as an object of derision. He's even a wax figure in the Berlin branch of Madame Tussauds.

But 21st-century Germans still treat the subject with extraordinary sensitivity. The Bavarian state government holds the copyright to Hitler's political manifesto—*Mein Kampf*—and won't allow any version to be published in German, even one annotated by historians (although it is readily available on the Internet and in the US). Any visit to Hitler's mountain retreat in Berchtesgaden includes a stop at the Nazi Documentation Center, where visitors see Nazi artifacts carefully placed in their historical context.

Many visitors to Berlin are curious about Hitler sites, but few artifacts of that dark period survive. The German Resistance Memorial is presented in German only and difficult for the tourist to appreciate (though it has a helpful audioguide in English; see page 721). The Topography of Terror is a fascinating exhibit located in a rebuilt hall on the same spot where the SS and Gestapo headquarters once stood (with complete English descriptions). Hitler's bunker is completely gone (near Potsdamer Platz). The best way to learn about Hitler sites is to take a Third Reich tour offered by one of the many local walking-tour companies (see "Tours in Berlin," page 659).

It's a balancing act, but when it comes to *der Führer,* Germans seem to be confronting their regrettable past.

for it, daily 10:00-18:00, Pariser Platz 4a, www.thekennedys.de, tel. 030/2065-3570.

• *Leave Pariser Platz and begin strolling...*

▲▲Unter den Linden

The street called Unter den Linden is the heart of former East Berlin. In Berlin's good old days, Unter den Linden was one of Europe's grand boulevards. In the 15th century, this carriageway

Eastern Berlin's Unter den Linden

HAUPTBAHNHOF & EurAide

500 meters

1/2 Mile

ORANIENBURGER

KUNSTHAUS TACHELES

Hauptbahnhof

Oranienburger Tor

FRIEDRICHSTR.

JOHANNIS-

Washington Platz

LUISENSTR.

SCHUMANNSTR.

REINHARD. STR.

ALBRECHTSTR.

ZIEGEL-

ALT-MOABIT

KAPELLE-UFER

ERNST-BISMARCK-STR.

MARIENSTR.

AM WEIDENDAMM

Spree River

HUMBOLDTHAFEN

(TUNNEL)

ELEVATED RAILWAY

Friedrich-strasse

PLANK.

OTTO-VON-BISMARCK-ALLEE

SCHIFFBAUERDAMM

GEORGENSTR.

CHANCELLERY

Bundestag ⓤ

PARLIAMENT

❸

REICHSTAG

DOROTHEEN-STR.

NEUSTÄDTISCHE KIRCHSTR.

MITTELSTR.

FRIEDRICH-STRASSE

HAUS DER KULTUREN DER WELT

Platz der Republik

❷ ❶

Bus #100 Ⓑ

WALK BEGINS

SCHADOW

❾

⓫

To Bahnhof Zoo via Bus #100

SCHEIDEMANNSTR.

❹

Pariser

UNTER DEN

To Victory Column

BRANDENBURG GATE

❺

Platz

❻

Unter den Linden

❿

KOMISCHE OPER

STRASSE DES 17 JUNI

❼

BEHRENSTRASSE

MEMORIAL TO THE MURDERED JEWS OF EUROPE

Französische Strasse Ⓤ

Former Course of The Wall

❽

HANNAH-ARENDT-STRASSE

JÄGERSTR.

TAUBENSTR.

T i e r g a r t e n

IN DEN MINISTER-GÄRTEN

Mohren-strasse

MAUERSTR.

GLINKAP

MOHRENSTR.

ENTLASTUNGS

LENNÉSTR.

To Kulturforum

EBERTSTRASSE

Mohren-strasse Ⓤ

To Potsdamer Platz

VOSSSTR.

To Museum of the Wall at Checkpoint Charlie

❶ Reichstag
❷ Memorial to Politicians Who Opposed Hitler
❸ Spree Riverfront
❹ Berlin Wall Victims Memorial
❺ Brandenburg Gate
❻ Pariser Platz
❼ US Embassy
❽ Memorial to the Murdered Jews of Europe
❾ The Kennedys Museum
❿ Russian Embassy
⓫ Berlin Story Bookstore

led from the palace to the hunting grounds (today's big Tiergarten). In the 17th century, Hohenzollern princes and princesses moved in and built their palaces here so they could be near the Prussian king.

Named centuries ago for its thousand linden trees, this was the most elegant street of Prussian Berlin before Hitler's time, and the main drag of East

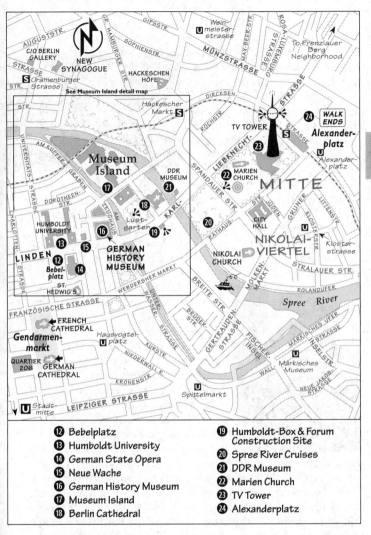

BERLIN

⑫ Bebelplatz
⑬ Humboldt University
⑭ German State Opera
⑮ Neue Wache
⑯ German History Museum
⑰ Museum Island
⑱ Berlin Cathedral
⑲ Humboldt-Box & Forum Construction Site
⑳ Spree River Cruises
㉑ DDR Museum
㉒ Marien Church
㉓ TV Tower
㉔ Alexanderplatz

Berlin after his reign. Hitler replaced the venerable trees—many 250 years old—with Nazi flags. Popular discontent actually drove him to replant the trees. Today, Unter den Linden is no longer a depressing Cold War cul-de-sac, and its pre-Hitler strolling café ambience has returned. Notice how it is divided, roughly at Friedrichstrasse, into a business section that stretches toward the Brandenburg Gate, and a culture section that spreads out toward Alexanderplatz. Frederick the Great wanted to have culture, mainly the opera and the university, closer to his palace, and to keep business (read: banks) farther away, near the city walls.

➲ Self-Guided Walk: As you walk toward the giant TV Tower, the big building you see jutting out into the street on your right is the **Hotel Adlon.** In its

heyday, it hosted such notables as Charlie Chaplin, Albert Einstein, and Greta Garbo. This was the setting for Garbo's most famous line, "I vant to be alone," uttered in the film *Grand Hotel.* Damaged by the Russians just after World War II, the original hotel was closed with the construction of the nearby Wall in 1961 and later demolished. The grand Adlon was rebuilt in 1997. It was here that the late Michael Jackson shocked millions by dangling his baby, Blanket, over the railing (second balcony up, on the side of the hotel next to the Academy of Art). See how far you can get inside.

Descend into the Brandenburger Tor S-Bahn station ahead of you. It's one of Berlin's former **ghost subway stations.** During

the Cold War, most underground train tunnels were simply blocked at the border. But a few Western lines looped through the East. To make a little hard Western cash, the Eastern government rented the use of these tracks to the West, but the stations (which happened to be in East Berlin) were strictly off-limits. For 28 years, the stations were unused, as Western trains slowly passed through and passengers saw only eerie DDR (East German) guards and lots of cobwebs. Literally within days of the fall of the Wall, these stations were reopened, and today they are a time warp (looking essentially as they did when built in 1931, with dreary old green tiles and original signage). Walk along the track (the walls are lined with historic photos of the Reichstag through the ages) and exit on the other side, following signs to *Russische Botschaft* (the Russian Embassy).

The **Russian Embassy** was the first big postwar building project in East Berlin. It's built in the powerful, simplified Neoclassical style that Stalin liked. While not as important now as it was a few years ago, it's as immense as ever. It flies the Russian white, blue, and red. Find the hammer-and-sickle motif decorating the window frames—a reminder of the days when Russia was the USSR.

Continuing past the Aeroflot airline offices, look across Glinkastrasse to the right to see the back of the **Komische Oper** (Comic Opera; program and view of ornate interior posted in window). While the exterior is ugly, the fine old theater interior—amazingly missed by WWII bombs—survives.

Back on the main drag, on the left at #40, is an entertaining bookstore, Berlin Story. In addition to a wide range of English-language books, this shop has a modest (but overpriced) museum and a wide range of nostalgic knickknacks from the Cold War. The West lost no time in consuming the East; consequently, some are feeling a wave of *Ost*-algia for the old days of East Berlin. At election time, a surprising number of the former East Berlin's voters still opt for the extreme left party, which has ties to the bygone Communist Party, although the East-West divide is no longer at the forefront of most voters' minds.

One symbol of that communist era has been given a reprieve. As you continue to Friedrichstrasse, look at the DDR-style pedestrian lights, and you'll realize that someone had a sense of humor back then. The perky red and green men—*Ampelmännchen*—were recently under threat of replacement by far less jaunty Western-style signs. Fortunately, after a 10-year court battle, the DDR signals were kept after all.

At **Friedrichstrasse,** look right. Before the war, the Unter den Linden/Friedrichstrasse intersection was the heart of Berlin. In the 1920s, Berlin was famous for its anything-goes love of life. This was the cabaret drag, a springboard to stardom for young and vampy entertainers like Marlene Dietrich. (Born in 1901, Dietrich starred in the one of the first German talkies—*The Blue Angel*—and then headed straight to Hollywood.) Over the last few years, this boulevard—lined with super department stores (such as Galeries Lafayette) and big-time hotels (such as the Hilton and Regent)—is attempting to replace Ku'damm as the grand commerce-and-café boulevard of Berlin. More recently, western Berlin is retaliating with some new stores of its own. And so far, Friedrichstrasse gets little more than half the pedestrian traffic that Ku'damm gets in the West. Why? Locals complain that this area has no daily life—no supermarkets, not much ethnic street food, and so on. Consider detouring to Galeries Lafayette, with its cool marble-and-glass, waste-of-space interior (Mon-Sat 9:30-20:00, closed Sun; check out the vertical garden on its front wall, belly up to its amazing ground-floor viewpoint, or have lunch in its recommended basement cafeteria).

If you continued down Friedrichstrasse, you'd wind up at the sights listed under "South of Unter den Linden," on page 699—including the Museum of the Wall at Checkpoint Charlie (a

10-minute walk from here). But for now, continue along Unter den Linden. At the corner, the **VW Automobil Forum** shows off the latest models from the many car companies owned by VW (free, corner of Friedrichstrasse and Unter den Linden, VW art gallery and handy VW WC in the basement).

As you explore Berlin, you may see big, colorful **water pipes** running overground. Wherever there are big construction projects, streets are laced with these drainage pipes. Berlin's high water table means that any new basement with lots of pumping out.

Continue down Unter den Linden a few more blocks, past the large equestrian statue of Frederick the Great, and turn right into the square called **Bebelplatz.** Stand on the glass window set into the pavement in the center.

Frederick the Great—who ruled from 1740 to 1786—established Prussia not just as a military power, but as a cultural and intellectual heavyweight as well. This square was the center of the "new Athens" that Frederick envisioned. His grand palace was just down the street (explained later).

Look down through the glass you're standing on: The room of empty bookshelves is a memorial repudiating the notorious Nazi **book burning.** It was on this square in 1933 that staff and students from the university threw 20,000 newly forbidden books (like Einstein's) into a huge bonfire on the orders of the Nazi propaganda minister Joseph Goebbels. A plaque nearby reminds us of the prophetic quote by the German poet Heinrich Heine. In 1820, he wrote, "Where they burn books, at the end they also burn people." The Nazis despised Heine because he was Jewish before converting to Christianity. A century later, his books were among those that went up in flames on this spot.

Great buildings front Bebelplatz. Survey the square counterclockwise:

Humboldt University, across Unter den Linden, is one of Europe's greatest. Marx and Lenin (not the brothers or the sisters) studied here, as did the Grimms (both brothers) and more than two dozen Nobel Prize winners. Einstein, who was Jewish, taught here until taking a spot at Princeton in 1932 (smart guy). Used-book merchants set up their tables in front of the university, selling books by many of the authors whose works were once condemned to Nazi flames just across the street.

The former **state library** (labeled *Juristische Fakultät,* facing

Bebelplatz on the right with your back to Humboldt University) is where Vladimir Lenin studied during much of his exile from Russia. If you climb to the second floor of the library and go through the door opposite the stairs, you'll see a 1968 vintage stained-glass window depicting Lenin's life's work with almost biblical reverence. On the ground floor is Tim's Espressobar, a great little café with light food, student prices, and garden seating (€3 plates, Mon-Fri 8:00-20:00, Sat 9:00-16:00, closed Sun, handy WC).

The round, Catholic **St. Hedwig's Church**—nicknamed the "upside-down teacup"—was built by the pragmatic Frederick the Great to encourage the integration of Catholic Silesians after his empire annexed their region in 1742. (St. Hedwig is the patron saint of Silesia, a region now shared by Germany, Poland, and the Czech Republic, and covered in the Görlitz chapter.) When asked what the church should look like, Frederick literally took a Silesian teacup and slammed it upside-down on a table. Like all Catholic churches in Berlin, St. Hedwig's is not on the street, but stuck in a kind of back lot—indicating inferiority to Protestant churches. You can step inside the church to see the cheesy DDR government renovation.

The **German State Opera** was bombed in 1941, rebuilt to bolster morale and to celebrate its centennial in 1943, and bombed again in 1945. Now it's being renovated (through 2013).

Continue down Unter den Linden. The next square on your right holds the **Opernpalais,** formerly a Prussian royal residence. Preening with fancy prewar elegance, it hosts the recommended but pricey Operncafé. With the best desserts and the longest dessert bar in Europe, it's popular with Berliners for *Kaffee und Kuchen.*

Cross Unter den Linden to the university side. The Greek-temple-like building set in the small chestnut-tree-filled park is the **Neue Wache** (the emperor's "New Guardhouse," from 1816).

 Converted to a memorial to the victims of fascism in 1960, the structure was transformed again, after the Wall fell, into a national memorial. Look inside, where a replica of the Käthe Kollwitz statue, *Mother with Her Dead Son,* is surrounded by thought-provoking silence. This marks the tombs of Germany's unknown soldier and an unknown concentration camp victim. The inscription in front reads, "To the victims of war and tyranny." Read the entire statement in English (on wall, left of entrance). The memorial, open to the sky,

incorporates the elements—sunshine, rain, snow—falling on this modern-day *pietà*.

• *After the Neue Wache, the next building you'll see is Berlin's pink-yet-formidable Zeughaus (arsenal). Dating from 1695, it's considered the oldest building on the boulevard and now houses the...*

▲▲▲German History Museum (Deutsches Historisches Museum)

This fantastic museum is a two-part affair: the pink former Prussian arsenal building and the I. M. Pei-designed annex. The main building (fronting Unter den Linden) houses the permanent collection, offering the best look at German history under one roof, anywhere. The modern annex features good temporary exhibits surrounded by the work of a great contemporary architect. While this city has more than its share of hokey "museums" that slap together WWII and Cold War bric-a-brac, then charge too much for admission, this thoughtfully presented museum—with more than 8,000 artifacts telling not just the story of Berlin, but of all Germany—is clearly the top history museum in town.

Cost and Hours: €6, daily 10:00-18:00, Unter den Linden 2, tel. 030/2030-4751, www.dhm.de.

Audioguide: For the most informative visit, invest in the excellent €3 audioguide, with six hours of info to choose from.

Touring the Museum: The permanent collection packs two huge rectangular floors of the old arsenal building with historical objects, photographs, and models—all well-described in English and intermingled with multimedia stations to help put everything in context. From the lobby, head upstairs (to the "**first floor**") and work your way chronologically down. This floor traces German history from 1 B.C. to 1918, with exhibits on early cultures, the Middle Ages, Reformation, Thirty Years' War, German Empire, and World War I. You'll see a Roman floor mosaic, lots of models of higgledy-piggledy medieval towns and castles, tapestries, suits of armor, busts of great Germans, a Turkish tent from the Ottoman siege of Vienna (1683), flags from German unification in 1871 (the first time "Germany" existed as a nation), exhibits on everyday life in the tenements of the Industrial Revolution, and much more.

History marches on through the 20th century on the **ground floor,** including the Weimar Republic, Nazism, World War II, Allied occupation, and a divided Germany. Propaganda posters trumpet Germany's would-be post-WWI savior, Adolf Hitler. Look for the model of the impossibly huge, 950-foot-high, 180,000-capacity domed hall Hitler wanted to erect in the heart of Berlin, which he planned to re-envision as Welthauptstadt Germania, the "world capital" of his far-reaching Third Reich.

Another model shows the sobering reality of Hitler's grandiosity: a crematorium at Auschwitz-Birkenau concentration camp in occupied Poland. The exhibit wraps up with chunks of the Berlin Wall, reunification, and a quick look at Germany today.

For architecture buffs, the big attraction is the **Pei annex** behind the history museum, which complements the museum with

often-fascinating temporary exhibits. From the old building, cross through the courtyard (with the Pei glass canopy overhead) to reach the annex. A striking glassed-in spiral staircase unites four floors with surprising views and lots of light. It's here that you'll experience why Pei—famous for his glass pyramid at Paris' Louvre—is called the "perfector of classical modernism," "master of light," and a magician of uniting historical buildings with new ones. (If the museum is closed, or you don't have a ticket, venture down the street—Hinter dem Giesshaus—to the left of the museum to see the Pei annex from the outside.)

• *Back on Unter den Linden, head toward the Spree River. Just before the bridge, wander left along the canal through a tiny but colorful arts-and-crafts market (weekends only; a larger flea market is just outside the Pergamon Museum). Continue up the riverbank two blocks and cross the footbridge over the Spree. This takes you to...*

Museum Island (Museumsinsel)

This island is filled with some of Berlin's most impressive museums (all part of the Staatliche Museen zu Berlin). The complex

was originally built around 1871, when Germany was newly unified as one nation—and Berlin dubbed itself the "Athens on the Spree River." The island's imposing Neoclassical buildings host five grand museums: the **Pergamon Museum** (classical antiquities, including the top-notch Pergamon Altar, with its temple and frieze); the **Neues Museum** ("New Museum," famous for its Egyptian collection with the bust of Queen Nefertiti); the **Old National Gallery** (Alte Nationalgalerie, 19th-century art, mostly German Romantic and Realist paintings); the **Altes Museum** ("Old Museum," more antiquities); and the **Bode Museum** (European statuary and paintings through the ages, coins, and Byzantine art). The entire

BERLIN

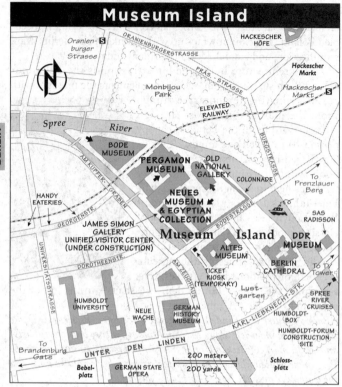

Museum Island

ensemble is being renovated, and when the project is finished, this will be one of the most impressive museum zones in Europe.

• *The museums of Museum Island, worth the better part of a sightseeing day, are described in more detail below. To bypass the museums and other sights on Museum Island for now, skip ahead to the "Museum Island to Alexanderplatz" section on page 697.*

The Museums of Museum Island

A formidable renovation is under way on Museum Island. When complete, a grand entry and unified visitors center will serve the island's five venerable but separate museums, and tunnels will lace the complex together (intended completion date: 2015, www.museums insel-berlin.de). In the meantime, pardon their dust.

Cost: The €16 Museum Island Pass combo-ticket—covering all five museums— is a far better value than buying individual

€8-12 entries (prices can vary depending on special exhibits). All five museums are also included in the city's €19 Museumspass (both passes described on page 651). Special exhibits—including the much-touted 2012 "Pergamon: Panorama of the Ancient Metropolis"—are extra.

Hours: Pergamon, Altes, and Bode museums open daily 10:00-18:00, Thu until 22:00; Old National Gallery open same hours except closed Mon; Neues Museum open daily 10:00-18:00, Thu-Sat until 20:00; tel. 030/266-424-242, www.smb.museum.

Required Reservation for Pergamon and Neues Museums: Visiting either the Pergamon Museum or the Neues Museum requires a *Zeitfensterticket* ("time-window ticket") that gives you a 30-minute time slot for entering the museum (included with admission; separate appointments required for each museum). Once inside, you can stay as long as you like. Reserve your time online (www.smb.museum) or in person at any Museum Island ticket office.

Crowd Control: You can usually get a time slot within about an hour, often sooner—except at the busiest times (Sat and Sun mornings), when you may have to wait longer. The least-crowded times are evenings when the museums are open late (Thu evening for the Pergamon Museum, Thu-Sat evenings for the Neues).

The temporary kiosk on Bodestrasse functions as the ticket booth for the Neues Museum and comes with avoidable lines. Long ticket-buying lines also plague the Pergamon Museum. Avoid them by purchasing your museum pass (and getting your assigned entry time) at one of the island's three never-crowded museums: Altes, Bode, or Old National Gallery. (From Unter den Linden, Altes is most convenient; if coming from Prenzlauer Berg, try the Bode.)

Planning Your Time: I'd start at the Bode, where I'd ask for an entry time to the Pergamon Museum in about an hour, and a ticket to the Neues Museum for 1.5 hours after that. Tickets and appointments in hand, spend any time left before your Pergamon time slot browsing the Bode. Then enjoy the Pergamon collection, where the art is earth-shaking but easy to see in an hour. If you have any extra time before your Neues appointment, nip into the time-tunnel Old National Gallery. Step into the Neues Museum within 30 minutes of your entry time, and be prepared to linger. For lunch nearby, follow the elevated train tracks away from the Pergamon down Georgenstrasse (see suggestions on page 749).

Getting There: The nearest S-Bahn station is Hackescher Markt, about a 10-minute walk away. From hotels in the Prenzlauer Berg, ride tram #M-1 to the end of line, and you're right at the Pergamon Museum.

▲▲▲Pergamon Museum (Pergamonmuseum)

The star attraction of this world-class museum, part of Berlin's Collection of Classical Antiquities (Antikensammlung), is the fantastic and gigantic Pergamon Altar. The Babylonian Ishtar Gate (slathered with glazed blue tiles from the 6th century B.C.) and the museum's many ancient Greek, Mesopotamian, Roman, and early Islamic treasures are also impressive.

Audioguide: Make ample use of the superb audioguide (included with admission)—it will broaden your experience. Punching #10 on the audioguide gets you the "Pergamon in 30 Minutes" general tour. Or follow my quicker, more succinct self-guided tour, next.

◐ Self-Guided Tour: With your timed entry and museum pass, walk boldly by the long line of people who don't have or read guidebooks, and go directly in.

There's a lot to see in this museum (everything is well-described by posted English information and the included audioguide). The best plan for the casual visitor is to focus on a few highlights.

From the entrance, walk straight ahead to find the museum's namesake, the **Pergamon Altar.** Actually a 65-foot-wide temple, this "altar" comes from the second-century B.C. Greek city of Pergamon (near the west coast of today's Turkey). The Pergamon Altar was just one component of a spectacular hilltop ensemble—temples, sanctuaries, palaces, theaters, and other buildings erected to honor the gods—modeled after the Acropolis in Athens. (See a model of the complete Pergamon Acropolis to the right, as you face the stairs.)

Pergamon was excavated from 1878 to 1886 by German archaeologist Carl Humann, who unearthed fragments of the temple's frieze all over the site (many pieces had been "recycled" as building materials in later structures). The bits and pieces were brought here to Berlin, reassembled on this replica of the temple, and put on display in this purpose-built museum in 1930.

The temple replica re-creates the western third of the original building. Stairs lead up to a chamber with a small sacrificial altar, where priests and priestesses sacrificed and burned animals, while toga-clad Greeks assembled in awe at the foot of the stairs below.

Surviving pieces of a 269-foot-long frieze that wrapped around the entire temple dramatically spill onto the stairs and around the room. Called the **Gigantomachy Frieze,** it shows the Greek gods under Zeus and Athena defeating the giants in a dramatic pig pile of mythological mayhem. Imagine how much more evocative these sculptures once were, slathered in color-ful paint, gold, and silver trim.

So what's the fight about? Long before the time of man, an epic struggle pitted the titans against the gods. When the gods won, they thrust their foes into a miserable underworld (the mythologi-cal equivalent of purgatory) and settled in for a comfy period of rule atop Mount Olympus. But the troublesome race of giants—children of the earth goddess Gaia, mother of the titans—sought revenge. The giants had legs of slither-ing snakes that kept them in contact with the ground, allowing Gaia to make them immortal. This frieze captures a pivotal event, when the giants Alkyoneus and Porphyrion led a rebellion of their race against the gods. (The people of Pergamon appreciated the parallels between this story and their own noble struggle against unenlightened barbarians.)

With your back to the altar steps, look at the right end of the frieze to find panels with Zeus and Athena, locked in combat with the giants. Faint surviving labels on the cornice above the statues—in Greek, of course—help identify the combatants; the modern English letters below may prove more helpful.

Find the **Athena** panel. Athena (faceless, in the center, with the shield) and Nike (all that's left are her wings, right arm, and

left leg) pull the chief giant Alkyoneus (his snake legs curling around his bicep) up by his hair—breaking his connection to the earth, the source of his immor-tality. Below them, Gaia—the mother of the giants—rises up from her subterranean realm to lend a hand. (See the fear in Gaia's and Alkyoneus' tortured eyes.) Alkyoneus would survive this brush with Athena, only to be killed soon after by Hercules. (The statue of Hercules is missing—all that survives is one pathetic paw of his lion pelt.)

The **Zeus** panel shows the (headless) king of the gods raining lightning bolts down on his enemies—including the snake-legged

Porphyrion, with his back(side) toward us. Notice Zeus' disembodied right hand up above, ready to pitch some serious heat. Fans of Greek mythology can take a slow walk along the entire length of the frieze, identifying their favorite gods and giants...the gang's all here. Before long, the giants will be history, and the gods can go back about their usual business of conspiring against each other and impregnating mortals.

Facing the altar stairs, go through the door to your left. The intricate, ancient Greek **mosaic floor** is finely assembled from miniscule pebbles, with a particularly impressive floral motif decorating the border. In the otherwise undecorated box in the middle, in what looks like an ancient Post-It note, you can see where the artist "signed" his work. The Athena statue standing in the middle of the room is a replica of one that once stood at the center of Athens' Acropolis. Turn

around to see the doorway you just came through, surrounded by the original, double-decker ornamental entryway to the Pergamon Acropolis. Ancient pilgrims who had come from far and wide to worship the gods in Pergamon passed through here on their way to the altar.

Return to the altar room, cross straight through it, and go out the door on the far side. From Pergamon, flash-forward 300 years (and travel south 110 miles) to the ancient Roman city of

Miletus. Dominating this room (on your right) is the 95-foot-wide, 55-foot-high **Market Gate of Miletus**—destroyed by an earthquake centuries ago and now painstakingly reconstructed here in Berlin. The exquisite mosaic floor from a Roman

villa in Miletus has two parts: In the square panel, the musician Orpheus strokes his lyre to charm the animals; in stark contrast, in the nearby rectangular mosaic (from an adjacent room), hunters pursue wild animals.

Step through the market gate and all the way back to 575 B.C., to the Fertile Crescent—Mesopotamia (today's Iraq). The Assyrian ruler Nebuchadnezzar II, who amassed a vast empire and enormous wealth, wanted to build a suitably impressive processional entryway to his capital city, Babylon, to honor the goddess Ishtar.

His creation, the **Ishtar Gate,** inspired awe and obedience in anyone who came to his city. This is a reconstruction, using some original components. The gate itself is embellished with two animals: a bull and a mythical dragon-like combination of lion, cobra, eagle,  and scorpion. The long hall leading to the main gate—designed for a huge processional of deities to celebrate the new year—is decorated with a chain of blue and yellow glazed tiles with 120 strolling lions (representing the goddess Ishtar). To get the big picture, find the model of the original site in the center of the hall.

These main exhibits are surrounded by smaller galleries. Upstairs is the **Museum of Islamic Art.** It contains fine carpets,  tile work, the Aleppo Room (with ornately painted wooden walls from an early 17th-century home in today's Syria; since it was commissioned by a Christian, it incorporates Arabic, Persian, and biblical themes), and the Mshatta Facade (walls and towers from one of the early eighth-century Umayyad "desert castles," from today's Jordan).

Special Exhibit: Through September of 2012, a temporary rotunda in front of the Pergamon Museum will house a special installation titled **Pergamon: Panorama of the Ancient Metropolis.** This 360-degree wraparound panorama will re-create the ancient Greek hilltop sanctuary that contained the Pergamon Altar, circa A.D. 129 (complete with a massive painting of the landscape, lighting effects to simulate day and night, and sound effects). Inside the main museum, an extensive collection of rarely exhibited artifacts from Pergamon will be on display (not covered by the Museum Island ticket, www.pergamon-panorama.de).

▲▲Neues (New) Museum and Egyptian Collection

Oddly, Museum Island's so-called "new" museum features the oldest stuff around. There are three collections here: the Egyptian Collection (with the famous bust of Queen Nefertiti; floor 0 and parts of floors 1-2), the Museum of Prehistory and Early History (floor 3 and parts of floors 1-2), and some items from the Collection of Classical Antiquities (artifacts from ancient Troy—famously excavated by German adventurer Heinrich Schliemann—and Cyprus, just off the entrance).

The top draw here is the Egyptian art—clearly one of the world's best collections. But let's face it: The main reason to visit is to enjoy one of the great thrills in art appreciation—gazing into the still-young-and-beautiful face of Queen Nefertiti. If you're in a pinch for time, make a beeline to her (floor 2, far corner of Egyptian Collection in room 210; for more on the museum, see www.neues-museum.de).

Audioguide: The fine audioguide (included with admission) celebrates new knowledge about ancient Egyptian civilization and offers fascinating insights into workaday Egyptian life as it describes the vivid papyrus collection, slice-of-life artifacts, and dreamy wax portraits decorating mummy cases.

Touring the Museum: After being damaged in World War II and sitting in ruins for some 40 years, the Neues Museum was recently rebuilt. Everything is well-described by posted English information and the audioguide.

To tour the whole collection, begin by going all the way to the top (floor 3) where you'll find the **prehistory section.** The entire floor is filled with Stone Age, Ice Age, and Bronze Age items. You'll see early human remains, tools, spearheads, and pottery.

The most interesting item on this floor (in corner room 305)

is the tall, conehead-like **Golden Hat,** made of paper-thin hammered gold leaf. Created by an early Celtic civilization in Central Europe, it's particularly exquisite for something so old (from the Bronze Age, around 1000 B.C.). The circles on the hat represent the sun, moon, and other celestial bodies—leading archaeologists to believe that this headwear could double as a calendar, showing how the sun and moon sync up every 19 years.

Down on floor 2, you'll find **early history** exhibits on migrations, barbarians, and ancient Rome (including larger-than-life statues of Helios and an unidentified goddess) as well as a fascinating look at the Dark Ages after the fall of Rome.

Still on floor 2, cross to the other side of the building for the **Egyptian** section. On the way, you'll pass through the impressive Papyrus Collection—a large room of seemingly empty glass cases. Press a button to watch a 3,000-year-old piece of primitive "paper" (made of aquatic reeds) imprinted with primitive text trundle out of its protective home.

Then, finally, in a room all her own, is the 3,000-year-old bust of **Queen Nefertiti** (the wife of King Akhenaton, c. 1340 B.C.)—the most famous piece of Egyptian art in Europe. Called "Berlin's most beautiful woman," Nefertiti has all the right beauty marks: long neck, symmetrical face, and the perfect amount of makeup. And yet, she's not completely idealized. Notice the fine wrinkles that show she's human (though these only enhance her beauty). Like a movie star discreetly sipping a glass of wine at a sidewalk café, Nefertiti seems somehow more dignified in person. The bust never left its studio, but served as a master model for all other portraits of the queen. (That's probably why the left eye was never inlaid.)

BERLIN

How the queen arrived in Germany is a tale out of *Indiana Jones.* The German archaeologist Ludwig Borchardt uncovered her in the Egyptian desert in 1912. The Egyptian Department of Antiquities had first pick of all the artifacts uncovered on their territory. After the first takings, they divided the rest 50/50 with the excavators. When Borchardt presented Nefertiti to the Egyptians, they passed her over, never bothering to examine her closely. Unsubstantiated rumors persist that Borchardt misled the Egyptians in order to keep the bust for himself—rumors that have prompted some Egyptians to call for the return of Nefertiti (just as the Greeks are lobbying the British to return the Parthenon frieze currently housed in the British Museum). Although this bust is not particularly representative of Egyptian art in general—and despite increasing claims that her long neck suggests she's a Neoclassical fake—Nefertiti has become a symbol of Egyptian art by popular acclaim.

The Egyptian Collection continues with other sculptures, including kneeling figures holding steles (stone tablets inscribed with prayers). On floor 1, a fascinating exhibit examines how depictions of the human image evolved during the 3,000-year span of ancient Egyptian culture. You'll also see entire walls from tombs and (in the basement—floor 0) a sea of large sarcophagi.

▲Old National Gallery (Alte Nationalgalerie)

This gallery, behind the Neues Museum and Altes Museum, is designed to look like a Greek temple. Spanning three floors, it

BERLIN

focuses on art (mostly paintings) from the 19th century: Romantic German paintings (which I find most interesting) on the top floor, and French and German Impressionists and German Realists on the first and second floors. You likely won't recognize any specific paintings, but it's still an enjoyable stroll through German culture from the century in which that notion first came to mean something. The included audioguide explains the highlights.

Touring the Museum: Start on the third floor, with Romantic canvases and art of the Goethe era (roughly 1770-1830), and work your way down. Use the audioguide to really delve into these romanticized, vivid looks at life in Germany in the 19th century and before. As you stroll through the Romantic paintings—the museum's strength— keep in mind that they were created about the time (mid-late 19th century) that Germans were first working toward a single, unified nation. By glori-

fying pristine German landscapes and a rugged, virtuous people, these painters evoked the region's high-water mark—the Middle Ages, when "Germany" was a patchwork of powerful and wealthy merchant city-states. Linger over dreamy townscapes with Gothic cathedrals and castles that celebrate medieval German might. Still lifes, idealized portraits of tow-headed children, and genre paintings (depicting everyday scenes, often with subtle social commentary) strum the heartstrings of anyone with Teutonic blood. The Düsseldorf School excelled at Romantic landscapes (such as Carl Friedrich Lessing's *Castle on a Rock*). Some of these canvases nearly resemble present-day fantasy paintings. Perhaps the best-known artist in the collection is Caspar David Friedrich, who specialized in dramatic scenes celebrating grandeur and the solitary hero. His *The Monk by the Sea (Der Mönch am Meer)* shows a lone figure standing on a sand dune, pondering a vast, turbulent expanse of sea and sky.

On the second floor, you'll find one big room of minor works by bigger-name French artists, including Renoir, Cézanne, Manet, Monet, and Rodin. Another room is devoted to the Romantic Hans von Marées, the influential early Symbolist Arnold Böcklin, and other artists of the "German Roman" (Deutschrömer) movement—Germans who lived in, and were greatly influenced by, Rome. Artists of the Munich School are represented by naturalistic canvases of landscapes or slice-of-life scenes.

On the first floor, 19th-century Realism reigns. While the Realist Adolph Menzel made his name painting elegant royal gatherings and historical events, his *Iron Rolling Mill (Das Eisenwalzwerk)* captures the gritty side of his moment in history—the emergence of the Industrial Age—with a warts-and-all look at steelworkers toiling in a hellish factory. The first floor also hosts a sculpture collection, with works by great sculptors both foreign (the Italian Canova, the Dane Thorvaldsen) and German (Johann Gottfried Schadow's delightful *Die Prinzessinnen,* showing the dynamic duo of Prussian princesses Louise and Frederike).

Bode Museum
At the "prow" of Museum Island, the Bode Museum (designed to appear as if it's rising up from the river), is worth a quick look. Just inside, a grand statue of Frederick William of Brandenburg on horseback, curly locks blowing in the wind, welcomes you into the lonely halls of the museum. This fine building contains a hodgepodge of collections: Byzantine art, historic coins, ecclesiastical art, sculptures, and medals commemorating the fall of the Berlin Wall and German reunification.

Altes (Old) Museum
The least interesting of the five museums, this building features the rest of the Collection of Classical Antiquities (the best of which is in the Pergamon Museum)—namely, Etruscan, Roman, and Greek art. I'd skip it.

Other Sights on and near Museum Island
In addition to the five museums just described, Museum Island is home to the following sights. One more sight (the DDR Museum) sits just across the river.

Lustgarten—For 300 years, the island's big central square has flip-flopped between being a military parade ground and a people-friendly park, depending upon the political tenor of the time. During the revolutions of 1848, the Kaiser's troops dispersed a protesting crowd that had assembled here, sending demonstrators onto footpaths. Karl Marx later commented, "It is impossible to have a revolution in a country where people stay off the grass."

Until recently, it was *verboten* to relax or walk on the Lustgarten's grass. But in 1999, the Lustgarten was made into a park (read the history posted in the corner opposite the church). On a sunny day, it's packed with relaxing locals and is one of Berlin's most enjoyable public spaces.

Berlin Cathedral (Berliner Dom)—This century-old church towers over Museum Island. Inside, the great reformers (Luther, Calvin, and company) stand around the brilliantly restored dome like stern saints guarding their theology. Frederick I rests in an ornate tomb (right transept, near entrance to dome). The 270-step climb to the outdoor dome gallery is tough but offers pleasant, breezy views of the city at the finish line. The crypt downstairs is not worth a look.

Cost and Hours: €7 includes access to dome gallery, €10 with audioguide, not covered by Museum Island ticket, Mon-Sat 9:00-20:00, Sun 12:00-20:00, until 19:00 Oct-March, closes early—around 17:30—on some days for concerts, interior closed but dome open during services, tel. 030/2026-9136, www.berliner-dom.de. The cathedral hosts many organ concerts (often on weekends, tickets from about €10 always available at the door).

Humboldt-Forum Construction Site (Former Site of Hohenzollern Palace)—Across Unter den Linden from Berlin Cathedral is a big lawn that for centuries held the Baroque palace of the Hohenzollern dynasty of Brandenburg and Prussia. Much of that palace actually survived World War II but was replaced by the communists with a blocky, Soviet-style "Palace" of the Republic—East Berlin's parliament building/entertainment complex and a showy symbol of the communist days. The landmark building fell into disrepair after reunification and was eventually dismantled in 2007. After much debate about how to use this prime real estate, the German parliament decided to construct the Humboldt-Forum, a huge public venue filled with museums, shops, galleries, and concert halls behind a facade constructed in imitation of the original Hohenzollern palace. With a €1.2 billion price tag, many Berliners consider the reconstruction plan a complete waste of money.

The temporary **Humboldt-Box** has been set up to help the public follow the construction of the new Humboldt-Forum. The multiple floors of the futuristic "box" display building plans and models for the project (€4, daily 10:00-22:00, tel. 01805-030-707, www.humboldt-box.com). On the top floor, a terrace-café with unobstructed views over Berlin serves coffee, desserts, and light food until 18:00, and a dinner menu after that (€5-15 lunch dishes, €15-22 dinners).

Spree River Cruises—The recommended Spree River boat tours depart from the riverbank near the bridge by the Berlin Cathedral. For details, see page 664.

• *Directly across the bridge from Museum Island, down along the riverbank, look for the...*

▲**DDR Museum**—Although this exhibit began as a tourist trap, it has expanded and matured into a genuinely interesting look at life in former East Germany (DDR). It's well-stocked with kitschy everyday items from the communist period, plus photos, video clips, and concise English explanations. The exhibits are inter-active—you're encouraged to pick up and handle anything that isn't behind glass. You'll crawl through a Trabant car (designed by East German engineers to compete with the West's popular VW Beetle) and pick up some DDR-era jokes ("East Germany had 39 newspapers, four radio stations, two TV channels...and one opin-ion.") The reconstructed communist-era home lets you tour the kitchen, living room, bedrooms, and more. You'll learn about the Russian-imported *Dacha*—the simple countryside cottage (owned by one in six East Germans) used for weekend retreats from the grimy city. (Others vacationed on the Baltic Coast, where nudism was all the rage, as a very revealing display explains.) Lounge in DDR movie chairs as you view a subtitled propaganda film or clips from beloved-in-the-East TV shows (including the popular kids' show *Sandmännchen—Little Sandman*). Even the meals served in the attached restaurant are based on DDR-era recipes.

Cost and Hours: €6, daily 10:00-20:00, Sat until 22:00, just across the Spree from Museum Island at Karl-Liebknecht-Strasse 1, tel. 030/847-123-731, www.ddr-museum.de.

Museum Island to Alexanderplatz

• *Continue walking down Unter den Linden. Before crossing the bridge (and leaving Museum Island), look across the river. The pointy twin spires of the 13th-century Nikolai Church mark the center of medieval Berlin. This **Nikolaiviertel** (Viertel means "quarter") was restored by the DDR and trendy in the last years of communism. Today, it's a lively-at-night riverside restaurant district.*

As you cross the bridge, look left in the distance to see the gilded **New Synagogue** dome, rebuilt after WWII bombing (described on page 713).

Across the river to the left of the bridge, directly below you, is the **DDR Museum** (described earlier). Just beyond that is the giant **SAS Radisson Hotel** and shopping center, with a huge aquarium in the center. The elevator goes right through the middle of a deep-sea world. (You can see it from the unforgettable Radisson hotel lobby—tuck in your shirt and walk past the guards with the con-fidence of a guest who's sleeping there.) Here in the center of the old communist capital, it seems that capitalism has settled in with a spirited vengeance.

In the park immediately across the street (a big jaywalk from the Radisson) are grandfatherly statues of **Marx and Engels** (nick-named "the old pensioners"). Surrounding them are stainless-steel monoliths with evocative photos that show the struggles of the workers of the world.

Walk toward **Marien Church** (from 1270), just left of the base of the TV Tower. An artist's rendering helps you follow the interesting but very faded old "Dance of Death" mural that wraps around the narthex inside the door.

The big red-brick building past the trees on the right is the **City Hall,** built after the revolutions of 1848 and arguably the first democratic building in the city.

The 1,200-foot-tall **TV Tower** (Fernsehturm) has a fine view from halfway up (€11, daily March-Oct 9:00-24:00, Nov-Feb 10:00-24:00, www.tv-turm.de). The tower offers a handy city orientation and an interesting view of the flat, red-roofed sprawl of Berlin—including a peek inside the city's many courtyards *(Höfe).* Consider a kitschy trip to the observation deck for the view and lunch in its revolving restaurant (mediocre food, €12 plates, horrible lounge music, reservations smart for dinner, tel. 030/242-3333). The retro tower is quite trendy these days, so it can be crowded (your ticket comes with an assigned entry time). Built (with Swedish know-how) in 1969 for the 20th anniversary of the communist government, the tower was meant to show the power of the atheistic state at a time when DDR leaders were having the crosses removed from church domes and spires. But when the sun shined on their tower—the greatest spire in East Berlin—a huge cross was reflected on the mirrored ball. Cynics called it "The Pope's Revenge." East Berliners dubbed the tower the "Tele-Asparagus." They joked that if it fell over, they'd have an elevator to the West.

Farther east, pass under the train tracks into **Alexanderplatz.** This area—especially the former Kaufhof department store (now

Galeria Kaufhof)—was the commercial pride and joy of East Berlin. Today, it's still a landmark, with a major U- and S-Bahn station. The once-futuristic, now-retro "World Time Clock," installed in 1969, is a nostalgic favorite and a popular meeting point. Stop in the square for a coffee and to people-watch. It's a great scene.

• *Our orientation stroll or bus ride (this is the last stop for bus #100) is finished. From here, you can hike back a bit to catch the riverboat tour, take in the sights south of Unter den Linden, venture into the colorful Prenzlauer Berg neighborhood, or consider extending this foray into eastern Berlin.*

Karl-Marx-Allee

The buildings along Karl-Marx-Allee in East Berlin (just beyond Alexanderplatz) were completely leveled by the Red Army in 1945. As an expression of their adoration to the "great Socialist Father" (Stalin), the DDR government decided to rebuild the street better than ever (the USSR provided generous subsidies). They intentionally made it one meter wider than the Champs-Elysées, named it Stalinallee, and lined it with "workers' palaces" built in the bold "Stalin Gothic" style so common in Moscow in the 1950s. Now renamed after Karl Marx, the street and its restored buildings provide a rare look at Berlin's communist days. Distances are a bit long for convenient walking, but you can cruise Karl-Marx-Allee by taxi, or ride the U-Bahn to Strausberger Platz (which was built to resemble an Italian promenade) and walk to Frankfurter Tor, reading the good information posts along the way. Notice the Social Realist reliefs on the buildings and the lampposts, which incorporate the wings of a phoenix (rising from the ashes) in their design. Once a "workers' paradise," the street now hosts a two-mile-long capitalist beer festival the first weekend in August.

The **Café Sibylle,** just beyond the Strausberger Platz U-Bahn station, is a fun spot for a coffee, traditional DDR ice-cream treats, and a look at its free informal museum that tells the story of the most destroyed street in Berlin. While the humble exhibit is nearly all in German, it's fun to see the ear (or buy a €10 plaster replica) and half a moustache from what was the largest statue of Stalin in Germany (the centerpiece of the street until 1961). It also provides a few intimate insights into apartment life in a DDR flat. The café is known for its good coffee and *Schwedeneisbecher mit Eierlikor*—an ice-cream sundae with a shot of egg liqueur, popular among those nostalgic for communism (Mon-Fri 10:00-20:00, Sat-Sun 11:00-20:00, Karl-Marx-Allee 72, at intersection with Koppenstrasse, a block from U-Bahn: Strausberger Platz, tel. 030/2935-2203).

Heading out to Karl-Marx-Allee (just beyond the TV Tower), you're likely to notice a giant colorful **mural** decorating a blocky communist-era skyscraper. This was the Ministry of Education, and the mural is a tile mosaic trumpeting the accomplishments of the DDR's version of "No Child Left Behind."

South of Unter den Linden

The following sights—heavy on Nazi and Wall history—are listed roughly north to south (as you reach them from Unter den Linden).

▲▲Gendarmenmarkt

This delightful, historic square is bounded by twin churches, a tasty chocolate shop, and the Berlin Symphony's concert hall (designed by Karl Friedrich Schinkel, the man who put the Neoclassical stamp on Berlin and Dresden). In summer, it hosts a few outdoor cafés, *Biergarten*s, and sometimes concerts. Wonderfully symmetrical, the square is considered by Berliners to be the finest in town (U6: Französische Strasse; U2 or U6: Stadtmitte).

The name of the square—part French and part German (after the *Gens d'Armes*, Frederick the Great's royal guard who were headquartered here)—reminds us that in the 17th century, a fifth of all Berliners were French émigrés—Protestant Huguenots fleeing Catholic France. Back then, Frederick the Great's tolerant Prussia was a magnet for the persecuted (and for their money). These émigrés vitalized Berlin with new ideas and know-how...and their substantial wealth.

Of the two matching churches on Gendarmenmarkt, the one to the south (bottom end of square) is the **German Cathedral** (Deutscher Dom). This cathedral (not to be confused with the Berlin Cathedral on Unter den Linden) was bombed flat in the war and rebuilt only in the 1980s. It houses the thought-provoking Milestones, Setbacks, Sidetracks *(Wege, Irrwege, Umwege)* exhibit, which traces the history of the German parliamentary system—worth ▲. The parliament-funded exhibit—while light on actual historical artifacts—is well done and more interesting than it sounds. It takes you quickly from the revolutionary days of 1848 to the 1920s, and then more deeply through the tumultuous 20th century. As the exhibit is designed for Germans rather than foreign tourists, there are no English descriptions—but you can follow the essential, excellent, and free 1.5-hour English audioguide or buy the wonderfully detailed €10 guidebook. If you think this museum is an attempt by the German government to develop a more sophisticated and educated electorate in the interest of stronger democracy, you're exactly right. Germany knows (from its own troubled history) that a dumbed-down electorate, manipulated by clever spin-meisters and sound-bite media blitzes, is a dangerous thing (free, Tue-Sun May-Sept 10:00-19:00, Oct-April 10:00-18:00, closed Mon year-round, tel. 030/2273-0431).

The **French Cathedral** (Französischer Dom), at the north end of the square, offers a humble museum on the Huguenots (€2, Tue-Sat 12:00-17:00, Sun 11:00-17:00, closed Mon, enter around the right side) and a viewpoint in the dome up top (€3, daily 10:30-19:00, last entry at 18:00, 244 steps, enter through door facing square). Fun fact: Neither of these churches is a true cathedral, as they never contained a bishop's throne; their German title of *Dom* (cathedral) is actually a mistranslation from the French word *dôme* (cupola).

Fassbender & Rausch, on the corner near the German Cathedral, claims to be Europe's biggest chocolate store. After 150

years of chocolate-making, this family-owned business proudly displays its sweet delights—250 different kinds—on a 55-foot-long buffet. Truffles are sold for about €0.60 each; it's fun to compose a fancy little eight-piece box of your own for about €5. Upstairs is an elegant hot chocolate café

with fine views. The window displays feature giant chocolate models of Berlin landmarks—Reichstag, TV Tower, Kaiser Wilhelm Memorial Church, and so on. If all this isn't enough to entice you,

I have three words: "Erupting Chocolate Volcano" (Mon-Sat 10:00-20:00, Sun 11:00-20:00, corner of Mohrenstrasse at Charlottenstrasse 60, tel. 030/2045-8440).

Gendarmenmarkt is buried in what has recently emerged as Berlin's "Fifth Avenue" shopping district. For the ultimate in top-end shops, find the corner of Jägerstrasse and Friedrichstrasse and wander through the **Quartier 206** (Mon-Fri 10:30-19:30, Sat 10:00-18:00, closed Sun, www.quartier206.com). The

adjacent, middlebrow **Quartier 205** has more affordable prices.

Nazi and Cold War Sites on Wilhelmstrasse
Fragment of the Wall—Surviving stretches of the Wall are virtually nonexistent in downtown Berlin. One of the most conve-

nient places to see a bit is at the intersection of Wilhelmstrasse and Zimmerstrasse/Niederkirchnerstrasse, a few blocks southwest of Gendarmenmarkt. Many visitors make the short walk over here from the Checkpoint Charlie sights (described later), then drop into the museum listed next.

▲▲**Topography of Terror (Topographie des Terrors)**—Coincidentally, the patch of land behind the surviving stretch of

Wall was closely associated with a different regime: It was once the nerve center for the most despicable elements of the Nazi government, the Gestapo and the SS. This stark-gray, boxy building is one of the few memorial sites that focuses on the perpetrators rather than the victims of the Nazis. It's a chilling but fascinating experience to see just how seamlessly and bureaucratically the Nazi institutions and state structures merged to become a well-oiled terror machine. There are few actual artifacts; it's mostly written explanations and photos, like reading a good textbook standing up. And, while you could read this story anywhere, to take this in atop the Gestapo headquarters is a powerful experience. The exhibit's a bit dense, but WWII historians (even armchair ones) will find it fascinating.

Cost and Hours: Free, daily 10:00-20:00, outdoor exhibit closes at sunset in winter, Niederkirchnerstrasse 8, tel. 030/254-5090, www.topographie.de.

Background: This location marks what was once the most feared address in Berlin: the headquarters of the Reich Main Security Office *(Reichssicherheitshauptamt)*. These offices served as the engine room of the Nazi dictatorship, as well as the command center of the SS *(Schutzstaffel,* whose members began as Hitler's personal bodyguards), the Gestapo *(Geheime Staatspolizei,* secret state police), and the SD *(Sicherheitsdienst,* the Nazi intelligence agency). This trio (and others) were ultimately consolidated under Heinrich Himmler to become a state-within-a-state, with talons in every corner of German society. This elite militarized branch of the Nazi machine was also tasked with the "racial purification" of German-held lands, especially Eastern Europe—the Holocaust. It was from these headquarters that the Nazis administered concentration camps, firmed up plans for the "Final Solution to the Jewish Question," and organized the domestic surveillance of anyone opposed to the regime. The building was also equipped with dungeons, where the Gestapo detained and tortured thousands of prisoners.

The Gestapo and SS employed intimidation techniques to coerce cooperation from the German people. The general public knew that the Gestapo was to be feared: It was considered omnipotent, omnipresent, and omniscient. Some political prisoners underwent "enhanced interrogation" right here in this building. The threat of *Schutzhaft* ("protective custody," usually at a concentration camp) was used to terrify any civilians who stepped out of line—or who might make a good example. But Hitler and his cronies also won people's loyalties through propaganda. They hammered home the idealistic notion of the *Volksgemeinschaft* ("people's community") of a purely Germanic culture and race, which empowered Hitler to create a pervasive illusion that "We're all in this together." Anyone who was not an Aryan was *Untermensch*—subhuman—and must be treated as such.

Touring the Museum: The complex has two parts: indoors, in the modern boxy building; and outdoors, in the trench that runs along the surviving stretch of Wall. Visit the indoor exhibit first.

Inside, you'll find a visitor center with an information desk and an extensive **Topography of Terror** exhibit about the SS and Gestapo, and the atrocities they committed in Berlin and across Europe. A model of the government quarter, circa 1939, sets the stage of Nazi domination in this area. A timeline of events and old photographs, documents, and newspaper clippings illustrate how Hitler and his team expertly manipulated the German people to build a broadly supported "dictatorship of consent."

The exhibit walks you through the evolution of Hitler's regime: the Nazi takeover; institutions of terror (Himmler's "SS

State"); terror, persecution, and extermination; atrocities in Nazi-occupied countries; and the war's end and postwar. Some images here are indelible, such as photos of SS soldiers stationed at Auschwitz, gleefully yukking it up on a retreat in the countryside (even as their help-

less prisoners were being gassed and burned a few miles away). The exhibit profiles specific members of the various reprehensible SS branches, as well as the groups they targeted: Jews, Roma, and Sinti (Gypsies); the unemployed or homeless; homosexuals; and the physically and mentally ill (considered "useless eaters" who consumed resources without contributing work).

Downstairs is a WC and a library with research books on these topics. Before heading outside, ask at the information desk to borrow the free audioguide that describes the outdoor exhibits.

Outside, in the trench along the Wall, you'll find the exhibit **Berlin 1933-1945: Between Propaganda and Terror,** which overlaps slightly with the indoor exhibit but focuses on Berlin. The chronological survey begins with the

post-WWI Weimar Republic and continues through the ragged days just after World War II. One display explains how Nazis invented holidays (or injected new Aryan meaning into existing ones) as a means of winning over the public. Other exhibits cover the "Aryanization" of Jewish businesses (they were simply taken over by the state and handed over to new Aryan owners); Hitler's plans for converting Berlin into a gigantic "Welthauptstadt (World Capital) Germania"; and the postwar Berlin Airlift, which brought provisions to some 2.2 million West Berliners whose supply lines were cut off by East Berlin.

With more time, explore the grounds around the blocky building on a **"Site Tour."** Posted signs explain 15 different locations, including the scant remains of the prison cellars.

German Finance Ministry (Bundesministerium der Finanzen)—Across the street (facing the Wall chunk) are the

former headquarters of the Nazi Luftwaffe (Air Force), the only major Hitler-era government building that survived the war's bombs. Notice how the whole building gives off a monumental feel, making the average person feel small and powerless. Walk into the stark courtyard. After the war, this was the headquarters for

the Soviet occupation. Later the DDR was founded here, and the communists used the building to house their—no joke—Ministry of Ministries. Walk up Wilhelmstrasse (to the north) to see an entry gate (on your left) that looks much like it did when Germany occupied nearly all of Europe. On the north side of the building (farther up Wilhelmstrasse, at corner with Leipziger Strasse) is a wonderful example of communist art. The mural, Max Lingner's *Aufbau der Republik* (*Building the Republic*, 1953), is classic Socialist Realism, showing the entire society—industrial laborers, farm workers, women, and children—all happily singing the same patriotic song. Its subtitle: "The importance of peace for the cultural development of humanity and the necessity of struggle to achieve this goal." This was the communist ideal. For the reality, look at the ground in the courtyard in front of the mural to see an enlarged photograph from a 1953 uprising here against the communists...quite a contrast. Placards explain the events of 1953 in English.

Stasi Museum—This modest exhibit, roughly between the Topography of Terror and Checkpoint Charlie, tells the story of how the communist-era Ministry for State Security (*Staatssicherheit*, a.k.a. Stasi) infiltrated all aspects of German life. Soon after the

Wall fell, DDR authorities scrambled to destroy the copious illicit information their agents and informants had collected about the people of East Germany. But the government mandated that these records be preserved as evidence of DDR crimes, and the documents are now managed by the Federal Commissioner for Stasi Records. A timeline traces the history of the archives, and wraparound kiosks profile individual "subversive elements" who were targeted by the Stasi. There are a few actual artifacts, but the exhibit is mostly dryly written texts and reproduced photographs that don't do much to personalize the victims—making this museum worth a visit only for those with a special interest in this period. Temporary exhibits are upstairs.

BERLIN

Cost and Hours: Free, Mon-Sat 10:00-18:00, closed Sun, Zimmerstrasse 90-91, tel. 030/232-450, www.bstu.bund.de.

Other Stasi Sites: If you're interested in this chapter of East German history, you may find it more satisfying (but time-consuming) to visit two other sites affiliated with the Stasi: a different **Stasi Museum,** in the former State Security headquarters (€5, Mon-Fri 11:00-18:00, Sat-Sun 14:00-18:00, Ruscherstarsse 103, U-5: Magdalenenstrasse, tel. 030/553-6854, www.stasi museum.de); and the **Stasi Prison,** where "enemies of the state" served time (€4, visits possible only with a tour; English tours daily at 14:30—call to confirm before making the trip; German tours Mon-Fri at 11:00, 13:00, and 15:00, Sat-Sun hourly 10:00-16:00; Genslerstrasse 66, reachable on various trams from downtown— see website for specifics, tel. 030/9860-8230, www.stiftung-hsh .de). There's also a good Stasi Museum in the former State Security branch in Leipzig (see page 572 in Leipzig chapter).

Checkpoint Charlie

This famous Cold War checkpoint was not named for a person, but for its checkpoint number—as in Alpha (#1, at the East-West

German border, a hundred miles west of here), Bravo (#2, as you enter Berlin proper), and Charlie (#3, the best known because most foreigners passed through here). While the actual checkpoint has long since been dismantled, its former location is home to a fine museum and a mock-up of the original border crossing. The area has become a Cold War freak show and—as if celebrating the final victory of crass capitalism—is one of Berlin's worst tourist-trap zones. A McDonald's stands defiantly overlooking the former haunt of East German border guards. You can even pay an

The Berlin Wall (and Its Fall)

The 96-mile-long "Anti-Fascist Protective Rampart," as it was called by the East German government, was erected almost overnight in 1961 to stop the outward flow of people from East to West (3 million had leaked out between 1949 and 1961). The Wall *(Mauer)* was actually two 12-foot-high concrete barriers whose rounded, pipe-like top (to discourage grappling hooks) was adorned with plenty of barbed wire. Sandwiched between the walls was a no-man's-land (or "death strip") between 30 and 160 feet wide. More than 100 sentry towers kept a close eye on the Wall. On their way into the death strip, would-be escapees would trip a silent alarm, which alerted sharpshooters.

During the Wall's 28 years, border guards fired 1,693 times and made 3,221 arrests, and there were 5,043 documented successful escapes (565 of these were East German guards). Officially, 136 people were killed at the Wall while trying to escape. One of the first, and most famous, was 18-year-old Peter Fechter. On August 17, 1962, East German soldiers shot and wounded Fechter as he was trying to climb over the Wall. For more than an hour, Fechter lay bleeding to death while soldiers and bystanders on both sides of the Wall did nothing. In 1997, a German court sentenced three former border guards to two years in prison for manslaughter.

As a tangible, almost too-apt symbol for the Cold War, the Berlin Wall got a lot of attention from politicians both East and West. Two of the 20th century's most repeated presidential quotes were uttered within earshot of the death strip. In 1963, US President John F. Kennedy stood in front of the walled-off Brandenburg Gate and professed American solidarity with the struggling people of Berlin: *"Ich bin ein Berliner."* A generation later in 1987, with the stiff winds of change already blowing westward from Moscow, President Ronald Reagan came here to issue an ultimatum to his Soviet counterpart: "Mr. Gorbachev, tear down this wall."

The actual fall of the Wall had less to do with presidential proclamations than with the obvious failings of the Soviet system, a general thawing in Moscow (where Gorbachev introduced *perestroika* and *glasnost,* and declared that he would no longer employ force to keep Eastern European satellite states under Soviet rule)—and a bureaucratic snafu.

By November of 1989, it was clear that change was in the air. Hungary had already opened its borders to the West that summer, making it next to impossible for East German authorities to keep people in. A series of anti-regime protests had swept nearby Leipzig a few weeks earlier, attracting hundreds of thousands of supporters (see page 571). On October 7, 1989—on the 50th anniversary of the official creation of the DDR—East German premier Erich Honecker said, "The Wall will be standing in 50 and even in 100 years." He was only off by 99 years and 11 months. A similar rally in East Berlin's Alexanderplatz on November 4—with a half-million protesters chanting, *"Wir wollen raus!"* (We want out!)—persuaded the East German politburo to begin a gradual process of relaxing travel restrictions.

The DDR's intention was to slightly crack the door to the West, but an inarticulate spokesman's confusion inadvertently threw it wide open. The decision was made on Thursday, November 9, to tentatively allow a few more Easterners to cross into the West—a largely symbolic reform that was intended to take place gradually, over many weeks. Licking their wounds, Politburo members left town early for a long weekend. The announcement about travel restrictions was left to a spokesman, Günter Schabowski, who knew only what was on a piece of paper handed to him moments before he went on television for a routine press conference. At 18:54, Schabowski read the statement dutifully, with little emotion, seemingly oblivious to the massive impact of his own words: "exit via border crossings...possible for every citizen." Reporters, unable to believe what they were hearing, began to prod him about when the borders would open. Schabowski looked with puzzlement at the brief statement, shrugged, and offered his best guess: *"Ab sofort, unverzüglich."* ("Immediately, without delay.")

Schabowski's words spread like wildfire through the streets of both Berlins, its flames fanned by West German TV broadcasts (and Tom Brokaw, who had rushed to Berlin when alerted by NBC's bureau chief). East Berliners began to show up at Wall checkpoints, demanding that border guards let them pass. As the crowds grew, the border guards could not reach anyone who could issue official orders. (The politburo members were effectively hiding out.) Finally, around 23:30, a border guard named Harald Jäger at the Bornholmer Strasse crossing decided to simply open the gates. Easterners flooded into the West, embracing their long-separated cousins, unable to believe their good fortune. Once open, the Wall could never be closed again.

The carnival atmosphere of those first years after the Wall fell is gone, but hawkers still sell "authentic" pieces of the Wall, DDR flags, and military paraphernalia to gawking tourists. When it fell, the Wall was literally carried away by the euphoria. What managed to survive has been nearly devoured by decades of persistent "Wall-peckers."

Americans—the Cold War victors—have the biggest appetite for Wall-related sights, and a few bits and pieces remain for us to seek out. Berlin's best Wall-related sights are the Museum of the Wall at Checkpoint Charlie (see page 708) and the Berlin Wall Memorial along Bernauer Strasse, with a long stretch of surviving Wall (near S-Bahn: Nordbahnhof; page 716). Other stretches of the Wall still standing include the short section at Zimmerstrasse/Wilhelmstrasse (near the Topography of Terror exhibit; page 701) and the longer East Side Gallery (near the Ostbahnhof; page 711).

exorbitant €10 for a full set of Cold War-era stamps in your passport. (For a more sober and intellectually redeeming look at the Wall's history, head for the out-of-the-way Berlin Wall Memorial at Bernauer Strasse, north of here near the Prenzlauer Berg neighborhood and described on page 716. Local officials, likely put off by the touristy crassness of the Checkpoint Charlie scene, have steered local funding to that area.)

▲Checkpoint Charlie Street Scene and Other Wall Sites—

Where Checkpoint Charlie once stood, notice the thought-provoking post with larger-than-life **posters** of a young American soldier facing east and a young Soviet soldier facing west. The rebuilt **guard station** now hosts two actors playing American guards who pose for photos. (Across the street is Snack Point Charlie.) A **photo exhibit** stretches down the street, with great English descriptions telling the story of the Wall. While you could get this information from a book, it's poignant to stand here in person and ponder the gripping history of this place.

A few yards away (on Zimmerstrasse), a **glass panel** describes the former checkpoint. From there, a double row of **cobbles** in Zimmerstrasse traces the former path of the Wall. These innocuous cobbles run throughout the city, even through some buildings.

Farther down on Zimmerstrasse, before Charlottenstrasse, find the **Memorial to Peter Fechter** (set just off the sidewalk, barely inside the Wall marker), who was shot and left for dead here in the early days of the Wall. For more on his sad story, see "The Berlin Wall (and Its Fall)" sidebar.

▲▲Museum of the Wall at Checkpoint Charlie (Mauermuseum Haus am Checkpoint Charlie)—While the famous border checkpoint between the American and Soviet sectors is long gone, its memory is preserved by one of Europe's most cluttered museums. During the Cold War, the House at Checkpoint Charlie stood defiantly—spitting distance from the border guards—showing off all the clever escapes over, under, and through the Wall. Today, while the drama is over and hunks of the Wall stand like trophies at its door, the museum survives as a living artifact of the Cold War days. The yellowed descriptions, which have scarcely changed since that time, tinge the museum with nostalgia. It's dusty, disorganized, and overpriced, with lots of reading involved, but all that just adds to this museum's borderline-kitschy charm. If you're pressed for time, this is a decent after-dinner sight.

Cost and Hours: €12.50, assemble 20 tourists and get in for

€8.50 each, €3.50 audioguide, discount with WelcomeCard but not covered by Museumspass, daily 9:00-22:00, U6 to Kochstrasse or—better from Zoo—U2 to Stadtmitte, Friedrichstrasse 43-45, tel. 030/253-7250, www.mauermuseum.de.

Touring the Museum: Exhibits narrate a gripping history of the Wall, with a focus on the many ingenious **escape**  **attempts** (the early years—with a cruder wall—saw more escapes). You'll see the actual items used to smuggle would-be Wessies—a VW bug whose trunk hid a man, two side-by-side suitcases into which a woman squeezed, a makeshift zip line for crossing over (rather than through) the border, a hot-air balloon in which two families floated to safety (immortalized in the Disney film *Night Crossing*), an inflatable boat that puttered across the dangerous Baltic Sea, primitive homemade aircraft, two surfboards hollowed out to create just enough space for a refugee, and more. One chilling exhibit lists some 43,000 people who died in "Internal Affairs" internment camps during the transition to communism (1945-1950). Profiles personalize various escapees and their helpers, including John P. Ireland, an American who posed as an eccentric antiques collector so he could transport 10 different refugees to safety in his modified Cadillac.

You'll also see **artwork** inspired by the Wall and its fall, and a memorial to Rainer Hildebrandt, who founded this museum shortly after the Wall went up in 1961 (he died in 2004, but the museum lives on as a shrine to his vision). On the **top floor** (easy to miss), that vision broadens to the larger themes of freedom and persecution, including exhibits on Eastern European rebellions (the 1956 uprising in Hungary, 1968's Prague Spring, and the Solidarity movement in 1980s Poland) and Gandhi's protests in India—plus a hodgepodge of displays on world religions and Picasso's *Guernica*. Fans of "the Gipper" appreciate the room honoring President Ronald Reagan, displaying his actual cowboy hat and boots. The small movie theater shows various Wall-related films (a schedule is posted), and the displays include video coverage of those heady days when people power tore down the Wall.

▲▲Jewish Museum Berlin
(Jüdisches Museum Berlin)

This museum is one of Europe's best Jewish sights. The highly conceptual building is a sight in itself, and the museum inside—an overview of the rich culture and history of Europe's Jewish community—is excellent, particularly if you take advantage of

the informative and engaging audio-guide. Rather than just reading dry texts, you'll feel this museum as fresh and alive—an exuberant celebration of the Jewish experience that's accessible to all. Even though the museum is in a nondescript residential neighborhood, it's well worth the trip.

Cost and Hours: €5, sometimes extra for special exhibits, discount with WelcomeCard, daily 10:00-20:00, Mon until 22:00, last entry one hour before closing, closed on Jewish holidays. Tight security includes bag check and metal detectors. The excellent €3 audioguide—with four hours of commentary on 151 different items—is essential to fully appreciate the exhibits. Tel. 030/2599-3300, www.jmberlin.de.

Getting There: Take the U-Bahn to Hallesches Tor, find the exit marked *Jüdisches Museum,* exit straight ahead, then turn right on Franz-Klühs-Strasse. The museum is a five-minute walk ahead on your left, at Lindenstrasse 9.

Eating: The museum's restaurant, Liebermanns, offers good Jewish-style meals, albeit not kosher (€9 daily specials, lunch served 12:00-16:00, snacks at other times, tel. 030/2593-9760).

Touring the Museum: Designed by American architect Daniel Libeskind (the master planner for the redeveloped World Trade Center in New York), the zinc-walled building has a zigzag shape pierced by voids symbolic of the irreplaceable cultural loss caused by the Holocaust. Enter the 18th-century Baroque building next door, then go through an underground tunnel to reach the museum interior.

Before you reach the exhibit, your visit starts with three **memorial spaces.** Follow the Axis of Exile to a disorienting slanted garden with 49 pillars (evocative of the Memorial to the Murdered Jews of Europe, across town). Next, the Axis of Holocaust, lined with artifacts from Jews imprisoned and murdered by the Nazis, leads to an eerily empty tower shut off from the outside world. The Axis of Continuity takes you to stairs and the main exhibit. A detour partway up the long stairway leads to the Memory Void, a thought-provoking space of "fallen leaves": heavy metal faces that you walk on, making unhuman noises with each step.

Finish climbing the stairs to the top of the museum, and stroll chronologically through the 2,000-year **story of Judaism** in Germany. The exhibit, on two floors, is engaging, with lots of actual artifacts. Interactive bits (for example, spell your name in Hebrew, or write a prayer and hang it from a tree) make it lively for kids. English explanations interpret both the exhibits and the design of the very symbolic building.

The top floor focuses on everyday life in Ashkenaz (medieval German-Jewish lands). The nine-minute movie "A Thousand Years Ago" sets the stage for your journey through Jewish history. You'll learn what garlic had to do with early Jews in Germany (hint: It's not just about cooking). The Middle Ages was a positive time for Jewish culture, which flourished in many areas of Europe. But around 1500, many Jews were expelled from the countryside and moved into cities. Viewing stations let you watch nine short, lively videos that pose provocative questions about faith. Moses Mendelssohn's role in the late-18th-century Jewish Enlightenment, which gave rise to Reform Judaism, is highlighted. The Tradition and Change exhibit analyzes how various subgroups of the Jewish faith modified and relaxed their rules to adapt to a changing world.

Downstairs, on the middle floor, exhibits detail the rising tide of anti-Semitism in Germany through the 19th century—ironically, at a time when many Jews were so secularized that they celebrated Christmas right along with Hanukkah. Berlin's glory days (1890-1933) were a boom time for many Jews, though it was at times challenging to reconcile the reformed ways of the more assimilated western (German) Jews with the more traditional Eastern European Jews. The exhibit segues into the **dark days** of Hitler—the collapse of the relatively tolerant Weimar Republic, the rise of the Nazis, and the horrific night of November 9-10, 1938, when, throughout Germany, hateful mobs destroyed Jewish-owned businesses, homes, synagogues, and even entire villages—called "Crystal Night" (Kristallnacht) for the broken glass that glittered in the streets.

The thought-provoking conclusion brings us to the present day, with the question: How do you keep going after six million of your people have been murdered? You'll see how German society has reacted to the Holocaust blood on their hands (one fascinating exhibit has footage of a 1975 sit-in of German Jews to protest a controversial play with a stereotypical Jewish villain), and listen to headphone commentary of Jewish people describing their experiences growing up in postwar Germany, Austria, and Switzerland.

More Sights South of Unter den Linden

East Side Gallery—The biggest remaining stretch of the Wall is now "the world's longest outdoor art gallery." It stretches for nearly a mile and is covered with murals painted by artists from around the world. The murals (classified as protected monuments) got a facelift in 2009, when the city invited the original artists back to re-create their work for the 20th anniversary of the fall of the Wall. This segment of the Wall makes a poignant walk. For a quick look, take the S-Bahn to the Ostbahnhof station (follow signs to Stralauerplatz exit; once outside, TV Tower will be to your right; go left and at next corner look to your right—the Wall is across the busy street). The gallery is slowly being consumed by developers. If you walk the entire length of the East Side Gallery, you'll find a small Wall souvenir shop at the end and a bridge crossing the river to a subway station at Schlesisches Tor (in Kreuzberg). The bridge, a fine example of Brandenburg Neo-Gothic brickwork, has a fun neon "rock, paper, scissors" installment poking fun at the futility of the Cold War.

Kreuzberg—This district—once abutting the dreary Wall and inhabited mostly by poor Turkish guest laborers and their families—is still run-down, with graffiti-riddled buildings and plenty of student and Turkish street life. It offers a gritty look at melting-pot Berlin, in a city where original Berliners are as rare as old buildings. Berlin is the largest Turkish city outside of Turkey itself, and Kreuzberg is its "downtown." But to call it a "little Istanbul" insults the big one. You'll see *Döner Kebab* stands, shops decorated with spray paint, and mothers wrapped in colorful scarves. But lately, an influx of immigrants from many other countries has diluted the Turkish-ness of Kreuzberg. Berliners come here for fun ethnic eateries. For an easy dose of Kreuzberg, joyride on bus #129 (catch it near Jewish Museum). For a colorful stroll, take the U-Bahn to Kottbusser Tor and wander—ideally on Tuesday and Friday between 12:00 and 18:00, when the Turkish Market sprawls along the Maybachufer riverbank.

North of Unter den Linden

There are few major sights to the north of Unter den Linden, but this area has some of Berlin's trendiest, most interesting neighborhoods. I've listed these roughly from south to north, as you'd approach them from the city center and Unter den Linden. On a sunny day, a stroll (or tram ride) through these bursting-with-life areas can be as engaging as any museum in town.

Hackescher Markt

This area, in front of the S-Bahn station of the same name, is a great people scene day and night. The brick trestle supporting the train track is another classic example of the city's Brandenburg Neo-Gothic brickwork. Most of the brick archways are now filled with hip shops, which have official—and newly trendy—addresses such as "S-Bahn Arch #9, Hackescher Markt." Within 100 yards of the S-Bahn station, you'll find Hackeschen Höfe (described next), recommended Turkish and Bavarian restaurants, walking-tour and pub-crawl departure points, and tram #M1 to Prenzlauer Berg.

Hackeschen Höfe (a block in front of the Hackescher Markt S-Bahn station) is a series of eight courtyards bunny-hopping through a wonderfully restored 1907 *Jugendstil* (German Art Nouveau) building. Berlin's apartments are organized like this—courtyard after courtyard leading off the main roads. This complex is full of trendy restaurants (including the recommended Turkish eatery, Hasir), theaters, and cinemas (playing movies in their original languages). This is a wonderful example of how to make huge city blocks livable. Two decades after the Cold War, this area has reached the final evolution of East Berlin's urban restoration. (These courtyards also serve a useful lesson for visitors: Much of Berlin's charm hides off the street front.)

Oranienburger Strasse

Oranienburger Strasse is anchored by an important and somber sight, the New Synagogue. But the rest of this zone (roughly between the synagogue and Torstrasse) is colorful and quirky—especially after dark. The streets behind Grosse Hamburger Strasse flicker with atmospheric cafés, *Kneipen* (pubs), and art galleries. At night (from about 20:00), techno-prostitutes line Oranienburger Strasse. Prostitution is legal throughout Germany. Prostitutes pay taxes and receive health care insurance like anyone else. On this street, they hire security guards (lingering nearby) for safety—and they all seem to buy their Barbarella wardrobes at the same place.

▲**New Synagogue (Neue Synagoge)**—A shiny gilded dome marks the New Synagogue, now a museum and cultural center.

Consecrated in 1866, this was once the biggest and finest synagogue in Germany, with seating for 3,200 worshippers and a sumptuous Moorish-style interior modeled after the Alhambra. It was desecrated by Nazis on Crystal Night (Kristallnacht) in 1938, bombed in 1943, and partially rebuilt in 1990. Only the dome and facade have been restored—a window overlooks the vacant field marking what used to be the synagogue. On its facade, a small plaque—added by East Berlin Jews in 1966—reads "Never forget" *(Vergesst es nie)*. At that time East Berlin had only a few hundred Jews, but now that the city is reunited, the Jewish community numbers about 12,000.

Inside, past tight security, the small but moving permanent

exhibit called Open Ye the Gates describes the Berlin Jewish community through the centuries (filling three big rooms on the ground floor and first floor, with some good English descriptions). Examine the cutaway model showing the entire synagogue (pre-destruction) and an exhibit of religious items. Stairs lead up (past temporary exhibits, with a separate entry fee) to the dome, where there's not much to see except the unimpressive-from-the-inside dome itself and ho-hum views—not worth the entry price or the climb.

Cost and Hours: Main exhibit-€3.50, dome-€2, temporary exhibits-€3, €7 combo-ticket covers everything, audioguide-€3; March-Oct Sun-Mon 10:00-20:00, Tue-Thu 10:00-18:00, Fri 10:00-17:00—until 14:00 in Oct and March-May, closed Sat; Nov-Feb Sun-Thu 10:00-18:00, Fri 10:00-14:00, closed Sat; Oranienburger Strasse 28/30, enter through the low-profile door in the modern building just right of the domed synagogue facade, S-Bahn: Oranienburger Strasse, tel. 030/8802-8300 and press 1, www.cjudaicum.de.

Nearby: A block from the synagogue (to the right as you face it), walk 50 yards down **Grosse Hamburger Strasse** to a little park. This street was known for 200 years as the "street of tolerance" because the Jewish community donated land to Protestants so they could build a church. Hitler turned it into the "street of death" *(Todes Strasse)*, bulldozing 12,000 graves of the city's oldest Jewish cemetery and turning a Jewish nursing home into a deportation center. Because of the small but growing radical Islamic element in Berlin, and a smattering of persistent neo-Nazis, several police officers and an Israeli secret agent keep watch over this park and the Jewish high school nearby.

Other Sights on Oranienburger Strasse—This is an enjoyable zone to explore by day or night. Spice up your stroll with these stops.

Next door to the New Synagogue (to the left as you face it) is every local kid's favorite traditional candy shop, **Bonbonmacherei,** where you can see candy being made the old-fashioned way (Wed-Sat 12:00-20:00, closed Sun-Tue, at Oranienburger Strasse 32, in the Heckmann Höfe—another example of a classic Berlin courtyard).

Just beyond the candy shop, across Tucholskystrasse, is the stately old red-brick facade of the former Imperial Post Office. Today this complex hosts an innovative avant-garde photography gallery called **C/O Berlin,** with pricey rotating exhibits on

Stolpersteine (Stumbling Stones)

As you wander through the Hackeschen Höfe and Oranienburger Strasse neighborhoods—and throughout Germany—you might stumble over small brass plaques in the sidewalk called *Stolpersteine. Stolpern* means "to stumble," which is what you are meant to do. These plaques are placed in front of former homes of residents who were killed during World War II. The *Stolpersteine* serve not only to honor the victims, but also to stimulate thought and discussion on a daily basis (rather than only during visits to memorial sites) and to put an individual's name on the mass horror.

More than 25,000 of these plaques have been installed across Germany. They're made of brass so they stay polished as you walk over them, instead of fading into the sidewalk. On each plaque is the name of the victim who lived in that spot, and how and where that person died. While some Holocaust memorials formerly used neutral terminology like "perished," now they use words like "murdered"—part of the very honest way in which today's Germans are dealing with their country's past. Ironically, the city of Munich banned *Stolpersteine*, saying that the plaques were insulting and degrading to victims of persecution, who would continue to be trod on by "Nazi boots." Installation of a *Stolperstein* can be sponsored for €95 and has become popular in schools, where students research the memorialized person's life as a class project.

two floors (usually one big-name exhibit plus lesser-known, more out-there photographers) and occasional installations outside the building (€10—price may vary with exhibits, daily 11:00-20:00, Oranienburger Strasse 35-36, tel. 030/2844-4160, www.co-berlin .com).

Two blocks farther down (across from the intersection with Auguststrasse) is the run-down, graffiti-slathered **Tacheles building.** This building—which may be gone by the time you read this—has long hosted an arts collective called Kunsthaus Tacheles. You're welcome to climb the stairs and poke around. Severely damaged in World War II, the condemned building was taken over by a community of squatters in 1990, shortly before its planned demolition. They managed to secure landmark status for the place and proceeded to convert the damaged husk of a building into living and studio space for artists. The building owner (now eager to develop this prime real estate into a fancy hotel) tried to evict the artists in early 2011, but they were spared thanks to a €1 million donation from an anonymous supporter. The owner still wants the artists out, and the latest ploy was to cut the unwanted tenants off from the outside world by—no joke—surrounding the entrances with a 10-foot-high wall (a bold suggestion in a city that knows a thing or two about the divisiveness of a wall). Will the artists prevail, or will the building fall? Stay tuned.

▲Prenzlauer Berg

Young, in-the-know locals agree that Prenzlauer Berg (PRENTS-low-er behrk) is one of Berlin's most colorful neighborhoods (roughly between Helmholtzplatz and Kollwitzplatz and along Kastanienallee, U2: Senefelderplatz and Eberswalder Strasse; or take the S-Bahn to Hackescher Markt and catch tram #M1 north). Tourists call it "Prenzl'berg" for short, while Berliners just call it "der Berg." This part of the city was largely untouched during World War II, but its buildings slowly rotted away under the communists. After the Wall fell, it was overrun with laid-back hipsters, energetic young families, and clever entrepreneurs who breathed life back into its classic old apartment blocks, deserted factories, and long-forgotten breweries. Ten years of rent control kept things affordable for its bohemian residents. But now landlords are free to charge what the market will bear, and the vibe is changing. This is ground zero for Berlin's baby boom: Tattooed and pierced young moms and dads, who've joined the modern rat-race without giving up their alternative flair, push their youngsters in designer strollers past trendy boutiques and restaurants. You'll count more kids here than just about anywhere else in town. Locals complain that these days the cafés and bars cater to yuppies sipping prosecco, while the working class and artistic types are being pushed out. While it has changed plenty, I still find Prenzlauer Berg a celebration of life and a joy to stroll through. Though it's a few blocks farther out than the neighborhoods described previously, it's a fun area to explore and have a meal (see page 753) or spend the night (see page 738).

▲Berlin Wall Memorial
(Gedenkstätte Berliner Mauer)

While tourists flock to Checkpoint Charlie, local authorities have been investing in this site to develop Berlin's most substantial

attraction relating to its gone-but-not-forgotten Wall. Exhibits line up along a two-block stretch of Bernauer Strasse, stretching northeast from the Nordbahnhof S-Bahn station. You can enter two different museums; see several fragments of the Wall, plus various open-air exhibits and  memorials; and peer from an observation tower down into a preserved, complete stretch of the Wall system (as it was during the

Cold War). To prepare for a visit here, be sure to read "The Berlin Wall (and Its Fall)" sidebar on page 706.

Cost and Hours: Free; Visitor Center and Documentation Center open Tue-Sun 9:30-19:00, Nov-March until 18:00, closed Mon; outdoor areas open 24 hours daily; last English movie starts at 18:00, memorial chapel closes at 17:00; Bernauer Strasse 111, tel. 030/4679-86666, www.berliner-mauer-gedenkstaette.de.

Getting There: Take the S-Bahn (line S-1, S-2, or S-25—all handy from Potsdamer Platz, Brandenburger Tor, or Friedrichstrasse) to Nordbahnhof. The Nordbahnhof's underground hallways have history exhibits in English (explained later). Exit by following signs for *Bernauer Strasse,* and you'll pop out across the street from a long chunk of Wall and kitty-corner from the Visitor Center.

Background: The Berlin Wall, which was erected virtually overnight in 1961, ran right along Bernauer Strasse. People were

suddenly separated from their neighbors across the street. This stretch was particularly notorious because existing apartment buildings were incorporated into the structure of the Wall itself. Film footage and photographs from the era show Berliners worriedly watching workmen seal off these

buildings from the West, brick by brick. Some people attempted to leap to freedom from upper-story windows, with mixed results. One of the unfortunate ones was Ida Siekmann, who fell to her death from her third-floor apartment on August 22, 1961, and is considered the first casualty of the Berlin Wall.

Touring the Memorial: From the Nordbahnhof station (which has some interesting Wall history in itself), head first to the Visitor Center to get your bearings, then explore the assorted Wall fragments and other sights in the park across the street. Work your way up Bernauer Strasse to the Documentation Center, Wall System, and memorial chapel.

Nordbahnhof—This S-Bahn station was one of the "ghost stations" of Cold War Berlin. As it was a dogleg of the East mostly surrounded by the West, Western subway trains had permission to use the underground tracks to zip through this station (without stopping, of course) en route between stops in the West. Posted information boards show photos comparing 1989 with 2009, and explain that East German border guards, who were stationed here to ensure that nobody got on or off those trains, were literally locked into their surveillance rooms to prevent them from escaping. (But one subway employee and his family used the tunnels to walk to the West and freedom.)

Follow signs down a long yellow hall to Bernauer Strasse. Climbing the stairs up to the Bernauer Strasse exit, ponder that the doorway at the top of these stairs (marked by the *Sperrmauer 1961-1989* plaque) was a bricked-off no-man's-land just 25 years ago. Stepping outside, you'll see the Wall park directly across the street, and the Visitor Center in a low rust-colored building kitty-corner across the street.

Visitor Center (Bezucherzentrum)—This new, small complex has a helpful information desk, a bookstore, and two good movies that provide context for a visit (they run in English at the top of each hour, about 30 minutes for the whole spiel): *History of the Wall* offers a great 12-minute overview of why the Wall was built and how it fell. That's followed by *Walled In!*, an animated 12-minute film illustrating the Wall as it functioned here at Bernauer Strasse (Wall wonks will find it fascinating). Before leaving, pick up the brochure explaining the outdoor exhibits, and ask about any new exhibits.

Wall Fragments and Other Sights—Across the street from the Visitor Center is a long stretch of Wall. The park behind it is scattered with a few more Wall chunks as well as monuments and memorials honoring its victims. To get your bearings, find the small model of the entire area when the Wall still stood (just across the street from the Nordbahnhof). While most items are explained by English plaques, the brochure from the Visitor Center helps you better appreciate what you're seeing. The rusty "Window of Remembrance" monument honors slain would-be escapees with their names, dates of death, and transparent photos viewable from both sides. Before it was the no-man's-land between the walls, this area was the parish graveyard for a nearby church; ironically, DDR officials had to move a thousand graves from here to create a "death strip."

Berlin Wall Documentation Center (Dokumentations-zentrum Berliner Mauer)—This "Doku-Center" has two movies, a small exhibit, and a viewpoint tower overlooking the preserved Wall section. The two **films** shown on the ground floor are different from those screened at the Visitor Center: *The View*, dating from 1965, tells the story of an elderly West Berlin woman who lived near the Wall, and could look into the death strip and the East from her window (in German only). *Mauerflug* features aerial photography of Berlin from the spring of 1990—after the Wall had opened, but while most of the 96-mile-long barricade still stood, offering an illuminating look at a divided city (English subtitles).

Upstairs is an **exhibit** with photos and videos detailing the construction of the Wall that began August 13, 1961. At the model of the Wall along Bernauer Strasse, notice how existing buildings were incorporated into the structure. Headphones let you listen to propagandistic, high-spirited oompah music from East Germany that celebrated the construction of the wall: "It was high time!" There's also a list of the 163 people who died attempting to cross the Wall. From the top-floor **viewpoint** look down at the Wall itself (described next).

Wall System—This is the last surviving intact bit of the "Wall system" (with both sides of its Wall—capped by the round pipe that

made it tougher for escapees to get a grip—and its no-man's-land, or death strip). The guard tower came from a different part of the Wall; it was actually purchased on that great capitalist invention, eBay (somewhere, Stalin spins in his grave). A strip of photos and descriptions explains what you're seeing. Plaques along the sidewalk below you mark the locations of escapes or deaths.

Just beyond the Wall section (to the left), and also viewable from the tower, is a modern, cagelike church (described next).

Chapel of Reconciliation (Kapelle der Versöhnung)—This marks the spot of the late-19th-century Church of Reconciliation, which survived WWII bombs...but did not survive the communists. When the Wall was built, this church wound up, unusable, right in the middle of the death strip. It was torn down in 1985, supposedly because it got in the way of the bor-

der guards' sight lines. (This coincided with a period in which anti-DDR opposition movements were percolating in Christian churches, prompting the nonbeliever regime to destroy several houses of worship.) If you're interested, walk around the chapel for a closer look (it closes at 17:00). Notice the larger footprint of the original church in the field around it. The chapel hosts daily prayer services for the victims of the Wall.

More Wall Sights—Over the next few years, the Memorial plans to gradually add more open-air exhibitions about the Berlin Wall farther along Bernauer Strasse. Eventually the chain of sights will stretch all the way to Eberswalder Strasse and Oderberger Strasse, near the heart of Prenzlauer Berg.

Natural History Museum (Museum für Naturkunde)

This museum is worth a visit just to see the largest dinosaur skeleton ever assembled. While you're there, meet "Bobby" the stuffed ape, and tour the new Wet Collections, displaying shelf after shelf of animals preserved in ethanol (about a million all together). The museum is a magnet for the city's children, who love the interactive displays, the "History of the Universe in 120 Seconds" exhibit, and the cool virtual-reality "Jurascope" glasses that put meat and skin on all the dinosaur skeletons.

Cost and Hours: €6, €3.50 for kids, Tue-Fri 9:30-18:00, Sat-Sun 10:00-18:00, closed Mon, last entry 30 minutes before closing, Invalidenstrasse 43, U6: Naturkundemuseum, tel. 030/2093-8591, www.naturkundemuseum-berlin.de.

Sights in Central Berlin

Tiergarten Park and Nearby

Berlin's "Central Park" stretches two miles from Bahnhof Zoo to the Brandenburg Gate.

Victory Column (Siegessäule)—The Tiergarten's newly restored centerpiece, the Victory Column, was built to commemorate the Prussian defeat of Denmark in 1864...then reinterpreted after the defeat of France in 1870. The pointy-helmeted Germans rubbed it in, decorating the tower with French cannons and paying for it all with francs received as war reparations. The three lower rings commemorate Bismarck's victories. I imagine the statues of Moltke and other German military greats—which lurk in the trees nearby—goose-stepping around the floodlit angel at night.

Originally standing at the Reichstag, in 1938 the tower was moved to this position and given a 25-foot lengthening by Hitler's architect Albert Speer, in anticipation of the planned re-envisioning of Berlin as "Germania"—the capital of a worldwide Nazi empire. Streets leading to the circle are flanked by surviving Nazi guardhouses, built in the stern style that fascists loved. At the memorial's first level, notice how WWII bullets chipped the fine marble columns. From 1989 to 2003, the column was the epicenter of the Love Parade (Berlin's city-wide techno-hedonist street party), and it was the backdrop for Barack Obama's summer 2008 visit to Germany as a presidential candidate. (He asked to speak in front of the Brandenburg Gate, but German Chancellor Angela Merkel wanted to save that symbol from "politics.")

Climbing its 270 steps earns you a breathtaking Berlin-wide view and a close-up of the gilded bronze statue of the goddess Victoria (go ahead, call her "the chick on a stick"—everybody here does). You might recognize Victoria from Wim Wenders' 1987 arthouse classic *Wings of Desire*, or the *Stay (Faraway, So Close!)* video

he directed for the rock band U2.

Cost and Hours: €2.20; April-Oct Mon-Fri 9:30-18:30, Sat-Sun 9:30-19:00; Nov-March Mon-Fri 10:00-17:00, Sat-Sun 10:00-17:30; closes in the rain, WCs for paying guests only, no elevator, bus #100, tel. 030/8639-8560. From the tower, the grand Strasse des 17 Juni leads east to the Brandenburg Gate.

Flea Market—A colorful flea market with great antiques, more than 200 stalls, collector-savvy merchants, and fun German fast-food stands thrives weekends on Strasse des 17 Juni (Sat-Sun 6:00-16:00, right next to S-Bahn: Tiergarten).

German Resistance Memorial (Gedenkstätte Deutscher Widerstand)—This memorial and museum, located in the former Bendlerblock military headquarters just south of the Tiergarten, tells the story of several organized German resistance movements and the more than 42 separate assassination attempts against Hitler. An ill-fated scheme to kill Hitler was plotted in this building (the actual attempt occurred in Rastenburg, eastern Prussia; the event was dramatized in the 2009 Tom Cruise film *Valkyrie*). The conspirators, including Claus Schenk Graf von Stauffenberg, were shot here in the courtyard. While there are no real artifacts, the spirit that haunts the place is multilingual.

Cost and Hours: Free, Mon-Fri 9:00-18:00, Thu until 20:00, Sat-Sun 10:00-18:00, free and good English audioguide—passport required, €3 printed English translation, no crowds, near Kulturforum at Stauffenbergstrasse 13, enter in courtyard, door on left, main exhibit on third floor, bus #M29, tel. 030/2699-5000, www.gdw-berlin.de.

Potsdamer Platz and Nearby

The "Times Square of Berlin," and possibly the busiest square in Europe before World War II, Potsdamer Platz was cut in two by the Wall and left a deserted no-man's-land for 40 years. Today, this immense commercial/residential/entertainment center, sitting on a futuristic transportation hub, is home to the European corporate headquarters of several big-league companies.

▲Potsdamer Platz

The new Potsdamer Platz was a vision begun in 1991, when it was announced that Berlin would resume its position as the capital of Germany. Sony, Daimler, and other major corporations have turned the square once again into a center of Berlin. Like great Christian churches built upon pagan holy grounds, Potsdamer Platz—with its corporate logos flying high and shiny above what was the Wall—trumpets the triumph of capitalism.

While Potsdamer Platz tries to give Berlin a common center, the city has always been—and remains—a collection of towns. Locals recognize 28 distinct neighborhoods that may have grown together but still maintain their historic orientation. While Munich has the single dominant Marienplatz, Berlin will always have Charlottenburg, Savignyplatz, Kreuzberg, Prenzlauer Berg, and so on. In general, Berliners prefer these characteristic neighborhoods

to an official city center. They're unimpressed by the grandeur of Potsdamer Platz, simply considering it a good place to go to the movies, with overpriced, touristy restaurants.

While most of the complex just feels big (the arcade is like any huge, modern, American mall), the entrance to the complex and Sony Center are worth a visit, and German-film buffs will enjoy the Deutsche Kinemathek museum (described later).

For an overview of the new construction, and a scenic route to the Sony Center, start at the Bahnhof Potsdamer Platz (east end of Potsdamer Strasse, S- and U-Bahn: Potsdamer Platz, exit following *Leipziger Platz* signs to see the best view of skyscrapers as you emerge). Find the green hexagonal **clock tower** with the traffic lights on top. This is a replica of the first automatic traffic light in Europe, which once stood at the six-street intersection of Potsdamer Platz. On either side of Potsdamer Strasse, you'll see enormous cubical entrances to the underground Potsdamer

Platz train station. Near these entrances, notice the slanted **glass cylinders** sticking out of the ground. The mirrors on the tops of the tubes move with the sun to collect light and send it underground (saving piles of euros in energy costs). A line in the pavement indicates where the **Berlin Wall** once stood. On the right side of the street, notice the re-erected slabs of the Wall. Imagine when the first piece was cut out (see photo and history on nearby panel). These hang like scalps at the gate of Fort Capitalism...look up at the towering corporate headquarters: Market forces have won a clear victory. Now descend into one of the train station entrances and follow signs to *Sony Center*. As you walk through the passage, notice the wall panels with historical information.

You'll come up the escalator into the **Sony Center** under a grand canopy (designed to evoke Mount Fuji). At night, multi-

colored floodlights play on the underside of this tent. Office workers and tourists eat here by the fountain, enjoying the parade of people. The modern Bavarian Lindenbräu beer hall—the Sony boss wanted a *Bräuhaus*—serves traditional food (€11-17, daily 11:00-24:30, big €8 salads, three-foot-long taster boards of eight different beers, tel. 030/2575-1280). Across the plaza, Josty Bar is built around a surviving bit of a venerable hotel that was a meeting place for Berlin's rich and famous before the bombs (€10-17 meals, daily 10:00-24:00, tel. 030/2575-9702). CineStar is a rare cinema that plays mainstream movies in their original language (www.cinestar.de).

Sights near Potsdamer Platz

▲**Deutsche Kinemathek Film and TV Museum**—This exhibit is the most interesting place to visit in the Sony Center. The early pioneers in filmmaking were German (including Fritz Lang, F. W. Murnau, Ernst Lubitsch, and the Austrian-born Billy Wilder), and many of them also became influential in Hollywood—making this a fun visit for cinephiles. Your admission ticket gets you into several floors of exhibits (including temporary exhibits on floors 1 and 4) made meaningful by the included, essential English audioguide.

Cost and Hours: €6, includes 1.5-hour audioguide, Tue-Sun 10:00-18:00, Thu until 20:00, closed Mon, tel. 030/2474-9888, www.deutsche-kinemathek.de.

Nearby: The Kino Arsenal theater downstairs shows offbeat art-house films in their original language.

Touring the Museum: From the ticket desk, ride the elevator up to the third floor, where you can turn left (into the film section, floors 3 and 2) or right (into the TV section, floors 3 and 4).

In the **film section,** you'll walk back in time through a fun mirrored entryway. The exhibit starts with the German film industry's beginnings, with an emphasis on the Weimar Republic period in the 1920s, when Berlin rivaled Hollywood. Influential films included the early German Expressionist masterpiece *The Cabinet of Dr. Caligari* (1920) and Fritz Lang's seminal *Metropolis* (1927). Three rooms are dedicated to Marlene Dietrich, who was a huge star both in Germany and, later, in Hollywood. (Dietrich, who performed at USO shows to entertain Allied troops fighting against her former homeland, once said, "I don't hate the Germans, I hate the Nazis.") Another section examines Nazi use of film as propaganda, including Leni Riefenstahl's masterful documentary of the 1936 Berlin Olympics and her earlier, chillingly propagandistic *Triumph of the Will* (1935). The postwar period was defined by two separate East and West German film industries. The exhibit's finale reminds us that German filmmakers are still highly influential and successful—including Wolfgang Petersen *(Das Boot, Air Force One, The Perfect Storm)* and Werner Herzog (the documentary *Grizzly Man* and the drama *Rescue Dawn*). (If this visit gets you curious about German cinema, see the recommendations in the Appendix.)

The **TV section** tells the story of *das Idioten Box* from its infancy (when it was primarily used as a Nazi propaganda tool) to today. The 30-minute kaleidoscopic review—kind of a frantic fast-forward montage of greatest hits in German TV history, both East and West—is great fun even if you don't understand a word of it (it plays all day long, with 10-minute breaks). Otherwise, the TV section is a little more challenging for non-German speakers to appreciate. Upstairs (on the fourth floor) is a TV archive where you can dial through a wide range of new and classic German TV standards.

Panoramapunkt—Across Potsdamer Strasse from the Film and TV Museum, you can ride what's billed as "the fastest elevator in Europe" to skyscraping rooftop views. You'll travel at nearly 30 feet per second to the top of the 300-foot-tall Kollhoff Tower. Its sheltered but open-air view deck provides a fun opportunity to survey Berlin's ongoing construction from above.

Cost and Hours: €5.50, €9.50 VIP ticket lets you skip the line, audioguide-€2.50, daily 10:00-20:00, until 22:00 in summer, last elevator 30 minutes before closing, in red-brick building at Potsdamer Platz 1, tel. 030/2593-07080, www.panorama punkt.de.

Kulturforum

Just west of Potsdamer Platz, Kulturforum rivals Museum Island as the city's cultural heart, with several top museums and Berlin's concert hall—home of the world-famous Berlin Philharmonic orchestra (admission to all Kulturforum sights covered by a single €8 Bereichskarte Kulturforum combo-ticket—a.k.a. Quartier-Karte—and also by the Museumspass; info for all museums: tel. 030/266-424-242, www.kulturforum-berlin.de). Of its sprawling museums, only the Gemäldegalerie is a must (S- or U-Bahn to Potsdamer Platz, then walk along Potsdamer Platz; or from Bahnhof Zoo, take bus #200 to Philharmonie).

▲▲**Gemäldegalerie**—Literally the "Painting Gallery," Germany's top collection of 13th- through 18th-century European paintings (more than 1,400 canvases) is beautifully displayed in a building that's a work of art in itself. The North Wing starts with German paintings of the 13th to 16th centuries, including eight by Albrecht Dürer. Then come the Dutch and Flemish—Jan van Eyck, Pieter Brueghel, Peter Paul Rubens, Anthony van Dyck, Frans Hals, and Jan Vermeer. The wing finishes with German, English, and French 18th-century artists, such as Thomas Gainsborough and Antoine Watteau. An octagonal hall at the end features an impressive stash of Rembrandts. The South Wing is saved for the Italians—Giotto, Botticelli, Titian, Raphael, and Caravaggio.

Cost and Hours: Covered by €8 Kulturforum combo-ticket, Tue-Sun 10:00-18:00, Thu until 22:00, closed Mon, audioguide included with entry, clever little loaner stools, great salad bar in cafeteria upstairs, Matthäikirchplatz 4.

☉ Self-Guided Tour: I'll point out a few highlights, focusing on Northern European artists (Germans, Dutch, and Flemish), with a few Spaniards and Italians thrown in. To go beyond my selections, make ample use of the excellent audioguide.

The collection spreads out on one vast floor surrounding a central hall. Inner rooms have Roman numerals (I, II, III), while adjacent outer rooms are numbered (1, 2, 3). After showing your ticket, turn right into room I and work your way counterclockwise (and roughly chronologically) through the collection.

Rooms I-III/1-4 kick things off with early German paintings (13th-16th centuries). In Room 1, look for the 1532 portrait of wealthy Hanseatic cloth merchant Georg Gisze by **Hans Holbein the Younger** (1497-1543). Gisze's name appears on several of the notes stuck to the wall behind him. And, typical of detail-rich Northern European art, the canvas is bursting with highly

BERLIN

symbolic tidbits. Items scattered on the tabletop and on the shelves behind the merchant represent his lofty status and aspects of his life story. In the vase, the carnation represents his recent engagement, and the herbs symbolize his virtue. And yet, the celebratory flowers are already beginning to fade and the scales behind him are unbalanced, reminders of the fleetingness of happiness and wealth.

In room 2 are fine portraits by the remarkably talented **Albrecht Dürer** (1471-1528), who traveled to Italy during the burgeoning days of the early Renaissance and melded the artistic harmony and classical grandeur he discovered there with a Northern European attention to detail. In *Portrait of Hieronymus Holzschuher* (1526), Dürer skillfully captured the personality of a friend from Nürnberg, right down to the sly twinkle in his sidelong glance. Technically the portrait is perfection: Look closely and see each individual hair of the man's beard and fur coat, and even the reflection of the studio's windows in his eyes. Also notice Dürer's little pyramid-shaped, D-inside-A signature. Signing one's work was a revolutionary assertion of Dürer's renown, at a time when German artists were considered anonymous craftsmen.

Lucas Cranach the Elder (1472-1553), whose works are in room III, was a court painter for the prince electors of Saxony and a close friend of Martin Luther (and his unofficial portraitist). But

The Fountain of Youth (1546) is a far cry from Cranach's solemn portrayals of the Reformer. Old women helped to the fountain (on the left) emerge as young ladies on the right. Newly nubile, the women go into a tent to dress up, snog with noblemen in the bushes (right foreground), dance merrily beneath the trees, and dine grandly beneath a landscape of phallic mountains and towers. This work is flanked by Cranach's Venus nudes. I sense a pattern here.

Netherlandish painters (rooms IV-VI/4-7) were early adopters of oil paint (as opposed to older egg tempera), whose flexibility allowed them to brush the super-fine details for which they are famous. **Rogier van der Weyden** (room IV) was a virtuoso handler of the new medium. In *Portrait of a Young Woman* (c. 1400-1464), the subject wears a typical winged bonnet, addressing the viewer

directly with her fetching blue eyes. The subjects (especially women) of most portraits of the time look off to one side; some art historians guess that the confident woman shown here is Van der Weyden's wife. In the same room is a remarkable, rare trio of three-panel altarpieces by Van der Weyden: The *Marienaltar* shows the life of the Virgin Mary; the *Johannesaltar* narrates the life of John the Baptist—his birth, baptizing Christ (with God and the Holy Spirit hovering overhead), and his gruesome death by decapitation; and the *Middelburger Altar* tells the story of the Nativity. Savor the fine details in each panel of these altarpieces.

BERLIN

Flash forward a few hundred years to the 17th century and Flemish (Belgian) painting (rooms VII-VIII/9-10), and it's apparent how much the Protestant Reformation—and resulting Counter-Reformation—changed the tenor of Northern European art. In works by **Peter Paul Rubens** (1577-1640)—including *Jesus Giving Peter the Keys to Heaven*—calm, carefully studied, detail-oriented seriousness gives way to an exuberant Baroque trumpeting of the greatness of the Catholic Church. In the Counter-Reformation world,

the Catholic Church had serious competition for the hearts and minds of its congregants. Exciting art like this became a way to keep people in the pews. Notice the quivering brushstrokes and almost too-bright colors. (In the same room are portraits by Rubens' student, Anthony van Dyck, as well as some hunting still lifes from Frans Snyders and others.) In the next rooms (VIII and 9) are more Rubens, including the mythological *Perseus Freeing Andromeda* and *The Martyrdom of St. Sebastian by Arrows* (loosely based on a more famous rendition by Andrea Mantegna).

Dutch painting from the 17th century (rooms IX-XI/10-19) is dominated by the convivial portraits by **Frans Hals** (c. 1582-1666). His 1620 portrait of Catharina Hooft (far corner, room 13) presents a startlingly self-possessed baby (the newest member of a wealthy merchant family) dressed with all the finery of a queen, adorned with lace and jewels, and clutching a golden rattle. The smiling nurse supporting the tyke offers her a piece of fruit, whose blush of red perfectly matches the nanny's apple-fresh cheeks.

But the ultimate Dutch master is **Rembrandt van Rijn** (1606-1669), whose powers of perception and invention propelled him to fame in his lifetime. Displayed here are several storytelling scenes (room 16), mostly from classical mythology or biblical stories, all employing Rembrandt's trademark chiaroscuro technique (with a strong contrast between light and dark). In *The Rape of Persephone*, Pluto grabs Persephone from his chariot and races toward the underworld, while other goddesses cling to her robe,

trying to save her. Cast against a nearly black background, the almost overexposed, action-packed scene is shockingly emotional. In the nearby *Samson and Delilah* (1628), Delilah cradles Samson's head in her lap while silently signaling to a goon to shear Samson's hair, the secret to his strength. A self-portrait (room X) of a 28-year-old Rembrandt wearing a beret is paired with the come-hither 1637 *Portrait of Hendrickje Stoffels* (the two were romantically linked). *Samson Threatens His Father-in-Law* (1635) captures the moment just after the mighty Samson (with his flowing hair, elegant robes, and shaking fist) has been told by his wife's father to take a hike. I wouldn't want to cross this guy.

Although **Johannes Vermeer** (1632-1675) is today just as admired as Rembrandt, he was little known in his day, probably because he painted relatively few works for a small circle of Delft collectors. Vermeer was a master at conveying a complicated story through a deceptively simple scene with a few poignant details—

whether it's a woman reading a letter at a window, a milkmaid pouring milk from a pitcher into a bowl, or (as in *The Glass of Wine*, room 18) a young man offering a drink to a young lady. The young man had been playing her some music on his lute (which now sits, discarded, on a chair) and is hoping to seal the deal with some alcohol. The woman is finishing one glass of wine, and her would-be suitor stands ready—almost *too* ready—to pour her another. His sly, somewhat smarmy smirk drives home his high hopes for what will come next. Vermeer has perfectly captured the exact moment of "Will she or won't she?" The painter offers some clues—the coat of arms in the window depicts a woman holding onto the reigns of a horse, staying in control—but ultimately, only he (and the couple) know how this scene will end.

Shift south to Italian, French, and Spanish painting of the 17th and 18th centuries (rooms XII-XIV/23-28). Venetian cityscapes by Canaletto (who also painted Dresden) and lots of bombastic Baroque art hang in room XII. Room XIII features big-name

Spanish artists Murillo, Zurbarán, and the great **Diego Velázquez** (1599-1660). He gave the best of his talents to his portraits, capturing warts-and-all likenesses that are effortlessly real. His 1630 *Portrait of a Lady* conveys the subject's subtle, sly Mona Lisa smile. Her figure and face (against a dull gray background) are filtered through a pleasant natural light. Notice that if you stand too close, the brushstrokes get muddy—but when you back up, the scene snaps into perfectly sharp relief.

From here, the collection itself takes a step backwards—into Italian paintings of the 13th-16th centuries (rooms XV-XVIII/29-41). This section includes some lesser-known works by great Italian Renaissance painters, including Raphael (rooms XVII and 29, including five different Madonnas, among them the *Terranuova Madonna*, in a round frame) and Sandro Botticelli (Room VIII).

New National Gallery (Neue Nationalgalerie)—This gallery features 20th-century art, with ever-changing special exhibits (covered by €8 Kulturforum combo-ticket, Tue-Fri 10:00-18:00, Thu until 22:00, Sat-Sun 11:00-18:00, closed Mon, café downstairs, Potsdamer Strasse 50).

Museum of Decorative Arts (Kunstgewerbemuseum)—Wander through a mazelike floor plan displaying a thousand years of applied arts—porcelain, fine *Jugendstil* (German Art Nouveau) furniture, Art Deco, and reliquaries. There are no English descriptions and no crowds (covered by €8 Kulturforum combo-ticket, Tue-Fri 10:00-18:00, Sat-Sun 11:00-18:00, closed Mon, Herbert-von-Karajan-Strasse 10).

▲**Musical Instruments Museum (Musikinstrumenten Museum)**—This impressive hall is filled with 600 exhibits spanning the 16th century to modern times. Wander among old keyboard instruments and funny-looking tubas. Pick up the included audioguide and free English brochure at the entry. In addition to the English commentary, the audioguide has clips of various instruments being played (just punch in the number next to the instrument you want to hear). This place is fascinating if you're into pianos.

Cost and Hours: €4 but included in €8 Kulturforum ticket, Tue-Fri 9:00-17:00, Thu until 22:00, Sat-Sun 10:00-17:00, closed Mon, low-profile white building east of the big yellow Philharmonic Concert Hall, tel. 030/2548-1178.

Philharmonic Concert Hall—Poke into the lobby of Berlin's yellow Philharmonic building and see if there are tickets available during your stay. The interior is famous for its extraordinary acoustics. Even from the outside, this is a remarkable building, designed by a nautical engineer to look like a ship—notice how different it looks from each angle. Inexpensive and legitimate tickets are often sold on the street before performances. Or you can buy tickets from the box office in person, by phone, or online (ticket office open Mon-Fri 15:00-18:00, Sat-Sun 11:00-14:00, info tel. 030/2548-8132, box office tel. 030/2548-8999—answered daily 9:00-18:00, www.berliner-philharmoniker.de). For guest performances, you must buy tickets through the organizer (see website for details).

Sights in Western Berlin

Throughout the Cold War, Western travelers—and most West Berliners—got used to thinking of western Berlin's Kurfürstendamm boulevard as the heart of the city. But those days have gone the way of the Wall. With the huge changes the city has undergone since 1989, the real "city center" is now, once again, Berlin's historic center (the Mitte district, around Unter den Linden and Friedrichstrasse). While western Berlin still works well as a home base, it's no longer the obvious place from which to explore Berlin. After the new Hauptbahnhof essentially put Bahnhof Zoo out of business in 2006, the area was left with an identity crisis. Now, more than 20 years after reunification, the west side is back and has fully embraced its historical role as a chic, classy suburb.

In the Heart of Western Berlin

A few interesting sights sit within walking distance of Bahnhof Zoo and the Savignyplatz hotels. For a detailed map of this area, see page 746.

▲**Kurfürstendamm**—Western Berlin's main drag, Kurfürstendamm boulevard (nicknamed "Ku'damm"), starts at Kaiser Wilhelm Memorial Church and does a commercial cancan for two miles. In the 1850s, when Berlin became a wealthy and important capital, her "new rich" chose Kurfürstendamm as their street. Bismarck made it Berlin's Champs-Elysées. In the 1920s, it became a chic and fashionable drag of cafés and boutiques. During the Third Reich, as home to an international community of diplomats and journalists, it enjoyed more freedom than the rest of Berlin. Throughout the Cold War, economic subsidies from the West made sure that capitalism thrived on Ku'damm. And today, while much of the old charm has been hamburgerized, Ku'damm is still a fine place to enjoy elegant shops (around Fasanenstrasse), department stores, and people-watching.

▲**Kaiser Wilhelm Memorial Church (Gedächtniskirche)**—
This church was originally dedicated to the first emperor of Germany. Reliefs and mosaics show great events in the life of Germany's favorite *Kaiser*, from his coronation in 1871 to his death in 1888. The church's bombed-out ruins have been left standing as a poignant memorial to the destruction of Berlin in World War II.

Cost and Hours: Church—free, daily 9:00-19:00; Memorial Hall—free, Mon-Sat 10:00-18:00, shorter hours on Sun. Located on Breitscheidplatz, U2/U9 and S-Bahn: Zoologischer Garten or U1/U9: Kurfürstendamm, www.gedaechtniskirche.com.

Touring the Church: The church is actually an ensemble of buildings: a new church, the matching bell tower, a meeting hall, and the bombed-out ruins of the old church, with its Memorial Hall. Note that the church is likely to be undergoing renovation when you visit (though the interior should still be open to visitors). Slated for completion around the fall of 2012, the renovations will strengthen the foundations of all four buildings and make it possible for visitors to get to the top of the church for the first time in 60 years. Until then, an aluminum tent surrounds the building to prevent dust contamination and to make it easier to work in inclement weather. (In fact, in an attempt to revitalize the western part of the city, the entire area around the church and Breitscheid Platz will be under reconstruction.)

Under a Neo-Romanesque mosaic ceiling, the **Memorial Hall** features a small exhibit of interesting photos about the bombing and before-and-after models of the church. After the war, some Berliners wanted to tear down the ruins and build it anew. Instead, it was decided to keep what was left of the old church as a memorial and stage a competition to design a modern, add-on section. The winning entry—the short, modern church (1961) next to the Memorial Hall—offers a meditative world of 11,000 little blue windows. The blue glass was given to the church by the French as a reconciliation gift. For more information on both churches, pick up the English flier (€0.50).

As you enter the **church,** a peaceful blue oasis in the middle of the busy city, turn immediately right to find a simple charcoal sketch of the Virgin Mary wrapped in a shawl. During the Battle of Stalingrad, German combat surgeon Kurt Reuber rendered the Virgin on the back of a stolen Soviet map to comfort the men in his care. On the right are the words "Light, Life, Love" from the gospel of John; on the left, "Christmas in the cauldron 1942"; and at the bottom, "Fortress Stalingrad." Though Reuber died in captivity a year later, his sketch had been flown out of Stalingrad on the last medical evacuation flight, and postwar Germany embraced it as a symbol of the wish for peace. Copies of the drawing, now known as the *Stalingrad Madonna,* hang in the Berlin Cathedral, in England's Coventry, and in Russia's Volgograd (formerly Stalingrad) as a sign of peaceful understanding between the nations. As another act of reconciliation, every Friday at 13:00 a "Prayers for Peace" service is held simultaneously with the cathedral in Coventry.

Nearby: The lively square between the churches and the Europa Center (a once-impressive, shiny high-rise shopping center built as a showcase of Western capitalism during the Cold War) usually attracts street musicians and performers—especially in the summer. Berliners call the funky fountain "the wet meatball."

The Story of Berlin—Filling most of what seems like a department store right on Ku'damm (at #207), this sprawling history exhibit tells the stormy 800-year story of Berlin in a creative way. While there are almost no real historic artifacts, the exhibit does a good job of cobbling together many dimensions of the life and tumultuous times of this great city. It's particularly strong on the story of the city from World War I through the Cold War. However, for similar information, the German History Museum on Unter den Linden is a far better use of your time and money (see page 684).

Cost and Hours: €10, daily 10:00-20:00, last entry 2 hours before closing, tel. 030/8872-0100, www.story-of-berlin.de. Times for the 30-minute bunker tour are posted at the entry.

▲**Käthe Kollwitz Museum**—This local artist (1867-1945), who experienced much of Berlin's stormiest century, conveys some powerful and mostly sad feelings about motherhood, war, and suffering through the stark faces of her art. This small yet fine collection (the only one in town of Kollwitz's work) consists of three floors of charcoal drawings, topped by an attic with a handful of sculptures.

Cost and Hours: €6, €1 pamphlet has necessary English explanations of a few major works, daily 11:00-18:00, a block off Ku'damm at Fasanenstrasse 24, U-Bahn: Uhlandstrasse, tel. 030/882-5210, www.kaethe-kollwitz.de.

▲**Kaufhaus des Westens (KaDeWe)**—The "Department Store of the West" has been a Berlin tradition for more than a century. With a staff of 2,100 to help you sort through its vast selection of 380,000 items, KaDeWe claims to be the biggest department store on the Continent. You can get everything from a haircut and train ticket (third floor) to souvenirs (fourth floor). The theater and concert box office on the sixth floor charges an 18 percent booking fee, but they know all your options (cash only). The sixth floor is a world of gourmet taste treats. The biggest selection of deli and exotic food in Germany offers plenty of classy opportunities to sit down and eat. Ride the glass elevator to the seventh floor's glass-domed Winter Garden, a self-service cafeteria—fun but pricey.

Hours and Information: Mon-Thu 10:00-20:00, Fri 10:00-21:00, Sat 9:30-20:00, closed Sun, S-Bahn: Zoologischer Garten or U-Bahn: Wittenbergplatz, tel. 030/21210, www.kadewe.de.

Nearby: The Wittenbergplatz U-Bahn station (in front of KaDeWe) is a unique opportunity to see an old-time station. Enjoy its interior with classic advertisements still decorating its venerable walls.

Berlin Zoo (Zoologischer Garten Berlin)—More than 1,500 different kinds of animals call Berlin's famous zoo home...or so the zookeepers like to think. The big hit here is the lonely panda bear (straight in from the entrance).

Cost and Hours: €13 for zoo, €13 for world-class aquarium, €20 for both, kids half-price, daily mid-March–mid-Oct generally 9:00-19:00, mid-Oct–mid-March generally 9:00-17:00, aquarium closes 30 minutes earlier; feeding times—*Fütterungszeiten*—posted just inside entrance, the best feeding show is the sea lions—generally at 15:15; enter near Europa Center in front of Hotel Palace or opposite Bahnhof Zoo on Hardenbergplatz, Budapester Strasse 34, tel. 030/254-010, www.zoo-berlin.de.

Erotic Art Museum—This offers two floors of graphic art (especially East Asian), old-time sex-toy knickknacks, and a special exhibit on the queen of German pornography, the late Beate Uhse. This amazing woman, a former test pilot for the Third Reich and groundbreaking purveyor of condoms and sex ed in the 1950s, was the female Hugh Hefner of Germany and CEO of a huge chain of porn shops. She is famously credited with bringing sex out of the bedroom and onto the kitchen table, "where it belonged." FYI: You'll see much more sex for half the price in a private video booth next door.

Cost and Hours: €5, Mon-Sat 9:00-24:00, Sun 13:00-24:00, last entry at 23:00, hard-to-beat gift shop, at corner of Kantstrasse and Joachimstalerstrasse, a block from Bahnhof Zoo, tel. 030/8862-6613.

Charlottenburg Palace Area

The Charlottenburg district—with a cluster of museums across the street from a grand palace—is an easy side-trip from downtown. The palace isn't much to see, but if the surrounding museums appeal to you, consider making the trip. To get here, ride U2 to Sophie-Charlotte Platz and walk 10 minutes up the tree-lined boulevard Schlossstrasse (following signs to *Schloss*), or—much faster—catch bus #M45 (direction Spandau) direct from Bahnhof Zoo.

Eating near Charlottenburg Palace: For a Charlottenburg lunch, the **Bräuhaus Lemke** is a comfortable brewpub restaurant with a copper and woody atmosphere, good local microbeers (*dunkles* means "dark," *helles* is "light"), and traditional German grub (€8-15 meals, daily 10:00-24:00, fun for groups, across from palace at Luisenplatz 1, tel. 030/3087-8979). Or consider lunching like the Russians, who have been part of Charlottenburg ever since Frederick the Great invited them in the 18th century. The small **Samovar** serves traditional Russian specialties in a comfortable, intimate setting (€6-20 meals, €3.40 Russian tea, daily 11:00-22:00, just past Bräuhaus Lemke at Luisenplatz 3, tel. 030/341-4154).

▲**Charlottenburg Palace (Schloss Charlottenburg)**—If you've seen the great palaces of Europe, this Baroque palace, also known as the Altes Schloss, comes in at about number 10 (behind Potsdam, too). It's the largest former residence of the royal Hohenzollern family in Berlin and contains the biggest collection of 17th-century French fresco painting outside France. The **Neue Flügel** (a.k.a. the Knobelsdorff Wing) has a separate entry fee and features a few royal apartments. Go upstairs and take a substantial hike through restored-since-the-war gold-crusted white rooms.

Cost and Hours: Palace—€12, includes audioguide, Tue-Sun 10:00-18:00, until 17:00 Nov-March, closed Mon, last entry 30 minutes before closing, tel. 030/320-911; Neue Flügel—€6, more during special exhibitions, free English audioguide, Wed-Mon 10:00-17:00, closed Tue, last entry at 16:30, when facing the palace walk toward the right wing, tel. 030/3209-1442, www.spsg.de. Note the only WC is within the castle, mid-tour.

▲**Museum Berggruen: Picasso and His Time**—While this tidy little museum is a pleasant surprise, it's expected to close for

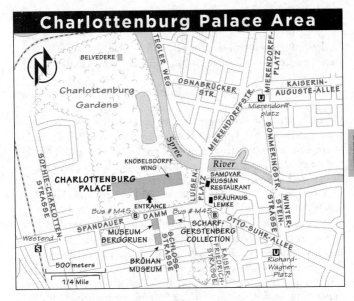

Charlottenburg Palace Area

renovation through 2012. If it's open, climb three floors through a fun and substantial collection of Picassos. Along the way, you'll see plenty of notable works by Henri Matisse. Enjoy a great chance to meet Paul Klee.

Cost and Hours: €8 combo-ticket includes the Scharf-Gerstenberg Collection, covered by Museumspass, open Tue-Sun 10:00-18:00, closed Mon, Schlossstrasse 1, tel. 030/326-95815, www.smb.museum.

▲**Bröhan Museum**—Wander through a dozen beautifully furnished *Jugendstil* and Art Deco living rooms, a curvy organic world of lamps, glass, silver, and posters. English descriptions are posted on the wall of each room on the main floor. While you're there, look for the fine collection of Impressionist paintings by Karl Hagemeister.

Cost and Hours: €6, Museumspass doesn't cover special exhibits, Tue-Sun 10:00-18:00, closed Mon, Schlossstrasse 1A, tel. 030/3269-0600, www.broehan-museum.de.

▲**Scharf-Gersternberg Collection**—This small museum houses a collection of more than 250 works of Surrealist and pre-Surrealist art. The *Surreal Worlds* exhibit shows just how freaky and weird the world looked to artists like Salvador Dalí, Paul Klee, and Francisco de Goya. Be sure to check out Dalí's film of his birth from an egg on the beach.

Cost and Hours: €8 combo-ticket includes Museum Berggruen—described earlier, open Tue-Sun 10:00-18:00, closed Mon, Schlossstrasse 70, tel. 030/3435-7315, www.smb.museum.

Nightlife in Berlin

Berlin is a happening place for nightlife—whether it's clubs, pubs, jazz music, cabaret, hokey-but-fun German variety shows, theater, or concerts.

Sources of Entertainment Info: *Berlin Programm* lists a non-stop parade of concerts, plays, exhibits, and cultural events (€2, in German, www.berlin-programm.de); *Exberliner Magazine* (€2.50, www.exberliner.com) doesn't have as much hard information, but is colorfully written English (both sold at kiosks and TIs). For the young and determined sophisticate, *Zitty* and *Tip* are the top guides to alternative culture (in German, sold at kiosks). Also pick up the free schedules *Flyer* and *030* in bars and clubs. Visit KaDeWe's ticket office for your music and theater options (sixth floor, 18 percent fee but access to all tickets; see page 733). Ask about "competitive improvisation" and variety shows.

Berlin Jazz—To enjoy live music near my recommended Savignyplatz hotels in western Berlin, consider **A Trane Jazz Club** (all jazz, great stage and intimate seating, €7-18 cover depending on act, opens at 21:00, live music nightly 22:00-2:00 in the morning, Bleibtreustrasse 1—see map on page 746, tel. 030/313-2550, www.a-trane.de). **B-Flat Acoustic Music and Jazz Club,** in the heart of eastern Berlin, also has live music nightly—and shares a courtyard with a tranquil tea house (shows vary from free to €10-12 cover, open Mon-Thu from 20:00 with shows starting at 21:00, Fri-Sat from 21:00 with shows at 22:00, closed Sun, a block from Rosenthaler Platz U-Bahn stop at Rosenthaler Strasse 13—see map on page 750, tel. 030/283-3123, www.b-flat -berlin.de).

Berliner Rock and Roll—Berlin has a vibrant rock and pop scene, with popular venues at the Spandau Citadel and at the outdoor Waldbühne ("Forest Stage"). Check out what's playing on posters in the U-Bahn, in *Zitty*, or at any ticket agency. Great Berlin bands include Wir Sind Helden, The Beatsteaks, Jennifer Rostock, and the funky ska band Seeed.

Cabaret—**Bar Jeder Vernunft** offers modern-day cabaret a short walk from my recommended hotels in western Berlin. This variety show—under a classic old tent perched atop a modern parking lot—is a hit with German-speakers, but can still be worthwhile for those who don't speak the language (as some of the music shows are in a sort of "Denglish"). Even some Americans perform here periodically. Tickets are generally about €22-25, and shows change regularly (performances start Mon-Sat at 20:00, Sun at 19:00, seating can be a bit cramped, south of Ku'damm at Schaperstrasse 24—see map on page 746, U-3 or U-9: Spichernstrasse, tel. 030/ 883-1582, www.bar-jeder-vernunft.de).

German Variety Show—To spend an evening enjoying Europe's largest revue theater, consider "YMA—Too Beautiful to Be True" at the **FriedrichstadtPalast**. It's a passionate visual spectacle, a weird ballet that pulsates like a visual poem (€17-105, Tue at 18:30, Thu-Sat at 19:30, Sat also at 15:30, Sun at 15:30, no shows Mon or Wed, Friedrichstrasse 107—see map on page 750, U6: Oranienburger Tor, tel. 030/2326-2326, www.show-palace .eu). The Friedrichstrasse area around the Palast and to the south has been synonymous with entertainment for at least 200 years. The East German government built the current Palast in 1984 on the ruins of an older theater, which itself was a horse barn for the Prussian Army. The current exterior is meant to mimic the interior design of the older theater.

Nightclubs and Pubs—Oranienburger Strasse's trendy scene (page 713) is being eclipsed by the action at Friedrichshain (farther east). To the north, you'll find the hip Prenzlauer Berg neighborhood, packed with everything from smoky pubs to small art bars and dance clubs (best scene is around Helmholtzplatz, U2: Eberswalder Strasse; see page 716).

Dancing—Cut a rug at **Clärchens Ballhaus,** an old ballroom that's been a Berlin institution since 1913. At some point everyone in Berlin comes through here, as the dance hall attracts an eclectic Berlin-in-a-nutshell crowd of grannies, elegant women in evening dresses, yuppies, scenesters, and hippies. The music (swing, waltz, tango, or cha-cha) changes every day, with live music on Friday and Saturday (from 23:15, €4 cover; dance hall open daily from 10:00—12:00 in winter—until the last person goes home, in the heart of the Auguststrasse gallery district at Auguststrasse 24—see map on page 750, S-Bahn: Oranienburger Strasse, tel. 030/282-9295, www.ballhaus.de). Dancing lessons are also available (€8, Mon-Tue at 19:00, Thu at 19:30, 1.5 hours). The "Gypsy" restaurant, which fills a huge courtyard out front, serves decent food and good pizza.

Art Galleries—Berlin, a magnet for new artists, is a great city for gallery visits. Galleries—many of which stay open late—welcome visitors who are "just looking." The most famous gallery district is in eastern Berlin's Mitte neighborhood, along **Auguststrasse** (branches off from Oranienburger Strasse at the ruined Tacheles building). Check out the Berlin outpost of the edgy-yet-accessible art of the New Leipzig movement at **Galerie Eigen+Art** (Tue-Sat 11:00-18:00, closed Sun-Mon, Auguststrasse 26, tel. 030/280-6605, www.eigen-art.com). The other gallery area is in western Berlin, along **Fasanenstrasse.**

Pub Crawls—Various companies offer pub crawls to some of Berlin's fun watering holes. The (unrelated) binge-drinking death of a 16-year-old in Berlin a few years ago reinforced the tours' strict

18-year-old minimum age limit. Pub crawls depart around 20:15, cost €12, generally visit four bars and two clubs, and provide a great way to drink it up with new friends from around the world while getting a peek at Berlin's bar scene...or at least how its bars look when invaded by 50 loud tourists. **Insider Tour** and **Sandeman's New Europe** (see contact info on pages 662 and 663) offer pub crawls, or look around town for fliers from other companies.

Sleeping in Berlin

When in Berlin, I used to sleep in the former West, on or near Savignyplatz. But now the focus of Berlin is in the East. I like the lively, colorful district in the heart of the *Kiez* (literally "gravel," meaning a homey, homogenous neighborhood in Berlin), and I've listed some suggestions in eastern Berlin's popular Prenzlauer Berg neighborhood.

Berlin is packed and hotel prices go up on holidays, including Green Week in mid-January, Easter weekend, the first weekend in May, Ascension weekend in May, German Unity Day (Oct 3), Christmas, and New Year's. Keep in mind that many hotels have limited staff after 20:00, so if you're planning to arrive after that, let the hotel know in advance.

In Eastern Berlin
Prenzlauer Berg

If you want to sleep in the former East Berlin, set your sights on the colorful and fun Prenzlauer Berg district. After decades of neglect, this corner of eastern Berlin has quickly come back to life. Gentrification has brought Prenzlauer Berg great hotels, tasty ethnic and German eateries (see "Eating in Berlin," later), and a happening nightlife scene. Think of all the graffiti as just some people's way of saying they care. The huge and impersonal concrete buildings are enlivened with a street fair of fun little shops and eateries.

This loosely defined area is about 1.5 miles north of Alexanderplatz, roughly between Kollwitzplatz and Helmholtzplatz, and to the west, along Kastanienallee (known affectionately as "Casting Alley" for its generous share of beautiful people). The closest U-Bahn stops are U-2: Senefelderplatz at the south end of the neighborhood, U-8: Rosenthaler Platz in the middle, or U-2: Eberswalder Strasse at the north end. Or, for less walking, take the S-Bahn to Hackescher Markt, then catch tram #M1 north.

$$$ Precise Hotel Myer's Berlin rents 52 simple, small rooms. The gorgeous public spaces include a patio and garden. This peaceful hub—off a quiet garden courtyard and tree-lined street, just a five-minute walk from Kollwitzplatz or the nearest U-Bahn

---

Sleep Code

(€1 = about $1.40, country code: 49, area code: 030)
S = Single, **D** = Double/Twin, **T** = Triple, **Q** = Quad, **b** = bathroom, **s** = shower only. Unless otherwise noted, credit cards are accepted, English is spoken, and breakfast is included.

To help you sort easily through these listings, I've divided the accommodations into three categories, based on the price for a standard double room with bath:

$$$ Higher Priced—Most rooms €125 or more.
  $$ Moderately Priced—Most rooms between €85-125.
    $ Lower Priced—Most rooms €85 or less.

Prices can change without notice; verify the hotel's current rates online or by email. For other updates, see www.ricksteves.com/update.

---

stop (Senefelderplatz)—makes it hard to believe you're in a capital city. Their four classes of rooms range from three to five stars, hence the wide price range (Db-€95-200, price also depends on season—check rates online for your dates, air-con in some rooms, elevator, pay Internet access and Wi-Fi, Metzer Strasse 26, tel. 030/440-140, fax 030/4401-4104, www.myershotel.de, myers @precisehotels.com).

$$$ Hotel Jurine (zhoo-REEN—the family name) is a pleasant 53-room business-style hotel whose friendly staff aims to please. In good weather, you can enjoy the breakfast buffet on the lush backyard patio (Sb-€90-110, Db-€130-160, extra bed-€37, rates vary by season, check website for discounts July-Aug, skip breakfast to save a few euros, elevator, free Wi-Fi, parking garage-€13.50, Schwedter Strasse 15, 10-minute walk to U2: Senefelderplatz, tel. 030/443-2990, fax 030/4432-9999, www .hotel-jurine.de, mail@hotel-jurine.de).

$$ Hotel Kastanienhof feels less urban-classy and more like a traditional small-town German hotel. It's wonderfully located on the Kastanienallee #M1 tram line, with easy access to the Prenzlauer Berg bustle. Its 35 slightly overpriced rooms come with helpful service (Sb-€79-94, Db-€105-140, extra bed-€29, reception closed 22:00-6:30—call ahead to make arrangements to get key if you'll arrive late, elevator, pay cable Internet in rooms, parking-€9, 20 yards from the #M1 Zionskirche tram stop at Kastanienallee 65, tel. 030/443-050, fax 030/4430-5111, www.kastanienhof.biz, info@kastanienhof.biz).

$$ The Circus Hotel, run by the popular hostel listed later, caters to youth hostelers who've outgrown the backpacker lifestyle.

BERLIN

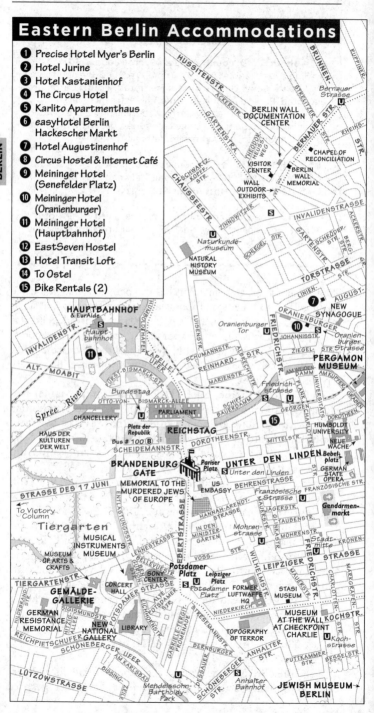

Eastern Berlin Accommodations

1. Precise Hotel Myer's Berlin
2. Hotel Jurine
3. Hotel Kastanienhof
4. The Circus Hotel
5. Karlito Apartmenthaus
6. easyHotel Berlin Hackescher Markt
7. Hotel Augustinenhof
8. Circus Hostel & Internet Café
9. Meininger Hotel (Senefelder Platz)
10. Meininger Hotel (Oranienburger)
11. Meininger Hotel (Hauptbahnhof)
12. EastSeven Hostel
13. Hotel Transit Loft
14. To Ostel
15. Bike Rentals (2)

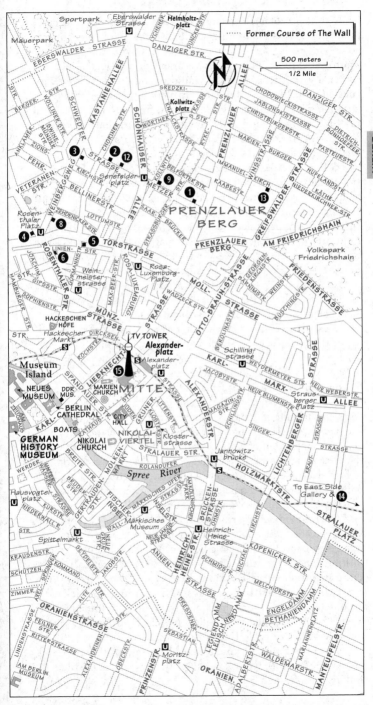

BERLIN

Each of its 60 colorful, trendy rooms has a unique bit of decoration. It overlooks a busy intersection, so there's some nighttime noise—try asking for a quieter back room. Owing to its idealistic youth-hostel roots, it's very service-oriented, with lots of included extras, a very "green" attitude, and occasional special events for guests (Sb-€70, small standard Db-€80, larger Db-€90, junior suite Db-€100, breakfast-€4-8, elevator, free Internet access and Wi-Fi, mellow ground-floor restaurant, Rosenthaler Strasse 1, directly at U8: Rosenthaler Platz, tel. 030/2000-3939, www.circus -berlin.de, info@circus-berlin.de).

$ **Karlito Apartmenthaus** offers nine well-located, modern, and comfortable apartments on a tranquil side street and above a hip café near Hackescher Markt. All of the sleek, Ikea-esque units have miniature balconies and are fully equipped (Sb-€62-77, Db-€72-85, price depends on season, extra person-€15, up to 2 children under 8 sleep free with 2 paying adults, breakfast in Café Lois-€5, elevator, free Wi-Fi, bike rental-€8/day, Linienstrasse 60—check in at Café Lois around the corner on Gormannstrasse, 350 yards from S-Bahn: Hackescher Markt, even closer to U8: Rosenthaler Platz, mobile 0179-704-9041, www.karlito -apartments.de, info@karlito-apartments.de).

$ **easyHotel Berlin Hackescher Markt** is part of an unapologetically cheap Europe-wide chain where you pay for exactly what you use—nothing more, nothing less. Based on parent company easyJet's sales model of nickel-and-dime air travel, the hotel has inexpensive base rates (small Db-€25-55, larger Db-€35-55, depending on season, it's cheaper to book earlier), then charges you separately for optional extras (breakfast, Wi-Fi, using the TV, and so on). The 124 orange-and-gray rooms are very small, basic, and feel popped out of a plastic mold, but (if you skip the extras) the price is right, and the location—at the Hackescher Markt end of Prenzlauer Berg—is wonderful (air-con, elevator, after booking online call to request a quieter back room, Rosenthaler Strasse 69, tel. 030/4000-6550, www.easyhotel.com).

Near Oranienburger Strasse: $$$ **Hotel Augustinenhof** is a clean hotel with 66 spacious rooms, nice woody floors, and some of the most comfortable beds in Berlin. While not exactly in Prenzlauer Berg, the hotel is on a side street near all of the Oranienburger Strasse action. Rooms in front overlook the courtyard of the old Imperial Post Office, rooms in back are a bit quieter, and all rooms have old, thin windows (official rates: Sb-€119, Db-€151, but you'll likely pay closer to Db-€99, elevator, free Wi-Fi or cable Internet in rooms, Auguststrasse 82, 50 yards from S-Bahn: Oranienburger Strasse, tel. 030/308-860, fax 030/308-86100, www.hotel-augustinenhof.de, augustinenhof @albrechtshof-hotels.com).

Hostels in Eastern Berlin

Berlin is known among budget travelers for its fun, hip hostels. These range from upscale-feeling hostels with some hotelesque private rooms comfortable enough even for non-hostelers, to more truly backpacker-type places where comfort is secondary to socializing. These are scattered around eastern Berlin, including some (Circus, Meininger, and EastSeven) in the Prenzlauer Berg area just described.

Comfortable Hostels with Hotelesque Rooms

$ Circus is a brightly colored, well-run place with 230 beds, a trendy lounge with upscale ambience, and a bar downstairs. It has typical hostel dorms as well as some very hotel-like private rooms; for a step up in quality, see the listing for the Circus Hotel, earlier (€19/bed in 8- to 10-bed dorms, €23/bed in 4- to 5-bed dorms, S-€43, Sb-€53, D-€56, Db-€70, T-€75, 2-person apartment with kitchen-€85, 4-person apartment-€140, breakfast-€4-8, no curfew, elevator, pay Internet access, free Wi-Fi, laundry, Weinbergsweg 1a, U8: Rosenthaler Platz, tel. 030/2000-3939, www.circus-berlin .de, info@circus-berlin.de).

$ Meininger is a Europe-wide budget-hotel chain with several locations in Berlin. With sleek, nicely decorated rooms, these are a great-value budget option, even for non-hostelers. They have three particularly appealing branches: in Prenzlauer Berg (Schönhauser Allee 19 on Senefelderplatz), at Oranienburger Strasse 67 (next to the Aufsturz pub), and near the Hauptbahnhof, at Ella-Traebe-Strasse 9 (rates vary by availability, but usually €18-19/bed in 6-bed dorms, Sb-€52, Db-€70, Tb-€86; rates at Hauptbahnhof location about €5-10 more; all locations: breakfast-€5.50, elevator, 24-hour reception, pay Internet access, free Wi-Fi in lobby, tel. 030/666-36100, www.meininger-hostels.de).

Backpacker Havens

$ EastSeven Hostel rents the best cheap beds in Prenzlauer Berg. It's sleek and modern, with all the hostel services and more: 60 beds, 24-hour reception, inviting lounge, fully equipped guests' kitchen, lockers, garden, and bike rental. Children are welcome. Easygoing people of any age are comfortable here (€18/bed in 8-bed dorms, €22/bed in 4-bed dorms with private bathroom—or €20/bed in dorm with bathroom down the hall, S-€38, D-€52, T-€66, private rooms have bathrooms down the hall, includes sheets, towel-€1, continental breakfast-€2, pay Internet access, free Wi-Fi, laundry-€5, 100 yards from U2: Senefelderplatz at Schwedter Strasse 7, tel. 030/9362-2240, www.eastseven.de, info @eastseven.de).

$ Hotel Transit Loft, actually a hostel, is located in a refurbished factory. Its 62 clean, high-ceilinged, modern rooms and wide-open lobby have an industrial touch. The reception—staffed by friendly, hip Berliners—is open 24 hours, with a bar serving drinks all night long (€21/bed in 4- to 6-bed dorms, Sb-€59, Db-€69, Tb-€89, includes sheets and breakfast, elevator, cheap Internet access, free Wi-Fi, fully wheelchair-accessible, down alley facing inner courtyard at Immanuelkirchstrasse 14A; U2/U5/U8 or S-Bahn: Alexanderplatz, then tram #M4 to Hufelandstrasse and walk 50 yards; tel. 030/4849-3773, fax 030/4405-1074, www.transit-loft.de, loft@hotel-transit.de).

$ Ostel is a fun retro-1970s-DDR apartment building that re-creates the lifestyle and interior design of a country relegated to the dustbin of history. All the furniture and room decorations have been meticulously collected and restored to their former socialist glory—only the psychedelic wallpaper is a replica. Guests buy ration vouchers (€7.50/person) for breakfast in the attached restaurant. Kitschy, sure—but also clean and memorable (€15/bed in a 4- or 6-bed "Pioneer Camp" room or in 12-bunk dorm—includes lockers, S-€33, Sb-€40, D-€54, Db-€61, 4-person apartments-€120, includes sheets and towels, 24-hour reception, free Wi-Fi in lobby, bike rental, free parking, free collective use of the people's barbeque, right behind Ostbahnhof station on the corner of Strasse der Pariser Kommune at Wriezener Karree 5, tel. 030/2576-8660, www.ostel.eu, contact@ostel.eu).

In Western Berlin:
Near Savignyplatz and Bahnhof Zoo

While Bahnhof Zoo and Ku'damm are no longer the center of the action, this western Berlin neighborhood is still a comfortable and handy home base (thanks to its easy transit connections to the rest of the city and proximity to the starting point of various guided tours). The streets around the tree-lined Savignyplatz (a 10-minute walk behind the station) have a neighborhood charm, with an abundance of simple, small, friendly, good-value places to sleep and eat. The area has an artsy aura going back to the cabaret days in the 1920s, when it was the center of Berlin's gay scene. The hotels and pensions I list here—which are all a 5- to 15-minute walk from Bahnhof Zoo and Savignyplatz (with S- and U-Bahn stations)—are generally located a couple of flights up in big, run-down buildings. Inside, they're clean and spacious enough so that their well-worn character is actually charming. Asking for a quieter room in back gets you away from any street noise. Of the accommodations listed here, Pension Peters offers the best value for budget travelers.

$$$ Hecker's Hotel is a modern, four-star business hotel with 69 big, fresh rooms and all the Euro-comforts. Their "superior" rooms cost €10 more than their "comfort" rooms, and—while the same size—have more modern furnishings and air-conditioning. Herr Kiesal promises free breakfasts (otherwise €16/person) for those reserving direct with this book (Sb-€95, Db-€180, all rooms €200 during conferences but generally only €100 July-Aug, look for deals on their website, non-smoking rooms, elevator, Wi-Fi, parking-€12-18, between Savignyplatz and Ku'damm at Grolmanstrasse 35, tel. 030/88900, fax 030/889-0260, www .heckers-hotel.com, info@heckers-hotel.com).

$$ Hotel Askanischerhof, the oldest B&B in Berlin, is posh as can be, with 16 sprawling, antique-furnished living rooms you can call home. Photos on the walls brag of famous movie-star guests. It oozes Old World service and classic Berlin atmosphere (Sb-€110, Db-€120, Tb-€130, elevator, Wi-Fi, free parking, Ku'damm 53, tel. 030/881-8033, fax 030/881-7206, www.askanischer -hof.de, info@askanischer-hof.de).

$$ Hotel Astoria is a friendly three-star business-class hotel with 32 comfortably furnished rooms and affordable summer and weekend rates (Db-€108-126, often Db-€80 in summer, check their website for deals, non-smoking floors, elevator, Internet access, parking-€9, around corner from Bahnhof Zoo at Fasanenstrasse 2, tel. 030/312-4067, www.hotelastoria.de, info@hotel astoria.de).

$$ Hotel Carmer 16, with 30 bright and airy (if a bit dated) rooms, is both business-like and homey, and has an inviting lounge and charming balconies (Db-€93 for those reserving direct with this book, extra person-€20, some rooms have balconies, family suites, elevator and a few stairs, Wi-Fi, Carmerstrasse 16, tel. 030/3110-0500, fax 030/3110-0510, www.hotel-carmer16.de, info @hotel-carmer16.de).

$$ Hotel-Pension Funk, the former home of a 1920s silent-movie star, is a delightfully quirky time warp. Kind manager Herr Michael Pfundt offers 15 elegant old rooms with rich Art Nouveau furnishings (S-€42, Ss-€60, Sb-€72, D-€72, Ds-€85, Db-€105, extra person-€25, cash preferred, Wi-Fi, a long block south of Ku'damm at Fasanenstrasse 69, tel. 030/882-7193, www.hotel -pensionfunk.de, berlin@hotel-pensionfunk.de).

$$ Hotel Bogota is a slumbermill just steps off Ku'damm, renting 115 rooms in a sprawling maze of a building that used to house the Nazi Chamber of Culture. A creaky, well-worn place with big, simple rooms and old furniture, it has the feel of a once-grand hotel (S-€49, Ss-€62, Sb-€98, D-€77, Ds-€84, Db-€89-150, extra bed-€21, look for Web deals and great last-minute prices in

BERLIN

Western Berlin

1. Hecker's Hotel
2. Hotel Askanischerhof
3. Hotel Astoria
4. Hotel Carmer 16
5. Hotel-Pension Funk
6. Hotel Bogota
7. Pension Peters
8. Restaurant Marjellchen
9. Rest. Leibniz-Klause
10. Dicke Wirtin Pub
11. Die Zwölf Apostel Rest.
12. Zillemarkt Restaurant
13. Technical University Mensa
14. Ullrich Supermarkt
15. Schleusenkrug Beer Garden
16. Winter Garden Buffet
17. A Trane Jazz Club
18. Bar Jeder Vernunft
19. Internet Café
20. Fat Tire Bikes

summer, children under 12 free, elevator, 10-minute walk from Savignyplatz at Schlüterstrasse 45, tel. 030/881-5001, fax 030/883-5887, www.hotel-bogota.de, info@hotel-bogota.de).

$ Pension Peters, run by a German-Swedish couple, is sunny and central, with a cheery breakfast room and a super-friendly staff who go out of their way to help their guests. With its sleek Scandinavian decor and 34 renovated rooms, it's a good choice. Some of the ground-floor rooms facing the back courtyard are a bit dark—and cheaper for the inconvenience (Sb-€58, Db-€79, big Db-€85, extra bed-€15, family room-€85, these special prices offered only with this book in 2012—mention when you reserve, up to 2 kids under 13 free with 2 paying adults, cash preferred, Wi-Fi and Internet access, 10 yards off Savignyplatz at Kant-strasse 146, tel. 030/312-2278, www.pension-peters-berlin.de, info @pension-peters-berlin.de, Annika and Christoph with help of his sister, Daisy).

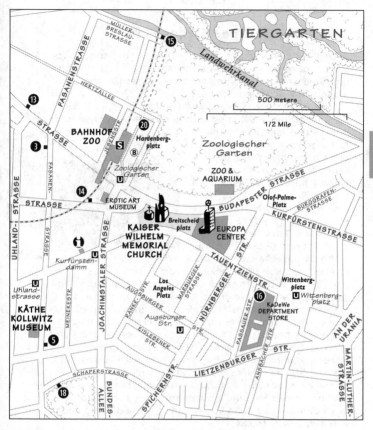

Eating in Berlin

There's a world of restaurants to choose from in this ever-changing city. Your best approach may be to select a neighborhood and browse until you find something that strikes your fancy, rather than seeking out a particular restaurant.

Don't be too determined to eat "Berlin-style." The city is known only for its mildly spicy sausage and for its street food (*Currywurst* and *Döner Kebab*—see the sidebar on the next page). Germans—especially Berliners—consider their food old-school; when they go out to eat, they're not usually looking for the "traditional local fare" many travelers are after. Nouveau German is California cuisine with scant memories of wurst, kraut, and pumpernickel. If the kraut is getting the wurst of you, take a break with some international or ethnic offerings—try one of the many Turkish, Italian, pan-Asian, and Balkan restaurants.

BERLIN

Berliner Street Fare

In Berlin, it's easy to eat cheap, with a glut of *Imbiss* snack stands, bakeries (for sandwiches), and falafel/kebab counters. Train stations have grocery stores, as well as bright and modern fruit-and-sandwich bars.

Sausage stands are everywhere (I've listed a couple of local favorites). Most specialize in **Currywurst,** created in Berlin after World War II, when a fast-food cook got her hands on some curry and Worcestershire sauce from British troops stationed here. It's basically a grilled *Bockwurst*-type pork sausage smothered with curry sauce. *Currywurst* comes either *mit Darm* (with casing) or *ohne Darm* (without casing). If the casing is left on to grill,  it gives the sausage a smokier flavor. (*Berliner Art*—"Berlin-style"—means that the sausage is boiled *ohne Darm*, then grilled.) Either way, the grilled sausage is then chopped into small pieces or cut in half (East Berlin style) and topped with sauce. While some places simply use ketchup and sprinkle on some curry powder, real *Currywurst* joints use tomato paste, Worcestershire sauce, and curry. With your wurst comes either a toothpick or small wooden fork; you'll usually get a plate of fries as well, but rarely a roll. You'll see *Currywurst* on the menu at some sit-down restaurants, but local purists say that misses the whole point: You'll pay triple and get a less authentic dish than you would at a street stand under elevated S-Bahn tracks.

Other good street foods to consider are *Döner Kebab* (Turkish-style skewered meat slow-roasted and served in a sandwich) and *Frikadelle* (like a hamburger patty; often called *Bulette* in Berlin).

Colorful pubs—called *Kneipen*—offer light, quick, and easy meals and the fizzy local beer, *Berliner Weiss.* Ask for it *mit Schuss* for a shot of fruity syrup in your suds.

In Eastern Berlin
Near Unter den Linden
At the Opera House (Opernpalais): The **Operncafé** is perhaps the classiest coffee stop in Berlin, with a selection of 65—count 'em: 65—different decadent desserts (daily 9:00-21:00, across from university and war memorial at Unter den Linden 5, tel. 030/202-683). The **Schinkel Klause Biergarten** serves good €10-19 meals on its shady terrace with a view of the Unter den Linden scene when

sunny, or in its cellar otherwise (daily 11:30-22:00, tel. 030/2026-8450).

Cheap Eats on Friedrichstrasse: **Bier's Curry und Spiesse,** under the tracks at the Friedrichstrasse S-Bahn stop, is a great, greasy, cheap, and generous place for an old-fashioned German hot dog. This is the local favorite near Unter den Linden for €2 *Currywurst.* Experiment with variations (the *Flieschspiess* is excellent) and sauces—and don't hold the *Zwiebeln* (fried onions). You'll munch standing at a counter, where the people-watching is great (daily 10:00-5:00 in the morning; from inside the station, take the Friedrichstrasse exit and turn left).

Near the Pergamon Museum: Georgenstrasse, a block behind the Pergamon Museum and under the S-Bahn tracks, is lined with fun eateries filling the arcade of the train trestle—close to the sightseeing action but in business mainly for students from nearby Humboldt University. **Deponie3** is a trendy Berlin *Kneipe* usually filled with students. Garden seating in the back is nice if you don't mind the noise of the S-Bahn passing directly above you. The interior is a cozy, wooden wonderland of a bar with several inviting spaces. They serve basic salads, traditional Berlin dishes, and hearty daily specials (€4-8 breakfasts, good €8 brunch Sun 10:00-15:00, €5-11 lunches and dinners, open daily from 9:00, sometimes live music, Georgenstrasse 5, tel. 030/2016-5740). For Italian food, a branch of **Die Zwölf Apostel** is nearby (daily until 24:00; described later, under "Near Savignyplatz").

In the Heart of Old Berlin's Nikolai Quarter: The *Nikolaiviertel* marks the original medieval settlement of Cölln, which would eventually become Berlin. The area was destroyed during the war but was rebuilt for Berlin's 750th birthday in 1987. The whole area has a cute, cobbled, and characteristic old town...Middle Ages meets Socialist Realism. Today, the district is pretty soulless by day but a popular restaurant zone at night. **Bräuhaus Georgbrau** is a thriving beer hall serving homemade suds on a picturesque courtyard overlooking the Spree River. Eat in the lively and woody but mod-feeling interior, or outdoors with fun riverside seating—thriving with German tourists. It's a good place to try one of the few typical Berlin dishes: *Eisbein* (boiled ham hock) with sauerkraut and mashed peas with bacon (€10 with a beer and schnapps). The statue of St. George once stood in the courtyard of Berlin's old castle—until the Nazis deemed it too decadent and not "German" enough, and removed it (€10-13 plates, three-foot-long sampler board with a dozen small glasses of beer, daily 10:00-24:00, 2 blocks south of Berlin Cathedral and across the river at Spreeufer 4, tel. 030/242-4244).

In City Hall: Consider lunching at one of Berlin's many *Kantine.* Located in government offices and larger corporations,

BERLIN

Eastern Berlin Eateries & Nightlife

1. Operncafé & Schinkel Klause Biergarten
2. Bier's Curry und Spiesse
3. Deponie3 Pub
4. Die Zwölf Apostel
5. Bräuhaus Georgbrau
6. Die Kantine im Roten Rathaus
7. Lutter & Wegner Rest.; Augustiner am Gendarmenmarkt
8. Beisl am Tacheles
9. Galeries Lafayette Food Circus
10. Aroma Espresso Bar
11. Hasir Turkish Restaurant
12. Weihenstephaner Bavarian Restaurant
13. Aufsturz Pub
14. Prater Biergarten
15. Zum Schusterjungen Speisegaststätte
16. La Bodeguita del Medio Cuban Bar Restaurant
17. Konnopke's Imbiss
18. Restaurant "Die Schule"
19. Kauf Dich Glücklich
20. Fleischmöbel Pub
21. Gugelhof Restaurant
22. Luigi Zuckermann Deli & Transit Restaurant
23. Metzer Eck Pub
24. Lemongrass Scent
25. Humboldt-Box Café
26. To Café Sibylle

Map: Eastern Berlin Eateries & Nightlife

BERLIN

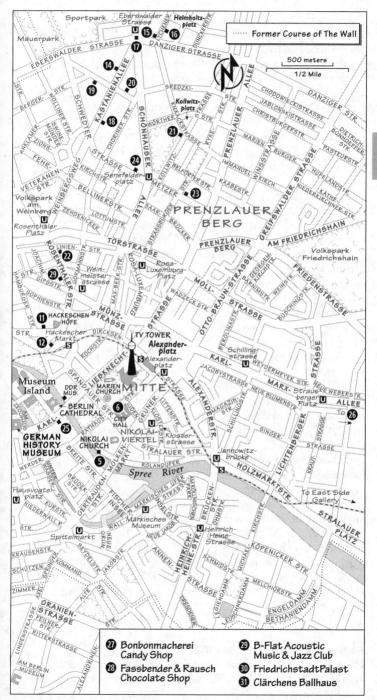

..... Former Course of The Wall

500 meters
1/2 Mile

Sportpark
Eberswalder Strasse
Helmholtz-platz
Mauerpark
EBERSWALDER STRASSE
DANZIGER STRASSE
Kollwitz-platz
PRENZLAUER BERG
Senefelder-platz
Volkspark am Weinberg
Rosenthaler Platz
TORSTRASSE
PRENZLAUER BERG
AM FRIEDRICHSHAIN
Volkspark Friedrichshain
Rosa-Luxemburg-Platz
Hackeschen Höfe
Hackescher Markt
TV TOWER
Alexander-platz
Museum Island
DDR MUS.
MARIEN CHURCH
MITTE
Schilling strasse
Straus-berger Platz
To 26
BERLIN CATHEDRAL
CITY HALL
NIKOLAI-VIERTEL
Kloster-strasse
GERMAN HISTORY MUSEUM
NIKOLAI CHURCH
Jannowitz-brücke
Spree River
ROLANDUFER
HOLZMARKTSTR.
To East Side Gallery
Hausvogtei-platz
Spittelmarkt
Märkisches Museum
Heinrich-Heine-Strasse
STRALAUER PLATZ
ORANIEN-STRASSE
AM BERLIN MUSEUM

27 Bonbonmacherei Candy Shop

28 Fassbender & Rausch Chocolate Shop

29 B-Flat Acoustic Music & Jazz Club

30 FriedrichstadtPalast

31 Clärchens Ballhaus

Kantine offer fast, filling, and cheap lunches, along with a unique opportunity to see Germans at work (though the food can hardly be considered gourmet). There are thousands of *Kantine* in Berlin, but the best is **Die Kantine im Roten Rathaus,** in the basement of City Hall. For less than €4, you can get filling German dishes like *Leberkäse* (German-style baloney) or stuffed cabbage (Mon-Fri 11:00-15:00, closed Sat-Sun, Rathausstrasse 15).

Near Gendarmenmarkt, South of Unter den Linden

The twin churches of Gendarmenmarkt seem to be surrounded by people in love with food. The lunch and dinner scene is thriving with upscale restaurants serving good cuisine at highly competitive prices to local professionals (see map on page 750 for locations). If in need of a quick-yet-classy lunch, stroll around the square and along Charlottenstrasse. For a quick bite, head to the cheap *Currywurst* stand behind the German Cathedral.

Lutter & Wegner Restaurant is well-known for its Austrian cuisine (*Schnitzel* and *Sauerbraten*) and popular with business-people. It's dressy, with fun sidewalk seating or a dark and elegant interior (€9-18 starters, €16-22 main dishes, daily 11:00-24:00, Charlottenstrasse 56, tel. 030/202-9540). They have a second location, called **Beisl am Tacheles,** near the New Synagogue (Oranienburger Strasse 52, tel. 030/2478-1078).

Augustiner am Gendarmenmarkt, next door to Lutter & Wegner, lines its sidewalk with trademark Bavarian white-and-blue-checkerboard tablecloths; inside, you'll find a classic Bavarian beer-hall atmosphere. Less pretentious than its neighbor, it offers good beer and affordable Bavarian classics in an equally appealing location (€6-12 light meals, €10-15 bigger meals, daily 9:00-24:00, Charlottenstrasse 55, tel. 030/2045-4020).

Galeries Lafayette Food Circus is a French festival of fun eateries in the basement of the landmark department store. You'll find a good deli and prepared-food stands, dishing up cuisine that's good-quality but not cheap (most options €10-15, cheaper €8-10 sandwiches and savory crepes, Mon-Sat 10:00-20:00, closed Sun, U-Bahn: Französische Strasse, tel. 030/209-480).

Near Checkpoint Charlie: **Aroma Espresso Bar** is a touristy joint, handy for made-to-order sandwiches. Israeli-born Sagi makes his own bread daily and piles on the fixin's for €4-6. This is a popular stop for walking-tour groups: If you get here when they do, expect a line (Mon-Sat 7:30-19:00, Sun 8:00-19:00, in summer until 20:30, Friedrichstrasse 200, tel. 030/206-16693).

At and near Hackescher Markt

Hasir Turkish Restaurant is your chance to dine with candles, hardwood floors, and happy Berliners savoring meaty Anatolian specialties. As Berlin is the world's largest Turkish city outside of Asia Minor, it's no wonder you can find some good Turkish restaurants here. But while most locals think of Turkish food as fast and cheap, this is a dining experience. The restaurant, in a courtyard next to the Hackeschen Höfe shopping complex (see page 713), offers indoor and outdoor tables filled with an enthusiastic local crowd. The service can be a bit questionable, so bring some patience (€6-10 starters, €14-20 main dishes, large and splittable portions, daily 11:30-1:00 in the morning, in late evening the courtyard is dominated by an unpleasantly loud underground disco, a block from the Hackescher Markt S-Bahn station at Oranienburger Strasse 4, tel. 030/2804-1616).

Weihenstephaner Bavarian Restaurant serves upmarket Bavarian traditional food for around €10-15 a plate; offers an atmospheric cellar, an inner courtyard, and a busy people-watching street-side terrace; and, of course, has excellent beer (daily 11:00-24:00, Neue Promenade 5 at Hackescher Markt, tel. 030/8471-0760).

Aufsturz, a lively pub, pours more than 100 different beers and 40 varieties of whiskey, and dishes up "traditional Berliner pub grub"—like nachos—and great potato soup for under €5. The traditional "Berlin board" for €17 can easily feed three voracious carnivores (daily from 12:00 until at least 2:00 in the morning, a block beyond the New Synagogue at Oranienburger Strasse 67, tel. 030/2804-7407).

In Prenzlauer Berg

Prenzlauer Berg is packed with fine restaurants—German, ethnic, and everything in between. Even if you're not staying in this area, it's worth venturing here for dinner. (For more on Prenzlauer Berg, see page 716; for restaurant locations, see the map on page 750.) Before making a choice, I'd spend at least half an hour strolling and browsing through this bohemian wonderland of creative eateries. Because Prenzlauer Berg sprawls over a wide area, I've organized my listings by neighborhood.

Near Eberswalder Strasse

The area surrounding the elevated Eberswalder Strasse U-Bahn station (on the U2 line, at the confluence of Kastanienallee, Danziger Strasse, Ebwerswalder Strasse, and Schönhauser Allee) is the epicenter of Prenzlauer Berg—a young, hip, and edgy place to eat and drink. While a bit farther north than other areas I recommend (and a 10- to 15-minute walk from most of my recommended hotels), it's worth the trip to immerse yourself in quintessential Prenzlauer Berg.

Prater Biergarten offers two great eating opportunities: a rustic indoor restaurant and a mellow, shady, super-cheap, and family-friendly outdoor beer garden (with a playground)—each proudly pouring Prater's own microbrew. In the beer garden—Berlin's oldest—you step up to the counter and order (simple €3-5 plates and an intriguing selection of beer munchies, daily in good weather 12:00-24:00). The restaurant serves serious traditional *Biergarten* cuisine and good salads (€7-17 plates, Mon-Sat 18:00-24:00, Sun 12:00-24:00, cash only, Kastanienallee 7, tel. 030/448-5688).

Zum Schusterjungen Speisegaststätte ("The Cobbler's Apprentice") is a classic old-school, German-with-attitude eatery that retains its circa-1986 DDR decor. Famous for its filling €7-10 meals (including various types of schnitzel and Berlin classics such as pork knuckle), it's a no-frills place with quality ingredients and a strong local following. It serves the eating needs of those Berliners lamenting the disappearance of solid traditional German cooking amid the flood of ethnic eateries. While it was recently sold, the new owners promise to keep the kitsch (small 40-seat dining hall plus outdoor tables, daily 12:00-24:00, corner of Lychener Strasse and Danziger Strasse 9, tel. 030/442-7654).

La Bodeguita del Medio Cuban Bar Restaurant is purely fun-loving Cuba—graffiti-caked walls, Che Guevara posters, animated staff, and an ambience that makes you want to dance. Come early to eat or late to drink. This restaurant has been here since 1994—and in fast-changing Prenzlauer Berg, that's an eternity. The German-Cuban couple who run it take pride in their food, and the main dishes are big enough to split. You can even puff a Cuban cigar at the sidewalk tables (€5-10 tapas, €6 Cuban ribs and salad, Tue-Sun 18:00-24:00, closed Mon, a block from U2: Eberswalder Strasse at Lychener Strasse 6, tel. 030/4050-0601).

Konnopke's Imbiss, a super-cheap German-style sausage stand, has been a Berlin institution for more than 70 years—it was family-owned even during DDR times. Berliners say Konnopke's cooks up some of the city's best *Currywurst* (less than €2). Located beneath the U2 viaduct, the stand was demolished in summer of 2010 during roadwork. Berliners rioted, and Konnopke's was rebuilt in a slick  glass-and-steel hut (Mon-Fri 10:00-20:00, Sat 12:00-20:00, closed Sun; Kastanienallee dead-ends at the elevated train tracks, and under them you'll find Konnopke's at Schönhauser Allee 44A). Don't confuse this with the nearby Currystation—look for the real Konnopke's.

Restaurant "**Die Schule**" is a modern place with a no-frills style where you can sample traditional German dishes tapas-style. Assemble a collection of little €2.50 plates of old-fashioned German food you might not try otherwise (good indoor and outdoor seating, €24 full 3-course dinner, daily 11:00-22:00, Kastanienallee 82, tel. 030/780-089-550).

After-Dinner Dessert and Drinks: There are oodles of characteristic funky pubs and nightspots in the area around Helmholtzplatz (and elsewhere in Prenzlauer Berg). Oderberger Strasse is a fun zone to explore; I've listed two places on this street that I particularly like. **Kauf Dich Glücklich** makes a great capper to a Prenzlauer Berg dinner. It serves an enticing array of sweet Belgian waffles and ice cream (best pistachio ice cream in Berlin) in a candy-sprinkled, bohemian lounge on a great Prenzlauer Berg street (daily 11:00-23:00, indoor and outdoor seating—or get your dessert to go, wait possible on busy nights, Oderberger Strasse 44, tel. 030/4435-2182). **Fleischmöbel** ("Meat Furniture") is a fun place to drink with locals, despite the lack of beer on tap. Here you'll find strong cocktails, cool classic rock, and a big blackboard. It's a bit hipster-pretentious, but offers a good glimpse into the Prenzlauer Berg lifestyle. Its two smallish rooms unashamedly offer a bit of 1960s retro in an increasingly trendy part of town; on warm evenings, tables fill the sidewalk out front (daily 12:00 until "whenever," Oderberger Strasse 2).

Near Kollwitzplatz

This square, home of the DDR student resistance in 1980s, is now trendy and upscale, popular with hip parents who take their hip kids to the leafy playground park at its center. It's an especially good area to prowl among upmarket restaurants—walk the square and choose. Just about every option offers sidewalk seats in the summer (great on a balmy evening). It's a long block up Kollwitzstrasse from U2: Senefelderplatz.

Gugelhof, right on Kollwitzplatz, is an institution famous for its Alsatian German cuisine. You'll enjoy French quality with German proportions. It's highly regarded, with a boisterous and enthusiastic local crowd filling its minimalist yet classy interior. In good weather, outdoor seating sprawls along its sidewalk. Their fixed-price meals are fun, and they welcome swapping (€20-30 three-course meal, €5-10 starters, €12-20 main dishes, daily 16:00-24:00, reservations required during peak times, where Knaackstrasse meets Kollwitzplatz, tel. 030/442-9229).

Near Rosenthaler Platz, Closer to Hackescher Markt

Surrounding the U8: Rosenthaler Platz station, a short stroll or tram ride from the Hackescher Markt S-Bahn station, and an easy walk from the Oranienburger Strasse action, this busy neighborhood has a few enticing options.

Luigi Zuckermann is a trendy young deli with Israeli/New York style. It's a great spot to pick up a custom-made deli sandwich (choose your ingredients at the deli counter), hummus plate, salad, fresh-squeezed juice, or other quick, healthy lunch. Linger in the interior, grab one of the few sidewalk tables, or take your food to munch on the go (€5-8 meals, Sun-Thu 8:00-24:00, Fri-Sat open 24 hours, Rosenthaler Strasse 67, tel. 030/2804-0644).

Transit is a stylish, innovative, affordable Thai/Indonesian/pan-Asian small-plates restaurant at the bustling Hackescher Markt end of Prenzlauer Berg. Sit at one of the long shared tables and dig into a creative menu of €3 small plates and €7 big plates. Two people can make a filling meal out of three or four dishes (daily 11:00-late, Rosenthaler Strasse 68, tel. 030/2478-1645).

Near Senefelderplatz (near Recommended Hotels on Metzer Strasse and Schwedter Strasse)

While neither of these places—in a sedate corner of Prenzlauer Berg near the Senefelderplatz U-Bahn stop—is worth going out of your way for, they're handy if you're staying at several of my recommended accommodations.

Metzer Eck is a time-warp *Kneipe* with a family tradition dating to 1913 and a cozy charm. It serves cheap basic typical Berlin food with five beers on tap, including the Czech Budvar (€5-8 meals, Mon-Fri 16:00-24:00, Sat 18:00-24:00, closed Sun, Metzer Strasse 33, on the corner of Metzer Strasse and Strassburger Strasse, tel. 030/442-7656).

Lemongrass Scent, with a gaggle of inviting sidewalk tables, offers tasty and affordable "Asian street kitchen" food near several recommended hotels (two-course weekday lunch special for less than €5, €3-4 starters, €5-8 main dishes, Mon-Fri 11:30-24:00, Sat-Sun 12:00-24:00, Schwedter Strasse 12, tel. 030/4057-6985).

In Western Berlin

Near Savignyplatz

Many good restaurants are on or within 100 yards of Savignyplatz, near my recommended western Berlin hotels (for locations, see map on page 746). Savignyplatz is lined with attractive, relaxed, mostly Mediterranean-style places. Take a walk and survey these; continue your stroll along Bleibtreustrasse to discover many trendier, more creative little eateries.

Restaurant Marjellchen is a trip to East Prussia. Dine in a soft, jazzy elegance in one of two six-table rooms. While it doesn't have to be expensive (€10-18 main courses, €27 two-course meals), plan to go the whole nine yards here, as this can be a great Prussian experience with caring service. The menu is inviting, and all the recipes were brought to Berlin by the owner's mother after she was expelled from East Prussia. Reservations are smart (daily 17:00-23:30, family-run, Mommsenstrasse 9, tel. 030/883-2676).

Restaurant Leibniz-Klause is a good place for a dressy German meal. You'll enjoy upscale presentation on white tablecloths, hunter-sized portions, service that's both friendly and professional, and no pretense—but annoying commercial radio taints the atmosphere. Their *Berliner Riesen-Eisbein* ("super-pork-leg on the bone"), with sauerkraut and horseradish, will stir even the tiniest amount of Teutonic blood in your veins (€15-22 plates, good indoor and outdoor seating, daily from 12:00 until late, on the corner of Leibnizstrasse at Mommsenstrasse 57, tel. 030/323-7068).

Dicke Wirtin is a pub with traditional old-Berlin *Kneipe* atmosphere, six good beers on tap, and solid home cooking at reasonable prices—such as their famously cheap *Gulaschsuppe* (€4). Their interior is fun and pubby, with soccer on the TV; their streetside tables are also inviting. Pickled eggs are on the bar—ask about how these can help you avoid a hangover (€5 daily specials, Bavarian Andechs beer on tap, open daily from 12:00, dinner served from 18:00, just off Savignyplatz at Carmerstrasse 9, tel. 030/312-4952).

Die Zwölf Apostel ("The Twelve Apostles") is popular for good Italian food. Choose between indoors with candlelit ambience, outdoors on a sun-dappled patio, or overlooking the people-parade on its pedestrian street. A local crowd packs this restaurant for €12 pizzas and €15-30 meals (long hours daily, cash only, immediately across from Savignyplatz S-Bahn entrance, Bleibtreustrasse 49, tel. 030/312-1433).

Zillemarkt Restaurant, which feels like an old-time Berlin *Biergarten,* serves traditional Berlin specialties in the garden or in the rustic candlelit interior. Their *Berliner Allerlei* is a fun way to sample a bit of nearly everything (cabbage, pork, sausage, potatoes and more for a minimum of two people...but it can feed up to five). They have their own microbrew (€10 meals, daily 12:00-24:00, near the S-Bahn tracks at Bleibtreustrasse 48A, tel. 030/881-7040).

Technical University Mensa puts you in a thriving, modern student scene. It feels like a student union building (because it is), with shops, a travel agency, a lounge, kids making out, and lots of international students to chat with. The main cafeteria *(Mensa)* is upstairs—bustling with students and lots of eating options. Streetside is a cafeteria with a more limited selection. Even with the non-student surcharge, eating here is very cheap (€3-5 meals, Mon-Fri 11:00-14:30, closed Sat-Sun, general public entirely welcome but pays the highest of the three prices, coffee bar downstairs with Internet access, just north of Uhlandstrasse at

Hardenbergstrasse 34).

Supermarket: The neighborhood grocery store is **Ullrich** (Mon-Sat 9:00-22:00, Sun 11:00-22:00, Kantstrasse 7, under the tracks near Bahnhof Zoo). There's plenty of fast food near Bahnhof Zoo and on Ku'damm.

Near Bahnhof Zoo

Schleusenkrug beer garden is hidden in the park overlooking a canal between the Bahnhof Zoo and Tiergarten stations. Choose from an ever-changing self-service menu of huge salads, pasta, and some German dishes (€7-12 plates, €3-5 grill snacks, daily 10:00-24:00; standing in front of Bahnhof Zoo, turn left and walk 5 minutes, following the path into the park between the zoo and train tracks; tel. 030/313-9909).

Self-Service Cafeterias: The top floor of the famous department store, **KaDeWe,** holds the Winter Garden Buffet view cafeteria, and its sixth-floor deli/food department is a picnicker's nirvana. Its arterials are clogged with more than 1,000 kinds of sausage and 1,500 types of cheese (Mon-Thu 10:00-20:00, Fri 10:00-21:00, Sat 9:30-20:00, closed Sun, U-Bahn: Wittenbergplatz).

Berlin Connections

By Train

Berlin used to have several major train stations. But now that the Hauptbahnhof has emerged as the single, massive central station, all the others have wilted into glorified subway stations. Virtually all long-distance trains pass through the Hauptbahnhof—ignore the other stations.

EurAide is an agent of the German Railway that sells reservations for high-speed and overnight trains, with staff that can answer your travel questions in English (located in the Hauptbahnhof; see "Arrival in Berlin" on page 653).

From Berlin by Train to: Potsdam (2/hour, 30 minutes on RE1 train; or take S-Bahn from other points in Berlin, S-7 direct, S-1 with a change at Wannsee, 6/hour, 30-50 minutes—see page 764 for details), **Oranienburg** and Sachsenhausen Concentration Camp Memorial (hourly, 20 minutes; or take the S-1 line from Friedrichstrasse or other stops in town, 3/hour, 45-50 minutes), **Warnemünde** cruise-ship port (sporadic but roughly hourly, 3-4 hours, most include a transfer in Rostock), **Wittenberg** (a.k.a. *Lutherstadt Wittenberg*, hourly on ICE, 42 minutes; also every 2 hours on slower regional train, 1.25 hours), **Dresden** (every 2 hours, more with a transfer in Leipzig, 2.25 hours), **Leipzig** (hourly direct, 1.25-1.5 hours), **Erfurt** (hourly, 2.5-3 hours, transfer in Leipzig or Naumburg/Saale), **Eisenach** and Wartburg Castle (hourly, 3-3.5 hours, transfer in Leipzig or Naumburg/Saale), **Hamburg** (1-2/hour direct, 1.75-2 hours), **Frankfurt** (hourly, 4 hours), **Bacharach** (hourly, 6.5-7.5 hours, 1-3 changes), **Würzburg** (hourly, 4 hours, change in Göttingen or Fulda), **Rothenburg** (hourly, 5-6 hours, often via Göttingen or Fulda, then Würzburg, then Steinach), **Nürnberg** (hourly, 4.5 hours), **Munich** (1-2/hour, 6-6.75 hours, every 2 hours direct, otherwise change in Göttingen), **Köln** (hourly, 4.25 hours), **Amsterdam** (6/day direct to Amsterdam Zuid, 6.5 hours; plus 1 night train/day to Amsterdam Centraal, 10 hours), **Budapest** (3/day including one overnight, 13 hours, these go via Czech Republic and Slovakia; if your railpass doesn't cover these countries, it's possible to go via Vienna but takes longer), **Copenhagen** (5/day, 6.75 hours, reservation required, change in Hamburg, 1/day direct departs at 11:26; also consider the direct overnight train-plus-ferry route to Malmö Central Station, Sweden, which is just 20 minutes from Copenhagen—covered by a railpass that includes Germany or Sweden), **London** (5/day, 10-11.5 hours, 2 changes—you're better off flying cheap on easy-Jet or Air Berlin, even if you have a railpass), **Paris** (5/day, 8-9 hours, change in Köln—via Belgium—or in Mannheim, 1 direct 12-hour night train), **Zürich** (hourly, 8.5 hours, transfer in Basel; 1 direct 12-hour night train), **Prague** (6/day, 4.5-5 hours, no over-night trains), **Warsaw** (4/day, 5.5 hours, reservations required on all Warsaw-bound trains), **Kraków** (1/day direct, 10 hours; 2 more with transfer in Warsaw, 8.5 hours), **Vienna** (8/day, most with 1 change, 2/day plus 1/night are direct, 9.5 hours; some via Czech Republic, but trains with a change in Nürnberg, Munich, or Würzburg avoid that country—useful if it's not covered by your railpass). It's wise but not required to reserve in advance for trains to or from Amsterdam or Prague. Train info: tel. 0180-599-6633, www.bahn.com. Before buying a ticket for any long train ride from Berlin (over 7 hours), consider taking a cheap flight instead (buy it well in advance to get a super fare).

Night trains run from Berlin to these cities: Munich, Paris, Amsterdam, Vienna, Budapest, Malmö (Sweden, near Copenhagen), Basel, and Zürich. There are no night trains from Berlin to anywhere in Italy or Spain. A *Liegeplatz,* a.k.a. *couchette* berth (€13-36), is a great deal; inquire at EurAide at the Hauptbahnhof for details. Beds generally cost the same whether you have a first- or second-class ticket or railpass. Trains are often full, so reserve your *couchette* a few days in advance from any travel agency or major train station in Europe.

By Plane

Berlin is in the process of whittling down to a single air-port. A new airport, called Willy Brandt Berlin-Brandenburg

International, opens in 2012 and will handle all air traffic for the area. Connections into downtown will likely be similar to your options from Schönefeld Airport (explained below), which is next to the new airport.

Until the new airport opens, **Tegel Airport** handles most flights from the United States and Western Europe (4 miles from center, no subway trains, catch the faster bus #X9 to Bahnhof Zoo, or bus #109 to Ku'damm and Bahnhof Zoo for €2.30; bus #TXL goes between Tegel Airport, the Hauptbahnhof—stop is out the *Washingtonplatz* entrance, and Alexanderplatz in eastern Berlin; bus #128 goes to northern Berlin; taxi from Tegel Airport costs €15 to Bahnhof Zoo, €25 to Alexanderplatz; taxis from Tegel levy a €0.50 surcharge).

Most flights from the east and discount airlines arrive at **Schönefeld Airport** (12.5 miles from center), at least until the adjacent **Willy Brandt Berlin-Brandenburg International Airport** opens. From the old Schönefeld arrivals hall, it's just a three-minute walk to the train station, where you can catch a regional express train into the city (ignore the S-Bahn, as there are no direct S-Bahn trains to the city center). Airport Express RE and RB trains go direct to Ostbahnhof, Alexanderplatz, Friedrichstrasse, Hauptbahnhof, and Bahnhof Zoo (€2.60, every 30 minutes, take trains in the direction of Nauen or Dessau, rail-pass valid). A taxi to the city center costs about €35. Similar train and taxi connections are expected at the new Willy Brandt airport when it opens.

The central toll telephone number for all airports is 01805-000-186. For British Air, tel. 01805-266-522; Delta, tel. 01803-337-880; SAS, tel. 01805-117-002; Lufthansa, tel. 01803-803-803.

Berlin, the Discount Airline Hub: Berlin is the continental European hub for discount airlines such as easyJet (lots of flights to Spain, Italy, Eastern Europe, the Baltics, and more—book long in advance to get incredible €30-and-less fares, www.easyjet.com). Ryanair (www.ryanair.com), Air Berlin (www.airberlin.com), and German Wings (www.germanwings.com) make the London-Berlin trip (and other routes) dirt-cheap, so consider this option before booking an overnight train. Consequently, British visitors to the city are now outnumbered only by Americans. For more on cheap flights, see page 841.

By Cruise Ship

The closest cruise-ship terminal to Berlin is 150 miles north, at Warnemünde on the Baltic Sea. Train connections run between the cruise center (Warnemünde station) and Berlin's Hauptbahnhof. Although trains run about every two hours, the trip is hardly worth it—the schedule is sporadic (very roughly hourly), the ride into Berlin takes three to four hours, and by the time you disembark, you won't have time to see much of anything before catching a return train. (The charming old Hanseatic town of Rostock, an easy S-Bahn ride from Warnemünde, could be more satisfying on a short visit.)

If you decide to go for it, board the local S-Bahn at the dock (direction Rostock Hauptbahnhof) and change at the Rostock train station for Berlin. A more convenient, 2.75-hour, direct connection between Warnemünde and Berlin leaves Friday and Saturday mornings at around 9:00 (on other days, this connection departs just before 7:00—likely too early for arriving cruise ships). To return to your ship, take the train to Rostock and transfer to the S-Bahn (direction Warnemünde). There's no need to book tickets in advance; it's easy to buy them at the station with cash or credit card.

A better option is a private excursion to Berlin. One of many excursion companies is **ship2shore,** which offers Berlin day trips starting at €99 per person (based on a minimum of 12 people). Their guides are great (tel. 030/243-58058, www.ship2shore.de, info@ship2shore.de). The recommended **Original Berlin Walks** walking-tour company also runs excursions from Warnemünde into Berlin (€760 for up to 3 people in a minibus, €60/additional person up to a maximum of 7—team up with others on your cruise to get the per-person cost down; see contact information on page 662).

NEAR BERLIN

Potsdam • Sachsenhausen Concentration Camp Memorial

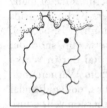

While you could spend days in Berlin and not run out of things to do, a few worthwhile side-trips are just outside the city center (less than 45 minutes by train from downtown Berlin). Frederick the Great's opulent palace playground at Potsdam is a hit with those who enjoy ornate interiors and pretty parks. At the opposite end of the city—and the sightseeing spectrum—Sachsenhausen Concentration Camp Memorial provides a somber look at the Nazis' mass production of death during the Holocaust. A third side-trip possibility—the small town of Wittenberg, with excellent Martin Luther-related sights—is also within a 45-minute train ride of Berlin, but covered in the Lutherland chapter.

Planning Your Time

Either Potsdam or Sachsenhausen can take anywhere from a half-day to a full day of your time, depending on your interests. Think twice before visiting Potsdam on a Monday (when Sanssouci Palace is closed) or a Tuesday (when the New Palace is closed); make your pilgrimage to Sachsenhausen any day but Monday (when the grounds are open but interior exhibits are closed).

Potsdam: It takes about an hour one-way from downtown Berlin to the palaces at Potsdam (including the train to Potsdam, then a bus to the palace of your choice). Touring either Sanssouci or the New Palace takes about an hour to an hour and a half, plus a potential wait for your Sanssouci entry time (aim to arrive at Sanssouci by 10:00 to avoid waiting in the ticket line) and about a half-hour on foot to connect them. Give yourself five hours round-trip to do the whole shebang (the two palaces are quite different but complementary, and connected by a pleasant stroll through the

park). On a quicker visit, you can make a beeline from the train station to your choice of palaces (Sanssouci is closer and more intimate, but may require a wait; New Palace is grander but at the far end of the park). It's tempting to stretch your Potsdam visit into a full day so you can linger in the park and tour other royal buildings, poke around the inviting town center of Potsdam, or visit nearby attractions (such as Cecilienhof, the site of the post-WWII Potsdam Conference).

If you're an avid cyclist, it's particularly enjoyable to combine a visit to Potsdam with a bike ride along skinny lakes and through green parklands back into the city (rent a bike in Berlin and bring it on the train; for details, see page 658).

Sachsenhausen: Two hours at the camp is enough for a quick walk through the grounds, but three hours is a minimum if you want to read the many worthwhile exhibits. Factoring in transit time, leave yourself at least six hours round-trip from central Berlin.

Both: For an exhausting day of contrasts, you could get an early start to visit Sachsenhausen (opens at 8:30), munch a picnic lunch on the train down to Potsdam (connected by the S-1 line in about 1.5 hours, with a change at Wannsee; several basic lunch options in Potsdam train station), and tour Frederick the Great's palaces before collapsing on an evening train back to Berlin.

Potsdam

Featuring a lush park strewn with the escapist whimsies of Frederick the Great, the sleepy town of Potsdam has long been Berlin's holiday retreat. And until the City Palace in downtown Berlin is rebuilt, it's your best opportunity to get a taste of Prussia's Hohenzollern royalty. While Potsdam's palaces are impressive, they don't quite crack Europe's top 10—perhaps because the audioguides don't

inject the Hohenzollerns' personalities into the place (or maybe the Hohenzollerns were really that boring). But Potsdam is convenient to reach from downtown Berlin, and it makes for a great break from the city's heavy history. It's also ideal on a sunny day, thanks to its strolling- and picnic-friendly park.

Getting to Potsdam

You have two easy train options for zipping from Berlin to Potsdam's Hauptbahnhof (main train station; round-trip covered by €6.80 Berlin transit day pass with zones ABC). Direct **Regional Express/RE1 trains** depart twice hourly from Berlin's Bahnhof Zoo (20 minutes to Potsdam), Hauptbahnhof (30 minutes), and Friedrichstrasse (35 minutes; any train to Brandenburg or Magdeburg stops in Potsdam). Note: Some RE1 trains continue past the Potsdam Hauptbahnhof to a stop called Park Sanssouci, a good choice closer to the palaces (check the schedule).

The **S-Bahn** is slightly slower, but more frequent and handier from some areas of Berlin. The S-7 line goes directly to Potsdam from Alexanderplatz, Hackescher Markt, Friedrichstrasse, Hauptbahnhof, Bahnhof Zoo, and Savignyplatz (6/hour, 30-45 minutes depending on starting point). The S-1 line, which requires a transfer at Wannsee, leaves from Potsdamer Platz, Brandenburger Tor, Friedrichstrasse, Oranienburger Strasse, and other city-center stations; after the line ends at Wannsee, cross the platform to an S-7 train, and ride it three more stops to Potsdam (6/hour, about 45-50 minutes total from downtown Berlin).

Orientation to Potsdam

Potsdam is about 15 miles southwest of Berlin. The city center is enjoyable to explore, but the big draws here are Frederick the Great's palaces, which surround the gigantic, sprawling Sanssouci Park at the northwest edge of town.

Tourist Information

A handy TI is inside Potsdam's train station (April-Oct Mon-Sat 9:30-20:00, Sun 10:00-16:00; Nov-March Mon-Sat 9:30-18:00, Sun 10:00-16:00; tel. 0331/2755-8830, www.potsdamtourismus .de). Another TI branch, closer to the town center at Luisenplatz, is less convenient for most visitors (April-Oct Mon-Fri 9:30-18:00, Sat-Sun 9:30-16:00; Nov-March Mon-Fri 10:00-18:00, Sat-Sun 9:30-14:00; Brandenburger Strasse 3, tel. 0331/505-8838). Get a map and ask about bus tours if you're interested (see "Tours in Potsdam," on the next page).

The **palace information office** is very helpful, with friendly English-speaking staff. It's across the street from the windmill near the Sanssouci entrance (daily April-Oct 8:30-18:00, Nov-March 8:30-17:00, tel. 0331/969-4200—then press 1, www.spsg .de; clean WC in same building, €0.30).

To supplement the English tour handouts and audioguides at the palaces, consider picking up the blue "official guide" booklets (available individually for each of the sights, €4 apiece at palace information office and gift shops).

Arrival in Potsdam

From Potsdam's **Hauptbahnhof** (main train station), you have several options for reaching the palaces. It's a long (but scenic) 45-minute **walk** (get directions and pick up a map at the TI), or—easier—you can take a bus or tram. To find the bus/tram stops, exit the station toward *Landtag/Friedrich-Engels-Strasse*; this takes you out the main door, where you'll find a row of stops. Various **buses** leave the station about every 10 minutes and connect to either palace (single ride-€1.80, all-day pass-€3.90, buy tickets at machine on board the bus, also covered by any Berlin pass with zones ABC). The convenient but packed bus #695 cruises through the appealing town center of Potsdam, stopping first at Sanssouci, then at the New Palace (3/hour, 15-20 minutes, leaves from lane 4). Bus #606 only goes to Sanssouci, and bus #605 stops only at the New Palace (3/hour apiece, 10-15 minutes, both leave from lane 5). If you're up for a hike, another option is to take **tram** #91 to Luisenplatz (3/ hour, 11 minutes, leaves from lane 1), then walk 20 minutes uphill through the park, which lets you enjoy a classic view of Sanssouci Palace.

If you arrive at Potsdam's **Park Sanssouci Station,** just walk straight out and head up the boulevard called Am Neuen Palais, with the big park on your right-hand side. In about 10 minutes, you'll reach the New Palace.

Tours in Potsdam

Local Tours—The Potsdam TI offers a bus tour of Potsdam sights, plus the interior of Sanssouci Palace. This normally wouldn't be worth the time...except that it's the only way to get into Sanssouci with a live, English-speaking guide (often with some German, too; €27 covers tour, palace, and park in 3.5 hours; April-Oct Tue-Sun at 11:00, no tours Mon or Nov-March; departs from Luisenplatz TI at 11:00 or from train station TI at 11:10; reserve by phone, in summer reserve at least 2 days in advance, tel. 0331/275-8899).

Various bus tours (including hop-on, hop-off options) conveniently connect this town's spread-out sights. Pick up brochures at the TI.

Tours from Berlin—Original Berlin Walks, Vive Berlin, and other companies offer inexpensive all-day tours from Berlin through Potsdam (1-3/weekly, small groups, English-language only, no reservations necessary, admissions and public transportation not included, doesn't actually go into Sanssouci Palace). **Original Berlin Walks'** tour leaves Berlin at 9:50 every Sunday from April through October (also on Thu June-Sept; €15, meet at taxi stand at Bahnhof Zoo, tel. 030/301-9194, www.berlinwalks .de). The guide takes you to Cecilienhof Palace (site of postwar Potsdam conference attended by Churchill, Stalin, and Truman), through pleasant green landscapes to the historic heart of Potsdam for lunch, and finishes outside Sanssouci Palace. Similar tours are run by **Vive Berlin** (€15, leaves Mon and Thu at 10:00 from outside Balzac Coffee on Potsdamer Platz, €24 bike tour leaves Sat at 10:00, tel. 0157/845-46696, www.viveberlintours.de).

Sights in Potsdam

Frederick the Great's Palaces

Frederick the Great was a dynamic 18th-century ruler who put Prussia on the map with his merciless military prowess. Yet he also had tender affection for the finer things in life: art, architecture, gardens, literature, and other distinguished pursuits (for more on Frederick, see the sidebar on page

646). During his reign, Frederick built an impressive ensemble of palaces and other grand buildings around Sanssouci Park, with the two top palaces located at either end. Frederick's super-Rococo Sanssouci Palace is dazzling, while his equally extravagant New Palace was built to wow guests and disprove rumors that Prussia was running out of money after the costly Seven Years' War.

Getting Between the Palaces: It's about a 30-minute walk between Sanssouci and the New Palace. To save time, you can hop on bus #695, which takes you between the palaces in either direction (covered by the cheaper €1.30 *Kurzstrecke* ticket, as well as by a Berlin transit pass with zones ABC). If you do walk, you'll find the park wilder, more forested, and less carefully manicured than other palace complexes, such as Versailles and Vienna's Schönbrunn.

▲▲**Sanssouci Palace**—*Sans souci* means "without a care," and this was the carefree summer home of Frederick the Great (built

1745-1747). Of all the palatial buildings scattered around Potsdam, this was his actual residence. While the palace is small and the audioguide does little to capture the personality of its former resident, it's worth seeing for its opulence.

Cost and Hours: €12, includes audioguide, April-Oct Tue-Sun 10:00-18:00, Nov-March Tue-Sun 10:00-17:00, last entry 30 minutes before closing, closed Mon year-round; in winter (Nov-March), entrance is with a live guided German tour only (departs about every 20 minutes)— about once an hour, they let English-speakers with audioguides tag along; tel. 0331/969-4200, www.spsg.de.

Crowd-Beating Tips: At this popular sight, your ticket comes with an appointed entry time. (Tickets are sold for the same day only.) For the most stress-free visit, come early: In the summer, if you arrive by 10:00 (when the ticket office opens), you'll get right in. If you arrive after 11:00, plan to stand in line to buy your ticket. You'll probably have to wait for your entry time, too—usually an hour or two later (pass this time visiting the Ladies' Wing and Palace Kitchen or exploring the sprawling gardens; if you have a very long wait, zip over to visit the New Palace, then come back to Sanssouci).

Touring the Palace: Your ticket covers three parts—The Ladies' Wing (to the left as you face the palace from the front/ garden side); the Palace Kitchen (to the right); and the living quarters and festival halls (the main, central part). You can visit the first two sights anytime, but you must report to the main part of the palace at the time noted on your ticket (you'll receive your audioguide there).

The **Ladies' Wing (Damenflügel),** worth a visit only if you have time to kill (and maybe not even then), contains apartments for ladies-in-waiting and servants. Borrow the dull English descriptions and walk past rooms cluttered with cutesy decor. The servants' quarters upstairs have been turned into a painting gallery.

At the **Palace Kitchen (Schlossküche),** see well-preserved mid-19th-century cooking equipment (with posted English information). Hike down the tight spiral staircase to the wine cellar, which features an exhibit about the grapes that were grown on the terraced vineyards out front.

The **Main Palace** was where Frederick the Great spent his summers. The dry audioguide narrates your stroll through the classic Rococo interior, where golden grapevines climb the walls and frame the windows. First explore the Royal Apartments, containing one of Frederick's three libraries (he found it easier to buy extra copies of books rather than move them around), the "study bedroom" where he lived and worked, and the chair where he died. The domed, central Marble Hall resembles the Pantheon in Rome (on a smaller scale), with an oblong oculus, inlaid marble floors, and Corinthian columns made of Carrara marble.

Finally you'll visit the guest rooms, most of which exit straight out onto the delightful terrace. Each room is decorated differently: Chinese, Italian, all yellow, and so on; the niche at the back was for a bed. As you exit (in the servants' quarters), keep an eye out for the giant portrait of Frederick by Andy Warhol.

▲▲**New Palace (Neues Palais)**—This gigantic showpiece palace (with more than 200 rooms) is, in some ways, more impressive than the intimate Sanssouci. While Frederick the Great lived primarily at Sanssouci, he built the New Palace later (1763-1769) to host guests and dazzle visiting dignitaries. And unlike at Sanssouci, there's rarely a long wait to buy tickets or enter the palace.

Cost and Hours: €6, includes audioguide, April-Oct Wed-Mon 10:00-18:00, Nov-March Wed-Mon 10:00-17:00, closed Tue year-round. To see the king's ho-hum apartments—eight small rooms that are a watered-down version of what you'll see at Sanssouci—you must take a required 45-minute tour in German (€5, offered May-Oct daily at 10:00, 11:00, 14:00, and 16:00).

During the off-season (Nov-March), the king's apartments are closed, and you can visit the rest of the New Palace by tagging along with a German tour (with an English audioguide; may have to wait up to 30 minutes for next tour). Tel. 0331/969-4200, www.spsg.de.

2012 Happenings: The New Palace is closed through the end of April 2012, after which it reopens with higher prices and a special exhibit (runs through Oct 2012).

Touring the Palace: The tour includes a pair of loaner slippers (to protect the floors) and a one-hour English audioguide that takes you through the ornate halls. From the Grotto Hall, decorated with seashells, you can peer into the lavish Marble Hall, used for fancy gatherings. Continue on through the eight suites of the Lower Princes' Apartments, which accommodated guests and royal family members. In the 19th and early 20th century, German emperors Frederick III (different from the earlier Frederick who built the place) and Wilhelm II (the last Kaiser) resided here. The Gentlemen's Bedchamber holds the red-canopy bed where Kaiser Frederick III died in 1888. The Ladies' Bedchamber is a reminder that noblemen and their wives slept separately.

Upstairs, the Upper Princes' Quarters include a small blue-tiled bathroom that was later installed for Kaiser Wilhelm II. You'll also find Wilhelm's bedroom, as well as a small painting gallery with portraits of Frederick the Great and Russia's Catherine the Great (who was actually a German princess). From up here, you also get a look into the sumptuous, 52-foot-high Marble Hall, with its ceiling painting of the Greek myth of Ganymede and the floors inlaid with Silesian marble. Through the windows, enjoy the views out into the gardens, which recede into the horizon.

Other Palaces—The two main palaces (Sanssouci and the New Palace) are just the beginning. The sprawling Sanssouci Park contains

a variety of other palaces and royal buildings, many of which you can enter. Popular options include the Italian-style **Orangerie** (the last and largest palace in the park, with five royal rooms that must be toured with a German guide, plus a view tower); the **New Chambers** (a royal guest house); the **Chinese House;** and other viewpoints, including the **Klausberg Belvedere** or the **Norman Tower.**

Cost and Hours: Each has its own entry fee and hours, some open weekends only (get a complete list from the Potsdam TI or the palace information office). If you have plenty of time and really want to see it all, you can buy a combo-ticket that covers all of the palaces at Potsdam (€19 for everything, €15 for all but Sanssouci, sold at palace ticket offices); www.spsg.de.

Bornstedt Royal Estate (Krongut Bornstedt)—Designed to look like an Italian village, this warehouse-like complex once provided the royal palaces with food and other supplies. Today the estate houses the Bornstedt Buffalo brewery and distillery, which delivers fine brews and (sometimes) schnapps, as it has since 1689. The brewpub's restaurant is a good place for lunch, serving local specialties (€10-16 plates). The kid-friendly grounds also house a wood-fired bakery with fresh bread and pastries. You can watch hatmakers, candlemakers, coopers, potters, and glassmakers produce (and sell) their wares using traditional techniques.

Cost and Hours: Free except during special events, daily 10:00-19:00, restaurant serves food until 22:00, Ribbeckstrasse 6, tel. 01805-766-488, www.krongut-bornstedt.de.

Getting There: From Sanssouci, walk toward the windmill and follow the street An der Orangerie about 500 yards.

More Sights in Potsdam

Potsdam Town—The easy-to-stroll town center has pedestrianized shopping streets lined with boutiques and eateries. For a small town, this was a cosmopolitan place: Frederick the Great imported some very talented people. For example, Dutch merchants and architects built the Dutch Quarter (Holländisches Viertel, at the intersection of Leiblstrasse and Benkertstrasse) with gabled red-brick buildings that feel like a little corner of Amsterdam. The city also has a good film museum and a museum of Prussian history (both near Breite Strasse). Even if you're just racing through Potsdam on your way to the palaces, you can still catch a glimpse of the town center by riding bus #695 (described earlier, under "Arrival in Potsdam"). Skip Potsdam's much-promoted Wannsee boat rides, which are exceedingly dull.

Cecilienhof—This former residence of Crown Prince William was the site of the historic Potsdam Conference in the summer of 1945. During these meetings, Harry Truman, Winston Churchill, and Joseph Stalin negotiated how best to punish Germany for dragging Europe through another devastating war. It was here that the postwar map of Europe was officially drawn, setting the stage for a protracted Cold War that would drag on for four and half decades. Designed to appear smaller and more modest than it actually is, Cecilienhof pales in comparison to the grand palaces concentrated around Sanssouci Park; it's only worth visiting if you're a WWII or Cold War history buff (or would like to visit the nearby Meierei brewpub).

Cost and Hours: €6, April-Oct Tue-Sun 10:00-18:00, Nov-March Tue-Sun 10:00-17:00, closed Mon year-round, tel. 0331/969-4224, www.spsg.de.

Eating: Try the brewery called **Meierei** ("Creamery") at Cecilienhof. Its nice beer garden offers spectacular views of the lake, solid German food, and great homemade beer. When you walk down the hill into the restaurant, note the big open field to the right—it used to be part of the Berlin Wall (€6-15 meals, daily 11:00-22:00, follow *Meierei* signs to Im Neuen Garten 10, tel. 0331/704-3211).

Getting There: First, go to the Reiterweg stop, at the northern end of Potsdam (from Sanssouci Palace, take bus #695; from the train station, ride tram #92 or #96). At Reiterweg, transfer to bus #603 (toward Höhenstrasse), and get off at the Schloss Cecilienhof stop.

Babelsberg—Movie buffs might already know that the nearby suburb of Babelsberg (just east of Potsdam) hosts the biggest film studio in Germany, where classics such as *The Blue Angel* and *Metropolis,* as well as recent hits *The Reader* and *Inglourious Basterds,* were filmed (for information about visiting, see www.filmpark-babelsberg.de).

NEAR BERLIN

Sachsenhausen Concentration Camp Memorial

About 20 miles north of downtown Berlin, the small town of Oranienburg was the site of one of the most notorious Nazi concentration camps (which collectively claimed the lives of millions of innocent people). Sachsenhausen's proximity to the capital gave it special status as the place to train camp guards and test new procedures. It was also the site of the Third Reich's massive coun-

terfeiting operation, depicted in the Oscar-winning 2007 movie *The Counterfeiters.* Today Sachsenhausen, worth ▲▲, is open to visitors as a memorial and a museum (Gedenkstätte und Museum

Sachsenhausen), honoring the victims and survivors, and teaching visitors about the atrocities that took place here.

Getting There

Take a train to the town of Oranienburg (20-50 minutes); from there, it's a 20-minute walk or a quick trip by bus or taxi to the camp. The whole journey takes just over an hour each way.

From downtown Berlin, a regional train speeds from Hauptbahnhof to Oranienburg (hourly, 20 minutes). Or you can take the S-Bahn (S-1) line from various stops downtown, including Potsdamer Platz, Brandenburger Tor, Friedrichstrasse, and Oranienburger Strasse (3/hour, 45-50 minutes depending on starting point). Note that the slower S-Bahn may not necessarily take longer if you factor in the time it takes to get to the Hauptbahnhof, find the correct platform, and wait for the train. The S-1 line also connects southward to Potsdam (with a change in Wannsee)—making it possible to connect Sachsenhausen and Potsdam's palaces in one extremely busy day.

Once at the Oranienburg train station, it's usually best to **walk** to the memorial (since the bus runs infrequently). Turn right out of the train station and head up Stralsunder Strasse for about two blocks. Turn right under the railroad trestle onto Bernauer Strasse, following signs for *Gedenkstätte Sachsenhausen*. At the traffic light, turn left onto André-Pican-Strasse, which becomes Strasse der Einheit. After two blocks, turn right on Strasse der Nationen, where you'll pass a memorial stone commemorating the death march (see page 774). This leads right to the camp, where you can enter the grounds through the gaps in the wall.

To avoid the walk, take a taxi or catch **bus #804** from in front of the Oranienburg station (hourly, every 2 hours on weekends, lane 4; bus #821 also possible but only 4/day; both covered by Berlin transit pass with zones ABC).

Orientation to Sachsenhausen

Cost and Hours: Free, mid-March–mid-Oct Tue-Sun 8:30-18:00, mid-Oct–mid-March Tue-Sun until 16:30; avoid visiting on Mon, when the grounds and visitors center are open but the exhibits inside the buildings are closed; Strasse der Nationen 22.

Information: The visitor center has WCs, a bookshop, and a helpful information desk. If visiting on your own, pick up the good €0.50 map of the camp. Also consider the €3 audioguide, with up to five hours of commentary (includes map). Tel. 03301/200-200, www.gedenkstaette-sachsenhausen.de.

Tours from Berlin: While you can visit Sachsenhausen on your

own, a tour helps you understand the camp's complicated and important story. Virtually all walking-tour companies in Berlin offer side-trips to Sachsenhausen. You'll meet in the city, then ride together by train to Oranienburg, and walk to the camp. (Bring along or buy lunch en route, as there's no place to eat at the camp.) The round-trip takes about six hours, much of which is spent in transit—but the time that you spend at the camp is made very meaningful by your guide's commentary.

Check the walking-tour companies' websites (see page 662), or compare brochures to find an itinerary that fits your schedule. Here are a few options: **Original Berlin Walks** (€15, April-Oct Tue-Fri and Sun at 10:00, runs less frequently off-season), **Vive Berlin** (free because they believe a visit here should be accessible to anyone, tipping the guide is encouraged; Tue, Fri, Sat, and Sun at 10:00), and **Insider Tours** (€15, Tue-Sun at 10:00).

Eating: You can't buy food at the camp. If you need lunch, bring it with you from Berlin, or buy it at the Oranienburg train station.

Background

Completed in July of 1936, Sachsenhausen was the first concentration camp built under SS chief Heinrich Himmler. It was custom-designed in the panopticon ("all-seeing") model popular in British prisons. The grounds were triangular so they could be observed from a single point, the main guard tower. The design was intended to be a model for other camps, but they soon discovered a critical flaw that prevented its widespread adoption: It was very difficult to expand without interfering with sight lines.

Sachsenhausen was not, strictly speaking, a "death camp" for the mass production of murder (like Birkenau); it was a labor camp, intended to wring hard work out of the prisoners. Many toiled in a brickworks, producing materials that were to be used in architect Albert Speer's grandiose plans for erecting new buildings all over Berlin.

Between 1936 and 1945, about 200,000 prisoners did time at Sachsenhausen; about 50,000 died here, while numerous others were transported elsewhere to be killed (in 1942, many of Sachsenhausen's Jews were taken to Auschwitz). Though it was designed to hold 10,000 prisoners, by the end of its functional life the camp had up to 38,000 people. In the spring of 1945, knowing that the Red Army was approaching, guards took 35,000 able-bodied prisoners on a death march, leading them into the forest for seven days and nights with no rations. Rather than "wasting" bullets to kill them, SS troops hoped that the prisoners would expire from exhaustion. On the eighth day, after 6,000 had already died, the guards abandoned the group in the wilderness, leaving them free. When Soviet troops liberated Sachsenhausen on April 22, 1945, they discovered an additional 3,000 prisoners who had been too weak to walk and were left there to die (all but 300 ended up surviving).

Just three months after the war, Sachsenhausen was converted into a Soviet Special Camp No. 7 for the USSR's own prisoners. It was a notorious "silent camp," where prisoners would disappear with no information. The prisoners were Nazis as well as anti-Stalin Russians. By the time the camp closed in 1950, 12,000 more prisoners had died here.

In 1961, Sachsenhausen became the first concentration camp turned into a memorial. The East German government did it largely for propaganda purposes: to deflect attention from the controversial construction of the Berlin Wall and to exalt the USSR as the valiant anti-fascist liberators of the camp and all of Germany (rather than commemorate the victims).

Since the end of communism, the country has redeveloped Sachsenhausen into a true memorial, with updated museum exhibits (scattered throughout the grounds in various buildings) and an emphasis on preservation—documenting and sharing the story of what happened here.

Self-Guided Tour

There's a lot to experience, but this outline covers the basics.

Entrance

First get your bearings in the **visitors center,** where you can peruse the bookshop, buy a map of the grounds, and rent an audioguide.

In the courtyard next to the visitors center, a **model** of the camp illustrates its unique triangular layout, containing the prisoners' barracks. This allowed guards stationed in tower A (at the main gate) to see everything going on inside those three walls. Along the left side of the triangle is the crematorium, called Station Z. (Nazis perversely joked that inmates entered the camp at A and exited at Z.) The smaller buildings outside the main triangle served as workshops, factories, and extra barracks that were added when the camp ran out of room.

Walk up the dusty lane called Camp Street. On the right is the SS officers' R&R building, nicknamed the **"Green Monster,"** where prisoners were forced to dress up and wait on SS officers. Officials mostly chose Jehovah's Witnesses because they had a strong pacifist code and could be trusted not to attempt to harm their captors.

Turn left through the fence into the courtyard in front of **guard tower A.** The clock on the tower is frozen at 11:07—the exact time that the Red Army liberated the camp (and a reminder that the Soviets—who were initially responsible for turning

the camp into this memorial—were the "good guys"). The building on the right—misnamed the **"New Museum"**—has an interesting DDR-era stained-glass window inside, as well as temporary exhibits and information on Oranienburg Concentration Camp (which preceded Sachsenhausen). To the left as you face the guard tower is the **SS commandant's house,** which is being turned into a museum about the administration of the camp.

Go through the gate cruelly marked *Arbeit Macht Frei*—"Work will set you free."

Main Grounds

Entering the triangular field, you can see that almost none of the original buildings still stand. Following the war, the Germans dismantled all of the barracks here in order to use them for building materials. Tracing the perimeter, notice the electric fence and barbed wire. A few feet in front of the wall is a gravel track called the **"neutral zone"**—any prisoner setting foot here would be shot. This became a common way for prisoners to attempt suicide. Guards quickly caught on: If they sensed a suicide attempt, they'd shoot to maim instead of kill. It was typical upside-down Nazi logic: Those who wanted to live would die, and those who wanted to die would live.

The daily **roll call** took place in the Appelplatz, the area in front of the guard tower. After a 4:15 wake-up call, prisoners would scramble to eat, bathe, and dress in time for the 5:00 roll call. Dressed in their standard-issue uniforms—thin, striped pajamas and wooden clogs—prisoners would line up while guards, in long coats with angry dogs, barked orders in German and accounted for each person, including those who had died in the barracks overnight. It could take hours, in any weather. One misbehaving prisoner would bring about punishment for all others. One day, after a prisoner escaped, SS officer Rudolf Höss (who later went on to run Auschwitz-Birkenau) forced the entire population of the camp to stand here for 15 hours in a foot of snow and subzero temperatures. A thousand people died.

To the far right, the wooden **barracks** (containing good museum displays and English descriptions) are reconstructed from original timbers. Barrack 38 focuses on the Jewish experience at Sachsenhausen, as well as the general mistreatment of German Jews under the Nazis (including anti-Semitic propaganda). Barrack 39 explains everyday life, with stories following 20 individual internees. You'll see how prisoners lived: long rows of

bunks, benches for taking paltry meals, latrines crammed wall-to-wall with toilets, and communal fountains for washing. Inmates would jockey for access to these facilities. The strongest, meanest, most aggressive prisoners—often here because they had been convicted of a violent crime—would be named *Kapo*, the head of the barrack. This was another example of depraved Nazi logic: The worst prisoners (rather than the best) were "promoted." Like many others, this camp had a prostitution ring—the Nazis brought in female inmates from the women's-only Ravensbrück concentration camp and forced them to "reward good prisoners" at Sachsenhausen.

NEAR BERLIN

Next to the barracks is the **camp prison,** where political prisoners or out-of-line inmates were sent. It was run not by the SS, but by the Gestapo (secret police), who would torture captives to extract information. Other prisoners didn't know exactly what went on here, but they could hear howls from inside and knew it was no place they wanted to be. This was also where the Nazis held special hostages, including three Allied airmen who had participated in a bold escape from a Nazi prisoner-of-war camp (the basis for *The Great Escape;* they later managed to escape from Sachsenhausen as well, before being recaptured) and Joseph Stalin's son, Yakov Dzhugashvili, who had been captured during the fighting at Stalingrad. (The Nazis offered to exchange the young man for five German officers. Stalin refused, and soon after, Yakov died here under mysterious circumstances.) The cells contain exhibits about the prisoners and the methods used by their captors. Outside, you'll find three posts (out of an original 15) with iron pegs near the top. Guards would execute people by tying their hands behind their backs, then hanging them on these pegs by their wrists until they died—a medieval method called *strappado.*

Walk around the semicircle toward the buildings in the middle of the camp. On the gravel **"boot-testing track,"** prisoners were forced to put on boots two sizes too small and walk in a circle all day, supposedly to "test" the shoes for fighting at Stalingrad. The patches of gravel show where each of the barrack buildings once stood. A marker represents the location of the gallows, where prisoners would be publicly executed as a deterrent to others.

Two buildings stand in the middle of the triangle. The one on the left is the **laundry building,** with special exhibits on topics such as Operation Bernhard, Sachsenhausen's counterfeiting ring. Nazi authorities created the world's largest counterfeiting operation by forcing inmates who were skilled forgers to create fake bills that would flood the US and British economies and devalue their currencies. The 2007 movie *The Counterfeiters* depicts the moral dilemma the prisoners faced: Do we create perfect fakes, which will ultimately work against our own cause? Or do we risk execution by intentionally doing bad work to sabotage the operation?

On the right is the **kitchen building,** with exhibits that trace chronologically the history of the camp. You'll learn how Sachsenhausen was actually built by prisoners, and see original artifacts including the gallows, a bunk from the barracks, uniforms, and so on. There are also photos, quotes, and a 22-minute film. The basement walls feature

some bizarre cartoons of vegetables preparing themselves to be eaten (these were drawn later by Soviets).

Memorial and Crematorium

Head back to the far end of the camp, dominated by the tower-

ing, 130-foot-tall, 1961 pro-communist DDR **memorial** to the victims of Sachsenhausen. The 18 triangles at the top are red, the color designated for political prisoners (rather than honoring the other Nazi victims who died here). At the base of the monument, two prisoners are being liberated by a noble Soviet soldier. The prisoners are unrealistically robust, healthy, and optimistic (they will survive and become part of the proud Soviet proletariat!). The podium in front was used by the East German army for speeches and rallies—exploiting Sachsenhausen as a backdrop for their propaganda.

Go through the gap in the fence to find the execution trench, used for mass shootings. Because this system proved too inefficient, the Nazis built Station Z, the **crematorium,** where they could execute and dispose of prisoners more systematically. Prior to the camp's liberation by Soviet troops, Nazi guards destroyed

the crematorium to remove evidence of their crimes; the ruins are inside the white building. The ramp took prisoners down into the "infirmary," while the three steps led up to the dressing room. This is where the Nazis tested Zyklon-B (used five times here, this was the chemical responsible for killing hundreds of thousands at Auschwitz). Most of the building's victims died in the room with the double row of bricks (for soundproofing; the Nazis also blasted classical music to mask noise). Victims would report

here for a "dental check," to find out if they had gold or silver teeth that could be taken. They would then stand against the wall to have their height measured—and a guard would shoot them through a small hole in the wall with a single bullet to the back of the skull. (The Nazis found it was easier for guards to carry out their duties if they didn't have to see their victims face-to-face.) Bodies were taken to be incinerated in the ovens (which still stand). Notice the statue of the emaciated prisoner—a much more accurate depiction than the one at the DDR monument. Outside, a burial ground is filled with ashes from the crematorium.

The Rest of the Camp

Return to the main part of the camp to visit the remaining sights. You can head left, up to the tip of the triangle (behind the big monument) to find the museum about the postwar era, when Sachsenhausen served as a **Soviet Special Camp**—the often-forgotten second act. Nearby is a burial ground for victims of that camp. At this corner of the triangle, the gate in the fence—called **tower E**—holds a small exhibit about the relationship between the camp and the town of Oranienburg.

Or you can turn right and walk along the wall toward the front corner. The long, green barracks were the **infirmary,** used for medical experiments on inmates (and explained by the exhibits inside). This was also where Soviet soldiers found the 3,000 remaining survivors when they liberated the camp. The small building in back was the morgue—Nazis used the long ramp for wheelbarrows bringing in the day's bodies. Behind that is a field with six stones, each marking 50 bodies for the 300 prisoners who died after the camp was freed.

While all of this is difficult to take in, as with all concentration camp memorials, the intention of Sachsenhausen is to share its story and lessons—and prevent this type of tragedy from ever happening again.

HAMBURG

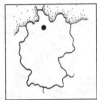

Hamburg is Germany's second-largest city, the richest judged by per-capita income, and its most important port. If you have German ancestors, chances are they left for America from here. Looking across the Elbe River from downtown, you can see giant container ships making their way down from the North Sea and docking under the huge derricks on the other side of the river.

Hamburg is popular with German tourists, who come here to enjoy Broadway-style musicals, eat fish, watch soccer games, and experience the nightlife of the Reeperbahn. Foreign visitors are in the minority, and you won't see as much English in the tourist industry here as in Munich or Rothenburg. Like many port towns, it can have rough edges, but a short stay can be memorable. As John Lennon said, "I might have been born in Liverpool—but I grew up in Hamburg."

Hamburg is unlike some other German cities in not having a quaint medieval downtown. While WWII bombs took a toll (see sidebar, page 790), what really destroyed Hamburg's medieval center was a huge fire in 1842. The city center today is a mixture of office buildings and (near the Binnenalster and Jungfernstieg promenade) brand-name shopping. The city shows off Germany's industrial prosperity in the 19th and 20th centuries more than its medieval heritage. Its fishy, maritime, Scandinavian feel is worlds away from the sun-drenched, Baroque joviality of Bavaria.

Planning Your Time

If you're on your way between Germany and Denmark, Hamburg is well worth a quick stop. If you're short on time, check your bag

HAMBURG

Hamburg

- **1** Hotel Wedina
- **2** Hotel Aussen Alster
- **3** Ibis Hotel Hamburg Alster
- **4** Motel One Hamburg-Alster
- **5** Hotel-Pension Alpha
- **6** Jugendherberge Hamburg "Auf dem Stintfang"
- **7** Kajüte Restaurant
- **8** Schifferbörse Restaurant
- **9** Café Koppel
- **10** Öz Urfa Kebap Salonu
- **11** Galeria Kaufhof (Grocery)
- **12** Launderette

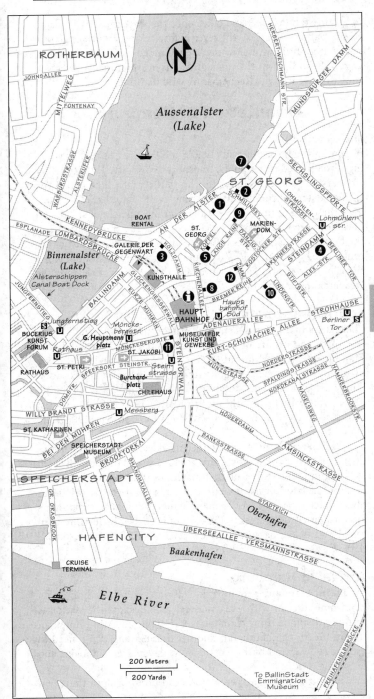

HAMBURG

in a train-station locker and take public transit to the City Hall and Reeperbahn, and cruise the river before taking an evening train out. With a full day, follow my "Self-Guided Tour" (described on page 788) to link up the top sights. An overnight stop gives you time to delve into the Reeperbahn's wild nightlife scene.

Orientation to Hamburg

(area code: 040)

Hamburg's sights are spread out and too far apart to rely on walking—you'll need to use public transport in this city. The city center sits between the Elbe River (to the south) and a lake called the Binnenalster (to the north). The ring road around this core follows the route of the old city walls. But most places of interest in Hamburg are just outside the central core: The train station and the St. Georg neighborhood (with good hotels) are just east of the center, the harbor and old warehouse district are to the south along the Elbe, and the St. Pauli district and the red light zone along the Reeperbahn lie to the west.

Tourist Information

Hamburg's main, though small, **TI** is in the train station, above the north end of platforms 3-4. It has good, free maps and sells Hamburg Cards (Mon-Sat 9:00-21:00, Sun 10:00-18:00, www .hamburg-tourism.de). A public transport info office is next door. There are also TIs at Landungsbrücken (Sun-Wed 9:00-18:00, Thu-Sat 9:00-19:00) and the airport (daily 6:00-23:00). For tourist information by phone, call 040/3005-1300 (Mon-Sat 9:00-19:00, closed Sun).

Hamburg Card: If you'll be seeing at least two or three museums, especially with a group, this card is a sound investment. Sold at TIs and public-transit ticket machines (see "Getting Around Hamburg," later), it comes with full-day public-transit privileges plus reduced-priced entry to many sights. While these discounts are meager (10-30 percent), the card only costs a little more than a plain transport pass (for single travelers: €8.90/1 day, €20.50/3 days; for groups of up to 5: €13.90/1 day, €34.50/3 days).

Arrival in Hamburg

By Train: Hamburg's main train station (Hauptbahnhof) has a handsome interior with a classic steel-arch design. The station is walking distance from Hamburg's City Hall and from hotels in the St. Georg neighborhood; to other destinations, you'll need to use the subway and buses. Fortunately, the station is a major hub for public transit.

From the platforms, escalators lead up to bridges that span

the tracks at the north and south ends of the building; at each end of each bridge is an exit to the city, making four exits in all. Most services are on the northern bridge, including the ticket counters in the *Reisezentrum* (Mon-Fri 6:00-21:30, Sat-Sun 8:00-21:00). You'll also find the city-run TI and a public-transport ticket office (both above tracks 3-4), several pay WCs (€0.50), and several banks of lockers (€3-5; one is above tracks 5-6).

By Plane: Hamburg's airport is a simple 25-minute ride from the train station on the S-1 **subway** line, which runs every 10 minutes for most of the day (first train around 4:30 in the morning, last around 24:00). A Hamburg *Grossbereich* ticket (€2.80) will cover your journey, but consider getting one of the public-transit day passes or the Hamburg Card if you'll be doing more travel that day.

If you're traveling *to* the airport, S-1 trains from the city divide at Ohlsdorf, one stop from the airport—one half of the train goes off in a different direction. Signs and bilingual announcements tell you which cars are going to the airport, and you have a chance to switch cars at Ohlsdorf if you're in the wrong part of the train.

Airport info: Tel. 040/50750, www.airport.de.

Helpful Hints

Laundry: At the **Express Wasch-Center,** a five-minute walk from the train station and convenient to St. Georg hotels, choose between self-service (€6/load) and full service (wash, dry, and fold—a steal at €9; Mon-Sat 8:00-20:00, closed Sun, just off Hansaplatz at Zimmerpforte 6, tel. 040/280-4655).

Bike Rental: Like many European cities, Hamburg has a government-run bike-sharing program. Called StadtRAD, it has 70 automated rental stations with distinctive red bikes. The first half-hour is free, but you must pay a €5 registration fee that gives you about 75 additional minutes of credit. To register, call 040/822-188-100 or go online at www.stadtrad hamburg.de.

Taxi: Call 040/211-211.

Bike Lanes and Pedestrians: Red-brick pavement on the sidewalk means it's a bike lane. Pedestrians make sure to stay on the gray part of the sidewalk—bicyclists show little tolerance or patience for tourists who stray onto the brick.

Getting Around Hamburg

You'll almost certainly need to use public transport in this spread-out city. Hamburg's subway system includes both U-Bahns (there are three lines, U-1 to U-3) and S-Bahns (technically commuter rail lines). Eurailpasses are good on the S-Bahn (but not the U-Bahn), but if you use a flexipass, it'll cost you a travel day. Buses and public ferries round out the system.

An HVV information office is next to the TI in the train station (Mon-Fri 6:00-21:00, Sat-Sun 7:00-21:00, tel. 040/19449, www.hvv.de). Buy tickets from the machines at each stop, which take coins and small bills; they're marked with the name of the system (HVV).

Single ticket prices depend on how far you're traveling; the shortest trips cost €1.30, longer ones €1.80, and the longest ones (within the *Grossbereich*—greater city limits, including the airport) cost €2.80. Key your destination into the ticket machines, and it will tell you the price of the ticket.

Day passes pay for themselves quickly and give you the run of the whole system (up to the greater city limits). For one person making two long trips or four short trips in a day, a *9-Uhr-Tageskarte* day pass usually saves money (€5.50, not valid Mon-Fri 6:00-9:00). Groups of up to five people can get a *9-Uhr-Gruppenkarte* for €9.60. If you have to use the system between 6:00 and 9:00 on weekdays, you'll have to buy the full-day pass (*Ganztageskarte*, €6.80). A three-day pass, only available for single travelers, costs €16.50 and is valid all day long.

Tours in Hamburg

Do-It-Yourself Orientation Tour: U-3 Subway

This circular subway line runs mostly above ground (often on old-style elevated tracks) and is good for a quick and cheap orientation to the city, bringing you back to your starting point in 45 minutes (covered by €2.80 single ticket, day pass, or Hamburg Card). From the train station (Hauptbahnhof), take the subway in the direction of Rathaus and St. Pauli. The first two stops are underground; then you'll emerge onto elevated tracks that run past downtown office buildings. At the Baumwall stop, you can see across to Speicherstadt, Hamburg's warehouse district. On the way to the next stop (Landungsbrücken), enjoy the view of the harbor and riverfront. The train dips underground again at St. Pauli and then re-emerges above ground for the northern arc of the ring, which runs through the pleasant but less interesting outer neighborhoods of the city. If you're short on time, just enjoy the short stretch between the Rathaus and Landungsbrücken stops.

Bus Tours

Several different companies run circular city bus tours with a multilingual commentary (about €15 for 90 minutes, generally a 10 percent discount with Hamburg Card). You can usually hop off the bus en route and complete the circuit later in the day. The best place to start is the train station—exit near track 3 from either the

Hamburg at a Glance

▲▲**The Reeperbahn** Hamburg's famous red light district, sizzling with Broadway-style theaters, night clubs, and Beatles sights. **Hours:** Always open. See page 790.

▲▲**Boat Rides** Plying Hamburg's humming harbor and stopping at a tony suburb with a hot beach scene. **Hours:** Daily 7:00-23:00. See page 793.

▲**BallinStadt Emigration Museum** Germany's version of Ellis Island, now housing history exhibits instead of emigrants. **Hours:** Daily April-Oct 10:00-18:00, Nov-March until 16:30. See page 795.

▲**Speicherstadt** Trendy riverside warehouse district with famous cafés and world's largest model railroad at the Miniatur Wunderland. **Hours:** District always open; Miniatur Wunderland open Mon 9:30-18:00, Tue 9:30-21:00, Wed-Thu 9:30-18:00, Fri 9:30-19:00, Sat 8:00-21:00, Sun 8:30-20:00. See page 793.

▲**City Hall** Hamburg's century-old Rathaus with mix of Neo-Renaissance, Neo-Gothic, and other architectural styles. **Hours:** English tours daily at 11:15, 13:15, and 15:15, also Sat at 17:15. See page 788.

Beatlemania Five floors about the Fab Four, including their formative Hamburg years. **Hours:** Daily 10:00-19:00. See page 791.

Hamburg History Museum Hamburg's history since its founding in A.D. 800. **Hours:** Tue-Sat 10:00-17:00, Sun 10:00-18:00, closed Mon. See page 797.

SS *Rickmer Rickmers* Century-old sailing ship expertly restored by a corps of volunteers. **Hours:** Daily 10:00-18:00. See page 792.

The Binnenalster Hamburg's inner lake with inviting waterside promenade and chic shops. **Hours:** Always open. See page 789.

HAMBURG

north or south bridge and you'll see double-decker buses waiting for you along Kirchenallee. Before boarding, make sure that you're on a bus with English commentary and check timetables if you plan to hop off and on. One company with frequent departures and English guides is **Die Roten Doppeldecker;** look for red buses with white *Stadtrundfahrt* lettering (departs April-Oct 9:30-17:00 every half-hour, less frequently Nov-March, tel. 040/792-8979, www.die-roten-doppeldecker.de).

Sights in Hamburg

Hamburg's sights are spread out, and you need public transportation to link them. Still, it's easy to get a good feel for the city in a day. In this section I've focused on the main areas that visitors find most interesting—City Hall and nearby, Landungsbrücken and the water, the Reeperbahn, and Speicherstadt—as well as a few other sights.

Self-Guided Tour: While you could see the sights in any order, consider this tour on public transit, using a day pass or Hamburg Card: Start at the Hauptbahnhof (train station). Walk 10 minutes down Mönckebergstrasse, or take the U-3 subway two stops, to the Rathaus (City Hall) and the Binnenalster. After checking out the sights, take the U-3 farther on to the St. Pauli stop, and walk the Reeperbahn, ending by the Beatlemania museum and Reeperbahn S-Bahn stop. Take the S-Bahn one stop back to Landungsbrücken. Here, get out on the water by taking the public #62 ferry toward Finkenwerder. Afterwards, return to Landungsbrücken, then continue one stop on the #62 ferry to Speicherstadt (Warehouse City) and tour this brick urban-renewal district. From Speicherstadt, return to the train station by crossing the bridge to the Baumwall station on the U-3 subway. It's easy to find a good place for lunch along the way (see recommendations in each section).

City Hall and the Binnenalster

▲**City Hall**—Hamburg's impressive, 647-room Rathaus was completed in 1897. The previous City Hall had burned down in the fire of 1842, and the new building was meant to showcase the wealth and grandeur of turn-of-the-century imperial Germany. Germans at the time were deeply entranced by their history (often viewed through romantic glasses—as at Bavarian King Ludwig's fantasy

castle Neuschwanstein). The City Hall shows off Neo-Renaissance, Neo-Gothic, and other then-popular historicist styles. While the building is called a "City Hall," Hamburg actually forms its own *Land* (state) within the Federal Republic of Germany, and the council that meets in the City Hall chambers calls itself a parliament. (Berlin and Bremen are the other two German cities with this semi-autonomous status.)

Cost and Hours: Free entry; tours-€3, 40 minutes; English tours daily at 11:15, 13:15, and 15:15, also Sat at 17:15; can be cancelled due to special events, more frequent German-language tours; tel. 040/428-312-470, www.hamburgische-buergerschaft.de.

Getting There: The City Hall has its own stop on the U-3 subway line (Rathaus). Enter the building through the archway and go into the lobby, where you'll find a desk selling tickets for tours.

Eating: Across the square from the City Hall, you can grab a quick meal at the **Schlemmer Markt,** which combines a sandwich and deli counter, food court with comfortable tables, and small supermarket under one roof (Mon-Sat 9:00-20:00, closed Sun, Rathausmarkt 7, tel. 040/410-9820).

• *Around the corner from the City Hall (walk to the canal and turn right) you'll find...*

The Binnenalster—This is the inner lake of two small, connected bodies of water that were formed by damming Hamburg's Alster River. Stand at the corner of the lake and look left along the waterside **Jungfernstieg,** the city's most elegant promenade and home to its top-of-the-line shops. Along the shore to the right, you can see the headquarters of Hamburg's most important shipping company, Hapag-Lloyd. Red-and-white Alsterschippern **canal boats** leave from the dock on Jungfernstieg for sleepy 50-minute tours round the lakes (€11, April-Sept leaves every half-hour from 10:00-18:00, less frequently in Oct, no tours Nov-March, tel. 040/357-4240, www.alstertouristik.de). Inside the huge Europa-Passage mall, the Thalia bookstore has armchairs (on floor 1) and, on floor 2, a café with a view of the water (Mon-Sat 10:00-20:00, closed Sun). The Jungfernstieg S-Bahn and U-Bahn stop is right at this corner of the lake.

The Reeperbahn and Nearby

Take New Orleans' Bourbon Street, the Strip in Las Vegas, and Amsterdam's streetwalker zone, mix them up in a cocktail shaker, and out pours the Reeperbahn. This is far and away Germany's most famous entertainment and red light district, yet it's also home to some Broadway-style musical theaters and Beatles-related sights. The quickest visit is a 10-minute walk down the street between the St. Pauli U-Bahn and Reeperbahn S-Bahn stops.

The Firebombing of Hamburg

With its port, munitions factories, and transportation links, Hamburg was a prime target for Allied bombers during World War II. After studying what the Luftwaffe did to Coventry in 1940, the British decided to use the same techniques against Hamburg on July 27, 1943. They hit targets first with explosive bombs to open roofs, break water mains, and tear up streets (making it hard for firefighters to arrive), then followed up with incendiary bombs.

But it had been a hot, dry summer, and when 700 RAF bombers concentrated their attack on a relatively small area, the result was a firestorm never seen before in the annals of war. A tornado of flames raged at up to 150 miles per hour, reaching temperatures of 1,500°F. Many inhabitants were baked to death huddling inside their air raid shelters. Some who went outside were sucked off their feet, disappearing into the super-heated vortex. The roads and sidewalks were on fire—those who tried to run across the roadways got their shoes stuck in boiling asphalt.

In three hours, the inferno killed about 42,000 people and reduced eight square miles of Hamburg to rubble and ashes. At the end of the eight-day bombing campaign, which included US raids, about one million survivors had fled the city. The firebombing of Dresden two years later is more famous, but almost double the number of people died in Hamburg. And while the earlier Nazi bombings of London, Rotterdam, and Coventry were deadly, some historians say the firebombing of Hamburg was World War II's first widespread destruction of a major city.

▲▲The Reeperbahn—As you stroll down the street, you'll see nightclubs, casinos, restaurants, fast-food joints, peep shows, erotic theaters, and sex shops with toys and gadgets of every description on display in the windows. This place is hopping with thousands of partiers in the evenings and until late at night—especially on Fridays and Saturdays. There's lots of action on the side streets, too.

Daylight makes the area feel seedy—the buildings look bleary-eyed and in need of makeup, and the sidewalks need to be swept. Nighttime is when it comes to life. Whatever time of day you go, a visit here is a must, even if you find it a little off-putting. The street is generally safe (as long as you don't go looking for trouble), and a police station is located prominently in the middle of the Reeperbahn.

Perhaps "street" isn't the right word for the Reeperbahn: It's actually a broad avenue with heavy car traffic that runs between the St. Pauli U-Bahn stop and the Reeperbahn S-Bahn stop. The east end of the avenue around the St. Pauli U-Bahn stop is gentrifying quickly, with high-rise buildings, chain hotels, and classier clubs going up. The west end, by the S-Bahn, is more run-down.

"Reeperbahn" literally means "roper's track"—it was once where the ropemakers worked who supplied Hamburg's shipping industry.

Eating: There are plenty of places to eat along the Reeperbahn, mostly fast food. For a little more quality and quiet, turn off onto the side streets to the north. Several pleasant cafés and restaurants cluster around the corner of Detlev-Bremer-Strasse and Seilerstrasse, near the St. Pauli U-Bahn stop; try **Don Benito** (€8-9 pizzas, €5 weekday lunch specials, quiet outdoor seating, tel. 040/3179-0650).

Herbertstrasse—Once the home of Europe's largest legal brothel, there's no organized prostitution anymore along the

Reeperbahn itself—it's been collected along a small parallel street called Herbertstrasse, two blocks to the south. You have to walk around the barriers at each end of Herbertstrasse to stroll down the street, which is lined wall-to-wall with glass-doored cabins where women try to entice prospective male customers. Traditionally, women (the "staff" excepted, of course) are not allowed on Herbertstrasse, although I've seen female tourists walk just around the barriers and gaze at the scene. Don't take photos here.

Beatlemania Museum—To relive the Beatles' Hamburg years in detail, visit the Beatlemania Museum at the corner of Reeperbahn and Grosse Freiheit, near the S-Bahn exit (use the stairway going

away from the city center). There are five floors of bilingual displays, with the top two focused on the Hamburg years and the bottom three on their subsequent career.

For some, the Reeperbahn's greatest significance is as the launching pad for the Beatles, who were unknowns when they arrived in Hamburg from Liverpool to play a season's worth of gigs in 1960. The group consisted of John, Paul, and George, plus drummer Pete Best (later replaced by Ringo Starr) and bassist Stuart Sutcliffe (who gave up music for art school in 1961, but died shortly thereafter).

Unpolished amateurs when they arrived, the band members became tight, hard-driving musicians by playing to a tough crowd night after night—they played 98 days straight at one point. While they were here, Ringo joined the band, and Sutcliffe's German girlfriend even gave them their signature haircuts. By the time they left Hamburg for good in 1962, the Beatles had released several hit singles, had made their first TV appearance back in England, and were just months away from international stardom.

Cost and Hours: €12, daily 10:00-19:00, last entry one hour before closing, Nobistor 10, tel. 040/3117-1818, www.beatlemania -hamburg.com.

Eating: The museum's café (daily 11:00-19:00) serves sandwiches and cakes; you can browse the gift shop or eat at the café without going into the museum, by going up the stairway to the right of the museum entrance.

Nearby: There is a monument to the now-gone Star Club, where the Beatles played a number of gigs, in a courtyard at Grosse Freiheit 37 (by St. Joseph's Catholic church); another one of their frequent venues, the Top Ten Club at Reeperbahn 136, still exists and is now called the Moondoo.

Landungsbrücken

Once Hamburg's passenger ship terminal, this is now the departure point for public ferries and harbor tours.

• *From the Landungsbrücken S-Bahn and U-Bahn stop, walk out toward the water. You'll see the old light-brown stone terminal building (now filled with shops). Beyond it are the piers, connected to shore by nine numbered bridges.*

As you walk down, you'll be assailed by employees of the many tour-boat companies, each pitching their trips—ignore them (most are German-only excursions). For getting out on the water, you have two main options (described later): an English-language tour daily at 12:00 for €15, or a ride on the public ferry boats (free with a public transport pass or Hamburg Card).

• *Look for an old sailing ship docked along the waterfront.*

SS *Rickmer Rickmers*—Moored near bridge 1 on the Landungsbrücken is a three-masted, steel-hulled ship built in Bremerhaven in 1896. The SS *Rickmer Rickmers* has been restored largely by volunteers and is open to the public. You can go aboard and explore the ship's four decks, including the crew quarters, engine room, and changing exhibits.

Cost and Hours: €4, daily 10:00-18:00, last entry 30 minutes before closing, tel. 040/319-5959, www.rickmer-rickmers.de. In front of the ship is a café, a little quieter than the others along the Landungsbrücken, where you can eat lunch while watching the ferries come and go.

▲▲**Boat Rides**—Of the many harbor tour boats, the only one with a live English guide is **Rainer Abicht**—look for the blue-and-white boats. Their waterside ticket windows are by Landungs-brücken bridge 4.

Cost and Hours: One-hour harbor tour in English-€15; March-Nov daily at 12:00, no English tours off-season; tel. 040/317-8220, www.abicht.de.

Hamburg's **public ferries,** which take the same tickets and passes as the S-Bahn and U-Bahn, give you almost as good a harbor tour at a much lower price (€2.80 for single ticket, or use day pass or Hamburg Card). Here's a great one-hour plan: go to bridge 3 and find the signs for ferry line #62 to **Finkenwerder.** It's a 28-minute trip downstream and another 28 minutes back—you can stay on the same boat (runs every 15 minutes from about 7:00-21:00, about every half-hour from 6:00-7:00 and 21:00-23:00). The big ferries, with both indoor and outdoor seating, have a bilingual map and guide printed on all the tables, which lets you follow along with the main sights en route.

Going toward Finkenwerder, the first stop is the old Fish Market (see page 797). The Finkenwerder stop itself is on the island with Airbus's test runway (closed to the public), used to develop the superjumbo A380. Consider breaking your journey at **Neumühlen,** the third stop, below hillside villas in the posh neighborhood of Övelgönne. Here you can see the modest "museum harbor" (Museumshafen) of retired boats (free and always open; German-only info and blueprints on bridge), enjoy Hamburg's beach (downstream from the ferry pier), or eat lunch at the two reasonably priced cafés by the ferry dock (Elbterrassen and Museumshafen Café). Bus #112, which terminates at the Neumühlen pier, runs every 15 minutes and is an alternative way to get from Övelgönne back to Landungsbrücken, St. Pauli, and the train station (it also gives you a look at the suburb of Altona).

For an even quicker trip on the water, take line #62 in the other direction to **Speicherstadt** and the Elbphilharmonie (5-minute trip, leaves every 15 minutes from Landungsbrücken bridge 1, boats run Mon-Fri 7:00-19:00, Sat-Sun 8:00-19:00). If you're coming back from Finkenwerder, just stay on board to reach Speicherstadt.

• *If you want to skip a boat ride, you can also reach Speicherstadt on dry land by taking the U-3 subway one stop from Landungsbrücken to Baumwall. Then walk across the bridge.*

Speicherstadt (Warehouse City)

This huge stand of red-brick riverside warehouses—rated ▲—was built in the 1880s and officially remained part of Hamburg's port zone until 2003. Long since impractical for goods storage (after the arrival of the modern container terminals across the river), the city nevertheless decided to renovate the area and preserve the warehouses as part of the urban landscape. The redevelopment is still a work in progress, and the new buildings are not yet fully occupied, but the project is a great source of pride and interest among locals and German tourists (it's the best-known waterfront revival effort in this mostly landlocked country). Now the old dockland zone just south of Speicherstadt, called HafenCity, is also being developed—from scratch—with interesting modern architecture and a planned fourth subway line.

• *For an atmospheric approach to Speicherstadt, go to the Landungs-brücken S-Bahn and U-Bahn stop and take public ferry #62 one stop upstream (leaves from bridge 1, transport passes valid). You'll disembark by the striking new Elbphilharmonie concert hall. You can also take the U-3 subway line to Baumwall and walk across the Niederbaumbrücke bridge to Speicherstadt. In either case, find the row of warehouses that faces the center city, along the street called Kehrwieder.*

The older, restored warehouses are each labeled with a letter, and in Block D you'll find **Speicherstadt Kaffeerösterei,** a café that serves cakes and desserts (they'll also make sandwiches) and sells coffee by the bag and small gifts (daily 10:00-19:00, tel. 040/3181-6161). As you walk into the café, you'll go through a flood gate (which can be closed in high water—all new building in Hamburg is well above water level due to the danger of tidal bores along the Elbe). On the wall on the right, check out the photographs of Speicherstadt when it was still lined with medieval-looking half-timbered warehouses. After 1881, when Hamburg joined the German customs union, these were torn down and the current, then-state-of-the-art buildings were built.

• *As you leave the café, look straight ahead across the canal into the city center. You'll see a single, short row of surviving half-timbered warehouses that still stand along Deichstrasse.*

Miniatur Wunderland—A few museums and theme-park-like attractions have moved into Speicherstadt's warehouses and cater mostly to German visitors. The most worthwhile is probably the Miniatur Wunderland, also in Block D, which claims to have the world's largest model railway, covering over 12,000 square feet with more than seven miles of track. Visit the Alps, Scandinavia, or the USA in miniature, marvel at the tiny airport (with model planes taking off), and watch night fall every 15 minutes. Wildly popular, there's often an hour's wait to get in, so you are strongly encouraged to reserve on their website at least a day in advance. If you can't reserve, arrive early (before 9:00) or late (after 18:00) for the shortest waits.

Cost and Hours: €12, Mon 9:30-18:00, Tue 9:30-21:00, Wed-Thu 9:30-18:00, Fri 9:30-19:00, Sat 8:00-21:00, Sun 8:30-20:00; but can open as early as 8:00 and close as late as 22:00 depending on demand; tel. 040/300-6800, www.miniatur-wunderland.com.

Nearby: Make sure to cross one of the side bridges in Speicherstadt to experience the long, industrial-feeling loading canals and to imagine this area when it was full of barges and dock-workers. On the Pickhuben bridge, a couple of blocks down from Block D at the corner of Pickhuben and Kannengieserort, a plaque shows photographs of the warehouses after they were bombed in World War II (see "Firebombing of Hamburg," on page 790).

More Sights in Hamburg

St. Michael's Church—Hamburg's best-known church, with its lantern-shaped tower, is worth a look if you have time. The interior is bright and wide; the decoration, unusually ornate for a Protestant church, recalls its Baroque origins (it was opened in 1768). A total rebuild after a 1906 fire (started by workers repairing the roof) lent the church a little of the flavor of an early-20th-century movie palace. Locals call the church "*der Michel.*" The church has fine acoustics (a special channel brings the organ's sound through an ornate, latticed grate in the ceiling) and hosts many concerts. You can climb to the top of its 350-foot-high tower.

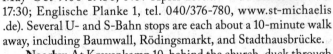

Cost and Hours: Free, tower-€4; daily May-Oct 9:00-19:30, Nov-April 10:00-17:30; Englische Planke 1, tel. 040/376-780, www.st-michaelis.de). Several U- and S-Bahn stops are each about a 10-minute walk away, including Baumwall, Rödingsmarkt, and Stadthausbrücke.

Nearby: At Krayenkamp 10, behind the church, duck through the archway for a glimpse of the **Krameramtswohnungen,** a few half-timbered buildings along a narrow lane that are rare survivors from 17th-century Hamburg. Tour-bus visitors crowd the tacky souvenir shops in the lane.

▲**BallinStadt Emigration Museum**—This museum, a German counterpart to Ellis Island, tells the story of emigration to America through Hamburg from the mid-19th century up through World War II. Especially after 1890, many emigrants from the Austro-Hungarian and Russian empires—today's Eastern Europe—went first to Hamburg, by train or even on foot, before boarding a ship

Hamburg and 9/11

One connection to America that Hamburg doesn't play up is its link to the 9/11 hijackers. Before moving to the US to go to flight school, Mohammed Atta and his co-conspirators lived in Harburg, a southern suburb of Hamburg, and Atta studied urban planning at the technical university there. Since they were fluent in English, well-educated, accustomed to living in the West, and smart enough to learn how to pilot an airplane, the Hamburg students were eagerly recruited by Al-Qaeda. The radical mosque that they attended used rented space at Steindamm 103, by the Lohmühlenstrasse U-Bahn stop in an ethnic neighborhood not far from Hamburg's main train station; the mosque is now closed, and no traces of it are visible.

to cross the ocean. The museum occupies the restored dormitory buildings that were opened in 1901 to house and quarantine emigrants before they were allowed on board. (Just as airlines look at your passport at check-in to make sure you'll be allowed into your destination country, shipping companies were once responsible for emigrants' return passage if they didn't pass a medical check on arrival—so the companies  had an incentive to make sure passengers were in good health.) Emigrants spent days here, or even a few weeks, in 22-40 bed dorm rooms; families could pay extra for a four-bed private room with sink.

The museum complex is named after Albert Ballin, who at the time it was built was director of the Hamburg-America Line (also known as HAPAG and now part of Hapag-Lloyd). Ballin, who was also the father of the modern cruise industry, was the son of Danish Jews who had moved to Hamburg, and he started his career working in his father's small emigration agency. Ballin committed suicide in November 1918, worried (rightly, as it turned out) that HAPAG's ships would be confiscated after Germany's impending defeat in World War I.

Though perhaps overpriced, the museum is engaging. Most exhibits include English text. At the end of the tour is a room where you can freely search a few online genealogy databases that you'd normally have to pay for.

Cost and Hours: €12, daily April-Oct 10:00-18:00, Nov-March until 16:30, last entry one hour before closing, tel. 040/3197-9160; www.ballinstadt.net.

Eating: The museum's reasonably priced restaurant is a good place to try *Labskaus,* a Hamburg specialty similar to corned beef hash; see page 800 (€7-10 main courses, daily 11:30-17:00).

Getting There: BallinStadt is right by the Veddel S-Bahn station, two stops from the train station on the S-3 or S-31 (going toward Harburg). From the S-Bahn platforms, follow the BallinStadt signs for five minutes to the museum, past the bus stop and roundabout.

Fish Market—Not strictly for fish, but rather more of a general food and flea market, it's a fun scene if you can get there before 9:30 on a Sunday morning (or stay up all night on the nearby Reeperbahn). Reach it from the Reeperbahn by foot (about 10 minutes), or from Landungsbrücken by ferry #62 (one stop to Altona/Fischmarkt) or bus #112 (to the Fischmarkt stop; market open Sunday only 5:00-9:30, mid-Nov-mid-March 7:00-9:30).

Hamburg History Museum—This is the place to learn about Hamburg's history and to view a model of the city as it looked in medieval times. The museum is close to the St. Pauli U-Bahn stop and is easy to combine with a visit to the Reeperbahn or St. Michael's Church.

Cost and Hours: €8, Tue-Sat 10:00-17:00, Sun 10:00-18:00, closed Mon, Holstenwall 24, tel. 040/428-132-2380, www .hamburgmuseum.de.

The Aussenalster—Walking and biking paths parallel the shore of Hamburg's larger lake, the Aussenalster, in the St. Georg district. You'll find these lanes between the lake and the street called An der Alster. They're especially pretty on sunny afternoons and evenings. If you're confident of your boating skills, you can rent a rowboat or a sailboat at the small marina.

Day Trips—Visitors disappointed by Hamburg's lack of a cute medieval old town should consider an outing to Lübeck, almost on the Baltic, 45 minutes northeast of Hamburg by train; or to Lüneburg, a small university town that got rich off local salt mines, 30 minutes to the south. Both have classic, well-preserved old centers with typical North German/Hanseatic brick architecture.

Sleeping in Hamburg

Hamburg has plenty of reasonably priced places to stay and only a few of the special events that send prices skyrocketing in Frankfurt or Köln. As the city is a popular musical theater destination for Germans, Friday and Saturday nights are usually more expensive than the rest of the week. Staying somewhere with good public transport links is a must in this not-very-walkable city. I've listed hotels in the St. Georg district, conveniently near the train station and the walking paths around the Aussenalster.

Sleep Code

(€1 = about $1.40, country code: 49, area code: 040)
S = Single, **D** = Double/Twin, **T** = Triple, **Q** = Quad, **b** = bathroom,
s = shower only. Unless otherwise noted, credit cards are
accepted, breakfast is included, and English is spoken.

To help you sort easily through these listings, I've divided
the accommodations into three categories based on the price
for a standard double room with bath:

$$$ Higher Priced—Most rooms €110 or more.
$$ Moderately Priced—Most rooms between €75-110.
$ Lower Priced—Most rooms €75 or less.

Prices can change without notice; verify the hotel's
current rates online or by email. For other updates, see www
.ricksteves.com/update.

Near the Train Station in the St. Georg District

The St. Georg neighborhood has good mid-range hotels, all an easy walk from the train station, coupled with lively street life. Lange Reihe, the main thoroughfare in this area, is trendy and gentrified (reach it via the station's north exit by track 3 onto Kirchenallee). As you walk off Lange Reihe toward the water (the Aussenalster), the buildings become more and more elegant, with an upper-class, diamonds-and-poodles feel. Just a few streets in the other direction is Steindamm, St. Georg's other major avenue (reached from the station's south exit); it's a raucous immigrant boulevard and feels like Queens compared to Lange Reihe's Manhattan.

$$$ Hotel Wedina—hip, informal, and design-conscious—has 59 rooms in four renovated townhouses on a quiet street a seven-minute walk from the station. Each building has a color and a theme (blue for literature, green for architecture, yellow for Mediterranean, and red for traditional). Three of the buildings are connected; the fourth, with reception, breakfast room, and a nice back garden, is across the street (very small Sb-€70, Db-€118, Tb-€155, also has 2-room apartments with kitchen, lots of stairs, free Internet access and Wi-Fi, parking-€15/day; Gurlittstrasse 23, tel. 040/280-8900, fax 040/280-3894, www.hotelwedina.de, info@hotelwedina.de). From the station, walk up Lange Reihe, then go left on Gurlittstrasse.

$$$ Hotel Aussen Alster, in a handsome townhouse with a refined, Upper-East-Side feel to it, has 27 pleasant rooms over a polished lobby and is a little more expensive than the other listings here. The hotel has loaner bikes for guests, as well as a sailboat and rowboat that you can take out on the Aussenalster, just a block away (Sb-€95-130, Db-€130-165, non-smoking, elevator, free Wi-Fi, parking-€14/day, Schmilinskystrasse 11, tel. 040/284-078-570, fax 040/284-078-5777, www.aussenalsterhotel.de, info @aussenalsterhotel.de). It's a 10-minute walk from the station up Lange Reihe, then left on Schmilinskystrasse.

$$ The **Ibis Hotel Hamburg Alster** is entirely lacking in character, but has 165 reliable rooms right by the station. Ask for a front-side, street-facing room—they're quieter than the back-facing ones, which overlook the train tracks (Sb-€78-99, Db-€88-124, rates vary with demand, check website for cheaper special rates, €10/person less without breakfast, non-smoking rooms, air-con, elevator, free Wi-Fi in lobby, sometimes free Wi-Fi in rooms if you reserve online, parking-€10/day; Holzdamm 4-12, tel. 040/248-290, fax 040/2482-9999, www.ibishotel.com, h1395@accor.com). Exit the station at the north end of track 3 to Kirchenallee, then turn left and walk five minutes, with the tracks on your left, onto Holzdamm.

$$ **Motel One Hamburg-Alster,** a monstrous (460-room), inexpensive hotel with cookie-cutter rooms, is part of a new Hamburg-based hotel chain. One stop by U-Bahn from the station or a 10-minute walk down the seedy, intensely ethnic Steindamm, it's an option if cozier places are booked (Sb-€76.50, Db-€99, higher during infrequent special events, prices include breakfast and in-room Wi-Fi—€7.50/person less without, non-smoking, air-con, elevator, free Wi-Fi by reception, parking-€11/day; Steindamm 102, tel. 040/4192-4970, fax 040/419-249-710, www.motel-one.com, hamburg-alster@motel-one.com). The hotel is right at the Lohmühlenstrasse U-Bahn stop.

$$ **Hotel-Pension Alpha,** a budget choice in an older but well-kept building, has 21 rooms almost in sight of the station. Some rooms have a private shower and sink but shared toilet (Ss-€43.50, Sb-€55.50, Ds-€79, Db-€92, Ts-€116.50, 3 percent more if paying with credit card, €6.50/person less without breakfast, pay Wi-Fi, Koppel 4, tel. 040/245-365, fax 040/243-794, www.alpha hotel.biz, info@alphahotel.biz). From the station, exit by track 3 north onto Kirchenallee and look for the red-brick church (St. Georg); the hotel is across the street that runs on the right side of the church.

Near Landungsbrücken

$ **Jugendherberge Hamburg "Auf dem Stintfang"** is a hostel with a super location and commanding view of the Elbe, atop a hill right behind the Landungsbrücken S- and U-Bahn station. It's big (357 beds), modern, and as most rooms have their own bath, competitive with staying in a hotel (bed in mixed 8-bed dorm with shared bath-€20, bed in 4-6 bed gender-segregated dorm with its own bath-€23, Db-€60, Tb-€75, Qb-€100, Quint/b-€125; €4/person extra for those 27 and over, €3 more if you're not a hostel member; includes breakfast and sheets, towels-€1.60, dinner-€7, laundry-€5.20/load, pay Internet access and Wi-Fi, Alfred-Wegener-Weg 5, tel. 040/313-488, fax 040/313-732, www.jugend herberge.de/jh/hamburg-stintfang, jh-stintfang@djh.de). From the train station, take the S-1 or S-3 three stops to Landungsbrücken, then follow the signs up the steep stairway, or take the long way, circling around back, if you have wheeled luggage.

Eating in Hamburg

Hamburg's food traditions have much in common with Scandinavia. Fish is a fixture on local menus, even if little of it is actually caught in the nearby North Sea. Herring is common in sandwiches, as a main dish, and at breakfast (often rolled up with pickled vegetables inside and secured with a toothpick, called *Rollmops*). *Labskaus*, a traditional northern German dish, is not unlike corned beef hash; it's typically served with pickles, red beets, a fried egg, and some-times a herring filet.

The following listings are near my recommended hotels in the St. Georg neighborhood, close to the train station. During the daytime it makes best sense to pick up lunch while sightseeing; see "Sights in Hamburg" for suggestions.

Kajüte sits on pontoons on the Aussenalster (opposite Hotel Bellevue) and is good if you're willing to pay a little more for atmosphere—come in the evening to watch sailboats and the set-ting sun across the water (€13-19 main courses, expensive drinks, reservations smart, indoor and outdoor seating, daily 11:00-22:00, An der Alster 10a, tel. 040/243-037).

Schifferbörse might not have the coolest location (across the street from the train station; exit by track 3), but it cooks up solid northern German food at fair prices, served in a traditional dining room carved with maritime motifs (€13-20 main courses, €7.50 weekday lunch specials, daily 11:30-23:00, Kirchenallee 46 between Bremer Reihe and Ellmenreichstrasse, tel. 040/245-240).

Café Koppel, a bright, inexpensive vegetarian café, occu-pies an art center reachable from St. Georg's main drag—Lange Reihe—by walking through an archway and across a courtyard. Choose between two indoor floors or quiet garden seating; there are a couple of main courses available every day (€6-8, chalked on the board) as well as soups and big salads (daily 10:00-23:00, Lange Reihe 75, tel. 040/249-235).

Of the many Turkish restaurants on and around Steindamm, several are a step up in comfort from your average *Döner Kebab* stand, offering nice main courses with table service and a printed menu (though still surrounded by sex shops). Try **Öz Urfa Kebap Salonu** at Steindamm 43, which has a handy pictorial menu, simple *Döner Kebabs* (€4-4.50), and main courses (€8-14; daily 8:00-4:00 in the morning, tel. 040/2805-5700).

Supermarket: The **Galeria Kaufhof** department store, by the train station, has a supermarket at basement level (Mon-Sat 10:00-20:00, closed Sun; exit the south bridge of the train station by track 14 toward Mönckebergstrasse and look for the entrance to your left). The **Edeka** supermarket inside the train station, on the upper level of the north bridge over the tracks, has longer hours, but is smaller and more expensive (daily 7:00-23:00).

Hamburg Connections

From Hamburg by Train to: Berlin (1-2/hour direct, 1.75-2 hours), **Leipzig** (hourly, 3-3.5 hours, some direct, others transfer in Berlin), **Köln** (hourly, 4 hours), **Frankfurt** (hourly, 4 hours), **Munich** (hourly, 6-6.5 hours), **Copenhagen** (direct trains almost every 2 hours, 5 hours). Train info: tel. 0180-599-6633, www.bahn.com.

GERMAN HISTORY

There was no Germany before 1871, but the cultural heritage of the German-speaking people stretches back 2,000 years.

Romans (A.D. 1-500)

German history begins in A.D. 9, when Roman troops were ambushed and driven back by the German chief Arminius. For the next 250 years, the Rhine and Danube rivers marked the border between civilized Roman Europe (to the southwest) and "barbarian" German lands (to the northeast). While the rest of Western Europe's future would be Roman, Christian, and Latin, Germany would follow its own pagan, *Deutsch*-speaking path.

Rome finally fell to the Germanic chief Theodoric the Great (a.k.a. Dietrich of Bern, A.D. 476). After that, Germanic Franks controlled northern Europe, ruling a mixed population of Romanized Christians and tree-worshipping pagans.

Charlemagne and the Franks (A.D. 500-1000)

For Christmas in A.D. 800, the pope gave Charlemagne the title of Holy Roman Emperor. Charlemagne, the king of the Franks, was the first of many German kings to be called *Kaiser* ("emperor," from "Caesar") over the next thousand years. Allied with the pope, Charlemagne ruled an empire that included Germany, Austria, France, the Low Countries, and northern Italy.

Charlemagne (Karl der Grosse, or Charles the Great, r. 768-814) stood a head taller than his subjects, and his foot became a standard measurement. The stuff of legend, Charles the Great had five wives and four concubines, producing descendants with names like Charles the Bald, Louis the Pious, and Henry the Quarrelsome. After Charlemagne died of pneumonia (814), his united empire did not pass directly to his oldest son but was

Why We Call Deutschland "Germany"

Our English name "Germany" comes from the Latin *Germania,* the Roman name for the lands north of the Alps where "barbarian" tribes lived. The French and Spanish call it *Allemagne* and *Alemania,* respectively, after the Alemanni tribe. Italians call the country *Germania,* but in Italy the German language is known as *tedesco.* Completely confused by all this, the Slavic peoples of Eastern Europe simply throw up their hands and call Germany *Německo* (Czech), *Niemcy* (Polish), or other variations of a word that basically means "people who can't speak right." The Hungarians borrowed this word from the Slavs and call anything German *német.*

To Germans, their country is *Deutschland,* their language is *Deutsch,* and they themselves are *Deutsche.* A few hundred years ago, this word was spelled *Teutsch* (later, the "t" changed to a "d"). The English word Teutonic, the Italian *tedesco,* and the Scandinavian *tysk* all come from this earlier form. *Alles klar?*

divided into (what would become) Germany, France, and the lands in between (Treaty of Verdun, 843).

The Holy Roman Empire (1000-1500)

Chaotic medieval Germany was made up of more than 300 small, quarreling dukedoms ruled by the Holy Roman Emperor. The title was pretty bogus, implying that the German king ruled the same huge European empire as the ancient Romans. In fact, he was "Holy" because he was blessed by the Church, "Roman" to recall ancient grandeur, and the figurehead "Emperor" of only a scattered kingdom.

Germany's emperors had less hands-on power than other kings around Europe. Because of the custom of electing emperors by nobles and archbishops, rather than by bestowing the title through inheritance, they couldn't pass the crown from father to son. In addition, there were no empire-wide taxes and no national capital. This system gave nobles great power: Peasants huddled close to their local noble's castle for protection from attack by the noble next door.

When Emperor Henry IV (r. 1056-1106) tried to assert his power by appointing bishops, he was slapped down by the nobles, and forced to repent to the pope by standing barefoot in the alpine snow for three days at Canossa (in northern Italy, 1077; see the sidebar on page 193).

Emperor Frederick I Barbarossa (1152-1190), blue-eyed and red-bearded (hence *barba rossa*), gained an international reputation

Church Architecture

History comes to life when you visit a centuries-old church. Even if you wouldn't know your apse from a hole in the ground, learning a few simple terms will enrich your experience. Note that not every church has every feature, and a "cathedral" isn't a type of church architecture, but rather a designation for a church that's a governing center for a local bishop.

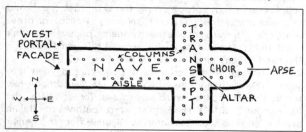

Aisles: The long, generally low-ceilinged arcades that flank the nave.

Altar: The raised area with a ceremonial table (often adorned with candles or a crucifix), where the priest prepares and serves the bread and wine for Communion.

Apse: The space beyond the altar, often bordered with small chapels.

Barrel Vault: A continuous round-arched ceiling that resembles an extended upside-down U.

Choir: A cozy area, often screened off, located within the church nave and near the high altar where services are sung in a more intimate setting.

Cloister: A square-shaped series of hallways surrounding an open-air courtyard, traditionally where monks and nuns got fresh air.

Facade: The outer wall of the church's main (west) entrance, viewable from outside and generally highly decorated.

Groin Vault: An arched ceiling formed where two equal barrel vaults meet at right angles. Less common usage: term for a medieval jock strap.

Narthex: The area (portico or foyer) between the main entry and the nave.

Nave: The long, central section of the church (running west to east, from the entrance to the altar) where the congregation stood through the service.

Transept: The north-south part of the church, which crosses (perpendicularly) the east-west nave. In a traditional Latin cross-shaped floor plan, the transept forms the "arms" of the cross.

West Portal: The main entry to the church (on the west end, opposite the main altar).

as a valiant knight, gentleman, bon vivant, and lover of poetry and women. Still, his great victories were away in Italy and Asia (on the Third Crusade, where he drowned in a river), while back home nobles wielded the real power.

This was the era of Germany's troubadours *(Meistersingers),* who traveled from castle to castle singing love songs *(Minnesang)* and telling the epic tales of chivalrous knights (Tristan and Isolde, Parzival, and the Nibelungen) that would later inspire German nationalism and Wagnerian operas.

While France, England, and Spain were centralizing power around a single ruling family to create modern nation-states, Germany remained a decentralized, backward, feudal battleground.

Medieval Growth

Nevertheless, Germany was strategically located at the center of Europe, and trading towns prospered. Several northern towns (especially Hamburg and Lübeck) banded together into the Hanseatic League, promoting open trade around the Baltic Sea. To curry favor at election time, emperors granted powers and privileges to certain towns, designated "free imperial cities." Some towns, such as Köln, Mainz, Dresden, and Trier, held higher status than many nobles, as hosts of one of the seven Electors of the emperor. To this day, every German town keeps careful track of whether it was "free" during the Middle Ages—or answered to a duke, king, archbishop, or elector in another place.

Textiles, mining, and the colonization of its eastern lands made Germany an economic powerhouse with a thriving middle class. In towns, middle-class folks (burghers), not the local aristocrats, began running things. In about 1450, Johann Gutenberg of Mainz invented moveable type for printing, a creation that would allow the export of a new commodity: ideas.

Religious Struggles and the Thirty Years' War (1500-1700)

Martin Luther—German monk, fiery orator, and religious whistle-blower—sparked a century of European wars by speaking out against the Catholic Church (see page 511).

Luther's protests ("Protestantism") threw Germany into a century of turmoil, as each local prince took sides between Catholics and Protestants. In the 1525 Peasant Revolt, peasants attacked their feudal masters with hoes and pitchforks, fighting for more food, political say-so, and respect. The revolt was brutally put down.

The Holy Roman Emperor, Charles V (r. 1519-1556), sided with the pope. Charles was the most powerful man in Europe, having inherited an empire that included Germany and Austria,

Typical Castle Architecture

Castles were fortified residences for medieval nobles. Castles come in all shapes and sizes, but knowing a few general terms will help you understand them.

Barbican: A fortified gatehouse, sometimes a stand-alone building located outside the main walls.

Crenellation: A gap-toothed pattern of stones atop the parapet.

Drawbridge: A bridge that could be raised or lowered, using counterweights or a chain-and-winch.

Great Hall: The largest room in the castle, serving as throne room, conference center, and dining hall.

Hoardings (or Gallery or Brattice): Wooden huts built onto the upper parts of the stone walls. They served as watch towers, living quarters, and fighting platforms.

The Keep (or Donjon): A high, strong stone tower in the center of the castle complex that was the lord's home and refuge of last resort.

Loopholes: Narrow slits in the walls (also called embrasures, arrow slits, or arrow loops) through which soldiers could shoot arrows at the enemy.

Machicolation: A stone ledge jutting out from the wall, fitted with holes in the bottom. If the enemy was scaling the walls, soldiers could drop rocks or boiling oil through the holes and down onto the enemy below.

Moat: A ditch encircling the wall, often filled with water.

Parapet: Outer railing of the wall walk.

Portcullis: A heavy iron grille that could be lowered across the entrance.

plus the Low Countries, much of Italy, Spain, and Spain's New World possessions. But many local German nobles took the opportunity to go Protestant—some for religious reasons, but also to seize Church assets and powers.

The 1555 Peace of Augsburg allowed each local noble to decide the religion of his realm. In general, the northern lands became Protestant, while the south (today's Bavaria, along with Austria) remained Catholic.

Unresolved religious and political differences eventually expanded into the Thirty Years' War (1618-1648). This Europe-wide war, fought mainly on German soil, involved Denmark, Sweden, France, and Bohemia (in today's Czech Republic), among others. It was one of history's bloodiest wars, fueled by religious extremism and political opportunism, and fought by armies of brutal mercenaries who worked on commission and were paid in loot and pillage.

By the war's end (Treaty of Westphalia, 1648), a third of all Germans had died, France was the rising European power, and

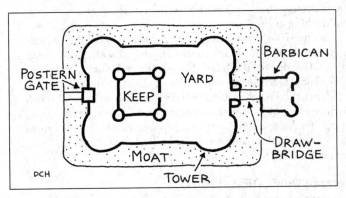

Postern Gate: A small, unfortified side or rear entrance used during peacetime. In wartime, it became a "sally-port" used to launch surprise attacks, or as an escape route.

Towers: Tall structures serving as lookouts, chapels, living quarters, or the dungeon. Towers could be square or round, with either crenellated tops or conical roofs.

Turret: A small lookout tower projecting up from the top of the wall.

Wall Walk (or Allure): A pathway atop the wall where guards could patrol and where soldiers stood to fire at the enemy.

The Yard (or Bailey or Ward): An open courtyard inside the castle walls.

the Holy Roman Empire was a medieval mess of scattered feudal states. In 1689, France's Louis XIV swept down the Rhine, gutting and leveling its once-great castles, and Germany ceased to be a major player in European politics until the modern era.

Austria and Prussia (1700s)

The German-speaking lands now consisted of three "Germanys": Austria in the south, Prussia in the north, and the rest in between.

Prussia—originally colonized by celibate ex-Crusaders called Teutonic Knights—was forged into a unified state by two strong kings. Frederick I (the "King Sergeant," r. 1701-1713) built a modern state around a highly disciplined army, a centralized government, and national pride. His grandson, Frederick II "The Great" (r. 1740-1786), added French culture and worldliness, preparing militaristic Prussia to enter the world stage. A well-read, flute-playing lover of the arts and liberal ideals, Frederick also ruled with an iron fist—the very model of the "enlightened despot."

Meanwhile, Austria thrived under the laid-back rule of the

Habsburg family. The Habsburgs gained power in Europe by marrying it. They acquired the Netherlands, Spain, and Bohemia that way (a strategy that didn't work so well for Marie-Antoinette, who wed the king of France).

In the 1700s, the Germanic lands became a cultural powerhouse, producing musicians (Bach, Haydn, Mozart, Beethoven), writers (Goethe, Schiller), and thinkers (Kant, Leibniz). But politically, feudal Germany was no match for the modern powers.

After the French Revolution (1789), Napoleon swept through Germany with his armies, deposing feudal lords, confiscating church lands, and forcing the emperor to hand over his crown (1806). After a thousand years, the Holy Roman Empire *(Reich)* was dead.

German Unification (1800s)

Napoleon's invasion helped unify the German-speaking peoples by rallying them against a common foreign enemy. After Napoleon's defeat, the Congress of Vienna (1815), presided over by the Austrian Prince Metternich, realigned Europe's borders. The idea of unifying the three Germanic nations—Prussia, Austria, and the German Confederation, a loose collection of small states in between—began to grow. By mid-century, most German-speaking people favored forming a modern nation-state; the only question was whether the confederation would be under Prussian or Austrian dominance.

Economically, Germany was becoming increasingly modern, with a unified trade organization (1834), railroads (1835), mechanical-engineering prowess, and factories booming on a surplus of labor.

Energetic Prussia took the lead in unifying the country. Otto von Bismarck (served 1862-1890), the strong minister of Prussia's weak king, used cunning politics to engineer a unified Germany under Prussian dominance. First, he started a war with Austria, ensuring that any united Germany would be under Prussian control. (The Austrian Empire would remain a separate country.) Next, Bismarck provoked a war with France (Franco-Prussian War, 1870-1871), which united Prussia and the German Confederation against their common enemy, France.

Fueled by hysterical patriotism, German armies swept through France and, in the Hall of Mirrors at Versailles, crowned Prussia's Wilhelm I as Emperor *(Kaiser)* of a new German Empire, uniting Prussia and the German Confederation (but excluding Austria). This Second Reich (1871-1918) featured elements of democracy (an elected *Reichstag*—parliament), offset by a strong military and an emperor with veto powers.

A united and resurgent Germany was suddenly flexing its

Germany in the Early 1800s

muscles in European politics. With strong industry, war spoils, overseas colonies, and a large and disciplined military, it sought its rightful place in the sun. Fueled by nationalist fervor, *Volk* art flourished (Wagner's operas, Nietzsche's essays), reviving medieval German myths and Nordic gods. The rest of Europe saw Germany's rapid rise—and began arming themselves to the teeth.

World War I and Hitler's Rise (1914-1939)

When Archduke Franz Ferdinand, the heir to the Austro-Hungarian Empire, was assassinated in 1914, all of Europe took sides as the political squabble quickly escalated into World War I. Germany and Austria-Hungary attacked British and French troops in France, but were stalled at the Battle of the Marne. Both sides dug defensive trenches, then settled in for four brutal years of bloodshed, boredom, mud, machine-gun fire, disease, and mustard gas.

Finally, at 11:00 in the morning of November 11, 1918, the fighting ceased. Germany surrendered, signing the Treaty of Versailles in the Hall of Mirrors at Versailles. The war cost the defeated German nation 1.7 million men, precious territory,

Germany During World War II
(1939-1945)

1939   Soldiers singing *"Muss ich denn, Muss ich denn zum Städtele hinaus"* ("I must leave, I must leave my happy home") march off to war. On September 1, Germany invades Poland to seize the free city of Danzig (Gdańsk), sparking World War II. Germany, Italy, and Japan (the Axis) would eventually square off against the Allies—which included Britain, France, the United States, and the USSR.

1940   The Nazi Blitzkrieg (lightning war) quickly sweeps through Denmark, Norway, the Low Countries, France, Yugoslavia, and Greece. With fellow fascists ruling Italy (Mussolini), Spain (Franco), and Portugal (Salazar), all of the Continent is now dominated by fascists, creating a "fortress Europe."

1941   Hitler invades his former ally, the USSR. Bombastic victory parades in Berlin celebrate the triumph of the Aryan race over the lesser peoples of the world.

1942   Allied bombs begin falling on German cities. That autumn and winter, German families receive death notices from the horrific Battle of Stalingrad. On the worst days, 50,000 men died (by comparison, America lost 58,000 total in Vietnam). Back home, Nazi officials begin their plan for the "final solution to the Jewish problem"—systematic execution of Europe's Jews in specially built death camps.

GERMAN HISTORY

colonies, their military rights, reparations money, and national pride.

A new democratic government called the Weimar Republic (1919) dutifully abided by the Treaty of Versailles, and tried to maintain order among Germany's many divided political parties. But the country was in ruins, its economy a shambles, and the war's victors demanded heavy reparations. Communists rioted in the streets, fascists plotted coups, and a loaf of bread cost a billion inflated Marks. War vets grumbled in their beer about how their leaders had sold them out. All Germans, regardless of their political affiliations, were fervently united in their apathy toward the new democracy. When the worldwide depression of 1929 hit Germany with brutal force, the nation was desperate for a strong leader with answers.

Adolf Hitler (1889-1945) was a disgruntled vet who had spent the post–World War I years homeless, wandering the streets of Vienna with sketchpad in hand, hoping to become an artist. In Munich, he joined other disaffected Germans to form the

1943 Germany fights a two-front war: against tenacious Soviets on the chilly Eastern Front, and against Brits and Yanks advancing north through Italy on the Western Front. Germany's industrial output tries desperately to keep up with the Allies'. The average German suffers through shortages, rationing, and frequent trips to the bomb shelter.

1944 Hitler's no-surrender policy is increasingly unpopular, and he narrowly survives being assassinated by a bomb planted in an office. After the Allies reach France on D-Day, Germany counterattacks with a last-gasp offensive (the Battle of the Bulge) that slows but does not stop the Allies.

1945 Soviet soldiers approach Berlin from the east, and Americans and Brits advance from the west. Adolf Hitler commits suicide, and families lock up their daughters to protect them from rapacious Soviet soldiers. When Germany finally surrenders on May 8, the country is in ruins, occupied by several foreign powers, divided into occupation zones, and viewed by the world as an immoral monster.

In the war's aftermath, German citizens were faced with the scope of the mass killings and atrocities committed by their leaders. Over 11 million people had been systemically murdered—6 million Jews as well as hundreds of thousands of disabled people, homosexuals, prisoners of war, political dissidents, and ethnic minorities.

National Socialist (Nazi) party. In stirring speeches, Hitler promised to restore Germany to its rightful glory, blaming the country's current problems on communists, foreigners, and Jews. After an unsuccessful coup attempt (the Beer Hall Putsch in Munich, 1923), Hitler was sent to jail, where he wrote an influential book of his political ideas, called *Mein Kampf (My Struggle)*.

By 1930, the Nazis—now wearing power suits and working within the system—had become a formidable political party in Germany's democracy. They won 38 percent of the seats in the Reichstag in 1932, and Hitler was appointed chancellor (1933). Two months later, the Reichstag building was mysteriously set on fire—an apparent act of terrorism with a September 11-sized impact—and a terrified Germany gave Chancellor Hitler sweeping powers to preserve national security.

Hitler wasted no time in using this Enabling Act to jail opponents, terrorize the citizenry, and organize every aspect of German life under the watchful eye of the Nazi party. Plumbers' unions, choral societies, schoolteachers, church pastors, filmmakers, and

Nazi Terminology

Many Nazi military terms are understood in English. "Nazi" is an abbreviation for *Nationalsozialismus* (National Socialism), Hitler's political party. Other terms you'll probably recognize are SS (short for *Schutzstaffel*, or "protective unit"), *Luftwaffe* (air force), and *Blitzkrieg* ("lightning war"). Nazis also devised the *Endlösung*, or "final solution" for doing away with Jewish people, by interning and killing them in *Konzentrationslager* (KZ, concentration camp). The *Widerstand* (resistance) stood up against the Nazis. Today, *Vergangenheitsbewaltigung* (coming to terms with the past) is a major issue in Germany. Many concentration camps and other wartime symbols have been turned into *Gedenkstätte* (memorials). You'll also see *Dokumentationzentrum* (documentation centers), where locals and visitors can learn about Nazi atrocities. The message of these sites is *Vergesst es nie*—"Never forget."

artists all had to account to a Nazi Party official about how their work furthered the Third Reich.

For the next decade, an all-powerful Hitler proceeded to revive Germany's economy, building the autobahns and rebuilding the military. Defying the Treaty of Versailles and world opinion, Hitler occupied the Saar region (1935) and the Rhineland (1936), annexed Austria and the Sudetenland (1938), and invaded Czechoslovakia (March 1939). The rest of Europe finally reached its appeasement limit, and World War II began (see timeline in sidebar on previous page).

Two Germanys (1945-1990)

After World War II, the Allies divided occupied Germany into two halves, split down the middle by an 855-mile border that Winston Churchill called an "Iron Curtain." By 1949, Germany was officially two separate countries. West Germany (the Federal Republic of Germany) was democratic and capitalist, allied with the powerful United States. East Germany (the German Democratic Republic, or DDR) was a socialist state under Soviet control. The former capital, Berlin, sitting in East German territory, was itself split into two parts, allowing a tiny pocket of Western life in the Soviet-controlled East. Armed guards prevented Germans from crossing the border to see their cousins on the other side.

In 1948, Soviet troops blockaded West Berlin. The Allies responded by airlifting food and supplies into the stranded city for nearly a year, forcing the Soviets to back off. In 1961, the East Germans erected a 12-foot-high concrete wall through the heart of Berlin. The Berlin Wall—built at the height of the Cold War

Benedict XVI, the German Pope

When Josef Ratzinger became the 265th pope in 2005, he introduced himself as "a simple, humble worker in the vineyard of the Lord." But the man has a complex history, a reputation for intellectual brilliance, a flair for the piano, a penchant for controversy for his unbending devotion to traditional Catholic doctrine...and a Bavarian accent.

Born in 1927 in the small Bavarian town of Marktl am Inn (southeast of Munich), young Josef went to school in nearby Traunstein, studying in the seminary. When Hitler took power, he lived life under Nazi rule as many Germans did—outwardly obeying leaders while inwardly conflicted. Like many Germans, he joined the Hitler Youth, was drafted into the Army, sprayed flak from anti-aircraft guns (guarding a BMW plant), and saw Jews transported to death camps. Near the war's end, he deserted, and subsequently spent a brief time in an American POW camp near Ulm.

After the war, Ratzinger became a priest and a professor of theology, first at Munster, then at the University of Tübingen. Originally a voice of liberal Catholicism, he became increasingly convinced that Church tradition was needed to offset the growing chaos of the world.

In 1977, he was made Archbishop of Munich. Ratzinger became Pope John Paul II's closest advisor and good friend. Every Friday afternoon for two decades, they met for lunch, intellectual sparring, and friendly conversation.

Under John Paul II, Ratzinger served as the Church's "enforcer" of doctrine, earning the nickname "God's Rottweiler." He spoke out against ordaining women, chastised Latin American priests for fomenting class warfare, reassigned bishops who were soft on homosexuality, reaffirmed opposition to birth control, and wrote thoughtful papers challenging the secular world's moral relativism.

The name of "Benedict" recalls both Pope Benedict XV (who healed World War I's divisions) and Europe's patron St. Benedict (c. 480-543), who symbolizes Europe's Christian roots.

between the United States and the USSR—was designed to prevent the westward flow of East German citizens (although officials claimed it was built to keep the West Germans out). The Berlin Wall came to symbolize divided Germany.

In West Germany, Chancellor Konrad Adenauer (who had suffered imprisonment under the Nazis) tried to restore Germany's good name, paying war reparations and joining international organizations of nations. Thanks to US aid from the Marshall Plan, West Germany was rebuilt, democracy was established, and its "economic miracle" quickly exceeded pre-WWII levels. Adenauer was succeeded in 1969 by the US-friendly Willy Brandt.

East Germany was ruled with an iron fist by Walter Ulbricht (who had been exiled by the Nazis). In 1953, demonstrations and protests against the government were brutally put down by Soviet—not German—troops. Erich Honecker (having endured a decade of Nazi imprisonment) succeeded Ulbricht as ruler of the East in 1971. Honecker was a kinder, gentler tyrant.

Throughout the 1970s and 1980s, both the US and the Soviet Union used divided Germany as a military base. West Germans debated whether US missiles aimed at the Soviets should be placed in their country. Economically, West Germany just got stronger while East Germany stagnated.

On November 9, 1989, East Germany unexpectedly opened the Berlin Wall (see sidebar on page 706). Astonished Germans from both sides climbed the Wall, hugged each other, shared bottles of beer, sang songs, and chiseled off souvenirs. At first, most Germans—West and East—simply looked forward to free travel and better relations between two distinct nations. But before the month was out, negotiations and elections to reunite the two Germanys had begun. October 3, 1990, was proclaimed German Unification Day, and Berlin re-assumed its status as the German capital in 1991.

Germany Today (1990-present)

Differences between "Ossies" (rude slang for former East Germans) and "Wessies" remain, but they're diminishing as the two economies seek equilibrium. Germany remains a major economic and political force in Europe. The country spent a decade under a center-right government led by Chancellor Helmut Kohl, followed by a decade under the center-left Chancellor Gerhard Schröder. Elections in 2005 resulted in no clear victory, and both major parties formed a "Grand Coalition," sharing power equally under Germany's first female chancellor, Angela Merkel. After strengthening her position in the country's 2009 elections, Chancellor Merkel formed a center-right coalition (pro-big business) with the conservative Liberal Democrats. Merkel topped Forbes' magazine's list of the world's most powerful women four years in a row (2006-2009).

Germany is fully integrated into the international community as a member of the European Union—an organization whose original chief aim was to avoid future wars by embracing Germany in the economic web of Europe. While many other European countries have been devastated by the economic crisis beginning in 2008, Germany—with the largest economy in the EU—has emerged relatively unscathed (though many Germans resent being compelled to bail out less fiscally responsible nations in the EU).

APPENDIX

Contents

Tourist Information

Germany's national tourist office **in the US** is a wealth of information. Before your trip, scan their website (www.cometogermany .com) for maps, Rhine boat schedules, and information on festivals, castles, hiking, biking, genealogy, cities, and regions. Most materials can be downloaded from their website; if you want tourist materials sent to you, a small donation is requested (tel. 212-661-7200).

In Germany, your best first stop in every town is generally the tourist information office—abbreviated **TI** in this book. Throughout Germany, you'll find TIs are usually well-organized and have English-speaking staff. TIs are good places to get a city map and information on public transit (including bus and train schedules), walking tours, special events, and nightlife. Many TIs have information on the entire country or at least the region, so try to pick up maps for destinations you'll be visiting later in your trip. If you're arriving in town after the TI closes, call ahead or pick up a map in a neighboring town.

As national budgets tighten, many TIs have been privatized. This means they have become sales agents for big tours and hotels, and their "information" is unavoidably colored.

While TIs are eager to book you a room, you should use their room-finding service only as a last resort. They are unable to give hard opinions on the relative value of one place over another. The accommodations stakes are too high to go potluck through the TI. Even if there's no "fee," you'll save yourself and your host money by going direct with the listings in this book.

Communicating

Hurdling the Language Barrier

German—like English, Dutch, Swedish, and Norwegian—is a Germanic language, making it easier on most American ears than Romance languages (such as Italian and French). These tips will help you pronounce German words: The letter *w* is always pronounced as "v" (e.g., the word for "wonderful" is *wunderbar*, pronounced VOON-der-bar). The vowel combinations *ie* and *ei* are pronounced like the name of the second letter—so *ie* sounds like a long *e* (as in *hier* and *Bier*, the German words for "here" and "beer"), while *ei* sounds like a long *i* (as in *nein* and *Stein*, the German words for "no" and "stone"). The vowel combination *au* is pronounced "ow" (as in *Frau*). The vowel combinations *eu* and *äu* are pronounced "oy" (as in *neu*, *Deutsch*, and *Bräu*, the words for "new," "German," and "brew"). To pronounce *ö* and *ü*, purse your lips when you say the vowel; the other vowel with an umlaut, *ä*, is pronounced the same as *e* in "men." (In written German, these can be depicted as the vowel followed by an *e*—*oe*, *ue*, and *ae*, respectively.) The letter Eszett (ß) represents *ss*. Written German capitalizes all nouns.

Though most young or well-educated Germans—especially those in the tourist trade and in big cities—speak at least some English, you'll get more smiles if you learn and use the German pleasantries. Study the German Survival Phrases on page 853. Give it your best shot. The locals will appreciate your efforts.

Telephones

Smart travelers use the telephone to book or reconfirm rooms, get tourist information, reserve restaurants, confirm tour times, or phone home. Generally, the cheapest way to call home is to use an international phone card purchased in Germany. This section covers dialing instructions, phone cards, and types of phones (for more in-depth information, see www.ricksteves.com/phoning).

How to Dial

Calling from the US to Germany, or vice versa, is simple—once you break the code. The European calling chart in this chapter will walk you through it.

Dialing Domestically Within Germany

Germany, like much of the US, uses an area-code dialing system. To make domestic calls, if you're calling within the same area code, you just dial the local number to be connected; but if you're calling outside your area code, you have to dial both the area code (which starts with a 0) and the local number.

Area codes are listed throughout this book, or you can get them from directory assistance (tel. 11833). For example, Munich's area code is 089 and the number of one of my recommended Munich hotels is 545-9940. To call the hotel within Munich, you'd dial 545-9940. To call it from Frankfurt, you'd dial 089/545-9940.

Local phone numbers in Germany can have different numbers of digits within the same city or even the same hotel (for example, a hotel can have a 6-digit phone number and an 8-digit fax number). One reason is that the German phone system allows direct dial to extension numbers, which are simply tacked onto the main number.

Be aware that some numbers, typically those that start with 018 (including some train and airline information numbers), are premium toll calls, costing more than a regular land-line call. The per-minute charge should be listed in small print next to the phone number. Mobile phone numbers start with 015, 016, or 017, and cost much more to call than land lines.

Dialing Internationally to or from Germany

If you want to make an international call, follow these steps:

• Dial the international access code (00 if you're calling from Europe, 011 from the US or Canada).

• Dial the country code of the country you're calling (49 for Germany, or 1 for the US or Canada).

• Dial the area code (without its initial 0) and the local number. (The European calling chart lists specifics per country.)

Calling from the US to Germany: To call the Munich hotel from the US, dial 011 (the US's international access code), 49 (Germany's country code), 89 (Munich's area code without the initial 0), then 555-9940 (the hotel's number).

Calling from any European country to the US: To call my office in Edmonds, Washington, from anywhere in Europe, I dial 00 (Europe's international access code), 1 (US country code), 425 (Edmonds' area code), and 771-8303.

European Calling Chart

Just smile and dial, using this key:
AC = Area Code, LN = Local Number.

European Country	Calling long distance within ...	Calling from the US or Canada to ...	Calling from a European country to ...
Austria	AC + LN	011 + 43 + AC (without the initial zero) + LN	00 + 43 + AC (without the initial zero) + LN
Belgium	LN	011 + 32 + LN (without initial zero)	00 + 32 + LN (without initial zero)
Bosnia-Herzegovina	AC + LN	011 + 387 + AC (without initial zero) + LN	00 + 387 + AC (without initial zero) + LN
Britain	AC + LN	011 + 44 + AC (without initial zero) + LN	00 + 44 + AC (without initial zero) + LN
Croatia	AC + LN	011 + 385 + AC (without initial zero) + LN	00 + 385 + AC (without initial zero) + LN
Czech Republic	LN	011 + 420 + LN	00 + 420 + LN
Denmark	LN	011 + 45 + LN	00 + 45 + LN
Estonia	LN	011 + 372 + LN	00 + 372 + LN
Finland	AC + LN	011 + 358 + AC (without initial zero) + LN	999 (or other 900 number) + 358 + AC (without initial zero) + LN
France	LN	011 + 33 + LN (without initial zero)	00 + 33 + LN (without initial zero)
Germany	AC + LN	011 + 49 + AC (without initial zero) + LN	00 + 49 + AC (without initial zero) + LN
Gibraltar	LN	011 + 350 + LN	00 + 350 + LN
Greece	LN	011 + 30 + LN	00 + 30 + LN
Hungary	06 + AC + LN	011 + 36 + AC + LN	00 + 36 + AC + LN
Ireland	AC + LN	011 + 353 + AC (without initial zero) + LN	00 + 353 + AC (without initial zero) + LN

European Country	Calling long distance within ...	Calling from the US or Canada to ...	Calling from a European country to ...
Italy	LN	011 + 39 + LN	00 + 39 + LN
Montenegro	AC + LN	011 + 382 + AC (without initial zero) + LN	00 + 382 + AC (without initial zero) + LN
Morocco	LN	011 + 212 + LN (without initial zero)	00 + 212 + LN (without initial zero)
Netherlands	AC + LN	011 + 31 + AC (without initial zero) + LN	00 + 31 + AC (without initial zero) + LN
Norway	LN	011 + 47 + LN	00 + 47 + LN
Poland	LN	011 + 48 + LN (without initial zero)	00 + 48 + LN (without initial zero)
Portugal	LN	011 + 351 + LN	00 + 351 + LN
Slovakia	AC + LN	011 + 421 + AC (without initial zero) + LN	00 + 421 + AC (without initial zero) + LN
Slovenia	AC + LN	011 + 386 + AC (without initial zero) + LN	00 + 386 + AC (without initial zero) + LN
Spain	LN	011 + 34 + LN	00 + 34 + LN
Sweden	AC + LN	011 + 46 + AC (without initial zero) + LN	00 + 46 + AC (without initial zero) + LN
Switzerland	LN	011 + 41 + LN (without initial zero)	00 + 41 + LN (without initial zero)
Turkey	AC (if there's no initial zero, add one) + LN	011 + 90 + AC (without initial zero) + LN	00 + 90 + AC (without initial zero) + LN

- The instructions above apply whether you're calling a land line or mobile phone.
- The international access codes (the first numbers you dial when making an international call) are 011 if you're calling from the US or Canada, or 00 if you're calling from virtually anywhere in Europe (except Finland, where it's 999 or another 900 number, depending on the phone service you're using).
- To call the US or Canada from Europe, dial 00, then 1 (the country code for the US and Canada), then the area code and number. In short, 00 + 1 + AC + LN = Hi, Mom!

Note: You might see a + in front of a European number. When dialing the number, replace the + with the international access code of the country you're calling from (00 from Europe, 011 from the US or Canada).

Prepaid Phone Cards

Insertable Phone Cards: This type of card can be used only at pay phones in Germany. It's handy and affordable for local and domestic calls, but more expensive than international phone cards (covered next) for international calls. They're sold in denominations starting at about €5 at TIs, tobacco shops, post offices, and train stations. To use the card, physically insert it into a slot in the pay phone. While you can use these cards to call anywhere in the world, it's only a good deal for making quick local calls from a phone booth. Note that insertable phone cards purchased in Germany don't work outside of the country.

International Phone Cards: These are the cheapest way to make international calls from Europe—with the best cards, it costs literally pennies a minute. They can also be used to make local calls.

You can use international phone cards from any type of phone, including the one in your hotel room (but ask at the front desk if there are any fees for toll-free calls). However, avoid using international phone cards at pay phones. Because the German phone company slaps on hefty surcharges, you'll get far fewer minutes for your money (for example, 10 minutes instead of 100 on a €5 card) than if you call from your hotel room or a mobile phone.

The cards are sold at small newsstand kiosks and hole-in-the-wall long-distance shops. Ask the clerk which of the various brands has the best rates for calls to America. Because cards are occasionally duds, avoid the higher denominations. Some shops also sell cardless codes, printed right on the receipt (since you don't need the actual card or receipt to use the account, you can write down the access number and code and share it with friends). Certain international phone cards work in multiple countries—if traveling to both Germany and Austria, try to buy a card that will work in both places.

To use the card, dial a toll-free access number, then enter your scratch-to-reveal PIN code. When using an international calling card, you must dial the area code even if you're calling across the street.

US Calling Cards: These cards, such as the ones offered by AT&T, Verizon, or Sprint, are the worst option. You'll nearly always save a lot of money by using an international phone card you've purchased in Germany.

APPENDIX

Types of Phones
Public Pay Phones
To make calls from public phones, you'll need a prepaid phone card (explained earlier). Coin-op phones are virtually extinct.

Hotel-Room Phones
Calling from your hotel room can be cheap for local calls (ask for the rates at the front desk first), but is often a rip-off for long-distance calls, unless you use an international phone card (explained on the previous page). Some hotels charge a fee for dialing supposedly "toll-free" numbers, such as the one for your international phone card—ask before you dial. Incoming calls are free, making this a cheap way for friends and family to stay in touch (provided they have a good long-distance plan for calls to Europe—and a list of your hotels' phone numbers). Even small hotels in Germany tend to have a direct-dial system, so callers can reach you in your room without going through reception. Ask the staff for your room's specific telephone number.

Mobile Phones
Many travelers enjoy the convenience of traveling with a mobile phone.

Using Your Mobile Phone: Your US mobile phone works in Europe if it's GSM-enabled, tri-band or quad-band, and on a calling plan that includes international calls. Phones from AT&T and T-Mobile, which use the same GSM technology that Europe does, are more likely to work overseas than Verizon or Sprint phones (if you're not sure, ask your service provider). Most US providers charge $1.29-1.99 per minute while roaming internationally to make or receive calls, and 20-50 cents to send or receive text messages.

You'll pay cheaper rates if your phone is electronically "unlocked" (ask your provider about this); then in Europe, you can simply buy a tiny **SIM card,** which gives you a European phone number. SIM cards are sold at mobile-phone stores and some newsstand kiosks for $5-15, and generally include several minutes worth of prepaid domestic calling time. When you buy a SIM card, you may need to show ID, such as your passport. Insert the SIM card in your phone (usually in a slot on the side or behind the battery), and it'll work like a European mobile phone. When buying a SIM card, always ask about fees for domestic and international calls, roaming charges, and how to check your credit balance and buy more time. When you're in the SIM card's home country, domestic calls are reasonable, and incoming calls are free. You'll pay more if you're roaming in another country.

Buying a European Mobile Phone: Mobile-phone shops all over Europe sell basic phones. The mobile-phone desk in a big department store is another good place to check. Phones that are "locked" to work with a single provider start at around $40; "unlocked" phones (which allow you to switch out SIM cards to use your choice of provider) start at around $60. You'll also need to buy a SIM card and prepaid credit for making calls.

Renting a European Mobile Phone: Car-rental companies and mobile-phone companies offer the option to rent a mobile phone with a European number. While this seems convenient, hidden fees (such as high per-minute charges or expensive shipping costs) can really add up—which usually makes it a bad value. One exception is Verizon's Global Travel Program, available only to Verizon customers.

Data Downloading on a Smartphone: Many smartphones, such as the iPhone, Android, and BlackBerry, work in Europe (note that you can use the AT&T iPhone in Europe, but not the Verizon model). For voice calls and text messaging, smartphones work the same as other US mobile phones (explained earlier). But beware of sky-high fees for data downloading (checking email, browsing the Internet, streaming videos, and so on).

The best solution: Disable data roaming entirely, and only use your device when you find free Wi-Fi. You can ask your mobile-phone service provider to cut off your account's data-roaming capability, or you can manually turn it off on your phone (look under the "Network" menu).

If you want Internet access without being limited to Wi-Fi, you'll need to keep data roaming on—but you can take steps to reduce your charges. Consider paying extra for a limited international data-roaming plan through your carrier, then use data roaming selectively (if a particular task gobbles bandwidth, wait until you're on Wi-Fi). In general, ask your provider in advance how to avoid unwittingly roaming your way to a huge bill. If your smartphone is on Wi-Fi, you can use certain apps to make cheap or free voice calls (see "Calling over the Internet," next).

Calling over the Internet

Some things that seem too good to be true...actually are true. If you're traveling with a wireless device (such as a laptop or smartphone), you can use VoIP (Voice over Internet Protocol) to make free calls over the Internet to another wireless device (or you can pay a few cents per minute to call from your computer to a telephone). If both devices have cameras, you can even see each other while you chat. The major providers are Skype (www.skype.com, also available as a smartphone app), Google Talk (www.google.com/talk), and FaceTime (this app comes standard on newer

Apple devices). If you have a smartphone, you can get online at a hotspot and use these apps to make calls without ringing up expensive roaming charges (though call quality can be spotty on slow connections).

Useful Phone Numbers

Emergencies
Police and Ambulance: tel. 112

Embassies
US Embassy in Berlin: Pariser Platz 2, tel. 030/83050; consular services at Clayallee 170, Mon-Fri 8:30-12:00, closed Sat-Sun and last Thu of month, tel. 030/8305-1200—calls answered Mon-Fri 14:00-16:00 only, www.usembassy.de, acsberlin@state.gov
Canadian Embassy in Berlin: Leipziger Platz 17, tel. 030/203-120, www.germany.gc.ca

Travel Advisories
US Department of State: US tel. 202/647-5225, www.travel.state .gov
Canadian Department of Foreign Affairs: Canadian tel. 800-267-6788, www.dfait-maeci.gc.ca
US Centers for Disease Control and Prevention: US tel. 800-CDC-INFO (800-232-4636), www.cdc.gov/travel

Directory Assistance
Directory Assistance: tel. 11833
International Directory Assistance: tel. 11834

Information
Train Info: tel. 0180-599-6633 (€0.14/minute); ask for an English speaker.
German Tourist Offices: Dial the local area code, then 19433.

Internet Access

It's useful to get online periodically as you travel—to confirm trip plans, check train or bus schedules, get weather forecasts, catch up on email, blog or post photos from your trip, or call folks back home (explained earlier, in "Calling over the Internet").

Some hotels offer a computer in the lobby with Internet access for guests. If you ask politely, smaller places may sometimes let you sit at their desk for a few minutes just to check your email. If your hotel doesn't have access, ask your hotelier to direct you to the nearest place to get online. Most of the towns where I've listed accommodations in this book also have Internet cafés. Many libraries offer free access, but they also tend to have limited opening hours and restrict your online time to 30 minutes, and may require reservations.

Traveling with a Laptop or Other Wireless Device: You can get online if your hotel has Wi-Fi or a port in your room for plugging in a cable. Some hotels offer Wi-Fi for free; others charge by the minute or hour. A cellular modem—which lets your laptop access the Internet over a mobile phone network—provides more extensive coverage, but is much more expensive than Wi-Fi.

Warning: Anytime you access the Internet—especially over a public connection (such as a Wi-Fi signal or at an Internet café)—you're running the risk that someone could be looking over your shoulder, literally or virtually. Be careful about storing personal information (such as passport and credit-card numbers) online. If you're not convinced it's secure, avoid accessing any sites (such as online banking) that could be sensitive to fraud.

Mail

While you can arrange for mail delivery to your hotel (allow 10 days for a letter to arrive), phoning and emailing are so easy that I've dispensed with mail stops altogether.

Get stamps at the neighborhood post office, newsstands within fancy hotels, and some mini-marts and card shops. Avoid standing in line at the post office by using the handy yellow stamp *(Briefmarke)* machines found just outside the building. Warning: These machines give change only in stamps, not in coins. A postcard stamp to the US or Canada costs €1.

You can mail one package per day to yourself worth up to $200 duty-free from Europe to the US (mark it "personal purchases"). If you're sending a gift to someone, mark it "unsolicited gift." For details, visit www.cbp.gov and search for "Know Before You Go."

Transportation

By Car or Public Transportation?

Cars are best for three or more traveling together (especially families with small kids), those packing heavy, and those scouring the countryside. Trains and buses are best for solo travelers, blitz tourists, and city-to-city travelers. While a car gives you the ultimate in mobility and freedom, enables you to search for hotels more easily, and carries your bags for you, the train zips you effortlessly from city to city, usually dropping you in the center and near the tourist office. A car is a worthless headache in cities such as Munich, Berlin, and Frankfurt.

I've included a sample itinerary for drivers (with tips and tweaks for those using public transportation) to help you explore Germany smoothly; you'll find it on page 10.

Trains

German trains are speedy, comfortable, and non-smoking. Though they're fairly punctual, frequent five-minute delays make very tight connections a gamble. They cover cities and small towns well, but a few out-of-the-way recommendations (such as Bavaria's Wieskirche) are only reachable by bus. If you have a railpass, you can hop on any train without much forethought (though for a small fee, you can reserve a seat on a fast train). Without a railpass, you can save a lot of money by understanding the difference between fast trains and cheaper "regional" trains. The German Railway is known as DeutscheBahn (DB).

Types of Trains

There are big differences in price, speed, and comfort between Germany's three levels of trains. ICE trains (white with red trim and streamlined noses) are the fastest, zipping from city to city in air-conditioned comfort, and costing proportionately more. Red regional trains (mostly labeled RB, RE, and IRE on schedules) are the slowest—the milk-run RB trains stop at every small station—but cost much less. Mid-level IC and EC trains are white with red trim but look older than the ICEs. If you have a railpass, take the fastest train available—railpass-holders don't pay a supplement for the fast ICE trains (with one exception, the "ICE Sprinter"). If you're buying point-to-point tickets, taking a slower train can save a lot of money.

Schedules

Schedules change by season, weekday, and weekend. Verify train times listed in this book at http://bahn.hafas.de/bin/query.exe/en. This website also includes bus and subways in cities.

At staffed train stations, attendants will print out a step-by-step itinerary for you, free of charge. You can also produce an itinerary yourself by using the computerized trackside machines marked *Fahrkarten* (usually silver, red, and blue). The touch-screen display gives you an English option; choose "Timetable Information," indicate your point of departure and destination, and then hit "Print" for a personalized schedule, including transfers and track numbers.

If you're changing trains en route and have a tight connection, note the numbers of the platforms (*Bahnsteig* or *Gleis*) where you will arrive and depart (listed on printed and online itineraries). This will save you precious time hunting for your connecting train.

If all else fails, call Germany's train information number from anywhere in the country: tel. 0180-599-6633 (€0.14/minute). Ask for an English speaker.

German Public Transportation

50 Kilometers
50 Miles

North Sea

To Copenhagen

Westerland • Tønder • Tinglev
Niebüll
Flensburg
Husum • Schleswig
Heide • Kiel
Rendsburg
Neumünster
Cuxhaven

Norden
Wilhelmshaven • Bremerhaven
Emden
Hamburg
Groningen • Leer
Weener • Oldenburg • Bremen
Lüneburg
Uelzen

NETHERLANDS

Den Helder

Haarlem
Amsterdam
Schiphol
Hengelo • Bad Bentheim
Celle • Wolfsburg
The Hague
Rheine • Osnabrück
Rotterdam • Utrecht
Hannover
Arnhem
Braunschweig
Emmerich
Münster
Antwerp
Duisburg • Essen
G E R M A
Brussels
Venlo • Hagen • Dortmund
Brussels
Mönchen-gladbach
Wuppertal
Göttingen
To Brussels
Düsseldorf
Kassel
Maastricht
Köln
Namur • Liege
Aachen
Siegen
Bonn • Siegburg
Marburg • Bebra
BELGIUM
Eisenach
Koblenz
Giessen
Fulda
Mosel-kern
St. Goar
LUX
Cochem • *Hahn*
Meiningen
Mainz
Frankfurt
Luxembourg
Beilstein
Trier • Bacharach
Worms
Darmstadt
Mannheim
Würzburg
Metz
Heidelberg
Steinach
To Paris
Saarbrücken
Rothenburg
Nürnberg
Forbach
ob der Tauber
Ansbach
Nancy
Baden-Baden Oos
Crailsheim
Dinkels-bühl
Karlsruhe
Ellwangen
Baden-Baden
Treucht-lingen
Strasbourg • Kehl
Nördlingen
FRANCE
Offenburg
Ingolstadt
Stuttgart
Colmar
Triberg
Dachau
Ulm
Titisee
Augsburg • Munich
Mulhouse
Bad Kroz
Freiburg • Singen
Buchloe
Ober-ammergau
Belfort
Staufen
Fried.
Kempten
Basel
Konstanz • Lindau
Füssen
SWITZERLAND
Zürich
Bregenz
Reutte
Murn. Garmisch
Feld-kirch
Bern
Mitten-wald
To Lausanne
To Luzern
To Lugano
LIECH.
Innsbruck
To Italy
To Interlaken

APPENDIX

Railpasses

The German Pass is a great value for rail travel within Germany if you're making several train journeys, or even just a Frankfurt-Munich round-trip. Railpasses are a better deal if you're under 26 (you qualify for a youth pass) or traveling with a companion (you save with the Twin pass). For shorter hops, a railpass probably isn't worth it if you learn how to get discounts on point-to-point tickets (explained later).

If you're traveling in a neighboring country, two-country Eurailpasses allow you to pair Germany with Austria, Switzerland, France, the BeNeLux region, Denmark, Poland, or the Czech Republic. The Eurail Selectpass gives you more travel in three, four, or five adjacent countries (but some Eastern European countries—like Poland—are not eligible). If you're planning a whirlwind tour of Europe, another possibility is the 23-country Eurail Global Pass. These passes are available in a Saverpass version, which gives a 15 percent discount on railpasses for two or more companions traveling together. For specifics, check the railpass chart on page 830 and visit www.ricksteves.com/rail.

Railpass travelers should know what extras are covered by their pass: for example, travel on any German buses marked "DeutscheBahn" or "DB" (run by the train company) and travel on city S-Bahn systems (except in Berlin, where only S-Bahn lines between major train stations are covered). Railpasses also cover or discount boats on the Rhine, Mosel, and Danube rivers, and give you a 20 percent dis-

count on the Romantic Road bus. Flexipass-holders should note that fully covered ("free") trips start the use of a flexi-day, while discounted trips do not. In other words, the flexipass day can also cover your train travel on that day (but if you're not planning to travel more that day, it makes sense to pay for, say, a short boat ride rather than start the use of a day of your pass).

Because it's so close to the border, traveling to or from Salzburg, Austria, on the main line from Munich counts as traveling within Germany, as far as your railpass is concerned (Salzburg is the official border station on that line).

When choosing how many flexi-days you need for your railpass, note that it can be worthwhile to buy an extra day (about $15-20 per person) even to cover short trips on regional trains—for instance, from Würzburg to Rothenburg.

Point-to-Point Tickets

Ticket fares are shown on the map on page 830 and at http://bahn
.hafas.de/bin/query.exe/en (no fare information for trains outside
Germany). The German Railway can charge a wide variety of fares
for the same journey, depending on the time of day, how far ahead
you purchase the ticket, and other considerations. Know your
options to get the best deal.

First Class vs. Second Class: First-class tickets usually cost
50 percent more than second-class tickets. While first-class cars
are always a bit more spacious and quiet than second class, the
main advantage of a first-class ticket is the lower chance that the
train will fill up. Riding in second class gets you there at the same
time, and with the same scenery. As second-class seating is still
comfortable and quiet, most of my readers find the extra cost of
first class isn't worth it—Germans themselves tell me they never
ride in first class unless someone else is paying for it.

Full-Fare Tickets: The most you'll ever have to pay for a
journey is the unrestricted *Normalpreis*. This full-fare ticket allows
you to easily change your plans and switch to an earlier or later
train, without paying a penalty. (If you buy a *Normalpreis* ticket for
a slower train, though, you can't use it on a fast one without paying
extra.)

Discount Fares: If you reserve a ticket on a fast train at least
three days in advance and are comfortable committing to particular departure times, you can usually save 25-75 percent over the
Normalpreis. But these tickets are more restrictive; you have to take
the train listed on the ticket. Changing one of these discounted
tickets costs at least €15.

Savings on Slow Trains: You can always save money on
point-to-point tickets if you're willing to skip Germany's high-
speed trains (IC, EC, and ICE) and limit yourself to regional
trains (labeled RB, RE, IRE, S, TR, or ALX). You may save even
more with three types of day passes valid only on these trains: the
various Länder-Tickets, the Schönes-Wochenende-Ticket, and the
Quer-durchs-Land-Ticket.

With a **Länder-Ticket,** up to five people traveling together get
unlimited travel in second class for one day for a very cheap price
(about €29-40, depending on area; a Länder-Ticket Single covers
one person for about €21). The catch: A Länder-Ticket only covers
travel within a certain *Land* (Germany's version of a US state, such
as Bavaria, Baden, or Rheinland-Pfalz). Also, these tickets don't
cover travel on weekdays before 9:00. Still, Länder-Tickets offer
big savings, don't require advance purchase, and are also valid on
local transport. For example, a Bayern-Ticket (the Bavarian version of a Länder-Ticket) not only gets you from Munich to Füssen,
but also covers the bus from Füssen to Neuschwanstein and back.

Railpasses

Prices listed are for 2011 and are subject to change. For the latest prices, details, train schedules, and easy online ordering, see my comprehensive Guide to Eurail Passes at www.ricksteves.com/rail. See Web site for more passes, including France-Germany and Germany-Czech passes.

"Saver" prices are per person for two or more people traveling together. "Youth" means under age 26. All passes for Germany cover KD Line boats on the Rhine and Mosel, 20% off Romantic Road bus ride.

GERMAN PASS

	Indiv. 1st Cl.	Indiv. 2nd Cl.	Twin 1st Cl.	Twin 2nd Cl.	Youth 2nd Cl.
3 days in 1 month	$338	$258	$260	$190	$206
4 days in 1 month	360	277	272	206	221
5 days in 1 month	394	297	303	221	236
6 days in 1 month	441	327	334	244	253
7 days in 1 month	488	359	366	268	268
8 days in 1 month	532	388	397	293	283
9 days in 1 month	585	424	428	315	300
10 days in 1 month	632	453	460	338	315

Twin price is per person for 2 traveling together. Odd-numbered groups must buy one individual adult, youth, or child pass. Youth passes are for travelers under 26 only. Kids 6–11 half of full adult (not Twin) fare. Kids 5 and under free. Also sold at main train stations in Germany.

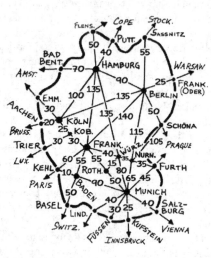

Map key:

Approximate point-to-point one-way second-class rail fares in US dollars. First class costs 50 percent more. Add up the approximate ticket costs for your trip to see if a railpass will save you money.

SELECTPASS

This pass covers travel in three adjacent countries. For four- and five-country options, please visit www.ricksteves.com/rail.

	Individual 1st Class	Saver 1st Class	Youth 2nd Class
5 days in 2 months	$502	$427	$327
6 days in 2 months	555	472	361
8 days in 2 months	656	558	427
10 days in 2 months	761	647	496

GERMANY–AUSTRIA PASS

	Indiv. 1st Cl.	Indiv. 2nd Cl.	Saver 1st Cl.	Saver 2nd Cl.	Youth 2nd Cl.
5 days in 2 months	$446	$383	$383	$328	$328
6 days in 2 months	491	420	420	361	361
8 days in 2 months	585	500	500	429	429
10 days in 2 months	683	580	580	500	500

The fare for children 4–11 is half the adult individual fare or Saver fare. Kids under age 4 travel free.

GERMANY–SWITZERLAND PASS

	Individual 1st Class	Saver 1st Class	Youth 2nd Class
5 days in 2 months	$476	$406	$335
6 days in 2 months	524	446	370
8 days in 2 months	618	530	436
10 days in 2 months	716	611	504

The fare for children 4–11 is half the adult individual or Saver fare. Kids under age 4 travel free.

BENELUX–GERMANY PASS

	Indiv. 1st Cl.	Indiv. 2nd Cl.	Saver 1st Cl.	Saver 2nd Cl.	Youth 2nd Cl.
5 days in 2 months	$469	$352	$352	$286	$286
6 days in 2 months	517	390	390	312	312
8 days in 2 months	611	460	460	368	368
10 days in 2 months	712	535	535	427	427

The fare for children 4–11 is half the adult individual fare or Saver fare. Kids under age 4 travel free.

DENMARK–GERMANY PASS

	Indiv. 1st Cl.	Indiv. 2nd Cl.	Saver 1st Cl.	Saver 2nd Cl.	Youth 2nd Cl.
4 days in 2 months	$382	$312	$312	$241	$239
5 days in 2 months	429	352	352	270	270
6 days in 2 months	476	390	390	296	296
8 days in 2 months	573	469	469	340	340
10 days in 2 months	688	523	523	385	385

The fare for children 4–11 is half the adult individual fare or Saver fare. Kids under age 4 travel free.

GERMANY–POLAND PASS

	Indiv. 1st Cl.	Indiv. 2nd Cl.	Saver 1st Cl.	Saver 2nd Cl.	Youth 2nd Cl.
5 days in 2 months	$462	$396	$396	$335	$336
6 days in 2 months	507	436	437	371	371
8 days in 2 months	601	517	517	439	439
10 days in 2 months	692	599	599	505	505

The fare for children 4–11 is half the adult individual fare or Saver fare. Kids under age 4 travel free.

GERMANY RAIL & DRIVE PASS

Any 2 rail days and 2 car days in 1 month.

Car Category	1st Class	2nd Class	Extra Car Day
Economy	$237	$194	$62
Compact	242	199	67
Intermediate	251	208	76
Intermediate Automatic	279	236	104
Full Size	329	286	154

Prices are per person, two traveling together. Extra rail day $60 in 1st Class, $47 in 2nd Class (max. 2).

To order a Rail & Drive pass, call your travel agent or Rail Europe at 800-438-7245. *These passes are not sold by Europe Through the Back Door.*

Some scenarios: From Munich to Nürnberg, ICE express trains take one hour and 10 minutes and cost €50, and RE regional trains take 35 minutes longer and cost €32. However, a Bayern-Ticket (Bavaria) lets one person ride the RE trains for only €21 (and just €29 covers up to five adults), as long as you leave after 9:00. Plus, if you return that day, there's no additional cost. The Baden-Ticket offers similar deals on the run from Freiburg to Baden-Baden, and the Rhineland-Pfalz-Ticket makes sense for longer day trips around the Rhine and the Mosel (for example, from Bacharach or Trier to Burg Eltz).

The **Schönes-Wochenende-Ticket** (€39) works much the same way, except that it's good only on Saturdays and Sundays, and covers regional trains all over Germany (rather than limiting you to one *Land*). It, too, is valid for up to five adults (no cheaper single version), but unlike the Länder-Tickets, doesn't cover buses and urban transport.

The **Quer-durchs-Land-Ticket** is essentially a weekday version of the Schönes-Wochenende-Ticket. This lets you ride for one weekday on any regional train anywhere in Germany for €42 (€6 for each additional passenger up to a maximum of 5 travelers, only valid after 9:00). For instance, two people could make the four-hour trip from Frankfurt to Trier on regional trains for €48 with a Quer-durchs-Land ticket and for €39 with a Schönes-Wochenende-Ticket. This trip would otherwise cost about €75 for two people. For even larger groups, these tickets save serious money.

Kids 6-14 travel free with a parent or grandparent, but the ticket needs to list the number of children (except if purchased from a regional-train ticket machine). Kids under 6 don't need tickets.

Buying Tickets

At the Station: Major German stations have a handy *Reisezentrum* (travel center) where you can ask questions and buy tickets (with a small markup for the personal service). Many smaller stations are unstaffed, so you'll have to buy tickets from the silver, red, and blue touch-screen machines (marked *Fahrkarten*, which means "tickets"). These generally user-friendly machines sell short- and long-distance train tickets, and print schedules for free (described earlier, under "Schedules"). Touch the flag to switch to English (although some screens are German-only). You can pay with bills or coins; the machines won't take your non-European credit card.

You'll also see the older, silver ticket machines with smaller screens and plenty of buttons; at some smaller stations, these machines are the only ticket-buying option. They sell same-day-only tickets to nearby destinations. In cities, they also sell local

public transport tickets.

To buy a ticket, press the flag button until it gives you a screen in English. Then look for your destination on the long list of towns on the left side of the machine. If your destination isn't on the list (because it's too far away), you can buy the ticket on board (let the conductor know where you boarded, and you won't even have to pay the small markup for buying a ticket on the train). If your destination *is* on the list, note its four-digit code and enter it on the number pad. The machine will automatically issue you a ticket for a one-way *(Einfache)* second-class fare, but you can alter that with the buttons below the keypad (press *Hin- und Rückfahrt* if you want a round-trip ticket, and *1./2. Klasse* for first class; also note the buttons for *Länder-Karte* day passes and children's tickets). Feed the machine cash (small bills are OK, but it won't take your non-European credit card), then collect your ticket and change. *Gut gemacht!* (Well done!)

In the Rhineland, you'll see a newer generation of these regional ticket machines, which are yellow and have touch screens, but still sell only same-day tickets.

On the Train: You can buy a ticket on board from the conductor for a long-distance journey (by paying a small markup), but if you're riding a local (short distance) train, you're expected to board with a valid ticket...or you can get fined. Note that ticket-checkers on local trains aren't necessarily in uniform.

Online: You can buy German train tickets online and print them out yourself or (for a fee) have them delivered by mail; visit http://bahn.hafas.de/bin/query.exe/en and create a login and password. If you print out your own ticket, the conductor will also ask to see the ID that you specified in the booking (typically the credit card you paid with).

Getting a Seat
As you board or exit a train, you'll usually have to push a button or flip a lever to open the door. Watch and imitate.

It costs €2.50 extra per person to reserve a seat, which you can do at a station ticket desk, a touch-screen machine, or online. German trains generally offer ample seating, but some do fill up on popular routes, especially on holiday weekends. If your itinerary is set, and you don't mind the small fee, seat reservations are worth it for the peace of mind—and a few fast trains require reservations (slower regional trains, however, don't accept them). With rare exceptions, it doesn't make sense to go through a US agent to make a seat reservation in advance of your trip; just do it online or at a German station.

On ICE trains, families with small children can book special compartments called *Kleinkindabteil,* which have room for strollers and diaper changing, for the regular seat-reservation price.

If you have a seat reservation, while waiting for your train to arrive, note the departure time and *Wagen* (car) number and look along the train platform for the diagram (*Wagenstandanzeiger)* that shows what sector of the platform the car will arrive at (usually A through F). Stand in that sector to avoid a last-minute dash to the right car or a long walk through the train to your seat. This is especially important for ICE trains, which are often divided into two unconnected parts.

If you're traveling without a reservation and are looking for a free seat, check the displays (or, in older trains, the slips of paper) that mark reserved seats. If you have a hard time finding an unreserved seat, take a closer look at the reservations—if you find a seat that's reserved for a leg of the journey that doesn't overlap with yours, you're free to take the seat. For example, if you're traveling from Frankfurt to Würzburg on a Munich-bound train, and you find a seat reserved only from Würzburg to Munich, it's all yours—you'll be getting off the train as the reservation-holder boards in Würzburg.

In stations without elevators, make sure to take advantage of the luggage belts along the stairs to each platform. They start automatically when you put your bag on the bottom or top of the belt.

Bikes on Board

Your bike can travel with you for €4.50 per day on regional trains or €9 per trip on fast trains. Deutsche Bahn's helpful website even has a list of bike-rental shops that are in or near train stations. Rentals usually run about €10 to €15 a day, and some rental outfits offer easy "pick up here and drop off there" plans.

Renting a Car

To drive in Germany, you'll need your driver's license. It's recommended, but not required, that you also have an International Driving Permit (sold at your local AAA office for $15 plus the cost of two passport-type photos; see www.aaa.com); however, I've frequently rented cars in Germany and traveled problem-free with just my US license.

To rent a car in Germany, you likely have to be 21 years old (most companies will not rent to anyone under that age), and restrictions and "underage fees" can apply if you're 21-24. There's generally not a maximum age limit, but if you are 70 or older, it's smart to ask. If you're considered too young or old, look into leasing (explained later), which has less-stringent age restrictions.

Research car rentals before you go. It's cheapest to arrange most car rentals from the US. Call several companies, and look online to compare rates, or arrange a rental through your home-town travel agent. Most of the major US rental agencies—such as Enterprise, Alamo/National, Avis, Budget, Dollar, Hertz, and Thrifty—have offices throughout Europe. It can be cheaper to use a consolidator, such as Auto Europe (www.autoeurope.com) or Europe by Car (www.ebctravel.com), which compares rates at several companies to get you the best deal. However, my readers have reported problems with consolidators, ranging from misinformation to unexpected fees. Because you're going through a middle-man, it can be more challenging to resolve disputes that arise with the rental agency.

Regardless of the car-rental company you choose, always read the contract carefully. The fine print can conceal a host of common add-on charges—such as one-way drop-off fees, airport surcharges, or mandatory insurance policies—that aren't included in the "total price," but can be tacked on when you pick up your car. You may need to query rental agents pointedly to find out your actual cost.

For the best rental deal, rent by the week with unlimited mileage. To save money on gas, ask for a diesel car. I normally rent the smallest, least-expensive model with a stick shift (cheaper than an automatic). An automatic transmission adds about 50 percent to the car-rental cost over a manual transmission. Almost all rent-als are manual by default, so if you need an automatic, you must request one in advance; beware that these cars are usually larger models (not as maneuverable on narrow, winding roads).

For a three-week rental, allow $900 per person (based on two people sharing) for a small economy car with unlimited mileage, including gas, parking, and insurance. For trips of this length, look into leasing; you'll save money on insurance and taxes.

You can sometimes get a GPS unit with your rental car or leased vehicle for an additional fee (around $15/day; be sure it's set to English and has all the maps you need before you drive off). Or, if you have a portable GPS device at home, consider taking it with you to Europe (buy and upload European maps before your trip). GPS apps are also available for smartphones, but downloading maps on one of these apps in Europe could lead to an exorbitant data-roaming bill.

Big companies have offices in most cities; ask to be picked up at your hotel. Small local rental companies can be cheaper but aren't as flexible.

Compare pickup costs (downtown can be cheaper than the airport), and explore drop-off options. Returning a car at a big-city train station can be tricky; get precise details on the car drop-off location and hours. Note that rental offices usually close from midday Saturday until Monday.

When you pick up the car, check it thoroughly and make sure any damage is noted on your rental agreement. Find out how your car's lights, turn signals, wipers, and gas cap function, and know what kind of gas the car takes. When you return the car, make sure the agent verifies its condition with you.

Car Insurance Options

When you rent a car, you are liable for a very high deductible, sometimes equal to the entire value of the car. Limit your financial risk in case of an accident by choosing one of these three options: Buy Collision Damage Waiver (CDW) coverage from the car-rental company, get coverage through your credit card (free, if your card automatically includes zero-deductible coverage), or buy coverage through Travel Guard.

CDW includes a very high deductible (typically $1,000-1,500). Though each rental company has its own variation, basic CDW costs $15-25 a day (figure roughly 25 percent extra) and reduces your liability, but does not eliminate it. When you pick up the car, you'll be offered the chance to "buy down" the deductible to zero (for an additional $15-30/day; this is sometimes called "super CDW").

If you opt for **credit-card coverage**, there's a catch. You'll technically have to decline all coverage offered by the car-rental company, which means they can place a hold on your card (which can be up to the full value of the car). In case of damage, it can be time-consuming to resolve the charges with your credit-card company. Before you decide on this option, quiz your credit-card company about how it works.

Finally, you can buy collision insurance from Travel Guard ($9/day plus a one-time $3 service fee covers you up to $35,000, $250 deductible, tel. 800-826-4919, www.travelguard.com). It's valid everywhere in Europe except the Republic of Ireland, and some Italian car-rental companies refuse to honor it. Note that various states differ on which products and policies are available to their residents.

For more on car-rental insurance, see www.ricksteves.com/cdw.

Leasing

For trips of two and a half weeks or more, consider leasing (which automatically includes zero-deductible collision and theft insurance). By technically buying and then selling back the car, you save lots of money on tax and insurance. Leasing provides you a new car with unlimited mileage and a 24-hour emergency assistance program. You can lease for as little as 17 days to as long as 6 months. Car leases must be arranged from the US. One of many reliable companies offering affordable lease packages is Europe by Car (US tel. 800-223-1516, www.ebctravel.com).

Driving

Remember to bring your driver's license. Seat belts are mandatory for all, and two beers under those belts are enough to land you in jail. You're required to use low-beam headlights if it's overcast, raining, or snowing.

Road Rules: Be aware of German rules of the road; for example, seat belts are mandatory for all, and kids under age 12 (or less than about 4.5 feet tall) must ride in an appropriate child-safety seat. It's illegal to use a mobile phone while driving—pull over or use a hands-free device. For more information about driving, ask your car-rental company, or check the US State Department website (www.travel.state.gov, click on "International Travel," then specify your country of choice and click "Traffic Safety and Road Conditions").

Tips: Your US credit and debit cards are unlikely to work at toll booths, self-service gas pumps, and automated parking garages. Be sure to carry sufficient cash in euros.

Use good local maps and study them before each drive. Learn which exits you need to look out for, which major cities you'll travel toward, where the ruined castles lurk, and so on. Every long drive between my recommended destinations is via the autobahn (super-freeway), and nearly every scenic backcountry drive is paved and comfortable.

Learn the universal road signs (explained in charts in most road atlases and at service stations). To get to the center of a city, follow signs for *Zentrum* or *Stadtmitte*. Ring roads go around a city.

The Autobahn: The shortest distance between any two points is the autobahn (no speed limit, toll-free). Blue signs direct you

Note: Your times may vary based on traffic, construction, and road conditions.

m = miles
h = hours
...... = ferry

North Sea

To Copenhagen 200m 4h

Flensburg

95m · 1.25h

NETHERLANDS

Hamburg

Amsterdam

165m · 2.5h

265m · 4.25h

G E R

310m · 4.5h

360m · 5.5h

Brussels

90m · 1.5h

40m · .75h

Aachen   Köln

230m · 3.5h

Erfurt

BELGIUM

55m · .75h

140m · 2.25h

30m
.5h

25m
.5h

Koblenz

55m
1h

Cochem

Bacharach

Frankfurt

60m · 1h

125m · 2h

200m · 3.25h

LUX.

70m · 1h

60m · 1h

Würzburg

Trier

175m · 2.5h

135m · 2.5h

100m · 1.5h

40m
.5h

Rothenburg

70m · 1.25h

Nürnberg

135m · 2h

Strasbourg

40m
1h

Baden-Baden

150m · 2h

100m · 1.75h

FRANCE

60m · 1.25h

200m · 3.25h

Colmar

260m · 4h

35m
1h

Freiburg

175m · 3.75h

Munich

Füssen

95m · 1.75h

95m · 2.25h

70m · 1.5h

100m...

Zürich

55m · 1h

70m · 1.25h

Appenzell

70m · 1.75h
(via Reutte)

Bern

SWITZERLAND

LIECH.

Innsbruck

20m
.25h

To Brenner Pass

Driving: Distance & Time

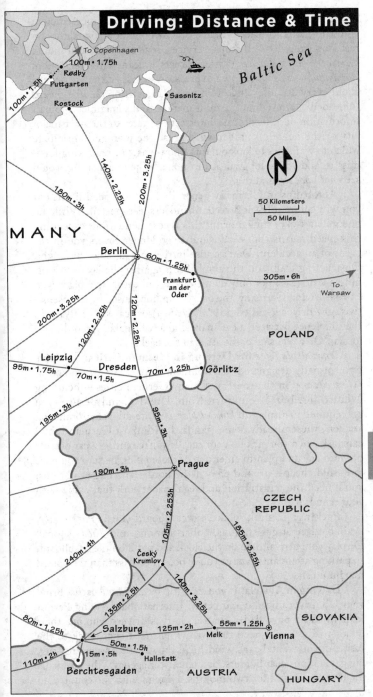

Baltic Sea

To Copenhagen
100m • 1.75h
Rødby
Puttgarten
100m • 1.5h
Rostock
Sassnitz

MANY

140m • 2.25h
180m • 3h
200m • 3.25h

50 Kilometers
50 Miles

Berlin
60m • 1.25h

Frankfurt an der Oder

305m • 6h
To Warsaw

120m • 2.25h
200m • 3.25h
120m • 2.25h
120m • 2.25h

POLAND

Leipzig
95m • 1.75h
70m • 1.5h
Dresden
70m • 1.25h
Görlitz

195m • 3h

95m • 3h

190m • 3h
Prague

CZECH REPUBLIC

105m • 2.253h
185m • 3.25h

240m • 4h
Český Krumlov

140m • 3.25h

135m • 2.5h
SLOVAKIA

80m • 1.25h
Salzburg
125m • 2h
Melk
55m • 1.25h
Vienna

110m • 2h
15m • .5h
50m • 1.5h
Hallstatt
AUSTRIA
HUNGARY
Berchtesgaden

to the autobahn. To understand the complex but super-efficient autobahn, look for the *Autobahn Service* booklet at any autobahn rest stop (free, lists all stops, services, road symbols, and more). Learn the signs: *Dreieck* ("three corners") means a Y-intersection; *Autobahnkreuz* is where two expressways cross. Exits are spaced about every 20 miles and often have a gas station (*bleifrei* means "unleaded"), a restaurant, a mini-market, and sometimes a tourist information desk. Exits and intersections refer to the next major city or the nearest small town. Peruse the map and anticipate which town names to look out for. Know what you're looking for— miss it, and you're long autobahn-gone. When navigating, you'll see *nord, süd, ost,* and *west.*

Autobahns in Germany generally have no speed limit, but you will commonly see a recommended speed posted. While no one gets a ticket for ignoring this recommendation, exceeding this speed means your car insurance no longer covers you in the event of an accident. Don't cruise in the passing lane; stay right. Obstructing traffic on the autobahn is against the law—so running out of gas is not only dangerous, it can earn you a big ticket. In fast-driving Germany, the backed-up line caused by an insensitive slow driver is called an *Autoschlange,* or "car snake." What's the difference between a car snake and a real snake? According to locals, "On a real snake, the ass is in the back."

***Umweltplakette* for Driving in German Cities:** To drive into specially designated "environmental zones" or "green zones" *(Umweltzone)* in the centers of many German cities—including Munich, Freiburg, Frankfurt, Köln, Dresden, and Berlin—you are required to display an *Umweltplakette.* Literally "environmental sticker," these already come standard with most German rental cars (ask when you pick up your car). If you're renting a car outside of Germany and plan to enter one of these cities, be sure you have one (sold cheap—around €5—at the border and at gas stations; you'll need the registration and legal paperwork that came with your rental).

Parking: To park, pick up a cardboard clock (*Parkscheibe,* available free at gas stations, police stations, and *Tabak* shops). Display your arrival time on the clock and put it on the dashboard, so parking attendants can see you've been there less than the posted maximum stay.

Driving in Austria: If you side-trip by car into Austria, bring your US driver's license and get an International Driving Permit (explained on page 834). Austria charges drivers who use their major roads. You'll need to have a *Vignette* sticker stuck to the inside of your rental car's windshield (buy at the border crossing, big gas stations near borders, or a rental-car agency). The cost is €8 for 10 days, or €22 for two months. Dipping into the country on regular roads—such as around Reutte in Tirol—requires no special payment. In Austria, green signs direct you to the autobahn, and autobahn speed limits are enforced.

Cheap Flights

If you're considering a train ride that's more than five hours long, a flight may save you both time and money. When comparing your options, factor in the time it takes to get to the airport and how early you'll need to arrive to check in. One of the best websites for comparing inexpensive flights is www.skyscanner.net. Other comparison search engines include www.kayak.com, www.wegolo.com, and www.whichbudget.com.

Well-known cheapo airlines include easyJet (www.easyjet.com) and Ryanair (www.ryanair.com). Those based in Germany are Air Berlin (www.airberlin.com), Germanwings (www.germanwings.com), and TUIfly (www.tuifly.com). Airport websites may list small airlines that serve your destination.

Be aware of the potential drawbacks of flying on the cheap: nonrefundable and nonchangeable tickets, minimal or nonexistent customer service, treks to airports far outside town, and stingy baggage allowances with steep overage fees. If you're traveling with lots of luggage, a cheap flight can quickly become a bad deal. To avoid unpleasant surprises, read the small print before you book.

Resources

Resources from Rick Steves

Rick Steves' Germany 2012 is one of many books in my series on European travel, which includes country guidebooks, city and regional guidebooks, Snapshot guides (excerpted chapters from my country guides), Pocket Guides (full-color little books on big cities), and my budget-travel skills handbook, *Rick Steves' Europe Through the Back Door*. Most of my titles are available as ebooks. My phrase books—for German, French, Italian, Spanish, and Portuguese—are practical and budget-oriented. My other books include *Europe 101* (a crash course on art and history), *Mediterranean Cruise Ports* (how to make the most of your time in port), and *Travel as a Political Act* (a travelogue sprinkled with tips for bringing home a global perspective). A more complete list of my titles appears near the end of this book.

Video: My public television series, *Rick Steves' Europe*, covers European destinations in 100 shows, with four episodes on

Germany. To watch episodes, visit www.hulu.com/rick-steves -europe; for scripts and other details, see www.ricksteves.com/tv.

Audio: My weekly public radio show, *Travel with Rick Steves*, features interviews with travel experts from around the world. All of this audio content is available for free at Rick Steves Audio Europe, an extensive online library organized by destination. Choose whatever interests you, and download it for free to your computer or mobile device via www.ricksteves.com/audio europe, iTunes, or the Rick Steves Audio Europe smartphone app.

Maps

The black-and-white maps in this book are concise and simple, designed to help you locate recommended places and get to local TIs, where you can pick up more in-depth maps of cities or regions (usually free). Better maps are sold at newsstands and bookstores. Before you buy a map, look at it to be sure it has the level of detail you want.

European bookstores, especially in touristy areas, have good selections of maps. For drivers, I'd recommend a 1:200,000- or 1:300,000-scale map. Train travelers usually manage fine with the freebies they get with the train pass and from the local tourist offices.

Other Guidebooks

If you're like most travelers, this book is all you need. But if you're heading beyond my recommended destinations, $40 for extra maps and books is money well spent.

The following books are worthwhile, though most are not updated annually; check the publication date before you buy.

Lonely Planet's guide to Germany is thorough, well-researched, and packed with good maps and hotel recommendations for low- to moderate-budget travelers. The similar Rough Guide is written by insightful British researchers.

Students and vagabonds like the highly opinionated Let's Go series, which is updated by Harvard students. Let's Go is best for backpackers who have railpasses, stay in hostels, and are interested in the youth and nightlife scene.

The popular skinny green Michelin Guides are excellent, especially if you're driving. Michelin Guides are known for their city and sightseeing maps, dry but concise and helpful information on all major sights, and good cultural and historical background. English editions are sold in Europe at gas stations and tourist shops.

Begin Your Trip at www.ricksteves.com

At ricksteves.com, you'll discover a wealth of free information on European destinations, including fresh monthly news and helpful tips from thousands of fellow travelers. You'll find my latest guidebook updates (www.ricksteves.com/update), a monthly travel e-newsletter (easy and free to sign up), my personal travel blog, and my free Rick Steves Audio Europe smartphone app (if you don't have a smartphone, you can access the same content via podcasts). You can even follow me on Facebook and Twitter.

Our **online Travel Store** offers travel bags and accessories specially designed by me to help you travel smarter and lighter. These include my popular carry-on bags (roll-aboard and backpack versions), money belts, totes, toiletries kits, adapters, other accessories, and a wide selection of guidebooks, planning maps, and DVDs.

Choosing the right **railpass** for your trip—amid hundreds of options—can drive you nutty. We'll help you choose the best pass for your needs and ship it to you for free, plus give you a bunch of free extras.

Rick Steves' Europe Through the Back Door travel company offers **tours** with more than three dozen itineraries and about 450 departures reaching the best destinations in this book...and beyond. We offer a 14-day tour of Germany, Austria, and Switzerland; a 12-day "unguided" tour (covering hotel and transportation) of those countries; and a 12-day tour of Berlin, Prague, and Vienna. You'll enjoy great guides, a fun bunch of travel partners (with small groups of generally about 24-28), and plenty of room to spread out in a big, comfy bus. You'll find European adventures to fit every vacation length. For all the details, and to get our Tour Catalog and a free Rick Steves Tour Experience DVD (filmed on location during an actual tour), visit www.ricksteves.com or call the Tour Department at 425/608-4217.

APPENDIX

Recommended Books and Movies

To learn more about Germany past and present, check out a few of these books and films.

Nonfiction

Germany: A New History (Schulze) is a one-volume compendium covering 2,000 years. *Inside the Third Reich*, based on 1,200 manuscript pages, is an authoritative account of 1933 through 1945, written by Albert Speer, Hitler's main architect. *Stasiland: True Stories from Behind the Berlin Wall* (Funder) relays the secrets of the Stasi, the East German Ministry for State Security. *In the Garden of Beasts* (Larson) chronicles 1930s Berlin through the eyes of America's ambassador to Nazi Germany.

For more on modern Germany, including cultural insights, pick up *Culture Shock! Germany* (Lord), *When in Germany, Do as the Germans Do* (Flippo), and *Of German Ways* (Rippley). Gourmets may want to grab *The Marling Menu-Master for Germany*.

Memoirs: Günter Grass stirred up controversy with his 2007 memoir, *Peeling the Onion*, which revealed he was a soldier in the dreaded Waffen-SS. *A Time of Gifts* (Fermor) tells of the author's walking tour of Europe—and Germany—in the 1930s. In *A Tramp Abroad*, Mark Twain recounts his amusing European adventures, including some in Germany.

Fiction

Classics of German fiction include the works of Thomas Mann (*Buddenbrooks* and *The Magic Mountain*) and Hermann Hesse (*Narcissus and Goldmund* and *Siddhartha*).

Some of the best modern German literature has wrestled with the country's warmongering past. *All Quiet on the Western Front*, a classroom classic by Erich Maria Remarque, speaks with eloquence about World War I. First published before World War II, *Address Unknown* (Kathrine Kressmann Taylor) is a novella with a cautionary tone about what would follow. In *The Tin Drum*, Günter Grass broke the post-WWII silence, creating a landmark work of literature in the process. *The Silent Angel* is a complex love story set after the war (by Nobel Prize winner Heinrich Böll).

A book of science fiction and time travel, *1632* (Flint) sends West Virginians back to 17th-century Germany. *The Good German* (Kanon), set during the postwar years, is part thriller, part historical fiction. *Berlin Noir* (Kerr) is filled with stories of secrets and crime.

For recent material, consider the following books, published since the mid-1990s. Esther Freud, the daughter of artist Lucien Freud, set *Summer at Gaglow* during the Great War. *Stones from the River*, the story of a dwarf in Nazi Germany, and *Floating in*

My Mother's Palm, which takes place in a small town on the Rhine, have brought Ursula Hegi accolades. Told by a sympathetic narrator, *The Reader* (Schlink) challenges readers to think, "What if my loved ones had been Nazis?" *Saints and Villains* (Giardina) is the fictionalized account of Dietrich Bonhoeffer, a Protestant theologian who protested against Hitler's rise. *Marrying Mozart* (Cowell) reveals a more intimate side of the famous composer.

Films

Leni Riefenstahl's *Triumph of the Will* (1935) is infamous Nazi propaganda turned film classic. *The Tin Drum* (1979) is based on Günter Grass' seminal novel, and *The Good German* (2006) is based on Joseph Kanon's thriller (both described earlier).

Other meditations on the war years—films filled with allegory and metaphor about the Nazis' rise to power—include *Mephisto* (1981) and Rainer Werner Fassbinder's *The Marriage of Maria Braun* (1979). *Downfall* (2004) tells of the Führer's final days. *Schindler's List* (1993)—about a factory owner's inspirational efforts to save his Jewish employees from deportation to concentration camps—won Steven Spielberg the Best Picture and Best Director Oscars.

Shoah (1985) is a 9.5-hour Holocaust documentary that includes no wartime footage, only interviews with those who lived through it. The well-respected *Das Boot* (1981) has a strong pacifist message, as do the films about the students who defied Hitler—and were ultimately sentenced to die: *The White Rose* (1982) and the beautiful, devastating *Sophie Scholl: The Final Days* (2005). *Cabaret* (1972), which made Liza Minnelli a star, is about the crazy Berlin scene in 1931, during the last days of the Weimar Republic as the Nazis were rising to power.

But German film is not composed of only dramatic, war-themed movies. Set in Berlin, *Wings of Desire* (1987) is Wim Wenders' best film, showing an angel who falls in love and falls to earth. *Immortal Beloved* (1994) made Beethoven into a flesh-and-blood man (with a secret lover). A different kind of music film, *Backbeat* (1994) chronicles the years the Beatles played in Hamburg just before becoming famous. *Run Lola Run* (1998) was an art-house phenomenon, combining action, love, and mobsters with a time-twisting plot. Jewish refugees settle in 1930s Kenya in *Nowhere in Africa* (2001). *Good Bye, Lenin!* (2003) is a funny, poignant look at a son's struggle to re-create long-gone Eastern Europe for his mother, while the former GDR's harsh secrets are exposed in *The Lives of Others* (2006).

Holidays and Festivals

This list includes many—but not all—big festivals in major cities, plus national holidays observed throughout Germany. Many sights and banks close on national holidays—keep this in mind when planning your itinerary. Before planning a trip around a festival, make sure you verify the dates by checking the festival's website or contacting the Germany national tourist office (see the beginning of the appendix). Austria's Salzburg has music festivals nearly every month.

For sports events, see www.sportsevents365.com for schedules and ticket information.

Here is a sampling of events and holidays in 2012:

Early Jan	Perchtenlaufen (winter festival, parades), Tirol and Salzburg, Austria
Feb 16-21	Fasching (carnival season, balls, parades in the days leading up to Ash Wednesday), throughout Germany
April 6	Good Friday
April 8	Easter; Easter Festival, Salzburg
May 1	May Day with maypole dances, throughout Austria and Germany
May 25-28 (Pentecost weekend)	Carnival of Cultures (www.karneval -berlin.de), Berlin; also Meistertrunk Show (historic play and market, medieval costumes, parties in the *Biergartens*, www.meistertrunk.de), Rothenburg
May 28	Pentecost Monday (Pfingstmontag), southern Germany
June	Fressgass' Fest (www.frankfurt.de), Frankfurt
June 7	Corpus Christi (Fronleichnam), southern Germany
Late June	City Festival (www.elbhangfest.de), Dresden; Frankfurt Summertime Festival (arts); Midsummer Eve Celebrations, Austria
July 14	Lichter Festival (fireworks and music, www.koelner-lichter.de), Köln
July 15-24	Kinderzeche Festival, Dinkelsbühl (www.kinderzeche.de)
Late July-Aug	Salzburg Festival (music, www .salzburgerfestspiele.at)
Aug 15	Assumption (Mariä Himmelfahrt), Munich

2012

JANUARY
S	M	T	W	T	F	S
1	2	3	4	5	6	7
8	9	10	11	12	13	14
15	16	17	18	19	20	21
22	23	24	25	26	27	28
29	30	31				

FEBRUARY
S	M	T	W	T	F	S
			1	2	3	4
5	6	7	8	9	10	11
12	13	14	15	16	17	18
19	20	21	22	23	24	25
26	27	28	29			

MARCH
S	M	T	W	T	F	S
				1	2	3
4	5	6	7	8	9	10
11	12	13	14	15	16	17
18	19	20	21	22	23	24
25	26	27	28	29	30	31

APRIL
S	M	T	W	T	F	S
1	2	3	4	5	6	7
8	9	10	11	12	13	14
15	16	17	18	19	20	21
22	23	24	25	26	27	28
29	30					

MAY
S	M	T	W	T	F	S
		1	2	3	4	5
6	7	8	9	10	11	12
13	14	15	16	17	18	19
20	21	22	23	24	25	26
27	28	29	30	31		

JUNE
S	M	T	W	T	F	S
					1	2
3	4	5	6	7	8	9
10	11	12	13	14	15	16
17	18	19	20	21	22	23
24	25	26	27	28	29	30

JULY
S	M	T	W	T	F	S
1	2	3	4	5	6	7
8	9	10	11	12	13	14
15	16	17	18	19	20	21
22	23	24	25	26	27	28
29	30	31				

AUGUST
S	M	T	W	T	F	S
			1	2	3	4
5	6	7	8	9	10	11
12	13	14	15	16	17	18
19	20	21	22	23	24	25
26	27	28	29	30	31	

SEPTEMBER
S	M	T	W	T	F	S
						1
2	3	4	5	6	7	8
9	10	11	12	13	14	15
16	17	18	19	20	21	22
23/30	24	25	26	27	28	29

OCTOBER
S	M	T	W	T	F	S
	1	2	3	4	5	6
7	8	9	10	11	12	13
14	15	16	17	18	19	20
21	22	23	24	25	26	27
28	29	30	31			

NOVEMBER
S	M	T	W	T	F	S
				1	2	3
4	5	6	7	8	9	10
11	12	13	14	15	16	17
18	19	20	21	22	23	24
25	26	27	28	29	30	

DECEMBER
S	M	T	W	T	F	S
						1
2	3	4	5	6	7	8
9	10	11	12	13	14	15
16	17	18	19	20	21	22
23/30	24/31	25	26	27	28	29

Aug (last weekend)	Museum Riverbank Festival (www.frankfurt-tourismus.de), Frankfurt
Sept (first two weeks)	Rheingau Wine Festival (www.frankfurt-tourismus.de), Frankfurt
Early Sept	Reichsstadt Festival (fireworks), Rothenburg
Sept	Berlin Festwochen (arts festival, www.berlinerfestspiele.de)
Sept 22-Oct 7	Oktoberfest (www.oktoberfest.de), Munich
Oct 3	German Unity Day (Tag der Deutschen Einheit), Germany
Oct 31	Reformation Day celebration, Wittenberg
Nov 1	All Saints' Day (Allerheiligen), southern Germany

Nov	Berlin Jazz Festival (www.berliner festspiele.de); St. Martin's Day Celebrations (feasts), Bavaria
Dec	Christmas markets throughout Germany, particularly in Nürnberg, Munich, Rothenburg, and Freiburg
Dec 6	St. Nicholas Day (Nikolaustag; parades), throughout Germany
Dec 24	Christmas Eve (Heilige Abend), when Germans celebrate Christmas
Dec 25	Christmas
Dec 31	New Year's Eve (Silvester; fireworks), throughout Germany, particularly Berlin

Conversions and Climate

Numbers and Stumblers

- Europeans write a few of their numbers differently than we do. 1 = 1, 4 = 4, 7 = 7.
- In Europe, dates appear as day/month/year, so Christmas is 25/12/12.
- Commas are decimal points and decimals commas. A dollar and a half is 1,50, one thousand is 1.000, and there are 5.280 feet in a mile.
- When pointing, use your whole hand, palm down.
- When counting with fingers, start with your thumb. If you hold up your first finger to request one item, you'll probably get two.
- What Americans call the second floor of a building is the first floor in Europe.
- On escalators and moving sidewalks, Europeans keep the left "lane" open for passing. Keep to the right.

Metric Conversions (approximate)

A kilogram is 2.2 pounds, and 1 liter is about a quart, or almost four to a gallon. A kilometer is six-tenths of a mile. I figure kilometers to miles by cutting them in half and adding back 10 percent of the original (120 km: 60 + 12 = 72 miles, 300 km: 150 + 30 = 180 miles).

1 foot = 0.3 meter	1 square yard = 0.8 square meter
1 yard = 0.9 meter	1 square mile = 2.6 square kilometers
1 mile = 1.6 kilometers	1 ounce = 28 grams
1 centimeter = 0.4 inch	1 quart = 0.95 liter
1 meter = 39.4 inches	1 kilogram = 2.2 pounds
1 kilometer = 0.62 mile	32°F = 0°C

Clothing Sizes

When shopping for clothing, use these US-to-European comparisons as general guidelines (but note that no conversion is perfect).

- Women's dresses and blouses: Add 30
  (US size 10 = European size 40)
- Men's suits and jackets: Add 10
  (US size 40 regular = European size 50)
- Men's shirts: Multiply by 2 and add about 8
  (US size 15 collar = European size 38)
- Women's shoes: Add about 30
  (US size 8 = European size 38-39)
- Men's shoes: Add 32-34
  (US size 9 = European size 41; US size 11 = European size 45)

Germany's Climate

First line, average daily high; second line, average daily low; third line, average days without rain. For more detailed weather statistics for destinations in this book (as well as the rest of the world), check www.worldclimate.com.

J	F	M	A	M	J	J	A	S	O	N	D
GERMANY • Berlin											
35°	37°	46°	56°	66°	72°	75°	74°	68°	56°	45°	38°
26°	26°	31°	39°	47°	53°	57°	56°	50°	42°	36°	29°
14	13	19	17	19	17	17	17	18	17	14	16
GERMANY • Munich											
35°	38°	48°	56°	64°	70°	74°	73°	67°	56°	44°	36°
23°	23°	30°	38°	45°	51°	55°	54°	48°	40°	33°	26°
15	12	18	15	16	13	15	15	17	18	15	16

Temperature Conversion: Fahrenheit and Celsius

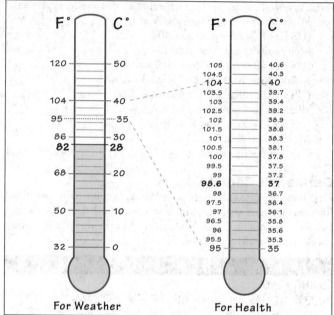

For Weather   For Health

Europe takes its temperature using the Celsius scale, while we opt for Fahrenheit. For a rough conversion from Celsius to Fahrenheit, double the number and add 30. For weather, remember that 28°C is 82°F—perfect. For health, 37°C is just right.

APPENDIX

Packing Checklist

Whether you're traveling for five days or five weeks, here's what you'll need to bring. Pack light to enjoy the sweet freedom of true mobility. Happy travels!

- ❑ 5 shirts: long- and short-sleeve
- ❑ 1 sweater or lightweight fleece
- ❑ 2 pairs pants
- ❑ 1 pair shorts
- ❑ 1 swimsuit
- ❑ 5 pairs underwear and socks
- ❑ 1 pair shoes
- ❑ 1 rainproof jacket with hood
- ❑ Tie or scarf
- ❑ Money belt
- ❑ Money—your mix of:
  - ❑ Debit card (for ATM withdrawals)
  - ❑ Credit card
  - ❑ Hard cash (in easy-to-exchange $20 bills)
- ❑ Documents plus photo-copies:
  - ❑ Passport
  - ❑ Printout of airline eticket
  - ❑ Driver's license
  - ❑ Student ID and hostel card
  - ❑ Railpass/car rental voucher
  - ❑ Insurance details
- ❑ Daypack
- ❑ Electronics—your choice of:
  - ❑ Camera (and related gear)
  - ❑ Computer/mobile devices (phone, MP3 player, ereader, etc.)
  - ❑ Chargers for each of the above
  - ❑ Plug adapter
- ❑ Empty water bottle

- ❑ Wristwatch and alarm clock
- ❑ Earplugs
- ❑ Toiletries kit
  - ❑ Toiletries
  - ❑ Medicines and vitamins
  - ❑ First-aid kit
  - ❑ Glasses/contacts/sunglasses (with prescriptions)
- ❑ Sealable plastic baggies
- ❑ Laundry soap
- ❑ Clothesline
- ❑ Small towel
- ❑ Sewing kit
- ❑ Travel information (guide-books and maps)
- ❑ Address list (for sending postcards)
- ❑ Postcards and photos from home
- ❑ Notepad and pen
- ❑ Journal

If you plan to carry on your luggage, note that all liquids must be in 3.4-ounce or smaller containers and fit within a single quart-size sealable baggie. For details, see www.tsa.gov/travelers.

Hotel Reservation

To: _____ _____
           hotel   *email or fax*

From: _____ _____
              name   *email or fax*

Today's date: _____ / _____ / _____
                      day   *month*   *year*

Dear Hotel _____ ,
Please make this reservation for me:

Name: _____

Total # of people: _____   # of rooms: _____   # of nights: _____

Arriving: _____ / _____ / _____   My time of arrival (24-hr clock): _____
                 day   *month*   *year*   (I will telephone if I will be late)

Departing: ____ / ____ / ____
                  day   *month*   *year*

Room(s): Single____   Double ____   Twin ____   Triple ____   Quad____

With: Toilet ____   Shower ____ Bath ____   Sink only ____

Special needs: View____ Quiet____ Cheapest ____ Ground Floor____

Please email or fax confirmation of my reservation, along with the type of
room reserved and the price. Please also inform me of your cancellation
policy. After I hear from you, I will quickly send my credit-card information
as a deposit to hold the room. Thank you.

_____
Name

_____

_____
Address

_____
City   **State**   **Zip Code**   **Country**

APPENDIX

*Before hoteliers can make your reservation, they want to know the informa-
tion listed above. You can use this form as the basis for your email, or you can
photocopy this page, fill in the information, and send it as a fax (also available
online at www.ricksteves.com/reservation).*

German Survival Phrases

When using the phonetics, pronounce ī as the long I sound in "light."

English	German	Phonetics
Good day.	Guten Tag.	**goo**-tehn tahg
Do you speak English?	Sprechen Sie Englisch?	**shprehkh**-ehn zee **ehng**-lish
Yes. / No.	Ja. / Nein.	yah / nīn
I (don't) understand.	Ich verstehe (nicht).	ikh fehr-**shtay**-heh (nikht)
Please.	Bitte.	**bit**-teh
Thank you.	Danke.	**dahng**-keh
I'm sorry.	Es tut mir leid.	ehs toot meer līt
Excuse me.	Entschuldigung.	ehnt-**shool**-dig-oong
(No) problem.	(Kein) Problem.	(kīn) proh-**blaym**
(Very) good.	(Sehr) gut.	(zehr) goot
Goodbye.	Auf Wiedersehen.	owf **vee**-der-zayn
one / two	eins / zwei	īns / tsvī
three / four	drei / vier	drī / feer
five / six	fünf / sechs	fewnf / zehkhs
seven / eight	sieben / acht	**zee**-behn / ahkht
nine / ten	neun / zehn	noyn / tsayn
How much is it?	Wieviel kostet das?	**vee**-feel **kohs**-teht dahs
Write it?	Schreiben?	**shrī**-behn
Is it free?	Ist es umsonst?	ist ehs oom-**zohnst**
Included?	Inklusive?	in-kloo-**zee**-veh
Where can I buy / find...?	Wo kann ich kaufen / finden...?	voh kahn ikh **kow**-fehn / **fin**-dehn
I'd like / We'd like...	Ich hätte gern / Wir hätten gern...	ikh **heh**-teh gehrn / veer **heh**-tehn gehrn
...a room.	...ein Zimmer.	īn **tsim**-mer
...a ticket to ___.	...eine Fahrkarte nach ___.	ī-neh **far**-kar-teh nahkh
Is it possible?	Ist es möglich?	ist ehs **mur**-glikh
Where is...?	Wo ist...?	voh ist
...the train station	...der Bahnhof	dehr **bahn**-hohf
...the bus station	...der Busbahnhof	dehr **boos**-bahn-hohf
...tourist information	...das Touristeninformationsbüro	dahs too-**ris**-tehn-in-for-maht-see-**ohns-bew**-roh
...toilet	...die Toilette	dee toh-**leh**-teh
men	Herren	**hehr**-rehn
women	Damen	**dah**-mehn
left / right	links / rechts	links / rehkhts
straight	geradeaus	geh-**rah**-deh-ows
When is this open / closed?	Um wieviel Uhr ist hier geöffnet / geschlossen?	oom **vee**-feel oor ist heer geh-**urf**-neht / geh-**shloh**-sehn
At what time?	Um wieviel Uhr?	oom **vee**-feel oor
Just a moment.	Moment.	moh-**mehnt**
now / soon / later	jetzt / bald / später	yehtst / bahld / **shpay**-ter
today / tomorrow	heute / morgen	**hoy**-teh / **mor**-gehn

In the Restaurant

I'd like / We'd like...	Ich hätte gern / Wir hätten gern...	ikh **heh**-teh gehrn / veer **heh**-tehn gehrn
...a reservation for...	...eine Reservierung für...	ī-neh reh-zer-**feer**-oong fewr
...a table for one / two.	...einen Tisch für ein / zwei.	ī-nehn tish fewr īn / tsvī
Non-smoking.	Nichtraucher.	**nikht**-rowkh-er
Is this seat free?	Ist hier frei?	ist heer frī
Menu (in English), please.	Speisekarte (auf Englisch), bitte.	**shpī**-zeh-kar-teh (owf **ehng**-lish) **bit**-teh
service (not) included	Trinkgeld (nicht) inklusive	**trink**-gehlt (nikht) in-kloo-**zee**-veh
cover charge	Eintritt	**īn**-trit
to go	zum Mitnehmen	tsoom **mit**-nay-mehn
with / without	mit / ohne	mit / **oh**-neh
and / or	und / oder	oont / **oh**-der
menu (of the day)	(Tages-) Karte	(**tah**-gehs-) **kar**-teh
set meal for tourists	Touristenmenü	too-**ris**-tehn-meh-**new**
specialty of the house	Spezialität des Hauses	shpayt-see-ah-lee-**tayt** dehs **how**-zehs
appetizers	Vorspeise	**for**-shpī-zeh
bread	Brot	broht
cheese	Käse	**kay**-zeh
sandwich	Sandwich	**zahnd**-vich
soup	Suppe	**zup**-peh
salad	Salat	zah-**laht**
meat	Fleisch	flīsh
poultry	Geflügel	geh-**flew**-gehl
fish	Fisch	fish
seafood	Meeresfrüchte	meh-rehs-**frewkh**-teh
fruit	Obst	ohpst
vegetables	Gemüse	geh-**mew**-zeh
dessert	Nachspeise	**nahkh**-shpī-zeh
mineral water	Mineralwasser	min-eh-**rahl**-vah-ser
tap water	Leitungswasser	**lī**-toongs-vah-ser
milk	Milch	milkh
(orange) juice	(Orangen-) Saft	(oh-**rahn**-zhehn-) zahft
coffee	Kaffee	kah-**fay**
tea	Tee	tay
wine	Wein	vīn
red / white	rot / weiß	roht / vīs
glass / bottle	Glas / Flasche	glahs / **flah**-sheh
beer	Bier	beer
Cheers!	Prost!	prohst
More. / Another.	Mehr. / Noch ein.	mehr / nohkh īn
The same.	Das gleiche.	dahs **glīkh**-eh
Bill, please.	Rechnung, bitte.	**rehkh**-noong **bit**-teh
tip	Trinkgeld	**trink**-gehlt
Delicious!	Lecker!	**lehk**-er

APPENDIX

For more user-friendly German phrases, check out *Rick Steves' German Phrase Book and Dictionary* or *Rick Steves' French, Italian & German Phrase Book*.

INDEX

St. Peter's Cemetery (Salzburg): 187

St. Peter's Church (Munich): 53–56

St. Peter's Church (Salzburg): 187–188

St. Peter's Fountain (Trier): 447

St. Sebastian Cemetery (Salzburg): 201

St. Thomas Church (Leipzig): 574–577

St. Wolfgang's Church (Rothenburg): 308

Stahleck Castle: 385

Stasi Museum (Berlin): 704–705

Stasi Museum in the "Runde Ecke" (Leipzig): 572–574

Staufen: 270–278

Stein Terrasse (Salzburg): 200

Steingasse stroll (Salzburg): 199–200

Sterrenberg Castle: 381

Stolpersteine (Berlin): 715

Story of Berlin: 732

Südmeile (Leipzig): 580

Swabian Gate (Freiburg): 261

Swimming: Cochem, 425; Rothenburg, 297

T

Taxis: Hamburg, 785; Munich, 41; Reutte, 157; Rothenburg, 297; tipping, 17

Tegelberg Gondola: 141

Tegelberg Luge: 141–142

Telephones: calling over the Internet, 822–823; dialing to or from Germany, 817–820; dialing within Germany, 817; European calling chart, 818–819; general information, 816; hotel-room phones, 821; mobile phones, 821–822; prepaid phone cards, 820; public pay phones, 821; useful phone numbers, 823

Tennis: 425

Theaterplatz (Dresden): 596–598

Theft: credit and debit cards, 16; general information, 12

Thuringian Folk Museum (Erfurt): 532

Time zones: 12

Tipping: 16–17

Tirol: general information, 119–120; transportation, 120–122

Tirolean folk evening (Reutte): 162

TIs. *See* tourist information

Topography of Terror: 701–704

Toppler Castle: 308–309

Toscanini Hof (Salzburg): 188

Tourist information: Bacharach, 392; Baden-Baden, 236; Berchtesgaden, 225; Berlin, 650–652; Cochem, 421; Dresden, 594; Erfurt, 517; Frankfurt, 349; Freiburg, 253–254; Füssen, 124; general information, 815–816; Görlitz, 628; Hamburg, 784; Köln, 460; Leipzig, 564; Munich, 38–39; Nürnberg, 483; Potsdam, 765; Reutte, 156; Rothenburg, 294–296; Salzburg, 172; St. Goar, 405; Staufen, 270; Trier, 441; Wittenberg, 542–543; Würzburg, 332–333

Tourist season: 5–8

Tours: Berchtesgaden, 226–227; Berlin, 658–664; Frankfurt, 353–354; Hamburg, 786–788; Köln, 463; Munich, 45–49; Nürnberg, 484–486; Potsdam, 766; Rothenburg, 297–298; Salzburg, 177–181; Trier, 444

Town Church of St. Mary's (Wittenberg): 549–553

Town Hall (Görlitz): 636

Toy Museum (Nürnberg): 496

Tradesman's House (Rothenburg): 308

INDEX

MAP INDEX

Audio Europe

Rick's free app and podcasts

The FREE **Rick Steves Audio Europe**™ app for iPhone, iPad and iPod Touch gives you 29 self-guided audio tours of Europe's top museums, sights and historic walks—plus more than 200 tracks filled with cultural insights and sightseeing tips from Rick's radio interviews—all organized into geographic-specific playlists.

Let **Rick Steves Audio Europe**™ amplify your guidebook.

With Rick whispering in your ear, Europe gets even better.

Thanks Facebook fans for submitting photos while on location! From top: John Kuijper in Florence, Brenda Mamer with her mother in Rome, Angel Capobianco in London, and Alyssa Passey with her friend in Paris.

Find out more at ricksteves.com

Join a Rick Steves tour

Enjoy Europe's warmest welcome... with the flexibility and friendship of a small group getting to know Rick's favorite places and people. It all starts with our free tour catalog and DVD.

Great guides, small groups, no grumps.

▶ Plan Your Trip

Browse thousands of articles and a wealth of money-saving tips for planning your dream trip. You'll find up-to-date information on Europe's best destinations, packing smart, getting around, finding rooms, staying healthy, avoiding scams and more.

▶ Eurail Passes

Find out, step-by-step, if a railpass makes sense for your trip—and how to avoid buying more than you need. Get free shipping on online orders

▶ Graffiti Wall & Travelers Helpline

Learn, ask, share—our online community of savvy travelers is a great resource for first-time travelers to Europe, as well as seasoned pros.

Rick Steves' Europe Through the Back Door, Inc.

ricksteves.com

urn your travel dreams into affordable reality

▶ Free Audio Tours & Travel Newsletter

Get your nose out of this guide book and focus on what you'll be seeing with Rick's free audio tours of the greatest sights in Paris, London, Rome, Florence, Venice, and Athens.

Subscribe to our free Travel News e-newsletter, and get monthly articles from Rick on what's happening in Europe.

▶ Great Gear from Rick's Travel Store

Pack light and right—on a budget—with Rick's custom-designed carry-on bags, roll-aboards, day packs, travel accessories, guidebooks, journals, maps and DVDs of his TV shows.

130 Fourth Avenue North, PO Box 2009 • Edmonds, WA 98020 USA
Phone: (425) 771-8303 • Fax: (425) 771-0833 • www.ricksteves.com

Credits

Researchers

To help update this book, Rick relied on...

Ian Watson

Ian has worked with Rick's guidebooks since 1993, after starting out with Let's Go and Frommer's guides. Originally from upstate New York, Ian speaks several European languages, including German, and makes his home in Reykjavík, Iceland.

Marijan Kriškovic

Born and raised in Slovenia and Croatia, Marijan got hooked on *Kaffee und Kuchen* (coffee and dessert) while visiting German relatives. He lives in Ljubljana with his girlfriend, Barbara, and cat, John Travolta III. Whether leading a Rick Steves tour or at home, Marijan is probably drinking *Kaffee* and eating *Kuchen* right now.

Cameron Hewitt

Cameron writes and edits guidebooks for Rick Steves. For this book, Cameron revisited revitalized Berlin and got *Ost*-algic in the former DDR. When he's not traveling, Cameron lives in Seattle with his wife Shawna.

Contributors

Gene Openshaw

Gene is the co-author of 10 Rick Steves books. For this book, he wrote material on art, history, and contemporary culture. When he's not traveling, Gene enjoys composing music, recovering from his 1973 trip to Europe with Rick, and living everyday life with his daughter.

Images

The following list identifies the chapter-opening images and credits their photographers.

Location	Photographer
Introduction: Füssen	Rick Steves
Munich: Marienplatz	Rick Steves
Bavaria and Tirol: Neuschwanstein Castle	Dominic Bonuccelli
Salzburg and Berchtesgaden: Salzburg Overview	Dominic Bonuccelli
Baden-Baden and the Black Forest: Baden-Baden	Cameron Hewitt
Rothenburg and the Romantic Road: Rothenburg	David C. Hoerlein
Würzburg: Residenzplatz	Ian Watson
Frankfurt: Frankfurt Scene from Bridge	Rick Steves
Rhine Valley: Bacharach and the Rhine	Dominic Bonuccelli
Mosel Valley: Beilstein	Cameron Hewitt
Trier: Trier	Ian Watson
Köln and the Unromantic Rhine: Köln's Cathedral	Cameron Hewitt
Nürnberg: Market Square	Rick Steves
Lutherland: Erfurt	Cameron Hewitt
Leipzig: Leipzig	Cameron Hewitt
Dresden: Zwinger	Cameron Hewitt
Görlitz: Church of St. Peter	Lee Evans
Berlin: Gendarmenmarkt	Cameron Hewitt
Near Berlin: Potsdam's new Palace	Cameron Hewitt
Hamburg: Hamburg	Cameron Hewitt

Acknowledgments

Thanks to Gene Openshaw for writing the tour of Munich's Alte Pinakothek; to Cameron Hewitt for writing the original versions of the Dresden, Nürnberg, Leipzig, and Lutherland chapters; to Ian Watson for writing the Hamburg chapter; and to Lee Evans for writing the original version of the Görlitz chapter.

Rick Steves' Guidebook Series

City, Regional, and Country Guides

*Rick Steves' Amsterdam,
    Bruges & Brussels*
Rick Steves' Best of Europe
Rick Steves' Budapest
*Rick Steves' Croatia
    & Slovenia*
Rick Steves' Eastern Europe
Rick Steves' England
*Rick Steves' Florence
    & Tuscany*
Rick Steves' France
Rick Steves' Germany
Rick Steves' Great Britain
*Rick Steves' Greece: Athens
    & the Peloponnese*
Rick Steves' Ireland

Rick Steves' Istanbul
Rick Steves' Italy
Rick Steves' London
Rick Steves' Paris
Rick Steves' Portugal
*Rick Steves' Prague
    & the Czech Republic*
*Rick Steves' Provence
    & the French Riviera*
Rick Steves' Rome
Rick Steves' Scandinavia
Rick Steves' Spain
Rick Steves' Switzerland
Rick Steves' Venice
*Rick Steves' Vienna,
    Salzburg & Tirol*

Snapshot Guides

Excerpted from country guidebooks, the Snapshots Guides cover many of my favorite destinations, such as *Rick Steves' Snapshot Barcelona, Rick Steves' Snapshot Scotland,* and *Rick Steves' Snapshot Hill Towns of Central Italy.*

Pocket Guides

My new Pocket Guides are condensed, colorful guides to Europe's top cities, including Paris, London, Rome, and more. These combine the top self-guided walks and tours from my city guides with vibrant full-color photos, and are sized to slip easily into your pocket.

Rick Steves' Phrase Books

French
French/Italian/German
German
Italian
Portuguese
Spanish

More Books

Rick Steves' Europe 101: History and Art for the Traveler
Rick Steves' Europe Through the Back Door
Rick Steves' European Christmas
Rick Steves' Mediterranean Cruise Ports
Rick Steves' Postcards from Europe
Rick Steves' Travel as a Political Act

Avalon Travel
a member of the Perseus Books Group
1700 Fourth Street
Berkeley, CA 94710

Printed in Canada by Friesens. First printing December 2011.

ISBN 978-1-59880-988-6
ISSN 1553-6866

For the latest on Rick's lectures, guidebooks, tours, public radio show, and public television
series, contact Europe Through the Back Door, Box 2009, Edmonds, WA 98020, tel.
425/771-8303, fax 425/771-0833, www.ricksteves.com, rick@ricksteves.com.

Europe Through the Back Door Reviewing Editors: Cameron Hewitt, Jennifer Madison
  Davis, Cathy Lu
ETBD Editors: Cathy McDonald, Gretchen Strauch, Suzanne Kotz, Tom Griffin,
  Samantha Oberholzer
ETBD Managing Editor: Risa Laib
Research Assistance: Cameron Hewitt, Ian Watson, Marijan Krišković, Rick Garman
Avalon Travel Senior Editor and Series Manager: Madhu Prasher
Avalon Travel Project Editor: Kelly Lydick
Copy Editor: Judith Brown
Proofreader: Lisa Noël Chrisman
Indexer: Claire Splan
Production and Typesetting: McGuire Barber Design
Cover Design: Kimberly Glyder Design
Graphic Content Director: Laura VanDeventer
Maps and Graphics: David C. Hoerlein, Lauren Mills, Laura VanDeventer, Twozdai
  Hulse, Kat Bennett, Mike Morgenfeld, Brice Ticen
Front Matter Color Photos: p. I, Bavarian Beer Maid © Rick Steves; p. xii, Burg Eltz ©
  Dominic Bonuccelli
Front Cover Photo: Marienplatz, New Town Hall and Frauenkirche turrets, Munich ©
  Wilfried Krecichwost/Getty Images/Royalty Free
Additional Photography: Rick Steves, David C. Hoerlein, Cameron Hewitt, Ian Watson,
  Dominic Bonuccelli, Gretchen Strauch, Karoline Vass, Robyn Cronin, Lee Evans

ABOUT THE AUTHOR

RICK STEVES

Since 1973, Rick Steves has spent 100 days every year exploring Europe. Rick produces a public television series (*Rick Steves' Europe*), a public radio show (*Travel with Rick Steves*), and an app and podcast (*Rick Steves Audio Europe*); writes a bestselling series of guidebooks and a nationally syndicated newspaper column; organizes guided tours that take over ten thousand travelers to Europe annually; and offers an information-packed website (www.ricksteves.com). With the help of his hardworking staff of 80 at Europe Through the Back Door—in Edmonds, Washington, just north of Seattle—Rick's mission is to make European travel fun, affordable, and culturally enlightening for Americans.

Foldout Color Map ▶

The foldout map on the opposite page includes:
• A map of Germany on one side
• City maps, including Berlin, Munich, Salzburg, and Vienna on the other side